P9-EEL-944

Short Story Criticism

Guide to Gale Literary Criticism Series

When you need to review criticism of literary works, these are the Gale series to use:

If the author's death date is:	You should turn to:
After Dec. 31, 1959 (or author is still living)	***CONTEMPORARY LITERARY CRITICISM*** for example: Jorge Luis Borges, Anthony Burgess, William Faulkner, Mary Gordon, Ernest Hemingway, Iris Murdoch
1900 through 1959	***TWENTIETH-CENTURY LITERARY CRITICISM*** for example: Willa Cather, F. Scott Fitzgerald, Henry James, Mark Twain, Virginia Woolf
1800 through 1899	***NINETEENTH-CENTURY LITERATURE CRITICISM*** for example: Fyodor Dostoevski, Nathaniel Hawthorne, George Sand, William Wordsworth
1400 through 1799	***LITERATURE CRITICISM FROM 1400 TO 1800 (excluding Shakespeare)*** for example: Anne Bradstreet, Daniel Defoe, Alexander Pope, François Rabelais, Jonathan Swift, Phillis Wheatley
	SHAKESPEAREAN CRITICISM Shakespeare's plays and poetry
Antiquity through 1399	***CLASSICAL AND MEDIEVAL LITERATURE CRITICISM*** for example: Dante, Homer, Plato, Sophocles, Vergil, the Beowulf Poet

---

Gale also publishes related criticism series:

CHILDREN'S LITERATURE REVIEW
This series covers authors of all eras who have written for the preschool through high school audience.

SHORT STORY CRITICISM
This series covers the major short fiction writers of all nationalities and periods of literary history.

POETRY CRITICISM
This series covers poets of all nationalities and periods of literary history.

DRAMA CRITICISM
This series covers dramatists of all nationalities and periods of literary history.

ISSN 0895-9439

Volume 8

Short Story Criticism

Excerpts from Criticism of the Works of Short Fiction Writers

Thomas Votteler
Editor

Laurie DiMauro
Cathy Falk
David Kmenta
Marie Lazzari
Thomas Ligotti
Sean R. Pollock
David Segal
Bridget Travers
Associate Editors

STAFF

Thomas Votteler, *Editor*

Laurie DiMauro, Cathy Falk, David Kmenta, Marie Lazzari, Thomas Ligotti, Sean R. Pollock, David Segal, Bridget Travers, *Associate Editors*

Jennifer Brostrom, Ian A. Goodhall, Elizabeth P. Henry, Susan Peters, James Poniewozik, Debra A. Wells, *Assistant Editors*

Jeanne A. Gough, *Permissions & Production Manager*
Linda M. Pugliese, *Production Supervisor*
Maureen Puhl, Jennifer VanSickle, *Editorial Associates*
Donna Craft, Paul Lewon, Lorna Mabunda, Camille Robinson, Sheila Walencewicz, *Editorial Assistants*

Maureen Richards, *Research Supervisor*
Paula Cutcher-Jackson, Mary Beth McElmeel, Judy L. Gale, Robin Lupa, *Editorial Associates*
Jennifer Brostrom, Tamara C. Nott, Amy Kaechele, *Editorial Assistants*

Sandra C. Davis, *Permissions Supervisor (Text)*
Maria L. Franklin, Josephine M. Keene, Denise M. Singleton, Kimberly F. Smilay, *Permissions Associates*
Rebecca A. Hartford, Michele M. Lonoconus, Shalice Shah, Nancy K. Sheridan, *Permissions Assistants*
Shelly Rakoczy, *Student Co-op Assistant*

Margaret A. Chamberlain, *Permissions Supervisor (Pictures)*
Pamela A. Hayes, *Permissions Associate*
Keith Reed, *Permissions Assistant*

Mary Beth Trimper, *Production Manager*
Mary Winterhalter, *Production Assistant*

Arthur Chartow, *Art Director*
C. J. Jonik, *Keyliner*

The paper used in this publication meets the minimum requirements of American National Standard for Information Sciences—Permanence Paper for Printed Library Materials, ANSI Z39.48-1984 ∞™

835 Penobscot Bldg.
Detroit, MI 48226-4094

Library of Congress Catalog Card Number 88-641014
ISBN 0-8103-2557-8
ISSN 0895-9439

Printed in the United States of America

Published simultaneously in the United Kingdom
by Gale Research International Limited
(An affiliated company of Gale Research Inc.)

Contents

Preface vii

Acknowledgments ix

Authors to Be Featured in Forthcoming Volumes xiii

Raymond Carver (1938-1988) 1

Kate Chopin (1851-1904) 63

Paul Laurence Dunbar (1872-1906) 116

Gabriel García Márquez (1928-) 152

Bret Harte (1836?-1902) 207

Henry James (1843-1916) 262

W. Somerset Maugham (1874-1965) 354

Grace Paley (1922-) 386

Kurt Vonnegut, Jr. (1922-) 423

Appendix: Select Bibliography of General Sources on Short Fiction 441

Literary Criticism Series Cumulative Author Index 447

SSC Cumulative Nationality Index 499

SSC Cumulative Title Index 501

Preface

Short Story Criticism (SSC) presents significant passages from criticism of the world's greatest short story writers and provides supplementary biographical and bibliographical materials to guide the interested reader to a greater understanding of the authors of short fiction. This series was developed in response to suggestions from librarians serving high school, college, and public library patrons, who had noted a considerable number of requests for critical material on short story writers. Although major short story writers are covered in such Gale series as *Contemporary Literary Criticism (CLC), Twentieth-Century Literary Criticism (TCLC), Nineteenth-Century Literature Criticism (NCLC),* and *Literature Criticism from 1400 to 1800 (LC),* librarians perceived the need for a series devoted solely to writers of the short story genre.

Scope of the Work

SSC is designed to serve as an introduction to major short story writers of all eras and nationalities. Since these authors have inspired a great deal of relevant critical material, *SSC* is necessarily selective, and the editors have chosen the most important published criticism to aid readers and students in their research.

Approximately ten to fifteen authors are included in each volume, and each entry presents a historical survey of the critical response to that author's work. The length of an entry is intended to reflect the amount of critical attention the author has received from critics writing in English and from foreign critics in translation. Every attempt has been made to identify and include excerpts from the most significant essays on each author's work. In order to provide these important critical pieces, the editors will sometimes reprint essays that have appeared in previous volumes of Gale's Literary Criticism Series. Such duplication, however, never exceeds twenty percent of an *SSC* volume.

Organization of the Book

An *SSC* author entry consists of the following elements:

- The **author heading** cites the name under which the author most commonly wrote, followed by birth and death dates. If the author wrote consistently under a pseudonym, the pseudonym will be listed in the author heading and the author's actual name given in parentheses on the first line of the biographical and critical introduction.

- The **biographical and critical introduction** contains background information designed to introduce a reader to the author and the critical debates surrounding his or her work. Parenthetical material following the introduction provides references to other biographical and critical series published by Gale, including *CLC, TCLC, NCLC, Contemporary Authors,* and *Dictionary of Literary Biography.*

- A **portrait of the author** is included when available. Many entries also contain illustrations of materials pertinent to an author's career, including holographs of manuscript pages, title pages, dust jackets, letters, or representations of important people, places, and events in the author's life.

- The list of **principal works** is chronological by date of first publication and lists the most important works by the author. The first section comprises short story collections, novellas, and novella collections. The second section gives information on other major works by the author. For foreign authors, the editors have provided original foreign-language publication information and have selected what are considered the best and most complete English-language editions of their works.

- **Criticism** is arranged chronologically in each author entry to provide a useful perspective on changes in critical evaluation over the years. All short story, novella, and collection titles by the author featured in the entry are printed in boldface type to enable a reader to ascertain without difficulty the works discussed. Also for purposes of easier identification, the critic's name and the publication date of the essay are given at the beginning of each piece of criticism. Unsigned criticism is preceded by the title of the journal in which it appeared.

- Critical essays are prefaced with **explanatory notes** as an additional aid to students and readers using *SSC.* The explanatory notes provide several types of useful information, including: the reputation of a critic, the importance of a work of criticism, and the specific type of criticism (biographical, psychoanalytic, structuralist, etc.).

- A complete **bibliographical citation,** designed to help the interested reader locate the original essay or book, follows each piece of criticism.

- The **further reading list** appearing at the end of each author entry suggests additional materials on the author. In some cases it includes essays for which the editors could not obtain reprint rights.

Beginning with volume six, *SSC* contains two additional features designed to enhance the reader's understanding of short fiction writers and their works:

- Each *SSC* entry now includes, when available, **comments by the author** that illuminate his or her own works or the short story genre in general. These statements are set within boxes or bold rules to distinguish them from the criticism.

- A **select bibliography of general sources on short fiction** is included as an appendix. Updated and amended with each new *SSC* volume, this listing of materials for further research provides readers with a selection of the best available general studies of the short story genre.

Other Features

A **cumulative author index** lists all the authors who have appeared in *SSC, CLC, TCLC, NCLC, LC,* and *Classical and Medieval Literature Criticism (CMLC),* as well as cross-references to other Gale series. Users will welcome this cumulated index as a useful tool for locating an author within the Literary Criticism Series.

A **cumulative nationality index** lists all authors featured in *SSC* by nationality, followed by the number of the *SSC* volume in which their entry appears.

A **cumulative title index** lists in alphabetical order all short story, novella, and collection titles contained in the *SSC* series. Titles of short story collections, separately published novellas, and novella collections are printed in italics, while titles of individual short stories are printed in roman type with quotation marks. Each title is followed by the author's name and the corresponding volume and page numbers where commentary on the work may be located. English-language translations of original foreign-language titles are cross-referenced to the foreign titles so that all references to discussion of a work are combined in one listing.

A Note to the Reader

When writing papers, students who quote directly from any volume in the Literary Criticism Series may use the following general forms to footnote reprinted criticism. The first example pertains to material drawn from periodicals, the second to material reprinted from books:

[1] Henry James, Jr., "Honoré de Balzac," *The Galaxy* 20 (December 1875), 814-36; excerpted and reprinted in *Short Story Criticism,* Vol. 5, ed. Thomas Votteler (Detroit: Gale Research, 1990), pp. 8-11.

[2] F. R. Leavis, *D. H. Lawrence: Novelist* (Alfred A. Knopf, 1956); excerpted and reprinted in *Short Story Criticism,* Vol. 4, ed. Thomas Votteler (Detroit: Gale Research, 1990), pp. 202-06.

Suggestions Are Welcome

Readers who wish to suggest authors to appear in future volumes, or who have other suggestions, are invited to contact the editors by writing to Gale Research, Inc., Literary Criticism Division, 835 Penobscot Building, Detroit, MI, 48226-4094.

Acknowledgments

The editors wish to thank the copyright holders of the excerpted criticism included in this volume, the permissions managers of many book and magazine publishing companies for assisting us in securing reprint rights, and Anthony Bogucki for assistance with copyright research. We are also grateful to the staffs of the Detroit Public Library, the Library of Congress, the University of Detroit Library, Wayne State University Purdy/Kresge Library Complex, and the University of Michigan Libraries for making their resources available to us. Following is a list of the copyright holders who have granted us permission to reprint material in this volume of SSC. Every effort has been made to trace copyright, but if omissions have been made, please let us know.

COPYRIGHTED EXCERPTS IN *SSC,* VOLUME 8 WERE REPRINTED FROM THE FOLLOWING PERIODICALS:

America, v. 119, September 14, 1968. © 1968. All rights reserved. Reprinted with permission of America Press, Inc., 106 West 56th Street, New York, NY 10019.—***American Quarterly,*** v. XI, Summer, 1959 for "For Daisy Miller to Julia Bride: 'A Whole Passage of Intellectual History' " by Peter Buitenhuis. Copyright 1959, renewed 1987 by American Studies Association. Reprinted by permission of the publisher and the author.—***Antaeus,*** n. 47, Autumn, 1982. Copyright © 1982 by *Antaeus.*—***Arizona Quarterly,*** v. 36, Autumn, 1980 for "For Better or Worse Tennessee and His Partner: A New Approach to Bret Harte" by Linda Burton; v. 42, Winter, 1986 for "Imagery as Action in 'The Beast in the Jungle' " by James W. Gargano. Copyright © 1980, 1986 by Arizona Board of Regents. Both reprinted by permission of the publisher and the respective authors.—***The Atlantic Monthly,*** v. 222, September, 1968 for "The Volunteer Fireman" by Charles Nicol. Copyright 1968 by The Atlantic Monthly Company, Boston, MA. Reprinted by permission of the author.—***Books Abroad,*** v. 47, Summer, 1973. Copyright 1973 by the University of Oklahoma Press. Reprinted by permission of the publisher.—***Canto: Review of the Arts,*** v. 2, Summer, 1978 for a review of "Furious Seasons, and Other Stories" by Ann Beattie. Copyright © 1978 by Canto, Inc. All rights reserved. Reprinted by permission of the author.—*The* ***Centennial Review,*** v. XXVI, Summer, 1982 for "Miss Tina Did It: A Fresh Look at 'The Aspern Papers' " by Joseph J. Waldmeir. © 1982 by *The Centennial Review.* Reprinted by permission of the publisher and the author.—***Critique: Studies in Contemporary Fiction,*** v. XXIX, Summer, 1988; v. XXX, Summer, 1989. Copyright © 1988, 1989 Helen Dwight Reid Educational Foundation. Both reprinted with permission of the Helen Dwight Reid Educational Foundation, published by Heldref Publications, Albemarle Street, N.W., Washington, DC 20016.—***Delta,*** France, May, 1982./ May, 1982 for "The Desires of Women, the Presence of Men" by Diane Cousineau. Reprinted by permission of the author.—***The Denver Quarterly,*** v. 22, Summer, 1987. Copyright © 1987 by the University of Denver. Reprinted by permission of the publisher.—***enclitic,*** v. 11, Fall, 1988. Copyright © 1988 by *enclitic,* Inc. Reprinted by permission of the publisher.—***fiction international,*** n. 6/7, 1976. Copyright © 1976 by the Editors. Reprinted by permission of the publisher.—***Genesis West,*** v. 2, Fall, 1963. Copyright © 1963 by The Chrysalis West Foundation, Inc. All rights reserved. Reprinted by permission of the publisher.—***Hispanic Journal,*** v. 9, Fall, 1987. © copyright, 1987 IUP Indiana University of Pennsylvania. Reprinted by permission of the publisher.—***The Hudson Review,*** v. XXXVII, Spring, 1984. Copyright © 1984 by The Hudson Review, Inc. Reprinted by permission of the publisher.—***The Iowa Review,*** v. 10 Summer, 1979 for " 'Will You Please Be Quiet, Please?': Voyeurism, Dissociation, and the Art of Raymond Carver" by David Boxer and Cassandra Phillips. Copyright © 1979 by The University of Iowa. Reprinted by permission of the publisher and David Boxer.—***The Journal of Negro History,*** v. LII, January, 1967. Reprinted by permission of The Association for the Study of Afro-American Life and History, Inc. (ASALH).—***The Kenyon Review,*** v. V, Autumn, 1943 for "In the Country of the Blue" by R. P. Blackmur. Copyright 1943 by Kenyon College. Renewed 1970 by the Literary Estate of R. P. Blackmur. All rights reserved. Reprinted by permission of the Literary Estate of R. P. Blackmur.—***Latin American Literary Review,*** v. XIII, January-June, 1985. Reprinted by permission of the publisher.—***London Review of Books,*** v. 4, September 16-October 6, 1982 for "Angel Gabriel" by Salman Rushdie. Appears here by permission of the *London Review of Books* and the author.—***The Mississippi Quarterly,*** v. XXV, Spring, 1972. Reprinted by permission of the publisher.—***Negro American Literature Forum,*** v. 8, Spring, 1974 for "The Fiction of Paul Laurence Dunbar" by A. Robert Lee. Copyright © Indiana State University 1974. Reprinted with the permission of Black American Literature Forum and the author.—***The New Criterion,*** v. IV, November, 1985 for "Is It All Right to Read Somerset Maugham?" by Joseph Epstein. Copyright © 1985 by The Foundation for Cultural Review. Reprinted by permission of the author.—***The New Republic,*** v. 192, February 4, 1985; v. 192, April 29, 1985. © 1985 The New Republic, Inc. Both reprinted by permission of *The New Republic.*—***The New York Times,*** August 19, 1968 by The New York Times Company. Reprinted by permission of the publisher.—***The New York Times Book Review,*** February 15, 1981; February 21, 1988. Copyright © 1981, 1988 by The New York Times Company./ September 1, 1968; February 20, 1972; May 15, 1988. Copyright © 1968,

1972, 1988 by The New York Times Company. All reprinted by permission of the publisher./ August 12, 1934; April 19, 1959. Copyright 1934, renewed 1962; copyright 1959, renewed 1987 by The New York Times Company. Both reprinted by permission of the publisher.—***The New Yorker,*** v. LXI, May 20, 1985 for "Living Death" by John Updike. © 1985 by the author. Reprinted by permission of the publisher.—***Nineteenth-Century Fiction,*** v. 22, December, 1967. © 1967 by The Regents of the University of California. Reprinted by permission of The Regents./ v. VIII, September, 1953. Copyright 1953, renewed 1981 by The Regents of the University of California. Reprinted by permission of The Regents.—***Papers of the Michigan Academy of Science, Arts and Letters,*** v. 46, 1961 for "The Christ Motif in 'The Luck of Roaring Camp' " by Allen B. Brown. Copyright 1961 by The University of Michigan. Renewed 1989 by Sheridan Baker. Reprinted by permission of the publisher.—***The Paris Review,*** v. 25, Summer, 1983. © 1983 The Paris Review, Inc./ v. 23, Winter, 1981. © 1981 The Paris Review, Inc. Reprinted by permission of the publisher.—***Partisan Review,*** v. XLVIII, 1981 for "Mrs. Hegel-Shtein's Tears" by Marianne Dekoven; v. XLIX, 1982 for "Absent Talkers" by Alain Arias-Misson. Copyright © 1981, 1982 by *Partisan Review.* Both reprinted by permission of the respective authors./ v. XVI, February, 1949. Copyright 1949, renewed 1976 by *Partisan Review.* Reprinted by permission of the publisher.—***Philological Quarterly,*** v. 64, Winter, 1985 for "Beyond Hopelessville: Another Side of Raymond Carver" by William L. Stull. Copyright 1985 by The University of Iowa. Reprinted by permission of the publisher and the author.—***The Quarterly Review,*** v. 304, October, 1966.—***Saturday Review,*** v. LI, April 27, 1968. © 1968 *Saturday Review* magazine. Reprinted by permission of the publisher.—***Shenandoah,*** v. XXXII 1981 for an interview with Grace Paley by Joan Lidoff. Copyright 1981 by Washington and Lee University. Reprinted from *Shenandoah* with the permission of the Editor and the Literary Estate of Joan Lidoff.—***The Southern Humanities Review,*** v. XI, Winter, 1977. Copyright 1977 by Auburn University. Reprinted by permission of the publisher.—***The Southern Literary Journal,*** v. X, Spring, 1978. Copyright 1978 by the Department of English, University of North Carolina at Chapel Hill. Reprinted by permission of the publisher.—***South Atlantic Quarterly,*** v. LIX, Winter, 1960. Copyright © 1960, renewed 1988 by Duke University Press, Durham, NC. Reprinted by permission of the publisher.—***The South Dakota Review,*** v. 15, Spring, 1977; v. 24, Autumn, 1986. © 1977, 1986, University of South Dakota. Both reprinted by permission of the publisher.—***Studies in American Jewish Literature,*** v. 2, 1982; n. 3, 1983. © 1982, 1983 State University of New York. All rights reserved. Both reprinted by permission of the publisher.—***Studies in Short Fiction,*** v. XI, Summer, 1974; v. 19, Winter, 1982; v. 25, Fall, 1988. Copyright 1974, 1982, 1988 by Newberry College. All reprinted by permission of the publisher.—***The Times Literary Supplement,*** n. 4112, January 22, 1982; n. 4312, November 22, 1985. © The Times Supplements Limited 1982, 1985. Both reproduced from *The Times Literary Supplement* by permission.—***Western American Literature,*** v. VIII, November, 1973. Copyright, 1973, by the Western Literature Association. Both reprinted by permission of the publisher.

COPYRIGHTED EXCERPTS IN *SSC,* VOLUME 8 WERE REPRINTED FROM THE FOLLOWING BOOKS:

Allen, Elizabeth. From ***A Woman's Place in the Novels of Henry James.*** St. Martin's Press, 1984. © Elizabeth Allen 1984. All rights reserved. Used with permission of St. Martin's Press, Inc. In Canada by Macmillan, London, Basingstoke.—Andreas, Osborn. From ***Henry James and the Expanding Horizon: A Study of the Meaning and Basic Themes of James's Fiction.*** University of Washington Press, 1948. Copyright 1948, by The President and Regents of the University of Washington. Renewed 1976 by Lowell W. Andreas. Reprinted by permission of the publisher.—Bell-Villada, Gene H. From ***García Márquez: The Man and His Work.*** The University of North Carolina Press, 1990. © 1990 The University of North Carolina Press. All rights reserved. Reprinted by permission of the publisher and the author.—Bender, Bert. From ***A Singer in the Dawn: Reinterpretations of Paul Laurence Dunbar.*** Edited by Jay Martin. Dodd, Mead & Company, 1975. Copyright © 1975 by Jay Martin. All rights reserved. Reprinted by permission of the author.—Bone, Robert. From ***Down Home: Origins of the Afro-American Short Story.*** Columbia University Press, 1988. Copyright © 1975 by Robert Bone. All rights reserved. Used by permission of Columbia University Press.—Booth, Wayne C. From ***The Rhetoric of Fiction.*** The University of Chicago Press, 1961. © 1961 by The University of Chicago. Renewed 1989 by Wayne C. Booth. Reprinted by permission of the publisher.—Chénetier, Marc. From "Living On/Off the 'Reserved': Performance, Interrogation, and Negativity in the Works of Raymond Carver," in ***Critical Angles: European Views of Contemporary American Literature.*** Edited by Marc Chénetier. Southern Illinois University Press, 1986. Copyright © 1986 by the Board of Trustees, Southern Illinois University. All rights reserved. Reprinted by permission of the author.—Cowdery, Lauren T. From ***The Nouvelle of Henry James in Theory and Practice.*** Revised edition. UMI Research Press, 1986. Copyright © 1986, 1980 Lauren Tozek Cowdery. All rights reserved. Reprinted by permission of the author.—Curtis, Anthony. From ***Somerset Maugham.*** Profile Books Ltd., 1982. © Anthony Curtis 1982. Reprinted by permission of the author.—Dupee, F. W. From ***Henry James.*** Sloane, 1951. Copyright, 1951. by William Sloane Associates, Inc. Renewed 1979 by F. W. Dupee. Reprinted by permission of William Sloane Associates, a division of William Morrow and Company, Inc.—Edel, Leon. From an introduction to ***Ghostly Tales of Henry James.*** Edited by Leon Edel. Grosset & Dunlap, 1963. Copyright ©, 1949, by the Trustees of Rutgers University Press. Introduction © 1963 by Leon Edel. Reprinted by permission of Rutgers University Press.—Ewell, Barbara. From ***Kate Chopin.*** The Ungar Publishing Company, 1986. Copyright © 1986 by The Ungar Publishing Company. Reprinted by permission of the publisher.—Geismar, Maxwell. From ***Henry James and the Jacobites.*** Houghton Mifflin Company, 1963. Copyright © 1962, 1963 by Maxwell Geismar. All rights reserved. Reprinted by permission of Houghton Mifflin

Company.—Gloster, Hugh M. From ***Negro Voices in American Fiction.*** The University of North Carolina Press, 1948. Copyright, 1948, by The University of North Carolina Press. Renewed 1976 by Hugh M. Gloster. Reprinted by permission of the publisher and the author.—Janes, Regina. From ***Gabriel García Márquez: Revolutions in Wonderland.*** University of Missouri Press, 1981. Copyright © 1981 by The Curators of the University of Missouri. All rights reserved. Reprinted by permission of the publisher.—Klinkowitz, Jerome. From ***Kurt Vonnegut.*** Methuen, 1982. © 1982 Jerome Klinkowitz. Reprinted by permission of the publisher.—Loggins, Vernon. From ***The Negro Author: His Development in America to 1900.*** Columbia University Press, 1931. Copyright 1931 Columbia University Press. Renewed 1959 by Vernon Loggins. Reprinted by permission of the Literary Estate of Vernon Loggins.—Loss, Archie K. From ***W. Somerset Maugham.*** Ungar, 1987. Copyright © 1987 by Archie K. Loss. All rights reserved. Reprinted by permission of the publisher.—Maugham, W. Somerset. From ***The Summing Up.*** Garden City Publishing Co., Inc., 1938. Copyright, 1938 by W. Somerset Maugham. All rights reserved.—Maugham, W. Somerset. From a preface to ***The Complete Short Stories: East and West, Vol. I.*** Doubleday, 1952. Copyright 1921, 1934 by Doubleday, a division of Bantam Doubleday Dell Publishing Group, Inc. Copyright, 1923, 1924, 1926, 1927, 1928, 1930, 1931, 1932, renewed 1961 by W. Somerset Maugham. All rights reserved. Reprinted by permission of A. P. Watt Ltd. on behalf of The Royal Literary Fund.—Maugham, W. Somerset. From a preface to ***The Complete Short Stories: The World Over, Vol. II.*** Doubleday, 1952. Copyright 1951, 1952 by W. Somerset Maugham. All rights reserved.—Minta, Stephen. From ***Gabriel García Márquez: Writer of Columbia.*** Jonathan Cape, 1987. Copyright © 1987 by Stephen Minta. Reprinted by permission of the author.—Morrow, Patrick. From ***Bret Harte.*** Boise State College, 1972. Copyright 1972 by the Boise State College Western Writers Series. All rights reserved. Reprinted by permission of the publisher and the author.—Newman, Judie. From "Kate Chopin: Short Fiction and the Arts of Subversion," In ***The Nineteenth-Century American Short Story.*** Edited by A. Robert Lee. London: Vision Press, 1986. © 1985 by Vision Press Ltd. All rights reserved. Reprinted by permission of the publisher.—Paley, Grace. From ***Enormous Changes at the Last Minute.*** Farrar, Straus, Giroux, 1974. Copyright © 1960, 1962, 1965, 1967, 1968, 1971, 1972, 1974 by Grace Paley. All rights reserved.—Pattee, Fred Lewis. From ***The Development of the American Short Story: An Historical Survey.*** Harper & Brothers, 1923. Copyright 1923 by Harper & Row, Publishers, Inc. Renewed 1950 by Fred Lewis Pattee. Reprinted by permission of HarperCollins Publishers, Inc.—Revell, Peter. From ***Paul Laurence Dunbar.*** Twayne, 1979. Copyright 1979 by Twayne Publishers. All rights reserved. Reprinted with the permission of Twayne Publishers, a division of G. K. Hall & Co., Boston.—Rhode, Robert D. From ***Setting in the American Short Story of Local Color: 1865-1900.*** Mouton, 1975. © copyright 1975 Mouton & Co., Publishers. Reprinted by permission of Mouton of Gruyter, a Division of Walter de Gruyter & Co.—Saltzman, Arthur M. From ***Understanding Raymond Carver.*** University of South Carolina Press, 1988. Copyright © University of South Carolina 1988. Reprinted by permission of the publisher.—Schatt, Stanley. From ***Kurt Vonnegut, Jr.*** Twayne, 1976. Copyright 1976 by Twayne Publishers. All rights reserved. Reprinted with the permission of Twayne Publishers, a division of G. K. Hall & Co., Boston.—Schleifer, Ronald. From "Grace Paley: Chaste Compactness," in ***Contemporary American Writers: Narrative Strategies.*** Edited by Catherine Rainwater and William J. Scheick. University Press of Kentucky, 1985. Copyright © 1985 by The University Press of Kentucky. Reprinted by permission of the publisher.—Seyersted, Per. From ***Kate Chopin: A Critical Biography.*** Louisiana State University Press, 1969. © The Norwegian Research Council for Science and the Humanities 1969. Reprinted by permission of Louisiana State University Press.—Skaggs, Peggy. From ***Kate Chopin.*** Twayne, 1985. Copyright 1985 by Twayne Publishers. All rights reserved. Reprinted with the permission of Twayne Publishers, a division of G. K. Hall & Co., Boston.—Spiller, Robert E., and others. From "Delineation of Life and Character" in ***Literary History of the United States, Vol. II.*** Edited by Robert E. Spiller and others. The Macmillan Company, 1948. Copyright, 1946, 1947, 1948, by Macmillan Publishing Company. Renewed 1976 by Robert E. Spiller, Willard Thorp, Thomas H. Johnson & Courtlandt Canby (C of Henry Seidel Canby). All rights reserved. Reprinted with permission of the publisher.—Tracy, Laura. From a conclusion to ***"Catching the Drift": Authority, Gender, and Narrative Strategy in Fiction.*** Rutgers University Press, 1988. Copyright © 1988 by Rutgers, The State University. All rights reserved. Reprinted by permission of the publisher.—Wakefield, John. From "Paul Laurence Dunbar, 'The Scapegoat' (1904)," in ***The Black American Short Story in the 20th Century: A Collection of Critical Essays.*** Edited by Peter Bruck. B. R. Grüner Publishing Co., 1977. © 1977 by B. R. Grüner Publishing Co. Reprinted by permission of B. R. Grüner Publishing Co., an imprint of John Benjamins Publishing Company.—Whitehead, John. From ***Maugham: A Reappraisal.*** London: Vision Press, 1987. © 1987 by John Whitehead. All rights reserved. Reprinted by permission of the publisher.—Williams, Kenny J. From ***They Also Spoke: An Essay on Negro Literature in America, 1787-1930.*** Townsend Press, 1970. Copyright © 1970 by Kenny J. Williams. Reprinted by permission of the author.—Zabel, Morton Dauwen. From an introduction to ***In the Cage & Other Tales.*** By Henry James, edited by Morton Dauwen Zabel. Copyright © 1958, renewed 1986 by Morton Dauwen Zabel. All rights reserved. Used by permission of Doubleday, a division of Bantam Doubleday Dell Publishing Group, Inc.

PHOTOGRAPHS AND ILLUSTRATIONS APPEARING IN *SSC,* VOLUME 8 WERE RECEIVED FROM THE FOLLOWING SOURCES:

© Jerry Bauer: **pp. 1, 423,** Courtesy of Tess Gallagher: **p. 8;** Photograph by Bob Adelman: **pp. 22, 38, 56;** Reprinted by permission of HarperCollins Publishers, Inc.: **p. 152;** Cover of ***No One Writes to the Colonel, and Other Stories,*** by Gabriel García Márquez. Illustration copyright © 1968 by Harper & Row Publishers, Inc. Reprinted by permission of HarperCollins Publishers, Inc.: **p. 163;** Jacket of ***Innocent Erendira, and Other Stories,*** by Gabriel García

Márquez. Jacket illustration copyright © 1978 by Harper & Row, Publishers, Inc. Reprinted by permission of HarperCollins Publishers, Inc.: **p. 188;** BBC Hulton/Bettmann Newsphotos: **p. 354;** Humanities Research Center Library, The University of Texas at Austin: **p. 363;** Courtesy of the Rank Organisation: **p. 373;** Photograph by Layle Silbert: **p. 386;** © Thomas Victor: **p. 413;** Courtesy of Charles Scribner's Sons: **p. 427.**

Authors to Be Featured in Forthcoming Volumes

Chinua Achebe, b. 1930. (Nigerian novelist, short story writer, and poet)—Achebe is widely regarded as one of the most important figures in contemporary African literature. In his acclaimed novel *Things Fall Apart* and the short stories of *Girls at War* and *The Sacrificial Egg,* Achebe fuses folklore, proverbs, and idioms from his native Ibo tribe with Western political and religious idealogies to examine the social and psychological legacy of European colonization in Africa.

Conrad Aiken, 1889-1973. (American poet, novelist, and short story writer)—A renowned poet, Aiken is also the author of several volumes of short stories noted for their psychologically acute portrayals of disturbed protagonists. One of his best-known stories, "Silent Snow, Secret Snow," is among the most often-anthologized in world literature.

James Baldwin, 1924-1987. (American novelist, essayist, dramatist, and short story writer)—Baldwin, who emerged in the 1960s as one of the civil rights movement's most eloquent spokesmen, is widely regarded as an important figure in contemporary American literature. In the short stories of his acclaimed collection, *Going to Meet the Man,* Baldwin vividly exposed some of the polarized racial and sexual attitudes prevalent in American society during the 1960s, while challenging readers to confront and resolve these issues.

Colette, (Sidonie Gabrielle Colette), 1873-1954. (French novelist, short story writer, and journalist)—One of the most prolific French authors of the twentieth century, Colette focused in her writings upon the unusual aspects of such traditional themes as human nature, sexual love, and the innocence of childhood. Her short story collections, including *Animal Dialogues, The Kepi,* and *Gigi, and Other Stories,* are often praised for their deft blending of sensuous detail, metaphorical language, and intense emotion.

Joseph Conrad, 1857-1924. (Polish-born English novelist, novella and short story writer, essayist, and autobiographer)—Conrad is a major writer of modern narrative fiction whose work is considered to have significantly affected the development of twentieth-century literature. His well-known novella *The Heart of Darkness* and his short story "The Secret Sharer" are often anthologized and are widely considered among the best works of their genres in the English language.

Graham Greene, 1904-1991. (English novelist, short story writer, dramatist, editor, essayist, travel writer, scriptwriter, and children's author)—Acclaimed as a novelist of suspenseful thrillers that focus upon moral issues of good and evil, Greene is also highly regarded as a short story writer. In such stories as "The Hint of an Explanation" and "The Basement" Greene combines in-depth characterizations, intriguing plot twists, and elements of mystery to create works that appeal to both popular and critical audiences.

Hermann Hesse, 1877-1962. (German novelist, short story writer, poet, and essayist)—Internationally revered for his works *Demian, Steppenwolf,* and *Siddhartha,* Hesse also wrote a considerable body of shorter fiction, much of which has been collected in his *Stories of Five Decades.*

Katherine Mansfield, 1888-1923. (New Zealand short story writer, critic, and poet)—During her brief career, Mansfield helped shape the modern short story form with her poetic, highly descriptive tales that emphasize mood over plot. Although she lived in London for most of her adult life, such acclaimed stories as "Prelude" and "A Doll's House" are set in her native New Zealand and evoke vivid images of her childhood.

Edna O'Brien, b. 1932. (Irish novelist, short story writer, dramatist, and scriptwriter)—Perhaps best known for her controversial novels, which have been banned in Ireland for their candid treatment of such topics as love, death, female sexuality, and the nature of sin, O'Brien has also published several volumes of short fiction. In these works, which include *A Scandalous Woman, and Other Stories, Returning,* and *Lantern Slides,* O'Brien frequently employs realistic descriptions and a female perspective to evoke memories of her childhood in rural Ireland.

Leo Tolstoy, 1828-1910. (Russian novelist, dramatist, short story writer, essayist, and critic)—Considered among the most important figures in world literature, Tolstoy is best known for his novels *War and Peace* and *Anna Karenina.* In his works of short fiction, including *The Death of Ivan Ilyich* and "God Sees the Truth, but Waits," Tolstoy employed a simple narrative approach to mystical experience and philosophical truth, while creating multidimensional portraits of Tsarist Russian society.

Raymond Carver

1938-1988

American short story writer, poet, and scriptwriter.

Carver is widely recognized as an important influence in contemporary American short fiction. His stories, often set in blue-collar communities of the Pacific Northwest, portray characters on the edge of bankruptcy, both emotionally and financially, and are distinguished by an unadorned, controlled style. While Carver is frequently aligned with minimalist writers, a classification largely based on the truncated prose and elliptical delineation of characters and events in his collection *What We Talk about When We Talk about Love,* many of his short stories in such later collections as *Cathedral* and *Where I'm Calling From: New and Selected Stories* are praised for their expansive treatment of character and the detailed realism of their depictions of everyday life.

Carver was born in northwestern Oregon and later moved with his family to Washington state, where his father worked in a sawmill. Married in 1957 and the father of two children before he reached the age of twenty, Carver worked sundry menial jobs and frequently moved with his wife and children between small towns in the Pacific Northwest. In 1958 Carver located in Paradise, California, where he attended Chico State College while working at night. The following year he began studying creative writing under John Gardner, who was then unknown as a novelist and who taught Carver the importance of craft and integrity in writing. At Chico State Carver founded the literary magazine *Selection,* in which he published his first short story, "The Furious Seasons," a Faulknerian tale written in a stream-of-consciousness style unlike any of his subsequent writings. In 1960 Carver moved to Arcata, California, and began attending classes at Humboldt State College, where he published stories in the school literary magazine, *Toyon.* He received his bachelor's degree in 1963 and later that year accepted a grant to study at the University of Iowa Writer's Workshop; Carver, however, wrote very little there and failed to complete the graduate program. He returned to California, working at various jobs and publishing only one story between 1965 and 1970, "Will You Please Be Quiet, Please?," which was selected for Martha Foley's *Best American Short Stories* in 1967. That same year Carver secured a white-collar job at a textbook publishing company, a position from which he was fired in 1970 after a company reorganization. Unemployment proved beneficial to Carver as he subsequently received income through severance pay and unemployment benefits, and was afforded sufficient time to write. In 1976 Carver published his first collection of short stories, *Will You Please Be Quiet, Please?,* which was nominated for a National Book Award.

Despite Carver's growing popular and critical success in the 1970s, his personal life was in turmoil due to his alcoholism and marital difficulties. In 1977 Carver stopped drinking and the same year met poet and short story writer Tess Gallagher, with whom he began living after separating from his wife and who significantly influenced his later writings. During the late 1970s and throughout the 1980s Carver revised earlier stories and wrote new pieces for such collections as *What We Talk about When We Talk about Love* and *Cathedral.* He received several awards and grants, including the prestigious Mildred and Harold Strauss Living award in 1983, which stipulated that he write full-time and give up his teaching post at Syracuse University in order to earn a tax-exempt salary for five years. In 1987 Carver was diagnosed with lung cancer. During his last year he continued writing and published the collection *Where I'm Calling From.* He died in 1988.

Carver's first short story collection, *Will You Please Be Quiet, Please?,* conspicuously displays an affinity with the works of American realist writer Ernest Hemingway in its terse, economical prose style. The majority of stories in this volume depict jobless, melancholy protagonists whose unremarkable lives reflect emptiness and despair. Short stories in his next collection, *Furious Seasons,* again portray ordinary, often unhappily married characters and convey a sense of unease. Like Hemingway, Carver created tension in his short stories through omission and understatement, thereby forcing conclusions about a story's meaning upon the reader. Critics observe that abrupt endings of such stories as "Neighbors"—the protagonists cling to one another in the hallway of their apartment in unspoken terror—leave the reader wondering what will happen next. Ann Beattie commented on the tableau effect of the ending of a Carver story, stating that "his language freezes moments in time with a clarity and complexity that allows us all the advantages his doomed characters are denied." Many critics have noted the often grim nature of Carver's stories, observing that the characters have no control over the circumstances of their lives and that they are subject to random, unsettling losses, as in the Kafkaesque story "The Father," which exemplifies the fear of losing one's identity. "Will You Please Be Quiet, Please?" is uncharacteristic of Carver's early stories in its expression of hope and the sense that the protagonist has reached a new understanding of his life.

Perhaps Carver's best-known work is *What We Talk about When We Talk about Love.* The stories of this collection, which reach extremes of stark understatement, have been denoted minimalist masterpieces by some critics and laconic, empty failures by others. Such works as "So Much Water So Close to Home" and "Everything Stuck to Him" (previously titled "Distance") are revised versions of earlier works that Carver pared down even further than he had the originals. Shortly before *What We Talk About* was published, Carver expressed his literary stance in his essay "A Storyteller's Shoptalk" (later published as "On Writing"): "Get in, get out. Don't linger. Go on." While "in" the story, Carver chose exact details to amplify the underlying terror of seemingly banal events. Dominant "obsessions" (Carver preferred this term to that of theme) in *What We Talk About* are the feelings of dislocation and lost identity that his characters experience as well as an awareness of random, uncontrollable changes in their lives. He expressed these concerns by depicting his characters as isolated from others and mirrored this alienated sense of being through minimal language, evoking his characters' inability to communicate their circumstances. Alain-Arias Misson noted: "The magic of Carver's stories is not *in* the language but *around* it: in the brooding sense of the unsayable." Carver's colloquial dialogue, replete with mundane observations that are suggestive of unsatisfied emotions and desires, often controls the story while other narrative elements, such as description, setting, and characterization are minimal.

Carver deeply admired the works of Anton Chekhov and throughout his career adhered to the Russian short story writer's standards of stylistically controlled narratives; yet, only in Carver's later writings did the humanist viewpoint of Chekhov become explicit. Carver noted this difference in his writing after *What We Talk About,* stating in an interview that "there was an opening open when I wrote ['Cathedral']. I knew I'd gone as far the other way as I could or wanted to go, cutting everything down to the marrow, not just to the bone." Most critics agree that *Cathedral* does exhibit much more detailed, descriptive prose than Carver's earlier fiction and denotes a change from a rather bleak vision of contemporary life to a more hopeful one. "Cathedral," which portrays an abrasive narrator who is insensitive, at times mocking, toward his wife's blind friend, contains an ending different from those of Carver's previous stories. By the story's conclusion, the narrator alters his attitude and experiences an epiphany when the two men draw a picture of a cathedral together in order for the blind man to discover what one looks like. In addition to new stories that feature characters who display personal insight and redemptive qualities, Carver revised and even rewrote earlier stories, conveying this same change. Often cited as an example is "A Small, Good Thing," a story that had appeared in *What We Talk About* under the title "The Bath." William L. Stull maintains that the original version is exemplary of the "existential realism" prevalent in the earlier volume, and that the revision portrays a "humanist realism" wherein Carver, though still narrating a tragic story, elicits more sympathy for his characters. Carver's last collection of short stories, *Where I'm Calling From,* also exhibits this new outlook. The final short story that he wrote, "Errand," chronicles the death from tuberculosis of Chekhov. A lyrical story that captures the dignity with which Chekhov faced death, "Errand" marks the height of Carver's hopeful vision.

Carver's literary career helped shape the direction of contemporary American short fiction. The stark, terse narratives of understated despair characteristic of his early works have been especially influential in reviving interest in the short story. Although some critics find his later stories sentimental, most consider that they represent a significant departure toward more insightful portraits of contemporary life and demonstrate of his continued artistic development.

(For further information on Carver's life and career, see *Contemporary Literary Criticism,* Vols. 22, 36, 53, 55; *Contemporary Authors,* Vols. 33-36, rev. ed., 126; *Contemporary Authors New Revision Series,* Vol. 17; *Dictionary of Literary Biography Yearbook: 1984; Dictionary of Literary Biography Yearbook: 1988.*)

PRINCIPAL WORKS

SHORT FICTION

Put Yourself in My Shoes 1974
Will You Please Be Quiet, Please? 1976
Furious Seasons, and Other Stories 1977
What We Talk about When We Talk about Love 1981
The Pheasant 1982
Cathedral 1983
Fires: Essays, Poems, Stories (essays, poetry, and short stories) 1983
If It Please You 1984
The Short Stories of Raymond Carver 1985
Those Days: Early Writings (short story and poetry) 1987
**Where I'm Calling From: New and Selected Stories* 1988

OTHER MAJOR WORKS

Near Klamath (poetry) 1968
Winter Insomnia (poetry) 1970

At Night the Salmon Move (poetry) 1976
Two Poems (poetry) 1982
This Water (poetry) 1985
***Where Water Comes Together with Other Water* (poetry) 1985
***Ultramarine* (poetry) 1986
A New Path to the Waterfall (poetry) 1989

*The new short stories from this volume were published in England as *Elephant, and Other Stories* in 1988.

**These works were published together in England as *In a Marine Light* in 1987.

Tom Bracken (essay date 1976)

[*In the following review, Bracken offers a favorable appraisal of* Will You Please Be Quiet, Please?]

[***Will You Please Be Quiet, Please?*** is] the first offering in a series of McGraw-Hill books in association with Gordon Lish, *Esquire*'s fiction editor—and a fine volume it is too: a riveting, marvelous read, commanding the kind of stunned silence one feels when every five or six years a Richard Yates, Joyce Carol Oates, or Gail Godwin cuts through our literature's murk, the merely trendy experiments on one hand and warmed-over "seriousness" on the other. Here suddenly is fiction that matters, a voice that matters (although the "style" is purely serviceable, a non-style, really). How is it his writing reaches out and affects us, shakes us—when there are, after all, so many good story writers with distinct voices and workmanlike methods?

One suspects that like Yates and Oates, Carver is of the people originally, both the genteel lower middle class and the *out*-of-work working class. He has a perfect ear and eye for their dialects and tics, their chain-smoking and televiewing and sex-substitute snack foods, their trashy daydreams. As in Yates and Godwin, a seemingly involuntary affection slips in under the unrelentingly tough-minded eye. An acid eye.

In a wide and mostly successful range of experiments with form, the twenty-two stories in this collection present a world of swing-shift honchos, salesmen, school teachers, grad school bar flies, who have broken whatever covenant their culture ever had with meaningful love and work; their wry, dreamy lives punched back and forth between outworn love and work ethics. With the exception of the deservedly well-known **"Will You Please Be Quiet, Please?"**—a most head-on, brutal, and loving marital infidelity story—there is little redemption or transcendence in the lives in this book. Unlike preceding generations of workers who sought oblivion from it all in the Protestant work ethic, these people, like the subjects in Studs Terkel's *Working,* know-without-knowing that the hour is late and, so, find their opiates as catch can. Most often, the location is our last utopia, the Pacific Northwest. Dad has been laid off at the aircraft factory. It's three a.m. and the sound on the TV is turned down, the screen pattern rolling. Who can sleep? And where's Mom? Out whoring, probably—and hating it; that, or she's sitting at the window wishing she were. For amusement, one stares under the coffee table at the cat licking and devouring a mouse. "It's just nature," someone mutters.

Because the "nature"—human and otherwise—that lies at the heart of the abyss, to which many of these poisonously comic stories drag us, has no more salvation in it than nature has for a head hunter, Carver, God bless him, forces himself to write from the gut and the ornery heart. He succeeds in showing us locked into our taboos of sexual and class privacy, desperately lured by strangers, by the forbidden, maintaining or breaking taboos as our compulsions and inhibitions dictate, but never feeling right about ourselves. What drives Carver characters up the wall isn't intellectualized "alienation" from others (that's stale beer in the working class when you're down-and-out and the marriage has blown); it's being cut off from ourselves that's the killer. We can not grab the handle of the "nature" lying at the center of us, the fatality controlling the mechanism of our deepest appetites. As the compulsive eater says in **"Fat,"** the lead story, "There is no choice," our slobdom is predetermined by the mysteries of appetite. When the characters aren't selling out—their values, or some faint, vestigial heritage of the blood—they *lease* out, bit by bit, as does Lee Waite, the reservation Indian in **"Sixty Acres."**

Carver's sense of comic situation is as rich as Stanley Elkin's, his style as beautifully tight and spare as Jerry Bumpus'. Carver seems to be one old-line conventional social realist to gobble up the lessons of the new fictionists and experimentalists, and forge new art of it: brief stories that are homey distillations of recognizable characters and situations, the silly voyeurisms and fetishes on our own block. Never does he take recourse in the shock-value black humor tricks or supernatural gore of other compressed stories making the big sale to the commercial markets, or what remains of them. The book is a bit crowded, and—for various reasons of slightness, posturing self-imitation, lack of unity—the 6th, 7th, 13th, 18th and 19th stories would be better off yanked, especially those which introduce the heart-of-the-heart of the male carnivore then duck or sentimentalize. An odd slip for Carver; this is his home territory. But who's to carp? Story for story, ***Will You Please Be Quiet, Please?*** is one of the most startlingly alive collections in recent years. Raymond Carver is not just tough, but—for this promising and important McGraw-Hill series—a tough act to follow. (pp. 169-70)

Tom Bracken, in a review of "Will You Please Be Quiet, Please?," in fiction international, *No. 6/7, 1976, pp. 169-70.*

Ann Beattie (essay date 1978)

[*Beattie is an American short story writer and novelist. Her works, written in a flat, dispassionate style that is often compared with Carver's, frequently chronicle the disillusionment of the 1960s generation. In the following discussion of* Furious Seasons, and Other Stories, *Beat-*

tie focuses on the "doomed" nature of Carver's characters.]

The first story I read by Raymond Carver appeared in *Esquire* several years ago. It was called **"Neighbors."** It was about a couple who look after their neighbors' apartment while they are away. During the story, each enters the apartment separately. The cat they are supposed to feed is forgotten, as Bill dresses in the woman's clothes, masturbates, and snoops around. His flush-faced wife no doubt does much the same. They don't tell each other what they do, but as the time they spend in the neighbors' apartment lengthens, and as these routines are repeated, their energy begins to bond them together, re-vitalizing their own marriage. They are on the brink of something, when Arlene makes the mistake of locking the key in the apartment. No matter that they might get the superintendent to let them in—by this point in the story the reader, too, has forgotten the real and practical world; in their horror and surprise they clutch each other in the hallway: "They leaned into the door as if against a wind, and braced themselves."

Strange story. I finished it and was awed and repelled; I felt as though I had been down on my knees watching it all through a keyhole. Stylistically, Carver's short declarative sentences produce a clever effect: his matter-of-factness, his detached observation of events, gains power as the events become increasingly odd and discomfiting. Author and reader stare together as Bill and Arlene embrace. It is not the physical union they or we expected, and it is an embrace that can, at best, only allow them temporarily to withstand the gust of wind.

I was delighted when McGraw-Hill, in association with Gordon Lish, brought out Carver's first collection of stories, ***Will You Please Be Quiet, Please?*** I was delighted again when I came upon ***Furious Seasons*** recently, published by Capra Press. The new book is just as good as the first; his subject matter is at once ordinary and very odd, and his writing is excellent. Again, Carver writes about marriages—the odd binding and bonding, the unspoken things understood (or not understood) between two people. One can no more imagine a happy past for the married couples we meet than a happy future: could Bill and Arlene possibly have been smiling young people, marching down the aisle to "The Wedding March?" or consider Leo and Toni in **"What Is It?"**, another of the best stories from the first collection, who have to sell their big luxury car quickly, before it is repossessed, because they have declared bankruptcy. Toni sells not only the car, but her body as well, while Leo—who has silently known all along that this is the way it will be—paces through his house, waiting. He thinks about biting off the rim of his glass. He watches an appropriately ironic television show. And, we are told, "he understands that he is willing to be dead." Toni returns after having sex with the used-car salesman, blames Leo because they are bankrupt, and collapses in bed. The end of the story which, like the ending of **"Neighbors,"** seems almost mythic, is too perfect to paraphrase, and to quote it would spoil the story. It is as clear and as stark as a light shone in your eyes, and it causes something beyond sadness.

But let's back up a second to that sentence of Carver's: "He understands that he is willing to be dead." It's a magnificent sentence, one that stands out even amid his invariably precise and well-phrased writing. Whatever Carver's characters are "willing to be," it never happens: what they don't will (lost key, bankruptcy) is sure to undo them. Moreover, the characters are detached from themselves; their minds are separated from what actions they will (or can) take. In the title story, **"Will You Please Be Quiet, Please?"**, a man whose wife has confessed her adultery wanders through the night: "He understood that things had been done. He did not understand what things now were to be done." Understanding leaves the characters helpless, still at the mercy of the wind, or whatever is going to overcome them. Yet there they are, as real and as incomprehensible as the people who posed for Diane Arbus's camera—or who talked about their lives to Bill Owens in *Suburbia.*

Carver's characters are a pretty closed-mouthed lot. When we do hear an honest statement (Toni's "Bankrupt!") it does not seem to help, or to end anything. The characters merely state the obvious, and the obvious is no road to salvation. Time and again in ***Furious Seasons*** we feel the undertow below the waves, the steam that can't escape. In **"Distance,"** a young wife and mother insists that her husband stay at home with her and their infant daughter instead of going hunting with a friend. At first we are made to think he goes anyway—we see him drive to meet the friend—but when he gets there he announces that he's only come to say he can't go. He returns to wife and child and we find them leaning on each other like Bill and Arlene at the end of **"Neighbors,"** laughing about the husband's having spilled the breakfast his wife cooked him when he came home: "They leaned on each other and laughed about it until tears came, while outside everything froze, for a while anyway." End of story. But wait: the story is told by the young man—now an older man—to his grown daughter, in Milan. There is no mention of the wife, but we know that after the incident he tells his daughter about how the mother had other men, and he had other women. There is no mention of their being married now. The daughter "sips Strega" as she listens, as though it's just another café story. But it soon becomes apparent to the reader that there was bitterness as well as joy in those tears on that day in the past, and that when the frozen world melted, things were not changed for the better. If the daughter is uncomfortable, Carver does nothing to emphasize it, but we become more and more uncomfortable. In another story, **"The Fling,"** we see again parent and child, in a story/confession that goes a step beyond **"Distance."** Here, a father confesses to his grown son his adultery, which has resulted in his own divorce from the son's mother and in his lover's husband's suicide. Here, the emphasis is also on the son, who clearly is not humane enough to respond to his father's pain, even when the father articulates it better than the father in **"Distance."** He sends his father off (the story takes place at an airport) and prepares to return to his life, wondering what his father could expect from someone like him—a book salesman in the Midwest, separated from his own wife.

It is difficult to read Carver's stories and not be reminded of Hemingway: stoicism here is not so much a form of bravery, though, as it is resignation. It's a bad world out there, with the sun shining on bad days and winds ready to topple you. Silence seems as appropriate a response as anything else. As in Hemingway, marriage—women—has ruined the good times. Compare Nick Adams's sad realization in Hemingway's "Cross Country Snow" that there will be no more fun skiing because his wife is pregnant and he will have to return to the States with the awareness of Carver's young man in **"Distance"** that he must think of his wife and family instead of sport. Or compare Hemingway's "An Alpine Idyll," a story about a peasant who keeps his dead wife by him, using her mouth to hang a lantern from in the shed as he chops wood, until the snow melts and he can bring her to town—with Carver's **"So Much Water So Close To Home,"** in which a man goes fishing with friends, and they discover the body of a young girl, dead and drowned; they decide to anchor her body so it won't float away, and notify the police of her death only when their trip is over. In Hemingway's story the event is important and interesting in itself—it is really an anecdote—but in Carver's story there is the further complexity of the husband-wife relationship: the already disturbed wife clearly identifies with the dead girl, and what she perceives to be her husband's cold imperviousness to the girl's death epitomizes for her what is wrong with their own relationship. So too, in **"Distance,"** the discussion of how geese are loyal to one another (they are monogamous, and will never pair off again if a partner dies) becomes not just a fact both interesting and sad, but a reflection of the lack of such real, sure devotion with the young couple:

> "That's a sad fate," the girl said. "It's sadder for it to live that way, I think, alone but with all the others, than just to live off by itself somewhere."
>
> "It is sad," the boy said, "but it's a part of nature like everything else."
>
> "Have you ever killed one of those marriages?" she asked. "You know what I mean."
>
> He nodded. "Two or three times I've shot a goose . . . then . . . I'd see another one turn back from the rest and begin to circle and call over the goose that lay on the ground."
>
> "Did you shoot it too?" she asked with concern.
>
> "If I could," he answered. "Sometimes I missed."

The marriages in Carver's fiction miss, too, but this is only metaphorically the jungle: when things go wrong in the natural order of marriage, a clean shot can't end the problem. Carver's aim, though, is true: unflinchingly, he follows the characters to their doom. Sometimes it is the world itself that kills the things of the world, as when a mute's black bass that he has made into pets, feeding and communing with them, are killed when the river floods in **"Dummy."** But more often the stories are about how people mindlessly hunt things (even in **"Dummy,"** the viciousness of nature only echoes people's viciousness to the mute): the brief, horrifying description of the maimed deer in **"Pastoral"**; the discussion of how geese are shot in **"Distance."** ***Furious Seasons*** is an apt title for this collection of stories: nature is humanized, and humanity is defined in terms of nature. The title story itself is one of the finest stories in the collection. As in many of the others, the reader knows or suspects more than all but the main character is silently aware of, and as is also typical of many of Carver's stories, the last scene, perceived by a character who knows less than we do, is a strange tableau indeed; we sympathize both with the central character, and with those who watch him. Carver's most poetic writing often comes at the very end of a story—his language freezes moments in time with a clarity and complexity that allows us all the advantages his doomed characters are denied: the intellectual level of the story manifests itself concretely, so that we not only understand with our heads, but feel in our hearts.

Carver's restraint, and his measured prose, produces effects that are dazzling; nobody writes like him, and the stories in ***Furious Seasons,*** like those in the previous collection, are some of the most impressive of contemporary short fiction. The truth of them will make the reader restless and uneasy. There is a quality about them that defies paraphrase; the cumulative effect is overpowering, and the perfectly chosen words with which he ends the stories streak out like beams of light—no mean accomplishment in stories so obsessed with life's darkness. (pp. 178-82)

Ann Beattie, in a review of "Furious Seasons, and Other Stories," in Canto: Review of the Arts, *Vol. 2, No. 2, Summer, 1978, pp. 178-82.*

David Boxer and Cassandra Phillips (essay date 1979)

[*In the following excerpt, Boxer and Phillips analyze short stories in* Will You Please Be Quiet, Please?, *discussing the themes of voyeurism and dissociation.*]

After growing up in rural Oregon and Washington, Raymond Carver migrated to northern California, in the early sixties, to pursue higher education at Chico State College. There he was discovered by one of his teachers, who happened to be the writer John Gardner, himself fresh out of graduate school. Gardner knew that promising young writers need nurturing. Carver was soon using his mentor's campus office on weekends for his writing. But writing wasn't all he was doing there, as he confessed, with amusement and some chagrin, many years later: "In his office on the weekends I used to go through his manuscripts and steal titles from his stories . . . I mean take his titles, which struck me as awfully good, as I recall, and rephrase them, and put them on my own stories." When Gardner caught on to what his young protegee was up to, Carver got a scolding, and was informed that the invasion of another writer's privacy and the pilfering of his words were basic improprieties.

This incident curiously resembles one of Carver's own best stories, **"Neighbors,"** from the collection ***Will You Please Be Quiet, Please?,*** a 1977 National Book Award nominee. In the story, a young couple, Bill and Arlene Miller, are tending the plants and cat of their vacationing neighbors, Jim and Harriet Stone. The unglamorous Millers—he a bookkeeper, she a secretary—wistfully envy the "fuller and brighter life" of the peripatetic Stones. They find themselves drawn to the vacant apartment and further to the closets, cupboards and drawers of their neighbors. The different world across the hall comes to dominate the Millers' thoughts, and it ignites their sex life. Totemically, the Millers are shedding their own dull skins for the bright feathers of their neighbors.

Much as Carver himself poked through Gardner's papers, filching his teacher's titles, Bill Miller sips the Stones' Chivas Regal, nibbles at food left in the refrigerator, pockets a pill bottle from the medicine chest, and dresses himself in Harriet's as well as Jim's clothing. Carver, we may speculate, was trying on the identity of a teacher and writer whom he admired and wanted to be like. The Millers' experiment is similar, if more insidious.

This connection between life and art seems more than coincidental; through many of the stories of Raymond Carver is woven a double strand of voyeurism and dissociation. The term "voyeurism" is used advisedly here, to mean not just sexual spying, but the wistful identification with some distant, unattainable idea of self. Dissociation is a sense of disengagement from one's own identity and life, a state of standing apart from whatever defines the self, or of being unselfed. As his dissociated characters tentatively reach out toward otherness, Carver ambushes them, giving them sudden, hideously clear visions of the emptiness of their lives; even the most familiar takes on the sharp definition of the strangely unfamiliar. They become voyeurs, then, of their own experience.

While it can't be said that each of the twenty-two stories in ***Will You Please Be Quiet, Please?*** (the very title suggests a backing off from involvement) incorporates voyeurism and dissociation, most contain elements of one, the other or both. Further, these ideas suggest a way of looking at Carver the artist, whose unique voice embodies the very cadences of anomie. His characters are the unemployed and the unhappily employed, laconic members of the non-upwardly mobile working and middle classes. Their marriages are without intimacy, their needs unexpressed, unrealized or sublimated into vague dreams of change for the better. They are the folks next door, familiar representatives of "the real America." Typically, Carver writes about characters whose lives are in suspended animation, verging on disarray: the salesman between jobs, the writer between stories, the student between semesters, the husband or wife between marriages, and the insomniac, caught between waking consciousness and the escape of sleep. Carver's chosen task is to convey through the most fitting language and symbols the special moments when these people have sudden, astonishing glimpses behind the curtain which separates their empty lives from chaos.

We see these dynamics at work in **"Neighbors,"** whose ominous subtext is, at first, hidden behind Carver's ironic, deadpan style. There are, in fact, early clues that the Millers' idyll across the hall is leading them to a confrontation with unacknowledged regions of their own selves. On Bill Miller's first trip to the apartment, he not only feeds Kitty and waters the plants, but he lingers, strolling absently from room to room. In the bathroom, he swipes the bottle of pills and "looked at himself in the mirror and then closed his eyes and then looked again" as if taking his bearings. By the third day of the Stones' absence, Bill, ostensibly sick, has stayed home from work. Before long, he skulks back into the neighbors' world, making a leisurely survey of their belongings and finally settling himself on their bed.

> He tried to remember when the Stones were due back, and then he wondered if they would ever return. He could not remember their faces or the way they talked and dressed.

Again the mirror serves as a reference point as Bill tries on several of both Stones' outfits, including Harriet's black and white check skirt and burgundy blouse.

Arlene is similarly mesmerized by the apartment, returning from one unaccounted for hour there "with lint clinging to the back of her sweater, and the color . . . high in her cheeks." She's forgotten to feed Kitty or water the plants, but she has found "some pictures." "Maybe they won't come back," she says, echoing the thought of her husband. But when they excitedly return together to the apartment, Arlene realizes that she's left the Stones' key inside. The door is locked. Carver ends the story on a forbidding note: "They stayed there. They held each other. They leaned into the door as if against a wind, and braced themselves". Surely, it is an ill wind, despite the couple's touching moment of closeness. Carver's characteristic short stabs of language convey panic, and the sort of detail of action that might be reported by an eyewitness.

"Neighbors," then, is about two rather hollow and thoroughly "average" people who encounter something in themselves they don't quite understand. They cast away from the terra firma of their mousy existence without charting a destination. The old life on one side of the hall seems more dissatisfying than ever, but the new life is on the other side of a locked door. In limbo, dissociated from both lives, the Millers have only each other. Carver has already shown us how very tenuous that link is. Arlene and Bill are a couple who exchange few words during dinner, and who watch TV after dinner. If they rarely disagree, it is more a matter of emotional anemia than connubial concord. When Bill returns from one of his forays into the Stones' apartment, he can't tell Arlene what he's been up to:

> "What kept you?" Arlene said. She sat with her legs turned under her, watching television.
>
> "Nothing. Playing with Kitty," he said, and went over to her and touched her breasts.
>
> "Let's go to bed, honey," he said.

The Millers' sex life catches fire, but only because of the fantasies they project for themselves in the apartment across the hall.

It is hardly gratuitous that Carver places a great number of his characters before mirrors and windows. Mirrors, we know, have the disconcerting capacity of making one a stranger to oneself. Bill Miller looks in the bathroom mirror in the Stones' apartment and sees only his own reflection there. He closes his eyes and opens them. Again, it is himself. But who is that? Wearing the Stones' clothes,

Bill again seeks some kind of confirmation from the mirror, though Carver never tells us exactly what he sees. The symbol of the mirror is used similarly in the title story, **"Will You Please Be Quiet, Please?".** Ralph Wyman, who has just learned of his wife's infidelity two years before, attempts to escape the revelation on an odyssey through the seediest part of town. Drunk, he sees his face in a bar restroom mirror and touches it. Later, when he's returned home, he locks himself in the bathroom and makes faces in the mirror.

If the mirror is an emblem of Carverian dissociation, the window, appropriately, is a complementary symbol of voyeurism. Dressed in one of Harriet Stones' outfits, Bill Miller drifts to the living room window, pulls the curtain aside and peers out "for a long time." In doing so, he's looking at the world as a different person, Harriet Stone, might.

In one of Carver's wittiest stories, **"The Idea,"** the voyeur motif is carried to an extreme. The first person narrator, a fiendishly prudish woman, sits in vigil each night by her kitchen window, waiting for the neighbors to enact their ritualized sexual fantasy.

> Then I saw him. He opened the screen and walked out onto his back porch wearing a T-shirt and something like Bermuda shorts or a swimsuit. He looked around once and hopped off the porch into the shadows and began to move along the side of the house. . . . He stopped in front of the lighted [bedroom] window and looked in.

He is, of course, playing the peeping Tom as his wife ("the trash!") seductively takes off her clothes within. The vehemence of the narrator's righteous indignation—and her devotion to the spectacle—is Carver's wry comment on the close kinship of puritanism and prurience. The narrator allows that she and her husband, Vern, "get jumpy" after watching the libidinous couple, but so desiccated is their own sex life that the "appetite" of the evening becomes one for food, great quantities of it. Vern's interest in the neighbors is more wholesome: "Maybe he *has* something there. . . . You don't know," he ventures, to his wife's chagrin. The narrator gets her comeuppance at the end of the story in the form of an infestation of ants. In her febrile mind, the ants become the immoral equivalent of the couple next door. Even after dispatching the modest column she had seen near the garbage can, she can't stop thinking about the little creatures: "Pretty soon I imagined them all over the house." As the images of the neighbors at their sexual play and the ants—"a steady stream of them, up one side of the can and down the other, coming and going"—fuse in her mind, she unwittingly reenacts the scene next door, exposing her own nastiness:

> I turned on every light in the house until I had the house blazing.
>
> I kept spraying.
>
> Finally I raised the shade in the kitchen and looked out. . . .
>
> "That trash," I said. "The idea!"
>
> I used even worse language, things I can't repeat.

(pp. 75-8)

The relationship between voyeurism and literature—the reading as well as writing of it—has yet to be fully explored. In the absence of a larger framework, we've found it useful to think of the voyeur as a thief, who possesses what he observes. Looking itself becomes experience, not merely vicarious experience. It is a transforming act, one which changes the character of that which is seen. This notion is operative, in different ways, both for the reader, whose understanding of the text is tied to his own way of perceiving, and for the writer, who takes his observations and shapes them as he wills. (p. 79)

In Carver's works, the gulf between the seer and the seen—that is, between writer and subject—is very small indeed. His voice barely impinges upon the story being told, unlike the way a Barthelme's or Pynchon's might. Carver stays as close to the simple truth of his observations as a writer possibly can. He seems to have appropriated what he's writing about and to have kept the stolen thing closely intact out of fascination or respect. And so, as we read his stories, we feel we're accomplices in this faintly stealthy act of appropriation. Like the writer, we're voyeurs, peering into the distrubed lives of these unsuspecting characters. This is what is unique about Carver, his thorough but subtle manipulation of the metaphor of the voyeur at every level of his writing.

The voyeuristic quality of Carver's style comes through brilliantly in the story, **"What's in Alaska?".** Carl and Mary are visiting their neighbors, Jack and Helen, for an evening of pot smoking from Jack's new water pipe. Earlier we've learned that Mary has been offered a job in Alaska, a place Carl admits he's "always wanted to go to." But Carl's sense of well-being has been shaken by Mary's criticism of his new "soft beige-colored shoes that made his feet feel free and springy." Moreover, Carl has "watched" his wife embracing Jack in the kitchen. Let's examine a typical stretch of dialogue from this story:

> "What did you read?" Jack said.
>
> "What?" Helen said.
>
> "You said you read something in the paper," Jack said.
>
> Helen laughed. "I was just thinking about Alaska, and I remembered them finding a prehistoric man in a block of ice. Something reminded me."
>
> "That wasn't in Alaska," Jack said.
>
> "Maybe it wasn't, but it reminded me of it," Helen said.
>
> "What *about* Alaska, you guys?" Jack said.
>
> "There's nothing in Alaska," Carl said.
>
> "He's on a bummer," Mary said.
>
> "What'll you guys *do* in Alaska?" Jack said.
>
> "There's nothing to do in Alaska," Carl said. He put his feet under the coffee table. Then he

Room Service

Anton Chekov's sister, Maria, born in 1863, three years younger than the writer, visited him in a Moscow clinic during the last days of March 1897. The hospitalization—it was the first such treatment for the tuberculosis that would kill him in 1904 at the age of 44—followed a hemorrhage that occured the evening of March 21st in the dining room of the Hermitage, Moscow's most fashionable restaurant. (Chekov, who was not wealthy by any reckoning, and never ostentatious, nevertheless owned two houses by this time and was building a third at Yalta.) He had gone to dinner at the invitation of his friend and confidant, Alexei Suvorin, an immensely rich newspaper and magasine publisher, a reactionary, a self-made man whose father had fought at Borodino as a private and who, like Chekov, was the grandson of a serf.

Chekov, meticulously dressed as usual, his usual pince-nez in evidence, had just been seated at the table and was doing something with his napkin when blood began gushing out of his mouth. Suvorin and two waiters helped him to the gentlemens' room and tried, unsuccessfully, to stanch the flow of blood with ice packs. Chekov was agonizingly embarrassed about what had happened. Later, back at his hotel, he persisted in denying the gravity of the situation. "He laughed and jested as usual,"

Carver took meticulous care revising his works, writing numerous drafts for his short stories. Above are two early versions of his O. Henry Prize-winning story "Errand."

moved them out under the light once more. "Who wants a new pair of shoes?" Carl said.

"What's that noise?" Helen said.

They listened. Something scratched at the door.

"It sounds like Cindy," Jack said. "I'd better let her in."

"While you're up, get me a Popsicle," Helen said. She put her head back and laughed.

"I'll have another one too, honey," Mary said. "What did I say? I mean *Jack,*" Mary said. "Excuse me. I thought I was talking to Carl."

"Popsicles all around," Jack said. "You want a Popsicle, Carl?"

"What?"

"You want an orange Popsicle?"

"An orange one," Carl said.

"Four Popsicles coming up," Jack said.

There's a transcribed quality to this conversation (which in its entirety is twelve pages long), as if Carver had been sitting in the corner noting down each comment, pause and peal of laughter. He has it down exactly, the directionless quality, the silliness, the halting rhythm of talk among people under the influence of marijuana. But there's more to this conversation than a technical prowess which conveys the illusion of eavesdropping. What seems to be casual talk, virtually empty of "communication," is really very deliberately and finely wrought. The typical out-of-synch effect of marijuana operates on a metaphorical level with Carl's own existential out-of-synch feelings. By tuning in obliquely to Carl's sullenness and the "bummer" he's on, by including the business about his shoes and the comments on Alaska and Mary's slip of the tongue (and embarrassed explanation), the conversation resonates with the meaning of the story itself. Carl, for instance, like the prehistoric man in Helen's newspaper story, is in a kind of emotional "block of ice." Even the seemingly innocuous episode of the Popsicles is endowed with meaning when the cat drags in a dead mouse and proceeds to lick it slowly "from head to tail" under the coffee table. The evening is bound to be a bummer for all. This is realistic writing of a different sort—a probe stuck beneath the skin of dissociation itself. Passivity is the strength of this language; little seems to be said, yet much is conveyed. If Carver's eye is that of the voyeur, his voice is that of dissociation.

At its most distinctive, Carver's language is unadorned, and, except for occasional bolts of metaphor, as laconic and unmannered as the outward lives of his characters. He flattens his prose to mirror the flatness of his characters' lives. The words in the stories are by and large those of the characters, we think, until we look a little closer: humor, irony and glimmers of the absurd affirm the writer's authority. Carver has perfected a style precisely calibrated with the emotional movement, or stasis, as the case may be, of his singularly ordinary characters. Nor, with few exceptions, does he choose to interpret the thoughts or actions of his subjects. The colloquial language, the first-person persona pieces, the dialogue's recorded quality, all suggest that the writer consciously has slipped into the lives of his characters and caught them at unguarded moments. Carver is the writer as voyeur, a chronicler of overheard conversations and secretly witnessed actions.

Thus it is that compared to the more "mannered" writers of the sixties and seventies—Barth, Pynchon, Barthelme, for example—Carver's style seems ingenuously simple, almost photo-realistic. Even the prose of Grace Paley and Leonard Michaels, both considered exemplars of lean, taut language, seems positively lush, almost Baroque in resonances and allusiveness, when held up to that of Carver. The temptation is to classify Carver as a throwback to an earlier era, say, of Anderson, Lardner and Hemingway. Although he derives from and to some extent reminds us of these earlier writers, there's a crucial difference. The sensibility here is clearly post-modern: beyond the flat quality of the Hemingway hero struggling to preserve an identity in the drear vastness of the wasteland, beyond the psychological frameworks of Anderson's stories, beyond the comic satire of Lardner. Carver's simple language is a disguise, as is Harold Pinter's, for the emotional violence lurking beneath neutral surfaces.

That Carver is designing in his use of images of voyeurism and dissociation is supremely evident in the story **"Put Yourself in My Shoes."** Here the central character, who is both voyeuristic and disengaged, is a writer. The very title suggests the writer's dilemma: how can someone literally see something from another's point of view; how does the writer convey that the trick has been done?

Myers has quit his job with a textbook publishing firm (Carver once worked for one) to write full-time. "He was between stories and he felt despicable." As Myers drives to meet his wife Paula at a bar in town,

> he looked at the people who hurried along the sidewalks, with shopping bags. He glanced at the gray sky, filled with flakes, and at the tall buildings with snow in the crevices and on the window ledges. He tried to see everything, save it for later.

This passage is reminiscent of one in **"Neighbors,"** describing the intensity with which Bill Miller peruses objects in the Stones' apartment:

> He looked out the window, and then he moved slowly through each room, considering everything that fell under his gaze, carefully, one object at a time. He saw ashtrays, items of furniture, kitchen utensils, the clock. He saw everything.

Although it's the Christmas season, Myers isn't part of the holiday bustle. Like his spiritual neighbor, Bill Miller, he's an observer, detached but curious; in short, another voyeur. (Unlike Miller, however, his detachment serves him creatively in his business as a writer.)

At the bar, Paula proposes they drop in on the Morgans, from whom they sublet a house the previous year, and whom they've never met. The Morgans are a stuffy, voluble academic couple. Myers, in contrast, is one of Carver's laconic sorts, and it's the diplomatic Paula who explains to the interested Morgans that her husband is a writer. When Edgar Morgan takes it upon himself to tell Myers stories which the writer "should be able to use," we begin to be aware of the multi-level irony on which this wry story is hinged. Not only is Myers coolly observing the Morgans, much in the way he made mental notes on the street scene, but Carver himself is meanwhile fashioning a story about a writer in the field. **"Put Yourself in My Shoes"** takes on the character of an aesthetic statement, one which puts forth the necessity of the writer's detachment, voyeurism, even cynicism.

It soon becomes clear that the Morgans' stories, intended to stimulate the writer, are merely amusing him to the point of rudeness. Inevitably, the Morgans leap on their former tenants, cataloguing with relish the Myers' transgressions during their tenancy. As the Myerses move toward the door, Morgan chuckles, tellingly accusing them of appropriating his two-volume set of *Jazz at the Philharmonic.* "I'd like this *writer* to tell me exactly what he knows of their whereabouts, Mr. Myers?" Morgan should be accusing Myers of taking with him something less concrete, but more valuable—the Morgans themselves. Isn't this, after all, the bread and butter of the writer, this cool treachery? Once safely in the car, Paula is eager to discuss the disastrous evening. But Myers remains detached: "He did not answer. Her voice seemed to come to him from a great distance . . . He was silent and watched the road." The final line of the story—as Carver's are wont—signifies much: "He was at the very end of a story." At the end, Carver and Myers merge.

If Carver the artist has cast himself in the role of the voyeur, he's played, as we've suggested earlier, an even more subtle trick on the reader. With all but the window pane removed, the reader too becomes a voyeur, a peeping Tom comfortably out of danger of getting caught. (Isn't this one of the appeals of all fiction?) But Carver has laid a trap for us too, for, along with the characters, we may experience the benignly familiar suddenly becoming strange and even frightening. In the title story, the pattern on a table cloth, a woman tossing her hair, and a man about to play a song on a jukebox suddenly loom as terrifying. An out-of-work salesman in **"They're Not Your Husband"** overhears two men making lewd remarks about his wife's expansive bottom, which then becomes his obsession and his undoing. In **"Are You a Doctor?"** a wrong number touches off a chain of events which threatens to undermine the complacency of a faithful, middle-aged husband. The effect is somewhat similar to that of reading Kafka. But what Kafka projects through the lens of a nightmarish reality, Carver, at his most distinctive, forces us to see through the most conventional and habitual experiences of everyday life. It is the familiar, the seemingly "known," which is the true mask of the terrifying.

Nowhere is this message more explicit than in **"The Father,"** a two-page story which could be read as Carver's homage to Kafka. A family, consisting of grandmother, mother, and three little girls, clusters around a crib watching and playing with the new baby, a boy. The father, meanwhile, sits in the kitchen, his back to them, in the aloof style of a man bored with women-talk. The five females are debating who the baby resembles in the fatuous way that such things are discussed. One of the girls declares, "*I* know! *I* know! . . . He looks like *Daddy!*" But if the baby looks like Daddy, asks another, then who does Daddy look like? The answer, terrifying to the children, is "Daddy doesn't look like *anybody!*" At this point, all turn to look at the father sitting in the kitchen. His reaction, described in the last sentence, reveals that even daddies hover close to the existential abyss: "He had turned around in his chair and his face was white and without expression." His is the face of fear; it is drained of expression and identity. The comfortable fellow known as Daddy has been erased. The story is mannered; we can't help but think of Kafka and other writers of the real unreal. But Carver also tells us something about his own obsession with the theme of dissociation, disconnection from the familiar in the most common surroundings. And if this story doesn't make that theme new for us in the way it is made new in Carver's more representative stories, it at least points a way to an understanding of precisely why we feel the ground shift beneath us in reading Carver.

In the more representative—i.e., less consciously stylized—stories, Carver is even more unsettling with his dissection of the mundane. Like most of us, his characters aren't heroes. They don't teach us how to behave nobly or honorably or even intelligently in moments of crisis. Like the voyeurs they are or resemble, Carver's characters shy away from dramatic confrontation, they avoid existential tests of character. These people are completely removed from Mailer's or Hemingway's preoccupation with masculine assertion. Although there are showdowns in these stories, no one really wants them to occur. Betraying wives are threatened with bodily harm, but rarely do their husbands actually make good on their threats. (An exception to this occurs in the title story, but even that scene, a flashback, becomes the prelude to erotic reconciliation.) In **"Bicycles, Muscles, Cigarets,"** where Carver waxes uncharacteristically sentimental, Evan Hamilton has a brief wrestling match with another neighborhood father who challenges his son's honesty. But even as fists begin to fly, Hamilton "couldn't believe it was happening." Leo, the deceived husband in **"What Is It?"** waits up all night for his errant wife, but backs off when she invites him to slug her. He's content, finally, to undress her as she sleeps and roll her, naked, under the covers. We see another example of capitulation in the climax of **"Sixty Acres,"** in which the main character, Lee Waite, confronts two smug boys who have been poaching ducks on his land, an inheritance from his Indian father. He puts the boys off the land, but does nothing more, and feels about his actions that "something crucial had happened, a failure." Carver's third-person narrator comments: "But nothing had happened."

Nothing happens because in the main Carver's dissociated characters prefer it that way. Living in a world of unarticulated longing, a world verging on silence, they may even, like the couples in **"Neighbors"** and **"Will You Please Be Quiet, Please?"**, consider themselves "happy." But such happiness is fragile, Carver tells us. Something or someone always happens along to disturb the uneasy equilibrium, forcing a sudden confrontation with a hidden or suppressed part of the self. The disturbance itself acts as a trigger to larger revelations of self-alienation.

In the story **"Are You a Doctor?"**, for instance, Clara Holt, a divorcee with a sick child, accidentally dials the unlisted number of Arnold Breit, a middle-aged man who is not a doctor. At first Arnold resists the temptation to become involved with the tenacious Clara and only reluctantly surrenders his name over the phone. But the temptation to dress himself in an alien persona triumphs over middle-aged inertia. Arnold accepts Clara's invitation to her apartment, a model of suburban-village tackiness, but finds neither the woman nor the setting romantic. After a fumbled embrace, Arnold retreats to the familiarity of his own apartment and life. But something has changed. At Clara Holt's instigation, Arnold has entered into a kind of voyeur's fantasy life, adopted a new, strange and exciting identity (Carver's narrator, of course, reveals how much at variance the fantasy is from the reality). The change is conveyed cunningly at the end of the story. The phone rings and Arnold, believing it may be Clara calling again, his heart pounding with anticipation, picks it up: " 'Arnold. Arnold Breit speaking,' he said." The use of his name here signifies much, for when Arnold answers the phone at the beginning of the story, he is expecting the caller to be his wife and automatically responds, " 'Hello, dear.' " This time it *is* his wife calling. She's surprised, as well she might be:

> "Arnold? My, aren't we formal tonight!" his wife said, her voice strong, teasing.
>
> "I've been calling since nine. Out living it up, Arnold?"
>
> He remained silent and considered her voice.
>
> "Are you there, Arnold?" she said. "You don't sound like yourself."

Arnold's brief but strange encounter with Clara Holt has been transforming. The "new" Arnold finds he has nothing to say to his wife, whose voice he "considers" as if it were curiously alien. In turn, Arnold no longer sounds like himself. Receiver in hand, he's vouchsafed a different vision of himself. The "awakening" is ironic, of course.

It is in moments like the conclusion of **"Are You a Doctor?"** that Carver's characters realize, with varying degrees of understanding, their aloneness, their dissociation even from their families. And it's appropriate that many of these "awakenings" occur in bed, during bouts of insomnia when the spouse lies soundly asleep, unknowing. Where there should be greatest intimacy, there is, instead, a dark and final sense of isolation.

"What's in Alaska?", for example, ends with a scene in which Mary has fallen asleep, leaving Carl awake with his new doubts. These uncertainties are made manifest in a Jamesian fashion, with Carl looking into the dark hallway and seeing, he thinks, "a pair of small eyes" (which reminds us of the neighbors' cat who so blissfully licked the mouse like a Popsicle). **"The Ducks,"** a story about a vaguely discontented working class couple, has a strikingly similar ending. After a half-hearted attempt at lovemaking, "she" falls asleep and "he" remains fitfully awake. He wanders to a window—it's raining outside—and back to bed, where he tries to awaken his wife. The final lines of the story are: " 'Wake up,' he whispered. 'I hear something outside'." Though less forbidding, the "something" bears a close resemblance to Carl's two little eyes in the dark hallway. In **"The Student's Wife,"** Nan spends a sleepless night crying, praying, pacing and reading magazines, as her husband, the student, snores in the bedroom. The existential terror of the night culminates, ironically, with the breaking dawn:

> She had seen few sunrises in her life and those when she was little. She knew that none of them had been like this. Not in pictures she had seen nor in any book she had read had she learned a sunrise was so terrible as this.

(pp. 79-85)

After first reading Carver, one familiar with both authors is likely to be struck by the resemblances in subject matter and style between Carver and Grace Paley. Like Carver, Paley is a writer who's interested in unassuming, ordinary people. Although not her most typical story, Paley's "The Burdened Man" seems a tale that Carver would have relished telling in his own inimitable fashion. Both writers experiment with persona pieces, though the kinds of self-revealing language they use to portray their first-person narrators are necessarily different: her people are mostly New Yorkers and his the less insouciant dwellers of the Western suburbs and countryside. They also share a particularly contemporary fondness for the darker shades of humor and irony, and a more traditional delight in common language and idiom. They share an important thematic goal too: to give voice to the feelings and desires, expressed and unexpressed, of those who, for one reason or another, cannot tell their own stories.

But a re-reading of both Paley and Carver reveals one crucial difference. Carver, like many of his post-modern contemporaries—Harold Pinter and Leonard Michaels, for example—writes at once comically and bleakly. Most of his stories have static or unhappy endings. (There are exceptions, like the title story, still to be discussed.) Paley, on the other hand, refuses to allow the bleakness of the modern condition to eclipse life's often ironic but nevertheless real joys and delights. Her characters have ingenuity; they are creative, capable of transforming adversity into another victory for love, friendship, family. They experience pain, frustration, and anger, but they rise from the depths to win out over the alienating elements of urban life. And they seem to have one quality that Carver's people almost uniformly lack—the courage to be themselves.

Carver's characters, on the bottom, often (not always) sink lower. In **"Collectors,"** one of Carver's strangest and most compelling stories, a man—the narrator—is shown at the lowest ebb of his life. He has no job, no family, no interests in anything but is waiting for a letter from "up north" about a job. "I lay on the sofa and listened to the rain. Now and then I'd lift up and look through the curtain for the mailman." Like Carver's other window images, this one suggests a kind of lonely voyeurism. Into this state of suspended animation pops a very pushy and talkative vacuum cleaner salesman who "collects" from the narrator his remaining dregs of self, much as the miraculous vacuum cleaner the salesman demonstrates "collects" the "bits and pieces" of a person's body:

> "You'll be surprised to see what can collect in a mattress over the months, over the years. Every day, every night of our lives, we're leaving little bits of ourselves, flakes of this and that, behind. Where do they go, these bits and pieces of ourselves? Right through the sheets and into the mattresses, *that's* where! Pillows, too. It's all the same."

At the end, the salesman also pockets ("collects") a letter, dropped through the mail slot, which may or may not be addressed to the narrator, an act the narrator is helpless to prevent.

The vacuum cleaner salesman introduces himself as Aubrey Bell, a name suggesting the kind of noisy intrusiveness Carver's laconic characters desperately avoid. Not only does Bell poke his machine into the corners and crevices of the narrator's rooms, but he continually challenges the narrator to give his name. The narrator, unlike Arnold Breit, refuses to surrender this last vestige of self to the curious salesman, who may be making off with it anyway at the end. Although none quite as strange as the vacuum cleaner salesman, there are many other Bell-like characters in Carver's stories. Clara Holt, for instance, brings the ringing of the telephone and subsequently much greater "noise" into Arnold Breit's life. In many stories, it's the sound of the wife's voice that ripples the quiet surface of the marriage. In **"What's in Alaska?"**, Mary starts Carl on his "bummer" first by criticizing his new shoes, then by telling him that he's "on a bummer tonight." Carl's reply is one that speaks for all of Carver's fragmented egos: "All I'm saying is I don't know why you said that. If I wasn't on a bummer before you said it, it's enough when you say it to put me on one."

Carl's complaint also reminds us of the title and title story of Carver's collection, **"Will You Please Be Quiet, Please?"** This title, as suggested earlier, indicates a desire for detachment, and the sort of clenched politeness that masks the impulse to shout, "Shut up!" In the midst of pressuring his wife, Marian, to tell the full tale of her infidelity, Ralph Wyman feels the temptation to withdraw from revelation, to "leave it at that." He has a womb-like vision of such a withdrawal: "He thought fleetingly that he would be someplace else tonight doing something else, that it would be silent somewhere if he had not married." Ralph finally leaves the house and goes to skid row in an unsuccessful attempt to escape the noise of his wife's confession. When he returns home at dawn, he locks himself in the bathroom. Marian rattles the door knob and begs to be let in. Ralph pleads in return, "Will you please be quiet, please?"

The title story is Carver's longest and most complex. It's placed last in the collection. It's also one of only three or four stories which end other than bleakly. Carver seems to endow his more complex, introspective "heroes,"

Ralph Wyman in this story, Al in **"Jerry and Molly and Sam"** (a serio-comic piece worthy of more comment than this reference in passing), with at least the possibility of brighter futures. After a night of hellish revelation, in which Ralph confirms the suspicions he's long held of his wife's unfaithfulness, he returns to the marital bed. It's a different kind of bedroom scene from those discussed earlier. Marian soothes away the pain of Ralph's self-revelation. And he responds in kind, not by forgiving her, for it isn't Ralph's place to forgive. Rather, he discovers an ability to grow and change, and the strength to discard the cherished but unrealistic vision of Marian and himself, and to accept his own as well as Marian's sensual nature. Much of this is conveyed in the imagistic description, at the end of the story, of release and sensual movement:

> He tensed at her fingers, and then he let go a little. Her hand moved over his hip and over his stomach and she was pressing her body over his now and moving over him and back and forth over him. He held himself, he later considered, as long as he could. And then he turned to her. He turned and turned in what might have been a stupendous sleep, and he was still turning, marveling at the impossible changes he felt moving over him.

This story is a different sort of fish, more writerly than most of Carver's, and richer in background information and authorial guidance. At the same time, we find here a sort of confluence of Carverian themes and images: the theme of marital crisis (which over half the twenty-two stories in the collection involve), the encounter with the dissociated self, and the kind of alienation that makes of one an observer. There are also marvelous scenes, including the one of the locked bathroom, in which Carver brings his distinctively plain style (and voyeur's intensity) to a story in the tradition of Cheever and Updike.

This is also, it seems, a very Jamesian story. Ralph Wyman is Carver's most introspective character. From college days he has pursued self-knowledge, and at one turn in the road had the feeling he was "on the brink of some kind of huge discovery about himself," a discovery which "never came." This is the period of "lowest ebb" for Ralph, when he becomes the fraternity drunk and acquires the sobriquet, "Jackson," after the name of the bartender at a college hangout. But Ralph gives up his dissolute ways, decides to become a teacher, joins in college activities and politics, and marries Marian Ross, "a handsomely pale and slender girl who took a seat beside him in a Chaucer class."

Ralph is deceived. He has paved over, not rid himself of "Jackson," the Dionysian side of him which continues to haunt his conscious mind. Carver, from the beginning, shows us the naivete of Ralph's pursuit of innocence and simplicity. On his honeymoon in Mexico, Ralph had been "secretly appalled by the squalor and open lust he saw and was anxious to return to the safety of California." But on the honeymoon Ralph has an even more disturbing "vision," one which "had nothing to do with Mexico." It is, significantly, a voyeur's vision of his wife, Marian,

> . . . leaning motionless on her arms over the ironwork balustrade of their rented *casita* as Ralph came up the dusty road below. Her hair was long and hung down in front of her shoulders, and she was looking away from him, staring at something in the distance. She wore a white blouse with a bright red scarf at her throat, and he could see her breasts pushing against the white cloth. He had a bottle of dark, unlabeled wine under his arm, and the whole incident put Ralph in mind of something from a film, an intensely dramatic moment into which Marian could be fitted but he could not.

What Ralph has perceived here so intensely is the threateningly mysterious sensuality of his own sensible-seeming wife (in many of Carver's stories, the sexual assertiveness of the woman represents a threat to the delicate male ego). Marian (or Woman, perhaps) inherits, from Ralph, those very traits of "squalor and open lust" he cannot face in himself, but also cannot fully suppress. As life becomes calmer, and as Ralph begins to feel "enormously happy," he becomes possessed by the need to replay the imagined scenes of Marian's abasement at a suburban party: ". . . Ralph thought about it more and more. Increasingly, ghastly images would be projected on his eyes, certain unthinkable particularities."

The voyeurism in this story is tinged with narcissism. It is almost as if Ralph were standing in front of a mirror which was reflecting not his but Marian's image, acting out "certain unthinkable particularities" for Ralph's benefit. Marian's long tale of the unfaithful wife, her "confession," which is delivered in the most elaborate, vividly recalled detail, suggests that she's conscious of the game they're playing, and has need of it too. The double nature of voyeurism, which hints at the intimate bond between "voyeur" and "victim," is conveyed in this conjunction of "window" and "voyeur" images:

> She went into the living room and turned on the lamp and bent to pick up a magazine from the floor. He watched her hips under the plaid woolen skirt. She moved in front of the window and stood looking out at the streetlight. She smoothed her palm down over her skirt, then began tucking in her blouse. He wondered if she wondered if he were watching her.

The revelation of Marian's unfaithfulness is self-revelation for Ralph. Even Ralph's accusation, "Christ! . . . But you've always been that way, Marian!", reveals more about him than about his wife. The self-discovery is underscored in the next line the narrator delivers: "And he knew at once that he had uttered a new and profound truth." Then follows Ralph's desperate all-night walk on the wild side of Eureka, the small northern California city where the Wymans live. He gets drunk, loses his money in a poker game, is mugged, and confronts ghastly nighttown images of dissociation and sensual corruption. In the course of his wanderings, he becomes "suddenly aware that he had come a long way that evening, a long way in his life. *Jackson,* he thought. He could be Jackson."

At dawn, he takes his battered soul and body home. His young daughter asks innocently, "What did you do to your face, Daddy?" But the image of self-alienation isn't complete until Ralph locks himself in the bathroom:

> He looked at himself in the mirror a long time. He made faces at himself. He tried many expressions. Then he gave it up. He turned away from the mirror. . . .

For Ralph this is a mirror which reflects hope, not despair. Ralph may not have "found himself" yet, but at least he's rid of the smug, "enormously happy" Ralph who couldn't face confusion and contradiction except by dissociating himself from them. Moreover, the "new" faceless Ralph is protean: he can accept the "many expressions" life gives us to wear. He can even "give up" and "turn away" from the mirror. Thus he is prepared for the final revelation of the concluding bed scene, and perhaps the one genuine epiphany in this collection of Carver's stories, the moment in which Ralph "turned and turned . . . marveling at the impossible changes he felt moving over him."

Carver has "turned" too. He's come full circle in this last story to show us how self-revelation can point a way back to understanding and intimacy. Yet even in this rare hopeful tale, the relationship between Kafkaean dissociation and voyeurism remains strong. The character is an unwilling witness of something "taboo," an act which stretches his perceptions. The voyeuristic glimpse leads to a rupture in the seemingly calm surface of life, and a disaffection with the self. It is an awakening to the possible terrors of existence. What changes ultimately will come about Carver is careful not to explain, for his stories finally are as open-ended as life itself. But he does tell us that life continually presents us with small but important tests, and that little can be taken for granted. "I learned a good deal about this and that from all my snooping" in John Gardner's office, Carver recalls, revealing more than he realizes about the sources of his art, as well as his success as a writer of fiction. He tells us this more explicitly in his story **"Put Yourself in My Shoes,"** in which we see the writer's observations transformed in his mind and art into revelations of larger experience. In this case, the larger experience is that of the writer, the artist. He's also made us aware, if we weren't before, of the close kinship between reading and voyeurism. For these things alone, he deserves the accolades he's already earned and will continue to earn. But he's done one thing more. Carver the artist and Carver the voyeur have conspired to convince us that we're reading about real people in real situations. His accuracy hits home; we put ourselves in the shoes of his characters, and we find, often, that the fit is alarmingly close. Reading Raymond Carver's stories is like peering into the windows of life through very powerful binoculars. (pp. 86-90)

David Boxer and Cassandra Phillips, "'Will You Please Be Quiet, Please?': Voyeurism, Dissociation, and the Art of Raymond Carver," in The Iowa Review, *Vol. 10, No. 3, Summer, 1979, pp. 75-90.*

Carver on the origin of his style:

I have a poor memory. By this I mean that much that has happened in my life I've forgotten—a blessing for sure—but I have these large periods of time I simply can't account for or bring back, towns and cities I've lived in, names of people, the people themselves. Large blanks. But I can remember some things. Little things—somebody saying something in a particular way; somebody's wild, or low, nervous laughter; a landscape; an expression of sadness or bewilderment on somebody's face; and I can remember some dramatic things—somebody picking up a knife and turning to me in anger; or else hearing my own voice threaten somebody else. Seeing somebody break down a door, or else fall down a flight of stairs. Some of those more dramatic kinds of memories I can recall when it's necessary. But I don't have the kind of memory that can bring entire conversations back to the present, complete with all the gestures and nuances of real speech; nor can I recall the furnishings of any room I've ever spent time in, not to mention my inability to remember the furnishings of an entire household. . . . I make up the conversations in my stories. I put the furnishings and the physical things surrounding the people into the stories as I need those things. Perhaps this is why it's sometimes been said that my stories are unadorned, stripped down, even "minimalist." But maybe it's nothing more than a working marriage of necessity and convenience that has brought me to writing the kind of stories I do in the way that I do.

Raymond Carver in his 1982 essay "Fires."

Adam Mars-Jones (essay date 1982)

[Mars-Jones is an English short story writer and critic. In the following review of What We Talk about When We Talk about Love, *he comments on Carver's writing style, discerning a highly restrained quality in his short stories which Mars-Jones considers to be characteristic of minimalism.]*

[***What We Talk about When We Talk about Love***] contains seventeen stories, all brief (less than ten pages each on average) and all dealing with the walking wounded of American suburbia, those who are obscurely defeated by broken marriage, accident, illness, bad bingo luck, flood and drink. His characters utter broken sentences and try to communicate their sense of loss, but articulateness is the first thing to go; expression brings them no relief.

To match his subjects Carver has devised a style of careful starkness and understatement, one which insists on its own neutrality and draws attention to its omissions. Description, character-drawing and plot-development are all foreshortened, and the stories conclude as often with depressive epiphanies as with more conventional resolutions. He is rewarded with a blurb which refers to "zero-degree stories", but things aren't really as terminally modern as all that.

Minimalism, after all, is a style (as artificial in its way as Henry James's maximalism) and not the opposite of a style; No Comment is rightly always classified as a comment. So when in the title story a wife, having corrected her husband's misuse of the word "vessel" (to mean *feudal dependant*), misuses it herself in identical fashion, we don't need to be nudged; and when her husband accepts this implied apology for her interference by tacitly adopting the correct word, he completes a delicate marital negotiation that doesn't need to be spelled out for our benefit. It seems to speak for itself.

That's the trick, though: to throw your voice so that it seems to be coming from the furniture, and Carver is an expert ventriloquist. The artificial inhumanity he adopts enables him to sidle unnoticed into areas of feeling which he couldn't approach directly.

This is partly a matter of cultural fashion. Few people nowadays would respect a book which announced *I want you to care for life's losers. For the little guy. For all of us. I want to break your heart.* But by cultivating a bleakness of manner which gives way at crucial moments to a rationed sympathy, Carver can achieve all these effects without being seen to solicit them.

Minimalism is well suited to the short-short-story form, since everything is over before the diminishing returns show up; there is only so much mileage in the poetry of inarticulateness, and the day of the autistic three-decker novel is not yet. But even with a volume of stories, doubts creep in. The first few pieces seem thin and perfunctory, and there is a recurring pattern, in **"Gazebo"**, **"Sacks"** and **"The Calm"**, of endings which lurch suddenly sideways, moving off in a direction that seems almost random.

Perhaps there is a reason for this. Endings and titles are bound to be a problem for a writer like Carver, since readers and reviewers so habitually use them as keys to interpret everything else in a story. So he must make his endings enigmatic and even mildly surrealist, and his titles for the most part oblique. Sometimes he over-compensates.

These reservations apply least to a run of five excellent stories in the middle of the book (**"Tell The Women We're Going"**, **"After The Denim"**, **"So Much Water So Close to Home"**, **"The Third Thing That Killed My Father Off "**, and **"A Serious Talk"**), where Carver really seems to hit his stride. The situations here are a little fuller and a little more conventional than elsewhere, so that Carver's restraint and scruple stand out all the more by contrast. **"After The Denim"**, for instance, merely describes, with a characteristic neutral precision, a couple's evening out playing bingo. The story has two narrative surprises, first that the Packers' marriage is a happy one, and second that Edith Packer is very ill. Both the characters are fully aware of these two facts; it is only the reader who is kept in ignorance, by a technique which withholds necessary information while seeming simply to reserve judgment.

The pathos of the story is enhanced by its being delayed and the reader is grateful for the few cues he is given. Carver's fiction, in fact, doesn't need to break the mould of the traditional story to achieve its effects. In the final analysis, he keeps more than he abandons.

In one story he even keeps a tone of voice which clashes with his preferred starkness; true, the narrator of **"The Third Thing That Killed My Father Off "** tells a tale of obsession, loss and disconnection, but he remains remarkably unaffected by it. "I'll tell you what did my father in," he begins, but having done so he ends by saying, "But as I said, Pearl Harbor and having to move back to his dad's place didn't do my dad one bit of good, either." This throwaway ending is the nearest Carver comes to exploring the comic potential of his material, and in a sense he is right to be wary of it. If any incident, properly considered, is a microcosm of defeat and loss, why insist on every moment of heartbreak? If three things can kill your father off, why not three thousand or three million?

The stories in ***What We Talk about When We Talk about Love*** use a drastic underwriting to distance the reader and then suddenly involve him, after pretending not to mind one way or the other. This technique is best suited to conventional material; it can accommodate both the lurid and the quirky, and can make tired situations seem fresh and exciting. Elsewhere it can tail off into sentimentality (as in the title story) or, worse, slickness **("Popular Mechanics")**. But in a *handful* of fine pieces Carver's coolness pays real dividends; his most impressive stories are as subtly rhetorical as they are shrewdly calculated, and none the worse for that.

Adam Mars-Jones, "Words for the Walking Wounded," in The Times Literary Supplement, *No. 4112, January 22, 1982, p. 76.*

Alain Arias-Misson (essay date 1982)

[Arias-Misson is a Belgian fiction writer, poet, artist, and critic. In the following essay, he discusses Carver's use of dialogue and narrative voice as evocative of the isolation felt by characters in What We Talk about When We Talk about Love.]

It seems odd that stories that are all of talk should be muffled by a roominess of silence. The unsaid makes a vacuum in the middle of the language into which the meaning of the talkers' existence is sucked. The flotsam, the drift of American life, is not represented in a *trôp-plein,* a spillover of language as in Barthelme, for instance, but in a loss, a stripping down, a mine stripping of the voice, a minus sign, a subtraction from the language. The linguistic space of the stories is mostly margin: the whiteness of the page that follows each attempt at speech swallows the words. In **"So Much Water So Close to Home"** the narrator's husband has returned from a weekend fishing trip with his buddies. At the river site they had found the naked body of a girl floating near shore caught in branches, which they did not report until two days later on their return. In the midst of the gossip and newspaper reports, husband and wife are locked in speech incommunicado.

> "What are you staring at me for?" he says. "What is it?" he says and lays down his fork.
>
> "Was I staring?" I say, and shake my head. The telephone rings.
>
> "Don't answer it," he says.
>
> "It might be your mother," I say.
>
> "Watch and see," he says.

In the blanks, what is not said presses about the lonely figures of Carver's stories. The silence that seeps in on the voices is the circumstance, the climate of the voice in America, its authenticity devastated by the detritus of mass culture. In **"Gazebo,"** a couple managing a motel lock themselves in and potential guests out following her discovery of his infidelity, in a ritual of purgation and separation:

> ". . . Who knows what I was missing all those years? You were my everything, just like the song."
>
> I go, "You're a wonderful woman, Holly, I know you've had the opportunities."
>
> "But I didn't take them up on it!" she goes. "I couldn't go outside the marriage."
>
> "Holly, please," I go. "No more now, honey. Let's not torture ourselves. What is it we should do?"

These voices admirably convey the loneliness, the attrition of the person by junk language; the brittleness of their lives is exposed in the exteriority of the speech line. The magic of Carver's stories is not *in* the language but *around* it: in the brooding sense of the unsayable. The trivial speech rhythms exhaust the inner throat, their diction injures the inner ear like t.v.-spiel. Unlike mechanical reproduction however, spoken language here is high artifice, distilled from real speech, fermented. In **"Gazebo,"** when the couple have reached a breaking point, the narrator says: "There was this funny thing of anything could happen now that we realized everything had." And the title story of the book is drawn from the sentence, "it ought to make us ashamed when we talk like we know what we're talking about when we talk about love." Here colloquialism verges on the incantatory. Otherwise the extrusion of interiority into the shell of stereotype, the privation of image and metaphor, lays an air of desolation thickly about the stories. Ellipsis is the predominant mode of Carver's voices, an anguished contraction of the speech-muscles. At the end of **"Gazebo"**:

> I hear a car start. Then another. They turn on their lights against the building and, one after the other, they pull away and go out into the traffic.
>
> "Duane," Holly goes.
>
> In this too she is right.

Like the sentences, the stories end on an edge with their "lives" left hanging in an air of uncertainty. A muted miniature apocalypse breaks silently about these personages.

Carver has the ability, rare today in the zero temperature of *voix blanches,* to give a voice to his characters. The first-person narrator who tells about half the stories wears a male or female voice with equal grace. The voice, similar to his (or her) characters, multiplies through the "unspoken" text with its colloquial tone and clumsy diction. The reader is drawn into the voices implicitly or, as in the beginning of **"Sacks,"** explicitly: "I want to pass along to you a story my father told me when I stopped over in Sacramento last year." In the stories told in third-person narrative the text is similarly contaminated by the colloquial style: "Two orderlies came in. They wheeled a thing like a bed. They unhooked the boy from the tube and slid him onto the thing with wheels." The story, **"The Bath,"** is about a child interned in a hospital in a coma and the emotional foundering of his parents. The author, wholly internalized in the voice of the narrator, is also "unconscious." This absent narrator will be seen to be a model for his characters. The fiction, saturated with the colloquial voice, has no other resources left (imagery, metaphor) except as they pertain to this voice. The unbroken voice, its closure, the unself-conscious speech, this narrative purity is bottled up like some rare life form in a vacuum, no longer viable in the corrupt atmosphere of self-conscious fiction. The void in language circumscribed here is the doubling back of the novel upon its voice.

These stories are not simply the texture of talk but *about* talk. ***What We Talk About When We Talk About Love.*** As the title says, about *talk.* Carver has *not* given a voice to his characters; he has given his characters to a voice. The *voix blanche* turned inside out like a glove. Like the absent narrator, they are not included in the text but their traces are clearly perceivable in its rhythms, diction, grammar. The characters are the pronouns and the proper names given existence by the verb "said." They have been sucked into the vacuum of their speech. So obsessive is the speech rhythm that the characters are lonely, lost, trapped in it. The author himself, emptied into the absent narrator, cannot reflect on his text, be conscious of his language, illuminate his fiction from the "outside."

Irresistible pressures build within this vacuum chamber of the voice to produce paradoxical fictional solutions. In **"So Much Water So Close to Home,"** the narrator and her husband, still incommunicado, go for a drive and drink beer in the picnic grounds just outside town. Observing men fishing in the pond there, she thinks: "So much water so close to home." She sees herself, "I'm right in it, eyes open, face down, staring at the moss on the bottom, dead." She goes alone to the murdered girl's funeral, and when she gets back: "First things first," he says as he unbuttons her blouse. "He says something else. But I don't need to listen. I can't hear a thing with so much water going." End of story. There is no psychological movement in the paralysis of the couple, their impotence to breach the silent wall behind the talk. The only shaping is obtained through the sparse water/death-sex images and the "solution" of the final sentence. This metaphor is achieved with so deft a touch that at first it slips by unnoticed. Its intensity is so alien to the ordinary flow of the voice—stripped of metaphor or image—that the reader checks back to see if the faucet has been left running in the kitchen. A metaphorical identity has been astonishingly realized. In **"What We Talk About When We Talk About Love,"** the conversation of two couples drinking and talking meanders about two conceptions of love, negative and positive. The talk is marked as if by a luminous marker. "The afternoon sun was like a presence in this room, the spacious light of ease and generosity." And the final, most moving image of the book: "I could hear everyone's heart. I could hear the human noise we sat there making, not one of us moving, not even when the room went dark." The metaphor collects, condenses the story into a powerful complex of love, fear, loneliness, death. The imagery is incompatible with the rhetoric of banality that dominates the story. It shines through—or darkens—the ordinariness of the talk. In Carver's stories the operative element is literary in the specific sense, a solution *of* language, not *in* it; all the more notable as it wrenches us out of a quasi-naturalistic environment. The metaphor of the story does not accompany, elucidate a psychological, dramatic progression as in the realistic novel. At a point of anguish in the enclosed lives, of frustration with the unspeaking language, the metaphor operates a *passage through* to an apocalyptic moment, an unsuspected transcendence of the text. So heteronomous is this poetic language that one may detect a third voice behind narrator and author—the poet in Carver, like us unable to tolerate a muted, incommunicable universe, intrudes on, breaks with, the textual voices. When the iron-clad ordinariness of the speech of the stories is invulnerable or the revelatory image insufficiently sharp—its gleaming edge blunted by the molecular cohesiveness, the sheer gravity of the talk—then the image appears irrelevant and the story fails. When it is fully achieved as in the above stories and others, when it appears as the inevitable if unpredictable precipitate of the fiction-solution—then it so jars us out of our received patterns of reading that we perceive a remarkably novel fictional experience. (pp. 625-28)

Alain Arias-Misson, "Absent Talkers," in Partisan Review, *Vol. XLIX, No. 4, 1982, pp. 625-28.*

Michael Gorra (essay date 1984)

[*In the following excerpt, Gorra negatively appraises* Cathedral, *finding fault with Carver's laconic style.*]

Carver has been so extravagantly admired in the last few years that an encounter with his work becomes an encounter with his critics as well, and it seems important to question the terms those critics have used. Do his admittedly deft stories face up, as Howe says they do [see Further Reading list], to "the waste and destructiveness that prevail beneath the affluence of American life"? Carver is the chief practitioner of what's been called "American minimalism," a mannerist mode in which the intentional poverty, the anorexia, of the writer's style is mimetic of the spiritual poverty of his or her characters' lives, their disconnection from anything like a traditional community. It is a prose so attenuated that it can't support the weight of a past or a future, but only a bare notation of what happens, now; a "slice of life" in which the characters are seen without the benefit of antecedents or social context. They rarely have last names.

Such a world is confusing, not just for a reader who expects characters to come with surnames, but for the characters themselves. If nothing can be expected on the basis of the past, then each new moment can bewilder a character, freeze him or her into a confusion of inaction. Carver in particular is famous for the passivity with which his characters confront, or fail to confront, their experience. **"Preservation"** in [***Cathedral***] stands for me as the archetypal Carver story. Sandy's husband has been unemployed for three months and no longer bothers to look for work. He spends his days on the sofa, waiting for her to come home from her own job. One afternoon Sandy finds that the refrigerator has lost its Freon. She unloads the contents of the freezer onto the kitchen table where, as the food defrosts, a puddle forms and slowly begins to drip onto the floor:

> She looked down at her husband's bare feet. She stared at his feet next to the pool of water. She knew she'd never again in her life see anything so unusual. But she didn't know what to make of it yet. She thought she'd better put on some lipstick, get her coat, and go ahead to the auction. But she couldn't take her eyes from her husband's feet. She put her plate on the table and watched until the feet left the kitchen and went back into the living room.

And the story ends. Yet why should it end there? It is in no way an ending in their lives; dinner still has to be eaten, the floor mopped, the auction attended. Their lives will presumably continue in precisely the same way. What makes this extremely thin slice better than one further down the loaf, what makes Carver's choice of an ending anything more than arbitrary? What makes the sight of her husband's foot next to a puddle "the most interesting thing" Sandy will ever see? What makes this moment count? To answer that one would need to know, with far more specificity than Carver provides, how Sandy feels about her husband's unemployment, her own job, her own life. One needs the details of her personal history even if her feelings about that history are confused and inarticulate. For this ending to work one needs the social detail, the context, that Carver's deliberately undersuggestive prose won't provide, and the story collapses under the weight of its own crust.

Carver doesn't persuade me that life is this pregnant with emptiness because in reading I feel that his style, like that of most minimalists, dictates rather than embodies his characters' predicament. Carver's fiction is entirely without the mingled sense of possibility and inevitability that seems to me essential for short fiction—the sense that out of all the things that could happen, this one has. Everything for which his minimalism has been praised coalesces into the negation of that sense. His stories both take place in and are mimetic of a vacuum, a vacuum based upon the elision at the center of his work. He writes almost exclusively about alcoholics, or about characters who, even when they don't drink, have the responses and desperation of alcoholics. That subject explains the absence of the quality I've described above, explains the seeming randomness of his world, in which every moment is a painful ending and none a new beginning. For Carver's characters all the choices have been made long before the story begins. What we read is an enactment of their consequences, an enactment that will be repeated again and again. The "slice of life" metaphor is in this case grimly appropriate.

The difficulty is that Carver is rarely open about his subject. He doesn't hide the whiskey bottles, but he does avoid naming the narrow range within which his work lies, and so leaves himself open both to an interpretation of the sort

Howe performs upon him, and to a criticism of the sort I've mounted above. It's difficult, in reading Carver, to know the degree to which he's attempted to extend these very private stories into public terms, the degree to which he intends alcoholism to provide a statement about American life as a whole. I suspect that such an extension is largely a product of his supporters' attempt to couple American minimalism to their own political programs, while minimalism's harshest critics (e.g. *The New Criterion*) have attacked that coupling in the service of their programs as well. Certainly Carver hasn't indulged in the false historicity of such statements as "This was in 1972, in Philadelphia," with which Ann Beattie concluded a story in *Secrets and Surprises.* I still don't like his aesthetic. I see no reason why alcoholics can't have last names (Sandy's husband doesn't even have a first one). But the odd and encouraging thing about Carver's work is that when he is open about his subject his prose does carry a density of detail that allows it to graze the edge of the terms with which Howe sees him. **"Where I'm Calling From"** describes a week spent at a "drying out facility" and possesses an unsentimental yet tender awareness of the world his characters have lost. It is easily the best story in this collection, and makes me think that if he confronted his subject he might in fact manage to turn the alcoholic into Everyman. (pp. 155-57)

Michael Gorra, "Laughter and Bloodshed," in The Hudson Review, *Vol. XXXVII, No. 1, Spring, 1984, pp. 151-64.*

When I was 27, back in 1966, I found I was having trouble concentrating my attention on long narrative fiction. For a time I experienced difficulty in trying to read it as well as in attempting to write it. My attention span had gone out on me; I no longer had the patience to try to write novels. It's an involved story, too tedious to talk about here. But I know it has much to do now with why I write poems and short stories. Get in, get out. Don't linger. Go on.

Carver, from his essay "A Storyteller's Shoptalk" in The New York Times Book Review *(15 February 1981).*

William L. Stull (essay date 1985)

[*Stull is an American educator and critic who has written extensively on Carver and has coedited* Conversations with Raymond Carver *(1990) with Marshall B. Gentry. In the following essay, he examines Carver's short stories, noting that they exemplify two types of realism: "existential realism," which is often associated with the remote, minimalist style of the stories in* What We Talk about When We Talk about Love, *and "humanist realism," a more subjective and expansive narrative technique that is employed in Carver's later works.*]

By now, most of us have a fair idea of what we talk about when we talk about the stories of Raymond Carver: sorry tales more transcribed than told in a spare, unforgiving prose that resonates with what David Boxer and Cassandra Phillips have called "the very cadences of anomie" [see excerpt dated 1979]. Rooted in what had previously been literary *terra incognita,* Carver was until the mid-1970s a steady and respected contributor to quarterlies and small presses. Now, with three major collections of his stories published—***Will You Please Be Quiet, Please?*** (1976), ***What We Talk About When We Talk About Love*** (1981), and ***Cathedral*** (1983)—he stands in peril of becoming, as Robert Houston has observed, an Influence [see Further Reading list]. And because what has come to strike most of us as the typical Carver story has been elliptical, understated, and studiously opaque, his influence extends not only to how we write but to how we read. Ironically, Carver, who has an abiding distrust of "formal innovation" in fiction, has probably done more than Barth, Barthelme, and Coover combined (busy innovators, all) to reshape contemporary reading habits. Thus, when we talk about Raymond Carver not as an author but as an Influence, we are likely talking not about individual stories individually assessed but rather about the expectations we bring to (and take back from) one kind of Carver story. Whether these preconceptions actually do justice to Carver's work, particularly his work since ***What We Talk About,*** remains to be seen.

Although Carver has been publishing fiction since the early 1960s, most readers took their measure of him from his second collection of stories. As reviewers were quick to point out, ***What We Talk About*** has an arresting unity of style and subject: "Seventeen tales of Hopelessville, its marriages and alcoholic wreckage, told in a prose as sparingly clear as a fifth of iced Smirnoff "[Donald Newlove, *Saturday Review* (April 1981)]. It is of such glib summations that Influences are made. But despite its compelling immediacy, ***What We Talk About*** is, as James Atlas noted, a narrower book (in the physical and moral senses alike) than Carver's first collection [see Further Reading list]. The cause of this constriction is partly historical. Where ***Will You Please Be Quiet, Please?*** gathers most all of Carver's stories from the formative years 1963-75, ***What We Talk About*** concentrates on work written or rewritten during half that time, the leaner years 1975-80. But the constriction is also aesthetic. Carver's first volume shows him experimenting with a wide range of themes and styles, while his second proves him the master of a single, singularly bleak, vision.

The setting of ***What We Talk About*** is indeed Hopelessville, U.S.A., the contemporary counterpart of Sherwood Anderson's Winesburg, Ohio. And because Hopelessville is, for most of us, familiar territory, our tendency to identify ourselves—and Raymond Carver—with it uncritically is understandable, if shortsighted. Both before and since ***What We Talk About,*** Carver has done more than chronicle what a character in **"One More Thing,"** the last story in the book, calls "a long line of low-rent tragedies." Even a glance at the final paragraph of the earlier title story,

"Will You Please Be Quiet, Please?" (first published in 1966), points toward a place beyond Hopelessville, a place where love can soothe us after the talking stops:

> He tensed at her fingers, and then he let go a little. It was easier to let go a little. Her hand moved over his hip and over his stomach and she was pressing her body over his now and moving over him and back and forth over him. He held himself, he later considered, as long as he could. And then he turned to her. He turned and turned in what might have been a stupendous sleep, and he was still turning, marveling at the impossible changes he felt moving over him.

To set this passage next to the closing paragraph of the later title story, **"What We Talk About When We Talk About Love,"** is to juxtapose heaven and hell:

> I could hear my heart beating. I could hear everyone's heart. I could hear the human noise we sat there making, not one of us moving, not even when the room went dark.

Where the earlier story ends with a sensuous evocation of "letting go" and turning toward another, the latter culminates (far too strong a word) in anxious isolation, enervation, and stasis. Universal darkness is descending, and the "human noise" of heartbeats fades out like a transistor radio with a dying battery. The expansive, lyrical cadences of the earlier story will probably surprise those who know only the bare, repetitive, dispassionate writing of ***What We Talk About.*** Both stories drift toward sleep, but where the sleep of the lovers is "stupendous," the sleep of the talkers about love is merely stupified.

Admittedly, **"Will You Please Be Quiet, Please?"** is an exceptional story, both within Carver's first two collections and within recent fiction at large. Much, indeed most, of his work to date has been bleak, spare, and unforgiving. At its narrowest, when Carver seems most the Influence, his writing can be acerbic, mannered, and predictable. Such is the case in what are surely the weakest stories in ***What We Talk About,*** **"Tell the Women We're Going"** and **"Popular Mechanics."** The first is a clockwork parable ("Bill Jamison had always been best friends with Jerry Roberts.") of largely motiveless malignity, a tale of two nice young men, one of whom bludgeons two girls to death with a stone. **"Popular Mechanics"** is an amalgam of Hemingway and Kafka (two of Carver's mentors, to be sure), but worthy of neither. There, in a blackly humorous reenactment of the two harlots' struggle over a child in 1 Kings 3:16-28, a pair of feuding parents grapple over their baby. The tug of war ends not with Solomonic wisdom, but with a sick joke: "In this manner, the issue was decided." The Latin root of "decide" (*de-caedere,* to cut off) indicates just what fate the hapless "issue" suffered.

More often, however, in ***What We Talk About*** Carver concerns himself with what Gary L. Fisketjon aptly termed "the terrifying implications of Normal Life." [in *The Village Voice* (18 September 1978)]. Like Aristotelian essence and Sartrean existence, speech and feeling, talk and love, run at odds throughout the collection. When characters struggle to express their inmost feelings, as in **"Sacks," "A Serious Talk,"** and the title story, words either fail them outright or fail to move their auditors. "Maybe he wanted me to say something," concludes the son in **"Sacks"** after his father has agonized to explain the affair that ended his marriage. In **"A Serious Talk,"** the story of a man's disruption of his ex-wife's Christmas, "There were things he wanted to say, grieving things, consoling things, things like that." Instead of saying them, however, he steals her pies, nearly sets the house on fire, and cuts her telephone cord. "He hoped he had made something clear." The title story, a postmodern rendition of Plato's *Symposium,* demonstrates that the more we talk about love, the less of it we feel. The two couples' conversation (a coda to the book) fades into "human noise" and darkness as the speakers sink deeper and deeper into gin-soaked anesthesia. For the Raymond Carver of ***What We Talk About,*** the chronicler of Hopelessville, these failures of communication bespoke a heartfelt pessimism, a conviction that things never are and never can be what they should be.

To be sure, angst and anomie permeate many of the stories in Carver's first collection, ***Will You Please Be Quiet, Please?*** **"The Father,"** a Kafkaesque vignette of fewer than five hundred words, is practically a textbook piece on existential fear and trembling. There, a child inquires about her new baby brother, "But who does he look like, who does he look like?" This seemingly innocent question quickly precipitates an identity crisis that leaves the father paralyzed with dread: "He had turned around in his chair and his face was white and without expression." As Boxer and Phillips have shown [see excerpt dated 1979], this sort of dissociation—"a sense of disengagement from one's own identity and life"—is among Carver's leitmotifs. Thus, at the close of **"Are You a Doctor?"** (a story whose title immediately raises existential doubts), a husband finds himself estranged not only from his wife but from himself: " 'Are you there, Arnold?' she said. 'You don't sound like yourself'." Dissociated from themselves, abandoned or betrayed by others, the citizens of Hopelessville lead lives of talky desperation.

And just as we know what to talk about when we talk about Raymond Carver, so we know what *not* to talk about. From him we have come to expect no writerly embellishments or authorial asides, no epiphanies or revelations in the manner of Joyce or O'Connor, no divine presence or forgiveness. Carver is a rigorous reviser of even his published work, and until recently, at least, his inclination has been to condense rather than expand stories. (It is instructive to compare a minimalist fiction like **"Mr. Coffee and Mr. Fixit"** in ***What We Talk About*** with its fuller, far more explicit precursor **"Where Is Everyone?"** in the Spring 1980 *TriQuarterly.*) As he made plain in "A Storyteller's Shoptalk" [in *The New York Times Book Review* (15 February 1981)], an informal apologia published shortly before ***What We Talk About*** and since reprinted as "On Writing" in ***Fires,*** Carver was following a trail blazed by Hemingway in stories like "Hills Like White Elephants." This route is the modernist *via negativa* of brevity, understatement, and crafted omission:

> What creates tension in a piece of fiction is partly the way the concrete words are linked together to make up the visible action of the story. But

> it's also the things that are left out, that are implied, the landscape just under the smooth (but sometimes broken and unsettled) surface of things.

Carver's motto was "No tricks," a vow that banished from ***What We Talk About*** much of the traditional rhetoric of fiction. In keeping with the dictum he quoted from Ezra Pound, "Fundamental accuracy of statement is the ONE sole morality of writing," Carver, who is also a poet, embraced an aesthetic of accuracy, objectivity, and authorial neutrality: no tricks. This is the fierce, implicitly moral aesthetic of Eliot's "A Game of Chess" and Stevens' "The Credences of Summer":

> Let's see the very thing and nothing else.
> Let's see it with the hottest fires of sight.
> Burn everything not part of it to ash.

It is, moreover, the precisionist aesthetic of Carver's contemporaries the Superrealist painters and sculptors, with whose art his writing bore close comparison. It is easy, for example, to illustrate many of Carver's tales of middle-American discontent with Photo-Realist paintings, suburban street scenes like Robert Bechtle's *1971 Buick* (1972) and working-class interiors like Ralph Going's *Pee Wee's Diner* (1977). Indeed, Bechtle's shadowy, intrusive *Hoover Man* (1966) bears a striking resemblance to Aubrey Bell, the relentless vacuum-cleaner salesman in **"Collectors,"** just as John de Andrea's life-size polychromed plastic *Man Leaning and Woman* (1971) seems cast from the same mold as the disaffected lovers in **"Gazebo."** In stories like **"Mr. Coffee and Mr. Fixit"** Carver used talk, his medium, at once minimally and hyperrealistically. Such writing was so sharply focused, banal, and therefore lifelike as to seem more recorded than written. Here, the speaker, an ex-alcoholic (nearly all Carver's character's are "ex-s" of one sort or another) recalls the rival for his wife's affections:

> Ross was a little guy. But not too little. He had a mustache and always wore a button-up sweater.
>
> His one wife jailed him once. The second one did. I found out from my daughter that my wife went bail. My daughter Melody didn't like it any better than I did. About the bail. It wasn't that Melody was looking out for me. She wasn't looking out for either one of us, her mother or me neither. It was just that there was a serious cash thing and if some of it went to Ross, there'd be that much less for Melody. So Ross was on Melody's list. Also, she didn't like his kids, and his having so many of them. But in general Melody said Ross was all right.
>
> He'd even told her fortune once.

Like the Superrealist images of Bechtle, Goings, and de Andrea, such talk seems at once familiar and disturbing: in Freud's terms, "uncanny." This haunting verisimilitude, moreover, accounts for much of the unsettling immediacy of ***What We Talk About When We Talk About Love.***

In keeping with his precisionist aesthetic, furthermore, Carver in these stories practiced what the art critic Linda Chase has called existential rather than humanist realism [in her *Photo Realism* (1975)]. In ***What We Talk About*** as in Sartre's *Le Mur* (1939), this moral and aesthetic orientation suggests a subject as well as a style: Hopelessville. It calls for characters who are more often cowardly than heroic, for Erostratus instead of Achilles. Despite the constant threat of violence in ***What We Talk About,*** stories like **"A Serious Talk"** and **"One More Thing"** end not with a bang but a whimper, a hasty retreat, a failure to connect. In Carver's two studies of Sartrean *nausée,* **"So Much Water So Close to Home"** and **"I Could See the Smallest Things,"** sensitive women capitulate to their stolid spouses rather than rebel. In the former, having savored the full brutality of her husband's refusal to let the corpse of a murdered girl cut short his fishing trip, the wife nonetheless beats a hasty sexual retreat to him. In the latter, when a woman suddenly associates her husband's phlegmy snores with the slugs she has seen her neighbor poisoning by moonlight, she seeks to obliterate her insight:

> I thought for a minute of the world outside my house, and then I didn't have any more thoughts except the thought that I had to hurry up and sleep.

Pity and fear abound in these stories, but Carver, writing of disasters rather than tragedies, affords the reader no catharsis, the characters no exit.

The foregoing is, I believe, a fair summary of what we commonly talk about when we talk about Raymond Carver. If he were less an artist and more an Influence, the talk might well end here. But as the ending of **"Will You Please be Quiet, Please?"** suggested—and as the best of his recent work confirms—there is another side of Raymond Carver. As Sartre himself took pains to show in *L'Existentialisme est un humanisme* (1946), existentialism and humanism are not incompatible. Carver's work before and since ***What We Talk About*** proves this to be the case in fiction no less than in philosophy. The winner of the 1983 O. Henry Award was Carver's **"A Small, Good Thing,"** an expansion of **"The Bath,"** a story in ***What We Talk About.*** A study of Carver's revisions reveals not only another side of his realism, the humanist side, but also another spirit in his work, a spirit of empathy, forgiveness, and community tacitly founded on Judeo-Christian faith.

As published in ***What We Talk About,*** **"The Bath"** is so representative a sample of existential realism, of the Raymond Carver we expect to read, that it is easy to dismiss as one of the author's lesser efforts. The plot—more a "story" in E. M. Forster's terms—is fragmentary. In preparation for her son Scotty's eighth birthday party, Ann Weiss goes to the bakery and orders a custom-made cake. Two days later, on the morning of his birthday, Scotty is struck by a hit-and-run driver and hospitalized. The cake forgotten, Ann and her husband hold an anxious vigil over the unconscious child. Despite the doctor's reluctance to use the word, Scotty appears to be in a deep coma. To break the tension, each parent once goes home briefly to bathe and change clothes. While at home, both receive upsetting anonymous telephone calls alluding to a cake and to Scotty. We—not they—recognize the caller as the baker, angry at his customers' negligence, unaware that their child lies near death.

"The Bath" exemplifies well the existential realism of ***What We Talk About.*** The situation—a life-or-death crisis—is rendered in studiously neutral tones. Characterization and detail are minimal. Mrs. Weiss is introduced as "the mother," Scotty as "the child." Only the nameless baker is described in any physical detail, and he bears a striking resemblance to Duane Hanson's life-size polyester and vinyl sculpture *Dishwasher* (1973):

> He was an older man, this baker, and he wore a curious apron, a heavy thing with loops that went under his arms and around his back and then crossed in front again where they were tied in a very thick knot. He kept wiping his hands on the front of the apron as he listened to the woman, his wet eyes examining her lips as she studied the samples and talked.

In keeping with the minimalist style of ***What We Talk About,*** the narrator, like the baker, offers only "the barest information." Phenomenological precision—"fundamental accuracy of statement"—is Carver's first concern, and most of **"The Bath"** is given over to objective description and inconclusive talk. Carver's narrator, although omniscient, is neither intrusive nor judgmental. When the worried mother talks to herself, he comments only, "She was afraid." Of the father he observes, "The man had been lucky and happy. But fear made him want a bath." Carver focuses relentlessly on two existential issues. First, what is the unconscious child's actual condition? Is he in a coma? " 'I wouldn't call it that,' " says the doctor hardly a reassuring reply. Second, who is the anonymous caller? At the end of the story, from the parents' viewpoint, both issues remain unresolved. At one point the parents pray, an act that unites them in silence, but there is no indication that their prayers are heard. The universe, like the baker, is unforgiving.

"A Small, Good Thing" is twice again as long as **"The Bath,"** which is not only develops but continues. More important, the revision *completes* the original by turning the sum of its fragmentary parts into a coherent whole that has a powerful dramatic structure, a beginning, middle, and end. Almost classical in its development, the revision nicely illustrates the other side of Carver's realism, the humanist side. Humanist realism, what we think of as the classic realism of Balzac, Henry James, and the early James Joyce, is surely no less truthful than existential realism. It differs, however, from its postmodern counterpart in both philosophical orientation and fictive techniques. Existential realism, the now almost classical realism of Sartre in *La Nausée* (1938) and Camus in *L'Étranger* (1942), the "new" realism of Robbe-Grillet in *Le Voyeur* (1955) and Butor in *La Modification* (1957), the Superrealism of Carver in ***What We Talk About,*** treats reality phenomenologically, agnostically, and objectively. Whether dead or in occultation, God—the archetype of the author—is absent from the world, which is discontinuous, banal, and, by definition, mundane. Existential fact rather than metaphysical truth is the artist's *donnée.* Hence, as Pound proleptically enjoined, "Fundamental accuracy of statement is the ONE sole morality of writing." The style of existential realism is, therefore, studiously objective, impersonal, and neutral (whatever the author's private judgments may be). In his "Shoptalk," Carver put the matter succinctly: "Get in, get out. Don't linger. Go on." Since the writer refuses to speculate, generalize, or judge—to deal in essences—the full burden of interpretation passes to the reader. In Carver's most radical work of this sort—in **"Gazebo," "Sacks,"** and **"What We Talk About,"** for example—the dialogue seems almost unedited, the descriptions photographed. Humanist realism, in contrast, takes a more expressive, more "painterly" approach to its subjects, as the titles of two of its classics indicate: *The Portrait of a Lady* and *A Portrait of the Artist as a Young Man.* Such realism treats reality metaphysically, theologically, and subjectively. Here, as Protagoras said, "Man is the measure of all things." The artist's godlike presence illuminates every particle of the world and charges it with meaning. In art, this is the luminous realism of Winslow Homer, Andrew Wyeth, and Edward Hopper, whose *Sun in an Empty Room* (1963) is suffused with the unseen but all-seeing creator's presence. In writing, it is the numinous realism of Tolstoy in *The Death of Ivan Ilych,* of Joyce in *Dubliners,* and of Flannery O'Connor in *Everything That Rises Must Converge,* as well as the more earthbound psychological realism of Turgenev and Chekhov. In this respect, it is highly significant that Carver set Chekhov's "and suddenly everything became clear to him" next to Pound's dictum in the "Shoptalk." Humanist rather than existential realism has in fact been the mode of some of Carver's best work before and since ***What We Talk About:*** of **"Put Yourself in My Shoes," "Bicycles, Muscles, Cigarets,"** and the title story of his first collection; of nearly all the stories in ***Cathedral,*** a book whose title suggests a religious undercurrent. As Carver admitted in a 1983 *Paris Review* interview, "I knew I'd gone as far the other way as I could or wanted to go, cutting everything down to the marrow, not just to the bone." In his most recent work, essence informs existence, truth caps fact, and, as William Dean Howells observed, "Morality penetrates all things, it is the soul of all things." That Carver the writer (not Carver the Influence) practices both existential and humanist realism testifies to his artistic scope and integrity. For him as for Joseph Conrad, the object of realism remains simultaneously visual and visionary: "to make you *see.*"

In **"A Small, Good Thing,"** the minimally developed characters of **"The Bath"** take on flesh, blood, and consciousness. The baker is no longer a plastic stereotype; he is "not jolly," "not rude, just abrupt." Carver early introduces Ann Weiss by name and sets forth her essence—her preconceptions, her need for community: "She was a mother and thirty-three years old, and it seemed to her that everyone, especially someone the baker's age—a man old enough to be her father—must have children who'd gone through this special time of cakes and birthday parties. There must be that between them, she thought." The account of Scotty's accident remains spare, but Carver slows down and develops the parents' reactions to the trauma. He carefully sketches the father's consciousness: "Until now, his life had gone smoothly and to his satisfaction—college, marriage, another year of college for the advanced degree in business, a junior partnership in an investment firm. Fatherhood. He was happy and, so far, lucky—he knew that." Even the secondary characters—Dr. Francis, Dr. Parsons, the black family Ann passes in the waiting room—are given essential identities.

Moreover, instead of highlighting, as in **"The Bath,"** the existential isolation that suffering imposes, Carver here works in the manner of George Eliot, enlarging rather than contracting human sympathies. In the original version of the story, the parents' prayers are acts of private desperation rather than communal faith. In the revision, praying together restores and reunites the couple: "For the first time, she felt they were together in it, this trouble. She realized with a start that, until now, it had only been happening to her and to Scotty. She hadn't let Howard into it, though he was there and needed all along. She felt glad to be his wife." Likewise, in **"The Bath"** the narrator keeps his distance as Ann anxiously waits for the doctor: "She was talking to herself like this. We're into something now, something hard." In the revision, Carver penetrates Ann's soul: "She stood at the window with her hands gripping the sill, and knew in her heart that they were into something now, something hard." Then, in a striking addition, he expands the parents' sympathies for one another: "But they seemed to feel each other's insides now, as though the worry had made them transparent in a perfectly natural way." This spiritual transparency makes a stark contrast to the existential opacity of the original characters. Furthermore, Carver recasts and develops Ann's encounter with a black family whose son (Nelson in the original, Franklin in the revision) has been, like hers, senselessly injured. The original version of their meeting briefly shows the sufferers isolated by their private pain. The revision, however, presents a minor epiphany. Social and racial differences notwithstanding, Ann feels deeply drawn to these characters whose plight mirrors her own: "She wanted to talk more with these people who were in the same kind of waiting she was in. She was afraid, and they were afraid. They had that in common."

With these and other rhetorical colorations, Carver involves us with the Weisses during the "terrible minutes" of their ordeal. But even as he makes the characters more sympathetic, he remains true to the harsh existential premises of the story, which here becomes a plot. As the doctor concedes, Scotty is in a coma. The disturbing telephone calls continue. Finally, at what is the turning point of the revision, the child dies:

> The boy looked at them, but without any sign of recognition. Then his mouth opened, his eyes scrunched closed, and he howled until he had no more air in his lungs. His face seemed to relax and soften then. His lips parted as his last breath was puffed through his throat and exhaled gently through the clenched teeth.

The cause of this deadly spasm is a "hidden occlusion," "a one-in-a-million circumstance" that epitomizes all Thomas Hardy meant by "Crass Casualty," the inscrutable indifference of the universe. The powerful rhetoric of the passage—the scrupulously balanced antitheses evoking simultaneous tension and release, pity and fear—bears comparison with treatments of similar scenes in the classics of humanist realism, including Hardy's *Jude the Obscure.* Were this the end of the story, **"A Small, Good Thing"** would still rank among Carver's finest work to date. But where **"The Bath"** was the inconclusive, fragmentary tale of an existential disaster, **"A Small, Good Thing"** is a fully developed tragedy. Carver therefore completes the story with a final scene of dramatic recognition, reversal, confrontation, and catharsis.

Stunned, the parents drive home from the hospital. As Ann sits down to call relatives and Howard aimlessly collects Scotty's toys, the telephone rings:

> "Hello," she said, and she heard something in the background, a humming noise. "Hello!" she said. "For God's sake," she said. "Who is this? What is it you want?"
>
> "Your Scotty, I got him ready for you," the man's voice said. "Did you forget him?"
>
> "You evil bastard!" she shouted into the receiver. "How can you do this, you evil son of a bitch?"
>
> "Scotty," the man said. "Have you forgotten about Scotty?"

Before Ann can identify the voice, the man hangs up. By now she has transferred all her rage at Scotty's death to this brutal caller. Then, shortly before midnight, another hang-up call jogs her memory: "It came to her then. She knew who it was. Scotty, the cake, the telephone number." Along with this recognition comes a reversal as the parents take the initiative by driving to the shopping center.

When the Weisses confront their adversary, the threat of violence is palpable. Ann's fists are clenched; the baker taps a rolling pin against his palm. But the tension evaporates when Ann tells the baker that Scotty is dead. Her fearsome anger gives way to nausea at the injustice of the facts, then to tears.

With this cathartic scene of suffering, the tale of yet another "low-rent tragedy" might well seem told. Both the original crises of **"The Bath"** have now been resolved: the child is dead, the caller known. But in **"A Small, Good Thing"** Carver goes farther still, beyond Hopelessville, beyond even the limits of humanism, toward a final vision of forgiveness and community rooted in religious faith.

Unlike his precursors in ***What We Talk About,*** the unfeeling son in **"Sacks,"** the insensitive husband in **"So Much Water So Close to Home,"** the baker recognizes and acknowledges the enormity of his behavior. He asks the Weisses to forgive him for the brutal way in which he has compounded their tragedy. More important, in an epiphany that recalls Carver's quotation from Chekhov ("and suddenly everything became clear to him"), the baker sees the spiritual indifference, the acedia, into which he has fallen:

> "Listen to me. I'm just a baker. I don't claim to be anything else. Maybe once, maybe years ago, I was a different kind of human being. I've forgotten, I don't know for sure. But I'm not any longer, if I ever was. Now I'm just a baker. That don't excuse my doing what I did, I know. But

Yakima, Washington, where Carver spent his boyhood and early adult years, as it appeared in 1989. Yakima and its environs serve as the setting for many of Carver's short stories.

> I'm deeply sorry. I'm sorry for your son, and sorry for my part in this," the baker said.

Silently, the Weisses accept this confession and apology. The baker then gives them the only consolation he can offer, his fresh bread: " 'Eating is a small, good thing in a time like this,' he said." The story ends in forgiveness and communion rather than the rage and isolation that pervade ***What We Talk About.*** Indeed, the possibility of successful communication, of talk that works, is one of the story's major themes. As the Weisses savor the baker's bread, they regain a taste for life; as the baker tells them of his doubts and loneliness, he recovers his lost humanity. "They talked on into the early morning, the high, pale cast of light in the windows, and they did not think of leaving."

Thus, what began in **"The Bath"** as an existential chronicle of Hopelessville becomes in **"A Small, Good Thing"** a rich demonstration of what George Eliot called "the secret of deep human sympathy." Love has been the overarching subject of Carver's stories, and it remains the abiding preoccupation of his most recent work. At the close of **"Will You Please Be Quiet, Please?"** (heretofore his most "hopeful" story), Carver showed wordless erotic love quelling jealousy and self-doubt. In **"A Small, Good Thing,"** he demonstrates the greater power of a second kind of love, brotherly love, to bind people together in their fallible mortality. Moreover, a subtle but pervasive pattern of religious symbols in **"A Small, Good Thing"** suggests the presence of a third kind of love in Carver's work since ***What We Talk About,*** Christian love.

The subject of **"The Bath"** is a coma—a form of death in life. **"A Small, Good Thing"** develops this subject through death itself into an account of spiritual rebirth. As the titles of the two versions suggest, the story is concerned with the two most basic Christian sacraments, baptism and communion. While their innocent child (a Christlike figure, to be sure) lies suspended between life and death, each of the parents bathes. Carver calls attention to this seemingly incidental action by making it the title of the original story. Saint Paul's commentary on baptism explicates Carver's sacramental image and prefigures the theme of the revised story. "Therefore we are buried with him by baptism into death: that like as Christ was raised up from the dead by the glory of the Father, even so we also should walk in newness of life" (Rom. 6:4). Newness of life—salvation—is indeed the burden of **"A Small, Good Thing,"** where Carver's unobtrusive religious symbolism expands into an understated allegory of spiritual rebirth. The child Scotty dies—painfully, irrationally, unjustly—in a sacrifice that recalls not only the crucifixion but also Christ's teachings. As Jesus makes clear again and again in the Gospels, the child is the emblem of perfect faith:

"Whosoever shall not receive the kingdom of God as a little child, he shall not enter therein" (Mark 10:15). This admonition, restated in Mark 9:35-37 and Matthew 18:1-6, weighs heavily on the baker in Carver's story, a childless man who has lost the power of Christian sympathy. As he confesses, "I don't know how to act anymore, it would seem." Whereas Scotty lies in a physical coma, the baker has lapsed into spiritual death in life: "He that loveth not his brother abideth in death" (1 John 3:14). With unwitting cruelty, he torments the Weisses, taunting them and taking the name of the Christlike child in vain. When he belatedly realizes the full force of his insensitivity, it is as though he has heard Christ's words in Matthew 18:6—"But whoso shall offend one of these little ones which believe in me, it were better for him that a millstone were hanged about his neck, and that he were drowned in the depth of the sea."

In harassing the Weisses, the baker has violated the most basic Judeo-Christian ethics. He has failed to love his neighbor as himself (Lev. 19:18, Gal. 5:14); he has spurned the Lord's Prayer—"And forgive us our debts, as we forgive our debtors" (Matt. 6:12); he has broken the golden rule (Matt. 7:12). Nevertheless, in the climactic confrontation scene, the baker finds himself forgiven. The Weisses leave judgment to heaven and thereby fulfill Christ's "new commandment": "That ye love one another; as I have loved you, that ye also love one another" (John 13:34). By thus turning the other cheek instead of avenging themselves, they too begin to arise from the spiritual death in life that Scotty's ordeal has laid upon them. And it is at this point, in the quietly moving final paragraphs of the story, that the second sacramental symbol, the "small, good thing" of the title, works a small miracle. In breaking bread together, the characters reenact the central rite of Christianity, the Lord's Supper. "It's a heavy bread, but rich," the baker says—an apt description of the Eucharist: "For the bread of God is he which cometh down from heaven, and giveth life unto the world" (John 6:33). With a palpable sense of "newness of life," the characters talk on into the dawn. The story ends with a sunrise—a classic symbol of the Resurrection: "The night is far spent, the day is at hand: let us therefore cast off the works of darkness, and let us put on the armor of light" (Rom. 13:12). What Carver first published as an existential tale of crass casualty he thus offers anew as a story of spiritual rebirth, a minor masterpiece of humanist realism.

This exegesis of the religious subtext in **"A Small, Good Thing"** necessarily distorts the subtle and haunting effect of the prize-winning story. Nevertheless, the distortion is justifiable if it offsets the equally distorted image of Raymond Carver as the consummate existential realist, the chronicler of Hopelessville, the Influence. The other side of Raymond Carver—the humanistic, expressive, even lyrical side—demands attention. Carver has described the stories in ***Cathedral*** as "more generous" than his previous work, and if the promise of **"A Small, Good Thing"** continues to hold true, we can safely expect still larger, better things from him. Mona Simpson recently asked Carver whether he is a religious man. "No," he answered, "but I have to believe in miracles and the possibility of resurrection." (pp. 1-13)

William L. Stull, "Beyond Hopelessville: Another Side of Raymond Carver," in Philological Quarterly, *Vol. 64, No. 1, Winter, 1985, pp. 1-15.*

Michael J. Bugeja (essay date 1986)

[In the following essay, Bugeja studies stories in Cathedral, *maintaining that some of them contain flawed endings and observing that the volume as a whole represents a shift for Carver toward more fully developed and hopeful stories.]*

Cathedral, Raymond Carver's third collection of short stories, has been hailed as a breakthrough for the 47-year-old fiction writer. Critics note that Carver has moved from his "minimalist" stance, a style some call too easy, and now writes a more mainstream fiction. To a degree this is true. The stories in his latest collection are longer and more traditionally developed than earlier works, but one wonders whether they simply reflect a development in Carver's talent rather than a conscious change in style. And despite the brilliance of Carver's prose, several stories in ***Cathedral*** suffer from a common problem: endings.

Consider two versions of the same story: **"The Bath,"** which first appeared in Carver's second book, ***What We Talk About When We Talk About Love,*** and **"A Small, Good Thing,"** one of the ***Cathedral*** stories. On the surface, the significant difference between the two versions is the new, riskier ending tacked onto **"A Small, Good Thing."** In both stories, the occasion is a boy's eighth birthday and the ordering of a cake from the bakery at a shopping center. On the day the cake is to be picked up for the party that afternoon, the boy is struck by the car of a hit-and-run driver. He is able to make it home to his mother, but then collapses and is taken to the hospital, where he slips into a coma. The mother and father stand vigil, each taking turns going home to bathe, feed the dog, and do other domestic things that need doing. During these intervals, the baker—angry because the cake has not been picked up—makes harassing telephone calls. The parents, confused by tragedy, have no idea who is calling. The boy's symptoms worsen, and so does the tenor of the telephone calls. This is where the first version ends. In the second version, the boy dies and the parents figure out that the baker has been calling and pay him a visit (more about that later).

In comparing both versions, one is struck more by the caliber of revisions that prepare us for the new ending than by the skill in which the second ending is rendered. Carver makes changes on nearly every page, adding material and revising passages. Some revisions improve phrasing and diction. Fragments become complete sentences and awkward locutions are smoothed over or excised. However, the important changes occur in technique. Examples:

> The mother decided on the spaceship cake, and then she gave the baker her name and her telephone number. The cake would be ready Monday morning, in plenty of time for the party Monday afternoon. This was all the baker was willing to say. No pleasantries, just this small exchange, the barest information, nothing that was not necessary. (Fourth paragraph, **"The Bath"**)

> She gave the baker her name, Ann Weiss, and her telephone number. The cake would be ready on Monday morning, just out of the oven, in plenty of time for the child's party that afternoon. The baker was not jolly. There were no pleasantries between them, just the minimum exchange of words, the necessary information. He made her feel uncomfortable, and she didn't like that. While he was bent over the counter with the pencil in his hand, she studied his coarse features and wondered if he'd ever done anything else with his life besides be a baker. She was a mother and thirty-three years old, and it seemed to her that everyone, especially someone the baker's age—a man old enough to be her father—must have children who'd gone through this special time of cakes and birthday parties. There must be that between them, she thought. But he was abrupt with her—not rude, just abrupt. She gave up trying to make friends with him. She looked into the back of the bakery and could see a long, heavy wooden table with aluminum pie pans stacked at one end; and beside the table a metal container filled with empty racks. There was an enormous oven. A radio was playing country-Western music. (Second paragraph, **"A Small, Good Thing"**)

The second version reflects a desire on Carver's part to put less distance between the narrative persona and the fiction. In **"The Bath,"** we learn the mother's first and last names through dialogue separated by several pages, the last name being withheld from the reader until the final few sentences. Through most of the first story, Ann Weiss is known only as "the mother." Thus, the earlier version has to rely on action and dialogue, with little help from point of view or commentary. The change in stance in **"A Small, Good Thing"** brings us closer to the fiction and anticipates a rather dramatic death scene, during which the boy awakens from his coma only to die. More importantly, the focusing of point of view through Ann heightens the tension in the second version. Her perceptions are crucial because later she will identify the baker through the country music she overhears and will confront him in the workplace she observes. Finally, she is wrong about the baker initially; they share no common bond through children. But that fact becomes ironic in the conclusion, when we learn how lonely the baker is and how much he regrets making the telephone calls. He serves them "a small, good thing"—hot rolls—and the baker and parents partake in a kind of communion for the dead child. While the symbol of "breaking bread" may be a tad too pat, it works because again Carver has prepared for it: the story revolves around a birthday cake, the boy was struck down while eating potato chips, and every few pages thereafter the parents are urged to eat, though they obviously are not hungry . . . until the ending.

Despite such fine preparation, the ending is flawed. In the first version, the narrative ends with the baker still trying to have the cake picked up, and the cryptic dialogue succeeds when the mother mistakes the caller for a hospital official. The strategy does not call for development of the baker's character. In the second version, it does. Yet Carver in the new ending characterizes the baker through dialogue, which may have worked in **"The Bath"** but falls short in **"A Small, Good Thing."** Confronted by the angry parents in the early morning hours, when bakers work in solitude, this one is caught off-guard, and he responds in the manner we have grown accustomed to: he grabs a rolling pin and threatens, "Careful, careful." Then Ann tells him that her son is dead, and the father tells him "shame on you," and the baker at once becomes sympathetic. "Let me say how sorry I am," he says, and then launches into a monologue in which we learn that he has no children and once was a better individual. He serves them the hot rolls and the narrative persona takes over, distancing itself from Ann's hitherto successful point of view:

> Then he began to talk. They listened carefully. Although they were tired and in anguish, they listened to what the baker had to say. They nodded when the baker began to speak of loneliness, and of the sense of doubt and limitation that had come to him in his middle years. He told them what it was like to be childless all these years. . . .

The closer Carver keeps to Ann, the better the fiction works. When he resorts to such commentary (a summation, really), the pace of the thirty-page story quickens to overdrive. The scene at the bakery is less than one-sixth the length of the fiction, and much of the scene is devoted to anger on Ann's part and uncertainty on the baker's. Thus, his two-page monologue has the effect of a neat wrap-up. By drawing out the scene in the same mode as the rest of the story, keeping close to Ann and characterizing the baker through her, Carver would have gained not only through pacing but through plausibility as well. A heinous accident has occurred and somehow the police are not involved nor the harassing telephone caller mistaken for the hit-and-run driver, despite passages like this:

> "Hello," she said, and she heard something in the background, a humming noise. "Hello!" she said. "For God's sake," she said. "Who is this? What is it you want?"
>
> "Your Scotty, I got him ready for you," the man's voice said. "Did you forget him?"
>
> "You evil bastard!" she shouted into the receiver. "How can you do this, you evil son of a bitch?"
>
> "Scotty," the man said. "Have you forgotten about Scotty?" Then the man hung up on her.

We do not question the above dialogue because we are swept by the power of Ann's story. If the police are not involved, they are not involved, simple as that, and if the caller is anonymous, he remains so: that is the beauty of good fiction. However, when the wrap-up occurs, the narrative persona loses some authority, the reader feels uneasy, and —justified or not—we reconsider such passages.

The same uneasy feeling occurs in **"Feathers,"** another long story that Carver wraps up with flash-forward commentary. Like **"A Small, Good Thing,"** the fiction before the ending is masterful, a story about a young couple, Fran and Jack, visiting with another couple, Olla and Bud, who live in the country with a baby and a peacock. Jack and Bud work together, and Fran at first is reluctant to have dinner at the farm: "She heard me before on the subject of Bud. But she didn't know him and she wasn't interested in knowing him. 'We could take a bottle of wine,' she said. 'But I don't care. Why don't you take some wine?' She shook her head. Her long hair swung back and forth over her shoulder. Why do we need other people, she seemed to be saying." Fran and Jack end up going, overcoming the weirdness of Olla (whose plaster-of-Paris cast of her once jaggedy teeth is displayed to remind her "how much I owe Bud"). Fran later comes to accept a peacock in the house (Olla thinks it's better than a watchdog), and—more importantly—she shows real emotion for what has to be the ugliest baby in the world. The evening becomes special, and after Fran and Jack go home, she tells her husband, "Honey, fill me up with your seed!"

Now comes the wrap-up, five paragraphs that color all the reader has learned about the couple. Fran has "a kid" and regrets the evening with Olla and Bud:

> "Goddamn those people and their ugly baby," Fran will say, for no apparent reason, while we're watching TV late at night. "And that smelly bird," she'll say. "Christ, who needs it!" Fran will say. She says this kind of stuff a lot, even though she hasn't seen Bud and Olla since that one time.

Then the reader is told that the kid "has a conniving streak in him. But I don't talk about it. Not even with his mother. Especially her." It continues in this vein for several sentences and then nostalgically recalls the night when all was well with them by Olla and Bud's.

It is an ending the reader is unwilling to accept. It is pat. Again we are compelled to reconsider earlier passages, such as this one, when the narration skips from the past to the present tense to describe Fran's blond hair:

> Now and then she threatens to cut if off. But I don't think she'd do that. She knows I like it too much. She knows I'm crazy about it. I tell her I fell in love with her because of her hair. I tell her I might stop loving her if she cut it.

Jack then returns to the past tense to tell the rest of his story, and the lapse to the present tense is interpreted to be current commentary. We do not question the moment of narration until we read the wrap-up. If we have assumed the fiction is close to the present, that assumption goes awry in the ending when we learn that Fran "cut her hair a long time ago. She's gotten fat on me, too. We don't talk about it. What's to say?" Thus, although Carver prepares us throughout the story for the new-found desire of Jack and Fran to conceive a child, he does not ready the reader for flash-forward commentary. In the passage about Jack's passion for Fran's hair, the past tense would have helped, however slightly, to signal the coming turn in the story. By itself, this is a small concern. But confusion about the moment of narration generates surprise in the ending and makes us wonder why Carver employed such a strategy in the first place.

One has to wonder, too, about why Carver opted to print **"The Train"** in this collection. The story is a sequel to John Cheever's classic "The Five-Forty-Eight." Essentially, Carver writes a new ending for the Cheever story. No matter how much one writer admires another, the act of writing a sequel prompts a comparison of the two stories, and in such a comparison, **"The Train"** suffers.

Cheever evokes a sense of nightmare in "The Five-Forty-Eight." Through a series of flashbacks that further the narrative, he sets up the main character, Blake, as an unsavory business man who has taken advantage of a former secretary, Miss Dent. The secretary, whose sanity we question, has a pistol and follows Blake through the city to the train, seeking vengeance. The mode of the story is nightmare, the sense of meeting a person one has wronged; the feeling of being followed in an impersonal city; the journey of a vehicle that cannot be stopped, whose passengers share the same destiny; the realization that nobody—even nearby acquaintances—can help; the total submission to the will of an enemy. To drive home the point, Cheever notes that Miss Dent has a "gift for dreams." He ends the story with appropriate imagery, the stuff of nightmares: Blake is escorted from the train to a deserted spot outside the station, forced to his knees and, fearing death, made to fall forward in the dirt, a final degradation.

Carver's story, dedicated to Cheever, begins, "The woman was called Miss Dent, and earlier that evening she'd held a gun on a man." He picks up as Miss Dent heads back to the station, presumably to make the return trip to the city. In the waiting room, she overhears the absurd conversation of an Italian-sounding woman in a rose-colored knit dress and an old man in a white silk cravat. An excerpt:

> "It's that girl I feel sorry for," the woman said. "That poor soul alone in a house filled with simps and vipers. She's the one I feel sorry for. And she'll be the one to pay! None of the rest of them. Certainly not that imbecile they call Captain Nick! He isn't responsible for anything. Not him," the woman said.

The old man half-listens, saying non-committal things like "Don't worry about me." The conversation steers toward Miss Dent when the woman says "Is this woman with the handbag going to worry about you?" Miss Dent, however, keeps her distance. The woman becomes more absurd—"Kentucky Fried Chicken at the North Pole! Colonel Sanders in a parka and boots. That tore it! That was the limit!"—and her annoyance with Miss Dent becomes more focused: "You don't say much. . . . But I'll wager you could say a lot if someone got you started. Couldn't you? But you're a sly boots. You'd rather just sit with your prim little mouth while other people talk their heads off. Am I right? Still waters. Is that your name?" Eventually, Miss Dent is moved to speak out and contemplates telling the couple that she has a gun in her handbag, but at that moment the train arrives.

To this point, the story succeeds, if not in comparison with Cheever's, at least on its own merits. The weird conversation is intriguing and skillfully wrought, and the ignorant goading of a woman who has a weapon within reach triggers a tension that is the hallmark of any Carver story. But as in **"A Small, Good Thing,"** the ending is weakened by a change in point of view away from Miss Dent to passengers on the arriving train. The change occurs in two long paragraphs that end the story. The passengers see Miss Dent and the others climb aboard and feel sure

> that whatever these people's business had been that night, it had not come to a happy conclusion. But the passengers had seen things more various than this in their lifetime. The world is filled with business of every sort, as they well knew. This still was not as bad, perhaps, as it could be. For this reason, they scarcely gave another thought to these three. . . . Instead, the passengers gazed out at the station and went back to thinking about their own business, those things that had engaged them before the station stop.

Such a strategy in an eight-page story calls attention to itself, no matter how skilled the author is in changing point of view. Tobias Wolff pulls it off in a considerably longer story, "An Episode in the Life of Professor Brooke," and succeeds because the change comes in a short, last paragraph that also serves as a flash forward, putting a neat cap on a story that could use one. Not so in **"The Train."** When Miss Dent is ready to confront the woman and man, a strategy we are prepared for, she doesn't and the reader is denied. Conveniently, the train arrives. The tension that the woman's antagonism generates is lost because Miss Dent does not confront the couple. She curiously lives up to the "sly boots/still waters" image and boards the train, undercutting the tension Carver meant to convey on a larger scale through the ignorance of the passengers. At best, **"The Train"** seems an indulgence; at worst, an exercise.

Perhaps the story with the weakest ending is **"Preservation."** It is told through Sandy, whose husband has lost his job and exiles himself to the sofa. Occasionally he reads a coffee-table book, *Mysteries of the Past,* staring long at a photograph of a two-thousand-year-old man recovered from a peat bog. The story is almost lyric, developing Sandy through interior monologue. The narrative proper begins when Sandy comes home from work to find the refrigerator has broken down and most of the food inside has spoiled. Now we are in familiar Carver territory: a small, domestic problem will serve as a catalyst to illuminate larger issues. The couple cannot afford a new refrigerator, and the husband is put on the spot:

> "We have to have one," she said. "Don't we need a fridge? Maybe we don't. Maybe we can keep our perishables on the window sill like those people in tenements do. Or else we could get one of those little Styrofoam coolers and buy some ice every day."

The husband relents, and they decide to look in the classifieds. They come across an entry about an auction, and the husband doesn't want to leave the house to go to it. Sandy encourages him, recalling how much she used to like attending auctions with her late father, whom she misses. The husband agrees, reluctantly, and they plan to go to it after she cooks some of the unthawed meat stacked with other food items on the table. Then the ending:

> Sandy cleared the newspaper away and shoved the food to the far side of the table. "Sit down," she said to her husband once more. He moved his plate from one hand to the other. But he kept standing there. It was then she saw puddles of water on the table. She heard water, too. It was dripping off the table and onto the linoleum.
>
> She looked down at her husband's bare feet. She stared at his feet next to the pool of water. She knew she'd never again in her life see anything so unusual. But she didn't know what to make of it. She thought she'd better put on some lipstick, get her coat, and go ahead to the auction. But she couldn't take her eyes from her husband's feet. She put her plate on the table and watched until the feet left the kitchen and went back into the living room.

The ending resolves nothing in the story. It indicates that the husband has taken up post again at the sofa. Sandy, always free to come and go as she pleases, probably will attend the auction. For the time being, however, she is mesmerized by her husband's feet, a curious image the reader can only connect to the photograph of the two-thousand-year-old man. But Carver has done little to charge that symbol and color the ending through it. The reader is forced to conclude the cycle of the forlorn man on the sofa is beginning again, this time with dire consequences. The reader must work harder than the author to come up with any meaning, a situation Carver's readers are unaccustomed to and one that rarely occurs.

Despite weak endings in four stories, ***Cathedral*** is a good book for all that Carver's fiction has come to represent about modern life—the futility of coping with alcoholism, eking out a living, saving a marriage, and re-learning to love. In addition, the collection has a handful of stories with genuine upbeat endings. Such stories enhance ***Cathedral*** not only because they show hope in an unforgiving world but because they help define emotional boundaries.

The effect is powerful in book form. **"Where I'm Calling From," "Fever,"** and the title story **"Cathedral"** resist the sense of tragedy so prevalent in **"Vitamins," "Careful,"** and **"The Compartment."** The latter stories seem more hopeless in book format than perhaps originally intended, and the upbeat fiction more optimistic, with other stories wavering between those poles. Thus, in ***Cathedral,*** Carver evokes a wider range of emotions in the reader while creating a milieu more realistic than the ones in ***Will You Please Be Quiet, Please?,*** his first uneven book, and in ***What We Talk About When We Talk About Love.***

"Vitamins" and **"Careful"** concern familiar Carver motifs—love (or the lack of it) and alcoholism. As we saw in comparisons of passages from **"The Bath"** and **"A Small, Good Thing,"** the writing in these newer stories is more sophisticated than the writing in ***What We Talk About When We Talk About Love,*** although **"Vitamins"** and **"Careful"** would fit well in that collection. **"The Compartment,"** again about love, is mostly interior monologue about a father's ambivalent feelings toward his son. A flashback to a fight scene that opens the story has as much tension as an early Carver short-short, **"Popular Mechanics,"** which features a man and a woman literally pulling apart a baby. The author of **"The Compartment,"** however, would never let such a powerful scene stand alone as a story; he integrates it within the larger context of a more developed fiction. This is the nature of the new Carver covering old ground, whether it is the rewriting of a story like **"The Bath"** or in the re-telling of familiar themes through more complex strategies. More important to the overall success of ***Cathedral,*** however, is the story critics have described as fuller and more optimistic than ones in his previous two books.

"Where I'm Calling From" features a narrator at a drying-out facility. Initially, the narrator is unable to tell his story: "I've been here once before. What's to say? I'm back." The strategy calls for the narrator to encourage a new-found friend, J. P., "to keep talking " about his wife, who taught him how to be a chimney sweep. J. P.'s story then is told second-hand through the narrator, a move that helps characterize the narrator as well as J. P. In addition, it puts more time and distance between the narrator and the fiction and avoids the sentimentality associated with love and chimney sweeps. In the passage below, the narrator relates how J. P. met his wife at a friend's house where she was sent to clean a chimney:

> When she'd finished her work, she rolled her things up in the blanket. From J. P.'s friend, she took a check that had been made out to her by his parents. And then she asks the friend if he wants to kiss her. "It's supposed to bring good luck," she says. That does it for J. P. The friend rolls his eyes. He clowns some more. Then, probably blushing, he kisses her on the cheek. At this minute, J. P. made up his mind about something. He put his beer down. He got up from the sofa. He went over to the young woman as she was starting to go out the door.
>
> "Me, too?" J. P. said to her.
>
> She swept her eyes over him. J. P. says he could feel his heart knocking. The young woman's name, it turns out, was Roxy.

The chimney sweep story is interwoven with scenes from the facility. When J. P. and the narrator first arrive, they have no appetite. But as J. P.'s love for Roxy becomes apparent—despite the setbacks caused by J. P.'s alcoholism—the narrator becomes more articulate about his own life and circumstances. The more the friends talk, the more they seem to recover. As the Roxy story unwinds, both men regain their appetite and desire to live again. The narrator, however, is still unable to communicate with his estranged wife or girlfriend. The storylines merge when Roxy visits J. P., who introduces her to the narrator in a touching scene that ends, appropriately, with a kiss from a chimney sweep:

> She moves over. She takes me by the shoulders—I'm a big man—and she plants this kiss on my lips. "How's that?" she says.
>
> "That's fine," I say.
>
> "Nothing to it," she says. She's still holding me by the shoulders. She's looking me right in the eyes. "Good luck," she says, and then she lets go of me.

After the kiss, the narrator is able to tell more of his own story, and the fiction concludes with him making up his mind to telephone his wife and girlfriend—a sign that he is on the road to recovery.

A similar ending occurs in **"Fever,"** a third-person story whose chief character, Carlyle, is learning to cope with the breakup of his marriage, while being father and mother to two children. Carlyle has another concern—finding a competent babysitter—the type of problem that can mushroom to colossal proportions in a Carver story. This one seems destined to do so. But the estranged wife, an aspiring artist who has run off with another school teacher and mutual friend, solves the problem long-distance via telephone. She puts her husband on to Mrs. Webster, a motherly figure who temporarily frees Carlyle from his troubles, as the narrative persona tells us in this passage: "He believed his life was beginning again. Though he hadn't heard from Eileen since that call six weeks ago, he found himself able to think about her without being angry or else close to tears."

At this point we sense that circumstances are too right for a Carver story and that something will occur to destroy the serenity that depends on Mrs. Webster. Two things happen: Carlyle comes down with fever on the very day his babysitter tells him that she will be leaving with her husband for Oregon. She explains that her stepson has invited her and her husband to help with a mink ranch, a proposition they cannot refuse. She says of her husband: "Jim won't have to worry anymore about what's going to happen to us. . . . He was sixty-two last week. He hasn't had anything for some time." The love the Websters share evokes a sympathetic response from Carlyle, who once thought he would grow old with his wife and now realizes that will never occur. The realization bonds Carlyle to the old woman, and he tells her about his love for Eileen and how the love went wrong. It is an ending skillfully handled through dialogue and commentary and one that never leaves Carlyle's point of view. Finally, the Websters must leave and Carlyle feels something end in his life. The last paragraph hints at the same kind of hope found in **"Where I'm Calling From":**

> As the pickup lurched forward, he lifted his arm once more. He saw the old couple lean toward him briefly as they drove away. Then he brought his arm down and turned to his children.

The story, one of the best in the collection, also contains humor associated with Carlyle's wife. She has adopted a new lifestyle in California and writes rambling letters that proclaim "That which is truly bonded can never become unbonded." She studies Carlyle's karma and advises him in telephone calls. She leaves absurd messages for him—"what goes around, comes around"—with Mrs. Webster. But despite the wife's weirdness, she is often on target, from knowing that Carlyle needs a good sitter to sensing his sickness: "I know, don't ask me how, that things are not going so well right now. You're sick, aren't you?" Such humor serves a purpose. It creates an atmosphere similar to tragicomedy, a feeling that although things will worsen in the fiction, the characters will emerge better for it.

That same sense of humor, however black, carries the title

story. The occasion is the visit of Robert, a blind man who just lost his wife and who once employed the narrator's wife as a reader. The narrator is jealous. He doesn't have to tell us. As in **"Where I'm Calling From,"** exposition is funneled to us second-hand, revealing more about the state of the narrator's mind than of Robert's personal past:

> They'd married, lived and worked together, slept together—had sex, sure—and then the blind man had to bury her. . . . Imagine a woman who could never see herself as she was seen in the eyes of her loved one. A woman who could go on day after day and never receive the smallest compliment from her beloved. A woman whose husband could never read the expression on her face, be it misery or something better. Someone who could wear makeup or not—what difference to him? She could, if she wanted, wear green eye-shadow around one eye, a straight pin in her nostril, yellow slacks and purple shoes, no matter. And then to slip off into death, the blind man's hand on her hand, his blind eyes streaming tears—I'm imagining now—her last thought may be this: that he never even knew what she looked like, and she on an express to the grave.

Robert arrives, and the narrator's jealousy worsens because his wife shows the blind man extra attention. Carver undercuts that jealousy with humor, leading us through a hilarious dinner scene that begins: "We dug in. We ate everything there was to eat on the table. We ate like there was no tomorrow. We didn't talk. We ate. We scarfed. We grazed that table. We were into serious eating." After dinner, Robert and the wife reminisce and the narrator feels left out. He strikes back, again with humor, rolling a joint and offering some to the blind man when the wife goes upstairs to get ready for bed. Once the wife returns and comes to accept Robert's sharing a joint with her husband, she tokes along with them until she falls asleep. The narrator continues his antics:

> I wish my wife hadn't pooped out. Her head lay across the back of the sofa, her mouth open. She turned so that her robe had slipped away from her legs, exposing a juicy thigh. I reached to draw her robe back over her, and it was then that I glanced at the blind man. What the hell! I flipped the robe open again.

Forced now to keep each other company, the narrator watches television and describes a documentary about cathedrals for the blind man. He has a difficult time. He asks Robert if he knows the difference between a cathedral and a Baptist church. And the blind man replies that the men who make building cathedrals their life's work never live to see the completion of that work—a phrase that resounds through the whole fiction. It reverberates off the narrator's previous commentary about Robert's late wife and pivots the action toward one of the better endings in the book.

Robert asks the narrator to get some heavy paper and a pen. He puts his hand over the narrator's hand and asks him to draw a cathedral. The blind man gives encouragement and advice: "You got it bub. I can tell. You didn't think you could. But you can, can't you? You're cooking with gas now. You know what I'm saying? We're going to really have us something here in a minute. . . . Put some people in there now. What's a cathedral without people?" The process continues until Robert tells the narrator to close his eyes and keep drawing, a feeling the narrator says "was like nothing else in my life up to now." The blind man has given the narrator a new kind of vision, a moral one, and the narrator is changed by the experience.

This is the achievement of ***Cathedral,*** a book that overcomes weak endings in certain stories and goes on to mark new terrain for Carver. In the title story and in **"Where I'm Calling From"** and **"Fever,"** he manages to elevate common characters to a higher plane, and he does so by stressing humanity. Lesser characters learn from people like Robert, Roxy, and Mrs. Webster, ordinary but well-meaning characters who touch another's life and somehow change it for the better. Alongside more tragic stories, these emerge as stronger and more memorable. They are better written, surely, and are more in the mainstream tradition, but they also exhibit an energy that should keep Carver at the fore of American contemporary fiction for a long time to come. (pp. 73-87)

Michael J. Bugeja, "Tarnish and Silver: An Analysis of Carver's 'Cathedral'," in The South Dakota Review, *Vol. 24, No. 3, Autumn, 1986, pp. 73-87.*

Marc Chénetier (essay date 1986)

[*In the following excerpt, Chénetier argues for an analysis of Carver's short stories based on rhetorical structure.*]

Somewhere between Sherwood Anderson and Ring Lardner, if that axis had been prolonged through the refractive experimental wave of the 1960s and 1970s; somewhere between William Carlos Williams and Charles Bukowski, if literary categories had not prohibited the practice of genre solecism; somewhere between Grace Paley, Tillie Olsen, and the last works of Richard Brautigan, if gender politics had not befuddled the eye in search of the common revelations hidden under daily trivia; somewhere between George Bellows, Edward Hopper, and Jasper Johns, should *ut pictura poesis* apply: there writes Raymond Carver. Not that such rough localizations necessarily echo his own set of debts and reverences. A card above his writing desk highlights one of Ezra Pound's admonitions: "Fundamental accuracy of statement is the ONE sole morality of writing." Hemingway, Tolstoy, and John Gardner, for different reasons (conciseness, a taste for the implicit, and personal contacts, respectively), loom large on Carver's mental and artistic horizon. But his existential and aesthetic concerns clearly have much in common with writers preoccupied with picturing the amazement of the quotidian. Whence the near-exclusive attention given to the thematic layout of his work by his few reviewers and critics. After each collection, reviews cautiously appear, sketching one or two of Carver's concerns and tentatively announcing the arrival of a "new realism." Repetition is the order of the reviewing day. Of serious investigation, there is precious little: there are courageous assessments by Thomas Le Clair [see Further Reading list] and Alain Arias-Misson [see excerpt dated 1982] and one long interesting article on ***Will You Please Be Quiet, Please?*** where David Boxer and Cassandra Phillips foreground and analyze major thematic features [see excerpt dated 1979].

Overall, "what Carver talks about" has dominated presentations to such an extent that the last thing one is tempted to do is add yet another examination of a writer advertised as a mere witness to the lame joys and devastating limbic sorrows of lower-middle America. But Carver's is a voice that brings to contemporary fiction more than a low-key and unlyrical commentary on protagonists "butchered out of their souls a thousand years" (as Allen Ginsberg puts it in *Howl*), a voice that never endeavors merely to bring forth a picture of the American mind paralyzed by the contradictions of might and want or of soul-handicapped gropings for a minimal sense of self, a voice that owes its richness and worth to the revisiting of rhetorical possibilities rather than to the talented redaction of another installment of Gogol's *Dead Souls*.

Needless to say, Carver's "world," unique and idiosyncratic to the point of having preemptively ruined a whole generation of young epigones, is worth exploring. But its conscientious exploration leads to further and, in critical terms, more fertile interrogations. Should Carver's "world" be so explicitly and "realistically" accurate, other explorers of the way in which "the other half" lives were not missing. But his fiction is not tit-for-tat, sign-for-thing journalistic investigation into the existence of mainstream alienation and marginality of the self. Narratives that begin with a bang and move on to strange muteness, that document hollowness by omission, have a "message" that amply transcends the linear and sequential deciphering of the words appearing on the page.

On the most immediate of levels, Carver's stories are studies in embarrassment. The violent economy of his short stories ("Get in. Get out. Don't linger. Go on.") forces the reader *in medias res,* almost kicking him upon the stage. The curtain opens, the suspended heartbeats of cleaved lives abruptly resume as Carver, using imperative and unjustified deictics bludgeons presence upon the reader: "*This* old station wagon with Minnesota plates pulls into a parking space in front of *the* window"; "*That* morning *she* pours Teacher's over *my* belly and licks it off." But past the opening lines the text proceeds to unravel into misdirection, hesitatingly gropes its way into rough-dug channels over whose less than abrupt shoulders it constantly threatens to flow.

The "selves" depicted in his pages have so little sense of attachment, belonging, and identity that the very plurality of the main protagonist in **"Fat"** forces him to refer to himself in the first person plural (" 'We're ready to order now', he says"). Loose, at large, and often utterly lost, their existence depends, for the duration of each story, on the concentrated exploration of the potential meanings attached to a single incident, whether minor or traumatically unsettling. Thus, for a minute, can a provisional sense of identity be chosen from among the variety of open-ended experiences which constitute their patchy lives. Identity is process and this process is what Carver's stories trigger, from crisis to crisis. There is hardly any sense ever given of the reasons why or ways in which one ever reached the opening of these superficially anecdotal moments; sudden entrances upon the page point to the characters' absence of control over lives consistently rendered through a language of vagueness and pointlessness.

Suspended between mysterious and unclear origins or causes and what I shall describe as preseismic endings, the stories are themselves explorations of mystery and vague sketches of revelation. [In "On Writing"] Carver designates a sentence by Chekhov as the epitome of the effect he strives for: "And suddenly everything became clear to him." But such blossoming knowledge is all but transitive for Carver: "I find these words filled with wonder and possibility. I love their simple clarity, and the hint of revelation that's implied. There is mystery, too: What has been unclear before? Why is it just now becoming clear? What's happened? Most of all—what now? There are consequences as a result of such sudden awakenings. I feel a sharp sense of relief—and anticipation." To use another natural metaphor, Carver's stories follow the ripples made by a stone in water. The reader is too late to catch a glimpse of the stone before it sinks and must be content with the detailed analysis of the ripples it has produced on the surface of the pond. Nor is he ever allowed to witness the agonizing break of the ripples against the shore. Carver's stories, with rare exceptions, are totally comprised in the surface covered and organized by the rings, excluding both the original point of impact ("Everything has changed since Harry's death," one story begins, but one never knows either about Harry or his death) and the final slushy smack against the bank ("He said, 'I just want to say one more thing'. But then he could not think what it could possibly be."). Carver's devotion to the circumscribed surface on which the wider and wider circles of ever fainter and fainter suggestion are the only evidence of clean brutal shocks may account for the lack of solidity of all information and the lability of diegetic arrangements, for the feeling of helpless drift conveyed by bobbing protagonists. Going from A to B without delimiting A or B leaves us with pure change, the space in between, natural change, as in "furious *seasons,*" moods and meteorological alterations, the endless process of reorganization and drive for coherence whereby nature attempts to equate being and meaning, the suspended seconds between blinding thunderbolt and crashing thunderclap. Such between-ness constitutes an important part of Carver's sense of "reserve."

Let us shift from water to fire for a final set of metaphors; the author himself suggests it whose most beautiful stories (**"Dummy," "So Much Water So Close to Home,"** and **"Distance"**) use the creeks and streams of *Near Klamath* and mix them with the *Fires* of creation, influences, and feverish anger into the *bona fide* "ordeals" of his characters' lives. Tidal waves and volcanic rumblings, sparks and ominous drops, flares and drownings scan one important and inconspicuous thematic dominant of a fictive world both irresistibly awash and timidly agleam.

One might say that Carver fuses his stories so that they

detonate a few minutes after one has read them. The explosion never takes place between the covers of a collection, even though two examples may act as the useful exceptions that confirm the rule. The explicit violence that concludes **"Tell the Women We're Going"** is one; it considerably weakens the story. Another, less explicit, concludes the tiny masterpiece called **"Mine"** in ***Furious Seasons*** and **"Popular Mechanics"** in ***What We Talk About:*** parents fighting over possession of a baby pull its limbs in different directions. The last lines hint at the possibility of some atrociously revisited judgment of Solomon [brackets indicate the version contained in ***Furious Seasons***]:

> She would have it, this baby ["whose chubby face gazed up at them from the picture on the table"]. She grabbed for the baby's other arm. She caught the baby around the wrist and leaned back. But he would not let go ["He would not give."]. He felt the baby slipping [going] out of his hands and pulled back very hard. ["and he pulled back hard. He pulled back very hard."] In this manner, the issue was decided. ["In this manner they decided the issue."]

The changes brought about by the revision of the tale point to Carver's masterful handling of ambiguity and suspension. The presence of the picture in the first version allowed metonymy to be a refuge against horror; but what active mode was still necessary in the original last sentence to make aggressivity manifest is replaced, in the more recent version, by a passive "the issue was decided" that takes out of the ending a modicum of the active violence born of the disappearance of the picture.

Such delicate balances are engineered to keep the reader tottering on the brink of certainty, which is much closer to it than the characters themselves ever get. Such is the ironic and distancing power of a voice of which Alain Arias-Misson [see excerpt dated 1982] could quite accurately say that "Carver has not given a voice to his characters; he has given his characters to a voice."

And this is still as dangerously explicit as Carver ever gets. On the whole, his stories end in relative indeterminacy, but only after he has made sure that the reader will take the ultimate step they seem to require. By means of ellipsis and the implicit, they acquire an inescapably preseismic nature. Intimations of the nefarious lurk at all times as an important part of what Iuri Lotman would call the "arch-seme" of the texts. Carver has gone on record as repudiating the word "theme," an understandable stand on the part of a writer operating on the thin edge between meanings nascent and gone, pursuing cruelly indefinite states of "dis-ease," as he calls the evils to which William Kittredge's characters fall prey. He would rather talk of "obsessions," he tells us in the afterword to ***Fires,*** and he describes in similar terms his permanent elusive quest for the meaning of his own productions. Stories written as explorations in "process" rather than in "fixed positions" need take us clearly away from established notions of theme. One is constantly reminded of stories by Flannery O'Connor ("A View From the Woods," for example), in which grace has no currency. Incipient change, hints, possible directions, and aborted realizations replace plainly affirmative statements. **"Pastoral"** ended, before it was reworked as **"The Cabin"** for ***Fires,*** with the following sentence: "He stared at the wordless distorted things about him." The creation of stories devoid of a fixed telos invites repeated revision. Carver has identified with the process O'Connor described in her essay "Writing Short Stories." He does not know any more than she did how his stories will end as he begins writing them. Shortened, prolonged, altered, simplified, or made more analytical each revision, Carver's texts are not rewritten for improvement so much as because they programmatically demand to be. When prolonged, their original texture is of necessity altered to redistribute inklings towards a modified telos dictated by the rereading of a *primus lector inter lectores pares.* **"The Bath,"** an extraordinarily threatening story in ***What We Talk About*** thus becomes the longer and mellower **"A Small Good Thing"** of ***Cathedral,*** signalling in this latest volume a movement away from threatening ambiguity, a working towards hope rather than horror, and the abandonment of features Carver may have come to consider akin to the narrative "gimmicks" he has always denounced.

The "reserve" in his texts thus seems to have shifted ground, and with that shift has come another in the arch-seme itself, if not in the referential contents of the tales. The accent used to fall on the apparently unaccentuated part of the canvas, over the spots where the ground was bare, devoid of color, the place where fears and desires could be projected as hinges. Now, however, a certain affirmative explicitness—however damning—has invaded ***Cathedral;*** from the title story to the new version of **"A Small Good Thing,"** in the form of the rather dark pigments covering the ground. In places, then, where the arch-seme used to consist of the very set of mutely deductive unifying suggestions underlying the disconnected fragments of the text, a certain chromatism of the brush may now be attempting to connect them through harmonic—and more harmonious—echoes. A spark of hope in **"Fever"** and in **"Cathedral"** tends to give a potentially new agenda to stories whose ultimate promise seems to remain that blindness unavoidably undercuts all awakenings. Commenting on Carver's characters, a reviewer wrote that the "only way for them to validate themselves is through the performance of some act—any act—that gives them the illusion of free will" [see Atlas entry in Further Reading list]. One could also suggest that if such blind gropings are intransitive they aim at modifying the orientation of a field of forces felt to be adverse, forces materialized by objects, appearances, conversations, attitudes, and behaviors that seem to demand that one be constantly on one's guard, uncommitted, and more or less passively receptive to their message of anguish. What is, threatens, and what is not, threatens even more. Moving away from present visible menaces one is just as much at risk to fall into hidden pits and suggested abysses. Gesticulations on the surface may be gestures for survival, but they tend to be just as effective as mindless thrashing over ice floes or quicksands. A strictly phatic use of language may signal presence with insistence but it hardly gives it any dynamism or sense of direction. Thus performing may spell disaster too and the "quietistic" form of the short story, in which Osip Mandelstam saw the canonical form of lower class alienation and which he opposed to the "Napoleonic" mastery of the novel, is particularly adapted to the need for cover of Carver's characters.

A sense of menace is the arch-seme that not only goes into or comes out of Carver's stories but also activates them and invites their constant reexploration and rewriting. Whatever "thematic" dressing that foundation is given matters far less than the problematic that provides the energy for discursive exploration. [In "On Writing" Carver states]:

> I think a little menace is fine to have in a story. For one thing, it's good for the circulation. There has to be tension, a sense that something is imminent, that certain things are in relentless motion, or else, more often, there simply won't be a story. What creates tension in a piece of fiction is partly the way the concrete words are linked together to make up the visible action of the story. But it's also the things that are left out, that are implied, the landscape just under the smooth (but sometimes broken and unsettled) surface of things.

Discussing Carver's stories one cannot *know* "what we talk about when we talk about them" without considering the rhetorical model governing the manner in which, time after time, Carver performs them. The way they are *about* anything is what must now concern us.

The promotional material on the jacket of ***Cathedral*** not unexpectedly emphasizes the pervasive atmosphere of stories that ominously mine the motherlode of threat. It uses for that effect terms with which no one could disagree, but contains, one objective that may lead astray the reader on the lookout for the underpinnings of Carver's art: "uninflected." I would like to argue here that the portion of the canvas left uncovered by the pigments of his prose contains nonetheless a complex weave of inflections, an underlying fabric whose warp and woof confer on the texts their direction and pattern while providing the power, and drawing the limits, of their meaning. These stories whose conclusions are inflected rather than inflicted upon us suggest that rhetorical considerations may be better suited to our analysis than thematic queries concerned with whatever is shown.

The interesting feature of Carver's writings is that they do not point to or at events, actions, and states of being to make plain their significance through a positivistic gesture of monstration so much as they define spheres from within and without, reveal limits and porous partitions between what is and what might be, explore the osmotic layer of contact between hypothetic realizations and tangential absences. Carver likes to define fiction as the bringing of the news from one world into another. But this process of communication is rather one that relies on suggestion, through ellipsis and indeterminacy, than one that endeavors to fill us in on what lies in the other world through a process of translation, be it metaphorical or grounded in referential illusion.

In "On Writing," Carver says: "The words can be so precise they may even sound flat, but they can still carry." Out of flatness, hollowness, and the systematized emptying of referentiality from lexicon and structure alike, he comes close indeed to a definition of literature by Umberto Eco in *L'Opera Aperta* that marks one step toward the question of negativity: "The determinate denotation of an indeterminate object."

Carver's strategic goal is to designate what is left out of a landscape of people and objects qualified by Thomas LeClair as "Hopper-plain." The tactical operations lexically bear on the use of indefinites (the recurrence of "it," "what," "something," and "thing" is paramount here); a permanent recycling of words from one sentence to the next that generates semantic abrasion and anaphorically carries the reader away from the original and already moderately contextualized occurrence; the use of objects as unexplained and disquieting symptoms (a word printed in hand on a banknote, the bridle in the story of that title, or the set of false teeth sitting on top of the T.V. set in **"Feathers"**).

Syntactically, parataxis feeds the elliptic and so does the uniformization of tense in narratives that weave memories, present situations, and speculations on becoming. The possibilities for bifurcation abound, lodged under the elliptic hinges between passages that seem to eliminate the idea of progression by their use of circular and repetitious dialogue; most passages must rely on the drastic reorientation of attention generated by alineas and permanent "reprises" to wrench themselves away from the burrowing effect of voices apparently unable to get away from under their own weight by logical subordination or anything resembling reasoning. Events and gestures, however minor and unmotivated, dominate the articulative possibilities of the characters to such an extent that their frequent randomness, taking over all responsibility for the concatenation of paragraphs, points systematically to the collagelike quality of an apprehension of the real unable to rely on the analytic and organizing powers of consciousness. Indeterminacy thus complements the sense of a lack of control and direction; reified paragraphs assume the dramatic consecution of minds jerked or brutalized from one moment into the next, haphazardly pushed into realization by novel dispositions of the familiar.

The overall structure of the stories promotes the impression founded on this local analysis. In generalizing the use of what Roman Ingarden might call "spots of indeterminacy" and of what Wolfgang Iser might call "blanks" into the self-defeating "progressions" of narratives devised to get as close as possible to Cynthia Ozick's "foreknowledge of nakedness" (but no closer), Carver has extensive recourse to diegetic itineraries that fold back upon themselves, to analeptic recollection, circularity, and phatic redundancy. One might say that these are stories without an elsewhere, stories that extend no opportunity to transcend experience. Discourses biting their own tail parallel the self-enclosed circularity of lives that can merely recycle their problems into pretenses of temporary solution. Most of the characters' lives, unable to debouch outside of a past that has merely cornered them, are told by drilling out of the pregnant event motivating the story all that could pass for worthy relevance. In **"Careful,"** a conversation that would account for the original situation does *not* take place and is metaphorically relayed by a plugged up ear.

"Vitamins" is the story of an affair that does *not* take place, the energy-providing goods that the protagonist's wife peddles being ironically denied by flattened lives. **"The Compartment"** presents a crucial trip the ultimate justification for which vanishes along the way and makes room for a nonjourney strewn with nonincidents. Such slackening of the narrative spring, one that slowly unwinds without ever snapping into action, may be considered to render mimetically existential itineraries. But formal analysis reveals the paradoxical accomplishment of an author who has simultaneously "fused" his stories in the ways described above and has made his structures exercises in defusing the usual sources of narrative energy.

The dialogue, for example, demonstrates an increase of tension by hollowing out the conative with the absurdly extreme ingrowth of phatic conversation: "She said, 'I think I'll go upstairs and put on my robe. I think I'll change into something else. Robert, you make yourself comfortable,' she said. 'I'm comfortable,' the blind man said. 'I want you to feel comfortable in this house,' she said. 'I am comfortable,' the blind man said." **"Feathers," "Preservation,"** and **"Where I'm Calling From,"** to cull three examples at random from ***Cathedral,*** dramatize the sort of time-stuffing achieved by oral language so desperate to have nothing to hitch on to that it is compelled to maintain an endless recycled babble, a recourse as hollow and as minimally life-preserving as inflatable jackets. (pp. 164-76)

The systematic emptying of the narrative moment through a variety of tactical suggestions of indeterminacy makes us mistake wonderment about what got the characters there for a sense of impending threat. We are not afraid of what may lurk ahead so much as we are afraid of our growing consciousness that present disasters and stases cannot be mended through the efforts of the lame disabled consciousness that allowed them to happen in the first place. Carver's sense of menace is not necessarily born of the vast and vacant spaces lying beyond the final period of each story, even though that area may be where the reader initially projects his or her own misgivings. Much rather, Carver is most threatening when one can say of a character, whose minimal articulateness we know will not allow him to disentangle himself from that impenetrable brush, what [Imamu Amiri Baraka] could say, twenty years ago of "speculative hipsters": "He had got, finally, / to the forest / of motives."

Such reaching for mute causes and moot consequences prepares us for an examination of negativity in Carver's work, that which [Wolfgang] Iser defines as the "nonformulation of the not-yet comprehended" [*The Act of Reading* (1980)]. Negativity, then, is the unformulated double, the background or reverse side suggested by omission, concealment, and cancellation. But before we examine negativity, we must turn to another set of linguistic elements constituting what we might tentatively describe as the most visible and practical windows opened by the text onto its necessary obverse, or else as the combination of beckoning signs and black holes that forcefully draw us into or through the fabric in quest of what it simultaneously covers, denies, implies, rejects, and suggests. Which is where, of course, "reserve" takes on an altogether new meaning: what we might call the "WH factor" does not only consist of Carver's strategic indeterminacy but also of his insistent use of interrogations, interrogative structures, and indefinite centers one can only define and fill with queries. *What, why, when,* and *which* scan writings that are always, in one manner or another, interrogations and wonderments. There is, of course, the astonishing number of titles with questions: **"Where Is Everyone?", "Why Don't You Dance?", "Will You Please Be Quiet, Please?", "Are You A Doctor?", "What's in Alaska?", "What Do You Do in San Francisco?", "Why Honey?", "How About This?"**, and **"What Is It?".** Such stories, mostly included in ***Will You Please Be Quiet, Please?,*** systematically pit the implicit and the subterraneous against explicit narratives aiming at some kind of resolution. Going unanswered, such questions linger in the mind during and after the reading of the texts, inciting one to look among the blanks and negations for answers feeding on transcended literal meaning, activating another multifarious set of questions where none is explicitly made to appear, and compelling to recycle mere suggestions and possibilities into new keys successively placed at the opening of the score. In which case, of course, less becomes more as willful expansion of what is merely hinted at becomes the necessary requisite for implementing the temptation of all transitive readings.

But such "questions" can also do without their final characteristic typographical mark. As a matter of fact, the passage from ***Will You Please*** to ***What We Talk About*** seems marked by a transition from recognizable questions to implicit ones. "What we talk about," being constantly defined by the very vagueness of such a lack of definition, is a recurrent notion that operates "en creux," the vague geometrical locus determined by the various points where thrusts at definition come to expire. A sense of internal puzzlement replaces the typographical marker where it does not appear; one could describe the internal shift in economy from ***Will You Please*** to ***What We Talk About*** as one regulated by an injection of ellipsis and irresolutions into texts stripped of their avowedly interrogative program. Sparer, more trimmed and elusive, more elliptic, sketchier (a sizeable number of them are reworked from the contents of ***Furious Seasons,*** and always in a reductive manner) the stories contained in ***What We Talk About*** have lost the questions of their titles and compensated them by a larger proportion of blanks within them or in their ending. For example, **"Why Don't You Dance?"**, the only questionlike title in ***What We Talk About,*** ends in a significant way that leaves the question operational while shutting the story down: "She kept talking. She told everyone. There was more to it, and she was trying to get it talked out. After a time, she quit trying." Conversely, the story entitled **"Mr. Coffee and Mr. Fixit"** in ***What We Talk About*** has a question for its title in ***Fires;*** there, in its much longer version as **"Where Is Everyone?"**, it makes plain a number of details that remain quite puzzling in the shortened text. Simultaneously, in ***What We Talk About*** parataxis is pushed to limits it never quite reached in ***Fires.*** The barest skeleton necessary for suggestion remains and a number of incidents that can be read as explanation in **"Where Is Everyone?"** are left as mere questions or unclear allusions in **"Mr. Coffee and Mr. Fixit"**. The thermos jug filled with vodka, the death of the father, the side affair with Beverly, and all the details that made for "understanding" or "answering" a story in the interrogative mode have been toned down and have lodged the interrogations dismissed from the title at the heart of the text itself.

The ratio of question-titles to internal explicitness appears rather constant and seems to confirm Roland Barthes's definition: "A question is never anything but its own scattered answer, dispersed in fragments among which meaning erupts and escapes at the same time." Judging by the ends of the stories, the tendency seems to be that the more clearly formulated the question is, the less diffuse and uncertain the answer becomes; the most plainly "affirmative" title will be the one that retains the greatest level of explicit indeterminacy. To borrow categories from Barthes's *S / Z,* even though both the proairetic and the hermeneutic codes can be traced in all stories, they are all too often superposed and alternately but nonexplicitly activated. The interrogative mode, foregrounded or clandestine, in turn activates one or the other at the expense of the one left dormant. Where the hermeneutic code is foregrounded by interrogative sentences, the proairetic assumes a more stabilized form. Let the proairetic dominate and the entire text—from lexicon to overall structure via syntactic choices—is activated as a tantalizing hermeneutic device. But in neither case is resolution clearly brought about. Diversely implanted in the mind of the reader, all manners of questions remain while Carver interrupts rather than ends his narratives. All hollow spots must be invested by the reading mind in sympathy or solidarity with the protagonists' inability to choose and decide. Very much like Samuel Beckett, in a text that derives its title from systematic use of the "WH Factor" (*What Where*), Carver always whispers: "Make sense who may. I switch off."

Eerily echoing Carver's definition of fiction ["Good fiction is partly a bringing of the news from one world to another"], Wolfgang Iser writes: "Fiction may be defined as a form of communication since it brings into the world something which is not already there." And he adds: "That which literature brings into the world can only reveal itself as negativity." It is within this context of negativity that Carver's fictions may perhaps be assessed in the most satisfactory manner. In effect, Carver's voice does not feel justified to damn or judge the various fictitious situations it depicts. Irony, always a bearer of blasting torches and sardonic piques, is not suited to the purposes of a writer who merely wants to make plain a consciousness of the abyss without pushing his characters into it as sacrificial and vaguely redemptive victims. His art is therefore one that wants to make manifest whatever, precisely, cannot be pointed at; whatever ails his protagonists may have causes they are unable to discover and consequences that we cannot fathom more than they. By activating in the midst of a rather meagre diegetic landscape a suggestive structure pointing, so to speak, to having-beens or might-bes, Carver makes plain the essential negative thrust of his endeavors. This process, to particularize a more general view of Iser,

> does not consist in giving a determinate solution to the determinate problems posed, but in the transformation of events into the discovery of the virtual cause. Meaning thus emerges as the reverse side of what the text has depicted. The world of the text appears in a state of alienation, and this alienation effect indicates that meaning is potentially there, awaiting redemption from its potentiality. In consequence of this, the unwritten text is constituted by a dialectic mutation of the written. . . . Meaning coincides with the emergence of the reverse side of the represented world. . . . We see the twofold structure of negativity—as the cause of the deformation it is also the potential remedy, and is thus the structural basis for communication.

Carver exploits negativity rather than irony to invalidate the reality his texts manifest. By pointing consistently to that which "has not yet been comprehended"—and another suggestion of his stories is that the characters themselves, not being quite equipped for the task, are pushed all the deeper into the process of alienation—Carver favors contact between the struggling nature of the object of representation and the decoding attitudes of the reader at the reception end of the line. The mediating effects of the interrogative structure, of the elements of indeterminacy, and of the undecidable prolongation of the diegetic end transform his narratives into far less and far more than what most reviewers and critics have been tempted to pigeonhole as "realism" or "minimalism."

Even thematically, lessons have to be drawn from Carver's refusal to designate his characters' fate as failure or incompletion. His work goes squarely against the grain of a tradition that considers literature as a generally cathartic or resolutive gesture, a tradition that culminates with the modernist hypostatization of Art as redeeming construct. Adorno [in *Aesthetische Theorie* (1970)], militating against the expulsion of negativity from art, which he read as a form of quietism, argued in favor of an art, such as Raymond Carver's, that refused to defuse the contradictions and quandaries out of which it was born, against a pre-Lacanian, vulgar-Freudian vision of expression as outlet, overflow, respite, or evacuation. . . . Irresolute endings, texts strewn with puzzling gaps, and opening situations progressively destabilized toward a sense of loss and disorientation thus add an aesthetic, moral, and ideological impact to a set of systematic formal disruptions. Nestled at the center of a paragraph that thrives on vagueness and the indefinite, a sentence in **"Fever"** may well be Carver's ultimate aesthetic statement of the question:

> She also sent Carlyle long, rambling letters, in which she asked for his understanding in this matter—*this matter* [Carver's italics]—but told him that she was happy. Happy. *As if, Carlyle thought, happiness was all there was to life* [my italics]. She told him that if he really loved her, as he said he did, and as she really believed—she loved him too, don't forget—then he would understand and accept things as they were.

Such refusal to let the text solve the issues that gave it birth can perhaps be best exemplified, both technically and hermeneutically, by two privileged tropic gestures in the works: halving and the status of metaphor.

Reading Carver, one cannot but be struck by abundant occurences of what I will call here "halving." Interestingly enough, Boxer and Phillips's article on "dissociation" exploits a number of images and dramatic situations pointing to "a sense of disengagement from one's own identity and life, a state of standing apart from whatever defines the self, or of being unselfed." It also notices that most of the existential states of what I would personally refuse to call "selves" are states of "suspended animation," being *between* semesters, stories, marriages, jobs, alcoholic bouts, sleeping, and waking. But such disconnection from the familiar flow of a "normal" existence cannot only be traced to practical matters of life organization. Thematically exploiting the fact, underlined by Iser, that "if the basic reference of the text is to the penumbra of excluded possibilities, one might say that the borderlines of existing systems are the starting point for the literary text," Carver makes a point of having his characters choose, as refuge, places of the body and mind that stand halfway between possibilities, places through which the flow of information "from one world to another" will be channeled in a privileged manner, birds of omen flying through high passes. The impossibility of exhausting or even of getting at tantalizing meanings tends to place all characters in a position of extended reaching, makes them teeter on verges and cuts driven through their experience. They beckon to the other lying on the opposite slope with a vaguely hopeful gesture of completion, to "the other life," as the title of a poem puts it, where "my wife is in the other half of this mobile home." The "Poem for Karl Wallenda, Aerialist Supreme" depicts him "midway between hotel and hotel," a reminder of the couple provisionally caught on the landing between two doors in **"Neighbors."** Similarly, all moments are taken as dividing time into an unsolvable past and an improbable future. The abundance of connecting devices such as "next morning" or "afterwards" as paragraph openers makes plain the perpetual division operated in time and space by lives in quest of what escaped. Subrevelatory moments will occur over a double gate **("I Could See the Smallest Things")** or during the meetings of parallel couples, meetings that formally evidence the precariousness of balances as much as they dramatically trigger debilitating comparisons and promote an extensive recourse to the vicarious (**"Neighbors,"** of course, but also **"They're Not Your Husband"** or **"What's in Alaska?"** in ***Will You Please*** and **"Feathers," "The Train," "Fever,"** or **"Cathedral"** in ***Cathedral***). As the narrator of **"What Do You Do in San Francisco?"** puts it: "The situation was close enough to get me thinking." Things half-told go along with stories halved by revision, stories where halving is either the dramatic outcome (**"Mine"** in ***Furious Seasons,*** and **"Nobody Said Anything,"** where a trout has replaced the fated baby), the dramatic source of tension (the half-realized affair of **"Are You a Doctor?"**), or a part of the circumambient decor (the half-light of **"Sixty Acres"** drowning incomplete actions and realizations, the half-glances exchanged in all the stories); there are stories in which mirrors and the vicarious are tentatively used as doomed processes of completion. Desire and contradiction are the paralyzing forces that prevent these characters from getting away from vague pains and half-realized torments. The following passage features a rare density of binary structures that spells out the character's indecision before it is made plain in the conclusive sentence:

> My wife *brought me up here the first time.* That's when we were still *together,* trying to make things work out. *She brought me here* and she stayed around for *an hour or two,* talking to Frank Martin in private. *Then* she left. *The next morning* Frank Martin got me aside and said "We can help you. If you want help and want to listen to what we say." But I didn't know *if they could help me or not.* Part of me wanted help. But there was another part.

Divided within or severed from a counterpart ("Whatever they did from now on, each would do it without the other," uncertain of or cut off from their reasons and motives, questions without answers, most characters emphasize the other half of the bed, the next room, next-door life, previous days, tomorrows, and coming opportunities as well as favor half-truths while failing to articulate anything *in toto.* The vaguely ominous nature of objects is born out of their belonging and not belonging, of their potential for otherness, and their power of defamiliarization. Reversals, parallels, contradictions, and paradoxes (from **"Dummy"** fished out of his own fish pond to **"The Lie"** via **"What We Talk About When We Talk About Love"** and **"The Fling"**) perpetually suggest that surfaces tend to have two sides and that the one we see is not the one that matters; they encourage us to turn all things over to look at their underbelly and install negativity at the heart of the written. All indefinites accrue to negative definition, and one is always closer to the stilled "endurance" of Faulknerian fame than to more traditional triumphant resolutions. Blind and silent, the fish of this poem is content with such provoked balance of forces as its minimal, repetitious, and non-affirmative stemming gesture can afford: "There's one that comes— / heavy, scarred, silent like the rest, / that simply holds against the current, // closing its dark mouth against / the current, closing and opening / as it holds the current." Equally blind and silenced by impoverished languages fed them by the media that fascinates them and shapes their reactions, Carver's characters are such fish, blind, scarred, half-way up or down river, face down in the water, contemplating a bottom obscured by the pale emission of their own paltry roe, reserving judgment, and moving laterally towards the edges.

It can be argued that the metaphorical process can be considered either as ally or enemy of negativity. Inasmuch as it makes manifest the unstoppable dissemination of meaning in the doomed movement of seizure of what must always remain radically other, the metaphorical can indeed be seen as a downstream representation of the unformulated that structures the text upstream and thereby appears as an inverted effect of negativity. [According to Iser, since it] "would be impossible for language to formulate both the deformation of human situations and the remedy in one and the same instant", [therefore] "language can never explicitly state the meaning: it can only make itself felt by way of the apparent deformations and distortions which the formulated text reveals." The metaphorical can be taken as such deformation and resorted to for effects that remain programmatically negative.

However, such distortion can also be apprehended from the point of view of its powers of translation, as the inscription into the text of what must remain more indefinite for negative purposes, the embodiment of that which must not be defined, the necessary hostage of the symbolic. Carver's refusal of metaphor strengthens a strategy that makes use of open-endedness not as a perpetual possibility for redefinition but as the programmatically limnal quality of the utterance, what A. R. Ammons calls "boundaried vacancies" [*Collected Poems, 1951-1971*]. With Carver, the metaphorical perpetually rests on this side of its realization. His reliance on "thing," "it," "what," and "whatever it was" betrays a desire not to bridge the space that separates negativity from articulate meaning. Given the context of the stories and their thematic drive, metaphor would appear as translation against the logics of a text feeding on grounds where no obvious meaning is supposed to grow, as the defining instrument of the negative spring. Jumping, so to speak, over negativity into the known and the controlled would necessarily signify that meaning has been reestablished by short-circuiting the devices that kept it strategically at bay. Looking at a disturbing moon, the woman narrating **"I Could See The Smallest Things"** dismisses the necessity of such a jump: "A big moon was laid over the mountains that went around the city. It was a white moon and covered with scars. *Any damn fool could imagine a face there.*" Not that overall situations cannot, in Carver's stories, be constructed metaphorically. Indeed, when the protagonist of **"The Compartment"** loses in turn his watch, the belongings in his suitcase, and his destination, one gets a clear sense of allegorical treatment that flirts with the metaphorical. Similarly, the overall ominous signified of "ugliness" hovers over **"Feathers,"** a story that pits horrid baby and false teeth against the archetypal peacock to point out potential and realized existential bifurcations. But the texts themselves retain a flatness and an indeterminacy, an untranslated quality of experience that at the most allows for illustrative similes but will not resort to metaphorical mutation. The quest for meaning appears legal when undertaken laterally, "on the side," but appears unacceptable, because denaturing, when conducted "from above." Meaning can be plucked from neighboring things, in the margins, by comparison, in the same plane, as happens with lives vicariously lived or characters in search of missing halves. Complements are allowed in, but all obvious supplements are ruled out. Language retains throughout Carver's collections such deliberate flatness of tone that any word slightly out of the ordinary bounds or kelter sounds odd and vaguely metaphorical in itself (for example, "regarded" for "looked at," in several instances, and "assessment" in **"Careful"**). The heavy rhetorical inflections of the texts condemn the metaphorical index to remain at an hypothetical zero degree above which it is seldom allowed to rise. Even plain demonstrative signifiers are relegated by characters to the reserve wherefrom it is not always necessary to retrieve them: "We both knew it was a peacock, sure, but we didn't say the word out loud. We just watched it." By the same token, the prodigious recreation of the shapes of cathedrals in **"Cathedral,"** when a seeing man lets a blind man's hand ride his own over the contours of a drawing, seems to indicate that the "always-already" metaphorical nature of language can be dispensed with and make way for the greater powers of performative communication. Passing on to his characters' handling of their narratives a lesson taught students by one of the rare artists in his stories, a lesson he may have taught himself, Carver could I suppose account for the quality of their speech by making of its impoverishment the reason of their inability to transcend their fate. But he could also, making of paltry necessity an interesting set of virtues, make it that of his own refusal to make things easy on us: "You've got to work with your mistakes until they look intended."

To my mind, the features of Carver's writing examined in this essay throw into question his present reputation as a "realist." Even though he has clearly reintroduced a modicum of social depiction in his stories, it seems clear that his strategic choices favor the work as construct over an obsolete mimetic conception of the use of literary language. A text that feeds on reader's reaction and filling in, that operates by substraction of explicitness and clearly outlined conclusions, cannot be said to rely on traditional categories of representation. What mimetic dimensions the texts retain have to do with a somewhat imitative exploration of the radical "béance" or gap that yawns at the heart of experience, in the presentation, rather than the representation, of a world of fractures, a world whose chief activity is a linguistically deprived attempt at making minimal sense. Thus, if Carver can be said to be a "minimalist"—a term he resents—the adequacy of the term must be attributed to a quality of experience more than to a representational mode. The dominant rhetorical inflections of his texts make sure that, as Adorno put it, "everything . . . as regards form and material, spirit and matter, has emigrated from reality into the works, and in them has been deprived of its reality." Denouncing the easy and abusive association of many literary products with *bona fide* mimesis, Iser rightly refuses

> the assumption that such texts are simply copies of a depraved world. If the deformations are signs of a hidden cause, [he adds,] and if this cause has to be rooted out by the reader's conscious mind, then, clearly, the *function* of the text (and hence the function of its negativity) far transcends that of simply copying reality. Negativity brings about the deformations which are the basic question posed by the text—a question that sets the text in the context of reality. Actualization of the virtual cause then opens up the possibility of finding the answer (which is potentially present in the formulated problems of the text). Negativity, then, embraces both the question and the answer, and is the condition that enables the reader to construct the meaning of the text on a question-and-answer basis.

Furthermore, as if to demonstrate that no writer could come out of the 1960s and 1970s unaffected by two decades of innovative experimentalism, Carver—however keen his ear and eye and whatever his imitative talents—does not only write in defiance of traditional concepts of realism in literature. He also stands neatly within the boundaries of a literary world that gradually sets itself free from the honored premises of modernism. His practical recognition of the irresolutive nature of the text removes him from a tradition expectant of meaning equated with the resolution of the opening tensions. Seemingly removed from the most vanguard experiments of our time, important aspects of Carver's prose could nonetheless be described by this assessment [by Ammons] of Samuel Beckett's revolt against classical and psychological aesthetics:

> With Beckett . . . we become aware that meaning as a relief from tension embodies an expectation of art which is historical in nature and consequently loses its claim to be normative. The density of negations not only lays bare the historicity of our concept of meaning but also reveals the defensive nature of such a traditional expectation—we obviously anticipate a meaning that will remove the illogicalities, conflicts and indeed, the whole contingency of the world in the literary work. To experience meaning as a defence, or as having a defensive structure, is, of course, also a meaning, which, however, the reader can only become conscious of when the traditional concept of meaning is invoked as a background, in order for it to be discredited.

Another contemporary helps us give a measure of Carver's achievement. Speaking of the things that he left out, A. R. Ammons invites us to hear "the hum of omissions," "the chant of vacancies, din of / silences," claims that he is "aware / of them, as you must be," as the reader of Raymond Carver's stories must be

> . or you will miss
> the non-song
>
> in my singing: it is not that words *cannot* say
> what is missing: it is only that what is missing
> cannot
> be missed if
> spoken: read the parables of my unmaking . . .

(pp. 177-90)

Marc Chénetier, "Living On/Off the 'Reserve': Performance, Interrogation, and Negativity in the Works of Raymond Carver," in Critical Angles: European Views of Contemporary American Literature, *edited by Marc Chénetier, Southern Illinois University Press, 1986, pp. 164-90.*

Michael Vander Weele (essay date 1987)

[*In the following excerpt, Vander Weele examines what he considers the inadequacy of language to express the desires of the characters in Carver's short fiction.*]

The doomsayers in our society are mostly specialists: on the environment, on population, on agriculture, employment, energy and other resources, and on the proliferation of nuclear arms. Their projections are numbing and, perhaps unfortunately, hardly imaginable. Concurrent to this industry of well-intentioned expertise, Raymond Carver has been writing stories which also require us to think about the ills of our society and our relationship to them. Carver's characters and their "low-rent tragedies" have the advantage, in our struggle between hope and despair, of being more imaginable than the projections that threaten only to numb us. Their speech, for all its strangeness, we recognize as our own.

Carver's stories are, mostly, about speech. They are also about desire. They are about the conditions of speech in an age that realizes too keenly that "the truth about our desire is that it is never our own." That expression comes from Geoffrey Hartman, a leading critic at Yale, but its force is felt as well by the characters who populate Carver's fiction: "people who read *Popular Mechanics* and *Field and Stream,* people who play bingo, hunt deer, fish and drink. They work at shopping centers, sell books, have milk routes, or try, drunkenly, to manage a motel." What I wish to investigate is the vocabulary of desire Carver gives these everyday characters. If their speech gives us the shock of self-recognition, do we recognize ourselves in the desires of these characters?

My first sense that we share a peculiarly modern desire with Carver's characters came in rethinking Dickens's classic fiction of desire, *Great Expectations.* Pip's character, for most of the novel, is created out of his desire to become a gentleman. That desire affects his estimation of himself and others. It affects his manners as well as his most deeply held beliefs. Pip's character, then is determined by what he lacks. The famous turn in the novel comes when Pip's character no longer is determined by desire for what he lacks but by suffering. Pip learns the ideal of suffering for others from his belated admiration for Joe and concern for Magwitch. Specific desire—here, to become a gentleman—takes a specific correction. One can hardly read Carver, however, and still read the turn in Dickens's novel with unflagging interest. And this is so even if one is sympathetic, as I am, to Dickens's effort to show the correction of character through the ideal of self-sacrifice. Such a turn doesn't seem to address the questions we face. How can desire be so specific—or how can specific desires be taken so seriously—in the first place? Doesn't such desire come from a different world than our own? And what does the difference say about the world we inhabit?

Our world seems closer to that of Dickens's French contemporaries. In *Mimesis,* Erich Auerbach described the "unconcrete despair" in *Madame Bovary* both socio-historically and linguistically. The surface irritations of life in Flaubert's novel, according to Auerbach, suggest a despair that is beyond specifics, is not tied down but is free-floating. ("Nothing happens, but that nothing has become a heavy oppressive, threatening something.") Baudelaire gives the same sense of unspecified despair in his famous Spleen poems, and connects it in "To the Reader" to an enervated will:

> As mangy beggars incubate their lice,
> We nourish our innocuous remorse
>
> . . . . .
>
> Cradled in evil, that Thrice-Great Magician,
> The Devil, rocks our souls, that can't resist;
> And the rich metal of our own volition
> Is vaporized by that sage alchemist.

Some have found Baudelaire's belief in God and the devil reducible to a dandiacal posture, but it is at least unquestionable that he knew boredom had the force of spiritual sin—and he knew we would know it that way too:

> In each man's foul menagerie of sin
> There's one more damned than all. He never gambols,
> Nor crawls, nor roars, but, from the rest withdrawn,
> Gladly of this whole earth would make a shambles
> And swallow up existence with a yawn . . .
>
> Boredom! He smokes his hookah, while he dreams
> Of gibbets, weeping tears he cannot smother.
> You know this dainty monster, too, it seems—
> Hypocrite reader!—You!—My twin!—My brother!

(pp. 108-10)

Carver's characters feel caught in something beyond their comprehension. In **"Why Don't You Dance?"**—the opening story of ***What We Talk About When We Talk About Love***—a middle-aged man has prepared a yard sale subsequent, we may suppose, to the break-up of his marriage. A young couple, out to furnish a small apartment, buy many of the man's possessions so cheaply it is almost a gift. We wonder if they will also inherit the strangeness or coldness of this house turned inside out, this house without walls or roof, without interior or reserve as it finds itself arranged on the front yard, lamps blazing, TV on, record-player playing as the old man and young girl dance on the driveway with the neighbors, they hope, looking on. The action of this story is framed by the old man's puzzlement at the beginning:

> In the kitchen, he poured another drink and looked at the bedroom suite in his front yard. The mattress was stripped and the candy-striped sheets lay beside two pillows on the chiffonier. Except for that, things looked much the way they had in the bedroom—nightstand and reading lamp on his side of the bed, nightstand and reading lamp on her side.
>
> His side, her side.
>
> He considered this as he sipped the whiskey.

and by the young girl's puzzlement at the end:

> Weeks later, she said: "This guy was about middle-aged. All his things right there in his yard. No lie. We got real pissed and danced. In the driveway. Oh, my God. Don't laugh. He played us these records. Look at this record-player. The old guy gave it to us. And all these crappy records. Will you look at this shit?"
>
> She kept talking. She told everyone. There was more to it, and she was trying to get it talked out. After a time, she quit trying.

The tragedy of Carver's "low-rent tragedies" is not, finally, the broken marriages or drunken violence we meet in his stories, but the characters' inability to go beyond their puzzlement over the significance of such events. They have neither the understanding nor the conditions for such speech. It remains an unrealized desire.

Though Carver's prose is spare to begin with, nowhere is it more so than in the setting for his stories. In **"Sacks,"** ***(Talk),*** for example, we don't know in which Midwestern city the son is looking out his hotel window, nor why he speaks to *us,* nor why he even wants to pass along the story his father told him, since he didn't care to hear that story in the first place and seems not to have made anything of it. We may guess that he has had problems with his family, but not much is told about that either. The lack of context defeats teleological or mechanistic explanations. The son's will remains inscrutable. The father is unable to understand how his sexual escapade could have happened to him. He can only figure this through talking with someone: "You're an educated man, Les," he says to his son. "You'll be the one to figure it out." "It," here, is the father's sudden desire and capitulation to his desire for the neighborhood Stanley Products woman, a woman half his age, with two young children and a husband at home:

> Well, I kissed her then. I put her head back on the sofa and I kissed her, and I can feel her tongue out there rushing to get in my mouth. You see what I'm saying? A man can go along obeying all the rules and then it don't matter a damn anymore. His luck just goes, you know?

This adultery is bad enough, to be sure. The son's father feels bad about the two kids and the husband. But the tragedy lies in not being able to figure how things like this happen, how the rules one lived by suddenly sustain one no longer. A mechanistic explanation is possible: the shared story about the "big holdup back East," the excitement that spills over from one forbidden act to another. Yet this hardly seems a sufficient reason. How could such a transitory rush overcome one unless one's beliefs, thought, and speech had already gone stale?

While the father, as with most of Carver's characters, seems at least part victim, what is he victim of? It's not a mental handicap, as with Nathan's paranoid schizophrenia in *Sophie's Choice;* nor is it the psychological scarring of a Sophie by a historical force as horrific as the Holocaust. It seems related to the lack of control sensed in society and documented by our doomsayers. It also seems related to Baudelaire's description of boredom as *the* modern sin. Unattached desire and unconcrete despair lead to the "dainty monster" who "swallow[s] up existence with a yawn."

The moral vocabulary of an earlier age may help us understand the modern situation as Carver represents it in the characters he brings to—but not over—the threshold of understanding. I have in mind something like the distinction John Donne made, through use of the Latin terms *voluntas* and *velleitas,* between passive willingness and a will examined through discourse. Donne described *velleitas* as an unexamined or passive willingness. *Voluntas,* on the other hand, is the "discoursed and examined will." "Discoursed" may mean, in Donne's time, either to turn over in one's own mind or to hold discourse with another. The context suggests the latter meaning:

> . . . our will is ever understood to be a will rectified, and concurrent with God. This is *Voluntas,* a discoursed and examined will. That which is upon the first sight of the object, is *Velleitas,* a willingnesse, which we resist not, onely because we thought not of it. And such a willingnesse had Christ, when suddenly he wished that the cup might pass: but quickly conformed his will to his Father's.

We may say, using this distinction between an unexamined willingness and a will examined through discourse, that Carver regularly situates his characters so that they realize the need to move from a more passive willingness to an active, discoursed will. But they seldom accomplish this movement. The responsibility for such a failure is not described by Carver. It may be social, referring to the anonymous social influences of our institutions, or, despite the social influences, it may be personal, as with Baudelaire's "boredom." It likely is both. Carver concerns himself less with the cause and more with the failure of language in this movement toward an examined and discoursed will. That failure, the title of Carver's second major collection of stories makes clear, is a failure of *our* language as well: ***What We Talk About When We Talk About Love.*** The "we" of that title is part of a complex social discourse between author and reader. It refers to us, implicates us as readers equally with author and characters.

This failure of discourse ends the last story in this collection, **"One More Thing":**

> L. D. put the shaving bag under his arm and picked up the suitcase.
>
> He said, "I just want to say one more thing."
>
> But then he could not think of what it could possibly be.

The personal and social aspects of this failure of discourse may be seen more fully in the details of **"Sacks."** The father wishes to tell the son his story about Sally Wain and what overcame him that day. They exchange small talk, then the father takes a deep breath and begins his story. It is just at that moment that the son's eyes, whether from insensitivity or embarrassment, focus on the ashtray between them and he reads HARRAH'S CLUB/RENO AND LAKE TAHOE/GOOD PLACES TO HAVE FUN. The ironic juxtaposition of such an advertising logo with the father's speech shows the difficulty of achieving a will examined through discourse. This ashtray interrupts the tale once more, just before the father tells the seduction scene. The father coughs and takes one of his son's cigarettes. The son's eyes settle on the ashtray once again and read what it says. Misreading may be an important part of this reading. With one vowel change, we have a last hurrah or the last advertisement for Harrah's before the father continues his story. How does a man tell of a Sally Wain, of her children and husband, in such a setting?

The woman at the bar draws the attention not only of the son but also of the father. She dances; arms on hips, with a man's arm linked on either side to one of hers. She may also link father and son. They may both have known

Portrait of Carver in 1984, Syracuse, New York.

woman in this way, enticing because forbidden, stripped of any relationship to others. These details point to the social context—more, the social responsibility—for the failure of speech. The father realizes that he needs to think through the significance of his actions. He's brought this far, but seems unable to go further. He is responsible for his own actions, to be sure, but he also seems a victim unable to say more than that he senses something important needs to be said. The son is also responsible for this inability. He is either too insensitive or too unwilling to help build a context for meaningful speech.

When the father first met his son, he handed him a white confectionary sack with some almond roca candy for his wife and jelly beans for his children. He told his son to be sure to remember them. At the end of the story the son, who has told us the father's tale, recalls that he didn't remember the sack. It doesn't matter:

> That was the last I've seen of him. On the way to Chicago, I remembered how I'd left his sack of gifts on the bar. Just as well. Mary didn't need candy, Almond Roca or anything else.
>
> That was last year. She needs it now even less.

What the sack holds is the father's intention, a gesture, a gift. The father wants to show that he still cares for the son's family. But to the son, the sack is indeed a white confectionary sack holding a little candy inside. His wife doesn't need, say, the extra calories.

Perhaps the son is not so obtuse as this reading suggests. The father's tale may stir the son's consciousness of his own culpability. The son wants to keep his distance, not share in the interpretive effort of communication, and thus he wills not to recognize the gesture or gift. What is true of the bag of candy is also true of the father's speech. The son does not or will not recognize the father's speech as a gift of trust. He is anxious to have this speech come to an end rather than open onto discourse. He is anxious to have his plane bring him back to Chicago. And he effectively stymies the possibilities of discourse by insisting upon the exteriority of this speech, just as he views the sack with candy as nearly empty inside. The father knows that there is something important to get at within this language. He doesn't know *what* it is. The possibility of looking, which is the same, here, as a speaking that depends upon a common pursuit of the truth, is denied by the son. This denial is apparent when the father tells of being in bed with Sally when her husband pulls into the driveway:

> " 'My God,' she screams. 'It's Larry!'
>
> "I must have gone crazy. I seem to remember thinking that if I run out the back door he's going to pin me up against this big fence in the yard and maybe kill me. Sally is making a funny kind of sound. Like she couldn't get her breath. She has her robe on, but it's not closed up, and she's standing in the kitchen shaking her head. All this is happening all at once, you understand. So there I am, almost naked with my clothes in my hand, and Larry is opening the front door. Well, I jump. I just jump right into their picture window, right in there through the glass."
>
> "You got away?" I said. "He didn't come after you?"
>
> My father looked at me as if I were crazy. He stared at his empty glass. I looked at my watch, stretched. I had a small headache behind my eyes.
>
> I said, "I guess I better be getting out there soon." I ran my hand over my chin and straightened my collar. "She still in Redding, that woman?"
>
> "You don't know anything, do you?" my father said. "You don't know anything at all. You don't know anything except how to sell books."

Worse than the son's apparent lack of interest is his question about the plot of the story. The father needs to know how he allowed himself to break up the lives of this young family. He's interested in the meaning, not the suspense or intrigue, of such a tale.

What can we say about Carver's language of desire? Desire itself often seems featureless or, if concrete, not very hopeful: "There were gardens and such, wildflowers in bloom, and little houses set back from the road. I said, 'I wish we had us a place out here.' It was just an idle thought, another wish that wouldn't amount to anything" (**"Peacock,"** ***Cathedral***). These desires are closer to the passivity, the unexamined and undiscoursed willingness, Donne described through the Latin term of *velleitas.* The desires seem, in advance, to be ineffective. There is both personal and social responsibility for such hopelessness. The hopelessness is much larger than any desire, and is not tied to any specific desire. The mechanistic explanation for the desires that are acted upon is most often a kind of voyeurism or illicit activity which gives one a sudden rush that masquerades as life. But for voyeurism to have such power, the life of assumed beliefs, thoughts, and feelings must be peculiarly weak. These beliefs, thoughts, and feelings—or their loss—are only with the greatest difficulty examined or given speech. Carver's characters seldom overcome such difficulty, but his readers are usually left questioning the possibilities of a sympathetic and examining discourse. Do we know how to create the language and situation for such discourse, for example, about love?

"Free will" may seem as other-worldly today as the turn in Dickens's novel. Near the end of last century, Nietzsche already described "free will" as "hundred-times-refuted theory." He did his best to bury it by analyzing the complicated ingredients of the will and showing that the emotion of command is not experienced apart from the emotion of resistance or constraint. But Nietzsche refutes a notion of "free will" quite different from the discoursed and examined will Donne had described. After the Enlightenment the will was thought to operate freely in response to the regularities of nature and society, whose careful observation could lead to man and woman's control over their environment and to their subsequent progress. Nietzsche rightly questioned whether "Nature's conformity to law" reflected some objective reality or only the object of our desires. But the discussion of will Donne raised is not couched in terms of power, much less autonomy. How does one achieve a discoursed and examined will without dependence upon others?

The lack of such a will is what Carver's fiction makes us consider. His fiction shows characters gain consciousness that they lack this will examined in discourse with others; and it positions his characters so that the question of lack and remedy shifts from the unresolved character to the puzzled, sympathetic reader. There are only a few exceptions where the characters reach some resolution by the end of the story. One of them comes in **"A Small, Good Thing" (*Cathedral*)**, a story Carver expanded from his earlier publication of **"Bath" (*Talk*).**

Howard and Ann's son, Scotty, is hit by a car on his way to school on the morning of his eighth birthday. Scotty returns home, but is taken to the hospital when he loses consciousness. Howard and Ann meet at the hospital and keep a bedside vigil. Neither trusts the doctor's optimistic prognosis. Late that night Howard goes home to bathe and change clothes. As he walks into the house, the phone rings. It is the baker from whom Ann had ordered an expensive cake with Scotty's name on it and a decorator's space ship with launching pad. Howard doesn't know any of this, however, nor does the baker explain it to him. The voice only says that there's a cake to be picked up and paid for. "I don't know anything about a cake,' [Howard] says. 'Jesus, what are you talking about?' " " 'Don't hand me that,' the voice said." Howard hangs up. The telephone rings again when Howard's in the bath. He grabs a towel and runs through the house to pick up the phone, thinking about Scotty at the hospital. When he picks up the phone, there's no sound at the other end. Then the caller hangs up.

A day and a half later Ann finally goes home. The phone rings. The conversation is confused and full of gaps:

> "Mrs. Weiss," a man's voice said. It was five o'clock in the morning, and she thought she could hear machinery or equipment of some kind in the background.
>
> "Yes, yes! What is it?" she said. "This is Mrs. Weiss. This is she. What is it, please?" She listened to whatever it was in the background. "Is it Scotty, for Christ's sake?"
>
> "Scotty," the man's voice said. "It's about Scotty, yes. It has to do with Scotty, that problem. Have you forgotten about Scotty?" the man said. Then he hung up.

Ann hurriedly calls the hospital, but there was no change in Scotty's condition.

Later that day Scotty dies. Howard and Ann return home. She calls the relatives; he gathers up toys. Then the telephone rings again. Ann picks it up on the first ring.

> "Hello," she said, and she heard something in the background, a humming noise. "Hello!" she said. "For God's sake," she said. "Who is this? What is it you want?"
>
> "Your Scotty, I got him ready for you," the man's voice said. "Did you forget him?"
>
> "You evil bastard!" she shouted into the receiver. "How can you do this, you evil son of a bitch?"
>
> "Scotty," the man said. "Have you forgotten about Scotty?" Then the man hung up on her.

Around midnight, when Howard answers the phone again, the line goes dead. Suddenly Ann knows who the caller is. Consumed with the idea of revenge, she makes Howard drive her to the bakery.

Rather than give the tension another turn, Carver relieves it. He gets his characters around a card table in the back of the bakery, with the baker apologizing and feeding Howard and Ann warm rolls and coffee ("Eating is a small, good thing in a time like this"). The baker begins to talk.

> They listened carefully. Although they were tired and in anguish, they listened to what the baker had to say. They nodded when the baker began to speak of loneliness, and of the sense of doubt and limitation that had come to him in his middle years. He told them what it was like to be childless all these years. To repeat the days with the ovens endlessly full and endlessly empty.

Though the focus is on the baker and his discovery that he is not the human being he once thought he was, he also restores life to Howard and Ann:

> "Smell this," the baker said, breaking open a dark loaf. "It's a heavy bread, but rich." They smelled it, then he had them taste it. It had the taste of molasses and coarse grains. They listened to him. They ate what they could. They swallowed the dark bread. It was like daylight under the fluorescent trays of light. They talked on into the early morning, the high, pale cast of light in the windows, and they did not think of leaving.

Such an ending runs the risk of seeming sentimental in our time, just as the turn in Dickens's novel seems to easy to us today. Yet Carver is the right author to accept this risk, spare as his prose is and effective in holding back the emotion one senses behind the cool lines. In the blind man and the narrator in **"Cathedral,"** the housekeeper and the teacher in **"Fever"** (***Cathedral***), and the hospitalized old couple and the doctor in the cover story of ***What We Talk About When We Talk About Love,*** we see the strange, potentially enabling pull people can have on each other, without seeing its fulfillment. The doctor doesn't find an answer to his question, only senses that the answer is involved with the hospitalized septuagenarians. The teacher only knows, without knowing quite why, that at last he can let his estranged wife go. The narrator of **"Cathedral"** rises with the spirit of the blind man as, with eyes closed and pen on paper, he leads the blind man's hand over what he imagines the contours of a cathedral would be. But most of the communication in this story comes through shared non-verbal work, as expression that stops short of the effort and commonality of speech.

The language of Carver's characters usually obstructs rather than aids the accomplishment of discourse. The situations in which language must be forged and to which it must be addressed—these situations usually are not enabling but recalcitrant, with little interior or reserve. What is most frightening about the desire expressed by Carver's characters is that they seem so little capable of correction. While they could be replaced by other similar desires, they are not definite enough to correct. Their indefiniteness, on the other hand, is massively oppressive.

Language, both its situation and its words, is the necessary condition for correction. Carver's fiction suggests the dependency of discourse on a sympathetic attentiveness to language as gesture as well as form. Carver is expert at showing, in ways sympathetic to his characters, the lack of such attentiveness and the societal influences that make such an attentiveness difficult. This expertise has no statistics or projections for its subject, but points to the most basic of our problems. It is a problem of recognizably personal as well as social responsibility. We all experience something of the fears and desires chronicled in Carver's poem, "The Mailman as Cancer Patient" (***Fires***). We often feel that the causes of our fears and desires are as indefinite as the causes of cancer. Who can tell what in them is social, and what is personal? The mailman will not hear the disease discussed, but walks through empty rooms. His wife, though she also thinks of crazy things, keeps on working:

> Yet sometimes at night
> the mailman dreams he rises from his bed
> puts on his clothes and goes
> out, trembling with joy. . . .
> He hates those dreams
> for when he wakes
> there is nothing left; it is
> as if he had never been
> anywhere, never done anything;
> there is just the room,

the early morning without sun,
the sound of a doorknob
turning slowly.

Desires, joys, fears—all remain unexamined and unspoken. And their indefiniteness is ominous.

Carver's attitude toward such characters as this mailman sometimes stops at a Hemingway-like admiration for the one who endures, as, for example, in his description of one in "Fish" ***(Fires)*** that comes "heavy, scarred, / silent like the rest, / that simply holds against the current, / opening and closing its dark mouth / against the current." At other times Carver leaves us situated, like his characters, at the point of consciousness that there is a recognition we should work towards. Carver doesn't underestimate the effort involved. But he knows in what direction it lies. I quote from the last lines of "This Word Love" ***(Fires)***, with which he closes his latest collection of stories, essays and poems:

But this word *love*—

this word grows dark, grows
heavy and shakes itself
and begins to eat through this paper.

Listen

(pp. 111-22)

Michael Vander Weele, "Raymond Carver and the Language of Desire," in The Denver Quarterly, *Vol. 22, No. 1, Summer, 1987, pp. 108-22.*

Marilynne Robinson (essay date 1988)

[*Robinson is an American novelist whose works, including* Housekeeping *(1981), are noted for their highly lyrical prose style. In the following review of* Where I'm Calling From, *she provides an overview of Carver's short stories and places them within the tradition of American realism.*]

Of the 37 stories in Raymond Carver's new collection, ***Where I'm Calling From,*** 30 have been collected before in four earlier volumes—two of them, **"What We Talk About When We Talk About Love"** and **"Cathedral,"** as title stories. I take this volume to invite a new look at Mr. Carver's career, a conviction encouraged in me by the fact that I would like to offer one. To be blunt, I propose to abduct Raymond Carver from the camp of the minimalists.

For 150 years or so, every kind of art whose style has caused it to be identified as "modern" has been interpreted in the same way—as a contemplation of, and protest against, a world leached of pleasure, voided of meaning, spiritually and culturally bankrupt, etc. This is supposedly the "modern condition," which we are schooled to accept as an objectively existing thing, like the Rock of Gibraltar. No matter that, by every measure, this teeming nation is, as it always has been, rapt as Byzantium, its man in the street entirely accustomed to viewing his life in cosmic terms. Such structuring and valuing habits of mind, we tell ourselves, are just what our age and culture lack, a deficiency our arts boldly mirror, being more or less helpless to do otherwise. The idea of "the modern" is now so very old it has had to be repackaged as "the post-modern" and covered with assurances that the new product is starker, more cynical, altogether more abysmal than the one we are accustomed to.

Assumptions about what writers must or should be doing tend to preclude curiosity about what they are doing in fact. Raymond Carver is generally taken to epitomize this arid tradition, to spearhead a new version of it called "minimalism."

Including him in this canon is intended as high praise, the assumption being commonplace that a serious writer cannot have any higher object than to make these bones walk yet again. So, on the basis of the strength students and critics sense in his work, Mr. Carver has been more or less dragooned. Then other critics berate in his person the hopeless and diminished landscape they find in contemporary fiction, seeing him through the eyes of his imitators and admirers.

In fact, Mr. Carver stands squarely in the line of descent of American realism. His weaknesses are for sentimentality and sensationalism. His great gift is for writing stories that create meaning through their form. Much attention has been paid to his prose, and to his preoccupation with very ordinary lives and with disruption, divorce, displacement, sadness, the thankless business of cadging income from small and unlikable jobs. He should be famous for the conceptual beauty of his best stories, and disburdened of his worst, which could then pass into relative neglect.

The narrative foreground in Mr. Carver's fiction is typically muted or flattened. The stories have in common a sort of bafflement, justified in the best ones by the fact that their burdens are truly mysterious. Anecdotes—for want of a better world—looming and untranslatable like remembered dreams (which they sometimes are) figure so largely in these stories as to suggest that they are analogues to fiction itself, and also to consciousness, specifically to consciousness as it is shared, collective or bonding. It has been usual for a long time to lament the absence of myth in modern life, as if intuitions of the primordial and essential were the products of culture and would be dispelled with the loss of certain images and illusions, as if the forces myth describes were not real or powerful *enough* to impose themselves on our attention all unbidden. The bafflement in the best of these stories does not render an absence of meaning but awkwardness in the face of meaning, a very different thing.

Mr. Carver uses his narrow world to generate suggestive configurations that could not occur in a wider one. His impulse to simplify is like an attempt to create a hush, not to hear less but to hear better. Nothing recurs so powerfully in these stories as the imagination of another life, always so like the narrator's or the protagonist's own that the imagination of it is an experience of the self, that fuddled wraith. It is as if the replication of the conditions of one's life in another's rescued one from the terrors of accident and randomness, as if the germ of myth or archetype were found at work in the tepid plasma of unstructured experience. This seems to me to express the rationale of Mr. Carver's own artistic practice.

In **"Neighbors,"** a couple, the Millers, look after the apartment next to their own while the couple who live in it are away. The Millers are, in a way, seduced by the apartment, a perfectly ordinary place except for odds and ends brought back from the vacations that make their neighbors' life seem to the Millers "fuller and brighter" than their own. The unguarded intimacy of the closed apartment stimulates the attraction between the Millers, makes them feel amorous and happy. What they experience amounts to an objectification of their own life, a little sweetened by reachable enhancements.

In **"Why Don't You Dance?"** a man whose marriage has collapsed puts his furniture up for sale in the front yard, where he has arranged it as it was inside his house, running out an extension cord so that the television and the record player work. A young couple come along and try out the furniture, stay for drinks and then, at the man's suggestion, dance together in the driveway. The intimacy of marriage is voided, exposed, reenacted and distanced, all at once. The moment may be said to suggest memory, art, the astonishing bond of intimacy among a world of strangers, the ghostliness of one's attachment of any place or relationship.

"So Much Water So Close to Home" is about the marriage of a man terrified of his own insensitivity and a woman of great emotional fragility, whose fears are focused around the undercurrent of violence in the husband's character. The husband, Stuart, has had a part in an incident involving neither guilt in law nor guilt as it is measured by finer instruments, at least so far as he can bring himself to acknowledge. He and three friends have gone deep into the mountains to fish, and have found the body of a young woman floating face down in the stream. After a little liquor and reflection they tether the body to a tree by a wrist and leave it as they found it, for three days, until they are done with their fishing. The story is told by Stuart's wife, who describes the men cooking and drinking and playing cards into the night while to one side the white body floats on the cold water. It is nightmarish, and the tranced state of the men, lingering there, is full of dark suggestion, which, in the wife's mind, shades into the crime itself. Clearly Stuart knows before he tells her about the incident—as he must since it is reported in the newspaper—that she will be deeply disturbed by it. He attempts expressions of love, but they are crude, and they reinforce her fears rather than comforting her. As she becomes more disturbed and withdrawn she becomes more dependent on his loyalty and love, which are real, though intermitted by anger and frustration at her recoil from him and at his own clumsiness.

The story is pure Carver. It establishes a very simple and striking visual paradigm, the woman in the fishing stream, which it is the work of the rest of the story to explicate. The center of the narrative is profound and emotional identification of the wife with the drowned woman, and also between husband and wife. Stuart knows early that his wife is again sliding into illness. She sees his fear and pities him. Marriage is the most characteristic and complex form of these imaginative extensions of the self that so preoccupy Mr. Carver.

To do justice to **"What We Talk About When We Talk About Love"** is not possible in a small space. It is an extraordinary example of the discovery of meaning in visually suggestive anecdotes—of a suicide with a bandaged head, knights encumbered in dying by the weight of armor, an old couple in bandages, casts and traction, and a beekeeper in helmet and gloves and padded clothes. This series of analogous images rises out of a conversation among two married couples drinking gin together at a kitchen table, who know from their combined experience that love is homicidal, self-destructive, symbiotic and (possibly) fugitive. When one of the men, at the end, imagines himself murdering his former wife, the implication is that he loves her still. Again, the fiction offers patterns, parables, which seem charged with suggestion, and which elude the powers of interpretation of those who recognize meaning in them. The story concludes: "I could hear my heart beating. I could hear everyone's heart. I could hear the human noise we sat there making, not one of us moving, not even when the room went dark."

In **"Bicycles, Muscles, Cigarettes,"** a man comes to the defense of his young son, who is in trouble with neighbors. The boy expresses his affection for his father by telling him that he hopes not to forget his grandfather, and he wishes he could have known his grandfather at his father's age, and his father at his own age, yearning to imagine himself into their lives, simply to intensify his pleasure in his own. In **"Distance,"** a divorced man tells his grown daughter, whom he sees only on rare occasions, a story about her infancy, calling himself and her mother "the boy" and "the girl." At the end of the story they both regret the loss of the galled, warm, commonplace life they have conjured.

In **"Fat,"** a waitress becomes fascinated with a man so obese he refers to himself in a regal and melancholy plural. The woman begins to imagine herself massive like him, so that her husband seems "a tiny thing and hardly there at all." Such configurations of identification, distancing and displacement recur again and again.

An interesting, though problematic, story is titled **"The Calm."** A man has violated the *comme il faut* of deer hunting, having "gut shot" a deer and then failed to stalk it down and end its misery. The story about the hunt is told by the man himself, who seems unaware of the impression he is making on his hearers. Apparently the man has neither read Hemingway nor absorbed enough of the local ethos, though he is local himself, to understand how his revelations reflect upon him. No reader will suffer a moment's doubt, however.

The calm of the title is created by a barber, who quiets the indignation of the others. At the end of the story, in a sort of coda, the narrator, who has watched from the barber's chair, says it was during all this he decided to leave his wife. This ending seems arbitrary, but it is not, if his leaving her is a violation of the way things should be, like the miserable business with the deer. Mr. Carver is as obsessed with marriage as any writer since William Blake, and he never treats its disruption lightly. The calm brought on by the absolving neutrality of the barber, in which judgment is dispelled and ugliness dissipated, allows the narrator to make his choice. The barber looks into the mirror at the narrator's face, "but if the barber saw something, he didn't offer comment." There is just such a calm in society, not to be disparaged, very much to be marveled at, though it permits most forms of betrayal and self-disgrace. It is the condition of moral autonomy.

As in **"Fat"** and **"Why Don't You Dance?"** we are given to know that a moment in vernacular experience has been understood and repeated as significant, providing one term in an analogy. In **"Why Don't You Dance?"** the point of view actually pivots, belonging to the divorced man at the beginning and the young woman at the end. The household objects, set out like a ritual site, signify for both of them because, literally and figuratively, they are a common possession.

The last seven stories here, previously uncollected, are more rueful and humorous, written in more elegant prose and more elegiac than the earlier ones. In **"Boxes,"** the weakening of an old woman's ties with life manifests itself in her continually moving, never able to feel at home and at ease. **"Whoever Was Using This Bed"** is about a couple, awakened by a phone call, who talk through the night about the aches and anxieties that press at such times but are lost in the amnesia of daylight consciousness. Finally they come to the question of whether or not the plug should be pulled if one of them were hopelessly ill. It is a funny, very natural conversation. Their insomnia, and the rumpled bedclothes, bring to mind the extreme of intimacy their marriage implies, even to the point of one possibly choosing to end the other's life.

In the story called **"Intimacy,"** a writer visits his former wife, a woman furious that her life with him has been cannibalized to make fiction and that he has become a success publishing the darkest passages of their marriage. She is aware of giving him new material, even in her wrath, and the story, with the writer as narrator, means she has done just that. But he falls to his knees in her living room and stays there immobilized until it occurs to her to say she forgives him. Then she can send him away. Divorce never really takes in Mr. Carver's stories. Marriage is, in essence, an innocent friendship, desperately vulnerable to derangement and bad luck, but always precious in itself, its lost pleasures always loyally remembered. As he leaves her house, he sees children tossing a football. "But," he says, "they aren't my kids, and they aren't her kids either."

"Menudo" is about a man caught miserably in an infidelity, on the point of losing his second wife when he has not really recovered from the loss of his first. **"Elephant"** is a wonderful little story that should put paid, if anything ever will, to a clamor in certain quarters for a Carver story about grace and transcendence. The narrator, a sort of suburban Père Goriot, is being bled of his substance by a former wife, a mother who is "poor and greedy," a shiftless son, a shiftless daughter with two children and a live-in good-for-nothing, and a brother who calls with hard-luck stories. The man is impoverished, exhausting his credit, working and worrying, trying to meet their endless demands. Then he dreams that his father is carrying him, as a child, on his shoulders. The image brings him a great release. He thinks of his daughter, "God love her and keep her," and hopes for the happiness of his son, and is glad that he still has his mother, and that his former wife, "the woman I used to love so much," is alive somewhere. Then perhaps he dies. He is carried past the place where he works at astonishing speed in a "big unpaid-for car." Whether it is death that has stopped for him, or an uncanny freedom, the exhilaration of the ending has a distinctly theological feel.

The last story, **"Errand,"** is about the death of Chekhov, a very formal piece in which that estimable man is shown to have brought credit to himself in the manner of his dying. A writer generally invokes another writer when he wishes to invite comparison. Mr. Carver, whose stories are merely narrative occasions within which some highly charged image floats like a holograph, reminds me of Chekhov scarcely at all, except in that Mr. Carver's work, like Chekhov's, creates the terms in which it should be interpreted.

Raymond Carver is not an easy writer to read. His narratives are often coarse. Sometimes he seems intent on proving that insensitive people have feelings, too. And while the impulse is generous, the experience of looking at the world through the eyes of a character as crude as the narrator of **"Cathedral,"** for example, is highly uncongenial.

Carver on a change in his writing:

The stories in ***What We Talk About*** are different to an extent. For one thing, it's a much more self-conscious book in the sense of how intentional every move was, how calculated. I pushed and pulled and worked with those stories before they went into the book to an extent I'd never done with any other stories. When the book was put together and in the hands of my publisher, I didn't write anything at all for six months. And then the first story I wrote was **"Cathedral,"** which I feel is totally different in conception and execution from any stories that have come before. I suppose it reflects a change in my life as much as it does in my way of writing. When I wrote **"Cathedral"** I experienced this rush and I felt, "This is what it's all about, this is the reason we do this." It was different than the stories that had come before. There was an opening up when I wrote the story. I knew I'd gone as far the other way as I could or wanted to go, cutting everything down to the marrow, not just to the bone. Any farther in that direction and I'd be at a dead end—writing stuff and publishing stuff I wouldn't want to read myself, and that's the truth. In a review of the last book, somebody called me a "minimalist" writer. The reviewer meant it as a compliment. But I didn't like it. There's something about "minimalist" that smacks of smallness of vision and execution that I don't like. But all of the stories in the new book . . . were written within an eighteen-month period; and in every one of them I feel this difference.

Raymond Carver in a 1983 interview with Mona Simpson for The Paris Review.

In **"Feathers,"** a story centered on a fine moment in which an ugly baby and a bedraggled peacock frolic together under the dinner table, the reader's attention is drawn to an annoying plaster cast of terribly crooked teeth, displayed like a trophy in the living room of this strange household. In this story, as in **"Cathedral,"** characters are overcome by an esthetic experience or realization. *Mutatis mutandis,* it is Henry James—beauty is the mode of address of the world to the human soul.

But there is lump as well as leaven in Mr. Carver, and the lumpishness is more irksome because it feels intentional. The characters sometimes seem set up, or condescended to. It is this condition from which they are rescued in the course of the story. Mr. Carver is rather like the poet William Carlos Williams, who declared there were "no ideas but in things," and who turned banality's pockets out and found all their contents beautiful.

The process of Mr. Carver's fiction is to transform our perception. Perhaps what he does cannot be done in another way. And, viewed from sufficient distance, an interesting problem can take its place among the beautiful things. (pp. 1, 35, 40-1)

Marilynne Robinson, "Marriage and Other Astonishing Bonds," in The New York Times Book Review, *May 15, 1988, pp. 1, 35, 40-1.*

Norman German and Jack Bedell (essay date 1988)

[*In the following essay, German and Bedell offer an explication of "Popular Mechanics."*]

The reviewers of Raymond Carver's 1981 collection of stories, ***What We Talk About When We Talk About Love,*** praise his "laconic and spare" style [see Atlas in Further Reading list] for its "fierce compression" [Meredith Marsh, *The New Republic* (25 April 1981)] and liken it to that of Anderson, Hemingway, Cheever, and Updike [see excerpt dated 1979]. Apart from these labels, only one critic, Robert Houston, attempts to explain the reason for the style [see Further Reading list].

Houston says that "Carver's characters never have 'epiphanies.' . . .Yet there *is* revelation, a revelation that Carver locates not in the characters but in the reader. . . ." Since Carver does not editorialize, the reader must discover for himself the morals—or, if you prefer, meanings—of the stories. Carver is, however, involved in morality, unlike his characters, who have experienced what David Boxer and Cassandra Phillips call "Carverian dissociation." Carver's narrative art is detached from the emotions of his characters, but he disguises his concern for man's moral deficiencies so as to intrude as little as possible between the fiction and the reader. The actions of the characters are sufficient to carry his themes.

Detachment, in fact, is one of the fictive stances by which Carver achieves startling effects. As James Atlas says, the stories' "minimality gives them a certain bleak power." Because the endings of the stories are truncated, the reader-as-literary-detective must often supply the conclusion.

A case in point is **"Popular Mechanics,"** at little more than a page long, the shortest short-short story in ***What We Talk About.*** Ambrose Bierce's definition of love in *The Devil's Dictionary* ("a temporary insanity curable by marriage") might aptly have served as an epigraph to the story, for, despite its misleading title, its theme is the deterioration of love.

Puzzling though the title **"Popular Mechanics"** may be, Carver is not overly subtle or obscure about its intended meaning. The title, also the title of a magazine for do-it-yourselfers, should conjure up in the reader's mind, by story's end, physical laws such as "for every action there is an equal but opposite reaction." Before the tug of war begins between the young husband and wife for the baby, "they knocked down a flowerpot that hung behind the stove." A passage from Robinson's "Mr. Flood's Party" may serve as an informing contrast: "As a mother lays her sleeping child / Down tenderly, fearing it may awake, / He set the jug down slowly at his feet / With trembling care, knowing that most things break." The flowerpot should have reminded the parents in Carver's story that they, too, live in a world where most things, even children, break.

The man tries to "break [his wife's] grip" by holding "on to the baby and [pushing] with all his weight." Here, the greater force is bound to win. Next, he works "on her fisted fingers with one hand and with the other hand he gripped the screaming baby up under an arm near the shoulder." Obviously, he is trying to gain an advantage through leverage.

As the child slips from her, the wife catches "the baby around the wrist and [leans] back." The husband then feels "the baby slipping out of his hands and he [pulls] back very hard." In the tug of war, the woman first has the advantage, then the man, then the woman again, based on laws involving force, mass, and leverage.

The conclusion of the story is understated: "In this manner, the issue was decided." Based on mechanical laws, what can the reader know about the outcome of the contest of wills turned into a contest of strength?—that the husband "won," and that the baby lost. The grim conclusion, the breaking or dislocating of the baby's arm, occurs in the reader's mind, after some thought. The metaphor Carver works in the story is that of the baby as wishbone. And wishbones break. W. D. Snodgrass uses the same image in poem 3 of the sequential title poem to *Heart's Needle,* when the divorcing parents lift the child over a puddle by pulling it in opposite directions: "The child between them on the street / Comes to a puddle, lifts his feet / And hangs on their hands." The persona later calls the child "love's wishbone." An argument for influence, or extreme fortuity, can be made based on the fact that a similar incident is mentioned in Snodgrass's poem: "I tugged your hand, once, when I hated / Things less: a mere game dislocated / The radius of your wrist." Earlier, working a different image, Snodgrass says, "something somewhere has to give."

The final line of **"Popular Mechanics,"** "the *issue* was decided," is a gruesome pun implying that the *argument* as well as the fate of the parents' offspring (issue) was decided. These two "popular mechanics" deal with their marital problem much as do-it-yourselfers might fix their cars: not with finesse, but by force. In the heat of the moment, both peaceful legal means and concern for the baby are forgotten.

Carver seems to be retelling and altering the story of Solomon and the two mothers (who were also prostitutes) to highlight a disconcerting fact of contemporary culture. In I Kings 3, two women have babies born three days apart. One woman's baby dies, and she exchanges her dead baby for the other woman's living baby. The just woman goes before Solomon with her complaint. Wisely, Solomon suggests dividing the baby with a sword and giving each woman half of the child. The just woman, with true motherly concern, urges Solomon not to slay the child, but to give it to the other woman, who in her turn says, "Let it be neither mine nor thine, but divide it."

In Carver's story, the baby's welfare is obviously not the "issue." Had the parents been tested by Solomon, they would have been served an equal share of their baby. In updating the story, Carver exposes a trait common to all in some degree, a selfish cruelty that often causes innocents to suffer. Interestingly, Snodgrass's "Heart's Needle: 3" concludes, "Love's wishbone, child, although I've gone / As men must and let you be drawn / Off to appease another, / It may help that . . . / Solomon himself might say / I am your real mother."

Ironically, the parents adore the icon of their baby but are careless with the baby itself. Early in the story, the husband is about to pack the baby's picture in his suitcase when the wife sees it and takes it to the living room. The argument over the baby's image turns into a struggle over the real baby, who, though identified as a boy, is usually referred to as "the baby," "this baby," or "it" ("She would have it, this baby"), thus disturbingly impersonalizing the child as an object to fight over—to the parents, a victory symbol and little else.

As Carver's other stories testify, this kind of squabble is too often the decadent result of "true love." In the opening sentence of **"Popular Mechanics,"** the ideal of marriage is contrasted with the reality via a meteorological metaphor: "Early that day the weather turned and the snow was melting into dirty water." What was snowy pure is now corrupt.

In the expository first paragraph of the story, the light that seeps in on the characters from the outside world is fading rapidly. As the light dims, the civility of the parents wanes. After packing his belongings, the man need only turn off the light to put an end to this segment of his life. At the climax of the fight, when the baby is endangered, "the kitchen window [gives] no light."

Volume of sound is inversely proportional to amount of light in the story. The darker the setting gets, the louder the characters become. Yet, despite the shrill voices of the parents, the reader senses a histrionic air, a faking or exaggerating of emotions. Impervious to his wife's ravings, the husband simply keeps packing. Both have screamed at the other so often that they are immune to hostility—immune, even, to the baby's genuine screaming. The only remnant of true vitality in the house is the flowerpot behind the stove, and it is broken through carelessness. The breaking pot symbolizes the breakup of the marriage. Another reading is that the flowerpot contains no life—at least no plant is mentioned. Tucked away "behind the stove," away from the light, any once-potted flower would long since have withered. The empty pot is like the house, a lifeless hull.

The bedroom, the kitchen, the living room—places of warm familial gatherings and intimacy—constitute the story's settings. In a typically Carverian liminal emblem of people on the verge, the author situates the woman "in the doorway of the kitchen." Before and after this scene, the narrator says, "Streaks of [dirty water] ran down from the little shoulderhigh window that faced the backyard" and "The kitchen window gave no light." In both passages, the window-as-threshold reminds the reader of the intimacy-distance dichotomy that Carver works throughout the story.

The turning off and on of lights and emotions in the story represents the ease with which contemporary lovers step in and out of marriages. The violence and hatred of the characters are the "popular mechanics," or *modus vivendi,* of present-day relationships. Here and in many of his stories, Carver paints a dark vision of the present state of human relations. (pp. 257-60)

Norman German and Jack Bedell, "Physical and Social Laws in Ray Carver's 'Popular Mechanics'," in Critique: Studies in Contemporary Fiction, *Vol. XXIX, No. 4, Summer, 1988, pp. 257-60.*

Paul Skenazy (essay date 1988)

[In the following excerpt, Skenazy provides a retrospective of Carver's career.]

Raymond Carver was 50 when he died on August 2, 1988 of cancer. His wife, writer Tess Gallagher, tells us that he hid his condition from the public to allow him to complete *A New Path to the Waterfall,* a book of poetry. In May and June of this year, I and others reviewed his collection of fiction, ***Where I'm Calling From: New and Selected Stories,*** casually certain that it represented a kind of stocktaking at midcareer. But now that book of thirty previously published tales and seven uncollected stories seems more Carver's effort to prepare his estate, be his own executor and anthologist. Carver took advantage of the opportunity to republish; he revised stories, reordered them from their position in previous collections, and even altered some titles. ("I see this as an instance in which I am in the happy position of being able to make the stories better than they were," he said of some earlier revised publications.) Along with the new poetry collection and ***Fires*** (a selection of poems, stories and essays and a *Paris Review* interview, published in 1983), ***Where I'm Calling From*** represents a job of self-editing, something comparable to Henry James' New York edition, if in an appropriately more compact and commonplace form.

Carver has been praised as an "alchemist" and "full-grown master" who writes "fables for this decade." His influence on new writers is pervasive, some say pernicious. Before him, wisdom had it that short fiction was small fiction—apprentice work, preparation for a novel and the big-time. He is credited and charged with being the source of our story renaissance; he himself has said that "the resurgence of interest in the short story has nothing less than revitalized the national literature." He's cited as encouraging its emphasis on blue-collar households and everyday life: the laconic voice, the simplified vocabulary and syntax, the working class characters and blowsy despair—what Tom Jenks calls "downside neo-realism," *Granta* labeled "dirty realism," and others memorialize as "K-Mart minimalism."

For a man eulogized for reshaping American writing, Carver had a relatively short career, in the relatively disrespected form of what we still pejoratively label the "short" story. He first gained some national notice when a story appeared in the *Best American Short Stories* volume of 1967. He started selling his work to the slick magazines like *Harper's* and *Esquire* in 1971. (He didn't appear in the *New Yorker* until the 1980s.) The thirty previously published stories in ***Where I'm Calling From*** are selected from the fifty-one that appear in his three collections with major New York publishers: ***Will You Please Be Quiet, Please?*** (1976), ***What We Talk About When We Talk About Love*** (1981), and ***Cathedral*** (1983). (***Furious Seasons*** appeared in 1977 from Capra Press in Santa Barbara; the seven stories were subsequently published in the later collections, frequently revised.)

There are reasons to talk about Carver's career as being disrupted in midsentence. There are other reasons to find some appropriate if horrible and clumsy fit to his death—the brevity of his writing life, the truncated ending, and the startled reactions of readers are so like the effect of the individual stories themselves. Referring obliquely to Carver, Alan Cheuse talks about "the life force that injures people into art." Cheuse is seduced by a sentimental faith in the superiority of the sufferer: pain amplifies. Carver has said that "Good fiction is partly a bringing of the news from one world to another," and we've come to depend on a bunch of writers nowadays as ambassadors to anguish: people who can transcribe their difficult experiences and unsatisfied longings and represent them as cultural soundings. Carver is doubtless the beneficiary of such reading habits, though he rarely seems to fall prey to such romanticism himself in his presentation of people. Carver makes metaphor of his torments, but stops short of insisting on their magnitude, their political or social import. Instead, he's one of those writers able to convert personal unhappinesses and struggles into small story lines, deliberately and persuasively misrepresent them in the abrasive circumstances of characters. His domestic melodramas are arranged to imply only themselves. Yet they are so starkly presented against such a vacant backdrop of place and time that it is hard for a reader not to try to find broader national meaning in the individual states of mind and soul—failure, defeat, incommunicable hurt, and shock that so much hope has dwindled to so little significance.

Carver practices his art to create the pretense of unfiltered life. His method emerges from his working class childhood and itinerant married years. He was never a natural; he found his form by default. Son of a sawmill worker and a waitress, he grew up in small Oregon towns on fishing and hunting and men's magazines. He married in his teens and had two children, and he and his wife did odd jobs to support themselves. In his autobiographical essay "Fires," he describes a moment in a laundromat one Saturday when he loses the chance to get some clothes into a dryer and realizes something of the frustrations of a life so little his own:

> Up to that point in my life I'd gone along thinking, what exactly, I don't know, but that things would work out somehow—that everything in my life I'd hoped for or wanted to do, was possible. But at that moment, in the laundromat, I realized that this simply was not true. I realized—what had I been thinking before?—that my life was a small-change thing for the most part, chaotic, and without much light showing through. At that moment I felt—I knew—that the life I was in was vastly different from the lives of the writers I most admired. . . . At that moment I saw accommodations would have to be made. The sights would have to be lowered.

Carver's voice comes from outside our tradition; he doesn't so much inherit literary forms as take advantage of them. His early stories and his literary credos owe much to Hemingway ("Get in, get out. Don't linger. Go on."), and he repeatedly pays homage to Chekhov, but the work is even more firmly shaped by his children, his drinking, his financial struggles. One of Carver's stories (**"The Student's Wife"**) ends when a woman who has quietly and desperately spent a sleepless night next to her snoring husband greets the sunrise: "Not in pictures she had seen nor in any book she had read had she learned a sunrise was so terrible as this." What's so powerful about the woman's insight is Carver's insistence on the distinction between our traditions of art and her terror: the books have shunned and slighted such truly quiet desperation.

It is Carver's task to depict these tiny, damning confinements of the spirit. Lowering his sights to accommodate the facts of his life, Carver finds in the story a form that can attend to the world glimpsed through a peephole rather than observed through the more formally framed windows of the spacious house of fiction: "I . . . limited myself to writing things I knew I could finish in one sitting, two sittings at the most." Like so many of his characters, he is out of place in the canon, someone who offhandedly misappropriates the conventions. **"Put Yourself in My Shoes,"** the closest Carver ever comes to metafiction, begins with Myers, a writer "between stories," vacuuming cat hairs when the phone rings. He lets his wife Paula talk him into dropping in on the Morgans, an academic pair whose house Myers and Paula lived in while the couple was abroad on sabbatical. The professor urges stories on Myers: of a man, leaving his wife for a younger woman, who is seriously wounded by a can of tomato soup his son throws at him, of a woman who dies suddenly while in the Morgans' apartment in Germany. Finally, Morgan proposes "the *real* story"—of his resentment against Myers and Paula for keeping a cat in the house, for using "*personal* possessions" and breaking dishes, for stealing a record album. Driving away, the writer is silent: "He was at the very end of a story."

This is warped self-scrutiny. The realist reveals his lack of standing, the landed Morgans reveal their complete identification with their property, and both families uncomfortably attempt to deny their common literary residence. From the cliches of empathy offered in the title to the last ambiguous line, Carver establishes a chain of voyeurism that extends beyond the depicted relationships and conversations to the reader. There's a certain shame and violation in the writer's position, his invasion and temporary possession of an environment that is not his and where he doesn't belong—first as housesitter, later as uninvited guest, afterwards as chronicler. The writer and his wife live off the academics, care for as they abuse their property, and seem to provide just the sort of objects of scorn and disaster the Morgans need to make their own stories worth telling. Meanwhile, we overhear and oversee the proceedings from our own bleak perspective. The story Carver tells belies the artistic myths we foster. As the uninvoked audience to this ugly spat, we realize that it says more about the emotional dependence we have on certain sacred objects, and about the unconsidered circumstances that demand the attention of most of us much of the time, than our conceptions of the writer allow.

Carver's fictional folk are the kind who don't quite fit in. Their gestures fall short, their clothes need pressing, their rent and car payments are due. They've "bungled" things, as one character puts it. They "sign up for it all," as someone else says, only to find themselves bit players in "another tragedy in a line of low-rent tragedies." Their dismalness comes from wives or husbands who leave or have affairs, rent that comes due, or some other intimation of betrayals private or cosmic. If they haven't lost their jobs, they work with fiberglass insulation, pitch vitamins or vacuum cleaners door-to-door. They live in hotel rooms and apartments and houses needing repairs, exchange cleaning in a dentist's office or a motel for rent, squat on a friend's ranch. They're in debt, and without too much worth reselling. The abandoned husband in **"Why Don't You Dance?"** has a yard sale of his furniture, which he sets up in room arrangements on the grass exactly as it once was inside his house. The husband in **"Are These Actual Miles?"** sends his wife off to sell the car before it's repossessed, knowing the price she'll get will include sex.

The trademark Carver tale is a kind of mundane ghost story in which these people are haunted by the presence of some lost, almost forgotten, not-really-expected possibility. They'd like to believe their problems will end with the right kiss, the right kid, the right job. They don't know where they're about to be off to or what might come next. They dream of some sign, some gesture to suggest that someone out there might notice or think it matters what move they make. A man lies around his house while he waits to "hear from up north" about work. Another has just gotten the promise of a job in Alaska when he thinks he sees his wife fondling his best friend. A woman talking to the man who's just betrayed her recalls her dream of a future that will never come when they would be old, ("Dignified. And in a place") A man imagines things'll be better if the wife loses weight so he doesn't have to overhear derogatory comments on her rear from customers in the restaurant where she works.

Carver's own problems with alcohol are contagious. Almost all his characters are looking for a fix. A lot of them are addicts—of drink, of love, of possessions. They stuff themselves with whatever is at hand. Whole stories involve small groups of people isolated in a room, drinking or smoking dope and eating for hours, talking against the grain of their lives. But the thirst, or hunger, that prompts the scene seems symptomatic of a desire for something more than the temporary respite of a melancholy stupor. It is linked to a sense of failure and a recognition of the gap between American possibilities and their own hard lot, but the problem is not only, or most importantly, financial. Nor is it exactly spiritual, though there's a dread of the unknown that makes many of the characters terrified of their own loneliness. They suffer from friendlessness and abandonment and feel a deep-seated frustration that tends to violence. The wrestling with economics and the battered emotions point only obliquely to the strains that the combined struggles with work and love place on intimacy. Seldom do the characters themselves recognize the factors that direct their actions; such interpretations come more often to the reader through (even occasionally despite) them.

For the best and worst of reasons, then, the lives behind Carver's voices are stifled, and we experience the frustrations in guarded references and occasional brief memories. The stories frequently end in a static tableau. A couple bleakly hug in a hallway in **"Neighbors"**; in **"What We Talk About When We Talk About Love,"** friends planning to go out to dinner drink and argue themselves into a state of inertia: "Now what?" one person mutters to the others. For the most part, the action is not so much imminent as forgone, proceeding from what has already happened. We read about the period of waiting, the consequences and reactions and adjustments. The story tells us about the state of shock as events are absorbed—absorbed rather than analyzed, recovered, or otherwise altered.

Especially in his first stories, Carver insists we notice how "every day, every night of our lives, we're leaving little bits of ourselves, flakes of this or that, behind," as a two-bit peddler puts it. Carver's method is analogical; people don't know who they are, or might be, until they see themselves mirrored in others. They want to be saved from themselves, made over from the outside. Often this is because their encounters remind them that they are no longer who they once were. A man who is asked to tend his neighbors' apartment in **"Neighbors"** retreats there for liquor, tries on the man's and woman's clothes, and finds that his sex life with his wife picks up. A waitress is fascinated by the immense appetite and delicate manners of a customer until she must admit to herself: "I know now I was after something. But I don't know what," and can only imagine that "My life is going to change. I feel it." After a wrong number almost leads to a rendezvous in **"Are You a Doctor?,"** the story ends with a long-distance phone call in which a wife tells her husband: "You don't sound like yourself."

Carver has tapped into our dependence on and identification with surrounding objects, or ongoing relations, for self-possession; the mildest disturbance of the shape of things leaves his people in need of outer substantiation. When forced to sell off property they own to make payments, the characters seem to be disposing of their identities as well, as if the objects are all that keep them stable inside middle-class routines, values, or assumptions. As they inventory someone else's life—the clothes and cupboards of the neighbor's apartment, the furniture that's left—a broken marriage, a woman killed in the woods—they find something approaching a tangible expression of their selves, magnified and distorted.

Then they struggle to translate their projected alternative self into language. They become storytellers—inadequate chroniclers—of their otherwise unexamined existences, as if the words would give credence to the emotion. In **"Why Don't You Dance?,"** the young woman who buys the rooms of furniture at the yard sale struggles to find form for the feelings that are the true cost of the pieces: "She kept talking. . . . There was more to it, and she was trying to get it talked out." Again and again, the characters look for words, seem to be trying to speak their way across a lifetime on a fraying rope of sound. A man about to leave his wife says he has "one more thing" to say, "but then he could not think what it could possibly be." Another man frustrated by his inability to convey his contradictory sentiments cuts through his wife's phone line as he departs.

Carver identifies the vagueness and dislocations of these often battered lives—the cliches that contain inexpressible confusions, the intimations of something more or at least different. The voyeurism of his characters seems parable-like, but with the meaningful part of the likeness absent, out of focus, off stage, barely glimpsed. Such distortion, however, reminds the readers of their own role as eavesdroppers on these brief keyhole chats with gloom. We are implicated by our efforts to provide meaning to the actions of these often unknowing people. The foreboding that Carver manages to instill in his short tales comes from the way we are forced to fill in the gap between the barren surface of events and the almost operatic emotional release and response that they often produce. The inexact fit between everyday circumstances and their soap opera consequences gives mystery and intensity to the commonplace predicaments. We find ourselves a little bereft, brought up short by endings which require us to measure the riot in the regret, the lethargy in the frustration, the artistry in the banality.

The problem with minimalism is obviously that it isn't enough. Like most excessive states, it is a reaction, a kind of austerity program in a time of rhetorical inflation. It is a way of cleaning house, making do with less, the literary equivalent of functionalist architecture. It offers an art of elimination, an effort one can associate with creating boundaries around private pain and avoiding public high-mindedness. The precisionist language suggests both poverty and simplicity: a dearth of alternatives and a willful discarding of the inessential. Echoing Hemingway's dictum about the hidden seven-eighths of the iceberg that a good story suggests, in "On Writing" Carver talks about how tension in fiction comes not only from "the visible action of the story" but "also the things that are left out, that are implied, the landscape just under the smooth (but sometimes broken and unsettled) surface of things." It's true, as critics have noted, that Carver's tales often leave so much out they exclude us too: don't supply enough for the reader to invade the events, or the characters to penetrate the reader's attention. They come sometimes at too high a pitch, when the flat surfaces and deadpan voice are forced to carry too heavy a burden of outrage. They are sometimes too insular, or seem evasive and unfinished. (This is particularly true of the hunting stories, which especially in their revised form often lack the resonance of the tales of people talking themselves into their lifelong indecisions.) Doris Grumbach objected to the "stinginess" of many of the stories in ***What We Talk About When We Talk About Love,*** and Michael Gorra complained that Carver's slices of life were far too lean when characters walked around with only first names, as they do in most of the pieces in that book [see excerpt dated 1984]. The technical spareness is frequently conflated with the material; Bharati Mukherjee recently used a *New York Times Book Review* essay to rail against minimalism's "dangerous social agenda": "Minimalism is nativist, it speaks in whispers to the initiated, . . . as though it were designed to keep out anyone with too much story to tell."

Minimalism like Carver's sometimes seems to imply a direct correlation between financial and emotional and cultural deprivation: a starvation of the senses and spirit that is unconditional and unrelieved, and which only finds outlet in desperation and passivity. But to claim that Carver's tales map some of the territory of failure is not to proclaim that he has revealed it all. And Mukherjee's reminder that minimalism has its antecedents in the Marlboro Man's stoic self-control shouldn't blind us to other equally significant sources, from Twain's restoration of the language to the longstanding intimacy of the story form with domestic rituals and everyday rhythms one finds as far back as Sarah Orne Jewett, Kate Chopin, Mary Wilkins Freeman, Sherwood Anderson. Carver admits to his own dissatisfactions with the confinements of his method, speaking of the self-conscious calculation of ***What We Talk About*** as a kind of experiment in reduction (much like the denatured color confinements self-imposed on analytic cubism), realizing in retrospect that he was approaching a "dead end": "I knew I'd gone as far as . . . I could or wanted to go, cutting everything down to the marrow, not just to the bone." He wrote nothing after the book's publication until **"Cathedral,"** a story he says came to him as a revelation, an "opening up" that "reflects a change in my life as much as it does in my way of writing."

The last, newer stories in ***Where I'm Calling From*** are about a third again as long as the earlier ones and more stately in cadence. They are autumnal, filled with fallen leaves that crunch underfoot, ex-wives to be revisited, concerns about annihilation that have to be talked out. Carver's (relative) verbal abundance serves as something of a cushion for the characters to fall back on. The suffering so long a part of his work is often alleviated or at least eased by a more forgiving acceptance of life's limits, sadnesses, and occasional compensations. Revelations occasionally appear, extraordinarily rendered if in the cautious and vague vocabulary appropriate to instants of pleasure in a world of uncertainty: "He felt something come to an end. It had to do with . . . the life before this." And in **"Cathedral"** itself comes an image that seems to speak back to the alienated vacuuming writer of **"Put Yourself in My Shoes."** The narrator is surprised to meet Robert, a blind man (and old friend of his wife's) who undermines all the speaker's ideas of blindness "from the movies." An evening of polite antagonism between the two men ends when a TV show about cathedrals prompts the narrator to help Robert realize their structure by joining hands with him to draw one. As they draw Robert urges the narrator to close his own eyes too: "I didn't feel like I was inside anything. 'It's really something,' I said."

The lesson here is more than of the blind leading the blind, because it reaches back to the implications of identitylessness and voyeuristic selfhood that are part of Carver's revelations about our culture. The object of so many of his protagonists is to get outside their own lives, through drink or talk or sex or some other saving grace. The stylistic minimalism mirrors the dearth of real alternatives available to these characters, despite the ready promises of each new fix. But here, the narrator has literally "opened up," as Carver says his art did in the writing. Going blind, he is no longer inside himself, if not quite outside, no longer alone if not quite intimate. The communion in sightless shaping of the cathedral's structure provides a scope which is a little more abundant, accomodating, even religious. It is a momentary possibility amid the downcast pessimism of most of Carver's tales. But it suggests another, more gracious and faithful kind of realism that Carver was struggling to believe in—another kind of ending.

Carver has always been the bard of people living in limbo, caught in the middle: in-between lives, alliances, decisions. A lot of critics talked about ***Cathedral*** when it appeared as a "transitional" volume, but the same can be said of Carver's career as a whole. Carver's insistence on rewriting stories even after publication encourages this sense one feels throughout his work that for all the deadendedness of the characters who inhabit his world, the dedication and curiosity that compels Carver's language about them is neverending. In "Fires," Carver suggests that revision "gradually takes me into the heart of what the story is *about.* I have to keep trying to see if I can find that out. It's a process more than a fixed position."

Carver insisted on remaining surprised by life; that's why, for all their dreariness and squalid conditions and threats of violence, one leaves his best pieces with a startled feeling of discovery and pleasure. It is not that he allows you distance from his defeated corps of citizens; on the contrary, your curiosity about them is an admission of complicity. But Carver never denies the most hapless of his people their vain, and so often misguided, cliches about future prospects.

Some damned conjunction of artistry and fate dictated Carver's choice of ***Where I'm Calling From*** as his title for this collection. On the surface, the words seem a diminished kind of declaration of presence, even faith, in location. But inside the story of that name, "where I'm calling from" is a drying-up hospital, one of those halfway houses so frequent in Carver. It's New Year's day, the narrator is there for the second time, he's got the shakes. A friend he made at the facility just went off with his wife, and the unnamed speaker is lonely, remembering a morning when he awoke next to his own wife, went naked to a window to see his landlord painting the side of his house, and could return to the warmth of his marriage bed. He wants to talk to his wife, who threw him out a few weeks before, even though she'll ask him "where I'm calling from, and I'll have to tell her." He wants to avoid fighting with her, and avoid promises about the future: "There's no way to make a joke out of this." Then after he talks to her, he wants to call his girlfriend and tell her "It's me."

There's a brave, sentimental, pathetically limited affirmation to all this, both in the story and in Carver's choice of the line as a title for this collection. ***Where I'm Calling From*** is an admission of failure and a grim offering of hope and possibility. It's the document, and the place, where things might, with some luck and cunning and will, alter, where one might be transformed into someone else, something more and better—expansive without addiction. It is based on a place where, biographically, Carver was not saved. But the experiences there marked a moment in what eventually became what he liked to call his "resurrection," the "state of grace" he claims came into his life in the last years. As a published volume, it is the document in which he has remade his life's work in prose for the last time.

In-between women, in-between homes, in-between drinks, the narrator locates himself in his disintegration. In-between times of his life, the writer views his past from the vantage of his salvation, aware of his impending death. It is all transition, all the uncertain and momentary and impermanent, all a story between drafts. (pp. 77-83)

Paul Skenazy, "Life in Limbo: Ray Carver's Fiction," in enclitic, *Vol. 11, No. 1, Issue 21, Fall, 1988, pp. 77-83.*

William L. Stull (essay date 1988)

[In the following excerpt, Stull discusses Carver's short stories that were published while Carver was an undergraduate student.]

Without revealing the urgency of his condition, during the last months of his life Raymond Carver told interviewers what he hoped might be his epitaph. "I can't think of anything else I'd rather be called than a writer," he said, "unless it's a poet. Short-story writer, poet, occasional essayist." To remember Raymond Carver the writer, to help scholars better understand where he was calling from, and to mark a shared twenty-fifth anniversary, . . . [Three of Carver's early uncollected stories were published] in the Spring 1963 issue of *Toyon* (vol. 9, no. 1), a student magazine that Carver edited shortly after his midyear graduation from Humboldt State College in Arcata, California.

Named for a hardy coastal shrub, *Toyon* survives, and Humboldt State (now University) has since established an annual Raymond Carver Short Story Contest in honor of its famous graduate.

Over the course of his life Raymond Carver published eighty-five separately titled works of fiction. ***Where I'm Calling From*** gathers those that he judged "most durable": thirty stories from his previous books, seven never before collected. The earliest story included is **"The Student's Wife,"** a Chekhovian study of character as mood that made its first appearance in the Fall 1964 issue of *Carolina Quarterly.* Where was Carver calling from in 1963, shortly before the first of his "most durable" works appeared in print? . . . [Part of the answer lies in] Raymond Carver's very first publications, which form the background of the *Toyon* stories.

Although Carver was not yet twenty-five years old when he edited *Toyon,* he had already published three important works of fiction. His first story to appear in print was **"The Furious Seasons,"** a work that, considerably revised, gave the title to ***Furious Seasons and Other Stories*** some seventeen years later. **"The Furious Seasons"** appeared in the second issue of *Selection* (Winter 1960-61), a student magazine that Carver had founded at Chico State College in the late 1950s. The story is a Gothic tale of incest and murder told in studiously Faulknerian fashion, with past and present tenses reversed for psychological effect. Carver's teacher at Chico State, the soon-to-be famous John Gardner, had told him, "Read all the Faulkner you can get your hands on and then read all of Hemingway to clean the Faulkner out of your system." With **"The Furious Seasons,"** Carver began working out Gardner's advice.

Carver's second published story proved less baroque and therefore more indicative of his work to come. Entitled **"The Father,"** it is a Kafkaesque tale of fewer than five hundred words, most of them unmediated dialogue, that charts the collapse of a young husband's identity. Carver had transferred from Chico to Humboldt State in the fall of 1960, and he wrote **"The Father"** for a newly arrived instructor named Richard C. Day. "I thought to myself that if I was lucky I might get to work with one real writer in my teaching career," Day later said. "And here he was in my first class." A writer himself, Day became Carver's friend and confidant. Moreover, as faculty adviser to *Toyon,* the college literary magazine, he saw to it that **"The Father"** appeared in the Spring 1961 issue. Slightly revised, this seminal fable is wedged between two later, longer stories in ***Will You Please Be Quiet, Please?***

Carver's third story appeared in print only weeks before his own issue of *Toyon* went to press. Published in the Winter 1963 *Western Humanities Review,* it is a Hemingway imitation called **"Pastoral."** Closely modeled on "Big Two-Hearted River" (1925), the ironically titled story is a fishing tale with dark undercurrents of anxiety and guilt. Mr. Harold, Carver's western Nick Adams, returns out of season and alone to fish at Castlerock, a vacation spot that he and his wife had earlier enjoyed together. (Following Hemingway's practice, Carver shapes the story as an "iceberg," its marital conflict seven-eighths submerged.) In the course of his abortive getaway, Harold is accosted by a pack of vicious young hunters, one of whom aims his rifle at the unarmed fisherman's crotch. Harold saves himself by asking for mercy, but he leaves the river feeling unheroic, homeless, and alone. All but unrevised, **"Pastoral"** appears in ***Furious Seasons*** (1977). Five years later, however, Carver rewrote the text for ***Fires*** (1983). There, retitled **"The Cabin,"** the story ends more hopefully, with an outcome truer to Carver's mature style and more consonant with Hemingway's original.

Carver was appointed editor of the 1963 *Toyon* shortly before his February graduation date. He was slated to begin a year's study at the Iowa Writers' Workshop in the fall, and during the spring he solicited manuscripts and assembled the issue. The finished journal appeared in May, and it included fifteen pieces of student writing. (A mildly scatological quotation from Brecht's *Mother Courage* is listed on the contents page as "filler.") Two stories, **"Poseidon and Company"** and **"The Hair,"** are attributed to Raymond Carver. A third story, **"The Aficionados,"** and a poem, "Spring, 480 B.C.," are credited to one John Vale. A contributor's note identifies Vale as "the pseudonym of an H.S.C. student who wishes to remain anonymous." What blows the cover off the punning pseudonym is that fact that "Spring, 480 B.C." went on to become one of Raymond Carver's best-known poems. Years later, Carver explained that he had failed to receive enough worthy submissions to make an issue. Torn between hubris and modesty, the editor included four of his own writings, two of them under Vale's name, to fill the journal's pages. For students of the American short story, Carver's ruse has a happy ending, since it preserved formative work that has not survived in manuscript.

It has become a truism to say that Raymond Carver is a literary descendant of Ernest Hemingway. **"The Aficionados,"** the story that opens Carver's *Toyon,* at once confirms this truism and complicates the Carver-Hemingway relationship. Attributed to Carver's pseudonymous alter ego, **"The Aficionados"** is a Hemingway parody, a "veiled" attack on a father figure to whom Carver had only recently paid homage. (It is perhaps worth noting that Hemingway's suicide had occurred less than two years before this parody appeared.) By means of a shocking *coup de grâce,* **"The Aficionados"** subverts Hemingway's famous "code" of masculinity. Carver suggests that within the myth of the hero lies an antithetical myth, the myth of the scapegoat. (Fittingly, it is the Hemingway "bitch goddess" who wields the instrument of the matador's destruction.) Bound up with the Hemingway code is, of course, the Hemingway style, whose tics and mannerisms "John Vale" skewers unerringly. In a travesty of Hemingway's most famous simile, for example, Carver likens the hills not to white elephants but to "great-breasted reclining women." The satire in **"The Aficionados"** is both dry and pointed, but its "thrust" (literalized in the final scene) proves less destructive than corrective. Having learned from Hemingway at his best, Carver distances himself from "Papa" at his worst. Inserted between **"Pastoral"** (1963) and **"The Cabin"** (1983), **"The Aficionados"** creates a richly dialectical pattern of influence: a process of imitation, rebellion, and reassessment spanning twenty years.

To a one, Carver's best-known stories—**"What We Talk About When We Talk About Love," "Cathedral,"** and **"Where I'm Calling From"**—concern the ways we live today. Relentlessly contemporary in their settings, themes, and speech patterns, they regularly attain the startling verisimilitude of recent photorealist painting. As a teenager, however, Carver devoured the futuristic fantasies of Edgar Rice Burroughs and the historical novels of Thomas B. Costain. English was his major at Humboldt State, but he supplemented it with courses in ancient and modern history. "I have a good memory," says the protagonist in **"Blackbird Pie"** (1986), one of Carver's last-written stories. The speaker proves his point by effortlessly recalling the Council of Trent, the Treaty of Utrecht, the fall of Carthage, and half a dozen battles from Thermopylae to Tannenberg. "Things stick in my head," he says.

For the most part, Carver confines his historical interests to his poetry. "Spring, 480 B.C.," for example, although credited to John Vale in *Toyon,* is but the first of Carver's several poems on the ancient hero-tyrants Xerxes and Alexander. (The series includes "Wine" and "Thermopylae" in *A New Path to the Waterfall.*) The single prose exception to the rule is the . . . classical vignette entitled **"Poseidon and Company."** Carver attached his own name to the story in *Toyon,* and he liked it well enough to republish it, with a slightly variant ending, in the Spring 1964 issue of *Ball State Teachers College Forum.* Although neither version rises above the level of learned ingenuity, both offset Carver's reputation as a relentless chronicler of contemporary life. Because the youthful protagonist is left unnamed, **"Poseidon and Company"** poses something of a riddle. Readers who recall the *Iliad,* however, will have no trouble identifying the dreamy boy as Homer, the blind poet who would grow up to immortalize Aias (Ajax) and Achilles as Poseidon's company in the Trojan War.

"The Hair," the last of Carver's *Toyon* stories, is easily the best. More than any other early work, it indicates the shape of Carver's fiction to come. "It marked him as a writer," recalled Professor Day, for whose class it was written. Over the course of an outwardly normal workday, the hair caught in the unnamed protagonist's teeth erodes his composure. Whether actual or imaginary, it defamiliarizes his experience, disrupts his routine, and isolates him from his wife. By nightfall he feels feverish, and toward midnight he wakes up screaming. Clearly, the minor irritant has precipitated a major crisis. But what is the trouble? Neither the protagonist nor his baffled spouse can say. Here, as in much of Carver's later writing, the event exceeds explanation—and therein lies its meaning.

"There's a Chekhovian clarity to Ray Carver's stories," Michael Koepf observed in 1981, "but a Kafkaesque sense that something is terribly wrong behind the scenes." Carver's trademark synthesis of simplicity and strangeness can be glimpsed in **"The Father,"** but the first story to achieve it fully is **"The Hair."** To be sure, the theme of identity undone is Kafkaesque. Following Chekhov, however, Carver "allows nothing to 'happen' but only smoothly and imperceptibly to 'become.' " No matter how discomfiting the action, the narrator's voice remains level and restrained, recalling Chekhov's early accounts of normality disrupted—"An Upheaval," for example, or "Panic Fears."

With uncanny accuracy and comprehensiveness, **"The Hair"** anticipates the "obsessions" of Carver's future work. (He disliked the word *theme.*) Prominent among these matters are voyeurism and dissociation (symbolized, as here, by windows and mirrors); the breakdown of communication between spouses; and what Gary Fisketjon has aptly termed "the terrifying implications of Normal Life." Like **"The Student's Wife"** (1964), the first of Carver's "most durable" stories, **"The Hair"** is a tale of rude awakening. In it, as in **"Why Don't You Dance?"** (1981), the central conflict is so fully objectified as to be unspeakable—a thing, not a word. Parallels of this sort abound, but surely the clearest descendant of **"The Hair"** is **"Careful"** (1983). There, the alcoholic protagonist's wax-stopped ear becomes the emblem of a host of "blockages," including his refusal to hear the truth about his drinking.

Raymond Carver never included **"The Hair"** in any of his major-press books. Nearly a decade after publishing the story in *Toyon,* however, he returned to it. Carver revised **"The Hair"** extensively—adding further details, giving the characters names, and slightly restructuring the opening. He was by then teaching at the University of California, Santa Cruz, and the revision appeared in a local alternative newspaper, *Sundaze,* dated January 7-20, 1972. The *Sundaze* text of **"The Hair"** can be read in ***Those Days*** (1987), a small-press book of Carver's early writings, printed in limited edition.

"What lasts is what you start with," reads one of the epigraphs to *A New Path to the Waterfall.* Raymond Carver's too-early death prevents him from commenting on [his formative stories]. . . . ***Those Days,*** however, contains work of similar vintage, and in his Preface, Carver judged it "Not bad, considering." Among his considerations were these words:

> The thing is, if a writer is still alive and well (and he's always well if he's still writing) and can look back from a great distance to a few early efforts and not have to feel *too* abashed or discomfited, or even ashamed of what he finds he was doing then—then I say good for him. And good, too, whatever it was that pushed him along and kept him going. The rewards being what they are in this business, few enough and far between, he ought perhaps even be forgiven if he takes some little satisfaction in what he sees: a continuity in the work, which is of course to say, a continuity in the life.

(pp. 465-69)

William L. Stull, "Raymond Carver Remembered: Three Early Stories," in Studies in Short Fiction, *Vol. 25, No. 4, Fall, 1988, pp. 461-69.*

Arthur M. Saltzman (essay date 1988)

[In the following excerpt, Saltzman examines the concepts of minimalist fiction and the characteristics of

Carver's short stories that adhere to tenets of minimalism.]

Raymond Carver's characters work for a living. They fret about mortgages and dream about vacations. They watch television, talk on the telephone, live among brand names, wonder about their neighbors. They know about pollution, laugh and cry at the movies, shake their heads at the news. They are bowlers, hunters, fishermen, cardplayers. Their families are dear to them, but there are inevitable misunderstandings, silences, infidelities—all the standard rifts and fractures love is prey to. Carver's characters smoke and drink more than they know they should. They complain about their misfortunes, harbor resentments, fear the future. Vaguely unhappy, vaguely lonesome, they tread water. They wonder if they are leading the right lives.

Carver's characters inhabit the world immediately recognizable as proletarian America, a terrain of fast food, used cars, and garish billboards. How so steadfastly pedestrian a literary environment as this has achieved so substantial an impact on contemporary American fiction is the chief motivation behind the critical fascination Raymond Carver has occasioned to date. He has been credited with the restoration of a presumably moribund form—literary realism. The well-wrought ambushes and exposures that constitute his celebrated collections of short stories have earned Carver the reputation of being among the leaders of a new movement in short fiction that is characterized by flatness of narrative tone, extreme spareness of story, an obsession with the drab and quotidian, a general avoidance of extensive rumination on the page, and, in sum, a striking restraint in prose style. This movement, whose most notable practitioners also include Ann Beattie, Elizabeth Tallent, Tobias Wolff, Mary Robison, and Frederick Barthelme, is typically referred to as "minimalism," a designation that highlights the spartan technique and the focus on the tiny fault lines that threaten to open out into violence or defeat.

The controversy surrounding such fiction is apparent in the more disparaging headings it has garnered which brand it as formulaic and faddish: "K-Mart Realism," "Hick Chic," "Freeze-Dried Fiction," "TV Fiction," "Hi-Tech Fiction," "Postliterate Literature," "Lo-Cal Literature," "White Trash Fiction," "Postalcoholic Blue-Collar Minimalist Hyperrealism," "Around-the-house-and-in-the-yard Fiction," "Coke Fiction." The thinly concealed indictment has less to do with the ordinariness of subject matter—the battle to establish literary attention for things so small was won generations ago—than with the possible failure of artistic nerve or the surrender to inhibition, as though what is really minimal about minimalism is the withered muse behind it or the decision to cater to the lowest common denominator of the contemporary reading public. Reviewers who praise Carver's refreshing readability and admire his expert delineation of the underside of the American Dream also seem eager to press Carver into service against postmodern elitists such as William Gaddis, Joseph McElroy, and Thomas Pynchon, who, so the argument usually concludes, pride themselves on creating texts so pure that few readers dare violate them. If minimalism is a reaction against postmodern pyrotechnics, what positive alternative direction for fiction does it present? Carver and company must stand trial for abdicating postmodern excesses only to succumb to an arid reserve—narrative voice shell-shocked by a hostile reality into a muddled monotone.

James Atlas, for example, claims that Carver's stories are severe to the point of anorexia. He laments a style that is "so aggressive in the suppression of detail, that one is left with a hunger for the richness, texture, excess, just as the cubed glass high-rises of Manhattan frustrate the eye's longing for nuance" [see Further Reading list]. John Barth, himself a devout "maximalist" author, perhaps inadvertently furthers the suspicion of writers like Carver by noting that a central reason for their popularity is probably the decline in literacy and the diminishment of reading habits among the television generation, which is to say that the general reader cannot handle more than the minimalists require of him ["A Few Words about Minimalism," *New York Times Book Review* (28 December 1986)]. By extension there is the question of whether the obvious influence of minimalism upon the "M.F.A. Mafia," as Jerome Klinkowitz terms them, is really due to the sheer convenience of the "less is more" philosophy. If the glib aesthetic of the 1960s was that anything and anyone could be proclaimed a work of art, the "happening" fiction of the 1980s may mark a comparable trend. Charles Newman [in *Salmagundi* 63-64 (Spring-Summer 1984)] goes so far as to diagnose the spread of minimalism to be part of "the classic conservative response to inflation—underutilization of capacity, reduction of inventory, and verbal joblessness," which simply rivets literary evolution to its inevitable socioeconomic context. The "cultural weightlessness" of minimalism—its assumptions of sociopolitical impotence and enervated sensibilities—is, in Newman's estimation, a methodology by which characters and authors alike are held captive: "Now it seems that the narrator is dragged down by his characters, adopting their limitations and defects, so that the reader is let off the hook by an author who refuses to attribute to him any curiosity—a strange deflection in which the reader does not blame the writer but rather feels superior to the characters" [*The New York Times Book Review* (12 July 1987)].

To counter these accusations effectively, we must begin by recognizing that while minimalist fiction obviously departs from the stylistic preening and playfulness of the works of Raymond Federman, Gilbert Sorrentino, and Ronald Sukenick, it does retain a concern with the intricacies of craft. Like Stanley Elkin and William Gass, for instance, Raymond Carver is a diligent refiner of sentences; the difference, however, is that whereas the former are masters of fusion and rhythmic embellishment, Carver is a surgeon who concentrates on taking sentences and "paring them down to where they seem solid somehow." Much has been written about Carver's attempts to develop a style relevant to the plague of inarticulateness that his characters endure. Proceeding only so far as the vernacular will allow, experience is bounded by the impoverished vocabulary of consciousness. Dialogues are brief, hedged, and in the shadow of what they need to be about. Gass discovers in such radical divestment of development faddishness swollen to creed: "Images are out. It is fraudulent to poeticize. Kept simple, short, direct, like a punch, the sentences avoid subordination, qualification, subtlety. Subordination requires judgment, evaluation; it creates complexity, demands definition" [*The New York Times Book Review* (11 October 1987)]. The numbing nature of contemporary life—postatomic and atomized, where communication dwindles as information proliferates—is inherent in the verbal incapacity that pervades these stories:

> "I can't think of anything else. You go now. Tell me what you'd like."
>
> "I don't know. Lots of things," he mumbled.
>
> "Well, tell me. We're just talking, aren't we?"
>
> "I wish you'd leave me alone, Nan."
>
> **—"The Student's Wife"**
>
> "What's wrong with here?" Jack said. "What would you guys do in Alaska? I'm serious. I'd like to know."
>
> Carl put a potato chip in his mouth and sipped his cream soda. "I don't know. What did you say?"
>
> After a while Jack said, "What's in Alaska?"
>
> "I don't know," Carl said. "Ask Mary. Mary knows. Mary, what am I going to do up there?"
>
> **—"What's in Alaska?"**
>
> "What are you staring at me for?" he asks. "What is it?" he says and lays his fork down.
>
> "Was I staring?" I say and shake my head stupidly, stupidly.
>
> **—"So Much Water So Close to Home"**
>
> "We're just talking. I just asked you how well you knew me. Would I"—how should he put it?—"am I trustworthy, for instance? Do you trust me?" It wasn't clear to him what he was asking, but he felt on the edge of something.
>
> "Is it important?" she said. She looked at him steadily. . . .
>
> He shrugged. "If you don't think it is, then I guess it isn't."
>
> **—"The Pheasant"**
>
> There were things he wanted to say, grieving things, consoling things, things like that.
>
> **—"A Serious Talk"**
>
> He said, "I just want to say one more thing."
>
> But he could not think what it could possibly be.
>
> **—"One More Thing"**

Crises arise in these stories when words are called to account for being inadequate to the task of conveying intentions.

The initial definition of minimalism as a kind of reassumption of traditional realism succeeding the stylistic libertinism of postmodernism is a reaction to, and welcoming of, the comparative hospitality of minimalist fictions to the common reader. Whereas the occasional dour academic might feel his solitary way along the dark and airless corridors of William Gaddis or Thomas Pynchon, the public wants literature that opens windows onto the world they know. In keeping with this logic, the prodigality of post-realist or surfictionist splinter groups has lost its momentum, and, as confirmed by the healthy sales statistics mounted by the new breed of short story writers, fiction has begun to regain its sanity.

Closer to the mark, however, is a definition of minimalism that treats it as another postmodern tributary in the multifarious progress of American literary history. Although their "experiments" with language are subtler than those of the more notorious desecrators of literary realism, the minimalists share their suspicion of the referential adequacy of words; at the same time, they share their clinical appreciation of the cadences of sentences. Raymond Carver, Ann Beattie, Mary Robison, Tobias Wolff, and writers like them are just as mannered and, in effect, just as subversive in their rigid jurisdiction over expansiveness as, at the other extreme, so-called maximalist writers like John Barth, T. Coraghessan Boyle, William Gaddis, William Gass, Joseph McElroy, Thomas Pynchon, and Ronald Sukenick are in their supermagnification and overregistration. It would be naïve, as well as inappropriate to the judiciously sucked-clean style of minimalism, to decide that it has miraculously come into being over the past decade or has that it has been so utterly innocent of the inroads and departures of postmodernism. (That so many minimalist authors teach or have taught in university classrooms further attests to the likelihood that they proceed in full awareness of their literary historical context.)

In short, if one of the main achievements of postmodern innovation in literature has been to broaden the scope of what and how a story can "be about," surely minimalism rates attention as a resulting option. As Kim A. Herzinger declares, minimalist writers "may well be creating literary constructs as formally rigorous and linguistically savvy as their postmodern predecessors. They are not, it seems to me, involved in a backbench effort to return to a pre-modern or pre-postmodern 'realism' " and could not achieve such a return even if they desired to, not after over half a century's worth of distrust of the representative powers of their medium. "Where the traditional 'realists' had a world and used a complex of ideas and emotions—done up in language—to describe it, the 'minimalists' have a complex of ideas and emotions—done up in language—which they use the world to describe" [*Mississippi Review* 40-41 (Winter 1985)]. As a radical divestiture of the sheer density to which realism conventionally ascribes—think of the weighty Henry James, William Dean Howells, or Theodore Dreiser, whose assiduous descriptions bespeak confident, noble enterprise—minimalism represents a challenge to the authenticity of received notions of what constitutes significant delivery of information.

Carver's suspicion of language, although its manifestation is understated when compared with the radical innovations of the postmodernists, reflects his social outlook and also has something to do with his trusting in fragments. Typically attributed to Donald Barthelme, this creed is manifested quite differently by Carver: instead of overloading the page with a blizzard of cultural detritus the way Barthelme does, Carver abstains from verbal indulgence altogether. While Barthelme's proliferation of referents ends up leveling out all input, Carver's technique shows how even the most modest foray into the world at large overwhelms the ability to absorb anything at all. His initial interest in the short story may have been economically motivated—it provides quicker tangible rewards—but it exhibits the contours of his artistic philosophy:

> To write a novel, it seemed to me, a writer should be living in a world that makes sense, a world that the writer can believe in, draw a bead on, and then write about accurately. A world that will, for a time anyway, stay fixed in one place. Along with this there has to be a belief in the essential *correctness* of that world. A belief that the known world has reasons for existing, and is worth writing about, is not likely to go up in smoke in the process. This wasn't the case with the world I knew and was living in.

Coherence and communicability would constitute authorial arrogance, a betrayal of reality.

Taking this idea further, Carver chooses to investigate the uninspiring conditions under which meaning might be achieved these days. In other words, his prose defamiliarizes the daily—one feels as though he were trying to negotiate his cellar stairs in the dark—by holding for inspection what is typically consigned to the voiceless background of fiction. To create what Stanley Elkin calls "the strange displacements of the ordinary" [*The Dick Gibson Show* (1971)], Carver chooses the opposite tactic from Elkin's: he rejects the lavish for the lean. There are none of the luscious, coiling sentences of Elkin, William Gass, or John Hawkes in his landscape; to get the fish Carver drains the lake. The correlative in painting is superrealism, as seen in the polished gleam of Richard Estes's surfaces that are made alien by their insistent foregrounding. In theater, where "minimalism" has greater currency as a critical term, there is the formidable example of Samuel Beckett's lifelong combat with the inexpressible and his reduction of stage event, property, and personality (in such play pieces as *Not I, Ohio Impromptu,* and *Breath*) to reach dramatic bedrock. Carver, too, believes in the richness of a glimpse and in the artistic legitimacy of being awestruck and left gaping by contemporary American life.

Carver probes into the furtive silences that lurk just behind the routines people keep. The dull captivity people endure in his stories is no guarantee of security. Underground streams of unease steal just beneath the narrative. If Carver's laconic surface is indebted to Hemingway, his atmosphere recalls Franz Kafka and Harold Pinter; the way someone pushes his food about the plate or hangs up the phone can be charged with menace. The tantalizing fragility of Carver's works is not due to a weak-willed abandonment of amplitude and depth, as some of his detractors suggest; rather, it results from his uncanny talent for catching lives at the moment they have begun to fray.

This brings to light another of Carver's "trademarks": the open-endedness, or lack of resolution, of his stories. "It would be inappropriate and, to a degree, impossible to resolve things neatly for these people and situations I'm writing about," Carver declares, going on to state that "satisfying" the reader's expectations and fulfilling the story's structural demands are by no means equivalent to providing unambiguous answers to the problems of plot. Here, too, it is instructive to note how Carver's fiction parallels the notorious distrust of totalization observed by Mas'ud Zavarzadeh in *The Mythopoeic Reality* and evidenced throughout the terrain of postmodern fiction. A principal lesson of the postmodernists is that epiphany is not something that is discovered in the world but created in the text; it does not originate from divine intervention but from literary convention, and self-evident works of art delight in exposing that contrivance to a sophisticated readership. Revelation is not a spiritual achievement but a linguistic one, and the role of language is not simply to commemorate the experience but to constitute it. Facing a worldly reality that, according to the consensus of recent fiction, is decentered and unsystematic at best and nonsensical at worst, the focused and stable meaning that epiphany suggests has been outdated for generations. A "totalizing fiction" which professes an integrated, even absolute, vision of reality is as antiquated as the myth of the hieratic author that it complements.

Carver is just as wary of granting his struggling characters any artificial lucidity or of rushing to restore composure to situations that have leaked out of hand. In his essay "On Writing" he observes, "What creates tension in a piece of fiction is partly the way the concrete words are linked together to make up the visible action of the story. But it's also the things that are left out, that are implied, the landscape just under the smooth (but sometimes broken and unsettled) surface of things." One recollects Robert Frost's paradoxical dictum: "All metaphor breaks down somewhere. That is the beauty of it." That is also the truth of it. Healing the ruptures—the divorces, deaths, and disappointments, all the creeping doubts like private ghosts—would be aesthetically unconscionable, not to mention beyond the scope of the characters who suffer them in Carver's fiction. Thus, his endings are often abrupt, truncated. To illustrate, here are representative examples from his first collection, ***Will You Please Be Quiet, Please?:***

> I feel depressed. But I won't go into it with her. I've already told her too much.
>
> She sits there waiting, her dainty fingers poking her hair.
>
> *Waiting for what?* I'd like to know.
>
> It is August.
>
> My life is going to change. I feel it.
>
> —**"Fat"**

> They stayed there. They held each other. They leaned into the door as if against a wind, and braced themselves.
>
> —**"Neighbors"**

> "Daddy doesn't look like *anybody!*" Alice said.
>
> "But he has to look like *somebody,*" Phyllis said, wiping her eyes with one of the ribbons. And all of them except the grandmother looked at the father, sitting at the table.

He had turned around in his chair and his face was white and without expression.

—**"The Father"**

. . . "I hate tricks," Carver admits. "At the first sign of a cheap trick or a gimmick in a piece of fiction, a cheap trick or even an elaborate trick, I tend to look for cover." While he appears to be echoing his mentor, John Gardner, whose *On Moral Fiction* is a book-length diatribe against what he considers stylistic preciousness and self-indulgent dazzle, Carver also appears to be referring to stories that sell out their difficulties for the comforts of closure. If postmodern fiction promotes a collaborative version of meaning that is elusive and negotiable, Carver's fiction is similarly collaborative, in that readers are challenged to complete for themselves the fragments that have been entrusted to them.

But it would be a mistake to glibly equate these achievements with artlessness, as though Carver's particular brand of realism were just the prose entry among such signs of the times as microwave ovens, computer chips, and Reaganomics. Carver strips the page to its essentials, down to the story's core. Where a Henry James or a William Faulkner might endlessly delve, Carver merely hints. He constructs a life style out of a few mundane objects littering the room and charges the casual phrase with massive implication, blunt as a blackjack. ("I will show you fear in a handful of dust," warned T. S. Eliot in *The Waste Land.*) In an often cited passage [from "On Writing"] Carver claims, "It's possible, in a poem or a short story, to write about commonplace things and objects using commonplace but precise language, and to endow those things—a chair, a window curtain, a fork, a stone, a woman's earring—with immense, even startling power." Carver stays faithful to the gross tokens of American culture—the stuff of waitresses, fishermen, salesmen, mail carriers; like Saul Bellow's Augie March, he is "a sort of Columbus of those near at hand." "Low-rent tragedies," as one Carver character calls them, seldom make the papers, so it is up to fiction to recover them.

To do so Carver abjures the "vague or blurred" and avoids "smoked-glass prose." William Carlos Williams, another devoted chronicler of the importance and the futility of average Americans, advises that "the difficulty is to catch the evasive life of the thing, to phrase the words in such a way that stereotype will yield a moment of insight. That is where the difficulty lies." The artist's dilemma is how to lift "to the imagination those things which lie under the direct scrutiny of the senses, close to the nose. It is this difficulty that sets a value upon all works of art and makes them a necessity."

Raymond Carver helps ventilate the contemporary literary scene with his plain-dealing, "post-postmodern" style and consequent reavowal of extratextual reality. The world he addresses is defined by odd jobs and compromised aspirations. Carver is just as appreciative of what is no less valuable for being anonymous. In the words of John Gardner, whom Carver gratefully credits as a formative influence, "Art rediscovers, generation by generation, what is necessary to humanness." Through a meticulous regard for how the plainest people live, Carver makes his own small-change world possible for art. (pp. 3-18)

Arthur M. Saltzman, in his Understanding Raymond Carver, *University of South Carolina Press, 1988, 190 p.*

Adam Meyer (essay date 1989)

[*In the following essay, Meyer analyzes different versions of Carver's short stories written for his early, middle, and late collections, positing that Carver's minimalist style belongs to the middle period while his early and later collections display more expansive narratives.*]

At this point in his career, there can be little doubt that Raymond Carver is "as successful as a short story writer in America can be" [see Facknitz, *Studies in Short Fiction* 23 (1986) in Further Reading list], that "he is becoming an influence" [see Robert Houston in Further Reading list]. Still, despite (or perhaps because of) this position, Carver remains a controversial figure. Much of the debate about Carver's merits centers around a similar debate about minimalism, a style that a few years ago was very hot and very hotly criticized, and that, now that it is cooling off, is under even more fervent attack. Much of the controversy is sparked by a confusion of terminology. As hard as it is accurately to define minimalism, for the same reasons we cannot entirely pin down such terms as realism, modernism, or post-modernism. It is even harder to say who is or is not a minimalist, as demonstrated by Donald Barthelme's being called a minimalist as often as he is called one of the post-modernists against whom the minimalists are rebelling. Nevertheless, Carver is generally acknowledged to be "the chief practitioner of what's been called 'American minimalism' " [see excerpt dated 1984]. Now that this has become a pejorative appelation, however, his admirers are quickly trying "to abduct [him] from the camp of the minimalists" [see Robinson excerpt dated 1988]. If he is to be successfully "abducted," however, it will not be because the label is no longer popular, but because it no longer fits.

The fact of Carver's membership in the minimalist fraternity has never been fully established. Many critics, as well as Carver himself, noted that his latest volume of new stories, ***Cathedral,*** seemed to be moving away from minimalist writing, that it showed a widening of perception and style. This is certainly true, but it is not the whole story. If we look back over Carver's entire output, an overview encouraged by the recent publication of his "selected" stories, ***Where I'm Calling From,*** we see that his career, rather than following an inverted pyramid pattern, has actually taken on the shape of an hourglass, beginning wide, then narrowing, and then widening out again. In other words, to answer the question "Is Raymond Carver a minimalist?" we must also consider the question "Which Raymond Carver are we talking about?," for he did not start out as a minimalist, and he is one no longer, although he was one for a period of time in between.

This hourglass pattern emerges when we read all of Carver's stories chronologically, or, to a lesser extent, when we read ***Where I'm Calling From*** from cover to cover.

Carver's evolution can perhaps be best understood when we examine several stories that have been published at different times in different versions. Carver, an inveterate rewriter, has stated that he would "rather tinker with a story after writing it, and then tinker some more, changing this, changing that, than have to write the story in the first place." Sometimes this tinkering results in only minor changes, as Carver makes clear when he cites admiration for Evan Connell's statement, "he knew he was finished with a short story when he found himself going through it and taking out commas and then going through the story again and putting commas back in the same places" (*F*). At other times, however, the result is an almost entirely different work. While the rewriting process is not unusual in itself, Carver's unwillingness to stop even after a piece has been published is not typical. One significantly revised publication that has elicited much critical commentary is **"A Small, Good Thing,"** which appears in ***Cathedral.*** It is a retelling of **"The Bath,"** a story from Carver's most minimalistic volume, ***What We Talk About When We Talk About Love,*** that transforms the piece into something far removed from that style. In fact, this change was responsible for alerting many readers and critics to the "new" Carver presented in ***Cathedral*** as a whole.

The basic situation in both stories is the same. A woman goes to a baker to order a special cake for her son Scotty's birthday party. The morning of his birthday, however, he is struck by a hit-and-run driver and becomes comatose. The baker, knowing only that the cake has not been picked up, calls the house and leaves threatening messages. The presentation of these events is very different in the two works, so by comparing them we can come to understand some of the salient features of minimalism. Most obviously, **"The Bath,"** ten pages long, is approximately one-third the length of **"A Small, Good Thing,"** an indication of the further development of the rewritten version. The characters in both stories are usually referred to by nouns or pronouns (the boy, the mother, he, she), but in **"The Bath"** we do not learn the mother's full name, Ann Weiss, until the last page, whereas she announces it to the baker in the second paragraph of **"A Small, Good Thing."** This might seem like a small thing, but it is indicative of a larger change. If we juxtapose the two versions of this early encounter between Mrs. Weiss and the baker, we clearly see a fundamental change in Carver's narrative strategy. In **"The Bath,"** Carver writes:

> The mother decided on the spaceship cake, and then she gave the baker her name and her telephone number. The cake would be ready Monday morning, in plenty of time for the party Monday afternoon. This was all the baker was willing to say. No pleasantries, just this small exchange, the barest information, nothing that was not necessary.

In **"A Small, Good Thing,"** Carver rewrites:

> She gave the baker her name, Ann Weiss, and her telephone number. The cake would be ready on Monday morning, just out of the oven, in plenty of time for the child's party that afternoon. The baker was not jolly. There were no pleasantries between them, just the minimum exchange of words, the necessary information. He made her feel uncomfortable, and she didn't like that. While he was bent over the counter with the pencil in his hand, she studied his coarse features and wondered if he'd ever done anything else with his life besides be a baker. She was a mother and thirty-three years old, and it seemed to her that everyone, especially someone the baker's age—a man old enough to be her father—must have children who'd gone through this special time of cakes and birthday parties. There must be that between them, she thought. But he was abrupt with her—not rude, just abrupt. She gave up trying to make friends with him. She looked into the back of the bakery and could see a long, heavy wooden table with aluminum pie pans stacked at one end; and beside the table a metal container filled with empty racks. There was an enormous oven. A radio was playing country-Western music.

The first version is sparse and elliptical, giving the reader only "the barest information, nothing that [is] not necessary," while the second offers a more expansive view, providing physical details of the characters and the bakery, as well as exploring the mother's thoughts. The revision also hints more fully at the conflict that will be developed later in the story. Kim Herzinger's definition of minimalism [in *Mississippi Review* 40-41 (1985)], "equanimity of surface, 'ordinary' subjects, recalcitrant narrators and deadpan narratives, slightness of story, and characters who don't think out loud," clearly fits the first paragraph, but it does not entirely account for the second, particularly in its exploration of the character's inner thoughts.

The most significant change from **"The Bath"** to **"A Small, Good Thing,"** however, is in their endings. Minimalist stories have been heavily criticized for their tendency to end "with a sententious ambiguity that leaves the

Carver and Tess Gallagher in 1984.

reader holding the bag," and **"The Bath"** certainly follows this pattern. It ends literally in the middle of one of the baker's telephone calls: " 'Scotty,' the voice said. 'It is about Scotty,' the voice said. 'It has to do with Scotty, yes.' " (*What*). At this point in the story, Scotty's medical condition is still uncertain, and, although the reader has figured it out, the parents still do not know who is making the horrible calls. This ending, then, is very much up in the air, and the reader leaves the story with a feeling of uneasiness and fear. **"A Small, Good Thing,"** however, goes beyond this point in time. Scotty dies. The parents come to realize that the baker has been making the harrassing calls, and they confront him. Once they explain the situation, the baker, feeling deep remorse for having bothered them, offers them some fresh rolls, telling them that "[e]ating is a small, good thing in a time like this." The story now ends on a note of communion, of shared understanding and grief: "They talked on into the early morning, the high, pale cast of light in the windows, and they did not think of leaving." The result is a story that has moved far beyond its minimalistic origins. Carver said in an interview that

> [t]he story hadn't been told originally, it had been messed around with, condensed and compressed in **"The Bath"** to highlight the qualities of menace that I wanted to emphasize. . . . But I still felt there was unfinished business, so in the midst of writing these other stories for ***Cathedral*** I went back to **"The Bath"** and tried to see what aspects of it needed to be enhanced, re-drawn, re-imagined. When I was done, I was amazed because it seemed so much better.

Most critics agree with this evaluation of **"A Small, Good Thing,"** which won the O. Henry award as the best short story of 1983. "The revision completes the original by turning the sum of its fragmentary parts into a coherent whole that has a powerful dramatic structure, a beginning, middle, and end," writes William Stull [see excerpt dated 1985], and Marc Chenetier feels that it signals "a movement away from threatening ambiguity, a working towards hope rather than horror, and the abandonment of features Carver may have come to consider akin to the narrative 'gimmicks' he has always denounced" [see excerpt dated 1986]. Indeed, as indicated earlier, nearly all of the stories in ***Cathedral*** show this movement away from the "gimmicks" of minimalism.

By looking at a story that has been published in three different versions, we get a fuller picture of the whole of Carver's evolution, his movement at first toward and then away from minimalism. **"So Much Water So Close to Home"** first appeared (in book form) in Carver's second volume, the small press book ***Furious Seasons*** (1977). It was reprinted in his second "major" volume, ***What We Talk About When We Talk About Love*** (1981) and appeared a third time in another small press book, ***Fires: Essays, Poems, Stories*** (1983). Most recently, it appeared as one of the selected stories in ***Where I'm Calling From*** (1988). The basic plot is the same in each publication. Stuart Kane and his buddies go fishing. As soon as they arrive at their campsite, they find a dead girl floating in the river. They decide to tie her to a tree so that she will not be lost downstream and then proceed to fish and drink for the remainder of the weekend. The story is told from the point of view of Stuart's wife, Claire, and is largely concerned with the strain that this event puts on their marriage, as she, empathizing with the dead girl, feels that her husband should have abandoned his trip and reported the body immediately.

A comparison of the way this material is treated in the first and second versions shows the several ways in which, according to John Barth [in *The New York Times Book Review* (28 December 1986)], a story can be minimalistic. First, Barth says, "there are minimalisms of unit, form and scale: short . . . paragraphs, super-short stories"; Carver's story is reduced by half in the revision, and long paragraphs, such as the one in which Claire explains the circumstances of the body's discovery, are broken up into many smaller ones (in this case, five). Second, "there are minimalisms of style: a stripped-down vocabulary; a stripped-down syntax that avoids periodic sentences"; this can be seen in Carver's alteration of "They fish together every spring and summer, the first two or three months of the season, before family vacations, little league baseball and visiting relatives can intrude" to "They fish together every spring and early summer before visiting relatives can get in the way" (*What*). Third, and most important, "there are minimalisms of material: minimal characters, minimal exposition . . . , minimal *mises en scene,* minimal action, minimal plot"; this third of Barth's observations is the one on which I wish to concentrate and illustrate here, for it is the key to seeing the change in Carver's aesthetic.

In the first version (*FS,* 1977), we are given long descriptions of the fishing trip, of Claire's reactions to her husband's behavior, of her thoughts about their past relationship, of the physical separation she imposes upon him, of the identification and subsequent funeral of the dead girl, and of many other actions and thoughts on several characters' parts. In the second version (*What,* 1981), however, these passages are either considerably reduced or eliminated altogether. As a result, this second version, since it stays on the surface of events and does not really allow us to get inside of the characters, seems to confirm the criticism that Carver's work is cold or unfeeling, that he lacks sympathy for his characters. For example, the last line of the opening paragraph in the first version—Claire's "Something has come between us though he would like to believe otherwise" (*FS*)—sets up, even sums up, much of the emotional conflict that is to be examined in the story. Its elimination in the second version leaves us unsure of the real motivations of the characters, thus diminishing our understanding of what is actually going on and, consequently, our concern for the people involved.

There are many more examples of such revisions, excisions that require more inference on the reader's part rather than providing him with more information. Consider, for instance, a long passage from the first version in which Claire thinks back on her previous life:

> The past is unclear. It is as if there is a film over those early years. I cannot be sure that the things I remember happening really happened to me. There was a girl who had a mother and father—

> the father ran a small cafe where the mother acted as waitress and cashier—who moved as if in a dream through grade school and high school and then, in a year or two, into secretarial school. Later, much later—what happened to the time in between?—she is in another town working as a receptionist for an electronic parts firm and becomes acquainted with one of the engineers who asks her for a date. Eventually, seeing that's his aim, she lets him seduce her. . . . After a short while they decide to get married, but already the past, her past, is slipping away. The future is something she can't imagine.

This passage, continuing in much the same vein for the rest of the page, provides us with valuable information about the character, her background, and her feelings about herself and her marriage. Therefore, when this is replaced by "I sit for a long time holding the newspaper and thinking" (*What*), we are obviously missing out on a key to understanding the actions within the story. We also miss out on fully comprehending the developing relationship between Stuart and Claire when several scenes showing her physical revulsion toward her husband, the way "his fingers burn" (*FS*) when he touches her, are reduced or eliminated. A long argument about her refusing to sleep in the same bed with him (*FS*), for example, becomes "That night I make my bed on the sofa" (*What*), again making it harder for the reader to grasp what is going on in the story. Unlike the first version, these elliptical revisions result [according to Gorra] in a minimalistic story whose "prose [is] so attenuated that it can't support the weight of a past or a future, but only a bare notation of what happens, now; a slice of life in which the characters are seen without the benefit of antecedents or social context."

Not only does the first version provide a fuller understanding of the main characters, it also presents important and detailed pictures of some of the minor characters who are all but eliminated in the revision. We have already seen how the baker's transformation from a mere voice on the other end of the telephone in **"The Bath"** to a fully realized person with his own history and concerns in **"A Small, Good Thing"** adds a whole new dimension, a fuller sense of humanity to that story, and the same is true here. For example, Carver's revision of **"So Much Water So Close to Home"** eliminates an important scene in which the couple's son, Dean, questions his father, only to be told to be quiet by his mother (*FS*). More significantly, Carver dramatically redraws his portrait of the victim. Although it seems like a minor detail, there is a world of difference in the reader's perception when a character is called "Susan Miller" rather than "the body." The ***Furious Seasons*** version of **"So Much Water So Close to Home"** contains the following scene, a description of a television news report in which the dead girl's parents go into the funeral home to identify the body:

> Bewildered, sad, they shuffle slowly up the sidewalk to the front steps to where a man in a dark suit stands waiting and holding the door. Then, it seems as if only a second has passed, as if they have merely gone inside the door and turned around and come out again, the same couple is shown leaving the mortuary, the woman in tears, covering her face with a handkerchief, the man stopping long enough to say to a reporter, "It's her, it's Susan."

There is also a description of what she looked like, her high school graduation picture flashed on the screen, and what she did for a living. In this way, she and her family become alive for the reader, who is now able to identify with them just as Claire does. When all we are told is that "the body has been identified, claimed" (*What*), however, we fail to reach this sort of understanding. We also therefore fail to understand fully Claire's motivation in attending her funeral.

Once again, the ending has been radically changed in the rewrite. In the first version, Claire returns from the funeral. Stuart attempts to initiate physical contact with her, but she rebuffs him, even stomping on his foot. He throws her down, makes an obscene remark, and goes away for the night. He sends her flowers the next morning, attempting to make up, but she "moves[s her] things into the extra bedroom" (*FS*). At the end of the story, still not understanding his actions, she says to him, " 'For God's sake, Stuart, she was only a child' " (*FS*). Her sense of continued sympathy for Susan and incomprehension of Stuart's behavior, her further separation from him, is perfectly in keeping with the previous actions and motivations of the characters. She had said earlier that her real fear was that "one day something [would] happen that should change something, but then you see nothing is going to change after all" (*FS*), yet it is clear at the end of the story that a fundamental alteration of her marital relationship has occurred. In the second version of the story, however, when Stuart attempts to initiate sexual activity with her, she allows herself to be symbolically raped; the sentence "I can't hear a thing with so much water going" (*What*) clearly recalls the rape and murder of the other girl. She even goes so far as to participate actively in the violation. " 'That's right,' I say, finishing the buttons myself. 'Before Dean comes. Hurry' " (*What*). Her motivation here is unclear, made even more so by its having been so understated in the earlier parts of the story. We do not understand what has caused her to change her mind about Stuart, nor why she is seemingly willing to return to the status quo. The ending is not ambiguous, like the ending of **"The Bath,"** but it is rather illogical and unconvincingly forced.

As we have seen, then, the revision of this story makes it more minimal than it had been, reduces it rather than enlarges it. When Carver assembled the stories for ***Fires,*** however, he decided to republish the first version (with some minor changes) rather than the second. As he explains in the afterword to the volume, "I decided to stay fairly close to the versions as they first appeared . . . , which is more in accord with the way I am writing stories these days [i.e., the stories in ***Cathedral***]" (*F*). Elsewhere Carver has stated that ***What We Talk About When We Talk About Love*** is a very "self-conscious book in the sense of how intentional every move was, how calculated. I pushed and pulled and worked with those stories before they went into the book to an extent I'd never done with any other stories." The end result, however, was not entirely satisfactory. "I knew I'd gone as far the other way as I could or wanted to go," he said, "cutting everything down to the marrow, not just to the bone," so he began to move in the other direction, first in ***Fires*** and then in ***Cathedral.*** Carver's movement away from minimalism is also apparent in his selection of the stories to be included in ***Where I'm Calling From.*** Only seven of the seventeen stories in ***What We Talk About When We Talk About Love*** are included, compared with eight of the twelve in ***Cathedral.*** Even more tellingly, Carver chooses four stories that appear "minimalized" in ***What We Talk About When We Talk About Love*** but reprints them in their other, fuller forms—for example, **"A Small, Good Thing"** rather than **"The Bath"** and the third **"So Much Water So Close to Home"** rather than the second.

This movement at first toward but then away from minimalism can also be traced in **"Distance,"** otherwise known as **"Everything Stuck to Him"** (in *What*), another story that is printed in all four volumes (*FS, What, F, Where*). While the changes here are much less dramatic than those in the three versions of **"So Much Water So Close to Home,"** the pattern is similar. The location of the story, for instance, is given in the first version as "Milan . . . in his apartment in the Via Fabroni near the Cascina Gardens" (*FS*), in the second as simply "Milan" (*What*), and in the third as "Milan . . . in his apartment on the Via Fabroni near the Cascina Gardens" (*F*). The lack of specificity in the second version indicates that it has been "minimalized," but Carver ultimately rejects this in favor of the fuller, more detailed description. The story is selected for ***Where I'm Calling From*** in this third version.

An even better example of these changes in Carver's aesthetic, however, is the story **"Where Is Everyone?,"** which was first published in the journal *TriQuarterly* in the spring of 1980. It reappeared, under the title **"Mr. Coffee and Mr. Fixit,"** in ***What We Talk About When We Talk About Love*** (1981). In the transition it was reduced by a third, Carver having cut from it the same sort of material that he excised in the second publication of **"So Much Water So Close to Home."** The story does not have much of a plot in either case. It is rather unusual among Carver's stories in that it is almost entirely composed of the narrator's reminiscences of past events, such as his wife's affair with an unemployed aerospace worker, his children and their actions, his father's death, and his widowed mother's sexual activities. The story is difficult to follow both chronologically and emotionally in both versions, but in the earlier, fuller version we are given many more clues. As Marc Chenetier points out:

> In its much longer version as **"Where Is Everyone?,"** it makes plain a number of details that remain quite puzzling in the shortened text. . . . The barest skeleton necessary for suggestion remains and a number of incidents that can be read as explanation in **"Where Is Everyone?"** are left as mere questions or unclear allusions in **"Mr. Coffee and Mr. Fixit."** . . . All of the details that made for "understanding" or "answering" a story in the interrogative mode have been toned down and have lodged the interrogations dismissed from the title at the heart of the story itself.

The two stories begin similarly, but they diverge sharply in a passage in which the narrator recalls his relationship with his children. "I hated my kids during this time," he says. "One afternoon I got into a scuffle with my son. . . . I said I would kill him." He goes on to explain the way the children, Katy and Mike, tried to take advantage of the situation, but he indicates that they were also deeply hurt by it, as seen by Mike's locking his mother out of the house one morning after she had spent the night at her lover's house and then beating her up when he does let her in. Not only is this passage missing from the revised version, but the son has been eliminated from the story altogether, and the daughter, whose name has been changed from Katy to Melody, just as the wife's has gone from Cynthia to Myrna, is little more than a stick figure who only appears in one brief paragraph. The result again is to provide the reader with less information about the state of the family; we get hints, but that is all. The narrator is also more reticent about himself. His comparing the situation to a scene in a novel by Italo Svevo (*TQ*), for instance, provides some insight into his personality and sets him apart from the standard, even stereotypical, Carver character. Not only does he read, a rarity in itself, but he reads novels by obscure Italian writers. This reference is eliminated in the revision, once more depriving us of a fact that might help us to make sense of the character's actions. The same is true of the sentence " 'No one's evil,' I said once to Cynthia when we were discussing my own affair" (*TQ*). This fact, as well as the way it seems to slip out without the narrator's being fully aware of having divulged it, opens up a whole new level of interest and awareness, one that remains blocked off when the line is deleted, as it is in the second version.

This obscuring of the central characters and their relationships continues throughout **"Mr. Coffee and Mr. Fixit."** In **"Where Is Everyone?,"** although the narrator says that "conversations touching on love or the past were rare" (*TQ*), they do exist and are presented to us. At one point, for example, Cynthia says to the narrator, "When I was pregnant with Mike you carried me into the bathroom when I was so sick and pregnant I couldn't get out of bed. You carried me. No one else will ever do that, no one else could ever love me in that way, that much. We have that, no matter what. We've loved each other like nobody else could or ever will love the other again" (*TQ*). This glimpse of the past, besides being touching, appearing as it does in the midst of anger and violence, explains the tie that binds the couple together despite their problems. Ironically, the other important interpersonal relationship in the story exists between the narrator and his wife's lover, Ross, even though they have never met. In **"Mr. Coffee and Mr. Fixit,"** there are a few elliptical references to this feeling of connection on the narrator's part: "But we had things in common, Ross and me, which was more than just the same woman" (*What*); or "I used to make fun of him when I had the chance. But I don't make fun of him anymore. God bless you and keep you, Mr. Fixit" (*What*). The rationale behind these statements is obscure. Here is another example of a peculiar bind that Carver can get himself into; when [according to Robert Towers in *New York Review of Books* (14 May 1981)] he "omit[s] what other writers might regard as essential information, it is often hard to know what has precipitated a given situation." In **"Where Is Everyone?,"** these passages are expanded, and the connection becomes easier to see. For example, the narrator had once suggested that Mike join the Army. Cynthia disagreed, but Ross spoke in favor of the idea. "I was pleased to hear this," the narrator says, "and to find out that Ross and I were in agreement on the matter. Ross went up a peg in my estimation. . . . He [had] told her this even after there'd been a pushing and shoving match out in his drive in the early morning hours when Mike had thrown him down on the pavement" (*TQ*). The narrator was more than willing to admit to his wife that Ross was "[o]ne of *us*" (*TQ*) at the time, and now he realizes that his anger toward Ross was really only jealousy because "he was something of a fallen hero to my kids and to Cynthia, too, I suppose, because he'd helped put men on the moon" (*TQ*). In the longer version, then, Ross, like the minor characters we have examined in the other stories, emerges as a person in his own right, more than just the lover of the narrator's wife. We can now see how the narrator comes to identify with him (they are, after all, two men in similar positions) and eventually to forgive him. When all we see is the forgiveness, though, we do not understand how it came to be.

Once again the endings are significantly different from one version to the other. In **"Where Is Everyone?,"** the narrator returns to his mother's house to spend the night. She reluctantly informs him of his wife's affair. He tells her, "I know that. . . . His name is Ross and he's an alcoholic. He's like me" (*TQ*). She responds, "Honey, you're going to have to do something for yourself" (*TQ*) and wishes him good night. The story ends with the following description:

> I lay there staring at the TV. There were images of uniformed men on the screen, a low murmur, then tanks and a man using a flame thrower. I couldn't hear it, but I didn't want to get up. I kept staring until I felt my eyes close. But I woke up with a start, the pajamas damp with sweat. A snowy light filled the room. There was a roaring coming at me. The room clamored. I lay there. I didn't move. (*TQ*)

This ending is somewhat ambiguous, but it does point to an apocalyptic change in the narrator's life, the sort that has resulted in his having reached the level of understanding he possesses at the time, about three years later, when he is narrating these events. **"Mr. Coffee and Mr. Fixit,"** however, ends in this manner:

> "Honey," I said to Myrna the night she came home. "Let's hug awhile and then you fix us a real nice supper."
>
> Myrna said, "Wash your hands." (*What*)

This ending so lacks any kind of summation, let alone consummation, that it baffles the reader. We do not even know when "the night she came home" is—Is it at the time of the events or at the time of their narration? What will be the effect of the things of which we have been told on the lives of those involved? We simply have to guess, with little to go on. Once asked about his endings, Carver stated, "I want to make sure my readers aren't left feeling cheated in one way or another when they've finished my stories. It's important for writers to provide enough to satisfy readers, even if they don't provide 'the' answers, or clear resolution." The ending of **"Mr. Coffee and Mr. Fixit,"** however, far from being satisfying, is the sort that, "rather than suggest[ing] depth . . . only signal[s] authorial cop out "[according to Peter La Salle in *America* (30 January 1982)]. This is undoubtedly one of the reasons that, as in the case of **"So Much Water So Close to Home,"** when Carver compiled the material for ***Fires,*** he returned, nearly word for word, to the original fuller version. Still one of his less successful pieces, as he tacitly admits by not selecting it for ***Where I'm Calling From,*** **"Where Is Everyone?"** is certainly better in that less minimal form.

John Biguenet finds **"Mr. Coffee and Mr. Fixit"** to be such a good example of everything he dislikes about minimalism that he uses it as the principal illustration in his satirical article "Notes of a Disaffected Reader: The Origins of Minimalism" [in *Mississippi Review* 40-41 (1985)]. After providing a summary of the story that is almost as long as the story itself, he writes:

> It sounds like parody, doesn't it? Fifteen years ago it would have been parody. But it's not parody; it's paraphrase. If paraphrase is literature purged of style, then paraphrase is a kind of minimalism, and since the absence of style is a style itself, a disaffected reader might argue that paraphrase is an apt description of minimalist style. The reader, like a child with crayons hunched over a coloring book, authors the story.

In **"Where Is Everyone?,"** however, Carver has already colored in the story for us, and we must keep in mind that it is this fuller, more expansive, more "authorly" version that he ultimately chooses to stand by. As we have seen by comparing the three versions of this story, as well as the various versions of other stories we have examined, Carver has undergone an aesthetic evolution, at first moving toward minimalism but then turning sharply away from it. The stories in ***What We Talk About When We Talk About Love,*** including **"The Bath,"** the second **"So Much Water So Close to Home,"** and **"Mr. Coffee and Mr. Fixit,"** do indeed follow Barth's definition of the "minimalist esthetic, of which a cardinal principle is that artistic effect may be enhanced by a radical economy of artistic means, even where such parsimony compromises other values: completeness, for example, or richness or precision of statement." In the final analysis, however, Carver rejects this minimalist aesthetic. In ***Fires*** and ***Cathedral,*** and in the selected (and, incidentally, the new) stories in ***Where I'm Calling From,*** he is clearly opting for "completeness, richness, and precision." Therefore, if [according to Stull] "most readers [take] their measure of him from his second collection of stories [i.e., *What*]," they get a distorted picture of the actual scope and direction of his writings, which "both before and since" that volume are quite different. Carver has said that he does not consider himself a minimalist, that "there's something about minimalist that smacks of smallness of vision and execution that I don't like," but this statement alone is not enough to remove the label. What should be enough, however, is the content of the work itself; rather than simply expressing his dissatisfaction with those stories he felt "were becoming too attenuated," he rewrote them or returned to an earlier version of them, so that they were more in keeping with his real style. It is no coincidence that, as he has moved away from his archminimalist phase to a more natural form, he has no longer felt this need to rewrite. "I feel that the stories in ***Cathedral*** are finished in a way I rarely felt about my stories previously," he told an interviewer shortly after the publication of that volume, and in a profile written at the time of the publication of ***Where I'm Calling From,*** he expresses regret at having "mutilated" some of his earlier stories when he says, "I used to revise even after a story was printed. I guess now I have a little more confidence." As this most recent collection makes abundantly clear, Raymond Carver may have been a minimalist, but he used to be and has once again become much more. (pp. 239-50)

Adam Meyer, "Now You See Him, Now You Don't, Now You Do Again: The Evolution of Raymond Carver's Minimalism," in Critique: Studies in Contemporary Fiction *Vol. XXX, No. 4, Summer, 1989, pp. 239-51.*

FURTHER READING

Aarons, Victoria. "Variance of Imagination." *The Literary Review* 27, No. 1 (Fall 1983): 147-52.

Review of *What We Talk about When We Talk about Love,* finding that "the moral and social implications of Carver's stories are clear: we make the wrong choices and fail to create fulfilling relationships with people because we fail to communicate with them."

Adelman, Bob, and Gallagher, Tess. *Carver Country: The World of Raymond Carver.* New York: Charles Scribner's Sons, 1990, 160 p.

Collection of photographs, letters, poems, and excerpts from Carver's short stories.

Atlas, James. "Less is Less." *The Atlantic* 247, No. 6 (June 1981): 96-8.

Examines Carver's style in *What We Talk about When We Talk about Love.* Atlas maintains that Carver attempts to mimic the vapid nature of contemporary life.

Bonetti, Kay. "Ray Carver: Keeping it Short." *The Saturday Review* 9, No. 10 (September-October 1983): 20-3.

Interview with Carver in which he discusses his life, writing process, and views on contemporary literature.

Carlin, Warren. "Just Talking: Raymond Carver's Symposium." *Cross Currents* XXVIII, No. 1 (Spring 1988): 87-92.

Interprets "What We Talk about When We Talk about Love" as a "theological dialogue" through which the characters reach a new understanding of themselves and their relationships to one another rather than attaining a definition of love.

Carver, Maryann; Kinder, Chuck; Kittredge, William; et al. "Glimpses: Raymond Carver." *The Paris Review* 33, No. 118 (Spring 1991): 260-303.

Collection of reminiscences of Carver's personal and literary development by his first wife, Maryann, and his friends, including William Kittredge, Richard Ford, and Mona Simpson.

Facknitz, Mark A. R. "Missing the Train: Raymond Carver's Sequel to John Cheever's 'The Five-Forty-Eight'." *Studies in Short Fiction* 22, No. 3 (Summer 1985): 345-47.

Discusses "The Train," Carver's sequel story to John Cheever's "The Five-Forty-Eight," finding that Carver's tale fails to further delineate the characters.

———. " 'The Calm,' 'A Small, Good Thing,' and 'Cathedral': Raymond Carver and the Rediscovery of Human Worth." *Studies in Short Fiction* 23, No. 3 (Summer 1986): 287-96.

Considers the "The Calm," "A Small, Good Thing," and "Cathedral" transitional stories of Carver's career wherein Carver portrays empathy between characters, a quality not present in his earlier works.

Gentry, Marshall Bruce, and Stull, William L., eds. *Conversations with Raymond Carver.* Jackson: University Press of Mississippi, 1990, 259 p.

Collection of interviews from 1977 to 1988, offering a thorough survey of Carver's views on his literary and personal development.

Houston, Robert. "A Stunning Inarticulateness." *The Nation* 233, No. 1 (4 July 1981): 23-5.

Appraises stories collected in *What We Talk about When We Talk about Love,* focusing on Carver's delineation of characters, which, Houston maintains, typically avoids a traditional epiphany.

Howe, Irving. "Stories of Our Loneliness." *The New York Times Book Review* (11 September 1983): 1, 42-3.

Positive review of *Cathedral,* noting a perceptiveness in Carver's depiction of "the waste and destructiveness that prevail beneath the affluence of American life." Howe concludes that "*Cathedral* shows a gifted writer struggling for a larger scope of reference, a finer touch of nuance."

Le Clair, Thomas. "Fiction Chronicle: January to June, 1981." *Contemporary Literature* 23, No. 1 (Winter 1982): 83-91.

Comments on Carver's style, maintaining that it is an "artifice" that mirrors the lives of his characters.

McInerney, Jay. "Raymond Carver: A Still, Small Voice." *The New York Times Book Review* (6 August 1989): 1, 24-5.

Reminiscences of McInerney's tutelage under Carver, highlighting Carver's encouraging manner toward students and his sincere humility.

Rubins, Josh. "Small Expectations." *The New York Review of Books* XXX, No. 18 (24 November 1983): 40-2.

Review of *Cathedral,* drawing several parallels between Carver's stories in this collection and the works of Dickens and noting that a "Dickensian tension, the sense of holding back a wave of emotionalism, of heartbreak or rage or faith, galvanizes much of *Cathedral*—with character after character poised on the edge of some abyss, the verge of despair."

Shute, Kathleen Westfall. "Finding the Words: The Struggle

for Salvation in the Fiction of Raymond Carver." *The Hollins Critic* XXIV, No. 5 (December 1987): 1-9.

Compares "The Bath" with its revised version, "A Small, Good Thing," and revisions of "So Much Water So Close to Home," asserting that after *What We Talk about When We Talk about Love* Carver's short stories display a more hopeful vision and depict characters who are more concerned with communication.

Stull, William L. "Visions and Revisions." *The Chariton Review* 10, No. 1 (Spring 1984): 80-6.

Praises Carver's devotion to revision, as exemplified by *Fires,* which contains revised and rewritten versions of early stories.

———. "Raymond Carver: A Bibliographical Checklist." *American Book Collector* 8, No. 1 (January 1987): 17-30.

Bibliography of works by Carver, including writings published in anthologies and periodicals.

Weber, Bruce. "Raymond Carver: A Chronicler of Blue-Collar Despair." *The New York Times Magazine* (24 June 1984): 36, 38, 42-6, 48-50.

Biographical portrait, discussion of theme and style in Carver's fiction, and commentary on Carver's influence on the short story genre.

Wolff, Tobias. "Raymond Carver: Had His Cake and Ate It Too." *Esquire* 112, No. 3 (September 1989): 240-42, 244, 247-48.

Reminiscences of Wolff's friendship with Carver.

Kate Chopin

1851-1904

(Born Katherine O'Flaherty) American short story writer, novelist, poet, and essayist.

A popular local colorist during her lifetime, Chopin is best known today for her psychological novel *The Awakening* and for such often-anthologized short stories as "Désirée's Baby" and "The Story of an Hour." In these, as in many of her best works, Chopin transcended simple regionalism and portrayed women who seek spiritual and sexual freedom amid the restrictive mores of nineteenth-century Southern society. Although reviewers and readers throughout the late nineteenth and early twentieth centuries condemned Chopin's frank treatment of such then-taboo subjects as female sexuality, adultery, and miscegenation, since the 1950s serious critical attention has been focused on her pioneering use of psychological realism, symbolic imagery, and sensual themes.

Chopin was born to a prominent St. Louis family. Her father died in a train accident when Chopin was four years old, and her childhood was most profoundly influenced by her mother and great-grandmother, who descended from French-Creole pioneers. Chopin also spent much time with her family's Creole and mulatto slaves, becoming familiar with their unique dialects. She read widely as a child, but was an undistinguished student at the convent school she attended. She graduated at age seventeen and spent two years as a belle of fashionable St. Louis society. In 1870 she married Oscar Chopin, a wealthy Creole cotton factor, and moved with him to New Orleans. For the next decade, Chopin pursued the demanding social and domestic schedule of a Southern aristocrat, her recollections of which would later serve as material for her short stories. In 1880, financial difficulties forced Chopin's growing family to move to her father-in-law's home in Cloutierville, a small town in Natchitoches Parish located in Louisiana's Red River bayou region. There, Chopin's husband oversaw and subsequently inherited his father's plantations. Upon his death in 1883, Chopin insisted upon assuming his managerial responsibilities, which brought her into contact with almost every segment of the community, including the French-Acadian, Creole, and mulatto sharecroppers who worked the plantations. The impressions she gathered of these people and Natchitoches Parish life later influenced her fiction.

In the mid-1880s Chopin sold most of her property and left Louisiana to live with her mother in St. Louis. Family friends who found her letters entertaining encouraged Chopin to write professionally, and she began composing short stories. These early works evidence the influence of her favorite authors: the French writers Guy de Maupassant, Alphonse Daudet, and Molière. At this time Chopin also read the works of Charles Darwin, Thomas Huxley, and Herbert Spenser in order to keep abreast of trends in scientific thinking, and she began questioning her Roman Catholic faith as well as the benefits of certain imposed mores and ethical restraints. After an apprenticeship marked by routine rejections, Chopin began having her stories published in the most popular American periodicals, including *America, Vogue,* and the *Atlantic.* Between 1894 and 1897 she published the collections *Bayou Folk* and *A Night in Acadie,* the success of which solidified her growing reputation as an important local colorist. Financially independent and encouraged by success, Chopin turned to longer works. Although she had published the novel *At Fault* in 1890, that work displays many of the shortcomings of an apprentice novel and failed to interest readers or critics. Publishers later rejected a novel and a short story collection, *A Vocation and a Voice,* on moral grounds, citing what they considered their unseemly promotion of female self-assertion and sexual liberation. Undaunted, Chopin completed *The Awakening,* the story of a conventional wife and mother who, after gaining spiritual freedom through an extramarital affair, commits suicide when she realizes that she cannot reconcile her new self to society's moral restrictions. The hostile critical and public reaction to the novel largely halted Chopin's career; she had difficulty finding publishers for later works and was ousted from local literary groups. Demoralized, she wrote little during her last years. A cerebral hemorrhage abruptly ended her life at the age of fifty-three.

The stories in *Bayou Folk,* Chopin's first collection, largely reflect her skills as a local colorist and often center on the passionate loves of the Creoles and Acadians in her native Natchitoches Parish. For example, "A Lady of Bayou St. John" portrays a young widow who escapes the sexual demands of a suitor by immersing herself in memories of her dead husband, while "La Belle Zoraïde" chronicles a mulatto slave's descent into madness after her mistress sells her lover and deprives her of their child. Recent critics occasionally detect in *Bayou Folk* the melodramatic conventions of popular magazine fiction. Nevertheless, they laud Chopin's meticulous description of setting, precise rendering of dialects, and objective point of view. In addition, commentators perceived in several stories universal themes that transcend the restrictions of regional fiction. One such story, the often-anthologized "Désirée's Baby," examines prejudice and miscegenation in its portrayal of Armand Aubigny, a proud aristocratic planter, and his wife Désirée. When she gives birth to a son possessing African characteristics, Aubigny assumes that Désirée is of mixed racial heritage and turns her and their son out of his house. However, while burning his wife's possessions, Armand discovers a letter written by his mother, which reveals that she and therefore Armand belonged to the race "cursed by the brand of slavery."

In *A Night in Acadie* Chopin continued to utilize the Louisiana settings that figured in *Bayou Folk.* However, the romanticism of the earlier collection is replaced by a greater moral ambivalence concerning such issues as female sexuality, personal freedom, and social propriety. Bert Bender observed that Chopin's "characters transcend their socially limited selves by awakening to and affirming impulses that are unacceptable by convention. Unburdened of restricting social conventions, her characters come to experience the suffering and loneliness, as well as the joy, of their freedom; for the impulses that they heed are a mere part of a world in which change and natural selection are first principles." For example, in "A Respectable Woman" a happily married woman becomes sexually attracted to Gouvernail, a family friend invited by her husband to visit their home for a week. Disturbed by her feelings, she is relieved when Gouvernail leaves, but as the following summer approaches, she encourages her husband to contact him again, ambiguously promising that "this time I shall be very nice to him." Chopin later expanded upon this essentially amoral perception of adultery in "The Storm," a story written near the end of her career, which portrays a woman's extra-marital affair as a natural impulse devoid of moral significance.

Chopin also explored the connection between selfhood and marriage in *A Night in Acadie.* Several stories reflect her contention that security and love cannot compensate for a lack of control over one's destiny. In "Athénaïse," for instance, the title character, a naive young bride, leaves Cazeau, her devoted yet insensitive husband, twice; first returning home to her parents, then traveling to New Orleans. Although Cazeau retrieves her from her parents, he refuses to follow her to the city after drawing an unsettling parallel between his actions toward her and his father's treatment of a runaway slave, a connection between slavery and marriage that is often made in Chopin's fiction. A month after arriving in New Orleans, however, Athénaïse learns that she is pregnant, and, thinking of her husband, experiences "the first purely sensuous tremor of her life." Now accepting her role as wife and mother, she reconciles with Cazeau. While some critics contend that Chopin likely formulated this conclusion, like other happy endings to her stories, to appease the moral sensibilities of her editors and publishers, most regard it as an appropriate ending to an incisive portrait of the limitations and rewards of marriage.

Early reviewers of *A Night in Acadie* objected to the volume's sensuous themes. Similar concerns were later raised by publishers who rejected Chopin's next volume, *A Vocation and a Voice.* Although Chopin continuously pursued its publication until her death, the volume did not appear as a single work until 1991. In these stories Chopin largely abandons local setting to focus upon the psychological complexity of her characters. Tales such as "Two Portraits," "Lilacs," and "A Vocation and a Voice," examine contrary states of innocence and experience and ways that society divides rather than unites the two. In "The Story of an Hour," the best known work in the collection, Chopin returns to the issue of marriage and selfhood in her portrayal of Mrs. Mallard, a woman who learns that her husband has died in a train accident. Initially overcome by grief, she gradually realizes that his "powerful will" no longer restricts her and that she may live as she wishes. While she joyfully anticipates her newfound freedom, however, her husband returns, the report of his death a mistake, and Mrs. Mallard collapses upon seeing him. Doctors then ironically conclude that she died of "heart failure—of the joy that kills." In evaluating *A Vocation and a Voice,* Barbara C. Ewell observed: "[The] collection, which includes some of Chopin's most experimental stories, reveals how intently she had come to focus her fiction on human interiority, on the interplay of consciousness and circumstance, of unconscious motive and reflexive action. Such psychological elements, combined with technical control, indicate a writer not only in command of her craft but fully in tune with the intellectual currents of her time. In many ways, *A Vocation and a Voice* represents the culmination of Chopin's talents as a writer of the short story."

Once considered merely an author of local-color fiction, Chopin is today recognized for her pioneering examination of sexuality, individual freedom, and the consequences of action—themes and concerns important to many later twentieth-century writers. While their psychological examinations of female protagonists have made Chopin's short stories formative works in the historical development of feminist literature, they also provide a broad discussion of a society that denied the value of sensuality and female independence. Per Seyersted asserted that Chopin "was the first woman writer in America to accept sex with its profound repercussions as a legitimate subject of serious fiction. In her attitude towards passion, she represented a healthy, matter-of-fact acceptance of the whole of man. She was familiar with the newest developments in science and in world literature, and her aim was to describe—unhampered by tradition and authority—man's immutable impulses. Because she was vigorous, intelligent, and eminently sane, and because her background had made her morally tolerant, and socially secure, she could write with a balance and maturity, a warmth and humor not often found in her contemporaries."

(For further information on Chopin's life and career, see *Twentieth-Century Literary Criticism,* Vols. 5, 14; *Contemporary Authors,* Vol. 104, 122; *Dictionary of Literary Biography,* Vols. 12, 78; and *Concise Dictionary of American Literary Biography, 1865-1917.*)

PRINCIPAL WORKS

SHORT FICTION

Bayou Folk 1894
A Night in Acadie 1897
Kate Chopin: The Awakening, and Other Stories (short stories and novel) 1970
The Storm, and Other Stories, with The Awakening (short stories and novel) 1974
The Awakening, and Selected Short Stories of Kate Chopin (short stories and novel) 1976
A Vocation and a Voice 1991

OTHER MAJOR WORKS

At Fault (novel) 1890
The Awakening (novel) 1899
The Complete Works of Kate Chopin 2 vols. (novels, short stories, poetry, and essays) 1970
A Kate Chopin Miscellany (letters, essays, diary entries) 1979

The Atlantic Monthly (essay date 1894)

[*In the following excerpt from a review of* Bayou Folk, *the critic commends the originality of Chopin's regional fiction.*]

To the noticeable group of Southern writers of fiction it is a pleasure to add a new name. Miss [Grace] King has written enough to make her Balcony Stories a confirmation of her power; Mrs. Chopin's ***Bayou Folk*** is, we believe, her first collection, though most, if not all of the stories which compose it have appeared in periodicals. It sometimes happens, however, that a distinctive power is not fully recognized until scattered illustrations of it are brought into a collective whole. In this case the reader perceives that Mrs. Chopin has taken for her territory the Louisiana Acadie; that she has chosen to treat of a folk that, despite long residence among no very distant kinsmen, has retained and perpetuated its own native characteristics. Mrs. Chopin shows us a most interesting group in her several stories. Her reproduction of their speech is not too elaborate, and the reader who at once shuts up a book in which he discovers broken or otherwise damaged English would do well to open this again; for the writer is discreet enough to give suggestions of the soft, harmonious tongue to which the Bayou folk have reduced English speech, and not to make contributions to philology. What he will find, both in speech and manner, is a sensitiveness to passion, a keen feeling for honor, a domesticity, an indolence which has a rustic grace, and a shiftlessness which laughs at its penalties.

One in search of the pleasure which stories may bring need not suspect from this that he has fallen upon a writer who is afflicted with a purpose to add to our stock of knowledge concerning obscure varieties of the human race. Mrs. Chopin simply deals with what is familiar to her, and happens to be somewhat new in literature. She deals with it as an artist, and the entire ease with which she uses her material is born not less of an instinct for story-telling than of familiarity with the stuff out of which she weaves her stories. The first story is the longest in the book, but, like the shortest, is an episode, as it were. All of the stories are very simple in structure, but the simplicity is that which belongs to clearness of perception, not to meagreness of imagination. Now and then she strikes a passionate note, and the naturalness and ease with which she does it impress one as characteristic of power awaiting opportunity. Add to this that a pervasive humor warms the several narratives, that the persons who appear bring themselves, and are not introduced by the author, and we have said enough, we think, to intimate that in this writer we have a genuine and delightful addition to the ranks of our story-tellers. It is something that she comes from the South. It is a good deal more that she is not confined to locality. Art makes her free of literature. (pp. 558-59)

A review of "Bayou Folk," in The Atlantic Monthly, *Vol. LXXIII, No. CDXXXVIII, April, 1894, pp. 558-59.*

The Nation, New York (essay date 1894)

[*In the excerpt below, the reviewer notes the artistry of Chopin's style in the stories collected in* Bayou Folk.]

Of writing many stories of Louisiana life there is no end. It is not surprising, for the material embraces all that is most picturesque, whether the scenes of action be New Orleans or the inland parishes, whether Creoles or negroes be the actors. Kate Chopin has written of the ***Bayou Folk*** dwelling in Natchitoches Parish, who are of every race and admixture of race that can be evolved from stems American, French, Spanish, Indian, Negro. Her stories are among the most clever and charming that have seen the light. Her pen is an artist's in choice of subject, in touch, and in forbearance. There is never a word nor an idea too much, and in the score of sketches in which the same names often recur, there is no repetition, nevertheless, of herself or of others. Hers is good work, and as interesting as the good often is not.

A review of "Bayou Folk," The Nation, *New York, Vol. LVIII, No. 1513, June 28, 1894, p. 488.*

The Nation, New York (essay date 1898)

[*In the following excerpt, an early reviewer praises Chopin's vivid depiction of Louisiana life.*]

Kate Chopin tells a story like a poet, and reproduces the spirit of a landscape like a painter. Her stories [in ***A Night in Acadie***] are to the bayous of Louisiana what Mary Wilkins's are to New England, with a difference, to be sure, as the Cape jessamine is different from the cinnamon rose, but like in seizing the heart of her people and showing the traits that come from their surroundings; like, too, in giving without a wasted word the history of main crises in their lives. That Cape jessamine is sometimes a thought too heavy is perhaps inevitable in the heated South. But enough there is of artistic in the best sense to hold the reader from cover to cover, transported for the time to a region of fierce passions, mediæval chivalry, combined with rags and bad grammar, a soft, sliding Creole accent, and the tragedies and comedies that loom with special meaning in a sparsely settled country.

A review of "A Night in Acadie" in The Nation, *New York, Vol. LXVI, No. 1719, June 9, 1898, p. 447.*

Fred Lewis Pattee (essay date 1923)

[*A historian, critic, poet, and novelist, Pattee was a pioneer in the study of American literature. In such works as* A History of American Literature, With a View to the Fundamental Principles Underlying Its Development *(1896) and* The First Century of American Literature *(1935), Pattee called for the recognition of American literature as distinct from the English tradition and contended that literature is the popular expression of a people, rather than the work of an elite. In the following excerpt from his historical survey* The Development of the American Short Story, *Pattee laments the critical neglect of Chopin and praises her as a multi-talented author.*]

[In American short story chronicles, Chopin] must be rated as a vivid episode, as brief and intense as a tropic storm. Her two volumes of short tales, ***Bayou Folk*** and ***A Night in Acadie,*** are still in their original editions and totally unread, and her name is forgotten save by a few, and yet there are few pieces in the American short-story collections that surpass in restrained intensity, in finesse, in the inevitableness of startling climax, some of the best of her tales.

To no novelist of her period, not even to Miss Wilkins, was fiction-writing a more spontaneous thing. She was of Celtic temperament, her father pure Irish, her mother partly French. Nothing in her early years, save, perhaps, this racial inheritance, prepared her for art. . . . She never won popularity; her later books were issued by various publishers, and when, in 1899, her novel, *The Awakening,* was greeted with hostile criticism, she abandoned literature as temperamentally as in the first place she had entered it. She must be rated as a genius, taut, vibrant, intense of soul, yet a genius in eclipse, one, it is to be feared, that is destined to be total.

The materials in Mrs. Chopin's two volumes are more strange even than those used by [George Washington] Cable and Miss [Grace] King, but the tales are far more than mere strange materials. Without a thought, undoubtedly, of what she was really doing, she struck always universal chords. The tales are more than mere snapshots in the Red River canebrakes: they are glimpses into the universal heart of humanity. Open, for instance, to the tale **"Athénaïse."** The young Creole maiden, after only two months of marriage, has run away from her husband, though he has done not a thing that even the most assiduous divorce lawyer could find against him. And this is her explanation:

> No, I don't hate him. It's jus' being married that I detes' an' despise. I hate being Mrs. Cazeau, an' I want to be Athénaïse Miché again. I can't stan' to live with a man; to have him always there; his coats and pantaloons hanging in my room; his ugly bare feet—washing them in my tub, befo' my very eyes. Ugh!

And she simply deserted him even as you and I may have dreamed, in our own lives, and what came of it is what might have come to you and me had we dared, like her, to go to the extremes of our impulses.

[Despite] crudenesses—she can even write passages like this: "He noticed that they were handsome eyes; not so large as Elvina's, but finer in their expression. They started to walk down the track"—nevertheless, in a few of her stories she has been surpassed in technique not even by Aldrich or Bunner. Local color she used with restraint only to intensify her characterization. Here, as with Miss King, was a chief source of her strength. Like Dickens, she could make even the most insignificant of her characters intensely alive. The reader knows them and feels them and sees them. Madame Celestin with her unconscious coquetry, her pathetic helplessness, her wavering, her delicious femininity, completely fascinates the solid old judge. He becomes young again, he will get her divorce—he is certain of it, he will marry her himself—he goes to propose to her, but Madame Celestin—the astounding last sentence of the story, so natural yet so dramatically final, is the very soul of art—and of life.

Her sense of dramatic values was strong. Unconsciously to the reader, she worked ever toward some unforeseen climax. The culmination of the story, **"Désirée's Baby,"** is peculiarly effective. The young planter, Armand Aubigny, rich, handsome, proud of his family name, married the beautiful Creole Désirée, who had come as a stranger into the community, and the two lived in a heaven of love and happiness until the baby was born. Then came a ghastly suspicion, growing with every day into more complete certainty: manifestly there had been a reversion to a negro ancestor. The neighborhood began to whisper and the love of Armand turned swiftly into hate. His wife had deceived him. Without defense or explanation, her head held high, her dainty wedding slippers on her feet, Désirée, her baby in her arms, marched into the swamp along the bayou and was never seen again, and in sullen rage Armand burned all traces of the woman and her child, even the costly wedding finery and the dainty layette. She had brought the first blot upon the proud family name. The tragedy is over;

the reader is about to close the book, when Armand, who is clearing the old bureau of all of Désirée's belongings, happens upon an old letter in his mother's handwriting. It had been written to his own father: "But, above all," the letter ended, "night and day, I thank the good God for having so arranged our lives that our dear Armand will never know that his mother, who adores him, belongs to the race that is cursed with the brand of slavery." The sentence closes the story, but not for the reader.

Without models, without study or short-story art, without revision, and usually at a sitting, she produced what often are masterpieces before which one can only wonder and conjecture. (pp. 325-27)

Fred Lewis Pattee, "The Revolt of the 'Nineties," in his The Development of the American Short Story: An Historical Survey, *Harper & Brothers Publishers, 1923, pp. 309-36.*

Joseph J. Reilly (essay date 1937)

[*A respected educator and critic, Reilly authored* James Russell Lowell As a Critic *(1915) and* Of Books and Men *(1932). In the following excerpt, he asserts that Chopin is "incomparably the greatest writer of her sex."*]

Optimists like to believe that, in the long run, justice is accomplished in literary history, the unworthy dislodged, the truly great seated among their peers, the neglected called to their place in the sun. Among those last must be numbered that writer of mixed French and Irish stock, Kate Chopin, whose work includes two striking volumes of short stories, ***Bayou Folk*** (1894) and ***A Night in Acadie*** (1897). What Hamlin Garland did for the Middle West, Mary Wilkins Freeman for New England, Thomas Nelson Page for the middle South, and Miss Murfree for the Tennessee mountain folk, Mrs. Chopin did for the dwellers along the sluggish marshy streams that meander among the sugar plantations of upstate Louisiana. Leaving New Orleans to Grace King and the pre-war days to G. W. Cable, she sought her material without distinction of class, and her people's knowledge of ante-bellum opulence was largely a tradition.

Mrs. Chopin, like H. C. Bunner, was a student of Maupassant. Her Celtic blood and romantic spirit rejected his icy cynicism and her human sympathy kept her point of view from the rigorous impersonality of his. But her innate talent for story-telling was enriched by studying his virtues and making them her own. Her beginnings are direct, almost laconic: her first sentence starts the reader off like a shot from a pistol; her endings are infallibly "right"; her descriptions whether of things, nature or people, are done with a few sharp strokes; her characterizations are never blurred: her people are not names but three-dimensional and quick with life. And, finally, she mastered the secret of economy in words.

The important thing with Mrs. Chopin as with Maupassant is character rather than situation and, particularly, the response of men—and even more of women—to the passion of love. Maupassant's interest is in the blasé, the sophisticated, when confronted by the ingenuous and unspoiled, while Mrs. Chopin's is in young men and women at the dawn of romantic passion. (p. 606)

The young men and girls of Kate Chopin's tales are unspoiled. They have not toyed with their emotions until they become their victims nor are they afraid of the promptings of their hearts. They are not unduly introspective; they have no need to be, for their instincts, like homing birds, fly straight and true, even though they sometimes make pretense of fluttering away. Hence these girls are capable of simple and supreme loyalty which triumphs over everything but contempt and abuse. For them love is the great, the crucial and transfiguring experience, the door swinging open to whatever earthly paradise there be, glorified by the abiding satisfactions of the heart.

Mrs. Chopin touches passion with a deft hand. In the use of young women, she is sensitively aware of its revelations, its hesitancies, its fears, while she senses how deeply the young men are troubled by its bitter-sweet torment and bewildered by its divine illogic, and always she treats these things with a certainty and convincingness which owe as much to reverence as to art. Thus 'Polyte, young plantation storekeeper, half in love with Azèlie with the red curved lips, the "dark, wide, innocent, questioning eyes, and black hair plastered smooth back from the forehead and temples," discovers her one night stealing from his supplies. Shocked, he lets her go. "He sat for a long time motionless. Then, overcome by some powerful feeling that was at work within him, he buried his face in his hands and wept, his whole body shaken by the violence of his sobs. . . . After that 'Polyte loved Azèlie desperately. The very action which should have revolted him had seemed, on the contrary, to inflame him with love."

Of course Mrs. Chopin does not confine herself to this sole *motif* nor, when treating it, is she concerned with a single formula. Love dawns and its loyalties find expression in infinite ways; in recounting them she sometimes hints at twists of thought whose subtleties she, like Maupassant, leaves the reader to divine. Thus it is with 'Polyte, instanced above; thus it is with Madame Delisle who, on the brink of eloping with the charming M. Sépincourt, learns of her husband's death in battle and at a stroke dismisses Sépincourt from her life and dedicates her youth and beauty to hallowing the memory of the dead.

These subtleties sometimes take another direction as with the middle-aged Mamzelle Fleurette, a sentimental soul strongly attracted to Lacodie, the perky little locksmith who comes to her shop each evening to buy a paper. She checks the feeling rigorously but when he dies and his widow remarries she feels that Lacodie has been forfeited to her and exultingly takes charge of his grave and hangs his picture in her room. Chicot, a half-starved, dull-witted old Negro, is faithful as a dog to an impoverished, worn-out old woman because she bears the adored family name of Boisduré. She dies: his loyalty experiences a curious recoil, abandoning her and centering itself in the large, vague glory of the name she bore. The withered form "was doubtless that of some Boisduré of *les Attakapas;* it was none of his." Tony Bocage, a giant boatman, smitten by Claire Duvigne, a city belle, is hired to take her for a pleasure row and on returning "is stirred by a terrible, an overmastering regret that he had not clasped her in his arms when they were out there alone, and sprung with her into the sea." He resolves not to miss a second chance. So Maupassant might have written, without elaborating on Tony's thoughts or curiously delving into his mind, content with a statement at once laconic and authoritative. But Tony's story in Mrs. Chopin's hands takes another turn into a new—and convincing—subtlety, fashioned to her own pattern, for she was a student of Maupassant's art, not of his psychology. When you finish the tale and learn of Tony's final contentment your memory will recall certain poems of Browning, especially "Evelyn Hope" in which death does not quench but kindle the lovers' faith.

Maternal instinct provides the theme for some of the finest stories. We have it in Mme. Carambeau, long at feud with her son for marrying an American girl, in Mamzelle Aurélie, self-centered and middle-aged, who, on sending back home four children she has mothered for a fortnight, "let her head fall down upon her bended arm and began to cry. Not softly, as women often do. She cried like a man, with sobs that seemed to tear her very soul." Most notably this theme appears in the tale of Athenaïse who, scarcely out of school and married to the widower Cazeau, resents his having married her and hides away from him in a city *pension.* Passion, beauty, and exquisite understanding conspire with unerring characterizations and an ending poignantly tender and exquisitely right to make this story a masterpiece.

Only one of her tales outranks it, a tragedy miniature in proportions, overwhelming in effect, told in a bare 2,000 words, every one significant from the crisp opening sentence to the final closing one which matches O. Henry's "Furnished Room" in the suddenness of its surprise and in the irony and pathos of its devastating revelation. It is called **"Désirée's Baby"** and is one of the world's great short stories. All Mrs. Chopin's gifts are here in their perfection: directness of approach, sureness of touch, the swift strokes which give the setting and introduce and realize the characters, the amazing economy of words which even she never equaled and Maupassant never surpassed. In a sentence or two she probes the psychology of Désirée and her husband to the quick, after first opening the way by what seem to the unwary scarcely more than casual phrases. The sense of impending tragedy comes early (as it must in so brief a thing) with perfect naturalness and in the turn given a sentence by two words. It is deepened by the picture of Désirée's house where friends visit her and her baby: "The roof came down steep and black like a cowl, reaching out beyond the wide galleries that encircled the yellow stuccoed house. Big, solemn oaks grew close to it, and their thick-leaved, far-reaching branches shadowed it like a pall." As one reads, recollections of other short story masters arise, with whose power and skill in evoking the spirit of tragedy this perfect tale takes its place, Poe, Hawthorne and Thomas Hardy.

From Kate Chopin's two volumes of short stories a modest book containing a dozen tales could be made, which would be an enriching addition to our all-too-few masterpieces. She is incomparably the greatest American short story writer of her sex. Her work deserves wider appreciation. May it soon have proper recognition! (pp. 606-07)

Joseph J. Reilly, "Stories by Kate Chopin," in The Commonweal, *Vol. XXV, No. 22, March 26, 1937, pp. 606-07.*

Robert E. Spiller and others (essay date 1948)

[*In the following excerpt from the critical study* Literary History of the United States, *Chopin's stories are ranked with those of Sarah Orne Jewett and Grace King.*]

The writing career of Kate Chopin, one of the shortest in the annals of the ordinarily long-lived regional writers, began in 1899 with some indifferent poetry and followed a meteoric course which ended a year or two before her death in 1904. What she did in that time had, however, an intensity, courage, vigor, and independence which sets her work in sharp contrast to the pale antidotes to [George Washington] Cable which Miss [Grace] King had chosen to offer. An exact contemporary of Miss King, Katherine O'Flaherty was born in St. Louis of Irish and French parents, was graduated from a convent into the active life of a Missouri belle, married Oscar Chopin at nineteen, entered New Orleans society, bore six children, moved to a Red River plantation, saw her husband die of swamp fever, returned to St. Louis, fended off several potential suitors, and in 1890, at the age of thirty-nine, published her first novel. She subsequently wrote nearly a hundred short stories, about half of which were collected in two volumes, ***Bayou Folk*** (1894) and ***A Night in Acadie*** (1897). The best of these describe the Acadians in the mid-Louisiana parishes of Natchitoches and Avoyelles, regions with which Mrs. Chopin had become acquainted during her plantation days. Many of them (and there is possibly a connection here with Mrs. Chopin's own mild unconventionality) turn upon acts of rebellion: Zaida's attempted elopement during the Cajun ball at Père Foché's; the refusal of Athenaise to settle into a dull marriage; young Polydore feigning rheumatism to escape work; Chicot, the *neg creol,* whose professed paganism contradicted his Christian practice. At their best the bayou tales displayed a clean economy of line, and were rounded off with a kind of Gallic finesse which suggested that Mrs. Chopin's study of Maupassant had not gone unrewarded. She knew, better than many of her contemporaries among the regionalists, how to begin, develop, and conclude a story without waste motion or observable self-consciousness. Her feeling for character was supported by an almost instinctive grasp of form and pace. Like Miss [Sarah Orne] Jewett, she knew how to use dialect for flavoring; with her it never became an obstacle. Miss [Mary Noailles] Murfree might have learned from her the art of subordinating environment to character. [Mrs. Chopin also] knew where sentiment ends and sentimentality begins. Yet many of her stories fell short of excellence because she wrote too swiftly and impulsively, leaned too heavily upon the suggestions of the moment, and impatiently shrugged off the burden of correction and revision. She rarely resorted to mere trickery, though it is a trick which mars her frequently anthologized (and not very typical) study in race relations, **"Désirée's Baby,"** which satisfies the reader's sense of justice while disappointing him with a contrived conclusion. Even her failures are readable, and at her subtle and economical best, she challenges the workmanship of Mary Wilkins Freeman, analyzing the more exotic and passionate Cajun character or painting the humble romances of canebrake and cotton field with something of that control and candor which her Northern contemporary brought to her studies of New England nuns and village choristers. (pp. 858-59)

Robert E. Spiller and others, "Delineation of Life and Character," in Literary History of the United States, *Vol. 11, edited by Robert E. Spiller and others, The Macmillan Company, 1948, pp. 843-61.*

Per Seyersted (essay date 1969)

[*A professor of American literature at the University of Oslo, Seyersted is the author of* Kate Chopin: A Critical Biography, *and the editor of* The Complete Works of Kate Chopin, *published simultaneously in 1969. These works introduced Chopin's previously unpublished or uncollected writings and sparked new interest in her short stories and* The Awakening. *In the following excerpt from* Kate Chopin: A Critical Biography, *Seyersted examines Chopin's treatment of the social and sexual issues of her day.*]

Kate Chopin was never a feminist in the dictionary sense of the term, that is, she never joined or supported any of the organizations through which women fought to get "political, economic, and social rights equal to those of men." Not only did she shy away from societies and issues in general, but she probably regarded the New World feminists as unrealistic when they so closely allied themselves with efforts to elevate men to their own supposedly very high level of purity; she undoubtedly concurred with the early George Sand, who felt that woman largely had the same drives as man and therefore also should have his "rights." (p. 102)

[If] Mrs. Chopin saw that the problems confronting her sex were too complicated to admit of easy solutions, she was also well acquainted with the manifold tendencies in the women themselves. It seems more than an accident that her three earliest extant stories are each in turn devoted to one of what we might call the three main types of women: the "feminine," the "emancipated," and the "modern" (to use the terminology of Simone de Beauvoir's *The Second Sex*), and that the tension between the two leading components of this triad was to reverberate through her whole *oeuvre.*

"Euphrasie," Kate Chopin's first tale from 1888, is the story of a feminine or traditional heroine, that is, a woman of the kind who accepts the patriarchal view of her role very pointedly expressed, for example, in the marriage sermon of Father Beaulieu of Cloutierville: "Madame, be submissive to your husband. . . . You no longer belong to yourself."

In a society where man makes the rules, woman is often kept in a state of tutelage and regarded as property or as a servant. Her "lack of self assertion" is equated with "the perfection of womanliness," as Mrs. Chopin later expressed it in a story. The female's capital is her body and her innocence, and she should be attractive and playful enough for the man to want her, while showing a reticence and resistance which can gratify his sense of conquest, or "the man-instinct of possession," as the author termed it in another tale. What man wishes, writes Simone de Beauvoir, "is that this struggle remain a game for him, while for woman it involves . . . [a recognition of] him as her destiny." In the man's world, woman should accept a special standard for the "more expansive" sex, and for herself, she should eagerly welcome the "sanctity of motherhood." As Mme. de Staël's Corinne is told: Whatever extraordinary gifts she may have, her duty and "her proper destiny is to devote herself to her husband and to the raising of her children."

Euphrasie is a dutiful daughter, and also a loyal fiancée as she tries to hide even from herself that she has suddenly fallen in love with someone else than the man she is engaged to. In the tradition of the feminine woman, she accepts the role of the passive, self-obliterating object as she makes no attempt to influence her fate, and she is willing to break her heart and proceed with the marriage, even though she considers it immoral to kiss her fiancé when she does not love him. (It is interesting to note that the author, in her very first story, on this point echoes George Sand; she does not openly offend by saying in so many words that Euphrasie should have kissed the other man when it becomes evident that they are mutually attracted, but that is what she implies.) As behooves a feminine woman, she lets the men decide her destiny: When her fiancé learns the truth by accident, he sets her free, thus—in Euphrasie's words—saving her from the sin a marriage to him would have meant to her.

As has been noted before, Kate Chopin put this story aside for a few years and destroyed the next two she wrote. The original draft of **"Euphrasie"** is lost, and we do not know why she titled the tale after the girl's fiancé when she later revised and shortened it. Nor do we know anything about the two other stories, except that the first was set on Grand Isle, and that the second, **"A Poor Girl,"** was offensive to editorial eyes, perhaps because the author already here was too open about untraditional urges in women.

The next of Kate Chopin's tales which has come down to us is **"Wiser than a God."** It is the story of Paula Von Stoltz, a young woman who works hard to become a concert pianist. She loves the rich George Brainard, but when he asks her to follow a calling that asks "only for the labor of loving," she replies that marriage does not enter into the "purpose of [her] life." George insists that he does not ask her to give up anything; she tells him, however, that music to her is "something dearer than life, than riches, even than love." This is too contrary to George's idea of woman's role; calling Paula mad, he lectures her and declares that even if the one who loved him had taken the vows as a nun, she would owe it to herself, to him, and to God to be his wife. But Fräulein Von Stoltz leaves to become an internationally renowned pianist, and her later constant companion is a composer who is wise enough not to make any emotional demands on her.

Paula largely answers to Simone de Beauvoir's definition of the emancipated woman, that is, a female who "wants to be active, a taker, and refuses the passivity man means to impose on her"; who insists on the active transcendence of a subject, the *pour soi,* rather than the passive immanence of an object, the *en soi;* and who attempts to achieve an existentialist authenticity through making a conscious choice, giving her own laws, realizing her essence, and making herself her own destiny.

The pride indicated in Paula's family name does not manifest itself in a haughty attitude toward her admirer; she is soft-spoken compared to the impetuous, youthful George who insists that she is throwing him into "a gulf . . . of everlasting misery." But she speaks up when she realizes they are in two different worlds, that he represents the patriarchal view of woman, and she the view of Margaret Fuller that women so inclined should be allowed to leave aside motherhood and domesticity and instead use their wings to soar toward the transcendence of a nonbiological career. (pp. 103-05)

"Euphrasie" proves that it is not female submission as such which the author leaves out in her writings, but only the concessions to sentimentality and conventionality, the violations of the logic in the various types of heroines. The author combines in these two tales a detachment and objectivity with a tender understanding and respect for both the feminine and the emancipated young lady.

In the third story we have from Mrs. Chopin, **"A Point at Issue,"** she turns to modern woman, that is, the female who insists on being a subject and man's equal, but who cooperates with the male rather than fighting him, without any of the antagonism often attributed to her emancipationist sister. (p. 105)

Unlike Paula of the previous story, Eleanor Gail of **"A Point at Issue"** does wed her suitor, Charles Faraday; they decide, however:

> . . . to be governed by no precedential methods. Marriage was to be a form, that while fixing legally their relation to each other, was in no wise to touch the individuality of either; that was to be preserved intact. Each was to remain a free integral of humanity, responsible to no dominating exactions of so-called marriage laws. And the element that was to make possible such a union was trust in each other's love, honor, courtesy, tempered by the reserving clause of readiness to meet the consequences of reciprocal liberty.

The Latin proverb which Kate Chopin gave as a motto for the previous story: "To love and be wise is scarcely granted even to a god," should more appropriately have been put at the head of **"A Point at Issue."** While Euphrasie disregards the conflict between love and reason because she has been indoctrinated with the idea of leaving the responsibility for her life to a man, and Paula avoids it by devoting herself to art and making her own decisions, Eleanor is the one really to be put to the test, as she, like her husband, believes that she can both love and be wise as they share a life in "Plymdale" as equals. (pp. 105-06)

Faraday agrees with his wife that she shall spend a year or two alone in Paris learning French. Once he tells her in a letter how a girl had momentarily charmed him, feeling no qualms in doing so as he saw it as unimportant, and, besides, "Was not Eleanor's large comprehensiveness far above the littleness of ordinary women?" While he thinks no more of the matter, Eleanor cannot escape old-fashioned jealousy; nor can Charles when he joins her in Paris for the summer and one day sees her with another man, who later turns out to be a painter doing her portrait. For a moment he wants to kill the "villain," but reason takes over, even before he learns that his jealousy was unfounded.

As a result of these incidents, both retreat one step from their advanced stand. Eleanor rejoins her husband in America, and, being unable to forget how jealousy made her suffer like a "distressed goddess," she has gained insight into her own nature and knows that, as she tells Charles, "there are certain things which a woman can't philosophize about." He has learned nothing from *his* agony, however, while Eleanor's affliction causes him to slip into the traditional attitude of the male when he patronizingly concludes: "I love her none the less for it, but my Nellie is only a woman, after all." And the author adds: "With a man's usual inconsistency, he had quite forgotten the episode of the portrait."

In her first two stories, Kate Chopin had betrayed a possible involvement with marriage only when she in **"Wiser than a God,"** with what looks like mild irony, speaks of "the serious offices of wifehood and matrimony" which constitute all of life to the woman Brainard eventually marries. When there is a somewhat more pronounced suggestion of an engagement in the third tale, it is again on the issue of woman and matrimony. The author by no means makes it clear that she speaks only for Eleanor when she writes: "Marriage, which marks too often the closing period of a woman's intellectual existence, was to be in her case the open portal through which she might seek the embellishments that her strong, graceful mentality deserved." It is interesting to note the surprising juxtaposition of marriage and death with which the story opens when it informs us that the wedding announcement of the Faradays was printed side by side with a "somber-clad" advertisement for "marble and granite monuments."

The impression we are left with by this tale is that Kate Chopin sympathizes with Eleanor even more than with Euphrasie and Paula and that she wishes the Faradays success in their venture to live as perfect equals. She appears to favor female emancipation, not the "quasi-emancipation" she authorially attributes to women showing their protest by wearing strange clothes, but the true, inner kind of growth and independence. She also seems to favor the couple's lack of preconceptions as they attempt to make "innovations into matrimony" by introducing a marital liberty. But Mrs..Chopin saw the complexities of this point at issue: "Reason did good work," she observes in connection with Eleanor's fight with jealousy, "but against it were the too great odds of a woman's heart, backed by the soft prejudices of a far-reaching heredity." Among the inherited factors imposing themselves upon

A photograph of five-year-old Kate O'Flaherty, taken the year of her father's death.

even a modern woman and a modern man are fundamental impulses, such as jealousy, and notions, such as that of male supremacy.

The idea of man's superiority is emphasized as Charles falls back into the age-old concept that his wife is "only a woman." It is perhaps a little surprising to find inconsistency attributed to him, a quality which traditionally typifies the so-called changeable women; however, it serves to stress his male overevaluation of himself: As a female, Eleanor is not expected to know much; therefore she can allow herself to feel that "she knew nothing," and at the same time be open for learning. Charles, on the other hand, is a man, thus a superior being, and as such he does not need to be taught anything.

With her three first stories, Kate Chopin had stated her major theme: woman's spiritual emancipation—or her "being set free from servitude, bondage, or restraint," as the term has been defined—in connection with her men and her career. (pp. 106-08)

In dealing with basic human drives, Kate Chopin did not have the naturalists' emphasis on heredity. **"Mrs. Mobry's Reason"** is her only treatment of this subject, and her interest here is not so much in the hereditary madness as in the awakening love which brings it out. This theme of activated passion inspired many of her tales. In **"A Harbinger,"** Diantha's eyes lose their baby look when Bruno gives her a kiss and she is ready to be "gathered [as a] wild flower." In **"La Belle Zoraïde,"** the heroine catches fire the moment she beholds "the stately movements of [Mézor's] splendid body swaying and quivering through the figures of the dance."

Mildred Orme of **"A Shameful Affair"** is Mrs. Chopin's first heroine who is awakened to both a spiritual and a sensuous emancipation. She spends a summer on a Missouri farm, where a young man first annoys her with his indifference and then stirs her with the boldness of his glance. While he remains inactive, one day she follows him when he is out fishing. She borrows his pole, and a fish bites; he tries to help her, and in the confusion, he gives the girl her first kiss. Then, embarrassed, he hurriedly leaves the scene. (pp. 108-09)

[**"A Shameful Affair"**] does not dwell sensuously on the kiss itself, and from the last in that Mildred does not blame the man. She realizes that her eyes had "gleamed for an instant unconscious things into his own," and she is not "wildly indignant" as traditional feminine modesty should prompt her to be. She also decides that "she would avoid nothing. She would go and come as always." When Mrs. Chopin went on to say that the heroine was nevertheless ashamed of the "hideous truth" that the kiss had been the most delicious thing she had ever known, it was perhaps because the author felt her protagonist had already sinned enough against the legend of female purity.

Later, the man calls himself a "consummate hound" and asks whether Mildred can forgive him some day, thus giving her a chance to play the conventional role of woman as the innocent party who makes no advances in sexual relations. But her answer shows that she is not satisfied with being only a passive object. In a striking illustration of the type of the emancipated woman, she claims instead the role, or at least the responsibility, of being an active subject when she replies: "some day—perhaps; when I shall have forgiven myself." The man is horrified when he realizes what a violation of the current rules for female attitudes, for womanly reticence this answer represents. (pp. 109-10)

This story was written in 1891. Other facets of emancipation are dealt with in further tales from the same year. One of these, **"The Going Away of Liza,"** is a maudlin, unsuccessful piece of writing, yet of a certain interest as the heroine is the author's first to leave her husband. (In calling him Abraham, Mrs. Chopin evokes the prototype of the patriarch.) Liza's reason is that she considers him commonplace and unable to give her the joys of existence which she craves. She goes to the city, but after months of "sin or suffering," she returns to the safety of their home on the farm.

Other Kate Chopin heroines are more successful in their attempts to defy conventions and decide over their own lives. Marianne of **"The Maid of Saint Phillippe"** refuses to become a traditional housewife and joins the Cherokees for a hunter's life instead. Eva Artless of **"An Embarrassing Situation,"** the author's one-act comedy, also takes her life in her own hands. She is a modern Eve, "brought up on unconventional and startling lines," and by suddenly visiting the man she admires, she puts him in a situation which can only be saved by that offer of marriage she is hoping for. Melicent of *At Fault* and Clarisse of **"At the 'Cadian Ball,"** meanwhile, are examples of women who manipulate their men by the less elaborate engineering of simply blowing hot and cold.

In this, Mrs. Chopin's second phase, we also find examples of traditional women who fill their serving or submissive role with loyalty and unselfish devotion. Mentine of **"A Visit to Avoyelles,"** for instance, is happy to toil faithfully for the husband who misuses her, although it makes her lose her beauty even faster than the hard-working Cajun women do in general. The heroine of **"Madame Célestin's Divorce,"** on the other hand, is a Catholic prepared to brave the scandal it would create if she left her husband.

As Kate Chopin was warming up, she was getting closer to an open, amoral treatment of woman's sexual self-assertion. That the Creole female may be tempted to trespass beyond her traditional chastity or fidelity is seen in Mme. Delisle of **"A Lady of Bayou St. John,"** who only at the last moment gives up her intention to desert her husband for a lover. In **"A Respectable Woman,"** a story written just before ***Bayou Folk*** was to appear, the question of infidelity is left open. Mr. Baroda is visited by Gouvernail, a New Orleans newspaper man. Mrs. Baroda is first openly irritated at his presence, but later secretly attracted to him: "she wanted to draw close to him . . . as she might have done if she had not been a respectable woman." To escape temptation, she leaves, and on her return she tells her husband, in words wonderfully ambiguous to the reader: "I have overcome everything! you will see. This time I shall be very nice to him."

The success of ***Bayou Folk*** launched Kate Chopin on the third phase of her career, and in **"The Story of an Hour"** she gave her most startling picture of female self-assertion. She does not say what Mrs. Mallard would do with her life now that she believed she could live for herself rather than for her husband. In **"Lilacs,"** her next story, however, it is clear that Mme. Farival has lovers. As a French artiste living in Paris, she is in a way outside the realm of American literary censors; but even so, she is "punished" in that the convent, where she had gone to school, no longer permits her to come for her yearly retreat. That Nathalie of **"The Kiss,"** who is fully American, also loses in that the lover she had planned to keep after marrying a rich nonentity refuses to acquiesce, is no more than could be expected in the America of 1894. What is new, however, is the author's amoral, detached attitude toward infidelity, and the wonderful light touch with which she ends such a story: "Well, she had Brantain and his million left. A person can't have everything in this world; and it was a little unreasonable of her to expect it."

Also in this period of Kate Chopin's career do we find an interplay between her self-assertive and self-forgetting heroines. Mamzelle Fleurette of **"A Sentimental Soul,"** for example, defies her confessor and instead heeds only her own conscience, and Dorothea of **"The Unexpected"** abandons her rich fiancé when he becomes ill, refusing to serve as his nurse. The widow Mrs. Sommers of **"A Pair of Silk Stockings,"** on the other hand, is used to thinking only of her children, and Azémia of the story **"Ti Frère"** marries her stupid suitor because she realizes he needs "a friendly hand to lead him." In **"Regret,"** meanwhile, we meet a self-centered woman who learns to think of others.

Just as Mrs. Chopin was occupied with the duality of the egotistic and the altruistic, she also devoted a few stories to the double attraction of the sensuous and the religious, a common literary theme at the time. We find it in **"Two Portraits,"** for example, where the author shows how Alberta, a young girl, may later develop into either a nun, who has the "glow of a holy passion" in her eyes as she devotes herself to God, or a wanton, whose body is made for love and who lives accordingly. The next time she presented such a juxtaposition—in **"A Vocation and a Voice"**—there was no longer any doubt that the protagonist chose the flesh rather than the spirit. **"A Mental Suggestion,"** meanwhile, describes passion fighting a different kind of struggle. Mrs. Chopin had a certain interest in what she called projected mental energy, and in this story she deals with the powers of hypnosis as they are first used to induce love, and then—in vain—to quench it.

If Kate Chopin was only half serious in this latter treatment of the power of love, she is deeply involved in **"Athénaïse,"** a story dealing with the fundamentals of woman's existence, that is, the influence on her life of husband and children, marriage and liberty.

Athénaïse is an example of the not uncommon phenomenon, the immature girl who marries merely because it is customary and only to find that she would rather be a Miss again. Not that she hates Cazeau, her husband, but she just "can't stan' to live with a man." Feeling marriage to be a galling yoke and a trap set for unsuspecting girls, she flees to her parents. In their opinion, however, there is nothing like marriage to develop and form a woman's character, particularly when she is guided by "a master hand, a strong will that compels obedience." Cazeau realizes that the marriage had been a blunder, but since he believes it to be their duty to make the best of it, he fetches her home. On the way, they pass "a great solitary oak-tree, with its seemingly immutable outlines, that had been a landmark for ages." It was here, Cazeau suddenly recalls, that as a small boy he had seen his father allow Black Gabe to rest, the runaway slave he had just recaptured and was taking back to thralldom.

In revolt against her husband and against a society which does not accept "a constitutional disinclination for marriage" as a reason for dissolving it, Athénaïse runs away again. Cazeau knows he can once more force her to come back and "compel her cold and unwilling submission to his love and passionate transports." But he refuses to undergo again "the humiliating sensation of baseness that had overtaken him in passing the old oak-tree" and tells her to return only if it is her own will to do so.

Meanwhile, Athénaïse is living incognita in a New Orleans pension. Here she becomes friendly with Gouvernail, the newspaper editor we have met before. The author tells us that he is part of a "congenial set of men and women,—*des esprits forts,* all of them, whose lives were irreproachable, yet whose opinions would startle even the traditional 'sapeur,' for whom 'nothing is sacred'." Then she adds with light irony: "But for all his 'advanced' opinions, Gouvernail was a liberal-minded fellow; a man or woman lost nothing of his respect by being married." The editor falls in love with Athénaïse: "He hoped some day to hold her with a lover's arm. That she was married made no particle of difference to Gouvernail." But at the same time he respects her for not being "the woman to be loved against her will," feeling—with George Sand—that "so long as she did not want him, he had no right to her,—no more than her husband had."

After a few weeks in the city, Athénaïse becomes ecstatic when she understands that she is pregnant. As she whispers her husband's name, the thought of him causes the "first purely sensuous tremor of her life" to sweep over her. Finally knowing her mind, which has come to her "as the song to the bird," she hurries home to nest-making and wifehood. (pp. 110-13)

It is easy to join Reedy of the *Mirror* when he sees Athénaïse as becoming "a wife in very deed and truth." But in spite of the happy end, the story contains a deep protest against woman's condition (while not forgetting its sensuous joys). Athénaïse's early "sense of hopelessness, [her] instinctive realization of the futility of rebellion against a social and sacred institution," is supported by the story's subtle symbolism.

Kate Chopin's names are sometimes emblematic. (An example is that of the chivalrous hero of a sketch she called **"Dr. Chevalier's Lie."**) Here, Cazeau's name would seem to stand for the *casa* or chateau in which woman lives her hemmed-in existence, and his stern manner, his jangling spur, and his snarling dogs to represent the authority which forces her to submission. Athénaïse, whose name perhaps refers to Athena, the patroness of spinning and weaving, is indirectly compared to a slave. (The word "emancipation," of course—the title of Kate O'Flaherty's early fable—is used to describe the releasing from bondage not only of women, but also of slaves.) Gabe then stands for the Archangel Gabriel, the herald of pregnancy, and the oak-tree for marriage and motherhood, woman's eternal destiny which makes her the tree of life rather than the free bird envisaged by Margaret Fuller.

"Athénaïse" is one of Kate Chopin's most important efforts. Not even in **"The Story of an Hour"** had she treated the female condition with such seriousness as here. She had opened her career by presenting the three main types of women, but we note that Eleanor of **"A Point of Issue"** was followed by no other clear-cut representative of her category, possibly because the author doubted that man could accept woman as his equal. Instead, Mrs. Chopin concentrated on the feminine and the emancipated females, and the fact that she often created these two opposites in pairs, exemplifying—in the course of a few weeks—first the one and then the other, would suggest that she was keeping up a running dialogue with herself on woman's lot. In one of these pairs (**"Madame Célestin's Divorce"** and **"An Idle Fellow"**), the author first deals with a Catholic attempting to go against the Church, and then with a person searching for God.

> I am very tired. I have been studying in books the languages of the living and those we call dead. . . . Now my brain is weary and I want rest.
>
> I shall sit here on the door-step beside my friend Paul. He is an idle fellow with folded hands. He laughs when I upbraid him, and bids me, with a motion, hold my peace. He is listening to a thrush's song that comes from the blur of yonder apple-tree. He tells me the thrush is singing a complaint. She wants her mate that was with her last blossom-time and builded a nest with her. She will have no other mate. . . .
>
> Paul is a strange fellow. . . . He knows the reasons that turn [people] to and fro and cause them to go and come. I think I shall walk a space through the world with my friend Paul. He is very wise, he knows the language of God which I have not learned.

Besides being a possible reference to Kate Chopin's own situation, **"An Idle Fellow"** is a central document in her demonstration of woman's various roles. With her meaningful use of names, the figure with folded hands is very likely Paul of the Bible who bids woman hold her peace. "Let your women keep silence," as he said, and also: "Wives, submit yourselves unto your own husbands." He is, to be sure, an unconventional Paul who drinks "deep the scent of the clover-field and the thick perfume from the rose-hedge," but this sexual symbolism is warranted when we recall that Paul, when he said it was Eve, not Adam, who "was in the transgression," added that "she shall be saved in childbearing."

Against the docile acceptance of these Biblical teachings as seen in the speaker of **"An Idle Fellow,"** Mrs. Chopin poses the views of the emancipated female. Of the many such women in the author's work, the clearest antithesis to Paul is Paula of **"Wiser than a God."** Refusing wifehood and motherhood in order to live for her non-biological career, she is a proud, defiant answer to the patriarch who condemns woman to be merely an object.

Kate Chopin's first extant tale was written in 1889. The story vividly expresses Paula's views, but artistically it is poor. . . . [However], the author quickly progressed beyond the apprentice stage. By the time she wrote **"An Idle Fellow"** in 1893, she was already an accomplished writer, and when she portrayed Athénaïse two years later, the *Century* was just publishing a story by her (**"Regret"**) which shows unquestionable artistic mastery. (pp. 113-15)

Per Seyersted, in his Kate Chopin: A Critical Biography, *Louisiana State University Press, 1969, 246 p.*

Robert D. Arner (essay date 1972)

[In the following excerpt, Arner refutes the critical contention that Chopin's often-anthologized "Desirée's

Baby" is a flawed work by examining its theme, structure, and imagery.]

[In his essay "Kate Chopin's *The Awakening* in the Perspective of Her Literary Career"], George Arms confessed bewilderment "at the appearance of **'Désirée's Baby'** in so many anthologies, even while admitting its elegance as a well-made tale in the manner of Maupassant." He compared the story to Mark Twain's *Pudd'nhead Wilson* as a work which raises "the question of identity in a racial context" and preferred Twain on the grounds that "his novel makes a complex and pragmatic inquiry not present in Mrs. Chopin's story." Nor is Arms alone in the opinion that **"Désirée's Baby"** is, for one reason or another, flawed and superficial. . . . Per Seyersted, the most thorough and most sympathetic of Mrs Chopin's critics to date, agrees; the conclusion, he says, is "somewhat contrived," though he quickly adds that it possesses a "bitter, piercing quality" that Maupassant himself could not have surpassed [*Kate Chopin: A Critical Biography*]. With respect to Arms's comments, it might be observed that to fault a story of several pages for not dealing with issues in as much depth or from as many perspectives as a novel of more than a hundred pages is at best questionable critical procedure; it is to demand of one genre what we normally expect of another. But even were the validity of Arms's comparison admitted . . . I feel that he has seriously misjudged the complexity of Kate Chopin's tale. In the same way, it seems to me that the claim that Mrs. Chopin betrays the reader's confidence as, for instance, O. Henry so frequently does by attempting to force on him a conclusion she has not prepared for rests on a too hasty reading of the story. In spite of Mrs. Chopin's announced distrust of striving for literary effect and artistic unity—what she termed the "polishing up process"—**"Désirée's Baby"** gives evidence of a careful craftsmanship that goes well beyond formal elegance and fuses theme, structure, and imagery into one of the most successful of her works.

"Désirée's Baby" is the story of a foundling adopted by the Valmondés, at the entrance to whose plantation she is found as a baby. The Valmondés name her Désirée, and when she grows to womanhood she is wooed and wed by a neighbor's son, Armand Aubigny, a descendant of one of the oldest and proudest families in Louisiana. Local rumor has it that Armand treats his slaves cruelly and inhumanely. Désirée bears him a son, but when the boy exhibits Negroid traits Armand spurns both wife and child. His explanation is simple and characteristic: " 'It means that the child is not white,' " he tells Désirée; " 'it means that you are not white.' " In despair Désirée writes to her mother to find out if the accusation is true. Madame Valmondé's brief reply speaks volumes in its careful omissions: " 'My own Désirée. Come home to Valmondé; back to your mother who loves you. Come with your child.' " Instead Désirée takes the baby and disappears into the tangled wilderness around the bayou. Some weeks later, as Armand is systematically attempting to purify his house from all traces of Désirée and the baby, he comes upon the fragment of a letter lodged in a drawer that, ironically, used to contain Désirée's love letters to him. This letter, however, was written by his mother, whom he has never seen that he remembers, to his father, and its final words are also the last words in the story: " 'But, above all, night and day, I thank the good God for having so arranged our lives that our dear Armand will never know that his mother, who adores him, belongs to the race that is cursed with the brand of slavery.' "

Far more is at stake in this ending than the simple discovery that the parent who has driven his wife and child to exile and death on the suspicion that his wife had Negro blood is himself the tainted and guilty party. That indeed might satisfy our sense of justice, but Kate Chopin has more to say on the issues of race and slavery. For one thing, the story makes a point made by a number of other Southern writers both before and after Mrs. Chopin: that there is no absolute distinction between white and black, but rather an imaginary line drawn by white men and crossed at their own choosing. Because the line is so indelibly fixed in the white man's mind, however, acts of renunciation are difficult to perform and no single act is sufficient to redeem the South from the curse of its racial caste system. Thus, though Armand's father marries a woman technically a Negress, the fact remains a secret until the end of the story and no positive results are produced by the marriage. On the other hand, the sins of the fathers are repeatedly visited upon the children, for Armand inherits not only his father's slaves but also a set of rigid social codes prescribing his attitude toward the Negro and reestablishing the relationship between white and black as one between master and slave, possessor and the possessed. Trusting in the absoluteness of this relationship, Armand condemns his wife and child to exile and, as things turn out, to death. But the racial code is proved to be a fiction at the end, as Armand's own mixed parentage establishes, and the victimizer ends up the victim of his own inflexible inhumanity. Of the two discoveries Armand makes at the conclusion of the story, that he is part Negro and that the idea of white racial purity is a myth, the second is the harder to live with, since it deprives him of all semblance of justification for his treatment of Désirée and the baby. He learns, in fact, that his relationship to his father is precisely the same as the one he imagined existed between his son and himself. It is this profound irony of sacrificer become the sacrifice, a reversal of racial identity, that underlies the story and determines—in fact, almost necessitates—the ironic reversal at the end. Form is wed inseparably to theme, and both originate in the realities of the Southern social system.

The antidote to the poison of racial abstraction that destroys Désirée, the baby, and Armand is love, a deeply personal relationship which denies the dehumanizing and impersonal categorization of people into racial groups. The possibility that love may offer individual salvation from the evils of racial definition is suggested first of all by Armand's father's marriage to a Negress and, second, by Madame Valmondé's open acceptance of Désirée and her child even after she believes that the girl is part black. Love demands that people be seen as individuals, not as members of a social caste or as extensions of one's own ego. But the story makes clear that Armand does not really love Désirée; he thinks of her as a possession, a rich prize to display to his friends and to flatter his vanity, and when he thinks that she is black the value of the prize entirely disappears. In the antebellum South anyone can own a black girl, however beautiful she may be. Armand sees his marriage to Désirée solely in terms of what he brings to the union, and it is strongly hinted that one factor influencing his decision to marry her is that, knowing she is adopted, he thinks of himself as indisputably her superior in rank and breeding. She will not be in a position to question his authority but must submit to his judgement in all matters, which in fact she does. This motivation is perhaps hidden from Armand, but the violence and destructiveness of his passion for Désirée is revealed to the reader in a group of key similes. He falls in love with her, Mrs. Chopin writes, "as if struck by a pistol shot." And a few lines further on, she expands on the same theme: "The passion that awoke in him that day, when he saw her at the gate, swept along like an avalanche, or like a prairie fire, or like anything that drives headlong over all obstacles." When Armand is reminded by Monsieur Valmondé that Désirée is nameless and of obscure origin, he dismisses the objections impatiently: "What did it matter about a name when he could give her one of the oldest and proudest in Louisiana?" These passages not only serve to define Armand's willful and headstrong character, but also suggest the role of *hubris* in the story, since Armand's passionate intensity and his pride in possession make him a willing agent of his own destruction. The Southern racial caste system has already begun to victimize Armand by accentuating the flaws in his personality which, but for the circumstances of his being born a master in a slaveholding society, might have remained dormant. As it is, a pride nurtured by artificial racial distinctions ultimately destroys Armand's chances for happiness and personal salvation. Character and environment unite to produce one part of the tragic denouement of the tale.

The several racial themes of **"Désirée's Baby"** are reinforced by two major patterns of images which, circulating throughout the story, unobtrusively contribute both unity and density of meaning. The first of these is the contrast between light and shadow, whiteness and blackness. Armand is associated with darkness from the outset. His estate is a place of terror and his house inspires fear. . . . [It] functions as a symbolic projection onto the landscape of Armand's personality. Armand himself is described, with more than a hint of irony in the first adjective, as having a "dark handsome face." In contrast, Désirée is surrounded by images of whiteness. Recovering from labor, she lies "in her soft white muslins and laces, upon a couch." She stands next to Armand "like a stone image: silent, white, motionless" after she has given him her mother's letter and is awaiting his reaction. On the day she walks into the wilderness around the bayou, she wears "a thin white garment"; her hair radiates a "golden gleam" in spite of its brown color. The reader who has paid attention to these details has little reason to object that the ending of the story comes as a surprise; it has been carefully and deliberately foreshadowed throughout.

A third important color in the story is yellow. Armand's plantation house is yellow and, in view of the association between his personality and the atmosphere surrounding the house, this fact acquires significance. Zandrine, Désirée's nurse during her convalescence, is also yellow. On a racial scale of values, so are La Blanche, a pale Negress mentioned several times in the story, and her son, the boy against whose color Désirée compares her son's color when she first suspects that her baby may be part Negro. So, of course, is Désirée's baby—and so is Armand. In fact, all the Negroes mentioned by name in the story are "yellow" rather than pure black. That so much yellow color is associated with the Aubigny estate, both with its buildings and, more important, with its slaves, is another means of foreshadowing the revelation of Armand's true racial identity. But it is also a subtle indictment of the white man's double standards and a measure of his racial guilt: black women may be concubines, but not wives. (The story, it might be noted along these same lines, contains the tantalizingly ambiguous remark that Armand heard his son crying "as far away as La Blanche's cabin.") Mrs. Chopin's arrangement of characters along a spectrum ranging from white to black as a means of underscoring, somewhat paradoxically, the theme that no real or final distinction based on color can be made between slave and master calls to mind a similar technique employed by Gertrude Stein in "Melanctha," though Miss Stein is of course working toward different ends. And it suggests a link between Mrs. Chopin's short story art and the art of the impressionists (we know that she was at least passingly familiar with their work and interested in it): truth is revealed in shifting modulations and tones of color.

The second major figurative pattern in **"Désirée's Baby"** has to do with the opposition between God or Providence and Satan. It is closely related to the contrast between the kingdom of light and the kingdom of darkness. As early as the third paragraph we are introduced to the idea that Désirée's fate has in some way been pre-ordained by God. Madame Valmondé, speculating on Désirée's origins, comes to the comforting conclusion that "she had been sent by a beneficent Providence to be the child of her [Madame Valmondé's] affection, seeing she was without child of the flesh." Later, this idea of Providential interference in the affairs of men is echoed ironically in Madame Aubigny's belief that God has so arranged things that Armand will never know his mother was a Negress. It transpires that God had other plans all along, however. Through no fault of her own, Désirée brings grief, not happiness, to Madame Valmondé, and she is the agent who, indirectly to be sure, brings Armand to a recognition of his mixed parentage. Thus the ironic reversal at the end of the story is counterpointed by a reversal and a defeat of each mother's expectations. By associating Désirée with Providential design in this poetic and oblique way, Kate Chopin seems to be indicating that God, and not the author, is the ironist who has spun this plot. Not only Armand's character and the social structure of the slaveholding South have a hand in forcing him to confront the reality of the shadow within, but also Providence itself seems to have taken an interest in the arrangements.

Armand himself dimly senses the connection between Désirée and Divinity. In a moment of self-pity, he imagines "that Almighty God had dealt cruelly and unjustly with him; and felt, somehow, that he was paying Him back when he stabbed thus into his wife's soul." By insulting and injuring Désirée, Armand believes that he hurts and insults God as well; he casts both of them out of his house. In this context, Mrs. Chopin's apparently insignificant comment, "the very spirit of Satan seemed suddenly to have taken hold of him," takes on a new dimension of meaning. Armand makes a most excellent earthly representative of Satan. His treatment of his wife is an act of defiance against both God and man (not, of course, against man in Armand's artificial social environment, but as a denial of the human power of love). He shares with Satan the sin of pride: racial and aristocratic pride specifically, but also a pride in his own power to rebel against God. The connection between Armand and Satan is subtly made not only in the sentence already cited, but also in Mrs. Chopin's careful arrangement of characters and her use of fire symbolism in the final scene: "In the centre of the smoothly swept backyard was a great bonfire. Armand Aubigny sat in the wide hallway that commanded a view of the spectacle; and it was he who dealt out to the half dozen negroes the material which kept this fire ablaze." Armand presides over the holocaust, intended to be a ritual of purification from guilt but really a ritual that re-affirms the impossibility of escaping the consequences of the slave system, enthroned in state like the very Prince of Darkness himself.

As Armand's character is defined both by his actions and by the images clustered around him, so is Désirée's. She is called the "idol of Valmondé," a metaphor which strengthens her associations with Divinity and Providence. Her face is "suffused with a glow that was happiness itself," as if joy were an indwelling vital principle, in contrast to Armand's face, which is frequently "disfigured by frowns." And her appearance when she walks into the thickets surrounding the bayou as a sacrifice to Southern racial codes lacks only the halo for complete beautification. . . . (pp. 131-38)

If the pattern of character and conflict built around this second set of images seems somehow familiar to us, it is probably because we have seen it, or something very like it, before. It represents another of the apparently endless variations on a theme made popular in Western romance literature by Samuel Richardson's *Clarissa,* a book which one critic has identified as the prototype of all subsequent stories of sentimental love. Mythopoeic in its power, *Clarissa* is the story of a young virginal maiden who is lustily and lustfully pursued through hundreds of pages by the villain, Lovelace, who, when he cannot seduce her, resorts to rape. Dishonored—she suspects that some dark part of her had acquiesced to the deed—Clarissa wastes away and dies. Lovelace is killed in a duel shortly thereafter, and on this note of villainy deservedly punished the novel closes. Throughout, Lovelace is associated with darkness and evil; he is driven by deep and unsearchable urges to seek Clarissa's ruin and his own destruction. Only marriage to Clarissa could have saved him from his evil inner nature, but Richardson, with fidelity to reality and an awareness of the irreconcilable differences between the characters he has created, forbids *Love*-lace that salvation.

Richardson's novel is far more complicated than this brief summary suggests and his psychological insights surpass those of Mrs. Chopin in this tale, but in spite of these and other differences **"Désirée's Baby"** owes much to the popularized Richardsonian tradition. In the "dark handsome face" of Armand Aubigny we can still dimly trace the features of Lovelace. Both men are aristocrats and both are excessively proud of their nobility, though Armand shares none of Lovelace's pride in intellectual attainments or his nearly godless faith in the power of reason. Both men possess enormous sexual energy, but while Lovelace's is directed toward seducing Clarissa, Armand's finds an outlet in the sadistic mistreatment of his slaves; the sexual pursuit central to *Clarissa* is reduced in **"Désirée's Baby"** to a few veiled innuendos concerning the master's relationship with his slaves. Armand's darkness is associated with sensuality and aggressiveness, in contrast to Désirée's whiteness, which represents purity and, in spite of her marriage, inviolability and gentleness. Désirée is unmistakably Kate Chopin's version of the Pure Maiden, the Saviour Woman; she suffers at the hands of a villain to whom, for all his villainy, she is powerfully attracted. Her suffering and her death, however, seem unimportant in the end. The reader has little doubt that she will be rewarded in heaven (whence she came?), that Armand will be punished. Désirée is the superego, to put the case in Freudian terms, to Armand's id. For a brief while she acts as the civilizing and humanizing consciousness for his primitive and animalistic unconscious. She provides him with a socially accepted and sanctified outlet for his brutal passions, a sexual surrogate, as it were, for his will to dominate. During this brief period of marital felicity, significantly, Armand stops mistreating his slaves. But when he discovers, or thinks he discovers, that Désirée is tainted with the blackness that confirms in his mind her essential similarity to his inner sensual and aggressive self, she loses her efficacy for him as a means to grace. Marriage to her was not salvation but, in both racial and psychological terms, surrender to the self within and therefore damnation. Predictably, Armand reverts to his old ways; if anything, he is more cruel to his slaves than formerly, linking them to his "betrayal" by a woman but unaware that they are projections, literally and symbolically, of the darkness that lurks within him.

Combining as it does racial themes with a transmuted seduction theme—what we might term the *Uncle Tom's Cabin* tradition and the *Clarissa* tradition—**"Désirée's Baby"** turns out to be a surprisingly rich and complex story, one of the best of its kind in American literature. Its richness is the more remarkable and its integration of elements the more noteworthy because Kate Chopin seldom reworked her stories, preferring, as she said, "the integrity of crudities to artificialities"—truth instead of beauty. But the excellence of this tale invites speculation as to how many of Mrs. Chopin's other stories would prove equally rewarding if given a close reading. Above all, the story testifies eloquently to the truth of Fred Lewis Pattee's assertion that Mrs. Chopin "must be rated as a genius, taut, vibrant, intense of soul. . . . Without models, without study or short-story art, without revision, and usually at a sitting, she produced what often are masterpieces before which one can only wonder and conjecture." (pp. 138-40)

Robert D. Arner, "Pride and Prejudice: Kate

Chopin's 'Désirée's Baby'," in The Mississippi Quarterly, *Vol. XXV, No. 2, Spring, 1972, pp. 131-40.*

Bert Bender (essay date 1974)

[In the following excerpt, Bender explicates "A Vocation and a Voice," "Athénaïse," and "The Storm," characterizing them as lyrical "songs of the self."]

If she is mentioned at all, Kate Chopin is safely categorized in literary histories as a local colorist. Some of her own titles (***Bayou Folk,*** 1894, and ***A Night in Acadie,*** 1897) and that of her first biography (*Kate Chopin and Her Creole Stories,* 1932 [see Further Reading]) imply that the classification may be just. But it is bitterly ironic that she should be so classified; for her fiction probes far more deeply into human nature than "local color" implies, and her entire career represents a struggle to break through restricting classifications. Her works, themselves, were the ultimate breakthrough: in the face of genteel traditions of the 1890's, she wrote of people who break free from traditional moral and social structures to experience and express socially unacceptable feelings. Her stories are lyric celebrations of life. In them, a character's feelings are associated with natural "songs" and "voices" or with images of objects and events in nature. In these celebrations, typically, a character awakens to ecstatic knowledge of his own sexual being; or a wife, having become aware that she resents the restricting presence of the husband and children whom she nevertheless loves, experiences at least fleeting moments of ecstatic freedom.

Such sentiments were disturbing to American readers at the turn of the century. As two other minority writers, Paul Laurence Dunbar and Charles Chesnutt, found, the public preferred harmless dialect stories to serious fiction of protest. Like them, Kate Chopin found that her stories of the quaint life on the Louisiana bayous were more acceptable than the more serious and searching fiction that she dared to write during the last part of her career. Her last novel, *The Awakening* (1899), shocked many of its reviewers (one said that it was "too strong drink for moral babes, and should be labeled 'poison' "), and others simply refused to review it at all. The bad publicity it received caused her to be ostracized by some of her friends and to be refused membership in the St. Louis Fine Arts Club, and the novel was quickly banned from the public libraries in St. Louis. Partly because of their unconventional morality, some of her best stories were unpublished until 1969, when her complete works were issued. (pp. 257-58)

The best of Kate Chopin's stories are thematically as unconventional as *The Awakening.* And—at a time when American short fiction was dominated by formal prescriptions for what Brander Matthews called the "Short-story" [*Lippincott's Magazine,* 36 (October 1885)], her lyrical stories were unconventional in their form. Toward the end of the nineteenth century, the production of the "Short-story" in America was a substantial industry. In a perversion of Poe's idea that composition should proceed "with the precision and rigid consequence of a mathematical problem" [*Selected Writings of Edgar Allan Poe* (1956)], the "Short-story" was mass-produced; its essential element was plot, and it culminated in O. Henry's stories with snap endings. The form was produced and defended by such genteel taste-makers as Matthews, Frank Stockton, H. C. Bunner, and Thomas B. Aldrich (each an editor as well as a writer), and its prevailing tone was of light comedy. The "Short-story" was particularly well suited to the complacent reiteration of American values—values which held that business enterprises, machines, and even machined art could bring a kind of progress. As H. S. Canby concluded in 1901, "Men of genius found through the short story a new voice, and the attempt to perfect, to give laws and form to the instrument, progressed because of the men who tried" [*Dial* 31 (16 October 1901)].

The lyrical voice embodied in Kate Chopin's short fictions is the antithesis of both the formal rigidity and the genteel, comic tone of the "Short-story." Variations on the theme of awakening to ecstatic self-realization, her stories are fictional songs of the self. In them, she affirms aspects of the self that conventions denied, affirms them in a way that resembles Whitman when he sings approvingly of "forbidden voices, / Voices of sexes and lusts." But her stories do not locate, as *Leaves of Grass* does, a mythic self as the synthetic, integrating center of a larger democratic context. The characters depicted in her fictions are tragically cut off from their social surroundings, because, like D. H. Lawrence's characters, their awakened identities are at odds with social conventions. The original title of *The Awakening* was "A Solitary Soul," and it suggests that for Kate Chopin, the freedom and ecstasy of self-affirmation are necessarily accompanied by isolation. Her characters transcend their socially limited selves by awakening to and affirming impulses that are unacceptable by convention.

Madam Victoire Verdon Charleville, Chopin's great-grandmother, whose unconventional views on marriage and women's rights greatly influenced Chopin's writings.

Unburdened of restricting social conventions, her characters come to experience the suffering and loneliness, as well as the joy, of their freedom; for the impulses that they heed are a mere part of a world in which change and natural selection are first principles.

Many of her characters are like the typical nineteenth-century romantic characters whose impulsive, unmediated awareness is approvingly opposed to traditional learning and knowledge from books. With Whitman, they would address their souls:

> Not words, not music or rhyme I want . . . not custom or lecture, not even the best,
> Only the lull I like, the hum of your valved voice.

And with Whitman they are aware always of the

> Urge and urge and urge,
> Always the procreative urge of the world.

A typical character in her works is Paul, in the brief sketch, **"An Idle Fellow"** (1893, 300 words). The narrator of the sketch emphasizes that he is brainweary, and he tells of his determination to rest and refresh himself by accompanying his strange friend, Paul. The narrator begins: "I am tired. At the end of these years I am very tired. I have been studying in books of languages of the living and those we call dead. Early in the fresh morning I have studied in books, and throughout the day when the sun was shining; and at night when there were stars, I have lighted my oil-lamp and studied in books. Now my brain is weary and I want rest." Paul, the idle fellow, is the model by whom the narrator hopes to be healed. Perfectly in tune with nature, Paul, like Whitman, listens "to a thrush's song," a "complaint" for a lost mate. Drinking "deep the scent of the cloverfield and the thick perfume from the rosehedge," Paul knows intuitively "the reasons that turn people to and fro and cause them to go and come."

The central figure in the story **"A Vocation and a Voice"** (1896) is a youth who frees himself from the restricting conventions of work and orthodox religion to achieve a knowledge of his intuitive, animal self. The mythic dimension of his quest for self-knowledge is evident in the first words of the story when he asks, trying to find his way back to his place of work, "Is this Adams Avenue?" Told that he is in "Woodland Park," he begins to wonder and to relish his freedom in nature. He lapses into a "blessed state of tranquility and contemplation" and realizes repeatedly how good it is "to be out in the open air": "He belonged under God's sky in the free and open air." But in meeting the girl Suzima, a travelling fortune teller, he comes to feel the disturbing excitement of sexual arousal and, eventually, his own frightening, violent rage when he is moved to protect the girl: "He felt as if he had encountered some hideous being with whom he was not acquainted and who said to him: 'I am yourself.' He shrank from trusting himself with this being alone. His soul turned toward the refuge of spiritual help, and he prayed to God and the saints and the Virgin Mary to save him and to direct him." He finds refuge from his frightening self-knowledge in a monastery, where symbolically he is granted permission "to build, with his own hands, a solid stone wall around the 'Refuge.' " Inevitably, though, while working one day "out in the open air," he succumbs to his animal impulses. He suddenly stops his work on the wall and lifts "his head with the mute quivering attention of some animal in the forest, startled at the scent of approaching danger." Having sensed the presence of Suzima, he comes finally to a full knowledge of himself: "He knew that he had pulses, for they were clamoring, and flesh, for it tingled and burned as if pricked with nettles."

The opposed forces in this story are, on the one hand, work, conventionality, orthodox religion, and the will; and on the other hand, idleness, unconventionality, a kind of pantheistic religion, and impulsiveness: or, as in the title of the story, **"A Vocation and a Voice."** For the natural impulses that work on the youth are represented primarily by Suzima's voice, the tracing and echoing of which embody the lyric quality of the story. The lull of her voice awakens in the youth the lull and hum of his own soul's voice, and the repeated sounding of Suzima's voice reminds the reader that in Kate Chopin's world, the throb of man's natural but often unrecognized impulses is as beautifully mysterious as D. H. Lawrence's blood consciousness.

With her "mystic cards and Egyptian wisdom," Suzima is an "interpreter of dreams." The boy is immediately struck with the full, free beauty of her voice, but not until he has a sexual encounter with Suzima does he fully feel the frightening significance of the voice. The sexual experience had brought him into touch with "the universe of man and all things that live"; Suzima's voice is therefore able to "penetrate his whole being and . . . complete the new and bewildering existence that had overtaken him." Despite his initial frightened attempt to wall out his life, then, the lull of Suzima's voice finally penetrates even the monastic walls to bring him to himself and help him accept the knowledge of his "pulses" and his "flesh": "The voice drew nearer and nearer; the woman drew nearer and nearer. She was coming; she was here. She was there, passing in the road beneath. . . . She was alone, walking with uplifted throat, singing her song. . . . He was conscious of nothing in the world but the voice that was calling him and the cry of his own being that responded."

Like the men in **"An Idle Fellow"** and **"A Vocation and a Voice,"** Kate Chopin's women must struggle to know and accept themselves, but their predicament is more excruciating because of what she called the "matrimonial yoke." Her stories openly criticize the unnaturalness of institutionalized marriage, but her characters do not contend with marriage in a uniform way. Some accept it after considerable anguish; some flee from it (even, like Edna Pontellier in *The Awakening,* into death); and some manage to find illicit but naturally innocent nourishment outside of the marriage. Regardless of the outcome, the predicament of the lonely, restricted women in these stories is like that of the lyric poet who in his loneliness turns his back to his audience. And in each case, Kate Chopin consoles herself by lyrically associating her characters' disruptive impulses with such natural and sanctifying impulses as a bird's song or a flower's blossoming.

"Athénaïse" (1895) is the story of a girl who, having yielded to custom by marrying prematurely, finds the "galling matrimonial yoke" unbearable. Incapable of either "patient resignation, a talent born in the souls of many women" or of "philosophical resignation," she is given to a kind of innocent rebelliousness. Her husband, Cazeau, is not unusually abusive; it is simply that she has married before having come naturally to know herself: "People often said that Athénaïse would know her own mind some day, which was equivalent to saying that she was at present unacquainted with it. If she ever came to such knowledge, it would be by no intellectual research, by no subtle analyses or tracing the motives of actions to their source. It would come to her as the song to the bird, the perfume to the flower." That there is no *reason* for her discomfort in her marriage merely adds to the exasperation of her husband and her father. Only her brother understands, for—since he has no authority over her—they relate freely, albeit with incestuous overtones. She explains to her brother that Cazeau is neither abusive nor drunken; nor does she hate him the way her brother does. She adds, "with a sudden impulse," that "It's jus' being married that I detes' an' despise. I hate being Mrs. Cazeau, an' would want to be Athénaïse Miché again. I can't stan' to live with a man; to have him always there; his coats an' pantaloons hanging in my room; his ugly bare feet—washing them in my tub, befo' my very eyes, ugh!" The institution of marriage, itself, is oppressive to her—the simple fact that her husband (as his name suggests) is head of the household: "her husband's looks, his tones, his mere presence, brought to her a sudden sense of hopelessness, an instinctive realization of the futility of rebellion against a social and sacred institution." Even though Cazeau is not harshly authoritative, he has, as Athénaise's father happily realizes, "a master hand, a strong will that compels obedience." And the nature of their relationship (and of marriage in general for Kate Chopin) is suggested by the repeated mention of Cazeau's spurs and by a scene in which the institutions of slavery and marriage are symbolically linked. Returning home with Athénaïse after she had first run away to her parents' home, Cazeau is reminded of an experience he had had in his youth with a runaway slave:

> The sight of a great solitary oak-tree, with the seemingly immutable outlines, that had been a landmark for ages—or was it the odor of elderberry stealing up from the gully to the south? or what was it that brought vividly back to Cazeau, by some association of ideas, a scene of many years ago? He had passed that old live-oak hundreds of times, but it was only now the memory of one day came back to him. He was a very small boy that day, seated before his father on horse-back. They were proceeding slowly, and Black Gabe had run away, and had been discovered back in the Gotrain swamp. They had halted beneath this big oak to enable the negro to take a breath; had agreed at the time that Black Gabe was a fool, a great idiot indeed, for wanting to run away from him.

But even a "kind and considerate master" is a master, and therefore oppressive. In his recollection of Black Gabe, even Cazeau, himself, seems to recognize the nature of his marriage: "The whole impression was for some reason hideous, and to dispel it Cazeau spurred his horse to a swift gallop." When Athénaïse runs away again, he refuses to pursue her; he has decided that "for the companionship of no woman on earth would he again undergo the humiliating baseness that had overtaken him in passing the old oak-tree in the fallow meadow."

Athénaïse finally does come to herself when, alone in a New Orleans boarding house, she has time and freedom. She is helped to her self-knowledge by the gentle wisdom of a newspaperman who, though he woos her, knows that he has "no right to her" until she wants him. Ironically, his very gentleness works against him and for Athénaïse, for she "could not fancy him loving anyone passionately, rudely, offensively, as Cazeau loved her." So in a way she is prepared for the miraculous change that comes over her "as the song to the bird, the perfume and color to the flower": she is stunned to learn from a black maid that she is pregnant, and, breathing unevenly, she begins to feel an immediate change in herself:

> Her whole being was steeped in a wave of ecstasy. When she finally arose from the chair in which she had been seated, and looked at herself in the mirror, a face met hers which she seemed to see for the first time, so transfigured was it with wonder and rapture.
>
> One mood quickly followed another, in this new turmoil of her senses, and the need of action became uppermost. . . . Cazeau must know. As she thought of him, the first purely sensuous tremor of her life swept over her. She half whispered his name, and the sound of it brought red blotches into her cheeks. She spoke it over and over, as if it were some new, sweet sound born out of darkness and confusion, and reaching her for the first time. She was impatient to be with him. Her whole passionate nature was aroused as if by a miracle.

Athénaïse's awakening to an ecstatic knowledge and acceptance of her biological destiny is by no means Kate Chopin's general solution for woman's anxieties. Athénaïse's nervous and impulsive discomfort with the lack of freedom in marriage is, however, for Chopin, a general condition in the institution; and Athénaïse's salvation in pregnancy is certainly the most socially acceptable of Kate Chopin's solutions to the problem. In other stories, some of which were not published during her lifetime, she writes more openly and perhaps more truthfully of socially unacceptable feelings about marriage and of equally unconventional developments from these feelings. Never in America had anyone written—in the words of one reviewer of *The Awakening*—with such "searching vision into the recesses of the heart" of a woman; "it is disturbing—even indelicate," the reviewer continued, to write of such feelings, even though they do "perhaps . . . play an important part in the life behind the mask."

"The Story of an Hour" (1894) was refused by the influential and genteel editor of *The Century*, R. W. Gilder (who had also rejected, among other things, Stephen Crane's "Maggie"), for the story is built around the lyrical expression of a woman's shockingly unorthodox feelings about her marriage. Louise Mallard's feelings come to her, as is usual in these stories, by way of natural undercurrents that are associated with songs and with objects in nature. As the original title of the story suggests (**"The Dream of an Hour"**), such feelings are subliminal, as they necessarily must have been in the 1890's. Kate Chopin's dreams of freedom, like those of Dunbar and Chesnutt, provide the lyrical impulse in her fiction.

In the story, Louise Mallard weeps "At once, with sudden, wild abandonment" when she is told that her husband has been killed in a railroad accident. There is no doubt that she has loved him deeply, but after the "storm of grief" subsides in her, she begins to awaken to a new life that is first suggested to her by a view from her window of "the tops of trees that were all acquiver with the new spring life. The delicious breath of rain was in the air. In the street below a peddler was crying his wares. The notes of a distant song which someone was singing reached her faintly, and countless sparrows were twittering in the eaves."

"There were patches of blue sky showing here and there through the clouds that had met and piled one above the other in the west facing the window." Gradually and fearfully, then, she realizes that a subtle change is overtaking her, but she is powerless to beat it "back with her will." Finally, she lets the "little whispered word . . . 'free, free, free!' " escape from her lips, and she realizes that henceforth "there would be no powerful will bending hers in that blind persistence with which men and women believe they have a right to impose a private will upon a fellow creature. A kind intention or a cruel intention made the act seem no less a crime as she looked at it in that brief moment of illumination."

The "strongest impulse of her being," she realizes, is the "possession of self-assertion," and she whispers repeatedly, "Free! Body and soul free!" But the story comes to an abrupt and ironic end. Mrs. Mallard is brought word that her husband is safe, and she collapses. The doctors conclude that she has died "of heart disease—of joy that kills."

A final story, **"The Storm"** (1898, unpublished until 1969), is another treatment of unconventional, impulsive behavior in marriage; and again, the impulses are associated with (and sanctioned by) larger impulses in nature—with the storm of the title. An actual storm strands Calixta's husband and son while they are away to town, and it parallels a "storm" of sexual energy that brings Calixta together with Alcée Laballiére, a former suitor who in passing by seeks shelter from the storm. With its 1,800 words, the story moves with the pace and rhythm of a natural change of weather. In five parts, it begins quietly with the approach of the storm: "The leaves were so still that even Bibi thought it was going to rain"; it crescendos in the second, the longest part; and it subsides in three short parts as quietly as it begins, ending with, "so the storm passed. . . ."

There is no suggestion that the marriage of Calixta and Bobinôt is in any way unhappy. Bobinôt is gentle and unauthoritative; he is "accustomed to talk on terms of perfect equality" with his little son, four-year-old Bibi; and, delayed by the storm and concerned for his wife's safety, he purchases a small gift, "a can of shrimps, of which Calixta was very fond." When Bobinôt and Bibi arrive home after the storm, the return is genuinely joyful for all three; there are kisses, exclamations of relieved concern, and plans for a shrimp feast.

Calixta's adulterous encounter had been accidental and innocent. It is simply that mysterious natural forces larger than the individuals or the marriage institution have worked to refresh all the parties of both marriages, Laballiére's as well as Calixta's. Kate Chopin's principle here, as usual, is that freedom nourishes. The love scene occurred in the stifling heat of the cabin as the storm's tempo built; the lightning and thunder brought on a corresponding rise of sexual desire as Alcée tried to calm Calixta by touching her. Then, "there was nothing for him to do but to gather her lips in a kiss." The scene—marred only by the wooden (and ironically conventional) diction of one short paragraph, in which "he possessed her" and "her mouth was a fountain of delight"—deserves to be quoted fully for its lucid simplicity and grace:

> They did not heed the crashing torrents, and the roar of the elements made her laugh as she lay in his arms. She was a revelation in that dim, mysterious chamber; as white as the couch she lay upon. Her firm, elastic flesh that was knowing for the first time its birthright, was like a creamy lily that the sun invites to contribute its breath and perfume to the undying life of the world.
>
> The generous abundance of her passion, without guile or trickery, was like a white flame which penetrated and found response in depths of his own sensuous nature that had never yet been reached.
>
> When he touched her breasts they gave themselves up in quivering ecstasy, inviting his lips. Her mouth was a fountain of delight. And when he possessed her, they seemed to swoon together at the very borderland of life's mystery.
>
> He stayed cushioned upon her, breathless, dazed, enervated, with his heart beating like a hammer upon her. With one hand she clasped his head, her lips lightly touching his forehead. The other hand stroked with a soothing rhythm his muscular shoulders.
>
> The growl of the thunder was distant and passing away. The rain beat softly upon the shingles, inviting them to drowsiness and sleep. But they dared not yield.

"The Storm" is remarkable not only for the freedom it asserts in the face of the suffocating conventionality of the 1890's, but for the lyrical ease with which it unites human and universal rhythms to celebrate "the procreative urge of the world." The story realizes Kate Chopin's dream of woman's renewed birthright for passionate self-fulfillment. But surely it is a tragic comment on her life and work that only recently—with a gradual but widespreading awakening of woman's consciousness, nearly three-quarters of a century after her death—has our culture been prepared to see Kate Chopin's dreams as anything but nightmares. (pp. 259-66)

Bert Bender, "Kate Chopin's Lyrical Short Stories," in Studies in Short Fiction, *Vol. XI, No. 3, Summer, 1974, pp. 257-66.*

Cynthia Griffin Wolff (essay date 1978)

[*Wolff is an American author and educator. In the following excerpt, she asserts that "Désirée's Baby" is "the most vivid and direct statement of [Chopin's] major concern—the limits of fiction."*]

For many years, **"Désirée's Baby"** was the one piece of Chopin's fiction most likely to be known; even today, despite the wide respect that her second novel has won, there are still readers whose acquaintance with Chopin's work is restricted to this one, widely-anthologized short story. [Daniel S.] Rankin, who did not feel the need to reprint **"Désirée's Baby"** in *Kate Chopin and Her Creole Stories,* nonetheless judged it "perhaps . . . one of the world's best short stories." Unfortunately, Rankin left future critics a terminology with which to describe the value of this and the other studies in ***Bayou Folk:*** it had the "freshness which springs from an unexplored field—the quaint and picturesque life among the Creole and Acadian folk of the Louisiana bayous." In short, it was excellent "regional" work—hence limited to certain circumscribed triumphs.

Critics' tendency to dismiss Chopin's fiction as little more than local color began to diminish by the late 1950's; nevertheless, old habits died hard. **"Désirée's Baby"** continued to be the most frequently anthologized of her short fictions, and while the comments on it strained after some larger tragic significance, the definition of that "tragedy" was still formulated almost exclusively in "regional" terms. (pp. 123-24)

Other critics, still acknowledging the importance of regional elements in the tale, seek to discover the reasons for its persistently compelling quality by examining the structure. Thus Larzer Ziff observes that "the most popular of Mrs. Chopin's stories, while they make full use of the charming lilt of Creole English and the easy openness of Creole manners, concern themselves, as do Maupassant's, with some central quirk or turn in events which reverses the situation that was initially presented" [*The American 1890s* (1968)]. He cites the conclusion of **"Désirée's Baby"** as an example: "So, characteristically, does the Chopin story depend on a twist." Taking a similar view, Per Seyersted remarks the "taut compression and restrained intensity" of the tale and then notes (with some asperity) that "the surprise ending, though somewhat contrived, has a bitter, piercing quality that could not have been surpassed by [Maupassant] himself" [*Kate Chopin: A Critical Biography* (1969)]. Yet, in the final analysis, these judgments are no more satisfactory than those that grow from the more narrow definition of Chopin as "local colorist": if significant effects are seldom achieved merely through a deft management of dialect and scenery, it is also the case that a "trick" or "surprise" conclusion is almost never a sufficient means by which to evoke a powerful and poignant reaction from the reader.

Thus **"Désirée's Baby"** remains an enigma. We still tend to admire it and to demonstrate our admiration by selecting it to appear in anthologies; yet the admiration is given somewhat grudgingly—perhaps because we cannot fully comprehend the story. The specifically Southern elements of the story seem significant; however, the nature of their force is not clear. The reversal of the situation that concludes the tale is important (although to a discerning reader it may well be no surprise), but, contrary to Seyersted's remarks, the story's full impact patently does not derive from this writer's "trick." And while the story has been accepted as characteristic of Chopin's work, it is in several ways unusual or unique—being the only one of her fictions to touch upon the subject of miscegenation, for example. We might respond to this accumulation of contradictions by assuming that a mistake has been made somewhere along the line—that the tale has been misinterpreted or that it is not really representative of Chopin's fiction. Yet such an assumption would not explain the force of those many years of readers' response; in the end, it would not resolve the persistent enigma of **"Désirée's Baby."** Alternatively, we might try to understand why critics' judgments of the story have been so different, presuming such judgments to be insufficient but not, perhaps, fundamentally incorrect. But more importantly, we must expand our vision of the story in order to see precisely those ways in which it articulates and develops themes that are central to other of Chopin's works.

A majority of Chopin's fictions are set in worlds where stability or permanence is a precarious state: change is always threatened—by the vagaries of impassive fate, by the assaults of potentially ungovernable individual passions, or merely by the inexorable passage of time. More generally, we might say that Chopin construes existence as necessarily uncertain. By definition, then, to live is to be vulnerable; and the artist who would capture the essence of life will turn his attention to those intimate and timeless moments when the comforting illusion of certainty is unbalanced by those forces that may disrupt and destroy. Insofar as Chopin can be said to emulate Maupassant, who stands virtually alone as her avowed literary model, we might say that she strives to look "out upon life through [her] own being and with [her] own eyes"; that she desires no more than to tell us what she sees "in a direct and simple way." Nor is Chopin's vision dissimilar to Maupassant's, for what she sees is the ominous and insistent presence of the margin: the inescapable fact that even our most vital moments must be experienced on the boundary—always threatening to slip away from us into something else, into some dark, undefined contingency. The careful exploration of this bourne is, in some sense, then, the true subject for much of her best fiction.

Certainly it is the core subject of **"Désirée's Baby"**—a story that treats layers of ambiguity and uncertainty with ruthless economy. Indeed, the tale is almost a paradigmatic study of the demarcating limits of human experience, and—since this subject is so typically the center of Chopin's attention—our continuing intuition that this story is a quite appropriate selection to stand as "representative" of her work must be seen as fundamentally correct. What is more, if we understand the true focus of this fiction, we are also in a position to comprehend the success of its conclusion. The "twist" is no mere writer's trick; rather, it is the natural consequence—one might say the necessary and inevitable concomitant—of life as Chopin construes it.

At the most superficial level in **"Désirée's Baby,"** there are distinctions that attend coloration, differences of pigment that carry definitions of social caste and even more damning implications about the "value" of one's "identity." The problem of race is managed quite idiosyncratically in this tale: we have already noted that this is the only one of Chopin's many stories to treat miscegenation directly or explicitly; however, we can be ever more emphatic—this is the only story even to probe the implications of those many hues of skin that were deemed to comprise the "negro" population. Yet from the very beginning Chopin focuses our attention upon this element with inescapable determination: she chooses not to use dialect conversation; she reduces the description of architecture and vegetation to a minimum—leaving only the thematically necessary elements. The result is a tale where the differences between "black" and "white" remain as the only way to locate the events—its only "regional" aspects, if you will—and we cannot avoid attending to them.

Yet for all this artistic direction, Chopin is clearly not primarily interested in dissecting the *social problem* of slavery (as Cable might be); rather, she limits herself almost entirely to the personal and the interior. Thus the dilemma of "color" must ultimately be construed emblematically, with the ironic and unstated fact that human situations can *never* be as clear as "black and white."

In the antebellum South, much private security depended upon the public illusion that whites lived within a safe compound, that a barrier of insurmountable proportions separated them from the unknown horrors of some lesser existence, and that these territorial boundaries were clear and inviolable. The truth, of course, was that this was an uncertain margin, susceptible to a multitude of infractions and destined to prove unstable. At its very beginning, the story reminds us of inevitable change ahead: Désirée is presumed to have been left "by a party of Texans"—pioneers en route to the territory whose slave policies were so bitterly contested when it was annexed that they proved to be a significant precursor to the Civil War that followed. Chopin's touch is light: the implications of this detail may be lost to a modern audience, but they would have loomed mockingly to a reader in 1892, especially a Southern reader.

Even within the supposedly segregated social system there is abundant evidence of violation. " 'And the way he cried'," Désirée remarks proudly of her lusty child; " 'Armand heard him the other day as far away as La Blanche's cabin'." What color is La Blanche, we might wonder, and what was Armand's errand in her cabin? "One of La Blanche's little quadroon boys . . . stood fanning the child slowly," and he becomes a kind of nightmare double (perhaps a half-brother, in fact) for Désirée's baby—a visual clue to the secret of this infant's mixed blood; eventually, his presence provokes the shock of recognition for Désirée. "She looked from her child to the boy who stood beside him, and back again; over and over. 'Ah!' It was a cry that she could not help; which she was not conscious of having uttered." None of the "blacks" is referred to as actually dark-skinned; even the baby's caretaker is a "yellow nurse."

In the end, only Armand's skin is genuinely colored—a "dark, handsome face" momentarily brightened, it would seem, by the happiness of marriage. And if this description gives a literal clue to the denouement of the story's mystery, it is even more effective as an index to character. Armand has crossed that shadowy, demonic boundary between mercy and kindness on the one hand and cruelty on the other. His posture towards the slaves in his possession has always been questionable—his "rule was a strict one . . . and under it his negroes had forgotten how to be gay, as they had been during the old master's easygoing and indulgent lifetime." Little wonder, then, that when his wife's child displeases him, "the very spirit of Satan seemed suddenly to take hold of him." His inhumanity towards Désirée and the servants alike bespeaks an irreversible journey into some benighted region; and the bonfire, by whose light he reads that last, fateful letter, is no more than a visible sign of the triumph of those powers of darkness in his soul. Thus when Désirée exclaims wonderingly, " 'my skin is fair. . . . Look at my hand; whiter than yours, Armand'," her comment *may* be relevant to the parentage of each; however, within the context of the story, it figures more reliably as a guide to the boundaries of humane behavior.

Underlying this insistent preoccupation with the literal question of color, then, is Chopin's ironic perception of the tenuous quality of such distinctions: it is simplistic to call "quadroons" and "yellows" "blacks" and "negroes." And if we move from this overt level into the labyrinth of the human soul, we will discover a man who has become lost in the wilderness of his own "blackest" impulses—a master who reverts to tyranny and is possessed by Satan, by the only absolute darkness in the tale. The lesser existence into which Armand sinks stems not from his Negroid parentage, but from a potential for personal evil that he shares with all fellow creatures (as the leit motif imagery of salvation and damnation suggests). Thus the horror that underlies Chopin's tale—and the ultimate mystery of "black and white" as she defines it—is not *really* limited to the social arrangements of the Southern slave system at all.

A world of evil is one sort of wilderness that lies along the margins of our most mundane activities, but it is not the only horror that lies in wait. Our moments of most joyful passion, too, threaten us with a form of annihilation: to be open to love is to be vulnerable to invasions that we can neither foresee nor fully protect ourselves against. Thus Chopin's rendering of the love between Désirée and Armand is an insistent compression of opposites. Armand is supposed to have fallen in love at first sight: "That was the way all the Aubignys fell in love, as if struck by a pistol shot. . . . The passion that awoke in him that day, when he saw her at the gate, swept along like an avalanche, or like a prairie fire, or like anything that drives headlong over all obstacles." The difference in Armand's life between love and some other force—something equally turbulent but more reckless and cruel—is no more than a hair's breadth or the fluttering of an eye. Linguistically, the two forces cannot be separated at all.

In Désirée's case, the peril of emotional entanglement has different origins; yet if anything, it is even more dangerous. She has been God's gift to her adoptive parents, the child of love as her name implies, helpless and delicate and unable to comprehend anything but love in its purest manifestations, "beautiful and gentle, affectionate and sincere,—the idol of Valmondé." Of the other side of love—of violence and baser passions—she is entirely innocent. In fact, innocence is her most marked characteristic, a kind of childlike, helpless ignorance. "It made [Madame Valmondé] laugh to think of Désirée with a baby. Why, it seemed but yesterday that Désirée was little more than a baby herself." Repeatedly, Chopin displays her infantine charm: Désirée couched with her baby, for example, "in her soft white muslins and laces," looking like nothing so much as a child herself. The vulnerability of such innocence is captured in her naive questions, in her trusting tendency to turn to her husband who has rejected her, even in the fragility of her garments that were surely intended only for one whose life might be protected from harsh contingencies. When Désirée married, she came to live at her husband's plantation, L'Abri (The Shelter); and such a home seems right, even necessary, for this delicate creature, even though the physical realities of the estate belie its name. "The roof came down steep and black like a cowl, reaching out beyond the wide galleries that encircled the yellow stuccoed house. Big, solemn oaks grew close to it, and thick-leaved, far-reaching branches shadowed it like a pall." However, Désirée must accept this refuge at mere face value: she cannot bring herself to see the ominous possibilities in those ancestral trees that portend both life and death.

In the end, Désirée cannot withstand the shock of being forced to acknowledge the contingencies whose existence she has ignored for so long. When Armand's love slips into cruelty, when L'Abri echoes with sibilant mockery, Désirée loses her own tenuous grasp on the balance of life. For her there seems only one choice, one final boundary to cross; and the alternatives are measured by the line between civilization and the patient, hungry bayou that lies just beyond. Madness, murder, death—all these wait to claim the love-child who could not keep her stability in the face of life's inescapable contrarieties.

> She took the little one from the nurse's arms with no word of explanation, and descending the steps, walked away, under the live-oak branches. . . . Désirée had not changed the thin white garments nor the slippers which she wore. . . . She walked across a deserted field, where the stubble bruised her tender feet, so delicately shod, and tore her thin gown to shreds. She disappeared among the reeds and willows that grew thick along the banks of the deep, sluggish bayou; and she did not come back again.

Much of the effect of this tale derives from the understatement that Chopin employs to render Désirée's annihilation and Armand's inescapable, internal hell. Even more, perhaps, the effect comes from the economy with which she captures the precariousness of the human condition—the persistent shadow-line that threads its way through all of the significant transactions of our lives. This is, perhaps, the most consistent theme in all of Chopin's fictions. We can see it in her choice of subject—preoccupation with marriage that may be either destructive or replenishing, the relationship between mother and child that is both hindering of personal fulfillment and necessary for full womanly development, and the convulsive effects of emergent sexuality. We can see it even more subtlely (but more insistently) in her imagistic patterns. (pp. 124-31)

The vision in all of Chopin's best fiction is consummately interior, and it draws for strength upon her willingness to confront the bleak fact of life's tenuous stabilities. Read quite independently, **"Désirée's Baby"** may be judged a superb piece of short fiction—an economical, tight psychological drama. However, seen in the more ample context of Chopin's complete work, the story accrues added significance as the most vivid and direct statement of her major concern—the fiction of limits. (p. 133)

Cynthia Griffin Wolff, "Kate Chopin and the Fiction of Limits: 'Désirée's Baby'," in The Southern Literary Journal, *Vol. X, No. 2, Spring, 1978, pp. 123-33.*

Judie Newman (essay date 1985)

[*In the following excerpt from* The Nineteenth-Century American Short Story, *Newman uses Chopin's story "Charlie" to examine how theme and technique interact in her fiction.*]

The emergence of the short story as a form in nineteenth-century America is perhaps not altogether surprising. It has been noted, especially by Frank O'Connor, that the short story flourishes in 'marginal' cultures and areas and that it deals very often with submerged population groups and with figures who find themselves situated within 'frontier' or 'outsider' conditions. . . . [O'Connor's case is] supported by the dominance, in nineteenth-century American short fiction, of 'local colour' writing. Local colour, while catering to an emergent sense of nationhood after the Civil War, which stimulated interest in the far-flung corners of the Union, tended to treat isolated communities, separated from their readers by creed, origins or language, groups which were marginalized by geography and the dominant culture.

One such submerged or 'outsider' group, especially in the nineteenth century, was that of women, who, if they wrote at all, tended to operate in the local colour field. Yet who now reads 'regional', local colour story-telling like Grace King's *Balcony Stories* (1893), or Ruth McEnery Stuart's *A Golden Wedding and Other Tales* (1893), both set in Louisiana? Or Tennessee local colour fiction like that of Mary Noailles Murfree, especially *In The Tennessee Mountains* (1884)? Even the fine New England stories of Sarah Orne Jewett—work like *A White Heron* (1886), *The King of Folly Island* (1888), *A Native of Winby* (1893), *The Life of Nancy* (1895) and above all *The Country of the Pointed Firs* (1896)—receive insufficient critical attention.

An exception to this critical neglect has been Kate Chopin (1851-1904), whose career among other things illustrates the changes in critical fashion from the 1890s to the present. In the '90s Chopin enjoyed success essentially as a local colourist, despite her abhorrence of the term, publishing two collections, ***Bayou Folk*** (1894) and ***A Night in Acadie*** (1897), which take for their subject-matter the life of the Acadians in Louisiana. With the appearance, however, of her novel *The Awakening* (1899), a frank account of a woman's sexual and spiritual awakening, adultery and suicide, late nineteenth- and early twentieth-century interest in her took a different direction. Guardians of taste proclaimed themselves at once shocked and deeply offended, especially at such explicitness in a woman. The novel was publicly condemned and duly banned from libraries, and Chopin erased from the literary scene. In 1923, the critic Fred Pattee praised Chopin but he, too, saw her erasure as final: 'She must be rated as a genius, taut, vibrant, intense of soul, yet a genius in eclipse, one, it is to be feared, that is destined to be total' [*The Development of the American Short Story*; see excerpt dated 1923]. Only one story continued to attract attention, **"Désirée's Baby"**, usually anthologized for its treatment of miscegenation. Chopin's re-emergence was to be based essentially upon her novel; Edmund Wilson devoted a chapter of *Patriotic Gore* (1962) [see Further Reading] to Chopin, and in 1969 Per Seyersted produced both a major critical biography [see excerpt dated 1969] and the standard edition of Chopin's complete works. This renewed attention was largely the result of the interest in Chopin's sexual frankness and different depictions of women. As Kenneth Eble has commented, on *The Awakening:* 'Quite frankly, the book is about sex. Not only is it about sex, but the very texture of the writing is sensuous, if not sensual, from the first to the last' [*Western Humanities Review,* (Summer 1956)]. But with the increasing sophistication of feminist criticism the interest in sex has broadened to an interest in gender, with spirited discussions of Chopin's attitudes to motherhood, marriage and male possession. (pp. 150-52)

The direction and measure of Chopin's own feminism have been hotly debated. Historical fact indicates that Chopin took no part in emancipatory movements, that she was happily married and devoted to her six children. The evidence of her stories is various. While **"The Storm"** suggests that adultery is good for you, or while **"The Story of an Hour"** portrays a wife who dies of grief when her husband is NOT killed in a railroad accident, or while in her first published story, **"Wiser than a God"**, the heroine chooses a career instead of a husband, other tales are less readily to be construed in 'propagandist' terms. Athénaïse, in the story of that title, vigorously condemns the institution of marriage: 'It's jus' being married that I detes' an' despise. I hate being Mrs. Cazeau, an' would want to be Athénaïse Miché again.' Yet when Athénaïse discovers her pregnancy all is forgiven in an orgy of baby-clothes buying and a return to her husband's arms, ending quite literally in an erotic clinch. **"Regret"** takes as its theme the regret of a betrousered old maid for the children she has never had. Many stories end conventionally in matrimony (**"Miss Witherwell's Mistake"**, **"Aunt Lympy's Interference"**, **"A Family Affair"**).

Where the heroine is initially portrayed as suffering within the institution of marriage she frequently reaffirms its value after a brief excursus (for example in **"A Visit to Avoyelles"**, **"Madame Célestin's Divorce"**, **"A Lady of Bayou St. John"**). To some extent this conventionality may be explained by cultural gate-keeping on the part of male editors and publishers. Certainly more explicit stories tended to be rejected: **"The Storm"**, for instance, remained unpublished until 1969. But Chopin's own distaste for idealized or cut-and-dried solutions and her attraction to transient states and the contingent individual, makes her position difficult to define. Without an awareness of the subtleties of Chopin's craft, the issue of her feminism is unlikely to be either fully understood or resolved. While the direction of interest in her fiction has shifted of late, from exotic 'Cajun' customs, to race, sex and gender, much criticism nonetheless remains thematic. As Patricia Hopkins Lattin aptly remarks: 'Kate Chopin criticism has been slow to mature from discussions of the author's unusual, sometimes revolutionary themes to analysis of the craft behind these themes' [*Mississippi Quarterly* 33, (1980); see Further Reading list].

It is the function of the present essay to examine how theme and technique interact in Chopin's stories, using as a departure-point **"Charlie"**, a miniature *Bildungsroman* which foregrounds the issue of a woman's place in society as it charts the development of Charlotte Laborde from adolescence to womanhood. Ostensibly the story records the taming of an independent spirit, Charlotte's feminization and acculturation to patriarchal norms. Charlie enters the story rebelliously, bounding off her horse and into the schoolroom, a sweating, grubby figure in 'trouserlets' and the strongest possible contrast to her six demure sisters. Her name and apparel are masculinized, her father sees her as 'that ideal son he had always hoped for' and the local people remember her as the heroine who saved the levee in her father's absence. Charlie has a pistol and is a good shot, but when she inadvertently wounds Firman Walton, a visiting stranger, in the arm she is disgraced. Sent to school in New Orleans to be 'sivilized', Charlie enthusiastically takes to fashion and accomplishments, a process assisted by her infatuation with Walton. When her father in his turn loses an arm in an accident, and Walton marries her sister, Julia, Charlie takes over the running of the plantation as her father's helpmeet, and accepts an eventual marriage to the inarticulate Mr. Gus. On a psychological level her development thus appears to be recessive. Charlie is also a writer, though from the examples given her poetry does not promise over much. She has used her gift to prevent her father's remarriage, by means of a 'touching petition', and she ends up as her father's scribe, writing letters at his dictation. Indeed, the Oedipal/Electral content of the story seems wincingly apparent in the excursions Charlie makes with Mr. Laborde, especially the emphasis on his youth and good looks, and on the heroine's final assumpion of the maternal rôle as mistress of the plantation and surrogate mother to the twins. Chopin's fiction thus appears to be coercive, supporting rather than subverting the norms of her society.

Yet such a bare outline belies the psychology behind the tale which is carefully structured to subvert the rôles constructed by and for the heroine, and to argue that Charlie finally transcends the script offered by her culture. Chopin establishes the subversive meaning of the story by drawing on a complex of images associated with the hand. Two incidents set the plot in motion, each involving the wounded arm of a male figure, while Charlie's development involves her written hand, hands given in marriage, her father's 'hands' (employees) and such apparently minor props as hand-cream, handkerchiefs, gloves and rings. In the first movement of the story Charlie is established as inhabiting a narcissistic fantasy world. Taking refuge with the Bichou family, Charlie regales them with news and stories 'colored by her own lively imagination', informing Xenophore that she is going to the woods to write poetry, slay panthers and shoot tigers and bears. She sees herself as protected by her diamond ring: 'all I have to do is to turn the ring three times, repeat a Latin verse, and presto! I disappear like smoke'. Significantly, from a psychological point of view, the ring is her mother's engagement ring, which Charlie has invested with magical protective powers. Once in the wood, which is really only a 'shady grove', Charlie tears up her writing-pad for target practice and in her shooting wounds Firman Walton. As a result she is doubly disarmed. Her father makes her 'stand and deliver her firearm' and in an effort to attract Walton she abandons her male dress.

The episode suggests that Charlie is more a Tom Sawyer than a Huck Finn, and that the masculinized 'derring-do' rôle which she has assumed is counter-productive. Importantly her play-acting injures both men and women. Her father suffers from wounded feelings and Walton is actually hurt. In addition two women suffer at Charlie's hands, a mother and a bride. Expelled from the schoolroom Charlie procures writing materials to offer a highly coloured account of the 'adventures' which occasioned her delay. In fact she has been supervising the delivery of a new bicycle. Chopin hints mysteriously here at a preceding accident. Charlie has earlier given her old bicycle to Ruben's bride, who has not been seen in public since its presentation. Charlie warns Zenophore darkly not to tamper with the bicycle: 'I reckon you heard about Ruben's bride'. Charlie's unwillingness to specify what did happen hints at an indelicate accident. When her efforts at writing prose fail to win Charlie's readmittance to the female group in the schoolroom, she turns to poetry with no better results. Interrupted by Aunt Maryllis scolding her son, Charlie launches a missile at her with the words: 'If there are going to be any bones broken around here, I'll take a hand in it'. (pp. 152-55)

Chopin ironizes Charlie's writing succinctly here. The would-be poet is particularly irritated at the interruption 'as she was vainly striving after a suitable rhyme for "persecution" '. Charlie's self-absorbed writing, as the earlier petition to her father implies, is coercive, potentially dangerous and a threat to sexual development, whether her own or others'. Far from applauding Charlie as an independent creator, Chopin underlines the fact that the products of her creative imagination are linked to a narcissistic desire to maintain the emotional status quo. As the engagement ring suggests, Charlie would like to remain at the Oedipal stage, an ideal son and a loving daughter. Her fantasies injure maternal and paternal figures, the lover and the bride. Writing will not gain her access to the female world, and is a weapon turned as much against herself as against men.

Banished to New Orleans, however, Charlie acts from a different prepared script, much enjoying a fortnight with her Aunt Clementine who 'provided entertainment such as Charlie had not yet encountered outside of novels of high life'. Plunging into the rôle of society lady, Charlie takes to the delights of jewellery and dress. Her attitude to the engagement ring changes: 'Hitherto she had worn it for the tender associations which made her love the bauble. Now she began to look upon it as an adornment'. Charlie applies cream to whiten her hands, sleeping at night in a pair of her father's old gloves. Ostensibly Charlie has merely exchanged the rôle of ideal son for that of ideal daughter. When her father consigns her to the seminary he 'kissed her fervently'. When he visits her he comes alone, and carries her off with him for a day at the lake.

> He did not tell her how hungry he was for her,
> but he showed it in a hundred ways. He was like
> a schoolboy on holiday; it was like a conspiracy;
> there was a flavor of secrecy about it too.

Despite the erotic language, however, the fixation is on the father's not the daughter's side. Mr. Laborde's misreading of the situation is indicated by reference to Charlie's hands. When Walton is about to impose his company on the pair, Laborde assumes that Charlie does not like him because 'She gave her whole attention to her gloves'. When Charlie draws off a glove and offers a hand for her father's inspection, his eyes are drawn only to the ring: 'No stones missing, are there?' Charlie's interest, however, has transferred itself to Walton. She asks her father to admire the whiteness of the hand: 'do you think it's as white as—Julia's, for instance?' Julia, Charlie's rival, is noted for her hands which are described in the opening of the tale as 'as white as lilies'. Mr. Laborde is blind to these implications: 'He held the hand fondly in both of his, but she withdrew it, holding it at arm's length'.

Just in case the reader were in any doubt as to Charlie's major focus of erotic interest, the scene is preceded by a description of Charlie writing lines of poetry, inspired by Walton, which she secretes in a locket. Chopin's description implies the limitations Charlie must now assume: 'Charlie wrote some lines of poetry in the smallest possible cramped hand'. In bedecking herself for Walton Charlie has written herself into a rôle which is as cramping as the preceding one. (pp. 155-57)

Ironically the sickly idyll in New Orleans is abruptly terminated by an accident at the sugar mill on the plantation. Chopin's indirection here again serves a subtle purpose. The reader is encouraged to see Charlie as returning to her father's arms. Charlie, fearing her father's death, dwells upon the fact that he will not be there at the station 'with outstretched arms', that he will never again be as he was at the lake 'clasping her with loving arms'. Events prove the premonition all too true. Mr. Laborde has actually lost his right arm, though the reader gleans this information only near the close of the story when he embraces Charlie with 'the arm that was left to him'. Instead of her father's embrace, Charlie is met by Gus who 'took her hand'. The text emphasizes in its imagery that Charlie does not simply return to her father as a socialized young lady. On her return the house is pervaded by 'a sweet, sickening odor . . . more penetrating than the scent of the rain-washed flowers', but this is the odour of anaesthetic, administered while the mangled arm is being amputated, a scent which undermines the associations of sweetness with young girls in flower. When Aunt Clementine outlines her plans to take the girls out into the world, she employs the conventional image: 'She had plans for separating these blossoms so that they might disseminate their sweetness'. Charlie, however, interrupts her aunt, rejecting her plans, and with them the image of woman as sweetness and light.

Nor is this decision merely governed by the desire to remain with her father. After the announcement of Julia's engagement, Charlie's speech to her father looks like a return to an earlier self: 'from now on I'm going to be—to be your right hand—your poor right hand'. But several points suggest that Charlie has now evolved a more mature relation to her father, and that her return marks an expansion of possibilities for her, rather than a limiting rôle. Firstly, Charlie burns the cramped lines of poetry. Secondly, she removes the ring and sends it to Julia, an action which indicates that she is now free from the desire to replace her mother. Thirdly, the reader's attention is drawn to the discrepancy between Charlie's real feelings and her family's image of them. Both her sisters and the servants misread Charlie's fury at the engagement as the result of a dislike for Walton. Irene says that 'She can't bear him'. Blossom reiterates that 'Miss Charlie f 'or hate dat man like pizen'. Earlier in the story Irene had watched Gus and Charlie in conversation and had assumed that she was rejecting a proposal of marriage. (In fact the two parties were discussing a remedy for horse-gall.) Now, however, Charlie no longer inhabits the fictions of others. Her acceptance of Gus marks her entry into a world distinct from her own and others' fantasies. Significantly Gus, an active practical man, is described as having no connection with the 'fevered' modern day. Unlike Walton, who is seen in a fever, he will not treat Charlie like a hothouse flower. . . . Far from retreating into the embrace of a patriarchal culture, Charlie has avoided the worst extremes of young ladyhood or of unproductive rebellion. At the close she has integrated the rôles of active male and mature woman, taking power into her own hands. The story takes the reader through three alternatives—the aggressive female-as-male, the milk and water miss who conforms, the Oedipal fantasy—to a more workable position. At the end of the story Charlie's femininity is emphasized: 'Now, with all the dignity and grace which the term implied, she was mistress of Les Palmiers'. But Charlie's accommodation to the rôle is an active one. The fantasies to which she contributed and which others orchestrated around her have been transcended.

"Charlie" offers a useful instance of Chopin's strengths and preoccupations, especially the contrast between a fantasy world of romance and the world of reality which recurs as a key focus. Chopin repeatedly places romantic dreams of escape in an ironic context, and turns 'convention' against itself. In **"Athénaïse",** the heroine's husband may have yielded to fiction when he envisages married life as 'w'at the story-books promise after the wedding'. But when Athénaïse rebels, she merely takes on a different rôle in another man's scenario. Her brother, Montéclin, engineers her escape as if it were an elopement, complicating the arrangements unnecessarily to cater to his spirit of adventure. . . . Alone in New Orleans Athénaïse is seen looking at pictures in a magazine, her eyes drawn particularly to one which reminds her of Montéclin: 'It was one of Remington's Cowboys'. When she decides to return, it is Montéclin who comments that 'the affair had taken a very disappointing, an ordinary, a most commonplace turn, after all'. The reader is distanced from any similar judgement by the preceding irony at his expense. Heroines who appear to conform often, in fact, escape from the images prepared for them by others to generate their own scripts.

In **"Miss Witherwell's Mistake",** for instance, Francis Witherwell is parodied as a female littérateur who combines local colour stories with journalism of the household hints variety. When she is not penning treatises on "Security Against the Moth" or "The Wintering of Canaries" Miss Witherwell excels in tales of passion 'acted beneath those blue and southern skies traditionally supposed to foster the growth of soft desire'. Miss Witherwell's contributions are assured their place in the Boredomville *Battery* by her own financial backing and investment in the paper. When her niece, Mildred, is sent to visit her, to help her forget an unsuitable (because impoverished) lover, Miss Witherwell is somewhat taken aback, despite her tales of passion, since for her 'two such divergent cupids, as love in real life, and love in fiction, held themselves at widely distant points of view'. The lovers are reunited, however, by Miss Witherwell—firstly when she sends Mildred to correct the errors in her proofs, and secondly when Mildred fictionalizes their story to her aunt and asks for advice on an ending. She asks whether the lovers should marry. Miss Witherwell's response is telling: 'The poison of the realist school has certainly tainted and withered your fancy in the bud, my dear, if you hesitate a moment. Marry them, most certainly, or let them die'. The happy ending in life is therefore a result of the correction of errors in fiction, as Mildred uses the conventions against her aunt.

Another Mildred, in **"A Shameful Affair",** has gone to the country 'to follow exalted lines of thought', but when she finds that the farm does not conform to its image in 'humorous fiction', she becomes bored, throws her book aside, and walks by the river where she is promptly kissed by Fred Evelyn. When, however, Fred presents himself in the conventional rôle of 'the most consummate hound that walks the earth', Mildred does not act the part of outraged virtue, but admits her own desire for him, leaving the hero all ablush. In **"A Family Affair"** Bosé arrives with the full paraphernalia of the young lady, bustles about in housewifely fashion, acts the 'ministering angel' to her aunt and captures the heart of the young doctor. The rôle of housewife and nurse is only assumed, however. Bosé departs with her mother's share of the family inheritance, her aim from the start. In other stories fictional conventions and conventional fictions are similarly exploded. **"The Storm"** ends: 'So the storm passed and everyone was happy', offering a happy ending which runs counter to the reader's expectations of a tale of adultery. In **"Ma'ame Pélagie"** the dismantling of the plantation legend brings happiness to Pauline, while in **"The Story of an Hour"** the correction of an erroneous newspaper report has less fortunate consequences.

Other Chopin stories highlight the tragic implications of being bound to a fictionalized rôle or image. In **"La Belle Zoraïde"** the slave Zoraïde prefers, in her insanity, a pretend-child (a bundle of rags) to her real infant, whom her mistress has removed. Zoraïde's story is narrated to Madame Delisle, who completely ignores its tragic content, considering it simply as a comfortable fiction to lull her to sleep. The story foreshadows **"A Lady of Bayou St. John"** in which Madame Delisle figures as a wife whose remembrance of her husband, absent in the Civil War, has grown faint, and who is tempted to take a lover. When the husband dies, however, Madame Delisle erects a shrine to his memory, preferring, as Zoraïde does, a fictional image to reality. More shockingly, in **"Fedora"**, the heroine constructs a false self-image with disastrous consequences. Although Fedora is only 30, she cultivates a severe expression and affects superior years and wisdom. When she falls in love with Young Malthers she is unable to escape the fixed image, and instead implants a passionate kiss upon Malthers's sister, who is his image in features and expression. The Sapphic overtones to the tale are less important than its analysis of damaging narcissism.

Chopin's concern is not simply with what women do to themselves, but also with what society does to them. Several of her stories hinge upon the juxtaposition of opposed images of women. **"Two Portraits"** contrasts two women, each named Alberta, each described in an identical opening paragraph, one 'The Wanton', the other 'The Nun'. The story implies that the contrast between these two socially learned rôles is not so very great. The tale ends with the nun quivering and swooning in sensual ecstasy before the image of Christ. In **"Lilacs"** two rôles are internalized in one woman, Adrienne Farival, who returns each year at lilac time to her convent school to assume an innocence which, in reality, she has long left behind. Carefully costumed in drab brown, bearing gifts for the chapel, Adrienne paints herself as a respectable woman. Sister Agathe commends her to 'your household duties . . . and your music, to which, you say, you continue to devote yourself'. In fact Adrienne is a Parisian chanteuse and dancer, of suspect virtue. (The reader notes the swift replacement of a Monsieur Henri by Monsieur Paul.) When Adrienne returns a year later to the convent she is denied admission, her gifts are returned and the actress confronts a hostile house: 'she saw only the polished windows looking down at her like so many cold and glittering and reproachful eyes'. The irony of the story is primarily directed at the harsh behaviour of the Mother Superior, who is herself not free from Adrienne's evident weakness for the male. Adrienne notes that the nun has replaced the image of Saint Catherine with the Sacré Coeur, embellished the

Kate and Oscar Chopin at the time of their wedding in 1870. Chopin wrote in her diary: "In two weeks I am going to be married, married to the right man. It does not seem as strange as I thought it would—I feel perfectly calm, perfectly collected."

statue of Saint Joseph, but allowed that of the Virgin to grow shabby. Though Chopin is arguing for an integration of rôles in Adrienne, her most biting censure is reserved for a woman like the Mother Superior who bolsters the social standard by excluding what Adrienne herself has become.

While contemporary readers must beware of imposing an anachronistic feminist image on Kate Chopin, it is nonetheless clear that her stories go beyond the conventions of both the fiction and the society of her day. Chopin's analysis of the way in which women perceive themselves, or allow others to perceive them, is subtle and wide-ranging in its implications. Her touch is light, unprescriptive and often humorous. The 'techniques' of her stories serve—subvertingly and with striking artfulness—to render the whole complex problematic of fitting self to image. While she is no polemicist, her stories suggest that women are amply capable of enlarging the rôles available to them, and that active accommodation transcends empty conformity or withdrawal into one or another pre-ordained fantasy. (pp. 157-62)

Judie Newman, "Kate Chopin: Short Fiction and the Arts of Subversion," in The Nineteenth-Century American Short Story, *edited by A. Robert Lee, London: Vision Press, 1986, pp. 150-63.*

Peggy Skaggs (essay date 1985)

[*In the following excerpt from her critical study* Kate Chopin, *Skaggs reviews the principal characteristics of Chopin's short fiction.*]

The critical praise Chopin received during her lifetime resulted largely from her short stories, most of which belong to the local-color tradition. ***Bayou Folk*** (1894), her first collection of short stories, contains twenty-three such tales, all but four having been published previously in popular journals. The stories are set in Louisiana, most of them in Natchitoches Parish, and since many of the characters appear in more than one tale, a loose unity develops. Most of the stories, somewhat superficial and sentimental, reveal their origin as popular magazine fiction. Yet even in these early stories Chopin's characters are struggling to find a place of their own in their communities; some are trying to cope with their need for love; and a few are already reaching timidly for autonomy, thus foreshadowing later strong characters, including Edna in *The Awakening.*

The ***Bayou Folk*** stories fall loosely into five groups: those that feature self-reliant young girls as protagonists; those that study the lingering dislocations caused by the Civil War; those that center upon emancipated black people who in seeking a place in society deny even their freedom; those that examine love between the sexes; and those that hint at the theme of male possessiveness. To some extent these concerns overlap, several stories treating more than one. And many of the stories address, at least obliquely, Lear's question—the question that lies at the heart of most of Chopin's later, more important fiction and that finally comes into clear focus in *The Awakening*—"Who am I?"

Several of the stories portray exceptionally self-reliant young girls. In **"A Rude Awakening,"** for example, Lolotte, barely seventeen years old, tries valiantly to care for three younger brothers but in doing so loses her identity and almost loses her life. Trying to substitute for her lazy father, old Sylveste, Lolotte attempts to drive a team and wagon to the landing. The team runs away, wrecking the wagon and leaving no trace of the girl. Guilt-ridden, Sylveste abandons his careless ways and takes a job with Joe Duplan, a neighboring planter. Duplan finally finds Lolotte in a New Orleans hospital suffering from amnesia, a rather common disorder in Chopin's characters. Upon seeing the planter, the girl remembers who she is; and Duplan returns her to her father, admonishing him never to forget again "that you are a man!" Here the story ends, with Lolotte, the self-reliant child, now having a role in caring for her brothers that is more appropriate to her age and strength, because her father has "awakened" to his responsibilities.

Similarly, in **"A Gentleman of Bayou Têche"** Martinette's father, Evariste, depends upon his young daughter. The two Acadians, so impoverished that even the Negroes look down upon them, are overjoyed because a man wants to hire Evariste to pose for a painting. But when old Aunt Dicey jealously tells Martinette that "Dey gwine sot down on'neaf the picture: 'Dis heah is one dem low-down 'Cajuns o' Bayeh Têche!'," Martinette orders her father not to pose. So Evariste goes fishing instead, and thus happens to be at the bayou when the painter's son almost drowns. Of course, Evariste rescues the child, and the grateful father promises to label his picture "A hero of Bayou Têche." But Evariste does not consider himself a hero; finally, the painter tells Evariste to caption the picture himself, and the Acadian tells him to write "Dis is one picture of Mista Evariste Anatole Bonamour, a gent'man of de Bayou Têche," showing that he has a healthy sense of his own dignity as a human being.

Not very different from Lolotte and Martinette, though even younger, a little barefooted girl named Fifine in **"A Very Fine Fiddle"** sells her father's violin, getting for it "a fiddle twice as beautiful . . . and a roll of money besides . . . enough to put shoes on all the little bare feet and food into the hungry mouths." Equally pragmatic is Boulotte in **"Boulôt and Boulotte,"** who at the age of twelve gets her first pair of shoes but carries them home in her hand so she will not "ruin it in de dus'." **"A Turkey Hunt"** presents Artemise, a young black protagonist less easily understood than these Acadian girls. In fact, "Pages might be told of her unfathomable ways." But she has one outstanding characteristic, a placid self-containment that suggests she feels quite complete within herself. (pp. 12-13)

[These young girls] demonstrate such self-sufficiency that one can scarcely imagine their growing up to be the helpless, self-effacing mothers and wives that society would push them to become. Serious conflicts must develop inside a person who must respond to such grossly contradictory expectations.

The stories that examine the lingering effects of the Civil War center on the theme of dislocation. The title character in **"Old Aunt Peggy,"** for example, is a freed slave who, by her own choice, remains virtually unchanged by the war or emancipation, clinging to the place where she feels secure and giving up entirely any active role in life.

One of Chopin's several studies of mental disorder that resulted from the war, **"Beyond the Bayou"** features Jacqueline, who has refused to cross the bayou for thirty years because she had been frightened "out of her senses" when P'tit Maître came wounded to her cabin during the war. But thirty years later, when P'tit Maître's son Chéri is accidentally wounded near Jacqueline's cabin, love gives her the courage to cross the bayou for help. As a result, "a look of wonder and deep content crept into her face as she watched for the first time the sun rise upon the new, the beautiful world beyond the bayou." Love has great healing power in Chopin's fictive world.

Ma'ame Pélagie, in a story of the same name, "adjusts" to the dislocations of the war much as Old Aunt Peggy and Jacqueline do. A fifty-year-old spinster with an air of queenly authority, Ma'ame lives with her sister, Pauline, near Valmêt, the family's mansion that the war had destroyed. They manage the plantation prosperously, working hard and saving every cent they make toward Ma'ame's one goal in life, restoring Valmêt. Their happiest moments occur on pleasant afternoons when they drink their black coffee on the portico of the old ruin, "with only each other and the sheeny, prying lizards for company, talking of the old times and planning for the new." The "new" times they plan for, however, would be no newer than Aunt Peggy's.

Eventually the ladies' niece, La Petite, comes to live with them, bringing new life and love into their sterile world. But La Petite soon declares that she is going back to her father's home because living as her aunts do is for her "a sin against myself." Love for La Petite proves stronger even than Ma'ame's need to restore her former place in the world; and so, sacrificing all her dreams, she decides to eradicate the old ruin and build a modern, new home.

Within a year, the faces of the sisters reveal the results. The younger sister seems revitalized: her "cheek was as full and almost as flushed as La Petite's. The years were falling away from her." But the older sister shows a different effect: "In her deep, dark eyes smouldered the light of fires that would never flame. She had grown very old." Pauline, only five years old when the sisters had lost their way of life, needed only the opportunity to find a new place in the new world. But Ma'ame Pélagie, twenty when the holocaust came, had lost her home, her way of life, and also the man she loved. Such losses proved too great to overcome. (pp. 14-15)

[These characters], then, have much in common because the war thirty years before had dislocated each in some fundamental way, leaving her or him unable to find a secure, productive place in the new order.

Many of these ***Bayou Folk*** stories, set in the South approximately thirty years after the Emancipation Proclamation, feature black people coping in various ways with the special identity problems that accompanied their freedom. For example, as noted above, Old Aunt Peggy simply withdraws from the struggle and waits to die. Others, as will be noted later, find happier places in society to replace the one lost through freedom.

Two stories, however, portray blacks who cope only by trying to hang onto their old identity as slave members of white families. In **"For Marse Chouchoute"** a young black protagonist named Wash suffers fatal injuries while doing a job that Chouchoute, a young white boy, should be doing. As he dies, Wash cries out, "I boun' to git well, 'ca'se who—gwine—watch Marse—Chouchoute?"

In much the same way, **"The Bênitou's Slave"** also develops the theme that a person needs to feel that he or she belongs somewhere. Uncle Oswald, who had belonged to the Bênitou family fifty years before, spends his life trying to get back to his "own" family. At last an unlikely coincidence leads Uncle Oswald to meet the tiny remainder of his old family—a little milliner and her daughter. They agree to let Uncle Oswald stay with them, making him happy because now he feels that he belongs. He knows now who he is: "My name's, Oswal', Madam; Oswal'—dat's my name. I b'longs to de Bênitous."

Much as one may deplore the stereotyped "befo' de wa' " image of the black men in these two stories, their actions do represent one direction sometimes taken in the search for an identity to replace one lost through emancipation. Chopin understands a basic need of the emancipated black man and the "emancipated" woman: both need deeply to find a new place in society. Both have for centuries been encouraged by white men to "know their place" and to "stay in their place." And both have encountered difficulty in finding a new place after becoming free. So the stories of these two self-effacing Negro characters illuminate later female creations by Chopin, notably the similar character of Adéle Ratignolle in *The Awakening,* the most nearly perfect of the "mother-women . . . who idolized their children, worshiped their husbands, and esteemed it a holy privilege to efface themselves as individuals. . . . "

The remainder of the stories in ***Bayou Folk*** revolve around love between the sexes and the complex ways in which love affects one's feelings about oneself.

In **"Love on the Bon-Dieu"** Chopin again displays her interest in mental disorders. A young couple, Lalie and Azenor, become acquainted through a priest, Lalie's only contact with any person other than the mad grandmother with whom she lives. Lalie tries to explain her situation to Azenor: "Po' ole Grand'mère! . . . I don't b'lieve she know mos' time w'at she's doin'. Sometime she say' I ain't no betta an' one nigga, an' she fo'ce me to work. Then she say she know I 'm goin' be one canaille like maman, an' she make me set down still, like she would want to kill me." Yet despite her grandmother's irrational attacks on her sense of who she is, Lalie seems unusually self-confident, perhaps because her grandmother clearly needs her.

But when Lalie falls ill, Azenor decides that he must take her away. Although he has no idea of where to take her, he feels that "there must be one somewhere with the spirit of Christ" who will make a place for her. Lifting her in his arms, however,

> he saw that she held . . . the pretty Easter-egg he had given her! He uttered a low cry of exultation. . . .
>
> No need now to go . . . begging admittance for her. . . . He knew now where her place was.

So, Lalie and Azenor in finding each other discover both place and love.

In **"A No-Account Creole"** the protagonist, Euphrasie, almost waits too long before discovering her right place in life. Placide Santien, with a possessive attitude much like that of Léonce Pontellier in *The Awakening* and of numerous other Creole gentlemen in Chopin's fiction, has regarded Euphrasie as his own ever since she was placed in his arms on his sixth birthday. Years later, asking her to marry him, he demands to know: "Do you love anybody better? . . . Any one jus' as well as me?" She replies honestly, "You know I love papa better, Placide, an' Maman Duplan jus' as well." But knowing no reason to refuse to marry Placide, she accepts. Soon, however, Wallace Offdean arrives, and Euphrasie discovers within herself strange, new feelings—almost another person—as she becomes better acquainted with Offdean.

One night Placide kisses her passionately on the lips. Afterwards, "She . . . sobbed a little and prayed a little. She felt that she had sinned, . . . a fine nature warned her that it was in Placide's kiss." Placide, upon learning Euphrasie's feelings, frees her to marry Offdean, her true love.

Chopin comes close in this story to having her protagonist marry a man she does not love because of having committed herself before knowing her own heart. Later, in *The Awakening,* the writer will confront directly the problems involved in exactly such a marriage, that of Edna and Léonce Pontellier, whose marriage "was purely an accident." (pp. 16-18)

Even in these earliest stories, Chopin almost always creates with great economy a unified effect. But **"In and Out of Old Natchitoches"** begins developing in one direction and then does an abrupt about-face. The author apparently creates a dilemma for her characters that she is either unwilling to confront or unable to resolve in her own mind. The first part of this story places the central character, Mademoiselle Suzanne St. Denys Godolph, in conflict with Alphonse Laballière. Suzanne, a school teacher of proud Creole stock, refuses to accept as a pupil a mulatto child whom Alphonse, of equally aristocratic old South blood, tries to force into her school, either simply to prove that he can do so or, perhaps, to express his disgust that such a high-born lady would actually lower herself so far as to accept paid employment.

To resolve this dramatic situation, Chopin simply changes focal points in mid-story. Suzanne moves to New Orleans, where she falls a bit in love with a distant cousin, Hector Santien. Alphonse follows, uncovers the cousin's secret identity as a notorious gambler, and saves the girl in spite of herself.

After exposing the cousin's vice-filled life, Alphonse returns to Natchitoches on the same train with Suzanne: "He went to her . . . and held out his hand; she extended her own unhesitatingly. She could not understand why. . . . It seemed as though the sheer force of his will would carry him to the goal of his wishes." This scene echoes Euphrasie's earlier decision to marry Placide because "she saw no reason why she should not," and it foreshadows Edna's later decision to marry Léonce when he "pressed his suit."

A bit more daring, **"In Sabine"** focuses on 'Tite Reine, a miserable young wife whose husband mistreats her cruelly. Before her marriage, she had been a charming girl, with "her trim, rounded figure; her . . . saucy . . . coquettish eyes, her little . . . imperious ways . . . her . . . nickname of 'Tite Reine, little queen." But that picture contrasts sadly with the girl Grégoire Santien finds when he visits her in Sabine Parish only a year after her marriage: "her eyes were larger, with an alert, uneasy look in them. . . . her shoes were in shreds." Worse, her "little imperious ways" have changed into a habitual response to her husband's call: "I 'm comin', Bud. Yere I come. W'at you want, Bud?" Taking mercy on the poor girl, Grégoire plies Bud with whiskey so that 'Tite Reine may escape to the safety of her old home. Happy to see her escape, the reader does not wonder much about what sort of place she will find awaiting her as a "feme sole" back on Bayou Pierre.

"La Belle Zoraïde," a sad love story, centers upon a pampered slave girl, who certainly has a secure place but no love and no autonomy at all. Madame Delarivière has reared Zoraïde, the beautiful black protagonist, in her own image: "As charming and as dainty as the finest lady of la rue Royale," Zoraïde does no work that might roughen her hands. In fact, she has her own little black servant. Madame often tells Zoraïde about the wedding that will someday join her with M'sieur Ambroise, the body servant of Doctor Langlé. But Zoraïde finally tells Madame that she loves Mézor, a field hand. Madame exclaims, "That negro! that negro! . . . but this is too much!" Zoraïde, nevertheless, pleads with simple logic: "Am I white, nénaine? . . . Doctor Langlé gives me his slave to marry, but he would not give me his son. Then, since I am not white, let me have from out of my own race the one whom my heart has chosen."

Of course, Madame forbids Zoraïde and Mézor to marry, but she cannot prevent their loving, as the black woman narrating the story to her own white mistress points out. Zoraïde becomes pregnant and breaks the news to Madame, saying, "Kill me if you wish, nénaine: forgive me if you will; but when I heard le beau Mézor say to me, 'Zoraïde, mo l'aime toi,' I could have died, but I could not have helped loving him."

At this point, Madame induces Dr. Langlé to sell Mézor. Then when Zoraïde delivers her child, Madame takes the baby away and tells Zoraïde that it was stillborn. Having thus disposed of Zoraïde's lover and baby, Madame returns to her plan to marry the girl to Dr. Langlé's body servant, and the slave girl seems to submit "as though nothing mattered any longer in this world." But Zoraïde manages to elude her owner's plans again.

Shortly before the scheduled wedding, the young woman

begins carrying in her arms a "senseless bundle of rags shaped like an infant." All treatments, even returning to her arms her own child, prove useless, and the poor girl lives out her days imagining herself the mother of a pile of rags. "She was never known again as la belle Zoraïde, but ever after as Zoraïde la folle." **"La Belle Zoraïde"** thus illustrates one of Chopin's best themes: that tragedy results when a person is robbed of her right to be her own person and to love whom she will.

Madame Delisle, the title character of **"A Lady of Bayou St. John,"** like Zoraïde finds her identity in an imaginary role. Madame's husband, Gustave, goes away to the war, leaving a beautiful but childish wife behind. Sepincourt, a neighbor, and the lonely lady fall in love and decide to run away together. But that very night Madame learns that her husband has died. Sepincourt impatiently waits until he can without indecency again speak of his love; but when he does go to her, she greets him "precisely as she . . . welcomed the curé, . . . clasping his two hands warmly, and calling him *'cher ami.'* Her whole attitude . . . brought the bewildering conviction that he held no place in her thoughts." Nevertheless, he declares: "I have come now . . . to ask you to be my wife, my companion, the dear treasure of my life." But having discovered a new, satisfying role as a widow, a new place in life wherein she feels comfortable, she answers:

> "can you not understand, *mon ami,* . . . that now such a thing . . .is impossible to me?"
>
> "Impossible?"
>
> "Yes, impossible. Can you not see that now . . . my very life, must belong to another? . . . "
>
> "Would you . . . wed your young existence to the dead?" he exclaimed with . . . horror. . . .
>
> "My husband has never been so living to me as he is now," she replied.

The narrator emphasizes Madame's kinship with poor "Zoraïde la folle," as both women live out their lives wrapped in the mantle of an illusory identity: "Madame still lives on Bayou St. John. She is rather an old lady now. . . . The memory of Gustave still fills . . . her days." Surely, Madame is also "la folle."

"Madame Célestin's Divorce" suggests the mysterious power of love and the tenacity with which a woman may cling to a place where she feels she belongs. Madame—who, significantly, has no name except her husband's—attracts the love of another man, Lawyer Paxton, while her husband is on one of his prolonged absences. Paxton encourages her to divorce Célestin—who drinks, lies, leaves home periodically, and neglects his family in every way. If she divorces Célestin, she will encounter the disapproval of family, community, and church; but she is prepared to "face it and brave it." Lawyer Paxton plans to settle in a new location, where he and a new family can make a new start.

But one morning, looking "unusually rosy" and wearing a pink bow, Madame Célestin tells Paxton: "I reckon you betta neva mine about that divo'ce. . . . You see, Judge, Célestin came home las' night. An' he 's promise me on his word an' honor he's going to turn ova a new leaf." Thus, Madame's love for Célestin and perhaps her sense of belonging with him have preserved their marriage, such as it is, thereby accomplishing what the combined disapproval of family, community, and church could not. (pp. 18-21)

"At the 'Cadian Ball" and **"Désirée's Baby"** treat related ideas that become increasingly important in Chopin's later works. The theme of masculine pride in "owning" a beautiful wife from the highest social stratum possible—what Chopin later calls "the man-instinct of possession"—ties these two stories together and relates them to some of the writer's most mature works as well.

In at least two important ways **"At the 'Cadian Ball"** foreshadows later Chopin works. First, it lays the groundwork for its sequel, **"The Storm,"** an almost perfect short story written six years later and so startlingly frank that Chopin never even tried to have it published. And second, the story introduces Alcée Laballière, a man in many ways like Léonce Pontellier in *The Awakening.* The two men share the qualities of kindness and decency as well as a French Creole heritage, social prominence, wealth, and pride in their aristocratic backgrounds. But most important, each man believes that the woman he marries should be, like the largest and brightest jewel ornamenting a monarch's crown, his most prized possession. (p. 22)

"At the 'Cadian Ball" begins with a description of "big, brown, good-natured" Bobinôt, an Acadian farmer, who loves a Spanish girl named Calixta, described as he visualizes her: "Her eyes . . . the . . . most tantalizing that ever looked into a man's; . . . that broad, smiling mouth and tiptilted nose, that full figure; that voice like a rich contralto song . . . taught by Satan." Bobinôt thinks at first that he will not go to the ball, even though he knows that Calixta will be there, because "what came of those balls but heartache . . . ?" When he hears that the handsome, young planter Alcée Laballière may attend, however, Bobinôt changes his mind. A breath of scandal had stirred the year before when Calixta and Alcée were both at Assumption, but no one talks of it now. Still, Bobinôt thinks of Alcée: "A drink or two could put the devil in his head . . . ; a gleam from Calixta's eyes, a flash of her ankle, a twirl of her skirts could do the same." So Bobinôt decides to go to the ball after all.

Next the story introduces Alcée and Clarisse. Alcée, gambling heavily by having planted nine hundred acres of rice, will either make or lose a very great deal of money, and he works hard because of the high stakes and the dramatic challenge. Clarisse, his distant cousin and his mother's godchild, lives with the Laballière family. She is "dainty as a lily; . . . slim, tall, graceful. . . . Cold and kind and cruel by turn, and everything that was aggravating to Alcée." Clarisse's guests often fill the big plantation house. But Alcée "would have liked to sweep the place of those visitors, often. Of the men, above all, with . . . their swaying of fans like women, and dandling about hammocks. He could have pitched them over the levee into the river, if it had n't meant murder. That was Alcée." However, he treats Clarisse gently until one day when his passion overcomes him: "he came in from the rice-field, and, toil-stained as he was, clasped Clarisse by the arms and panted a volley of hot, blistering love-words into her face. No man had ever spoken love to her like that." Clarisse, the true blue blood, handles the situation with haughty ease: " 'Monsieur!' she exclaimed, looking him full in the eyes, without a quiver. Alcée's hands dropped and his glance wavered before the chill of her calm, clear eyes." But she continues: " *'Par exemple!'* she muttered disdainfully, as she turned from him, deftly adjusting the careful toilet that he had so brutally disarranged."

A day or two later a storm destroys the rice crop. Although he maintains an icy silence, Alcée looks ill and gray. "Clarisse's heart melted with tenderness; but when she offered her soft, purring words of condolence, he accepted them with mute indifference." One night soon, however, Clarisse happens to see Alcée ride away sometime around midnight. She forces from his servant the information that Alcée is going to the 'Cadian ball to have a "li'le fling" that will take his mind off his troubles. Clarisse reacts with contempt.

Both of the two couples—Bobinôt and Calixta, Alcée and Clarisse—seem to belong together. In each instance, the two share similar social statuses, financial resources, goals in life, ideals, value systems, life-styles.

But in another sense, Alcée and Calixta belong together too. The young planter really goes to the ball to rekindle the fire that he and Calixta had merely banked at Assumption the preceding year. And as soon as they see each other, the passion flames anew. They stroll into the garden and exchange teasing, bantering words. . . . At this point, a servant interrupts to give Alcée a message from "some one in de road" who wants to see him. The gentleman declares that he would not go out to the road "to see the Angel Gabriel" and threatens to break the black man's neck should another interruption occur.

But Clarisse herself interrupts Alcée and Calixta next, declaring that she "could n't stan' it" if Alcée does not come home and adding, "Not to frighten you. But you mus' come." Whereupon, "Alcée swung himself over the low rail and started to follow Clarisse . . . without a glance back at the girl. He had forgotten he was leaving her there." Calixta, left alone thus abruptly, lets Bobinôt walk her home and volunteers that if he still wants to marry her, "I don' care, me," thus making the young Acadian man indescribably happy. And at about the same time Clarisse is telling Alcée that she loves him, thus making the young Creole gentleman equally ecstatic.

The reader knows that both men have been treated only coldly by their chosen brides. Why, then, do Bobinôt and Alcée feel such joy to be marrying Calixta and Clarisse? Both couples, again, have much in common in terms of social status and life-styles. But these men do not wish to marry other women who share these elements with them, so why Calixta and Clarisse, who clearly feel no passion for their prospective husbands? Surely at least part of the answer must lie in the feeling of each that he has won a prized possession, one that any man in similar circumstances would be proud to "own." Bobinôt and Alcée demonstrate, too, that such possessiveness may motivate the humble as well as the aristocratic man. In a later story, **"Her Letters,"** a similar feeling, which Chopin then calls "the man-instinct of possession," drives a widowed husband to distraction and finally to suicide by drowning.

"Désirée's Baby," Chopin's most famous story, also pivots around male possessiveness and related matters of identity. First, the foundling Désirée appears at the Valmondés' plantation with no identity at all; but the family accepts her affectionately, and she finds there a secure place and abundant love. When she grows up, however, and becomes the object of Armand Aubigny's love, her foster father reminds the young man that the girl is "nameless." But Armand declares himself indifferent to that fact: "What did it matter about a name when he could give her one of the oldest and proudest in Louisiana?"

The question of identity arises again when Madame Valmondé looks at Désirée's month-old child and exclaims, "This is not the baby!" The older woman then asks Désirée what Armand thinks of the child, and the happy young mother glowingly replies, "Oh, Armand is the proudest father in the parish, I believe, chiefly because it is a boy, to bear his name."

The fact that the infant has Negro forebears gradually becomes apparent to everyone, last of course to Désirée. When she realizes the situation, Désirée demands of Armand, "look at our child. What does it mean? tell me." And he answers coldly, "It means . . . that the child is not white; it means that you are not white." And, if she "is not white," of course, Armand Aubigny's pride in having Désirée and their son to bear his name has turned to bitter ashes.

Désirée writes to Madame Valmondé, begging her, "For God's sake tell them it is not true. You must know it is not true." If her racial identity is reestablished, Désirée believes that she will be able to resume her former place in her husband's affections. The older woman, however, replies briefly: "My own Désirée: Come home to Valmondé; back to your mother who loves you. Come with your child." But when Armand tells her that he wants her to go, Désirée feels that the world really has no place for her and her baby. So she takes the infant and walks into the swamp, never to return.

Eventually Armand discovers that the black ancestry comes from himself and not from Désirée, thus concluding the story with an ironic reversal that demonstrates powerfully the irrationality of racism.

This reversal also points up an interesting fact about Chopin's view of the respective places of man and woman in the world. Désirée certainly understands that if she has an "untainted" bloodline, as she attempts to establish and as the physical evidence clearly suggests she does have, then Aubigny must necessarily have a "tainted" one. Yet, although functioning within the same bigoted tradition that causes Armand to send her coldly away to perish, Désirée wants only to regain her place as the beloved wife of this "tainted" man and the mother of his child of mixed blood.

Further, at no time does the truth occur to anyone except Désirée herself, again despite the clear physical evidence apparent to anyone who might really look at the two parents. Manifestly, in Chopin's view of life as revealed here Désirée, even leaving out of consideration her past status as a foundling, has far more to lose than Aubigny does, because her place and even her name depend upon a man's regarding her as a prized possession. Had the truth been known in time, Armand's pride would still have been wounded, but surely he would not have been destroyed, as Désirée and the baby are.

Chopin, then, seems already in this first collection of short stories, sentimental and superficial as many of them are, to be moving toward the study of women in search of themselves. Even though Désirée and several others do find a sufficient sense of identity in viewing themselves as prized possessions of the men to whom they belong, in a few of the stories in Chopin's next volume the inevitable dissatisfaction with such a place in life will begin to emerge. And in the third collection, ***A Vocation and a Voice,*** this dissatisfaction will become the dominant theme of the best stories.

But Chopin's interest, even in these earliest stories, extends well beyond the "woman-question" to encompass the entire, complex matter of human identity, memorably expressed by Shakespeare's Lear when he stands naked on the heath in the center of the tempest crying "Is man no more than this?" Whether describing self-reliant young girls, analyzing the lingering dislocations of the Civil War, portraying emancipated black people who deny their freedom, examining the effects of love upon individual human personalities, or exploring the phenomenon of masculine possessiveness, Chopin creates in the stories of ***Bayou Folk*** characters struggling to fulfill the needs for self-knowledge, for love, and especially for a place in life where they can feel they belong.

• • • • •

In her second volume of stories, ***A Night in Acadie,*** Chopin shifts emphases and concentrates particularly on love—all kinds of love: filial, fraternal, paternal, maternal, marital, sexual—although she continues to examine the various other facets of human identity as well.

Nine of the twenty-one stories center around children. Orrick Johns in a 1911 review of Chopin's ***Bayou Folk*** and ***A Night in Acadie*** says, "no such knowledge of children and no such love of them is to be found in other books." This evidence that Chopin knew and loved children should be considered when analyzing Edna's ambivalent attitude toward her young sons in *The Awakening.* The children in the ***Acadie*** stories affect the lives of adults in varied ways. They heal, pacify, enlighten, comfort, and love. Even when they act mischievously, good often results.

In **"After the Winter,"** for example, the interference of children brings M'sieur Michel, the protagonist, back into contact with humanity after twenty-five years of alienation. **"Ripe Figs"** reveals beautifully the differing perspectives on time of the child and the adult, expressing in one short page virtually the essence of the generation gap. And **"A Matter of Prejudice"** tells of a proud Creole woman who for ten years had refused to visit her son Henri because he is married to an "American" woman. Finally, a child's love heals this breach between the generations.

"Mamouche" carries the name of one of its central characters, a mischievous waif who turns up one rainy night at Doctor John-Luis's door and eventually brings to that bachelor physician the fulfillment he had not even known he lacked. Mamouche also figures in bringing fulfillment to two adults in **"The Lilies"** when he lets down the fences that separate the Widow Angèle's calf from Mr. Billy's crops. The crops suffer, but the story ends with a hint that marriage between the impoverished Widow and the wealthy but lonely Mr. Billy may follow.

"Odalie Misses Mass" tells of a little girl who stops by to "show herself" dressed up for mass on Assumption day to Aunt Pinky, her "old friend and protegée." Finding that the ill, old black woman has been left alone while everyone else has gone to church, Odalie stays with her. After mass Odalie's mother finds both the child and the old woman asleep; but Aunt Pinky never awakens. Odalie's childish conceit, her obvious delight in displaying her new outfit, and the love that makes her miss the big occasion after all rather than leave Aunt Pinky alone—these qualities illustrate what Johns means in saying that Chopin knew and loved children.

Two stories develop the idea that a woman needs to feel maternal love, even if she has never borne a child. In **"Polydore"** Mamzelle Adelaide—a kind, naive, middle-aged spinster—tries faithfully to fulfill her promise made years before to Polydore's dying mother to look after the boy. Now a stupid, lazy lad of fourteen, Polydore pretends one day to be ill, thus causing Mamzelle to go out into the heat and consequently to develop a severe fever. Polydore feels dreadfully guilty. At last he confesses to Mamzelle "in a way that bared his heart to her for the first time. . . . she felt as if a kind of miracle had happened. . . . She knew that a bond of love had been forged. . . . she drew him close to her and kissed him as mothers kiss." Thus through maternal love Mamzelle's good but heretofore emotionally impoverished life gains warmth and beauty.

"Regret" develops more fully this theme that to experience life richly a woman needs a child or children to love and care for. Although in the beginning Mamzelle Aurélie, the protagonist, feels perfectly satisfied, circumstances force her to recognize that her life lacks something.

Mamzelle, one of Chopin's most memorable women, "possessed a good strong figure, ruddy cheeks, . . . and a determined eye. She wore a man's hat . . . and an old blue army overcoat . . . and sometimes topboots." Far from regretting her spinster status, "Mamzelle Aurélie had never thought of marrying. . . . and at the age of fifty she had not yet lived to regret it." Neither does she think of herself as lonely, although "she was quite alone in the world, except for her dog Ponto, and the negroes . . . and the fowls, a few cows, a couple of mules, her gun . . . and her religion." But when her neighbor Odile must go away on an emergency, Mamzelle offers to care for Odile's children.

Mamzelle soon discovers that "children are not little pigs; they require . . . attentions which were wholly unexpected by Mamzelle Aurélie, and which she was ill prepared to give." In time she learns that "Marcélette always wept when spoken to in a loud and commanding tone," that Ti Nomme picks all the choicest flowers in the garden and cannot sleep without being told at least one story, that Elodie must be rocked and sung to sleep—in short that each child is an individual and that each must have all the privileges and attention that individuality involves. In fact, Mamzelle confides to her cook: "I tell you . . . I'd rather manage a dozen plantation' than fo' chil'ren. It's terrassent! Bonté! Don't talk to me about chil'ren."

The spinster quickly adjusts, however. She learns to accept Ti Nomme's "moist kisses—the expressions of an affectionate and exuberant nature." In a few days she becomes accustomed "to the laughing, the crying, the chattering." And by the end of two weeks, "she could sleep comfortably with little Elodie's hot plump body pressed close against her."

But then Odile reclaims her brood. Mamzelle watches them leave: "The excitement was all over. . . . How still it was when they were gone!" She goes back into the house, now empty as never before: "The evening shadows were creeping and deepening around her solitary figure. She let her head fall down upon her bended arm, and began to cry. . . . She cried like a man, with sobs that seemed to tear her very soul." Mamzelle again lacks that important part of a woman's life, the maternal relationship; but worse, perhaps, she can never again perceive herself as the strong, self-sufficient, satisfied planter.

Five of the stories in ***A Night in Acadie*** feature unselfish characters who sacrifice themselves for someone they love. In **"A Dresden Lady in Dixie,"** a little Acadian girl named Agapie hides a beautiful Dresden figurine from the big plantation house in her soapbox full of treasures. After it is found there everyone is heartbroken, especially Agapie and her family. But then Pa-Jeff, an old black man to whom Agapie has been kind, learns of the crisis. Sympathizing with her and her family in their shame and feeling secure in his own reputation for utter honesty, Pa-Jeff makes up a story about himself as the center of a controversy between "De Sperrit" and "Satan." "Satan," he says, made him take the figurine and hide it in the child's box; but "De Sperrit" moves him to confess his "guilt" and clear the child's name. Consequently, "Agapie grew up to deserve the confidence and favors of the family. She redoubled her acts of kindness toward Pa-Jeff; but somehow she could not look into his face again." Although sentimentality mars this story, Agapie's suffering could have been portrayed so vividly only by a writer who understood and loved children.

The protagonist in **"Tante Cat'rinette"** acts from a love as unselfish as Pa-Jeff 's. While still a slave Cat'rinette had saved the life of her master's daughter, and the father in gratitude had named the daughter "Cat'rine . . . Das Miss Kitty," freed Cat'rinette, and given her a house. But now, thirty-five years later, things have changed. Miss Kitty lives in poverty, and the town has condemned Tante Cat'rinette's house, wanting to pay her $1,000 and then demolish it. The old woman, however, refuses to sell and fears that mysterious powers will destroy her house if she leaves it even for a moment. But one day she learns that Miss Kitty is seriously ill and too poor to hire a physician.

That night very late, Cat'rinette dares to leave her house to visit the woman she deeply loves. Miss Kitty, drowsing restlessly, reacts "instinctively" to Cat'rinette's touch: " 'It's Tante Cat'rinette!' she exclaimed. . . . 'They all said you wouldn' come'."The old woman stays all night, caring for Miss Kitty and the baby and thus enabling both Miss Kitty and her husband, Mr. Raymond, to get a few hours of rest. Just before daybreak she leaves, to return home before those fearful forces can seize her house. But she promises to return each night.

On her way home Tante Cat'rinette has a vision in which "Vieumaite," an image of her old master, tells her to take the city's offer, lend the money to Mr. Raymond, move into Miss Kitty's home where she can care for the younger woman properly, live there until she dies, and then by her will leave whatever remains of the $1,000 to Miss Kitty. Thus Cat'rinette's love for Miss Kitty leads her to solve everyone's problems. The little house she had received as a mark of honor long ago now has become a symbol of her importance to the family she loves and with whom she feels she belongs. (pp. 23-30)

In **"Ozème's Holiday"** Chopin illustrates unselfish love while also revealing the importance of image to Ozème, an Acadian plantation hand. Although a hard worker, he values his reputation as a happy-go-lucky fellow. One October day, when the cotton is bursting in the fields, he sets out for a week's vacation on Cane River. Along the way, however, he discovers an old black woman and her son who are both ill; so he spends his week picking their cotton for them. Yet when he gets home, he makes up a story about the "sporting time" he has had. Ozème's compassion for down-and-out strangers causes him to sacrifice his own interests. Yet he acts irresponsibly in timing his vacation and he lies in telling about his week's "sporting" activities in order to maintain his image as a devil-may-care fellow. (pp. 30-1)

"Cavanelle," an interesting study of fraternal love, tells how one man brings meaning and purpose to his own existence by giving himself to another. The protagonist, Cavanelle, loving as selflessly as Pa-Jeff, Tante Cat'rinette, Chicot, and Ozème, dedicates himself to his ill sister, Mathilde, whom he believes to be a great singer. The narrator, shocked at Mathilde's pathetic musical performance and Cavanelle's seeming deafness, wonders, "is Cavanelle a fool? is he a lunatic?" But then she answers her own questions: "I realized that Cavanelle loved Mathilde intensely, and we all know that love is blind, but a god just the same." Cavanelle, like Chopin's other self-sacrificing characters, acts from a deep, fulfilling, humane kind of love.

The seven remaining stories in ***A Night in Acadie*** focus primarily on romantic love, and some of them feature strange relationships indeed. A few are little more than sketches. For example, **"Caline"** simply paints a portrait of a young country girl whose perception of life is changed forever by a passing train. When it develops mechanical problems near where she lies asleep, a young man gets off, paints her portrait, and then resumes his journey. Soon she goes to the city and begins to look into the face of every passerby, seeking the face that "awakened" her that day.

The title story of the volume, **"A Night in Acadie,"** portrays a girl named Zaïda, who in her headstrong determination to live her own life foreshadows Edna Pontellier. The protagonist, a young bachelor named Telèsphore, meets Zaïda on a train and decides to go with her to Foché's ball. The way the girl moves and acts captures Telèsphore's interest: "She carried herself boldly" with "an absence of reserve . . . yet . . . no lack of womanliness." Yet later when he "tried to think of her he could not think at all. . . . his brain was not so occupied with her as his senses were." Zaïda in her bold, sensuous ways and in her effect on Telèsphore reminds the reader a bit of Calixta as Chopin portrayed her in 1892 in **"At the 'Cadian Ball,"** but she suggests more forcefully the 1898 Calixta in **"The Storm."**

As events develop, Telèsphore learns that Zaïda plans to run away and marry a rascal named André Pascal. Unable to stop her, Telèsphore goes along to prevent her riding alone at midnight to "Wat Gibson's—a kine of justice of the peace or something," where Zaïda says the wedding is scheduled for 1:00 A.M. Arriving at the trysting place, they learn that André has been drinking and "sho' raisin' de ole Nick" all day "down to de P'int."

Eventually, drunk and belligerent, André arrives. Zaïda declares, "You might stan' yere till the day o' judgement on yo' knees befo' me; I ain't neva goin' to marry you." And he retorts insultingly, "The hell you ain't!" Immediately, Telèsphore knocks Pascal down. . . . (pp. 31-2)

[Zaïda] watches the combat in the highest excitement, doing nothing to prevent the maiming or even death of either combatant, determined "to see fair play" between the man she had only that day met and the insulting drunk she had meant to marry despite the objections of family and friends. Zaïda's attitude toward the fight has some of the intense detachment that forms a strange part of Edna Pontellier's attitude toward life.

In an anticlimactic denouement, Telèsphore, after winning the fight, asserts his masculine authority and drives Zaïda home. Zaïda "was like a little child and followed whither he led." Chopin apparently modified this story in an attempt to please R. W. Gilder, influential editor of the *Century.* She wrote to him: "I have made certain alterations which you thought the story required to give it artistic or ethical value. . . . The marriage is omitted, and the girl's character softened and tempered by her rude experience." The original ending having been lost, one can only speculate on its content; but it seems to have been less edifying and more consistent with Zaïda's character. At any rate, this bold, sensuous, self-assertive girl exhibits until the end of the fight qualities suggestive of both the voluptuous Calixta and the headstrong Edna Pontellier.

Another strange romance is that of Mamzelle Fleurette, the heroine in **"A Sentimental Soul."** Robert Arner calls Mamzelle "As unlikely a rebel as anyone may wish to meet." A devoutly religious spinster, Mamzelle falls secretly in love with a married man, Lacodie, who loudly voices his radical political opinions and intentions to overcharge the prosperous. (p. 33)

Mamzelle seems as unlikely to be a lover as a rebel, but through her Chopin creates her most beautiful description of falling in love: "Mamzelle Fleurette was in . . . trouble . . . so bitter, so sweet, so bewildering, so terrifying! . . . She thought the world was growing brighter and more beautiful; she thought the flowers had redoubled their sweetness and the birds their song, and that the voices of her fellow-creatures had grown kinder and their faces truer."

Recognizing her problem at last, Mamzelle hurries to confession, where she shocks the priest: "A slap in the face would not have startled Father Fochelle more forcibly." Determining that Lacodie is unaware of Mamzelle's love for him, the priest scolds her and tells her to "keep Satan at bay."

Soon Lacodie develops a fever and dies. Father Fochelle forbids that Mamzelle even go to the funeral, "and she did not question his authority, or his ability to master the subtleties of a situation utterly beyond reach of her own powers." (pp. 33-4)

In the meantime Lacodie's young, pretty widow has begun taking in washing to support herself and her child. Spring comes. She grows flowers and buys a bird. Then she begins to sing with the bird. Soon she marries again.

The widow's remarriage shakes Mamzelle's very soul: "A terrible upheaval [was] taking place in [her] soul. She was preparing for the first time in her life to take her conscience into her own keeping." And so, Mamzelle Fleurette becomes a rebel as well as a lover. She goes to a church across town from her own neighborhood and confesses to a priest she does not know. She tells him "all her little venial sins, which she had much difficulty in bringing to a number of any dignity," but she does not mention "her love for Lacodie, the dead husband of another woman." After confession, "Mamzelle Fleurette did not ride back to her home; she walked. The sensation of walking on air was altogether delicious; she had never experienced it before." That feeling of "walking on air" does not come to Mamzelle when she first feels love for a man, delightful as she finds that experience; only when she takes "her conscience into her own keeping" does she experience it. Thus Mamzelle's need for autonomy in making her own decisions and choices becomes a minor theme in **"A Sentimental Soul."**

In **"At Chênière Caminada,"** another story of thwarted love, a shy young fisherman named Tonie falls in love with Claire Duvigné—a beautiful, popular girl who, like Lacodie, dies. Far from grieving for her as Mamzelle does for Lacodie, however, Tonie rejoices because now Claire will not marry anyone else.

An instinctive coquette, Claire had sensed Tonie's unspoken passion one day when she hired a ride in his boat. But "She did not dream that under the rude, calm exterior . . . his reason [was] yielding to the savage in-

Chopin in 1876 with her first four sons: Fred, George, Jean, and Oscar.

stinct of his blood." As a matter of fact, Tonie had come very close to killing both Claire and himself while they were alone on the lake that day. Apparently Chopin was already associating death in the ocean with human passion in 1893, five years before Edna Pontellier would yield her body to the erotic embrace of the sea in *The Awakening.* (pp. 34-5)

Finally, two stories feature wives who experience difficulty in abiding by their marriage vows. In **"A Respectable Woman"** Mrs. Baroda is a happily married woman who feels "a little provoked" about her husband's friend Gouvernail visiting their plantation at a time when "She was looking forward to a period of . . . undisturbed tête-à-tête with her husband." But she finds Gouvernail disturbingly attractive, despite her strong love for her husband. . . .

Recognizing what is happening, she escapes to the city and remains there until he leaves the plantation. The narrator says: "Mrs. Baroda was greatly tempted . . . to tell her husband—who was also her friend—of this folly. . . . But she did not. . . . she knew there are some battles in life which a human being must fight alone." In this story, written in January 1894, Mrs. Baroda evidences no romantic naïveté and no lack of sexual satisfaction within her marriage, two commonly suggested motives for the infidelity of Edna in *The Awakening.* She simply feels strong sexual attraction toward another man besides her husband. She has no motivation for being unfaithful except a physically healthy body. On the contrary, she has every reason for being faithful to her beloved husband.

And of course she does flee the scene to make sure that she remains faithful. But before the year's end, she suggests that Gouvernail be invited for another visit. Her husband declares his delight that she has "overcome" her "dislike" for his friend. She laughingly tells him, "after pressing a long, tender kiss upon his lips, 'I have overcome everything! . . . This time I shall be very nice to him'." And the reader understands that she is going to risk losing everything—her husband, her marriage, her very happiness—simply because passion aroused demands its fulfillment.

"Athénaïse" is another story about marriage from a woman's perspective. The protagonist, Athénaïse, has recently married Cazeau, a soft-spoken but severe-looking widower. When his bride does not return one evening after visiting her parents, "He did not worry much about Athénaïse . . . ; his chief solicitude was manifestly for the pony she had ridden." Cazeau, being very busy, has little time to concern himself about Athénaïse's absence, but on the third afternoon after her departure "the task of bringing his wife back to a sense of her duty" becomes even more important than his other work. Cazeau realizes that "The marriage had been a blunder; he had only to look into her eyes to feel that, to discover her growing aversion." But he expects to make the best of the situation and to see to it that Athénaïse does the same.

Meanwhile, Athénaïse, younger than Cazeau, less experienced, and miserable in the married state, has returned to her parents' home and announced that she will never return to her husband's. . . . (pp. 35-6)

Athénaïse explains to her uncomprehending family that she does not dislike her husband but simply the condition of being married: "It's jus' being married that I detes' an' despise. I hate being Mrs. Cazeau, an' would want to be Athénaïse Miché again." She still sees herself as Athénaïse Miché, the young girl she had been until two months before; and she finds it impossible to perceive herself as Mrs. Cazeau, a married woman with a completely new role to play in life and even a new name to which she must learn to answer.

When confronted by her husband on the third day of her truancy, Athénaïse "appeared neither angry nor frightened, but thoroughly unhappy, with an appeal in her soft dark eyes . . . that wounded and maddened him at once. But whatever he might feel, Cazeau knew only one way to act toward a woman." He simply tells her what to do. And confronted thus, Athénaïse yields helplessly: "Her husband's . . . mere presence, brought to her a sudden sense of hopelessness, . . . of the futility of rebellion against a social and sacred institution." Cazeau, in knowing "only one way to act"—to tell Athénaïse what to do—foreshadows Léonce's first response to Edna's rebellion in *The Awakening.* Cazeau's basic kindliness and decency also resemble those of Léonce. And further, the young wife's hopelessness also predicts a scene in the later story when Edna throws her wedding ring onto the floor and stomps it with her foot.

Some sense of how Athénaïse feels comes to Cazeau, however, as they ride home: "The sight of a great solitary oak-tree . . . brought vividly back to Cazeau . . . a scene of many years ago," when he had been a small boy. He and his father were on horseback, returning a runaway slave to their plantation: "Black Gabe was moving on before them at a little dogtrot. . . . They had halted beneath this big oak to enable the negro to take breath; for Cazeau's father was a kind . . . master, and every one had agreed . . . that Black Gabe was a fool . . . for wanting to run away from him." The memory makes Cazeau distinctly uncomfortable, and he resolves that never again will he force Athénaïse to return to him: "For the companionship of no woman on earth would he again undergo the humiliating sensation of baseness that had overtaken him in passing the old oak-tree." Thus Chopin specifically links the institution of marriage as practiced in 1895 with the institution of slavery.

The girl does flee again; but this time she goes to New Orleans rather than to her father's home. Cazeau "knew that he could again compel her return . . . but the loss of self-respect seemed to him too dear a price to pay for a wife." So he does not attempt to contact her.

Athénaïse spends a rather lonely month in New Orleans, but the "comforting, comfortable sense of not being married" makes up for the loneliness. Her neighbor in the boarding house happens to be Gouvernail, the same bachelor who attracts Mrs. Baroda in **"A Respectable Woman."** He helps Athénaïse to pass the time, and she drifts toward a probable love affair with him: "He was patient; . . . That she was married made no . . . difference to Gouvernail. . . . When the time came that she wanted him, . . . he felt he would have a right to her. So long as she did not want him, he had no right to her,—no more than her husband had." Perhaps some of Gouvernail's attractiveness to women results from his feeling, unusual in Chopin's male characters, that women have the right to want a man or not.

At any rate, the discovery that she is pregnant saves Athénaïse from being awakened sexually by Gouvernail. The news transforms her completely: "Her whole being was steeped in a wave of ecstasy. When she . . . looked at herself in the mirror, a face met hers which she seemed to see for the first time, so transfigured was it with wonder." Learning to view herself as mother seems much easier for Athénaïse than learning to view herself as wife. She thinks: "Cazeau must know. As she thought of him, the first purely sensuous tremor of her life swept over her. . . . She was impatient to be with him. Her whole passionate nature was aroused as if by a miracle." She takes the earliest train home to Cazeau, and on the long trip she "could think of nothing but him." When she arrives, "he felt the yielding of her whole body against him. He felt her lips for the first time respond to the passion of his own." Thus Athénaïse finds that prospective motherhood not only offers a role in which she feels comfortable but also releases her pent-up love for Cazeau.

Yet she has paid a price for fulfilling these two emotional needs. She has sacrificed her name and more; she has sacrificed also her autonomy, her right to live as a discrete individual. Athénaïse Miché exists no longer.

• • • • •

In Chopin's third collection of stories, the proposed but unpublished ***A Vocation and a Voice,*** the characterizations become firm, and the drive toward autonomy becomes insistent in many characters. As Robert Arner points out, had this collection been published Chopin's works probably would not have been neglected as they have been, for these stories exhibit "a strength and a maturity, a firmness of line and a level of artistic achievement" that critics would have found difficult to ignore. Most of these stories turn inward, studying human emotions and values more deeply than do the stories in ***Bayou Folk*** and ***A Night in Acadie.*** They treat a number of topics—religion, suicide, illusions, the fickleness of people and of fate, the power of sex, and the impulse toward self-assertion. And most look deeply into some character or human experience, trying to fathom exactly what comprises the fulfilled person or the adequate life.

Five of the stories indicate that Chopin was thinking about religion—its significance, scope, and meaning to the human psyche. Two of these, **"An Idle Fellow"** and **"A Scrap and a Sketch,"** espouse a sort of Emersonian nature religion; the other three insist that the fully realized person needs to experience harmony among his or her sensual, sensuous, and spiritual parts.

The narrator in **"An Idle Fellow,"** a "bookworm," describes the wisdom of Paul, who sits drinking "the scent of the clover" and reading in the eyes of passersby "the story of their souls." Paul personifies Emerson's concepts of the relative value of books and nature as teachers of the self and interprets a bird's song much like the one Whitman "translates" in "Out of the Cradle Endlessly Rocking."

"The Night Came Slowly" shares with **"An Idle Fellow"** this theme of the powers of nature. The narrator, wanting "neither books nor men," asks: "Can one of them talk to me like . . . the Summer night? . . . My whole being was abandoned to the soothing and penetrating charm of the night." But a man and his "Bible Class" come into the woods and break the spell. The narrator sneers: "What does he know of Christ? . . . I would rather ask the stars: they have seen him." So only nature can teach with authority.

Chopin joins **"The Night Came Slowly"** with **"Juanita"** by publishing them under one title, **"A Scrap and a Sketch,"** and by proposing to present them together again in this third collection under the title "Sketches," thus suggesting that the reader should look for a thematic link between the two. That the stories are related is further suggested by the fact that both appear as diary entries within a two-day period in July 1894.

Juanita, a two-hundred-pound girl dressed in a dirty "Mother Hubbard," mysteriously attracts men from far and near—among others a city gentleman, a wealthy Missouri farmer, a Texas millionaire. But one day a poor, shabby, one-legged beggar appears. Juanita bears his child out of wedlock and "lavishes . . . her undivided affections" upon him. Love thus proves again to be a strange force, indeed, and a woman's soul as unfathomable as the universe. That Chopin links **"Juanita"** with **"The Night Came Slowly"** emphasizes the naturalness of sex and the fact that it, like other aspects of nature, exerts a force so vast, complex, and mysterious as to defy comprehension, much less control, by human creatures.

"An Idle Fellow" and **"A Scrap and a Sketch"** suggest that, to hear the "language of God," one must listen to nature. But Archibald, the protagonist in **"A Morning Walk,"** receives in the church important truths about himself. As a scientist he lives close to nature, but it has never spoken to him the "language of God" until one spring morning when he follows a lovely young girl named Lucy to church and hears the minister preach on the words of Jesus, "I am the Resurrection and the Life." Archibald can understand when the preacher speaks "the language of God," not only because he has long been intimate with nature but also because Lucy has stirred his sensuous and sensual feelings on this lovely spring morning. With the preacher's text comes a "vision of life . . . the poet's vision, of the life that is within and the life that is without, pulsing in unison, breathing the harmony of an undivided existence." . . . [For] Archibald, the sensuous, the sensual, and the spiritual come together in harmony, making it possible for him to embrace all of experience. (pp. 37-40)

[In **"Two Portraits,"** a woman finds] it impossible to breathe "the harmony of an undivided existence." Chopin had earlier given other titles to **"Two Portraits,"** at one time calling it "The Nun and the Wanton" and at another "The Nun, the Wife and the Wanton." All three titles, of course, suggest that the protagonist, Alberta, exists in a divided state. This story emphasizes the maternal influence in determining the sort of person a child becomes.

Chopin first sketches the character of Alberta the Wanton, a young woman whose substitute mother, a prostitute, alternates between beating Alberta and indulging the child's every whim. Alberta also becomes a prostitute at an early age, and she takes good care of her body "for she knows it brings her love to squander and gold to squander." Someone tells Alberta to save her gold, warning her that she will not always remain young and beautiful. But Alberta, like a good many Chopin characters, knows a way to escape that which she cannot face: "with death and oblivion always within her reach" she need never fear the "degradation" of age and "ugliness." Alberta the Wanton, possessing no spiritual dimension, can end her existence whenever the "ugliness" of age threatens "degradation."

After completing her portrait of Alberta the Wanton, Chopin puts the same raw materials into a different environment and creates by contrast Alberta the Nun, who needs a physical dimension as badly as her twin needs a spiritual one. Whenever the child tries to experience God with her senses, the mother figure tells her that one reaches God with the soul, not the body. This "holy woman" teaches Alberta "that the soul must be made perfect and the flesh subdued." Consequently, when this Alberta matures, she feels an overpowering impulse toward the spiritual; and so she enters the convent, where she sees "visions" that seem to be at least as sensual as they are spiritual. Their effects are described through such terms as "ecstacy," "roused," "awakened," "pressed her lips," "quivering contemplation," "abandon herself," and "swooned in rapture." Thus Alberta the Nun, with her attention riveted upon heaven, remains as pathetically unfulfilled as Alberta the Wanton, whose total existence centers upon the flesh. Both lack a necessary dimension. (p. 41)

Perhaps Chopin felt that a person can fully control his or her own life only through the decisive act of ending it. At any rate, she created a number of suicidal characters, several of them in this group of stories. Alberta the Wanton, for example, knows that for the totally physical person escape through suicide always remains possible. When Chopin's characters do reach out to embrace "death and oblivion," they usually choose to drown. (p. 42)

"Her Letters" tells the story of a marriage, largely

through a man's behavior and thoughts during a few years following his wife's death. The wife has lived a double life. To her husband, "She had never seemed . . . to have had a secret. . . . He knew her to have been cold and passionless, but true, and watchful of his . . . happiness."

But in the first scene of the story, she fondles a bundle of letters. One she kisses "again and again. With her sharp white teeth she tore the far corner . . . where the name was written; she bit the torn scrap and tasted it." Only the letters remain of her affair with a man who "had changed the water in her veins to wine, whose taste had brought delirium." For four years she has "been feeding upon [the letters] . . . they had sustained her . . . and kept her spirit from perishing."

Yet she loves her husband, too. Knowing that she will soon die, "She shrank from inflicting the pain . . . which . . . those letters would bring . . . to one . . . whose tenderness and years of devotion had made him . . . dear." Finding herself unable to part with her treasured letters—"How desolate and empty would have been her remaining days without them."—she arrives at a daring plan that reveals much about both her husband and herself. She wraps the bundle and on it writes: "I leave this package to the care of my husband. With perfect faith in his loyalty and his love, I ask him to destroy it unopened."

His reaction when he finds the letters sheds light on the nature of both the man and the marriage: "If he had come upon that bundle of letters in the first flush of his poignant sorrow there would not have been an instant's hesitancy. To destroy it promptly and without question would have seemed a welcome expression of devotion—a way . . . of crying out his love." But she has been dead for a year before he finds the bundle, and so he at first feels mystified. . . . Gradually, of course, the ensuing question comes to him: "What secret save one could a woman choose to have die with her?" And he now reacts rapidly: "As quickly as the suggestion came to his mind, so swiftly did the man-instinct of possession stir in his blood."

Thus Chopin reveals with great subtlety that masculine possessiveness constitutes the pivotal problem with husband, wife, and marriage. In fact, Chopin treats such possessiveness in most of her best works about man-woman relationships, including **"At the 'Cadian Ball," "In Sabine," "Désirée's Baby," "At Chênière Caminada," "Athénaïse," "The Story of an Hour," "Wiser Than a God," "The Gentleman from New Orleans,"** and of course *The Awakening*— in which the action is motivated by Edna's reaction to the possessiveness of Lèonce, Alcée, and finally Robert.

The husband in **"Her Letters,"** nevertheless, does behave as his wife knew he would; that is, he destroys the letters, not by burning for fear that he might accidentally read a word or phrase as they burn, but by casting them into the river. He thereupon becomes a driven man, however, seeking the answer to his mystery in every conversation and contact. Finally, after years of such torture, "He no longer sought to know from men and women what they . . . could not tell him. Only the river knew. He went and stood again upon the bridge where . . . the darkness . . . had . . . engulfed his manhood." And so, feeling that his "manhood" has been forever "engulfed" with the letters, he throws himself also into the water.

The river affects the widower in much the same hypnotic, erotic way that it affects the narrator in **"An Egyptian Cigarette"** and that the sea affects Edna in *The Awakening*. . . . In all three accounts, the sirens of the water seem to promise caresses, rapture, and peaceful repose to those who accept the invitation to shed their individuality (or, in Edna's case, the struggle to establish it) and become one with the elements.

Three of the stories projected for ***A Vocation and a Voice*** focus on people's illusions—both the futility of illusions, on the one hand, and their power in an individual's life, on the other.

In **"The White Eagle"** the protagonist gropes her way through the misfortunes of a lonely life, always carrying with her an old cast-iron eagle that had "sheltered her unconscious dreams" in childhood. Eventually she dies and someone places the eagle at the head of her grave, where he perches with a seemingly wise but actually vacuous look. The bird seems to symbolize the dreams, hopes, and illusions of the character. Although her dreams remain unfulfilled and in a sense as meaningless as the bird's expression, without them this woman would have been utterly alone and defenseless against life's misfortunes.

"Two Summers and Two Souls" links an ephemeral infatuation with a man's illusion that no commitment should ever be broken. The result is predictably tragic. A summer romance leads a young man to beg a girl whom he has known for only five weeks to marry him. She asks for time to consider, and he returns home. A year later he is shocked to receive a letter from the girl declaring that she loves him too and wants to marry him. But to him, "It was as if one loved, and dead and forgotten had returned to life; with the strange illusion that the rush of existence had halted while she lay in her grave; and with the still more singular delusion that love is eternal." But the man never considers telling her that this is a different summer and he a different soul. He goes to her, "As he would have gone unflinchingly to meet the business obligation that he knew would leave him bankrupt." Thus the girl's illusion that love is eternal and the man's illusion that one should never break a commitment lead the two into a tragic union.

In **"The Recovery"** a blind woman recovers her sight after fifteen years of blindness, but in doing so loses an important illusion. Accustomed to living in a dark world and to thinking of herself as she looked at twenty, the woman as a result of her recovery faces a crisis. (pp. 43-5)

For a while she coyly postpones looking into the mirror, but at last she does confront her own image. The sight stuns her: " 'Mother!' she cried, involuntarily, turning swiftly; but she was still alone. . . . The eyes, above all, seemed to speak to her. Afflicted as they had been, they alone belonged to that old, other self that had somewhere vanished." All the beauty of the June day, seeing again the dear faces of those she loves—nothing compensates for the loss of "that old, other self."

[Three] stories deal with the fickleness of fate and of people, aspects of life that no serious observer can overlook.

"The Blind Man" shows the vagaries of fate when a streetcar strikes down a wealthy man with perfect hearing and sight instead of a poor, blind beggar with no defense against traffic hazards and nothing to lose except life itself. This story also juxtaposes the world's cold indifference toward the constant suffering of the beggar with its shocked horror at the sudden death of the rich man. In **"Elizabeth Stock's One Story,"** the fickleness of both fortune and people conspire to rob a good woman of her job, her health, and finally her life. (pp. 45-6)

"Ti Démon" reveals the importance of both chance and a person's name in shaping his life. The protagonist is a mild person whose mother had fondly dubbed him Ti Démon when, as a crying infant, he kept her awake nights. The name sticks with him through many years of gentle behavior until finally one night his fickle fiancée and a man he thinks is his friend betray him. He becomes so angry that he actually does behave violently for the only time in his life. Thereafter, people regard him with awe and terror, saying, "he's dangerous him—they call him Ti Démon." His mother's whimsy in nicknaming him, the faithlessness of those he loves, and the caprices of public opinion severely circumscribe his life.

"Ti Démon" illustrates that human fickleness, sometimes compounded by the caprices of fortune, may shape one's reputation and character. But in seven stories of this group Chopin suggests that another power—the power of sex—often exerts the strongest force in forming personality and character. In **"The Unexpected"** the thought of sexual contact with her fiancé—formerly handsome and well built but now wasted from illness—repels the protagonist so strongly that she gains unwelcome insights into herself. In **"A Mental Suggestion"** sexual love transforms the protagonist into a better person. In **"Suzette," "Fedora,"** and **"The Godmother,"** however, sexual feelings nudge the protagonists toward strange, unnatural, or even cruel behavior. And finally, in the title story, sexual magnetism virtually determines the protagonist's life-style, his knowledge of himself, even his name.

"Suzette" explores some unpleasant aspects of infatuation. The title character is prinking before a small mirror when Ma'ma Zidore tells her that one of her suitors, Michel Jardeau, has drowned. Suzette feels sure that Michel has taken his own life because of his hopeless love for her, but she scarcely reacts at all. . . . The young coquette idly wonders why she does not care, although a year before she had loved Michel "desperately." At that time he had "seemed to care for little Pavie Ombre"; but at a barbecue "sudden infatuation" for Suzette had seized him, and he "stayed beside her the whole day long; turning her head with his . . . soft touches. . . . after that day he cared no longer for . . . any woman . . . besides Suzette. What a weariness that love had finally become to her, only herself knew." Meanwhile Pavie continues loving Michel. Upon hearing of his death, she first falls "in a white, dead faint." Then she wails and sobs, "indifferent to those who might hear her in passing along the road." And nearby Suzette continues preening herself until she hears cattle approaching. Then she rushes to the window and rivets her attention on one of the cowboys driving the herd. But he does not even glance at her. "Suzette turned from the window—her face gray and pinched, with all the warmth and color gone out of it. She flung herself upon the bed and there she cried and moaned with wrenching sobs between." So Suzette and Michel alike seem to want only to attract the objects of their desire physically, not to develop knowing, loving relationships with them. (pp. 46-7)

The drive to know love and to satisfy it physically may shape a woman's character, whether the drive is frustrated or fulfilled. **"Fedora"** features a thirty-year-old spinster who has forged a place for herself among her brothers, her sisters, and their guests by assuming an elderly air of stern authority: "Fedora was tall and slim, and carried her head loftily, and wore eye-glasses and a severe expression." She has for eight years known young Malthers, now a big, handsome man of twenty-three, to whom she suddenly finds herself strongly attracted: "the sudden realization came home to her that he was a man—in voice, in attitude, in bearing, in every sense—a man." From that moment "She wanted him by her, though his nearness troubled her. There was uneasiness, restlessness, expectation when he was not there within sight or sound. There was redoubled uneasiness when he was by—there was inward revolt, astonishment, rapture." But of course, young Malthers feels no such passion for Fedora; indeed, he would surely be astonished to learn that the spinster is even capable of such feelings.

When Malthers's sister comes to visit, Fedora announces that she will meet the girl's train, because "the brute was restive, and shouldn't be trusted to the handling of the young people." The girl, Fedora finds, looks disturbingly like her brother, but in miniature. She sits "lower in the cart than Fedora, who drove, handling whip and rein with accomplished skill." Fedora, "in her usual elderly fashion," tells Miss Malthers that she hopes the girl will come to her "freely and without reserve" with all her wants and needs. Fedora "had gathered the reins into one hand, and with the other free arm she encircled Miss Malthers' shoulders. When the girl looked up into her face with murmured thanks, Fedora bent down and pressed a long, penetrating kiss upon her mouth."

Robert Arner discusses well the homosexual overtones of Fedora's actions. But he does not mention Chopin's emphasis on Fedora's lust for Mr. Malthers nor the spinster's conflicting needs for a place where she feels that she belongs and for sexual love. Her attitude toward the small girl who looks like the man for whom she yearns seems to be an attempt to reconcile these conflicting forces. (pp. 47-8)

The title story, **"A Vocation and a Voice,"** makes clear that Chopin knew the strength of sexual attraction. Although "many editors" refused the story, written in 1896, the *St. Louis Mirror* did publish it on 27 March 1902. The story features a homeless, loveless, even nameless protagonist who is called only "the boy" until almost the end of the narrative. **"A Vocation and a Voice"** essentially tells the story of the boy's search for his own identity, for his answer to Lear's question, "Who am I?"

Mrs. Donnelly, with whose family the boy lives as "an alien member" in "The Patch," has sent him on an errand to a distant part of the city; as he makes his way on foot back toward "The Patch," he progresses slowly because "With him was a conviction that it would make no difference to any one whether he got back to 'The Patch' or not." Having "a vague sense of being unessential which always dwelt with him," the boy haphazardly goes along with a gypsy couple he encounters. He enjoys camping out and contributes his share to the group's welfare by doing various chores.

By calling him only "the boy," the narrator emphasizes his youthful innocence: "He was rather tall, though he had spoken with the high, treble voice of a girl." Further, "The young girls did not attract him more than the boys or the little children." As the story unfolds, his namelessness poignantly emphasizes the universality of his experiences—the loss of innocence and the accompanying search for place, love, and knowledge of self.

Suzima, the female half of the nomadic couple he joins, appears "robust and young—twenty or thereabouts—and comely, in a certain rude, vigorous fashion." When the boy happens along, she is beating out a grass fire while cursing her absent husband, who makes a habit of getting drunk whenever camp-breaking time arrives. (pp. 49-50)

The boy finds a place, of sorts, with this make-shift family as they make their leisurely way southward. "The days were a gorgeous, golden processional, good and warm with sunshine, and languorous." They stop for a month near a village, where the boy renews his close contact with the Catholic church. When Suzima and Gutro decide to move on at the end of a month, the village priest tries to get the boy to stay. But the boy refuses: " 'I got to go,' he murmured. . . . Yes, he wanted to lead an up-right, clean existence before God and man. . . . He liked the village, the people, the life which he had led there. Above all he liked the man whose kindly spirit had been moved to speak and act in his behalf. But the stars were beginning to shine and he thought of the still nights in the forest. A savage instinct stirred within him." Perhaps the man is beginning to awaken within the boy. (p. 50)

This idyllic existence continues until one day the boy happens upon Suzima bathing nude in a little stream. "He saw her as one sees an object in a flash from a dark sky—sharply, vividly. Her image, against the background of tender green, ate into his brain and into his flesh with the fixedness and intensity of white-hot iron." Afterward the woman at first acts "less kind" to him, but they soon become lovers.

The sexual experience produces an immediate, dramatic effect: "A few days had wrought great changes with the boy. That which he had known before he now comprehended, and with comprehension sympathy awoke. He seemed to have been brought in touch with the universe of men and all things that live. He cared more than ever for the creeping and crawling things, for the beautiful voiceless life that met him at every turn; . . . that silently unfolded the mysterious, inevitable existence." Thus the boy who began the story without place, love, or knowledge of himself has found all three.

But inevitably his love for Suzima and his new comprehension of life soon make his place as "the boy" in this household untenable. A quarrel between Gutro and Suzima sets off the explosion: "Suddenly, the man, in a rage, turned to strike her with a halter that he held uplifted, but, quicker than he, the boy was ready with a pointed hunting knife that he seized from the ground." Although the fracas causes no serious physical injuries, its results nevertheless reach far.

The boy thus encounters an abrupt challenge not only to his delicious new feeling of understanding and sympathy with all of life but even to his long-held concept of his own inner person: "He had always supposed that he could live in the world a blameless life . . . He had never dreamed of a devil lurking unknown to him, in his blood, that would some day blind him, disable his will and direct his hands to deeds of violence. . . . He felt as if he had encountered some hideous being with whom he was not acquainted and who had said to him: 'I am yourself'." This new concept of himself he finds unbearable, and so he enters a monastery, the "Refuge," where he succeeds for years in hiding from the "devil lurking . . . in his blood."

At the Refuge the boy acquires a new sense of who he is and, at last, even a name—Brother Ludovic: "He often felt that he had been born anew, the day whereupon he had entered the gate of this holy refuge. That hideous, evil spectre of himself lurking outside, ready at any moment to claim him should he venture within its reach, was, for a long time, a menace to him. But he had come to dread it no longer, secure in the promise of peace which his present life held out to him." Thus he comes to feel secure in his new place and in his knowledge of himself.

Brother Ludovic has a great dream, to build a solid stone wall around the Refuge. He works feverishly at this task that will take a lifetime to complete. "He liked to picture himself an old man, grown feeble with age, living upon this peaceful summit all enclosed by the solid stone wall built with the strength of his youth and manhood."

But he learns that this self-image, too, lacks completeness. One day while working on his wall, "Suddenly Brother Ludovic stopped, lifting his head with the mute quivering attention of some animal in the forest, startled at the scent of approaching danger. . . . The air was hot and heavy. . . . He could hear soft splashing at the pool. An image that had once been branded into his soul . . . unfolded before his vision with the poignancy of life." These strong appeals to the senses of smell, sight, hearing, and touch remind the reader that Brother Ludovic remains a physical being as well as a spiritual one. Then a distant sound draws nearer, and the images grow more sensual. . . . Finally, the sexual magnetism overwhelms Brother Ludovic: "He was conscious of nothing in the world but the voice that was calling him and the cry of his own being that responded. Brother Ludovic bounded down from the wall and followed the voice of the woman." Thus Brother Ludovic learns that he needs more from life than a secure place, even the "Refuge"; that nothing, not even rock walls, will contain the force of sexual attraction; and that he may never know fully that complex person who dwells within himself.

Despite the distinctly masculine point of view in **"A Vocation and a Voice,"** the boy exhibits universal, conflicting needs that transcend the limitations of gender. In Chopin's day society allowed, although it did not encourage, a writer to examine these human needs from the masculine point of view. But when the same author later offered in *The Awakening* a female character, Edna Pontellier, engaged in a similar struggle to find herself, the public and most literary critics ostracized Chopin and her works, bringing to a virtual conclusion her literary career.

"The Story of an Hour" Per Seyersted calls Chopin's "most startling picture of female self-assertion" [see excerpt dated 1969]. In it Mrs. Mallard, a lady with a weak heart, learns that her husband has been killed. She weeps "with sudden, wild abandonment"; and when "the storm of grief had spent itself," she goes to her room alone, where she sits for a time encased in her grief. The lines of Mrs. Mallard's "fair, calm face . . . bespoke repression." She feels something approaching her, something almost tangible:

> There was something coming to her. . . . What was it? She did not know. . . . But she felt it . . . reaching toward her through the sounds, the scents, the color that filled the air.
>
> . . . She was beginning to recognize this thing that was approaching to possess her, and she was striving to beat it back with her will. . . .
>
> When she abandoned herself a little whispered word escaped her. . . . She said it over and over under her breath: "free, free, free!"

Mrs. Mallard knows that she will cry again for the loss of a kind, loving husband. She clearly has had the first two of those three qualities—love, place, and autonomy—which Chopin associates with the full life. But the narrator exclaims:

> What did it matter! What could love, the unsolved mystery, count for in face of this possession of self-assertion which she suddenly recognized as the strongest impulse of her being!
>
> "Free! Body and soul free!" she kept whispering.

The stories Chopin wanted to include in this volume do indeed bring her characters into clear focus, and some of these characters refuse to settle quietly for lives of only partial fulfillment. Mrs. Mallard, for example, discovers that no amount of love and security can compensate for a lack of control over her own existence. (pp. 50-3)

Peggy Skaggs, in her Kate Chopin, *Twayne Publishers, 1985, 130 p.*

Barbara C. Ewell (essay date 1986)

[*Ewell is a professor of English at Tulane University in New Orleans. In the following excerpt from her critical study* Kate Chopin, *Ewell traces the development of Chopin's short fiction from vivid examples of local color to complex studies of universal human behavior.*]

Barely two weeks after Chopin finished *At Fault* she began work on a second novel, which she completed on November 27, 1890. *Young Dr. Gosse and Théo,* according to her letter to Stone and Kimball of Chicago, was prefaced with "a Parisian scene: the story proper opens ten years later and is acted in America." But we know no more of it. Chopin sent the manuscript to ten different publishers before she destroyed it sometime after 1895. Her friend William Schuyler had written tantalizingly in 1894 that it was "her very strongest work" [*A Kate Chopin Miscellany* (1979)].

But even though Chopin's second novel could find no home, the Louisiana stories she began writing in the spring of 1891 continued to be accepted. Like Sarah Orne Jewett, Mary E. Wilkins Freeman, Louisa Alcott, and Rose Terry Cooke, her national audience was largely created in children's magazines, like *Youth's Companion* and *Harper's Young People.* Though slanted toward juvenile interests, these were actually family journals with large circulations and discriminating editorial staffs where even an authority like *Harper's* William Dean Howells might notice a new author's work. In fact, he did; and Chopin's children later recalled his letter praising her sketch **"Boulôt and Boulotte"** in the December *Harper's Young People* and encouraging her to write more like it.

Barely a vignette, **"Boulôt and Boulotte"** (September 20, 1891) contains many of the elements that came to define Chopin's art at its best. It is a very simple story: twelve-year-old Boulôt and Boulotte, "little piny-woods twins," set out one Saturday to buy new shoes, but return with their purchases in hand rather than on their feet. Confronted by their waiting brothers and sisters, bumbling Boulôt awkwardly acknowledges he hadn't thought of wearing the new shoes; but his unflustered sister witheringly remarks, "You think we go buy shoes for ruin it in de dus'? *Comment!*" Chopin actually manages to inject suspense into this meager event, confining our point of view to that of the expectant siblings and briefly, at least, withholding the specific reason for their shocked reactions. Howells must also have appreciated the sharp domestic realism of the piece and its lack of sentimentality, despite the tempting combination of children and poverty. But the most characteristic feature of the story, in terms of Chopin's early success, is its skillful, economic use of local color and dialect. The latter, which is confined to the climax, contributes both atmosphere and humor, while the distinctive setting is evoked with brief geographical allusions and unusual names for both people and things, like "picayunes" and "socoes."

This mastery of local-color effects perhaps indicates why Chopin's early stories were selling so well. Local color had been an extremely popular mode of fiction throughout the 1880s. Initiated with Bret Harte's and Mark Twain's stories of the West in the 1860s, the genre was enthusiastically taken up by writers throughout the country, eager to capitalize on the special flavors of their regions. Characterized by picturesque settings, phonetically spelled dialects, eccentric characters, sentimentality, humor, or a dash of romance, the fashion attracted writers like Jewett,

Freeman, and Cooke in New England; Hamlin Garland, Alice French, Edward Eggleston, E. W. Howe, and Constance Fenimore Woolson in the Midwest; Mary Noailles Murfree, Thomas Nelson Page, and Joel Chandler Harris in the South. Louisiana, with its rich mixture of cultures—French, Spanish, Afro-American, Native American, and Anglo-Saxon—proved uniquely fertile, counting George Washington Cable, Lafcadio Hearn, Ruth McEnery Stuart, Grace King—and Kate Chopin—among its interpreters. (pp. 51-3)

Though Rankin suggests that Chopin resisted identification as a local colorist and vehemently objected to "the conventional groove" in fiction, she clearly learned much from these writers. Particularly admiring Jewett for her "technique and nicety of construction," Chopin was equally adept at creating unassuming dramas of great intensity. She also shared Jewett's affection for French writers, especially Flaubert, Daudet, and of course, Maupassant, but their lightness of tone and careful phrasing would have been found in Cable or King as well. The poetic rhythms of stylists like Hearn, in his evocative *Chita: A Memory of Last Island* (1889), are likewise apparent, especially in her later work. And while she praised James Lane Allen's "A Kentucky Cardinal" as "a refreshing idealistic bit," her own fiction tended to the more biting realism of Mary Wilkins Freeman, whom she called "a great genius" [*Miscellany*]. Freeman's portrayal of strong, unconventional characters and skillful use of dialect clearly influenced Chopin, though her Louisiana settings rarely lent themselves to the harsh isolation of Freeman's stories. Instead, Chopin tended to focus on more romantic situations, sharpening them with her realistic perspective and intense characterizations. Like Cable and King, Chopin could not resist the glamorous and eccentric variety of Louisiana's heterogeneous population, but quite unlike them, she insisted on writing about their present realities rather than their idealized pasts. In this respect, she had more in common with Ruth Stuart, with whom she also shared a lively sense of humor and sympathy for plain, back-country folk.

Chopin's particular slant on Louisiana was the Cane River country. Its bayous and cotton fields, 'Cadians and Creoles, Native and Afro-Americans, were the raw material of about half the stories that she wrote in 1891—and they were the ones that sold first. Never a slow learner, Chopin in the next two years wrote only one short story set outside Louisiana, a sharp social satire that remained unpublished until 1897. That most of her early sales were to children's magazines also influenced the kind of stories she was writing. The moral tone and the relatively high incidence of youthful characters reflect Chopin's sense of her best market. However, she regularly sent stories to other journals like *Harper's* and *Century,* and the latter's acceptance of **"A No-Account Creole"** with a "flattering letter" and a hundred dollars in the summer of 1891 was certainly encouraging. Other acceptances, by Boston's *Two Tales* and the new *Vogue,* followed, with the latter's inaugural issue in January 1893 featuring two stories, including **"Désirée's Baby,"** destined to be her most famous tale. As for the novel, her failure to sell *Young Dr. Gosse* evidently convinced her that the genre was no longer congenial to her talents. Her success with Louisiana short stories persuaded her to continue in that vein.

By the spring of 1893, Chopin was ready to collect some of her stories into one volume. After negotiation on its contents, Houghton Mifflin, on March 24, 1894, brought out ***Bayou Folk,*** a collection of twenty-three tales and sketches—"faithful, spirited representations," the blurb ran, "of [the] unfamiliar characters and customs . . .of these semi-aliens" [*Publisher's Weekly* (17 March 1894)].

Though its contents reflect a broad range of story lengths and themes, the Louisiana settings and occasionally recurring characters give this created world a loose unity with its own peculiar logic. Whether writing about conventional romances and love triangles, echoes of the war and reconstruction, the stereotyped tangles of Afro-and Euro-American relationships, or cross-generational conflicts, Chopin frequently presents themes and situations from multiple vantages, achieving an unobtrusive internal dialogue that carries over from story to story and is characteristic of her fiction.

The most explicit such dialogue occurs in the first three stories [**"A No-Account Creole," "In and Out of Old Natchitoches,"** and **"In Sabine"**]: each deals with one of the "Santien boys," a family introduced in *At Fault,* and each presents his triangular relationship with a woman and another man. Though written over five years, their place at the head of the collection focuses the continuity Chopin seems to have perceived in her work, even as their increasing sophistication dramatizes her rapid growth as a writer. (pp. 53-5)

The internal dialogue established in these introductory stories—and the self-contained world it implies—is continued more randomly in the fourth selection, which is the first of several domestic sketches involving fathers and daughters. Composed with three other short pieces (including **"Boulôt and Boulotte"**), **"A Very Fine Fiddle"** (September 13, 1891) is little more than a vignette, though rich with local detail. Young Fifine's initiative in selling her shiftless father's violin brings sudden prosperity, but at the questionable cost of her father's music. Chopin's touch here is light and skillful; the poignance of Cléophas' closing words suggests both the magnitude of his loss and the ambivalent price of material comfort.

A somewhat earlier and less successful story, **"A Rude Awakening"** (July 13, 1891), elaborates this basic situation of an energetic daughter trying to compensate for the incompetence of her father. But the tale's spirited figures (Aunt Minty and the worthless Sylveste) and unsentimental portrait of poverty do not redeem the awkward plot and obtrusive moralizing.

A third and more elaborate version of this motif, which also expands the political implications of poverty, occurs in the penultimate story, one of four published for the first time in ***Bayou Folk.*** **"A Gentleman of Bayou Têche"** (November 5-7, 1893) is the story of Evariste Bonamour. Though as poor as Cléophas and Sylveste, he is not shiftless, and his motherless daughter, Martinette, seeks for him not money but respect. She will not have him mocked in a portrait which her neighbor, Aunt Dicey, insists will be insultingly captioned: "Dis heah is one dem low-down 'Cajuns o' Bayeh Têche!"

The story's democratic assertion that poverty does not abrogate one's claim to be a gentleman occurs in the context of ubiquitous class and racial prejudice. Though pointedly poorer than Mr. Hallet's black servants, Martinette is "puffed up" over her father's modeling. At the same time, Dicey and her son, Wilkins, openly disdain the Bonamours' simplicity; Wilkins's "visible reluctance and ill-disguised contempt" in serving them are clearly intensified by the fact that the Bonamours' color admits them to Hallet's table, despite their poverty and unsophistication. And Sublet, an outsider oblivious to the human realities of the situation, views the entire group with the snobbery of an aesthete looking for quaint diversion.

Though Chopin clearly faults all these perspectives, her story also achieves a self-reflexive irony that, characteristically, calls her own perspective, and thus that of her readers, into question. Most tellingly, this is her only borrowing of G. W. Cable's Têche setting, and that fact, coupled with Sublet's view of these people as merely "bits of 'local color,' " questions the appropriateness of the entire genre. Though Chopin was critical of local colorists' exploitations of their material, she herself was, as a writer, also an outsider. And though she may have been more sensitive to her subject(s) than some, she must also have recognized herself as not greatly unlike Hallet who, though a fairly positive figure, remains patronizing—in both the best and worst senses. For Chopin, local color was a means of specifying her characters and enlarging their reality. Her consistent focus on action and personality instead of setting implies such a function. That she had second thoughts about her own exploitation of the genre—even a sensitive exploitation—seems clear. Certainly she never saw it as an end, and, indeed, she would eventually abandon it.

Still Chopin had "no objection to a commonplace theme if it be handled artistically or with originality" [*Miscellany*], and she often relied on staple texts of Southern local-color ficton, especially "the wa' "—the Civil War, that is. Unlike Page or Allen or King, however, Chopin wrote relatively few stories that commented directly on the war's aftermath and even fewer that recollected antebellum days. Of those dozen or so tales, nine are included in ***Bayou Folk,*** her most conventional and best-selling collection. Placed fifth here, **"Beyond the Bayou"** (November 7, 1891) establishes Chopin's most familiar theme in these period stories: the war's devastating effects and the restorative powers of affection. In this tale, Jacqueline, or La Folle, dramatically overcomes the psychic and geographic confinement imposed by a violent childhood experience.

The rather extensive revisions of this relatively early story are instructive of Chopin's increasing skill. Though some changes, like the elimination of translations, reflect the transition from a children's magazine to an adult collection, others significantly diminish the melodrama of La Folle's "only mania" (her fear of crossing the bayou) to a simple fact. The role of the landscape is also enhanced, becoming, much as in Mary N. Murfree's fiction, an index of character as well as—more characteristically for Chopin—a structure for thematic contrasts. The bayou, for instance, is a psychological as well as a physical barrier, and crossing it marks La Folle's transition from solitude to the communal life of the plantation. She is catapulted there by her love for a child, a symbol of human continuity and community, just as war, their opposite, had initially thrust her into neurotic isolation.

Chopin in 1876, wearing a favorite riding outfit. Neighbors in Cloutierville often disapproved of her "tight-fitting clothes, her chic hats and [the] good deal of lavender in all her costumes."

La Folle's two trips "beyond the bayou" are also contrasted: as the first to save Chéri is terrifying, so the second the next morning is serenely beautiful. Chopin's revisions here intensify the soothing, sensual patterns of the landscape and eliminate the abstractions of the new morning's "green and white and blue and silvery shinings," which had been contrasted with the "interminable red" of La Folle's mad vision. In their place are concrete details and subtle physical parallels such as the confining crescent of the bayou and the "silver bow" of the river; the "big abandoned field" and "the woods that spread back into unknown regions," now displaced by a "broad stretch of velvety lawn" and a well-cultivated, aromatic flower garden. Such contrasts sympathetically dramatize the transformation of La Folle's psyche. In fact, her "exultation" and "deep content," the rewards of her freedom, are much more unambiguous than Chopin would later permit. Even so, the revised story amply demonstrates how well Chopin could handle conventional material—black women's devotion to white children, the lingering irrationality of war, or the power of love—both "artistically" and "with originality." (pp. 60-3)

[Another reconstruction tale, **"Ma'ame Pélagie,"**] is Chopin's only explicit treatment of the popular Southern mythology of the golden days "befo' de wa' " and its consequences. Known as "Madame" though never married, Pélagie Valmêt and her sister Mam'selle Pauline have lived in poverty for thirty years beside the ruins of their once splendid mansion on the Côte Joyeuse—that strip of rich bottomland along the "coast" of the Red River, famed for its joyous prosperity. With her grand dreams of rebuilding, Pélagie is, in some ways, one of Chopin's strongest characters, ably managing a large plantation, once defying an enemy army, and loving faithfully not only her lost sweetheart Felix but also her sister. Nevertheless, as much as that of . . . La Folle; Pélagie's world is an illusion of the past.

The conflict facing her, that of choosing between a beloved past and the present needs of a beloved sister, is skillfully expressed in the architectural imagery. Emotionally as well as physically, Pélagie has lived with her sister "in the shadow of the ruin" (an earlier title). As cramped by Pélagie's dream as they are by their tiny three-room cabin, the two women refresh themselves with memories that, especially for Pauline, are shadowy indeed. But when their niece, La Petite, brings them a whiff of an "outside and dimly known world," Pauline begins to share the girl's view of her aunts' existence as a "dream-life" and "a sin" against one's self and life. A fine dream sequence dramatizes the power of the myth La Petite challenges. In it, Pélagie relives one last time the festivities and tragedies of that decaying shell. The present realities of moonlight and bats and trumpet vines mingle poignantly with vividly remembered flames of chandeliers and war, together with the double pain of a soldier's new buttons pressed upon a breaking heart. But when the night fades, Venus, the star of love, not the romantic moon, guides Pélagie back to her sister and the present. With fictional as well as material economy, the ruin is at last turned to positive ends: the shapely wooden house Pélagie builds rests "upon a solid foundation of bricks"—the red bricks of the once glorious Valmêt mansion.

Pélagie's story is Chopin's version of the female tragedy of war—the loss of youth and beauty and love and home, all those elements that define a woman's existence far more explicitly than a man's. Léandre, the Valmêt son, has quite readily abandoned "the big plantation with all its memories and traditions" and has contentedly made a new life for himself in the city. Only the women remain behind, bereft of the things that gave their lives meaning and unable either to forge new meanings or to relinquish the memory of the old. But while Chopin portrays their plight with sympathetic understanding, she does not, like other Southern writers, prefer that lost era to the present. For Chopin, that past, for all its beauty, remains lost, and to dwell there is to deny what *is* valuable—present life. Ma'ame Pélagie grows old quickly when her dream vanishes; but life flourishes around her. The purpose of the past, Chopin insists, is to nourish the present, even at its own expense.

Chopin's adaptation of such conventional material to her own evolving purposes is also evident in stories that deal with Afro-Americans. Southern local-color fiction had, of course, created several stereotypes: ex-slaves nostalgic for the good old days, cheerful pickaninnies, loyal mammies and uncles, tragic mulattoes, and cruel villains. Though Chopin only once portrayed the last of these—and then obliquely in **"Désirée's Baby"**—the others often appear, especially in her early work. ***Bayou Folk*** includes eight of the ten stories focusing on people of color written before the collection's 1894 appearance; only two other stories, both written in 1896, ever repeat that emphasis, as Chopin had by then ceased to use Afro-Americans as central characters. While, like Alphonse in **"In and Out of Old Natchitoches,"** she never quite overcame her racial biases, this group of stories reveals a gradual lessening of stereotypical views—and language—in favor of more realistic and sympathetic portrayals. (pp. 65-7)

Chopin had more success, and perhaps more sympathy, with characters of mixed blood. In the South, of course, mulattoes, quadroons, octaroons, and other offspring of mixed parentage occupied an anomalous social position, considered black by whites and often resented for their color by Afro-Americans. While it was not included in ***Bayou Folk*** and remained unpublished, **"A Little Free Mulatto"** (February 28, 1892) was Chopin's first attempt to address directly the problems of racial identification and segregation that recur in this collection. Its focus is the plight of little Aurélia, whose parents' pride in their mixed race prohibits her association with either "the white children up at the big-house, who would often willingly have had her join their games" or with "the little darkies who frolicked all day long as gleefully as kittens before their cabin doors." The child is at last transported to "paradise" when her family moves to "L'Isle des Mulâtres," an actual colony of "free mulattoes" along the Cane River, now known as Isle Brevelle. Though Chopin's sketch depicts the universality of racial pride and the pain of its isolation, it also implies her belief in the propriety of segregated communities. Aurélia's family, for instance, finds deep satisfaction in "an atmosphere which is native to them"; and the pointedly Afro-American dialect of their brief dialogue seems calculated to diminish their dignity at least in our eyes, if not in the happy Aurélia's. (p. 68)

Chopin seems to have found a better vehicle for her, at best, equivocal feelings about race in **"Désirée's Baby"** (November 24, 1892), the story on which her reputation rested until the 1950s. (p. 69)

Like the best of her mentor Maupassant's work in this mode, the ending not only inverts our expectations but seems inevitable in doing so. From the brooding atmosphere of the ironically named house, "L'Abri" (the shelter), to Armand's arrogance and his "dark, handsome face" beside his wife's gray eyes and fair skin, the groundwork is carefully laid for this reversal, offering the attentive reader a dreadful comprehension that the almost too convenient discovery of the letter stunningly confirms.

Apart from its calculated construction, **"Désirée's Baby"** also offers characters with mythical dimensions. Like the hero of classical tragedy, Armand is the proud man who comes to know himself too late as the source of "evil"—identified here with the "black blood" that Southern aristocrats like himself so feared in their legitimate offspring. More profound than any mere social stigma, however, that blackness becomes the mark of universal human darkness, that demonic region where "the very spirit of Satan" takes hold. Like Othello, whose plight as a dark foreigner marrying a fair woman resembles Armand's own situation, he is the victim of his emotional volatility. His passions are instant and furious: he falls in love "as if struck by a pistol shot," his passion sweeps along "like an avalanche, or like a prairie fire, or like anything that drives headlong over all obstacles." The violence of these similes is later echoed in the consumptive bonfire that destroys Armand's wife's and son's possessions as ruthlessly and vengefully as he had their persons. Recalling Ahab, another nineteenth-century rebel, Armand also proudly revolts against a God who has dared to injure *him,* the bearer of "one of the oldest and proudest [names] in Louisiana," a title whose very limits expose his folly. Like Melville's hero, Armand seeks a surrogate for his vengeance, but his "last blow at fate"—sending Désirée away without a word—recoils on himself in the destruction of what he most loves, the very beings who had briefly transformed his brooding spirit.

The tragic Désirée also implies depths beyond her narrative function. Like Desdemona, she is essentially passive, an innocent victim trapped by circumstances she hardly comprehends. A foundling herself, Désirée's identity is literally and metaphorically only what is given. Once she has become Armand's wife, an Aubigny, she can neither recover herself as a child of the Valmondés nor exist in any other dimension. The innocent maid who is rejected instead of cherished, Désirée has no place in life; she must die. Other ironic details abound: the adopted child of mysterious origins is "desired" while that of Armand's flesh is unwanted; Armand's mother believes the knowledge of her race will be concealed to good purpose; the stone pillar that first shelters and then becomes identified with Désirée—"silent, white, motionless"; the inverted imagery of Providence and Satan, or of black and white, including "La Blanche," the quadroon maid, whose pale skin indicts both her mistress and her master.

But the element that gives the story its impact is its exploration of the powerful feelings about race and miscegenation that persist in American culture. Rooted in separatism, these fears are partly engendered by a misguided notion of innocence. Armand's pride is that of the "pure," whose tragedy lies in not learning soon enough that none of us are truly set apart, free from the blemishes we perceive in others. To act on such premises, as he does, ensures a rigorous isolation indeed: spiritual death. Of course, Chopin's association of black with Satanic evil and the discovery that the cruel villain of the piece *is* Afro-American reveals her continuing ambivalence about race. Even so, her portrayal of the senseless destruction that arises from unexamined pride and fears comments powerfully on the ironic, wasteful nature of prejudice. This insight she explores again in **"La Belle Zoraïde."**

Published with its companion piece, **"A Lady of Bayou St. John,"** in *Vogue,* **"La Belle Zoraïde"** (September 21, 1893) is Chopin's most sympathetic version of a stock figure in local-color fiction, the tragic mulatto. Placed near the end of ***Bayou Folk,*** the tale draws together several of the volume's major themes: madness, triangular relationships, and racial pride and prejudice. Manna-Loulou's account of **"La Belle Zoraïde,"** the beautiful quadroon, and her love for "le beau Mézor," a black slave, is a tragedy precipitated by Zoraïde's selfish white mistress, Madame Delarivière. As in **"Désirée's Baby,"** the calamity issues from an irrational hatred of blackness and an egotistical, destructive desire for control. But while Zoraïde is more powerless than Désirée, she refuses to be shaped by others' definitions of herself. She is, she insists, "not white." And when her beloved Mézor, "straight as a cypress-tree and as proud looking as a king," is sold away and their child vindictively taken from her, Zoraïde withdraws into madness. Loved for her white beauty and despised for her black attachments, she will not endure the enforced split of her being. Zoraïde prefers instead her own private world with its senseless rag "piti" ("petite" or "little one") to the selfish, racist insanity around her. Her retreat, then, though tragic and limited, is nonetheless authentic self-assertion.

An unusual frame tale reasserts these themes and accents its layered, fictional self-consciousness. The highly crafted opening, for example, moves unobtrusively from an outdoor panorama to an interior, focusing on characters from the earlier companion piece. A passing boatman's sad patois song recalls to Manna-Loulou another old song and the story of Zoraïde, as she turns from the window to her mistress lying "in her sumptuous mahogany bed," waiting to be entertained by her personal Scheherazade. But just as this young madame's vanity and selfishness echo Madame Delarivière's, so Manna-Loulou's interjection about the incorrigibility of "negroes" betrays a self-consciousness beneath her subservient exterior and emphasizes the story's multiple awarenesses. Certainly the servant sees, as we do, more in the story than her mistress, who fastens sentimentally on the plight of the orphaned child. Her apparent obliviousness to the tragedy of a woman unable to love whom she chooses is echoed in her larger blindness to the personal and structural injustice that occasions such pain. Finally, Chopin's curious coda, which repeats the women's final conversation "in the soft Creole patóis, whose music and charm no English words can convey," redoubles this narrative layering, calling attention not only to the fictiveness of this reality but also to its obliqueness, full of half-hidden, hardly understood messages. Such technical and thematic subtleties mark the tale as one of Chopin's best. (pp. 70-3)

[Perhaps] Chopin's most artful combination of sexual politics and social prejudice occurs in her second *Two Tales* story, **"At the 'Cadian Ball"** (July 15-17, 1892). Set in St.

James Parish, a cane-growing region a short way up the Mississippi River's "coast" from New Orleans, two interlocking love stories are adeptly woven around the occurrence of the title. Big, brown Bobinôt loves "that little Spanish vixen" Calixta, who has also attracted the attentions of Alcée Laballière, a local planter. In the contest for her favors at the ball, the simple farmer is no match for the suave gentleman planter. But when Alcée's elusive kinswoman, Clarisse, suddenly appears to summon him home, he responds like "one who awakes suddenly from a dream." The ball finally ends as a disappointed Calixta listlessly yields her hand to a grateful Bobinôt, while Clarisse tells an ecstatic Alcée that she will marry him.

The narrative's subtle unfolding of the lovers' conflicts incorporates excellent local detail. For example, Chopin's survey of the ball—its midnight gumbo, the fiddlers and cardplayers, *le parc aux petits* for sleeping babies, the dancers and the gossipy chatter—establishes the gay communal context in which partners can be chosen. Similarly, secondary characters, like Bruce, Alcée's manservant, economically move the plot forward; and the black man's colorful monologue, which reluctantly reveals far more than he intends to the persistent Clarisse, exemplifies Chopin's mastery of a genre piece.

But it is the tale's psychological and social perception that distinguishes it. All four lovers want precisely what they cannot have, and, while three eventually achieve their desires, none, we suspect, will find much satisfaction in their accomplishments. The unpredictabilities of passion and the barriers of class complicate and unsettle the neat symmetry of the final couplings. And in an unpublished sequel, **"The Storm,"** Chopin confirms these expectations, even as the later story reverses society's earlier triumph over personal desire.

The ways in which class constrains female passion and the price of violating class limits are a central issue. Because she is only a simple 'Cadian, with Spanish blood to boot, Calixta enjoys an apparent freedom of self-expression, including fighting, swearing, and inviting "a breath of scandal" when she visits neighboring Assumption Parish. But while she enjoys exploiting her attractions, Calixta's frankly sexual appeal has clear bounds: she can charm Alcée, but she cannot claim him. As with 'Tite Reine earlier, her failure is the conventional punishment for any woman who dares to be too openly passionate: she is deserted by the rich hero and deemed lucky to get anyone, even stodgy Bobinôt.

But if Chopin does not sanction Calixta's reckless spirit, her criticism of the upper-class alternative is only more subtly depicted. Though Clarisse also focuses male attention, her role as Creole Lady—"Cold and kind and cruel by turn"—deftly conceals her pleasure in it. When Alcée, in a fit of passion, one day clasps her by the arms and pants "a volley of hot, blistering love-words into her face," she instantly chills him with "her calm, clear eyes" and disdainfully adjusts "the careful toilet that he had so brutally disarranged." Clarisse is the classic tease, the woman whose power—whose hope—lies in manipulation to defeat her rival for the male.

Of course, Clarisse's success also depends on Alcée's complicitous assent to the paradigms of feminine behavior. For him, Calixta is never more than a "little fling," a diversion from his troubles with nice (and other) women, and he forgets her as soon as he hears Clarisse's voice. Indeed, his gentlemanly expectations of winning a "real lady" blind him, finally, to anything but the patent illusion of his conquest.

The lower-class Bobinôt, on the other hand, lacks even the support of these mythologies. Though as jealous as Clarisse, he must rely on his own patient fidelity and the other woman's initiative to achieve his ends. Only after Calixta is abandoned, "almost ugly after the night's dissipation," does he have any chance with her, and even then because Calixta is as willing to spite Alcée for his rejection as Alcée was to requite Clarisse's coyness. Bobinôt's powerlessness also implies male fears of emasculation when the force of female sexuality is freed from its ladylike disguise. Certainly, Calixta's "business-like manner" in proposing to Bobinôt indicates her resignation from a game in which her natural assets are useless against the more respectable artifice of femininity.

But while this plot . . . apparently confirms conventional models of female behavior, its costs suggest a deep ambivalence, echoed in the tale's final image. The end of the ball concludes the courtships, ending the dance figures that have left Alcée and Clarisse, Bobinôt and Calixta, together as partners. In the distance, there is the "rapid discharge of pistol-shots," a harmless signal, we are assured, that *"le bal est fini"*; but the ominous note of violence reverberates with the other disquieting events that have marked the 'Cadian ball. Placed among ***Bayou Folk***'s final and best stories, **"At the 'Cadian Ball"** thus symbolically disturbs the uncertain realities that lie beneath these quaint local-color surfaces and exposes the hidden power of Chopin's finest art.

Bayou Folk represents Chopin's most sophisticated use of local-color themes—themes she had consciously exploited for commercial success; but it also reveals her recognition of their limits. For Chopin, the stereotypes of Southern aristocracy, of antebellum nostalgia, of Afro-American subservience and loyalty, even of romantic love, seem in her best work a bit frayed at the edges. That fraying was acceptable and even refreshing in a genre grown increasingly stale and, by the 1890s, playing itself out. But it also reflected a challenge both to fiction and to the society it describes. By insisting on the ambivalences concealed in these pious stereotypes, Chopin was actually forging her own, more Jamesian brand of realism and thus preparing the way for a more overt critique of the superficialities of human behavior. (pp. 76-9)

[Chopin expressed] impatience with both social judgmentalism and thoughtless idealism. In her diary entries of 1894, she rails at both, exclaiming over the moral pretensions of the "ladies & gentlemen sapping the vitality from our every day existence" and at the reformer who "does not ever realize the futility of effort" [*Miscellany*]. For Chopin, the concrete substance of life was what mattered, and she had little time for those who cared only for its appearances or too superficially for its ideal possibilities.

With the splendid success of ***Bayou Folk*** behind her as encouragement, she set out in the years following its publication to explore that substance with increased vigor and trenchancy. (p. 84)

• • • • •

Eighteen ninety-four was productive and busy for Kate Chopin. Continuing to write and sell stories, she was also occupied with promotional visits and readings for her new collection. That May, for example, having accepted yet another invitation to an "immensely uninteresting" gathering of society people, she confessed in her journal that "the commercial instinct" made her do it; "I want the book to succeed," she confided. In fact, the book was selling well. By June she had received "more than a hundred press notices." Prestigious journals like *The Nation* were calling her stories "among the most clever and charming that have seen the light" [see excerpt dated 1894]; *Atlantic Monthly* praised her "distinctive power" and her "clearness of perception," and concluded that she was "a genuine and delightful addition to the ranks of our storytellers" [see excerpt dated 1894].

But mere acclaim did not satisfy her. She pointed out that among those notices, there were only a "very small number which show anything like a worthy critical faculty. . . . I had no idea the genuine book critic was so rare a bird." A discriminating reader herself, Chopin had hoped for an audience appreciative of her achievements and critics who could see past the quaint, attractive surfaces of dialect and local color. Early on, she had recognized that the way to national recognition lay in exploiting the unique subject of the bayou country. But she also knew that the real quality of her fiction rested not in surfaces but in her ability to convey "human existence in its subtle, complex, true meaning, stripped of the veil with which ethical and conventional standards have draped it"—her injunction to midwestern writers that June.

Chopin was keenly aware of the limitations of superficial art. After all, her discovery of "life, not fiction" in Maupassant had inspired her to write. The "naturalness and ease" of her local-color fiction were indeed, as the *Atlantic Monthly* editor had suspected, indicators "of power awaiting opportunity." The success of her collection gave her precisely the opportunity—confidence and an audience—that her fictional powers required. (pp. 85-6)

Kate Chopin was quite conscious of the demands of her craft and the fiction she approved. That she took her art seriously is further confirmed by a brief private comment from the "Impressions" she began recording that summer of 1894. Meditating on her previous decade, the loss of Oscar and her mother, her return to St. Louis and the beginning of her writing career, she describes these as "ten years of my growth—my real growth" [*Miscellany*]. And while she asserts her willingness to exchange them for her loved ones, she declares that she "cannot live through yesterday," lingering lovingly at gravesides. At forty-three, she had acquired a sense of which things fade and which endure, and she had no intention of pursuing the former.

Given such convictions, it can be no coincidence that immediately after the success of ***Bayou Folk,*** Chopin turned, for the first time in nearly two years, to non-Louisiana settings and to characters and themes much less conventional than those that had created the national audience she now enjoyed. Having caught the public's ear at last, Chopin apparently felt freed of the confines of local color and immediately set about to clarify the "subtle, complex, true meanings" that alone would give her art permanence. Paris, St. Louis, and the Missouri hills join New Orleans and Natchitoches as locales, and the unfamiliar settings that had initially sold her work now recede to simply an essential context of a specific reality. Recurring themes assume a new prominence: the unresolved tensions between a developing self and a rigid social code, the consequences of sexual awareness and its repressions, the nature and cost of self-assertion, the role of perception in human behavior. And while the first of these stories were to remain uncollected, their composition clearly affected Chopin's later Louisiana tales.

One index of Chopin's experimentalism is the difficulty she had in placing some of these new stories. *Century,* Chopin's usual first choice for her better work, rejected **"The Story of an Hour,"** as did *Vogue* at first; after the success of ***Bayou Folk,*** *Vogue* reconsidered and purchased it for ten dollars. **"Lilacs"** was read by eight editors before the New Orleans *Times-Democrat* accepted it, two years after its composition. **"Cavanelle"** and **"A Sentimental Soul"** had similar difficulties; the latter was finally purchased by the *Times-Democrat* in 1895, continuing what had become a tradition of carrying a Chopin story at Christmas.

Despite *Vogue*'s reluctance, **"The Dream of an Hour"** (as it was editorially titled) [April 19, 1894], is quite remarkable, ranking with *The Awakening* as one of Chopin's most memorable statements of female self-assertion. It was the first of her experimental tales, and Seyersted sees it as a direct response to her collection's success, an expression of "release from what she evidently felt as repression or frustration, thereby freeing forces that had lain dormant in her" [Seyersted, *Kate Chopin: A Critical Biography* (1969)].

"The Story of an Hour" recounts Louise Mallard's unexpected response to the reported death of her husband, Brently, in a train accident. Grieving alone in her room, she slowly recognizes that she has lost only chains: 'Free! Body and soul free!' she kept whispering." Then when her husband suddenly reappears, the report of his death a mistake, she drops dead at the sight of him—of "heart disease," the doctors announce, "of joy that kills."

Chopin's handling of details illustrates how subtly she manages this controversial material. Louise Mallard's heart disease, for example, the key to the final ironies and ambiguities, is introduced in the first sentence, like the loaded gun of melodrama. But her illness gradually deepens in significance from a physical detail—a symptom of delicacy and a reason to break the bad news gently—to a deeply spiritual problem. The more we learn about Brently Mallard's overbearing nature and the greater his wife's relief grows, the better we understand her "heart trouble." Indeed, that "trouble" vanishes with Brently's death and returns—fatally—only when he reappears.

But Chopin also exposes Louise's complicity in Mallard's subtle oppression. Her submission to his "blind persistence" has been the guise of Love, that self-sacrificing Victorian ideal. Glorified in fiction Chopin had often decried, this love has been, for Louise and others, the primary purpose of life. But through her new perspective, she comprehends that "love, the unsolved mystery" counts for very little "in face of this possession of self-assertion which she suddenly recognized as the strongest impulse of her being!" As Chopin often insists, love is not a substitute for selfhood; indeed, selfhood is love's precondition. Such a strong and unconventional assertion of feminine independence likely explains *Century*'s rejection. Its editor, R. W. Gilder, had zealously guarded the feminine ideal of self-denying love, and was that very summer publishing editorials against women's suffrage as a threat to family and home.

The setting, too, reflecting Chopin's local-color lessons, buttresses her themes. Louise stares through an "open window" at a scene which is "all aquiver with the new spring life." A renewing rain accompanies her "storm of grief," followed by "patches of blue sky." Then, explicitly "through the sounds, the scents, the color that filled the air," "it" comes "creeping out of the sky" upon her. Louise at first dutifully resists and then helplessly succumbs. The sense of physical, even sexual, release that accompanies her acquiescence to this nameless "thing" underpins a vision of freedom that Chopin characteristically affirms as a human right—as natural as generation, spring, or even death.

The transforming power of that insight is echoed in Louise's altered view of the future, whose length "only yesterday" she had dreaded, but to which she now "opened and spread her arms . . . in welcome." But it is a false vision. The habit of repression has so weakened Louise that her glimpse of freedom—her birthright—does not empower her, but leaves her unable to cope with the everyday reality to which she is abruptly restored. In her conventional marriage, the vision is truly illusory.

Chopin skillfully manipulates the point of view to intensify the final revelation and the shifting perspectives on Louise's life. "Mrs. Mallard" appears to us at first from a distance; but the focus gradually internalizes, until we are confined within her thoughts, struggling with "Louise" toward insight. As she leaves the private room of her inner self, our point of view retreats; we see her "like a goddess of Victory" as she descends the stairs, and then, as the door opens, we are identified with the unsuspecting Brently, sharing his amazement at his sister-in-law's outcry and his friend's futile effort to block his wife's view. The final sentence, giving the doctors' clinical interpretation of her death, is still more distant. That distance—and the shift it represents—is crucial. To outsiders, Louise Mallard's demise is as misunderstood as is her reaction to Brently's death. That even the respected medical profession misinterprets her collapse indicts the conventional view of female devotion and suggests that Louise Mallard is not the only woman whose behavior has been misread.

Such shifting perspectives and the effort to balance the desire for freedom with realistic limitations also characterize Chopin's next story, **"Lilacs"** (May 14-16, 1894). Described to a prospective editor as one of her best, it is her only tale set entirely in France. Its focus is Madame Adrienne Farival's annual visit to the convent of her childhood at lilac time. One year, however, she is turned away by the Mother Superior, who has learned that Madame is no pious widow, but "Mademoiselle," a professional singer in Paris.

The story's two very different environments afford an intriguing double view of Adrienne. At the convent, where she seeks a lost childhood innocence, she is part of a pastoral idyll, inhabiting a lush, spring garden of simplicity and generous female affection. But the shift to Paris reveals a different Adrienne, "clad in a charming negligé . . . reclining indolently in the depths of a luxurious armchair" in a lavish, disordered apartment. This is no innocent, but a petulant, extravagant sensualist, a star of the Paris theater. Each mutually complicating background reveals very different dimensions of Adrienne's sensuous and spontaneous but ultimately childish character.

By her second visit, our response to Adrienne has altered with that of the sisters. Instead of a jubilant welcome, she receives the Mother Superior's "bitter reproachful lines," made cruel by Adrienne's evident need for serenity, but undeniably deserved by her duplicity. This ambivalence is focused in the glimpse of her friend Sister Agathe's convulsive sorrow; the stern suppression of the nun's spontaneous affection is the painful inverse of Adrienne's irresponsible freedom.

Though Chopin attempts to balance the conflicting demands of discipline and freedom, she obviously distrusts the suppression of feeling. Such suppression was one reason she thought so little of religious life, even though her childhood friend Kitty Garesché had joined a religious community. A few days after she had completed **"Lilacs"** she described a recent convent visit, declaring that she "would rather be that dog" than a nun, since it was "a little picture of life and that what we had left was a phantasmagoria." That entry tellingly continues with Chopin's recollection of her own first experience of childbirth, concluding "It must be the pure animal sensation; nothing spiritual could be so real—so poignant" [*Miscellany*]. But while Chopin impugned sensual repression, she also recognized the power of the opposing moral forces. Even Adrienne accepts the Mother Superior's banishment as just, if unkind. The bitter defeat of Adrienne's defiance is captured in the story's concluding gesture:

> After a short while, a lay sister came out of the door with a broom, and swept away the lilac blossoms which Adrienne had let fall upon the portico.

For Adrienne, discarding these harbingers of spring and renewal marks the end of innocence; but for the sisters, too, it signals the shutting out of human warmth and sensuous affection. Adrienne's irresponsibility will not again sully their closely guarded innocence, but neither will her reckless spirit liberate them from the rigid morality they defend at such a high cost.

Chopin's impatience with the superficial morality of much

organized religion resurfaces in her next sketch, originally written in her diary. **"The Night Came Slowly"** (July 24, 1894) juxtaposes the mysticism of the night and nature with the daytime visit of an unpleasant young evangelist. As in **"Lilacs,"** the sensuousness of nature represents a more authentic access to God and the spirit than any arrogant human scheme. Chopin's particularly unsympathetic treatment of the "young fool" and his "Bible Class" emphasizes her insistence on a more transcendental path: "I would rather ask the stars [about Christ]," she concludes; "they have seen him."

A day or two later, Chopin developed this opposition of morality to human spontaneity in another diary sketch. After some changes, **"Juanita"** (July 26, 1894) eventually appeared with **"The Night Came Slowly"** in the short-lived, avant-garde magazine *Moods* (Philadelphia). Its focus is a five-foot-ten, two-hundred-pound country woman, whose attractiveness to men the narrator finds incomprehensible. Despite stories of Texas suitors with millions, however, Juanita chooses a poor, one-legged man. That they are married when she bears his child is unclear, but Chopin's conclusion is nonchalant: "For my part I never expected Juanita to be more respectable than a squirrel; and I don't see how any one else could have expected it." Reflecting Chopin's eye for the grotesque, as well as the picturesque, the sketch implies the curious couple's harmony with nature if not with human morality: "They go off thus to the woods together where they may love each other away from all prying eyes save those of the birds and squirrels. But what do the squirrels care!" The tonal ambivalence, like that in **"Lilacs,"** accentuates the tension Chopin perceived between moral appearances and nature's serene reality. (pp. 87-93)

[By October, 1894, Chopin] had "ready another collection of Creole tales" which she hoped "to have published in book form after they have made their slow way through the magazines. Two-thirds of the stories in ***A Night in Acadie*** (1897) were already complete and soon to be in print; others would be added. But the final collection is only superficially "another collection of Creole tales"; her confident experiments with settings and themes, and the lessons of her translations and essays, had left their mark. Fully half of the stories Chopin collected for ***A Night in Acadie*** were actually written before ***Bayou Folk*** appeared. Since she had deliberately overlooked them for the earlier volume, it seems probable that, in gathering these remaining Louisiana tales now, she counted on them to fill out any slightness and to balance her newer, bolder stories.

Certainly, the impression of ***A Night in Acadie*** is very different from that of ***Bayou Folk.*** Chopin's bayou world persists, but its romance and charm seem diminished, its happy endings muted. In fact, there are both fewer love stories and fewer tragic conclusions than before. Melodrama, too, has faded, implying a greater moral ambivalence than in ***Bayou Folk.*** But although this second collection contains some of Chopin's most distinguished work, contemporary reviewers were not very enthusiastic. *Nation* found the collection "sometimes a thought too heavy" [see excerpt dated 1898] and *Critic* believed it "marred by one or two slight and unnecessary coarsenesses." William Marion Reedy, however, observed more astutely in his *Mirror* that the collection was clearly about "the same old human nature that is old as mankind." (p. 94)

"Azélie" (July 22-23, 1893), is the earliest of several rather elusive love stories included in ***A Night in Acadie,*** one of a series of tales of mid-and late 1893 that explore obsessive love, especially for remote or unattainable objects. Though devoted to her worthless Popa, Azélie lacks the moral sense of other daughters in Chopin. But her deficiency only intensifies the infatuation of 'Polyte, the local plantation's store manager. Passive and essentially amoral (like the later **"Juanita"**), Azélie is indifferent to the overzealous attentions of the youth, who feels his love for her a degradation, but irresistible. Like other reformers, usually female, 'Polyte thinks he can "rescue her from . . . the demoralizing influences of her family and her surroundings." But Azélie won't cooperate, and instead, 'Polyte follows her blindly to the moral "graveyard" "yonda on Li'le river—w'ere Azélie." 'Polyte's attraction is perhaps closer to lust than love, given his oblivion to her moral failings (including theft) and his preoccupation with her physical proximity, but his loss of self is no less complete. Chopin's oblique approach to his obsession and her detached, bemused tone invite puzzlement at the hidden, chaotic forces at work on poor 'Polyte.

In **"At Chênière Caminada"** (October 21-23, 1893), physical passion is better transmuted into romance. When the painfully shy Tonie Bocaze (who reappears in *The Awakening*) hears the lovely Mlle. Claire Duvigné play the organ at Chênière Caminada, a Gulf Coast resort, he is immediately smitten. As uncultivated and instinctual as a Lawrentian hero, Tonie obeys the sudden dictates of love as naturally as those of hunger and thirst. But these mortal desires remain unsatisfied because their object is, for him, as remote as heaven itself. In fact, Tonie's passion is too literally mortal. Recalling an afternoon as Claire's hired sailor, he is "stirred by a terrible, an overmastering regret, that he had not clasped her in his arms when they were out there alone, and sprung with her into the sea." For her part, Claire artfully and willingly engages in romantic poses, including one that causes her death. But in dying she at last becomes "that celestial being whom our Lady of Lourdes had once offered to [Tonie's] immortal vision." Thus, like **"A Lady of Bayou St. John,"** Tonie can fully indulge his romantic desires for his beloved. Claire's death thus unites what for Chopin were the twin transcendences of romance and religion. As in several later tales (**"Lilacs," "Two Portraits,"** and **"A Sentimental Soul"**), this coupling deepens her presentation of the conflict between body and spirit, art and innocence.

"A Respectable Woman" (January 20, 1894) moves Chopin's fiction still closer to an open examination of desire. Offering perhaps her most ambivalent conclusion, it details the growing attraction of Mrs. Baroda for her husband's unassuming old friend, Gouvernail, another recurring character. Though she at first flees temptation, and later opposes his second visit, she eventually encourages her husband to invite his friend again, enigmatically remarking that "This time I shall be very nice to him."

Despite its effect of surprise, this concluding equivocation is carefully anticipated. Indeed, one subtext here is precisely the ambiguous role of perception in behavior. Mrs. Baroda's initial displeasure provokes—and is provoked by—her unconscious and negative image of this man she has never met, an image instantly dissipated by Gouvernail's attractive reality. Acting the part of unconscious coquette, Mrs. Baroda exhausts her resources to secure his attentions and then so confuses her emotions that only flight can resolve her adolescent dubieties.

Gouvernail is no less oblique. Under the oak, talking "freely and intimately" of the past and present, he recites an "apostrophe to the night" from Whitman, a passage whose context is unmistakably erotic. As his reserve falls away, he remarks his pleasure in this "little whiff of genuine life" out in the country, which life is for him clearly physical. The erotic tension is left sharply unresolved, the surfaces as calm as the Southern night itself. But the compelling conflict between respectability and desire is reiterated in other tensions, between Mr. Baroda's unconscious serenity and his wife's flustered confusion, between their evident affection and the turbulence of adulterous passion. That tension is further heightened by Gaston's eagerness for Gouvernail's return—and his own cuckolding. Delicate enough to tease our doubts as to whether Mrs. Baroda has finally overcome her desire or her respectability, the story eloquently delineates the electric communications of sexuality. And its poised withholding of judgment attests to Chopin's mastery of tone and authorial distance. (pp. 96-9)

[Ten] tales of ***A Night in Acadie*** were all written after the flush of ***Bayou Folk***'s success and the experimentation that followed it. Many reflect Chopin's increasing self-confidence and more direct approach to her characteristic themes in a familiar setting. At the same time, contemporary, non-Louisiana tales parallel the concerns of those later incorporated into ***A Night in Acadie,*** particularly her increasing interest in duality and sexual repression. Accordingly, these intervening stories will also be treated here.

"Cavanelle" (July 31-August 6, 1894), her first Creole story in five months, is rich in mannered, picturesque detail. Its extensive revisions, some of which delete identifying references, and Chopin's contemporaneous composition of two other unusual personal narratives, **"The Night Came Slowly"** and **"Juanita,"** indicate her experimentation not only with point of view (only nine of her sketches use first person), but also with the close translation of life into art. Certainly, Cavanelle is vividly drawn—"an innocent, delightful humbug" of a New Orleans merchant whose fractured speech patterns reveal his characteristic nervous energy. His one passion is his sister Mathilde, for the sake of whose wonderful voice—an illusion of his affection—he has devotedly scrimped. But when the young girl dies, Cavanelle immediately assumes the care of his Aunt Félicie—"a noble woman who has suffer' the mos' cruel affliction, an' deprivation, since the war." The female narrator then recognizes that Cavanelle's heroic devotion is its own end.

The narrator's ruminations and changing assessments of the little man give the tale an unusually meditative quality, as if she were turning a memory, trying to divine its meaning. The narrative is marked by her self-conscious lapses—not recalling which color streetcar she rode to Cavanelle's house, or what piece Matilde sang—as well as by digressive fantasies about the maid's voodoo practices or Cavanelle's self-indulgences after Matilde's death. Though her assessment of Cavanelle is identically phrased at the beginning and end of her account ("Cavanelle was an angel"), its meaning is deepened by these intervening reflections. The initial sense of saintliness includes, by the end, an awareness of Cavanelle's personal need for self-sacrifice, irrespective of the good consequences for his relatives. Devotion to others is Cavanelle's peculiar means of self-assertion.

The value of other-centeredness, a notion running counter to several stories of the spring and summer, also shapes Chopin's next tale, **"Regret"** (September 17, 1894), which specifically examines the limits and costs of self-sufficiency. Mamzelle Aurélie, never married, is near fifty when the unexpected, temporary care of four small children causes her to reevaluate her complacent solitude. Unlike the hero of Maupassant's tale of the same name, Aurélie has had no remorse, remaining unmarried simply because she has "never been in love." But if Aurélie's experience challenges her unconventional independence, the source of that challenge is also unconventional—the importance of the sensual life.

What the children reveal to Aurélie is exactly the sensual dimensions of her unrecognized loss. Their sticky fingers and moist kisses, their needs for aired nightgowns and clean feet, for mended clothes and rocking, disorient her orderly, almost abstract existence. The persistent animal imagery associated with the children further underlines Aurélie's limited comprehension of their bodiliness. "Little children are not little pigs," she learns, whose only need is food, nor can they, like chickens, be shooed into shelter at bedtime. But their physical demands have an emotional component with which Mamzelle only gradually comes to terms. And the depths of that revelation, the sensual dimension of love, leave her full of regret when the children depart.

Chopin intensifies the poignancy of Mamzelle's sorrow both in the affectionate portraits of the children's exactions and in the emotionally charged settings. Initially, Mamzelle's isolation is rather neutral, mirrored by her remote farm, which she inhabits "quite alone" except for her dog, her gun, and her religion. But the children rupture the contentment of that solitude. And the final, sudden stillness over the sad disarray left by her little guests and the evening shadows "creeping and deepening around her solitary figure" effectively dramatize her revelation. Mamzelle cries "like a man, with sobs that seemed to tear her very soul." But this recollection of her earlier masculine independence now seems woefully incomplete. An inverse of Louise Mallard, Aurélie has glimpsed a life that has revealed the insufficiency of her own. Though neither woman copes very well with the reality that remains, Aurélie's survival hints the superiority of independence.

Just two days later, Chopin again focused on the choices women face, arriving at still more acrid conclusions. **"The**

Kiss" (September 19, 1894), a non-Louisiana story not included in ***A Night in Acadie,*** features the lovely and ruthless Nathalie, who, like Lily Bart in Wharton's *House of Mirth,* finds her plots to marry a rich man almost foiled by a more passionate admirer. But Nathalie is far less refined than Lily, and when she discovers that she cannot have both love and money, she readily settles for the latter. Unlike Aurélie, Nathalie foresees the loss of sensual love, but her faint regret also articulates the older woman's plight: "Well, she had Brantain and his million left. A person can't have everything in this world; and it was a little unreasonable of her to expect it." Neither woman can combine independence and sensual satisfaction. But while Aurélie's ignorance sympathetically confirms conventional notions of female fulfillment, Nathalie's calculating violation of that code provokes condemnation. Indeed, the bitter realism of Nathalie's preference of security to romance, which invokes Maupassant, jars against the comic urbanity of its Howellsian plot. This curious hybrid underscores a subtle ambivalence about female roles, a duality that continued to shape Chopin's work. (pp. 101-04)

Occupied in October by essays, Chopin followed them with two stories that again pick up these conflicting threads of self-assertion and social or religious convention. **"A Sentimental Soul"** (November 18-22, 1894) is Mlle. Fleurette, whose shy passion for one of her customers, Lacodie, occasions a moral crisis. Characteristically, Chopin unfolds the shopkeeper's affection gradually, showing her nervous attentions and slow awakening to love while coyly concealing the source of trouble: "He was the husband of another woman." As in **"Lilacs,"** a natural longing for sensuous affection is opposed to a rigid moral scheme, embodied both in Mamzelle's intense scruples—"murder was perhaps blacker, but she was not sure"—and in her stern confessor, Father Fochelle. Mamzelle's long-repressed emotions at last find an outlet when Lacodie dies and his fat, attractive young wife quickly remarries. Though forbidden by Father Fochelle to indulge her romantic fantasies, Mamzelle longs to be Lacodie's bereaved and perfect lover. Given her childish dependence on external religious authority, choosing the sentimental role of spiritual widow has revolutionary implications: "for the first time in her life to take her conscience into her own keeping."

As with most great moral acts, this one is reflected in a small gesture; she goes to confession in a distant parish, and she does not submit her decision to the new priest's scrutiny. Her reaction is pure elation: "The sensation of walking on air was altogether delicious; she had never experienced it before." Though she has not escaped the categories of sentimental romance, Mamzelle's growth is real. Taking responsibility for her life and giving it even this very limited purpose is, after all, no small achievement. Indeed, as Chopin once rather wryly remarked of a friend who had declared that she lived for euchre: "Well—after all—something to live for—that is the main thing!" [*Miscellany*].

Chopin's next story, **"Her Letters"** (November 29, 1894), set in St. Louis and thus excluded from ***A Night in Acadie,*** explores the consequences of the secret adultery Mamzelle Fleurette did not have the courage to commit. Unable to

A sketch of Chopin in 1900 by her son Oscar, who worked as an illustrator and cartoonist for the St. Louis Post-Dispatch.

destroy her four-year-old love letters, the unnamed woman of the story is as sentimental as Mamzelle. Both her sustenance ("some god-given morsel") and a corrosive (whose every passionate word "had long ago eaten its way into her brain"), these letters substantiate a hidden, sensual life—her real life—and she prefers the memory of that life and love to the empty reality of her marriage.

Chopin's technique of gradual unfolding is especially apt here. Tantalizing us with the woman's "dread of possibilities" and her "premonition of danger" in going away, Chopin only clarifies her plight well into the story with the mention of the "dear one." The characters' anonymity deepens this sense of mystery and distance, which intensifies in the ironic contrast between our intimate perspective on the woman and the misperceptions of her character by her husband and closest friends. Chopin's skillful use of setting echoes this dual perspective: an external bleakness ("a leaden sky in which there was no gleam, no rift, no promise") set against a glowing interior, with its wood fire brightening and illumining the luxurious apartment to its furthermost corner. The repetition of this scene a year later—both of gestures and emotional conflict—dramatizes the very different consequences of the woman's secret life for herself and for her husband. Indeed, the final irony is that, even destroyed, her letters do exactly what she had feared they might. But their mortal power has in fact sprung from the weakness of the couple's love; while she has preferred her hidden life to his well-being, his "man-instinct of possession" has violated her right to that independent self. As the last of 1894's probing tales, **"Her Letters"** is an austere comment on the conflicts engendered by social and sexual roles, as well as perhaps an intriguing aside on Chopin's own romantic interlude in Cloutierville. Increasingly, as in this tale, the hidden self is the reality that conventions and superficial perceptions only conceal or distort. And while stories like **"Ozème's Holiday"** suggest the humor of such distortions, their ominous, destructive power defines a stronger current in Chopin's fiction. (pp. 104-07)

The second story in ***A Night in Acadie,*** **["Athénaïse"]** gathers several of the collection's most significant themes. An 1893 allusion to its subject, the marriage of Athénaïse Miché (in **"In and Out of Old Natchitoches"**), suggests that Chopin had the story in mind for some time. When Athénaïse returns home abruptly after only two months of marriage, her brother Montéclin helps her to flee to New Orleans. In a variation on Suzanne St. Denys Godolph's visit to the city in the earlier tale, Athénaïse arouses the interests of the sensitive Gouvernail, the very one who recited poetry to Mrs. Baroda (**"A Respectable Woman"**). While Gouvernail patiently awaits some response to his affection, Athénaïse discovers that she is pregnant, and without hesitation, returns to her husband, Cazeau, "her whole passionate nature" aroused for the first time, "as if by a miracle."

With its complex heroine and sophisticated critique of marriage and female sexuality, **"Athénaïse"** marks a major step on the way to *The Awakening.* While nineteenth-century ladies, in fiction and in real life, were expected to dislike any passionate expression, a lawful wedding ceremony was supposed to translate the virginal bride to the more respectable ecstasies of motherhood. In **"Athénaïse,"** Chopin frankly examines this maidenly reticence as a function not only of sexual apprehension, but of the formidable nature of wedlock itself. That she links Athénaïse's sexual awakening with motherhood complicates her criticism of the institution of marriage, even as it probably eased *Atlantic Monthly*'s acceptance of this superb tale.

In fact, the sanctity of marriage is prejudiced throughout the narrative's early sections: by Athénaïse's brother's helpful litany of legitimate motives for divorce—abuse, drunkenness, hatred; by their parents' observation about its "formation of a woman's character"; by her father's admiration for compelled obedience; and by Athénaïse's own view of it as a trap for young girls, even as she acknowledges "the futility of rebellion against a social and sacred institution." But the most damning evidence against marriage is perceived by Cazeau as he follows the reluctant Athénaïse home. By "some association of ideas," he suddenly recalls a childhood scene when his father had recaptured a runaway slave, Black Gabe. The memory leaves a hideous impression, and the parallel arouses a profound consciousness of the humiliation that masterhood involves. His own self-respect requires that he relinquish the right to compel another human being to do his will.

Gouvernail has a similar view of the freedom necessary for love, but, for him, wedlock is not the indissoluble bond that Cazeau glumly feels he and Athénaïse must make the best of. Rather, it is a spiritual affair, based only on the lovers' mutual desire, or, as one essayist had put it in 1889: "[a] true marriage is a natural concord and agreement of souls . . .the death of love is the end of marriage." Gouvernail is simply waiting for "the death of love" of Athénaïse for Cazeau, so that he might propose a "true marriage" of souls. But while both he and Cazeau differently allow Athénaïse the freedom to choose their affection, she herself—as even neighbors recognize—is simply unacquainted with her own mind and cannot yet realize that freedom.

Athénaïse's immature notions of freedom are mingled with romantic illusions about marriage. Headstrong, like many of Chopin's finest heroines, she weds Cazeau without much forethought. But the romance of the prospect hardly prepares her for the reality of married life. (pp. 108-09)

Later in New Orleans, restored to the irresponsible leisure of childhood, she delights in the familiar, "comforting, comfortable sense of not being married!" For Athénaïse, marriage not only represents a loss of freedom, but a loss of innocence. Her appreciation of Gouvernail's chaste attentions in contrast to Cazeau's way of loving ("passionately, rudely, offensively") underlines her romantic illusions. Indeed, Gouvernail's courtliness is only a style of hard-won restraint; his passions are as turbulent as Cazeau's and would doubtless be expressed in a similar way if Athénaïse would respond. Athénaïse's problem is that she has not recognized her own sensuality, the agreeable passion that would ameliorate the normal disillusionments of marriage: its invasions of privacy, its limitations on behavior, and for women, especially, its literal transformation of identity.

That pregnancy brings about Athénaïse's self-recognition is a double-edged insight. On the one hand, it affirms the emotional fulfillment of motherhood and suggests that biological experience must precede the acceptance of social roles. But Chopin's insistence on the sensual component of Athénaïse's change is significant. Knowledge of her pregnancy steeps her in "a wave of ecstasy," and when she thinks of Cazeau, "the first purely sensuous tremor of her life swept over her." Athénaïse's awakened sensibilities bring with them self-possession, too. As she had once thrown away the keys to Cazeau's house and its responsibilities, so now she demands money of his city merchant with "an air of partnership, almost proprietorship." At last, Athénaïse does "know her own mind"—and body. Her pregnancy has not only made her receptive to sexuality but offered her a new power that she did not, and could not, have as a maiden. (pp. 110-11)

Chopin's resolution of Athénaïse's dissatisfactions with marriage has suggested to some that the conclusion "contradict[s] the theme of escape" in the story, while others read irony and restlessness into the final scene on the Cazeaus' darkened porch. But Chopin, though demonstrably aware of the limitations of marriage, was equally sensitive to the deeply satisfying pleasures of motherhood and the rich sensuality of reproduction. . . . That she could combine both awarenesses in a single story attests to the complexity of her insight and the maturity of her skills.

"Athénaïse" is technically as well as thematically adept. The settings, ranging from the rural Cane River to the bustling French Quarter and the quiet nooks of New Orleans's West End, contribute unobtrusively to mood and theme. The presentation of consistent and well-developed characters also profits enormously from her earlier experiments with delayed exposition, which demands constant reevaluations of their nature. Cazeau, for example, is first seen worrying more about the pony his wife has ridden home than about her. His physical description as "tall, sinewy, swarthy, and altogether severe looking" with thick black hair "gleam[ing] like the breast of a crow" does little to soften this unsympathetic first impression, and we are well into the story before we discover that he feels Athénaïse's absence "like a dull, insistent pain." From that point, our response to Cazeau's stern exterior is much modified as he struggles with his powerful love for his willful and petulant young wife, and his dashed hopes that their days together "would be like w'at the story-books promise after the wedding." By the final scene, Cazeau's own deeply romantic nature, his blunt integrity, and his sensitivity are equally manifest. But the unfolding of Cazeau and other characters is as gradual and even misleading as the processes of self-discovery themselves.

With **"Athénaïse,"** ***A Night in Acadie*** was essentially complete. Only two later works, including the title story, were incorporated into the collection. And Chopin's work throughout the remainder of 1895 reaffirms her gradual abandonment of local color even as it reflects her continued fascination with the later themes of duality and sexual repression. (pp. 111-12)

[***A Night in Acadie***] was in many ways her final statement on the genre that had brought her national prominence. Chopin continued to use Louisiana settings effectively, but her dependence on them ceased. The confident experimentation following ***Bayou Folk***'s success had definitively widened her range of themes and settings. The very unevenness of ***A Night in Acadie,*** gathering early tales excluded from her first collection together with many outstanding later stories, reflects this transition. The final effect of ***A Night in Acadie*** is one of increasing subtlety and reach in Chopin's talent as well as a new sense that evoking the quaintness of Louisiana was no longer her primary intent. Chopin was on a new course in her fiction, en route to an examination of human life more honest than she, or many others, had yet dared. (p. 123)

Barbara C. Ewell, in her Kate Chopin, *The Ungar Publishing Company, 1986, 216 p.*

FURTHER READING

Arner, Robert D. "Kate Chopin's Realism: 'At the 'Cadian Ball' and 'The Storm'." *The Markham Review* 2, No. 2 (February 1970): 1-4.

Traces the development of Chopin's use of realism in her fiction through a comparison of these two stories.

———. "Characterization and the Colloquial Style in Kate Chopin's 'Vagabonds'." *The Markham Review* 2, No. 6 (May 1971): 110-11.

Analyzes a passage from "Vagabonds" that exemplifies what the critic considers Chopin's masterful use of Louisiana dialects.

Bonner, Thomas Jr. *The Kate Chopin Companion.* New York: Greenwood Press, 1988, 245 p.

Exhaustive dictionary identifying the characters, settings, and events of Chopin's fiction. Also includes Chopin's translations of short stories by such French authors as Guy de Maupassant and Adrien Vely.

Dyer, Joyce. "Symbolic Setting in Kate Chopin's 'A Shameful Affair'." *Southern Studies: An Interdisciplinary Journal of the South* XX, No. 4 (Winter 1981): 447-52.

Examines Chopin's juxtaposition of fertility images from the natural world with the protagonist's sexual awakening.

———. "The Restive Brute: The Symbolic Presentation of Repression and Sublimation in Kate Chopin's 'Fedora'." *Studies in Short Fiction* 18, No. 3 (Summer 1981): 261-65.

Contends that "Fedora" is among Chopin's most incisive studies of sexual repression and sublimation.

———."Gouvernail, Kate Chopin's Sensitive Bachelor." *Southern Literary Journal* 14, No. 1 (Fall 1981): 46-55.

Discusses the function of the recurring character Gouvernail in *The Awakening* and several short stories. Dyer contends that Gouvernail grew increasingly cynical with each appearance in Chopin's works; he is therefore properly omitted from her later, happily resolved stories.

Fletcher, Marie. "The Southern Woman in the Fiction of Kate Chopin." *Louisiana History* VII, No. 2 (Spring 1966): 117-32.

Discussion of Chopin's female characters. Fletcher notes that while Chopin strove to depict realistic characters, her Southern women frequently adhere to traditional values, particularly with regard to the expression of sexuality.

Lattin, Patricia Hopkins. "Kate Chopin's Repeating Characters." *The Mississippi Quarterly* XXXIII, No. 1 (Winter 1979-80): 19-37.

Argues that recurring characters throughout Chopin's fiction contribute to the complexity and sophistication of her art.

Miner, Madonne M. "Veiled Hints: An Affective Stylist's Reading of Kate Chopin's 'Story of an Hour'." *The Markham Review* 11 (Fall 1981): 29-32.

Close grammatical analysis of "The Story of an Hour" that focuses on the reader's response to the tale.

Rankin, Daniel S. *Kate Chopin and Her Creole Stories.* Philadelphia: University of Pennsylvania Press, 1932, 313 p.

First biography of Chopin, valued for its insights based upon interviews with her family and friends. Also contains several well-known stories by Chopin, including "The Story of an Hour" and "Two Portraits."

Rocks, James E. "Kate Chopin's Ironic Vision." *Louisiana Review* 1, No. 2 (Winter 1972): 110-20.

Study of Chopin's literary methods and themes, focusing on her use of irony.

Schuyler, William. "Kate Chopin." *The Writer* VII, No. 8 (August 1894): 115-17.

Biographical sketch that expresses regard for Chopin and her work.

Toth, Emily. "Kate Chopin and Literary Convention: 'Désirée's Baby'." *Southern Studies* XX, No. 2 (Summer 1981): 201-08.

Examines how Chopin subverts the stereotype of the "tragic Octoroon" through her portrayal of Armand Aubigny.

———. *Kate Chopin.* New York: Morrow, 1990, 528 p.

Detailed biography of Chopin.

Wilson, Edmund. "Novelists of the Post-War South: Albion W. Tourgée, George W. Cable, Kate Chopin, Thomas Nelson Page." In his *Patriotic Gore: Studies in the Literature of the American Civil War,* pp. 587-93. New York: Oxford University Press, 1962.

Brief overview of Chopin's career that praises "The Story of an Hour" and *The Awakening.*

Paul Laurence Dunbar

1872-1906

American poet, short story writer, novelist, librettist, and essayist.

Dunbar is considered one of the first important black authors in American literature. In his fiction and poetry he depicted the social conditions of emancipated slaves and expressed the emotions of black Americans during the late nineteenth century. Many of his short stories, often following the "plantation" tradition of Thomas Nelson Page and other nineteenth-century white writers who portrayed black characters as oafish, simple-minded, and devoted slaves, were written at a time when appeasing white audiences was crucial to the literary success of black authors. Accordingly, Dunbar has been labeled an accommodationist by many reviewers, yet recent criticism has focused on Dunbar's attempts to insert strains of social protest into his stories. His protest fiction, while not as well known as the plantation tales, nevertheless constitutes an impressive quantity of Dunbar's oeuvre and is widely believed to be his most powerful writing.

Born in Dayton, Ohio, Dunbar was the son of former slaves. As a child he listened to his mother's stories about her early life on Kentucky plantations, and later incorporated much of this information into his writing. However, because his mother had understandably omitted the more brutal aspects of slavery from her stories, Dunbar tended to glorify plantation life, an aspect of his work that has been widely criticized. He began writing stories and poems as a child, and teachers recognized and encouraged his talent. As a high school student Dunbar continued to write, composing several plays for his drama club and acting as editor of the school newspaper. He also founded the *Dayton Tattler,* a short-lived black newspaper that was printed by his friend and classmate, the future aviator Orville Wright. Following graduation in 1891, Dunbar was unable to afford the expense of a college education, and he applied for work at newspaper offices and other businesses. Despite his growing reputation in Dayton as a gifted writer, many jobs were closed to black applicants, and for several years Dunbar could only find work as an elevator operator. While on duty, he often recited his poetry to passengers in his lift, and in his spare time he continued to write and publish poems and short stories, although he rarely received payment for them.

During the early 1890s, Dunbar also gave occasional readings, one of which was enthusiastically received at a meeting of the Western Association of Writers (WAOW). Three members later visited Dunbar to find out more about his life, and, one of the men, appalled by the prejudice to which Dunbar was subjected, wrote a letter to the press praising Dunbar and his work that was reprinted in newspapers across the country. Shortly after the article appeared, Dunbar was admitted as a WAOW member, and his popularity as a speaker increased. Encouraged by this publicity, he privately published *Oak and Ivy,* a collection of poetry that he sold from his elevator post. Much of the verse in this collection was black American dialect poetry, which was highly popular with white audiences. Dunbar believed that if he could win over white readers with the humor of his dialect verse, he could gradually display his abilities as a serious author. However, his poems and stories written on contemporary themes and in standard English were not embraced by white society, and Dunbar found himself trapped in the role of dialect poet. He often described himself as "a black white man," and among papers found after his death was the note: "It is one of the peculiar phases of Anglo-Saxon conceit to refuse to believe that every black man does not want to be white." Throughout his short but prolific career, Dunbar wrote numerous poems, novels, and short stories that addressed American racial problems and social oppression, but these never surpassed the popularity of his dialect poems and plantation tales. At the age of thirty-three, bitter, alcoholic, and suffering from tuberculosis, Dunbar died at his mother's home in Dayton.

Dunbar's four collections of short stories illuminate his struggle with artistic honesty and commercial success; his later work and its emphasis on social protest clearly reveal his choice for truth over popular themes. *Folks from Dixie,* his first volume, strongly imitated the sentimental Southern plantation tradition. Many of the tales, influenced by the stories Dunbar's mother told him, portray idealized master-slave relationships in the Civil War era. At the time of the book's publication, reviewers found the discussions of the spiritual, moral, and domestic lives of black people very revealing, and many commented on the stories in which Dunbar disregarded the plantation tradition and focused on psychological and social themes. "Jimsella," for example, concerns Mandy and Jim, a black couple who move to New York City after emancipation is declared. The squalor of tenement life is difficult for them to cope with, and Jim deserts Mandy, but returns after Mandy gives birth to their daughter. "At Shaft 11," a frequently analyzed story, examines the problems connected with labor unions through a detailing of a West Virginia coal mine strike. Fearful of white reaction to this story's controversial topic, however, Dunbar diminished its impact by idealizing the white owners of the mines and making the protagonist an enlightened white miner.

Dunbar's next volume, *The Strength of Gideon, and Other Stories,* is considered by many critics to be his best collection of short fiction and his strongest statement of racial concerns. The few plantation stories that are included—such as the title work—often focus upon the psychological dilemma of slaves who have been emancipated but are unsure of how to handle their new freedom. The most esteemed tales are those involving social or political injustice, and one, "The Ingrate," contains what is regarded as Dunbar's most forceful attack on slavery. Based on his own father's escape from a Southern plantation and set during the Civil War, this work revolves around Joshua, a slave who yearns for freedom, manages to flee to Canada, and then decides to join the Union army so that he can fight for the emancipation of all slaves. Another story, "One Man's Fortunes," is also based on personal experience. Bert, a black youth, graduates from school and disregards social convention by applying for a job with a white lawyer. He is rejected after numerous attempts and finally reconciles himself to working as a janitor. Soon, the lawyer runs for a judicial post and entices the young man to work for him in order to solicit black votes. After the election bid is successful, Bert is fired and replaced with a white assistant. Defeated, Bert ponders: "I wonder if it can be true . . . that a colored man must do twice as much and twice as well as a white man before he can hope for even equal chances with him? That white mediocrity demands black genius to cope with it?" A similar theme of oppression is found in "Mr. Cornelius Johnson, Office-Seeker." The black protagonist of the title works for the Alabama Republican Party and moves to Washington, D.C. to accept a promised political post. Continually dodged and ignored by government representatives, Cornelius is progressively stripped of his dignity. After a year, during which he is forced to sell his clothes and mortgage his home in order to stay in the city, the Senate refuses his appointment.

Although his later short story collections deal almost exclusively with racial oppression and exploitation, Dunbar understood the need to cater to white audiences and continued to accept and employ the limitations of the dialect story. *In Old Plantation Days* is a radical shift back to this style; Dunbar largely avoided racial themes in this collection, but wrote social protest articles for various newspapers and magazines during this time. Nearly all of the collection's tales are set on the fictional plantation of Stuart Mordaunt during the antebellum era. In these stories, the institution of slavery is never questioned, and many of the works portray Mordaunt's black servants as fiercely loyal. Accordingly, many modern critics consider *In Old Plantation Days* to be Dunbar's weakest short fiction. However, several stories, including "The Last Fiddling of Mordaunt's Jim," have been praised for their effective blend of folkloristic elements and strong narrative skills. Dunbar's final short story collection, *The Heart of Happy Hollow,* chiefly contains tales of postbellum black life which, like those in *The Strength of Gideon,* are strongly concerned with racial problems. Included in *The Heart of Happy Hollow* are two stories about lynching, one of which, "The Lynching of Jube Benson," is esteemed by critics as a courageous, moving work of social protest. A white physician, Dr. Melville, is so disturbed when two younger friends express a strong interest in lynching that he shares a traumatic story with them. Melville tells the men that many years ago, his fiancée was raped and murdered, and the community quickly determined Jube Benson, his black house servant, to be the guilty party. In a fury, the townspeople lynch Jube immediately; only minutes later the real murderer is apprehended—a white man who had concealed his identity by blackening his face and hands. Although Melville considered Jube a close friend, he admits with shame that he was almost eager to believe in Jube's guilt and have him lynched. "Why did I do it," the doctor says in retrospect. "I don't know. A false education, I reckon, one false from the beginning." The pathos of the story, which is reiterated throughout *The Heart of Happy Hollow,* along with the collection's ironic and satiric elements, have led critics to perceive the book as one of Dunbar's most fully realized achievements in short fiction.

In general, discussion of Dunbar's works has more often been a reflection of racial issues in American history than a dispassionate assessment of his literary production. It was not until the 1960s that critics began to pay more attention to Dunbar's achievements and, in so doing, resurrected Dunbar as an important voice in American literature. Recent criticism has focused more on understanding Dunbar's compromises rather than simply attacking him for his accommodationist stance. Much of this criticism has demonstrated the tragedy of Dunbar's position—that of a man who was deeply ashamed of the only work he could sell, who perceived his own inadequacies, and who believed he collaborated in the defamation of his own people. A. Robert Lee asserted: "Caught in the historical paradox of his time, endowed with invention but not genius, [Dunbar] was occasionally able to perceive and arrest the brutal particulars of black historical experience. Where he gave in to the costume formulas of romance and resorted to wooden dialogue he clearly writes fiction both weak and ineffective; but where he sought faithfully to portray the live psychology of race, he is able to break through, to seize his reader with a sense of place and time, of human beings bound up in racial calamity."

(For further information on Dunbar's life and career, see *Twentieth-Century Literary Criticism,* Vols. 2, 12; *Contemporary Authors,* Vols. 104, 124; *Dictionary of Literary Biography,* Vols. 50, 54, 78; *Concise Dictionary of American Literary Biography, 1865-1917;* and *Black Writers.*)

PRINCIPAL WORKS

SHORT FICTION

Folks from Dixie 1898
The Strength of Gideon, and Other Stories 1900
In Old Plantation Days 1903
The Heart of Happy Hollow 1904
The Best Stories of Paul Laurence Dunbar 1938

OTHER MAJOR WORKS

Oak and Ivy (poetry) 1893
Majors and Minors (poetry) 1895
Lyrics of Lowly Life (poetry) 1896
Clorindy; or, The Origin of the Cakewalk [with Will Marion Cook] (libretto) 1898
Dream Lovers: An Operatic Romance (libretto) 1898
The Uncalled (novel) 1898
Lyrics of the Hearthside (poetry) 1899
Poems of Cabin and Field (poetry) 1899
Jes' Lak White Folks [with others] (libretto) 1900
The Love of Landry (novel) 1900
Uncle Eph's Christmas (drama) 1900
Candle-Lightin' Time (poetry) 1901
The Fanatics (novel) 1901
In Dahomey: A Negro Musical Comedy [with others] (libretto) 1902
The Sport of the Gods (novel) 1902; also published as *The Jest of Fate: A Story of Negro Life,* 1903
Lyrics of Love and Laughter (poetry) 1903
When Malindy Sings (poetry) 1903
Li'l Gal (poetry) 1904
Christmas Is a Comin', and Other Poems (poetry) 1905
Howdy, Honey, Howdy (poetry) 1905
Lyrics of Sunshine and Shadow (poetry) 1905
A Plantation Portrait (poetry) 1905
Joggin' erlong (poetry) 1906
The Life and Works of Paul Laurence Dunbar (poetry and short stories) 1907
The Complete Poems of Paul Laurence Dunbar (poetry) 1913
Speakin' o' Christmas, and Other Christmas and Special Poems (poetry) 1914
The Letters of Paul and Alice Dunbar: A Private History (letters) 1974
The Paul Laurence Dunbar Reader (poetry, short stories, essays, journalism, and letters) 1975
I Greet the Dawn: Poems by Paul Laurence Dunbar (poetry) 1978

George Preston (essay date 1898)

[The following essay is a review of Dunbar's first short story collection, Folks from Dixie. *The review, in which Preston hails the work as "the first expression in national prose fiction of the inner life of the American negro," is typical of the critical response Dunbar needed in order to continue publishing his stories.]*

This little book [***Folks from Dixie***] comes with more importance than many larger works, and deserves especial attention for several reasons. It has claims on purely literary grounds. It is well written, it is better than well thought, it is most profoundly felt. The stories are firm, clear-cut, and interesting enough in themselves to lift the volume above the level of the books of the month.

In addition to this, and beyond it, the work is notable as the first expression in national prose fiction of the inner life of the American negro. For, strangely enough, although his figure and his characteristics have formed prominent and picturesque factors of national literature for nearly half a century, never until now has he spoken a word for himself. It should, perhaps, be said that Mr. Dunbar's poems, published about a year ago, were the first utterance from behind the impenetrable curtain separating the black American from the white. But the poems were mostly far-off musical murmurings of the same sad and humorous truths now distinctly and forcibly told in these simple tales.

The marked difference between these new stories from the inside and the old ones from the outside is hardly apparent, however, at a glance. The first story in particular is quite familiar; there seems nothing more to be told concerning the peculiarities of the negro idea of "getting religion"—which is, after all, rather more satisfactory and certainly more definite than our own. The coloured seeker gets religion or he does not; it is almost as simple as passing through a hole in a fence. At all events, he is never left on the fence, as the white brother too often is. Several of the stories prove this more or less interestingly and conclusively, and **"The Trial Sermon on Bull-Skin"** is among the best of the kind.

But the force and originality of the work are revealed more fully in four slight sketches. These alone would win a place apart for the author as one having authority. In them he makes a complete departure from the lines that other writers have traversed, and enters where they have not attempted to tread. In them he reveals the spiritual, moral, social, and domestic life of his race, as they have never been revealed, for the reason that they have never before been described from within. Surely no one standing without could see and feel **"The Ordeal at Mt. Hope"** as the author sees and feels it. The beautiful maternity of the grotesque black mother and the grim dignity of the repulsive black father; the appeal to mercy and justice for their degraded son, "who was an epitome of the evil as his parents were of the sorrows of the place;" the squalor, the ignorance, and the vice of the race's environment—all blended in a deep, far cry of *Weltschmerz.* Well might the young preacher, whose ordeal is the struggle to raise his people, feel the uselessness of preaching;

> that he would only be dashing his words against the accumulated evil of years of bondage as the ripples of a summer sea beat against a stone wall. . . . It was not the wickedness of this boy he was fighting, nor the wrong-doing of Mt. Hope. It was the aggregation of the evil done by the fathers, the grandfathers, the masters, and the mistresses of these people.

The humble nature of the efforts made by the preacher for the advancement of Mt. Hope shows the complete sincerity of Mr. Dunbar's knowledge of his sad subject.

There is the same unflinching frankness in **"The Deliberations of Mr. Dunkin,"** although the story is in quite another vein, and deals humorously with matters *à la mode* in fashionable coloured society. The author might say as one of the modish damsels of the story says: "I knows coloured folks, I kin shet my eyes an' put my han's on 'em in de da'k." And yet with all the story's unsparing revelations, the fundamental motives and emotions seem much like those which move most men and women of higher education and lighter complexions.

The sketch striking the deepest note of the universal is the one entitled **"Jimsella."** It covers only some eight or nine pages, and is almost entirely psychological, yet it rounds the common destiny of humanity. It contains but two characters, Jim and Mandy, unless the atom of a baby in its bundle of rags may be counted a third. The little tale is very short, very simple, and very piteous. The ignorant husband and wife drift from a plantation home of comparative comfort to the rigorous poverty of a New York tenement. Jim finds the change too hard to bear, and deserts Mandy. When he wanders back there is a baby in the bundle of rags, and after the first anger of the meeting has passed he asks the child's name.

> "I calls huh Jimsella, dat's what I calls huh, ca'se she's de ve'y spittin' image of you." . . .
>
> They were both silent for a while, and then Jim said: "Huh name ought to be Jamsella—don't you know Jim's sho't fur James?"
>
> "I don't keer what it sho't fur!" The woman was holding the baby close to her breast and sobbing now. "It wasn't no James dat come a-cou'in me down home. It was jes plain Jim."

And so the simple story passes, with the softening of the black father's heart to a tender, infinitely human close. The last of the work is better than the first, and the book will repay thoughtful rereading after it has been read solely for entertainment. (pp. 348-49)

George Preston, in a review of "Folks from Dixie," in The Bookman, *New York, Vol. VII, No. 4, June, 1898, pp. 348-49.*

The New York Times Book Review (essay date 1898)

[*In the following review of* Folks from Dixie, *the critic approves of Dunbar's objective characterizations while finding fault with his method of presenting dialect speech.*]

Of Mr. Dunbar's *Lyrics of Lowly Life* Mr. William Dean Howells has written:

> His brilliant and unique achievement is to have studied the American negro objectively, and to have represented him as he found him to be, with humor, with sympathy, and yet with what the reader must instinctively feel to be entire truthfulness. He reveals a finely ironical perception of the negro's limitations, with a tenderness for them which I think so very rare as to be almost quite new.

These words apply with equal force to Mr. Dunbar's volume of prose sketches, ***Folks from Dixie.*** Had it appeared anonymously we should welcome it as a very delightful addition to the dialect stories of the South, and as an unusually faithful and delicate delineation of character. There is a certain distinction in the style and a wise restraint in the handling which would be sufficiently remarkable whatever might be the authorship of the stories, but which, in the circumstances, rises into the region of the marvelous. We fear Mr. Dunbar wishes his critics were colorblind, and would judge his work as literature only, without insistence upon the note of personality. But he must forgive us for saying that in view of his race and the traditions of his childhood he has done two unique things: He has treated the negro "objectively," as Mr. Howells says, with perfect truth and sympathy, but without a trace of sentimentality; and he has treated the former slave owners we had almost said subjectively, not only without any touch of bitterness, but with a comprehension and tenderness so fine as to be beyond praise. Nothing could be more nobly conceived than the story of **"Nelse Hatton's Vengeance."** To have written it required rare qualities of head and of heart.

We think Mr. Dunbar falls into the common error of rather over-spelling his dialect. "Ovah" for "over," "ouah" for "our," seems needless, for those final "r's" are not often rolled, unless, perhaps, in the West. We have not happened to hear "wif" for "with," the usual corruption being "wid"—but it savors of impertinence to find fault with the dialect of a writer belonging to "the inner cult."

Again, to quote Mr. Howells, Mr. Dunbar "has evinced innate distinction in literature; in more than one piece he has produced a work of art," and we may add that just how artistic and finely felt are the things he has done can be fully appreciated by the Southern whites alone.

A review of "'Folks from Dixie'," in The New York Times Book Review, *June 18, 1898, p. 39.*

Vernon Loggins (essay date 1931)

[*Loggins was an American educator, editor, and biographer who wrote several biographical and critical works on American, English, and French authors. In the following excerpt, he traces the subjects and themes of Dunbar's short fiction collections.*]

Dunbar's first collection of short stories, ***Folks from Dixie*** (1898), contains some of his most characteristic and best work as a writer of fiction. There is no [framework for the grouping of the stories]. . . . Whatever unity the book as a whole has is told by the title, ***Folks from Dixie***; the characters, not all of them colored, are either still in Dixie or once lived there. Two of the stories, **"The Ordeal at Mt. Hope,"** an argument for industrial education, and **"At Shaft 11,"** an indirect plea for the Negro to stay out of labor unions, were designed for more than entertainment. The rest are pure tales. . . . [A] blending of kindliness and romance and sentimentality is in **"A Family Feud,"** a tale of ante-bellum days on two Kentucky plantations. . . . Dunbar's knowledge of plantation life in Kentucky probably came from his mother, who passed her childhood and early womanhood as a slave and who was throughout most of Dunbar's life his constant companion. At any rate, he had derived from some source a penetrating understanding of the primitive Negro's superstitions, religious zeal, romance, humor, and language. The following exhortation addressed by a preacher to a willful girl in **"Annie 'Lizer's Stumblin' Block"** gets to the very heart of Negro folk feeling:

> "You see, honey," Uncle Eben went on, "when you starts out on de Christian jou'ney, you's got to lay aside evry weight dat doeth so easy beset you an' keeps you f 'om pergressin'; y' ain't got to think nothin' 'bout pussunal 'dornment; you's jes' got to shet yo' eyes an' keep open yo' hea't an' say, Lawd, come; you must n't wait fu' to go to chu'ch to pray, nuther, you mus' pray anywhar an' ev'rywhar. Why, when I was seekin', I ust to go 'way off up in de big woods to pray, an' dere's whar de Lawd answered me, an' I'm a-rejoicin' to-day in de powah of de same salvation. Honey, you's got to pray, I tell you. You's got to brek de backbone of yo' pride an' pray in earnes'; an' ef you does dat, you'll git he'p, fu' de Lawd is a praar-heahin' Lawd an' plenteous in mussy."

It is such talk that makes ***Folks from Dixie*** a memorable volume. And it was his intimate knowledge of the folk ways of Negroes which enabled Dunbar to do some of the strongest work found in his later volumes of short stories, ***The Strength of Gideon*** (1900), ***In Old Plantation Days*** (1903), and ***The Heart of Happy Hollow*** (1904). (pp. 314-15)

Two of the stories in Paul Laurence Dunbar's ***Folks from Dixie,*** **"The Ordeal at Mt. Hope"** and **"At Shaft 11,"** have been pointed out as dealing with social problems. . . . [They belong to a field in which some] Negro novelists and short story writers between 1865 and 1900 ventured, that of fiction offering comment on the social status of the Negro, especially in relation to the white man. It was, as we might expect, the field in which the Negro was most voluminous, and, if not most pleasing, most vigorous. It was also the field in which he was most original.

In his later collections of short stories Dunbar dwelt more and more on racial problems. He said in the foreword to ***The Heart of Happy Hollow:***

> Happy Hollow; are you wondering where it is? Wherever Negroes colonize in the cities or villages, North or South, wherever the hod-carrier, the porter, and the waiter are the society men of the town; wherever the picnic and the excursion are the chief summer diversion, and the revival the winter-time of repentance, wherever the cheese cloth veil obtains at weddings, and the little white hearse goes by with black mourners in the one carriage behind, there—there—is Happy Hollow. Wherever laughter and tears rub elbows day by day, and the spirit of labour and laziness shake hands, there—there—is Happy Hollow.

But Happy Hollow was not to Dunbar a place for nothing more than sentimental tears and spontaneous laughter. It had its serious side, its sense of wronged justice, its tragedy. In a story of an educated colored youth's ruthless disillusionment, **"One Man's Fortune,"** included in ***The Strength of Gideon,*** a white lawyer is made to say:

> The sentiment of remorse and the desire for atoning which actuated so many white men to help Negroes right after the war has passed off without being replaced by that sense of plain justice which gives a black man his due, not because of, nor in spite of, but without consideration of his color.

The idea thus expressed was a guiding principle for Dunbar in writing stories on such themes as Negroes exploited by unscrupulous politicians, the economic relations existing between whites and blacks, and the effect of city life on country-bred Negroes. (pp. 320-21)

Vernon Loggins, "Fiction and Poetry, 1865-1900," in his The Negro Author: His Development in America to 1900, *1931. Reprint by Kennikat Press, Inc., 1964, pp. 305-52.*

Sterling Brown (essay date 1937)

[*Brown, a noted authority on black literary history, is also a poet, folklorist, and educator. His anthologies and criticism are considered among the most important contributions to the understanding of black literature. In the essay below, excerpted from his study* The Negro in American Fiction, *first published in 1937, Brown briefly describes Dunbar's typical settings and characters and stresses his conventional neglect of the harsh realities of black life during the late nineteenth and early twentieth centuries.*]

[In ***The Heart of Happy Hollow***] Dunbar has aptly described the typical setting for his fiction:

> Happy Hollow. . . . Wherever Negroes colonize in the cities or villages, North or South, wherever the hod-carrier, the porter, and the waiter are the society men of the town; wherever the picnic and the excursion are the chief summer diversion, and the revival the winter-time of repentance. . . . Wherever laughter and tears rub elbows day by day, and the spirit of labour and laziness shake hands, there—there—is Happy Hollow.

In Old Plantation Days (1903) repeats the Thomas Nelson Page formula [of sentimental plantation stories]. Negro house servants comically ape the "quality," or intervene in lovers' quarrels, or in duels between cavaliers.

One slave deceives his beloved master into believing that the good times of slavery still prevail. The planters, high-bred and chivalrous, and the slaves, childish and devoted, rival each other in affection and sacrifice. These anecdotes of slavery, but a step above minstrel jokes, are all too happy for words, and too happy for truth.

The harshness of Reconstruction and of Dunbar's own time is likewise conventionally neglected in his other volumes of short stories: ***Folks from Dixie*** (1898), ***The Strength of Gideon*** (1900), and ***The Heart of Happy Hollow*** (1904). Freedmen discover that after all their best friends are their kindly ex-masters. In **"Nelse Hatton's Revenge,"** an upstanding Negro gives his hard-earned money and best clothes to his destitute master, who had abused him when a slave. The venality of Reconstruction politicians, which certainly existed, is satirized; but the gains of Reconstruction, which certainly exist, are understressed. Probably with due cause, Dunbar feared the rising poor-whites; therefore, like many Negro spokesmen of the period, he idealized the ex-planter class, the "aristocrats," *without* due cause.

Dunbar's fiction veers away from anything more serious than laughter or gentle tears. **"At Shaft 11"** shows the difficulties of Negro strikebreakers; but, afraid of organized labor, Dunbar idealized owners, operators, and staunchly loyal Negro workers who get to be foremen, thus carrying over the plantation tradition formula into the industrial scene. **"The Ordeal at Mt. Hope"** faces the loose-living of a "Happy Hollow," and then is lost in sentimental compromise. Dunbar wrote two stories of lynching, **"The Lynching of Jube Benson"** and the unusually ironic **"The Tragedy at Three Forks."** But Dunbar usually places the hardships of Negro life in the city, as in **"Jimsella,"** with pastoral distrust of the city and faith in rural virtue. Fast livers, quacks, politicians and hypocritical race leaders are occasionally attacked. (pp. 77-8)

Sterling Brown, "Reconstruction: The Not So Glorious South," in his Negro Poetry and Drama and The Negro in American Fiction, *Atheneum, 1969, pp. 64-83.*

Hugh M. Gloster (essay date 1948)

[*Gloster is a noted critic of black literature. In the following excerpt, he focuses on stories by Dunbar that illustrate or are influenced by the plantation tradition.*]

Catering to the demands of publishers and readers of his time, Dunbar generally evaded [complex racial] themes . . . and usually specialized either in the treatment of white American life or in the perpetuation of the plantation tradition. Three of his novels—*The Uncalled* (1898), *The Love of Landry* (1900), and *The Fanatics* (1901)—deal almost entirely with white characters; and the fourth, *The Sport of the Gods* (1902), though a promising naturalistic study, illustrates the plantation-school concept that the Negro becomes homesick and demoralized in the urban North. With a few exceptions, moreover, the short stories comprising ***Folks from Dixie*** (1898), ***The Strength of Gideon*** (1900), ***In Old Plantation Days*** (1903), and ***The Heart of Happy Hollow*** (1904) follow the formulas of Thomas Nelson Page. (pp. 46-7)

[In most of his short stories] . . . Dunbar becomes a successful imitator of the plantation school. Like other resuscitators of the legendary South, he presents "the big house," peopled by high-spirited and indulgent blue-bloods, and "the quarters," inhabited by spoiled and satisfied slaves whose lives are made picturesque by conjuration, gambling, feasting, rivalries, love affairs, mimicry, and primitive religion. In this environment move such familiar types as the proprietary mammy, the pompous butler, the pretentious coachman, and the plantation exhorter. A wide social gulf divides the slaves in "the big house" from those in "the quarters." The relationship between master and slave is idealized as one of mutual affection and loyalty, and the best masters do not buy and sell slaves unless forced to do so because of financial strain. Furthermore, the patricians generally avoid flogging by delegating this unpleasant assignment to overseers or supervised Negroes. The overseer, being in most cases a representative of "poor white trash," is not portrayed sympathetically. A purveyor of these expected themes, Dunbar avoids penetrating social analysis of the South and suggests that Negroes who migrate to the North become maladjusted and demoralized individuals who remember the years before emancipation with pitiable nostalgia.

Folks from Dixie, Dunbar's first collection of short stories, contains twelve tales treating action before and after the Civil War. The majority of the narratives conform to the postulates of the plantation tradition. **"Anner 'Lizer's Stumblin' Block"** presents a slave woman who will not become converted until sure of the marital intentions of her lover. **"A Family Feud"** is a story of ante-bellum days told to the author by Aunt Joshy. **"The Intervention of Peter"** shows how an old Negro prevents a duel between two Southern gentlemen. **"The Colonel's Awakening"** mirrors the loyalty of two ex-slaves to their elderly demented master who has lost his wealth and sons in the Civil War. **"The Ordeal at Mt. Hope," "The Trial Sermons on Bull-Skin,"** and **"Mt. Pisgah's Christmas Possum"** furnish glimpses of Negro church life. Anticipating *The Sport of the Gods,* **"Jimsella"** describes the struggles of a Negro couple in New York, where "it was all very different: one room in a crowded tenement house, and the necessity of grinding day after day to keep the wolf—a very terrible and ravenous wolf—from the door." Several stories in ***Folks from Dixie,*** however, tend to diverge from plantation prescriptions. **"Aunt Mandy's Investment"** treats the machinations of a Negro shyster who fleeces gullible black folk. **"The Deliberation of Mr. Dunkin"** unfolds the wooing of a teacher by an affected member of the school board. **"Nelse Hatton's Revenge"** sets forth the kindness of an ex-slave to a former master whom he had earlier vowed to kill. Veering from plantation requirements more than any other story in the volume, **"At Shaft 11"** recounts the heroic part played by Sam Bowles, a Negro foreman, in a West Virginia mine strike and race riot.

The imprint of the plantation tradition is also strong upon ***The Strength of Gideon, and Other Stories,*** a collection of twenty narratives. The title story and **"Mammy Peggy's**

Pride" depict the loyalty of ex-bondmen to their former masters. **"Viney's Free Papers," "The Fruitful Sleeping of the Rev. Elisha Edwards," "The Case of 'Ca'line': A Kitchen Monologue," "Jim's Probation,"** and **"Uncle Simon's Sunday Out"** portray various experiences of plantation life. Illustrative of the unfitness of the Negro to cope with the inhospitable environment of the Northern metropolis are **"An Old Time Christmas," "The Trustfulness of Polly," "The Finding of Zach," "The Faith Cure Man," "Silas Jackson," "The Finish of Patsy Barnes,"** and **"One Man's Fortunes."** The last-named story records the failure of a Negro lawyer who learns "that the adages, as well as the books and the formulas, were made by and for others than us of the black race." Several stories of the volume, however, break rather sharply from typical plantation subject matter. **"Mr. Cornelius Johnson, Office-Seeker," "A Mess of Pottage,"** and **"A Council of State"** present the Negro in politics. **"The Ingrate"** portrays a slave who yearns for freedom:

> To him his slavery was deep night. What wonder, then, that he should dream, and that through the ivory gate should come to him the forbidden vision of freedom? To own himself, to be master of his hands, feet, of his whole body—something would clutch at his heart as he thought of it; and the breath would come hard between his lips.

Escaping to Canada, he rejoices in the work of the Abolitionists and joins the Union Army during the Civil War. A bloody tale of lynching and mob passion, **"The Tragedy at Three Forks"** is social protest that is a far cry from Dunbar's usual treatment of the Southern scene. After Jane Hunster, a white girl of a small Kentucky town, commits arson because of jealousy, her father hastily attributes the crime to a Negro:

> Look a here, folks, I tell you that's the work o' niggers. I kin see their hand in it.

Thereafter incendiary newspaper articles result in the seizure and lynching of two innocent Negroes. In a struggle for pieces of the mob's rope to be kept as souvenirs, Dock Heaters fatally stabs Jane's fiancé; and the one-sided justice of the South is indicated in the following persuasive reply to a demand that the murderer also be lynched: "No," cried an imperious voice, "who knows what may have put him up to it? Give a white man a chance for his life."

Most of the stories of ***In Old Plantation Days*** follow the pattern of those in Page's *In Ole Virginia* and have their setting on the plantation of Stuart Mordaunt, a typical master of the legendary South. **"Aunt Tempy's Triumph"** shows how a proprietary mammy, who thinks she owns the "plantation with all the white folks and niggers on it," succeeds in giving away the master's daughter in marriage. **"Dizzy-Headed Dick," "A Lady Slipper,"** and **"Who Stand for the Gods"** present slaves who intervene to assist white lovers. **"Aunt Tempy's Revenge," "The Trouble about Sophiny," "Ash-Cake Hannah and Her Ben," "The Conjuring Contest," "Dandy Jim's Conjure Scare," "The Memory of Martha,"** and **"The Easter Wedding"** deal principally with the love affairs of bondmen. The old-fashioned exhorter and plantation religious life are described in **"The Walls of Jericho," "How Brother Parker Fell from Grace," "The Trousers,"** and **"The Last Fiddling of Mordaunt's Jim."** Slave loyalty is exemplified in **"A Blessed Deceit"** and **"The Stanton Coachman." "The Brief Cure of Aunt Fanny"** reveals the rivalry between two plantation cooks, while **"A Supper by Proxy"** pictures a lavish feast prepared by Negroes in "the big house" in the absence of the master. **"Mr. Groby's Slippery Gift"** unfolds the loyalty of two slave brothers and the cruelty of an overseer. The last five stories of the volume shift to post-bellum times and urban scenes. **"The Finding of Martha,"** highly suggestive of Chesnutt's "The Wife of His Youth," sets forth the successful quest of a Negro preacher for his wife of slavery times. **"The Defection of Mary Ann Gibbs," "A Judgment of Paris," "Silent Samuel,"** and **"The Way of a Woman,"** all having their locale in the Negro ghetto of a Northern city, are chiefly concerned with competition in love. (pp. 51-5)

Though dealing chiefly with post-bellum Negro life, many of the sixteen tales of ***The Heart of Happy Hollow*** do not escape the influence of the plantation tradition. **"Cahoots"** sentimentalizes the life-long devotion of a slave to his master. **"The Wisdom of Silence"** portrays an ex-slave who, having grown prosperous and boastful, is humbled and thereafter aided by his former owner. **"One Christmas at Shiloh"** and **"A Matter of Doctrine"** present Negro ministers as suitors. **"Old Abe's Conversion"** traces the transformation of an old-fashioned exhorter into a progressive pastor. **"A Defender of the Faith"** and **"The Interference of Patsy Ann"** mirror the pathos of Negro life in a big city. **"The Mission of Mr. Scatters," "The Promoter,"** and **"Schwalliger's Philanthropy"** expose colored swindlers. **"The Scapegoat"** describes the craft of a Negro politician, while **"The Home-Coming of 'Rastus Smith"** limns a young Negro lawyer who adopts a supercilious attitude toward his mother and former sweetheart. **"The Boy and the Bayonet"** illustrates a lesson in military discipline. Misleadingly titled, **"The Race Question"** is the soliloquy of an old colored man at a race track. In **"The Lynching of Jube Benson"** a white physician, defending his opposition to mob violence, recounts the murder of a loyal and innocent Negro friend.

In his short stories, therefore, Dunbar generally accepts the limitations and circumscriptions of the plantation tradition. Glorifying the good old days in the accepted manner, he sentimentalizes master-slave relationships and implies that freedom brings social misery to the black man. Negro migrants to the urban North are usually represented as nostalgic misfits, some of whom fall prey to poverty, immorality, or disease, and others to disillusionment occasioned by political or professional reverses. **"The Ingrate"** and **"The Tragedy at Three Forks,"** both of which are effective examples of the use of irony, are possibly the only stories in the four volumes that entirely escape the tendency to idealize Dixie. Furthermore, the narratives give an unauthentic recording of life because of their neglect of the unpleasant realities of the Southland. These considerations lead directly to the observation that Dunbar usually catered to the racial preconceptions of his publishers and readers by employing the themes and stereotypes of the plantation tradition. Nevertheless, his literary reputation itself constituted a strong argument against Negro inferiority; and he helped to prepare the American audience for succeeding authors possessing greater originality and deeper social understanding. (pp. 55-6)

Hugh M. Gloster, "Negro Fiction to World War I," in his Negro Voices in American Fiction, *1948. Reprint by Russell & Russell, Inc., 1965, pp. 23-100.*

Darwin Turner (essay date 1967)

[*Turner is an American educator, poet, and critic specializing in black and Southern literature. In the excerpt below, he explores the ironic nature of Dunbar's short stories, arguing that Dunbar was "far more bitter and scathing, much more a part of the protest tradition than his reputation suggests."*]

At twenty-four, Paul Laurence Dunbar became a symbol of the creative and intellectual potential of the American Negro. He was envisaged thus by his earliest patrons, who hoped that his literary talent and his black skin would encourage the doubtful to contribute financially to the humanistic education of Negroes. He was envisaged thus by William Dean Howells, one of America's most respected literary critics, who praised *Majors and Minors,* Dunbar's second book, as "the first instance of an American Negro writer who evinced innate distinction in literature." Because he was one of America's most popular poets at the beginning of the twentieth century, he was acclaimed as a symbol by many early critics, who praised him excessively.

More recently, however, his image has been defaced by scholars who have censured him for tarnishing the symbol by perpetuating the derogatory caricatures of the minstrel show and the plantation tales. His reputation has suffered from such a scholar as Robert Bone, author of *The Negro Novel in America* who, from a study of Dunbar's novels, alleged that whenever he "had something to say which transcended the boundaries of the plantation tradition . . . he resorted to the subterfuge of employing white characters, rather than attempting a serious literary portrait of the Negro." His reputation has suffered also from those readers who, seeking to compress his thought into pithy phrases, have failed to reveal the significant changes in his subject-matter and attitudes. His reputation has suffered from those who have been blinded by a single work or who have failed to discern his attempts at ironic protest. The result has been the currently popular images of Dunbar as a disenchanted angel fluttering his wings against publishers' restrictions or as a money-hungry Esau willing to betray his birthright for a mess of popularity. Careful examination of Dunbar and of his works explains the reasons for his inability to write the kind of protest which some of his critics wish. Simultaneously, such scrutiny reveals Dunbar to be far more bitter and scathing, much more a part of the protest tradition than his reputation suggests.

Paul Laurence Dunbar's experiences, his political and economic philosophies, and his artistic ideals prevented his writing the acerbate criticism of the South which some readers desire. Paul Laurence Dunbar's cardinal sin is that he violated the unwritten commandment which American Society has handed down to the Negro: "Thou shalt not laugh at thy black brother" (Especially thou shalt not laugh at thy black brother who spoke dialect and was a slave). But Paul Laurence Dunbar could not identify himself with the slave or freedman about whom he wrote. Born free in Dayton, Ohio, elected president of the high school literary club and editor of the school newspaper by his white classmates, published and praised in America and in England, Dunbar judged the color of his skin to be a very thin bond linking him to the half-Christian, half-pagan slaves a mere two-hundred years removed from savagery, in his opinion. That bond of color was insufficiently tight to gag his chuckles about some of their ridiculous antics which his mother, an ex-slave, had narrated.

Even if Dunbar had been completely free to write scathing protest about the South, he could not have written it, or would have written it ineptly. His experiences and those of his family had not compelled him to hate white people as a group or the South as a region. After Dunbar was twenty, every major job he secured, every publication, and all national recognition resulted directly from the assistance of white benefactors. It is not remarkable that Dunbar assumed that successful Negroes need such help or that, knowing the actuality of Northern benefactors, he believed in the existence of their Southern counterparts. Dunbar was not a unique disciple of such a creed. In *The Ordeal of Mansart,* the militant W. E. B. DuBois has described the manner in which intelligent freedmen sought salvation with the assistance of Southern aristocrats.

As his personal experiences freed him from bitterness towards Caucasians as a group, so his family's experiences relieved bitterness towards the South. The experiences of his parents in slavery probably had been milder than most. His father had been trained in a trade and had been taught to read, write, and compute. As a semi-skilled worker occasionally hired out, he fared better than the average field hand. Irony rather than bitterness is the dominant tone in **"The Ingrate,"** a story Dunbar based on his father's life. Although Dunbar's mother had experienced unpleasantness (as what slave did not), her life as a house slave in Kentucky undoubtedly was easier than that of a slave in the deeper South.

Even had his experiences prompted protest against the South, his social and economic philosophies would have militated against it. Believing that America would prosper only if all citizens recognized their interdependence, he sought to win respect for Negroes by showing that, instead of sulking about the past, they were ready to participate in the joint effort to create a new America. In the poems of *Majors and Minors* (1895) and the stories of ***Folks from Dixie*** (1898), he repeatedly emphasized the ability and willingness of Negroes to forgive white Americans for previous injustices.

Dunbar's noble sentiments and protagonists reveal not only a naive political philosophy but also a romantic and idealized concept of society. He believed in right rule by an aristocracy based on birth and blood which assured

Dunbar as a young boy.

culture, good breeding, and all the virtues appropriate to a gentleman. He further believed that Negroes, instead of condemning such a society, must prove themselves worthy of a place in it by showing that they had civilized themselves to a level above the savagery which he assumed to be characteristic of Africa. Furthermore, having been reared in Dayton, Ohio, he distrusted big cities and industrialization. Provincially, he assumed the good life for the uneducated to be the life of a farmer in a small western or mid-western settlement or the life of a sharecropper for a benevolent Southern aristocrat. Neither a scholar, political scientist, nor economist, he naively offered an agrarian myth as a shield against the painful reality of discrimination in cities.

Artistic ideals also restricted Dunbar's protest. Even Saunders Redding, generally extremely perceptive in his study of Dunbar, has regretted Dunbar's failure to criticize his society more frequently in his poetry. Dunbar, however, regarded poetry—in standard English—as a noble language, best suited for expressing elevated ideas. Prose was his voice of protest. Protest is missing even from his first two books of poetry, which were privately printed.

In summary, Dunbar's experiences, his social and economic philosophies, and his artistic ideals limited his criticism of the South. This fact, however, should not imply, as some suppose, that Dunbar accepted the total myth of the plantation tradition. In reality, he was no more willing to assume the romanticized plantation to be characteristic of the entire South than he was willing to deny that some slaves had loved their masters or had behaved foolishly.

Nor should it be assumed that his hunger for fame and money silenced his protest against unjust treatment. Actually, he vigorously castigated conditions familiar to him in the North.

The legend of his enforced silence may have germinated from Dunbar's complaints about editors' reactions to his poetry. W. D. Howells had praised Dunbar's dialect poetry as his unique contribution to American literature. Dunbar subsequently felt that Howells' judgment caused editors to underestimate the worth of his non-dialect poetry. Dunbar complained also about his failure to improve as a writer. But no biographer has recorded a single complaint about restrictions in subject-matter or thesis. As candid as Dunbar was in correspondence, such silence implies an absence of restriction. In fact, evidence suggests occasional deference to Dunbar. An editor of *Century* sought Dunbar's judgment about whether the magazine over-emphasized the comic character of the Negro. Dunbar responded with his assurance that a laugh could not hurt the Negro, who has "a large humorous quality in his character."

Significantly, Dunbar was least silent at the very time at which he depended most upon continuing popularity with editors and readers. During 1900 and 1901, he derived his only income from royalties and public readings. His medical expenses, the support of his mother, and the cost of maintaining an attractive wife and a home in Washington increased both his expenditures and his worry about his ability to sustain the expenses. At such a critical time, he frequently spoke out as vigorously as his idol, Frederick Douglass, had spoken and as bitterly as any Negro has.

From 1898 until 1903 he identified himself with protest in articles to newspapers. In 1898 in the Chicago *Record,* he condemned the murder of Negroes in the race riots in Wilmington, North Carolina. When the Denver *Post* requested an article in 1899, he wrote "The Hapless Southern Negro." In 1900 he defended the Negro's intellectual potential in the Philadelphia *Times;* and in 1903, in the *Chicago Tribune,* he pointed out the irony that America condemned Russia's treatment of prisoners yet ignored the lynching, the re-enslavement, the disfranchisement, the unemployment and the discrediting of American Negroes. Four articles of protest may seem too few, but they refute the reputed silence.

Even more significant is his fiction in 1900 and 1901. Previously, his protests had been mild. In ***The Strength of Gideon, and Other Stories*** (1900), however, Dunbar slapped back. In **"A Mess of Pottage"** he pictured the Negro as an individual betrayed by both political parties. **"A Council of State"** is written in a similar tone. Intelligent Negro leaders have planned to campaign against the Republican administration which has made them "crushed men of a crushed race." When advised to be moderate, one leader answers:

> Conservatism be hanged! We have rolled that word under our tongues when we were being trampled upon; we have preached it in our churches when we were being shot down; we have taught it in our schools when the right to use our learnings was being denied us, until the very word has come to be a reproach upon a black man's tongue.

Their efforts are futile. Betrayed by a mulatto who has no sympathy for the Negroes she professes to represent, they are crushed by the white machine.

Another story is even more acerbate. Having worked faithfully for the Republican party in Alabama, Mr. Cornelius Johnson (in **"Mr. Cornelius Johnson, Office-Seeker"**) comes to Washington to obtain the minor political appointment he expects as a reward for his service. As the Congressman repeatedly postpones inquiry into the matter, Johnson is progressively stripped of the dignity in which he has cloaked his image. Insulted by white clerks who call him by his first name, forced to save money by moving from his hotel into a boarding house and by eating snacks in his room rather than dining out, compelled to secure money by pawning his clothes, Johnson finally mortgages his home in Alabama so that he may remain in Washington. His despair intensifies because "a body feels as if he could fight if only he had something to fight. But here you strike out and hit—nothing." After a year's delay he is informed that the Senate has refused to confirm his appointment. Ruined financially and emotionally, he cries to Washington, "Damn your deceit, your fair cruelties; damn you, you hard white liar."

Dunbar's characteristic irony occasionally seeps through the bitterness. In **"Mr. Cornelius Johnson,"** he mused wryly:

> In Alabama one learns to be philosophical. It is good to be philosophical in a place where the proprietor of a cafe fumbles vaguely around in the region of his hip pocket and insinuates that he doesn't want one's custom.

In **"A Council of State"** he mocked the elasticity of the word "colored" and the credulity of white people who accept as a leader of Negroes anyone who professes to be. Irony accompanies humiliation as "Mr." Cornelius Johnson is reduced to "Cornelius" in the office of his Congressman, and the mulatto "leader" of her people is assigned servant's errands by the white boss of the Republican machine. The irony, however, does not lighten the tone. These stories cannot be called pessimistic. The confirmed pessimist at least perceives an alternative outcome even while he positively affirms the inevitability of the undesired outcome. In these stories Dunbar, however, saw only destruction.

Dunbar recognized economic as well as political problems. The most thought-provoking story on the theme is **"One Man's Fortune,"** which Dunbar drew from his experiences in Dayton. Having graduated from a Northern college, Bertram Holliday seeks his fortune confident that he is "master of his fate" and "captain of his soul." Applying for employment as a clerk in the office of a white lawyer, he is advised to start at the bottom, to accept a position as waiter in a hotel. When Bert protests that waiting on tables will not provide legal experience, he is warned that, unprotected by the sympathy which Northerners once felt for Southern slaves, Negroes of a later generation can expect no justice in the North. Applying to an office which had advertised for a clerk, preferably with a high school education, he is told to seek a job in the shipping room. Similar rebuffs teach him that "all the addresses and all the books written on how to get on are written for white men. We blacks must solve the question for ourselves." Bert does not desire to go South to teach school. He believes that, since the South is training its own teachers, jobs for educated Northern Negroes must be developed in the North.

After taking work as a janitor in a factory, he is hired as a clerk by the lawyer who previously had rejected him. Now campaigning for a judiciary post, the lawyer wants Bert to solicit votes from Negroes in the community. After the lawyer has been elected, Bert is replaced by a white youth. Defeated, Bert accepts a teaching position in the South.

Contrasted with the fate of the idealistic protagonist is the success of his more realistic classmate, Davis, who argues that the Negro has no real opportunity in North America. Because his ancestors, savages two hundred years earlier, had been taught civilization in the lowest and most degrading contact with it, the Negro cannot assume the psychology which makes white men respond eagerly to challenges. The Anglo-Saxon heritage of seven centuries teaches, Davis insists, a love for struggle in a normal battle. The Negro, who lacks this frenzy, is forced into an abnormal battle. Instead of fighting to secure a position befitting his education, Davis works in a hotel until he saves enough money to purchase a barber shop, which he operates successfully by concealing his intelligence from his white customers.

In ***The Strength of Gideon, and Other Stories,*** economic problems and injustice also harass the uneducated. In **"The Finish of Patsy Barnes,"** Patsy and his mother have come North hoping to support themselves more easily than they had in Kentucky. His mother's illness forces Patsy to seek employment as a jockey. In this story, as in **"One Man's Fortune,"** Dunbar contrasted the Negroes' failure with the success of Irish immigrants already possessed of authority to employ or reject Negroes whose ancestors had populated America for generations. In **"An Old-Fashioned Christmas,"** Jimmy Lewis, a young newsboy, is arrested on Christmas Eve for shooting dice with a friend for five-cent stakes. Confined overnight, the tearful child is brought before a judge who explains that he must send Jimmy to jail to demonstrate New York City's intolerance of gambling. To free him, Jimmy's mother pays his fine with money she had saved to buy food appropriate for an old-fashioned Christmas dinner. Written in 1899, the story anticipates current condemnations of police brutality and money-blinded courts.

Dunbar also examined injustices in the South. The popularity of lynchings inspired the ironic **"The Tragedy at Three Forks."** Inflamed by editorial innuendo, townspeople lynch two Negroes for a crime committed by a white girl. However, when one white man kills another in the ensuing struggle for souvenirs, he is spared because the crowd agrees with an observer that a white man must be given a chance to explain his actions. Dunbar concluded his tale of the lynching.

> Conservative editors wrote leaders about it in which they deplored the rashness of the hanging but warned the Negroes that the only way to stop lynching was to quit the crimes of which they so often stood accused.
>
> (pp. 1-9)

In his final two works of protest fiction, **"The Wisdom of Silence"** and **"The Lynching of Jube Benson,"** he continued his criticism of the South. **"The Wisdom of Silence"** is ironic. By refusing assistance and by succeeding despite the efforts of loan sharks, Jeremiah Anderson angers his ex-master. As Dunbar says, nothing angers a person more than to be frustrated when he is prepared to say, "I told you so." Fortunately for the ex-master, Jeremiah's crops and barn are burned by persons unknown. Jeremiah is forced to receive and acknowledge help from his exmaster, "Thank e' Mas' Sam." In **"The Lynching of Jube Benson,"** a Southern doctor unsuccessfully attempts to explain why he lynched a faithful servant whom he suspected of rape.

> Why did I do it. I don't know. A false education, I reckon, one false from the beginning. I saw his black face glooming there in the half light, and I could only think of him as a monster. It's tradition. At first I was told that the black man would catch me, and when I got over that, they taught me that the devil was black, and when I had recovered from the sickness of that belief, here were Jube and his fellows with faces of menacing blackness. There was only one conclusion: This black man stood for all the powers of evil, the result of whose machinations had been gathering in my mind from childhood up.

His writings evidence Dunbar's protests against both the South and the North. His position, however, is difficult to appraise exactly because he vacillated and assumed seemingly contradictory stances. Some of his attitudes are difficult to explain. Although the illustrations in his collections of stories seem to caricature Negroes, Dunbar appreciated them so much that he secured an original for his home. Many readers disparage Page's plantation tales, which idealize a genteel, aristocratic society which never existed. Yet, Dunbar apparently considered the Negroes authentic, or at least conceivable. In "Negro Life in Washington," he described a living Negro whom he imagined to have emerged from one of Page's stories.

Perhaps the simplest explanation which offers any consistency is that readers have demanded too much of Dunbar as a symbol. Commanding him to speak for the Negro, they forget that Negroes speak with hundreds of different voices. Dunbar is merely one. Insensitive to the implications of creating comic Negro figures, he was extremely sensitive to the insults which a Northern society might inflict upon an educated Negro. Willing to criticize injustices of Northern or Southern society, he, nevertheless, supported outmoded economic and social ideals. Occasionally conscious of the ridiculous postures of white Americans, he was even more conscious and less tolerant of ridiculous behavior of Negro Americans. Ignorant of historical truths about Africa and about slavery, he respected as fact the myths current in his time. Because he recognized distinctions between Negroes he knew and Negro stereotypes of the plantation stories, he inferred the race's remarkable progress within a generation. In short, Paul Laurance Dunbar was a talented, creative, high school graduate whose views reflect the limited knowledge of many historians, economists, and social philosophers of his day. (pp. 12-13)

Darwin Turner, "Paul Laurence Dunbar: The Rejected Symbol," in The Journal of Negro History, *Vol. LII, No. 1, January, 1967, pp. 1-13.*

Kenny J. Williams (essay date 1970)

[In the essay excerpted below, Williams discusses Dunbar's short fiction reflecting the romantic, plantation, and naturalist literary traditions, and assesses the strengths and weaknesses of each.]

From 1896 until his death in 1906 Paul Laurence Dunbar was the subject of numerous essays and extensive readings—both public and private—as he became, for many people, the symbol of Negro authorship in the United States. Some referred to him as the very first Negro writer in America; others who had heard of Phillis Wheatley allowed that he was the second writer; but all agreed that he was the first truly to interpret Negro life in the country. In many ways Dunbar's success saddened him because he knew that there had been other writers before him and almost without exception it was his dialect poetry which drew white America to him. This poetry which was thought of as a "representative interpretation of Negro life" was such a small portion of his total output. (pp. 153-54)

Those who would now dismiss Dunbar's work fail to remember that he wrote at a time when the romantic tradition was still in vogue in America, at a time when stories of the ante-bellum South were still appearing in popular magazines. Dunbar, who himself was not a southerner, did not write from his own personal experiences, but rather from the stories which his mother, who had been a slave in Kentucky, told him; hence, the assertion that he wrote from personal observation and participation is not valid. He had not really known what the aftermath of slavery in the South was actually like. One of his literary models was James Whitcomb Riley with whom he developed a friendship, and much of what Dunbar wrote in terms of the plantation tradition was simply the Riley vernacular transposed into stories of the South. Furthermore, Dunbar was aware of the publishing situation in the 1890's and the early years of the twentieth century, and much of his work was geared toward popular tastes rather than toward social criticism. (p. 155)

For a well-known poet Dunbar produced an unusually large body of fiction, and it can be divided primarily into two types. There are those stories in which he appeared to concern himself mainly with white characters and their world, stories which do not deal with specific aspects of Negro life. In some of these stories the characters could have been anybody and the situations frequently applicable to white and black alike. Those who look at this fiction and deplore the lack of Negro characters are inadvertently supporting the thesis that the Negro artist must and should produce either works which are within the mold of social protest or which are circumscribed not only by the time and place but also by the race of the author. Dunbar was not, in this fiction, intent upon renouncing his race neither was he attempting to ignore those problems which he saw daily but rather he was operating within the framework of his own belief that the literary artist who happens to be a Negro is not bound by the limitations of purely racial subjects. With this view of literary art Dunbar produced *The Uncalled* (1898), *The Love of Landry* (1900), *The Fanatics* (1901), ***Ohio Pastorals,*** five short stories which appeared in *Lippincott's Monthly Magazine* from August (1901) to December (1901), and numerous short stories within his short story collections. (pp. 156-57)

Little can be said for the five stories which comprise ***Ohio Pastorals.*** **"The Mortification of the Flesh," "The Independence of Silas Bollender," "The White Counterpane," "The Minority Committee,"** and **"The Visiting of Mother Danbury"** are stories which employ some of the more popular techniques of the day and as they appeared in five successive issues of *Lippincott's Monthly Magazine* they are simply entertaining fillers in the magazine. No single characteristic distinguishes them from the host of magazine stories which were popular at the time.

The second type of fiction which Dunbar wrote was in the plantation tradition after the manner and formula of Joel Chandler Harris, Thomas Nelson Page, Irwin Russell, and George Washington Cable. In four collections of short stories, ***Folks from Dixie*** (1898), ***The Strength of Gideon, and Other Stories*** (1900), ***In Old Plantation Days*** (1903), and ***The Heart of Happy Hollow*** (1904), Dunbar presents a sentimental picture of the Old South. His portrait of ante-bellum days is similar to those which followed the conventional local color methods. This tradition presented imagined characters in typical situations when the South was thought of as being divided into two classes: the slaves and the masters. Seldom are the unpleasant aspects of life displayed. Of all of the men who dealt successfully with this world of masters and slaves, Dunbar was the only non-southerner in the group. As the observant outsider, Dunbar never permitted his characters to become clowns merely for the sake of humor. Even though he really did not know the characters about whom he wrote, from his mother's stories he was able to present them sympathetically and gently; his plantation stories (as much of his dialect poetry) show more obviously the influence of James Whitcomb Riley than they do of the plantation school of southern writers. When Dunbar wrote of the days following the Civil War when Negroes were migrating in large numbers to northern cities, he was insistent upon the contrast between the more pleasing side of life in the South with the harshness of life in northern cities. This was partially due to Dunbar's own belief in an agrarian way of life as opposed to that in an industrial community.

His first collection of short stories, ***Folks from Dixie,*** is most apparently influenced by the then-popular plantation tradition. Many of the stories are set in Kentucky where his mother had been enslaved. While the stories are typical of their genre, Dunbar demonstrates a far more sensitive understanding of his characters than Russell, Page, Cable, or Harris ever did. Thus while most of the twelve stories of the collection are traditional in the sense that they portray—in a large measure—the happy and contented relationship between master and slave, the differences (both social and intellectual) between house and field slaves, the narratives are presented with far greater knowledge of some of the basic problems which existed before and after the Civil War. Dunbar, who did not have first-hand knowledge of either slavery or those days following in the South, was content to employ the usual stereotypes: the young master or the considerate master who sold his slaves only in a financial crisis, the beautiful mistress who spent much time in the slaves' quarters taking care of the ill and educating the young, the poor white overseer who was hated by master and slave alike, the house slaves—especially the "Mammy" and the butler—who controlled everybody and everything in the "Big House," and the general aura of gentility which pervaded the idea of southern life and manners.

Although his stories in this collection included in varying degrees all of these stereotypes, he did analyze such themes as the effects of religion and church life in such stories as **"Anner 'Lizer's Stumblin' Block," "The Ordeal at Mt. Hope"** which was also a strong plea for industrial education, **"Mt. Pisgah's Christmas Possum,"** and **"The Trial Sermons on Bull-Skin."** The idealized portrait of loyalty and dedication is best exemplified in **"The Colonel's Awakening"** where ex-slaves aid their old master who has lost his mind, his fortune, and his sons during the Civil War. The same theme is evident in **"The Intervention of Peter"** where Peter, an old respected slave, prevents a duel between two southern "gentlemen," and in **"Nelse Hatton's Revenge"** where another ex-slave aids a former master who had seemed so terrible prior to the Civil War. He further explored the exploitation of Negroes by Negroes in such stories as **"Aunt Mandy's Investment,"** and in **"Jimsella"** he presented the problem of life in the North, a problem which he was to treat at greater length in *The Sport of the Gods.* Just as **"The Ordeal at Mt. Hope"** is a form of social protest so also is **"At Shaft 11"** where Dunbar pleads with Negroes to stay out of labor unions. The success of these stories, once one passes the superficialities of the local color tradition, is in Dunbar's ability to distinguish the true meaning of the actions of his characters from those actions which are assumed for the sake of expediency. No white writer of the plantation tradition was ever able to do this.

The Strength of Gideon, and Other Stories consists of twenty stories. Life on the plantation is treated in **"Viney's Free Papers," "The Case of 'Ca'line': A Kitchen Monologue," "Uncle Simon's Sunday Out," "The Fruitful Sleeping of the Rev. Elisha Edwards,"** and **"Jim's Proba-**

tion." Once again Dunbar portrays the loyalty of the ex-slaves for their old masters in such stories as **"Mammy Peggy's Pride,"** and in the title story of the collection **"The Strength of Gideon."** A number of the narratives of this collection deal with the inability of Negroes to adjust to northern urban environments and with the role of Negroes in politics during the days of Reconstruction. **"An Old Time Christmas," "The Trustfulness of Polly," "The Finding of Zach," "The Faith Cure Man," "Silas Jackson," "The Finish of Patsy Barnes,"** and **"One Man's Fortune"** portray the disillusionment with life in the North. **"One Man's Fortune"** is especially interesting today for it deals with a young man who had listened to all of the injunctions to "get an education" only to discover that education has little or no value for him. He becomes aware that society still looks at him as a Negro rather than as a man. Dunbar makes it clear that the initial effort toward aiding the freedman after the Civil War was soon replaced by a general spirit of indifference. Political aspirations are treated realistically in **"Mr. Cornelius Johnson, Office Seeker," "A Mess of Pottage,"** and **"A Council of State."** In **"The Ingrate"** Dunbar sympathetically presents the story of a slave who has escaped to Canada but who later returns to the United States in order to join the Union Army and to help others gain their freedom. The story, which is probably patterned after the life of his father, is significantly one of his strongest attacks on the institution of slavery.

With ***In Old Plantation Days*** Dunbar returns to the basic type of ***Folks from Dixie.*** While in his second collection of short stories Dunbar introduced far more realistic portrayals of character and situations as well as more stories of social protest, his third volume re-echoes the traditionalism of the first. Stuart Mordaunt's plantation is the background for most of the stories which adhere to the conventional concept of good masters, happy and contented slaves, and cruel overseers. A very few of the stories, most notably **"A Judgement of Paris," "Silent Samuel,"** and **"The Way of a Woman,"** deal with those days of adjustment in northern cities after the Civil War.

Dunbar concerned himself more with racial problems in ***The Heart of Happy Hollow*** than he had done in his earlier collections. . . . It is ironic that Dunbar should have called his village "Happy Hollow" because if one can say true happiness existed here, it was of the most hollow variety. People groped for a method which would alleviate, no matter how briefly, the problems of their lives in an environment which was essentially hostile. For this reason the small things of life took on added significance as the characters were bound together in their search for anything which would help them. The people of Happy Hollow were a serious lot, laughter was seldom, tears came often as they were often forced to mask their true feelings in order to survive. They were exploited by the unscrupulous and ignored by the supposedly sympathetic. With no one to whom they might turn, they lived—or rather, they existed—from day to day. The pathos of the collection is perhaps best exemplified by **"The Lynching of Jube Benson."** Dunbar firmly believed, as he demonstrated in so many of his stories, that the role of the writer was to tell a good story; consequently, he did not view fiction as primarily a social instrument. Yet, in spite of the functional restrictions which he placed upon his own work and upon himself, probably nowhere in American literature has the protest against lynching been more plaintively revealed. The anger and rancor occasioned by the action is submerged in the author's own sense of disbelief which is passed on to the reader who shares in the shock of the action. (pp. 160-65)

Whatever the shortcomings of [**"The Lynching of Jube Benson"**] may be, no man committed to the plantation tradition could have told it. (p. 172)

Kenny J. Williams, "The Masking of the Poet," in his They Also Spoke: An Essay on Negro Literature in America, 1787-1930, *Townsend Press, 1970, pp. 153-215.*

Bert Bender (lecture date 1972)

[*Bender is an American educator and critic. The following excerpted essay was originally presented as a lecture at the Centenary Conference on Paul Laurence Dunbar at the University of California, Irvine, in 1972. In the essay, Bender contends that Dunbar wrote several short stories dealing with the emotional discontent of black Americans resulting from racial, economic, and political oppression, and discusses "Anner 'Lizer's Stumblin' Block" and "The Lynching of Jube Benson" in depth.*]

Dunbar is usually remembered as "the first Negro poet to win national recognition and full acceptance in America." William Dean Howells's review of Dunbar's *Majors and Minors* (1895) served as the pronouncement from the established white literary community that "here was the first instance of an American Negro who had evinced innate distinction in literature." In his introduction to Dunbar's next collection of poems, *Lyrics of Lowly Life* (1896), Howells emphasized (in, from the perspective of the 1970s, an oddly condescending way) his preference for Dunbar's dialect poems, remarking that they "best preserved and most charmingly suggested" the "precious difference of temperament between the races which it would be a great pity to lose." Howells goes on to express his appreciation of Dunbar's "finely comical perception of the Negro's limitations, with a tenderness for them which I think so rare as to be almost quite new" and to predict (with unfortunate accuracy) that "this humorous quality which Mr. Dunbar had added to our literature . . . would most distinguish him, now and hereafter." To have been recognized in this way by the American literati was a financial help but an artistic restriction; for Dunbar wanted most to be remembered for his poetry in standard English, while he had to yield to the public demand for songs and for readings of his dialect poems. He went on, however, after *Lyrics of Lowly Life,* to publish four volumes of short stories and four novels. He depicted in his work, and he undeniably *had,* more faces than that of the smiling, humble, benevolently enslaved black. Perhaps the best comment on critical assessments which treat him as Howells did or as later critics have (who have disapproved of Dunbar's lack of militance) is his own poem "We Wear the Mask." Ironically, it is included in the volume which Howells introduced.

It is true that even in his fiction Dunbar often romanticizes plantation life in the South, as is suggested by the titles to three of his volumes of stories, ***Folks from Dixie, In Old Plantation Days,*** and ***The Heart of Happy Hollow.*** But this tendency in Dunbar is what Robert Hemenway [in *The Black Novelist*] has called his "interest in the pastoral idyll (and its antithesis, an evil, threatening city)"; his romanticizing "suggests that he was as much a victim of popular American mythology as his white countrymen. As a result, his fiction becomes a curious blend of white myths and black stereotypes, muted black protest and indirect white injustice."

But alongside his broadly humorous and—from the point of view of his white audience—harmless stories in dialect, Dunbar published stories which were more directly expressive of the emotional discontent in black America. These stories are informed by a lyric impulse—Dunbar's dream of freedom and equality for his people—and the impulse arises in reaction to various kinds of real oppression. There are stories about white oppression in the South (as in **"The Ingrate"** and **"The Lynching of Jube Benson"**), stories—in keeping with literary interests of the day—about economic oppression (as in **"Jimsella"** and **"At Shaft 11"**), and stories about oppressive superstitions and political struggles within the black community (as in **"The Scapegoat"** and **"The Faith Cure Man"**). These stories frequently attain a lyrical intensity by portraying the emotional light and dark of the black world, or by evoking the underlying, prayerful mood which is characteristic of much of our early black literature. Such a mood in Dunbar gives rise—as in his poem "Sympathy," in which he speaks of a singing caged bird—not to

> . . . a carol of joy or glee,
> But a prayer that he sends from his heart's deep
> core,
> But a plea, that upward to Heaven he flings—
> I know why the caged bird sings!

"Anner 'Lizer's Stumblin' Block" is one of Dunbar's stories that is set on a plantation but which focuses on a problem within the black community itself—the severely moralistic restrictions of evangelical religion. Only in the opening paragraphs is the black-white relationship mentioned, and then its function is to emphasize the darkness of the blacks' religion rather than to suggest either an oppressive or benevolent master-slave relationship:

> It was winter. The gray old mansion of Mr. Robert Selfridge, of Fayette County, Ky., was wrapped in its usual mantle of winter somberness, and the ample plantation stretching in every direction thereabout was one level plain of unflecked whiteness. At a distance from the house the cabins of the Negroes stretched away in a long, broken black line that stood out in bold relief against the extreme whiteness of their surroundings.

In this setting, Anner 'Lizer, the acknowledged belle of the estate, is contrasted to her lover, Sam Merritt. He is natural and physical, and he is an "unconscious but pronounced skeptic"; she, however, is religious, and, as the story proceeds, she becomes "more and more possessed by religious fervor." At the Baptist revival, "the weirdness of the scene and the touch of mysticism in the services" move her nearly to religious ecstasy. Though she prays both to keep Sam and to "get religion," she and Sam become separated. The mystical black religion is a barrier between Anner and Sam; she is required to deny her sexual being until she can publicly display her religious enthusiasm. Finally, after having been able neither to attract Sam nor to experience religious ecstasy, she is allowed to achieve both. She is reunited with Sam one night when she finds him alone in the woods, away from the strangely oppressive influence of the revival. Then, as a result of the consummation of her love with Sam, she finally "set the whole place afire by getting religion at home early the next morning." The ending is ironic; for, though the church had told her that Sam was her stumbling block to getting religion, "the minister announced that 'de Lawd had foun' out de sistah's stumblin' block an' removed it f'om de path.' " The story, then, is based on a struggle between oppressive religious fervor and natural, physical drives. It is impressive in its handling of Anner's psychology, but it is also impressive in the way it vividly dramatizes the fervor of the revival meeting and captures in the rhythmical dialect the strange mixture of fear, ecstasy, and incantation:

> Earnestly he besought the divine mercy in behalf of "de po' sinnahs, a-rollin' an' a-tossin' in de tempes' of dere sins. Lawd," he prayed, "come down dis evenin' in Sperit's powah to seek an' to save-ah; let us heah de rumblin' of yo' cha'iot wheels-ah lak de thundah f'om Mount Sinai-ah; oh, Lawd'ah, convert mou'nahs an' convict sinnahs-ah; show 'em dat dey mus' di an' cain't lib an' atter death to judg-a-ment; tu'n 'em aroun' befo' it is evahlastin' an' eternally too late." Then, warming more and more, and swaying his form back and forth, as he pounded the seat in emphasis, he began to wail out in a sort of indescribable monotone: "O Lawd, save de mou'nah!"
>
> "Save de mou'nah!" came the response from all over the church.
>
> "He'p 'em out of de miah an' quicksan's of dere sins!"
>
> "He'p, Lawd!"
>
> "And place deir feet upon de evahlastin' an' eternal rock-ah!"
>
> "Do, Lawd!"
>
> "O Lawd-ah shake a dyin' sinnah ovah hell an' fo'bid his mighty fall-ah!"
>
> "O Lawd, shake'em!" came from the congregation.
>
> By this time every one was worked up to a high state of excitement, and the prayer came to an end amid great commotion. Then a rich, mellow voice led out with:
>
> "Sabe de mou'nah jes' now,
> Sabe de mou'nah jes' now,
> Sabe de mou'nah jes' now,
> Only trust Him jes' now,
> Only trust Him jes' now,

> He'p de sinnah jes' now;"
>
> and so to indefinite length the mournful minor melody ran along like a sad brook flowing through autumn woods, trying to laugh and ripple through tears.

Though Anner began "to sway backward and forward like a sapling in the wind, and she began to mourn and weep aloud," she couldn't get religion. But the natural attraction that finally brings Anner and Sam together has its mystery, too. In what is a kind of symbolic dialectic, Dunbar depicts the reunion of Anner and Sam by completing the story's pattern of contrasted light and dark. Praying alone in the woods, Anner cried "aloud from the very fullness of her heart, 'O Lawd, sen' de light—sen' de light,' " and "as if in answer to her prayer, a light appeared before her." Remembering the church song "Let us walk in de light," she struggled through the darkness toward the light: "How it flickered and flared, disappeared and reappeared, rose and fell, even as her spirits, as she stumbled and groped her way over fallen logs and through briers." Anner finally breaks through to a clearing to find Sam, who is carrying a lighted taper which he is using to catch a treed coon. The story ends on an odd note of mixed allegory, comedy, and irony. Though Dunbar treats the restrictive Baptist religion ironically, he sees its undeniable hold on the people, for Anner returns to the church: life on the plantation remains pretty much the same. The tone of the story is like the "mournful minor melody" that Dunbar described in the revival meeting; like "a sad brook flowing through autumn woods," it tries "to laugh and ripple through tears."

In the better of his two stories of lynchings, **"The Lynching of Jube Benson,"** Dunbar treats the problem of racial injustice in an effective, indirect way—from the perspective of a white man who has taken part in a lynching. As the white man tells his story, it becomes clear that he is one who Dunbar optimistically imagines to have awakened from the world's dream that he speaks of in "We Wear the Mask." By focusing on obsessive images in the mind of the white man, Dr. Melville, Dunbar brings out the psychological reality of Dr. Melville's horror over having lynched an innocent man. As the doctor prepares to tell his story, he gazes "abstractedly into the fire," and then begins, "I can see it all very vividly now." The story unfolds, then, in a series of intense recollections that crescendo in the doctor's mind until he repeats at the end, "something kept crying in my ears, 'Blood guilty! Blood guilty!' "

Dr. Melville had fallen in love with his landlord's daughter, Annie, and he had been assisted in his courtship of Annie by the black handyman, Jube Benson, who became a loyal friend of the doctor. As the doctor tells his story, it becomes apparent that even now he is not completely free of the "false education" by which he tries to account for his guilt: It was "a false education, I reckon, one false from the beginning." For, ironically, Dunbar has him recall how Jube had been "a perfect Cerberus" in keeping other suitors from Annie. Then, recalling how he had fallen ill and how Jube had cared for him in his sickness, he describes the dreamlike "chimerical vision" he had of Jube. In his "fight with death" he had seen "only a black but gentle demon that came and went, alternating with a white fairy, who would insist on coming in on her head, growing larger and larger and then dissolving." Prepared, then, by his false education, he had seen, as he recalls—after Annie had been murdered and after the suspected Jube had been trailed down—Jube's "black face glooming there in the half light, and I could only think of him as a monster." Despite Jube's pleas in "the saddest voice" the doctor had ever heard, he was lynched by the mob. The doctor's vivid recollection haunts him:

> Hungry hands were ready. We hurried him out into the yard. A rope was ready. A tree was at hand. Well, that part was the least of it, save that Hiram Daly stepped aside to let me be the first to pull upon the rope. It was lax at first. Then it tightened, and I felt the quivering soft weight resist my muscles. Other hands joined, and Jube swung off his feet.
>
> No one was masked. We knew each other. Not even the culprit's face was covered, and the last I remember of him as he went into the air was a look of sad reproach that will remain with me until I meet him face to face again.

The lynchers learn too late that they have lynched the wrong man and that Annie had been murdered by a white man whose face was "blackened to imitate a Negro's." Realizing what he has done, Dr. Melville gasps, "God forgive me," but it is, of course, too late. Examining the skin under the dead girl's fingernails to find proof, he reads his "own doom" when he sees that the skin is white. With the cry ringing in his ears, "Blood guilty! Blood guilty!", he helplessly respects Jube's brother's fierce refusal to be helped home with the body. The story ends with the doctor sitting silently with his head in his hands and then rising to say, "Gentlemen, that was my last lynching." But Dunbar does not give us a naïvely optimistic ending. Rather, the tone is of qualified hope or prayer that the situation might improve. Though Dr. Melville appears to have unlearned much of his "false education," we see that his thinking is still slightly infected. The hope is that the men to whom Dr. Melville tells his story will be moved emotionally to see the injustice of their system. Dr. Melville tells his story in Gordon Fairfax's library, where a group of men have been discussing a recent lynching, and after one man has callously said, "I should like to see a real lynching." The scene implies that education and reasoning, alone, will not solve the problem. Something else is needed, like Dr. Melville's confessional display of his emotions. Dunbar's story, then, is operative in several ways; it is a *cri de coeur,* yet it is an effort to show the way; it is a longing dream of improvement, yet the dream is highly qualified; and, like Dunbar's "caged bird's song," it is a lyric plea to a higher power. (pp. 211-17)

Bert Bender, "The Lyrical Short Fiction of Dunbar and Chesnutt," in A Singer in the Dawn: Reinterpretations of Paul Laurence Dunbar, *edited by Jay Martin, Dodd, Mead & Company, 1975, pp. 208-22.*

A. Robert Lee (essay date 1974)

[*In the following excerpt, Lee praises several of Dunbar's short stories that depart from the plantation myth.*]

Dunbar's [short] fiction, four volumes of tales which in the main tell lightly ironic, rose-tinted versions of plantation culture before and in the immediate wake of the Civil War, and suitably leavened with touches of melodrama, amounts to an uneven mix. Often his characters veer close to comic-racial cartoons. But occasionally Dunbar's stories do explore those abrasive, and utterly unsentimental, truths which in historical fact characterized 19th-century Southern life, truths he usually permitted, whether by design or out of unawareness, only to simmer behind the "quaint," anecdotal features of his story-line. They are "folktales" crowded with a cast of "Uncles" and "Aunts," "High-yellas" and "exhorters," mammies, preachers, shuffling "house-niggers" and pliant fieldhands, whose "small" occasions, some touching, others doltish or infantile—whether of love, religion, rivalry or servitude—act as departure points for each plantation story.

Dunbar never wholly disencumbered himself of the sentimental plantation myth. After all, it had a hold on the minds of his white readership, though his second and fourth collections ***(The Strength of Gideon*** and ***The Heart of Happy Hollow)*** have a number of tales quickened with racially purposive comment. To call Dunbar a black counterpart of Joel Chandler Harris, creator of the Uncle Remus tales, would perhaps be an unduly harsh judgement; but in no active sense did his fiction, with the possible exception of his third and fourth novels, *The Fanatics* and *The Sport of the Gods,* constitute a "useable past" for Richard Wright, James Baldwin, Ralph Ellison, and the subsequent literary architects of American negritude.

Folks from Dixie (1898), using the plantation "frame," is an anthology of folk "doings"—comic snatches like **"Mt. Pisgah's Christmas Possum"** or **"The Deliberation of Mr. Dunkin,"** oozy sentiment like **"The Colonel's Awakening"** or **"A Family Feud,"** and sermonettes given fictional occasion like **"The Ordeal at Mt. Hope."** However, embedded in this collection is the rather impressive story **"At Shaft 11,"** a parable of racial strife with class overtones set in the hill coal-mines of West Virginia. Here Dunbar makes a stand for racial solidarity in the face of both capitalist management and white worker intransigence. A tale somewhat formulaic and overly symmetrical in its denouement (a black working-class leader is finally "paired" with his white counterpart betokening the strength of cross-racial class unity), it nevertheless signifies Dunbar's perception that white and black class interests might profitably blend across the color-line.

The Strength of Gideon, and Other Stories (1900), twenty tales in all, is again set largely in the South, though there are tales of Northern city life which register Dunbar's growing disaffection with urban living, a disaffection which culminates in *The Sport of the Gods.* Many of the stories, as before, smack of the mixture: plantation happenings, "conjuration" pieces, thinly-veiled warnings against migration into the urban North. Dunbar again and again asserts his faith in the agrarian life, a belief that the South, once weaned of racism and morally "reconstructed," would prove a region more amenable to black national interests than the industrial cities north of the Mason-Dixon line.

Amid the ironic but essentially soft-centered renderings of life under slavery in ***The Strength of Gideon, and Other Stories*** (1900) (**"Viney's Free Papers"** or **"Mammy Peggy's Pride,"** for instance), Dunbar included a couple of sourly sharp-edged stories which bristle with open indictments of racism. In **"One Man's Fortune,"** Bertram Holliday, a black mid-Westerner, is put through a harrowing sequence of job humiliations in perpetuation of the color-line. With uncharacteristic acidity Dunbar has his hero muse: "I wonder if it can be true . . . that a colored man must do twice as much and twice as well as a white man before he can hope for even equal chances with him? That white mediocrity demands black genius to cope with it?" And similarly in **"Mr. Cornelius Johnson, Office-Seeker,"** an Alabama office-seeker, callously rebuffed in Washington, D.C., as he awaits preferment in return for election support given to a white congressman, slowly degenerates into a broken man. His words, as he departs D.C., again flash anger and bitter denunciation in testimo-

Dunbar's beloved mother Matilda. The stories she told him of her years in slavery on southern plantations formed the basis for his short stories.

ny to the dead letters which most white promises have meant to the blacks of America: "Damn your deceit, your fair cruelties; damn you, you hard, white liar!" Despite angry outbursts of this kind, a number of lively portraits and an eye upon the twists of racial irony, Dunbar's claims in this volume are not the strongest, but they do argue consciousness, an alertness to the doublethink behind racial abuse.

With ***In Old Plantation Days*** (1903), a collection written under hasty commission, Dunbar returned to the plantation frame, assembling a diary of the lives and happenings of various black families and personalities who live on and around the estate of Ol Mas' Stuart Mordaunt. The hands are projected by Dunbar as artless comic puppets, occasionally half-human in feeling and depth, but mainly "entertainment," one-dimensional figures in a Southern fantasy-land bedecked in magnolia, happy slave cabins, and kindly white patriarchs. Pastime-reading for the undiscriminating perhaps, but Dunbar was lending his not uningenious pen to a dangerous, recurringly tiresome piece of racial-historical mythology.

His last collection, ***The Heart of Happy Hollow*** (1904), takes wider but sadly only a few deeper soundings in the ways of 19th-century black-folks living in small Southern towns. Most of the fourteen tales contribute to a kind of urban cameo, set pieces of pathos or opportunist sleight-of-hand. In **"The Scapegoat,"** for instance, Dunbar works through the turns of ward-politicking in the black community ("Little Africa") of a Southern hamlet; in **"Schwallinger's Philanthropy"** he etches the wiles of a race-track tout in a vein not dissimilar to Faulkner's *The Reivers.* The book is not without Dunbar's penchant for over-ripe sentiment (**"A Defender of the Faith"** and **"The Interference of Patsy Ann"**) for eulogizing a factitious Ol' South (**"Cahoots"** and **"The Wisdom of Silence"** especially), but a couple of the tales do have considerable cutting power.

In **"The Mission of Mr. Scatters"** Dunbar tells an allegory of imposture which reaches towards the ironies of Twain's classic "The Man Who Corrupted Hadleyburg." A Kentucky township is awakened from its "long post-bellum slumber" by a gorgeously dressed black con-man who exposes both the black community's complacent belief in Providence and the white squirearchy's sham-chivalry. With a sure sense of tone and of the intricate duplicities of white racial psychology during Reconstruction, Dunbar logs up his indictments with persuasive skill. In **"The Lynching of Jube Benson,"** the moral thrust is more direct and brutal. The plot is simple enough: a devoted black servant is accused of raping and killing the resident white belle. He is caught and hung only for it to be discovered he was not the rapist . . . . Apart from revealing a sure grasp of the process whereby racial typologies are created, Dunbar in this story breaks out from his more usual one-dimensionality into the live sexual and psychic tissue behind racial sadism. Dunbar could, and here is a notable instance, get beyond his "required" docility. (pp. 168-70)

Paul Laurence Dunbar can never be claimed for the major ranks of fiction, black or white. But to insist on his limitations should not eclipse the resources of his writing. Caught in the historical paradox of his time, endowed with invention but not genius, he was occasionally able to perceive and arrest the brutal particulars of black historical experience. Where he gave in to the costume formulas of romance and resorted to wooden dialogue he clearly writes fiction both weak and ineffective; but where he sought faithfully to portray the live psychology of race, he is able to break through, to seize his reader with a sense of place and time, of human beings bound up in racial calamity. (p. 172)

A. Robert Lee, "The Fiction of Paul Laurence Dunbar," in Negro American Literature Forum, *Vol. 8, No. 1, Spring, 1974, pp. 166-72.*

Robert Bone (essay date 1975)

[Bone is an American critic and educator with special interest in African-American writings. Bone has said of himself: "A white man and critic of black literature, I try to demonstrate by the quality of my work that scholarship is not the same thing as identity." He is the author of the informative critical histories The Negro Novel in America *(1958; rev. ed. 1965) and* Down Home: A History of Afro-American Short Fiction from Its Beginnings to the End of the Harlem Renaissance (1975). *In the following excerpt from a revised and expanded edition of the latter work, Bone examines the reasons behind Dunbar's accommodationist writing and illuminates the thematic concerns of his short story collections.]*

In *Doctor Faustus,* Thomas Mann describes a butterfly whose wings resemble a leaf, "not only in shape and veining, but in the minute reproduction of small imperfections, imitation drops of water, little warts and fungus growths, and more of the like. When this clever creature alights among the leaves and folds its wings, it disappears by adaptation so entirely that its hungriest enemy cannot make it out."

Protective mimicry is the key to Dunbar and his age. In the post-Reconstruction era, hungry enemies were everywhere, and they were determined to reduce the blacks to something like their former state of servitude. In the face of this onslaught, it often seemed the better part of valor to blend with one's surroundings, and to seek sanctuary through invisibility. Even the blemishes of the environment—including the fungus growths of racism—were incorporated into this ingenious adaptation. Thus the Negro minstrel troupes, who blackened their own dark skins with burnt cork, and distorted their own features to conform to the white stereotype.

In Paul Dunbar's shorter fiction, protective mimicry consisted (1) of imitating the Plantation School, and (2) utilizing the conventions of the minstrel stage. Some thirty of his stories are historical romances with settings in the antebellum South, while twenty more are minstrel travesties. These forms offered safety and protection to a black author because they were firmly established in the popular culture of the day. In so merging with his cultural surroundings, Dunbar was assured of popular success, but he paid an awesome price for this protective coloration. Like the black minstrels, he collaborated in the defamation of his own people.

Dunbar's protective adaptation to a hostile environment was not at all unique. His was an age of accommodation, presided over by the imposing figure of Booker T. Washington. The Founder of Tuskegee, whose racial policies were formulated in his Atlanta speech of 1895, dominated Negro thought and action for a generation. He exerted a profound influence on the cultural expression of American Negroes, including their imaginative literature. There is no point in trying to ignore or minimize this influence. Dunbar was Washington's disciple, and no amount of sophistry will transform an advocate of compromise and reconciliation into a racial militant. (pp. 42-3)

It cannot be denied that Dunbar wrote a handful of protest stories, representing approximately 7 percent of his output in the genre. But most of his tales are so accommodationist in tone as to be embarrassing to modern readers. Only by ignoring the overwhelming mass of evidence is it possible to classify him as a protest writer.

To rank Dunbar on some sort of militancy scale is to do him a disservice, for in any scrupulous and conscientious reckoning, he is bound to be the loser. This approach, moreover, is open to the charge of provincialism, insofar as it imposes the values of the present on the past. Every age has a right to be judged on its own terms; and every writer, by the canons of his chosen genre. That, in Dunbar's case, is the pastoral, rather than the protest mode. Ultimately we must weigh his substance as a pastoralist, assessing him by what is central, and not tangential to his art.

The challenge of Dunbar criticism is to disengage his art as far as possible from the imperatives of ideology, and judge it as an act of the imagination. This procedure will require us to be sympathetic, and yet critical; to make historical allowances, and yet to take his measure by the realistic standard of what was possible for a man of his time. If, for example, Dunbar's reputation suffers from comparison with that of his contemporary, [Charles] Chesnutt, that is because the latter strove to rise above his era and transform its consciousness, while the former was content for the most part to reflect the social prejudices of his age. (pp. 43-4)

Dunbar's accommodation to the minstrel tradition is well known. Over a period of years he collaborated with the black composer Will Marion Cook, on a number of music-hall entertainments familiarly known as "coon shows." Dunbar contributed most of the lyrics to *Clorindy; or, the Origin of the Cake-Walk* (1898), and some of the lyrics to *Jes' Lak White Folks* (1900) and *In Dahomey* (1902). In 1899 he wrote a vaudeville sketch called *Uncle Eph's Christmas* for Ernest Hogan, a veteran minstrel singer and former star of *Clorindy.* Here is a sample of the dialogue: "Pappy, where was de first possum perskivered?" "Don't you know dere's no sich word in the dictionumgary as perskivered?"

Dunbar persisted in these collaborations despite the active opposition of his wife. They became in fact a major source of conflict in his marriage. Alice Dunbar and her rather aristocratic family objected that such activities were beneath the dignity of a serious poet. They felt entirely justified in this opinion when a Boston reviewer of *Uncle Eph's Christmas* called Dunbar "Prince of the coon song writers." In January 1900, Alice accompanied her husband on a business trip to New York where she tried to break off his relationship with Hogan. A bitter quarrel ensued, and the breach in their marriage was never altogether healed.

Dunbar's insensitivity to the implications of the minstrel stereotype is nowhere more apparent than in the illustrations that adorn the four collections of his stories. The drawings of his white illustrator, Edward Windsor Kemble, are travesties of Negro life, blatantly racist in their impact. They are at best comic stereotypes and at worst vicious caricatures. It would be damaging enough if, against his better judgment, Dunbar had been forced to accept such a collaboration by his publishers. But what are we to say of a black writer who so admired these racist drawings that he asked the artist to let him frame the originals for his den?

Equally accommodationist was Dunbar's response to the Plantation School. These writers were the chief propagandists of the New South, and as such, their object was to win the acquiescence of the North in the disfranchisement of Southern blacks. To this end they portrayed the former slaves as feckless and irresponsible, and altogether incapable of self-government. For such childlike and dependent wards, freedom was illusory, and Negroes who migrated to the North were seized (especially at Christmas time) with paroxysms of nostalgia and regret. So ran the fantasies of Southern writers whose poetry and fiction amounted to a literary version of keeping the Negro in his place.

Dunbar's culpability in parroting the propaganda of his racial enemies is not to be denied. There are few clichés of the Plantation School, however anti-Negro in their implications, that he hesitates to use. In **"Viney's Free Papers"** he portrays a slave who revokes her manumission rather than confront the ambiguities of freedom. In **"Silas Jackson"** he warns against the folly of abandoning the South for the lure of "false ambitions" in the North. In **"An Old Time Christmas"** he depicts the yearning of Northern migrants for the old plantation, not scorning to support his point with a few lines from "Swanee River." Dunbar's images of Negro life in these and many other tales cannot be distinguished from those of Thomas Nelson Page.

In accordance with his tactic of accommodation, Dunbar was prepared, like Washington, to sacrifice the greater for the lesser good. Just as Washington renounced the ballot box and opera house in order to achieve a modest economic gain, so Dunbar renounced his highest ambitions as a writer and settled for a modest reputation as a dialect poet and local colorist. The point in each case was to win a limited acceptance by a gesture of propitiation. Like Washington, Dunbar was prepared to recognize his "place." As the black leader accepted a subordinate position for his people, so the black writer for his art. (pp. 52-4)

Dunbar's art, like Washington's politics, rested on pastoral assumptions. A pronounced anti-urban bias is evident throughout his work. Aspiration beyond a certain point is condemned as a form of hubris. Much of Dunbar's fiction constitutes a warning to younger blacks against "the false ideals and unreal ambitions" to which they might succumb in the Northern cities. The pastoral convention, in Dunbar's hands, served as a restraint on Negro aspiration. Some such restraint was essential to the black bourgeoisie, whose aspirations were restricted by the stubborn realities of caste.

Washington and Dunbar, though active in separate spheres, faced a common task. The reconciliation of Negro aspiration with the principle of white supremacy was the focal point of both careers. In this they embodied the historical dilemma of the social class from which they sprang. The rising Negro middle class found its journey up from slavery blocked at every turn by the artificial barriers of caste. They were torn, in consequence, between a desire to succeed, and a fear of retaliation in the event that they should succeed too well. It was to this agonizing conflict that Dunbar addressed himself in his short fiction.

At bottom Dunbar's stories represent a quest for a solution to the problem of Negro aspiration. Four alternatives were possible in Dunbar's time: (1) the Negro might accommodate to caste by curbing his ambition; (2) he might conceal his true motives behind a minstrel mask; (3) he might sound the protest note and challenge the restrictive practices of caste; (4) he might turn to illicit forms of aspiration when he found the normal channels closed. Dunbar explores all of these alternatives, not without considerable confusion and inconsistency. (pp. 56-7)

[Dunbar's] four collections contain a total of seventy-three stories, which may be divided, according to historical setting, into thirty-one antebellum and forty-two post-emancipation tales. The former are historical romances which conform in all respects to the plantation myth. The image of plantation life that they convey would cause no disturbance at a convention of the Knights of the White Camelia. These plantation tales may be found in all four volumes, but are concentrated in the third, ***In Old Plantation Days*** (1903). In terms of genre, they consist primarily of pastorals and travesties.

The stories with a post-emancipation setting deal somewhat more authentically with Negro life. Yet even here, stereotypes of the Plantation School and the minstrel tradition intrude between Dunbar and his material, obscuring his vision and distorting his sense of truth. Only in a handful of stories does he succeed in circumventing these false images. The settings of his post-emancipation tales include the rural South (principally smalltown Kentucky), metropolitan New York and Washington, and the generic "Little Africa." This euphemism for the urban ghetto reflects Dunbar's rather gingerly approach to material with which he felt considerably less at ease than the plantation scene.

To Dunbar's seventy-three collected stories must be added ten uncollected tales, which he himself has designated as ***Ohio Pastorals.*** These stories, most of which appeared in *Lippincott's* from 1901 to 1905, have a common setting in the Ohio village of Dorbury, and an overlapping cast of characters, all of whom are white. Linguistically they belong to the "b'gosh" and "I vum" school of country dialect. The Ohio pastorals are highly autobiographical, being transparent projections of the author's emotional conflict with his mother. As in his first novel, *The Uncalled* (1898), Dunbar assumes the mask of whiteness when writing of intensely personal emotions.

So much for an overview of Dunbar's short fiction. Six basic story-types encompass most of his output in the genre. First there are the pastorals (32), deriving essentially from the Plantation School. Next the travesties (20), deriving from the minstrel shows. Third, protestations of loyalty (8), which offer reassurance to the whites in the Washington tradition. Fourth, stories of uplift (6), which celebrate the success virtues. Fifth, protest stories (6), which challenge the artificial barriers of caste. Sixth, stories of illicit aspiration (5), which are close in spirit to the Brer Rabbit tales. We will now discuss these story-types *ad seriatum,* illustrating each with one or more representative tales.

In his short stories and his novels, Dunbar employs three distinct varieties of pastoral. According to their basic thrust, I have called them pastorals of release, pastorals of reconciliation, and pastorals of place. The first type predominates among the Ohio pastorals; the second, among the antebellum tales; the third, among the post-emancipation stories. (pp. 61-3)

The pastorals of release have their source in the strict authoritarian controls of Dunbar's youth. They celebrate his liberation from the Protestant ethic of hard work and self-denial, from the competitive pressures of the Negro middle class, or in other words, from his mother's tyranny. Truancy is the central metaphor of these stories, and in this respect they anticipate the fiction of Claude McKay. Their tone is one of genial humor, deriving from a leniency and mellowness of spirit. They advocate a tolerance of human weakness, and a generous forgiveness of venial sins. These stories are designed, in short, to mitigate the rigors of the puritan tradition.

"The Independence of Silas Bollender" will serve to illustrate the type. An Ohio farmer with a nagging wife defies her wishes and attends a country fair, where he indulges in the harmless pleasures that such occasions offer: "Anyway, he enjoyed himself. He ate gingerbread, rode the merry-go-round, and someone even saw him coming out of one of the many minstrel shows with a seraphic smile on his face." At the racetrack, however, a pickpocket relieves him of his watch and wallet, and he returns in disgrace to his morally complacent but forgiving spouse. This emotional syndrome of rebellion, guilt, and reconciliation is typical of Dunbar's Ohio pastorals.

The pastorals of reconciliation have their origin in this syndrome. Revolt against maternal domination produces guilt, which in turn necessitates a reconciliation with the mother. **"The White Counterpane,"** for instance, depicts the reconciliation of a mother and her son, after a breach occasioned by the son's marriage. It is the mother's recollection of her own courtship that effects the reconciliation:

". . . she sat for a space, her mind roaming the green pastures of the past." Sentimental memories of the past, in short, perform a harmonizing function. This motif, projected on the historical plane, accounts for most of Dunbar's antebellum tales.

Breach-and-reconciliation constitutes the plot of these plantation tales. Typically they open with a feud or bitter quarrel between two lovers or their families; between Blue-and-Grey, master-and-slave, or east-and-west plantations. In the end a reconciliation is effected, often through the intervention of a faithful servant. The moral injunction implicit in these tales is to forgive and forget. The spirit of dissension, or faction, or die-hard conservatism is condemned, while the virtues of conciliation and openness to change are celebrated.

The pastorals of place are concerned with exposing false ambition or restraining the aspiring mind. Working within the conventions of the Plantation School, Dunbar subscribes—or pretends to subscribe—to Southern agrarian values. He thus portrays the Great Migration as a moral disaster. At the same time, the Northern movement that he condemns functions in his fiction as a metaphor of social mobility. The moral of these stories is: know your place, be content with what you have, and resist the temptation to aspire above your station. The pastorals of place, in short, subserve the Washingtonian doctrine of limited aspiration.

Throughout Dunbar's fiction, the Northern city is depicted as a repository of false ideals. Anti-heroes, or negative exemplars, are created to embody these false values and illusory goals. Typically they are youthful migrants who succumb to the temptations of gambling, drinking, street crime, disease, or promiscuity. **"Silas Jackson"** is the purest story of its kind. It deals with a Virginia farmboy who becomes a waiter at a resort hotel. Eventually he is corrupted and destroyed by an opportunity to join a troupe of Negro singers in New York. Like Silas Bollender, he returns from his excursion in disgrace: ". . . spent, broken, hopeless, all contentment and simplicity gone, he turned his face toward his native fields."

A variation on the theme of false ambition is what might be called the carpetbagger theme. Here the protagonist is tempted by a get-rich-quick scheme which promises to bring success without the trouble of hard work. . . . [But] always the protagonist falls victim to his own avarice. In the end his Eldorado vanishes, and he is brought low. The moral of these tales is Washingtonian: only through hard work and sacrifice can the black man hope to improve his lot.

Some of Dunbar's overly ambitious blacks are undone by their own pretentiousness and pride. These are the boastful ones, who insist on flaunting their prosperity. Success turns their heads; they put on airs, become pompous, and adopt a condescending attitude toward their less fortunate brothers. In imitation of the white aristocracy they buy expensive clothes, assume fancy names, cultivate impressive manners, and in short become dandified. Such stories as **"The Wisdom of Silence," "Johnsonham, Jr."** and **"The Home-Coming of 'Rastus Smith"** warn the blacks to keep a low profile and do nothing to arouse the envy of their enemies.

Pastoral and travesty are closely related literary forms. Both employ the device of masquerade, but so to speak, in opposite directions. When a courtier pretends to be a shepherd, the result is pastoral, but when a shepherd pretends to be a courtier, the result is travesty. In travesty the masker "dresses up," while in pastoral he "dresses down." But in either case, the form depends on audience recognition that the masquerader is not what he pretends to be.

Travesty moves from the sublime to the ridiculous. A form of parody, it implies a moral norm beyond itself, of which it is a humorous burlesque. It posits an exalted sphere of human conduct from which its own sphere represents a falling-off. The victims of travesty are brash pretenders to that higher sphere. They are built up for a fall, which occurs when their pretensions are unmasked. The form depends, in short, on that deflationary movement known as *bathos* (from the Greek, *depth*), which may be defined as anticlimax, or comedown. It is through this reductive mechanism that the pretender is brought low.

In minstrel travesty, the moral norms of course are white. It is to white standards of dress, language, and deportment that the "darkies" of the minstrel stage aspire. Imitation of the white ideal is the crux of minstrel humor, for it is thought to be an imitation doomed in advance. The little girl, no matter how persuasively she dresses up, cannot be her mother. The Negro's imitation is *necessarily inferior:* that is the essential point. His pretensions are ludicrous in light of his inevitable failure. He is a comic figure insofar as he falls short of the white ideal.

Dunbar's travesties run true to form. They stress the imitative, or derivative, or secondhand features of Negro life. The key characters are those members of the black community—headwaiters, butlers, and body servants—who have the freest access to white culture. This dimension of Dunbar's art is closely related to the popular diversion of the cakewalk. He was familiar with the form through his efforts in the field of musical comedy. The cakewalk, in which Negro slaves parodied the elegance and formal manners of the Big House, was a standard ingredient of every minstrel show. If we recognize its equivalent in Dunbar's fiction, we cannot fail to be impressed with the affinity of his art to minstrelsy.

"A Supper by Proxy" is the purest of Dunbar's travesties. It presents us literally with a dress-up affair, in which slaves momentarily assume the outward semblance of their masters. A Virginia planter and his wife announce their intentions of making an extended trip to Philadelphia. During their absence, the house servants prepare a lavish banquet to which they invite the entire "black aristocracy" of the neighborhood. In the midst of the festivities, their childish world of make-believe is rudely shattered. Old master returns in disguise, and much to their chagrin the pretenders are unmasked.

"A Supper by Proxy" is a classic example of social travesty, whose comedy derives from the attempt to rise above one's station. He who imitates his betters, like Malvolio, runs the risk of ridicule. This is the source of humor in such post-emancipation tales as **"A Judgment of Paris," "The Deliberation of Mr. Dunkin,"** and **"The Way of a Woman."** What is really at issue in these tales is the former slave's desperate quest for a code of manners, a model of deportment, a standard of taste appropriate to his new status as a freedman. That this painful effort on the part of black folks to become "respectable" should be perceived as comical by Dunbar is a measure of his psychological assimilation to the white man's point of view.

Dunbar's religious travesties constitute a variation on the theme. Here a comic disproportion arises between saintly pretensions and human frailties. These stories contrast the high road of salvation with the low road of appetite. They move from a lofty spiritual plane to a mundane level of petty intrigue, ulterior motive, courtship rivalry, or venial sin. Thus a convert is not so much "under conviction" as in search of a husband (**"Anner 'Lizer's Stumblin' Block"**); or what seems to be a miracle turns out to be a prank (**"The Walls of Jericho"**). Often these stories have a bathetic ending which provides a naturalistic explanation for a seemingly supernatural event.

Most of Dunbar's religious travesties are antebellum tales whose common setting is the Virginia plantation of Stuart Mordaunt. The central figure in the Mordaunt series is old Parker, the plantation exhorter. Mordaunt's Jim, who represents the unregenerate element among the slaves, is Parker's foil. A devoted servant of the Lord, Parker is sometimes guilty of the sin of overzealousness. From time to time he is taken down a peg by being discovered in some embarrassing or apparently compromising position. These travesties derive from the folk form of the preacher tale, in which the black preacher's alleged pomposity, greed, unchastity, or hypocrisy provides a source of deflationary humor.

A few religious travesties have post-emancipation settings. Their plots generally turn on some form of rivalry in church governance. But the tone is comic; the issues trivial or insignificant. These stories proclaim above all that the lives of black folk are lacking in high seriousness. We are presented not with Negro church life, but a parody thereof. Dramatic conflict may be present, but it is unworthy of mature minds. Of these undignified portrayals, **"The Trial Sermon on Bull-Skin"** is perhaps the most representative, while **"Mt. Pisgah's Christmas' Possum"** is closest to the minstrel stereotype. (pp. 63-8)

Eight of Dunbar's tales are protestations of loyalty. . . . Some are set in the antebellum South; others follow the fortunes of a Southern family beyond the Civil War, in order to demonstrate the loyalty of former slaves through thick and thin. All reflect the house-servant orientation inherited by Dunbar from his mother. **"At Shaft 11"** constitutes a special case. This story, which deals ostensibly with labor strife in the West Virginia coalfields, has been praised as an extension of Dunbar's range and a clear break with the Plantation School. In actuality, the old plantation has simply been transposed from Virginia to West Virginia. Despite this metamorphosis, loyalty to white power remains the story's theme.

In its offensiveness to modern readers, **"The Strength of Gideon"** is typical of Dunbar's loyalty tales. Modeled closely after Thomas Nelson Page's "Meh Lady," the story is concerned with a loyal slave who is the mainstay of his master's womenfolk throughout the Civil War. Even as the Yankee troops advance, and his beloved Martha urges him to join her in deserting to the Yankee camp, Gideon remains loyal to his white folks. At the moment of decision, the voice of Duty, in the person of ole Missy, calls. Gideon's response must surely be the saddest line in Negro literature: "Yes, Mis' Ellen, I'se a-coming."

Six of Dunbar's stories are concerned with the theme of moral uplift. Inspirational in tone, they seek to redeem the darker brother from his backward ways. Their origin can thus be traced to the missionary impulse of the planter class, which would not rest content until its slaves were Christianized. This impulse toward salvation has been secularized in Dunbar, and amounts to little more than the inculcation of bourgeois values. These stories are little sermonettes on the dangers of gambling, alcohol, and sex, or the vices of shiftlessness, irresponsibility, and wife-desertion. They are dedicated to the dissemination of what might be called the Booker-T virtues. (pp. 69-70)

Despite his natural inclination to accommodate, Dunbar is not entirely lacking in rebelliousness. While ordinarily his true feelings are well masked, on occasion the mask slips, and we catch a glimpse of the authentic self. Six of his stories, for example, are concerned with voicing historic grievances, protesting current injustices, and defending his race from the ravages of the post-Reconstruction, repression. Two of these (**"The Ingrate"** and **"The Easter Wedding"**) attack the institution of slavery; two (**"The Tragedy at Three Forks"** and **"The Lynching of Jube Benson"**) are antilynching tracts; and two (**"One Man's Fortunes"** and **"A Council of State"**) are direct assaults on the barriers of caste and the bastions of white supremacy.

"One Man's Fortunes" is typical of Dunbar's protest tales. Autobiographical in origin, it reflects the young poet's bitterness, following his high-school graduation, when he was unable to find a decent job. Bert Halliday, the hero of the story, is a graduate of the state university who leaves his alma mater full of hope, but is brought to the verge of despair by a series of disillusioning encounters with white discrimination and hypocrisy. Thwarted ambition is the story's theme. The hero insists upon his due, and a lower level of aspiration, symbolized by teaching in the South, is accepted only under duress. (pp. 70-1)

If legitimate ambition is thwarted by the color line, then illicit forms of aspiration are certain to appear. A new type of hero is required to dramatize this theme. In Dunbar's early stories the heroes are paragons of virtue, as virtue would be understood by whites. In certain of his later tales, however, a hero of a different stamp appears. This is a man whose character and actions are shrouded in moral ambiguity. With his appearance, the moral certainties of melodrama are dissolved, and the outlines of a more sophisticated moral vision are revealed. Dunbar is striving to transcend the official (or white) morality of which he has been heretofore a captive, and an outlaw (or Negro) code is beginning to emerge.

Thus we have the confidence man, the racetrack tout, or the convicted felon cast in the heroic role. These are metaphors, or ritual masks, behind which lurks the elusive figure of Brer Rabbit. For it was the signifying Rabbit who first embodied this outlaw code. In a social order where the white man possesses all the power, writes all the laws, and formulates the moral code, the black man is pushed beyond the pale of conventional morality. He becomes a moral outlaw. So it is with Dunbar's disreputable heroes: the trickster with his signifying ways is a threat to the white man's moral order; the racetrack tout is a challenge to white respectability; the convict is a victim of the white man's law.

The figure of the trickster emerges slowly in Dunbar's fiction. His first treatment of the theme, **"Aunt Mandy's Investment,"** is little more than a sentimental portrait of the con man with a heart of gold. In **"The Mission of Mr. Scatters,"** however, we are confronted with a genuine rogue-hero. A similar progression may be seen in Dunbar's treatment of the racetrack milieu. In **"The Finish of Patsy Barnes"** an adolescent boy earns money for his mother's medical expenses by the "questionable" expedient of becoming a jockey. But in **"Schwallinger's Philanthropy"** a racetrack tout is developed as a full-fledged trickster-hero.

Dunbar's best story, **"The Scapegoat,"** represents the culmination of this tendency. The plot concerns a political boss in Little Africa who is betrayed by his white associates when the city is seized by a momentary passion for reform. Convicted of election-rigging, Robinson Asbury serves a year in the penitentiary. On emerging he announces his retirement from politics, but secretly he works for the defeat of the machine. On election day it rains black voters, and Asbury enjoys the full measure of revenge. In his slickness, duplicity, and ruthless survival code, Asbury is a lineal descendant of Brer Rabbit. The blunder committed by his enemies is to toss him back in the brier patch!

How shall we assess Dunbar's work in the short-story form? Much of it is inauthentic, in the sense that it reflects the white man's definitions of reality. Much of what remains is parochial or topical, and does not survive its own historical epoch. Very few of Dunbar's stories escape the limitations of a facile commercialism: they were mass-produced, written to standard specifications, and packaged for a quick sale. The truth is that Dunbar was a black businessman working in the literary line.

Despite these strictures, it cannot be denied that Dunbar played an important role in the evolution of the Afro-American short story. He established a pastoral tradition that would come to fruition in the era of the Harlem Renaissance. He was the founder, moreover, of a populist and anti-intellectual tradition that descends through Langston Hughes to the revolutionary writers of the Black Power movement. Finally, in his focus on the theme of Negro aspiration he identified a subject to which generations of black storytellers would return.

On balance, however, the verdict must be negative. In the short-story field, Dunbar will be remembered chiefly as a purveyor of dead forms. Plantation tales, minstrel travesties, loyalty sagas: these were the sterile fantasies of a nation engaged in a hollow ritual of self-justification. That they survived at all in the fiction of a black American is testimony to the coercive power of the white man's literary forms.

There is a moribund quality in Dunbar's art, attributable at least in part to the limitations of his age. To overcome those limitations, to make the most of his restricted possibilities, to stretch the imaginations of his contemporaries and thereby enlarge their moral horizons, it would have been necessary for Dunbar to adopt a sharply different literary stance. Romanticism would have had to yield to realism; loyalty to satire; pastoral to antipastoral. (pp. 71-3)

Robert Bone, "Paul Dunbar," in his Down Home: Origins of the Afro-American Short Story, *Columbia University Press, 1988, pp. 42-73.*

Michael Flusche (essay date 1977)

[In the essay excerpted below, Flusche offers the theory that Dunbar's powerless, unsuccessful protagonists reflect Dunbar's own frustrating experiences in white society.]

"My position is most unfortunate," Paul Laurence Dunbar once remarked, "I am a black white man." As the black author best known to white Americans in the 1890's, he was publishing two books a year; his short stories and poems were being carried regularly by *Lippincott's* and *Scribner's;* and Dodd, Mead & Company was paying him a retaining fee for first publication rights on his fiction. Yet his literary success did not soothe the malaise he felt from being a black author living in and writing for white America of the 1890's. In the back of his mind there was always the painful—but well founded—suspicion that his popularity sprang not from the quality of his work but from the color of his skin. As the first descendant of slaves consistently to place his writings with the leading journals, he always hoped, but was never able, to escape condescending tributes as the leading author of his race. (p. 49)

The demands of the marketplace made it imperative that through the point of view, the setting, the subject matter, or dialect, Dunbar place most of his short stories within or near the plantation tradition. Even the ten or twelve stories most laden with moonlight and magnolias, however, could not have been confused with those of Thomas Nelson Page. For in Dunbar there was no celebration of the Old Regime; he trotted out the stage pieces of a good plantation story, but with a distinct lack of enthusiasm. To be a popular success, Dunbar did not need to do more than recite the plantation formula—he could count on the readers' stock response to supply what was lacking.

Dunbar could accept the form of the tradition, for it allowed him to compromise between his readers' taste and his own ambition to prove to the world, as he wrote to a friend, "that after all we are more human than African." Once he had established his name he was confident that he could shape the world to his own vision; but first he must gain and hold his audience. For that reason he studded his stories with confused darkies giving their woolly heads a half-hearted scratch, with wise old uncles speaking in garbled tongues, and with happy multitudes whose supreme delight was possum, prepared in any manner. (p. 52)

Even as Dunbar wrote some genuinely funny stories, he knew that the shouts of joy he sent rippling across the fictional plantation were strained. Beneath the superficial joy of many of his stories, there is a persistent sense of failure. Three out of four protagonists do not of their own strength and efforts achieve what they seek; they are incapable of mastering life even on the most trivial level. One-third of the unsuccessful protagonists never reach their goal at all; the others, having reached an impasse, are saved from having to resolve the conflict by the dissolution of the antagonistic force or by outside intervention. The one constant in Dunbar's universe was that success, if it came at all, went not to the persistent but to the patient.

Of the protagonists in Dunbar's fiction who actually achieved their goals, about half were plantation mammies and female household slaves who enjoyed the well-established reputation of being great strategists of romance and reconcilers of lovers. It was no great innovation for Dunbar to follow this tradition. Successful male protagonists—white or black—however, presented Dunbar with considerable literary difficulties since aggression for males in his universe was taboo. The solution of the problem was to make them less than men. They were clownish, especially when proposing to a girl; or they were young boys, named "Patsy," for example; or they were old men. But they could not be fully developed, forceful, virile. Of the three most masculine successful figures, two were frauds, fast-talking impostors. The third was a young preacher whose eyes moistened at the thought of his mother and who was almost upon sight adopted by elderly Aunt Caroline.

The problem for Dunbar was more than just a matter of not offending his white readers, for most of his white protagonists appear just as effeminate or henpecked as his Negroes, possibly even more so. Nor was Dunbar simply staying safely within the bounds for male aggressiveness prescribed by the genteel literary taste of the period. The separation of aggressiveness and success seems, rather, to reflect Dunbar's own experience of impotence before the world in which he lived. . . . [He] wrote that some power deprived him of his ability to achieve his goals, and when he did overcome his fear, "I grope without direction and by chance."

In Dunbar's stories the most common reward for initiative was failure. . . . If success did come to Dunbar's protagonists, it normally was the result of another's action. **"The Vindication of Jared Hargot,"** a typical Dunbar success story, recounted the sad career of Hargot, a local poet who endured the ridicule of the local wags. Finally, however, the townspeople felt sorry for him and arranged a testimonial for the poet who had at least "piped sweetly in the smiling vale." This tribute was more condescension from the town than a victory for Hargot.

Almost more difficult for Dunbar than conceiving successful male protagonists was describing men who were strong and effective in the company of women. The pattern was almost everywhere the same in Dunbar's stories: in three, the male character was dominant; in five, the man and woman addressed each other as equals; in the rest, about twenty stories, the dominance of the female was either explicit or evident from the author's descriptions. In this regard there seemed to be no difference between his white and black characters.

Couples, whether married or courting, were unable to express any serious affection for one another; their relationship was either comical, maudlin, or explicitly unemotional. The ritual surrounding courtship and marriage raised a serious problem for Dunbar. His stories demanded that he have couples expressing interest in one another, but at the same time he had his characters deny that they were personally involved. Affection-free courting was not just a comic device for Dunbar; he went to great lengths to keep his characters from getting emotionally involved. Although the genteel and plantation traditions insisted that relationships of young lovers be near the platonic, they nowhere demanded that affection be denied. Dunbar went further, not only bowing to the apprehensions of his white readers about black sexuality but also expressing his own suspicions about personal relationships.

Females occupied a privileged position in Dunbar's fiction. They were not just charming and intelligent women so popular in nineteenth-century fiction. Their strengths were not just the domestic virtues. They were universally competent, observant, and resourceful. They set the standards of achievement and next to them men seemed bumblers. On one occasion [in **"One Christmas at Shiloh"**], a straying husband returned to his wife:

> "You will tek me back!" he cried, "you will fu'give me!"
>
> "Yes, yes, of co'se. I will, Madison, ef you has made a man of you' se'f."

(pp. 54-6)

The world that Dunbar created in his fiction reflects the difficulty he had in gaining the confidence of society. In Dunbar's experience, a clearly defined public position, a form of self-assertion, was dangerous and to be avoided. Success could come only to one who avoided all offensive gestures and alienated no one. The clearest fictional statement of this idea appears in *The Fanatics,* which seems at first to be a novel of national reconciliation, following the standard pattern of lovers from the North and South healing the wounds of the nation. It is soon evident, however, that national unity is not the problem under consideration so much as individual identity.

The exceedingly complex plot consists of a series of four loosely connected romances, plus the political reconciliation of two widowers. A scorecard for the characters would indicate that any person or family who took a definite position on a question such as secession or who took aggressive action for either side would meet with a tragic end, apparently demanded by the calculus in the mind of the divine monitor of human affairs. Obviously Dunbar could not imagine a successful character with a clear public identity.

If a person finds a well-defined role and identity an impediment or even a threat, and if by the color of his skin he is immediately identifiable, he may well be tempted to shuck off all identification, to become, in a way, invisible; only so could he then become an individual, with his own personal identification. Society imposed an identity on Dunbar; he was a Negro poet—and readers all thought they knew what that meant. He was the "Poet Laureate," the Robert Burns, of his race. But Dunbar did not want to think of himself as a Negro poet; he did not think that his dialect verse was his best. He may have wanted to be in some way like the hero of one of his better short stories, a complete individual, with no attachments to society.

This story, **"At Shaft 11,"** concerns a miners' strike in West Virginia. After the introduction of black strike-breakers, violence, and negotiation, the conflict was easily—incredibly—settled by one man, whom Dunbar was careful to describe. Jason Andrews, the foreman at Shaft 11, first entered the story at sunset, when it was neither night nor day, standing by his home up the hill away from the village. From the beginning, then, Dunbar suggests he was an independent man. When the strike first threatened, his wife cautioned him: "Jason, Jason, . . . don't you have nothin' to do with their goin's-on, neither one way nor the other." When the strike broke out, he followed his wife's injunction and sided with neither the strikers nor the company. News of the incoming Negro strike-breakers provoked a public discussion. Jason stood on the edge of the crowd, half in the shadow, listening to the talk, before he presented a carefully hedged defense of the Negroes: "As for the niggers, I ain't any friendlier to 'em than the rest of you. But I ain't the man to throw up a job and then howl when somebody else gets it." But Jason remained alone in his vague middle position; the workers would not follow his advice to refrain from violence. Ultimately fighting did break out, and Jason rode immediately to the telegraph office to wire for help. Once the strike was over Jason became the hero of the blacks and the whites; by his independent position, Dunbar felt Jason was able to avoid alienating either race.

The penalties for taking aggressive action that were operative in *The Fanatics* were also effective in **"At Shaft 11."** Jason Andrews, although he took no side, rode for help. In the course of the ride he injured his arm. The leaders of the two sides in the fight likewise suffered because of their actions, and the pattern of injuries to arms and shoulders suggests that to Dunbar there was an automatic association between aggression and retribution.

For Dunbar the ideal social role may have been an undefined middle position incapable of giving offense; but with regard to race, this obviously presented an insoluble dilemma. Because Dunbar could not fit between the categories of black and white, he described himself as a black white man. Optimistically he hoped that whites would take talented Negroes as individuals into their society, without regard for their color. Because he was accomplished and deserved to be accepted, he felt most sharply the whites' insistence that he remain a Negro. In spite of the color of his skin, he wrote on one occasion, "I am entirely white!" Among Dunbar's papers found after his death was one which carried the note: "It is one of the peculiar phases of Anglo-Saxon conceit to refuse to believe that every black man does not want to be white." He found an apt expression of this conflict between his ambitions and society's edicts in a folktale in which the slaves on a large plantation effectively supplant the white man by holding a huge feast at the big house while the master is away. Dunbar used this tale as the basis of one of his short stories, **"A Supper by Proxy,"** but as the slave explained in the conclusion that Dunbar tacked on, the master really had given the supper by proxy. Clearly Dunbar was reluctant to assert that slaves or their descendants ever intended to displace the master, or even that they would desire to live in the same style.

This illustration of "Aunt Ca'line" by the white artist E. W. Kemble is from Dunbar's Folks From Dixie. *Dunbar was later castigated by critics for including illustrations which they felt were racist depictions of black life. The renowned black critic Robert Bone described Kemble's drawing as "at best comic stereotypes and at worst vicious caricatures."*

Nevertheless, his sense of outrage found its way into his fiction on several occasions. But except for two stories concerning lynching, Dunbar's ambiguity and the predispositions of his readers hedged most of his complaints about racial injustice. For example, the four stories that treat most fully the economic hardship and corrupting ways of the city for unprepared Southern Negroes are as much object lessons in the fate of unsuspecting black emigrants from the South as they are protests against white injustice. If the Northern city was an unpleasant environment for blacks, many readers undoubtedly concluded, let them stay in the rural South.

Dunbar's scattered protests against racial injustice were lost in the midst of twenty volumes of poetry, novels, and short stories. Because the vast majority of his stories were humorous and confirmed the white man's image of the contented darky, Paul Dunbar's readers did not see all the implications which one of his poems had for the author:

> We wear the mask that grins and lies,
> It hides our cheeks and shades our eyes—
>
> . . . . . .
>
> We smile, but, O great Christ, our cries
> To thee from tortured souls arise.
> We sing, but oh the clay is vile
> Beneath our feet, and long the mile;
> But let the world dream otherwise,
> We wear the mask!

(pp. 56-8)

Michael Flusche, "Paul Laurence Dunbar and the Burden of Race," in The Southern Humanities Review, *Vol. XI, No. 1, Winter, 1977, pp. 49-61.*

John Wakefield (essay date 1977)

[*In the following excerpt, Wakefield—through a detailed discussion of "The Scapegoat"—analyzes how Dunbar inserted strains of social protest in his otherwise accommodationist stories.*]

When Dunbar was at the height of his fame, his contemporary Charles W. Chesnutt quit work as a full-time writer. In a letter to his publisher he observed, "My friend, Mr. Howells has remarked several times that there is no color line in literature. On that point I take issue with him." Dunbar continued his career as a professional writer, and in so doing accepted the limits imposed upon him by a publishing world dominated by white values. If we can judge from what the leading editor of his age found attractive in black writing, then we are led to the conclusion that a black writer was required to play the role of what Howells called the "exemplary citizen." The liberal editor was referring in this phrase to the public image projected by the writings of Booker T. Washington. Howells' approval indicates the kind of decorum required of a black writer by his nineteenth-century audience.

The kind of style that please Howells, he found in the writing of Dunbar, Washington, and the early Chesnutt. He admired above all its freedom from "bitterness." Unruffled by racial injustice, they wrote in a style that he characterized as showing a "sweet, brave, humor." Dunbar's career depended upon his being able to reproduce the desired tone. By confining himself to the stereotype themes of plantation fiction—racial reconciliation, black loyalty, and above all humour—Dunbar achieved this. He was, however, well aware of the genre's limitations. When questioned about the relationship of his work to his race, he replied, "I hope you are not one of those who would hold the Negro down to a certain kind of poetry—dialect and concerning only scenes of plantation in the South?" Dunbar's short stories showed that he rarely followed his own advice.

Dunbar's conversation in this respect was largely dictated by the hidden conventions of decorum ruling the black writer's relationship with his audience. While we can safely assume that a white audience imposed severe restrictions of style and subject-matter on a writer, we must not underestimate the demands of the black middle-class. James Weldon Johnson, Dunbar's friend and literary heir, claimed that both black and white audiences exerted pressures on the black writer. Dunbar, faced with what Johnson called "the problem of a double audience," had to be careful to respect the prejudices of both sides. (pp. 39-40)

Recent criticism of Dunbar's short stories has been rather influenced by the protest literature of the sixties. However, as Robert Bone has pointed out, there is not too much evidence that Dunbar was a frustrated protest writer [see excerpt dated 1975]. Bone dismisses Darwin T. Turner's references [see excerpt dated 1967] to Dunbar's stories of lynching, and his occasional letters of protest to newspapers, as unconvincing. Bone's view of Dunbar as a typical product of the so-called age of Booker T. Washington seems to push the argument too far in the opposite direction. Dunbar was a more complicated man than that. More recently Bernhard Ostendorf has re-focussed discussion on Dunbar's social dilemma as a writer: "Thus Dunbar was caught between theme, form, and audience." This seems to me a more promising approach to Dunbar, especially if the writer's style is related to the newspaper articles which Bone chooses to ignore.

My own feeling is that instead of approaching Dunbar in terms of genre and content, as Bone and Turner try to do, we might consider how Dunbar manoeuvred within the narrow confines of decorum. What we discover will represent only marginal victories for Dunbar. It will, however, reveal some of the problems of audience-writer relations that Dunbar had to contend with, and some of the rhetorical devices Dunbar developed. The bulk of Dunbar's first collection of short stories ***Folks from Dixie*** (1898) is a study in evasion. As the title suggests, it is a fight from contemporary problems to an idealized south, filled with stereotype blacks who scarcely ever refer to slavery. There is, however, one exception. The story of the mine strike **"At Shaft 11"** deals with a current conflict between black and white workers. Dunbar shows some ingenuity in dealing with this subject within the limits prescribed by decorum. . . . By playing the role of the white miner he tries to reconcile his audience to the reasonableness of the blacks. In a less interesting way he used this same strategy in at least three other stories from ***Folks from Dixie:*** **"A Family Feud," "The Intervention of Peter,"** and **"Nelse Hatton's Vengeance."** Nelse Hatton is a typical example of Dunbar's conception of the exemplary black. Instead of revenging himself on his old master, who turns up at his home after the emancipation, Hatton overcomes his former hatred and treats the white with hospitality. Dunbar's idealism leaves little to be desired, but it does leave his hero somewhat devoid of any normal human responses. Decorum clearly required that blacks purge themselves of anger. And this was equally valid for both the writer and his characters.

With the publication of Dunbar's second collection of short stories, some of his hesitance disappears. Social injustice does get discussed, and blacks are allowed to show anger. ***The Strength of Gideon*** (1900) represents Dunbar's only real attempt to break directly with the rules of decorum. Characteristically, the small group of stories in which Dunbar allows himself this liberty all deal with scenes from contemporary life, and none of them are told in dialect. One character in particular merits our attention. The newspaper editor Courtney of **"A Council of State"** forgets the text of a rather tame speech he has prepared and bursts into anger on the question of racial injustice. Here Dunbar as a former editor of a black newspaper comes closest in his fiction to playing himself. The sense of frustration felt by Courtney in following a carefully prepared text that will offend no-one in his audience reflects perhaps some of Dunbar's own hidden emotions:

> He started calmly, but as he progressed, the memory of all the wrongs, personal and racial that he had suffered; the knowledge of the disabilities that he and his brethren had to suffer, and the vision of toil unrequited, love rejected, and loyalty ignored, swept him off his feet.

Another embittered black, the disappointed politician of **"Mr. Cornelius Johnson, Office-Seeker,"** is more direct still:

> "Damn you! damn you!" he cried. "Damn your deceit, your fair cruelties; damn you, you hard, white liar!"

Dunbar, however, seems to have tired even of these momentary flashes of anger. In his next collection of stories ***In Old Plantation Days*** (1903) he reverted to the plantation fiction of his first publication ***Folks from Dixie.***

In **"The Scapegoat"** which appeared in Dunbar's last series of stories, ***The Heart of Happy Hollow,*** he finally turned away from any direct treatment of the race problem. In this story Dunbar attacks the black middle-class, thus reversing most of the assumptions upon which his career as a writer had been based. Dunbar's displays of anger in ***The Strength of Gideon*** were the result of his ability to identify with the ideals of the emerging black middle-class: the story of Asbury's betrayal and defeat at the hands of these "idealists" suggests that he had changed his mind.

The hero of **"The Scapegoat"** is a man who does not derive his virtues from the middle-class but from the poor blacks of Cadgers where he grew up. By emphasizing Asbury's shrewdness and cunning, Dunbar shows his determination to break with the image of the exemplary citizen:

> It was his wisdom rather more than his morality that made the managers after a while cast their glances toward him as a man who might be useful to their interests. It would be well to have a man—a shrewd powerful man—down in that part of the town who could carry his people's vote in his vest pocket and who at any time its delivery might be needed, could hand it over without hesitation.

Asbury's strengths enable him to ignore the rules of decorum. He has no obligations either to white patrons, or the black middle-class.

In **"The Scapegoat"** Dunbar appears to be drawing on the folktale. By taking the theme of intrigue and the black trickster-hero from his plantation stories and setting him in a contemporary urban situation, he could step outside the values imposed by the white literary code. The black folktale did not celebrate the values of the middle-class, but of the race. Robinson Asbury realizes that competing with the white man is but half the game. A talented black in a hostile society is a peculiarly vulnerable man. And so Asbury instinctively falls back on the wisdom of the black folktales that teach the importance of subterfuge and cunning.

In escaping from the limiting influences of the white literary code Dunbar was able to drop that "fine perception of irony" which had vitiated his early writing. Irony is present in **"The Scapegoat"** but it is an irony directed at the false, élitist idealism of the black middle-class. Instead of decorum, there is a spirit of amoral mischief ruling this story. (pp. 41-5)

Asbury provides the black with a strategy for survival. Dunbar had already shown in ***The Strength of Gideon*** stories that the idealistic black was the natural prey of the unscrupulous white patron. Asbury, shrewd and resourceful, regards virtue as the questionable luxury of those born into the black middle-class. Asbury, who has been a former bootblack and barber, understands human nature. His rise to fame as a local ward politician does not change him. Instead of moving uptown where the black rich live, he stays with the poor and identifies with them. Asbury scorns "the better class" blacks that run the politics of the town, and draws his political strength from the people. By refusing to observe the ideas of social decorum that characterize the black middle-class, Asbury overcomes the divisiveness that weakens the black community in politics. In fact he embodies Dunbar's own earlier criticism of the black middle-class of New York City who destroyed racial solidarity through their inability to identify with the poor of the ghetto:

> So if the better class Negro would come to his own he must lift not only himself, but the lower men, whose blood brother he is. He cannot afford to look down upon the citizens of the Tenderloin or to withdraw himself from them; for the fate of the blacks there degraded, ignorantly vicious as they may be, is his fate.

Asbury's character suggests, then, an implicit rejection of the politically impotent exemplary black. So thoroughgoing is his political realism, that Dunbar never allows him to discuss the subject of racial injustices. The empty rhetoric of the black press is not for him. Even the sign that hangs above his store "Equal Rights, Barber Shop" is designed primarily to attract customers, not to express an ideal. The ideals of the middle-class can be read any day in their newspapers, along with such trivia as "how Miss Boston entertained Miss Blueford to tea." Asbury has more practical concerns, and helps his customers by keeping their "policy returns, which was wise, if not moral." (pp. 45-6)

The first political campaign that Asbury enters brings him into immediate conflict with the black middle-class. Two lawyers called Bingo and Latchett, who also have political ambitions, hear news of Asbury's activities. Ironically, the innocent sign above the barber's shop angers them most of all. Political idealism, they feel, belongs properly to the middle-class:

> Is it any wonder, then, that they viewed with alarm his sudden rise? They kept their counsel, however, and treated with him, for its was best. They allowed him his scope without open revolt until the day upon which he hung out his shingle. This was the last straw. They could stand no more. Asbury had stolen their other chances from them, and now he was poaching upon the last of their preserves. So Mr. Bingo and Mr. Latchett put their heads together to plan the downfall of their common enemy.

Although as resourceful as Br'er Rabbit, Asbury has forgotten the art of the possum who lays low so as to avoid danger. Mr. Bingo, who never does anything openly, understands the value of this subterfuge at this stage better than Asbury.

An appeal to black ideals becomes a central theme in Mr. Bingo's campaign against Asbury. Bingo, who is not in the least idealistic, finds a suitable front in the form of a Mr. Issac Morton, the unsuspecting principal of a local school. Morton exemplifies for Dunbar the ineffectual idealism of the middle-class:

> Mr. Morton was really an innocent young man, and he had ideals which should never have been exposed to the air. When the wily confederates came to him with their plan he believed that his worth had been recognised, and at last he was to be what Nature destined him for—a leader.

Dunbar's attack on this form of idealism is recorded in the language of these worthy citizens. Their vocabulary is full of such terms as, "ideal," "moral," and "better class of people." Although this rhetoric is enough to win the support of the middle-class blacks, it fails to convince the black electorate as a whole. Mr. Bingo gives it up and goes downtown to pledge support to Asbury's faction. The conversation that takes place between the two men helps us to define what kind of "morality" Asbury stands for. Bingo begins by taking Asbury to task for living in the ghetto:

> "Well, it was well done, and you've shown that you are a manager. I confess that I haven't always thought that you were doing the wisest thing in living down here and catering to this class of people when you might, with your ability, to be much more to the better class."
>
> "What do they base their claims of being better on?"
>
> "Oh, there ain't any use discussing that."

Asbury ultimately wins the election for his side, but commits a few indiscretions in the effort. The losers challenge the legality of the ballot, and evidence of irregularity comes to light. Asbury, the most conspicuous black in the community, presents himself as the most obvious victim to quieten outraged public opinion:

> They began to look around them. They must purify themselves. They must give the people some tangible evidence of their own yearnings after purity. They looked around them for a sacrifice to lay upon the altar of reform. Their eyes fell upon Mr. Bingo. No, he was not big enough. His blood was too scant to wash away the political stains. Then they looked into each other's eyes and turned their gaze away to let if fall upon Mr. Asbury. They really hated to do it. But there must be a scapegoat. The god from the Machine commanded them to slay him.

Thus Asbury is obliged to bear the collective sins of the entire community. Asbury's only consolation at the trial lies in unmasking those who really played a hand in the fraudulent ballot. Although not entirely innocent himself, Asbury has never laid claim to any moral superiority. There is, thus, a kind of poetic justice in his revealing the deeper immorality of those around him:

> He did not mention the judge's name. But he had torn the mask from the face of every other man who had been concerned in his downfall.

In the second part of **"The Scapegoat"** Asbury returns from prison and starts playing possum. Although he is not a helpless animal from black folklore even an important black remains vulnerable. In the heat of his successful campaign Asbury had momentarily forgotten this. His first act on returning is to remove the sign "Equal Rights, Barber Shop" from his store. Doubtless he does this to openly demonstrate his retirement from the political scene, but there is another reason. Asbury has learned that conspicuous idealism—even if, as in his case, unintended—is the worst possible form of advertisement.

Like his vulnerable brethren from the black folktale, Asbury realizes that he is a natural prey to hostile forces and must behave accordingly. Indeed, as the story progresses he begins more and more to resemble the trickster-hero of the folktale. Despite the realistic setting of Cadgers and the details of the election campaign, Asbury is clearly a type. We neither know what he looks like, nor how he dresses. We know only that he is shrewd. The same may be said of Bingo. These two men act out a seemingly unequal contest of wit characteristic of the folktale. Bingo must lose because his social pretensions serve to identify him with the élite rather than the common people.

The exact relationship between **"The Scapegoat"** and black oral culture would probably be difficult to establish within clearly defined limits. And it would seem unwise to push the undoubted resemblances between them too far. What does seem to me more readily ascertainable is that Dunbar's rejection of decorum in favour of the black trickster's disguise can be traced to his early story **"The Ingrate."** This story records how Dunbar's father, Joshua, tricked his master and escaped from slavery. The details of the plot are for us unimportant. The main point of reference between **"The Scapegoat"** and **"The Ingrate"** is that both the main characters resort to the old trick of a slave trying to outwit his master: they disguise their intelligence under a display of outward weakness and humility. Thus we are told of Asbury that, "He came back with no flourish of trumpets, but quietly, humbly." He remains "quiet," and when Bingo visits to check on Asbury, the barber-lawyer's demeanor fools him, "Mr. Bingo expressed the opinion that Asbury was quiet because he was crushed." Asbury has to display that his shrewdness no longer poses a threat to his political enemies. Dunbar has adapted the behaviour of Josh from **"The Ingrate"** to meet contemporary needs. The lore of surviving on the plantation still has relevance. Josh plays his role as follows:

> But he met his master with an impassive face, always silent, always docile; and Mr. Leckler congratulated himself that so valuable and intelligent a slave should be at the same time so tractable. Usually intelligence in a slave meant discontent; but not so with Josh.

The one significant difference between the stories is that Asbury outsmarts a fellow black, and not a white man. But here I think we must note some apparent evasiveness on Dunbar's part. Open conflict between black and white was, according to the rules of decorum, impossible. Looked at more closely however, does not a hidden struggle exist between Asbury and the white man? . . . On the surface no overt conflict between Asbury and whites is to be seen. However, it was not the black middle-class that led to his downfall: the final decision to offer Asbury to the people of Cadgers as a scapegoat came from "The God of the Machine." Logically Asbury's desire for revenge should be directed at the white-black power structure behind the party. (pp. 46-9)

It would not do to confuse the character of Asbury with Dunbar. Nevertheless, the similarities between the two are compelling. Although Dunbar never faced his hero's defeat, he ran the same kind of dangers. Like Asbury, Dunbar's silence on civil rights was part of a strategy. Only by an almost scrupulous adherence to decorum could he save himself from falling prey to public opinion. Only by developing a constant vigilance could he steer a course between the prejudices of both black and white. If the story of **"The Scapegoat"** helps us to understand some of the problems facing the black as a public figure, it also argues the need for a reappraisal of Dunbar in terms of his age. (pp. 49-50)

John Wakefield, "Paul Laurence Dunbar, 'The Scapegoat' (1904)," in The Black American Short Story in the 20th Century: A Collection of Critical Essays, *edited by Peter Bruck, B. R. Grüner Publishing Co., 1977, pp. 39-51.*

Peter Revell (essay date 1979)

[*Revell is a British critic and librarian who has published several bibliographies and works of literary criticism. In the following essay, which is excerpted from his full-length study* Paul Laurence Dunbar, *Revell focuses on Dunbar's ironic protest stories, which he maintains are his most powerful works.*]

Though Dunbar worked in the short-story form throughout his writing career, his fame as a poet has tended to cause his achievements in prose to be overlooked. As a prose writer he is certainly uneven and occasionally meretricious, but he was also to some degree commercially successful. Having produced a number of stories on plantation themes during the 1890s that appealed to magazine readers, he found himself the victim of his own success in much the same way that the immense popular response to his dialect poetry had compelled him to work to a formula in order to satisfy the demands of magazine editors and the reading public they sought to please. (p. 107)

Such was Dunbar's success in the plantation form that it has often been supposed that his short stories are all of this type and that his work in this form was largely hack work undertaken to make money and to allow time for the more serious work of writing poetry. Other critics, better acquainted with the evidence, have maintained that Dunbar began by writing plantation stories, tried to establish himself as a writer of stories of social realism and protest, but reverted to plantation themes under pressure from the sources that supplied his income as a writer. But even this more informed view is to some extent a superficial judgment, perhaps suggested by the titles of the four collections of short stories published during Dunbar's lifetime. The first of these, ***Folks from Dixie*** (1898), is, as the title suggests, primarily a collection of plantation tales, but there are several stories set in other locales than the Southern plantation, postbellum in date, and realistic in their treatment of social problems. **"Jimsella"** deals with the difficulties encountered by a young black family from the South who are trying to make their way in a Northern city. **"Aunt Mandy's Investment"** is a cautionary tale of the swindling of poor black investors by a black confidence trickster, a real enough problem for many rural blacks from the South who had moved North with their families, taking their hard-earned savings with them. (Dunbar was to return to the theme of the black confidence trickster in several later stories and treat it from several points of view.) **"Nelse Hatton's Vengeance,"** perhaps the best of the ***Folks from Dixie*** stories, is set in a "little Ohio town which, for convenience, let us call Dexter." The same Ohio small-town setting, based on Dunbar's recollections of his youth in Dayton, Ohio, provides the locale of two of his novels. This early story is a notable anticipation of the ironic treatment of black-white relationships in the postbellum period that gives a special force to some of the later stories. **"At Shaft 11"** stands out among the other stories of this first collection as a bold attempt, though ultimately an artistic failure, to treat the problems of capital and labor and the exploitation of black and white workers in a West Virginia mine. Another story, **"The Deliberation of Mr. Dunkin,"** recalls some of Charles W. Chesnutt's stories written at about the same time—such stories as "A Matter of Principle" and "Uncle Wellington's Wives," from *The Wife of His Youth* (1899)—for its gentle satire on the jockeying for position and influence among the prominent citizens of the black community of a Middle Western small town. Chesnutt's satire frequently has an intraracial point to make and turns upon the particular pretensions of very light-skinned mulattos, such as the group calling themselves the Blue-Vein Society in "A Matter of Principle," while Dunbar's stories generally attach little importance to the relative skin color of the characters. There are, however, some notable exceptions to this generalization in Dunbar's political stories, as we shall have cause to note later. But leaving this matter aside, both Dunbar and Chesnutt in these stories depict black characters who are full citizens of an urban community and not in any sense plantation darkies.

If Dunbar's first collection promised a wider, bolder, more imaginative exploration of the life of Afro-Americans, the second collection, ***The Strength of Gideon and Other Stories*** (1900), came close to fulfilling that promise, and is the one book in which Dunbar most nearly achieves success as a writer of realism and social protest. Two of the stories, **"Mr. Cornelius Johnson, Office-Seeker"** and **"A Council of State,"** are in their way small masterpieces, in the line of, though much slighter than, those earlier masterpieces in the fictional portrayal of corruption in the political life of Washington, Henry Adams' novel, *Democracy* (1880) and the novel Mark Twain wrote with Charles Dudley Warner, *The Gilded Age* (1873). But these stories are written from the heart of the black experience of Washington politics, with a restrained power and a keen eye for the subtle and cynical manipulation of the race's political aspirations by party interests. We cannot doubt that much of the power of these stories derives from personal observation of the political scene and of the black community's part in it during Dunbar's years in Washington.

Only one story in this second collection, **"Uncle Simon's Sundays Out,"** is written on the plantation theme, and its comic hero is a character like the Uncle Julius of Chesnutt's stories collected in *The Conjure Woman* (1899), who is able to achieve his own desired ends by skillfully directing the wishes of his master and mistress while apparently displaying only a subservient attention to their well-being. Another story, **"An Old-Time Christmas,"** presents a possible but unlikely picture of an ex-slave woman in New York reminiscing about the good old days on the plantation when "Christmas lasted all the week and good cheer held sway," her thoughts accompanied by the words of Stephen Foster, floated up to her by a voice in the alley below:

> Still longing for the old plantation,
> An' for the old folks at home.

Such a passage as this must have particularly appealed to white readers in the South, but Dunbar turns even this unpromising beginning to good effect by describing how the woman has to put all her little treasure of money saved for Christmas to pay the fine on her small son, who is threatened with imprisonment for some petty misdemeanor. The story thus concludes with a moral lesson for white readers in the North, who are reminded of the difficult material conditions and the harshly unsympathetic attitude of the police and the law toward the black communities who live in their cities and serve in their homes.

Two more stories, **"The Strength of Gideon,"** which gives the collection its title, and **"Viney's Free Papers,"** have plantation settings. Certainly the second of these, which implies in its conclusion that the slave was happier as a slave without hope of freedom, is closer in spirit to the typical plantation tale of Page than almost anything else Dunbar wrote. But both stories are also deeply concerned with the slave's deep longing for freedom—**"The Strength of Gideon,"** uniquely among Dunbar's work, actually covers the period of emancipation—and in both the stock-character slave of the plantation tale who prefers the life of devoted loyalty to the white master over the challenges of freedom is contrasted with the character of the slave woman who ardently seeks the freedom that will give her a full life. The conflict becomes one between the woman's desire for freedom and her loyalty to her man. Gideon's Martha finally leaves him, with a hope that they may be reunited after the war:

> "Hunt me up when you do come," she said, crying bitterly, "fu' I do love you, Gidjon, but I must go. Out yonder is freedom."

But Ben's Viney in the other story gives up her chance of freedom and burns her free papers so that she can stay with her man. The message for white readers, particularly those in the South, is one frequently voiced by black leaders in the increasingly difficult post-Reconstruction years. It is that the South owes an ineradicable debt to the ex-slave, for the labor that established plantation, home, and city throughout the South and even more for the loyalty and devotion which ensured that the womenfolk of the Confederate fighting men should not come to harm in the chaotic conditions of the later years of the war. (pp. 109-12)

Dunbar's real concern in the ***Strength of Gideon*** stories is to assert the black man's humanity, a bold enough departure in writing for an audience accustomed to the stereotyped image of the black man presented by the plantation myth. In a newspaper article on "The Hapless Southern Negro," Dunbar had declared that the black people of the South were "strictly human":

> They have their idle, but they have their industrious. They have their criminal, but they have their virtuous. They have their high and they have their low. To sum it all up, they are strictly human.

In seeking to extend the range of his depiction of black characters, it was inevitable that Dunbar should occasionally depict types of subservience, idleness, and vanity that were the stock in trade of the typical plantation story. But there is remarkably little dependence on this stereotyped product in the ***Strength of Gideon*** collection, and an immense gain in maturity and depth in the representation of Afro-American life. The unevenness of Dunbar's short-story writing has perhaps caused these stories to be underrated by critics, who have generally conceded to Chesnutt the preeminent position among black writers of prose fiction in the period before the Harlem Renaissance. There can be no doubt that Chesnutt's achievement is far more consistent, that he is a polished stylist, that in the stories of *The Conjure Woman* (1899) he handled the plantation form with great subtlety, and that the plotting of some of the stories in *The Wife of His Youth* is forceful and dramatic. But Dunbar deserves credit for his attempts to extend the range of the black short story into a wide variety of locales, into various social levels and an extensive range of character types. The question how much was achieved in these stories of black humanity can best be deferred until the detailed consideration of some of them.

Dunbar's third collection, ***In Old Plantation Days*** (1903), . . . offered only a number of short and simple variations on the plantation theme, thus developing the least interesting stories from the first collection into a successful commercial formula. The reviewer in the *New York Times* thought that they were "good stories, such as tend to the encouragement of good feeling between the races—black and white," and drew attention to their adherence to the established pattern of the plantation tale:

> Thomas Nelson Page himself does not make "ole Marse" and "ole Miss" more admirable nor exalt higher in the slave the qualities of faithfulness and good humor. Appropriately, as the servant is in Dr. Page's stories the incidental feature to the portrayal of the master, so in these stories it is the master that is incidental, and the theme is the servant. If it is not the negro as he is, if it is not the negro as he ever was, it is certainly the negro as his old masters like to think of him—the negro as the remnant of old servants like to tell of him, the kind of negro which is and will remain the ideal link between the races.

This review indicates clearly enough the kind of response that the stories might be expected to produce from the white readers they were primarily written for. Though the stories were unflattering to race pride and were not, as the reviewer admitted, a true representation of the black Southerner, they express a conciliatory attitude toward white opinion which was not uncommon among black writers and speakers at the time. But if the stories of ***In Old Plantation Days*** represent Dunbar in a conciliatory mood, this is only one aspect of his response to the situation of the black man in America at that time. A mere four months before the review we have quoted appeared in the *New York Times,* Dunbar's letter attacking lynch law, disfranchisement, and peonage in the South and bitterly denouncing the complacency and hypocrisy of the North was published in the same newspaper. In a period when race prejudice in the South was most intense and public opinion in the North largely indifferent, black spokesmen chose whatever means and opportunities were available to them to improve the condition of their people.

Dunbar's fourth collection of stories, ***The Heart of Happy Hollow*** (1904), the last to be published in his lifetime, might from its title be thought to be another collection of plantation stories. But the author's brief foreword makes clear that he is writing of the inhabitants of the black quarter in "the cities or villages, north or south, wherever the hod carrier, the porter and the waiter are the society men of the town." As this remark suggests, the effort is more like that of the ***Strength of Gideon*** stories, to depict a broad panorama of black humanity in a variety of locales. The overall tone of the collection is, however, somewhat more subdued, and the aspiring young black politician and would-be lawyer are less evident than the poor but striving city-dweller, the old preacher, and the washerwoman. All the stories are postbellum in period, though one, **"Cahoots,"** is a reminiscence of slavery and the war in the style of Page. (pp. 113-15)

We have noted that almost all the stories in his four collected volumes are on black themes, though the range of styles varies from that of the simple plantation tale, designed to glorify the institutions of the Old South, to the protest story, condemning racial injustices in relatively outspoken terms. If we were to consider the four collections chronologically as expressions of racial consciousness, we would have to regard the ***Strength of Gideon*** collection, following on the rather unpromising beginning of ***Folks from Dixie,*** as the peak of his achievement. The third collection, ***In Old Plantation Days,*** exhibits a marked decline in this respect, followed by a partial recovery in the last collection, ***The Heart of Happy Hollow***. . . . In general the stories show an increasing competence in what was after all a difficult and complex task, that of entertaining a primarily white reading public while interesting them in the fortunes of black characters and, when opportunity offered, enlisting their sympathy for the problems of the race and drawing their attention to some of the injustices under which it suffered. A true estimate of Dunbar's achievement in the short story can best be obtained by studying some of the best of them more closely as expressions, from various points of view, of topics of racial interest. The stories make a much more coherent and consistent body of achievement when considered in this way. (pp. 115-16)

By comparison with [his] stories of racial injustice in the South, Dunbar's stories of the economic pressures endured by black citizens in the North are comparatively subdued. Only one of them calls for consideration as a protest story. **"One Man's Fortunes,"** which is said to have been based on Dunbar's personal experiences in trying to find work as a young man in Dayton, is a direct statement of protest against the racial discrimination and economic difficulties brought upon the educated Afro-American. Many of Dunbar's stories depicting the life of black citizens in the North and South during the last decades of the nineteenth century are involved with real, often desperate, economic hardship. Any truthful representation of their lives could hardly be otherwise, but Dunbar's primary intention in these stories seems to have been to present a picture of the ordinary lives of black citizens, in their homes, at their jobs, and in the hopes, the sacrifices, the love of family that express their spirit.

"One Man's Fortunes" follows the first few months of working life for three young friends who are graduates from a state university in the Middle West. One is white and goes straight into his father's business. The other two are black. One, Webb Davis, sees his path as predetermined by his African origin and his father's having been a slave; he will take things as he finds them and advance himself as he can. The other, Bertram Halliday, has a more idealistic outlook and a more optimistic view of his chances. "He had settled upon the law as a profession," but an interview with a prominent lawyer in his home town of Broughton (a Middle Western town of "between seventy and eighty thousand souls") is not promising. The lawyer advises that "the time has not come when a white person will employ a colored attorney," and "your people have not the money to spend in litigation of any kind." Halliday believes that his competence as a lawyer should be the only matter of concern: "I am an American citizen, there should be no thought of color about it." The lawyer advises that this is quite unrealistic. . . . (pp. 124-25)

[He] offers to speak on Halliday's behalf to a headwaiter he knows. For a time Halliday considers going South to teach, but decides instead to stay and fight it out. He finds work as an underjanitor in a factory, and then over a year later is summoned to the lawyer's office and offered a job there. He soon realizes that the lawyer is actuated by self-interest, since he is hoping to be elected to a seat on the bench and needs the black vote on his side. Halliday accepts the bargain, but two weeks after the election has brought the lawyer to office is dismissed and replaced by "a young white man about his own age." Halliday, "burning with indignation" but unable even to return to his old job, decides to do the thing he abhors, go South to teach. He sends word of his decision to his friend Webb Davis, who after graduation had "worked in a hotel, saved money enough to start a barber-shop and was prospering." Davis is not without sympathy, but

> "Thank heaven," he said, "that I have no ideals to be knocked into a cocked hat. A colored man has no business with ideals—not in *this* nineteenth century!"

The ambiguity of this conclusion, and many passages of a similar kind in the stories of politics and protest, probably account for the frequent misinterpretation of Dunbar's prose writing by both white and black critics. The words can be taken literally, as advice to be followed, suggesting an accommodationist but materialistic approach to white-dominated society as the only path to personal advancement. They can also be taken ironically, as a bitterly sardonic comment on the falsity of American democracy in the last decade of the nineteenth century. No doubt the modern reader should find both attitudes to life contained in these concluding words, for the ambiguity reflects the dilemma of Dunbar himself, dependent for material success on pleasing a predominantly white reading public, which had its own preconceived image of the black man in America, yet striving as he could to change that image and win for the people of his race the right to work, to be judged and rewarded as equal citizens of the great democracy.

The average uneducated black citizen at the end of the nineteenth century depended less for survival on the ideals of a democratic society tenuously relevant to himself than on the sheer will to live and on such faith and hope as he might derive from his religion. Some of the most memorable of Dunbar's stories are those in which these sources of strength are quietly celebrated.

"Jimsella," an early story collected in ***Folks from Dixie,*** describes Mandy Mason's marriage in the South and her journey to a Northern city with her man, Jim. There they encounter discouragements, problems, and harsh poverty. Jim is increasingly shiftless and discouraged, and seems likely to desert the family until Mandy brings him around through love of their newborn daughter, Jimsella. The story is important as an early example of the realistic treatment of life in a black quarter in the North and has often been interpreted—with other stories by Dunbar and his novel *The Sport of the Gods*—as an expression of antimigration propaganda, advocating the view, usually identified with Booker T. Washington, that the Southern black worker would find only hardship and poverty in the North and should stay in the South. But in fact the story implies that the problems can be overcome with the right spirit. Dunbar's line is always to suggest that individual qualities determine the individual's chances of triumphing against odds. Patience, quiet determination, warmth, and love are the qualities that ensure survival and, as we have noted, he offers little hope for betterment through social action or the existing political system.

Several stories emphasize the importance of the church in giving social cohesion to the black community, where family life is often under intense pressure of economic problems and the breaking up of families frequently denies the individual all hope of support. **"The Ordeal at Mt. Hope"** describes the efforts of a local preacher to raise the morale of a poor black community. His method is along lines that Booker T. Washington would have approved, by amelioration through effort within the existing social framework. His success is indicated when Elias, the scapegrace son of his landlady, decides to become a carpenter and "dat no-count Tom Johnson done opened a fish-sto', an' he has de boys an' men bring him dey fish all de time. He give 'em a little somep'n' fu' dey ketch, den he go sell 'em to de white folks."

This kind of small-business enterprise is one way up, but the plight of abandoned children is an altogether more serious problem. **"Old Abe's Conversion"** is a moving and impressive story from Dunbar's last collection that dramatizes the change in the work of the black minister, from the old religion of fervor, which provided the strength to survive the sufferings of slavery, to the new religion of social work, serving the needs of a people "freed" into a society that has given them no place—needs especially great among the young, who are often without guidance or hope.

"One Christmas at Shiloh" is an example of the manner in which Dunbar could on occasion take the elements of the plantation story and make something better of it. The characters of the story are all plantation figures, men and women who have come North after the war and now live in the black quarter of New York and are members of the congregation of Shiloh Chapel. The story traces the fortunes of Martha Maria Mixon, a "widder lady" but one of the "grass" variety who had left her shiftless husband behind and come North, where, being "industrious, careful, and hard-working, she soon became prosperous." At the end she is reunited with her husband, who has in the interval become a successful preacher. The characters are recognizably the comic figures of the typical plantation story, but they are now solid citizens and responsible members of their community.

In contrast, another story, **"The Wisdom of Silence,"** takes the more conservative line of Booker T. Washington that the freedman has a good future in the South if he will learn to live with his old masters. Jeremiah Anderson, a freed slave, leaves the plantation and prospers as a farmer, though he is fiercely independent of his old master and prefers to borrow from the moneylenders. He becomes boastful of his prosperity and is punished for his pride by the local white community, who burn his house and barn. He is saved from certain ruin at the hands of the moneylenders by the intervention of his wife, who persuades him to swallow his pride and borrow the money he needs from his old master. The implication is that of much of Washington's teaching, that the black man in the South must forget pride, even forget justice, and learn to take a secondary place, so that he is at least assured of a place. Such a view is distasteful to the modern reader, but there can be no doubt that it was accepted by many black citizens in Dunbar's time as good advice. It was also, of course, a view that the majority of white readers of magazine fiction would approve.

That to succeed one had to please the white community was a common view. A story like **"The Boy and the Bayonet"** is designed to illustrate the natural aspirations of an urban black family to be good citizens of their country and a credit to their community, without thought of any potential gain from white approval. Dunbar's account of the efforts of a mother and her son at a Washington high school to make sure that his company wins in the school cadet drill puts no particular emphasis on the fact that they are black, and leaves it for the reader to decide that they are just like any other family in their wish to work as members of a well-run, mutually dependent community.

Other stories offer memorable portraits of character types, good and bad. **"The Case of 'Ca'line,'"** subtitled "A Kitchen Monologue," builds the character through her own words, uttered with considerable vigor and colloquial gusto. **"The Race Question,"** not what the title jokingly implies, is the monologue of an old devotee of the race track who still finds his amusement there despite the claim that "I's Baptis' myse'f, an' I don't app'ove o' no sich doin's!"

The confidence man appears to have interested Dunbar as a character type, and several stories describe his varied activities among the black community, presumably as cautionary tales for such black readers as may chance to read them and as entertaining tales of rascality for white readers. The subjects are in general treated with humor and a measure of sympathy. **"Aunt Mandy's Investment"** describes the swindling of small investors in an enterprise called The Coloured American Investment Company by Mr. Solomon Ruggles, a man "possessed of a liberal amount of that shrewd wit which allows its possessor to feed upon the credulity of others." His wickedness is a little redeemed by his returning Aunt Mandy fifteen dollars in one week for her five-dollar investment, while absconding with all other funds. **"The Mission of Mr. Scatters"** depicts a black confidence trickster at work in a small Kentucky town with the spurious report of an inheritance. So eloquent is he that he is able to bend the local gentry to his wishes, largely by appealing to their sense of the values of the Old South, so that the mildly satirical tone of the story directs ridicule at the credulous white aristocracy as well as the gullible blacks. **"The Promoter"** and **"The Trustfulness of Polly"** are more serious tales and much more serious in their implications. The first describes the havoc wrought in the black district by a promoter of spurious property deals, a man who had "profited by the example of the white men for whom he had long acted as messenger and factotum." **"The Trustfulness of Polly"** describes the hardships brought upon one poor black family in New York by the husband's obsession with bringing off a win in the numbers racket. **"Schwalliger's Philanthropy"** is a humorous and sympathetic picture of a race-track tout who uses his inside knowledge of the corrupt practices of gamblers to recover the money of an old man who has fallen victim to a shell-game operator.

Only one character, Jason Buford of **"The Promoter,"** is presented as a completely sinister and evil figure among these varied portraits of the more rascally inhabitants of the black quarter. There are many characters who are wily and not strictly honest, often in conformity to a system not of their making, but few who are without some spark of sympathetic humanity. Violence and wrongdoing by force are not in their nature; they merely seek an easier path to the comforts of wealth than the difficult road society normally assigns to people of their race.

It is perhaps to be regretted that Dunbar did not more often attempt to depict the life of black entertainers (to use the word in a general sense) in the theater, vaudeville, and the sporting world, who at the turn of the century were beginning to claim a very substantial part in their professions. (pp. 125-30)

"Silas Jackson" is a cautionary tale of a waiter who discovers a talent for singing, has a quick success as a singer with a traveling opera company, but succumbs to the temptations of easy money and fast living and eventually finds that his talent has burned out; "all contentment and simplicity gone," he is compelled to return to the humble cabin in the South whence he came. Silas, who "had a cough, too," is perhaps a projection by Dunbar of the line his own life might have taken if he had followed up some of the opportunities open to him.

"The Finding of Zach" is notable . . . for its use of the contrast between simpleminded and worldly minded characters as a source of humor, a device turned to good effect in **"The Promoter," "The Mission of Mr. Scatters,"** and **"Schwalliger's Philanthropy."** Zach is being sought by his father, "a typical old uncle from the South," who makes his way to the "Banner Club" and there becomes the source of much "respectful amusement" among the patrons for being "such a perfect bit of old plantation life and so obviously out of place in a Tenderloin club room." Zach, as it happens, is "one of the wildest young bucks that frequented the club." The humor of the story turns upon the successful efforts of Mr. Turner, the genial and splendid proprietor of the Banner Club, to present the dissolute Zach to his father in a sober and respectable condition. Zach's father and Mr. Turner offer a total contrast between the simple rural ex-slave from Mississippi and the tough, urban sophisticate from the Tenderloin, but they are both men of integrity and endowed with a fundamental humanity that furthers the good in this imperfect world.

Generosity of spirit is the virtue celebrated in another brief story, **"Johnsonham, Jr.,"** a tale of two freedmen who had come North to better themselves and been sullen rivals ever since. When the wife of one of them dies in childbirth, their rivalry is forgotten. "All petty emotions had passed away before this great feeling which touched both earth and the beyond." In celebrating the qualities of generosity of spirit, family feeling, and a deep human compassion, often in the most adverse social conditions, Dunbar in these stories of black humanity moves into a wider human dimension than that afforded by his poetry, and strikes a note that attained its full resonance many years later in such a work as Gwendolyn Brooks's *In the Mecca.*

While a serious claim can be made for many of Dunbar's short stories as constituting collectively an assertion of black aspiration in his time, it must also be conceded that something like half of the more than one hundred stories he wrote are plantation tales substantially conforming to the traditional pattern. Given the popularity of this pattern among white readers, especially in the post-Reconstruction period, it was inevitable that Dunbar should write in this form. The question remains what use he made of it, and further what alternative uses might have been open to him.

One alternative that was open but effectively denied was the realistic portrayal of plantation life, supplying an accurate account of the social and economic conditions of the inhabitants of the quarters and of the big house, an account in which the romantic trappings and the humorous anecdotage were cut away to show the often meager and harsh reality beneath. A literary precedent for this mode of portraying antebellum plantation life already existed in the slave narratives and the antislavery novels of Mrs. Stowe and others. But the mood of the post-Reconstruction period was entirely against this kind of portrayal. Even Chesnutt, whose childhood and young manhood in North Carolina just after the War would have given him much firsthand knowledge, offers nothing like a firsthand realistic treatment in the stories of *The Conjure Woman,* but prefers to make greater use of the folklore element to suggest the shrewdness, resilience, and humor of the slave community, with only occasional hints in the retrospective narration to convey a sense of the harshness of the old regime. Dunbar lacked the knowledge to make an effective realistic portrayal even had he wished to, so his use of the plantation tale becomes a series of literary variations on a theme. Being unable to transcend or displace the tradition, he makes what use of it he can, generally by refining or modifying its elements.

A few stories are written entirely according to the pattern established by Thomas Nelson Page, though with considerably less force, since the style is direct narrative in place of the retrospective account, in the dialect of an old ex-slave, which Page frequently used to great effect. Dunbar's story **"The Colonel's Awakening"** depends upon the stock situation of an old colonel devoted to the memory of his sons, dead in the Civil War. He is himself kept alive only by the devotion of his servant whose task it is to maintain, by an elaborate ritual of preparation, the fiction that the sons are not dead and will one day return. The colonel dies

The last house Dunbar lived in, 219 North Summit Street, Dayton, Ohio, has been turned into a state memorial by the Ohio Historical Society.

when Ike the servant makes one error in keeping up this ritual. Another story, **"A Family Feud,"** is told in the words of an old family retainer, Aunt Doshy, and describes how a potentially destructive feud between two families is settled by love and marriage between the children of the families, with the black servants acting as messengers and even occasionally as purveyors of wise counsel. Both these stories employ situations and characters which are part of the commonplace stock in trade of the plantation tale. In both the black servants play a vital part in keeping the families who own them alive and thriving, but this too is part of the customary format of a story by Page. In Page's stories the slave or ex-slave is generally a person of great moral strength and integrity, though these qualities are exercised entirely to the benefit of the white aristocracy; but in Dunbar's stories in this vein, the characterization is too slight to convey much more than a sense of the slave's simpleminded devotion. The most that can be said for these stories is that they leave a residual impression that the white aristocracy owed a great deal to the devotion of their slaves, a claim often put forward by the more conciliatory element of black leadership in the South.

Even this qualified justification can hardly be advanced for the stories of ***In Old Plantation Days,*** in which the stylized and unreal world of Mordaunt's plantation provides an escapist setting for humorous stories of the eternal struggle between deviltry and righteousness, represented by those with an excessive fondness for the pleasures of cards, liquor, and loose women, and those who dedicate themselves to the service of religion and a good standard of family life. The life of the quarters appears for the most part as a closed world, watched over with some amusement but little interference by the family in the big house. There is not the least suggestion that the weaknesses of certain characters in the quarters might have been found among their masters. Mordaunt rules the people of the quarters as he might rule a large family of undisciplined but basically good-natured children, with good-humored, even-tempered indulgence, allowing considerable latitude in their behavior, but with an eye for their moral welfare and a firm support for the good characters among them. Brother Parker, Aunt Doshy, and Aunt Tempy are the leading characters among the devout, and are the pillars of rectitude in the life of the quarters. Yet they are also old people who recollect the passions of their own youth and understand, though they do not condone, the inevitable human tendency to wander from the straight and narrow path. In most stories the prime mover of deviltry is the younger slave Jim, whose path to eventual righteousness is set with many pitfalls.

Slavery as an institution is not questioned at all in these stories, and though the slaves are poor and their lives narrowly circumscribed there is not any suggestion of hardship in their lot. Both good and bad characters are depicted as comic in much of their behavior, but there is a raciness and vigor in their language and their attitude to life which impart a certain folk strength to their characterization. Some words of Brother Parker to one of the Mordaunt boys best illustrate this quality: "I been preachin' de gospel on yo' father's plantation, night aftah night, nigh on to twenty-five years, an' spite o' dat, mos' o' my congregation is in hell."

The folk element in black storytelling is frequently associated with tales of cunning and deception, the wiliness necessary for survival, as in the *Uncle Remus* stories of Joel Chandler Harris or the *Conjure Woman* stories of Chesnutt. But the characters of Dunbar's stories are more likely to survive by a kind of rugged simplicity than by cunning evasions. Similarly, the folk use of conjuring and the supernatural finds little place in Dunbar's work. One story, **"The Conjuring Contest,"** introduces the memorable character of "Doctah Bass," the conjure doctor, actually an old slave, who lives in his "bottle-filled, root-hung room," but the use of conjuring in the narrative itself is very superficial. The same is true of two other stories that involve conjuring, **"Dandy Jim's Conjure Scare"** and **"The Brief Cure of Aunt Fanny,"** but Dunbar's occasional use of the supernatural can be much more effective. **"The Walls of Jericho"** makes comic use of an apparently supernatural incident in describing how Brother Parker, losing his grip on the plantation flock because of a "sensational revivalist" who has moved into the district, regains his ascendancy with the help of "two of the young men of his master's household" who contrive to make "the walls of Jericho"—the trees around the clearing where prayer meetings are held—really fall in response to the revivalist's exhortations, causing total panic in his congregation.

A much better story is **"The Last Fiddling of Mordaunt's Jim,"** highly praised by Benjamin Brawley, and, if skill in narration be the only criterion, one of the best of Dunbar's stories. In the story, Brother Parker falls sick and Jim, fearing that his fiddling and encouragement of frivolity among the cabins has caused Parker's illness, puts his fiddle away. Parker recovers and Jim gets out his fiddle to celebrate the recovery. Parker sends for him and, instead of upbraiding him, asks his pardon for the things he had said about him. Jim is entirely contrite and goes back to his cabin, but he cannot rest. He hears during the night that Brother Parker is worse. Jim's wife, Mandy, goes to nurse him, and Jim bolts himself into the cabin alone:

> He had sat there, it seemed, a long while, when suddenly out of the stillness of the night a faint sound struck on his ears. It was as if some one far away were fiddling, fiddling a wild, weird tune.

The sound comes nearer and nearer until Jim, in an agony of fear, smashes his fiddle and cries out, "Lawd, Lawd, spaih me, an' I'll nevah fiddle ergin!" The music begins to recede, grows fainter and fainter, and passes on into silence. Soon after, Jim hears that Brother Parker has died. Jim is convinced that the devil had come for him and tried to fiddle his soul away to hell, and would have done "ef I hadn't a-wrassled in praih." From that moment Jim joins the company of the devout, but the final paragraph reveals that the sound of the fiddle "was only a belated serenader who had fiddled to keep up his spirits on a lonely road."

This effective use of the folk element, unique in Dunbar's work, depends upon the skill with which he combines the emotional power of the folk story of the devil fiddling the sinner away to hell with the emotional power of religion in the life of the quarters. The conclusion supplies a rational explanation of the events, but the explanation in no way diminishes the force of the story. The coincidence of the wayfarer passing at the moment of Parker's death conveys a sense of something unexplained after the rational explanations. The contrition and forbearance of Parker's deathbed apology to Jim lead us to feel that there is a truth and rightness in human nature that persists even in the limited world of the plantation. Or one might read the conclusion ironically, as a suggestion that Parker and Jim are alike duped by events, that their piety has little to do with reality. The story is essentially one of reconciliation between good and evil, but it leaves at the conclusion an uncertainty of response and a mingling of feelings which continue to work in the reader's mind. If Dunbar had worked with more persistence along the lines of this story, he might have reshaped the hackneyed and commonplace material of the plantation tale not into a formula for protest against white oppression but into a parable of the human condition.

In one story of antebellum days, **"The Ingrate,"** Dunbar turns away from the plantation setting to depict something of the social and economic realities of slavery. The story, known to be based on the experience of Dunbar's father, Joshua, in making his escape to the North, concerns the efforts of a slave named Joshua (a trained plasterer, as Dunbar's father was) to achieve freedom. Joshua has been hired out by his owner, Mr. Leckler, with the promise that he can retain some of his earnings toward buying his freedom, though Leckler intends that this event shall be postponed indefinitely. However, the irony is turned against Leckler when Joshua uses the liberty his outside employment gives him to forge a railroad pass and escape to freedom in Canada. Joshua's desire for freedom is a consuming passion:

> His fellow-servants laughed at him and wondered why he did not take a wife. But Joshua went on his way. He had no time for marrying or for love; other thoughts had taken possession of him. He was being swayed by other thoughts than the mere fathering of slaves for his master. To him slavery was deep night. . . . To own himself, to be master of his hands, feet, of his whole body—something would clutch at his heart as he thought of it.

When Joshua achieves freedom, he sees his individual liberty as an augury for the race, and "his heart swelled, for on the dim horizon he saw the first faint streaks of dawn." Again like Joshua Dunbar, he eventually becomes a sergeant in the Union Army and, as one of "this band of Uncle Sam's niggers," fights for the freedom of his brothers in the South.

The short stories of Dunbar deserve closer attention than they have generally received from critics. Even so discerning a critic as Hugh M. Gloster presents an overall judgment which is a serious oversimplification:

> In his short stories . . . Dunbar generally accepts the limitations and circumscriptions of the plantation tradition. Glorifying the good old days in the accepted manner, he sentimentalizes master-slave relationships and implies that freedom brings social misery to the black man. Negro migrants to the urban North are usually represented as nostalgic misfits, some of whom fall prey to poverty, immorality, or disease and others to disillusionment occasioned by political or professional reverses [see excerpt dated 1948].

While all of these points of criticism might be justified by particular stories or by applying particular interpretations to some stories, the criticism as a whole makes no allowance for the frequent irony of Dunbar's conclusions, and implies that protest must be loud and clear to be effective. Its effect upon white readers in Dunbar's time was, however, likely to be greater because of the bitter understatement which Dunbar often employed to force home a message that many white readers would have found unpalatable and would have rejected as overt statement. Such stories as **"One Man's Fortunes"** and **"A Council of State"** may express merely disillusionment from one point of view. From another, they suggest a determination to deliver some home truths to the white reader who sits comfortably in judgment behind the wall of his prejudices.

A more sympathetic judgment of Dunbar's stories might follow from considering them as the attempts of a serious artist to find a voice in traditional forms that were generally recalcitrant to change or had been debased to the formulas of light entertainment fiction. Even Dunbar's plantation stories, though they conform to the approved white product, do to a degree represent a refinement of the form. Brother Parker, Aunt Doshy, and even Jim are examples of the faithful or the happy-go-lucky slave of the accepted tradition, but they are an improvement on the ignorant, immoral, drunken, and criminal blacks portrayed in many stories, articles, poems, and cartoons of the period. . . . [When] he chose to forget the plantation formula, Dunbar's achievements in the short-story form merit far greater recognition and praise than they have so far received. From the variety of his settings, in the rural South, the Middle Western small town, and the big city of the North, and from the range of his characterizations, among farm laborers, politicians, professional men, small traders, preachers, entertainers, and many others, he created a broad outline of Afro-American life that, while sketchy and imperfect in some respects, offered a bold groundplan to future generations of writers of his race. (pp. 130-38)

Peter Revell, in his Paul Laurence Dunbar, *Twayne Publishers, 1979, 197 p.*

FURTHER READING

Baker, Houston A., Jr. "Paul Laurence Dunbar: An Evaluation." *Black World* XXI, No. 1 (November 1971): 30-7.

Discusses Dunbar's artistic environment, the critical ambivalence surrounding his works, and his overall contributions to black American literature.

Brawley, Benjamin. "Paul Laurence Dunbar." In his *The Negro in Literature and Art in the United States,* pp. 64-75. New York: Duffield & Co., 1930.

Provides biographical information and a chronological examination of Dunbar's major works.

———. *Paul Laurence Dunbar: Poet of His People.* 1936. Reprint. Port Washington, N.Y.: Kennikat Press, 1967, 159 p.

Critical biography based on Dunbar's letters and on personal interviews with his mother, former wife, friends, and acquaintances.

Cunningham, Virginia. *Paul Laurence Dunbar and His Song.* New York: Dodd, Mead & Co., 1947, 283 p.

Considered one of the most authoritative biographies on Dunbar. The book, which contains dialogue attributed to letters, scrapbooks, and personal reminiscences, traces his life, presenting a picture of a dutiful son, loyal friend, and brilliant writer.

Jones, Gayl. "Breaking Out of the Conventions of Dialect: Dunbar and Hurston." *Présence Africaine* 144 (1987): 32-46.

Analyzes Dunbar's attempts to blend black literature with black folklore through the use of dialect in "The Lynching of Jube Benson."

Martin, Jay, ed. *A Singer in the Dawn: Reinterpretations of Paul Laurence Dunbar.* New York: Dodd, Mead & Co., 1975, 255 p.

Collection of lectures and memorial poems read at the Centenary Conference on Paul Laurence Dunbar at the University of California, Irvine, in 1972. Contributors include Arna Bontemps, Addison Gayle, Jr., Nikki Giovanni, and Darwin T. Turner.

Story, Ralph. "Paul Laurence Dunbar: Master Player in a Fixed Game." *CLA Journal* XXVII, No. 1 (September 1983): 30-55.

Biographical and historical discussion of Dunbar's works and the difficulties he encountered as a black artist.

Gabriel García Márquez

1928-

(Full name: Gabriel José García Márquez; also wrote under the pseudonym Septimus) Colombian novelist, short story writer, journalist, critic, and scriptwriter.

García Márquez is one of the most significant authors of *el boom,* a flourishing of Latin American literature during the 1960s that brought international recognition to García Márquez and such authors as Carlos Fuentes, Mario Vargas Llosa, and Julio Cortázar. Marked by a style that has been termed "magical realism," the novels and short fiction of García Márquez are noted for rendering fantastic incidents through realistic detail and for combining historical allusion with imaginative hyperbole for satirical effect. Like his masterwork, the novel *Cien años de soledad* (*One Hundred Years of Solitude*), his short fiction, the bulk of which was written early in his career, has earned critical commendation for presenting mythic, exaggerated characters and dream-like events. Alfred Kazin observes: "Strange things happen in the land of [García] Márquez. As with Emerson, Poe, Hawthorne, every sentence breaks the silence of a vast emptiness, the famous New World 'solitude' that is the unconscious despair of his characters but the sign of [his] genius."

García Márquez was born in Aracataca in northern Colombia, where he lived for eight years with his maternal grandparents. The storytelling of his grandmother, the people of Aracataca, and local myths and superstitions played a major role in inspiring the events and settings of his fiction. García Márquez enrolled in the University of Bogotá in 1946 to study law, but when civil warfare in Colombia caused the institution to close in 1948, he transferred to the University of Cartagena and worked as a journalist for *El universal.* Devoting himself to journalistic and literary endeavors, he discontinued his law studies in 1950 and moved to Barranquilla to work for the daily paper *El heraldo.* At this time he wrote short stories that were published in regional periodicals, and through a circle of local writers he became acquainted with the works of such authors as Franz Kafka, William Faulkner, Virginia Woolf, and James Joyce. García Márquez returned to Bogotá in 1954, serving as a film critic and reporter for *El espectador,* and the next year his novella *La hojarasca* (*Leaf Storm*) was published. During this period García Márquez gained political notoriety for his account in the *Espectador* of the experiences of Luis Alejandro Velasco, a sailor who survived the shipwreck of a Colombian naval vessel in the Caribbean; the series of reports exposed the existence of contraband cargo onboard the ship and suggested the general incompetence of the nation's navy. Seeking to avoid governmental retribution García Márquez traveled throughout Europe during 1955, working as a foreign correspondent for the *Espectador.* In 1956, however, the military government of Colombia shut down the periodical and García Márquez subsequently settled in Paris, where he lived in poverty while writing short stories and his novella *El coronel no tiene quien le escriba* (*No One Writes to the Colonel*), which was published in the journal *Mito* in 1958 and appeared in book form in 1961.

García Márquez returned to South America in 1957 to work on the staff of a periodical in Caracas, Venezuela. After the Cuban revolution of 1959 he strongly supported the new government of Fidel Castro and worked for Castro's news agency, the Prensa latina, traveling on related business between Bogotá, Havana, and New York. He resigned from the agency two years later and moved to Mexico City, where he earned a living as a journalist and scriptwriter, and in 1962 his first collection of short fiction, *Los funerales de la Mamá Grande,* was published. In the mid-1960s García Márquez devoted himself to writing *One Hundred Years of Solitude,* a novel that earned him significant international acclaim and financial reward. Alternating residences between Mexico City and Barcelona, Spain, he continued to write short stories through the early 1970s, and a collection of his short fiction, *La increíble y triste historia de la cándida Eréndira y de su abuela desalmada,* appeared in 1972 to critical commendation. Two years later García Márquez founded the magazine *Alternativa,* and during the late 1970s he concentrated primarily on journalism, focusing on such issues as the opposition to the right-wing dictatorship of Augusto Pinochet in Chile and the role of Cuba in the guerilla warfare taking place in Angola. García Márquez subsequently resumed fiction writing, and his short novel *Crónica de una muerte anunciada* (*Chronicle of a Death Foretold*) appeared in 1981; the next year he received the Nobel Prize in literature. He continued to engage in both literary and journalistic work throughout the 1980s, including the writing of two major novels, *El amor en los tiempos del cólera* (*Love in the Time of Cholera*) and *El general en su laberinto* (*The General in His Labyrinth*), and traveled frequently between his residences in Mexico City, Barcelona, Colombia, and western Europe.

García Márquez's first short stories, written during the late 1940s and early 1950s, were later collected in *Ojos de perro azul.* Portraying dreamlike, often nightmarish states of consciousness, these works are regarded as displaying the influence of Kafka's fiction, and depict events that frequently focus on themes of death and the double self. Critics generally deem these early stories unsuccessful for their overly self-conscious use of unconventional narrative techniques. In his novella *Leaf Storm* García Márquez introduces Macondo, the fictional setting of several subsequent works, including *One Hundred Years of Solitude.* *Leaf Storm* recounts the story of a colonel and the inhabitants of a small town, dominated by a banana company, who come into conflict over the death of a solitary and unpopular doctor. The multiple narrative perspectives from which the story is narrated are considered to contribute to its theme of solitude and to reflect the influence of the novels of Faulkner. Likewise, the recurrence of the people and places of Macondo in Márquez's stories and novels has led commentators to compare the region with that of Yoknapatawpha County in Faulkner's novels.

The collection *Los funerales de la Mamá Grande* (translated in *No One Writes to the Colonel, and Other Stories*) features García Márquez's short fiction written during the early 1960s. Critics frequently commend the stories in this volume for presenting hyperbolic, archetypal characters, such as the deceased village matriarch in the title story (translated as "Big Mama's Funeral"), and for creating a sense of oppressive timelessness within Macondo and other unspecified rural locales in Latin America. In *No One Writes to the Colonel* García Márquez presents a retired military officer who waits unavailingly in a rural village for the mail to arrive with his pension check from the government. For its depiction of the stifling social and political institutions of an undenoted South American nation, the novella has been considered to represent Colombia in general, and in particular the state of the country during *la violencia,* a period of violent social and political crises that culminated during the 1950s.

Much of García Márquez's short fiction written after *One Hundred Years of Solitude* appears in *Eréndira* and critics note his use of complex narrative techniques, lengthy sentence structures, and whimsical digression in both the collection and novel. Similar to *Solitude,* the works in *Eréndira* exemplify the style of "magical realism," including the use of exaggerated or distorted characters and a fusion of naturalistic observation with the fantastic. For example, in "Un señor muy viejo con unas alas enormes" ("A Very Old Man with Enormous Wings") and "El ahogado más hermoso del mundo" ("The Handsomest Drowned Man in the World"), realistic detail is used to portray the occurrence of the extraordinary, such as the appearance in the latter work of a colossal dead man on the beach of a Caribbean town. The novella *Eréndira* (translated as *Innocent Eréndira*) portrays a monstrously heartless grandmother who forces her granddaughter into a life of prostitution after the child accidentally burned down her cottage. Depicting events within carnivalesque settings, the work mixes oneiric elements with political allegory to suggest the relationship between dictatorships and oppressed populaces in Latin America.

García Márquez's short novel, *Chronicle of a Death Foretold,* is noted for its sparse journalistic style, differing from that of most of his previous fiction, and recounts through a reportorial narrative voice a murder that occurred many years earlier. Indian-born English novelist Salman Rushdie praises this technique for "[making] the real world behave in precisely the improbably hyperbolic fashion of a Márquez story." While García Márquez's major novels, especially *One Hundred Years of Solitude,* have received more critical attention than his short fiction, his stories and novellas are regarded as important works in the development of his career and have contributed to García Márquez's high international stature.

(For further information on García Márquez's life and career, see *Contemporary Literary Criticism,* Vols. 2, 3, 8, 10, 15, 27, 47, 55; *Contemporary Authors,* Vols. 33-36, rev. ed.; *Contemporary Authors New Revision Series,* Vols. 10, 28; and *Dictionary of Literary Biography Yearbook: 1982.*)

PRINCIPAL WORKS

SHORT FICTION

La hojarasca 1955
[*Leaf Storm,* published in *Leaf Storm, and Other Stories,* 1972]

"Monólogo de Isabel viendo llover en Macondo"; published in the journal *Mito,* 1955; also published as "Isabel viendo llover en Macondo," 1967
["Monologue of Isabel Watching It Rain in Macondo," published in *Leaf Storm, and Other Stories,* 1972]

El coronel no tiene quien le escriba 1961
[*No One Writes to the Colonel,* published in *No One Writes to the Colonel, and Other Stories,* 1968]

Los funerales de la Mamá Grande 1962
[*Big Mama's Funeral,* published in *No One Writes to the Colonel, and Other Stories,* 1968]

No One Writes to the Colonel, and Other Stories 1968; contains the stories originally collected in *Los funerales de la Mamá Grande,* with the addition of the novella *No One Writes to the Colonel*

La increíble y triste historia de la cándida Eréndira y de su abuela desalmada 1972
[*Innocent Eréndira, and Other Stories* (selected translation), 1978]

Ojos de perro azul 1974

[*Innocent Eréndira, and Other Stories* (selected translation), 1978]
Innocent Eréndira, and Other Stories 1978; contains the stories originally collected in *La increíble y triste historia de la cándida Eréndira y de su abuela desalmada* and *Ojos de perro azul*
Crónica de una muerte anunciada 1981
[*Chronicle of a Death Foretold,* 1982]
Collected Stories 1985
Collected Novellas 1990

OTHER MAJOR WORKS

La mala hora (novel) 1962
[*In Evil Hour,* 1979]
Cien años de soledad (novel) 1967
[*One Hundred Years of Solitude,* 1970]
**Relato de un náufrago. . . .* (journalism) 1970
[*The Story of a Shipwrecked Sailor,* 1986]
El otoño del patriarca (novel) 1975
[*The Autumn of the Patriarch,* 1975]
Crónicas y reportajes (journalism) 1976
El amor en los tiempos del cólera (novel) 1985
[*Love in the Time of Cholera,* 1988]
El general en su laberinto (novel) 1989
[*The General in His Labyrinth,* 1990]

*This work was originally written in 1955.

Mario Vargas Llosa (essay date 1971)

[*A Peruvian-born novelist, short story writer, journalist, and critic, Vargas Llosa was a prominent writer of* el boom, *a period in Latin American literature initiating the heightened international recognition of the works of such Central and South American authors as Vargas Llosa, Carlos Fuentes, Julio Cortázar, and García Márquez. Vargas Llosa's fiction characteristically condemns the social and military institutions of contemporary Peru and his novels have been praised for their complex and experimental narrative structures. The following essay was originally published in Spanish in Vargas Llosa's seminal biographical and critical study,* García Márquez: Historia de un deicidio *(see Further Reading list). Here, he examines narrative technique and the theme of death in García Márquez's early short fiction.*]

García Márquez has described the difficulties that he encountered when he first began writing, back in 1947, a time when he was a student of Law and a dutiful reader of Kafka: "I was constantly faced with the problem of themes; I found myself having to seek out the story before being able to write it." These words provide a key to the ten short stories, written between 1947 and 1952, which together make up his literary prehistory. His dilemma was by no means unique; many a young author has begun to write believing that originality lies in a rejection of those raw materials of his craft readily accessible in his own life and milieu. So as not to "copy reality," he silences his personal and historical demons and imposes upon himself themes that appear clinically pure, incapable of being measured against real life, even though they may have little or nothing to do with his literary sensibilities. Only the cultural demons are now left to nourish the creative process, with the result that the young author, quite unwittingly, marches into the very snare which he has been hoping to avoid: those writings that show nothing of his life or his world will, in contrast, bear relentless testimony to the scope and nature of his reading. It is no easy matter to discover the future creator in these early tales. They are hardly to be considered the first steps of his literary vocation for they introduce tendencies quite alien to those that will govern the construction of fictional reality from ***La hojarasca*** **(*Leaf Storm*)** to **"El último viaje del buque fantasma" ("Last Voyage of the Ghost Ship").**

What is especially surprising in these texts, in contrast with the later writing, is their intellectualism. Cold and humorless—the first of them written under the devastating influence of Kafka, and the last under the influence (no less devastating) of Faulkner—they reveal a world of extreme sophistication, of mannerisms, of literary tics. The truth of the matter is that García Márquez has not yet come to grips with his literary vocation, for that vocation is in the making. He is already a rebel, to be sure, but not the revolutionary who, on returning to Aracataca with his mother, discovers the collapse of a world that had given him life, and who becomes conscious of a reality which he will dedicate himself thereafter to redeeming (exorcizing) with his pen. He is quite clear on this point: though unsure of the dates, he is able to recall that the trip to Aracataca with his mother took place when all of these stories, with the exception of **"La noche de los alcaravanes" ("The Night of the Curlews")**, had already been written. The new experience strengthened his nascent vocation, opened his eyes to the raw material of his art and transformed the diligent reader and servant of Kafka and Faulkner into a writer who would, in turn, have them serve him in the creation of his own special world.

Although the literary interest of these tales is minimal, they do arouse curiosity as portraits of the emotional and cultural life of the adolescent who, by the end of the forties, far removed from his beloved tropics, was resigning himself to a career in law and discovering—with awe—the great novelists of modern times. Ten short stories appeared that would never be gathered together as a book. Almost invariably they were given enigmatic titles: **"La tercera resignación" ("The Third Resignation")**, **"Eva está dentro de su gato" ("Eve inside Her Cat")**, **"Tubal-Caín forja una estrella" ("Tubal-Cain Forges a Star")**, **"La otra costilla de la muerte" ("The Other Rib of Death")**, **"Diálogo del espejo" ("Dialogue in a Mirror")**, **"Amargura para tres sonámbulos" ("Bitter Sorrow for Three Sleepwalkers")**, **"Ojos de perro azul" ("Blue-Dog Eyes")**, **"Nabo" ("Nabo")**, **"Alguien desordena estas rosas" ("Someone Has Disturbed the Roses")** and **"La noche de los alcaravanes" ("The Night of the Curlews").** The first five were written in Bogotá between 1947 and the middle months of 1948 and the remainder in Cartagena and Barranquilla.

The dominant theme in almost all of these is death. Sometimes the events of life are narrated from within death;

sometimes death is viewed from within life; sometimes there are recurring deaths within death. Most of the stories reach for a setting outside the limits of time and space, within an abstract reality. Throughout, the narrative perspective is subjective and internal: the world of life, or death, is viewed by a consciousness which in narrating narrates itself. Objectivity is lacking even in those stories which spring from an objectively real anecdote, like **"Bitter Sorrow for Three Sleepwalkers"** and **"Nabo."** Apart from these two, all are rooted firmly in an imaginary reality, by degrees which range from the mythic and legendary (**"The Night of the Curlews,"** a tale inspired by a popular superstition) to the truly fantastic. The consistency of this fictional reality is more than anything else psychological: actions, which are few, are dwarfed by bizarre sensations, extraordinary emotions, impossible thoughts. It is what the characters feel or think that is being related; almost never what they do.

An atmosphere of nightmare and neurosis pervades these tales, in which dreams and self-duplications are often important themes. The phenomenon of the double self first appears in **"The Other Rib of Death"** and **"Dialogue in a Mirror"**; here we catch an early glimpse of the great theme of recurring names, personalities and destinies of *One Hundred Years of Solitude.* The last of these stories, however, introduces a concrete element which allows it to be set directly within the "history" of the fictional reality: its curlews belong to a world which is already that of ***Leaf Storm.*** This may explain why **"The Night of the Curlews"** is the only one of the ten stories "resurrected" by *One Hundred Years of Solitude.* And yet in the previous story, **"Someone Has Disturbed the Roses,"** just as if the subconscious had surfaced to play tricks on the "abstracting" mind of the author, two local elements filter through into the narrative, soon to become established customs of the fictional society as it appears in ***Leaf Storm***: little wooden pegs are placed in the eyes of a dead child so that during the wake they will remain "open and unflinching"; "bread and aloe leaves" are hung for good luck at the entrance to a house, as happens in many homes in Macondo.

A pattern which we might term metaphysico-masturbatory is repeated in various of these ten tales: a solitary character tortures himself with thoughts of ontological disintegration, self-duplication and extinction. Naturally, not all of the stories follow the same lines, nor is their quality uniformly nil. The differences will be more apparent if we review each tale in turn from the point of view of its content and manner of narration.

"The Third Resignation" pulsates with an agonizing fear of death. In the very first lines, the omniscient narrator draws his reader into an imaginary reality by remarking that the persistent noise which the protagonist hears, "he had heard, for example, at the time of his first death." This fusion of the delirious and fantastic with the routine and trivial, as well as the congealed horror which sprouts droll asides ("He felt handsome wrapped in his shroud; fatally handsome"), are strongly reminiscent of Kafka. A seven-year-old child dies of typhoid, but the doctor manages to "prolong the boy's life even beyond death." In his coffin, the dead boy goes on growing for eighteen years under the loving care of his mother, who examines him each day with a tape measure. At twenty-five years of age he stops growing and suffers "his second death." His body begins to decompose and gives off a foul smell. He realizes that he will now have to be buried and is seized by an infinite dread because, with his conscious mind still alert, he has the impression that he is about to be buried alive. He pictures "life" within the grave, the slow disintegration of his flesh, of his bones, of the wood of his coffin and then how all this dust will rise to the surface, to a new life, as a tree, as a fruit. It will be like living over again. But by then he will probably be so resigned to his condition that he will die anew, this time "from resignation."

The slight narrative thread is lost among the descriptions of the dead character's sensations and the mass of grotesque detail: the living corpse is gradually being eaten away by mice, a maddening noise is torturing his eardrums, the stench of his own decay is offending his sense of smell. The omniscient narrator is so close to his protagonist, so involved in the intimacies of the latter, that the tale often appears a monologue by the dead man. Herein lies one of the few merits of the text: the flawless coherence of the spatial perspective, most unusual in one who has just begun to write. The language is hardly distinctive, but it has a certain flow and is well in keeping with its topic. The vocabulary is dense, disturbing in its impact on the senses, and the syntax tortuous. Certain of the narrative elements will recur in the work of García Márquez: the attempt to build a story around a corpse may be seen in ***Leaf Storm,*** in **"Los funerales de la Mamá Grande" ("Big Mama's Funeral")**, and, from all appearances, in *El otoño del Patriarca* (*The Autumn of the Patriarch*), while the idea that one can die again within death reappears in *One Hundred Years of Solitude* with the multiple deaths of Melquíades and Prudencio Aguilar ("that other death which exists within death," *One Hundred Years of Solitude*), and again in **"El mar del tiempo perdido" ("The Sea of Lost Time"),** whose "sea of dead men" has different depths which the cadavers travel according to the length of time they have spent in their present state—those nearest to the surface are the oldest, those who have attained greatest repose.

Six weeks after the first short story, came **"Eve inside Her Cat,"** the same in essence as its predecessor, though changed in appearance. Once again the subject is death and reincarnation, the agonizing desire that all should not end with the grave. Here Eve is a distant precursor of Remedios the Beauty; she is no less lovely a creature, and, like Remedios, she ascends one day to another life, transformed into a "pure spirit." The narrator follows her into this other realm or existence, which is "an easier, uncomplicated world, where all dimensions had been eliminated." At first Eve thinks she is in limbo, but then she has her doubts. She "lives" in darkness and is ubiquitous, being simultaneously in all parts of "real" life as well as in that other life (or death). When she was a person of flesh and blood, she was tormented by her beauty, a "sickness," which kept her awake at night and which resulted from the activities in her blood of "tiny, burning insects which, at the approach of dawn each day, would awaken and, in an excruciating subcutaneous adventure, swarm with trembling feet around that luscious lump of clay where her bodily beauty was centered." Suddenly, Eve feels the need to eat an orange; the yearning, while gratuitous, is overwhelming. She remembers then that pure spirits may enter a living being, and she decides to take the form of her cat (though fearing for a moment that as a cat she may prefer mice to oranges). But on trying to locate the animal she finds that he has ceased to exist, along with her home. Only then does she realize that three thousand years have passed since she began this other life (or death).

This summary may give the impression that the story is a humorous one. On the contrary, it is told with meticulous anguish. Apart from Eve, who is still alive within death like the protagonist of the previous tale, there is another corpse: a child who has died and whose memory is an additional torture for Eve. Death is present in all of the works of García Márquez, but never in such an obsessive or exclusive manner as in these first years of his career as a writer.

Two and a half months later there appeared **"Tubal-Cain Forges a Star,"** a story diffuse to the point of incoherence. The frail plot is lost among the mass of morbid ideas and sensations which constitute the narrative substance. These include repeated allusions to a persecution mania, to a schizophrenic impression of a double self and to suicide. Here again we encounter the Kafkan motif of the mice, present in the first two stories. The title is gratuitous: it is never clear whether the lone character is called Tubal-Cain, nor for that matter whether the story has a character at all. There are times when the tale seems to consist of a torrent of images sweeping across the troubled consciousness of a madman ("What is he saying? That I'm mad? Bah . . . One . . . But am I perhaps mad?"), or of the experiences of a sensibility excited by drugs (the character feels "beautiful and alone beneath the bitter heaven of cocaine" and hears voices that cry "We are the marijuanas; we are upside down!"), or of the disparate memories that race through the mind of a suicide victim during the brief instant when the rope is closing around his neck, since the final paragraph shows that the character dies from hanging (unless that, too, is another nightmarish dream): "The rope was tightening, tightening now around his throat, irrevocably. He could feel a straining, then a tremendous jolt as the vertebrae in the nape of his neck broke apart."

Death is as much in evidence here as in the earlier stories; there is even the possibility that this tale, like those before it, recounts the experiences of someone deceased ("I want them to leave me alone with my death, the death I first knew twelve years ago, when I came home stumbling, swollen with fever . . . "). As a whole the story makes tedious reading because of an unjustifiable preoccupation with technique, but there are successful moments, as in the depiction of certain hallucinatory states of mind: the protagonist, in the space of a few seconds, sees his father emerge from a picture and expand to enormous proportions ("He could see the body growing, assuming arbitrary shapes, bulging out along the ceiling which was now beginning to shake"), and then he sees him shrink again and finally disintegrate, now transformed into countless miniature beings: " . . . one tiny, solitary creature, who was about to double and multiply over the four corners of the room, in a wild scattering of matching figures, all of them alike, on the move, rushing about in complete confusion. . . . "

"The Other Rib of Death" opens with a surrealistic dream in which anguish and black humor are fused: the protagonist is traveling on a train which crosses a landscape of "still life, sown with unlikely, artificial trees, whose fruits are knives and scissors. . . . " Suddenly, without explanation, he takes a screwdriver and removes from his foot the head of a boil. Through the hole he can make out "the end of a greasy yellow cord." He pulls on the cord and out comes "a long, an immensely long ribbon, which issued forth of its own free will, without causing irritation or pain," at which point he sees his brother, "dressed up like a woman in front of a mirror, trying to extract his left eye with a pair of scissors."

Only the beginning of the tale is so colorful; next there comes a psychic drama aggravated by obsessions with death and with a double self. The narrative viewpoint is that of a character who, at daybreak, finds himself caught between a waking and a sleeping state, and who is assailed by strange sensations, dark terrors and somber visions. Soon after, a more precise and more unnerving experience stands out sharply against the whirl of images: the memory of a twin brother, who died from a tumor on the stomach. Masochistically, the character imagines the tumor, feels it growing within his very being, envisions it devouring muscles, vital organs, dragging him in turn toward his death. Then he is gripped by a terrifying fear of his brother, that "other" self, the double: "They were thus replicas. Two identical brothers, disturbingly repetitive." He begins to feel that the spatial limits separating his dead brother and himself are illusory, that the two share a common identity. He fears that "when putrefaction has taken hold of the dead man's body, he, the one still living, will also start to rot within his animate world." But what if the process were the reverse, with the influence emanating from "the one who had stayed alive"? In that case, perhaps, "both he and his brother would remain intact, achieving a balance between life and death which would ward off putrefaction." Or could it be "that the brother who was buried might remain incorruptible even when the rot of death was spreading through the body of the surviving brother with his fine, blue eyes"? These clammy questions are soon followed by a blissful sensation of peace, and the protagonist, now relaxed, closes his eyes "to await the coming day." Were all of these events simply the products of a restless imagination? Apparently so, for six months after this story comes **"Dialogue in a Mirror,"** a continuation of **"The Other Rib of Death,"** in which it is made quite clear that the events of the previous tale were merely "preoccupations and anxieties of the early morning hours."

The new text is as inconsequential as the last. The anonymous protagonist, on waking that same morning, touches his face and is soon absorbed in the discovery of his own body. Recognizing that complex biological unity as his own, he is both fascinated and perplexed, and begins exploring his body with his hands: "Just there, where his fingers touched—and beyond his fingertips, bone against bone—his irrevocable anatomical condition had hidden away a system of parts, a dense universe of tissues, of lesser worlds, which supported him, which elevated his carnal frame into a position which would be much less permanent than the ultimate and natural posture of his bones." But now awake, he gets out of bed and stands before the bathroom mirror, where he sees—or thinks he sees—the reflection of his dead twin brother. At this point he surrenders fully to a terrifying game of repetition and self-duplication: he is convinced that the gestures and contorsions of the face in the mirror are not his own but those of his brother, who is imitating his movements with perfect timing, or else whose movements he himself is imitating. There are moments when he seems to detect (or when perhaps he invents) a fleeting disharmony between his own movements and those of the reflection. Suddenly, while he is shaving, the person in the mirror cuts himself and begins to bleed; he touches his own skin, but can find no mark. At that same instant he remembers a word (Pandora) which he has been trying to recall throughout the story and he is filled with a sudden joy.

This tale, like the four that precede it, is set within an internal and subjective reality that is best termed abstract: all reference to time and place is eschewed; the language is studiously neutral; in the five stories an identical situation recurs (a solitary character, lying dead or asleep, is plagued by unnatural sensations); in each of them we note the same ambigüity with regard to the type of reality described. Is this an "imaginary" or an "objective" reality? The first of these terms seems more appropriate if the characters are indeed dead, and the second if the resurrections, repeated deaths and reduplications are merely the fantasies of disturbed minds. The rigorous coherence within incoherence which operates among the first five stories begins to weaken with the sixth, and the change is even greater in those that follow: García Márquez has begun to read Faulkner and the experience will leave a bright imprint on these last tales.

"Bitter Sorrow for Three Sleepwalkers" (appearing ten months later) signals a shift from the internal to the external and from the abstract to the concrete in the treatment of fictional reality. The tale is narrated in the first person plural by the three sleepwalkers of the title, but its subject is a young girl. More than a short story the work is a poetic tableau, an elegy for a girl who, sometime in the past, fell from a second story window into a stone yard and who, instead of dying, remained with "her vital organs in disarray and no longer responsive to her will, as if she were a warm corpse that had not yet begun to stiffen." From that moment on—a long time seems to have elapsed since the accident—she has been a solitary creature, living within a private, hallucinatory world ("She told us once that she had seen a cricket inside the glass of her mirror and that she had gone through the surface of the glass to get it"). But within this world she is gradually—even deliberately—destroying herself. One day she decides to stop moving, to remain seated on the concrete floor, and then she announces: "I shall never smile again." The three narrators, who speak of her with great sorrow and nostalgia (in all probability they are her younger brothers), believe that before long she will tell them: "I shall never see again," "I shall never hear again," and that "of her own free will, she would cut herself off sense by sense, until one day we would find her sitting with her back against the wall, looking as if she had gone to sleep for the first time in her life."

The language is less diffuse than in the earlier texts but it continues to be highly "literary," carefully wrought and reminiscent of certain of the author's (better) readings. The air of mystery and foreboding, of imminent revelation is achieved by means of a Faulknerian syntax, oblique and anticipatory, twisting and turning ("All of this—and even more—we would have believed that afternoon. . . . ," "We could have said that we were doing what we had been doing every day of our lives . . . "), and also by the intrusion—as if some deforming prism had been placed over the narrative material—of the character-narrator, whose sole function in the story is that of a "technical" advisor.

"Blue-Dog Eyes" recalls a story by Sartre ("Erostrate") because of its opening scene: a woman is undressing in a room, and a man watching her exclaims, "I always wanted to see you like this, with the skin of your belly full of deep holes. . . . " But then it turns out that this is an oneiric tale; the strange encounters between the couple take place in the precarious, impalpable world of dreams. At one point the narrator-protagonist sees a woman enter his room; her eyes fascinate him and he decides to give her the name "blue-dog eyes." They continue to meet thereafter in their respective dreams for several years. The woman attempts to track down in "real" life this friend or lover from her dream world ("Her life was given over to searching me out in reality; she would try to identify herself by means of the name 'blue-dog eyes' "). She passes through restaurants and along streets, repeating the words aloud, even writing them "on the steamed up windows of hotels, stations and public buildings." But her search proves futile, for the narrator is "the unique man, who remembers nothing of what he has dreamt when he wakes up." The tale becomes even more complex and bewildering. Has the woman really been looking for the narrator in "real" life? The man thinks so because this is what she tells him during their oneiric meetings, but it may be that what she thinks she does during her waking hours is something which she herself is dreaming; perhaps she too forgets what she has dreamt once she wakes up. Despite its ingenious plot, this is the most poorly executed, the most confusingly structured of all of the early stories of García Márquez.

More deserving of attention is **"Nabo,"** where, as in **"Bitter Sorrow for Three Sleepwalkers,"** we encounter a poetic creature living on the periphery of life: a mute child, unable to walk, who recognizes no one, who is a "dead and solitary girl that liked the phonograph." Of all the writings, this is the one most reminiscent of Faulkner, not only because of its form, but also for its subject matter. It appears to be set in the Deep South, with peasants who live in semi-slavery, estates with horses, aristocratic young ladies and their Black servants, and saxophone players in the public squares. The tale is made up of two parts or dimensions, skilfully drawn together into a single story by two alternating narrators: the omniscient narrator and a plural narratór-character (doubtless the brothers or parents of the child). The two parts of the story take place within different realms of reality—one the reality of external things, the other the fantasy or madness of the protagonist.

The "objective" portion of the story is as follows: Nabo, a young Black, is required to groom the horses on an estate and play the phonograph which keeps the idiot girl amused. The girl discovers—presumably thanks to Nabo—how to move the handle of the phonograph and is one day heard to pronounce the boy's name, "Nabo." The groom is in the habit of visiting the town square on Saturday nights to listen to a black saxophone player who one day gives up playing in the band and disappears forever. Then one morning Nabo is kicked in the head by a horse and remains "disturbed" for the rest of his life. He is bound hand and foot by his master and locked in a room, where food is passed to him from under the door. He lives in this state for fifteen years, like an animal, until one day in a fit of rage he breaks down the door of his cell and runs off—now huge and ferocious—in search of the stable and the horses, which have long since disappeared from the estate. During his escape he smashes mirrors and tears down everything within reach. The girl (now a woman) sees him running by and utters the only word she has ever learned, "Nabo."

The "subjective" portion is this: in the loneliness of his cell, Nabo relives incessantly in his pitiful mind the tragic instant when the horse's hoof shattered his forehead. He has no awareness of the passage of time; his mind revolves obsessively around this single memory. Suddenly, he hears a voice calling to him, urging him to follow. In the shadows he recognizes the saxophone player that he used to listen to in the square. The shadowy figure speaks to him affectionately, urging Nabo to leave with him: "We have been waiting for you in the group." The boy shows little enthusiasm, whereupon the man insists, assuring him that all that has happened was arranged by "them" in order to have him in "the group." But Nabo is not interested and talks about the horses and the comb that he had used to groom their tails. Finally the apparition suggests: "If finding the comb is all that keeps you from joining the group, then go and look for it." It is at this point that Nabo breaks down the door of his prison and escapes, now a "huge and bestial Negro."

This second level or dimension of the story has an ambiguity characteristic of literature involving an imaginary reality. The reader must make up his mind where he stands by eliminating one of the two interpretations possible. The specter of the dead saxophone player who comes and invites Nabo to go with him to the "group" (in other words, to the afterlife, to heaven) could be simply a hallucination occurring in the mind of the protagonist, in which case that part of the story would be taking place on a "subjective" plane within an "objective" reality. But there is another possibility, namely that the dead saxophone player really does appear in Nabo's dark cell as an emissary from the afterlife and that he is, consequently, not a mental vision but a miraculous or fantastic being. If this is indeed the case, then the present portion of the story is occurring within a subjective reality, and the events narrated by this tale are no longer objectively real, but part of an "imaginary" reality.

Also to be noted in **"Nabo"** are certain motifs which will soon become part of the stock in trade of this fictional reality. One of them is the theme of sequestration. The young girl in **"Bitter Sorrow for Three Sleepwalkers"** leads a "withdrawn" life, but Nabo even more so, and in his seclusion one may see a precedent for the estrangement of the doctor in ***Leaf Storm.*** Another motif is that of the girl or woman who is somehow "different," who lives on the periphery of life. The lovely idiot girls of **"Bitter Sorrow for Three Sleepwalkers"** and **"Nabo"** are first sketches of characters like Santa Sofía de la Piedad and Remedios the Beauty. What must be emphasized, however, is that with this last tale the author has begun to show a strong interest in telling a story; the technical complexities and careful manipulations of language are now subordinate to this interest, whereas in earlier cases the story seemed a pretext to justify extravagant displays of style. It matters little that the structure, language and even subject matter are still somewhat foreign. The faithful reader is becoming a writer: trading the abstract for the concrete, the psychic for the vital, he is showing an increasing ability to tell a story in a truly *convincing* manner.

In **"Someone Has Disturbed the Roses,"** there appears another cripple, as in **"Bitter Sorrow for Three Sleepwalkers"** and **"Nabo,"** but with a change of sex (this time it is a boy) and condition (he is dead). As in the first stories, the narrator is also dead: "Since it's Sunday and the rain has now stopped, I think I shall take a bunch of roses to my grave." A very devout woman, who grows and sells flowers, lives all alone in a house, one room of which serves as a chapel. Each Sunday she has the impression that an invisible gust of wind comes and disturbs the roses on the altar. In fact, it is not the wind, but the spirit of a young boy, who died forty years earlier after falling from a ladder—a boy with whom the woman had played when she was a child. The narrator of this story is none other than this spirit-invalid, who, after dying, sat and waited for twenty years in the room now containing the altar for someone to come and occupy the deserted house. One day he sees the woman moving in; even though twenty years have gone by, he is still able to recognize the girl who used to go bird-nesting with him in the stables. From this moment on—another twenty years elapse—he has "lived" with this woman, now in her old age, and has watched her sewing, sleeping and praying. Each Sunday the spirit tries, without success, to take a bunch of roses from the chapel to his grave on the hillside of the town; *he* is that "invisible wind" which disturbs the flowers on the altar.

This is the most successful of the ten stories—the best written and the most skilfully constructed. Despite its magical or fantastic air, it has a number of picturesque details drawn from an objective reality, certain of which will reappear in the Macondo of ***Leaf Storm*** (the "bread and aloe leaves" at the entrance to the house, the "wooden pegs" in the dead boy's eyes). In addition, the boy-sitting-in-a-chair-waiting is, as we know, the nuclear image of ***Leaf Storm:*** this is the plight which the narrator-grandchild has to suffer throughout the novel. Little by little, the amorphous reality of the early tales is beginning to take on a recognizable shape. It has begun to move within fixed limits, the same limits that will govern its development, its growth and regrowth in future years.

"The Night of the Curlews" is the dividing line between the prehistory and the history of the fictional reality. The story is based on a popular superstition from the Atlantic coast, which holds that curlews will peck out the eyes of anyone who imitates their song. Three men are drinking beer in the courtyard of a brothel where there are seven of these birds. One of the men begins to imitate the call of the curlew, whereupon "the birds swooped down to the table and pecked out the men's eyes." The tale is told by the three blind men and begins with their loss of sight. Casually, just as if nothing has happened, they join hands and try to adapt to a world through which they move now only by memory, touch and smell. Hand in hand, they pass through a labyrinth where they are met by the voices of women and children. One of the voices tells them that the newspapers have taken up their story, but that nobody believes it. The men can find no one to take them home. For three days now, they have been lost and unable to rest. Finally, they sit back and enjoy the sunshine, passive beings, "now having lost all notion of distance, time and direction."

The story is told not as an objectively real experience, but rather as one belonging to an imaginary reality: the note of mystery and surprise is intense, and innuendos are relied upon almost to excess. From a narrative standpoint the story is interesting in that it is presented almost entirely in dialogue—a technique by no means common in the work of García Márquez. Moreover, it is here that the curlews make their first appearance in the fictional reality; they will become a permanent part of the author's landscape from the first novel on. Of the ten stories, this one alone would be cannibalized by *One Hundred Years of Solitude*—just as if García Márquez wished to emphasize that only in this text had he begun in earnest his life as a substitute for God. (pp. 451-60)

Mario Vargas Llosa, "A Morbid Prehistory (The Early Stories)," translated by Roger Williams, in Books Abroad, *Vol. 47, No. 3, Summer, 1973, pp. 451-60.*

Alfred Kazin (essay date 1972)

[*A highly respected American literary critic, Kazin is best known for his essay collections* The Inmost Leaf *(1955) and* Contemporaries *(1962), and particularly for* On Native Grounds *(1962), a study of American prose writing since the era of William Dean Howells in the late 1800s. Having studied the works of "the critics who were the best writers—from Sainte-Beuve and Matthew Arnold to Edmund Wilson and Van Wyck Brooks" as an aid to his critical understanding, Kazin observes that "criticism focussed many—if by no means all—of my urges as a writer: to show literature as a deed in human history, and to find in each writer the uniqueness of the gift, of the essential vision, through which I hoped to penetrate into the mystery and sacredness of the individual soul." In the following review of* Leaf Storm, and Other Stories, *he contends that the works of the collection evidence the theme of the "New World," which presents parallels between the literature of Latin America and that of major authors of the United States.*]

When Gabriel García Márquez's utterly original *One Hundred Years of Solitude* came out here in 1970, I read it—I experienced it—with the same recognition of a New World epic that one feels about *Moby Dick.* Whatever else you can say about contemporary American novels, they are generally overpopulated and personally too scornful to remind the reader that ours was, until very recently, a New World. This is a subject, a climate of feeling, that requires a virtually empty continent, a powerful sense of wonder at how little men change even in the most bizarre moments of discovering a "Nature" beyond the usual conceptions of Nature, one or two characters who are too big for the society they are trying to create.

Above all, the "New World" as a subject requires an indifference to the ordinary laws of space, time and psychology that enforce realism. No one who has read *One Hundred Years of Solitude* will ever forget the sensation of tripping on sentences that in the most matter-of-fact way described what happens under the pressure cooker of total "newness." Verily, there has been nothing to compare the New World with but the New World itself.

Gabriel García Márquez comes from Colombia, a country whose 20th-century history has been dominated by the civil wars that are the background of everything he writes. His great novel was first published in Argentina, and he now lives in Barcelona. Unlike the subtle but timid Borges, who comes out of a library and may be remembered as the Washington Irving of Latin America, Márquez—born in 1928—reflects the incessant ironies of post-imperialist national development. He has extraordinary strength and firmness of imagination and writes with the calmness of a man who knows exactly what wonders he can perform. Strange things happen in the land of Márquez. As with Emerson, Poe, Hawthorne, every sentence breaks the silence of a vast emptiness, the famous New World "solitude" that is the unconscious despair of his characters but the sign of Márquez's genius. I am guessing but I wonder if the outbreak of creative originality in Latin America today, coming after so many years of dutifulness to Spanish and French models, doesn't resemble our sudden onrush of originality after we had decided really to break away from the spell of England.

However, Márquez is not a Protestant romantic of the time when it seemed that *all* the world would soon be new. He is a dazzlingly accomplished but morally burdened end-product of centuries of colonialism, civil war and political chaos; a prime theme in all his work is the inevitability of incest and the damage to the germ plasm that at the end of his great novel produces a baby with a pig's tail. He always writes backwards, from the end of the historical cycle, and all his prophecies are acerb without being gloomy. The farcically tragic instability and inhumanity of the continent where Nature is still too much for man and where the Spanish conquest is still unresolved, dominate his work. What makes his subject "New World" is the hallucinatory chaos and stoniness of the Colombian village, Macondo, through which all history will pass. What makes Márquez's art "New World" is the totally untraditionalist, unhindered technique behind this vision of the whole—from the white man's first scratches in the jungle to the white man's inability to stave off the sight of his own end.

Leaf Storm and Other Stories was Márquez's first book, begun when he was 19. In some of these beautiful early stories—**"The Handsomest Drowned Man in the World," "A Very Old Man with Enormous Wings," "The Last Voyage of the Ghost Ship,"**—Márquez's typical double vision of the natural world as inherently a fable, a story to be told and retold rather than something "real," expresses itself with perfect charm. The handsomest drowned man is a native of a fishing village who in death becomes super-large and magnificent, a young god, until he is recognized by his old neighbors. The very old man with enormous wings is an angel who wearily sinks to earth in a poor village and is treated as some bothersome fowl until he clambers off again. A young man constantly sees a great trans-Atlantic liner sinking before his eyes, but no one else can see it or find any record of this liner being on the high seas.

In each of these stories Márquez takes a theme that in a lesser writer would seem "poetic," a handsome conceit lifted out of a poem by Wallace Stevens but then stopped dead in its narrative tracks. Márquez manages to make a story out of each of these—not too ambitious, but just graceful enough to be itself. He succeeds because these are stories about wonders, and the wonders become actions. Márquez as a very young man was already committed to the subject of creatures working out *all* their destinies. In every Márquez work a whole historical cycle is lived through, by character after character. And each cycle is like a miniature history of the world from the creation to the final holocaust. Márquez is writing that history line by line, very slowly indeed in each piece of writing (the slowness of pace is part of his manner, his mystique; he sees things in a long-held, eerily powerful light).

The upsetting narrative sequence may remind us of the subtlest imaginations of the 20th-century. But I would guess that Márquez owes this technique to his vision of the mad repetitiousness of history in his country. A harsh mysteriously arid peasant village like Macondo experiences everything in his work, over and over again, like those characters in *One Hundred Years of Solitude* who promptly reappear after dying.

The title story itself encompasses so much of the perverse, insistent, weirdly lasting solitude that Faulkner describes that you realize what a bond exists between "American" writers, North and South, whose common experience is of a refractory landscape always too much for the most complicated persons who try to find shelter in it. A French doctor mysteriously appears one day in 1903 in the village of Macondo with a letter of "recommendation" from Colonel Aureliano Buendía. (Colonel Buendía will be a major figure in *One Hundred Years of Solitude* and another colonel, who takes in the French doctor, may be a first sketch of the fantastic José Arcádio Buendía who also married his first cousin.) But in ***Leaf Storm*** this colonel is a kindly old man who originally settled in the village as a refugee from the civil wars and lives there with his second wife, his daughter Isabel by his first wife, and his grandson.

The doctor is a queer one. He wears his belt outside the loops on his pants and his trunk holds two cheap shirts, a set of false teeth obviously not his own, a portrait, a formulary and some old French newspapers. When the colonel's wife hospitably asks what he would like to eat, he says "Grass" and explains "in his parsimonious ruminant voice: 'Ordinary grass, ma'am. The kind that donkeys eat.' "

The doctor earns the colonel's lasting gratitude by curing him of an illness. But later, when violence breaks out in the town and some wounded men are placed outside the doctor's door so that he can tend to them, he refuses even to go out to them on the grounds that he has forgotten medicine. "And he kept the door closed. . . . the anger turned into a collective disease which gave no respite to Macondo for the rest of his life."

The refusal somehow becomes the most important event in the town's history. Although a banana company establishes itself in Macondo and for a number of years excites and disturbs the inhabitants with visions of industrialization and prosperity before it leaves like a "leaf storm," the marvelous thing about the story is not the outward happening but the bond of hatred and silence that exists between the doctor and the town. They mentally, obsessively feed on each other. The kindly colonel, his daughter and grandson, who interweavedly relate the story, reflect in their stolid descriptions and reflections a sense of the ominousness that the doctor has brought to Macondo, and with which he colors all human relationships.

In 1928 the doctor hangs himself from a beam in his house. The colonel is the only person in town who will cut him down and bury him; the town officials try to balk the stranger even in death, refuse a death certificate and defy the colonel to get a coffin, to put the doctor in and to follow him to the cemetary. The Márquez touch: The coffin has to be opened again to put in a single shoe left on the bed. The town official refusing to give permission for burial, goes through the motions of hanging himself to prove that the doctor couldn't *really* have hanged himself. "When he gets to the coffin, he turns on his heels, looks at me, and says: 'I'd have to see him hanging to be convinced.' "

The colonel says: "I would have done it. I would have told my men to open the coffin and put the hanged man back up again the way he was until a minute ago. . . . Even though the act of moving a corpse who's lying peacefully and deservedly in his coffin is against my principles, I'd hang him up again just to see how far this man will go."

At the end the colonel finally gets the coffin out of the house and on its way to the cemetery. The town remains implacable, "lunching on the smell" of the stranger in death. The slow working out of the stranger's unfathomable life finally becomes a type of the strangeness and solitude that Macondo itself represents without knowing it. "By that time the banana company had stopped squeezing us and had left Macondo with the rubbish of the rubbish they'd brought with them. And with them went the leaf storm, the last traces of what prosperous Macondo had been like in 1915. A ruined village was there . . . occupied by unemployed and angry people who were tormented by a prosperous past and the bitterness of an overwhelming and static present." (pp. 1, 14, 16)

Alfred Kazin, in a review of "Leaf Storm, and Other Stories," in The New York Times Book Review, *February 20, 1972, pp. 1, 14, 16.*

Gabriel García Márquez with Peter H. Stone (interview date 1981)

[In the following excerpt from an interview, García Márquez elaborates on his influences and literary techniques.]

[Stone]: *[How] does it feel being a journalist again, after having written novels for so long? Do you do it with a different feel or a different eye?*

[García Márquez]: I've always been convinced that my true profession is that of a journalist. What I didn't like about journalism before were the working conditions. Besides, I had to condition my thoughts and ideas to the interests of the newspaper. Now, after having worked as a novelist, and having achieved financial independence as a novelist, I can really choose the themes that interest me and correspond to my ideas. In any case, I always very much enjoy the chance of doing a great piece of journalism.

What is a great piece of journalism for you?

Hiroshima by John Hersey was an exceptional piece.

Is there a story today that you would especially like to do?

There are many, and several I have in fact written. I have written about Portugal, Cuba, Angola and Vietnam. I would very much like to write on Poland. I think if I could describe exactly what is now going on, it would be a very important story. But it's too cold now in Poland; I'm a journalist who likes his comforts.

Do you think the novel can do certain things that journalism can't?

Nothing. I don't think there is any difference. The sources are the same, the material is the same, the resources and the language are the same. *The Journal of the Plague Year* by Daniel Defoe is a great novel and *Hiroshima* is a great work of journalism.

Do the journalist and the novelist have different responsibilities in balancing truth versus the imagination?

In journalism just one fact that is false prejudices the entire work. In contrast, in fiction one single fact that is true gives legitimacy to the entire work. That's the only difference and it lies in the commitment of the writer. A novelist can do anything he wants so long as he makes people believe in it.

In interviews a few years ago, you seemed to look back on being a journalist with awe at how much faster you were then.

I do find it harder to write now than before, both novels and journalism. When I worked for newspapers, I wasn't very conscious of every word I wrote, whereas now I am. When I was working for *El Espectador* in Bogotá, I used to do at least three stories a week, two or three editorial notes every day, and I did movie reviews. Then at night, after everyone had gone home, I would stay behind writing my novels. I liked the noise of the Linotype machines which sounded like rain. If they stopped, and I was left in silence, I wouldn't be able to work. Now, the output is comparatively small. On a good working day, working from nine o'clock in the morning to two or three in the afternoon, the most I can write is a short paragraph of four or five lines, which I usually tear up the next day.

Does this change come from your works being so highly praised or from some kind of political commitment?

It's from both. I think that the idea that I'm writing for many more people than I ever imagined has created a certain general responsibility that is literary and political. There's even pride involved, in not wanting to fall short of what I did before.

How did you start writing?

By drawing. By drawing cartoons. Before I could read or write I used to draw comics at school and at home. The funny thing is that I now realize that when I was in high school I had the reputation of being a writer though I never in fact wrote anything. If there was a pamphlet to be written or a letter of petition, I was the one to do it because I was supposedly the writer. When I entered college I happened to have a very good literary background in general, considerably above the average of my friends. At the university in Bogotá, I started making new friends and acquaintances, who introduced me to contemporary writers. One night a friend lent me a book of short stories by Franz Kafka. I went back to the pension where I was staying and began to read *The Metamorphosis.* The first line almost knocked me off the bed. I was so surprised. The first line reads, "As Gregor Samsa awoke that morning from uneasy dreams, he found himself transformed in his bed into a gigantic insect. . . . " When I read the line I thought to myself that I didn't know anyone was allowed to write things like that. If I had known, I would have started writing a long time ago. So I immediately started writing short stories. They are totally intellectual short stories because I was writing them on the basis of my literary experience and had not yet found the link between literature and life. The stories were published in the literary supplement of the newspaper *El Espectador* in Bogotá and they did have a certain success at the time—probably because nobody in Colombia was writing intellectual short stories. What was being written then was mostly about life in the countryside and social life. When I wrote my first short stories I was told they had Joycean influences.

Had you read Joyce at that time?

I had never read Joyce, so I started reading *Ulysses.* I read it in the only Spanish edition available. Since then, after having read *Ulysses* in English as well as a very good French translation, I can see that the original Spanish translation was very bad. But I did learn something that was to be very useful to me in my future writing—the technique of the interior monologue. I later found this in Virginia Woolf and I like the way she uses it better than Joyce. Although I later realized that the person who invented this interior monologue was the anonymous writer of the *Lazarillo de Tormes.*

Can you name some of your early influences?

The people who really helped me to get rid of my intellectual attitude towards the short story were the writers of the American Lost Generation. I realized that their literature had a relationship with life that my short stories didn't. And then an event took place which was very important with respect to this attitude. It was the Bogotazo, on the ninth of April, 1948, when a political leader, Gaitan, was shot and the people of Bogotá went raving mad in the streets. I was in my pension ready to have lunch when I heard the news. I ran towards the place, but Gaitan had just been put into a taxi and was being taken to a hospital. On my way back to the pension, the people had already taken to the streets and they were demonstrating, looting stores and burning buildings. I joined them. That afternoon and evening, I became aware of the kind of country I was living in, and how little my short stories had to do with any of that. When I was later forced to go back to Barranquilla on the Caribbean, where I had spent my childhood, I realized that that was the type of life I had lived, knew, and wanted to write about.

Around 1950 or '51 another event happened that influenced my literary tendencies. My mother asked me to accompany her to Aracataca, where I was born, and to sell the house where I spent my first years. When I got there it was at first quite shocking because I was now twenty-two and hadn't been there since the age of eight. Nothing had really changed, but I felt that I wasn't really looking at the village, but I was *experiencing* it as if I were reading it. It was as if everything I saw had already been written, and all I had to do was to sit down and copy what was already there and what I was just reading. For all practical purposes everything had evolved into literature: the houses, the people, and the memories. I'm not sure whether I had already read Faulkner or not, but I know now that only a technique like Faulkner's could have enabled me to write down what I was seeing. The atmosphere, the decadence, the heat in the village were roughly the same as what I had felt in Faulkner. It was a banana plantation region inhabited by a lot of Americans from the fruit companies which gave it the same sort of atmosphere I had found in the writers of the Deep South. Critics have spoken of the literary influence of Faulkner but I see it as a coincidence: I had simply found material that had to be dealt with in the same way that Faulkner had treated similar material.

From that trip to the village I came back to write ***Leaf Storm,*** my first novel. What really happened to me in that trip to Aracataca was that I realized that everything that had occurred in my childhood had a literary value that I was only now appreciating. From the moment I wrote ***Leaf Storm*** I realized I wanted to be a writer and that nobody could stop me and that the only thing left for me to do was to try to be the best writer in the world. That was in 1953, but it wasn't until 1967 that I got my first royalties after having written five of my eight books.

Do you think that it's common for young writers to deny the worth of their own childhoods and experiences and to intellectualize as you did initially?

No, the process usually takes place the other way around, but if I had to give a young writer some advice I would say to write about something that has happened to him; it's always easy to tell whether a writer is writing about something that has happened to him or something he has read or been told. Pablo Neruda has a line in a poem that says "God help me from inventing when I sing." It always amuses me that the biggest praise for my work comes for the imagination while the truth is that there's not a single line in all my work that does not have a basis in reality. The problem is that Caribbean reality resembles the wildest imagination.

Whom were you writing for at this point? Who was your audience?

Leaf Storm was written for my friends who were helping me and lending me their books and were very enthusiastic about my work. In general I think you usually do write for someone. When I'm writing I'm always aware that this friend is going to like this, or that another friend is going to like that paragraph or chapter, always thinking of specific people. In the end all books are written for your friends. The problem after writing *One Hundred Years of Solitude* was that now I no longer know whom of the millions of readers I am writing for; this upsets and inhibits me. It's like a million eyes are looking at you and you don't really know what they think.

What about the influence of journalism on your fiction?

I think the influence is reciprocal. Fiction has helped my journalism because it has given it literary value. Journalism has helped my fiction because it has kept me in a close relationship with reality.

How would you describe the search for a style that you went through after **Leaf Storm** *and before you were able to write* One Hundred Years of Solitude?

After having written ***Leaf Storm,*** I decided that writing about the village and my childhood was really an escape from having to face and write about the political reality of the country. I had the false impression that I was hiding myself behind this kind of nostalgia instead of confronting the political things that were going on. This was the time when the relationship between literature and politics was very much discussed. I kept trying to close the gap between the two. My influence had been Faulkner; now it was Hemingway. I wrote ***No One Writes to the Colonel,*** *The Evil Hour,* and **"Big Mama's Funeral"** which were all written at more or less the same time and have many things in common. These stories take place in a different village from the one in which ***Leaf Storm*** and *One Hundred Years of Solitude* occur. It is a village in which there is no magic. It is a journalistic literature. But when I finished *The Evil Hour,* I saw that all my views were wrong again. I came to see that in fact my writings about my childhood were *more* political and had more to do with the reality of my country than I had thought. After *The Evil Hour* I did not write anything for five years. I had an idea of what I always wanted to do, but there was something missing and I was not sure what it was until one day I discovered the right tone—the tone that I eventually used in *One Hundred Years of Solitude.* It was based on the way my grandmother used to tell her stories. She told things that sounded supernatural and fantastic, but she told them with complete naturalness. When I finally discovered the tone I had to use, I sat down for eighteen months and worked every day.

How did she express the "fantastic" so naturally?

What was most important was the expression she had on her face. She did not change her expression at all when telling her stories and everyone was surprised. In previous attempts to write *One Hundred Years of Solitude,* I tried to tell the story without believing in it. I discovered that what I had to do was believe in them myself and write them with the same expression with which my grandmother told them: with a brick face.

There also seems to be a journalistic quality to that technique or tone. You describe seemingly fantastic events in such minute detail that it gives them their own reality. Is this something you have picked up from journalism?

That's a journalistic trick which you can also apply to literature. For example, if you say that there are elephants flying in the sky, people are not going to believe you. But if you say that there are four hundred and twenty-five elephants in the sky, people will probably believe you. *One Hundred Years of Solitude* is full of that sort of thing. That's exactly the technique my grandmother used. I remember particularly the story about the character who is surrounded by yellow butterflies. When I was very small there was an electrician who came to the house. I became very curious because he carried a belt with which he used to suspend himself from the electrical posts. My grandmother used to say that every time this man came around, he would leave the house full of butterflies. But when I was writing this, I discovered that if I didn't say the butterflies were yellow, people would not believe it. When I was writing the episode of Remedios the Beauty going to heaven it took me a long time to make it credible. One day I went out to the garden and saw a woman who used to come to the house to do the wash and she was putting out the sheets to dry and there was a lot of wind. She was arguing with the wind not to blow the sheets away. I discovered that if I used the sheets for Remedios the Beauty, she would ascend. That's how I did it, to make it credible. The problem for every writer is credibility. Anybody can write anything so long as it's believed. (pp. 48-56)

You often use the theme of the solitude of power.

The more power you have, the harder it is to know who is lying to you and who is not. When you reach absolute power, there is no contact with reality, and that's the worst kind of solitude there can be. A very powerful person, a dictator, is surrounded by interests and people

Cover of the collection containing the English translations of the volume Los funerales de la Mamá Grande *and the novella* El coronel no tiene quien le escriba.

whose final aim is to isolate him from reality; everything is in concert to isolate him.

What about the solitude of the writer? Is this different?

It has a lot to do with the solitude of power. The writer's very attempt to portray reality often leads him to a distorted view of it. In trying to transpose reality he can end up losing contact with it, in an ivory tower, as they say. Journalism is a very good guard against that. That's why I have always tried to keep on doing journalism because it keeps me in contact with the real world, particularly political journalism and politics. The solitude that threatened me after *One Hundred Years of Solitude* wasn't the solitude of the writer; it was the solitude of fame, which resembles the solitude of power much more. My friends defended me from that one, my friends who are always there.

How?

Because I have managed to keep the same friends all my life. I mean I don't break or cut myself off from my old friends and they're the ones who bring me back to earth; they always keep their feet on the ground and they're not famous.

How do things start? One of the recurring images in The Autumn of the Patriarch *is the cows in the palace. Was this one of the original images?*

I've got a photography book that I'm going to show you. I've said on various occasions that in the genesis of all my books there's always an image. The first image I had of *The Autumn of the Patriarch* was a very old man in a very luxurious palace into which cows come and eat the curtains. But that image didn't concretize until I saw the photograph. In Rome I went into a bookshop where I started looking at photography books, which I like to collect. I saw this photograph and it was just perfect. I just saw that was how it was going to be. Since I'm not a big intellectual, I can find my antecedents in everyday things, in life, and not in the great masterpieces.

Do your novels ever take unexpected twists?

That used to happen to me in the beginning. In the first stories I wrote I had a general idea of the mood, but I would let myself be taken by chance. The best advice I was given early on was that it was all right to work that way when I was young because I had a torrent of inspiration. But I was told that if I didn't learn technique, I would be in trouble later on when the inspiration had gone and the technique was needed to compensate. If I hadn't learned that in time, I would not now be able to outline a structure in advance. Structure is a purely technical problem and if you don't learn it early on you'll never learn it.

Discipline then is quite important to you?

I don't think you can write a book that's worth anything without extraordinary discipline.

What about artificial stimulants?

One thing that Hemingway wrote that greatly impressed me was that writing for him was like boxing. He took care of his health and his well-being. Faulkner had a reputation of being a drunkard, but in every interview that he gave me he said that it was impossible to write one line when drunk. Hemingway said this too. Bad readers have asked me if I was drugged when I wrote some of my works. But that illustrates that they don't know anything about literature or drugs. To be a good writer you have to be absolutely lucid at every moment of writing and in good health. I'm very much against the romantic concept of writing which maintains that the act of writing is a sacrifice and that the worse the economic conditions or the emotional state, the better the writing. I think you have to be in a very good emotional and physical state. Literary creation for me requires good health, and the Lost Generation understood this. They were people who loved life.

Blaise Cendrars said that writing is a privilege compared to most work and that writers exaggerate their suffering. What do you think?

I think that writing is very difficult, but so is any job carefully executed. What is a privilege, however, is to do a job to your own satisfaction. I think that I'm excessively demanding of myself and others because I cannot tolerate errors; I think that it is a privilege to do anything to a perfect degree. It is true though that writers are often megalomaniacs and they consider themselves to be the center of the universe and society's conscience. But what I most admire is something well done. I'm always very happy when I'm traveling to know that the pilots are better pilots than I am a writer.

When do you work best now? Do you have a work schedule?

When I became a professional writer the biggest problem I had was my schedule. Being a journalist meant working at night. When I started writing full-time I was forty years old, my schedule was basically from nine o'clock in the morning until two in the afternoon when my sons came back from school. Since I was so used to hard work, I felt guilty that I was only working in the morning; so I tried to work in the afternoons, but I discovered that what I did in the afternoon had to be done over again the next morning. So I decided that I would just work from nine until two-thirty and not do anything else. In the afternoons I have appointments and interviews and anything else that might come up. I have another problem in that I can only work in surroundings that are familiar and have already been warmed up with my work. I cannot write in hotels or borrowed rooms or on borrowed typewriters. This creates problems because when I travel I can't work. Of course, you're always trying to find a pretext to work less. That's why the conditions you impose on yourself are more difficult all the time. You hope for inspiration whatever the circumstances. That's a word the romantics exploited a lot. My Marxist comrades have a lot of difficulty accepting the word, but whatever you call it, I'm convinced that there is a special state of mind in which you can write with great ease and things just flow. All the pretexts—such as the one where you can only write at home—disappear. That moment and that state of mind seem to come when you have found the right theme and the right ways of treating it. And it has to be something you really like too, because there is no worse job than doing something you don't like.

One of the most difficult things is the first paragraph. I have spent many months on a first paragraph and once I get it, the rest just comes out very easily. In the first paragraph you solve most of the problems with your book. The theme is defined, the style, the tone. At least in my case, the first paragraph is a kind of sample of what the rest of the book is going to be. That's why writing a book of short stories is much more difficult than writing a novel. Every time you write a short story, you have to begin all over again.

Are dreams ever important as a source of inspiration?

In the very beginning I paid a good deal of attention to them. But then I realized that life itself is the greatest source of inspiration and that dreams are only a very small part of that torrent that is life. What is very true about my writing is that I'm quite interested in different concepts of dreams and interpretations of them. I see dreams as part of life in general, but reality is much richer. But maybe I just have very poor dreams.

Can you distinguish between inspiration and intuition?

Inspiration is when you find the right theme, one which

you really like; that makes the work much easier. Intuition, which is also fundamental to writing fiction, is a special quality which helps you to decipher what is real without needing scientific knowledge, or any other special kind of learning. The laws of gravity can be figured out much more easily with intuition than anything else. It's a way of having experience without having to struggle through it. For a novelist intuition is essential. Basically it's contrary to intellectualism which is probably the thing that I detest most in the world—in the sense that the real world is turned into a kind of immovable theory. Intuition has the advantage that either it is, or it isn't. You don't struggle to try to put a round peg into a square hole.

Is it the theorists that you dislike?

Exactly. Chiefly because I cannot really understand them. That's mainly why I have to explain most things through anecdotes, because I don't have any capacity for abstractions. That's why many critics say that I'm not a cultured person. I don't quote enough.

Do you think that critics type you or categorize you too neatly?

Critics for me are the biggest example of what intellectualism is. First of all, they have a theory of what a writer should be. They try to get the writer to fit their model and if he doesn't fit they still try to get him in by force. I'm only answering this because you've asked. I really have no interest in what critics think of me; nor have I read critics in many years. They have claimed for themselves the task of being intermediaries between the author and the reader. I've always tried to be a very clear and precise writer trying to reach the reader directly without having to go through the critic.

How do you regard translators?

I have great admiration for translators except for the ones who use footnotes. They are always trying to explain to the reader something which the author probably did not mean; since it's there the reader has to put up with it. Translating is a very difficult job, not at all rewarding, and very badly paid. A good translation is always a recreation in another language. That's why I have such great admiration for Gregory Rabassa. My books have been translated into twenty-one languages and Rabassa is the only translator who has never asked for something to be clarified so he can put a footnote in. I think that my work has been completely recreated in English. There are parts of the book which are very difficult to follow literally. The impression one gets is that the translator read the book and then rewrote it from his recollections. That's why I have such admiration for translators. They are intuitive rather than intellectual. Not only is what publishers pay them completely miserable, but they don't see their work as literary creation. There are some books I would have liked to translate into Spanish, but they would have involved as much work as writing my own books and I wouldn't have made enough money to eat.

What would you have liked to translate?

All Malraux. I would have liked to translate Conrad, and Saint Exupéry. When I'm reading I sometimes get the feeling that I would like to translate this book. Excluding the great masterpieces, I prefer reading a mediocre translation of a book than trying to get through it in the original language. I never feel comfortable reading in another language, because the only language I really feel inside is Spanish. However, I speak Italian and French, and I know English well enough to have poisoned myself with *Time* magazine every week for twenty years.

Does Mexico seem like home to you now? Do you feel part of any larger community of writers?

In general, I'm not a friend of writers or artists just because they are writers or artists. I have many friends of different professions, amongst them writers and artists. In general terms, I feel that I'm a native of any country in Latin America but not elsewhere. Latin Americans feel that Spain is the only country in which we are treated well, but I personally don't feel as though I'm from there. In Latin America I don't have a sense of frontiers or borders. I'm conscious of the differences that exist from one country to another, but in my mind and heart it is all the same. Where I really feel at home is the Caribbean, whether it is the French, Dutch, or English Caribbean. I was always impressed that when I got on a plane in Barranquilla, a black lady with a blue dress would stamp my passport, and when I got off the plane in Jamaica, a black lady with a blue dress would stamp my passport, but in English. I don't believe that the language makes all that much difference. But anywhere else in the world, I feel like a foreigner, a feeling that robs me of a sense of security. It's a personal feeling, but I always have it when I travel. I have a minority conscience.

Do you think that it's an important thing for Latin American writers to live in Europe for awhile?

Perhaps to have a real perspective from outside. The book of short stories I'm thinking of writing is about Latin Americans going to Europe. I've been thinking about it for twenty years. If you could draw a final conclusion out of these short stories it would be that Latin Americans hardly ever get to Europe, especially Mexicans, and certainly not to stay. All the Mexicans I've ever met in Europe always leave the following Wednesday.

What effects do you think the Cuban Revolution has had on Latin American literature?

Up until now it has been negative. Many writers who think of themselves as being politically committed feel obligated to write stories not about what they want, but about what they think they should want. That makes for a certain type of calculated literature that doesn't have anything to do with experience or intuition. The main reason for this is that the cultural influence of Cuba on Latin America has been very much fought against. In Cuba itself, the process hasn't developed to the point where a new type of literature or art has been created. That is something that needs time. The great cultural importance of Cuba in Latin America has been to serve as a kind of bridge to transmit a type of literature which had existed in Latin America for many years. In a sense, the boom in Latin American literature in the United States has been caused by the Cuban Revolution. Every Latin American writer of that generation had been writing for twenty years but the European and American publishers had very little interest in them. When the Cuban Revolution started there was suddenly a great interest about Cuba and Latin America. The revolution turned into an article of consumption. Latin America came into fashion. It was discovered that Latin American novels existed which were good enough to be translated and considered with all other world literature. What was really sad is that cultural colonialism is so bad in Latin America that it was impossible to convince the Latin Americans themselves that their own novels were good until people outside *told* them they were.

Are there some lesser-known Latin American writers you especially admire?

I doubt there are any now. One of the best side effects of the boom in Latin American writing is that publishers are always on the lookout to make sure that they're not going to miss the new Cortázar. Unfortunately many young writers are more concerned with fame than with their own work. There's a French professor at the University of Toulouse who writes about Latin American literature; many young authors wrote to him telling him not to write so much about me because I didn't need it anymore and other people did. But what they forget is that when I was their age the critics weren't writing about me, but rather about Miguel Angel Asturias. The point I'm trying to make is that these young writers are wasting their time writing to critics rather than working on their own writing. It's much more important to write than to be written about. One thing that I think was very important about my literary career was that until I was forty years old, I never got one cent of author's royalties though I'd had five books published.

Do you think that fame or success coming too early in a writer's career is bad?

At any age it's bad. As I said before I would have liked for my books to have been recognized posthumously, at least in capitalist countries where you turn into a kind of merchandise.

Aside from your favorites, what do you read today?

I read the weirdest things. I was reading Muhammad Ali's memoirs the other day. Bram Stoker's *Dracula* is a great book and one I probably would not have read many years ago because I would have thought it was a waste of time. But I never really get involved with a book unless it's recommended by somebody I trust. I don't read any more fiction. I read many memoirs and documents, even if they are forged documents. And I reread my favorites. The advantage of rereading is that you can open at any page and read the part that you really like. I've lost this sacred notion of reading only "literature." I will read anything. I try to keep up to date. I read almost all the really important magazines from all over the world every week. I've always been on the lookout for news since the habit of reading the teletype machines. But after I've read all the serious and important newspapers from all over, my wife always comes around and tells me of news I hadn't heard. When I ask her where she read it, she will say that she read it in a magazine at the beauty parlor. So I read fashion magazines and all kinds of magazines for women and gossip magazines. And I learn many things that I could only learn from reading them. That keeps me very busy.

Why do you think fame is so destructive for a writer?

Primarily because it invades your private life. It takes away from the time that you spend with friends, and the time that you can work. It tends to isolate you from the real world. A famous writer who wants to continue writing has to be constantly defending himself against fame. I don't really like to say this because it never sounds sincere, but I would really have liked for my books to have been published after my death, so I wouldn't have to go through all this business of fame and being a great writer. In my case, the only advantage in fame is that I have been able to give it a political use. Otherwise, it is quite uncomfortable. The problem is that you're famous for twenty-four hours a day and you can't say, "Okay, I won't be famous until tomorrow" or press a button and say, "I won't be famous here or now." (pp. 60-70)

Do you have any long-range ambitions or regrets as a writer?

I think my answer is the same as the one I gave you about fame. I was asked the other day if I would be interested in the Nobel Prize, but I think that for me it would be an absolute catastrophe. I would certainly be interested in deserving it, but to receive it would be terrible. It would just complicate even more the problems of fame. The only thing I really regret in life is not having a daughter.

Are there any projects now underway you can discuss?

I'm absolutely convinced that I'm going to write the greatest book of my life, but I don't know which one it will be or when. When I feel something like this—which I have been feeling now for awhile—I stay very quiet so that if it passes by I can capture it. (p. 73)

Gabriel García Márquez and Peter H. Stone, in an interview in The Paris Review, *Vol. 23, No. 82, Winter, 1981, pp. 44-73.*

Regina Janes (essay date 1981)

[*Janes is an American critic, educator, and historian with special interests in the cultures of eighteenth-century England and India, and of twentieth-century Latin America. In the following excerpt from her* Gabriel García Márquez: Revolutions in Wonderland, *she discusses the narrative style of the works collected in* Innocent Eréndira, and Other Stories, *relating them to García Márquez's literary development following the 1967 publication of* One Hundred Years of Solitude.]

When he finished *One Hundred Years of Solitude*, García Márquez knew what his next novel would be. In 1968 he was learning how to construct an electric chair for the use of a character in that novel. In 1969 he had read so many histories and anecdotes of despots that he had to forget them all in order to write his own story of the solitude of the dictator. Originally, the novel was to take the form of the dictator's monologue before a tribunal of the people at the end of a reign of three hundred years in which, among other excesses, the dictator had served up his roasted minister of defense on a silver platter, in uniform and decoration, to ambassadors and bishops assembled for a gala banquet. Obviously, García Márquez made some changes, but he also knew from the beginning that the style of the work had to be different from that of *One Hundred Years of Solitude* and that it would be a denser and more difficult style. At one point, he joked that it would be in the style of Robbe-Grillet so that no one could understand it and he could be sure that it was a good novel.

Between the novels, he published two volumes of early reportage, *When I Was Happy and Undocumented* (1974) and *The Story of a Castaway Who Was Ten Days Adrift on a Raft without Food or Drink, Who Was Proclaimed a Hero of the Nation, Kissed by Beauty Queens, Enriched by Publicity, and then Abhorred by the Government and Forgotten Forever* (1970), and a volume of seven short stories, ***The Incredible and Sad Story of Innocent Eréndira and Her Heartless Grandmother*** (1972), that included, in addition to the title story (1972), the earlier **"Sea of Lost Time"** (1962), **"A Very Old Man with Enormous Wings"** (1968), **"The Handsomest Drowned Man in the World"** (1968), **"Death Constant beyond Love"** (1970), **"The Last Voyage of the Ghost Ship"** (1968), and **"Blacamán the Good, Vendor of Miracles"** (1968). It was an elegant volume, and it makes quite clear that García Márquez was writing himself out of the style of *One Hundred Years of Solitude* and into that of *The Autumn of the Patriarch* in 1968, while the two later stories seem to be something of a vacation from the intricacies of the dictator. Though the stories are very different from one another, they possess a common motif that suggests the discomfort of a suddenly fashionable author or "escritor de moda," as he styled himself in the preface to *The Story of a Castaway:* all treat an often uncomfortable relationship to crowds and focus on public figures, some of whom would rather not be public figures, though others seek it. Except for **"Death Constant beyond Love,"** they also share a determined resistance to interpretation. In most cases, the dynamics of the plotting suggest certain thematic possibilities, but, written in a wholly symbolic mode, the stories are devised to repel the impertinence of any interpretations imposed upon them through the intransigence of the irreducible, impenetrable events or images at the center. While a great deal may be said about these stories, they have been designed to escape the critic's web of exegesis.

The same is true of *One Hundred Years of Solitude,* of course; the sense we make of it is as much an artifact as the thing itself. But because it juxtaposes its incomprehensible premises (why incest?) with comprehensible lives, we read past the impenetrable episode to which we cannot assign meaning, content with those to which we can, trusting that someday, like the theory of relativity, it will make sense and we will be able to understand it as well as talk about it, quote it, and use it for analogies. The difficulty is more obvious in the shorter forms, which, being shorter, do not provide as many escape hatches from the absurd impossibility of the invention at their center: an old man with wings, a ghost ship that materializes, a beautiful drowned man, an immortal huckster, a heartless grandmother with green blood. In **"A Very Old Man with Enormous Wings"** and **"The Last Voyage of the Ghost Ship,"** an impossible event is made real; in ***Innocent Eréndira*** and **"Death Constant beyond Love,"** a possible event is made strange; and **"The Handsomest Drowned Man in the World"** and **"Blacamán the Good, Vendor of Miracles"** work both sides of the street. All of them deal with exploitation, credulity, and the force of illusion along the Atlantic litoral in the dry, dusty towns of the Guajira peninsula or in a city that combines the chained bay and slave port of Cartagena with the rotating light of Santa Marta. There are cross-references among the stories, images and characters that go back to *One Hundred Years of Solitude* and beyond it into the earliest fictions, devices the magpie author uses to suggest the integration of his fragmented world and to enhance the reflective power of the rhetorical surface by creating recognitions for the reader within the universe of the text.

In **"A Very Old Man with Enormous Wings"** and **"The Handsomest Drowned Man in the World,"** both subtitled "A Tale for Children," García Márquez wrote out the stylistic vein of *One Hundred Years of Solitude;* in **"Blacamán the Good, Vendor of Miracles"** and **"The Last Voyage of the Ghost Ship,"** he tried on parts of the style of *The Autumn of the Patriarch.* **"Death Constant beyond Love"** and ***Innocent Eréndira,*** while more similar to the stories in the style of *One Hundred Years of Solitude* than to those in the later style, seem to be moving in yet another direction and may augur the mode of the novel García Márquez has written and thus far refused to publish while Gen. Augusto Pinochet is still in power, ***Chronicle of an Expected Death.***

The most conspicuous of the stylistic innovations is in the management of the sentence and the paragraph. **"The Last Voyage of the Ghost Ship"** is a single sentence; **"Blacamán the Good, Vendor of Miracles"** is divided into seven paragraphs, but one-third of its sentences run over ten lines of text, and interminable as the paragraphs of *One Hundred Years of Solitude* often seem, there are more of them per page of text than in **"Blacamán,"** while sentences that run over ten lines of text are rare. The principal exception is Fernanda's monologue, a two-and-a-half-page sentence. The page-paragraph ratio in **"A Very Old Man with Enormous Wings"** and **"The Handsomest Drowned Man in the World"** is the same as in the novel, while **"Death Constant beyond Love"** and ***Innocent Eréndira*** go back to the shorter, more frequent paragraphs of the fictions prior to *One Hundred Years of Solitude* by the simple expedient of reintroducing and marking dialogue.

As the precedent in Fernanda's monologue indicates, one purpose of the inordinate sentence is to imitate the sound of a single voice. The method looks introspective, but is not. It is rhetorical, a representation of how the character consciously sees himself and represents himself to others. The character's self-presentation may betray him, as Fernanda's and Blacamán's do, but such betrayal follows from the character's ignorance of the implications of what he says or seems to think. The excessive sentence has other uses: to recall what someone else said in the past, imitating that voice; to represent an imagined interaction; to represent an interaction and dialogue taking place in the present. Only the first of these is present in Fernanda's monologue, which quotes other members of the family at some length and asks a question no one ever asked her, "Good morning, Fernanda, did you sleep well?" Since the question was never asked and no response is given, this does not constitute a full interaction, but it is as close an approach to one as occurs in the speech. Further, Fernanda quotes what others have said about her; in the later uses, the speaker will quote what others have said in his presence but not necessarily directly to or about him. Of course, all these quotations, interactions, and dialogues erupt in the sentence without quotation marks or other indicators (the sections italicized in the translation of **"The Handsomest Drowned Man in the World"** are not italicized in the original). And the obvious question is what purpose their presence serves.

Specific purposes vary from context to context, but the general object of the device is to create a sense of some immediate action while reducing the number of characters on stage or eliminating the individuality of characters to make them representative of a community. **"Blacamán the Good, Vendor of Miracles"** reduces us to two very similar characters, Blacamán the Good and Blacamán the Bad, though multitudes of others rush past or cluster about, and only Blacamán the Good speaks, telling his story in the first person. **"The Last Voyage of the Ghost Ship"** reduces us to a single nameless character whose story is related by an omniscient narrator and who interacts only with the ghost ship, his mother, a boatman, and the townspeople who beat him up. **"The Handsomest Drowned Man in the World"** reduces the named characters to one, Esteban, the drowned man, and uses an omniscient narrator who adopts the perspectives of the people of the village in order to render a divided, but finally communal, imagination, shifting from the children, to the men, the women, the young women, and the oldest woman to unite them finally, men and women, in a common awakening to "the narrowness of their dreams" and a common resolve to make everything "different from then on." The effect is to keep us locked inside the consciousness of a single character or community and to vary the rhetorical surface without allowing any other characters to assume an independent existence, separate from the all-embracing, all-consuming perspective adopted within the narrative.

The method communicates a very peculiar and particular obsessiveness, well illustrated in the difference between these stories and **"A Very Old Man with Enormous Wings,"** written with the omniscient narrator, sentential management, and structural arrangement of *One Hundred Years of Solitude.* In that story, as in **"The Handsomest Drowned Man in the World,"** an odd personage occupies the central place, a very old man with enormous wings who may be either a fallen angel or merely a winged Norwegian and who is just as unlikely and physically impossible as a beautiful drowned man. But both his fate and his relationship to other characters are very different from those in the later stories. Discovered in his backyard by Pelayo (who had been throwing into the sea Tobías's crabs from **"The Sea of Lost Time"**), he is first wondered at by Pelayo and Elisenda, his wife, who "interpret" him as a castaway by skipping over "the inconvenience of the wings"; he is next identified as an angel by the wise old neighbor woman resembling the aunt of García Márquez who, as town consultant on mysteries, at once identified an oddly shaped hen's egg brought for her inspection as a basilisk's egg and ordered it burned. (The wise old woman recommends clubbing the angel to death.) The angel is gawked at, investigated by the church with proper suspicion, made a carnival attraction, tormented by the curious who flock to see him, and then loses his celebrity to a woman turned into a spider, but not before he has enriched Elisenda and Pelayo, in whose house he stays, an intolerable inconvenience and a companion to their child, until he finally grows back his feathers and flies away. The story's splendor is the implicit contrast between what we expect angels to be like and what this one is, with his strong sailor's voice, his unbearable smell, parasite-infested wings, diet of eggplant mush, and clumsy first attempts at flight: this is an angel as buzzard.

Some of the changes worked in García Márquez's language by *One Hundred Years of Solitude* are evident in the differences between the opening of this story and that of **"The Sea of Lost Time."** The first paragraph of **"The Sea of Lost Time"** takes us from January when "the sea was growing harsh [and] beginning to dump its heavy garbage on the town" to the year when Mr. Herbert came and, instead of changing for the worse, the sea "grew smoother and more phosphorescent" and finally gave off "a fragrance of roses." That beautiful oddity ends the paragraph. In **"A Very Old Man with Enormous Wings,"** the first sentence makes a temporal loop like that which begins the novel, moving from the third day of rain to Pelayo's throwing the crabs in the sea, back to the night before and the newborn child's temperature, attributed to the stench. As should be evident, that sentence packs in several relationships, several times, and the thoughts as well as the actions of the characters. The phosphorescence and the garbage of the sea have been transferred to the sands of the beach, which "glimmered like powdered light" and "had become a stew of mud and rotten shellfish." The images are more specific. And the paragraph ends not with a beautiful but with a comic, paradoxical oddity, a very old man who could not get up, "impeded by his enormous wings." Other stylistic affinities with *One Hundred Years of Solitude* appear in hyperbole that causes a contradiction, the old man's wings are "forever entangled in the mud"; in absurd lists, the letters the priest receives from Rome, the ailments of those who seek cures from the angel, the ridiculous miracles he does perform; the quick movement between objective description and analysis and commentary by the narrator; the long period of time covered but only tentatively sketched by the story, from the recent birth of the child until sometime after he begins school; the finality and release of the conclusion, the angel came, and the angel went, without causation.

The difference between this story and the others from 1968 is that here, although the angel is central and every event bears on him, on his appearance, behavior, identity, fate, or effects, our attention to the angel is frequently interrupted by shifts of focus to other characters, sometimes named, often described at length, and by the obtrusiveness of the narrator, who is both at one with and apart from the characters in the story, like the narrator of *One Hundred Years of Solitude.* When Father Gonzaga enters, for example, we are treated to his suspicions of the angel, his observations upon him, his sermon to the gathered townspeople, and his promise to seek advice from higher authorities. A few pages later, there appears a synopsis of his correspondence about the angel, and in another few pages, the waning of the angel's popularity cures Father Gonzaga of his insomnia, and he disappears from the narrative. The full history of the woman who was turned into a spider for having disobeyed her parents constitutes another episode and provides a similar distraction, as does the imaginative excess of the ailments suffered by those who seek the angel's help and the cures he provides, the blind man who stayed blind but grew three new teeth, the leper whose sores sprouted sunflowers, the paralytic who did not recover the use of his limbs but almost won the lottery. Such details call attention to themselves, rather than to their cause, and the difference from García Márquez's management of hyperbole in **"The Handsomest Drowned Man in the World"** is instructive.

If episodic structure and narrative commentary distract us from the angel, everything in the other story keeps us focused on the drowned man. Even the inevitable description of the village, delayed until the third paragraph, is contained within a paragraph that begins and ends with how the villagers determined that the drowned man was a stranger. The sea itself, with which the story as inevitably begins, is no more than that through which the drowned man floats to shore, mistaken by the children first for an enemy ship, then for a whale. The drowned man is remarkable for his size to the children and for his weight to the men who carry him to the nearest house and hypothesize that it was perhaps in the nature of some drowned men to "keep on growing after death," like the boy in **"The Third Resignation."** Only when the women have removed the mud and scraped off the remora with fish scalers is his beauty discovered in a series of superlatives that link inextricably the appearance of the drowned man and the minds of those who observe him: "Not only was he the tallest, strongest, most virile, and best built man they had ever seen, but even though they were looking at him there was no room for him in their imagination." The superlatives continue, but they are very simple superlatives: the shoes of the man with the biggest feet will not fit, nor will the pants of the tallest man, nor the shirts of the fattest. The author's hold on Esteban is so secure that the reader scarcely notices the oddity of Esteban's exchange with the lady of the house as he declines to accept the chair that she is terrified he will break. This exchange takes place only in the imagination of the women sitting around him and is part of the transformation of their awe and passion into pity. Humanized, first by being named and then by speaking, Esteban becomes more immediate, more present, both to the women and to us. But why not use quotation marks? Partly because it is not necessary to use them, partly because García Márquez was practicing getting along without them, and partly because they would be disruptive. The sudden dialogue in the middle of a sentence or paragraph is an extension of that technique of *One Hundred Years of Solitude* in which, in the middle of a long paragraph, some properly identified person says something in properly punctuated speech. Here the characters are nameless save for Esteban and are divided into "the men" and "the women." As a result, a shift into unmarked speech can be assigned without difficulty or hesitation to the appropriate group. The two short sentences in quotation marks and separate paragraphs, "He has the face of someone named Esteban" and ' "Praise the Lord,' they sighed. 'He's ours,' " obviously merit the attention that separation secures for them.

More than **"A Very Old Man with Enormous Wings,"** which chronicles the cruelty of simple folk in their treatment of any out-of-the-way creature, **"The Handsomest Drowned Man in the World"** seems an optimistic tale for children in the new solidarity the drowned man creates among the villagers and the new determination for the future he bequeaths them, though it is elaborated only in fantasy. It makes the impossible real, in the figure of an oversize, beautiful drowned man, and it makes the possible strange, in an event that so galvanizes a community as to transform it forever. But it is the only fiction by García Márquez that is turned inside out by a later work. The later work is, of course, *The Autumn of the Patriarch.* Like Esteban, the patriarch has the huge size of a drowned man, must be scaled of underwater creatures to be readied for burial, and was too large, according to the history books, to get through doors. All his children were premature, "seven-monthers," and Esteban's too-small pants are those of a "seven-monther"; (the translation has "undersized child"; [translator Gregory] Rabassa had not seen the unfinished novel). Finally, devastatingly, as we are told that memories of Esteban will, so the belief in the patriarch has held his nation together for generations. If the flashes forward were not enough, there are unsettling recollections of ***Big Mama's Funeral*** in "the most splendid funeral they could conceive of" for their drowned man and the heartwarming assignment of relatives to Esteban "so that through him all the inhabitants of the village became kinsmen." The story should probably still be read as optimistic and therefore a tale for children, its hopefulness tempered even in its own conclusion by the extravagance of the villagers' fantasy that the scent of their rose gardens on the high seas will bring the captains of great ocean liners down from the bridge to point out to the insistent passengers in fourteen languages "over there, where the sun's so bright that the sunflowers don't know which way to turn, yes, over there, that's Esteban's village." But the parallels suggest García Márquez's awareness of the ambiguity of the power of illusion.

If we had any doubts about his awareness of that ambiguity, **"Blacamán the Good, Vendor of Miracles"** would dispel them. Blacamán is a species, though he has a very particular history, and his division into Blacamán the Good and Blacamán the Bad, realizing the potential relationship between Esteban and the patriarch, is, the story suggests, a trick of rhetoric. Reappearing in ***Innocent Eréndira*** playing Blacamán the Bad's opening trick of asking for a serpent in order to test his antidote on himself, Blacamán finally becomes a legend in **"Death Constant beyond Love,"** as Laura Farina's father sighs of Senator Onésimo

Sánchez (who of course figured in ***Innocent Eréndira***), "C'est le Blacamén de la politique." But Blacamán had already become a legend in his own story.

For Blacamán, Good or Bad, is the immortal huckster, the con man who never dies. If Blacamán the Good possesses the impossible ability to resurrect the dead and to live forever, he uses it only to keep Blacamán the Bad alive in his tomb "as long as I'm alive, that is, forever." And his greatest con may be persuading the reader to believe that he is Blacamán the *Good.* When the story opens, the unnamed speaker is describing seeing "him" for the first time. Not until the third of the interminable paragraphs does the speaker name Blacamán, whom he qualifies as Blacamán the Bad, while he himself is Blacamán the Good. Playing on our sympathies and perhaps our memory of the first and second Adams, the second Blacamán persuades us that he deserves to be called "the Good" because of his sufferings and his miraculous powers, gained through suffering. The two Blacamáns have separate histories, but both histories have political overtones, and both seem to be cyclic. Blacamán the Bad deceived the marines and gave the viceroys he embalmed a look of such authority as to enable them to continue ruling after their deaths; Blacamán the Good puts his audiences to sleep "with the techniques of a congressman" and blithely remakes history with the inscription on Blacamán the Bad's tombstone. While the story ends with Blacamán the Good at his apogee, he has related both Blacamán the Bad's fall and his earlier prosperity, while his own reappearance in ***Innocent Eréndira*** suggests that by then he too may have fallen on evil times.

A simple tale of the turning of fortune's wheel, the rhetoric is the richest since ***Big Mama's Funeral*** and for the same reason: to erect a barrier of words between the protagonist and the reader, to achieve distance through stylization. In the opening sentence, the details of the still nameless Blacamán the Bad's dress are so thoroughly specified that he almost disappears: "From the first Sunday I saw him he reminded me of a bullring mule, with his white suspenders that were backstitched with gold thread, his rings with colored stones on every finger, and his braids of jingle bells, standing on a table by the docks of Santa Maria del Darien in the middle of the flasks of specifics and herbs of consolation." When at the end of that sentence, we suddenly hear Blacamán's voice, the voice is not a personal one, but the eternal voice of the sideshow barker. The sort of detail that distracts us briefly from the angel in **"A Very Old Man with Enormous Wings"** is deployed here throughout; sometimes the details seem altogether meaningless. Why should Blacamán the Bad smuggle Blacamán the Good "disguised as a Japanese"? Sometimes they are disquietingly meaningful, as in the description of the Blacamáns' flight:

> the more lost we became, the clearer the news reached us that the marines had invaded the country under the pretext of exterminating yellow fever and were going about beheading every inveterate or eventual potter they found in their path, and not only the natives, out of precaution, but also the Chinese, for distraction, the Negroes, from habit, and the Hindus, because they were snake charmers.

Before the sentence ends, it has incorporated economic exploitation and an allusion to Carpentier's *Kingdom of This World* in the gringos' belief that the natives of the Caribbean have the power to change form. Such details shift us, in the very act of reading, from the text to the world outside the text, the fundamental act of satire.

"The Last Voyage of the Ghost Ship," apart from the management of its sentence, is much simpler rhetorically and, to my mind, altogether impenetrable. From the speaker's opening "Now they'll see who I am," the story unfolds the town's disbelief in the ghost ship that the boy sees on March nights and that at first he himself thought was an illusion, though years of watching it destroy itself on the shoals have now emboldened him to say "Now they'll see who I am," as he saves the ship from its customary destruction and guides it into the town, running it aground in front of the church where he has the pleasure of watching the townspeople contemplate openmouthed the largest ocean liner in the world, with its name *Halalcsillag* engraved in iron letters and the waters of the sea of death dripping down its side. With a little guidance, anyone can tell stories in a sentence, but the tale's real achievement is its evasion of interpretation by presenting so many possibilities and denying any evidence that binds the story to one. The allegorical structure is the human power to make real and visible to others what was at first only a private vision, discounted and ridiculed. And it applies equally well to art, politics, religion, science, and any human endeavor that originates in an individual and ends by making a difference to others. While such endeavors may begin in the individual's desire for identity and recognition and even in hostility and rage, they end by making something independent of the person in whom they originate, who may take pleasure in the effect and materiality of what he has made, but who is finally irrelevant to it, which finds its existence in the effect it has on others and which is finally only itself. In other fictions of this period, **"Death Constant beyond Love"** and **"The Handsomest Drowned Man in the World,"** ocean liners have figured as emblems of power, prosperity, and freedom that pass and do not enter those dismal villages, but shed a little radiance as they go; and this liner is evidently Scandinavian, like the Norwegian with wings. But if it is easy and appealing to make the boy an artist and his ship a book, it is just as easy to make him a politician and his ship a revolution. So perhaps it is best to leave them as a boy and a ship.

Why is the story told in a single sentence that is not for a moment either awkward or unclear? Apart from the desire to experiment for the patriarch's sake, the single sentence suggests the unity of the boy's obsession, from its casual origin when he himself is skeptical of the ship's existence, through the bitter single-mindedness he develops when others resist belief and beat him for his, to the astonishment and vindication he feels when a mystery snuffs out the harbor buoys and he is able to guide, control, and present the ship to the town. That a mystery snuffs out the buoys, giving the boy power over the ship, seems to be an acknowledgment of the mysterious sources of human creative power. We can point to the biographical origins and see the results, but we have no idea how it was done, even if the achievement is our own. Pointing out that **"The Last Voyage of the Ghost Ship"** originates in a simile at the end of ***Leaf Storm,*** "the coffin is floating in the light as if they were carrying off a dead ship to be buried" affords no explanation at all of the art of García Márquez.

In **"Death Constant beyond Love"** and ***The Incredible and Sad Story of Innocent Eréndira and Her Heartless Grandmother,*** García Márquez's manner makes another revolution, combining some ingredients from the mode of the fictions prior to *One Hundred Years of Solitude,* folding in certain of the later rhetorical practices, and baking them in a moderate oven with even heat to serve up something else again. **"Death Constant beyond Love"** is a very short story, ***Innocent Eréndira*** a very long one, and though they share certain characteristics, they are very different with respect to purpose and degree of realism. **"Death Constant beyond Love,"** for the first time in a long time, tells the realistic story of a man in a stressful, but thoroughly recognizable situation. ***Innocent Eréndira*** is in large part a political allegory, as the other is not, that makes strange and therefore endurable the too-possible predicament of the heroine, prostituted by her grandmother. The stories share, however, a new spaciousness, a movement away from the compression of *One Hundred Years of Solitude* and the later stories, effected by a minute, slow development of relationships among characters, articulated through dialogue, properly punctuated and paragraphed. This attention to the interaction of characters is closer to the earlier fictions than to the later and is accompanied by a reduction in the rapidity with which episodes succeed one another and by a reduction in the seeming independence of episodes or phrases from the rest of the rhetorical surface. At the same time, García Márquez does not abandon his smuggler's tricks but uses his characteristic imagery, paradoxes, and ironies to create complex characters who are neither purely victims nor merely objects of satire. Eréndira's grandmother pushes hard against this generalization, but I will argue that it holds. Resembling in their complexity the characters of *One Hundred Years of Solitude,* these characters are no longer divided from the reader by the multiplication of episode but are instead clearly visible in their frailty and their final responsibility for what becomes of them. In the middle of weaving the patriarch's tapestry of illusions of reality, García Márquez seems to be turning the web over to the side of show where life is "arduous and ephemeral" and love is "contaminated by the seeds of death."

Although it is not a political allegory, **"Death Constant beyond Love"** contains a significant political component through its protagonist, Senator Onésimo Sánchez, a hardworking, corrupt senator on his quadrennial campaign tour through the desert towns of his district. The story begins, as García Márquez's stories often do when he is about to unravel the self-serving illusions of politics, with a paragraph that summarizes the action in advance. To its representation of that common syndrome of the happily married, forty-two-year-old man terrified of time, finding a new intensity through an illicit and temporally circumscribed passion for a much younger woman, the author adds a literal death sentence: the senator has been told by his doctors that he will die in six months, and the senator has told no one. Now more than ever a disbeliever in the illusions he purveys, the senator not only accepts the eternal absence of the cardboard vision of progress, brick houses and an ocean liner moving past, that his men set up to provide a climax to his speech of promises, but he also recognizes that his own continued political existence depends on the absence of that progress and the continued collaboration between him and those in the town who live off the poverty of the rest. The certainty of death provides a final disillusionment, and the usually chaste senator accepts the offer of Laura Farina's favors in exchange for a favor to her father that he has been refusing for years. But it is only a shift of illusions. Death is more constant than love, and while Blacamán the Bad may have succeeded in deceiving death by feigning lovesickness, the senator cannot.

One Hundred Years of Solitude can be accused of sentimentalizing "love" in that harping on the absence of love implies that its presence would change things in an important way. Since the characters in the novel embrace most of the forms love takes among human beings, but the narrator tells us that only the child with a pig's tail is engendered in love, to associate with solitude all the other shapes that loves takes seems naive and sentimental. Fortunately for the novel, the author is a little sentimental but not naive: the only passion he grants the name of love issues in the child that ends the line, eaten by ants. So much for the ability of love to change the world: it does, but not in the way we might desire. For the senator, facing death, love is doubtless more comforting than his politics, as the physical position he adopts indicates, curled up like a child, his head on Laura Farina's shoulder, his face in her armpit. He is never represented making love to her, though it is pleasant to observe that the author's sexual technique has improved since *One Hundred Years of Solitude:* no longer merely explosive or playful, it has become slow, luxurious, and gentle.

Stylistically, the slowing of García Márquez's pace emerges in the paradoxes articulated by the narrator in the first paragraph (between the appearance of the town and the possibility of it containing someone able to change another's life, between the name of the town, its roselessness, and the rose the senator wears) and in his management in the second paragraph of a typical burlesque list. The usual elements are there, but separated by "real" time they no longer come at us pell-mell:

> The carnival wagons had arrived in the morning. Then came the trucks with the rented Indians who were carried into the towns in order to enlarge the crowds at public ceremonies. A short time before eleven o'clock, along with the music and rockets and jeeps of the retinue, the ministerial automobile, the color of strawberry soda, arrived.

Because this story is about politics, love, and venality, there are three kinds of flying creatures in it: the paper birds released during the campaign speech that fly out to sea; the paper butterfly the senator makes while talking to the town leaders and tosses into the fan's air current, which carries it out of the room and flattens it against the wall in the next room where Laura Farina, failing to scrape it off, is told by a drowsy guard that it is painted on the wall; and, after the town leaders have left, the thousands of banknotes flapping in the air when Laura Farina walks into the senator's room, to be told as he turns off the fan, " 'You see,' he said, smiling, 'even shit can fly'." Widely spaced, these parallel actions possess different symbolic implications appropriate to their different degrees of possibility and instance the use of the hyperbolic and the impossible in a realistic context that is stretched but not violated by them.

Stylistically, in its disposition of individual elements, ***Innocent Eréndira*** resembles **"Death Constant beyond Love,"** but it differs in its selection of elements and in their relation to verisimilitude. The story of ***Innocent Eréndira*** is tabloid stuff: girl prostituted by grandmother conspires to murder grandmother. Girl escapes, the lover she persuaded to carry out the murder is taken into custody. From the first appearance of a nameless, ungrandmothered Eréndira in **"The Sea of Lost Time"** to the story's elaboration of a two-page incident in *One Hundred Years of Solitude,* however, it is clear that García Márquez is interested in forced prostitution as a metaphor for economic exploitation, foreign or domestic, but more often foreign. Like economic exploitation, prostitution, even when forced, cannot occur without the acquiescence of the victim whom it corrupts by offering only an uneasy choice between poverty and dishonor. As in **"The Last Voyage of the Ghost Ship,"** Innocent Eréndira's prostitution works more as metaphor than as allegory since its conclusion offers too many possible readings to make an altogether successful allegory. The allegorist may decide that Eréndira's murder of her grandmother and flight with the gold represent nationalization, the return to the people of the profits of their oppression; or he may decide that murder and flight represent nationalization through the revolution, a necessary violence if the profits are to be returned to the people, but what is he to do with the disappearance of the people, never to be heard of again? Or the separation of the people from their revolutionary instrument, Ulises, whom they abandon? The committed allegorist will manage somehow, but it seems more sensible to regard the story as Eréndira's, whose history touches intermittently but not continuously another level of meaning.

Eréndira's history charts a course from pure passivity to her family tyrant, through resistance forcibly overcome by the first man to whom she is sold, rescue by the church that gives her a momentary happiness, lost when she is restored by her habit of obedience to her grandmother and followed by a mounting hatred for the old woman that issues in a failed attempt to elope with Ulises, the eventual murder of the grandmother by Ulises, and Eréndira's escape. Eréndira's transformation from passivity to resistance is not benign. Related as it is, with even less access than is usual in García Márquez to the internal consciousness of characters (a feature made necessary perhaps by the ugliness of the material with which he is working), the gradual welling up of resistance in Eréndira entails the loss of all positive affect and the submersion of all other feelings by the desire to rid herself of her oppressor. Pitiable as a victim, she is in large part responsible for her own submission and only less so for the deformation her character undergoes.

As to her grandmother, she too is a victim, though one we hold fully responsible for what becomes of her. And there would seem to be little to humanize that great white whale who gives orders in her sleep, procures a letter from Senator Onésimo Sánchez testifying to her high moral character so that she can prostitute her granddaughter unmolested, survives arsenic sufficient to exterminate a generation of rats and an exploding piano, and bleeds green, the color of our money, when she finally succumbs to Ulises's knife. But she has determination and her memories. She subdues a revolt of inconsiderate men who do not want to line up again at nine the next morning but want Eréndira now, and she comforts Eréndira with the prospect that the wealth she is now gaining will protect her from the mercies of men later in life and will make her independent with a house of her own. Even in her old age, faded and fat, it "could have been said that she had been the most beautiful woman in the world"; she dreams dreams and suffers nostalgia, though the longest of her dreams ends with her killing a man in a context that resembles **"The Woman Who Came at Six O'Clock."**

As in most of García Márquez's fictions, the rhetorical surface is made up of a mosaic of elements from heterogeneous sources. The phrase "I'm the domestic mail" was first said by a man García Márquez met in El Chocó in 1954, and Ulises's oranges with diamonds inside them may derive from an image García Márquez invented on the same trip—that if bananas were planted in El Chocó, they would grow with grains of platinum inside them. The missionary nuns' theft of Eréndira alludes to Vargas Llosa's *The Green House,* and Ulises's face of a traitor angel seems to allude to Asturias's Miguel Angel Face (Cara de Angel) in *El señor presidente,* perhaps as restitution for the many unkind things García Márquez has said about Asturias as man and as artist and perhaps as coals of fire for Asturias's accusing García Márquez of plagiarism. Alvaro Cepeda Samudio reappears driving the truck for which his physiognomy ordained him, and the narrator in the first person claims to have got the end of the story of Eréndira from Rafael Escalona, one of his own characters who is also a contemporary popular singer.

The odd appearance of the first-person narrator in ***Innocent Eréndira,*** briefly introducing himself and his source for a few sentences before disappearing under the surface again, suggests the importance to these stories of knowing the ending before the story begins to be told. The common effectiveness in the management of closure shared by these tales no longer depends on annihilating the world or the fiction. Instead, finality is achieved though ends are left open: we do not know where the man with wings or Eréndira goes, but they do escape; we do not know what will become of Esteban's village or what will be done with the ghost ship; Blacamán lives forever, and only the senator conclusively dies, weeping with rage. Congruent with the degree of artifice in the fictions, the endings confirm the fictitiousness of all endings save one but suggest with a chastened hopefulness the continuing, transforming power of ideas. (pp. 70-87)

Regina Janes, in her Gabriel García Márquez: Revolutions in Wonderland, *University of Missouri Press, 1981, 115 p.*

Salman Rushdie (essay date 1982)

[*Rushdie is an Indian-born English novelist and critic who created an international controversy with the publication in 1988 of his novel* The Satanic Verses, *a work considered blasphemous to many Muslims. As a reaction to the work, the government of Iran issued a death-edict against Rushdie; Britain subsequently placed the author under governmental protection. Numerous prominent authors worldwide objected to threats against Rushdie, signing a protest statement in early 1989 that condemned Iran's edict as a form of censorship and asserted the artistic merit of the* Verses, *a novel that continues to be the subject of conflicting aesthetic and religious opinions. (See* Contemporary Literary Criticism, *Vol. 59.) The* Verses, *as well as such novels by Rushdie as* Midnight's Children *(1981), characteristically blend fantasy, satire, allegory, and realistic detail, gaining praise for a style some critics have termed "magical realism," a denotation that has merited the comparison of his works with those of García Márquez. In the following excerpt from a review of* Chronicle of a Death Foretold, *Rushdie lauds García Márquez's literary technique, initiating his discussion with a sentence that resonates the style of many works by García Márquez.*]

We had suspected for a long time that the man Gabriel was capable of miracles, because for many years he had talked too much about angels for someone who had no wings, so that when the miracle of the printing presses occurred we nodded our heads knowingly, but of course the foreknowledge of his sorcery did not release us from its power, and under the spell of that nostalgic witchcraft we arose from our wooden benches and garden swings and ran without once drawing breath to the place where the demented printing presses were breeding books faster than fruitflies, and the books leapt into our hands without our even having to stretch out our arms, the flood of books spilled out of the print room and knocked down the first arrivals at the presses, who succumbed deliriously to that terrible deluge of narrative as it covered the streets and the sidewalks and rose lap-high in the ground-floor rooms of all the houses for miles around, so that there was no one who could escape from that story, if you were blind or shut your eyes it did you no good because there were always voices reading aloud within earshot, we had all been ravished like willing virgins by that tale, which had the quality of convincing each reader that it was his personal autobiography; and then the book filled up our country and headed out to sea, and we understood in the insanity of our possession that the phenomenon would not cease until the entire surface of the globe had been covered, until seas, mountains, underground railways and deserts had been completely clogged up by the endless copies emerging from the bewitched printing press, with the exception, as Melquíades the gypsy told us, of a single northern country called Britain whose inhabitants had long ago become immune to the book disease, no matter how virulent the strain . . .

It is now 15 years since Gabriel García Márquez first published *One Hundred Years of Solitude.* During that time it has sold over four million copies in the Spanish language alone, and I don't know how many millions more in translation. The news of a new Márquez book takes over the front pages of Spanish American dailies. Barrow-boys hawk copies in the streets. Critics commit suicide for lack of fresh superlatives. His latest book, ***Chronicle of a Death Foretold,*** had a first printing in Spanish of considerably more than one million copies. Not the least extraordinary aspect of the work of 'Angel Gabriel' is its ability to make the real world behave in precisely the improbably hyperbolic fashion of a Márquez story.

In Britain, nothing so outrageous has yet taken place. Márquez gets the raves but the person on the South London public conveyance remains unimpressed. It can't be that the British distrust fantasists. Think of Tolkien. (Maybe they just don't like good fantasy.) My own theory is that for most Britons South America has just been discovered. A Task Force may succeed where reviewers have failed: that great comma of a continent may have become commercial at last, thus enabling Márquez and all the other members of 'El Boom', the great explosion of brilliance in contemporary Spanish American literature, finally to reach the enormous audiences they deserve. (p. 3)

It seems that the greatest force at work on the imagination of Márquez . . . is the memory of his grandmother. Many, more formal antecedents have been suggested for his art: he has himself admitted the influence of Faulkner, and the world of his fabulous Macondo is at least partly Yoknapatawpha County transported into the Colombian jungles. Then there's Borges, and behind Borges the *fons* and *origo* of it all, Machado de Assis, whose three great novels, *Epitaph of a Small Winner, Quincas Borba* and *Dom Casmurro* were so far ahead of their times (1880, 1892 and 1900), so light in touch, so clearly the product of a fantasticating imagination (see, for example, the use Machado makes of an 'antimelancholy plaster' in *Epitaph*), as to make one suspect that he had descended into the South American literary wilderness of that period from some Dänikenian chariot of gods. And Garciá Márquez's genius for the unforgettable visual hyperbole—for instance, the Americans forcing a Latin dictator to give them the sea in payment of his debts, in *The Autumn of the Patriarch:* 'they took away the Caribbean in April, Ambassador Ewing's nautical engineers carried it off in numbered pieces to plant it far from the hurricanes in the blood-red dawns of Arizona'—may well have been sharpened by his years of writing for the movies. But the grandmother is more important than any of these. She is Gabriel García Márquez's voice.

In an interview with Luis Harss and Barbara Dohmann [see Further Reading list], Márquez says clearly that his language is his grandmother's. 'She spoke that way'. 'She was a great storyteller'. Anita Desai has said of Indian households that the women are the keepers of the tales, and the same appears to be the case in South America. Marquez was raised by his grandparents, meeting his mother for the first time when he was seven or eight years old. His remark that nothing interesting ever happened to him after the age of eight becomes, therefore, particularly revealing. Of his grandparents, Márquez said to Harss and Dohmann:

> They had an enormous house, full of ghosts. They were very superstitious and impressionable people. In every corner there were skeletons and memories, and after six in the evening you didn't dare leave your room. It was a world of fantastic terrors.

From the memory of that house, and using his grandmother's narrative voice as his own linguistic lodestone, Márquez began the building of Macondo.

But of course there is more to him than his granny. He left his childhood village of Aracataca when still very young, and found himself in an urban world whose definitions of reality were so different from those prevalent in the jungle as to be virtually incompatible. In *One Hundred Years of Solitude,* the assumption into heaven of Remedios the Beauty, the loveliest girl in the world, is treated as a completely expected occurrence, but the arrival of the first railway train to reach Macondo sends a woman screaming down the high street. 'It's coming', she cries, 'Something frightful, like a kitchen dragging a village behind it'. Needless to say, the reactions of city folk to these two events would be exactly reversed. García Márquez decided that reality in South America had literally ceased to exist: this is the source of his fabulism.

The damage to reality was—is—at least as much political as cultural. In Márquez's experience, truth has been controlled to the point at which it has ceased to be possible to find out what it is. The only truth is that you are being lied to all the time. García Márquez (whose support of the Castro Government in Cuba may prevent him from getting his Nobel) has always been an intensely political creature: but his books are only obliquely to do with politics, dealing with public affairs only in terms of grand metaphors like Colonel Aureliano Buendía's military career, or the colossally overblown figure of the Patriarch, who has one of his rivals served up as the main course at a banquet, and who, having overslept one day, decides that the afternoon is really the morning, so that people have to stand outside his windows at night holding up cardboard cutouts of the sun.

El realismo magical, 'magic realism', at least as practised by García Márquez, is a development of Surrealism that expresses a genuinely 'Third World' consciousness. It deals with what Naipaul has called 'half-made' societies, in which the impossibly old struggles against the appallingly new, in which public corruptions and private anguishes are more garish and extreme than they ever get in the so-called 'North', where centuries of wealth and power have formed thick layers over the surface of what's really going on. In the work of García Márquez, as in the world he describes, impossible things happen constantly, and quite plausibly, out in the open under the midday sun. It would be a mistake to think of Márquez's literary universe as an invented, self-referential, closed system. He is not writing about Middle Earth, but about the one we all inhabit. Macondo exists. That is its magic.

It sometimes seems, however, that Márquez is consciously trying to foster the myth of 'Garcíaland'. Compare the first sentence of *One Hundred Years of Solitude* with the first sentence of ***Chronicle of a Death Foretold:*** 'Many years later, as he faced the firing squad, Colonel Aureliano Buendía was to remember that distant afternoon when his father took him to discover ice' (*One Hundred Years*). And: 'On the day they were going to kill him, Santiago Nasar got up at five-thirty in the morning to wait for the boat the bishop was coming on' (***Chronicle***). Both books begin by first invoking a violent death in the future and then retreating to consider an earlier, extraordinary event. *The Autumn of the Patriarch,* too, begins with a death and then circles back and around a life. It's as though Márquez is asking us to link the books. This suggestion is underlined by his use of certain types of stock character: the old soldier, the loose woman, the matriarch, the compromised priest, the anguished doctor. The plot of *In Evil Hour,* in which a town allows one person to become the scapegoat for what is in fact a crime committed by many hands—the fly-posting of satiric lampoons during the nights—is echoed in ***Chronicle of a Death Foretold,*** in which the citizens of another town, caught in the grip of a terrible disbelieving inertia, once again fail to prevent a killing, even though it has been endlessly 'announced' or 'foretold'. These assonances in the Márquez oeuvre are so pronounced that it's easy to let them overpower the considerable differences of intent and achievement in his books.

For not only is Márquez bigger than his grandmother: he is also bigger than Macondo. The early writings look, in retrospect, like preparations for the great flight of *One Hundred Years of Solitude,* but even in those days Márquez was writing about two towns: Macondo and another, nameless one, which is more than just a sort of not-Macondo, but a much less mythologised place, a more 'naturalistic' one, insofar as anything is naturalistic in Marquez. This is the town of **"Los funerales de la Mamá Grande"** (the English title, **"Big Mama's Funeral",** makes it sound like something out of Damon Runyon), and many of the stories in this collection, with the exception of the title story, in which the Pope comes to the funeral, are closer in feeling to early Hemingway than to later Márquez. And ever since his great book, Márquez has been making a huge effort to get away from his mesmeric jungle settlement, to *continue.*

In *The Autumn of the Patriarch,* he found a miraculous method for dealing with the notion of a dictatorship so oppressive that all change, all possibility of development, is stifled: the power of the patriarch stops time, and the text is thereby enabled to swirl, to eddy around the stories of his reign, creating by its non-linear form an exact analogy for the feeling of endless stasis. And in ***Chronicle of a Death Foretold,*** which looks at first sight like a reversion to the manner of his earlier days, he is in fact innovating again. The ***Chronicle*** is about honour and about its opposite—that is to say, dishonour, shame. The marriage of Bayardo San Roman and Angela Vicario ends on their wedding night when she names the young Arab, Santiago Nasar, as her previous lover. She is returned to her parents' house and her brothers, the twins Pedro and Pablo Vicario, are thus faced with the obligation of killing Santiago to salvage their family's good name. It is giving nothing away to reveal that the murder does in fact take place. But the oddness and the quality of this unforgettable short fable lie in the twins' reluctance to do what must be done. They boast continually of their intention, so that it is a sort of miracle that Santiago Nasar never gets to hear about it; and the town's silence eventually forces the twins to perform their terrible deed. Bayardo San Roman, whose honour required him to reject the woman with whom he was besotted, enters a terrible decline after he does so: 'honour is love', one of the characters says, but for Bayardo this is not the case. Angela Vicario, the source of it all, appears to survive the tragedy with more calm than most.

The manner in which this story is revealed is something new for García Márquez. He uses the device of an unnamed, shadowy narrator visiting the scene of the killing many years later, and beginning an investigation into the past. This narrator, the text hints, is García Márquez himself—at least, he has an aunt with that surname. And the town has many echoes of Macondo: Gerineldo Márquez makes a guest appearance, and one of the characters has the evocative name, for fans of the earlier book, of Cotes. But whether it be Macondo or no, Márquez is writing, in these pages, at a greater distance from his material than ever before. The book and its narrator probe slowly, painfully, through the mists of half-accurate memories, equivocations, contradictory versions, trying to establish what happened and why; and achieve only provisional answers. The effect of this retrospective method is to make the ***Chronicle*** strangely elegiac in tone, as if García Márquez feels that he has drifted away from his roots, and can only write about them now through veils of formal difficulty. Where all his previous books exude an air of absolute authority over the material, this one reeks of doubt. And the triumph of the book is that this new hesitancy, this abdication of Olympus, is turned to such excellent account, and becomes a source of strength: ***Chronicle of a Death Foretold,*** with its uncertainties, with its case-history format, is as haunting, as lovely and as true as anything García Márquez has written before.

It is also rather more didactic. García Márquez has, in the past, taken sides in his fictions only where affairs of state were concerned: there are no good banana company bosses in his stories, and the idea of the masses, 'the people', is occasionally—for instance, in the last few pages of *The Autumn of the Patriarch*—romanticised. But when he has written about the lives of 'the people', he has thus far forborne to judge. In ***Chronicle,*** however, the distancing has the effect of making it clear that García Márquez is launching an attack on the macho ethic, on a narrow society in which terrible things happen with the inevitability of dreams. He has never written so disapprovingly before.

He gets away with that, too, because he never makes the error of allowing his characters and their motives to become one-dimensional. And there is, of course, the sheer beauty of his sentences and of his images (helped into English, once again, by Gregory Rabassa, who, along with Grass's translator, Ralph Manheim, must be the very best in the business), the dry wit, and the unequalled talent for rooting his fabulous imagination firmly in the real world.

Chronicle is speech after long silence. For a time García Márquez abjured fiction: whatever the reasons for his return to the form, we can only be grateful that he is back, his genius unaffected by the lay-off. (pp. 3-5)

Salman Rushdie, "Angel Gabriel," in London Review of Books, *Vol. 4, No. 17, September 16-October 6, 1982, pp. 3-5.*

García Márquez describes how he writes a story:

In my case, [a story] always begins with an image, not an idea or a concept. . . .

The image grows in my head until the whole story takes shape as it might in real life. The problem is that life isn't the same as literature, so then I have to ask myself the big question: How do I adapt this, what is the most appropriate structure for this book? I have always aspired to finding the perfect structure. One perfect structure in literature is that of Sophocles' *Oedipus Rex.* Another is a short story, "Monkey's Paw," by an English writer, William Jacobs.

When I have the story and the structure completely worked out, I can start—but only on condition that I find the right name for each character. If I don't have the name that exactly suits the character, it doesn't come alive. I don't see it.

Once I sit down to write, usually I no longer have any hesitations. I may take a few notes, a word or a phrase or something to help me the following morning, but I never work with a lot of notes. That's what I learned when I was young. I know writers who have books full of notes and they wind up thinking about their notes and never write their books.

Gabriel García Márquez, in an excerpt from an interview that was published in The New York Times Book Review, *21 February 1988.*

Lois Parkinson Zamora (essay date 1985)

[*In the following essay, Zamora examines the theme of the apocalypse as a structuring device in* Chronicle of a Death Foretold *and notes García Márquez's use of journalistic technique in the short novel.*]

[In ***Chronicle of a Death Foretold***], Gabriel García Márquez continues his novelistic exploration of the nature of time and time's end. . . . [The] end is neither communal nor political, as it is in *One Hundred Years of Solitude* and *The Autumn of the Patriarch,* but terribly individual and wholly inevitable. If the historical determinism in social and political institutions is the implicit subject of the earlier novels, this subject becomes explicit as García Márquez's focus narrows upon the fated nature of the individual existence in ***Chronicle of a Death Foretold.*** The novel depicts the life span not of a society or a political institution, as do the earlier novels, but rather that of a single human being. Alfred J. MacAdam asserts quite correctly [in *Modern Latin American Narratives: The Dreams of Reason* (1977)] that "the essential problem of *One Hun-*

dred Years of Solitude structurally and in its attitude toward history, is duration." I would amplify that observation to include the proposition that the essential problem in much of García Márquez's fiction is how duration ends. My discussion of ***Chronicle of a Death Foretold*** will concentrate upon this point.

García Márquez uses the paradigms of apocalypse to structure and direct *One Hundred Years of Solitude* and *The Autumn of the Patriarch.* In considering the apocalyptic nature of ***Chronicle of a Death Foretold,*** it is appropriate to begin with Frank Kermode's observation [in *The Sense of an Ending: Studies in the Theory of Fiction* (1967)] that the relationship between the individual human span and the span of history has become increasingly problematic with the lengthening of the scale of perceived history, an observation immediately applicable to García Márquez's latest novel, as in Hannah Arendt's discussion of that lack of a sense of beginning and end in modern history ["The Concept of History," in *Between Past and Future* (1969)]. If the individual's relation to the beginning and the end of time becomes more difficult to imagine as the former recedes and the latter fails to present itself, it is precisely the myth of apocalypse that provides for García Márquez a temporal pattern of initiation and conclusion. The end which the apocalyptic myth imposes on time is of course fictional, but it is with this fiction that the author relates his characters' histories to that of mankind and gives significance to their individual deaths by placing them in the mythic context of the universal death. Temporal ends and narrative endings are harmonized in the myth of apocalypse as they are in García Márquez's apocalyptic fictions.

The myth of apocalypse allows García Márquez an enlarged perspective on his characters' temporal situations by placing the reader beyond the end of history, whether that of Macondo or of Santiago Nasar. We, along with St. John of Patmos or Melqúiades of Macondo or the journalist/narrator of ***Chronicle of a Death Foretold,*** see how the beginning relates to the end, how the historical and fictive orders operate, from a privileged temporal and narrative position. The traditional apocalyptists, like García Márquez's narrators, were exiles, outsiders, who nonetheless had an urgent moral stake in the world they described, and hence felt themselves compelled to write, as God ordered St. John: "Write the things which thou hast seen, the things which are, and the things which shall be hereafter" (Revelation 1:19). For García Márquez the end is a fact of history and a necessary fiction as well: the alternating rhythms of civilization and cataclysm, of decay and regeneration, of disaster and millennium, which are the rhythms of apocalypse, underlie his fiction and inform his vision of human reality. Whether individual and collective ends coincide, as they do in *One Hundred Years of Solitude,* or whether the end is an individual predicament, as it is in ***Chronicle of a Death Foretold,*** García Márquez's vision is of a historical process which moves steadily toward conclusion.

In *One Hundred Years of Solitude,* García Márquez's apocalyptic vision of a foretold future remains unstated until the final pages of the novel, when we learn that Melquíades has written Macondo's history one hundred years before it happens. In ***Chronicle of a Death Foretold,*** however, that vision is immediately evident in both its title and its opening sentence: "On the day they were going to kill him Santiago Nasar got up at five-thirty in the morning to wait for the boat the bishop was coming in." Unlike Aureliano, whose imminent death before a firing squad is described in the first sentence of *One Hundred Years of Solitude,* Santiago is given no reprieve. His fate, we learn at the end of the novel, is sealed from the beginning. And if I have said that the end is not a communal one, as in the case of the Buendías and Macondo, Santiago Nasar's death is no less a group drama. The narrator's concern, even beyond questions of the moral responsibility of the murderers or the victim, is the role of the community in the death, and the nature of their communal guilt. It is precisely *because* Santiago's death is foretold, *because* everyone shares the foreknowledge of his end, that the narrator is moved to undertake his investigation. Why did no one prevent his death? Could no one intercede in the "announced" scenario of events leading to catastrophe? Does announcement imply irrevocability? And will the narrator's written account (the death "aftertold") modify the future, even if it cannot undo the past?

These tensions—between foreknowledge and human volition, between individual responsibility and communal destiny—are inherent in all apocalyptic narration. St. John exhorts his listeners to reform even as he shows that it is too late, revealing a pre-determined schedule of events in which individual and communal destinies are foretold and hence presumably final. Nevertheless, St. John's emphasis on the reforming power of language (Christ is imaged *as* the Word) implies that his own verbal account may yet modify the future. The title of this novel in its original Spanish—literally, "chronicle of an announced (or publicized) death"—is more direct in both syntax and diction than translator Gregory Rabassa's inverted "death foretold": however, the Biblical tone created by the inverted word order and the apocalyptic ring of "foretold" in the translated title are justified by the apocalyptic nature of the narration.

The structure of the narration is as apocalyptic as the questions its narrator poses. If Melquíades' narration hurtles forward at an increasingly dizzying pace to meet the end it describes, here too we are made to feel the pressure of time's movement toward Santiago's violent finale. The repeated re-tellings of the murder, including an account of the autopsy (which, as one of the participants says, was like killing him again), escalate in ferocity and pace until the final lurid description of Santiago's evisceration reaches a pitch of feverish intensity. And despite the novel's foretold ending, suspense mounts continuously until the final scene, in part because García Márquez exploits the most basic fact of human existence: the individual's end is by definition foretold, we all must die. So we hope, despite all evidence, that Santiago's death will be forestalled, perhaps because we recognize in his story the mortal weight of our own individual destiny. This rush of time toward Santiago's end seems the more precipitous in contrast to the curious immobility of time after the murder. We are told that for years the town has talked of nothing else, and even twenty-seven years later, the town's history seems paralyzed by the events of that Monday morning. The comment of one of the murdering twins to his brother describes the inevitability which we sense in both the murder and the narrative structure that contains it: " 'There's no way out of this,' he told him. 'It's as if it had already happened'."

Santiago's death is announced before is occurs, not only by his murderers and the rest of the town but also by events and by the very fabric of the physical environment. The apocalyptist seeks, or rather, creates, in the events and natural phenomena of the past and present the patterns by which to foretell the future. Similarly, the narrator of Santiago's death finds—or creates—premonitory patterns everywhere. The first paragraph of the novel describes Santiago's dream on the morning of his death. His mother, a respected prophetess (we are told that she has a well-earned reputation as an accurate interpreter of dreams if they are told to her on an empty stomach), fails to recognize the "ominous augury" in her son's dream. That the dream is an omen is never questioned by the narrator (or the townsfolk); that trees in dreams are to be interpreted as bad omens is presented as a universally held truth. The disemboweling of rabbits in the kitchen portends Santiago's disemboweling. Divina Flor's vision of Santiago going upstairs with a *rama de rosas* ("bouquet of red roses") prefigures the *racimo de entrañas* ("bough or bunch of entrails") which Santiago will carry a few minutes later. (Gregory Rabassa translates *racimo* as "roots," thus losing the ominous symmetry of the Spanish.) Clotilde Armenta, the local madam, remembers Santiago that morning as dressed in aluminum: " 'He already looked like a ghost,' she told me." The foretold future appears retrospectively to be latent in every action, object, appearance.

It is in ***Chronicle of a Death Foretold*** that García Márquez's journalistic training calls itself most clearly to his reader's attention. García Márquez has never stopped writing for periodicals and has often expressed his fascination with the relationship between journalism and literature, that is, between reality and its written versions, between facts and their narration, between detachment and creative participation. Futhermore, García Márquez's intention to use his Nobel Prize money to start a leftist newspaper in Bogotá has been widely publicized. Hence we understand that the title of the novel not only announces the apocalyptic perspective of the narrator but also suggests this problematic relation between journalism and literature, and the narrator's ambivalent stance between (or in) both realms. "Chronicle" is, after all, a word which more frequently names newspapers than novels, probably because it suggests an unmediated sequential account of events rather than an order which is contingent upon narrative structure or intent. Indeed, a part of García Márquez's journalism is anthologized under the title *Crónicas y reportajes (Chronicles and Reports).*

Hayden White, in an essay on the nature of narration, discusses the medieval chronicle, which typically lists in two vertical columns opposite each other the year and the events of that year. If no events are deemed of sufficient magnitude to merit chronicling in a given year, the space opposite that year testifies to that fact by its blankness. The chronicle, White states, "possesses none of the attributes which we normally think of as story; no central subject, no well-marked beginning, middle, and end, no peripeteia. . . . " ["The Value of Narrativity in the Representation of Reality," *Critical Inquiry* (Autumn 1980)]. It is above all the lack of an ending which characterizes the chronicle: time is represented as paratactical and endless; the list of years in the chronicle which White analyzes continues beyond the list of events, suggesting "a continuation of the series ad infinitum, or rather, until the Second Coming. But there is no story conclusion." The narrator of ***Chronicle of a Death Foretold*** returns to narrate the crime twenty-seven years after its occurrence, hoping to extract some conclusions about the murder and the nature of historical inevitability by imposing a long overdue ending—the narration itself—on the events which he describes. Though the narrator specifically assumes the stance of "chronicler," we will see that his narration achieves and embodies precisely what, according to White, the chronicle typically lacks, a narrative ending which implies a historical conclusion.

The death which the novel treats in fact actually occurred in the Colombian *departamento* ("state") of Sucre on January 22, 1951; the victim was an acquaintance of the author when he was a young newspaperman in the city of Barranquilla, on the Caribbean coast. The explicitly autobiographical narrator of this novel records the senseless death of Santiago Nasar with the care of an investigative journalist, and with the ostensible detachment of one. He hides his own passionate engagement with the moral and ethical issues of the murder behind the mask of a reporter, rarely stating a personal opinion. Perhaps his only subjective conclusion about the murder is that he believes that Santiago died without understanding his own death. It is hardly an idiosyncratic opinion, since the whole town believes that he was innocent of the crime of honor for which he was killed. Futhermore, his observation could be applied far more generally than to just Santiago. The narrator names several "victims" of the circumstances he recounts, implying an aspect of interchangeability in Santiago's fate; we sense that the comment also applies to the narrator himself, who in fact never reaches a satisfactory understanding of Santiago's death. That the narrator is himself twice mistaken for Santiago suggests his own identification with the victim, despite his tone of journalist detachment, and makes his observation relevant to his own death and ours, also foretold and unsearchable.

In his self-conscious role as impartial reporter, the narrator meticulously documents his sources. He willfully minimizes the apparent control he exercises over the structure of his narration by constantly citing his informants and quoting directly from myriad interviews—"he said," "she said," "he said that she said," "according to them," etc. Like the traditional apocalyptist, he is both listener and recorder, narratee and narrator, casting himself as the medium, the mere vehicle, for his story, which is explicitly called a revelation by one of the characters. His obsessive attention to the precise time of the occurence leading to the catastrophe also resembles traditional apocalyptic narrative and serves as well to remind the reader of the narrator's ostensible role as chronicler. We know minute by minute who does what during the hour before Santiago's murder, as if sequence might somehow reveal cause. So the narrator carefully disavows omniscience; he seems to hope that by refusing to acknowledge to himself or his readers his role as *creator* of a written verbal order, he can force events to speak for themselves, to yield their own objective truth.

There is in the novel a precedent for the narrator's effort. Referring to an earlier chronicle written by another investigator immediately after the murder, the narrator indirectly describes his own intent: "The investigating judge who came from Riohacha must have sensed [the fatal coincidences] without daring to admit it, for his impulse to give them rational explanation was obvious in his report." Futhermore, the judge is a reader of "the Spanish classics and a few Latin ones," as well as Nietzsche, reflecting García Márquez's own stated literary and philosophical preferences. In this foretold world, even the autobiographical narrator and his account are prefigured.

Of course the explanation of Santiago's death is *not* contained in the minute details which the journalist (or the investigating judge) presents, as the narrator knows too well. Despite the journalistic conventions to which he carefully adheres, the structure of his narrative is hardly a chronicle, in the original sense which I have discussed. Interviews and the actual events they treat—the distant past and a more recent past—conflate as the narrator shifts his focus frequently and without warning from the murder to its subsequent verbal versions. The time of the narration itself is yet another temporal layer in this complex, synchronic account. Futhermore, the end seems endlessly repeated, death tantalizingly un-do-able as descriptions of Santiago's bloody fate proliferate; like *The Autumn of the Patriarch,* variant versions of the protagonist's death serve to initiate and conclude several of the chapters, the narrative structure thus underlining García Márquez's thematic concern with the nature of ends and endings in these novels. And though I have said that the narrator is unwilling to acknowledge his role as creator, he does in fact recognize that the "shards of memory" with which he works are dangerously slippery, and that the backward movement of the mind through time is far less certain than the forward movement of clock and calendar toward the foretold death he wishes to chronicle.

García Márquez upon receiving the Nobel Prize in literature in 1982.

It is precisely the disjunction between the patterns of time and those of narration which occasions the definitive crack in the narrator's journalistic façade. The final chapter begins with the reference to the narrative impulse which the whole town shares:

> For years we couldn't talk about anything else. Our daily conduct, dominated then by so many linear habits, had suddenly begun to spin around a single common anxiety. The cocks of dawn would catch us trying to give order to the chain of many chance events that had made absurdity possible, and it was obvious that we weren't doing it from an urge to clear up mysteries but because none of us could go on living without an exact knowledge of the place and the mission assigned to us by fate.

Not only the narrator but also the entire town wants to use Santiago's death to foretell their own—"the place and mission assigned to us by fate." Their need to situate the individual end—Santiago's and their own—in the larger context of historical ultimacy links their efforts, like those of the narrator and García Márquez himself, directly to apocalyptic narration, which, as I have already said, responds to the human desire for conclusion. So they attempt to impose order on the "spinning" events of experience in the hope of understanding the providential plan for the whole. (This passage recalls the metaphoric description of the Buendías' history as a turning wheel on a wearing axle, a description which, like this one, evokes García Márquez's concern with historical patterns and their narrative embodiment.) The narrator, in the long paragraph which immediately follows the one I have just cited, provides the reader with the knowledge the townspeople seek, revealing the fated "place and mission" of one character after another from his vantage point beyond their "assigned" ends. This privileged position is due simply to the twenty-seven years which have elapsed since the murder: unlike the omniscient Melquíades, this narrator's apocalyptic perspective is personal rather than cosmic, his knowledge of their individual ends the product of mere survival.

Immediately after the paragraph which catalogues the ends of some of the townsfolk, the narrator proceeds to describe his own end, detailing the painstaking research required to write the novel which we are reading. It is clear that the novel itself is the "place and mission" of the narrator, and of Santiago as well, for the narrator understands that his written account is the only conclusion which might yet imbue Santiago's "senseless" death with meaning. If Melquíades' narration survives the end of Macondo and mitigates its tragic finality, so ***Chronicle of a Death Foretold*** is the extenuating circumstance of Santiago's murder, the end which does in fact confer meaning on the events it recounts. To invoke again Hayden White's definitions, *chronicle* gives way to *narrative* as the narrator imposes meaning on duration by creating an order which ends. The novel itself is the product and the emblem of that process.

Following upon the surreal imagery and baroque style of *The Autumn of the Patriarch* and the magical happenings and involuted syntax of *One Hundred Years of Solitude,* the spare, reportorial realism of ***Chronicle of a Death Foretold*** comes as something of a surprise. The style of course emphasizes the journalistic impulse behind the novel, and serves to foreground the conflict between fact and its narration which burdens the journalist/narrator. Indeed, twice he directly addresses that conflict, the first time when he describes his encounter with Angela Vicaria in a remote Indian village in the Guajira: "When I saw her like that in the idyllic frame of the window, I refused to believe that the woman there was who I thought it was, because I couldn't bring myself to admit that life might end up resembling bad literature so much." His second reference regards the investigative judge, who, like himself, does not think it legitimate that "life should make use of so many coincidences forbidden literature. . . . " In both instances, the usual relation of the terms is reversed: it is *life* which demands that we suspend our disbelief; only "bad literature," the journalist/narrator suggests, would so ignore the laws of probability and causality.

Although we imagine the magical realist *novelist,* García Márquez, with tongue in cheek as he gives such comments to his journalist/narrator, we see that those comments nonetheless closely resemble another made by the *journalist* García Márquez in the introduction to his series of newspaper articles, *Reláto de un náufrago (Story of a Castaway,* 1955). He writes that the castaway's account of his ten days at sea "was so detailed and fascinating that my sole literary problem was to find a reader who would believe it." And in a recent interview, García Márquez states: "the tricks you need to transform something which appears fantastic, unbelievable into something plausible, credible, those I learned from journalism. The key is to tell it straight. It is done by reporters and country folk." What concerns García Márquez and his journalist/narrator is not only that the event took place but also how that event may be reconstructed in a way that is both convincing and revealing.

There are examples in recent Brazilian fiction of such reconstruction which are far more politically motivated than García Márquez's. Forbidden to write about actual occurrences, Brazilian journalists like Márcio Souza (*The Emperor of the Amazon,* 1980) and Ivan Angelo (*The Celebration,* 1976) have written novels which aim to disseminate information about events otherwise suppressed by the authoritarian regime. *The Celebration* was published a year after the arrest and murder of Vladimir Herzog, a highly respected Brazilian journalist: the novel is both a response to and a record of this violent repression of journalistic expression and human rights. Of course the result of censorship has always been the repression of expression, but it is a satifying irony that it has also been a source of inspiration for Brazilian writers, who have reacted by altering the nature and purposes of literature. If government censors are creating fiction by editing reality, writers like Souza and Angelo are writing novels which document historical events even as they disguise those events in vivid, elliptical satires. Where newspapers cannot publish all the news that is fit to print, fiction may well become the medium which fulfills the function of journalism.

Such self-conscious mixing of the aims and techniques of journalism and fiction is, however, relatively rare in contemporary Latin American literature, although "documentary" and "testimonial" narratives have recently received critical attention. Mexican novelist Carlos Fuentes, for example, explicitly separates his novelistic activities from his journalism, and Julio Cortázar's *Libro de Manuel* (*Manual for Manuel,* 1974), juxtaposes, but does not integrate, newspaper articles and fictional narration. In contemporary U.S. fiction, on the contrary, Truman Capote and Norman Mailer, in their "non-fiction novels," raise the same kinds of questions about the relationship of genres that García Márquez raises, questions which were already being brilliantly formulated by John Dos Passos and James Agee in the twenties and thirties. As in ***Chronicle of a Death Foretold,*** it is murder and the irrationality with which fate selects its victims that attracts Capote and Mailer, whether in Capote's novella, *Handcarved Coffins,* in his novel, *In Cold Blood,* or in Mailer's *The Executioner's Song.* Perhaps like the journalist/narrator of García Márquez's novel, these North American writers wish to write the ending which the facts won't concede, to conclude the mystery with the text itself. Truman Capote in the introduction to his collection, *Music for Chameleons* (1980), writes that his integration of the techniques of journalism and fiction "altered my entire comprehension of writing, my attitude toward art and life and the balance between the two, and my understanding of the difference between what is true and what is *really* true." It is precisely the struggle to understand the distinction between what is true and what is *really* true, between fact and its creative embodiment, that is dramatized by the journalist/narrator of ***Chronicle of a Death Foretold.***

The journalist is by definition a public figure as the novelist is not, reporting as he must on events about the community to the community. I have already said that one of the narrator's primary concerns is with the nature of communal guilt, and I have referred to the communal narrative impulse which in some sense underlies and explains the motivation of the individual narrator. Another communal element, the extravagant fiesta, provides the background and the cultural logic for the murder. The constant din of a carnival which will prove itself both wedding and wake resounds throughout the novel (except during the final description of the murder, when the town falls deafeningly silent). The delirium of the fiesta is the necessary preliminary to Santiago's death, which might best be construed in terms of the culminating ritual sacrifice of the festivals of ancient Greece. Octavio Paz [in "Todos Santos, día de muertos," in *El laberinto de la soledad* (1950)] finds in the Latin American fiesta elements of the Dionysian festivals, relating the energy of their collective frenzy to death, their beauty to brutality. Indeed, mourning and merriment are explicitly linked in ***Chronicle of a Death Foretold,*** and the language and tone of their description is from classical tragedy: when Bayardo's sisters lament their brother's misfortunes, we are told that they go barefoot through the streets, tearing their hair out by the roots and wailing loudly "with such high-pitched shrieks that they seemed to be shouts of joy." Of course, we are already familiar with this dual sense of the Latin American fiesta in García Márquez's work. Before the massacre of the striking banana workers in *One Hundred Years of Solitude,* the narrator writes that the three thousand people "seemed more like a jubilant fair than a waiting crowd." José Arcadio Segundo lets out the shout of defiance which sets off the army's machine guns because, we are told, he is "intoxicated by the tension, by the miraculous depth of the silence, and futhermore convinced that nothing could move that crowd held tight in a fascination with death. . . . " The ensuing scene is described as "enchanted," and as "a kind of hallucination," descriptions which suit as well the scene of Santiago's death, also the culmination of a "jubilant fair."

Octavio Paz also explores the temporal nature of the Latin American fiesta. He asserts that in the ecstatic present of the fiesta, the past and future are integrated into "a complete and perfect today of dancing and revelry. . . . " Like the sacrifices of the ancient festivals, which symbolized both end and beginning, Santiago's end serves in turn to begin the process of artistic creation which is the novel itself. The symbolic day of the murder, Monday, looks both backward and forward: Melquíades writes, we remember, in a timeless room where it is always Monday, and the "absurd Monday" of the murder is also called an endless day. Although it is of course the beginning of the work week, Monday is likely also to be the end of the weekend in the world about which García Márquez writes. ("Santo lunes" is a popular expression which recognizes and ruefully excuses the frequent extension of Sunday into Monday, of fiesta into work, and raises Monday to the status of perpetual holy day/holiday, a status implicitly acknowledged in the Bishop's Monday morning visit to the town.) So Monday signifies the simultaneity of beginning and end, the conflation of past and future in a timeless present which characterizes both the murder and the fiesta that occur on that day. We learn that every Monday morning Santiago has a shot of cane liquor in his coffee to "help him bear the burden of the night before": though the frenzy of this particular fiesta has abated by Monday morning, the violence which follows is its direct result, indeed "the burden of the night before." Santiago strolls through the town early Monday morning, calculating the costs of the fiesta, not realizing that his own life will be foremost among them.

The motive for the murder, the protection of the honor of the bride and her family, seems to be the inevitable outgrowth of the communal delirium of the fiesta. The code of honor is traditional, inflexible, and in this case, irrationally acceded to by the entire town. Though condemned by the narrator, we are told that the court finds it a legitimate motive for murder, and those who did not intervene to prevent the murder console themselves later with "the pretext that affairs of honor are sacred monopolies." It is the thematic treatment of this irrational undertow of communally held moral and social traditions, more than its narrative technique or mythic structure, which links this particular work to William Faulkner's fiction. The theme of honor is central in Faulkner's work, and the Mississippian pursued it with an anguished detachment, as does the autobiographical narrator of his novel. For both writers, it is the element in which the barbaric past is located, the element which taints the present and truncates the future, whether of Sutpen or Quentin or Santiago. In ***Chronicle of a Death Foretold,*** the engagement of the townsfolk with the communal myth of honor gives to their ceaseless commentary the resonance of the chorus of Greek tragedy as they comment on the inevitable disaster that is unleashed when the traditional code is disobeyed. (The chorus of citizens in *The Autumn of the Patriarch* provides a similar background accompaniment, though theirs is less an ethical commentary then a political one.) Thus, in this most recent novel, more than in García Márquez's previous work, tragedy and apocalypse conjoin. The future of the hero is abruptly truncated for his transgression of a supposedly divinely sanctioned law, but that tragedy is molded and modified by the author's apocalyptic vision. Santiago's death is transformed into a narrative which gives meaning and coherence to an otherwise isolated, and hence senseless, moment in history.

In all of his fiction in the various ways I have discussed, Gabriel García Márquez uses the patterns of apocalypse to narrativize history. In *One Hundred Years of Solitude,* the apocalyptic myth suits the scope of his fictive vision: like apocalypse, Macondo is, after all, nothing less than a symbolic outline of the history of the world. *The Autumn of the Patriarch* and ***Chronicle of a Death Foretold*** are also concerned with cataclysmic ends, whether of a political system or an apparently innocent individual. García Márquez, through his surrogate authors in *One Hundred Years of Solitude* and ***Chronicle of a Death Foretold,*** and in his satiric portrait of contemporary Latin American dictators, places himself squarely in the current of that cataclysmic history, the better to probe the nature of our mortality. And if we lament Santiago's murder, or the obliteration of Macondo in a hurricane of minutes, hours, days, years, we may also rejoice in the permanence of the record of their ends. García Márquez poses his art against the terrible transience of human life: with words, he seems almost to overcome the temporal loss which he so poignantly describes.

It is the "almost" in the preceding sentence which García Márquez's 1982 Nobel Prize acceptance speech seems aimed at cancelling [see Ortega entry in Further Reading list]. Of course the Nobel speech is often the occasion of a strange mix of genres, as García Márquez recognized when he said of his speech before it was written that he wanted it to be "a political speech presented as literature." As if to dispel the misconception that because his novels are apocalyptic they necessarily reflect a view of a doomed future, García Márquez directly addresses the issue of his own literary apocalypticism and the apocalyptic nature of our times. He begins his speech by invoking the utopian visions and fantastic images inspired by the discovery of the New World: El dorado, the fountain of eternal youth, the giant of Patagonia, described by a sailor on Magellan's voyage, who when shown a mirror, "lost his sense, overwhelmed by his fear of his own image." With familiar temporal sweep, the author moves immediately from such beginnings to a consideration of ends, quoting a statement made by William Faulkner when he received the 1949 Nobel Prize for Literature:

> On a day like today, my teacher William Faulkner said in this place, "I refuse to accept the end of man." I would not consider myself worthy to occupy the same position as he if I were not fully conscious that for the first time since the beginning of humanity, the colossal disaster that he refused to accept thirty-two years ago is now nothing more than a possible scientific possibility. . . .

But even as he contemplates the end of humanity by nuclear holocaust, García Márquez oscillates back to envision its opposite, asserting that it is not too late to undertake the creation of "a new and leveling utopia of life where no one can decide the form of another person's death." Here we witness a marked shift in emphasis from the negative to the positive side of the apocalyptic myth and a shift as well in García Márquez's relation to the Latin American literary tradition of historical idealism. In *One Hundred Years of Solitude* and ***Chronicle of a Death Foretold,*** it is the fact of the survival of the narration itself which suggest temporal continuance and serves as saving counterbalance to communal and individual annihilation; in *The Autumn of the Patriarch,* mere survival is all that the people are justified in expecting, for the future in that novel does not by any means hold out the promise of "a new and leveling utopia." Thus the vision presented by García Márquez in his Nobel speech is decidedly more optimistic than any that has yet been embodied in his fiction (as was the vision presented by Faulkner when he accepted the prize for 1949). His speech offers, in fact, a resounding affirmation of historical and human potentiality: "Neither floods nor plagues nor famine nor cataclysm nor even the eternal wars throughout centuries and centuries have managed to reduce the tenacious advantage of life over death." Although it represents a shift in emphasis, García Márquez's speech remains a part of the apocalyptic tradition as I have described it, with its dialectic of cataclysm and millennium. It is precisely the expressed hope that historical renovation—even utopia—may yet be possible, despite enumerated past disruptions and present dangers, which is most characteristic of apocalyptic dicta.

García Márquez ends his speech with a playful yet profound revision of the concluding sentence of *One Hundred Years of Solitude* in which he invokes not the historical cataclysm of his novel's ending, but historical renewal instead. In his speech he describes a utopia where "races condemned to one hundred years of solitude will have at last and forever a second opportunity on earth." Here García Márquez dismisses the very idea of irrevocability, both historical and fictive; nothing need be irremediable, to use a word which often appears in his novels. By proposing in his Nobel speech this new version of the apocalyptic conclusion of his masterpiece, García Márquez enacts the renovating activity which he describes, calling into question the nature of both ends and endings and finality itself, be it the finality of Biblical hurricane, nuclear holocaust, or novelistic structure. (pp. 104-115)

Lois Parkinson Zamora, "Ends and Endings in García Márquez's 'Crónica de una muerte anunciada' ('Chronicle of a Death Foretold')," in Latin American Literary Review, *Vol. XIII, No. 25, January-June, 1985, pp. 104-16.*

John Simon (essay date 1985)

[*A Yugoslavian-born American film and drama critic, Simon has been both commended as a judicious reviewer and censured as a petty faultfinder. He believes that criticism should be subjective, and as Andrew Sinclair has observed, "He is as absolute and arrogant in his judgements as any dictator of culture, a rigidity that is his great strength and weakness." In the following review of García Márquez's* Collected Stories, *which was originally published in the* New Republic *in 1985, he condemns García Márquez's treatment of the fantastic and asserts that the events of his stories are unconvincing and his characterizations flat.*]

Frequently the history of literature (or the history of human gullibility) spews up a novel that becomes an "intellectual best-seller"—a book that all persons with literary or intellectual pretensions feel obliged to acquire, and some even to read. It may be the worst work by an established artist whose "best-seller time" has come. This was the case with Nabokov's *Ada,* even though the book was—is—unreadable. Or it may be the tome of a clever counterfeiter, a prestidigitator or *fumiste*—of skill but no substance—as in the case of Umberto Eco's *The Name of the Rose.* Or it may simply be the book of a mediocre but newly emerged writer of strange origin or bent that strikes even some usually judicious people as unusual, original, unique (never mind that it is factitious, trivial, and, to be honest about it, boring). Such a book is—was—Gabriel García Márquez's *One Hundred Years of Solitude,* which earned its author the Nobel Prize, won by such other prodigious Latin American writers as Miguel Angel Asturias (at least unpretentious) and the unspeakable Gabriela Mistral, but never by Jorge Luis Borges, the one who most deserved it.

To read *One Hundred Years of Solitude* is to dive into a mountain of cotton candy head first and brain last, and endlessly, suffocatingly, sickeningly try to eat one's way out of it. This book that, without false modesty, could call itself *One Thousand Years of Solitude* is repetitious beyond anything but an old-time movie serial, with characters that even a genealogical chart cannot individuate (why should it? since when is the writer's job done by a chart?); the same sticky-sweet mixture of fantasy and social satire stretches on and on. Its mischievousness loses whatever edge it might have through iteration, lip-smacking enjoyment of its own cleverness, and flights into a fancy that seems to me the evasion rather than the extension of truth.

I had no better luck with two short novels by this writer, *The Autumn of the Patriarch* and ***Chronicle of a Death Foretold.*** Still, it seemed possible that he could achieve more with less—in the short story, which might curb his passion for prolixity. And indeed there are in the ***Collected Stories*** a few relatively unassuming, predominantly realistic tales that qualify García Márquez as a potential Hispanic Somerset Maugham. There is even one concluding novella in the author's dubious surrealist manner that works well enough, aside from some straining for effect and misfired jokes. For the rest, despite the odd powerful image and some passages of acerb mockery, these stories are mostly exercises in epigonous surrealism, with fantasy squeezed as desperately and self-destructively as when a novice milkmaid mistakes a bull's scrotum for a cow's udder.

The earliest stories, from the collection ***Eyes of a Blue Dog,*** are the poorest, though here the author has the excuse of his early twenties. In several of them, the protagonist is either a corpse somehow still alive or a living person relentlessly verbose in death. Death-in-life, life-in-death—these parvenu archetypes are pounded in with elaborately contrived, carefully self-contradictory detail. "Madam," says the doctor in **"The Third Resignation,"** the opening story,

> your child has a grave illness: he is dead. Nevertheless . . . we will succeed in making his organic functions continue through a complex system of autonutrition. Only the motor functions will be different. . . . We shall watch his life through growth, which, too, shall continue on [sic] in a normal fashion. It is simply "a living death." A real and true death. . . .

Here the preposterous conceit—it has no satirical thrust—has at least a kind of fairy-tale diaphaneity. Presently, pseudo-psychological obfuscation sets in. The living corpse hears terrible noises inside his head: "The noise had slippery fur, almost untouchable," yet our cadaver-hero will "catch it" and "not permit it to enter through his ear again, to come out through his mouth, through each of his pores . . . " etc. But forthwith this "furry" noise "[breaks] its cutglass crystals, its ice stars, against the interior walls of his cranium." Nevertheless, our hero proposes to "Grab it. Squeeze it. . . . Throw it onto the pavement and step on it [until it is] stretched out on the ground like any ordinary thing, transformed into an integral death." Notice that the noise goes from soft and furry to hard and crystalline and back again to something squeezable, thence to something animate that can be stomped on and stamped out with an "integral death." A pious hope, that; in García Márquez no death is integral enough.

Surrealism is all very well if it has some fidelity to its own bizarre self. A Max Ernst must remain an Ernst; it cannot, must not, transform itself into a Tanguy, a Matta, a Wilfredo Lam, at the whim of its undisciplined creator. Let the image be as crazy and hellish as it wants to be, but let it stay in focus. Out of focus, hell itself is not hell any more. It is only an amorphous blur. Yet from García Márquez's paragraphs of chaos a fine image, at times, surfaces—such as that "silence, as if all the lungs of the earth had ceased breathing so as not to break the soft silence of the air."

In the second story, **"The Other Side of Death,"** a similarly living corpse is haunted by a smell instead of a sound. If, in the previous story, the author played around with tenses, here he fools with pronouns:

> They were traveling in a train—I remember it now [this "I" comes out of nowhere]—through a country-side—I've had this dream frequently—like a still life, sown with false, artificial trees bearing fruit of razors, scissors, and other diverse items—I remember now that I have to get my hair cut—barbershop instruments. He'd had that dream a lot of times but it had never produced this scare in him. There behind a tree was his brother, the other one, his twin, signaling—this happened to me somewhere in real life—for him to stop the train.

Note the confusion of "they," "I," and "he" in what is mostly a third-person-singular story. Note also the sloppiness of "other diverse items." And note the theme of the brother, the twin, the alter ego, that crops up with tiresome frequency in these stories—once it is even a mirror image that bleeds when the shaver does not—and later in the same paragraph another García Márquez favorite, the tumor. Here the character notices one on his middle toe, calmly takes a screwdriver out of his pocket "and extracts the head of the tumor with it." And, sure enough, this character, too, "gently wrapped in the warm climate of a covered serenity . . . felt the lightness of his artificial and daily death."

"Bitterness for Three Sleepwalkers" is even less scrutable. It may—just may—be about the death of a mother as perceived by her three sons. In any case, "she," whoever she is, seems to "become dissolved in her solitude" and to have "lost her natural faculty of being present." In **"Dialogue with the Mirror,"** a man "who had had the room before" meditates about the death of a brother. Again the story keeps shifting between a "he" and an "I" and ends with the man shaving before a mirror, which gives the author a chance to have lots of fun with "right" and "left" and "forward" and "backward." In the end the mirror image bleeds, while the man, unbloodied, smells kidneys in gravy and feels "satisfaction—positive satisfaction—that a large dog had begun to wag its tail inside his soul." In the title story, **"Eyes of a Blue Dog,"** a man and a woman inhabit each other's dreams but cannot find each other when awake, because the sleeper, upon waking, forgets the watchword "Eyes of a blue dog" with which to recognize the other. Kipling did this sort of thing better in "The Brushwood Boy."

There follows a straightforward story about a whore who has killed one of her johns and elicits a fake alibi from an ugly restaurateur who adores her and feeds her free of charge. Entitled **"The Woman Who Came at Six O'Clock,"** it is a neatly managed mood piece, situated in the bar-eatery before the evening's clients arrive, and containing such nice turns of phrase as "the man looked at her with a thick, sad tenderness, like a maternal ox." But in **"Nabo: The Black Man Who Made the Angels Wait,"** we are back in the thick of the old farrago with yet another figure hovering in a state that is neither life nor death, and a plot, if that is the word for it, obscurer than any. We get several more such stories, some with ghosts in them, and one, **"The Night of the Curlews,"** that is totally impenetrable. But it is the first to offer a favorite García Márquezian theme: the curious behavior of certain animals. In this instance it is curlews, which blind three men for no apparent reason.

In the stories from the next collection, ***Big Mama's Funeral,*** Macondo, the mythical locale of most of García Márquez's fiction, becomes more important yet. This Macondo can be anything from a pathetic hamlet to a good-sized town running to seed, and is peopled with the author's stock company of characters who pop up throughout his fiction, short or long. Here the writing is more assured, and some of the besetting mannerisms are kept relatively at bay. They are replaced, however, by new tricks no less annoying. Thus **"Tuesday Siesta"** is a potentially interesting story about a poor woman who travels wretchedly, with her small daughter, to a distant town where her son, caught in the act of robbery, was killed and buried. She carries a cheap bouquet to lay on his grave, and rouses the indolent priest, during the hot hour of the siesta, for the key to the cemetery. But the townsfolk, aroused by her presence, gather ominously around the priest's house as the story abruptly ends. In Luis Harss and Barbara Dohmann's *Into the Mainstream: Conversations with Latin-American Writers* [see Further Reading list], we read:

> What he first imagined in the story, says García Márquez, was the part he left out. Though not entirely. Somehow what has been omitted is implicit, therefore all the more vivid and powerful.

Would it were so. We know something about the mother, very little about the daughter, and nothing at all about the townspeople except that they love their siesta. There is not enough to make up for the missing confrontation. There is not even a dénouement, only an anticlimax of the thudding rather than the teasing variety. García Márquez has said that he considers revelations "a bad literary device" and consequently avoids them. The avoidance, I think, is mutual.

Finally, the stories from the ***Eréndira*** volume, written between 1968 and 1972, are in the author's maturest style and perfectly display its generous flaws and niggardly virtues. Here the surrealism has become formulaic: in **"A Very Old Man with Enormous Wings,"** a senile, motheaten angel falls out of the sky and confounds Macondo, which, however, loses interest when the sideshows of an itinerant carnival become more popular. Eventually, the angel just flies away. Conversely, in **"The Handsomest Drowned Man in the World,"** the sea washes up a gorgeous, oversized male corpse, impeccably preserved; as the townswomen all fall in love with him while dressing him in whatever large enough finery they can muster, he has to be tossed back into the waves.

The long and fairly controlled title novella, ***The Incredible and Sad Tale of Innocent Eréndira and Her Heartless Grandmother,*** is probably all the García Márquez one needs to read for a full sampling of his ideas, strategies, and techniques. A mélange of the surreal, scurrilous, and occasionally poetic, it tells of a monstrous, larger-than-life grandmother who, having always exploited her lovely granddaughter, Eréndira, now travels all over with her and prostitutes her to all comers until her alleged debt for supposedly causing their house to burn down is paid back by Eréndira, on her back. The debt is self-perpetuating, and it is only after many years of weird and grueling adventures that the girl, with the help of a lover, manages to do in the grandmother, who takes more killing than Rasputin. Gathering up her ill-gained fortune, Eréndira abandons the lovesick youth and vanishes. Along its way, the novella takes satirical potshots at government, religion, capitalism, family relations, passion, and whatnot, and generally maintains its narrative propulsion despite its curlicues and discontinuities. Though there is wit, horror, and even wistfulness aplenty, the supernatural elements contribute little beyond a superficial exoticism, and one must finally wonder whether the story's eccentricities do not cancel one another out.

Translated conscientiously, though sometimes ungrammatically, by Gregory Rabassa and (the ***Big Mama*** volume) S. J. Bernstein, these stories sorely lack a philosophical or emotional center. "In García Márquez's world, love is the primordial power that reigns as an obscure, impersonal, and all-powerful presence," wrote Octavio Paz in *Alternating Current.* Obscurity and impersonality, to be sure, abound in these ***Collected Stories,*** but they contain more obfuscatory deliquescence than concentrated power. And they seem to have precious little to do with love, unless you call love a minor writer's obsession with telling tall tales such as his beloved grandmother told him, a boy of eight, to make him sleep. "Nothing interesting has happened to me since," García Márquez has said, and we are compelled to believe him. But he has certainly learned his grandmother's lessons well: with his fabulating, he can put even grown-ups to sleep. (pp. 375-81)

John Simon, "Incontinent Imagination: Gabriel García Márquez, 'Collected Stories'," in his The Sheep from the Goats: Selected Literary Essays of John Simon, *Weidenfeld & Nicholson, 1989, pp. 375-81.*

John Updike (essay date 1985)

[A highly regarded American novelist, short story writer, critic, and poet, Updike is best known for his series of novels Rabbit Run *(1960),* Rabbit Redux *(1971),* Rabbit Is Rich *(1981), and* Rabbit at Rest *(1990), which chronicles life in Protestant, middle-class America. In such works he presents characters searching for meaning in their lives as they undergo domestic rituals and moral*

dilemmas. In the following excerpt from a review of García Márquez's Collected Stories, *he analyzes theme and style in the works of the volume.*]

[The works in García Márquez's ***Collected Stories***] are rich and startling in their matter and confident and elegant in their manner. For the reader who has exhausted the wonders of García Márquez's masterpiece, *One Hundred Years of Solitude,* they probably constitute (along with its fine precursor, ***Leaf Storm***) the next-best place to turn. They are—the word cannot be avoided—magical, though for this reader the magic sparkled unevenly through the spread of tricks and was blacker than he had expected. García Márquez did not begin, as some of his interviews have suggested, as a realist who then broke through to a new, matter-of-fact method of fantasy. Interviewed by Peter Stone in 1981, for *The Paris Review* [see excerpt dated 1981], he described the breakthrough:

> I had an idea of what I always wanted to do, but there was something missing and I was not sure what it was until one day I discovered the right tone—the tone that I eventually used in *One Hundred Years of Solitude.* It was based on the way my grandmother used to tell her stories. She told things that sounded supernatural and fantastic, but she told them with complete naturalness. When I finally discovered the tone I had to use, I sat down for eighteen months and worked every day.

The tone was brick-faced:

> In previous attempts to write *One Hundred Years of Solitude,* I tried to tell the story without believing in it. I discovered that what I had to do was believe in them myself and write them with the same expression with which my grandmother told them: with a brick face.

Yet the first story collected here, composed when García Márquez was a mere nineteen, with quite characteristic aplomb details the thoughts of a young man's corpse as it lies in the coffin:

> His body rested heavily, but peacefully, with no discomfort whatever, as if the world had suddenly stopped and no one would break the silence, as if all the lungs of the earth had ceased breathing so as not to break the soft silence of the air. He felt as happy as a child face up on the thick, cool grass contemplating a high cloud flying off in the afternoon sky. He was happy, even though he knew he was dead, that he would rest forever in the box lined with artificial silk.

The mature García Márquez's gift of linkage, his way of letting implausible threads intertwine and thicken into a substantial braid, already flourishes in these stories composed when he was a student and youthful journalist in Colombia. The next in order of composition takes up the thoughts of the dead boy's twin: "The idea of his twin brother's corpse had been firmly stuck in the whole center of his life." There is so much spiralling Faulknerian in direction that it is hard to know who is dead and who is merely imagining it pronouns float in and out of embodiments, and a host of creepy sensations flicker by—"Death began to flow through his bones like a river of ashes . . . The cold of his hands intensified, making him feel the presence of the formaldehyde in his arteries." Perhaps the parent of all these coffined boys is the corpse seen by the ten-year-old child at the beginning of ***Leaf Storm.***

> I've seen a corpse for the first time. . . . I always thought that dead people should have hats on. Now I can see that they shouldn't. I can see that they have a head like wax and a handkerchief tied around their jawbone. I can see that they have their mouth open a little and that behind the purple lips you can see the stained and irregular teeth. . . . I can see that they have their eyes open much wider than a man's, anxious and wild, and that their skin seems to be made of tight damp earth. I thought that a dead man would look like somebody quiet and asleep and now I can see that it's just the opposite. I can see that he looks like someone awake and in a rage after a fight. . . . When I discover that there are flies in the room I begin to be tortured by the idea that the [now closed] coffin's become full of flies. . . . I feel as if someone is telling me: *That's the way you'll be. You'll be inside a coffin filled with flies. You're only a little under eleven years old, but someday you'll be like that, left to the flies inside of a closed box.*

The ideas of living death, of a consciousness travelling within an immobilized body, of piecemeal dying within the garish trappings of Latin-American burial, of "chemical adventure," of "that somnambulism where the senses lose their value," of "an easier, uncomplicated world, where all dimensions had been eliminated" dominate these stories, with their disagreeable sweetish stench of precocity, of adolescent terror turned outward. Though this spectral field will be extended into a sociological realm of closed houses and frozen lives, a geographical limbo where only the bitter past animates thought, García Márquez's great theme of suspended motion is announced here at the outset, along with a smooth and dandified indifference to the conventions of realism.

He is not sure he had read Faulkner at the time of these early stories; he told his interviewer, "Critics have spoken of the literary influence of Faulkner, but I see it as a coincidence: I had simply found material that had to be dealt with in the same way that Faulkner had treated similar material." The similarities are remarkable, not only in the climate of class-ridden, aggrieved torpor but in the music of obsessive circling, of a trapped yet unquenchably fascinated sensibility; Faulkner even, in such stories as "Beyond" and "Carcassonne," like García Márquez drones into the life beyond the grave. The author the young Colombian did read was Kafka:

> At the university in Bogotá, I started making new friends and acquaintances, who introduced me to contemporary writers. One night a friend lent me a book of short stories by Franz Kafka. I went back to the pension where I was staying and began to read *The Metamorphosis.* The first line almost knocked me off the bed. . . . I didn't know anyone was allowed to write things like that. If I had known, I would have started writing a long time ago. So I immediately started writing short stories.

One story in this first collection moves out of the surreal into the orbit of Hemingway. **"The Woman Who Came at Six O'Clock"** gives us a nearly empty restaurant, a lot of unadorned dialogue, a woman of shady habits, a courteous barman, a whiff of criminal violence. But even here the sluggish tide of semi-death sweeps in, drowning reality: "Across the counter she couldn't hear the noise that the raw meat made when it fell into the burning grease. . . . She remained like that, concentrated, reconcentrated, until she raised her head again, blinking as if she were coming back out of a momentary death." Nonsense, of a sombre sort, nibbles at the edge of many a sentence, the rereading of which threatens to plunge us into a hopeless world of glutinous, twisted time:

> That's the way she's been for twenty years, in the rocker, darning her things, rocking, looking at the chair as if now she weren't taking care of the boy with whom she had shared her childhood afternoons but the invalid grandson who has been sitting here in the corner ever since the time his grandmother was five years old.

Spatial disorientation also occurs within the unpredictable prose:

> Then the three of us looked for ourselves in the darkness and found ourselves there, in the joints of the thirty fingers piled up on the counter.

These three have just been inexplicably rendered blind, so their disorientation has some rationale. Elsewhere, a woman's consciousness wanders for no clear reason into that of a cat and hangs for no less than three thousand years over the desire to eat an orange, and a black stableboy kicked by a horse lies interminably in the straw while the death angels wait and a "little dead and lonely girl," who seems also to be mute and over thirty, keeps recranking a gramophone. The stable story, **"Nabo: The Black Man Who Made the Angels Wait,"** ends with a monstrous run-on sentence in which García Márquez, at the age of twenty-three, in bravura fashion lays claim to his authorial power. A method of centrifugal revelation, wherein a set of images at first glance absurd or frivolous gradually coheres into a frozen, hovering world that we can recognize as the site of an emotion, of dread and pity: this is to become the method of *One Hundred Years of Solitude.*

The second, middle set of stories, all dated 1962, are more naturalistic, and but for the title story and **"One Day After Saturday"** are located not in Macondo but in El Pueblo—"the town," and a town differing from Macondo mostly in the relatively straightforward, staccato style with which it is described. Evidently García Márquez's lush early style had been chastised by his fellow-leftists. In his *Paris Review* interview, he said of this period of his writing,

> This was the time when the relationship between literature and politics was very much discussed. I kept trying to close the gap between the two. My influence had been Faulkner; now it was Hemingway. I wrote ***No One Writes to the Colonel,*** *The Evil Hour,* and **"Big Mama's Funeral,"** which were all written at more or less the same time and have many things in common. These stories take place in a different village from the one in which ***Leaf Storm*** and *One Hundred Years of Solitude* occur. It is a village in which there is no magic. It is a journalistic literature.

He lived, in the late fifties and early sixties, abroad, in Europe, Mexico, and Venezuela; for a time he worked for Castro's news agency, Prensa Latina, in its New York bureau. Yet the stories of ***Big Mama's Funeral*** seem scarcely political, but for their convincing rendition of stagnation and poverty, and the rather farcical condemnation of Big Mama's empire. They are brighter-humored, with more comic touches, than the earlier stories. Unreality breaks into squalor like the chickens of this perky sentence: "It was a green, tranquil town, where chickens with ashen long legs entered the schoolroom in order to lay their eggs under the washstand." There is a new, epigrammatic loftiness: "She bore the conscientious serenity of someone accustomed to poverty;" "She was older than he, with very pale skin, and her movements had the gentle efficiency of people who are used to reality." García Márquez, a well-travelled man of the world, is contemplating his remembered Caribbean backwater with a certain urbanity, preparing to make a totally enclosed microcosm, a metaphor, of it. The young author's eerie muddling of the concrete and the abstract, his will to catch hold of a terrible vagueness at the back of things, now works within single polished sentences: "But this morning, with the memories of the night before floating in the swamp of his headache, he could not find where to begin to live;" "When she finished the stems, Mina turned toward Trinidad with a face that seemed to end in something immaterial."

Several of these tales are García Márquez's best. **"There Are No Thieves in This Town,"** the longest of the lot, with magisterial empathy describes the confused, self-destructive behavior of a handsome young idler, Damaso, the love borne him by his considerably older wife, Ana, and the small-town boredom that stretches stupefyingly to the horizon. The town is so low on entertainment resources that Damaso's theft of three battered billiard balls creates an enormous vacuum; with no overt touches of the fabulous, an enchanted environment, shabby and stagnant yet highly charged, is conjured up. **"Artificial Roses,"** showing how a young girl's love secrets are detected by her blind grandmother, and **"Tuesday Siesta,"** sketching the arrival in town of the mother of a slain thief, are smaller but not inferior in their purity and dignity of treatment. **"Balthazar's Marvelous Afternoon,"** a parable of artistry in which the town rich man, José Montiel, defaults on paying for "the most beautiful cage in the world," sidles toward fantasy, and the prize-winning **"One Day After Saturday"** enters broadly into it, as the town suffers a plague of dying birds. **"Big Mama's Funeral"** (attended by the President of Colombia and the Pope) is firmly fantastical and celebrates Macondo, the territory of imagination where the author was to strike it rich. But not immediately: after 1962 García Márquez, living in Mexico City, undertook a new career as a screenwriter and wrote almost no fiction until January of 1965, when "the right tone" for his masterpiece came to him.

The third and last group of stories were mostly composed

after the completion and triumph of *One Hundred Years of Solitude,* and they have the strengths and debilities of an assured virtuosity. One of them, **"The Last Voyage of the Ghost Ship,"** is a single six-page sentence, and two of them, **"A Very Old Man with Enormous Wings"** and **"The Handsomest Drowned Man in the World,"** are subtitled "A Tale for Children." For the first time, we feel a danger of cuteness: "They wanted to tie the anchor from a cargo ship to him so that he would sink easily into the deepest waves, where fish are blind and divers die of nostalgia"; "The house was far away from everything, in the heart of the desert, next to a settlement with miserable and burning streets where the goats committed suicide from desolation when the wind of misfortune blew." Such imagery has become a mere vocabulary, used a bit glibly, though with flashes of the old murky power. García Márquez's conception of an angel as a dirty, muttering, helpless old man with bedraggled wings is ominous and affecting, and scarcely less so the drowned corpse so tall and beautiful and virile that "even though they were looking at him there was no room for him in their imagination." But the sea he keeps evoking has the unreality not only of sleep and dreams but of, in the words of the old song, a cardboard sea, a sea that indeed could be packed up and sold like the sea in his novel *The Autumn of the Patriarch.*

The longest and latest of these later stories, ***The Incredible and Sad Tale of Innocent Eréndira and Her Heartless Grandmother,*** has been made into a movie, with a script by the author and under his control, so the two forms of illusion can be fairly contrasted. Having seen the film before I read the prose, I was struck by how much that had seemed obscure was easily clarified—the photographer, for instance, who in the film appeared wholly gratuitous and of unrealized significance, is explained in the story as a natural adjunct of the carnival that grows up wherever the prostituted heroine is encamped. The comings and goings of Eréndira's young lover Ulises, baffling on the screen, make simple sense in print. On the other hand, Irene Papas, as the Grandmother, cannot look "like a handsome white whale" with "powerful shoulders which were so mercilessly tattooed as to put sailors to shame;" but she does, unavoidably, put a human face on this implacable character, and makes her more disturbing than she is in the book, where her cruelty remains a matter of literary premises and symbolist comedy. The scene of Eréndira's defloration, which in its written paragraph is swathed in subaqueous imagery, in the movie flays the eyes with its real girl, its real man with his three-day beard, its real shack, its real torrents of rain, its real brutality. The film, in short, had a power to stir and scare us quite unrelated to any cumulative sense it was making; its script was logically so loose that García Márquez could insert into it another story, **"Death Constant beyond Love,"** for the sake of its photogenic episodes of a painted-paper ocean liner and of peso notes that become butterflies. The one image in **"Death Constant beyond Love"** that penetrates into our own experience and lends it a negotiable significance—the frightened yet captivating odor of the heroine (not Eréndira), like "the dark fragrance of an animal of the woods . . . woods-animal armpit"—could not, of course, be captured on film. Thrown into real landscapes, with flesh-and-blood actors, the careless cruelty of "the incredible and sad tale" glared at the moviegoer confusingly, not quite action and not quite poetry. Seeing real human beings go through his motions, we realized how much stylized dehumanization García Márquez offers his readers.

There is a surplus of sadism in these later stories. Eréndira is made to submit to masses of men and her grandmother is prolongedly slain by a lover who is then spurned; the fallen angel is relentlessly abused and teased; and in **"Blacamán the Good, Vendor of Miracles"** a child is transformed into a miracle worker by a diet of pain:

> He took off the last rags I had on, rolled me up in some barbed wire, rubbed rock salt on the sores, put me in brine from my own waters, and hung me by the ankles for the sun to flay me . . . When [he fed me] he made me pay for that charity by pulling out my nails with pliers and filing my teeth down with a grindstone.

The child has his revenge: when he becomes a miracle worker, and his master is dead, he revives him in his tomb and leaves him inside, "rolling about in horror." He revives him not once but repeatedly: "I put my ear to the plaque to hear him weeping in the ruins of the crumbling trunk, and if by chance he has died again, I bring him back to life once more, for the beauty of the punishment is that he will keep on living in his tomb as long as I'm alive, that is, forever." Not a pretty tale, but then, we might be told, neither is life in Latin America. Nor were García Márquez's two post-*Solitude* novels, *The Autumn of the Patriarch* and ***Chronicle of a Death Foretold,*** pretty tales. The former seemed, to this reader eager for more tropical dazzlement, tortuous and repetitive, and the latter astringent and thin. Both left a sour taste.

Even before he won the Nobel Prize, García Márquez was worried about the effects of celebrity and fame: "It tends to isolate you from the real world," he explained to *The Paris Review.* "I would really have liked for my books to have been published after my death, so I wouldn't have to go through all this business of fame and being a great writer." Being a great writer is not the same as writing great. He writes slow: "On a good working day, working from nine o'clock in the morning to two or three in the afternoon, the most I can write is a short paragraph of four or five lines, which I usually tear up the next day." He writes, he informed the interviewer, "for my friends," and the knowledge of "millions of readers . . . upsets and inhibits me." The bold epic qualities of his masterpiece, his genial and handsome jacket photo, and his outspoken leftist political views combine to give a false impression of a robust literary extrovert; reading his collected stories suggests instead that his inspirations are extremely private and subtle. And, it may be, fragile. "The point of departure for a book for me," he recently told an interviewer from The *Times,* "is always an image, never a concept or a plot." He also confided, "When you are young, you write . . . on impulses and inspiration. . . . When you are older, when the inspiration diminishes, you depend more on technique. If you don't have that, everything collapses." To write with magical lucidity along the thin edge where objective fact and subjective myth merge is a precarious feat. Though he emphasizes technique—"Ultimately, literature is nothing but carpentry," he said to *The Paris Review*—there is much in the process beyond conscious control, however artfully monitored the promptings of the subconscious are. *One Hundred Years of Solitude* was a work of consummate ripeness. The author's sparse production in the eighteen years since its writing betrays the effort of fending off rot. (pp. 118, 121-25)

John Updike, "Living Death," in The New Yorker, *Vol. LXI, No. 13, May 20, 1985, pp. 118, 121-25.*

Susan Mott Linker (essay date 1987)

[In the following excerpt, Linker explicates García Márquez's allusions to the Bible, ancient legend, and classical mythology in the paired stories "Balthazar's Marvelous Afternoon" and "Montiel's Widow."]

Within the literary constructs of Gabriel García Márquez, **"La prodigiosa tarde de Baltazar"** and **"La viuda de Montiel"** represent both a unit and a transitional point. **"La viuda de Montiel"** completes the parabolic message introduced and developed in **"La prodigiosa tarde de Baltazar,"** following directly after **"La prodigiosa tarde de Baltazar"** in the collection ***Funerales de la Mamá Grande.*** Robert Sims has explored the story **"Funerales de la Mamá Grande"** as a transitional point in García Márquez's work [see Further Reading list], indicating the story's dual political and mythical content, and Sim's observations are likewise applicable to the story-unit of **"La prodigiosa tarde de Baltazar"-"La viuda de Montiel".** In it, the socio-political criticism is quite evident: Balthazar's negative attitudes toward the rich are understood after Montiel's meteoric rise to prosperity is explained in **"La viuda de Montiel".** What is not nearly so evident is the complex mythical framework of the two tales, veiled under the deceptively simple format of the confrontation between Balthazar and Montiel, artisan and businessman. It is through the use of a many-layered structure that is legendary, mythical and parabolic in nature that García Márquez reveals the message central to the two stories: the collapse of an old and established order under the challenge of a new social and philosophic system. It will be [my purpose], then, to explore the use of myth, legend and parable in **"La prodigiosa tarde de Baltazar"-"La viuda de Montiel"** in the prophesying of cosmic destruction and renewal.

In a 1967 interview concerning the philosophical orientation of his works, García Márquez spoke of the subversive function of literature. . . . [He noted] three elements fundamental to many of the works of the Colombian author: challenge, decline, and renewal. The type of challenge that Balthazar incarnates is that of change to static tradition, of the ideal to the material. It is, too, as Vargas Llosa has indicated [see Further Reading list], the challenge of "lo imaginario" to "lo real objetivo." From this confrontation, Balthazar will emerge the ultimate victor, but only when **"La prodigiosa tarde de Baltazar"** and **"La viuda de Montiel"** are considered as one prolonged unit.

Before embarking on a detailed examination of the mythico-legendary framework of the stories, it is first necessary to explore two interrelated elements in **"La prodigiosa tarde de Baltazar":** its title and Balthazar's name. In the title, the attention of the reader is drawn to the word "prodigious," a curious choice if one considers only the superficialities of the tale. In the etymology of the word (from the Latin, *prodigium,* "prophetic sign") and its original meaning can perhaps be found the key to understanding the thrust of the tale-unit of **"La prodigiosa tarde de Baltazar"-"La viuda de Montiel":** What occurred in the making and delivering of the Balthazar's cage is to be of prophetic significance. It will, indeed, foretell the events that unfold in **"La viuda de Montiel".** The threat of change will penetrate Montiel's defenses to strike at his most susceptible point, his inability to cope physically or psychologically with challenge and anger, and he will topple (as we see in **"La viuda de Montiel"**) not unlike Achilles, struck in the heel.

Balthazar's name, likewise, draws the attention of the alert reader. It is unique in García Márquez's works, and unlike many of the other names and characters he creates, has not appeared in previous works and will not reappear in *Cien años de soledad.* The most obvious derivation for the name is that of one of the Three Wise Men who sought Jesus at birth, and its mythical connections with **"La prodigiosa tarde de Baltazar"** will subsequently be more fully explored. Of more direct significance to the theme of prophecy is the connection of the name Balthazar with the Old Testament prophet Daniel (Belteshazzar), a name given the prophet by one of King Nebuchadnezzar's eunuchs (Daniel 1:7). It is Daniel-Belteshazzar who prophesies the end for King Belshazzar, son of Nebuchadnezzar (Daniel 5:5-29). Belshazzar has, Daniel informs us, "been weighed in the balances and found wanting" (Daniel 5:24), and he has, among other sins, "praised the gods of silver and gold, of bronze, iron, wood and stone" (Daniel 5:23). It is as if we were hearing Balthazar's invectives against the rich, and in **"La viuda de Montiel"** we learn that José Montiel has, like the Babylonian king, based his rise to prosperity on greed and violence. Like King Belshazzar, too, Montiel is destined to die, and his empire to end in disintegration, as prophesied by Daniel-Belteshazzar (Daniel 5:30).

The role of the dream or vision as a revelation is well established, and García Márquez also uses it as a prophetic tool in the story-unit. Balthazar's vision of prosperity and triumph over the rich is referred to as a "dream," an element that ties the story to the prophetic and messianic visions of Daniel, Jesus and Zoroaster, as will be seen later in more detail. In **"La viuda de Montiel",** amid the ruins of the business established by José Montiel, his wife Adelaida has a vision (dream?) of La Mamá Grande that foretells her death. . . . What is evident is that Adelaida's death (and that of her social class) will indeed be signalled when the will to rule—the strength of her arm—has been exhausted. Her name (from the German *adel-heit,* "of noble rank") ties her failure of will to the upper classes as a whole, and her dream represents yet another approach to the theme of decline and disintegration.

In **"La viuda de Montiel",** the function of Mr. Carmichael's corns and his umbrella (which never enters the house unopened) is also that of an augury, foretelling the collapse of Montiel's enterprise. As Vargas Llosa points out, the very rain itself is connected to the Biblical flood, and is indicative of collapse. . . . The gradual putrefaction of Montiel's unsold products hints, too, of an apocalyptic curse, and in the sound of distant thunder is sensed the inevitable end for Montiel's widow.

The link between these prophecies and the theme of renewal evolves out of the creation of Balthazar's cage, and the creative act itself has been clearly delineated by García Márquez. Balthazar has abandoned his regular work as carpenter and fallen into a nearly trance-like condition during two weeks of concentrated work on the cage; and during that time, he has neither shaven nor slept soundly, and has the appearance of a Capuchine monk. In the creation of the cage can be glimpsed many of the features characteristic of the mythical rites of renewal: the priestly figure of Balthazar, his solitary period of withdrawal, and his trance-like state. In his study on the relationship between mystical ecstasy and knowledge [in *Ecstasy: A Way of Knowing* (1974)], Andrew Greeley describes the creative process as "a fair analogue to the mystical experience," a trance which does not, however, prevent the artist from dealing with general reality, as we see in Balthazar's case.

There is little doubt that Balthazar's efforts have led to a monumental creation. The cage is . . . the biggest cage anyone has ever seen, with compartments for eating, sleeping and recreation. It is a vast domed cathedral, as strongly soldered as a penitentiary, extravagantly beyond the needs of modest troupials. It will magically redefine the real concept of cage, becoming a world in itself, and its violent rejection by Montiel is noteworthy. We can see in Balthazar's creative act, then, the type of *renovatio* that Mircea Eliade discusses in *Myth and Reality* [1963].

As in primitive rites of renewal, Balthazar's *renovatio* takes place in the new year, in the season of resurrection (in this case, early April). It is, as Graciela Maturo points out [in *Claves simbólicas de García Márquez* (1972)], a time framework that is the culmination of Christian mythical time, sanctifying and making possible the regeneration of the human spirit—one of the basic themes of the story-unit. The destruction of Montiel's empire, appropriately, occurs during the season of heavy rains, a prominent motif in many of García Márquez's works. Eliade ties the use of rain to what he terms "the myth of the destruction of the world," which frequently involves a flood, and culminates in world renewal.

Eliade also points out the possible political significance of the creative act of renewal:

> For in the course of time, cosmic renewal, the "Salvation" of the World, came to be expected from a certain type of King or Hero or Savior or even political leader. Although in strongly secularized form, the modern world still keeps the eschatological hope of a universal *renovatio* to be brought about by the victory of a social class or even of a political party or personality.

For García Márquez, that social class will be Balthazar's, and his personal victory over Montiel will represent the triumph of the spiritual and artistic realm. In Balthazar's creation of the cage, his condemnation of the rich, and his acceptance of the role of hero are found the factors that will ultimately produce Montiel's downfall in **"La viuda de Montiel"**.

As an integral part of the creation of the new world, there is also found the custom of the orgiastic celebration in primitive rites of renewal. It is a collective festival, not unlike that found at the end of **"La prodigiosa tarde de Baltazar"**, that serves as reconfirmation of the myth (in this case, the status of Balthazar as community and cosmic hero). Balthazar's drunken spree takes on Bacchic dimensions when we concieve of him in the role of hero-god, and his impulsive and impractical personality further connects him to the Dionysian cult, as studied by Luis Lozano in his contribution to *Explicación de "cien años de soledad"*. Furthermore, Lozano connects the Dionysian spirit with challenge to established order, a theme that is basic to the meaning of **"La prodigiosa tarde de Baltazar"-"La viuda de Montiel"**. Since the existence of Balthazar's Dionysian character implies that of its natural counter-part, the Apollonian personality, it is no surprise that José Montiel should stand for repressive order and tradition in the story-unit. It is Montiel who allied himself with dictatorial government and formulistic Church through his dealings with the mayor and his gift of the figure of St. Joseph to the church. Balthazar's other Apollonian counterpart, Ursula, serves as a level-headed balance for Balthazar's impulsiveness. As her name indicates, she represents

Cover of the English translation of La increíble y triste historia de la cándida Eréndira y de su abuela desalmada, *published in 1978.*

simultaneously the orderliness of the Ursuline nuns and the guiding qualities of the Pole Star.

Balthazar's celebration in the pool hall connects him to a particular aspect of Bacchic orgiastic rites: the creation of the god Bacchus. In her study [*Mythology* (1924)], Jane Ellen Harrison points out that "It is only in the case of Dionysus that we catch the god at the moment of his making, at the moment when the group ecstasy of the worshipper projects him." It is precisely during the celebration of the "sale" of the cage that the crowd of Balthazar's neighbors has created for him the role of hero, which he accepts, albeit with scant enthusiasm. . . . The fact that Balthazar did not sell the cage is of no importance. The belief of the townspeople in his triumph "projects" him as hero in the ecstasy of the pool-hall celebration.

This brings us, then, to an examination of the mythico-legendary framework of **"La prodigiosa tarde de Baltazar"-"La viuda de Montiel"**, and its connections with the theme of cosmic renewal. The function of myth in the renewal process is multiple. Levi-Strauss has described it [in *Structural Anthropology*] as a model of human behavior that offers solutions to problems and can overcome contradictions. Eliade sees myth as a model for human behavior that gives meaning and value to life, and awakens the consciousness of another world. Thus defined, myth has a great deal in common with parable, and as such has proven quite useful to García Márquez during a transitional period in which his stories incorporate both mythical elements and political content (the period during which the collection ***Funerales de la Mamá Grande*** was composed). Often rising out of times of societal crisis (as, for example, "la violencia" in Colombia), myth can offer the hero who will bring justice, transform society, or reestablish eternal human values, and, in doing so, sacrifice himself. In **"La prodigiosa tarde de Baltazar"-"La viuda de Montiel"**, the gift of the cage declares the value of the gratuitous act, in stark contrast to Montiel's self-serving materialism. Balthazar's creation is a reaffirmation of the Aristotelian Way of Excellence, an expression of Virtue that gives both meaning and value to life. His gift creates the belief in the community that Balthazar has triumphed monetarily over the miserly Montiel, and is enough to excite the imagination of the village, to awaken it to the vulnerability of Montiel and the prophecy of change.

The mythico-legendary bases for **"La prodigiosa tarde de Baltazar"-"La viuda de Montiel"** are multiple, and are woven into a texture of surprising tautness and apparent simplicity. When stripped down to their essentials, the two tales yield up the following points, termed by Levi-Strauss the "gross constituent units" of a myth: A simple, visionary man makes a marvellous object. A well-to-do neighbor tries to buy the object, but it has been made for, and is destined to, the son of a rich and repressive miser. The miserly father angrily refuses the gift, because he considers it an attack on his authority and position. The simple man leaves the gift with the furious miser, and celebrates his moral victory with friends and neighbors, who make of him a hero, and his victory their own. The miser eventually dies of a fit of anger, and his lands and business deteriorate and fail. His wife dies abandoned, and his children are scattered to other parts of the world.

The most obvious of the mythico-legendary traditions used by García Márquez as a framework for the stories is the tale of the Three Wise Men (the Magi) and the life of Christ. In particular, the story of the Magi offers numerous parallels with the basic plot line of **"La prodigiosa tarde de Baltazar".** Balthazar, one of the three Magi, brings a gift to Jesus (Pepe Montiel), son of Joseph (José Montiel), and, as in the Biblical tradition, it is the rich (Balthazar) who brings the gift to the impoverished (Montiel), in spiritual terms. The Magi are led by a brilliant star, and Balthazar is directed by Ursula, whose connection with the constellation Ursa Major is easily seen. The Wise Men are confronted by a suspicious and insecure Herod (Montiel), who is infuriated when the Magi circumvent his plan to find Jesus (Matthew 2:16). John of Hildeshiem's version of the tale of the Magi even goes so far as to tell us that after giving their gifts to the baby Jesus, the three kings, who had not had food or drink in thirteen days, "desported themselves," celebrating together in Bethlehem, details that bring to mind Balthazar's two weeks on the cage and his celebration in the pool hall. In addition, the same version of the legend also refers to the thirty gold pennies brought to Jesus by Melchior—which will later become the payment for Jesus' betrayal—a number seen in **"La prodigiosa tarde de Baltazar"** in the proposed price of Balthazar's cage.

The parallels between José Montiel (as revealed in **"La viuda de Montiel"** and **"La prodigiosa tarde de Baltazar"**) and the figure of Herod the Great are particularly intriguing. Herod's rule was characterized by ruthless police methods, and he often resorted to individual arrests and executions. Regarded as a foreigner by Palestinians, he was constantly suspicious of conspiracy. Montiel's connection with the abuses of local authorities is made clear in **"La viuda de Montiel"**, and in **"La prodigiosa tarde de Baltazar"** we are informed that he sleeps without benefit of a fan to hear possible intruders. Just as Montiel has achieved prosperity through the support of outsiders to the village, Herod required the protection of the Roman authorities to confirm his position in Palestine. John of Hildesheim's version of the legend makes specific mention of the fact that Herod was an alien, had been made king by the Romans, and was fearful "lest he should lose his kingdom because Christ was born."

In the story of the Three Kings there is also mention of the Roman emperor Octavian, whose name is found in that of Octavio Giraldo, the doctor who attempts to buy Balthazar's cage. If the figure of Giraldo is carefully examined, his connections with the formulistic Church are evident: his voice of a priest speaking Latin; the softness of his skin and his feminine qualities, as well as his surname (La Giralda). The supportive relationship of the Romans to Herod is therefore made analogous to the role frequently played by the Church in supporting the political and economic *status quo* in much of Latin America by a process of non-intervention. . . . When Giraldo learns that he has lost the cage to the son of José Montiel, his reaction is one of studied indifference—a quick sigh, a comment on Montiel's wealth, and then the matter is forgotten, much in the same way that the formulistic Church has divorced itself from the revolutionary dimensions of Christ's teachings.

In the parallels between the story of the Magi and **"La prodigiosa tarde de Baltazar"-"La viuda de Montiel"** is seen the challenge of established authority by a new and threatening force. . . . It is noteworthy that the Three Kings have come to be considered as symbolic of the three races of man or the three parts of the known world, thus inviting a comparison with the challenge of the mixed races, the *mestizo,* to the traditionally Creole power structure in Latin America. On a larger scale, the conflict between Balthazar and Montiel can be interpreted as representative of the age-old conflict between East and West, of Palestine and Rome (as also implied in García Márquez's ***Crónica de una muerte anunciada***). In that context, the figure of Balthazar as representative of Eastern spiritualism and Montiel of Western materialism takes on new meaning. Even the names of characters themselves lead to the points of the compass: Balthazar (travelling from the East); Ursula (from Ursa Major, most conspicuous of the northern constellations); Adelaida (as in the capital of southern Australia); Montiel (to whom Balthazar travelled in a westward direction); and Octavio Giraldo (the *giralda,* or weathervane). The blending of Christian and Islamic elements in the Giralda of Seville further makes the use of the surname Giraldo appropriate. The discovery of the points of the compass leaves the reader but a short step from their connection with the four points of the cross, long associated with Christian symbolism. And so the reader is led back once again to the theme of sacrifice and renewal.

Further consideration of the Magi leads the reader inevitably to the Persian Magi, a priestly caste dating in Persia from around 500 B.C., and followers of Zoroaster (Zarathustra), whose life-legends emulated those of Christ, and offer parallels with the figure of Balthazar. Zoroaster, too, is a figure who challenged an existing system of belief; like Balthazar, he had his first prophetic vision at the age of thirty; he neither married nor had children; he spent time in seclusion while writing the volumes of the Zendavesta beliefs; and his followers practiced the drinking of an intoxicating Haoma juice. More than anything else, we are told, Zarathustra as presented in the *Gathas* was a man who acted as a renewer and purifier, a man spending himself for others, much as Balthazar creates in the community a new vision, pays the costs of the celebration, and then is left consumed and debased in the street.

Another figure in which we find a combination of myth, legend and history is that of Jesus, who, like Zoroaster, brought the threat of change to an existing moral and religious system. The similarities between the figure of Christ and that of Balthazar are numerous, and for the most part, quite evident. Jesus' age when he begins his ministry, his marital status, profession and dress are only a few of the parallels with the figure of Balthazar. Balthazar's reluctant acceptance of his role as hero, his abandonment by his followers, his promise to return and degraded end would further suggest his connection with the sacrifice and resurrection of Jesus.

If the figure of Balthazar can be tied to that of Christ, in his gift of the cage must be seen the qualities of immortality and Grace. Its comparison to an ice factory would further link the cage to the alchemical traditions of the diamond-body of Christ, a theme discussed by Graciela Maturo in her study of the works of García Márquez. The cage is "sumamente bonita," the Aristotelian *summum bonum,* and in it are united the highest virtues of human effort and excellence. It is to be participated in by all, unless, as Aristotle informs us in the *Summum Bonum,* an individual has been "maimed for virtue," as in the case of Montiel Aristotle makes a clear distinction between the artisan moved to excellence by his sense of virtue and love of work and the "life of money-making," which he deems to be one of constraint (imprisonment?), and so characteristic of Montiel's existence. For Montiel the Pharisee, the cage signals spiritual imprisonment: His son gazes out from behind the bars of the cage as would a jailed criminal. In contemporary art, the cage has been used to express imprisonment, in particular the theme of the political prisoner. The gift of the empty cage thus becomes a symbolic condemnation of Montiel's involvement in political abuse and a reaffirmation of human freedom.

The etymological connections in Latin between *jaula* (cage) and *cueva* (cave) are close (both from *cavus,* an empty, hollow place), and bring to mind the Platonic image of the cave. The characterization in Plato of the cave as a world-prison symbolic of spiritual blindness links it to the concept of Montiel-cage. It is Balthazar who must " . . . be made to descend again among the prisoners in the den" to enlighten them, as an essential part of the founding of Plato's Whole State. The empty cage is, then, a highly ambiguous image, an amalgamation of imprisonment-spiritual blindness and freedom-light-virtue, and as such, symbolizes mankind's highest and lowest aspirations.

In José Montiel one can also see embodied the traditions of the Old Testament patriarch Joseph, whose wealth, like Montiel's was based on livestock and agriculture, and who through forced sale bought up land and cattle from Egyptians caught in a severe famine (Genesis 47:13-21), much as Don Chepe buys the land of political adversaries forced to leave the village. The language in **"La prodigiosa tarde de Baltazar"**, too, is Biblical in tone: the enumerations of the "mil jaulas de a sesenta pesos"; Balthazar's "Para eso la hice," that echoes Jesus' "I was sent for this purpose" (Luke 4:43); and in the wording of the abandonment of Balthazar, " . . . pero a la hora de la comida lo dejaron solo en el salón," reflective of Christ's abandonment by the disciples.

In the story-unit of **"La prodigiosa tarde de Baltazar"-"La viuda de Montiel"**, the theme of resurrection, although developed in a veiled fashion, is of central importance. Balthazar, champion of the poor, of simplicity and the imaginative and spiritual realm, is left in apparent defeat at the end of **"La prodigiosa tarde de Baltazar"**, but his challenge to Montiel's self-serving materialism is dispersed and multiplied, and will surreptitiously reappear in **"La viuda de Montiel"** in the form of the reprisals of the *pueblo* and the figure of Mr. Carmichael, the Black manager of the estate left by Montiel. The forces of change and decay, which are so fully developed in *Cien años de soledad* are thus seen in nuclear form in **"La prodigiosa tarde de Baltazar"-"La viuda de Montiel".** The eternal rebirth of Balthazar's challenge must inexorably lead to the decline and destruction of Montiel and his repressive system.

In the structural labyrinth of interconnected themes and figures of **"La prodigiosa tarde de Baltazar"-"La viuda de Montiel",** we find two other mythical figures related to the Magi and resurrection. The first, Dionysus, is convenient to García Márquez's tale not only because of the god's function within the orgiastic rite, but also because we can see in Dionysus a more profound meaning that connects him with the hero-figure of Balthazar: his function as the . . . liberator and savior. Dionysus' connections with the theme of resurrection are also seen clearly in his annual cycle of death and rebirth, and it significant that his sacrifice occurs, like Christ's, in the springtime (**"La prodigiosa tarde de Baltazar"** is set in early April). As with the Zoroastrians, the Dionysian cults sang hymns (dithyrambs) and ate bull's meat as part of the basic ritual, and it is Ursula who prepares meat and sings "una canción muy antigua" while awaiting Balthazar's return.

Another figure from Greek mythology also related to Balthazar and the theme of resurrection is that of the god Adonis. His connections with Balthazar are found in the gift of myrrh which many versions of the tale of the Magi attribute to King Balthazar. The demi-god Adonis was born from the bark of the myrrh tree, and his life symbolizes the regenerative cycles of plant life during the year. He is, therefore, a symbol of death, resurrection and immortality, and his close similarity to Dionysus can easily be seen. It is also perhaps through the consideration of myrrh that García Márquez's choice of Balthazar (rather than Melchior or Gaspar) can be understood. It is the aromatic and bitter myrrh that was used in embalming, and was widely understood to be symbolic of Christ's suffering and death. Balthazar's gift is, then, the bitter and death-dealing gift of change to José Montiel, whose name (*monte-hiel,* mountain of bitterness) further suggests the idea of myrrh and Golgotha, making Christ's sacrifice.

The framework of myth, legend and parable is a base drawn from multiple sources, all of which are prophetic of challenge, destruction and renewal: the legend of the Magi, the lives of Jesus, Zoroaster and Daniel, and the myths of Adonis and Dionysus. The story-unit is a transitional work that is a synthesis of characters and situations in partial development, some of which will later emerge in more fully developed form, as in **"Funerales de la Mamá Grande,"** *La mala hora* and *Cien años de soledad.*

García Márquez's use of Christian and classical mythology in no way lessens the impact of the central message of the unit, but rather enhances it. . . . The use of world myth and legend serves to universalize the major components of the work, and is essential to the understanding of the central message of **"La prodigiosa tarde de Baltazar"-"La viuda de Montiel"**: that the eternal rebirth of Balthazar's challenge must inevitably lead to the decline and disintegration of Montiel and the repressive system he symbolizes. It will be a multi-faceted triumph, that of the imaginative, chaotic and spiritual over the objective, materialistic and repressive. But if the cycle itself is Dionysian (as we have seen), the basic struggle must be eternal: Montiel will be supplanted by Don Sabas of *La mala hora,* Balthazar by Dr. Giraldo, and so the challenge is perpetuated. Finally, what Balthazar would seem to be prophesying is not a simple and direct triumph of certain artistic and social values, but the struggle and triumph of the spirit of human freedom and dignity through a tortuous and lengthy process of inexorable change—the struggle of mankind for rebirth into the Platonic Whole State. (pp. 89-98)

Susan Mott Linker, "Myth and Legend in Two Prodigious Tales of García Márquez," in Hispanic Journal, *Vol. 9, No. 1, Fall, 1987, pp. 89-100.*

Stephen Minta (essay date 1987)

[*In the following excerpt from his* Gabriel García Márquez: Writer of Colombia, *Minta discusses the novella* No One Writes to the Colonel *in relation to* la violencia, *a series of political crises in Colombia that reached a height of violence during the 1950s.*]

The central—almost the only—figure in Samuel Beckett's play *Happy Days* is a woman called Winnie. She is about fifty years old, and she spends the entire play buried in the earth, up to her waist in the first act, literally up to her neck in it in the second. From this unpromising and obviously declining position, anchored in the midst of an unbroken plain under a merciless light, she manages to sustain a dialogue with herself, constantly giving herself encouragement or reassurance, somehow getting through the day with the kind of routines that mark and condition a life, brushing her hair, going through the contents of her bag, and occasionally speculating on the way things are, though always in a manner designed to distance her from the possibility, or the threat, of change. Her world is apparently as self-contained as a world could be, drastically limited in space, essentially reduced to the dimensions of repetitious speech. Yet other worlds do intrude, memories of happier times and other places, above all the vague presence on stage of another character, Willie, a man in his sixties, someone with whom Winnie has had a long and progressively more limited relationship. Willie sits or crawls, mostly in silence, apparently more animal than human, yet still important to Winnie because, withdrawn and laconic as he is, he offers the last remaining hope that her voice will be heard by someone, that she may not, after all, be so totally alone.

The play contains much that is deeply moving, much, too, that is very funny—as a character in another of Beckett's plays remarks: 'Nothing is funnier than unhappiness.' However, the play also raises ethical questions that invite no easy response. What little remains of Winnie's life is being systematically destroyed; of that there is no doubt. Were the play to move to a third act, we should expect to find the central character fully absorbed into the earth and finally silenced. But how should the spectator respond to this process? In one way, Winnie's voluble adaptability to the increasing hopelessness of her situation, her determination to remain cheerful and to keep talking, her concern for order and appearances as a means of survival, all arouse in the audience not merely feelings of sympathy, but a sense of being witness to a struggle that is altogether heroic. If the encroaching mound of earth suggests the decline of old age and the inevitability of death, then Winnie's attitude, a warm and even passionate dramatization of old clichés ('One mustn't grumble', 'One should learn to make the most of things'), stands out as a message of a very positive kind, a refusal to surrender to the logic of despair. However, seen from another point of view, perhaps it is not so much the earth which is rising as Winnie who is falling? Perhaps she is falling, being sucked ever deeper into the morass, precisely because she is so relentlessly capable of making the most of things, of adapting with such apparent dexterity to a pattern of life that seems in the end to be a denial of life itself. At the end of the play, she watches as Willie tries to climb up the mound in which she is imprisoned. His errand is uncertain; perhaps he wants to kiss her, or perhaps to kill her and so end the misery of her private world or the torture of their shared existence. Winnie recognizes her complete helplessness, a passivity that has now become absolute: 'There was a time when I could have given you a hand', she says, 'and then a time before that again when I did give you a hand.' What has happened here? Does the problem lie in the nature of life itself, in the irresistible process of physical and mental decline? Or does it lie in Winnie's refusal or inability to countenance revolt, to take a stand, in her endless acceptance of life as it is given? Should we admire Winnie's resilience in the face of an unendurable pressure, or should we recoil in the face of her seemingly limitless capacity to reach an accommodation with the wretchedness of her condition? The play, clearly, will offer no resolution of this dilemma, recognizing that no resolution is possible outside the limits of an individual consciousness, but it does allow the complexities and the poignancy of the situation to emerge in a particularly challenging way.

García Márquez's long short story ***No One Writes to the Colonel,*** written while he was in Europe in the 1950s, presents the reader with rather similar problems, and, in a sense, the problems are more complex still, because—whether intentionally or otherwise—the moral ambiguities raised within the story are not subject to the same rigorously neutral control as exists within Samuel Beckett's play. García Márquez's story seems at times to be searching for some form of resolution of the dilemmas it contains, while at other times it appears to take refuge in the inscrutable nature of those same dilemmas. Moreover, the story deals with issues of both a personal and a social kind, whereas Beckett's concerns in *Happy Days* are almost exclusively personal. Whatever their differences, however, both the story and the play are deeply involved with the problems of how to live in a world which is seen as ultimately unacceptable and unendurable, and both are far more productive of thought than their relatively simple narrative structures would suggest. ***No One Writes to the Colonel*** is set in the tropical lowlands of Colombia, in a place which resembles Sucre, the inland river port in the department of the same name where García Márquez's family lived in the 1940s. The central figure of the story, the colonel of the title, is a man seventy-five years of age, a veteran of the War of a Thousand Days, the Colombian civil war of 1899-1902. We learn that the colonel fought on the losing Liberal side and that he was present at the signing of the Treaty of Neerlandia on 24 October 1902. This treaty . . . marked the end of the military ambitions of the Liberal general Rafael Uribe Uribe, while in García Márquez's fictional world this same act of surrender brings to an end the military career of Colonel Aureliano Buendía, described in ***No One Writes to the Colonel*** as the 'quartermaster general of the revolutionary forces on the Atlantic coast'.

The events in ***No One Writes to the Colonel*** take place in the year 1956, when Colombia had already suffered through nearly a decade of the *violencia;* it is also the year, as the story twice reminds us, of the Suez crisis in Europe. For the central figure of the story, the half-century that has elapsed since the end of the War of a Thousand Days has been generally uneventful, but it has been dominated by a single, inescapable passion: the colonel's desire to obtain the war veteran's pension that was promised by the government in the wake of the surrender at Neerlandia. Every Friday, when the mail arrives, brought by river launch from a town eight hours away, the colonel goes to see if there is any news of his pension, and, inevitably, there is none. As the postmaster succinctly puts it: 'El coronel no tiene quien le escriba,' the flat and dismissive statement that gives the story its title. Still the colonel refuses to give up hope and patiently keeps on waiting for the next Friday to come around. His desire for his war pension is doubly motivated. Most obviously, he is in desperate need of the money: the colonel and his wife are living in conditions of great material deprivation, and have long suffered from the effects of chronic undernourishment. . . . However, the colonel is also concerned with what he sees as the morality of the situation. He has an unshakeable sense that the war pension should be his by virtue of natural justice, that the cause he fought for in the civil war, 'to save the Republic', as he puts it in a conversation with his lawyer, was a just cause, that defeat was not humiliation, and that, however long the process may take, justice and truth must surely triumph in the end.

The colonel's optimism, which is not, in fact, quite as unwavering or as unreflective as some critics have suggested, has produced very different responses among readers. According to one editor of the story: 'A state of innocence and truth protect the colonel's inner life from the contaminating evils around him,' and the writer goes on to suggest that there is a general lesson here: 'A capacity for love and sacrifice are the safeguards of Man's happiness and, armed with these qualities, he can spiritually survive' (Giovanni Pontiero). According to another editor, however, the story 'shows a man who is victimized by his pride, dignity, and quixotic hopes as much as by the realities of history, government, and society' (Djelal Kadir [*Triple espera: Novelas cortas de Hispanoamérica* (1976)]). Clearly, the discrepancies reflect very different basic attitudes and values, and return us to the kind of dilemmas which face the audience in Beckett's *Happy Days.* Is the colonel's persistence in trusting to the future—a future in which we, as observers of his situation, can see little obvious reason for hope—a form of heroic madness in a world where values have become so distorted under the impact of endless violence, poverty, and repression that sanity appears a mockery? Or is the colonel's optimism a kind of suicide, a blank refusal to accept the reality of a world which is inevitably impinging upon him, an attempt to live according to values that are unsustainable except by an act of wilful blindness, a perverse effort to try to redeem the inadequacies of half a century by proving himself to have been right all along? These dilemmas are always near the surface of the tale, not least in the passages dealing with the relationship between the colonel and his wife. Where he is quixotic and optimistic, she is practical and, understandably, often near to despair, and, in one beautifully simple exchange between them, we see a confrontation between what are, in effect, two utterly distinct world views:

> 'You can't eat illusions,' said the woman.
>
> 'You can't eat them, but they feed you,' replied the colonel.

The general situation is complicated in a variety of ways by the fact that the couple have inherited from their dead son a fighting cock, an animal which, in the context of their society, represents potential wealth, either as an object to be sold immediately, or—more problematically—as an investment, which will pay off should the bird turn out to be a good fighter in the pit. Naturally enough, the colonel's wife is for selling the bird, putting their finances in order, and having something decent to eat; but the colonel, though hesitant at times, is driven by a desire to keep the bird. He knows that it costs more than they can afford to feed it, but, because it once belonged to their son, it represents an almost magical link with the past, it is wondrously and intensely alive, where so much else seems dead or dying, and it carries with it the possibility of hope, one that is more than simply financial, something strangely indefinable that appeals to the colonel more than the arid certainties of an immediate cash transaction. Inevitably, critics have argued that the fighting cock should be interpreted as a symbol of some kind, of revolt, of trust in the workings of fate or resignation to them, of the collective hopes of a people for whom chance alone appears to offer some possibility of release from their troubles, but this is a matter to which I shall return later.

The tale is told in an apparently simple and direct way, and, as we have seen, this directness was the result of a conscious decision which García Márquez took in the 1950s to move away from what he felt was the excessively literary style of his first novel, ***Leaf Storm,*** in order to try to deal more authentically with the rough realities of contemporary Colombia. The colonel of the story is never named. We are told that he grew up in the small town of Manaure, situated to the east of Riohacha, in the department of La Guajira in north-eastern Colombia. We learn nothing about how or why he came to fight on the Liberal side in the civil war; given that he is seventy-five years old in 1956, he would have been eighteen at the start of the War of a Thousand Days, and, according to his lawyer, he was a colonel by the time he was twenty. At some point he became associated with the town of Macondo, the legendary setting for *One Hundred Years of Solitude* which is generally identified with Aracataca, García Márquez's birthplace in the department of Magdalena. His distinctive, if problematical, honesty is reflected in his appointment at the time of the civil war as 'treasurer of the revolution in the district of Macondo'. He faithfully made the journey to the surrender at Neerlandia, travelling for six days with the funds of the rebel forces contained in two trunks tied to the back of a mule. He arrived just half an hour before the signing of the treaty, and obtained a receipt for the funds from Colonel Aureliano Buendía.

In an interesting passage from *One Hundred Years of Solitude,* this latter incident, which is only briefly described in ***No One Writes to the Colonel,*** is filled out in greater detail, and in a way that gives some insight into García Márquez's continuing thoughts about the character of his colonel some ten years after the writing of the story in which he first appears. In the later novel, the two trunks which the colonel brings to Neerlandia are revealed to contain solid gold; Aureliano Buendía is in the process of signing the final copy of the surrender document when:

> . . . a rebel colonel appeared in the doorway of the tent, leading by the halter a mule laden with two trunks. In spite of his extreme youth, he had an arid appearance and a patient expression. He was the treasurer of the revolution in the district of Macondo. . . . With a deliberation that was exasperating, he unloaded the trunks, opened them, and placed on the table, one by one, seventy-two gold bricks. Everyone had forgotten the existence of such a fortune. . . .

The passage is interesting because it suggests that the colonel's honesty, one of the most obvious aspects of his character, should not be viewed in a wholly simple light. Certainly, in a time of civil war, there is something remarkable about the way he has behaved; he could so easily, amidst all the chaos of defeat, have taken the Liberal gold for himself and lived for ever in comfort. But, at the same time, there is something exasperating about his meticulous concern for the details of his task. It has a hint almost of the bureaucratic, suggesting a form of honesty that is hard, at times, to distinguish from the simply obstinate. It might be said in reply, perhaps, that it is only such forms of honesty that are likely to survive under the pressure of war and the debasement of moral values, a point which brings the reader back once again to the difficult question of the appropriateness of the colonel's obstinate, absurd, or heroic resistance in the short story of which he is the subject. It is clear, at least, that the colonel is meant to be no simple hero, no mere moral counterweight to the chaos that surrounds him.

Following the Liberal defeat the colonel seems to have done very little, except to wait for his illusory pension. After the signing of the Treaty of Neerlandia he lives on in Macondo for a few years, but then the banana fever, symbolized by that same 'innocent yellow train' which appears in *One Hundred Years of Solitude,* comes to change the way of life in the town for ever. The colonel is unable to tolerate the invasion:

> In the drowsiness of siesta time, he saw a dusty, yellow train arrive, with men and women and animals suffocating in the heat, crowded together even on the roofs of the carriages. It was the

> banana fever. In twenty-four hours they transformed the town. 'I'm going,' the colonel said then. 'The smell of bananas is rotting my insides.'

So, we are told, he left Macondo in June 1906; fifty years later we find him settled in a remote and terrorized town further south, where he continues his life of endless expectation. Now, in 1906, he would have been only twenty-five years old, and the apparently uninterrupted period of passive waiting that has filled more than half a century of his existence seems scarcely credible. In reality, however, the story is told in a way that does not encourage the reader to reconstruct the past in any great detail. García Márquez is clearly not interested primarily in establishing a wholly plausible sequence of events to sustain the image of his central character. He is concerned above all with what the colonel is now, with what remains to him of life, with the psychology of waiting, and with his struggle to survive, spiritually and materially, in an increasingly enclosed world. Once, we learn, the colonel belonged to a veterans' association that included members of both political parties, but, as he says, 'all my comrades died waiting for the mail', and he is now left to face his problems alone.

Nothing very much happens in the course of ***No One Writes to the Colonel.*** Indeed, the story is constructed in such a way as to convince the reader that the chances of something ever happening in the town are extremely limited. What we are given is a sense of the unending pressures which weigh down upon the colonel's life: the forces of personal poverty, the tyranny of the climate, and the collective fear which is the mark of the years of the Colombian *violencia;* and it is only in the context of these seemingly invincible pressures that we can form any sense of the meaning—if there can be one—of the colonel's dogged resistance. The poverty in which he and his wife live is made explicit from the very opening lines of the story. He opens a tin of coffee and finds there is only a teaspoonful left; he uses a knife to scrape out the inside of the tin, in order that nothing should be wasted, and so another day begins. The dull precision of the gestures confirms the impression of an unending round of attempts to deal with a situation that has, imperceptibly over the years, become an impossible one. This search for a way out of the enclosed world of poverty colours the entire narrative.

The couple have nothing left to sell, except a clock and a picture, and no one wants to buy them, the clock because it is now old-fashioned, since clocks with luminous dials have begun to appear on the local market, and the picture because almost everyone in town has an identical one. The couple's poverty has become a powerful force of isolation, for they have struggled to maintain appearances, and this has led to desperate subterfuge: 'Several times I've put stones on to boil', his wife says, 'so the neighbours wouldn't know that we've gone for days without putting the pot on the stove.' Within their relationship, too, the long-term effects of poverty and the attempts to conceal it have been corrosive. When the colonel's wife goes to the local priest, Father Ángel, in an effort to raise some money on their wedding rings—and is rebuked by the priest with the cliché that 'it is a sin to trade with sacred things—she cannot tell her husband at first, and offers a half-hearted explanation for her absence. The colonel, sensing her hesitation, sees the moral clearly: 'The worst thing about a bad situation', he says, 'is that it makes one tell lies.' It would be a mistake, however, to conclude that the description of the couple's poverty conveys only despair. On the contrary, ***No One Writes to the Colonel*** represents García Márquez's first important attempt to explore the humorous dimensions of a serious subject, revealing an approach that is characteristic of much of his best work and one that is very different from the heavy and sombre style of his earliest writings. At various points in the story, the colonel is able to contemplate his predicament with a wry sense of detachment, and, on one occasion, faced with the interminable problem of where to find something to eat, he argues with unanswerable false logic: 'If we were going to die of hunger, we'd have died already by now.'

To the troubles of poverty are added the trials of the climate. The story takes place between the months of October and December, and the weather during those months provides a kind of external image of the colonel's inner struggle. Throughout the Caribbean lowlands of Colombia, there are two distinct seasons, marked not by variety in temperature, as in the temperate zones of the world, but by the presence or absence of rain. The rainy season is called winter, and lasts from late April to November or early December, while the dry season, summer, runs from December to April. The heaviest rains come in May and October, and García Márquez set two of his early stories in those months: the **"Monologue of Isabel Watching It Rain in Macondo"**, which dates back to 1952, describes the sudden onset of winter with a rainstorm in May, while ***No One Writes to the Colonel*** opens with a picture of the rains in October. In each case, there is a firm link between the coming of rain and a feeling of unease and disgust, allied to a sense of sadness, desolation, and disintegration. In the former piece, the approaching rainstorm produces an immediate physical reaction in the narrator: 'I felt shaken by the slimy sensation in my stomach,' she says, and then later, as the rains fall unceasingly, 'I felt changed into a desolate meadow, sown with algae and lichens, with soft and sticky toadstools, fertilized by the loathsome flora of dampness and shadow.' The colonel, too, experiences 'the feeling that toadstools and poisonous lilies were sprouting in his stomach', and his wife, thinking of a man who has recently died in the town, says 'it must be horrible to be buried in October', as if there is something truly terrifying about the rapacity of the earth under the tropical rain. As the rainy season gives way to summer towards the end of the story, the change, both physical and psychological, in the colonel's condition is immediately apparent. 'The whole year ought to be December,' he says, for with the onset of the dry season life seems possible once again.

However, throughout most of the story, the town is in the grip of the winter rains, suffocating and unhealthy. Such, too, is the quality of the political and social atmosphere. By 1956, the worst years of the *violencia* were over, and García Márquez was concerned, as we have seen before, not so much with detailing the horrors that had recently overtaken rural Colombia as with trying to understand the effects on those who had survived. There is nothing overtly dramatic, therefore, about this story of the *violencia.* On the contrary, the reader is quickly made aware of the dull and restricted nature of life in a community where repression has become institutionalized. Violence here has been so completely absorbed into the fabric of everyday life that most people seem hardly conscious of the forms it has taken. The colonel waits for curfew to be sounded in order to set his clock; we learn that it is years since elections have been held, and that it would be foolish to expect any change—as the local doctor puts it: 'We're too old now to be waiting for the Messiah.' The press is censored. It is possible to read about the Suez crisis, but not about what is happening in Colombia: 'Since there's been censorship', the colonel says, 'the newspapers don't talk about anything except Europe,' and he goes on to make a remark that, in its very naïvety, underlines something close to a simple truth: 'The best thing would be for the Europeans to come over here and for us to go to Europe. That way, everyone would know what's going on in their own country.' The colonel and the local doctor belong to a resistance group that is responsible for circulating clandestine information, and, later in the story, on a sweltering Sunday night, while the colonel is watching a game of roulette in the town's billiard hall, he is caught up in a police raid. He realizes he has a clandestine paper in his pocket. He comes face to face with the killer of his son, and in circumstances very like those in which his son was shot, but the moment of confrontation swiftly and safely passes, and García Márquez makes no attempt to heighten the sense of drama; for the clandestine paper, the police raid, even the son's violent and unnecessary death, have all become part of the regular and expected pattern of life in the town. It is perhaps this acceptance of violence as an inevitable condition of life, something like the weather which must be endured because it cannot be changed, that constitutes the saddest, and also the most dangerous, legacy of the Colombian *violencia.* It is, once again, only in the context of such an apparently closed and hopeless situation that we may try to understand the importance of the colonel's own affirmative view of life.

In many ways, ***No One Writes to the Colonel*** reveals a town that is not only isolated from the larger world, but also bitterly divided within. Cut off from the rest of Colombia, it yet reproduces all the most dismal features of contemporary Colombian life. The town is highly stratified, both socially and economically. We see the world of Don Sabas, 'with a two-storey house that isn't big enough to put his money in', and we learn that he is the only Liberal leader who has been able to survive the years of persecution, having come to an agreement with the local mayor (on terms that are fully clarified in *In Evil Hour*), and subsequently growing rich by buying up the property of his fellow partisans as they were systematically driven from the town or assassinated. By contrast, we get occasional glimpses of the poor parts of town, as when a funeral procession passes by and the women from the 'barrios bajos' watch it go, 'biting their nails in silence'. We see the world of the colonel's corrupt or ineffectual lawyer, with his endless complacent explanations of the intricacies of the Colombian bureaucracy, and a chair 'too narrow for his sagging buttocks'. There is also the local priest, Father Angel, a man concerned principally with the proper observance of the forms of religion, who uses the ringing of the church bells to propagate a system of ecclesiastical film censorship, and then sits at the door of his office to check on those who have disobeyed his instructions. For a year now the only films on offer have been condemned as 'bad for everyone', but the cinema still functions, showing films with mildly provocative titles like *Midnight Virgin.* We see the town's mayor, on the balcony of the police barracks, appropriately enough, dressed in his underwear, and with his swollen cheek unshaven, the latter detail also to be explained in the course of *In Evil Hour.*

Finally, on the margins of this society, there are the 'foreign' merchants, called variously Syrians or Turks. These names are widely applied in both Central and South America to a class of immigrants who came to the Caribbean in the late nineteenth century from Syria, Lebanon, and Palestine. They were mostly Christians fleeing from Turkish persecution, and they initially found work in the Caribbean region as itinerant salesmen. In recent times, their descendants have become fully integrated into the social and political life of a number of Latin American countries, but in García Márquez's writings they are invariably portrayed as alien, unassimilated, and exotic. In *One Hundred Years of Solitude,* the 'Street of the Turks' is described as the place 'where the Arabs languished who, in times past, used to exchange trinkets for macaws'; while in ***No One Writes to the Colonel,*** the extent to which the colonel's wife registers her decline in the society of the town is emphasized by her remark that, in the course of trying to sell off their unsellable picture, she has gone 'even to the Turks'.

This, then, is a town that seems altogether lost, a town described in a marvellous phrase as 'ravaged by ten years of history', dwelling in a kind of lethargy that appears to be beyond hope of reversal. This town, rendered mute by the excesses of its own familial savagery, stands, too, for so many others in the Colombia of the mid-1950s. The formal structures of social and political life offer no hope. If there is anything positive to be found, one must turn elsewhere. Some individuals, it seems clear, have managed to survive the horrors of the past without succumbing to the sterility of the present. There is the doctor who attends the colonel's wife, and who is also active in the local resistance; he shares much, incidentally, with the doctor of *In Evil Hour,* despite some superficial differences in the detail of their age and appearance. He refuses to accept payment from the colonel for his medical services, as he refuses to drink the coffee he knows the couple cannot afford to offer him, and, in both cases, his refusal is conveyed with an instinctive awareness of the importance of the couple's pride and dignity which allows the relationship between the three of them to remain as one between equals. The doctor has survived as a human being, events have not defeated him, and, if he declines to speculate on the coming of a Messiah, it is from a position of strength, not of despair.

Then, perhaps, there is the example of the colonel himself, though no final judgment is possible here because, as I have suggested, the colonel remains a controversial figure. Some would argue that his capacity to retain a faith in the future is all that matters in the context of the kind of world in which he is forced to live, and I think that might well be the best reading of his role in the story. According to such a reading, the problems surrounding the way the colonel thinks and acts are largely irrelevant. The fact that he is there, continuing to insist that his pension will arrive, that things will improve, that the fighting cock will bring an end to his financial problems, is enough in itself; and the question of whether he is right to have such faith, whether it makes any sense, whether or not it is even responsible in the circumstances, these are, arguably, all secondary issues. Such an approach is, I think, supported by the importance given to the colonel's sense of humour. It is difficult to account logically for the power of humour, but it is often far more influential in life than other things which ought logically to matter more. In the case of the colonel, his sense of humour allows him to express a detachment from the miserable conditions in which he is living, somehow making the misery less threatening, less all-encompassing. We are given a fine example of this process in the opening pages of the story. The colonel's wife is watching as he dresses to go to a funeral:

> 'You look as though you're ready for a special event,' she said.
>
> 'This burial is a special event,' the colonel said. 'It's the first death from natural causes that we've had in years.'

The positive value of such an attitude, in such adverse circumstances, is beyond analysis.

As soon as one tries to explore the detailed working out of the story, however, questions do arise, and they come to focus in the end on the colonel's concern for the fighting cock that he has inherited from his son. He longs to keep the bird, but comes very near to parting with it, under the general pressure of his financial situation and the constant pleading of his wife. He has reached the point when he has decided to sell the bird to Don Sabas; but then, while he is out of the house one day, the friends of his dead son, who have recently taken over the expense of feeding the bird, arrive to carry it off, saying that it belongs not simply to the colonel and his wife, but to the whole town. They take the bird to a trial fight in the cockpit, and there, almost by chance, the colonel comes to see it perform. This sequence of events implies that the author is seeking to turn the fighting cock into a symbol of some kind, a representative, perhaps, of the collective hopes of the people, an embodiment, as Vargas Llosa suggests, of the people's intense desire for change and renewal after the events of the past decade. It is clear, I think, that García Márquez is concerned in some way with developing the social dimensions of the colonel's private struggle, but a problem arises as soon as one looks at the description of the cock fight itself. The colonel perceives nothing but the sadness and absurdity of the event:

> He saw his fighting cock in the centre of the arena, alone, defenceless . . . with something like fear visible in the trembling of his feet. His adversary was a sad and ashen cock. . . .

The birds go through the motions of fighting, and the crowd respond with wild enthusiasm; but the colonel cannot share in the excitement:

> The colonel noticed the disproportion between the enthusiasm of the ovation and the intensity of the fight. It seemed to him a farce to which—voluntarily and consciously—the fighting cocks had also lent themselves.

This last observation seems more appropriate as a comment on the years of the Colombian *violencia* than as an affirmation of the possibilities of escape. Nevertheless, the colonel goes home applauded by all the poor people of the town, and the narrator tells us that 'that afternoon . . . the people had awakened'. The colonel reaffirms his intention not to sell his fighting cock, and later, when his wife challenges him by saying 'you're dying of hunger, completely alone', he answers, with an evident reflection of the communal enthusiasm, 'I'm not alone'. So something has obviously happened, but just how and why the enthusiasm of the crowd has transformed the sad farce of the cockpit into something vital and sustaining is not really clear. The tumult of the crowd reminds the colonel of happier and freer days in the town, in the time when there were elections and functioning political parties, but much remains unexplained. Perhaps one of the problems here stems from the choice of the fighting cock as a potential symbol. García Márquez has said that he originally intended to end the story with the colonel wringing the cock's neck and serving the bird up as soup, and that he changed his mind on this only at the last minute. Clearly, the tone of the remark reveals his exasperation in the face of some of the more sublime efforts of critics to turn the fighting cock into appropriate symbolic terms. But there may also be a frustrated realization that perhaps the bird was not the best possible symbol for some of the things he wanted to suggest.

A final problem of interpretation arises in connexion with the closing lines of ***No One Writes to the Colonel.*** One might have expected to look there for some confirmation of the general direction that the story has been taking, but, in fact, the conclusion resolves nothing. For the climactic note on which the story ends is in itself ambiguous and opaque in its implications. We are given what is in many ways a typical short story ending, one that seeks to imply, through the device of its restricted space, that far more is involved than could adequately be explained to the reader. The colonel's wife has returned to her regular line of questioning. Now that the fighting cock is not to be sold, what are they going to eat, and what will happen if, at the cock fights the following month, the bird turns out to be a loser? As dawn breaks one Sunday morning, the couple exchange the following words:

> 'He's a cock that can't lose.'
>
> 'But suppose he does lose?'
>
> 'There are still forty-five days to begin to think about that,' the colonel said.
>
> The woman grew desperate.
>
> 'And meanwhile, what do we eat?' she asked, and seized the colonel by the collar of his flannel night-shirt. She shook him hard.
>
> 'Tell me, what do we eat?'
>
> The colonel had needed seventy-five years—the

> seventy-five years of his life, minute by minute—to reach this point. He felt pure, explicit, invincible at the moment of replying: 'Shit.'

Once again, it is clearly stated that this is a moment of consequence, but it is difficult to say precisely why. We are told that a lifetime's experience has gone into the final word, *mierda,* but what does that really imply? In an obvious way, we could say that this is an act of rebellion, symbolized by the colonel's use of a word that would never have normally entered his vocabulary—earlier in the story, indeed, he has reacted in a predictably offended way on hearing the word uttered by Alfonso, one of the former companions of his dead son, though the point of this parallel is lost in the English version by J. S. Bernstein, who translates Alfonso's 'Mierda, coronel' as 'Goddamn it, Colonel'. For all that, it seems a rather limited act of rebellion in the circumstances. Some critics, sensing this, have argued that the ending of the story changes nothing. So Giovanni Pontiero writes: 'The colonel gives vent to his frustrations without attempting to answer his wife's anguished questions or resolve anything. We leave the town and its inhabitants exactly as we found them—still waiting for the miracle that will transform their lives.' For other critics, however, the colonel's act of self-assertion, if that is what it is, presages a radical change in his attitude towards his situation. Vincenzo Bollettino, for example, argues [in *Breve estudio de la novelística de García Márquez* (1973)] that the final word of the story is critical for an understanding of the whole work. At this point, he believes, the colonel finally comes face to face with the absurdity of existence, and thus of his own existence; he at last understands that death is the necessary and inevitable end of all life's struggles, and this newly acquired realization conditions the violence of his final dramatic affirmation. Bollettino writes: 'His life has been nothing but a desperate attempt to evade reality, taking refuge now in his pride as a soldier, now in his veteran's pension, now in his fighting cock, but all in vain. Sooner or later, he had to come face to face with reality. At least now he does not have to conceal the fact that life is "shit".'

These differences in the response to the final lines take us back to some of the fundamental differences of approach that I have tried to explore with regard to the work as a whole. Such differences are not, I think, reconcilable, for the story allows many possibilities to emerge and never appears to decide between them. Much, naturally, depends on the values and expectations that the individual reader brings to the work, though these will always be, in themselves, complex and difficult to define. A number of terms that I have used in the course of this discussion, such as optimism and resistance, carry a wide range of implications, both positive and negative, and frequently serve only to conceal the thing one wants to talk about. If the colonel's irrational and often infuriating optimism is thought of as fundamentally self-deluding, then one will more naturally look for an ending to the story which will suggest a break with the habits of the past—and this is the approach which writers like Vincenzo Bollettino take. If, on the other hand, the colonel's optimism is felt to be the only valid mechanism by which he can deal with a world that would otherwise be perceived as intolerable, then one will tend to see the ending of the story as a reinforcement of his determination to continue his struggle as before. The former view is certainly easier to defend logically, but I suspect that the latter may be the more profitable reading. The more one thinks about the position of the colonel and his town, the more one is likely to be drawn by a logic of despair, and yet the book does not seem to be a tale of despair, or even simply one that encourages a realistic acceptance of things. If neither the colonel, nor the reader, nor the author can precisely articulate the nature of the alternatives, that may be because of the nature of hope itself, always dependent, to some degree, on faith rather than reason. Such a view, of course, invites charges of pure sentimentality, but the fact remains that many of the colonel's long-term problems cannot be met by any obvious solutions, and I think that is what gives his struggle an enduring interest and complexity. A comparison with *In Evil Hour* makes the point very well. That story is also about an intolerable world, but a potential solution is held out strongly at the end of the book, as people take to the hills to continue their struggle by force of arms. Such a solution may be more immediately satisfying and uplifting than the ambiguities of ***No One Writes to the Colonel,*** but it is one that can make sense only in a limited range of situations. The colonel's problems, of poverty, old age, and a life unfulfilled, remain to be faced, intractable and apparently beyond redress, and in the end, perhaps, it is only with a recognition of the true nature and extent of those problems that one might come to understand the significance of the colonel's quixotic resistance to them:

> 'You can't eat illusions,' said the woman.
>
> 'You can't eat them, but they feed you,' replied the colonel.

The English translation of ***No One Writes to the Colonel*** provides, on the whole, a good sense of the original, but there are one or two places where the meaning is obscured, usually because a Spanish idiom has been too literally translated, or, perhaps, misunderstood. I give two examples here. When the colonel's wife sees her husband off one morning, she reminds him to make sure that the doctor calls round to visit her, saying: 'Pregúntale al doctor si en esta casa le echamos agua caliente.' This literally means: 'Ask the doctor if we pour hot water over him in this house,' and is more or less rendered thus in the English version: 'Ask the doctor if we poured boiling water on him in this house,' whereas something like 'Ask the doctor what we've done to scare him away' might have been more appropriate. Then, later, when the colonel's wife is talking to her husband about changing their lawyer, she says, in effect, 'what use is money to us when we're dead?': literally, 'we get nothing out of it if they put [the money] in our coffin the way they do with the Indians', a reference to the Indian custom of burying the dead with their possessions. The English version, 'we're not getting anything out of their putting us away on a shelf as they do with the Indians', is simply wrong. Lastly, and incidentally, the presence of a significant trio of names—those of Álvaro, Germán, and Alfonso—is obscured in the English version by the rendering throughout of the name Germán as Hernán. (pp. 65-82)

Stephen Minta, in his Gabriel García Márquez: Writer of Colombia, *Jonathan Cape, 1987, 186 p.*

Gene H. Bell-Villada (essay date 1990)

[*Bell-Villada is a Haitian-born American educator and critic who has written the study* García Márquez: The Man and His Work. *He has stated that his scholarly interests include "international relations, problems of culture, and relations between society and culture." In the following excerpt from the above-mentioned work, Bell-Villada examines the theme of love and the parody of traditional literary genres in* Innocent Eréndira *and* Chronicle of a Death Foretold.]

It was only when he was in his late fifties that García Márquez came to be regarded as one of the great writers of romantic love. While Caribbean magic and politics stand out as the subjects most commonly associated with his art, the truth is also that few novelists have written as wisely and in such full depth about that banal yet elusive world of male-female attraction, courtship, and love, with all its attendant pleasures and frustrations, its commitments and ambivalences, its private certainties and public prejudices, its erotic force and everyday suppressions, its subjective, complex subtleties and objective, simplifying ritualizations, its expectations and surprises, and its entire ensemble of ups and downs—its vastly contradictory textures—as has the Colombian novelist. Love in García Márquez's fiction is as it is in real life: both fearsome and joyous, all-consuming yet creative, ecstatic and serene, glorious yet somehow sad and funny as well.

The interest had long been with him. Some of García Márquez's most imaginative and touching early articles tell of lovers reunited after undergoing many trials, or of the ways in which the telephone has transformed old courtship habits. Commenting in February 1955 on the romance that had blossomed between renowned bullfighter Dominguín and an Italian beauty (who had written the Spaniard one of those innocent fan letters, "filled with the expressive and nonsensical foolishness of love"), the young journalist would conclude his brief column with the wry observation that "love remains, through the end of time, more powerful than a [raging] bull." These insights he was to include and develop in his magisterial "total" novels; *One Hundred Years of Solitude* is not only a town-and-family chronicle but also, as we saw earlier, a compendium of love stories; and *The Autumn of the Patriarch* anatomizes the tyrant's erotic disorders and ill-fated love life as much as it does his political history. To his interviewer for *Playboy,* a jolly García Márquez characterized himself as "a nymphomaniac of the heart."

The novella or short novel ***The Incredible and Sad Tale of Innocent Eréndira and Her Heartless Grandmother*** depicts successively love for sale, young love, and love unrequited, all amid the desolate sands of the Guajira desert. The lengthy title suggests a carnival barker's high bombast, and its two women in fact live mostly in tents (a circus tent, eventually). Save for **"Big Mama's Funeral"** no García Márquez narrative evokes with such fervor the atmosphere of plebeian festiveness and street revelry as does ***Eréndira*** (its shorter title). The basic plot, ironically, is as sad as the title indicates: a fourteen-year-old innocent is prostituted for two years by the "handsome white whale" of her grandmother, in payment for a million-peso "debt" incurred when the girl accidentally burned their house down. The novella thus first concentrates on the act of love commercialized and extorted by power.

For the grandmother, herself a whilom whore, love is and always has been just a business, and she typically reduces everything to (in Marx and Engels's phrase) "the icy water of egotistical calculation." When she first offers Eréndira to the widowered shopkeeper, the girl is examined for her dimensions and treated like so much merchandise—there is an entire page of haggling as to her "price." Throughout the story we see the old vixen computing labor costs, going to such absurd extremes as having Eréndira do the Indian servants' dirty wash so as to discount it from their pay, or trying to browbeat an ambulant, feisty photographer into defraying a fourth of the musicians' wages. The rotund adventuress shows that unctuous, informal, backslapping amicability ("Because I like you," she explains to the photographer) or the capacity for unwitting projection and false outrage (for example, accusing the widower of "lack of respect for virtue," or calling Eréndira's overeager customers "perverts" and "an inconsiderate bunch of slobs") ordinarily associated with unscrupulous businesspeople. On one level, then, ***Eréndira*** is a comic caricature of capitalism at its rawest, most "underdeveloped," and most interpersonally predatory. The matriarchal pimp and domestic tyrant even gives orders in her sleep.

Eréndira on the other hand is a classic portrait of pure innocence in absolute thrall to worldly power. Having fully internalized her oppression, the heroine *follows* orders and does housework in her sleep, routinely replying with a formulaic "Sí, abuela" ("Yes, grandmother") to the old despot's every utterance. These are in fact the only two words the oppressed will ever address directly to her oppressor (the sole exceptions being three scattered brief complaints to the malevolent matriarch about pains from overwork). When the grandmother, in order to retrieve Eréndira from the convent, pulls the trick of marrying her off to a pliable Indian boy, the victim "willingly" returns to her victimizer's clutches even while pointing at her nominal husband. Further along in her "career" Eréndira toys mentally with pumping boiling water into the evil ogress's bath but suddenly repents when called by her, and later, to her lover Ulises she will confess being incapable of murdering the old harridan "because she's my grandmother." In the end, in a kind of magical Freudism, Eréndira's face takes on instant maturity the moment her malefactress plops dead at the hands of Ulises. And yet she abandons her loving redeemer, for the sordid injustices she has endured have made her selfishly individualistic and opportunistic rather than compassionate or sympathetic (a common enough real-life result). The young maiden, it turns out, never loved her wooer and rescuer.

Eréndira is in fact a shrewd and very funny love story cum swashbuckling tale. Much of its wild humor, appropriately, derives from its being a broad parody of some venerated traditional genres: ancient myth, medieval romance, and above all fairy tale, along with movie melodrama (a kind of twentieth-century avatar). Numerous conventions are plundered from these formats and turned upside down. The "hero" Ulises, an angel-faced naïf and occasional bungler, is the farthest thing possible from the wily adventurer of Homeric fame. Neither is this tropical Ulises a navigator, nor a womanizer; indeed he is a virgin, and on their first night his experienced damsel has to teach *him* about love after he goes limp. Similarly, Eréndira's late father and grandfather share the noble name "Amadís," an obvious echo of the most celebrated of medieval Spanish romances of knight-errantry (famously satirized, of course, by Cervantes). García Márquez's Amadises were smugglers on the hot Guajira desert rather than gallant knights in an idealized Europe. The first Amadís rescued not a pure maiden from a tower but a heartless whore from an Antillean brothel, while the second was actually shot in a fight over a woman. The aging moll now lives reenacting past glories, dining at her long table decorated with silver candelabra and set for twelve, an empty aristocratic ritual aptly symbolizing her fake elegance.

It is the fairy-tale nature of ***Eréndira,*** however, that most gives the novella its distinctive details and flavor. The characters are instantly recognizable types. Eréndira herself is a kind of Cinderella, a paragon of girlish innocence, slaving under a tyrant who is cruel stepmother, wicked witch, and evil queen (indeed she sits on a throne, borne aloft by Indian servants) all rolled into one. Max Lüthi, a renowned expert on the genre, notes [in his *Once upon a Time: On the Nature of Fairy Tales*] that the fairy-tale hero frequently "breaks away from his home and goes out into the world." Likewise, when on a moonlit night Ulises's father demands to know where the boy is going, the latter responds, precisely, "Into the world," and moreover elicits a requisite paternal curse from his stereotypically ruddy, pipe-smoking, Bible-declaiming Dutch progenitor. The parting is further comically undercut when, in a follow-up scene, the paterfamilias declares sententiously, "He'll be back, beaten down by life," and his wise Guajiro Indian wife snaps in reply, "You're so stupid. He'll never come back."

The adventures involving the three principals are the familiar stuff of fairy tale, played by García Márquez for laughs. The youthful, wealthy enough "hero" falls in love at first sight with the young "maiden in distress"—in fact ends up in bed with her on their first meeting, she actually charging him her full fee (thereafter half, finally nothing) for her tender reciprocities. Later in the story an anguished Eréndira calls out Ulises's name (like Rapunzel in her tower) into the night, and from his distant orange plantation he miraculously—yet expectedly—hears her cry. His successive ordeals on her behalf culminate, true to form, in the final scene when he slays the dragonlike virago with a knife (though he could have simply shot the cad in her sleep), setting Eréndira free. But alas, there is no final wedding or "happily ever after" for this gallant, tearful paladin so casually abandoned by his ladylove. Indeed, only in the safety of the convent, in chapter 4, will Eréndira admit to being happy. She actually does marry—not at the end, however, but exactly midway through the novella, when the grandmother arranges the instant wedding with the Indian boy in order to spirit her away from the missionaries. The forced marriage-of-convenience lasts not forever but a few ceremonial minutes.

Fairy-tale narratives show a marked preference for the numbers three and seven. ***Eréndira,*** accordingly, has seven chapters containing some fundamental threes: three different men who first "initiate" the heroine; three "abductions" of Eréndira (by missionaries, by rival whores, and by Ulises); three oranges pilfered from the family farm by the hero just before the couple's abortive flight; and his three attempts at slaying the ogress, the third, with its hand-to-hand combat, being typically the fiercest. The naturalness with which the miraculous and fantastical are incorporated into the text as simply one more element in the story, is another fairy-tale trait. Ulises's ability to change glass objects to blue is diagnosed by his sagacious mother as a symptom of lovesickness, on the same order as his lack of appetite for bread; the oranges that grow with diamonds inside of them are appropriate for a social milieu of professional contraband; and the moribund grandmother's oozing green blood helps highlight the vixen's not being exactly human. (Possible associations: green is the color ordinarily attributed to dragons; and, in Spanish, *verde* is a common synonym for the sexual.) The special role assigned in ***Eréndira*** to hard objects—the gilded piano, the diamond-oranges, the gold vest—replicates the fairy-tale genre's bias for palpable mineral presences: gold rings, metal swords, glass slippers.

Moreover, with its purehearted lovers struggling against a slick and grotesque villain, ***Eréndira*** plays on the conventions of silver-screen romance and Perils-of-Pauline melodrama. Ulises utters lover's vows perfectly imaginable in the corniest celluloid tearjerker—for example, at his first encounter with Eréndira: "Everyone says you're very beautiful. And it's true." Or later, at Eréndira's request that he kill the witch: "For you, I'll do anything." The sordid context of these lines gives them their unmistakable parodic flavor. The story in fact was first drafted in 1968 as a film script, though a cinema version, directed by the Brazilian Ruy Guerra, did not appear until 1984. The garish decor of the novella's opening does suggest a set by Fellini, and Ulises in flight is actually described as brandishing a pistol "with the confidence of a movie gunfighter." (The revolver, naturally, turns out to be a hopeless dud at the height of the chase.) The final lines of the story are clearly inspired by the ending to Truffaut's *400 Blows*—in 1959, we might recall, García Márquez wrote an awestruck review of that landmark film. In ***Eréndira,*** however, the device too is altered: whereas the French youngster's long rush toward the sea ends on a quizzical freeze-frame there, García Márquez's adolescent girl first runs alongside the ocean and then heads back into the desert—still running.

Other moments in the story suggest the farcical rhythms and raw physicality of the animated cartoon genre. When a virginal Eréndira resists the widower's lusts by screaming and scratching at him, he slaps her off the ground, and she "with her long Medusa hair" floats momentarily in space—just as happens to cartoon characters before falling off some cliff. In his surprise initial visit to her, Ulises at first is seen sticking out his face from behind her bed, and she rubs her head with the towel "to prove that it wasn't an illusion"—humorous gestures recognizable to any comic book fan. The cruel murder of the hapless photographer in chapter 5 is told with a pratfall rapidity ("He flipped into the air and fell dead on top of his bicycle") that helps attenuate the sheer horror of the event. And the silent detonation of the gilded piano, along with the evil woman's caricaturesque understatement (she observes, "Pianos don't explode just like that") are reminiscent of the well-placed sticks of dynamite in countless Tom and Jerry short features. García Márquez thereby raises cartoon conventions to the level of a high art—appropriately, for in some of his earliest articles he wrote favorably of comic strips and promoted their literary legitimacy.

Like many of García Márquez's shorter works, ***Eréndira*** deftly combines a profound sadness with a (literally) explosive humor. On one hand, the sufferings of real-life Eréndiras admittedly go on by the thousands in our world day after day, just as devout lovers also exist who are abandoned once their good works have been completed. But the author also understands that, in literature, tales of woe make no converts and that social evils are often better lampooned knowledgeably than excoriated morally. Where righteous indignation would have failed, the narrative is saved by its funny side. The grandmother no doubt is malevolence incarnate, heartlessness made flesh, but she is also ridiculous both visually and psychologically—her honey-tongued hypocrisy being unforgettable. Similarly, the lovers' first-night chat consists of a series of one-line jokes only García Márquez could have dreamt up—such as Ulises's comparing the sea to "the desert but with water," or his alluding to a man who could walk on the waves, "but that was a long time ago." With its formal wizardry, its tropical adventures on the road, and its seriocomic, bittersweet flavor, ***Eréndira*** stands as one of García Márquez's most delightful and perfect shorter creations.

Chronicle of a Death Foretold also contains a parody love story—though little to laugh about. This is García Márquez's darkest book by far, the only major volume of his that isn't funny (while being thick with ironies). Its amorous element in turn comes enmeshed within a broad network of collective concerns such as class, rituals, honor, religion, and guilt—but also, in a twist of fate, finally exists for itself. The plot couldn't be simpler: Bayardo San Román, a mysterious, attractive, rich young man, shows up in August at an unnamed small town, seeking a wife. He takes a fancy to Ángela Vicario, who resists at first but is eventually talked into it by her middle-class parents. A monumental wedding feast is held six months later; that night, however, Bayardo returns Ángela to her family because she is not a virgin. Brutally interrogated by her mother as to the culprit, Ángela mentions Santiago Nasar, the only son of a locally successful Arab family. In revenge her twin brothers Pedro and Pablo murder Santiago with machetes in front of his house before the eyes of most townspeople, who remain shaken by the crime long thereafter. Following three years in prison the twins are acquitted on grounds of justifiable homicide; Bayardo drops out of sight; and Ángela suddenly falls in love with, and for the next seventeen years writes a weekly letter to her "husband," who one August day shows up with her two thousand letters, unopened, and says, "Well, here I am."

Its seemingly simple plot and prose notwithstanding, the five unnumbered chapters of ***Chronicle*** form a narrative in its way as complex as is *The Autumn of the Patriarch.* The impending crime is anticipated in the initial seven words; hearsay reports it at the end of chapters 1 and 3; the autopsy takes up the start of chapter 4; the terrible social aftermath to the crime opens chapter 5; and the actual murder—preceded by a breathtaking suspense sequence—is only rendered in all its horrific detail in the final five paragraphs of the text. We see the consequences of the murder long before the murder itself, and the immediate buildup to the murder, in turn, only toward the end. In the same fashion, each of the first three chapters ends with an allusion to Santiago by name, while the last of course tells of his annihilation.

The organization, as in *Patriarch,* is not as much chronological as by subject. The first chapter concentrates on Santiago's final ninety minutes of life; the second, on Bayardo and on the wedding night; the third, after some legal matters, on the Vicario brothers; the fourth, following the autopsy and a report concerning the fate of the respective families, on Ángela's late-budding love; and at last, the fifth, after an account of the townspeople's reactions, on the tense few minutes of pursuit and murder. The "Faulknerian" juggling of time is by now a seamless and perfectly natural literary device in García Márquez's arsenal.

The other literary artifice in ***Chronicle*** is in the telling itself, for it is a novel not only about a horrendous crime but about the narrator's task of piecing together the crime. While the volume could simply have been called "The Death of Santiago Nasar," the chosen title signals the book's being someone's account of that death too. The "Crónica" of the Spanish original is a standard journalistic term denoting a reportorial article, usually of a nonpolitical and even sensationalistic kind. It's a genre familiar enough to García Márquez the journalist, who in fact serves as the "chronicler" for this mock report and includes as "informants" his own real-life parents, four of his younger siblings, and his wife-to-be Mercedes. Self-portrayed as a resident of the town at the time of the murder, who now reconstructs the events after a twenty-seven-year interval, the novelist manages to evoke an immediate suspense as well as a serene hindsight in his readers, who in turn find themselves experiencing those febrile episodes from the two perspectives at once.

From the first page to the last, the various concentric and remote times that surround the murder alternate with the more recent testimony from the surviving witnesses. The text bristles with such indications as "he said to me," or "she admitted," or "many agreed that," and the like. One scholar has counted thirty-seven speaking characters who directly contribute to the narrator's investigation, their combined statements adding up to 102 such quotations, on average almost one per page. Another scholar tallies up nearly eighty characters putting in some sort of appearance—the equivalents of those countless fleeting street voices that comprise much of *The Autumn of the Patri-*

arch. Here, however, the lack of an omniscient narrator makes discrepancies inevitable. In an obvious instance, some witnesses remember that fateful morning as sunny and breezy, others as gray and drizzly. On the other hand, though most of them consider Santiago innocent of the drastic charges (as does, fairly emphatically, the chronicler), a large variety of contradictory speculations emerges as to why Ángela would frame him.

As is often pointed out, ***Chronicle*** shows many of the conventions of the classic detective story. Besides a crime, a motive, a victim, and an investigator, there is the role of the judiciary—a trial complete with judge, attorney, and an extensively-cited legal brief. In the same way, the autopsy scene enumerates Santiago's multiple wounds with a clinical exactitude. The text deploys certain other precise details typical of the genre. The unfolding clock time—5:30, 6:45, 6:58—is carefully spelled out; Santiago's gun collection—with brand names and models—is drily enumerated; and the twins' two sets of knives are meticulously described as to type and size. And there is, toward the end, the customary explanation and summing up of the crime and its consequences.

But this is a whodunit with a difference. The normal sequence of events, after all, is reversed. The identity and motive of the criminals is fully revealed halfway through the opening chapter; the criminal act is withheld until the closing pages. Santiago's formidable weaponry proves to be useless, and precisely because of his own state of bewildered innocence. Though the twins are legally acquitted, their honor killing has most probably visited its summary justice on the "wrong" party. An enormous gap thus remains in this detective story; the murder, strictly speaking, is no mystery at all, yet it gives rise in turn to the unsolved mystery of the sexual "culprit." The unrepentant killers turn themselves in, but it is their taciturn sister, unreliable and unforthcoming as a witness, who has in a sense pulled off the perfect crime.

What could have been just a naturalistic thriller about bloody deeds and rustic chivalry is given special depth and resonance through the intimations of Greek tragedy, religious ritual, and other archaic residues woven into García Márquez's text. Following the classic unities of place and action, the novel opens and closes inside the victim's home, and the book's every page bears the stamp of that one murder. Concerning unity of time, the central events cover the twelve hours that unfold between the wedding feast the day before (presumably about sundown, though there are no concrete indications) and next day's sunrise. The outer time frame of the physical novel is just over ninety minutes, from Santiago's arising upstairs at 5:30, to his falling dead in the kitchen at 7:05.

As in Sophocles's *Oedipus Rex,* there are dark omens and foreshadowings, some of them unwittingly from the victim-to-be. When the housemaid Victoria throws the rabbit's entrails to the dogs, a shocked Santiago exclaims, "Don't be a savage. What would it be like if those guts were from a human being?" And in fact Santiago at the end is clutching at his entrails. At the wedding, moreover, he compares its floral decorations to those for the dead and says, "I don't want flowers at my funeral." The terse observation, "That was the last time *x* saw him," appears four different times in the text, and the twins of course go announcing their plans, eight times in chapter 3 alone.

The almost incredible series of chance misses, in which countless individuals set out to forewarn Santiago yet are detained, misinformed, or simply ignored, seems, in the heat of the narrative, one of those bitter instances of every possible thing going mysteriously wrong. Seen whole, however, the random accidents add up to a chain of inevitability. Like King Oedipus, who only too late in the game realizes that the machinery he set in motion leads inexorably to him, a rich Santiago is sealed in his fate, seems moreover destined to remain oblivious to what is happening, and in his distraction even spurns armed assistance from the father of his fiancée. There are some additional and familiar ambiguities. Though he may not be specifically guilty of the deflowering, Santiago does impress us from the start as a proud and arrogant young man who casually abuses the maid's daughter, and later, to the narrator, mocks Ángela as "your cousin the ninny." In keeping with his social and sexual hubris, there is also in Santiago's dying moments a tragic and heroic grandeur—the way he walks a hundred yards with his usual good carriage, smiles at the astonished neighbors whose house he traverses, tells his aunt across the river that he has been killed, and arrives faithfully home before dropping finally dead.

Chronicle tells of two great collective events—the joyous wedding (complete with a serenade to the deserted mansion) and later the tragic murder, witnessed by the townsfolk who gather in the plaza as if for a parade. "We" is in fact the grammatical subject of the opening paragraph to chapter 5, after which the narrator recalls the effects of the crime on many of the individuals concerned—for example, the prompt death of Ángela's traumatized father, or the prostitution that was to be the lot of Santiago's fiancée. Here the cast of characters—with unique names such as Celeste Dangond and Poncho Lanao—fast multiplies as we learn of their respective involvements with the crime and/or their eventual fates. The communal ties with Santiago's death are thereby established and made real, are shown and itemized as well as told—and the murder looms more and more as a collective rite of sacrifice. Indeed the word "sacrifice" is actually employed on earlier occasions in referring to the Vicario twins' work as cattle slaughterers, a repeated usage that predisposes us to view the murder as another sacerdotal act by self-appointed ministers (their last name hinting at this role).

The ritualistic nature of the events is further underscored by the novel's religious intimations. The death in the Spanish title is "anunciada," with overtones of the Annunciation. The morning of the murder is at first dominated by the collective excitement over the arrival of the bishop, whose brief and perfunctory blessing disappoints them, and their emotional high pitch is retained for the deeds shortly to follow. Most of the key names in the book seem chosen for their religious connotations: Ángela, Pedro and Pablo (as in the apostles), their mother Purísima, their father Poncio ("Pontius"); Bayardo *San* Román (who is no saint); the Nasar hacienda *Divine Face* and their maid Divina Flor (with a parallel irony in the name of Santiago's sweetheart Flora); and the medical student Cristo (short for Cristóbal) Bedoya, who is unable to save his best friend. The combination "Santiago Nasar" is a striking paradox, Santiago being St. James, the Spanish slayer of Moors, here applied to an Arab (albeit a Christian). Of the García Márquez siblings, the one who most sees Santiago that day is his sister the nun (never mentioned by name), while Ángela herself is compared at one point to a nun. In all, the roster reads like a devotional gathering.

The archaic flavor of the action in ***Chronicle*** is heightened by its elusive remoteness in time and the presence of earlier sorts of technology. Though not specified, the period appears to be the 1920s, when Model-T Fords would be something novel. In addition, Bayardo's father had once waged war against Colonel Aureliano Buendía (that is, in the 1890s), and at the wedding there are waltz ensembles playing. Significantly, the only two automobiles mentioned are those belonging to the San Román outsiders; the only communications medium alluded to is the telegraph; and the bishop sails past in an old-fashioned paddleboat of a kind American readers would associate with Mark Twain and that were out of use in Colombia by 1950.

Chronicle's very first glance at ancient traditions is its epigraph ("the pursuit of love / is like falconry"), which comes from a seventeen-line lyric by the great medieval Spanish-Portuguese poet Gil Vicente (1456?-1536?). Though the disturbingly beautiful and deceptively simple poem of origin is all but untranslatable, its basic idea is to liken love to a sport that, with ill-chosen prey, can bring dangers, battles, and woes aplenty. The original Spanish, moreover, contains an important pun, for "altanería" signifies not only "falconry" but also "arrogance, hauteur."

From the start it is hence hinted that ***Chronicle*** will tell of the romantic chase as well as of human pride and power. Each of the two romantic males in the book are in fact characterized initially as arrogant and haughty. Santiago, a falconry expert, is even referred to once as "a sparrow hawk." This lively and imaginative set of notions receives a further twist halfway through the novel, when the narrator recalls warning Santiago at the brothel by citing to him (without identifying) the first three lines to Gil Vicente's same poem: "Halcón que se atreve / con garza guerrera / peligros espera," well rendered by Rabassa as "A falcon who chases a warlike crane / Can only hope for a life of pain"; nevertheless, "heron" rather than "crane" is the more accurate prey here. The second quotation within the book (and the opening of the poem) therefore emphasizes the conflictual side of romantic love, its "politics" as it were. As we have seen, for all their might and power, both Santiago and Bayardo will be unwittingly brought to heel by the warlike heron Ángela.

For indeed at the core of ***Chronicle*** is a love story, a narrative about the customs, clashes, illusions, and emotions of love. Briefly ignoring the Santiago material, we could summarize the novel thus: wealthy and attractive male courts local girl; estrangement occurs; reconciliation later follows. The initial portions of the love narrative are highly evocative of fairy-tale romance. With his narrow waist, silver buckles, and kid gloves, Bayardo at first resembles a medieval seigneur. His given name inevitably recalls the famous "knight without fear or blame" of fifteenth-century France. His personal traits are heroic—he hails from the highest local military stock, knows church Latin and Morse code, and is a champion swimmer. And his courtship is all pomp and ceremony—he buys Ángela's favorite house as her bridal gift, and their wedding feast harks back to society's most hallowed of shared erotic dreams.

These and many other romantic formulas are to be seriously subverted in the course of ***Chronicle.*** The trouble begins with Ángela, who at first does not like Bayardo, thinks him "conceited" and "stuck up" but, feeling intimidated, also finds him "too much of a man for me." And of course she doesn't love him, but her mother Pura, seeing economic gain, informs Ángela, "Love can be learned too." The disastrous night and the honor killing, in turn, elicit from the narrator's wise mother Márquez the resigned and telling equation, "Honor is love," to which most townsfolk agree. Ángela, however, proves to be a feisty, resilient sort who, though hard-pressured into the marriage, subtly resists—for example, she refuses to don her wedding gown until Bayardo's two-hour-late arrival. And of the chief actors she is the only one not to succumb to death or degradation, acquiring in her solitude as a seamstress in Riohacha a self-knowledge and a quiet dignity all her own.

In the process Ángela grows as a woman. She begins to feel for Bayardo precisely when being punished by her opportunistic mother, and the sentiment thereafter becomes an entity potent and enduring enough for her to write and mail to him the two thousand letters. Ironically, her flabby and balding Bayardo will prove to be an egotistical man less than worthy of the warrior "heron" he comes back to, while Ángela's belated passion turns out to be the only true and lasting bond of romantic sentiment depicted in the book. Love, an emotion in ***Chronicle***'s initial stages closely bound up with such matters as social prestige, virginity fetishism, and family honor, finally blooms as a genuine personal feeling, with its own internal dynamic and history, only after the entire paraphernalia of power and control has been swept aside and superseded—and also when the woman, now on some equal footing with the man, consents to him from the depths of her inner being.

Though Ángela's two thousand letters reportedly run the full gamut of emotions from those of secret lover and proper fiancée to abandoned wife, the only quotation furnished from those pages is the almost cliché-novelesque, "As proof of my love I send you my tears" (the spot being not tears at all but spilled ink). Love-by-letters is of course the most basic of amorous written traditions, with literary roots in the epistolary romance and with real-life implications of distance and deferred passion. The fact that here the recipient saves but never even opens his beloved's correspondence adds to the whole dark joke, and the one statement we see when the couple finally meet again in the flesh is not some joyous term of endearment but Bayardo's banal and fatuous, "Well, here I am."

These letters and what they stand for are among the many other amorous conventions more or less undetermined and parodied in ***Chronicle of a Death Foretold.*** There are Santiago's parallel love letters to Flora, violently thrown back at him in her misinformed hysteria minutes prior to his death. There is the bereaved love of the widower Xius, his own noble sentiment no match for Bayardo's flamboyant machismo. At the wedding there is a prelude to another such union in the narrator's impulsive proposal to the young girl Mercedes (which, by contrast, will lead to a long marriage in real life). One might normally consider the bottom end of the love scale to be the brothel of María Alejandrina Cervantes, but the whorehouse is actually a kind of refuge and erotic "school." The madam herself, her long name resonant with old heroic and literary echoes, is affectionately depicted as a woman of some authority, one with whom an adolescent Santiago could have fallen in love. If anything it is Santiago and his father who, in their dealings with the domestics and the lesser whores, are the most exploitative of their sexual power as rich males. In ***Chronicle,*** as in other García Márquez novels, the erotic takes on many forms, from the most spiritual and selfless to the most abusive and base.

The impact of ***Chronicle of a Death Foretold*** is further heightened by our knowledge that the narrative is based in part on some true events close to the author. The original crime occurred on Monday, 22 January 1951, in the town of Sucre, where García Márquez's family had been living for ten years. Here is a rudimentary summary of the real-life incidents.

After a year's romantic involvement, Miguel Reyes Palencia, twenty-nine, the scion of a landowning family, married a local schoolteacher named Margarita Chica Salas, twenty-two, on Saturday the twentieth at 7:00 A.M. He loved her, but had also been pressured into marriage by threats from Margarita's older brothers (not twins) José Joaquín and Víctor Manuel, commercial fishermen, who had heard slanderous rumors about the young couple. At the wedding night Miguel got completely drunk, then slept the entire day and night following the festivities. Early on Sunday the twenty-first he awoke in a bedroom at the Chica household, saw Margarita naked at his side, and found out she was not a virgin. He beat her, demanding her deflowerer's name, but she refused. He then returned her to Mrs. Chica, who, on her knees, implored him to wait a few weeks in order to avert scandal. Margarita's brother Víctor now showed up and asked; she named Cayetano Gentile and burst into tears.

Cayetano, twenty-four, tall, elegant, and good-looking, the son of successful Italian immigrants, was a third-year medical student. He and Margarita had been engaged once in the past, though this had not prevented him and Miguel Reyes Palencia from being drinking partners and close friends. On the morning that he was to die, Cayetano went down to the river port to see Miguel and Margarita off on their honeymoon trip, but the couple, strangely, had never showed up. There he also posted a letter to García Márquez's father Eligio in Cartagena, and ran into Gabo's brother Luis and sister Margot, who invited him over for breakfast. Cayetano graciously declined the offer, he being due at the family farm *El Verdún* that same day. He then went by to see his sweetheart Nydia Naser, not yet aware that José and Víctor Chica were at the general store across from his two-story house, waiting to hack him to death.

A crowd was gathering near Cayetano's home. His mother Julieta was inside, having been warned about the death threat by a little boy she knew. Seeing one of the Chica brothers running toward the house, but not her son approaching rapidly from the corner opposite, she slammed and locked both doors. Cayetano arrived at the front door and started banging and screaming. Julieta, thinking it the pursuers, scurried inside for protection. Cayetano now fled, curiously bypassing the hotel next door (where there was a policeman), and dashed into the following house, but Víctor reached his prey and knifed him fourteen times. The victim managed to rise up and walk home, his entrails dangling out. He died there amid relatives, saying "I'm innocent." The Chica brothers turned themselves in immediately, spent a year in jail, and were finally acquitted. Meanwhile the Chica family moved away, and Margarita, feeling disgraced, did not venture out for two years. Miguel in turn remarried, became an insurance agent, fathered twelve children, and nourished no regrets on the matter. Thereafter he saw Margarita just twice, first for the annulment, and years later on some obscure financial question. The townsfolk mostly thought Cayetano guiltless.

The crime would have a lasting impact on young Gabo, who was in Cartagena at the time. He knew all of the parties involved; Cayetano had been a friend since childhood, and Julieta was godmother to one of Gabo's younger brothers. A practicing journalist of three years, García Márquez considered writing an article or a novel about the incident, but his editor friend Germán Vargas suggested that he let the whole thing settle in his mind, and his mother also asked him to wait, not wanting to see her relatives and personal memories written up in a book of his. Besides, the apprentice author had not yet found an organizing principle for the narrative, and to this end he often rehearsed the story with friends, feeling that the plot still had, in the words of Alvaro Cepeda, "a leg missing." In fact it was Cepeda who, a couple of decades later, suggested adding the estranged lovers' reunion, and at that point it all fell into place for the novelist, who realized that it was not so much the account of "an atrocious crime" as "the secret history of a terrible love." In other words, a love story waiting to be told.

The love element is in fact what gives the recast plot its imaginative dimension. Both the groom and the accused lover become highly romanticized entities. Santiago's Arab origins, for one, make him additionally remote and exotic, as also does, for Ángela, her exile in faraway Riohacha. Geographically the real Sucre lies quite a way inland, but from ***Chronicle***'s unnamed town the shimmering Caribbean Sea, with its pirate legends and romantic ocean cruisers, is sighted more than once. The bride's avenging brothers are reborn as twins, a "magical" sort of condition, and their profession as butchers allows for their skill with the machetes and that repeated early use of the word "sacrifice." The bishop's visit is of course totally invented for the sake of religious "atmosphere."

Countless other details have been altered, and space permits us to cite only a few. In a perfect reversal, it is the narrator's mother who now becomes the victim's godmother, he even bearing her middle name, the mutual ties thereby being thickened, while it is Mrs. Vicario and not Ángela who has been the schoolteacher. Cayetano's sweetheart's last name "Naser" is actually retained in a variant form, but given to Santiago. The judiciary aspect, for artistic reasons, is also greatly magnified. Rather than the 322 out of 500 pages assiduously studied by the novel's sleuth-narrator, the only legal document that the author in reality managed to consult was the seven full pages of the brief for the defense. To add to the ironies, although García Márquez did converse with the Chica brothers' defense attorney, the man by that time was advanced in years and could scarcely remember the trial, which for him was just another honor-killing case—a far cry from the continued amazement that the learned and literate judge expresses (for us) in ***Chronicle.***

It is precisely this rustic code that ***Chronicle of a Death Foretold*** evokes, a code that, to younger and more modern readers (the author's own two children included) seems as remote as science fiction. In this regard the book is a subtle indictment of the machismo that forms part of such a code. García Márquez in his interviews often declares himself anti-*machista,* and the novel contains some passing attacks on such an ethic, notably from the shopkeeper Clotilde, who complains of women's solitude before men and specifically mentions Pedro's act of shaving with a butcher knife as "the height of machismo." Doing what the Andalusian Lorca also did with real nuptials and a peasant vendetta in *Blood Wedding,* the Colombian novelist brings off a poetical and quasi-"anthropological" reconstruction of a ritual murder, treats it with such dignified objectivity as to create from it a work of tragedy—but one that conveys its own moral critique as well. As we have seen, true love is depicted as coming into its own only when machismo and its associated values have been scrapped. (pp. 176-91)

Gene H. Bell-Villada, in his García Márquez: The Man and His Work, *The University of North Carolina Press, 1990, 247 p.*

FURTHER READING

Bell-Villada, Gene H. *García Márquez: The Man and His Work.* Chapel Hill: University of North Carolina Press, 1990, 247 p.

Provides biographical discussion, essays on García Márquez's major novels, and several essays on his short fiction. Bell-Villada's examination of the theme of love in *Innocent Eréndira* and *Chronicle of a Death Foretold* is excerpted above.

Berg, Mary G. "The Presence and Subversion of the Past in Gabriel García Márquez' *Eréndira.*" In *La chispa: Selected Proceedings,* edited by Gilbert Paolini, pp. 23-31. New Orleans: Eighth Louisiana Conference on Hispanic Languages and Literatures, Tulane University, 1987.

Contends that *Innocent Eréndira* subverts the traditions of Western culture and that the novella implies that "the ideals and roles designated by novels of chivalry, classic myths, a heritage of folk tales, history itself, are inappropriate for the modern age."

Box, J. B. H. *"El coronel no tiene quien le escriba."* London: Grant & Cutler, 1984, 109 p.

Explicates setting, character, imagery, and style in the novella.

Byk, John. "From Fact to Fiction: Gabriel García Márquez and the Short Story." *Mid-American Review* 6, No. 2 (1986): 111-16.

Focuses on the technique termed "magical realism" as manifested in García Márquez's early short stories.

Castillo, Debra A. "The Storyteller and the Carnival Queen: *Funerales de la Mamá Grande.*" *Romance Quarterly* 35, No. 4 (November 1988): 457-67.

Discusses the presentation in the novella of history, fictionality, and oral storytelling.

Chase, Cida S. " 'La violencia' and Political Violence in García Márquez's Short Fiction." *Journal of Popular Culture* 22, No. 1 (Summer 1986): 73-82.

Extrapolates on García Márquez's reaction to *la violencia* through an examination of his short fiction written before 1962.

Dauster, Frank. "The Short Stories of García Márquez." *Books Abroad* 47, No. 3 (Summer 1973): 466-70.

Examines García Márquez's short fiction in relation to *One Hundred Years of Solitude* and "the growth of the mythography of Macondo."

Davis, Mary E. "The Voyage Beyond the Map: 'El ahogado más hermoso del mundo'." *Kentucky Romance Quarterly* 26, No. 1 (1979): 25-33.

Discusses how the story "The Handsomest Drowned Man in the World" illustrates "the manner in which García Márquez utilizes a heroic figure to revolutionize mundane reality."

Fau, Margaret Eustella. *Gabriel García Márquez: An Annotated Bibliography, 1947-1979.* Westport, Conn.: Greenwood Press, 1980, 198 p.

Most extensive English-language bibliography of primary and secondary sources.

Fau, Margaret Eustella, and de Gonzalez, Nelly Sfeir. *Bibliographic Guide to Gabriel García Márquez, 1979-1985.* Westport, Conn.: Greenwood Press, 1986, 181 p.

Continuation of Fau's bibliography, cited above.

Fiddian, Robin W. "Two Aspects of Technique in *El coronel no tiene quien le escriba.*" *Neophilologus* 59, No. 3 (July 1985): 386-93.

Elaborates on García Márquez's use of Christian allusion and animal imagery in the novella.

Foster, David William. "García Márquez and the *Écriture* of Complicity: 'La prodigiosa tarde de Baltazar' " and "The Double Inscription of the *Narrataire* in *Los funerales de la*

Mamá Grande." In his *Studies in the Contemporary Spanish-American Short Story,* pp. 39-50, 51-62. Columbia: University of Missouri Press, 1979.

Chapters detail elements of style and narrative technique in García Márquez's short story and novella.

García Márquez, Gabriel. "Chronicle of a Film Foretold." *American Film* 9, No. 10 (September 1984): 12-13, 72.

Recalls an autobiographical event that inspired the novella *Innocent Eréndira* and the screenplay for the film *Eréndira,* and describes his experiences during the filming process.

Goetzinger, Judith. "The Emergence of a Folk Myth in *Los funerales de la Mamá Grande.*" *Revista de estudios hispanicos* 6, No. 2 (May 1972): 237-48.

Notes García Márquez's stylistic development as evidenced in the novella *Los funerales de la Mamá Grande,* contrasting the work with the other stories in the collection of the same title.

González, Eduardo. "Beware of Gift-Bearing Tales: Reading García Márquez According to Mauss." *Modern Language Notes* 97, No. 2 (March 1982): 347-64.

Analyzes the ritual of the gift exchange outlined by Marcel Mauss in *The Gift: Forms and Functions of Exchange in Archaic Societies* (1967) as presented in García Márquez's story "Balthazar's Marvelous Afternoon."

Guibert, Rita. "Gabriel García Márquez: New York City, June 3, 1971." In her *Seven Voices: Seven Latin American Writers Talk to Rita Guibert,* translated by Frances Partridge, pp. 305-37. New York: Alfred A. Knopf, 1973.

Interview in which García Márquez expounds on journalism, his literary art, and his views on contemporary Latin American politics.

Hamill, Pete. "Cuba Diving 1: Love and Solitude." *Vanity Fair* 51, No. 3 (March 1988): 124-31, 192.

Description of conversations with García Márquez in Havana in which the author discusses his personal relations with Cuban President Fidel Castro and compares his own "solitude of fame" with Castro's "solitude of power." García Márquez also describes his writing habits and the portrayal of love in his works, particularly *Love in the Time of Cholera.*

Harss, Luis, and Dohmann, Barbara. "Gabriel García Márquez; or, The Lost Chord." In their *Into the Mainstream: Conversations with Latin-American Writers,* pp. 310-41. New York: Harper & Row, 1967.

Recounts discussion with García Márquez on his childhood, the fictional world of Macondo, his political views, and his major works.

Janes, Regina. *Gabriel García Márquez: Revolutions in Wonderland.* Columbia: University of Missouri Press, 1981, 115 p.

Includes chapters on García Márquez's early short fiction and his major novels. Janes's discussion of the stories collected in *La increíble y triste historia de la cándida Eréndira y de su abuela desalmada* is excerpted above.

Kennedy, William. "The Yellow Trolley Car in Barcelona, and Other Visions: A Profile of Gabriel García Márquez." *The Atlantic* 231, No. 1 (January 1973): 50-9.

Recollections by the American novelist of conversations with García Márquez in Barcelona.

Latin American Literary Review, Special Issue: Gabriel García Márquez 13, No. 25 (January-June 1985).

Offers an essay by Dona M. Kercher on *Chronicle of a Death Foretold,* a discussion of *Leaf Storm* by Frank Dauster, essays on García Márquez's novels and journalism, several brief reflections on his works, and García Márquez's commentary on storytelling, translated as "Lost Tales." The essay by Lois Parkinson Zamora on *Chronicle* is excerpted above.

Malm, Ulf. "Reading Gabriel García Márquez: Hyperbole and Intertext in Four Stories." *Studia Neophilologica* 61, No. 1 (1989): 77-88.

Discusses the governing narrative principles of "The Man with Enormous Wings," "The Sea of Lost Time," "The Handsomest Drowned Man in the World," and *Innocent Eréndira.*

Mano, D. Keith. "A Death Foretold." *National Review* 35, No. 11 (10 June 1983): 699-700.

Views the events of *Chronicle of a Death Foretold* as uncompelling and faults García Márquez's characterizations.

McMurray, George R., ed. *Critical Essays on Gabriel García Márquez.* Boston: G. K. Hall & Co., 1987, 224 p.

Contains several reviews of and essays on García Márquez's short fiction, particularly his novellas, as well as discussions of the literary techniques of his major novels.

McNerney, Kathleen. *Understanding García Márquez.* Columbia: University of South Carolina Press, 1989, 180 p.

Provides information on García Márquez's life, novels, and short fiction, as well as a selected bibliography of primary and secondary sources.

Minta, Stephen. *Gabriel García Márquez: Writer of Colombia.* London: Jonathan Cape, 1987, 186 p.

Offers discussions of García Márquez's life, major novels and novellas, and two chapters on the fictional milieu of Macondo. Minta's examination of *No One Writes to the Colonel* in relation to Colombian politics is excerpted above.

Ortega, Julio, ed. *Gabriel García Márquez and the Powers of Fiction.* Austin: University of Texas Press, 1988, 97 p.

Contains critical essays that address *Chronicle of a Death Foretold* and *No One Writes to the Colonel,* as well as discussions of García Márquez's novels and a translation of his 1982 Nobel Prize lecture.

Peel, Roger M. "The Short Stories of Gabriel García Márquez." *Studies in Short Fiction* 8, No. 1 (Winter 1971): 159-68.

Focuses on the stories set in Macondo, asserting that "Macondo transcends its Colombian boundaries to become a reproduction of the whole nature of Latin America, presenting situations which are regional in their detail but universal in their implication."

Penuel, Arnold M. "The Sleep of Vital Reason in García Márquez's *Crónica de una muerte anunciada.*" *Hispania* 68, No. 4 (December 1985): 753-66.

Discusses the "rich mixture of mythical, religious, social, psychological, and historical elements" of *Chroni-*

cle of a Death Foretold and examines unconscious forces that motivate its characters.

———. "The Theme of Colonialism in García Márquez' *La increíble y triste historia de la cándida Eréndira y de su abuela desalmada.*" *Hispanic Journal* 10, No. 1 (Fall 1988): 67-83.

Maintains that *Eréndira* "is ultimately a complex literary statement, similar to a parable, on the nature of the relations between Spain and its American colonies and, by extension, on the nature of colonialism itself."

Simons, Marlise. "Love and Age: A Talk with García Márquez." *The New York Times Book Review* (7 April 1985): 1, 18-19.

Interview in Mexico City in which García Márquez elaborates on the two themes in his work and expounds on the writing process.

———. "García Márquez on Love, Plagues and Politics." *The New York Times Book Review* (21 February 1988): 1, 23-5.

Interview occasioned by the publication of the English translation of *Love in the Time of Cholera.* García Márquez discusses his writing style, journalism, politics, and cinema.

Sims, Robert Lewis. *The Evolution of Myth in García Márquez from "La hojarasca" to "Cien años de soledad."* Miami: Ediciones universal, 1981, 153 p.

Argues that prior to the appearance of *One Hundred Years of Solitude* García Márquez's short fiction and novels developed "from imitation and experimentation to originality and liberty, and [were] accompanied by a progressive accessibility to the polyvalent modalities of myth."

Smith, Gilbert. *"Innocent Eréndira, and Other Stories."* In *Magill's Literary Annual, 1979,* Vol. I, edited by Frank Magill, pp. 318-21. Englewood Cliffs, N.J.: Salem Press, 1979.

Deems *Innocent Eréndira* an uneven collection, faulting García Márquez's "frequent duplication of unusual perceptions" in the stories, while praising his use of metaphor.

Vargas Llosa, Mario. *García Márquez: Historia de un deicidio.* Barcelona: Barral editores, 1971, 667 p.

Seminal biographical and critical study of García Márquez by the Peruvian-born novelist, in the original Spanish. The essay on García Márquez's early short fiction has been translated and is reprinted above.

Williams, Raymond L. *Gabriel García Márquez.* Boston: Twayne Publishers, 1984, 176 p.

Critical study of García Márquez's career, including analyses of his early short fiction, a chapter addressing *Innocent Eréndira,* and one discussing *Chronicle of a Death Foretold.*

Bret Harte

1836?-1902

(Full name: Francis Brett Harte) American short story writer, poet, critic, journalist, editor, novelist, and dramatist.

One of the most influential and popular writers of the nineteenth century, Harte achieved fame and success for his works about the American western frontier. In such celebrated short stories as "The Luck of Roaring Camp," "The Outcasts of Poker Flat," and "Tennessee's Partner," he employed realistic description, stock characters, and local dialect and humor to nostalgically portray life in the California mining camps of the 1840s and 1850s. Although Harte lost much of his popularity later in his career, elements of his work—especially its regional flavor and use of such stereotyped characters as the ornery prospector, the cynical gambler, and the kind-hearted prostitute—influenced his contemporaries and later writers of popular Westerns.

Harte was born in Albany, New York. Although his education was disrupted by his family's frequent relocations, he was an avid reader whose favorite authors included Charles Dickens, Edgar Allan Poe, and Washington Irving. As a young adult, Harte moved to San Francisco to live with his mother, who had remarried following the death of Harte's father. There he worked at various times as a school teacher, a miner, and an express messenger for the Wells Fargo stagecoach lines before accepting a staff writing position at the *Northern Californian* weekly in Union, California. Returning to San Francisco in 1860, Harte worked as a printer for the *Golden Era* and published several sketches in that paper over the next few years. In 1864 he began contributing to the newly established *Californian,* later serving as its editor; in this capacity he commissioned Mark Twain, who was then a relatively unknown author, to write a weekly story for the journal. In 1868 Harte became the first editor of the *Overland Monthly,* where he published several of his most famous stories, including "The Luck of Roaring Camp" and "The Outcasts of Poker Flat." These stories, along with his poem "Plain Language from Truthful James" (also known as "The Heathen Chinee") met with great success and established him as a prominent literary figure and a unique voice of the American West. In 1871 he left California for Boston and signed a one-year contract for $10,000 with the *Atlantic Monthly,* which gave the magazine exclusive rights to a minimum of twelve stories and poems and made Harte the highest paid American writer of the time.

Although he was at the pinnacle of his success, Harte had difficulty fulfilling the agreement with the *Atlantic,* submitting only nine of the promised twelve pieces. When his contract was not renewed, he subsequently attempted lecturing and writing plays (including a collaboration with Mark Twain), but both of these endeavors proved unsuccessful. Discouraged by a loss of popularity among American readers and overwhelmed by increasing financial difficulties, Harte accepted a consul position in Krefeld, Germany in 1878, and in Glasgow, Scotland, two years later. In 1885, following the termination of his consular appointments, Harte moved to London, where he found a highly receptive audience for his fiction. He remained there for the rest of his life, publishing a volume of short stories almost yearly until his death in 1902.

In his stories Harte offered romanticized depictions of the California gold-rush era, featuring grotesque or idealized characters, detailed descriptions of regional settings, and a strong appeal to sentiment—qualities that earned him the title "Dickens among the pines." Just as Dickens had created larger-than-life caricatures, Harte invented such stock frontier characters as the seedy prospector and the hard-bitten gambler—individuals whose depraved exterior is essential to Harte's most common plot formula: to expose the "heart of gold" beneath the most coarse appearance. Thus, the cynical Jack Hamlin reveals an underlying concern for others in "An Heiress of Red Dog" and "Mr. Jack Hamlin's Meditation," a group of criminals place the welfare of a young couple above their own in

"The Outcasts of Poker Flat," and the callous miners in "The Luck of Roaring Camp" become the sensitive and self-sacrificing guardians of a child born to a prostitute.

In addition to characterization, Harte emphasized in his stories the "local color" of Californian landscape and culture. His realistic descriptions are often compared to the backdrops of a stage, reflecting the mood of the action and characters. In "Tennessee's Partner," for example, Harte presents an idealized view of friendship between two miners, while casting an aura of foreboding over Tennessee's trial for theft through his presentation of setting: "The little cañon was stifling with heated resinous odors, and the decaying driftwood in the bar sent forth faint, sickening exhalations." In his essay "The Rise of the Short Story," Harte associated his regionalism with a uniquely American form of fiction: "The secret of the American short story is the treatment of characteristic American life, with absolute knowledge of its peculiarities and sympathy with its methods; with no fastidious ignoring of its habitual expression or the inchoate poetry that may be found hidden even in its slang; with no moral determination except that which may be the legitimate outcome of the story itself. . . . "

Early in his career, Harte received virtually undisputed acclaim as a short story writer. During the 1870s, however, reviewers began to fault Harte's fiction for its reliance on coincidence, romantic situations, and melodrama. As a result his literary standing in the United States plummeted, and by the 1940s, the view of Harte as a Victorian sentimentalist was widely held, even though his works continued to please European audiences, particularly in England. Since the 1960s, however, some critics have reassessed the strengths of Harte's fiction, arguing that he is a romanticist whose works should be interpreted in terms of symbolism rather than realism. For example, some critics have noted the presence of Christian symbolism within "The Luck of Roaring Camp," viewing the adopted baby as a redeeming Christ figure. Commentators have also noted that as a regionalist writer and creator of standard American character types, Harte helped further the evolution of an independent American literature. Describing his influence, Granville Hicks wrote: "Harte, though he may not have been in any strict sense the founder of American regionalism, was the first writer to gain popularity after the Civil War by the exploitation of sectional peculiarities, and there is little doubt that his example directly inspired many of the writers of the seventies, eighties, and nineties."

(For further information on Harte's life and career, see *Twentieth-Century Literary Criticism,* Vols. 1, 25; *Contempoary Authors,* Vol. 104; *Dictionary of Literary Biography,* Vols. 12, 64, 74, 79; and *Concise Dictionary of American Literary Biography, 1865-1917.*)

PRINCIPAL WORKS

SHORT FICTION

Condensed Novels, and Other Papers 1867; also published as *Condensed Novels, and Other Papers* [enlarged edition], 1871
The Lost Galleon, and Other Tales (short stories and poetry) 1867
The Luck of Roaring Camp, and Other Sketches 1870
Mrs. Skaggs's Husbands, and Other Sketches 1872
An Episode of Fiddletown, and Other Sketches 1873
M'liss: An Idyl of Red Mountain 1873
Tales of the Argonauts, and Other Sketches 1875
The Twins of Table Mountain, and Other Stories 1879
Flip, and Other Stories 1882
Cressy 1889
The Heritage of Dedlow Marsh, and Other Tales 1889
A Sappho of Green Springs, and Other Stories 1891
Sally Dows, Etc. 1893; also published as *Sally Dows, and Other Stories,* 1893
The Bell-Ringer of Angel's, and Other Stories 1894
A Protegee of Jack Hamlin's and Other Stories 1894; also published as *A Protegee of Jack Hamlin's, and Other Stories* [enlarged edition], 1894
Barker's Luck, and Other Stories 1896
Stories in Light and Shadow 1898
Tales of Trail and Town 1898
Mr. Jack Hamlin's Mediation, and Other Stories 1899
Condensed Novels, Second Series: New Burlesques 1902
Trent's Trust, and Other Stories 1903

OTHER MAJOR WORKS

Poems (poetry) 1871
East and West Poems (poetry) 1871
Gabriel Conroy (novel) 1876
Two Men of Sandy Bar: A Drama (drama) 1876
Sue: A Play in Three Acts (drama) 1902

The Atlantic Monthly (essay date 1870)

[*The essay excerpted below discusses several of Harte's best-known short stories included in his collection* The Luck of Roaring Camp, and Other Sketches.]

The most surprising things in that very surprising publication, *The Overland Monthly,* have been the stories or studies of early California life, in which Mr. [Bret] Harte carried us back to the remote epochs of 1849 and 1850, and made us behold men and manners now passing or wholly passed away, as he tells us. Readers who were amazed by the excellent quality of the whole magazine were tempted to cry out most of all over **"The Luck of Roaring Camp,"** and the subsequent papers by the same hand, and to triumph in a man who gave them something new in fiction. We had reason indeed to be glad that one capable of seeing the grotesqueness of that strange life, and also of appreciating its finer and softer aspects, had his lot cast in it by the benign destiny that used to make great rivers run by large towns, and that now sends lines of railway upon the same service. But we incline to think that nothing worth keeping is lost, and that the flower born to blush unseen is pretty sure to be botanized from a bud up by zealous observers. These blossoms of the revolver-echoing cañon, the embattled diggings, the lawless flat, and the immoral bar might well have been believed secure from notice, and were perhaps the last things we should have expected to unfold themselves under such eyes as Mr. Harte's. Yet this happened, and here we have them in literature not overpainted, but given with all their natural colors and textures, and all their wildness and strangeness of place.

The finest thing that could be said of an author in times past was that he dealt simply, directly, and briefly with his reader, and we cannot say anything different about Mr. Harte, though we are sensible that he is very different from others, and at his best is quite a unique figure in American authorship, not only that he writes of unhackneyed things, but that he looks at the life he treats in uncommon lights. What strikes us most is the entirely masculine temper of his mind, or rather a habit of concerning himself with things that please only men. We suppose women generally would not find his stories amusing or touching, though perhaps some woman with an unusual sense of humor would feel the tenderness, the delicacy, and the wit that so win the hearts of his own sex. This is not because he deals often with various unpresentable people, for the ladies themselves, when they write novels, make us acquainted with persons of very shocking characters and pursuits, but because he does not touch any of the phases of vice or virtue that seem to take the fancy of women. We think it probable that none but a man would care for the portrait of such a gambler as Mr. John Oakhurst, or would discern the cunning touches with which it is done, in its blended shades of good and evil; and a man only could relish the rude pathos of Tennessee's partner, or of those poor, bewildered, sinful souls, The Duchess and Mother Shipton. To the masculine sense also must chiefly commend itself the ferocious drollery of the local nomenclature, the humor with which the most awful episodes of diggings life are invested by the character of the actors, and the robust vigor and racy savor of the miners' vernacular; not that these are very prominent in the stories, but that they are a certain and always noticeable quality in them. Mr. Harte could probably write well about any life he saw; but having happened to see the early Californian life, he gives it with its proper costume and accent. Of course, he does this artistically, as we have hinted, and gets on without a great use of those interconsonantal dashes which take the sinfulness out of printed profanity. You are made somehow to understand that the company swear a good deal, both men and women, and are not examples to their sex in any way; yet they are not offensive, as they might very well be in other hands, and it is the life beneath their uncouth exteriors that mainly interests. Out of this Mr. Harte has been able to make four or five little romances, which we should call idyls if we did not like them better than most recent poetry, and which please us more and more the oftener we read them. We do not know that they are very strong in plot; perhaps they are rather weak in that direction; but the world has outlived the childish age in fiction, and will not value these exquisite pieces the less because they do not deal with the Thrilling and the Hair's-breadth. People are growing, we hope,—and if they are not, so much the worse for people,—to prefer character to situations, and to enjoy the author's revelations of the former rather than his invention of the latter. At any rate, this is what is to be liked in Mr. Harte, who has an acuteness and a tenderness in dealing with human nature which are quite his own, and such a firm and clear way of handling his materials as to give a very complete effect to each of his performances.

Amongst these we think **"The Outcasts of Poker Flat"** is the best, for the range of character is greater, and the contrasts are all stronger than in the others; and, in spite of some sentimentalized traits, Mr. John Oakhurst, gambler, is the best figure Mr. Harte has created, if, indeed, he did not copy him from life. The whole conception of the story is excellent;—the banishment of Oakhurst, Uncle Billy, The Duchess, and Mother Shipton from Poker Flat, their sojourn in the cañon, where they are joined by the innocent Tommy Simson, eloping with his innocent betrothed; Uncle Billy's treacherous defection with the mule; the gathering snows, the long days spent round the camp-fire listening to Tommy's version of Pope's Homer; the approaches of famine, and the self-sacrifice of those three wicked ones for the hapless creatures whose lot had been cast with theirs. As regards their effort to adapt their conduct to Tommy's and Piney's misconception of their characters and relations, the story is a masterpiece of delicate handling, and affecting as it is humorous. Mr. Harte does not attempt to cope with the difficulties of bringing those curiously assorted friends again into contact with the world; and there is no lesson taught, save a little mercifulness of judgment, and a kindly doubt of total depravity. Perhaps Oakhurst would not, in actual life, have shot himself to save provisions for a starving boy and girl; and perhaps that poor ruined Mother Shipton was not really equal to the act ascribed to her: but Mr. Harte contrives to have it touch one like the truth, and that is all we can ask of him. . . .

> Only Mother Shipton—once the strongest of the party—seemed to sicken and fade. At midnight on the tenth day she called Oakhurst to her side. "I'm going," she said, in a voice of querulous weakness, "but don't say anything about it. Don't waken the kids. Take the bundle from under my head and open it." Mr. Oakhurst did so. It contained Mother Shipton's rations for the last week, untouched. "Give 'em to the child," she said, pointing to the sleeping Piney. "You've starved yourself," said the gambler. "That's what they call it," said the woman, querulously, as she lay down again, and turning her face to the wall, passed quietly away.

Even in **"Miggles,"** which seems to us the least laudable of these stories, the author, in painting a life of unselfish devotion, succeeds in keeping the reader's patience and sympathy by the heroine's unconsciousness of her heroism, and the simple way in which she speaks of it. She has abandoned her old way of life to take care of Jim, a paralytic, who in happier days "spent all his money on her," and she is partially hedged in by a pet grizzly bear which goes about the neighborhood of her wild mountain home with her. If you can suppose the situation, the woman's character is very well done. When the "judge" asks her why she does not marry the man to whom she has devoted her youthful life, "Well, you see," says Miggles, "it would be playing it rather low down on Jim to take advantage of his being so helpless. And then, too, if we were man and wife now, we'd both know that I was bound to do what I now do of my own accord." Of course all the people are well sketched; in fact, as to manners, Mr. Harte's touch is quite unfailing. The humor, too, is good, as it is in all these pieces. Miggles's house is papered with newspapers, and she says of herself and Jim: "When we are sitting alone, I read him these things on the wall. Why, Lord," says Miggles, with her frank laugh, "I've read him that whole side of the house this winter."

"The Idyl of Red Gulch" suffers from some of the causes that affect the sketch of Miggles unpleasantly, but it is more natural and probable, and the interview between Miss Mary and Tommy's mother is a skilful little piece of work. But we believe that, after **"The Outcasts of Poker Flat,"** we have the greatest satisfaction in **"Tennessee's Partner,"** though even in this we would fain have stopped short of having the partners meet in Heaven. Tennessee is a gambler, who is also suspected of theft. He has run away with his partner's wife, and has got himself into trouble by robbing a stranger near the immaculate borders of Red Dog. The citizens rise to take him, and in his flight he is stopped by a small man on a gray horse.

> The men looked at each other a moment in silence. Both were fearless, both self-possessed and independent; and both types of a civilization that in the seventeenth century would have been called heroic, but, in the nineteenth, simply "reckless." "What have you got there? I call," said Tennessee, quietly. "Two bowers and an ace," said the stranger, as quietly, showing two revolvers and a bowie-knife. "That takes me," returned Tennessee; and, with this gamblers' epigram, he threw away his useless pistol, and rode back with his captor.

Tennessee refuses to make any defence on his trial before Judge Lynch. "I don't take any hand in this yer game," he says, and his partner appears in court to buy him off, to the great indignation of the tribunal, which sentences Tennessee at once. "This yer is a lone hand played alone, without my pardner," remarks the unsuccessful advocate, turning to go, when the judge reminds him that if he has anything to say to Tennessee he had better say it now.

> Tennessee smiled, showed his white teeth, and saying, "Euchred, old man!" held out his hand. Tennessee's partner took it in his own, and saying, "I just dropped in as I was passing to see how things was getting on," let the hand passively fall, and adding that it was "a warm night," again mopped his face with his handkerchief, and without another word withdrew.

So Tennessee was hanged, and his body was given to his partner, who invited the citizens of Red Dog to attend the funeral. The body was borne to the grave in a coffin made of a section of sluicing and placed on a cart drawn by Jinny, the partner's donkey; and at the grave this pathetic speech was made:—

> "When a man," began Tennessee's partner, slowly, "has been running free all day, what's the natural thing for him to do? Why, to come home. And if he ain't in a condition to go home, what can his best friend do? Why, bring him home! And here's Tennessee has been running free, and we brings him home from his wandering." He paused, and picked up a fragment of quartz, rubbed it thoughtfully on his sleeve, and went on: "It ain't the first time that I've packed him on my back, as you see'd me now. It ain't the first time that I brought him to this yer cabin when he couldn't help himself; it ain't the first time that I and Jinny have waited for him on yon hill, and picked him up, and so fetched him home, when he could n't speak, and did n't know me. And now that it's the last time, why—" he paused, and rubbed the quartz gently on his sleeve—"you see it's sort of rough on his pardner. And now, gentlemen," he added, abruptly, picking up his long-handled shovel, "the fun'l's over; and my thanks, and Tennessee's thanks, to you for your trouble."

As to the **"Luck of Roaring Camp,"** which was the first and is the best known of these sketches, it is, like **"Tennessee's Partner,"** full of the true color of life in the diggings, but strikes us as less perfect and consistent, though the conception is more daring, and effects are achieved beyond the limited reach of the latter. As in **"Miggles,"** the strength and freshness are in the manners and character, and the weakness is in the sentimentality which, it must be said in Mr. Harte's favor, does not seem to be quite his own. His real feeling is always as good as his humor is fresh.

We want to speak also of the author's sentiment for nature, which is shown in sparing touches, but which is very fine and genuine. Such a picture as this: "A hare surprised into helpless inactivity sat upright and *pulsating* in the ferns by the roadside, as the *cortège* went by,"—is worth, in its wildness and freshness, some acres of word-painting. The same love of nature gives life and interest to **"High-Water Mark," "A Lonely Ride," "Mliss,"** and some other pieces (evidently written earlier than those we have just been speaking of), with which Mr. Harte has filled out his book. These pieces, too, have the author's characteristic cleverness; and the people in **"Notes by Flood and Field"** are almost as lifelike as any in his recent work. The dog "Boonder" is a figure entirely worthy to appear in the most select circles of Red Dog or Poker Flat. (pp. 633-35)

A review of "The Luck of Roaring Camp and Other Sketches," in The Atlantic Monthly, *Vol. XXV, No. 5, May, 1870, pp. 633-35.*

G. K. Chesterton (essay date 1902)

[Widely recognized for the sparkling wit of his prose, Chesterton was regarded as one of England's premier essayists during the first half of the twentieth century. In the following excerpt he examines characteristics of American humor and Harte's uniquely comic voice.]

There are more than nine hundred and ninety-nine excellent reasons which we could all have for admiring the work of Bret Harte. But one supreme reason stands out in a certain general superiority to them all—a reason which may be stated in three propositions, united in a common conclusion: first, that he was a genuine American; second, that he was a genuine humourist; and, third, that he was not an American humourist. Bret Harte had his own peculiar humour, but it had nothing in particular to do with American humour. American humour has its own peculiar excellence, but it has nothing in particular to do with Bret Harte. American humour is purely exaggerative; Bret Harte's humour was sympathetic and analytical.

In order fully to understand this, it is necessary to realise, genuinely and thoroughly, that there is such a thing as an international difference in humour. If we take the crudest joke in the world—the joke, let us say, of a man sitting down on his hat—we shall yet find that all the nations would differ in their way of treating it humourously, and that if American humour treated it at all, it would be in a purely American manner. . . . American humour, neither unfathomably absurd like the Irish, nor transfiguringly lucid and appropriate like the French, nor sharp and sensible and full of realities of life like the Scotch, is simply the humour of imagination. It consists in piling towers on towers and mountains on mountains; of heaping a joke up to the stars and extending it to the end of the world.

With this distinctively American humour Bret Harte had little or nothing in common. The wild, sky-breaking humour of America has its fine qualities, but it must in the nature of things be deficient in two qualities, not only of supreme importance to life and letters, but of supreme importance to humour—reverence and sympathy. And these two qualities were knit into the closest texture of Bret Harte's humour. Every one who has read and enjoyed Mark Twain as he ought to be read and enjoyed will remember a very funny and and irreverent story about an organist who was asked to play appropriate music to an address upon the parable of the Prodigal Son, and who proceeded to play with great spirit, "We'll all get blind drunk when Johnny comes marching home." The best way of distinguishing Bret Harte from the rest of American humour is to say that if Bret Harte had described that scene, it would in some subtle way have combined a sense of the absurdity of the incident with some sense of the sublimity and pathos of the theme. You would have felt that the organist's tune was funny, but not that the Prodigal Son was funny. But America is under a kind of despotism of humour. Every one is afraid of humour: the meanest of human nightmares. Bret Harte had, to express the matter briefly but more or less essentially, the power of laughing not only at things, but also with them. America has laughed at things magnificently, with Gargantuan reverberations of laughter. But she has not even begun to learn the richer lesson of laughing with them.

The supreme proof of the fact that Bret Harte had the instinct of reverence may be found in the fact that he was a really great parodist. This may have the appearance of being a parodox, but, as in the case of many other paradoxes, it is not so important whether it is a paradox as whether it is not obviously true. Mere derision, mere contempt, never produced or could produce parody. A man who simply despises Paderewski for having long hair is not necessarily fitted to give an admirable imitation of his particular touch on the piano. If a man wishes to parody Paderewski's style of execution, he must emphatically go through one process first: he must admire it, and even reverence it. Bret Harte had a real power of imitating great authors, as in his parodies on Dumas, on Victor Hugo, on Charlotte Brontë. This means, and can only mean, that he had perceived the real beauty, the real ambition of Dumas and Victor Hugo and Charlotte Brontë. To take an example, Bret Harte has in his imitation of Hugo a passage like this:

"M. Madeline was, if possible, better than M. Myriel. M. Myriel was an angel. M. Madeline was a good man."

I do not know whether Victor Hugo ever used this antithesis; but I am certain that he would have used it and thanked his stars if he had thought of it. This is real parody, inseparable from admiration. It is the same in the parody of Dumas, which is arranged on the system of "Aramis killed three of them. Porthos three. Athos three." You cannot write that kind of thing unless you have first exulted in the arithmetical ingenuity of the plots of Dumas. It is the same in the parody of Charlotte Brontë, which opens with a dream of a storm-beaten cliff, containing jewels and pelicans. Bret Harte could not have written it unless he had really understood the triumph of the Brontës, the triumph of asserting that great mysteries lie under the surface of the most sullen life, and that the most real part of a man is in his dreams. (pp. 428-30)

The same general characteristic of sympathy amounting to reverence marks Bret Harte's humour in his better-known class of works, the short stories. He does not make his characters absurd in order to make them contemptible: it might almost be said that he makes them absurd in order to make them dignified. For example, the greatest creation of Bret Harte, greater even than Colonel Starbottle (and how terrible it is to speak of any one greater than Colonel Starbottle!) is that unutterable being who goes by the name of Yuba Bill. He is, of course, the coach-driver in the Bret Harte district. Some ingenious person, whose remarks I read the other day, had compared him on this ground with old Mr. Weller. It would be difficult to find a comparison indicating a more completely futile instinct for literature. Tony Weller and Yuba Bill were both coach-drivers, and this fact establishes a resemblance just about as much as the fact that Jobson in *Rob Roy* and George Warrington in *Pendennis* were both lawyers; or that Antonio and Mr. Pickwick were both merchants; or that Sir Galahad and Sir Willoughby Patten were both knights. Tony Weller is a magnificent grotesque. He is a gargoyle, and his mouth, like the mouths of so many gargoyles, is always open. He is garrulous, exuberant, flowery, preposterously sociable. He holds that great creed of the convivial, the creed which is at the back of so much that is greatest in Dickens, the creed that eternity begins at ten o'clock at night, and that nights last for ever. But Yuba Bill is a figure of a widely different character. He is not convivial; it might almost be said that he is too great ever to be sociable. A circle of quiescence and solitude such as that which might ring a saint or a hermit rings this majestic and profound humourist. His jokes do not flow upon him like those of Mr. Weller, sparkling, continual and deliberate, like the play of a fountain in a pleasure garden; they fall suddenly and capriciously, like a crash of avalanches from a great mountain. Tony Weller has the noisy humour of London, Yuba Bill has the silent humour of the earth.

One of the worst of the disadvantages of the rich and random fertility of Bret Harte is the fact that it is very difficult to trace or recover all the stories that he has written. I have not within reach at the moment the story in which the character of Yuba Bill is exhibited in its most solemn grandeur, but I remember that it concerned a ride on the San Francisco stage coach, a difficulty arising from storm and darkness, and an intelligent young man who suggested to Yuba Bill that a certain manner of driving the coach in a certain direction might minimise the dangers of the journey. A profound silence followed the intelligent young man's suggestion, and then (I quote from memory) Yuba Bill observed at last:

> "Air you settin' any value on that remark?"
>
> The young man professed not fully to comprehend him, and Yuba Bill continued reflectively:
>
> " 'Cos there's a comic paper in 'Frisco pays for them things, and I've seen worse in it."

To be rebuked thus is like being rebuked by the Pyramids or by the starry heavens. There is about Yuba Bill this air of a pugnacious calm, a stepping back to get his distance for a shattering blow. . . . And the effect is inexpressively increased by the background and the whole picture which Bret Harte paints so powerfully: the stormy skies, the sombre gorge, the rocking and spinning coach, and high above the feverish passengers the huge dark form of Yuba Bill, a silent mountain of humour.

Another unrecovered and possibly irrecoverable fragment about Yuba Bill, I recall in a story about his visiting a lad who had once been his protégé in the Wild West, and who had since become a distinguished literary man in Boston. Yuba Bill visits him, and on finding him in evening dress lifts up his voice in a superb lamentation over the tragedy of finding his old friend at last "a 'otel waiter." Then, vindictively pursuing the satire, he calls fiercely to his young friend, "Hi, Alphonse! bring me a patty de foy gras, damme." These are the things that make us love the eminent Bill. He is one of those who achieve the noblest and most difficult of all the triumphs of a fictitious character—the triumph of giving us the impression of having a great deal more in him than appears between the two boards of the story. Smaller characters give us the impression that the author has told the whole truth about them, greater characters give the impression that the author has given of them, not the truth but merely a few hints and samples. In some mysterious way we seem to feel that even if Shakespeare was wrong about Falstaff, Falstaff existed and was real; that even if Dickens was wrong about Micawber, Micawber existed and was real. So we feel that there is in the great salt-sea of Yuba Bill's humour as good fish as ever came out of it. The fleeting jests which Yuba Bill throws to the coach passengers only give us the opportunity of fancying and deducing the vast mass of jests which Yuba Bill shares with his creator.

Bret Harte had to deal with countries and communities of an almost unexampled laxity, a laxity passing the laxity of savages, the laxity of civilised men grown savage. He dealt with a life which we in a venerable and historic society may find it somewhat difficult to realise. It was the life of an entirely new people, a people who, having no certain past, could have no certain future. The strangest of all the sardonic jests that history has ever played may be found in this fact: that there is a city which is of all cities the most typical of innovation and dissipation and a certain almost splendid vulgarity, and that this city bears the name in a quaint old European language of the most perfect exponent of the simplicity and holiness of the Christian tradition; the city is called San Francisco. San Francisco, the capital of the Bret Harte country, is a city typifying novelty in a manner in which it is typified by few modern localities. San Francisco has in all probability its cathedrals, but it may well be that its cathedrals are less old and less traditional than many of our hotels. If its inhabitants built a temple to the most primal and forgotten god of whose worship we can find a trace, that temple would still be a modern thing compared with many taverns in Suffolk round which there lingers a faint tradition of Mr. Pickwick. And everything in that new gold country was new, even to the individual inhabitants. Good, bad, and indifferent, heroes and dastards, they were all men from nowhere.

Most of us have come across the practical problem of London landladies, the problem of the doubtful foreign gentleman in a street of respectable English people. Those who have done so can form some idea of what it would be to live in a street full of doubtful foreign gentlemen, in a parish, in a city, in a nation composed entirely of doubtful foreign gentlemen. Old California, at the time of the first rush after gold, was actually this paradox of the nation of foreigners. It was a republic of incognitos: no one knew who any one else was, and only the more ill-mannered and uneasy even desired to know. In such a country as this, gentlemen took more trouble to conceal their gentility than thieves living in South Kensington would take to conceal their blackguardism. In such a country every one is an equal, because every one is a stranger. In such a country it is not strange if men in moral matters feel something of the irresponsibility of a dream. To plan plans which are continually miscarrying against men who are continually disappearing by the assistance of you know not whom, to crush you know not whom, this must be a demoralising life for any man; it must be beyond description demoralising for those who have been trained in no lofty or orderly scheme of right. Small blame to them indeed if they become callous and supercilious and cynical. And the great glory and achievement of Bret Harte consists in this, that he realised that they do not become callous, supercilious and cynical, but that they do become sentimental and romantic, and profoundly affectionate. He discovered the intense sensibility of the primitive man. To him we owe the realisation of the fact that while modern barbarians of genius like Mr. Henley, and in his weaker moments Mr. Rudyard Kipling, delight in describing the coarseness and crude cynicism and fierce humour of the unlettered classes, the unlettered classes are in reality highly sentimental and religious, and not in the least like the creations of Mr. Henley and Mr. Kipling. Bret Harte tells the truth about the wildest, the grossest, the most rapacious of all the districts of the earth—the truth that, while it is very rare indeed in the world to find a thoroughly good man, it is rarer still, rare to the point of monstrosity, to find a man who does not either desire to be one, or imagine that he is one already. (pp. 430-32)

G. K. Chesterton, "The Ways of the World: Bret Harte," in The Pall Mall Magazine, *Vol. XXVII, No. 3, July, 1902, pp. 428-32.*

Henry C. Merwin (essay date 1908)

[*In the excerpt below, Merwin discusses female characters in Harte's short fiction.*]

In Bret Harte's stories woman is subordinated to man just as love is subordinated to friendship. The principal figure in almost all the tragic tales is a man. There is no female character, moreover, that appears and reappears in one story after another, as do Yuba Bill, Jack Hamlin, and Colonel Starbottle; and, so far as we can judge from a writer of such reserve, the *gusto* which Bret Harte evidently felt in writing about these worthies was not evoked to the same degree by any of his heroines.

And yet what modern author has exhibited a more charming gallery of heroines, or has depicted the passion of love in so pure and wholesome a form! The critic must clear up his ideas about what constitutes nobility in woman, before he can fairly estimate the women described by Bret Harte. A sophisticated reader would be almost sure to underestimate them. Even that English critic who was perhaps his greatest admirer, makes the remark, literally true, but nevertheless misleading, that Bret Harte "did not create a perfectly noble, superior, commanding woman." No; but he created, or at least sketched, more than one woman of a very noble type. What type of woman is most valuable to the world? Surely that which is fitted to become the mother of heroes; and to that type Bret Harte's best women belong. They have courage, tenderness, sympathy, the power of self-sacrifice; they have even that strain of fierceness which seems to be inseparable, in man or beast, from the capacity for deep affection. They do indeed lack education, and inherited refinement. Bret Harte himself occasionally points out the deficiency in this respect of his pioneer women.

> She brushed the green moss from his sleeve with some towelling, and although this operation brought her so near to him that her breath—as soft and warm as the Southwest trades—stirred his hair, it was evident that this contiguity was only frontier familiarity, as far removed from conscious coquetry, as it was, perhaps, from educated delicacy.

And yet it is very easy to exaggerate this defect. In most respects the wholesomeness, the democratic sincerity and dignity of Bret Harte's women (and of his men as well) give them the substantial benefits of gentle blood. Thus he says of one of his characters, "He had that innate respect for the secrets of others which is as inseparable from simplicity as it is from high breeding;" and this remark might have been put in a much more general form. In fact, the essential similarity between simplicity and high breeding runs through the whole nature of Bret Harte's characters, and perhaps, moreover, explains why the man who loved the mining camps of California fled from philistine San Francisco and provincial Boston to cosmopolitan London.

Be this as it may, the defects of Bret Harte's heroines relate rather to the ornamental than to the indispensable part of life, whereas the qualities in which they excel are those fundamental feminine qualities upon which, in the last analysis, is founded the greatness of nations. Bret Harte's women have the independence, the innocent audacity, the clear common sense, the resourcefulness, typical of the American woman, and they have, besides, a depth of feeling which is rather primeval than American, which certainly is not a part of the typical American woman as we know her in the Eastern States.

Perhaps the final test of nobility in man or woman is the capacity to value *something,* be it honor, affection, or what you will, be it almost *anything,* but to value something more than life itself, and this is the characteristic of Bret Harte's heroines. They are as ready to die for love as Juliet was, and along with this *abandon* they have the coolness, the independence, the practical faculty, which belong to their time and race, but which were not a part of woman's nature in the age that produced Shakespeare's "unlessoned" girl.

Bret Harte's heroines have a strong family resemblance to those of both Turgénieff and Thomas Hardy. In each case the women obey the instinct of love as unreservedly as men of an archaic type obey the instinct of fighting. There is no question with them of material advantage, of wealth, position, or even reputation. Such considerations, so familiar to women of the world, never enter their minds. They love as nature prompts, and having once given their love, they give themselves and everything that they have along with it. There is a magnificent forgetfulness of self about them. This is the way of nature. Nature never counts the cost, never hoards her treasures, but pours them out, to live or die as the case may be, with a profusion which makes the human by-stander—economical, poverty-stricken man—stand aghast. In Russia this type of woman is frequently found, as Turgénieff, and to a lesser degree Tolstoi, found her among the upper classes, which have retained a primeval quality long since bred out of the corresponding classes in England and in the United States. For women of the same type in England, Thomas Hardy is forced to look lower down in the social scale; and this probably accounts for the fact that his heroines are seldom drawn from the upper classes.

Women of this type sometimes fail in point of chastity, but it is a failure due to impulse and affection, not to mere frivolity or sensuality. After all, chastity is only one of the virtues that women owe to themselves and to the race. The chaste woman who coldly marries for money is, as a rule, morally inferior to the unchaste woman who gives up everything for love.

It is to be observed, however, that Bret Harte's women do not need this defense, for his heroines, with the single exception of Miggles, are virtuous. The only loose women in Bret Harte's stories are the obviously bad women, the female "villains" of the play, and they are by no means numerous. Joan, in **"The Argonauts of North Liberty,"** the wives of **"Brown of Calaveras,"** and of **"The Bell-Ringer of Angels,"** respectively, the cold-blooded Mrs. Decker, and Mrs. Burroughs, the pretty, murderous, feline little woman in **"A Mercury of the Foothills"**—these very nearly exhaust the list. On the other hand, in Thomas Hardy and Turgénieff, to say nothing of lesser novelists, it is often the heroine herself who falls from virtue. Too much can hardly be made of the moral superiority of Bret Harte's stories in this respect. It is due not simply to his own taste and preference, but to the actual state of society in California, which, in this respect as in all others, he faithfully portrayed. The city of San Francisco might have told a different story; but in the mining and agricultural parts of the state the standard of feminine virtue was high. Perhaps this was due, in part at least, to the chivalry of the men, reacting upon the women,—to that feeling which Bret Harte himself called "the western-American fetich of the sanctity of sex," and, again, "the innate Far-Western reverence for women."

In all European societies, and now, to a lesser degree, in the cities of the United States, every man is, generally speaking, the enemy of every young and good-looking woman, as much as the hunter is the enemy of his game. How vast is the difference between this attitude of men to women and that which Bret Harte describes! The California men, as he says elsewhere, "thought it dishonorable and a proof of incompetency to rise by their wives' superior fortune." They married for love and nothing else, and their love took the form of reverence.

The complement of this feeling, on the woman's side, is a maternal, protecting affection, perhaps the noblest passion of which women are capable; and this is the kind of love that Bret Harte's heroines invariably show. No mother could have watched over her child more tenderly than Cressy over her sweetheart. The cry that came from the lips of the Rose of Tuolumne when she flew to the rescue of her bleeding lover was "the cry of a mother over her stricken babe, of a tigress over her mangled cub."

Let us recall the picture of the Rose as she first appears in the story,—summoned out of bed by her father, in the middle of the night, to help entertain his troublesome guest, the youthful poet. While the two men await her coming on the piazza, the elder confides some family secrets to his young friend.

> "But hush," said Mr. McCloskey—"that's her foot on the stairs. She's cummin'."
>
> She came. I don't think the French window ever held a finer view than when she put aside the curtains and stepped out. She had dressed herself simply and hurriedly, but with a woman's knowledge of her best points, so that you got the long curves of her shapely limbs, the shorter curves of her round waist and shoulders, the long sweep of her yellow braids, and even the delicate rose of her complexion, without knowing how it was delivered to you. . . . it was two o'clock in the morning, the cheek of this Tuolumne goddess was as dewy and fresh as an infant's, and she looked like Marguerite, without ever having heard of Goethe's heroine.

Bret Harte's heroines are almost all of the robust type. A companion picture to the Rose is that of Jinny in the story **"When the Waters were up at Jules."**

> Certainly she was graceful! Her tall, lithe, but beautifully moulded figure, even in its characteristic Southwestern indolence, fell into poses as picturesque as they were unconscious. She lifted the big molasses can from its shelf on the rafters with the attitude of a Greek waterbearer. She upheaved the heavy flour sack to the same secure shelf with the upraised palms of an Egyptian caryatid.

Trinidad Joe's daughter, also, was large-limbed, with blue eyes, black brows, and white teeth. It was of her that the doctor said, "If she spoke rustic Greek instead of bad English, and wore a cestus instead of an ill-fitting corset, you'd swear she was a goddess."

It is to be remembered that Bret Harte's nobler type of women, and in most cases of his men also, was drawn from the western and southwestern emigrants. The "great West" furnished his heroic characters,—California was only their accidental and temporary abiding place. The eastern emigrants came by sea, and very few women accompanied them. The western and southwestern emigrants crossed the plains, and brought their wives and children along. These people were of the muscular, farm type, with such health and such nerves as spring from an out-door life, from simple, even coarse food, from early hours and abundant sleep. The women shared the courage of their fathers and brothers. Bret Harte's heroines are womanly to their finger-tips, but they have nerves of steel. Such was Lanty Foster, in whose veins flowed "the blood that had never nourished cravens or degenerates, but had given itself to sprinkle and fertilize desert solitudes where man might follow; . . . whose first infant cry had been answered by the yelp and scream of panther; whose father's rifle had been leveled across her cradle, to cover the stealthy Indian who prowled outside."

Bret Harte's women show their primitive character in their love-affairs, in respect to which they are much like Shakespeare's heroines. "Who ever loved that loved not at first sight!"

John Ashe's betrothed and Ridgway Dent had known each other a matter of two hours or so, before they exchanged that immortal kiss which nearly cost the lives of both. Two brief meetings, and one of those in the dark, sufficed to win for the brave and clever young deputy sheriff the affections of Lanty Foster. In **"A Jack and Gill of the Sierras,"** a handsome girl from the East tumbles over a precipice, and falls upon the recumbent hero, part way down, with such violence as to stun him. This is hardly romantic, but the dangerous and difficult ascent which they make together furnishes the required opportunity. Ten minutes of contiguity suffice, and so well is the girl's character indicated by a few masterly strokes, that the reader feels no surprise at the result.

And yet there is nothing that savors of coarseness, much

less of levity, in these abrupt love-affairs. When Bret Harte's heroes and heroines meet, it is the coming together of two souls that recognize and attract each other. It is like a stroke of lightning, and is accepted with a primeval simplicity and un-selfconsciousness. The impression is as deep as it is sudden.

What said Juliet of the anonymous young man whom she had known something less than an hour?

> Go, ask his name: if he be marrièd
> My grave is like to be my wedding bed.

So felt Liberty Jones when she exclaimed to Dr. Rysdael, "I'll go with you or I'll die!"

It is this sincerity that sanctifies the rapidity and frankness of Bret Harte's love-affairs. Genuine passion takes no account of time, and supplies by one instinctive rush of feeling the experience of years. Given the right persons, time becomes as long and as short as eternity. Thus it was with the two lovers who met and parted at midnight on the hilltop.

> There they stood alone. There was no sound of motion in earth or woods or heaven. They might have been the one man and woman for whom this goodly earth that lay at their feet, rimmed with the deepest azure, was created. And seeing this they turned toward each other with a sudden instinct, and their hands met, and then their lips in one long kiss.

But this same perfect understanding may be arrived at in a crowd as well as in solitude. Cressy and the Schoolmaster were mutually aware of each other's presence at the dance before they had exchanged a look, and when their eyes met it was in "an isolation as supreme as if they had been alone."

Cressy is so real, so lifelike, that her first appearance in the story, namely her return to school, after the episode of a broken engagement, leaves the reader firmly convinced of her previous existence: This is what the youthful schoolmaster saw on that memorable morning:—

> In the rounded, untouched, and untroubled freshness of her cheek and chin, and the forward droop of her slender neck, she appeared a girl of fifteen; in her developed figure and the maturer drapery of her full skirts she seemed a woman; in her combination of naïve recklessness and perfect understanding of her person she was both. In spite of a few school-books that jauntily swung from a strap in her gloved hand, she bore no resemblance to a pupil; in her pretty gown of dotted muslin, with bows of blue ribbon on the skirt and corsage, and a cluster of roses in her belt, she was as inconsistent and incongruous to the others as a fashion-plate would have been in the dry and dog-eared pages before them.

(pp. 297-301)

Poor Cressy, like Daisy Miller, was the pathetic victim of circumstances, chief among which was the lack of a lover worthy of being her husband. Could any country in the world, except our own, produce a Cressy! She has all the beauty, much of the refinement, and all the subtle perceptions of a girl belonging to the most sophisticated race and class; and underneath she has the strong, primeval, spontaneous qualities, the wholesome instincts, the courage, the steadfastness of that pioneer people, that religious, fighting, much-enduring people to whom she belonged.

Cressy is the true child of her father; and there is nothing finer in all Bret Harte than his description of this rough backwoodsman, ferocious in his boundary warfare, and yet full of vague aspirations for his daughter, conscious of his own deficiencies, and oppressed with that melancholy which haunts the man who has outgrown the ideals and conventions of his youth. Hiram McKinstry, compared with the masterful Yuba Bill, the picturesque Hamlin, or the majestic Starbottle, is not an imposing figure; but to have divined him was a greater feat of sympathetic imagination than to have created the others.

It is characteristic, too, of Bret Harte that it is Cressy's father who is represented as acutely conscious of his own defects in education; whereas her mother remains true to the ancestral type, deeply distrusting her husband's and her daughter's innovations. Mrs. McKinstry, as the reader will remember, "looked upon her daughter's studies and her husband's interest in them as weaknesses that might in course of time produce infirmity of homicidal purpose and become enervating of eye and trigger finger. . . . 'The old man's worritts hev sorter shook out a little of his sand,' she had explained."

Alas that no genius has arisen to write the epic of the West, as Hawthorne and Mary Wilkins and Miss Jewett have written the epic of New England! Bret Harte's stories of the western people are true and striking, but his limitations prevented him from giving much more than sketches of them. They are not presented with that fullness which is necessary to make a figure in fiction impress itself upon the popular imagination, and become familiar even to people who have never read the book in which it is contained. Cressy, like Bret Harte's other heroines, flits across the scene once or twice, and we see her no more. Mrs. McKinstry is sketched only in outline, and yet she is a strong, tragic figure of a type now extinct or nearly so, as powerful and more sane than Meg Merrilies, and much more worthy of a permanent place in literature.

Bret Harte's heroines include to a remarkable degree almost everything that was interesting in feminine California. Even the aborigines have a place. The Princess Bob is an Indian. So is the Mermaid of Lighthouse Point; and in **"Peter Atherley's Ancestors"** we have a group of squaws, the youngest of whom is thus touchingly described:

> A girl of sixteen in years, a child of six in intellect, she flashed her little white teeth upon him when he lifted his tent-flap, content to receive his grave melancholy bow, or patiently trotted at his side, carrying things he did not want, which she had taken from the lodge. When he sat down to write, she remained seated at a distance, looking at him with glistening beady eyes like blackberries set in milk, and softly scratching the little bare brown ankle of one foot with the turned-in toes of the other, after an infantile fashion.

Next in point of time come the Spanish occupants of the soil. Bret Harte has not given us such an elaborate portrait of a Spanish girl as he has of that fascinating and gallant young gentleman Enrico Saltello; but there is a charming sketch of his sister Consuelo. It will be remembered that Consuelo, fancying or pretending to fancy a prearranged meeting between her American suitor and a certain Miss Smith, dashes off on the erratic Chu Chu, and is found by her agonized lover two hours later reclining by the roadside, "with her lovely blue-black hair undisheveled," and apparently unhurt, but still, as she declares, the victim of a serious accident. Thus she replies to her lover's tender inquiries as to the nature of her injuries:—

> "You comprehend not, my poor Pancho! It is not of the foot, the ankle, the arm, or the head that I can say 'She is broke!' I would it were even so. But," she lifted her sweet lashes slowly,—"I have derranged my inside. It is an affair of my family. My grandfather have once tumble over the bull at a rodeo. He speak no more; he is dead. For why? He has derrange his inside. Believe me, it is of the family. You comprehend? The Saltellos are not as the other peoples for this. . . . "
>
> (pp. 301-02)

Thackeray himself was not a greater master of dialect than Bret Harte, and as Thackeray seems to bring out the character of Costigan by his brogue, so Bret Harte, by means of her delightfully broken English, discloses the gentle, piquant, womanly, grave, non-humorous, but tenderly playful character of the Spanish señorita. Consuelo is not the only one. There are Donna Supelvida in *Gabriel Conroy;* Rosita Pico, the friend of Mrs. Demorest, in **"The Argonauts of North Liberty;"** Pepita Ramirez, by whose charms Stephen Masterton, the Methodist preacher, became **"A Convert of the Mission,"** and Carmen de Haro, in **"The Story of a Mine,"** whose voice was "so musical, so tender, so sympathizing, so melodious, so replete with the graciousness of womanhood, that she seemed to have invented the language."

The Mexican women are represented by the passionate Teresa, who met her fate, in a double sense, **"In the Carquinez Woods,"** finding there both a lover and her death; and even the charming daughter of a Spanish mother and an American or English father is not missing. Such marriages were frequent among the adventurous Anglo-Saxons who had settled in California long before the discovery of gold. It was said, indeed, that the señoritas preferred Americans as husbands, and this preference accounted in part for the bitter feeling against them entertained by the Spaniards. It was bad enough that they should acquire the land, without capturing the women also. José Castro, the military commander of the province, declared, in 1846, that such indignities could not be borne by Castilian blood. "A California Cavaliero cannot woo a Señorita, if opposed in his suit by an American sailor; and these heretics must be cleared from the land."

In **"Maruja"** we have the daughter of a New England whaling captain and a Spanish woman of good family, who unites the best qualities of both races.

> Her eyes were beautiful, and charged with something more than their own beauty. With a deep brunette setting even to the darkened curves, the pupils were as blue as the sky above them. But they were lit with another intelligence. The soul of the Salem whaler looked out of the passion-darkened orbits of the mother, and was resistless.

As to the American women who emigrated to California, Bret Harte's gallery contains a picture, or at least a sketch of every type. Of the western and southwestern women mention has already been made. The South is represented by Sally Dows, who appears not only in the story of that name, but also in **"Colonel Starbottle's Client."** Sally Dows is a "reconstructed" rebel, a rebel indeed who never believed in the war, but who stood by her kindred. She is a charming young woman, graceful, physically and mentally, coquettish but businesslike, cool and alluring, and always mistress of herself and the situation. The key to her character dawns at last upon her northern lover:

> Looking at her closely now he understood the meaning of those pliant graces, so unaffected and yet always controlled by the reasoning of an unbiased intellect; her frank speech and plausible intonations! Before him stood the true-born daughter of a long race of politicians! All that he had heard of their dexterity, tact, and expediency rose here incarnate with the added grace of womanhood.

In his portrayal of eastern women Bret Harte is less successful. . . . Moreover, the conventional well-bred woman of any race or clime did not interest him. Writers of fiction, as a rule, find their material in one particular class, and in the dependents or inferiors with whom that class comes especially in contact. Dickens is the historian of the London cockney, Thackeray of aristocratic and literary London, Trollope of the English county families, and to some extent, of Englishmen in public life, Rhoda Broughton of the county families and of academic society, George Eliot of the middle and farmer class, Thomas Hardy of the farmer and peasant class, Mr. Howells of the typical well-to-do American family. Bret Harte, on the other hand, drew his material from every class and condition—from the widow Hiler to Louise Macey, from Mrs. McKinstry to Cherry Brooks; but women did not usually attract him as subjects for literature, unless they were close to nature, or else emancipated from custom and tradition by some originality of mind or character.

He could indeed draw fairly well the accomplished woman of the world, such for example as Amy Forester in **"A Night on the Divide,"** Jessie Mayfield in **"Jeff Briggs' Love Story,"** Grace Nevil in **"A Mæcenas of the Pacific Slope,"** Mrs. Ashwood in **"A First Family of Tasajara,"** and Mrs. Horncastle in **"Three Partners."** But these women do not bear the stamp of Bret Harte's genius.

His army and navy girls are better, because they are redeemed from commonplaceness by their patriotism. Miss Portfire in **"The Princess Bob and Her Friends,"** and Julia Cantire in **"Dick Boyle's Business Card,"** represent those American families, more numerous than might be supposed, in which it is almost an hereditary custom for the men to serve in the army or navy, and for the women to become the wives and mothers of soldiers and sailors. In such families patriotism is a constant inspiration, to a degree seldom felt except by those who represent their country at home or abroad.

Bret Harte was patriotic, as many of his poems and stories attest, and his long residence in England did not abate his Americanism. "Apostates" was his name for those American girls who marry titled foreigners, and he often speaks of the susceptibility of American women to considerations of rank and position.

In **"A Rose of Glenbogie,"** after describing the male guests at a Scotch country house, he continues: "There were the usual half-dozen smartly-frocked women who, far from being the females of the foregoing species, were quite indistinctive, with the single exception of an American wife, who was infinitely more Scotch than her Scotch husband." And in the **"The Heir of the McHulisches"** the American consul is represented as being less chagrined by the bumptiousness of his male compatriots than by "the snobbishness and almost servile adaptability of the women. Or was it possible that it was only a weakness of the sex which no Republican nativity or education could eliminate?" What American has not asked himself this same question!

The only New England woman of whom Bret Harte has made an elaborate study, with the possible exception of Thankful Blossom, is that very bad person, Joan, in **"The Argonauts of North Liberty."** The subject had almost a morbid fascination for him. As Hawthorne pointed out in *The Scarlet Letter,* the man or woman whom we hate becomes an object of interest to us, almost as much as the person whom we love. An acute critic declares that Thackeray's wonderful insight into the characters and feelings of servants was due to the fact that he had a kind of horror of them, and was morbidly sensitive to their criticisms—the more keenly felt for being unspoken. So Joan represents what Bret Harte hated more than anything else in the world, namely, a narrow, censorious, hypocritical, cold-blooded Puritanism. Her character is not that of a typical New England woman; its counterpart would much more easily be found among the men; but it is a perfectly consistent character, most accurately worked out. Joan combines a prim, provincial, horsehair-sofa respectability with a lawless and sensual nature,—an odd combination, and yet not an impossible one. She might perhaps be called the female of that species which Hawthorne immortalized under the name of Judge Pyncheon.

Joan is a puzzle to the reader, but so she was to those who knew her. Was she a conscious hypocrite, deliberately playing a false part in the world, or was she a monstrous egotist, one in whom the soul of truth had so died out that she thought herself justified in everything that she did, and committed the worst acts from what she supposed to be the most excusable motives? Her intimates did not know. One of the finest strokes in the story is the dawning of suspicion upon the mind of her second husband.

> For with all his deep affection for his wife, Richard Demorest unconsciously feared her. The strong man whose dominance over men and women alike had been his salient characteristic, had begun to feel an indefinable sense of some unrecognized quality in the woman he loved. He had once or twice detected it in a tone of her voice, in a remembered and perhaps even once idolized gesture, or in the accidental lapse of some bewildering word.

And yet it would be unjust to say that Bret Harte had no conception of the better type of New England women. The schoolmistress in **"The Idyl of Red Gulch,"** one of the earliest and one of the best stories, is as pure and heroic a maiden, and as characteristic of the soil, as Hilda. The reader will remember the description of Miss Mary as she appeared playing with her pupils in the woods:

> The color came faintly into her pale cheek . . . felinely fastidious, and intrenched as she was in the purity of spotless skirts, collars and cuffs, she forgot all else, and ran like a crested quail at the head of her brood, until romping, laughing, and panting, with a loosened braid of brown hair, a hat hanging by a knotted ribbon from her throat, she came—upon Sandy, the unheroic hero of the tale.

In the culminating scene of this story, the interview between Miss Mary and the mother of Sandy's illegitimate boy, when the teacher consents to take the child with her to her home in the East and bring him up, although she is still under the shock of the discovery of Sandy's relation to him,—in this scene the schoolmistress exhibits true New England restraint, and a beautiful absence of heroics. It was just at sunset. "The last red beam crept higher, suffused Miss Mary's eyes with something of its glory, flickered and faded and went out. The sun had set on Red Gulch. In the twilight and silence Miss Mary's voice sounded pleasantly. 'I will take the boy. Send him to me to-night.' "

One can hardly help speculating about Bret Harte's personal taste and preferences in regard to women. Cressy and the Rose of Tuolumne were both blondes; and yet on the whole he certainly preferred brunettes. Even his blue-eyed girls usually have black hair. The Treasure of the Redwoods disclosed from the recesses of her sunbonnet "a pale blue eye and a thin black arch of eyebrow." One associates a contralto voice with a brunette, and Bret Harte's heroines, so far as the subject is mentioned, have contralto voices. Not one is spoken of as having a soprano voice. Even the slight and blue-eyed Tinka Gallinger "sang in a youthful, rather nasal contralto."

As to eyes, he seems to have preferred them gray or brown, a "tender gray" and a "reddish brown." Ailsa Callender's hair was "dark with a burnished copper tint at its roots, and her eyes had the same burnished metallic lustre in their brown pupils." Mrs. MacGlowrie was "a fair-faced woman with eyes the color of pale sherry."

A small foot with an arched instep was a *sine qua non* with Bret Harte, and he speaks particularly of the small, well-shod foot of the southwestern girl. He believed in breeding, and all of his heroines were well-bred,—not well-bred in the conventional sense, but in the sense of coming from sound, courageous, self-respecting, self-improving stock. Within these limits his range of heroines is exceedingly wide, including some that are often excluded from that category. He is rather partial to widows, for example, and always looks upon their innocent gayeties with an indulgent eye. It was thus that he saw the widow of the "Santa Ana" valley as she appeared at the first dancing party ever held in that region: "The widow arrived, looking a little slimmer than usual in her closely buttoned black dress, white collar and cuffs, very glistening in eye and in hair, and with a faint coming and going of color."

"The Blue Grass Penelope," Dick Spindler's hostess, and Mrs. Ashwood, in **"A First Family of Tasajara,"** are all charming widows. Can a woman be a widow and untidy in her dress, and still retain her preëminence as heroine? Yes, Bret Harte's genius is equal even to that. . . .

> For the widow had a certain indolent southern negligence, which in a less pretty woman would have been untidiness, and a characteristic hook-and-eye-less freedom of attire, which on less graceful limbs would have been slovenly. One sleeve-cuff was unbuttoned, but it showed the vein of her delicate wrist; the neck of her dress had lost a hook, but the glimpse of a bit of edging round the white throat made amends. Of all which, however, it should be said that the widow, in her limp abstraction, was really unconscious.

Red-haired women have been so popular in fiction during recent years that it was perhaps no great feat for Bret Harte in the **"Buckeye Hollow Inheritance"** to make a heroine out of a red-haired girl and a bad-tempered one too; but what other romancer has ever dared to represent a young and lovely woman as "hard of hearing"! There can be no question that the youngest Miss Piper was not quite normal in this respect, although, doubtless, for purposes of coquetry and sarcasm, she magnified the defect. In her memorable interview with the clever young grocery clerk (whom she afterward married) she begins by failing to hear distinctly the title of the book which he was reading when she entered the store; and we have this picture: "Miss Delaware, leaning sideways and curling her little fingers around her pink ear, 'Did you say the first principles of geology or politeness? You know I am so deaf; but of course it couldn't be that.' "

The same heroine was much freckled,—in fact her freckles were a part of that charm which suddenly overcame the bashful suitor of Virginia Piper, whom Delaware was endeavoring to assist in his courtship. "Speak louder, or come closer," she said. He came closer, so close in fact that "her soft satin cheek, peppered and salted as it was by sun freckles and mountain air," proved irresistible; and thereupon, abruptly abandoning his suit to the oldest, he kissed the youngest Miss Piper—and received a sound box on the ear for his temerity and fickleness. Freckles become positive enhancements of beauty under Bret Harte's sympathetic touch. Julia Porter's face "appeared whiter at the angles of the mouth and nose through the relief of tiny freckles like grains of pepper."

Bret Harte bestowed great care upon the details of the human face and figure. There are subtleties of coloring, for example, that have escaped almost everybody else. Who but Bret Harte has really described the light which love kindles upon the face of a woman? "Yerba Buena's strangely delicate complexion had taken on itself that faint Alpine glow that was more of an illumination than a color." And so of Cressy, as the Schoolmaster saw her at the dance. "She was pale, he had never seen her so beautiful. . . . The absence of color in her usually fresh face had been replaced by a faint magnetic aurora that seemed to him half spiritual. He could not take his eyes from her; he could not believe what he saw."

The forehead, the temples, and more especially the eyebrows of his heroines—these and the part which they play in the expression of emotion—are described by Bret Harte with a particularity which cannot be found elsewhere. To cite a few out of many examples: Susy showed "a pretty distress in her violet eyes and curving eyebrows;" and the eyebrows of the princess "contracted prettily in an effort to understand." Kate Howard "was silent for a minute, with her arched black brows knitted;" and of the unfortunate Concepcion de Aguello it is written:—

> The small mouth quivered, as for some denied caress,
> And the fair young brow was knitted in an infantile distress.

Even the eyelashes of Bret Harte's heroines are carefully painted in the picture. Flora Dimwood "cast a sidelong glance" at the hero, "under her widely-spaced heavy lashes." The eyes and eyelashes of that irrepressible child, Sarah Walker, are thus minutely and pathetically described: "Her eyes were of a dark shade of burnished copper,—the orbits appearing deeper and larger from the rubbing in of habitual tears from long wet lashes."

Bret Harte has the rare faculty of making even a tearful woman attractive. The Ward of the Golden Gate "drew back a step, lifted her head with a quick toss that seemed to condense the moisture in her shining eyes, and sent what might have been a glittering dewdrop flying into the loosened tendrils of her hair." The quick-tempered heroine is seen "hurriedly disentangling two stinging tears from her long lashes;" and even the mannish girl, Julia Porter, becomes femininely deliquescent as she leans back in the dark stage coach, with the romantic Cass Beard gazing at her from his invisible corner. "How much softer her face looked in the moonlight!—How moist her eyes were—actually shining in the light! How that light seemed to concentrate in the corner of the lashes, and then slipped—flash—away! Was she? Yes, she was crying."

One might go on indefinitely, quoting from Bret Harte's vivid and always brief descriptions of feminine feature and aspect; but doubtless the reader has not forgotten them, and I can only hope that he will not regret to have looked once more upon these familiar portraits painted in brilliant, and, as we believe, unfading colors. (pp. 302-07)

Henry C. Merwin, "Bret Harte's Heroines," in The Atlantic Monthly, *Vol. 102, No. 3, September, 1908, pp. 297-307.*

Henry Seidel Canby (essay date 1909)

[*A prolific American author whose works include* The Short Story in English, *Canby was one of the founders of the* Saturday Review of Literature. *In the following excerpt from his book on short fiction, he outlines Harte's contributions to the development of the popular American short story.*]

Bret Harte was certainly not the author of the best English stories of the nineteenth century, but it is a question whether, on the whole, his tales have not been the most widely read. Hawthorne never has been *widely* read in his short stories, except as the cumulative processes of time and the agencies of school-English have piled up the numbers of his readers. Poe's following in America has always been a large one, but in England, until recently, his success has been, at most, one of esteem. Bret Harte, however, was, and is, pretty generally known by all the reading classes, and very nearly as widely on one side of the water as the other. Thus, if we regard those years when the new short story was just getting a foothold, he appears as an advance agent of a fiction of American life for Englishmen, as well as of California habits for the Easterner, with an audience evenly distributed through much of the English-speaking world.

The circumstances of his sudden rise into popularity are well known. **"The Luck of Roaring Camp,"** published in the new *Overland Monthly* for August, 1868, by a reluctant staff, who feared that the tale was highly immoral, brought instant recognition from the East, and a more tardy one from his own people at home. **"The Outcasts of Poker Flat,"** and other tales, speedily following, gained more plaudits; reputation sought the prophet out even in his own country, and in 1871 he had achieved not only fame there but a call to the East. This success, which became English almost as speedily, was, in the main, a success by means of the short story, and so remains to-day. A share of it was due to such permanencies of genius as lead to imaginative observation, another to the material which California offered him, a part, and a large one, to the form in which this material was cast in the stories that he made from it. It is this last cause which is involved with the development of the short story.

So clearly distinguishable was the new kind of short story after Bret Harte had used it to advertise his Forty-niners, so little recognized as a type before, that it was natural for certain writers to refer to the Californian as the inventor of this form of narrative. How little this statement is true we know; yet how great were his services may be read between the lines in a response to his flatterers which he himself provided in *The Cornhill Magazine* of July, 1899. "The Rise of the Short Story" in that number is honest disclaimer. Not to me, writes, in effect, the romancer of Sandy Bar, but to conditions as I found and grasped them is credit due. Poe, Hawthorne, Longfellow (the Longfellow of *The Tales of a Wayside Inn*), wrote good short stories, so his argument runs, but their tales were not characteristic of American habits, life, and thought. Their work "knew little of American geography," and, all said, it was provincial. The war was the national mixing-pot, thus he continues, East learned West there, and North South, but, except for Hale in his *Man Without a Country,* the writers did not seize their opportunities. And then, in California, where life was as distinctly individual as the current fiction was unreal or European in its depiction of humanity, he felt the need of a sympathetic, truthful picture, took his chance, and wrote **"The Luck of Roaring Camp."** Life, in that story, said Harte, was treated as it was, with sympathy for its methods, with a welcome for its peculiarities, with no moral, and no more elimination than was artistically necessary. In a word, when the Americans broke away from European models, and began to give free expression to the thoughts and feelings of their native land, the result was—not what one expects him to write, original American fiction, but—the short story.

There are some things evidently dubitable in this statement, but a great deal that is true; and from the *apologia* is to be gleaned far more than the common statement that Harte developed American local color and with it floated a native short story. It is superficial to say that Poe and Hawthorne were un-American and provincial. But Harte was speaking in the language of his own practice, and must be interpreted before critically condemned. Presumably he meant that his predecessors were provincial because they did not write of the West, and un-American because they neglected the more external signs and marks of Americanism. Yet the unsound in this article is trivial when compared with the explanation of Bret Harte's success and his services to the short story which it provides. For, with the assistance of the clew which he gives us, we can account for the extent of his triumph, and follow the rise of one of the commonest varieties of our short story.

Bret Harte's technique, like O'Brien's, is, roughly, Poe's. The volume published at Boston in 1870, ***The Luck of Roaring Camp, and other Sketches,*** includes what are probably the three very best stories he wrote, **"The Luck of Roaring Camp," "The Outcasts of Poker Flat,"** and **"Tennessee's Partner."** Strangely enough, they are called "sketches," in contradistinction to the "stories," which, beside **"Mliss,"** embrace two very inferior narratives. Each of these three early masterpieces begins with the matter in hand, moves quickly to its conclusion, and emphasizes the climax by direction of narrative, by proportion, and by selection of incident. Each has unity of tone, and perfect unity of impression. Indeed, there is no better example of this last than **"Tennessee's Partner."** Whether Bret Harte learned this technique from Poe, or from the exigencies of journalism, is comparatively unimportant. He had to learn it, as the earlier **"Mliss,"** which, for all its pathos, suffers for lack of good telling, and other early narratives show.

Now this fashion of arranging one's materials was particularly well adapted to bring out contrasts in life, singular associations, vivid situations. The earlier American storytellers, each in his way, negatively or positively, had demonstrated that. But it was just such contrasts, associations, and situations in real life that the young Harte was ambitious to turn into literature. No distinctly Californian story had been written on the coast. *The Overland Monthly* wanted one. California life: the romance of the Argonauts, the revelry, chivalry, pocket-finding, shooting, love, hate, and sudden friendship of Roaring Gulch and Sandy Bar, it was all chiaroscuro, it was rapid, it had little past, and an unseen future, it was compounded of the strangest contrasts. The settled orders of the old world had broken rank and flung themselves in social confusion upon the gold-fields, and the society that resulted was like that of the farce-comedy, kaleidoscopic, capable of anything, a society in which a remarkable situation could instantly develop and give place as quickly to another. The novel as a beaker for so turbulent a mixture would never have succeeded; the life was too new, confusing, transient. The old and simple tale might have swept up certain episodes, but it would have lost the glitter, the brilliance, the vivid transitoriness of the unexpected situation. But the new short story, with its emphasis upon the climax, and that climax the heart of a situation, was the very means. Read these fine stories, compare them with the "local color" sketches of Bret Harte's contemporaries, and one sees why, to use his own language, he "turned the trick."

In this fortunate application of a method of telling to a life which only so could best be told, Bret Harte advanced upon Mr. Hale's first stories, where the grasp of a strong situation, rather than any way of emphasizing it, attracts attention; advanced upon O'Brien, whose skill was scarcely equal to his imagination, and became a pioneer by virtue of the new realms he conquered for the short story. But it is impossible to sum up his achievement without more consideration of the content of these short stories. It was the fresh life depicted in them which his contemporaries hailed, and although it is probable that if his California novelties had not been exhibited in just the proper showcase, to wit, the short story, they would have gained a hearing that at most was contemporary, yet it is erroneous to suppose that his triumph, like Poe's, was a triumph of technique. Tennessee's Partner, John Oakhurst, Yuba Bill, Kentuck are as long-lived, seemingly, as any characters in nineteenth century fiction. Mliss would join them if Harte could have given her an equally good narrative; the New England schoolmarm in the Sierras must be added, although she appears under too many names to be individual. What gives these characters their lasting power? Why does that highly melodramatic tragedy in the hills above Poker Flat, with its stagy reformations, and contrasts of black sinner and white innocent, hold you spell-bound at the thirtieth as at the first reading? Why does Tennessee's partner make you wish to grasp him by the hand? Bret Harte believed, apparently, that it was his realism which did it. He had put the Western miner into literature as he was—hence the applause. He had compounded his characters of good *and* evil as in life, thus approximating the truth, and avoiding the error of the cartoon, in which the dissolute miner was so dissolute that it was said, "They've just put the keerds on that chap from the start." But we do not wait to be told by Californians, who still remember the red-shirt period, that Roaring Camp is not realism. The lack of it is apparent in every paragraph describing that fascinating settlement. The man who would look for Yuba Bill at Sandy Bar, would search for Pickwick in London, and Peggotty on Yarmouth Beach. Not the realism, but the idealization, of this life of the Argonauts was the prize Bret Harte gained. After all, the latter part of the introduction to his first book was more pertinent than the first, which I have just been paraphrasing, for, at the end, he admits a desire to revive the poetry of a heroic era, and to collect the material for an Iliad of the intrepid Argonauts of California.

In this attempt, Harte sought out novel characters, and then idealized the typical and the individual which he found in them. So doing, he sat at the feet of a greater writer, one not more fortunate in materials, but far stronger, more versatile, more poignant in grasp. The debt which Bret Harte owed and acknowledged to Dickens has been often remarked upon, yet in no way can the value of these pictures of the gold-fields be better estimated than by emphasizing it again. What Dickens did in England, the ever-living personalities which he created by imagining English cockneys, English villains, English boys, with all their energies devoted to an expression of what was most individual, peculiar, and typical in them, just this Bret Harte endeavored to accomplish with his Californians. The truth by exaggeration was his art also. And the melodrama which accompanies contrasts more violent than life, the falsity which follows an attempt to make events illustrate a preconceived theory of human nature, were his faults as well. He looked upon the strange life about him with the eye of an incurable romancer, and gave us a Poker Flat which is just as false to the actual original in the Sierras, as it is true sentimentally. In this, his error, if you are foolish enough to call it so, was again the error of Dickens. But Mr. Pickwick is more valuable than any actual gentleman of his period, Kentuck will outlive the John Smiths of the California historical society. The sentimental romancer, when he is not banal, nor absurd, is an inestimable boon to the race he describes. He inspirits with the emotions which live for ever the body of contemporary verisimilitude: clothing, manners, speech, morals, which, without a soul, must die with their generation. Dickens did this for his London, and Harte, in his footsteps, performed a like service for the golden days of California. (pp. 288-95)

[However, in Harte's] innumerable later narratives the same character types appear with wearisome frequency. The virginal dew is dried from the cheeks of his untamed women; the Argonaut no longer glows with the colors of a dawning civilization. And although his biographer, T. Edgar Pemberton, strenuously asserts that the stories in other fields prove that he was not graveled for matter when he left California, still **"Unser Karl,"** ***The Desborough Connections,*** and his other old-world tales are no more than good magazine work. The classic aura is not upon them. For the situation must be very novel, very fresh, very significant of those human traits which can be seen in the lightning flash, "which doth cease to be ere one can say 'It lightens,' " else this kind of short story loses its place in great literature. In the narrowness of his genius which could not add new provinces when the old ones were exhausted, Harte was inferior to his master. He was far inferior in humor, far inferior in the breadth as well as the length of his creative powers. In pathos alone does he even approach an equal level.

On the other hand, it is exceedingly improbable that Dickens could have immortalized the Forty-niner. The short story was the only tool that was capable of such magic. Sandy Bar was no novelist's spoil; its life was too rapid. Nor would "sketches," like those by "Boz," have caught the day of the Argonauts; if one missed its vivid contrasts, one missed more than half. The new short story was the tool, and Dickens, it is quite certain, could never have restrained himself to its limits. In spite of his one experiment, *The Signal-Man,* the feat was against nature. But Harte, of a race keen to see the significance of events, quick of perception beyond comparison among Anglo-Saxon peoples, inclined to be superficial, inclined to hurry, inclined to be pleased with a novelty and to advertise it; Harte, with the view-point of Dickens, his own sense of form, and a genius for sympathetic study, was the man to turn into five talents the sum he had been lent.

And so, at the end, one is inclined to agree with Harte's own conclusion, as expressed in his *Cornhill* essay ["The Rise of the Short Story"]. He was certainly wise in coming to his own world for characters, for plot, and for setting. And one agrees, also, that to this step toward truth of portraiture is due much of the strength of the modern short story. But we must add to these statements. It was the use of the new short story technique that made Harte's shift to local subjects so fruitful in result; it was the high color, the novelty, the rich contrasts of California life, which put upon his success an emphasis that advertised the short story. It was his good fortune to look upon this variegated life with eyes which Dickens had opened to see personality, with senses by this insight made keen to feel the old primeval emotions stirring in unexpected places, with a resultant power to make poetry of that from which the realist made prose. In every way Bret Harte was a fortunate man.

Finally, he completes that development towards a popular form for the short story which, after the passing of Poe and of Hawthorne, O'Brien had begun. While the novel life of California was peculiarly get-at-able by means of the short-story technique, novel situations, unusual contrasts, strange contradictions everywhere could be exploited by the same method. Harte's stories raised a crop of "wild life" tales after them, but they were also followed by an equally flourishing growth of narratives in which the striking situations provided by the most civilized life were written into some kind of literature. In the decade after his first success, the short-story form became a usual, not the extraordinary tool. And as the peculiarly geographical development of our civilization, and the general shifting of social standards and social orders, which marks the end of the nineteenth century, proceeded, more and more fields were opened up for its use. So, after all, Harte was right; it was the treatment of life, as it was here in America, which began the vogue of the short story. (pp. 295-98)

Henry Seidel Canby, "The Mid-Century in America," in his The Short Story in English, *Henry Holt and Company, 1909, pp. 280-298.*

Henry Childs Merwin (essay date 1911)

[*In the essay excerpted below, Merwin assesses some of Harte's strengths and limitations as a writer, focusing on his short fiction.*]

Bret Harte's faculty was not so much that of imagining as of apprehending human character. Some writers of fiction, those who have the highest form of creative imagination, are able from their own minds to spin the web and woof of the characters that they describe; and it makes small difference where they live or what literary material lies about them. Even these authors do not create their heroes and heroines quite out of whole cloth,—they have a shred or two to begin with; but their work is mainly the result of creation rather than perception.

The test of creative imagination is that the characters portrayed by it are subjected to various exigencies and influences: they grow, develop, yes, even change, and yet retain their consistency. (p. 293)

A few great novels have indeed been written by authors who did not possess this faculty, especially by Dickens, in whom it was conspicuously lacking; but no long story was ever produced without betraying its author's deficiency in this respect if the deficiency existed. *Gabriel Conroy,* Bret Harte's only novel, is so bad as a whole, though abounding in gems, its characters are so inconsistent and confused, its ending so incomprehensible, that it produces upon the reader the effect of a nightmare.

In fact, the nearer Bret Harte's stories approach the character of an episode the better and more dramatic they are. Of the longer stories, the best, as everybody will admit, is **"Cressy,"** and that is little more than the expansion of a single incident. As a rule, in reading the longer tales, one remembers, as he progresses, that the situations and the events are fictitious; they have not the spontaneous, inevitable aspect which makes the shorter tales impressive. **"Tennessee's Partner"** is as historical as Robinson Crusoe. Bret Harte had something of a weakness for elaborate plots, but they were not in his line. Plots and situations can hardly be satisfactory or artistic unless they form the means whereby the characters of the persons in the tale are developed, or, if not developed, at least revealed to the reader. The development or the gradual revelation of character is the *raison d'être* for the long story or novel.

But this capacity our author seems to have lacked. It might be said that he did not require it, because his characters appear to us full-fledged from the start. He has, indeed, a wonderful power of setting them before the reader almost immediately, and by virtue of a few masterly strokes. After an incident or two, we know the character; there is nothing more to be revealed; and a prolongation of the story would be superfluous.

But here we touch upon Bret Harte's weakness as a portrayer of human nature. It surely indicates some deficiency in a writer of fiction if with the additional scope afforded by a long story he can tell us no more about his people than he is able to convey by a short story. The deficiency in Bret Harte was perhaps this, that he lacked a profound knowledge of human nature. A human being regarded as material for a writer of fiction may be divided into two parts. There is that part, the more elemental one, which he shares with other men, and there is, secondly, that part which differentiates him from other men. In other words, he is both a type of human nature, and a particular specimen with individual variations.

The ideal story-writer would be able to master his subject in each aspect, and in describing a single person to depict at once both the nature of all men and also the nature of that particular man. Shakspere, Sterne, Thackeray have this power. Other writers can do the one thing but not the other; and in this respect Hawthorne and Bret Harte stand at opposite extremes. Hawthorne had a profound knowledge of human nature; but he was lacking in the capacity to hit off individual characteristics. Arthur Dimmesdale and Hester, even Miriam and Hilda, are not real to us in the sense in which Colonel Newcome and Becky Sharp are real. Hawthorne's figures are somewhat spectral; they lack flesh and blood. His forte was not observation but reflection. He worked from the inside.

Bret Harte, on the other hand, worked from the outside. He had not that faculty, so strong in Hawthorne, of delving into his own nature by way of getting at the nature of other men; but he had the faculty of sympathetic observation which enabled him to perceive and understand the characteristic traits that distinguish one man from another.

"Barker's Luck" and **"Three Partners,"** taken together, illustrate Bret Harte's limitations in this respect. Each of these stories has Barker for its central theme, the other personages being little more than foils to him. In the first story, **"Barker's Luck,"** the plot is very simple, the incidents are few, and yet we have the character of the hero conveyed to us with exquisite effect. In **"Three Partners,"** the theme is elaborated, a complicated plot is introduced, and Barker appears in new relations and situations. But we know him no better than we did before. **"Barker's Luck"** covered the ground; and **"Three Partners,"** a more ambitious story, is far below it in verisimilitude and in dramatic effect. In the same way, **"M'liss,"** in its original form, is much superior to the longer and more complex story which its author wrote some years afterward, and which is printed in the collected edition of his works, to the exclusion of the earlier tale.

In one case, however, Bret Harte did succeed in showing the growth and development of a character. The trilogy known as **"A Waif of the Plains," "Susy,"** and **"Clarence,"** is almost the same as one long story; and in it the character of Clarence, from boyhood to maturity, is skilfully and consistently traced. Upon this character Bret Harte evidently bestowed great pains, and there are some notable passages in his delineation of it, especially the account of the duel between Clarence and Captain Pinckney. Not less surprising to Clarence himself than to the reader is the calm ferocity with which he kills his antagonist; and we share the thrill of horror which ran through the little group of spectators when it was whispered about that this gentlemanly young man, so far removed in appearance from a fire-eater, was the son of Hamilton Brant, the noted duellist. The situation had brought to the surface a deep-lying, inherited trait, of which even its possessor had been ignorant. In this character, certainly in this incident, Bret Harte goes somewhat deeper than his wont.

We have his own testimony to the fact that his genius was perceptive rather than creative. In those Scotch stories and sketches in which the Consul appears, very much in the capacity of a Greek chorus, the author lets fall now and then a remark plainly autobiographical in character. Thus, in **"A Rose of Glenbogie,"** speaking of Mrs. Deeside, he says, "The Consul, more *perceptive* than analytical, found her a puzzle."

This confirms Bret Harte's other statement, made elsewhere, that his characters, instead of being imagined, were copied from life. But they were copied with the insight and the emphasis of genius. The ability to read human nature is about the most rare of mental possessions. How little do we know even of those whom we see every day, and whom, perhaps, we have lived with all our lives! (pp. 293-97)

[Individual] character eludes us. But it did not elude Bret Harte. He had a wonderful faculty both for understanding and remembering its outward manifestations. His genius was akin to that of the actor; and this explains, perhaps, his lifelong desire to write a successful play. Mr. Watts-Dunton has told us with astonishment how Bret Harte, years after a visit to one of the London Music Halls, minutely recounted all that he had heard and seen there, and imitated all the performers. That he would have made a great actor in the style of Joseph Jefferson is the opinion of that accomplished critic.

The surprising quickness with which he seized and assimilated any new form of dialect was a kind of dramatic capacity. The Spanish-English, mixed with California slang, which Enriquez Saltello spoke, is as good in its way as the immortal Costigan's Irish-English.

> "To confer then as to thees horse, which is not—observe me—a Mexican plug. Ah, no! you can your boots bet on that. She is of Castilian stock—believe me and strike me dead! I will myself at different times overlook and affront her in the stable, examine her as to the assault, and why she should do thees thing. When she is of the exercise I will also accost and restrain her. Remain tranquil, my friend! When a few days shall pass much shall be changed, and she will be as another. Trust your oncle to do thees thing! Comprehend me? Everything shall be lovely, and the goose hang high."

Bret Harte's short stay in Prussia, and later in Scotland, enabled him to grasp the peculiarities of nature and speech belonging to the natives. Peter Schroeder, the idealist, could have sprung to life nowhere except upon German soil. "Peter pondered long and perplexedly. Gradually an explanation slowly evolved itself from his profundity. He placed his finger beside his nose, and a look of deep cunning shone in his eyes. 'Dot's it,' he said to himself triumphantly, 'dot's shoost it! Der Rebooplicans don't got no memories. Ve don't got nodings else.' "

What character could be more Scotch, and less anything else, than the porter at the railway station where the Consul alighted on his way to visit the MacSpaddens. " 'Ye'll no be rememberin' me. I had a machine in St. Kentigern and drove ye to MacSpadden's ferry often. Far, far too often! She's a strange, flagrantitious creature; her husband's but a puir fule, I'm thinkin', and ye did yersel' nae guid gaunin' there.' "

Mr. Callender, again, Ailsa's father, in **"Young Robin Gray,"** breathes Scotch Calvinism and Scotch thrift and self-respect in every line.

> "Have you had a cruise in the yacht?" asked the Consul.
>
> "Ay," said Mr. Callender, "we have been up and down the loch, and around the far point, but not for boardin' or lodgin' the night, nor otherwise conteenuing or parteecipating. . . . Mr. Gray's a decent enough lad, and not above instruction, but extraordinar' extravagant."

Even the mysteries of Franco-English seem to have been fathomed by Bret Harte, possibly by his contact with French people in San Francisco. This is how the innkeeper explained to Alkali Dick some peculiarities of French custom:

> "For you comprehend not the position of *la jeune fille* in all France! Ah! in America the young lady she go everywhere alone; I have seen her—pretty, charming, fascinating—alone with the young man. But here, no, never! Regard me, my friend. The French mother, she say to her daughter's fiancé, "Look! there is my daughter. She has never been alone with a young man for five minutes,—not even with you. Take her for your wife!" It is monstrous! It is impossible! It is so!"

The moral complement of this rare capacity for reading human nature was the sympathy, the tenderness of feeling which Bret Harte possessed. Sympathy with human nature, with its weaknesses, with the tragedies which it is perpetually encountering, and above all, with its redeeming virtues,—this is the keynote of Bret Harte's works, the mainspring of his humor and pathos. He had the gift of satire as well, but, fortunately for the world, he made far less use of it. Satire is to humor as corporal punishment is to personal influence. A satire is a jest, but a cutting one,—a jest in which the victim is held up to scorn or contempt.

Humor is a much more subtle quality than satire. Like satire, it is the perception of an incongruity, but it must be a newly discovered or invented incongruity, for an essential element in humor is the pleasurable surprise, the gentle shock which it conveys. A New Jersey farmer was once describing in the presence of a very humane person, the great age and debility of a horse that he had formerly owned and used. "You ought to have killed him!" interrupted the humane person indignantly. "Well," drawled the farmer, "we did,—almost." Satire is merely destructive, whereas sentiment is constructive. The most that satire can do is to show how the thing ought *not* to be done. But sentiment goes much further, for it supplies the dynamic power of affection. (pp. 297-300)

There is often in Bret Harte a subtle blending of satire and humor, notably in that masterpiece of satirical humor, the "Heathen Chinee." The poet beautifully depicts the naïve indignation of the American gambler at the duplicity of the Mongolian,—a duplicity exceeding even his own. " 'We are ruined by Chinese cheap labor!' "

Another instance is that passage in **"The Rose of Tuolumne,"** where the author, after relating how a stranger was shot and nearly killed in a mining town, records the prevailing impression in the neighborhood "that his misfortune was the result of the defective moral quality of his being a stranger." So, in **"The Outcasts of Poker Flat,"** when the punishment of Mr. Oakhurst was under consideration, "A few of the Committee had urged hanging him as a possible example and a sure method of reimbursing themselves from his pockets of the money he had won from them. 'It's agin justice,' said Jim Wheeler, 'to let this yer young man from Roaring Camp—an entire stranger—carry away our money.' But a crude sentiment of equity residing in the breasts of those who had been fortunate enough to win from Mr. Oakhurst overruled this narrower local prejudice."

Even in these passages humor predominates over satire. In fact,—and it is a fact characteristic of Bret Harte,—the only satire, pure and simple, in his works is that which he directs against hypocrisy. This was the one fault which he could not forgive; and he especially detested that peculiar form of cold and calculating hypocrisy which occasionally survives as the dregs of Puritanism. Bret Harte was keenly alive to this aspect of New England character; and he has depicted it with almost savage intensity in **"The Argonauts of North Liberty."** Ezekiel Corwin, a shrewd, flinty, narrow Yankee, is not a new figure in literature, but an old figure in one or two new situations, notably in his appearance at the mining camps as a vender of patent medicines. "That remarkably unfair and unpleasant-spoken man had actually frozen Hanley's Ford into icy astonishment at his audacity, and he had sold them an invoice of the Panacea before they had recovered; he had insulted Chipitas into giving an extensive order in bitters; he had left Hayward's Creek pledged to Burne's pills—with drawn revolvers still in their hands."

Even here, however, the bitterness of the satire is tempered by the humor of the situation. But in Joan, the heroine of the story, we have a really new figure in literature, and it is drawn with an absence of sympathy, of humor and of mitigating circumstances which is very rare, if not unique, in Bret Harte.

One other example of pure satire may be found in his works, and that is Parson Wynn, the effusive, boisterous hypocrite who plays a subordinate part in **"The Carquinez Woods."** With these few exceptions, however, Bret Harte was a writer of sentiment, and that is the secret of his power. Sentiment may take the form of humor or of pathos, and, as is often remarked, these two qualities shade off into each other by imperceptible degrees. (pp. 300-02)

A consummate example of this blending of humor and pathos is found in the story **"How Santa Claus Came to Simpson's Bar."** The boy Johnny, after greeting the Christmas guests in his "weak, treble voice, broken by that premature harshness which only vagabondage and the habit of premature self-assertion can give," and after hospitably setting out the whiskey bottle, with crackers and cheese, creeps back to bed, and is thus accosted by Dick Bullen, the hero of the story:—

> "Hello, Johnny! You ain't goin' to turn in agin, are ye?"
>
> "Yes, I are," responded Johnny decidedly.
>
> "Why, wot's up, old fellow?"
>
> "I'm sick."
>
> "How sick?"
>
> "I've got a fevier, and childblains, and roomatiz," returned Johnny, and vanished within. After a moment's pause he added in the dark, apparently from under the bedclothes,—"And biles!"
>
> There was an embarrassing silence. The men looked at each other and at the fire.

How graphically in this story are the characters of the Old Man and his boy Johnny indicated by a few strokes of humor and pathos! Perhaps this is the greatest charm of humor in literature, namely, that it so easily becomes the vehicle of character. (pp. 302-03)

The humor of the passage just quoted from **"How Santa Claus Came to Simpson's Bar,"** the humor that made Bret Harte famous, and still more the humor that made him beloved, was not saturnine or satirical, but sympathetic and tender. It was humor not from an external point of view, but from the victim's point of view. The Californians themselves saw persons and events in a different way; and how imperfect their vision was may be gathered from the fact that they stoutly denied the truth of Bret Harte's descriptions of Pioneer life. They were too close at hand, too much a part of the drama themselves, to perceive it correctly. Bret Harte had the faculty as to which it is hard to say how much is intellectual and how much is emotional, of getting behind the scenes, and beholding men and motives as they really are. (p. 305)

Henry Childs Merwin, in his The Life of Bret Harte with Some Account of the California Pioneers, *Houghton Mifflin Company, 1911, 362 p.*

Fred Lewis Pattee (essay date 1915)

[*Pattee was a highly respected literary critic and historian whose works frequently encouraged international recognition of a distinctly American literary canon. In the excerpt below, he provides an overview of Harte's career, focusing on his method of characterization, as well as the influences of both the work of Charles Dickens and Harte's years in California.*]

Harte's first story with other than a legendary theme was **"M'liss,"** written for the *Golden Era* sometime before 1867. For the student of his literary art it is the most important of all his writings, especially important because of the revision which he made of it later after he had evolved his final manner. It is transition work. The backgrounds are traced in with Irving-like care; the character of the schoolmaster is done with artistic restraint and certainty of touch. M'liss is exquisitely handled. There is nothing better in all his work than this study of the fiery, jealous little heart of the neglected child. It is not necessarily a California story; it could have happened as well even in New England. It is not *genre* work, not mere exploiting of local oddities; it is worked out in life itself, and it strikes the universal human chord that brings it into the realm of true art.

But even in the earlier version of the story there are false notes. The names of the characters strike us as unusual: M'liss, McSnagley, Morpher, Clytemnestra, Kerg, Aristides, Cellerstina. We feel that the author is straining for the unusual; and we feel it more when the Rev. Joshua McSnagley comes upon the scene:

> The reverend gentleman was glad to see him. Moreover, he observed that the master was looking "peartish," and hoped he had got over the "neuralgy" and "rheumatiz." He himself had been troubled with the dumb "ager" since last conference. But he had learned to "rastle and pray." Pausing a moment to enable the master to write his certain method of curing the dumb "ager" upon the book and volume of his brain, Mr. McSnagley proceeded to inquire after Sister Morpher. "She is an adornment to Christewanity, and has a likely growin' young family," added Mr. McSnagley.

Somehow it does not ring true. The author is thinking of the effect he hopes to produce. He must fill his reader with wonder. "A saintly Raphael-face, with blond beard and soft blue eyes, belonging to the biggest scamp in the diggings, turned toward the child and whispered, 'Stick to it, M'liss.' " That sentence is the key to the author's later manner. "Life in California is a paradox," he seems everywhere to say, "just look at this."

The transition from F. B. Harte the poet and romancer to Bret Harte the paradox maker and showman came through Dickens. It was the Dickens era in America. The great novelist had made his second tour of the country between November, 1867, and April, 1868, and his journeyings had been a triumphal progress. All classes everywhere were reading his books, and great numbers knew them literally by heart. (pp. 70-1)

[Dickens] never analyzed, he never sought the heart of things, or got at all below the surface of his characters; he was content simply to exhibit his marvelous creations with all their ludicrous incongruities, and the show is so entertaining and the showman exhibits it with such zest, such joyous abandon, that we stand like children and lose ourselves in wonder and enjoyment.

We can see now that the time was ripe for a California Dickens. There was a prepared audience—the whole nation was reading the great novelist of the people. California, moreover, was in the fierce light of the gold excitement—anything that came from it would find eager readers. It was a veritable Dickens land, more full of strange types than even the slums of London: Pikes, Greasers, Yankees, Chinese, gamblers, adventurers from all the wild places of the world, desperadoes, soldiers of fortune, restless seekers for excitement and gold. Everything was ready. Harte doubtless blundered into his success; doubtless he did not reason about the matter at all, yet the result remains the same: he came at the precise moment with the precise form of literature that the world was most sure to accept. It came about as the most natural thing in the world. Saturated with Dickens as he had been from his childhood, it is not strange that this motley society and its amazing surroundings should have appealed to him from the objective and the picturesque side; it is not strange that, even as did Dickens, he should have selected types and heightened them and peopled a new world with them; it is not strange that he should have given these types Dickens-like names: Miggles, McCorkle, Culpepper Starbottle, Calhoun Bungstarter, Fagg, Twinkler, Rattler, Mixer, Stubbs, Nibbles. His work is redolent of Dickens. Sometimes we seem to be reading a clever parody after the fashion of the ***Condensed Novels,*** as for instance this from **"The Romance of Madrono Hollow":**

> There was not much to hear. The hat was saying to the ribbons that it was a fine night, and remarking generally upon the clear outline of the Sierras against the blue-black sky. The ribbons, it so appeared, had admired this all the way home, and asked the hat if it had ever seen anything half so lovely as the moonlight on the summit? The hat never had; it recalled some lovely nights in the South in Alabama ("in the South in Ahlabahm" was the way the old man had heard it), but then there were other things that made the night seem so pleasant. The ribbons could not possibly conceive what the hat could be thinking about.
>
> (pp. 72-3)

"M'liss" is full of such echoes. A little later than **"M'liss,"** when he was required to furnish the *Overland* with a distinctly Californian story, he set about examining his field precisely as Dickens would have done. "What are some of the most unusual phases of this unique epoch?" he asked himself. During a short period women and children were rare in the remote mining districts. What would result if a baby were born in one of the roughest and most masculine of the camps? It is not hard to conjecture how Dickens would have handled the problem; **"The Luck of Roaring Camp"** is Harte's solution. The situation and the characters are both unique. They would have been impossible in any other place or at any other moment in the world's history. So with all of Harte's later stories: undoubtedly there may have been a Roaring Camp and undoubtedly there were Cherokee Sals and Kentucks, undoubtedly the gold rush developed here and there Jack Hamlins and Tennessees and Uncle Billys and Yuba Bills. The weakness of Harte is that he takes these and peoples California with them. Like Dickens, he selects a few picturesque and grotesque exceptions and makes of them a whole social system.

Harte had nothing of the earnestness and the sincerity of the older master; after a time he outgrew his manner, and evolved a style of his own—compressed, rapid, picturesque; but this early point of view he never changed. He sought ever for the startling and the dramatic and he elaborated the outside of it with care. He studied the map of California for picturesque names, just as Dickens studied the street signs of London. He passed by the common materials of human life to exhibit the strange phenomena of one single accidental moment in a corner of America.

Once he had begun, however, there was no possibility of stopping. The people demanded work like **"The Luck of Roaring Camp"** and would accept nothing else. It is pathetic to see him during the early years of his great fame, trying to impress upon the reading public that he is a poet after the old definition of the word. The *Atlantic* had paid him $10,000 to write for a year work like **"The Luck of Roaring Camp."** He gave four stories, and he gave also five careful poems of the Longfellow-Whittier type. By 1873 he had put forth no fewer than fourteen books, nine of them being poems or collections of his poetry. In vain. The public ordered him back to the mines and camps that even then were as obsolete as the pony express across the Plains.

Despite his biographers, the latter part of his life is full of mystery. After seven years of literary work in New York City, he went in 1878 as consul to Crefeld, Germany. Two years later he was transferred to Glasgow, Scotland, where he remained for five years. The rest of his life he spent in London, writing year after year new books of California stories. He never returned to America; he was estranged from his family; he seemed to wish to sever himself entire-

Hart during his years as editor of the Overland Monthly.

ly from all that had to do with his earlier life. He died May 5, 1902, and was buried in Frimby churchyard, in Surrey.

. . . . .

A novelist must rise or fall with his characters. What of Harte? First of all we must observe that he makes no attempts at character development. Each personage introduced is the same at the close of the story as at the opening. He has no fully studied character: we have a burning moment, a flashlight glimpse—intense, paradoxical, startling, then no more. We never see the person again. The name may appear in later sketches, but it never designates the same man. Colonel Starbottle is consistent from story to story only in make-up, in stage "business," and the well known "gags"—as, for instance, a succession of phrases qualified by the adjective "blank." "Yuba Bill" is Harte's synonym for stage driver, "Jack Hamlin" for gambler. We have a feeling constantly that the characters are brought in simply to excite wonder. Gabriel Conroy devotes his life for years to the finding of his sister Grace. He leaves his wife to search for her; he can think of nothing else; yet when at length he does find her among the witnesses in a courtroom he takes it as a mere commonplace. A moment later, however, when told that his wife, for whom we know he cares nothing at all, has given birth to a son, he falls headlong in a swoon.

His characters may perhaps be true to facts; he may be able to give the prototype in every case; and yet we are not convinced. The stories told by the college freshman at home during his first Christmas vacation may all be true, and yet they may give a very false idea of college life in its entirety. So it is with Harte. The very year that he landed in California a procession of one thousand children, each child with a flower in his hand, marched one day in San Francisco. **"The Luck of Roaring Camp"** gives no such impression. In all save the remotest camps there were churches and worshipers, yet who would suspect it from Harte's tales? California has never accepted Harte's picture of its life, just as the South has never accepted *Uncle Tom's Cabin.* It is not fair to picture an era simply by dwelling on its exceptions and its grotesque possibilities. Art must rest upon the whole truth, not upon half truths.

The truth is that the man had no deep and abiding philosophy of life; he had indeed no philosophy at all. In the words of his discerning biographer, Merwin,

> There was a want of background, both intellectual and moral, in his nature. He was an observer, not a thinker, and his genius was shown only as he lived in the life of others. Even his poetry is dramatic, not lyric. It was very seldom that Bret Harte, in his tales or elsewhere, advanced any abstract sentiment or idea; he was concerned only with the concrete; and it is noticeable that when he does venture to lay down a general principle, it fails to bear the impress of real conviction. The note of sincerity is wanting.

The fact that his rascals in a crisis often do deeds of sublime heroism must not deceive us, despite the author's protestations of a great moral purpose underlying his work. (pp. 73-5)

Harte makes his villains heroes at the crisis simply to add *finesse* to his tale. He is dealing with paradoxes; he is working for his reader's wonder. If in a moment where pity is expected, woman is harsh and man tender; if the reputed good man is a rascal at the supreme test, and the reputed rascal proves suddenly to be a saint, it adds to the effectiveness of the tale.

Everywhere there is the atmosphere of the theater. The painted backgrounds are marvels of skill. There are vast color effects, and picturesque tableaux. There is a theatric quality about the heroines; we can see the make-up upon their faces. Too often they talk the stagiest of stage talk as in the first parting scene between Grace Conroy and Arthur Poinset. The end is always a drop-curtain effect. Even **"Tennessee's Partner"** must have its appropriate curtain. We can imagine a double curtain for **"The Outcasts of Poker Flat":** the first tableau showing the two dead women in the snow, the second the inscription over the body of Oakhurst, the gambler. Instead of closing the book with a long breath as after looking at a quivering section of human life, we say, "How strange! What brilliant work!" and we feel like clapping our hands for a tableau of all the cast, the spot light, and the quick curtain.

Bret Harte had no real affection for the West; he never again visited it; he never even wrote to the friends he had left there. With Mark Twain it was greatly different. The West to him was home; he loved it; he recorded its deepest life with sympathy. To Harte it was simply a source of literary material. He skimmed its surface and found only the melodramatic and the sensational.

And yet after all the real strength of Bret Harte came from his contact with this Western soil. Irving and Dickens and the early models that had so molded him served only to teach him his trade; the breath of life in his works all came from the new life of the West. It would be impossible for one to live during seventeen years of his early life in an atmosphere like that of the west coast and not be transformed by it. Taking his work altogether there is in it far more of California than there is of Dickens or of all the others of the older writers. Only a few things of the life of the West seem to have impressed him. He lived fifteen years in San Francisco yet we see almost nothing of that city in his work; the dramatic career of the Vigilantes he touched upon almost not at all. He selected the remote mining camps for his field and yet he seems to have been impressed by very few of the types that were found in them. Only a few of them ring true at every point, Yuba Bill the stage driver is one. We feel that he was drawn by a master who has actually lived with his model. Yuba Bill is the typical man of the region and the period—masterful, self-reliant, full of a humor that is elemental. There is no prolonged study of him. We see him for a tense moment as the stage swings up to the station, and then he is gone. He is as devoid of sentimentality as even Horace Bixby. The company have been shouting "Miggles!" at the dark cabin but have got no reply save from what proves later to have been a parrot:

> "Extraordinary echo," said the Judge.
>
> "Extraordinary d—d skunk!" roared the driver

> contemptuously. "Come out of that, Miggles, and show yourself. Be a man."
>
> Miggles, however, did not appear.
>
> Yuba Bill hesitated no longer. Taking a heavy stone from the road, he battered down the gate, and with the expressman entered the enclosure. . . .
>
> "Do you know this Miggles?" asked the Judge of Yuba Bill.
>
> "No, nor don't want to," said Bill shortly.
>
> "But, my dear sir," expostulated the Judge, as he thought of the barred gate.
>
> "Lookee here," said Yuba Bill, with fine irony, "hadn't you better go back and sit in the coach till yer introduced? I'm going in," and he pushed open the door of the building.

That rings true. If one were obliged to ride at night over a wild, road-agent-infested trail there is no character in all fiction whom we would more gladly have for driver than Yuba Bill. We would like to see more of him than the brief glimpses allowed us by his creator.

The humor in Harte is largely Western humor. There is the true California ring in such conversations, for instance, as those in the earlier pages of **"Uncle Jim and Uncle Billy."** It is an atmosphere rather than a series of hits. One finds it in **"The Outcasts of Poker Flat":**

> A few of the committee had urged hanging him [Oakhurst] as a possible example, and a sure method of reimbursing themselves from his pockets of the sums he had won from them. "It's agin justice," said Jim Wheeler, "to let this yer young man from Roaring Camp—an entire stranger—carry away our money." But a crude sentiment of equity residing in the breasts of those who had been fortunate enough to win from Mr. Oakhurst overruled this narrower local prejudice.

This atmosphere of humor shimmers through all of the stories. There is never uproarious merriment, but there is constant humor. The conjugal troubles of the "old man" in **"How Santa Claus Came to Simpson's Bar"** are thus touched upon:

> His first wife, a delicate, pretty little woman, had suffered keenly and secretly from the jealous suspicions of her husband, until one day he invited the whole Bar to his house to expose her infidelity. On arriving, the party found the shy, *petite* creature quietly engaged in her household duties and retired abashed and discomfited. But the sensitive woman did not easily recover from her shock of this extraordinary outrage. It was with difficulty she regained her equanimity sufficiently to release her lover from the closet in which he was concealed and escape with him. She left a boy of three years to comfort her bereaved husband. The old man's present wife had been his cook. She was large, loyal, and aggressive.

His characters are exceptions and his situations are theatric, yet for all that he cannot be ignored. He caught the spirit of the early mining camps and with it the romantic atmosphere of the old Spanish Colonial civilization that was swept away by the Anglo-Saxon rush for gold. His name cannot fail to go down with the era he recorded, and to identify oneself forever with an era, even though that era be a brief and restricted one, is no small achievement. He is the writer of the epic of the gold rush of the middle century in America, and whatever the quality of that epic may be, it can never be forgotten. He said in 1868:

> It may not have been an heroic era; it may have been a hard, ugly, unworked, vulgar and lawless era; but of such are heroes and aristocracies born. Three hundred years, and what a glamor shall hang about it! . . . A thousand years, and a new Virgil sings the American Æneid with the episode of Jason and the California golden fleece, and the historians tell us it is a myth! Laugh, my pioneer friends, but your great-great-great-great-grandchildren shall weep reverential tears. History, as was said of martyrdom, is "mean in the making" but how heroic it becomes in the perspective of five centuries!

And in many ways his work is really of epic strength. He dealt with elemental men, often with veritable demigods, as Yuba Bill. His canvases are as broad as those even of Mark Twain. His human drama is played before a truly Western background. While Tennessee is being tried for his life, "Above all this, etched on the dark firmament, rose the Sierra, remote and passionless, crowned with remoter passionless stars." At moments of crisis the narrative always moves with power. The wolves and the fire in the story **"In the Carquinez Woods"** are intensely vivid and lurid in their presentation. The ride from Simpson's Bar is told with the graphic thrill of an eye-witness, and the description of the snow-storm at the opening of *Gabriel Conroy* reminds one of Thomas Hardy.

Finally, Harte was the parent of the modern form of the short story. It was he who started Kipling and Cable and Thomas Nelson Page. Few indeed have surpassed him in the mechanics of this most difficult of arts. According to his own belief, the form is an American product. We can do no better than to quote from his essay on "The Rise of the Short Story." It traces the evolution of a peculiarly American addition to literature.

> But while the American literary imagination was still under the influence of English tradition, an unexpected factor was developing to diminish its power. It was *humor,* of a quality as distinct and original as the country and civilization in which it was developed. . . . Crude at first, it received a literary polish in the press, but its dominant quality remained. It was concise and condense, yet suggestive. It was delightfully extravagant, or a miracle of under-statement. It voiced not only the dialect, but the habits of thought of a people or locality. It gave a new interest to slang. From a paragraph of a dozen lines it grew into half a column, but always retaining its conciseness and felicity of statement. It was a foe to prolixity of any kind; it admitted no fine writing nor affectation of style. It went directly to the point. It was burdened by no conscientiousness; it was often irreverent; it was de-

> void of all moral responsibility, but it was original! By degrees it developed character with its incident, often, in a few lines, gave a striking photograph of a community or a section, but always reached its conclusion without an unnecessary word. It became—and still exists as—an essential feature of newspaper literature. It was the parent of the American "short story."

Harte has described the genesis of his own art. It sprang from the Western humor and was developed by the circumstances that surrounded him. Many of his short stories are models. They contain not a superfluous word; they handle a single incident with graphic power; they close without moral or comment. The form came as a natural evolution from his limitations and powers. With him the story must of necessity be brief. He who depicts the one good deed in a wicked life must of necessity use a small canvas. At one moment in his career Jack Hamlin or Mother Shipton or Sandy does a truly heroic deed, but the author must not extend his inquiries too far. To make a novel with Mother Shipton as heroine would be intolerable. (pp. 76-80)

Bret Harte was the artist of impulse, the painter of single burning moments, the flashlight photographer who caught in lurid detail one dramatic episode in the life of a man or a community and left the rest in darkness.

In his later years Harte's backgrounds became less sharp in outline. His methods grew more romantic; his atmospheres more mellow and golden. The old Spanish dream of the days of his early art possessed him again, and he added to his gallery of real creations—M'liss, Yuba Bill, Jack Hamlin, Tennessee's Partner—one that perhaps is the strongest of them all, Enriquez Saltillo, the last of a fading race. Nothing Harte ever did will surpass that creation of his old age. In **"Chu Chu, The Devotion of Enriquez,"** and **"The Passing of Enriquez"** we have the fitting close of the work of the romancer of the west coast. For once at least he saw into the heart of a man. Listen to Enriquez as he makes his defense:

> Then they say, "Dry up, and sell out"; and the great bankers say, "Name your own price for your stock, and resign." And I say, "There is not gold enough in your bank, in your San Francisco, in the mines of California, that shall buy a Spanish gentleman. When I leave, I leave the stock at my back; I shall take it, nevarre!" Then the banker he say, "And you will go and blab, I suppose?" And then, Pancho, I smile, I pick up my mustache—so! and I say: "Pardon, señor, you haf mistake. The Saltillo haf for three hundred year no stain, no blot upon him. Eet is not now—the last of the race—who shall confess that he haf sit at a board of disgrace and dishonor!" And then it is that the band begin to play, and the animals stand on their hind legs and waltz, and behold, the row he haf begin.

It is the atmosphere of romance, for the mine which had caused all the trouble had been in the family three hundred years and it had become a part of the family itself. When it passed into the hands of the new régime, when his wife, who also was of the new régime, deserted him, then passed Enriquez. The earth that for three hundred years had borne his fathers opened at the earthquake and took him to herself. It was the conception of a true romancer. The work of Bret Harte opened and closed with a vision of romance, a vision worthy even of a Hawthorne. (pp. 81-2)

Fred Lewis Pattee, "Bret Harte," in his A History of American Literature Since 1870, *1915. Reprint by Cooper Square Publishers, Inc., 1968, pp. 63-82.*

Edward J. O'Brien (essay date 1923)

[*O'Brien was an American poet and critic who also edited numerous collections of short stories. In the following excerpt from his* The Advance of the American Short Story, *O'Brien discusses Harte's career and characterizes his role in the development of American literature, arguing that although Harte's fiction is often plagued by melodrama and false sentiment, he may well be considered one of the most representative and influential writers of his time.*]

In 1868, Harte was appointed editor-in-chief of *The Overland Monthly,* which had just been established, and it was in the second number of this periodical that he printed **"The Luck of Roaring Camp,"** and like Byron and Kipling woke to find himself famous. The inhibitions of frontier life are clear in Harte's account of the story's reception in the publishing offices before it appeared.

> He had not yet received the proof-sheets when he was suddenly summoned to the office of the publisher, whom he found standing, the picture of dismay and anxiety, with the proof before him. The indignation and stupefaction of the author can be well understood when he was told that the printer, instead of returning the proofs to him, had submitted them to the publisher, with the emphatic declaration that the matter there was so indecent, irreligious, and improper that his proofreader—a young lady—had with difficulty been induced to continue its perusal.

"The Luck of Roaring Camp" took the country by storm, despite the prudery of local Tartuffes. *The Atlantic Monthly* invited him to become a regular contributor, and he refused a professorship of literature in the new University of California. Story now followed story in quick and brilliant succession, and the first and best of his collections was issued in book form in 1869. He began to feel that he had outgrown California, and in 1870 bade it farewell forever. On his triumphal trip east he was fêted as a national hero in a manner only comparable to the later European journeys of Mark Twain. But his best work was already accomplished, and although the *Atlantic Monthly* subsidized him for a time at the rate of ten thousand dollars a year, it proved a bad bargain from an editorial point of view, for Harte's head was completely turned with praise. What would Poe have thought, and what passed through the lonely mind of Herman Melville at this moment? It is hard to tell, but the irony of life persists in laughing at fine artists.

Harte's writing, from being an art, soon descended to the level of a profession, and presently the transition was swift from a profession to a trade, although a gleam of the old fire lingered always, and is found in **"Colonel Starbottle for the Plaintiff "** as late as 1901, the year before his death. During the remainder of his life, he was a social butterfly, airy about his debts, and apparently still more airy about his wife and four children whom he left behind in 1878, when he accepted the American consulate at Crefield in Germany, and for whom he never sent. Did he consider that his family lacked his own social graces, we wonder, or did he find his wife an awkward realist? We do not know. Their outward relations seem to have remained harmonious, but Harte always took the easiest way, and for him the easiest way was that of a bachelor in English country houses.

Germany bored him, and he was transferred by political wire-pulling to the consulate at Glasgow, where he proved to be something of an absentee, and was encouraged to resign in 1885. He passed the rest of his life in England, having on the whole outlived his best talents, and died there on May 5, 1902. He had missed in England everything which Henry James had found.

In his preface to ***The Luck of Roaring Camp,*** Harte has summarized his artistic aims with tolerable clearness.

> I trust that in the following sketches I have abstained from any positive moral. I might have painted my villains of the blackest dye,—so black, indeed, that the originals thereof would have contemplated them with the glow of comparative virtue. I might have made it impossible for them to have performed a virtuous or generous action, and have thus avoided that moral confusion which is apt to arise in the contemplation of mixed motives and qualities. But I should have burdened myself with the responsibility of their creation, which, as a humble writer of romance and entitled to no particular reverence, I did not care to do.

(pp. 101-04)

Such were his aims, and it must be confessed that in his first volume, at least, he went far towards achieving them. These stories portray an interesting society which has long vanished, although the current Western story of commerce would not tend to make us conscious of the fact. They came at the psychological moment to ensure their success. The Civil War was over, and America was at the beginning of the transition period, when the sense of nationality and continental destiny was newly awakened, and there was a strong desire to realize and appreciate the life of the new frontiers. Harte, at the age of twenty-nine, stumbled upon a form of writing which satisfied this national craving without demanding from the reader any special reflection or subtlety of appreciation. The public response was like a literary Louisiana Purchase. The nation was flattered, and it repaid the compliment by flattering Bret Harte.

Unfortunately he had neither the strength of character nor the artistic integrity to resist the spell for any length of time. A drifting temperament with little moral courage and only too prone to follow the rule of *laissez faire,* he seems to have had much easy charm, a winning garrulity of speech, and a code of worldly wisdom. He was hardly noted for his sense of responsibility, and he could have had few deep friendships, but he must have had a host of acquaintances. Boynton has noted his capacity for sentimental self-pity, but he never allowed self-pity to embitter his pleasures. Pettie's portrait shows a week mouth, emphasized rather than concealed by a flowing moustache, and eyes which reveal no fixed purpose or surety of conviction.

Pemberton, his first biographer, exclaims: "What attention should be paid to a critic who prefers the subtleties of Henry James to the wholesome pathos of Bret Harte!" Unfortunately, the "wholesome pathos" of Bret Harte is often strikingly similar to the "wholesome pathos" of Paul Dombey and Little Nell.

At any rate he gave the American public what it wanted, and America gave him in return what he wanted,—adulation, money, and ease. He was the wicked fairy at the christening of the short story who bestowed on it the fatal gifts of type and of local color, and he rather more than paved the way for the advent of the surprise ending. Essentially an imitative talent without marked originality, and with a sense of the theater rather than a sense of drama, he was fortunate enough to find a life of seldom paralleled vividness to photograph. To-day he would be the most popular of moving-picture actors, and he would be well-satisfied. His imitativeness frequently borders with perilous closeness upon parody and, as we know, much of his prose and verse is avowed parody.

He has neither subtlety nor spiritual power, and he seldom avoids false sentiment for long. We may, moreover, regard him as the first American story-writer in an ever-lengthening series whose art has been profoundly corrupted by great financial rewards too easily won. He seldom resolved the conflict between his instinct to be truthful and his equally strong instinct to obscure the truth in a sentimental haze. His psychology is solid and reasonably satisfying when he is at his best, but it is never deeply apprehended, and at his worst we have the heresy of "types" presenting before us the stagy and creaking conventions of cheap Western melodrama. There are two kinds of simplification in literature: the subtle choice of the precise strokes which will tell, and the lazy blurring manner of the professional raconteur. We find both in Harte, and frequently together.

He established in America the sentimental convention of the strong, silent man, and that is largely the secret of his English vogue. Kipling, who learned from him everything that Harte had to teach, accepted the formula and carried it to a higher human level, but in Harte's work all later short stories of active event are already implicit. When he leaves the life of pioneer California, his work is negligible. His stories of European life are rubbish, and his tales of the Spanish missions, which are bad Irving, will cure insomnia.

What then is the merit of Bret Harte? Well, he is the typical "man of feeling," and at his best he combines sense and sensibility in his work. We also find swift and vivid narrative, unity rising to effective climax, and a worthy subject matter for a romantic epic. Pioneer life is rendered vividly for the first time. In an article entitled "The Rise of the

Short Story," he pleaded that his wish was to accept life as he found it, and to record it faithfully without provinciality and without passing a moral judgment. He implied that he believed himself to have been eminently successful in achieving this absence of provinciality, and seems to have considered that in this respect his work showed a marked improvement over the work of Hawthorne and Poe. There is a false glitter about his general plea, and not a little fatuousness, but I believe that his first intentions were thoroughly honest, and that for a short time they were successfully realized.

He built upon Poe's structure, but sought the unexpected rather than the marvelous. The feeling of this contrast has led critics to call him a realist, which is true if we allow for considerable qualification. He was conscious of the art with which Poe and Hawthorne utilized tone color for their effects, but he could seldom subdue his color to its appropriate place in the background. There is usually a glare, and I dare say this accounts for some of his popularity. One also feels that he was a little too anxious to present America with a literature which it would readily acknowledge, to question the value either of his methods or of his achievements. (pp. 105-10)

The parallel between the naked light of California and the lack of penumbra in Harte's short stories has not been pointed out, so far as I know. The two facts would appear to be related as cause and effect. His later stories, written under English skies, while he recalled the California of his youth, have sharper and sharper outlines. In his earlier stories, the fault is less noticeable, and occasionally, as in **"Tennessee's Partner,"** his sense of nature becomes almost pantheistic, so that the forest plays the part of a sympathetic Greek chorus to the action of the tale.

What conflict was Harte called upon as an artist to resolve? It was the essential conflict of pioneer society in new settlements which no writer who has experienced it has ever successfully sublimated, though it is a possible achievement. "It was, in one sense, a free life," says Van Wyck Brooks [in his *The Ordeal of Mark Twain* (1920)], half-paraphrasing Bret Harte.

> It was an irresponsible life, it implied a break with civilization, with domestic, religious and political ties. Nothing could be freer in that sense than the society of the gold-seekers in Nevada and California as we find it pictured in *Roughing It.* Free as that society was, nevertheless, scarcely any normal instinct could have been expressed or satisfied in it. The pioneers were not primitive men, they were civilized men, often of gentle birth and education. . . . In escaping responsibility, therefore, they had only placed themselves in a position where their instincts were blocked on every side. There were so few women among them, for instance, that their sexual lives were either starved or debased; and children were as rare as the 'Luck' of Roaring Camp, a story that shows how hysterical, in consequence of these and similar conditions, the mining population was. Those who were accustomed to the exercise of complex tastes and preferences found themselves obliged to conform to a single monotonous routine.

Now there was a magnificent opportunity here for a literary artist to sum up in a great gesture the whole pioneer conflict between suppressed instinct and environment, and to resolve and sublimate the struggle. Bret Harte admirably portrayed the picturesque side of this life, and showed no little sentimental sympathy with it in doing so, but he missed its epic tide, and to this day the pioneer west awaits its great chronicler. Such a man must possess all the narrative qualities of Bret Harte, all the human depth of Mark Twain, and a capacity for testing and transcending experience which both men lacked. Melville could have done it, but his life found expression in other channels. It has not been done in Australia, where the same opportunity offered. Now it is perhaps too late, for the chance would seem to have passed. Jack London had the experience, but he succumbed to the public, as most of Bret Harte's successors have succumbed.

In fact, Harte was a perfect type of the literature which was to follow him. Sharp-sighted, eager, nervous, superficial, anxious for quick results, and with a sentimental faith in his star, he may be taken to represent a common American ideal of the happy warrior. His heroism finds wish-fulfillment only in his writings, and it finds fulfillment there only in a fundamental romantic evasion of reality. The short story is in the market-place as soon as he publishes his first tale, and it is only a step to "O. Henry" and his school of protective coloration. Harte is far from being the greatest of American story writers, but he is probably the most representative of the characteristic qualities and weaknesses, and historically he may prove to have been our most influential man. (pp. 110-13)

Edward J. O'Brien, "Bret Harte and Mark Twain," in his The Advance of the American Short Story, *Dodd, Mead and Company, 1923, pp. 98-116.*

Fred Lewis Pattee (essay date 1923)

[In the following excerpt, Pattee outlines six distinctive characteristics of Harte's short stories: their colorful depiction of the West, a pervasive atmosphere of western humor, a "startling use of paradox and antithesis," a penchant for creating characters as types or composites of individuals, "a splashy type of impressionism," and an emphasis on literary technique.]

In July, 1867, Harte collected all that he deemed valuable of his parodies and sketches and legends and tales and issued them with the title, ***Condensed Novels and Other Papers.*** It was to be primarily a humorous publication: both the New York firm that accepted it and the readers who bought it classed it with Mark Twain's *The Jumping Frog and Other Sketches* which appeared at almost the same moment—the new California humor. But it was only the condensations that were humorous: the "Other Papers," the most of them solid and serious, were to be floated by the lightness of these vivacious parodies: "their introduction here," he was careful to assure his readers, "must rest solely upon the assumed popularity of the ***Condensed Novels.***" He did not claim for them any California characteristics, not even for the legends: he had intended them as serious literary exercises independent of time or place.

"Though based upon local scenery and local subjects, no one is better aware than their author of their deficiency in local coloring, a deficiency which he nevertheless believes is made up by such general interest and abstract fidelity as may make them applicable to any locality."

That Harte almost up to the date of **"The Luck of Roaring Camp"** deemed local-color studies inferior to Hawthorne-like sketches is forced upon anyone who reads straight through his early writings. That, however, he was early capable of such "local coloring" we have the best of evidence. As one toils through his early travesties, his conventional sketches and poems, his Irving-like legends, one stumbles all at once upon a discovery as thrilling as the finding of a nugget in a bank of clay. Once, for just a moment, it would seem, he forgot to be literary, forgot his traditions and his models and his proprieties, and let himself go. In the December, 1860, number of the *Era* appeared his sketch, **"The Work on Red Mountain"**—the first arresting title he had used. As one reads it, its conventional Irving-like opening, its introduction of its characters with their Dickens-like names—McSnagley, Kerg, Clytemnestra Morpher, Cellerstina Montmoressy—and its gargoyle-like characterization, suddenly one sits erect. The leading character has entered:

> "My name's M'liss—M'liss Smith! You can bet your life on that. My father's old Smith—old Bummer Smith—that's what's the matter with him. M'liss Smith—and I'm coming to school!"

It is a landmark. At this moment something new came into American fiction. Oliver Twist in an earlier period had confronted another schoolmaster, but there was nothing in the episode to compare with this. One was a cringing pauper in a civilization one large part of which fawned upon the other, and the demand of Oliver was but a spurt of audacity: the other was the incarnation of the wild lawlessness of a whole area, that primitive passion unchecked by convention or precedent, that irreverence and imperious self-assertion which had been born of the frontier and had culminated in the California of the gold-rush decade. Dickens never could have created M'liss; no European, no New Englander even, could have created her. She was uniquely Californian. She had grown up untutored in the wild gulches of "Smith's Pocket" with men elemental in their hates and loves and appetites and ideals of freedom. She was as unconventional as a coyote, and when crossed she was as fiercely alive. Told that Joshua once made the sun stand still, she burst out even in the awful presence of the school committee:

> "It's a damned lie. I don't believe it."

Wherever she appears the story is alive and compelling. It ends grippingly as a short story should end:

> "If you lock me up in jail," said M'liss, fiercely, "to keep me from the play-actors, I'll poison myself. Father killed himself—why shouldn't I? You said a mouthful of that root would kill me, and I always carry it here," and she struck her breast with her clenched fist. . . .
>
> "Lissy, will you go with me?"
>
> The child put her arms around his neck, and said, joyfully, "Yes."
>
> "But now—to-night?"
>
> "To-night" . . .
>
> The stars glittered brightly above them. For good or ill the lesson had been learned, and behind them the schoolhouse of Red Mountain closed upon them forever.

Unlike the rest of Harte's early work, the story struck fire. Californians recognized M'liss as one of themselves and asked for more. Harte humored them with a serial in the *Era* beginning September, 1863, an expansion of the earlier short story into a novel with proportions commensurate with their expectations. The result was a failure so complete that it may be described as a debacle. The vein of gold accidentally opened in his earlier tale he turned his back upon, and elaborately he sought to please his California readers with what he considered they would most enjoy, with strongly localized sensation. M'liss's letter to the schoolmaster proved to be a leaf torn from Bummer Smith's account book, and a jotting on the back gave the location of a new mine fabulously rich. It began to be whispered that the man had not committed suicide, but had been murdered on account of his secret—perhaps by M'liss. Immediately the plot spread out sensationally in all directions in dime novel fashion, until in the eighth installment it mastered its creator. A whole chapter he devotes to an explanation of his dilemma, closing it by begging his readers to send him letters suggesting ways out. Evidently none came, for, after floundering on for two installments more, the hodgepodge ends in chaos. It is like a "Condensed Novel" travesty of Nick Carter. Strange that the hand which had created **"M'liss"** should have produced nothing more like it for eight years, strange that he did not deem it worthy of inclusion in his 1867 volume, yet we of to-day can hardly realize how savage a thing **"M'liss"** seemed in 1860, how uncouth and how unliterary. Young Harte was not then seeking to be an innovator: he was seeking to learn the art of producing polite literature as the world in general defined such literature. Even after his great success, when he had settled in the East and knew fully the worth of the field he had discovered, he turned from it again and again to do work for which his soul longed in areas the very antipodes from those he felt himself condemned to cultivate.

But one could not live long in San Francisco during the decade of the 'sixties without unconsciously revising one's literary ideals. In 1863 Artemus Ward visited the Coast and did much toward precipitating in literary form the crude native humor of the region. In an editorial in the *Era,* December, 1863, Harte summed up the essence of his humor with comprehension and clearness. "It is," he said,

> the humor of audacious exaggeration—of perfect lawlessness; a humor that belongs to the country of boundless prairies, limitless rivers, and stupendous cataracts. In this respect Mr. Ward is the American humorist, *par excellence,* and "his book" is the essence of that fun which overlies the surface of our national life, which is met in the stage, rail car, canal and flatboat,

> which bursts out over campfires and around bar-room stoves—a humor that has more or less local coloring, that takes kindly to, and half elevates, slang, that is of to-day and full of present application. The showman has no purpose to subserve beyond the present laugh.
>
> (pp. 228-31)

In **"M'liss"** Harte had sprinkled only here and there the wild California flavors, in **"The Luck of Roaring Camp"** he made them the predominating characteristic. *The Overland Monthly* had been established to promote things Californian, but after the first issue, to quote Harte's own words, "its editor called the publisher's attention to the lack of any distinctive Californian romance in its pages and averred that, should no other come in, he himself would supply the omission in the next number." The result was **"The Luck of Roaring Camp,"** written deliberately to furnish a peculiarly Californian magazine with a peculiarly Californian tale. Its author had learned his art: the story would have satisfied Poe in the externals of technique, but it was not its art that gave it all in a moment its overwhelming vogue. It was its newness of atmosphere and background, its fresh wild humor, and, moreover, its *risqué* theme, for in 1868 the theme was indeed deemed upon the borders of propriety. The first proof reader upon it prudishly refused to proceed with such material. It insulted her. Then, too, its atmosphere of paradox, whether caught from Hugo or not, seemed new and startling.

Harte had found his formula: the voice of the East assured him so in no uncertain words, and, inspired by the new joys of recognition, he began to write with confidence. In half a dozen stories he reached remarkable levels. He was at his best: in all his later voluminous output there is nothing to compare in freshness and zest and artistry with this work poured out when the new wine of his first enthusiasm flowed clear. Various were the causes for his gradual failure, but the chief among them undoubtedly was the fact—to change the figure—that the mine he had discovered was a pocket and not a lode. Whatever might be his enthusiasm, he was fated to see diminishing returns. He who would confine himself to the social régime of a fleeting and squalid community in the wilds must soon run out of materials, or else repeat himself, especially if he work with that most material-exhausting of all literary forms, the short story. In later years Harte could only repeat in varied combinations his old characters and backgrounds and motifs, and always it was with a growing mechanicalness and loss of original freshness and charm.

Harte did perhaps six distinctive things for the short-story form. First, he threw over his stories, especially over his early masterpieces, a peculiar atmosphere of locality, one that to the readers of his day was startlingly new. He did for California what Dickens had done for London: he romanticized it; he gave it a mythology with a background perfectly in keeping. His methods of securing his localizing effect were unusual. Seemingly he made little of his setting: one may glance through one of his tales and be surprised to find only here and there a sentence touching upon landscape or surroundings, and yet one carries away from it local coloring as the dominating impression. Never does Harte, in notable contrast with many of his disciples, describe the landscape setting simply because it is unusual or unique. Always is it introduced as background, as scenery for his little theater, and, like all scenery, it is painted splashingly with swift impressionistic strokes. The tragedy of **"The Outcasts of Poker Flat"** is played before this drop curtain:

> The spot was singularly wild and impressive. A wooded amphitheatre surrounded on three sides by precipitous cliffs of naked granite, sloped gently toward the crest of another precipice that overlooked the valley.

"The Luck of Roaring Camp" opens with this setting:

> The camp lay in a triangular valley, between two hills and a river. The only outlet was a steep trail over the summit of a hill that faced the cabin, now illuminated by the rising moon.

It is like directions to a scene painter. Always is the scenery in accord or in contrast with the tragedy or the comedy enacting in the foreground. Tennessee is being tried for what the camp considers a capital crime, and the elements are in sympathy.

> The little cañon was stifling with heated resinous odors, and the decaying driftwood on the bar sent forth faint, sickening exhalations. The feverishness of the day, and its fierce passions, still filled the camp.

But

> Above all this, etched on the dark firmament, rose the Sierra, remote and passionless, crowned with remoter passionless stars.

Sometimes, not often, the background becomes a character in the plot and dominates the tale like a personality. The opening of the tale, **"Highwater Mark,"** reminds one strongly of the opening chapter of Hardy's *Return of the Native,* written years later:

> But if Dedlow Marsh was cheerless at the slack of the low tide, you should have seen it when the tide was strong and full. When the damp air blew chilly over the cold, glittering expanse, and came to the faces of those who looked seaward like another tide: when a steel-like glint marked the low hollows and the sinuous line of slough; when the great shell-incrusted trunks of fallen trees arose again, and went forth on their dreary, purposeless wanderings, drifting hither and thither, but getting no farther toward any goal at the falling tide or the day's decline than the cursed Hebrew in the legend; when the glossy ducks swung silently, making neither ripple nor furrow on the shimmering surface . . . .
>
> (pp. 233-35)

The second element emphasized by Harte was a saving dash of the new Western humor. In **"Tennessee's Partner"** he has recorded that in the gulches and the barrooms of early California "all sentiment was modified by a strong sense of humor." The statement is illuminating: without this peculiar quality in his work, which often is an atmosphere rather than a quotable entity, Harte would have been as sentimentally extreme as Dickens, his master. The funeral scene in **"Tennessee's Partner"** would have been mere gush. Even as it is, the last paragraph is mawkish sentimentality: the faithful partner dies of a broken heart and the two meet in heaven. And it is only this same atmosphere of humor that saves his melodrama from ridiculousness, for melodrama is everywhere present in his work. At times, as in **"The Rose of Tuolumne,"** it rises to all the shrillness of the Bowery villain play:

> Look! Do you see? This is his blood—my darling boy's blood!—one drop of which, dead and faded as it is, is more precious to me than the whole living pulse of any other man. Look! I come to you to-night, christened with his blood, and dare you to strike—dare you to strike him again through me, and mingle my blood with his. Strike, I implore you! Strike! if you have any pity on me, for God's sake! Strike! if you are a man! Look! Here lay his head on my shoulder; here I held him to my breast, where never—so help me my God—another man—Ah!—

The story is saved only by Mr. McClosky, a pure Bret Harte creation, and by its constant grim humor such as that which accounted for the deadly assault upon Dent by the explanation "that his misfortune was the result of the defective moral quality of his being a stranger, and was, in a vague sort of way, a warning to others, and a lesson to him."

The third characteristic was his startling use of paradox and antithesis. The world he presents is topsy-turvy. Of the dwellers in Roaring Camp he notes that

> The greatest scamp had a Raphael face, with a profusion of blonde hair; Oakhurst, a gambler, had the melancholy air and intellectual abstraction of a Hamlet; the coolest and most courageous man was scarcely over five feet in height, with a soft voice and an embarrassed, timid manner. . . . The strongest man had but three fingers on his right hand; the best shot had but one eye.

This became a mannerism with Harte. His heroes are men whom the world usually brands as villains. **"A Passage in the Life of Mr. John Oakhurst"** illustrates his method perfectly. There are two sets of characters, represented by Mrs. Decker, a pathetic invalid and a saintly soul, on the one hand, and by John Oakhurst, a notorious gambler, on the other. The two elements meet and the result furnishes the motif of the story. Oakhurst is everywhere regarded as a villain of melodramatic dye. Once, to be near the devout Mrs. Decker, he attended her church, and his appearance was considered by all the church members as an impertinence:

> One or two thought that the sexton was exceeding remiss in not turning him out after discovering who he was; and a prominent pewholder remarked, that if he couldn't take his wife and daughters to that church, without exposing them to such an influence, he would try to find some church where he could. Another traced Mr. Oakhurst's presence to certain broad Church radical tendencies, which he regretted to say he had lately noted in their pastor, Deacon Sawyer, whose delicately organized sickly wife had already borne him eleven children, and died in an ambitious attempt to complete the dozen, avowed that the presence of Mr. Oakhurst's various and indiscriminate gallantries was an insult to the memory of the deceased, that, as a man, he could not brook.

But Oakhurst proves to be the only *man* in the story and the only character that is in the least admirable. Whenever he appears, he satisfies our ideals of what a hero should be.

> However Mr. Oakhurst might hide his shapely limbs in homespun and home-made garments, there was something in his carriage, something in the pose of his beautiful head, something in the strong and fine manliness of his presence, something in the perfect and utter discipline and control of his muscles, something in the high repose of his nature—a repose not so much a matter of intellectual ruling as of his very nature—that, go where he would, and with whom, he was always a notable man in ten thousand.

But this is not enough: like his namesake in **"The Outcasts of Poker Flat,"** despite the fact that he is a beast of prey living richly upon his winnings, he is a saint: he sacrifices himself in the end for the sake of a principle. And the woman whom her husband worshiped as a saint proved to be as black inwardly as Oakhurst was black outwardly. She is the deliberate ruiner of at least two men; she has been all the time false to her husband, but when she meets the deluded man after she has learned the outcome of the tragedy, she is like an innocent child. He is bursting with the awful news concerning Oakhurst and Hamilton, but she sweetly begs him not to annoy her: She has a headache.

> Mr. Decker could not resist the petitionary grace of those white hands and that sensitive mouth, and took her in his arms. Suddenly he said, "What's that?"
>
> He was pointing to the bosom of her white dress. Where Mr. Oakhurst had touched her, there was a spot of blood.
>
> It was nothing; she had slightly cut her hand in closing the window; it shut so hard! If Mr. Decker had remembered to close and bolt the shutter before he went out, he might have saved her this. There was such a genuine irritability and force in this remark that Mr. Decker was quite overcome with remorse.

(pp. 235-38)

Everywhere it is the same: it is a mannerism. Trappington in **"A Secret of Telegraph Hill"** became a criminal because his mother took him so frequently to church when he was young. In the tale **"In the Carquinez Woods"** it is the courtesan Teresa who proves to be an angel in the hour of fire, and it is the eminently proper parson's daughter, whom the reader had supposed was to be the heroine, that is cursed by her dying lover as the veritable "daughter of hell." A moment of brightness in a life supposed by all to be unrelievably black; a deed of sacrifice that atones for a life of wickedness: that is the typical motif in the Bret Harte short story.

His fourth characteristic concerns his methods of characterization. He peopled his stories with highly individualized types, with picturesque extremes in an abnormal social régime. They are not photographs, they are not actual individuals, they are composites made up by fusing the unique qualities of many actual men or women into a single personality. Yuba Bill is the dream of a romancer who has known or has read about many California stage drivers. Colonel Starbottle is redolent of the make-up box: he changes from story to story. He is a gargoyle, and yet for all that he is alive, for Harte had learned from his master, Dickens, that art of creating what in reality is a realm of Munchausen, and then, miracle of miracles, of actually breathing into it the breath of life.

The fifth distinctive element in his work is a splashy type of impressionism. His treatment of background we have noted: he painted with broad strokes and strong colors, and he applied the method to his characters. Usually he works with extremes, with incarnated peculiarities, sharply emphasized. From him it was that Kipling learned the secret of the colorful impressionistic epithet, of the telling comparison, the single adjective that flashes a vivid picture. Harte describes a certain squaw as "a berry-eyed old woman with the complexion of dried salmon." Her daughter he describes as having also "berry eyes, and a face that seemed made of a moist laugh." Another character he pictures as "a stout, middle-aged woman of ungirt waist and beshawled head and shoulders."

Finally, like James and Aldrich, who were contemporaneous workers, he emphasized the technique of his art. He, too, had found Poe by way of France, he, too, was a conscious workman who knew the rules. Like Poe, too, he brought to the short story the training of the experienced magazine editor, and it was a training that kept him so long upon short, single-issue effects that he grew powerless to work effectively with the longer units. Again and again after the period of the serialized **"M'liss"** he tried to enter what was then considered the more serious field of fictional endeavor, the extended romance. One novel, *Gabriel Conroy,* he wrote, and at least sixteen novelettes which were issued as separate volumes, but not one of them is to be found in a list of his best writings. He was brilliant in short dashes, but he had not the patience to hold himself to a long and leisurely plot and to slow character development. There were other reasons for his failure: Harte lacked moral basis; he was superficial; he was theatric. He was temperamental, too, like Irving, and worked by impulse. Moreover, he dealt with materials impossible to be prolongated to novel length. If one is to make John Oakhurst or Mother Shipton heroic, one must deal with episodes: must make impressionistic sketches of vivid moments: to go farther would be to relate mere picaresque miscellany. It was only within narrow limits with single situations and highly colored materials that he could work at all effectively or artistically.

Unquestionably the influence of Harte upon the American short story has been greater than that exerted by any other American author, always excepting Irving. His influence was far greater than the quality of his work entitled him to exert. He was peculiarly fortunate: everything for a time conspired to give him the center of the stage. The imagination of the whole world had been fired by the California gold era and the field had been untouched by romancers: his material was timely to the moment. Dickens had just visited America and the fame of him and his work had penetrated every household; then had come the news of his death, and enormous space had been given to him in all the journals of the world and new editions had crowded upon one another, until everyone had his Dickens:—the reading public had been educated to appreciate the type of work that Harte was to give them. Moreover, he came at the moment when better art was demanded, when the feminized fiction of the mid-century was no longer satisfying the majority of the readers, and he gave them his work in a form that seemed to them to be peculiarly adequate. In him may be found all the elements that had characterized the popular fiction of the earlier period, and yet his fresh, wild materials, his new Western humor, and his peculiarly effective technique made him appear like the inspired creator of a new *genre.*

Great as has been his influence, however, he can never be a permanently commanding figure in American fiction. He lacked sincerity. One of his earliest reviewers characterized **"Mrs. Skagg's Husbands"** as a tale showing the "uncertain touch of a hand which has no sympathy with its work." It was a drastic arraignment, but, viewed in the calmness and perspective of today, it is seen to have been deserved. His work is not truth, it is extravaganza, and it is an extravaganza which touches not alone California manners and men, but all Americans generally as they have come from the mold of democracy, and it is not true. He wrote only to entertain. He would not report California; he would deliberately manufacture a California that would fill his reader with wonder. Nowhere is there realism; nowhere is there attempt to paint things as they are. Imagine reporting the robustly masculine Yuba Bill as saying not "damn," but "d——n." Imagine him "dancing about in an excess of fury" and giving vent to his feelings with: "Be a man, Miggles: Don't hide in the dark; I wouldn't if I were you, Miggles," and imagine a sane man talking this variety of talk to an ignorant street Arab of seven years:

> Melons, this is all irrelevant and impertinent to the case. *You* took those bananas. Your proposition regarding Carrots, even if I were inclined to accept it as credible information, does not alter the material issue. You took those bananas. The offense under the statutes of California is felony. How far Carrots may have been accessory to the fact either before or after, is not my intention at present to discuss. The act is complete. Your present conduct shows the *animo furandi* to have been equally clear.

It is vaudeville; it is posturing; it is mere smartness. In all of his work there is no experience, no genuine feeling, no sympathy of comprehension; it is the theater and not life. Moreover, the moral perspective of it is wrong. Men do not at will put on a new suit of morals as they put on a new suit of clothes. Ruled by emotion and not by principle, by the desire to create wonder and sensation in his reader rather than to interpret for him life, he tells not the truth, and the ultimate basis of all great fiction, be it long or be it short, is the Truth. (pp. 238-41)

Fred Lewis Pattee, "Bret Harte," in his The Development of the American Short Story: An Historical Survey, *Harper & Brothers Publishers, 1923, pp. 220-44.*

Harte on the origins of the American short story:

[While] the American literary imagination was still under the influence of English tradition, an unexpected factor was developing to diminish its power. It was humor—of a quality as distinct and original as the country and civilization in which it was developed. It was at first noticeable in the anecdote or "story," and after the fashion of such beginnings was orally transmitted. It was common in the barrooms, the gatherings in the country store, and finally at public meetings in the mouths of "stump orators." Arguments were clinched and political principles illustrated by "a funny story." It invaded even the camp meeting and pulpit. It at last received the currency of the public press. But where ever met it was so distinctly original and novel, so individual and characteristic, that it was at once known and appreciated abroad as an "American story." Crude at first, it received a literary polish in the press, but its dominant quality remained. It was concise and condensed, yet suggestive. It was delightfully extravagant—or a miracle of understatement. It voiced, not only the dialect, but the habits of thought of a people or locality. It gave a new interest to slang. From a paragraph of a dozen lines it grew into half a column, but always retaining its conciseness and felicity of statement. It was a foe to prolixity of any kind; it admitted no fine writing nor affectation of style. It went directly to the point. It was burdened by no conscientiousness; it was often irreverent; it was devoid of all moral responsibility—but it was original! By degrees it developed character with its incident, often, in a few lines, gave a striking photograph of a community or a section, but always reached its conclusions without an unnecessary word. It became—and still exists—as an essential feature of newspaper literature. It was the parent of the American "short story."

From "Short Stories: Bret Harte on Their Origin and His Own Part in It" in the New York Times, *June 9, 1900.*

Alfred C. Ward (essay date 1924)

[*In the excerpt below, taken from Ward's book* Aspects of the Modern Short Story: English and American, *the critic explains elements of popular appeal within Harte's fiction, contrasting his works with those of Nathaniel Hawthorne and Edgar Allen Poe.*]

There is no need to dig deeply in order to understand why Bret Harte's short stories carried him to immediate fame and fortune. The pleasant slumbers of Washington Irving, the shadowy sobriety of Hawthorne, and the sulphureous vapours of Poe, did not make for the gaiety of nations; nor did such characteristics warm the hearts of humanity or make the whole world kin. When these earlier writers dealt with human beings, it was usually at a distant remove, and in an allegorized or mesmerical medium.

Bret Harte's happy service was to bring readers at one leap into the vitalizing sunshine of golden California: where "sweet-scented grass, which the children loved to keep in their desks, intertwined with the plumes of the buckeye, the syringa, and the wood-anemone, and the dark blue cowl of the monk's-hood, or deadly aconite"; where the delicacy and confident innocence of Miss Mary the schoolmistress dwelt alongside the drunken debauchery of Sandy Morton and the curses of Mother Shipton.

What the "great reading public" loves, is not subtle gradations, but sharp contrasts of bright sunlight and deep shadow. It desires not only to see innocence and villany engaged in combat, but also to be led to believe that a goodly number among the devils of this world have embryonic angel's wings. The deep-drinking, hard-swearing, reckless gamblers of the Western gold-mining camps were depicted by Bret Harte as susceptible to strangely generous impulses, and as capable of being abashed and reformed (at least for a while) by speechless innocence or helpless need.

The type of literary critic who bases his judgments upon an unblemished record of human inexperience, finds no difficulty in dismissing Bret Harte's stories with a curl of the lip and an all-embracing condemnatory word: "Sentimentalism!" The themes used by Bret Harte are certainly ingenuous. Roaring Camp changes its character in one short year; and, ceasing to resemble an annexe of hell, becomes like unto a masculine Dorcas meeting—just because it has had to undertake the guardianship of a nameless infant whose despised and outcast mother died at its birth. Miggles, an attractive daughter of joy, retires from the public eye in order to devote herself lovingly and whole-heartedly to a paralyzed and dumb imbecile, who in the days of his strength had been her lover. When the outcasts of Poker Flat are snowed up, dissolute old Mother Shipton starves herself to death so that a girl companion shall have the week's meagre rations which the old woman has kept untouched. Tennessee's partner, notwithstanding that Tennessee has used him badly, is willing to sacrifice all his personal possessions if Judge Lynch will acquit Tennessee. And even after that fruitless offer of a bribe has imperilled his own neck, Tennessee's partner faithfully waits by "the ominous tree," so that he may carry the body of his friend on its last silent journey. When the drunken occupants of Simpson's Bar become moved at heart by the babbling of a sick boy on Christmas Eve, one of their number rides fifty perilous miles on horseback at dead of night in order to bring back a few poor toys to the child:

> And even so, bedraggled, ragged, unshaven and unshorn, with one arm hanging helplessly at his side, Santa Claus came to Simpson's Bar and fell fainting on the first threshold. The Christmas dawn came slowly after, touching the remoter peaks with the rosy warmth of ineffable love. And it looked so tenderly on Simpson's Bar that the whole mountain, as if caught in a generous action, blushed to the skies.

A writer of fiction who ventures to show the outcropping of human sensibility in natures free from the anaemic influences of urban civilization, is unlikely to escape the double charge of improbability and sentimentality. . . . Ambrose Bierce held strong views in regard to the demand for probability as a necessary factor in imaginative literature. At this point, it need only be suggested that not one of the situations, summarized above from Bret Harte's stories, violates human experience of probability. The nearer men and women approach to the rougher contacts of life and death, the more probable it becomes that they will obey illogically-generous impulses, and pursue those impulses with a simple-hearted consistency which the cultured misname sentimentality.

Apologetic is uncalled-for in any critical survey of Bret Harte's work, once his plots are accepted at their own high worth. He handles his chosen situations with assurance, and combines virility with delicacy of treatment as only an artist who is also a master-craftsman can. Moreover, it must be recognized that his stories have a much more complex organic unity than those of Poe or Hawthorne; and that, while their structure is of greater complexity, their aim is simpler and more direct.

The parabolic intention of Hawthorne, and the more violent impressionism of Poe, were secured by insistence upon a single particular factor; so that the resultant work, technically, was something of a monstrosity. Bret Harte's primary and paramount aim was to tell a story that would create the greatest possible interest in the greatest possible number of readers. The singleness of that aim involves many problems of craftsmanship: it means that the writer has to work out a method that will enable him to be all things to all men—usually an ignoble endeavour in the moral sphere, but representing a quest for perfection in the purpose of a literary artist. (pp. 45-9)

In a general view, the following points may be noted in ***The Luck of Roaring Camp*** volume:

(1) The "field" is much more closely circumscribed in time and place than in Poe and Hawthorne, who introduce little *locale.*

(2) Character-drawing plays a dominant part.

(3) Little use is made of the impressionistic method. Effects are allowed to "creep in *at the eye.*"

(4) Natural description is employed as a means of emphasis (see, for example, the passage quoted above from **"How Santa Claus Came to Simpson's Bar"**), for the purpose of heightening contrasts, and to suggest atmosphere.

(5) Pathos and humour greatly strengthen the human note.

From the particular view-point of technique, Bret Harte's beginnings are of special interest. Hawthorne employed the device of an introductory paragraph which quietly surveys the scene and leads up to the main theme. Poe usually strikes a bizarre chord which thrills along the blood.

Harte has a characteristic method of beginning with a staccato phrase which, as it were, calls the passer-by to halt, and provokes curiosity:

> There was commotion in Roaring Camp.
>
> We were eight including the driver. **("Miggles")**
>
> I do not think that we ever knew his real name. **("Tennessee's Partner")**
>
> Sandy was very drunk. **("The Idyl of Red Gulch")**
>
> His name was Fagg—David Fagg. **("The Man of No Account")**
>
> It had been raining in the valley of the Sacramento. **("How Santa Claus Came to Simpson's Bar")**

This is an effective device which has been perseveringly imitated by later and lesser short-story writers; but it is a dangerous method of beginning, because it can so easily degenerate into a barren verbal mannerism. Each one of the opening sentences reproduced is something much more valuable than a mere staccato phrase: each one of these sentences contains a promise. If we are told that there was commotion in Roaring Camp, it is surely an implied promise that the informant has interesting news to tell as to the why and wherefore of the commotion. Again, who is there among men that could learn either that "We were eight including the driver," or that "Sandy was very drunk," without immediately becoming possessed by a consuming desire to know more? To hold out an alluring promise or to rouse the tantalizing itch of curiosity in the first half-dozen words is one of the few irresistible ways of beginning a short story.

Even when Bret Harte's thrust is less immediate than usual, he contrives to be no less intriguing:

> A subdued tone of conversation, and the absence of cigar-smoke and boot-heels at the windows of the Wingdam stage-coach, made it evident that one of the inside passengers was a woman. **("Brown of Calaveras")**
>
> As I opened Hop Sing's letter, there fluttered to the ground a square strip of yellow paper covered with hieroglyphics, which, at first glance, I innocently took to be the label from a pack of Chinese fire-crackers. **("Wan Lee, the Pagan")**
>
> As Mr. John Oakhurst, gambler, stepped into the main street of Poker Flat on the morning of the 23rd of November 1850, he was conscious of a change in its moral atmosphere since the preceding night. **("The Outcasts of Poker Flat")**

It is probably true that most readers begin upon a short story in a more or less perfunctory mood, which necessitates the stimulation of their interest from the very outset—a reason sufficiently practical to incite the writer to study the technique of beginnings, altogether apart from any artistic impulse. The "average reader" approaches a novel in a spirit of endurance; he is prepared to begin slowly, and to condone an occasional flatness. But he will not abide such things in a short story.

Important as are beginnings, however, they are but beginnings; and the short-story writer is only on the threshold of his problem when he has succeeded in capturing the interest of the reader: there is still to be faced the much greater difficulty of maintaining the pitch of the story throughout, and of finishing at that one inevitable moment beyond which the reader's interest drops dead. The course of a successful short story is not analogous to a successful aeroplane-flight. In the former, there must be no graceful downward slide, concluding with a level run at diminishing speed. The reader may safely be left to make his own landing.

Bret Harte is perhaps less successful in endings than in beginnings; but his conduct of the main narrative of his stories is nearly always exemplary. He has occasional lapses, when he obtrudes his own personality quite gratuitously, and interpolates some comment that self-criticism should have deleted. An instance of this kind occurs in **"The Idyl of Red Gulch,"** when the author says, of Sandy:

> As I should like to present him in a heroic attitude, I stay my hand with great difficulty at this moment, being only withheld from introducing such an episode by a strong conviction that it does not occur at such times. And I trust that my fairest reader, who remembers that, in a real crisis, it is always some uninteresting stranger or unromantic policeman, and not Adolphus, who rescues, will forgive the omission.

Though this glimpse into the workshop is deplorably out of place as an interruption of **"The Idyl,"** it states a literary principle of the first importance in relation to Bret Harte's own work. Here he registers, in unambiguous language, his regard for those laws of probability which he may be thought sometimes to violate; and the more closely his stories are examined in the light of emotional experience, the greater is likely to be the admiration aroused by his ability to represent the universal in terms of the particular—to show some of the essential features of the whole human race through the peephole of a Californian mining-camp. (pp. 50-4)

Small though his community of splendid rapscallions is, Bret Harte secures wide variety both in theme and character; while the whole range of his stories is shot through and through by pathos and irony and humour, mingled as inextricably as these elements are usually found to be in actual life. The pen that could trip so amusingly in the rhyme of "The Heathen Chinee," could also agonize with Cherokee Sal in the hour when she lay under the primal curse of woman, isolated from all save her half-contemptuous masculine associates, in the rude cabin on the outer edge of Roaring Camp.

And that same pen could depict, without a false stroke, the pathos of the scene inside the hut when, with Cherokee Sal lying dead, a strange procession paced by the improvised crib wherein lay the two-hours-old infant:

> The door was opened, and the anxious crowd of men, who had already formed themselves into a queue, entered in single file. Beside the low bunk or shelf, on which the figure of the mother was starkly outlined below the blankets, stood a pine table. On this a candle-box was placed, and within it, swathed in staring red flannel, lay the last arrival at Roaring Camp. . . . The first man entered with his hat on; he uncovered, however, as he looked about him, and so unconsciously set an example to the next. In such communities good and bad actions are catching.
>
> (pp. 56-7)

When the winter of that year came, Roaring Camp found itself a "confusion of rushing water, crashing trees, and crackling timber," as the great flood leapt upon it and carried away the cabin where the child lived with Stumpy, his self-appointed foster-father: "the pride, the hope, the joy, The Luck, of Roaring Camp had disappeared." The men were returning from a vain search when a relief-boat came up the river, bearing as passengers a man and an infant who had been taken from the water two miles away:

> It needed but a glance to show them Kentuck lying there, cruelly crushed and bruised, but still holding The Luck of Roaring Camp in his arms. As they bent over the strangely assorted pair, they saw that the child was cold and pulseless.

A dead child in the arms of a dying man would lure a second-rate writer into maudlin outpourings, sending dignity and decent reserve to the four winds. Bret Harte's place among short-story writers must be gauged as much by the pitfalls he avoids as by his positive merits. He was a highly accomplished craftsman; he was also an artist whose delicacy and restraint are shown, not least, in his avoidance of the sunken reefs that beset the passage of those who adventure amidst emotional deeps. (p. 59)

Alfred C. Ward, "Bret Harte: 'The Luck of Roaring Camp'," in his Aspects of the Modern Short Story: English and American, *University of London Press, Ltd., 1924, pp. 45-59.*

Allen B. Brown (essay date 1961)

[In the following essay, Brown presents "The Luck of Roaring Camp" as a romantic story infused with Christian symbolism.]

"Bret Harte's **'The Luck of Roaring Camp,'** whatever one may think of its merits, must be admitted to be the most influential short story ever written in America." So states Fred Lewis Pattee in *The Cambridge History of American Literature.* This story has been and still is reprinted in many anthologies and textbooks of American literature. Edward J. O'Brien included it in *The Twenty-five Finest Short Stories.* Any novelty it once had cannot account for the continued life of this story, first published in 1868. Powerful appeal to the subconscious of most of its readers can.

A long period of overestimation was inevitably followed by detractions. One of the most severe is in Brooks, Purser, and Warren's *An Approach to Literature.* Harte is criticized for an excess of editorial comment, a hackneyed theme, oversimplifying characters and situation, and, above all, for sentimentality. Knickerbocker and Reninger in their *Interpreting Literature* have done their best to refute these charges by claiming that the characters *are* representative, that Harte did possess accurate information about California miners, and that their actions are sufficiently motivated. However, Knickerbocker and Reninger admit that the ending is too contrived. Pattee claims that Harte is less sentimental than Dickens, his favorite author.

My contention is that these well-known critics have missed the chief point, that **"The Luck of Roaring Camp"** is not primarily an early realistic story but a romantic, symbolic story akin to Hawthorne and Kafka and therefore of a type that can be respectably admired by today's scholars. George R. Stewart, Jr., Bret Harte's latest and most complete biographer, states that Harte was thoroughly grounded in the Bible. **"The Luck of Roaring Camp"** certainly bears this out. Harte's father was a Roman Catholic teacher of Greek in an Albany, New York, seminary; and Pattee has noted that Harte was a bookish boy who had read all of his father's considerable library, that some of his earliest stories are "pure Hawthorne" and even the style is sometimes like Hawthorne, and that "he had read much in the French." Harte has frequently been said to show the influence of Victor Hugo; and the subject matter, the teaching, the symbolism employed, the "unpadded, finely calculated" clear-cut style is not unlike some of the work of Maupassant.

The story is familiar. The son of the disreputable Cherokee Sal is the first child born in Roaring Camp. The hundred men there adopt the orphaned baby, contribute to its support, suckle it by an ass, hold a formal christening at which they name him Thomas Luck, and proceed to regenerate themselves under his beneficent influence. They vie in attending the child, and Nature herself is "his nurse and playfellow." Roaring Camp is unusually prosperous and becomes a model mining community. About a year later, a flash flood kills the three principal characters (The Luck, Stumpy, and Kentuck), but not before Kentuck is convinced that he will accompany the dead baby, that his salvation is secure.

Harte records in his introduction to ***The Luck of Roaring Camp and Other Tales*** that the printer of *The Overland Monthly,* a deacon, protested to the publisher that **"The Luck of Roaring Camp"** "was so indecent, irreligious, and improper that his proofreader—a young lady—had with difficulty been induced to continue its perusal." A number of other people agreed with the publisher and the printing department. After the story was published, over their united protests, a religious magazine strongly objected to it as "unfavorable to immigration" and "the investment of foreign capital." But let us look at the story itself. If it can be shown that this story has closely interwoven Christian symbolism as well as disreputable characters and hints at profanity—Christ himself preferred the company of the disreputable to the scribes and Pharisees—it may be easier to understand why this story laid tremendous hold upon all its readers and stirred many to subconscious resentment. They felt it a sacrilege.

The story has many Christian echoes and parallels. Roaring Camp, its miscellaneous inhabitants drawn even from distant Australia, is destroyed by flood and may easily represent the world in miniature. That the Son of God came to redeem our world, to all believers in Him, is the luckiest thing that ever happened. The Luck seems to have been born about Christmas Eve 1850. "A fire of withered pine boughs" and "staring red flannel" coupled with the gifts brought to the baby may suggest Christmas. Christ's function in the world, regeneration, is mentioned twice; and the miners and their surroundings are changed almost beyond recognition. They keep out all strangers and the legend arises that "they worship an Ingin baby." Theirs is a "pastoral happiness," which Cockney Simmons calls " 'evingly."

The Luck's mother, moreover, like the mother of Our Lord, is a disgraced virgin and again, like the Lady of Sorrows, suffers "martyrdom" fulfilling "the primal curse" and "punishment of the first transgression" and so "expiates her sin." Stumpy, who stands godfather to the child, is also like St. Joseph in being the head of two families. The men who attend her lying-in are as contemptuous as were the people of Bethlehem, and the new baby receives as rude a cradle, most appropriately for this "light of the world" a candle-box. Harte says The Luck is "introduced *ab initio,*" the same words that begin the Latin New Testament. There is another Biblical echo in calling Roaring Camp "a city of refuge." The hundred men, who act as a unit and as modern wise men, bring, along with many inappropriate things, considerable gold, and a Bible that Harte may intend as a clue to his whole story. Principally they illustrate that appearance may be the opposite of reality. I find it highly suggestive that one has a Raphael face and another is like Hamlet, often said to be a kind of Christ. Harte's calling attention to three fingers and one eye can suggest the holy Trinity and the Masonic emblem for God. Further use of the mystic three is the triangular shape of the valley, which lies between two hills and a river, the age-old symbol of life and death. The resolve to secure outside help is postponed for three months and The Luck's lullaby has ninety stanzas. The only outlet to the valley is a steep trail that is "lost in the stars above." As she dies, Cherokee Sal is said to leave "Roaring Camp, its sin and shame, forever" by that trail.

Now comes the passage that Brooks, Purser, and Warren [in their *An Approach to Literature*] find particularly objectionable and oversentimental. "The pines stopped moaning, the river ceased to rush, and the fire to crackle. It seemed as if Nature had stopped to listen too." They object:

> Now, we could admit that the pines might have stopped moaning, because of a lull in the breeze; but we know perfectly well that the river did not cease to rush, and that, if the sound of the pines had stopped, the sound of the river would have been more readily heard than before. Harte is deliberately falsifying his scene in order to play on the reader's emotions and to prepare him, thereby, to accept the regeneration of the camp.

The whole camp is regenerated (or at least improved) because, despite Brooks, Purser, Warren, Knickerbocker, and Reninger, the baby *is* a miracle worker. Here Harte makes use of the well-known legend, so beautifully expounded in Milton's hymn from "On the Morning of Christ's Nativity" (stanzas III-VII), that all nature held its breath when the Prince of Peace was born. Later, the baby, like St. Francis, talks to the birds; and, as Stumpy says, they were " 'a-jawing' . . . like two cherrybums."

The donkey, so often associated with Jesus, is mentioned several times. There is a hint at resurrection or the continuity of life in laying out the dead mother on the left (evil side) and the newly born on the right. The men all uncover to show their respect, and rough old Kentuck, who has some similarity to the Apostle Peter, is delighted with the infant's holy touch when The Luck wrestles with his finger as the angel did with Jacob. "The d—d little cuss!" exclaims Kentuck, a euphemism which Harte may well intend to mean doomed as well as damned in this world. Kentuck tries to demonstrate his unconcern by whistling, but pauses at a large redwood tree, which might represent the cross of Christ, and returns to join Stumpy beside the baby. The suggestion that the baby be sent to Red Dog, a hell compared to the regenerated Roaring Camp, forty (a favorite Biblical number) miles away is summarily rejected. No other region can share their new faith. Most appropriately, finery for the child, including a rosewood cradle, perhaps an allusion to love or the mystic rose, is ordered from Sacramento (twice forty miles away).

The men are superstitious, and it is felt that "a fresh deal" is called for. The christening is complete with choir, music, procession, banners, and altar. Stumpy ends their service by declaring " 'I proclaim you Thomas Luck, according to the laws of the United States and the State of California, so help me God'," as if "under a Christian roof." Kentuck, who had regarded his garments as a kind of snake's skin (long a symbol of regeneration and resurrection), becomes admirably clean and changes his shirt every day. "Nor were moral and social sanitary laws neglected." The baby, always surrounded with pine boughs or other evergreens, lies above as the men work below, receives gifts of every beautiful thing that they can find (they had never noticed Nature's beauty before), and becomes as grave, tractable, and quiet as we imagine the Baby Jesus must have been. Roaring Camp is "inviolate" and completely closed to strangers, although some think it would be best to extend his influence to others. This is comparable to the early Jewish Christians' attitude toward the Gentiles. Like Jesus, the baby ("the hope . . . of Roaring Camp") disappears but reappears with Kentuck (Peter), who has withstood the trial by water and now ventures confidently into the Unknown.

I have attempted to demonstrate that Harte was steeped in the Bible and Christian tradition, almost certainly patterned **"The Luck of Roaring Camp"** on earlier moral writers, that it is the suggestion of sacrilege which horrified his earliest readers and his religious teaching which charmed the rest. When one is aware of the dominance of the multitude of Christian symbols closely interwoven throughout the story, the action is never questionable and the ending is inevitable. Bret Harte's masterpiece has long puzzled readers and even many otherwise acute critics because it is stated not in inartistic allegory but in highly suggestive symbols. (pp. 629-33)

Allen B. Brown, "The Christ Motif in 'The Luck of Roaring Camp'," in Papers of the Michigan Academy of Science, Arts and Letters, *Vol. 46, 1961, pp. 629-33.*

J. R. Boggan (essay date 1967)

[In the excerpt below, Boggan challenges interpretations of "The Luck of Roaring Camp" as a Christian allegory, emphasizing natural, pagan themes within the work.]

[For] us to decide just what the moral outcome of Harte's position is in **"The Luck of Roaring Camp"** is certainly more of a complicated matter than many may have sentimentally thought. Is it true, for instance, as one reader has recently stated, that Harte is taking no position at all here, is being involved with "nothing in particular—except telling an entertaining story"? [Roy R. Male, ed., *Types of Short Fiction* (1962).] Or is it true, as other readers have suggested, that Harte fails here in his attempt to write a realistic local color tale—fails because he falsifies his story treatment in order to force the reader into an emotional acceptance of Christian regeneration and redemption? Or is it true, as at least one other reader has argued—a reader who rightly recognizes that the story is primarily symbolic rather than realistic—that Harte, having perhaps charmed a number of early readers with his "religious teaching," is undeniably taking a Christian point of view, and that, in order to understand this, one has only to consider "the multitude of Christian symbols" therein? [See Brown excerpt dated 1961.]

That there are, of course, a number of Christian allusions and Biblical echoes in the story is plain to see. Obviously, for example, the child born of Cherokee Sal at the beginning is, in one sense, the Christ child, the Saviour. Needing a foster father, he is born, if not in a manger, in a rude cabin, and if he does not receive the most valuable gifts of the Wise Men he does receive the most valuable gifts of the men of Roaring Camp. Moreover, in supposedly regenerating these men, he comes to be worshipped by them, and in dying in the flood at the story's end he can, at least in the person of Kentuck, inspire man's faith in the hereafter.

Having granted this obvious parallel, however, I intend in this essay to show that the ironic voice that tells us the story and intrudes to comment freely if somewhat ambiguously on the happenings in Roaring Camp is really *not* the voice of a Christian believer and that, despite the coming of little Luck, the men of Roaring Camp are *not* really regenerated.

What appears to be true, as Harte early points out in describing some of the men in Roaring Camp, is not true. Who would think, for example, that the "greatest scamp had a Raphael face," that the "coolest and most courageous man was scarcely over five feet in height, with a soft voice and an embarrassed, timid manner"? Who would think that the little child that is to lead the Camp to its "regeneration" would be born of a "very sinful woman"?

Understandably, then, one can't necessarily put one's faith in conventional, stereotyped notions. Appearances are often deceiving; good may or may not come of evil and vice versa. "Perhaps the less said of Cherokee Sal the better." And perhaps not. Apparently not, for the narrator is soon to speak sympathetically of her "terrible . . . loneliness." "She was a coarse and, it is to be feared, a very sinful woman." But to be thought, to be feared, very sinful is not necessarily to *be* very sinful; and one begins to understand, perhaps, that the voice speaking to us is not, though it may at times appear to be, the unqualified, fearful voice of the conventional Christian believer.

That the storyteller seems to be committed to Christianity, but is not, might be inferred again and again. Consider, for example, the following complementary passages:

> The camp lay in a triangular valley between two hills and a river. The only outlet was a steep trail over the summit of a hill that faced the cabin, now illuminated by the rising moon. The suffering woman might have seen it from the rude bunk whereon she lay—seen it winding like a silver thread until it was lost in the stars above. . . . for whether owing to the rude surgery of the camp, or some other reason, Cherokee Sal was sinking fast. Within an hour she had climbed, as it were, that rugged road that led to the stars, and so passed out of Roaring Camp, its sin and shame, forever.

The only way out of this small "city of refuge" (though not that kind of city unfortunately for Cherokee Sal lying in her rude cabin on the outer edge of the clearing, as much an outcast here as she might well have been in any society anywhere), the only way out for one living in Roaring Camp—or nearby Red Dog, or anywhere else in California, or the West, or the world—is the difficult, winding climb of life to the "summit" (if such it be) of death. The trail winds, one might say, like a "silver thread"—or an umbilical cord—to death. Dying there in her bunk, Sal "might" have looked at the sky, might have followed the trail until it was "lost in the stars"—lost, as we know, because the trail that goes down over the hill never really gets to the heavenly stars in the first place.

In a manner of speaking, then, Cherokee Sal, "sinking fast," paradoxically climbed "that rugged road . . . and so passed out of Roaring Camp, its sin and shame forever." Roaring Camp, then, having lost its outcast "very sinful woman," was left with its own sin and shame—perhaps its sense of the wrong its men had done her. In any event, the birth of the child was something the very nature of the men were ready and waiting for. There had been too many worthless killings; this was something "novel" to engage their attention, to excite their curiosity, to bet on. One could see very early, perhaps that these men might be willing to gamble their all. The congregation outside Sal's rude cabin rose to their feet as one man before the sharp cry of their god-child, while inside his candle-box the swathed infant lay, awaiting the "procession," the offertory of the Camp's collective conscience to begin.

Later, when it comes time for the christening ceremony (the life-giving waters, the sacrament of Baptism) Stumpy proclaims the child "Thomas Luck"—so help him God. Whether, of course, God does help Stumpy or whether that "helpless bundle" of Luck does ever go back on Stumpy are questions for the future. Right now it's enough to say that the men have been transformed from doubting Thomases into doting disciples and that Tommy was christened "as seriously as he would have been under a Christian roof, and [not that perhaps it did much good] cried and was comforted in an orthodox manner."

No sooner, though, had the men become regenerated, no sooner had they begun worshipping their god-child, idolizing him, giving him whatever little attentions they could, than there came to them, "forewarned" (as much as Noah ever was) by Red Dog under water, the unexpected deluge. Stumpy, eager for the water to put more gold into the gulches, loses his cabin and the tabernacle of his life, and Luck dies in the arms of his undying believer, Kentuck.

> A smile lit the eyes of the expiring Kentuck. "Dying!" he repeated. "He's a-takin' me with him. Tell the boys I've got the Luck with me now"; and the strong man, clinging to the frail babe as a drowning man is said to cling to a straw, drifted away into the shadowy river that flows forever into the unknown sea.

Again Harte suggests the conventional idea of a Heaven but does not commit himself to it. Just as, before, Cherokee Sal was "sinking fast," so now is a man drowning; just as, before, Cherokee Sal "passed out" of Roaring Camp, perhaps to follow a trail that was "lost in the stars," so now a man drifts away "into the shadowy river that flows forever into the unknown sea." For all we know, Cherokee Sal in her most secret moments might yet have been a believer; the regenerated Kentuck, we know, is. In terms of the analogy chosen by the narrator, however, the "frail babe" is of no more help to the dying man than a piece of straw. Of course, that's with regard to continuing his life in this world. As for the heavenly life to come (up out of the "unknown sea"), that's another matter.

Perhaps we're to infer that that flood isn't so destructive after all? Perhaps the same God who justly destroyed the wicked in Noah's time now justly rewards the good? Perhaps the baptismal waters, having been sprinkled over the Luck, now splash over his disciples? And yet we have no more reason to think that from evil (Eve, Cherokee Sal experiencing the "primal curse") comes good (the new Adam, the little child that shall lead them) than from good (the infant innocence of Luck) comes evil (the destroying flood). Just because the men of Roaring Camp—for various reasons: to ease a guilty conscience, to find relief from boredom, to seek excitement in a different kind of gamble, to experience paternal love for their flesh-and-blood child—feel the need to adopt themselves to this god of a candle-box, does it necessarily follow that this helpless little bundle, hanging on with a cry of pain to Kentuck's finger, is going to grow up tomorrow to be their protector-saviour? Moreover, if, as the storyteller seems to infer, Christ failed in his attempt to regenerate man, is that any reason to suppose that this infant child will do any better? Luck is the child of a reckless gambling man, and his name, after all, is not that of the supposed far-seeing Christ child but, rather just the opposite, that of blind Chance.

Of course, the child of luck cannot be compared exclusively with the Christ child. In fact, he need not be thought of as a child of organized religion at all. He need not be thought of, for instance, as those in the nearby society of Red Dog think of him—as some superstitious North American Injun god. He need not be thought of, though he is taken down and put beside the gold gulch, as Mammon, god of the riches of this world. He need not be thought of, there in his bower—"serenely happy, albeit there was an infantine gravity about him, a contemplative light in his round gray eyes"—as the Buddha who achieved his enlightenment under the bo tree. He need not be thought of as a Hindu holy man, practicing yoga though, as the narrator ironically says, "it is recorded" that he dropped over a bank "on his head in the soft earth, and remained with his mottled legs in the air in that position for at least five minutes with unflinching gravity."

Indeed, the whole upside-down point of all this is that Tommy Luck need not be thought of as representing any one of these religions, Christian or otherwise. To the storyteller one is no more superstitious, lucky or unlucky, than another since all are unbelievable. "I hesitate to record," he says, with mock concern, "the many other instances of his [Luck's] sagacity, which rest, unfortunately, upon the statements of prejudiced friends. Some of them were not without a tinge of superstition." Indeed—though maybe, like Saint Francis, little Luck can talk with the birds: " . . . and dern my skin," says the unconsciously irreverent Kentuck, "if he wasn't a-talkin' to a jaybird as was a-sittin' on his lap . . . [them] a-jawin' at each other just like two cherrybums."

Although it may not have seemed that way to us at first, we can now begin to see, perhaps, that the child of luck is surely as much the pagan child of Nature as he is the Christ child. On the day of the christening, the "procession . . . marched to the grove with music and banners," and the child was "deposited before a mock altar." Later, the men fix him up a "bower" and decorate it "with flowers and sweet-smelling shrubs" and such beautiful minerals as mica and quartz. The woods and hillsides yield treasures which, if they would not do for all high priests, "would do for Tommy." He was surrounded "by playthings such as never child out of fairyland had before"—which is not to say, of course, that he, or, for that matter, the Christ of the Magi, *was* a child out of fairyland—he might not have been.

Was it a myth, like many another, that "Nature took the fondling to her broader breast," that in that "rare atmosphere" some "subtle chemistry . . . transmuted ass's milk to lime and phosphorous"? "Strange to say" was it, that "the child thrived"? That "Jinny," the ass, could successfully nurse the Luck, says the storyteller, "was no less problematical" than that Romulus and Remus could be suckled by a she-wolf (and, he might have added, that Romulus could build up Rome and be made divine). In other words, Harte implies that, if the reader doesn't believe that little Luck could have survived under such maternal conditions, then he can't very well believe in the literal reality of any myth, pagan or Christian. Or, to put it another way, *is* the reader to believe in the literal reality of the story? Is he to read **"The Luck of Roaring Camp"** as a realistic (and consequently a sentimental) local color tale of the West? "Strange," indeed, that the child "thrived," for, if, on the day of his birth, all Nature seemed to stop in awe to listen to his cry, if for him "she would let slip between the leaves golden shafts of sunlight that fell just within his grasp," if for him she sent "wandering breezes," so, too, was it for him she sent the roaring flood. The pathetic fallacy is that one could believe blind, indifferent Nature to be benevolent. [The critic adds in a footnote: "Brooks, Purser, and Warren, in *An Approach to Literature,* accuse Harte of being unrealistic in his handling of nature, of 'deliberately falsifying his scene in order . . . to prepare . . . [the reader] to accept the regeneration of the camp.' It should be clear, however, that Harte is not writing a realistic story and that he does not intend the careful reader to think that the men of Roaring Camp are significantly regenerated."]

Repeatedly, then, it seems to me that Harte in no way commits himself to the idea that life, this one or the supposed hereafter, is worth looking forward to. Consider, for example, the deliberate juxtaposition of the dead Cherokee Sal (lying in her cabin under the blankets, on a shelf, waiting to be "committed to the hillside") with her newborn infant, "the d—d little cuss," the "last arrival at Roaring Camp" (lying in his box, swathed in "staring red flannel"). Thus, after several exhausted hours, in which the "sharp, querulous cry" of the child is heard, Stumpy, during the gift-giving ceremonies, is shown to be maintaining "a silence as impassive as the dead on his left, a gravity as inscrutable as that of the newly born on his right." Then, as Kentuck bends over the candle-box, the child turns and "in a spasm of pain" catches hold of his finger, much as if he wants now, in this life, the same kind of help that Kentuck, holding on to the helpless drowned babe, will want later, in the next.

It might be argued that, because the men's eyes have been "cleared and strengthened" to the beauties of Nature, to the mica and quartz, for example, that had heretofore been thought "trifles," a sense of the beautiful comes to those who worship. It might also be argued that, because the men embrace religion, they become better and so learn to love not only the Luck but their neighbor. But that Nature has beautiful things for an observer to see, that the one and only world we know yields up more treasures than ever "child out of fairyland had before," is scarcely proof that a hereafter exists or that the storyteller thinks it does. And though Stumpy the lounger accepts the responsibility of staying up all night in Sal's cabin, and though Kentuck, finger held high, repeats again and again his embarrassing refrain, is that any sign that either of them are better men than they were before? Stumpy, after all, wants religiously to be the proprietor of an office, while Kentuck, in the carelessness of his large nature, shows no more sentiment than what, presumably, he's felt all along.

If, however, Kentuck is a believer, perhaps we can infer that Tommy Luck, like the dying Christ, has worked his regeneration, has left his disciples, his myth, behind him? And yet, just as some unsentimental people may argue that the world today is little better for having had Christ or his religion in it, so Harte may argue that the men of Roaring Camp are little better for having had Luck and having worshipped him. If, in other words, the Camp felt it had to isolate itself from, say, the strangers in Red Dog in order for its men to be "saved," this need not suggest that the Luck had a divine mission but only that all men are dying.

The first "spasm of propriety" (coming the day after "the

spasm of pain" felt by the infant child) was "the first symptom of the camp's regeneration." This sudden, temporary contraction into decency—as if such a thing were purely involuntary, not to be helped—was accounted for only by a harsh "unkind allusion" to the defunct Cherokee Sal, namely, that Roaring Camp, so one man speaking for the rest had said, didn't want any more of her kind. And in such communities as Roaring Camp "good and bad actions are catching," says the narrator, as if, either way, he were talking of a disease. Thus when that first man in line enters—(what?)—the makeshift funeral parlor of Sal's rude cabin to see her lying starkly outlined under a sheet—or the lying-in hospital of her no longer used brothel to pay curious homage to her infant child—when that first man enters with his hat on, he uncovers himself and so "unconsciously" sets an example for the next man. But whether this action is good or bad depends solely on whether the majority in the society approves of such a custom as, say, a man (though not a woman) taking off his hat before going into a church, or Kentuck showing openly his unmanly sentiment for "the d—d little cuss," or on whether a man can forget himself for a moment and show himself touched by a woman's sufferings, or on whether a man can read his Bible in peace.

Consequently, if, despite their physical imperfections, the "aggregate force" of Roaring Camp, or of any other place, approve of one god over another, it is wise for one, unless he intends to become an outcast and consequently an evil person, "to bow to the majority"—much as Stumpy was "wise enough" to do when the crowd appointed him "extempore surgeon and midwife" to Sal (with the result, incidentally, that he soon won society's reward, could with priestly "authority and *ex-officio* complacency" suggest the hat be passed, as it were, for an acceptable offering). Right from the beginning, then, the Roaring Camp that smoked its pipe and literally awaited "the issue" was the Camp that rose as one man, as one congregation, to later fiercely put down Sandy Tipton's individual notion that they should send the infant to Red Dog "where female attention could be procured."

> "Besides," said Tom Ryder, "them fellows at Red Dog would swap it, and ring in somebody else on us." A disbelief in the honesty of other camps prevailed at Roaring Camp, as in other places.

And so, despite the distrust that remained to follow that first "spasm of propriety," the "work of regeneration began in Roaring Camp." Now many of these rehabilitated, spiritually reborn men got into the habit of "lounging in at Stumpy's," and this forced the rival establishment of "Tuttle's grocery" to import the kind of carpet and mirrors one might find in a rehabilitated saloon. Moreover, now that these people who, before, had been against a show of sentiment even when some of them felt it, were taking a good look at themselves, "the appearance of Roaring Camp tended to produce stricter habits of personal cleanliness." Thus Kentuck, though in the carelessness of his large nature being anything but prudish, had quickly to slough off his decaying, snake's-skin-like garments for "certain prudential reasons." That is, he, too, was wise enough to bow to the majority, to the "subtle influence of innovation," and to begin to appear regularly at the Luck's "in a clean shirt," his face "still shining from his ablutions."

But although "moral and social sanitary laws" were put into effect, how much really had the men changed for the good? Before, they had a "natural levity," now they smoke with "Indian gravity." Before, when their luck wasn't so good, they would habitually say, "D—n the luck!" and "Curse the luck!" Now, when the luck is with them, they don't say that anymore. Before, the men drank, now their eyes are "cleared and strengthened," now they sit around "drinking in the melodious utterances," the lugubrious lullaby of "Man-o'-War Jack," who has so decked out the exploits of the "*Arethusa,* Seventy-Four" (into ninety would-be comforting stanzas, each ending with a prolonged dying fall) that, as the infant Luck is about to close his eyes, the men are looking happily ahead to the future. "An indistinct idea that this was pastoral happiness pervaded the camp. 'This 'ere kind o' think . . . is 'evingly,' " said the Cockney Simmons. Of course (since gods and heavens are as persistently changeable over the years as the here and there emergent waters of the Arethusa or the rise and fall of the stanzas about the exploits of the ship that bears its name), one thinking man's pipe dream of a heaven on earth is apt to be different from another's; Simmons was reminded, as we, in a different time and place might not be, of Greenwich.

If, then, the men were content, "it is to be hoped that Tommy was." At any event, this was "the golden summer" of Roaring Camp. And yet, because their "claims had yielded enormously," because the Luck was with them, the Camp "was jealous of its privileges and looked suspiciously on strangers." Possessively the men begin to preempt the land around them, and, instead of giving encouragement to immigration (aside from the eminently respectable idea of inviting one or two "decent" families to "reside" with them), attain a "proficiency with the revolver." The "reserve" of Roaring Camp is thus kept "inviolate," is no longer the uncivilized "city of refuge" it was before—not by a long shot.

Thus, whether the Luck was not content after all and so did go back on Stumpy, or whether Stumpy himself was too concerned about the flood waters putting more gold into the gulches and so got more than he bargained for, the logical outcome of the story is that, like the good citizens of Harte's well-known Poker Flat (experiencing, at the expense of the outcasts, "a spasm of virtuous reaction, quite as lawless and ungovernable as any one of the acts that provoked it"), the men of Roaring Camp are no more regenerated, no more spiritually reborn, than is the Christ child in the person of little Luck. (pp. 271-80)

J. R. Boggan, "The Regeneration of 'Roaring Camp'," in Nineteenth-Century Fiction, *Vol. 22, No. 3, December, 1967, pp. 271-80.*

Patrick Morrow (essay date 1972)

[*Morrow is an American educator and critic. He has commented: "To me the primary function of criticism is explication and not attack." In the excerpt below from his monograph* Bret Harte, *Morrow responds to criticism of Harte's works by describing his use of parables in several stories and explaining his intentions as a writer of popular fiction.*]

In Harte's heyday of popularity, the early 1870's, one reader called his fiction "a whole new and strange world." Actually, Harte's strange new world was often nothing more than a new set and stage to dramatize the values of his East Coast reading public. Today, most critics believe that Bret Harte's fiction declined in quality as the author got older and farther removed in time and space from California. But in his University of Virginia dissertation, "The Later Literary Career of Bret Harte, 1880-1902," Donald E. Glover makes the fascinating assertion, backed up by extensive analysis, that Harte's later stories are *qualitatively* very similar to his earlier ones. If this is true, Harte may not have been writing increasingly inferior art, but creating the same product for a changing audience, one that became increasingly less sophisticated. This could explain why in the 1870's Hart was publishing in *The Atlantic, Lippincott's,* and a handful of the most respected literary journals, but why by 1895 he was for the most part publishing in such slick and conservative illustrateds as *Weekly Graphic, Windsor Magazine, The Strand,* and *Cosmopolitan.* The sophisticated literati had moved on to new forms and ideas. Over a thirty-year period Harte's successful, essentially unchanged literary product increasingly appealed to those who wanted familiarity instead of discovery. It is perhaps not coincidental that in the last decade or so of his life Harte published numerous stories in magazines aimed for children or adolescent girls.

At this point, we need to make some distinctions between high or serious literature and popular literature, realizing that these two exist on a continuum and are not two separate and mutually exclusive forms. Serious literature traditionally is the development and statement of a brilliant individual's consciousness delivered into artistry through great skill with words and mastery of form. Serious literature gives us a philosophical sense of the world, articulates new possibilities and perspectives, and often makes moral statements showing us the difference between good and evil, the genuine and the spurious. Typically, great writers tend to change, to mature and develop; witness Twain, James, and Faulkner. Popular writers tend to repeat the successful performance of a product; witness, to go outside literature, the portraits of Sir Joshua Reynolds or the concert tours of the Rolling Stones. Popular literature reinforces an audience's values and expectations, often with the skillful manipulation of cliché, stereotype, and formula. By means of popular art an audience can find both a justification of its covert and overt values and a dramatization of wish-fulfillment. Popular literature often restates old myths in new ways, creating a product that shows how people feel about things at a given time. Most of Harte's stories work in this way: they dramatize their intended audience's feelings and values far more than they show an artist's "world picture" and personal vision. The reader, then, must try to uncover in a popular work the *why* and *how* of its success. Questions about a popular work's "quality" are secondary, since by definition a lot of people are convinced that it is "good."

With this distinction between popular and serious literature in mind, let us examine one of Bret Harte's most famous stories, **"The Luck of Roaring Camp." "The Luck"** forms the prototype for Harte's most famous fiction. This story has been attacked, like many of Harte's tales, for being facile, filled with slick language, overdrawn in sentiment, and riddled with clichés. These statements contain much truth. But they are also judgments that measure Harte's fiction against the standards of High Art and Serious Literature. Actually, I believe Harte wrote **"The Luck"** as a "parable" instead of a "short story," a supposition which explains the lack of realism (except for touches of detail), psychological motivation, and organization around a central conflict. Parables are designed to illustrate truths, or perhaps to reinforce an audience's values and expectations; such tales are not typically well-wrought statements from an artistic consciousness. One critic, Allen B. Brown, sees **"The Luck"** as a parable of Christian redemption [see excerpt dated 1961]. But Brown, I believe, mistakes the motif for the message. True, Harte was more or less a Christian, but he had little except skepticism for organized religion and certainly no particular devotion to Christ. Harte did have a devotion to the Unitarian minister Thomas Starr King, but both men were oriented much more toward current issues and social injustice than toward religious or spiritual concerns. To me, the parable, although outfitted with Christian trappings, primarily illustrates the triumph of Victorian civilization over the raw, savage, anarchistic wilderness.

Using a mixture of picturesque and realistic details within a Romantic setting, the parable illustrates the ultimate nobility of all (white) men, especially in times of crisis. The story is mythic not realistic, and presents the age-old convention of a Mysterious Stranger as a rescue figure. The characters are carefully stereotyped into external villains and internal saints. Roaring Camp is an outpost, a "city of refugees," and clearly these anarchistic types need to be saved—regenerated—repatriated to civilization. Cherokee Sal, of course, must succumb to the conventions of Nineteenth-Century melodrama, but it is a shocker that in 1868 a woman of such "low vartue" would even be "on-stage" for so long. Her role as perverse madonna, who brings forth in miracles and mystery the faith-giving Tommy Luck, flouts decorum and propriety; but in a striking way she reaffirms Harte's keystone belief that potentially everyone has some good. Complete with crèche and adoring bucolics (the miners), Tommy is born as "the pines stopped moaning, the river ceased to rush, and the fire to crackle. It seemed as if Nature had stopped to listen too." Of course this is a cliché bedecked in purple prose—but consider the audience. They want a reconfirmation of the validity of their beliefs. The Luck is sent to redeem men fallen from a worthy civilization, and Harte concentrates not on developing the title figure, but on portraying his effect on other characters.

James Folsom in *The American Western Novel* indignantly berates Harte for turning the story into an "Eastern." Indeed, Folsom is correct. After the Luck arrives, Roaring Camp goes Middle Class. Stumpy turns from a profane miner into a devoted house-husband, lovingly cooing at the infant and calling him "the d—n little cuss." According to Harte, the Luck makes the camp regenerate and become more civilized as the miners take on parental roles, tidy up sleazy cabins, hold a christening, build new living quarters, and "produce stricter habits of personal cleanliness." Somewhat as in *Snow White and the Seven Dwarfs,* hard work and lyrical adoration create a chosen community during a halcyon summer. The luck is with them; gold claims yield enormous profits, and the "town fathers" want to move in "respectable families in the fall." Says the area's mail carrier,

> They've a street up there in Roaring that would lay over any street in Red Dog. They've got vines and flowers round their houses, and they wash themselves twice a day. But they're mighty rough on strangers, and they worship an Ingin baby.

The strangers have not reached the "highly civilized" plateau of "Roaring's" denizens who regard the white settlement of the area as an ideal goal, symbolized by the baby. How could anyone ask for a tale that more beautifully renders the myth of Manifest Destiny?

One serious problem with the Mysterious Stranger story, as the critic Roy R. Male notes, is what to do with the stranger once his function is completed. If he hangs around, he may move to the position of protagonist and the story becomes something else, in the case of **"The Luck of Roaring Camp"** possibly a *bildungsroman.* Male, and probably most contemporary readers, feel that the story's ending is bathos. But to the Victorian audience, with its very different values and expectations, the ending was "tinged with high pathos." Like his mother, Tommy is killed by a literary convention, a flood, which also drowns several miners, including Stump and Kentuck. These men receive some redemption in that they died better men than they were before The Luck's arrival. But Harte's real pitch is for repatriation, and he makes that pitch to the audience. The story should regenerate us by giving us renewed purpose, optimism, faith, belief in human potential, and if we are Victorian enough, a good cry. Serious literature produces a theme, but parables and Western Union deliver messages.

Similarly, **"Tennessee's Partner"** should not merely be dismissed as a mawkish story of implausible events and psychologically invalid characters existing together in a world of melodramatic conventions. **"Tennessee's Partner"** is a parable about the power of brotherly love. Harte treats the subject with high pathos and obscures some of the issues the story raises by plating them with his silvered rhetoric. He tends to substitute dramatic effect for character development. The brotherly love theme fascinated Harte, and among his other treatments of the partner relationship are **"Barker's Luck," "In the Tules,"** and **"Uncle Jim and Uncle Billy."** The custom of partnership was firmly rooted in mining camp folkways, as numerous historical studies have shown. Like so many of Harte's tales, **"Tennessee's Partner"** has a realistic basis carefully crafted into a romantic scenario that portrays man's goodness.

Numerous other Bret Harte stories follow this parable formula. **"The Outcasts of Poker Flat"** shows that, ultimately, there is good in even the worst people. This tale has a fair sampling of Harte's famous colorful and picturesque characters, including the slick gambler, the whore with a heart of gold, the ingènue, and "the innocent." **"Outcasts"** has little to do with such realistic conventions as character motivation. Rather, the tale describes the conversion of several characters from evil to good when they are isolated by an immense mountain snowstorm. **"Brown of Calaveras"** is a parable that demonstrates the nobility of duty over desire. This tale marks the first appearance of Jack Hamlin, whose masculine objectivity and laconic stoicism Harte used in some twenty other works. **"How Santa Claus Came to Simpson's Bar"** is a parable with the theme of "never give up." The town's miners, a rough but chivalrous bunch, contrive to rescue a deprived boy from having a solitary and disillusioning Christmas. On the edge of despair the boy is emotionally resurrected by Dick Bullen, who, after a tortuous mountain ride to a far-away town, returns with a present. Harte's use of parables spanned his career, and they may be found in his children's stories, and in his few fictional works with settings other than California.

Harte's later fiction has an unfair reputation for being inferior imitations of his earlier work, and stories such as **"In the Carquinez Woods"** (1883) are probably the reason. A lengthy Romance, its plot is simply incredible, even more far-fetched than the later Spanish "legend," **"Maruja."** *L'eau Dormant,* nicknamed "Low Dorman," is a young half-breed who lives in a redwood tree. Dorman saves a runaway waif named Teresa from being imprisoned for stabbing her lover. She, too, is a half-breed. The reader begins to perceive, through paragraphs of romantic descriptions and genteel euphemisms, that these two have set up housekeeping in the tree. Enter coincidence. Nellie Wynn, Dorman's scorned sweetheart and flirtatious daughter of the local minister, toys with the affections of Teresa's former lover, the local sheriff. And Sheriff Dunn, in turn, is Dorman's unknown father. The plot gets considerably more complex before being resolved by one of Harte's *deus ex natura* events, this time a forest fire which burns Dorman and Teresa to death. Apparently Harte intended to write a grand-scale tragic love story, but instead of creating complex characters, succeeded merely in creating a complex plot. By the early 1880's Harte's stories are being published in England and on the Continent before being printed in America. His audience now is clearly European, unfamiliar with California geography. The tale is silly and far-fetched, nearly his worst published effort. This inaccurate picture of the Carquinez Straits area—it is a grassy plain, not a redwood forest—ought to be one of the least disturbing inaccuracies in the tale.

Much of Harte's later fiction, though, is far better than **"Carquinez." "Mrs. Skagg's Husbands"** (1871) exhibits superfluous drama and a contrived plot, but the story makes some powerful statements about men/women relationships and about the conflict between Western land and Eastern money. **"An Ingènue of the Sierra"** (1893) is one of the best anecdotal parables about Yuba Bill, the gigantic, sharp-tongued stage driver. Gilbert Chesterton said in *Varied Types,* "There is about Yuba Bill this air of pugnacious calm, a stepping back to get his distance for a shattering blow. . . . to be rebuked [by Yuba Bill] is like being rebuked by the Pyramids or the starry heavens." During the 1890's Harte also wrote **"Colonel Starbottle's Client,"** one of his most ironic and humorous tales about this picturesque old Southern gentleman, who, attired in white goatee, blue linen coat, ruddy face, and pompous manner, would utter sentences like "I would, suh, be ready to hold mahself personally responsible, suh." These and other stories demonstrate that despite the drudgery of writing potboilers for a living, Harte could rise to his earlier level of accomplishment, particularly in drawing character types.

It is important to recognize that Bret Harte was not a great artist, but a skilled writer of popular fiction. Out of tall tales and barroom ballads he fashioned the local color story. His skill in using romance and melodramatic conventions, his careful craftsmanship, and his mastery of the written word enabled his parables to be the means by which Americans at the time understood the Western experience. But Harte did not merely write skillful parables which reinforced an approving audience's values; he also used the parable for making serious social criticism. Harte made a lucky strike in subject matter, but like many popular writers, he was critical of those who made him famous. He resented the constant pressure of producing enough of the same old stories to keep himself and his family reasonably secure and comfortable. Harte was a professional, and he took pride in not doing sloppy work; yet, sadly, his later letters reveal that he had ceased to respect most of what he wrote.

Three other facts point to a schism between Harte the human being and Harte the popular fiction writer. First, Harte's stories contain virtually no personal autobiographical incidents. Perhaps this omission was simply Victorian diffidence, but Harte did lead an interesting life. Like his idol, Longfellow, Harte may have found his experiences at odds with his ideals, and he may have chosen to write about the latter. Second, Harte's narrators manipulate and withhold information to the point of being condescending to the audience. The narrator's high diction also stresses the distance between himself and the story. Third, recognizing the nature of Harte's narrator opens the door to Bret Harte the literary critic, who from this position often attacked the very aspects which made his stories famous.

Professor Margaret Duckett, author of the most important recent criticism of Harte, has noted his concern with race relations. She regards **"Three Vagabonds of Trinidad"** (1900) as a story which condemns the idea of Manifest Destiny, an historical concept which Harte celebrated some thirty years before in **"The Luck of Roaring Camp."** In the story white townspeople brutally drive out a Chinese boy and an Indian. These two outcasts later befriend a proper little boy from Boston who betrays them to their enemies. Professor Duckett in an article on Harte's novella, ***The Crusade of the Excelsior,*** points to his historical perspective in this story to show that he attacks social and racial injustice. The story protests militarism and the exploitation, through the Church and government, of the gentle, pastoral Mexicans. The parable has some ironic twists in its obvious moral, "honesty is the best policy,"

Harte with members of his family. Clockwise: Harte, his daughter-in-law, his wife Anna, and his youngest daughter Ethel.

for the individuals who follow this moral in ***Crusade*** have their rights curtailed by a Church desperately trying to maintain orthodoxy.

One of Harte's best, although not most famous, stories is **"The Right Eye of the Commander."** On one level this is a tale about a naive frontier and an evil civilization, a story which appears to have had its origins in the New Testament and to have taken some of its imagery from the same source. The tale, set in the California of 1797, is the recounting of what happens when Commandante Hermenegildo Salvatierra receives a visitor named Pegleg Scudder of Boston, who gives the one-eyed commander a glass eye. In retelling this continuing story of civilization corrupting the frontier, Harte may have been thinking of *Matthew,* 18, 7:

> Unless you be converted, and become as children, you shall not enter into the kingdom of heaven.

Two verses later is an even more relevant passage:

> If thy eye scandalize thee, pluck it out, and cast it from thee. It is better with one eye to enter life than having two eyes to be cast into hell fire.

Harte, typically, tried to relate local Western incidents to universal truths.

In **"The Right Eye of the Commander,"** Harte attempts to deal with the problem of evil in a way reminiscent of Melville in "Benito Cereno" or *Moby Dick,* and of Hawthorne in "Ethan Brand." When Salvatierra mysteriously receives his glass eye, he becomes an instrument of evil, and a palor of evil falls upon everything he comes into contact with. He becomes selfish in trying to be "all things to all men," and deceptive by not revealing that the eye is a *glass* eye, thus hiding his sin. He begins to terrorize his subjects. Up to this point he was a "good" man—civilizing the Indians (as symbolized by Paquita) and commanding the respect of his men. But after this acceptance of evil his world drastically changes.

Harte's tale takes place in an atmosphere of mystery, isolation, and loneliness. Characteristic touches of satire and humor do not appear. We first see the commander gazing out toward the ocean; the preceding year had been "uneventful—the days had slipped by in a delicious monotony." It has been ten years since a foreign ship has wanted to dock in the bay, and Pegleg Scudder, the American captain who does dock, remains a mysterious stranger throughout the story. But he is not a rescue agent, a Christ-like angelic messenger of good will converting men from evil ways; instead he is demonic in his mystery. He represents as evil the force of civilization. The storms and secret midnight meetings symbolize his evil effect on the San Carlos community. Pegleg, a Flying Dutchman figure, creates dissension between the Comandante and his subjects. Harte closes with the revelation that Pegleg continues to trade his wares in other areas; consequently, this ending shows how the continued existence of evil dims the ultimate triumph of good. (pp. 14-24)

Patrick Morrow, in his Bret Harte, *Boise State College, 1972, 48 p.*

Roscoe L. Buckland (essay date 1973)

[*In the following excerpt, Buckland examines the role of Jack Hamlin, one of Harte's most popular recurring characters, in several of his short stories.*]

Jack Hamlin may have had his prototype in "Cherokee Bob," a well-known gambler in California, and he may also have been an idealized composite of gamblers Bret Harte had seen in mining camps and towns. Whatever may have been his model, Harte observed in the gambler, and developed in Jack Hamlin, a dashing hero for sentimental romance, a rogue for comedy of manners, and possibly a projection of unfulfilled desire.

Certainly Harte was not attempting to establish a biography the reader could reconstruct from the twenty stories in which Hamlin appears. He was not concerned with the chronological or geographical precision of the historical romance; he was creating local color out of the flush times of California. His chronology varies from story to story as he needed it to provide the time sequence of plot or to give the appearance of truth, as in the opening of a tall tale. His geography, especially in his later years, was reconstructed from his recollections of names of towns and camps, mountains, valleys and rivers to catch a spirit of romance and comedy. Friends of Hamlin appear again and again, and allusions to events in other stories tempt the reader into building elaborate cross references which simply do not work out. (pp. 111-12)

Hamlin first appears, very briefly, in **"The Idyll of Red Gulch,"** written for the *Overland Monthly* (December, 1869) where he is referred to as a gambler who threw a decanter at the head of a man who had mentioned a school teacher's pristine name in a bar-room. In the next story in which he appears, **"Brown of Calaveras"** (*Overland Monthly,* March, 1870), the basic formula of the Hamlin story plot (intervention, complication, and extrication) and the basic traits of Hamlin's character are set out. With a few important thematic developments this is the Hamlin story that Harte wrote again and again.

Without allowance for surprise elements and details of action and dialog essential to the meaning of incidents, the plot of **"Brown of Calaveras"** can be stated quite briefly. Brown's wife arrives suddenly from "back East." Hamlin is struck by her beauty and her manner. Brown is without money. Hamlin lets him win enough to become successful in business, but the wife grows tired of him and sends a note to Hamlin setting a time for them to run off together. When Hamlin arrives, Brown takes him to the spare bedroom to which he has been relegated and asks Hamlin's help. Hamlin listens while he debates to himself whether or not to keep the elopement date. Finally he advises Brown to shoot the man who is having an affair with his wife; to act like a man, and treat his wife like a woman. Then Hamlin rides away in a fury, but by morning he is singing like a lark.

Within this story we have the basic elements of the romantic Hamlin and the rogue Hamlin. He is a hard gambler, but he will let a man win a small fortune. He has a reputation with women and a cynical attitude toward them, but he is, romantically, looking for an ideal woman. He is a man with a gun; he is also a man of refined, expensive taste, and musical ability. He has a contemptuous attitude toward the "average man."

In addition to the apparently contradictory elements of character, there are the ambiguities of motivation and action common to the Hamlin stories. Why does Hamlin choose not to run away with Brown's wife? Has the contempt for Brown shifted to contempt for the woman? Has Hamlin realized the price would be too high? In the stories where Hamlin extricates himself from involvement or takes a hand in the action, such questions of motivation or shifts in attitude are what raise the stories above the level of their plots.

A comparison with the possible prototype, Cherokee Bob, gives further indication of the character Harte is creating in **"Brown of Calaveras."** Both are half-breeds. Hamlin has an Indian stoicism inherited from his mother; he is referred to once in the story as "Commanche Jack." Cherokee Bob was the son of a Hudson Bay Company Scotchman and an Indian woman of the southwest Red River country. Both men had pale faces. Both have long eyelashes and moustaches. But where Cherokee Bob's hair was long and straight, Hamlin's is long and curly. In moustache and hair Hamlin resembles Bret Harte more than Cherokee Bob. Both Jack and Bob are elegant in dress. Both are gamblers and both are gunmen. Cherokee Bob was a fabulous marksman. In **"Brown of Calaveras"** only the fact that Hamlin wears a gun is noted, but in later stories his reputation with a gun is cited again and again. Both were attracted by women of beauty and refinement—the carpenter's wife for whose love Cherokee Bob was bullet-ridden was such a woman.

Other comparisons, drawn from material in later stories, point up the romantic elements with which Harte invested his character. Hamlin is a man of considerable culture, evidently Louisiana culture. Cherokee Bob was a frontier man with no apparent interest in literature or the arts. Cherokee Bob had no physical afflications; Hamlin suffered from "lung fever," popular ailment of the sentimental romance.

The cultural side of Jack Hamlin is illustrated by his musical ability (of which there is no mention in the legend of Cherokee Bob). Harte uses Hamlin's musical ability as a plot device, as evidence of Hamlin's more refined background, and as a means of satiric comment. In **"A Sappho of Green Springs"** Hamlin is described as a gambler by vocation and a musician by taste. It is a taste which Harte developed rather intensively for Hamlin as one story followed another. In **"Brown of Calaveras"** he has a sweet, but uncultivated, tenor voice. In *Gabriel Conroy* we find that he had been the organist in the Second Presbyterian Church of Sacramento until the congregation objected to his gambling and he was asked to resign by a deacon, a successful liquor dealer. In **"The Convalescence of Jack Hamlin"** he says that he was the organist in Dr. Todd's church in Sacramento for a year or two. In **"An Apostle of the Tulles"** he plays the organ and sings in a fine tenor voice, having been organist and tenor in a church back in the states. In **"The Convalescence of Jack Hamlin"** he still sings like a skylark, but his repertoire ranges from "Come, Ye Disconsolate" to selections from *Il Trovatore.* There is in fact more information about his music than about his gambling, and his taste plays a bigger part in the action than his vocation. One reason may be that Bret Harte knew more about music than about gambling. He did not himself gamble; Anna Griswold, the woman Harte married, was an accomplished musician, and when he met her, she was lead contralto in Dr. Thomas Starr King's Unitarian Church choir in San Francisco.

There are numerous references to Hamlin's reputation as a gambler; he is shown playing poker or running a faro game, or traveling toward a new mining town. But these scenes are used to help set a scene or explain why *he* is where the action of the story is. (pp. 112-14)

Gambling is a handy occupation for the romantic, dashing hero. Unlike the rancher, or the businessman, or the miner, the gambler is free to be wherever he is needed at a moment's notice. He is by nature fortune's child: all things—money, women, even life itself—excepting only his reputation, are things lightly caught and lightly held. If ever he longs for or finds the woman to have and to hold, there is an inevitable pathos in the romance. The occupation is also handy for satire. The gambler, especially the well-dressed and refined gambler, can move through all the levels of society, from the most primitive mining camp to the finest saloon in San Francisco. He can consort with the best dressed ladies of either virtue. Bankers and prospectors come to him. Of all people, he knows best just who he is and where he is, and he can be contrasted with those who do not.

But the gambler who can serve these literary functions must be of a certain style. Bret Harte created, perhaps as much for himself as for his readers, a myth of California. He recounted it in lectures which he gave throughout the United States and England. In this mythic picture the gambling saloons are large and gilded, decorous and quiet, places of light and music. "The best-dressed men were gamblers; the best-dressed ladies had no right to that title," Harte reported in "The Argonauts of '49." In this lecture Harte mentions a gambler, Mr. John Oakhurst, who, out of sympathy for the wife of the man who had lost his savings, lets the man win three thousand dollars—the only time he has ever played a game that wasn't square.

In addition to what may be related to this myth, there are other qualities and habits which Harte ascribes to Hamlin, making comparisons between Harte and Hamlin almost inevitable. Hamlin dresses elegantly and formally in town and at work. On the trail, riding toward adventure, he dresses in the colorful velvet of the vacquero. Harte was always fashionably dressed, most often very correctly, occasionally somewhat too colorfully for proper taste. Hamlin is repeatedly, and approvingly, "cynical," "aloof," "cool," "disdainful," "contemptuous of the average man," "indifferent," and "careless." He is courteous, he is kind to children. But he can be insolent; he is sometimes contemptuous of landlords and tradesmen. He is often quite unkind even to his faithful Negro servant, Pete. These traits that Harte chose to give to Hamlin give some clues as to why people could be both attracted to and infuriated or puzzled by Bret Harte.

They also reveal a style of detachment from life that Harte would have liked to have been able to carry off. Jack Hamlin could make money easily and bestow it generously. His occupation required that he be on the move, in fact, that it be better not to return. Harte, especially in his later years, was writing so desperately that he found writing and literary discussion almost distasteful. This was the price he paid for his detachment—his "cynicism" "coolness," "disdainfulness," "indifference," and "carelessness." Harte left California, and never returned; he left the United States, and never returned. He left behind him a reputation for social and financial carelessness which he knew he could not afford to repeat so blatantly. A close look at Hamlin's attitude toward children shows it to be very similar to Harte's attitude toward the children he met in Germany. They are charming little people to pat or play games with; they are not charming when they become cunning, or avaricious, or possessive—and American children show more of these undesirable traits than do German children. When Harte left the United States he left his family, and for nearly the rest of his life managed to resist every opportunity to bring the family together again. His attitude as father could most favorably be described as ambivalent; his duty as husband he maintained by regular payments to his wife. There is little doubt that Harte preferred the detached state of bachelorhood with its attendant state of romantic possibilities; in real life he could not carry the reputation as lightly as he could have his rambling gambler carry it. The Hamlin stories may have provided an answer to what people were saying about him.

The romantic side of Jack Hamlin is best seen in *Gabriel Conroy* and in **"The Three Partners,"** long works in which Hamlin "takes a hand in the game." *Gabriel Conroy* may have received the highest price ever paid for an American novel up to 1876, and there "may have been worse novels," as Stewart says, but whatever, it was certainly the most overpriced novel ever written. Both *Gabriel Conroy* and **"The Three Partners"** are stories of wills and forged documents, long-lost relatives, devious schemes, trials and lawsuits, fortune hunters, and deep-dyed villains. In **"The Three Partners"** Hamlin helps save one of the three partners from the schemes of his wife and a shady character, finally killing the villain in a gun fight. In *Gabriel Conroy* Hamlin, again the dashing hero, careless of his doctor's advice, takes a hand to help the hero and the woman who finally turns out to be a heroine. While doing this he meets his ideal woman, the beautiful Indian girl, Doña Dolores, adopted by a Spanish grandée. This Beatrice and François Villon romance and Hamlin's deathbed scene must both have been very satisfying to readers of the sentimental romance. The women of both these stories are generally more believable than the men, and the motivations of the woman are in several cases psychologically rather intriguing.

The best of the Hamlin stories are the satirical stories—those which have as their subject religion and sex. The Hamlin resurrected after *Gabriel Conroy* is the cynical, worldly man he was in **"Brown of Calaveras,"** and the setting of most of the stories is more urbane. Throughout the works of Harte that deal with the "Anglo-Saxon" in California, there are two societies: the primitive mining camp with its rough and honest miners and its rough and honest women; and the cities, towns and ranches, with their merchants, capitalists, lawyers, promoters, and clergymen, and their wives of varying degrees of gentility and honesty. Between these two there is the brotherhood of those who make their way by bravery and wit: John Oakhurst, Colonel Starbottle, and Jack Hamlin with his physician, Dr. Duquesne, and his faithful, voluntary Negro servant, Pete, and the ladies they have known. In the later Hamlin stories the scene shifts from Red Gulch, Sandy Bar, or Simpson's Bar to Tasajara, the Tulles, Wingdam, Sacramento, or San Francisco. In these later stories there are fewer Susie O'Gradies and more colonel's ladies. Through these areas Hamlin travels with his "cynical" attitude toward women and his "contempt" for the average man, sometimes mediating to set things right, sometimes escaping a fate (marriage) worse than his gambling ways.

For example, **"An Heiress of Red Dog"** (ca. 1878) is set in a mining town that has seen better days. A husband whose wife is unfaithful and whose friends are seeking his money wills his fortune to a waitress, with the stipulation that none of it may be given to any man she may fall in love with. She has fallen in love with a no-good gambler, and has been supporting him with money that is her share, and her share only, of the fortune—what she earns by running a hotel she has bought with part of the fortune. Hamlin defends her reputation from the slurs of the town. He is repelled by her penuriousness until he learns the reason for it; then he goes out to make the no-good marry her. It is too late; the man dies of an overdose of drugs. The heiress dies, and the fortune goes to a relative of the no-good gambler. This is, I believe, Bret Harte's best story of the woman more to be pitied than censured. Through Hamlin, Harte makes some of his best statements about the position of the honest woman among hypocrites.

"An Apostle of the Tulles" (1896) is an ironic treatment of revivalist religion. Hamlin's part in the story is mainly notable for its almost sentimental picture of the virtuous side of the gambler, and useful as the thematic contrast between true and sham religion. The story involves a camp meeting, a lonely widow, a lynching, and the death-bed conversion of a down-beat gambler. The young apostle gives up preaching because he cannot do well at tent-show religion, failing to see that he really can inspire faith when he simply practices Christianity. He takes up the duty of caring for a lonely widow without realizing she wants love, not charity.

Another lonely widow is the heroine of **"A Sappho of Green Springs"** (1890). The plot of the story is the attempt of three men—Hamlin, an editor, and a lumberman named Bowers—to determine the identity of the poetess "White Violet." Hamlin discerns her identity and out of respect for her calls off the wager. Hamlin never sees her, but she has seen him. The honest, homespun lumberman finds her and marries her. Two years later at Hamlin's funeral, Mr. Bowers again sees the editor, who congratulates him on his marriage, but hopes that Mrs. Bowers has not given up writing. Mr. Bowers tells him she is not writing any more: "You'll excuse my sayin' it to a man of your profession, but it's what most folks will find is a heap better than readin' or writin' or actin' poetry—and that's—Rest." Mr. Bowers was right; Hamlin was "acting poetry." But they are gathered there because she has come to place white violets on Hamlin's bier. It is as though Harte felt that he had let Hamlin somehow overstep the boundaries of human charity.

In two stories, Hamlin makes religion and sex very closely related. In **"Mr. Jack Hamlin's Mediation,"** Jack stops at the house where a woman is waiting for her husband to return. She is a music hall woman Hamlin has known before. She is not leading a happy life because of her husband's excessive Christian tolerance. By advice to husband and wife, and threats to the hired girl, Hamlin arranges things so that the wife will be treated like a lady and secure from gossip. In **"The Bell-Ringer of Angels"** there is a similar situation, although with a much different ending. A man famous for his marksmanship has married a beautiful woman and brought her to his home where she will be removed from temptation. In the same camp, there are two brothers, the older of whom has brought his brother there to remove him from temptation. The husband protects his wife with his six-shooter; the older brother protects his ward with the Bible. The older brother and the wife have been in love before, but he manages to resist her advances. The younger brother cannot. Hamlin is in town and both husband and older brother seek to protect the wife from the notorious gambler, and ultimately the older brother shoots the younger, thinking he is Hamlin.

The plot depends upon the devices of mistaken action and mysterious reappearances after the shooting. Hamlin's part is to serve mainly in the mistaken action. The part is appropriate to his characer, and it is noted that upon first seeing the woman, he "recognizes" her—"the light and trifling of either sex are prone to recognize each other by some mysterious instinct." The ironies of situation give the story what force it has: the similarity of the bell-ringer and the older brother, the analogy of six-shooter and Bible, the woman who does not want to be saved—and finally, the motives of the two men.

What makes **"The Apostle of the Tulles," "The Mediation of Jack Hamlin,"** and **"The Bell-Ringer of Angels"** somewhat unusual is the relationship Harte establishes between religion and sex. Fundamentalist religion, and the revivalist preacher, even the preacher with the roving eye, were familiar subjects of Southwest humor, and a favorite subject for the satire of writers such as Irving and Cooper, who, like Harte, loved the good life. Also, Harte had had his own experience with social priggery when he wrote **"The Luck of Roaring Camp."** But the three stories make the further point that it is male obtuseness, augmented by religious dogma, that makes each man do the foolish thing he does and fail to see what is wanted of him. Each woman is different; each may have a somewhat different idea of sex, but each one wants her sex recognized—"to be treated like a woman."

In **"A Mercury of the Foothills"** Hamlin is involved with a woman more dangerous than the light and trifling sort, a woman more like the wife of Brown of Calaveras. She is the wife of a mining engineer whose work has taken him to the foothills. She and Hamlin had dallied in San Francisco; they have kept the affair alive by correspondence. When Hamlin comes riding out to see her, he finds that she is not the woman of his dreams. She is, in fact, planning to kill her husband, using a rattlesnake that has been made a pet by the boy whom she has beguiled into becoming her secret letter carrier. Hamlin kills the snake and warns the husband, who closes up his home and takes his wife to Sacramento.

Danger of a different sort lies in the woman in distress, especially the damsel in distress. In **"A Knight-Errant of the Foothills"** Hamlin helps rescue Don Jose Sepulveda from his family, their priest and an irate husband and his wife—a large poetess by the name of Dorothy Dewdrop, whose many poems of suffering and aspiration have convinced the old Don that the husband is a cold and soulless person. The story is an obvious, and rather amusing use and parody of *Don Quixote.* In **"A Protégée of Jack Hamlin"** Jack rescues a young lady from suicide (she has been betrayed by a no-good gambler). He sets her up in a ladies' finishing school, where he charms the ladies with his music. She becomes a successful painter. At the beginning of the story Hamlin was not in the least concerned with the "abstract morality" of her situation:

> For himself he did not indulge in that sort of game; the inexperience and vacillations of innocence were apt to be bothersome, and besides, a certain modest doubt of his own competency to make an original selection had always made him prefer to confine his gallantries to the wives of men of greater judgment than himself. . . .

But as Hamlin continues his attention to her and as her accomplishments increase, he becomes deeply attracted to her. When his illness requires some rest and quiet, he comes to her. Fortunately a woman arrives, the wife of a man of some distinction, whom Hamlin has known well in the past. She is in search of Hamlin. Hamlin departs, coughing into his handkerchief, with Pete to care for him. In **"A Ward of Colonel Starbottle's"** the old Colonel also takes on a protégé, and Hamlin helps rescue him from the snide remarks of friends and from the young ward, who has all the latent characteristics, however adolescent, of a woman like the wife of Brown.

Harte's stories are sometimes sentimental and the plots sometimes remind one of the stories parodied in ***Condensed Novels.*** But quite often the surprise ending works well with the thematic irony. With his music, his beautiful figure, and his "lung fever" Hamlin is the hero of the sentimental romance. But there is a roguishness, and that quality of "cynicism" that comes off quite well. Harte was not a great social critic, but he did have an eye for avarice, hypocrisy, and meanness.

The last of the Hamlin stories, **"The Convalescence of Jack Hamlin,"** was written in 1901, when Harte was being cared for in the home of Madame Van de Velde and was the subject of some gossip. In the story, Hamlin comes to the home of Seth Rivers, where the "ozone" will cure him of his lung fever. He effects the cure, and while doing so charms the pious neighbors with his manners and his music, confounds the women who want to convert him, and the men who want to run him out; rescues Mrs. Rivers from what amounts to blackmail by Deacon Turner, who has known her erring sister (and had helped her err) in Sacramento; and exposes the hypocrisy of Parson Greenwood in a poker game that Hamlin has deliberately rigged.

All of Hamlin is in this story: the gallantry and the charm, the scorn of the "average man," the calm and deadly threat, the "cynical" view of human nature, the sympathy for the persecuted woman, the love of children. All the furnishings are there: Dr. Duquesne and the Negro servant, Pete; the elegant clothing; the perfume and the scented soap; the reckless, galloping horsemanship; the reputation; the singing like a lark. Hamlin enters, plays a hand in the game, and is ready to move on to the next game.

This is the gayest of all the Hamlin stories. It was written when Bret Harte may well have known that he was a dying man. (pp. 115-22)

Roscoe L. Buckland, "Jack Hamlin: Bret Harte's Romantic Rogue," in Western American Literature, *Vol. VIII, No. 3, November, 1973, pp. 111-22.*

Donald E. Glover (essay date 1973)

[*Glover is an American scholar whose research has focused on fantasy literature. In the essay excerpted below, he reevaluates Harte's later works, citing the ultimately liberating influence derived from his desire to appease a European audience.*]

Harte's career conveniently falls into two major periods: the brief, glittering success of 1868-1872, and the long exile in England from 1880 to his death in 1902. These periods reveal the basic dichotomy and paradox which control his art and the critical response to his work as a whole. The majority of critics suggest that the important period in Harte's life and work ends with the production of **"The Outcasts of Poker Flat"** in 1869. His later career is tantalizing for the mystery surrounding his twenty year separation from his wife and his relationship with Mme. Van de Velde, but the scores of short stories that constitute his later works are traditionally thought of as sad and negligible repetitions of an earlier style and themes.

However, it was after 1878 that Harte won at least partial acceptance of his own image, the image of a Victorian man of taste who happened to have been "out West." This image led him on an Easterly course from the crude response in San Francisco to the brief plaudits of New York, and finally to acceptance in London—Mecca for American writers of that day. Harte was an expatriate more by necessity than by real inclination or choice, but like all artistic expatriates, he was looking for an audience which would appreciate his writing and flatter his artist's ego. In England, he met Hardy and George Eliot. He was the frequent guest of the Duke of Northampton; Sullivan asked for a libretto; the Prince of Wales requested an introduction. Harte even had the temerity to criticize Henry James, whom he had just met, for being "un-American."

> Met Henry James, Jr. the American novelist, who is creating quite a reputation here. He looks, acts, and thinks like an Englishman, I am sorry to say, excellent as his style is. I wish he had more of an American flavor.

Public and private interest was such that Harte was asked to lecture at Oxford and to present the "Response" to the Royal Academy Toast to Literature; magazines deluged his agent with requests for stories.

Feeling successful in Europe, for the first time Harte stopped writing about California, choosing German **("The Legend of Saamtstadt")** and later Scottish locales (the "St. Kentigern" stories narrated by an urbane consul) drawn from his experiences in Crefeld and Glasgow. More secure financially, and approved by his audience as something more than a local phenomenon, he wrote what he wanted: a disastrous series of plays (*The Luck of Roaring Camp* and *Thankful Blossom,* both in 1882) adapted from earlier successful stories. Here we see the paradox in his career. Although contemporary criticism in England showed that Harte was fully appreciated for his skill as a technician and wit, the English reader clearly wanted only local color stories dealing with the romantic Gold Rush era. The irony of Harte's dilemma now becomes apparent. The conflict is no longer between his own view of himself as artist and an unappreciative audience, but between his desire to escape the old materials and his English reader's insistence that he continue with stereotyped California materials. By 1890, the strain shows through in a letter to Mrs. Florence Henniker, daughter of Lord Houghton and Harte's literary protégé.

> You are quite right; I have been 'working hard' lately, but I fear that the 'numbness at the back of the head' will be reserved for my readers. My writing lately has *revealed* to me *hitherto* unknown depths of weariness and stupidity!

He tried to escape the boredom by writing more plays (unsuccessful); by experimenting with various themes, such as racial prejudice and the social outcast; and by completing the libretto for an opera, *The Lord of Fontenelle,* which was set to music by Emmanuel Moōr, but left unperformed. Harte frequently escaped from London to the country estates of friends like James Anthony Froude or Geraldine Webb and even made one trip to Switzerland. But sheer financial necessity forced him to write for the only audience who would pay—the very sort of story which he undoubtedly wrote best and which his American critics now thought him incapable of writing because of his distance from the source of inspiration.

What then of the later work, by far the bulk of his creative output? A study of these stories uncovers several factors that help put the total work in critical perspective. First, Harte continued to follow the pattern established in the early work: use of local color materials (now German, Scottish, English, and Californian), humor-tempering sentiment, melodramatic endings, simple characters and plot lines. Second, the development of his later writing was dictated by the reaction of his audience. During the period 1882-1885, he wrote for both American and English readers. By the late 1880's, he had turned, through financial necessity, almost entirely to an English public. The late stories clearly reflect the reactions of his readers and their effect on any innovations in technique and theme which he attempted. Third, between 1882 and 1902, Harte experimented with many other story types using appropriately developed styles. He returned to the theme of social criticism, especially attacking prejudice against minority groups in stories presented with increasing realism; he attempted international stories along the lines of James and Howells; he used a new, urbane tone with the consular narrator of the St. Kentigern stories. Each experiment met opposition from his readers and their continued demand for the favorite California Gold Rush story. Finally, forced by his financial dependence on a receptive audience, Harte adjusted his style and technique to produce highly colored, melodramatic stories combining humor, sentiment, and pathos with a strong dash of not always factually accurate local color.

The process of adapting his style to the demands of an English audience was a slow one for Harte, and one he frequently rebelled against, but it was this adaptation which brought into being a quite different kind of western story from that which he had produced in America in the 1870's. By observing selected works from the later period, we can recognize the process of change and its end product.

"In the Carquinez Woods" (1882) best serves as the example of Harte's indecision about his audience and his treatment of materials as he began adjusting to new demands from an English audience. The English magazine reader was, like his American counterpart ten years earlier, receptive to the glamour of the Golden West, but as Boynton points out, "So far as it [the reading public] was English, it had a pretty vague notion of the veracity of his replicas of the early California sketches."

As his first work commissioned by a major magazine in two years, **"In the Carquinez Woods"** represents an active return to magazine writing after the failure of the dramatic adaptation of **"The Luck of Roaring Camp,"** a production on which Harte had mistakenly placed high expectations. Critical reception of **"In the Carquinez Woods"** was mixed; most critics praised scene depiction and plotting, while the *Spectator* disliked its lack of moral force. The *Spectator* review, however, notes the appeal of "novel scene" and "novel states of society," personified by the hero, the half-breed Indian botanist Low, and the half-breed Mexican gypsy, Teresa.

The plot of this romance is incredible. L'eau Dormant, popularly known as Low Dorman, lives in a hollowed-out redwood tree. He saves the runaway Teresa from jail by stabbing her lover. They set up housekeeping in the tree. Low's ex-sweetheart, Nellie Wynn, frivolous daughter of the bigoted local minister, plays with the affections of Teresa's former lover, Sheriff Dunn—who in turn is Low's unknown father. In the *dénouement* of this intricate plot, a cataclysmic forest fire conveniently burns Low and Teresa to death.

Unlike the earlier stories, **"Carquinez Woods"** was conceived on a grand scale, appearing in four weighty installments. Long sections are devoted to developing the grandeur of the local setting, which critics are quick to point out is inaccurately portrayed as a redwood forest rather than the grassy plain it is in fact. These "slips" give presumed further evidence of Harte's fading memory. The description, however, clearly shows Harte manipulating his memories and materials for an effect to be produced on an audience unfamiliar with the actual geography of California.

The characters and plot, as well as setting of **"Carquinez Woods"** are intensified. Such characters are uncommon even in the context of **"The Outcasts of Poker Flat"** or **"The Luck,"** where local color figures are set against an indigenous background. In England, removed from the demands for local realism, Harte places his highly exaggerated characters before a vivid backdrop. The major characters are least credible; at times they are noble savages living in a pastoral setting. But they swiftly become merely savages living in a tree. As sensational personalities, however, they were eminently successful with English readers.

Although this story touches on the theme of social ostracism, one which appears throughout Harte's work and perhaps relates to his own father's position as the unrecognized son of a wealthy Jew, social inequality here is hidden by a sensational overlay of sentimental love and intrigue. It is quite unlike Harte's harsh and stark treatment of the same theme in **"Three Vagabonds of Trinidad"** (1900).

"Maruja" (1885) marks Harte's commitment to a new audience. Although he had used California-Mexican and Spanish materials earlier, he had never used these materials extensively, nor used a woman of aristocratic Spanish background as the heroine in such an extended plot. The intricacy and length of the plot required certain changes in Harte's technique.

He arouses interest by using a legendary curse, a picturesque heroine (based on Majendra Atherton, a woman known by the Hartes), a down-trodden hero, and an insane villain. The sensationalism of plot, with its dramatic encounters between father and abandoned son, its violent deaths, and its passionate love scenes, contributes to what the *Athenaeum* called a "quite new picture of old Spanish life." Harte manages to use the unwieldy materials well, combining them into fast-moving melodrama. The characters, however, remain stiff and inconsistent, Maruja, for example, shifting abruptly from heartless coquette to tender lover. There is less wrenching of coincidence for effect, although the chance meeting of West and his son strains credibility.

"Maruja" shows Harte moving a step away from the simple tales of the early seventies, from the integrated local color of setting, character, and action, toward the more artificial, albeit more dramatic, presentation of picturesque characters in a heightened California setting. Characters are more important and more fully developed, as seen in a comparison of Maruja and Teresa. Serial publication helped to enforce more rigid control of plot and suspense than in earlier, shorter works, and **"Maruja"** moves rapidly and smoothly to its conclusion with all the plot elements integrated.

Comparing Harte stories of the early seventies and mid-eighties, one sees that the tone of the early work, bordering on broad farce and sentimental melodrama, becomes more sophisticated as Harte's lovers move into polite society. Gone are the rude, grizzled miners and tawdry, golden-hearted prostitutes. A tone of refinement pervades all dialogue indicating both Harte's desire to meet his audience on their own level and his awareness of the success of the stories of his countrymen, Howells and James.

By 1889, with American criticism of his catering to English taste on the rise, Harte began, on commission, the first story in a trilogy: **"A Waif of the Plains"** (1889), **"Susy"** (1893), and **"Clarence"** (1895). This trilogy marks the high point of his later career. These three stories reveal a new sense of realism, a controlled use of coincidence and sentiment, and a fully developed grasp of effective dramatic scenes.

The major reviews of **"A Waif "** repeat the trans-Atlantic critical dichotomy. The *Nation* commented that the later work showed "aimless incompleteness." Strachey of the

Spectator captured the essence of Harte's appeal to the typical English reader.

> In none of his previous work . . . has Bret Harte exhibited more powerfully his rare faculty of bringing a scene vividly before us, or more skillfully his delicate appreciation of character in old and young alike.

Taking his traditional outcast orphan as central figure, Harte convincingly depicts Clarence Brant as a sensitive and independent boy rejected by those on whom he has an honest claim. His youthful enthusiasm and discouragement, however reminiscent of Oliver Twist, are handled with more realism. The setting gives ample local color material; yet, Harte shows restraint by depicting only scenes integral to plot movement. Local setting is carefully used for dramatic and realistic effect, as in the children's early sighting of an Indian for the first time, and later in a child's realistic view of the bloody bodies of savagely massacred whites. There is less coincidental and sensational matter, and greater realism in descriptions of death without the usual pathos and sentimentality. There are faults with the inconsistent characters and incomplete ending, but clearly Harte has developed the technical skill of narration well beyond the level of **"The Luck."**

"Susy" added sub-themes of squatter's rights, problems of Spanish land grants, and Mexican superstitions, and **"Clarence"** incorporated the Civil War as background effectively. Taken together, they indicate that Harte was equipped to meet the demands of novel writing as he had not been in 1875. More interesting, however, is the new realistic treatment of setting and character, the interest in new themes, and the new emotional restraint which diminishes his usual sentimentality.

Harte attempted to return to Scottish material in **"The Heir of the McHulishes"** (1893), and **"A Rose of Glenbogie"** (1894). Once again, the critics rejected his bid for a new subject matter. And, compared with other stories of this period which have an American setting, the Scottish stories do seem flat and artificial. Harte's talent was for action and natural description, not for recording social dialogue. His works are invariably dullest when two characters are placed face to face in a drawing room and required to talk. His style is most effective where it deals with dramatic episodes, characters in action, the humor of situation or event, and broad, sweeping melodrama; all of which Hollywood took from his stories into the silent Western movie and then into our era via television.

Although Harte continued to use the themes of social injustice and racial prejudice, and experimented with combinations of old and new material, only two stories during the last nine years of his career, **"An Ingénue of the Sierras"** (1893), and **"Dick Boyle's Business Card"** (1899), stand out as significant in this discussion. In **"Ingénue,"** Harte resurrected Yuba Bill, the irrepressible stage driver of the early stories. The dialect and humor are perfect as the plot moves to a surprise ending of O. Henry smoothness. There are no improbable actions forced upon the reader, who enjoys Bill's silent consternation as he slowly realizes that the ingénue he has been duped into helping is in fact a "she-devil." Harte united character with plot using local color only as a necessary background. Unlike his earlier successes, there is no hint of sentimentality; humor and irony remain the central focus.

"Dick Boyle's Business Card" stands at the end of Harte's career as evidence of the considerable achievement of his mature style. A traveling salesman rides with an Army Commandant's daughter, who is secretly conveying needed arms to a nearby fort. Indians attack while the soon-to-be lovers fall behind the wagon in conversation, and the hero kills an Indian and of course wins the lady. The story succeeds because Harte keeps tight rein on the emotional element. The narrative shifts deftly from the lovers to the Indian attack. The characters and situations are credible. Harte infuses the story with realism and humor and escapes the usual sentimental clichés of his earlier love stories.

We are left with essentially two views of Harte's later writing. One suggests that, ". . . he lived quietly in London, an overworked hack, scraping the bottom of the California barrel to turn his thousand words a day. . . . " The other states,

> California was all the subject he ever needed rather than the only subject he could think of, and the limitations of his accomplishment are rather those of his art than of the opportunities of his material. . . . His range was small, his heights and depths neither lofty nor profound, his mind not richly stocked with intellectual goods. But he has not been surpassed in what he did best. This is enough to guarantee his permanent place in American letters.

I prefer the second view. It avoids the pitfalls of the "native writer-spontaneous creation" trap and does justice to Harte fairly on his own ground. Early critics overestimated Harte as a literary artist who displayed great originality, sensitivity, and descriptive genius in his early stories, and whose later years were a tragic descent into despair, penury, and hackwork.

Perhaps his English readers assessed him more nearly at his real level. For them, he was not primarily a nationalistic writer; he was a *raconteur.* His fame rested neither on his personality nor on his anticipated novel. In England, free from the constricting demands for accurate local description, he allowed his inclination to bend realistic local color for the purpose of excellent story telling. (pp. 143-51)

Donald E. Glover, "A Reconsideration of Bret Harte's Later Work," in Western American Literature, *Vol. VIII, No. 3, November, 1973, pp. 143-51.*

Robert D. Rhode (essay date 1975)

[*Rhode is an American editor and scholar. In the excerpt below, from his book* Setting in the American Short Story of Local Color: 1865-1900, *Rhode explores the relationship between setting and character in Harte's short fiction.*]

Though Harte cannot properly be called a naturalist, he

had a scientific way of viewing life. He would not have attributed all conduct to environmental conditions, however; he frequently asserted that men owe much to their surroundings, that in the harmony between a creature and its habits lies more than meets the eye. This conviction grew upon him during the nineties and occasionally crops out in the mouths of his characters. For example:

> It must be the contact of the vulgar earth—this wretched, crackling material, and yet ungovernable and lawless earth—that so depraved them [the natives].

> Here was the old philosophy which accepted the prairie fire and cyclone, and survived them without advancement, yet without repining. Perhaps in different places and surroundings a submission so stoic might have impressed him; in gentlemen who tucked their dirty trousers in their muddy boots and lived only for the gold they dug, it did not seem to him heroic.

> Women prematurely aged by frontier drudgery and childbearing, girls who had known only the rigors and pains of a half-equipped, ill-nourished youth in their battling with the hard realities of nature around them.

One scheme by which Harte has successfully linked setting with characters and their actions is to use particular natural objects or scenes as stimuli to bring about attitudes or feelings. There need be no concordance between scene and character based on past experience; the response elicited may be purely psychological. In such case the setting appears as a motivating influence on character.

That Harte was aware of the literary possibilities in this setting-character relation is evident. He was himself emotionally responsive to California landscapes, which "kept me in a state of excitement". Likewise his characters are often emotionally aroused—sometimes even in a very emphatic way:

> Again, when he [a lone pioneer in the Tules] essayed to bathe his parched and crackling limbs in its [the Sacramento's] flood, he would be confronted with the dazzling lights of the motionless steamboat and the glare of stony eyes—until he fled in aimless terror.

> As he rode abstractedly forward under the low cottonwood vault he felt a strange influence stealing over him, an influence that was not only a present experience, but at the same time a far-off memory.

> "I should be over the ledge before you came back! There's a dreadful fascination in it even now".

He had swelled with strange emotions as he gazed at his ancestral hall.

Not one of the stories from which these selections are drawn develops an important emotional response of characters to the setting. Suggestions of this kind usually turn out to be purely stylistic or literary. Though Harte's practice of alluding to the awe-inspiring quality of the scenery may not always be objectionable, it usually is when it is so prolonged as to constitute a false lead. For example, in **"A Night on the Divide"** (1898) a cultivated but colorless young woman finds herself alone for a short while in a snow-covered mountain range. Her reaction is profound:

> The impressive and majestic solitude . . . seemed to descend upon her from the obscurity above. At first it was accompanied with a slight thrill of vague fear, but this passed presently into that profound peace which the mountains alone can give their lonely and perturbed children. It seemed to her that Nature was never the same, on the great plains where men and cities always loomed into such ridiculous proportions, as when the Great Mother raised herself to comfort them with smiling hillsides, or encompassed them and drew them closer in the loving arms of her mountains. The long white Canada stretched before her in a purity that did not seem of the earth; the vague bulk of the mountains rose on either side of her in a mystery that was not of this life. Yet it was not oppressive; neither were its restfulness and quiet suggestive of obliviousness and slumber; on the contrary, the highly rarefied air seemed to give additional keenness to her senses; her bearing had become singularly acute; her eyesight pierced the uttermost extremity of the gorge, lit by the full moon that occasionally shone through slowly drifting clouds. Her nerves thrilled with a delicious sense of freedom and a strange desire to run and climb.

The reader who faithfully follows this character's emotional response afterward seeks in vain for its purpose in the story. The passage adds nothing to the individuality of the heroine, who turns out to be a mere sounding board. The quotation is more suggestive of travelogue than adventure.

In **"Flip, a California Romance",** the reaction of a stranger to the landscape is more adequately handled, and the setting takes on a function essential to the story. Lance Harriot, an exhausted fugitive, is "maddened and upheld" by the influence of a spicy wood until he can find assistance. He has wandered into a remote valley that is famed for its extraordinary power of inducing "the wildest exaltation" upon any "man and beast" who enters it.

> The delicious spices of balm, bay, spruce, juniper, yerba buena, wild syringas, and strange aromatic herbs as yet unclassified, distilled and evaporated in that mighty heat, and seemed to fire with a mid-summer madness all who breathed their fumes. They stung, smarted, stimulated, intoxicated.

> It was said that the most jaded and foot-sore horses became furious and ungovernable under their influences; wearied teamsters and muleteers, who had exhausted their profanity in this fiery air, extended their vocabulary, and created new and startling forms of objurgation.

And in keeping with this legend, Harriot is made to experience a remarkable change of character. When he plunges into a stream for a bath, he enjoys a "startling transformation"; he not only washes himself, but "by the same operation" becomes "morally cleansed" of "every stain and ugly blot of his late misdeeds and reputation". But Harriot's change is prolonged; when he leaves the valley he carries with him new ambitions and new purposes. The plausibility of the story aside, the point can be made from this example that setting can be successfully capitalized in a story, if its link with character is convincing.

Another way in which Harte sometimes integrates setting and character is by bringing persons into contact with natural phenomena in such a manner as to affect their aesthetic or moral nature, touching them physically, or altering their status in the world. A single natural object, a huge boulder situated near a mine, is portrayed with considerable detail in **"A Millionaire of Rough and Ready"** (1887). Having discovered a rich vein of gold, a long-suffering prospector, Slinn, becomes paralyzed from shock as he waits for the coach beside the boulder marking the end of his claim and is unable to reveal his discovery. Years later his memory is revived by an accidental revisit to the same spot; but on a third visit to the locality he dies from shock and is unable to realize his hope of sudden riches.

"The Heritage of Dedlow Marsh" (1889) is the story of a young brother and sister struggling vainly to shake off the shackles of their narrow, dismal surrounding. Jim and Maggie have inherited from their eccentric father, Boone Culpepper, a vast tract of marshy land and a hatred for society. Long isolation at the old homestead has made these young people almost unsuitable for any other sort of life, as their stay at Logport proves to them. Logport society turns Jim into a frustrated lover and drunkard, driving him almost to suicide after the precedent of his father. Maggie blames her own ambitions for Jim's downfall; she should have known, she says,

> that there could be nothing in common between her folk [the family of Jim's lover] and such savages as we; that there was a gulf as wide as that Marsh and as black between our natures, our training and theirs; and even if they came to us across it, now and then, to suit their pleasure, light and easy as that tide—it was still there to some day ground and swamp them.

"A Convert of the Mission" (1896) is a good example of a character's adjustment to a new environment. A Protestant minister in poor health goes to a decadent Spanish town for a rest, where he becomes interested in a moonlit garden containing a beautiful senorita with a lovely voice. For a time he remains loyal to his own missionary instincts, but the whole spirit of the place so enthralls him that at last he becomes the convert, not the lady. A Catholic proselyte, he adopts the ways of the village and is found visiting the mission with his young lover. The motivation is skillfully handled, though the situations are artificial.

There is a suggestion of a third way in which setting has an influence upon characters in Harte's fiction, namely by representing to them a sign of Providence or a symbol of their own lives. This symbolic setting is not important or frequent enough in Harte's stories to deserve more than a mention, but it should not be overlooked. Though in none of Harte's stories is the setting as a whole symbolical, instances occur in which a particular scene symbolizes a general theme or truth to a particular character. The next-to-last scene in **"The Outcasts of Poker Flat",** for example, in which the pure woman and the wicked are found lying peacefully side by side under a blanket of snow, seems to symbolize to the searching party—and the reader—the absurdity of conventional morality. Toward the end of **"Miggles"** (*Overland,* June, 1869), another of Harte's earliest stories, there is a striking tableau which reflects, at least to one of the travellers, the patience and self-sacrifice of the heroine for her paralyzed lover:

> The storm had passed, the stars were shining, and through the shutterless window the full moon, lifting itself over the solemn pines without, looked into the room. It touched the lonely figure in the chair with an infinite compassion, and seemed to baptize with a shining flood the lowly head of the woman whose hair, as in the sweet old story, bathed the feet of him she loved.

In **"Snow Bound at the Eagle's"** the falling flakes of snow, Harte explains gratuitously, "seemed to illustrate the conviction that had been slowly shaping itself", namely, that all escape was blocked. In **"Jim's Big Brother from California"** the stars, we read, "might have represented the extreme mutations in fortune in the settlement that night". One more brief but rather effective touch of symbolism may be found in **"The Reincarnation of Smith",** wherein Smith, caught in an inextricable web of his own crimes and a hopeless love for a woman whom he has previously deserted as a wife, sees in a stream leading to the sea the only solution to his oppressive dilemma:

> Yes [he muses], it was pointing him the only way out,—the path to the distant ocean and utter forgetfulness again!

And thus in the story the river, having flooded the country, carries his body out to the sea.

A fourth and last way in which Harte successfully worked out the idea of a fundamental character-environment connection was by the use of a person to embody the special characteristics of a locality, to represent, in a sense, the genius of a place. According to this scheme, the scene is partly represented by description, but its essential nature is further revealed by the person filled with its essence. Character and setting are thus mutually invigorated, each making the other more intelligible.

Such was the formula in Harte's first successful story. After the lame **"My Metamorphosis"** in April, 1868, there appeared in December of the same year one of the most original stories yet produced in this country, **"The Work on Red Mountain".** The central character, M'liss, a little waif as "shaggy as a Shetland colt and sleek-souled as little Eva", is, to quote from Pattee [see excerpt dated 1923],

> the incarnation of the wild lawlessness of a whole area, that primitive passion unchecked by convention and precedent, that irreverence and imperious self-assertion which had been born of the frontier and had culminated in the California of the gold-rush decade. . . . She had grown up untutored in the wild gulches of "Smith's Pocket" with men elemental in their hates and loves and appetites and ideal of freedom.

M'liss is a strange product of a strange environment. She would be meaningless elsewhere, for Red Mountain is the key to her character; and the objects and scenes among which she lives gain in meaning because she is present to represent them. Harte must have felt that the favorable reception of this story was due to the strong local interest, for he rewrote it as a full-length serial three years later with even greater emphasis upon the locality. But the effort was a dismal failure, not because new material was added to expand it, but because, when he increased the bulk of the story, his erstwhile formula for connecting the setting to the character somehow escaped him.

With **"Flip, a California Romance"**, the case is somewhat better. Flip, the central character, is less civilized even than M'liss, but is drawn along the same lines. "She was redolent of the spices of the thicket, and to the young man's excited fancy seemed at that moment to personify the perfume and intoxication of her native woods". The tale rings surprisingly true for the most part, in spite of the unmistakeable learnings toward cheap melodrama at the end. For Flip is unique, not beautiful. When Harte says in **"A Maecenas of the Pacific Slope"** (1891) that his heroine "standing there, graceful, glowing and animated, . . . looked the living genius of the recreated apartment", he is using a mere figure of speech; but in **"Flip"** the girl and the spicy woods are by the force of repetition so completely fused that there can be no doubt of the connection.

One more example of this type will suffice. **"A Sappho of Green Springs"** (1891) is a story of a genuine local colorist, an anonymous poetess who has so perfectly reflected her natural surroundings that any one who knows the district well can find her exact locality with no further information than that contained in her verse. She finds material even in "the little flicks and checkers o' light and shadder down in the brown dust". Jack Hamlin, entering her particular valley, was sure at once that

> this was the "underbrush" which the poet had described: the bloom above and below, the light that seemed blown through it like the wind, the suggestion of hidden life beneath this tangled luxuriance, which she alone had penetrated,—all this was here. But more than that, here was the atmosphere that she had breathed into the plaintive melody of her verse.

As the story develops, the fact becomes clear that these particular woods and the poetess belong to each other and should never part. The character-setting link is fundamental in this story, not literary fancy. The story as a whole, however, is not efficiently shaped to bring it into full prominence.

From the foregoing examples, it is evident that Harte was experimenting with character-setting relationships in his stories. The failure of particular stories was sometimes a matter of shallowness of human interest, Dickensian sentimentality, or poor literary technique, but in many cases it can be traced to a malproportioned, discordant conjunction of setting with the other narrative elements, especially with his characters.

Harte's interpretation of the Western scene, viewed apart from his narrative art, aims in a general way to demonstrate its extraordinary aesthetic properties, to reveal the hazards and excitement under which its hardy inhabitants passed their lives without fear or perturbation, to illustrate the uncertainty of life and fortune in a land that is unknown and unpredictable. The Western environment, Harte seems to imply, has produced a stolid, stoical race, reckless in danger, unmindful of the sudden inversions of fortune, ridiculously rough in the exterior, but tender and sentimental in its interior aspects, however eccentric it appears to the uninitiated. The incongruity of a Westerner in another part of the world is a common motif among all of the [Western] local colorists . . . ; and the titles of Harte's stories alone will reveal his special satirical delight in finding, among his own Sierras, a Western prototype for the personages of heroic antiquity and classical mythology. (pp. 82-90)

Robert D. Rhode, "Setting in Close Relation to Character," in his Setting in the American Short Story of Local Color: 1865-1900, *Mouton, 1975, pp. 82-135.*

Charles E. May (essay date 1977)

[May is an American editor and critic who has written extensively on the short story. He has commented that he hopes to "establish the short story as a major narrative form, not just the poor little sister of the novel." Here he highlights the central role of sardonic humor in Harte's tale "Tennessee's Partner."]

Every student of American literature knows that Bret Harte wrote banal and sentimental short stories. The only point of debate seems to be which of his best-known sketches—**"The Luck of Roaring Camp," "The Outcasts of Poker Flat,"** or **"Tennessee's Partner"**—is the most banal and sentimental. Since 1870, indiscriminate readers have wept over the death scene of Kentuck with the "cold and pulseless" babe in his arms, have softened at the sacrifice of Mother Shipton for Piney Woods, and have marveled at the forgiveness that passes all understanding of Tennessee's Partner. T. Edgar Pemberton, an early Harte admirer, has asked of **"Tennessee's Partner"** [in his *Bret Harte: A Treatise and a Tribute* (1900)]: "Will anyone with the soul to understand it ever forget the exquisite pathos of the ending of that beautiful story?" Of those more critical readers who might answer his question with a disgusted and superior snort, Pemberton says, "Such people will always exist, and, most happily for humanity, Bret Harte does not appeal to them, but to the 'great heart of the nation.' "

Thirty years later in his career, after all the excitement of the epoch-making volume, ***The Luck of Roaring Camp and Other Sketches,*** had died down, Harte himself felt that he had not only spoken to the great heart of the nation, but he had also spoken of the habits of mind of its people. Although humbly denying that he had originated the short story in America, he was quite willing to accept credit for helping establish the "American short story." Poe and Hawthorne had written short stories, Harte says in his 1899 essay in the *Cornhill Magazine* ["The Rise of the Short Story"], but they had not written stories "characteristic of American life, American habits nor American thought."

And, indeed, serious scholars of American fiction have conceded that Harte's influence has been considerable. Arthur Hobson Quinn has said [in his *American Fiction: An Historical and Critical Survey* (1936)] that Harte taught nearly every American writer of short stories some of the essentials of his art. And Fred Lewis Pattee places him second only to Washington Irving in his influence on the form. Although Quinn admires Harte, especially for his "realistic . . . probing beneath the surface for the more profound causes of human conduct," while Pattee has reservations about Harte's work being more "extravaganza" than truth, both realize that Harte's most important saving grace was a sense of humor. Pattee says that without it, Harte would have been as sentimentally extreme as Dickens, his master [see excerpt dated 1923]; Quinn says that his sense of humor "preserved in him that sense of proportion which was one of his great gifts to the development of the short story." Harte would have been happy to accept this as his major contribution, for in his *Cornhill* article he singles out humor as the factor which finally diminished the influence of English models on the short story in America:

> It was *Humour*—of a quality as distinct and original as the country and civilization in which it was developed. It was at first noticeable in the anecdote or "story," and after the fashion of such beginnings, was orally transmitted. It was common in the barrooms, the gatherings in the "country store," and finally at public meetings in the mouths of "stump orators."

Pattee has noted that in **"Tennessee's Partner,"** Harte records an important clue to his appeal—that in the gulches and barrooms of early California, "all sentiment was modified by a strong sense of humor." Without humor, Pattee observes, the funeral scene in **"Tennessee's Partner"** would have been "mere gush." Even then, however, he adds, the last paragraph is "mawkish sentimentality." Pattee is not the only one who has noted Harte's sense of humor, but not found it strong enough in **"Tennessee's Partner."** In fact, most critics, even those who have called it the best of all Harte's stories, say that its chief effect is not humor at all, but pathos. Henry Childs Merwin, in an early biography of Harte, says the story's pathos results from the fact that Tennessee was unworthy of his partner's devotion:

> Had Tennessee been a model of all the virtues, his partner's affection for him would have been a bestowal only of what was due. It would not have been, as it was in fact, the spontaneous outpouring of a generous and affectionate character.

Of course, it is just that "spontaneous outpouring" which has caused more cynical or more critical readers of Harte's story to reject it as psychologically invalid, unrealistic, and just plain incredible.

An interesting early cynical response to the story was reported a few years ago by Bradford A. Booth [in his "Mark Twain's Comments on Bret Harte's Stories," *American Literature,* January 1954], who had access to the first edition of ***The Luck of Roaring Camp and Other Sketches*** from the library of one of America's most famous cynics: Mark Twain. Twain's annotations on the story focus on the central problem:

> But does the artist show a clear knowledge of human nature when he makes his hero *welcome back* a man who has committed against him that sin which neither the great nor the little ever forgive? & not only welcome him back but love him with the fondling love of a girl to the last, & *then* pine and die for the loss of him?

The problem has been stated in more detail since by those forerunners of a whole generation of close, critical readers—Cleanth Brooks and Robert Penn Warren [in their *Understanding Fiction*]. After asserting the usual theme of the story—"a man's intense loyalty to his friend"—Brooks and Warren proceed to question the credibility of many of Tennessee's Partner's actions. Would a man, they ask, who sees things in such concrete terms that he has no concept of abstract judicial law forgive Tennessee for stealing his wife? Would a man who felt that the townspeople had hanged his friend for "no good reason" actually invite them to the funeral and thank them for their trouble? Brooks and Warren's most serious question, however, is the most damaging one to Harte: "Has not Bret Harte taken a theme, which, perhaps he had seen successfully employed for pathetic effects in other fiction . . . without ever grounding the story in a presentation of the real psychological issues involved—without, in other words, trying to understand his main character?" A serious charge, indeed, and one that perhaps needs more careful examination. Perhaps it is the critics who have not understood.

Brooks and Warren base their judgment on the fact that Harte dodges the psychological problem of the reconciliation between the two partners by failing to bring into focus and make believable the wife-stealing episode. This episode, which Brooks and Warren say is one of the important psychological steps by which Tennessee's partner arrives at his subsequent actions, is simply not made credible. As a result the whole story loses its point. Of course, that depends on what one takes the point of the story to be. But Brooks and Warren go on confidently to suggest the reasons why Harte fails:

> By skimping it and moving away from it toward the final effort at pathos, Bret Harte has made the whole story seem anticlimatic and illogical. Either he was so little interested in the psychology of the situation that he did not investigate it, or he was aware that the issues involved were too complicated for him to handle.

Although it is obvious that Brooks and Warren think the latter reason is true, the story itself supports the former one. But regardless of the reason, whether the skimping of the scene makes the story anticlimatic and illogical depends not so much on the critic's viewpoint as it does on the storyteller's point of view, for it is his moral perspective which should direct the reader's response to the story. And this story has a dramatically defined narrator with a voice and purpose of his own.

After relating how Tennessee's partner went to San Francisco for a wife and was stopped in Stockton by a young waitress who broke at least two plates of toast over his head, the narrator says that he is well aware that "something more might be made of this episode, but I prefer to tell it as it was current at Sandy Bar—in the gulches and barrooms—where all sentiment was modified by a strong sense of humor." It is from this point of view—sentiment modified by humor—that the narrator also tells the episode which Brooks and Warren criticize. The incident of Tennessee's running off with his partner's wife is related in the same flippant phrases and in the same intonation as that of Tennessee's partner's somewhat hazardous wooing. But more importantly, it is this barroom point of view which dominates the whole story. And once we are willing to accept it, the story takes on a new and not so pathetic dimension. The narrator fully intends for this story to be, not the occasion for tears, but for sardonic laughter.

The first clue to the ironic discrepancy in the story comes in the title and in the first line in which the narrator explains the title's significance: "I do not think we ever knew his real name." The narrator then devotes the first full paragraph to a discussion of men in Sandy Bar being christened anew with names indicative of some aspect of dress or character. This should not be taken as gratuitous local color; for the whole story centers around a man who *seems* to have no character except in relation to his devotion to his partner, and who *seems* to have no name except a relative one.

The fact is, however, Tennessee's partner does have another name, a name that, from the barroom point of view, indicates his real character in the story. In the crucial courtroom scene, after Tennessee's partner has unsuccessfully tried to bribe the judge and jury, Tennessee himself calls his partner by another name: "For the first time that evening the eyes of the prisoner and his strange advocate met. Tennessee smiled, showed his white teeth, and saying 'Euchred, old man!' held out his hand." Knowing that euchre is a card game and that the capture and trial of Tennessee has been described in the terminology of cards, and knowing that the verb form of the word "euchre" is a colloquial expression which originated in American English around 1845 and which means to get the better of someone by scheming, we begin to suspect that there is something more in this story than the straining for pathetic effect.

The name that Tennessee calls his partner is the past tense form of the verb "euchre." That Tennessee's partner was not euchred is obvious. He was not beaten by scheming. Tennessee simply ran off with his wife. No, the euchred one in the story is Tennessee himself who has been beaten by his partner by quiet scheming and a poker face. In fact, it is probably that Tennessee himself gives his partner the name at that very moment during the trial because he has realized what his partner has done. This would not only explain Tennesse's understanding smile, but it would also explain his partner's nervous mopping of his face as he lets Tennessee's hand fall from his passively and withdraws without another word. The title of the story, had it been named after the true character of the central figure, might have been "Euchred," but that, of course, would have given the game away. It is little wonder that Harte considered this one of his favorite stories, for in it his typical American humor of the barroom and country store has euchred readers for a century—even Mark Twain, who knew cards and storytellers well enough to know better.

Brooks and Warren are certainly correct when they say that Tennessee's partner is a man "who evidently sees everything in very concrete and personal terms." When he loses his wife he takes it "simply and seriously." When Tennessee returns from his escapade and all the boys who gather in the canyon are "naturally indignant" that there is no shooting, Tennessee's partner looks at them in such a way as to indicate "a lack of humorous appreciation." In fact, the narrator gives us another clue here which should tip us off to the partner's potential for silent, yet deadly, revenge; for he is a "grave man, with a steady application to practical detail which was unpleasant in a difficulty." Tennessee's partner's steady application to practical detail proves unpleasant indeed to Tennessee in his difficulty at the trial. For surely, the partner, in his serious and practical way, knows that his attempt to bribe the judge and jury will clinch the case against Tennessee, knows that it will be the final trump in the card game which began with Tennessee's capture. The narrator tells us that the insult of the bribe attempt on Judge Lynch—"who, whether bigoted, weak, or narrow, was at least incorruptible—firmly fixed in the mind of that mythical personage any wavering determination of Tennessee's fate."

Further clues to the sardonic potential of the partner are suggested by the imagery with which the narrator describes him during the courtroom scene. When he enters the court, we note, with foreboding perhaps modified by humor, that his face is "sunburned into a preternatural redness," his trousers are "streaked and splashed with red soil," and he is mopping his face with a "red bandana handkerchief, a shade lighter than his complexion." Before we are tempted to pass this off as gratuitous caricature, we should note that Tennessee's partner's preternatural redness is referred to again in the story after the funeral oration when the men look back and see him sitting on Tennessee's grave, "his face buried in his red bandana handkerchief." This image of sorrow and pathos is ambiguously mixed with demonic humor, for "it was argued by others that you couldn't tell his face from the handkerchief at that distance, and the point remained undecided." Is Tennessee's partner lost in grief, his face in his red bandana? Or is his face glowing with that preternatural redness of his sardonic revenge?

Additional elements of the sardonic humor in the story point the way to its real meaning. For example, not to be missed in that scene of the partner sitting on Tennessee's grave is the fact that the grave itself is in a rough enclosure, "which in the brief days of Tennessee's partner's matrimonial felicity, had been used as a garden, but was now overgrown with fern." Harte makes use not only of colloquial expressions but colloquial pronunciation as well to indicate his satiric purpose. That the partner, when he comes to ask for the body, asks for the "diseased," that he says, "when the gentlemen were done with the 'diseased,' he would take him," is not to be ignored. For Tennessee has been a "disease," not only to his partner, but to the body politic of Sandy Bar as well. Furthermore, the partner invites the men to the "fun'l," and afterwards says, "the fun'l's over; and my thanks, and Tennessee's thanks, to you for your trouble." The "fun" that is the funeral is a sardonic fun, indeed, more serious and more complicated than we at first imagine.

When Tennessee's partner invites the men to the funeral, the narrator says, "Perhaps it was from a sense of humor, which I have already intimated was a feature of Sandy Bar—perhaps it was from something even better than that, but two thirds of the loungers accepted the invitation at once." That "something better," which sentimental readers have always been willing to accept as an indication of sympathy and perhaps regret on the part of the men, might be seen instead as the final necessary act in the ritual of complicity between the partner and the town in their vigilante justice on Tennessee. The "popular feeling" which had grown up against Tennessee in Sandy Bar could end no other way. At the trial, the narrator makes it abundantly clear that Tennessee's fate was sealed, that the trial is only to justify "the previous irregularities of arrest and indictment." The men have no doubt about his fate; they are "secure in the hypothesis that he ought to be hanged on general principles." It is this very knowledge that they are going to hang Tennessee not so much for a concrete wrong as on general principles that makes them begin to waver until the partner, who has suffered a concrete wrong by Tennessee, enters the game with his attempted bribe. As a result of his taking a hand, the town helps Tennessee's partner avenge himself on Tennessee, and the partner helps the town get rid of a bothersome blight on the body politic. The complicity here between the serious, slow partner and the townspeople is similar to that between the slow-witted idiot and the town to rid themselves of an obnoxious practical joker in Ring Lardner's "Haircut."

One final problem remains to be dealt with—the pining away and dying of Tennessee's partner at the conclusion. It can be understood more clearly now that we know the true psychology of the main character. He is a serious and simple man, with a steady application to practical detail. As Brooks and Warren well note, he sees things in very concrete terms. He takes the loss of his wife quietly and seriously. He accepts Tennessee back in the same manner. In his simple and serious way, however, he knows he must avenge himself. This is not to say that he is not close to Tennessee; they have been partners for four years. After his scheming has achieved his purpose, he cannot escape his responsibility for Tennessee's death. As he says to the men at the funeral, "You see, it's sort of rough on his pardner." That he begins to fail in health and seems to pine away and die for the loss of Tennessee out of simple dog-like devotion would indeed be psychologically incredible. It is surely hard to believe, as it was for Mark Twain, that Tennessee's partner would die of "rampant adoration," but not so hard to believe he would die of grief-stricken guilt.

The economical use of detail in the story as well as its combination of sardonic humor and moral complexity is similar to Poe's masterpiece, "The Cask of Amontillado." In its use of a narrator who quietly and cleverly controls his satiric intent, it is surely as well done as Ring Lardner's "Haircut" or Mark Twain's "Celebrated Jumping Frog." One brief incident in the story, typical of those details which many readers have passed over as gratuitous, but which really reflect on the true purpose of the story, takes place on the way to the "fun'l": "Jack Folinsbee, who had at the outset played a funeral march in dumb show upon an imaginary trombone, desisted from a lack of sympathy and appreciation—not having, perhaps, your true humorist's capacity to be content with the enjoyment of his own fun." Bret Harte surely exhibits the "true humorist's capacity" in **"Tennessee's Partner."** Because of the lack of reader appreciation, he has had to be content with the enjoyment of his own fun for over a hundred years. (pp. 109-17)

Charles E. May, "Bret Harte's 'Tennessee's Partner': The Reader Euchred," in The South Dakota Review, *Vol. 15, No. 1, Spring, 1977, pp. 109-17.*

Linda Burton (essay date 1980)

[*In the essay below, Burton cites evidence of a homosexual relationship between Tennessee and his partner in the story "Tennessee's Partner."*]

Bret Harte's literary reputation has never again reached the height of its early 1870s' popularity, which was largely stimulated by the acclaimed publications, all in the 1860s, of **"The Luck of Roaring Camp," "The Outcasts of Poker Flat,"** and **"Tennessee's Partner."** At best the Easterner Harte, known as "the first internationally famous writer of short stories about the West," is usually examined solely as a representative of Western local color, and his stories are often derided for their excessive sentimentality and lack of character development. Accordingly, very few critics have actually considered Harte's works deserving of serious study. Nevertheless, if we allow ourselves to look further into Harte's stories and consider them as being possibly more intricate than mere examples of Western local color, we find that they deserve careful attention—an attention obviously different from what they have already received. In particular, by studying closely Harte's most often anthologized story, **"Tennessee's Partner,"** we can observe that the story should not be dismissed, which it often is, as a poorly written, overtly sentimentalized narrative of one "pardner's" brotherly love for the other.

And yet most literary critics have consistently followed the brotherly love interpretation of **"Tennessee's Partner."** From T. Edgar Pemberton, who in 1903 described **"Tennessee's Partner"** as a "pathetic tale" of one man's devotion to his degenerate partner [see Further Reading list], to Richard O'Connor, who in 1966 described the relationship as a "loyalty-unto-death" situation [see Further Reading list], most critics have unquestioningly seen the story as a poorly written parable of brotherly love. In addition, Cleanth Brooks and Robert Penn Warren indict Harte for being "so thoroughly obsessed with the pathos of the partner's loyalty that he has devoted no thought to the precise nature of the basis of that loyalty" and, therefore, "has made the whole story seem anticlimactic and illogical" [*Understanding Fiction*]. Clearly, these interpretations tend to downgrade Harte's story as the critics cannot account for what is termed the story's unexplainable happenings, which are usually haphazardly attributed to a weakly developed plot and characters. However, by approaching Harte in a new way, in particular by considering the possibly homosexual relationship between Tennessee and his partner, we may be able to answer questions that have previously puzzled critics. Of course, it is difficult to determine whether or not Harte was fully conscious of the homosexual relationship that he depicts in the story. Perhaps a modern reader, in a time when homosexuality is openly analyzed and discussed, can actually ascertain more accurately than earlier readers what Harte either consciously or unconsciously was attempting to convey. Consequently, we may discern that the entirety of Harte's works needs further investigation.

Probably the most intriguing episode in **"Tennessee's Partner,"** which puzzles both critics and townspeople alike, occurs near the beginning of the story when Tennessee returns alone after having absconded with his partner's wife: "But to everybody's surprise when Tennessee one day returned from Marysville, without his partner's wife,—she having smiled and retreated with somebody else,—Tennessee's Partner was the first man to shake his hand and greet him with affection. The boys who had gathered in the cañon to see the shooting were naturally indignant." Even Brooks and Warren ask, "How could this man forgive Tennessee?" Or as Ratliff in Faulkner's *The Hamlet* notes, "A man takes your wife and all you got to do to ease your feelings is to shoot him." However, Tennessee's Partner cannot shoot his closest companion, Tennessee. In addition, shortly thereafter, the narrator explains that the townspeople believe Tennessee's Partner's "continued intimacy with Tennessee after the affair above quoted could only be accounted for on the hypothesis of a copartnership of crime." What the townspeople are oblivious to at this point in the story (and what critics have yet failed to notice) is that it is not a "copartnership of crime" that Tennessee and his partner share, but a partnership of homosexual love. Forgiveness, consequently, lies with the fact that the woman had little effect on the partners' love for each other; and after she left the scene, the two men lived alone together again, just as they had done before she and Tennessee's Partner were married.

Harte in his later years.

Likewise of interest is that Tennessee and his partner live together not only before and after the previously mentioned marriage but also *during* the marriage. As we are told, "Of their married felicity but little is known, perhaps for the reason that Tennessee, then living with his partner, one day took occasion to say something to the bride on his own account." The marriage, therefore, did not cause a rift between the two men because they continued to live together. Neither does Tennessee's Partner mourn excessively over the loss of his wife. After the bride and Tennessee "went to housekeeping without the aid of a justice of the peace, Tennessee's Partner took the loss of his wife simply," the reason being, of course, that his wife was not an important factor in his life. The question perhaps comes to mind as to why Tennessee's Partner and Tennessee became involved with this woman in the first place, and a likely answer is that they both were seeking their heterosexuality and, at the same time, attempting to deny their homosexuality by having a close relationship with a woman, something neither man obviously found successful. In this affair, as in most other aspects of their life together, they even share the same woman. Thus the two men could shake hands when Tennessee returned to Sandy Bar without the bride, since they were happy to be back together again with only each other to love.

Also of importance is the wifely role played by Tennessee's Partner as his relationship with Tennessee takes on the appearances of Tennessee as the erring, wayward husband and his partner as the loyal, virtuous wife. For example, when Tennessee is on trial for robbery, Tennessee's Partner comes to the courtroom to aid him by attempting to bribe the judge with "seventeen hundred dollars in coarse gold and a watch,—it's about all my pile." Thus Tennessee's Partner would relinquish all his worldly possessions to save his beloved Tennessee. After Tennessee's hanging, acting once more as the loyal wife might act, the Partner comes to fetch Tennessee's body home for burial. At this point, Tennessee's Partner tells the townspeople: "It ain't the first time that I've packed him home on my back, as you see'd me now. It ain't the first time that I brought him to this yer cabin when he couldn't help himself; it ain't the first time that I and Jinny have waited for him on yon hill, and picked him up and so fetched him home, when he couldn't speak and didn't know me." Critics, of course, have often been perplexed as to why Tennessee's Partner is evidently loyal to so obvious a degenerate as Tennessee. The answer certainly cannot lie simply with brotherly love; but when we note the sexual side of the partners' relationship, we can better understand the devotion of the wifely Tennessee's Partner to Tennessee. Tennessee's Partner, therefore, is devoted in much the same manner as a traditional wife to a husband.

Moreover, not only is Tennessee's Partner devoted to Tennessee, but he also shares Tennessee's name, as can be noted at the beginning of the story when the narrator tells us that "we never knew his [Tennessee's Partner's] real name." According to the narrator, "these appellatives were derived from some distinctiveness of dress . . . or from some peculiarity of habit." In addition, the people of Sandy Bar "never knew" Tennessee's Partner "by any other than this relative title." Of course, at the beginning of the story, the critic has no idea that the "peculiarity of habit" in this case might indicate the unusual closeness of Tennessee and his partner. Neither is there any indication that the narrator or townspeople are ever consciously aware of the homosexual element of the partners' relationship. Yet as it is a traditional social custom for a wife to assume her husband's name and become known by a relative title, Tennessee's Partner likewise shares Tennessee's name.

Finally another example of the partners' relationship, which along with all the other evidence points to Tennessee and his partner being, in fact, homosexual lovers, happens at the end of the story, the climax which critics have seldom found adequate since Tennessee's Partner pines to his death over his insoluable loss of Tennessee. The narrator relates, "But from that day his rude health and great strength seemed visibly to decline; and when the rainy season fairly set in, and the tiny grass-blades were beginning to peep from the rocky mound above Tennessee's grave, he took to his bed." Seemingly, Tennessee's Partner cannot bear to live without his Tennessee, and he approaches death with visions of Tennessee: " 'Thar! I told you so!—thar he is,—coming this way, too,—all by himself, sober, and his face a-shining. Tennessee! Pardner!' And so they met." Thus the story ends as Tennessee's Partner cannot endure living after the loss of his beloved Tennessee; and it is not just the loss of a partner that Tennessee's Partner cannot endure, but the loss of possibly the only person he has ever genuinely loved. Partners they certainly were, but lovers as well.

We can suggest, therefore, from all the evidence that the two partners experience simply more than brotherly love. By assuming the role of a wife and indeed functioning as Tennessee's lover, the character of Tennessee's Partner, as well as other elements of the plot, may be more fully understood. Realizing that the bond between them was more than friendship, we can fit together all the aspects of the story. We, moreover, find a well-constructed story, rather than a poorly constructed one. With his death, Tennessee's Partner retains a commitment to Tennessee not only of loyalty-unto-death, but a loyalty after death as well. Of course, this interpretation does not intend to imply that all of Harte's stories contain such relationships. Yet at the same time we can see the need for further detailed study of Harte and even possibly of Western fiction, especially as critics such as C. L. Sonnichsen continue to say: "Western fiction has traditionally been clean. Where the coyotes howl and the wind blows free was never a place for promiscuous sex, kinky sex, or perversion." By visiting Sandy Bar and looking at Bret Harte differently, we perceive him not only as a teller of local color tales but also as a definer of the complex relationships that exist among human beings. (pp. 211-16)

Linda Burton, "For Better or Worse, Tennessee and His Partner: A New Approach to Bret Harte," in Arizona Quarterly, *Vol. 36, No. 3, Autumn, 1980, pp. 211-16.*

FURTHER READING

Barnett, Linda D. "Bret Harte: An Annotated Bibliography of Secondary Comment." *American Literary Realism* 5, Nos. 3-4 (Summer-Fall 1972): 189-484.

Comprehensive annotated bibliography of writings about Harte.

Conner, William F. "The Euchring of Tennessee: A Reexamination of Bret Harte's 'Tennessee's Partner'." *Studies in Short Fiction* 17, No. 2 (Spring 1980): 113-20.

Rejects the standard interpretation of "Tennessee's Partner" as a sentimental tale of loyalty, suggesting instead that the sentimentality is only there to mask the real theme of frontier gamesmanship.

Duckett, Margaret. "Plain Language from Bret Harte." *Nineteenth-Century Fiction* 11, No. 4 (March 1957): 241-60.

Focuses on Harte's efforts to combat racial prejudice through his sympathetic portrayal of Chinese characters.

Gardner, Joseph H. "Bret Harte and the Dickensian Mode in America." *The Canadian Review of American Studies* 2, No. 2 (Fall 1971): 89-101.

Examines criticism comparing Harte's fiction to the works of Charles Dickens.

Harte, Geoffrey Bret. "Bret Harte: A Centenary Portrait." *The Cornhill Magazine* 154 (August 1936): 168-80.

Harte's grandson reflects upon his grandfather's life and literary career.

Heywood, J. C. "An American Humorist." In his *How They Strike Me, These Authors,* pp. 197-223. Philadelphia: J. B. Lippincott and Co., 1877.

Discusses Harte's writing style and use of humor, including excerpts from several short stories.

Krause, Sydney J. "Bret Harte: The Grumbling Realist's Friend and Foe." In his *Mark Twain as Critic,* pp. 190-224. Baltimore: Johns Hopkins Press, 1967.

Details Mark Twain's marginal notes in his personal copies of Harte's work.

Kuhlmann, Susan. "To the West." In her *Knave, Fool, and Genius,* pp. 33-48. Chapel Hill: University of North Carolina Press, 1973.

Study of the confidence man as a fictional type, with references to Harte's characters John Oakhurst, Jack Hamlin, and Yuba Bill.

Loomis, C. Grant. "Bret Harte's Folklore." *Western Folklore* 15, No. 1 (January 1956): 19-22.

Examines the relationship between legends of the American West and Harte's short fiction.

Morrow, Patrick. "Bret Harte (1836-1902)." *American Literary Realism* 3, No. 2 (Spring 1970): 167-77.

Overview of critical approaches to Harte's work, citing numerous articles.

O'Connor, Richard. *Bret Harte: A Biography.* Boston: Little, Brown and Co., 1966, 331 p.

Stresses the paradoxical and contradictory nature of Harte's life.

Pemberton, T. Edgar. *The Life of Bret Harte.* New York: Dodd, Mead and Co., 1903, 358 p.

Biography written by Harte's friend and collaborator that quotes extensively from Harte's letters to family members, friends, and acquaintances as well as from some of Harte's poems and tributes to other writers.

Schroeder, Fred E. H. "The Development of the Super-Ego on the American Frontier." *Soundings* 57, No. 2 (Summer 1974): 189-205.

Schroeder argues that "The Luck of Roaring Camp" depicts a progression from primitive to civilized society, reflecting Frederick Jackson Turner's theory on the significance of the American frontier and Freud's characteristics of civilization.

Smith, C. Alphonso. In his *The American Short Story,* pp. 27-32. Boston: Ginn and Company, 1912.

Overview of Harte's writing style and method of character development.

Stewart, George R. *Bret Harte: Argonaut and Exile.* Port Washington, N.Y.: Kennikat Press, 1935, 385 p.

Considered the definitive account of Harte's life. Stewart avoids the romanticizing tendency of earlier biographers.

Woodbury, George Edward. "The West." In his *America in Literature,* pp. 150-82. New York: Harper & Brothers, 1903.

Discusses Harte's artistic temperament and factors influencing his creativity.

Henry James

1843-1916

(Full name: Henry James, Jr.) American novelist, short story writer, essayist, critic, biographer, autobiographer, travel writer, and dramatist.

Considered one of the greatest novelists in the English language, James was also an accomplished writer of short fiction. Shunning what he called "the baseness of the arbitrary stroke," James wrote carefully stylized stories, emphasizing introspection and moments of revelation over plot. His use of highly self-conscious narrators and his treatment of the ambiguous relationship between fiction and reality helped prepare the way for the interior monologue techniques of such later writers as James Joyce and Virginia Woolf. In addition, James brought to literature a number of original themes, of which the most notable is the American abroad, or the "international" story. Many of James's best-known works, including the novella *Daisy Miller: A Study,* hinge upon this encounter of the New World with the Old. In other short works, particularly "The Figure in the Carpet," "The Real Thing," and *The Aspern Papers,* James dealt with such social and psychological concerns as the artist's role in society, the need for both morality and the appreciation of art in life, and the benefits of a developed consciousness receptive to the thoughts and feelings of others.

James was born in New York City, the second son of well-to-do, liberal parents. His father was an occasional theorist on religion and philosophy and a devotee of philosopher Emanuel Swedenborg; his older brother, William, was also a philosopher and a forerunner of psychological study in America. As James's father believed his children should be "citizens of the world," William and Henry spent much of their youth in France, England, Switzerland, and Germany, as well as New England, where they studied with tutors and governesses. This constant oscillation between various cultures had a profound effect on James, becoming a major theme of his fiction and an attraction throughout his life. In 1860 James moved with his family to Newport, Rhode Island. A back injury prevented him from serving in the Civil War, a situation that informed his early war-related stories, which are told from a spectator's perspective. After briefly attending Harvard Law School in 1862, James devoted himself to the study of literature, particularly the works of Honoré de Balzac and Nathaniel Hawthorne. During this time he began publishing short fiction and criticism in the *Continental Monthly,* the *North American Review,* and the *Atlantic Monthly.* He also met and developed a lifelong friendship with William Dean Howells, then an assistant editor at the *Atlantic.* Howells later became editor of the *Atlantic* and James's literary agent. Together, James and Howells were the leading proponents of realism in nineteenth-century American literature.

During a trip to Europe in 1869, James became acquainted with such literary figures as George Eliot, John Ruskin, Dante Gabriel Rossetti, and Alfred Lord Tennyson. That year also marked the death of James's beloved cousin, Minny Temple. Minny's death came as a profound shock to James, and she is thought to have provided the model for many of his literary heroines, including Daisy Miller. In 1870 James returned to the United States, where he wrote his first novel and published his first significant international story, "A Passionate Pilgrim." In 1875, unhappy with the cultural climate in America, James relocated permanently in Europe, spending a year in France, where he associated with a circle of writers that included Gustave Flaubert, Emile Zola, Guy de Maupassant, and Ivan Turgenev. James found the work and manners of the French writers vulgar, though he developed a deep admiration for Turgenev, who, like James, emphasized in his stories the development of character rather than plot. Although James had received recognition for his early stories and novels, the publication of *Daisy Miller* in 1879 earned him his first, and perhaps greatest, popular success. Initially refused publication by James Foster Kirk, James's American publisher, who denounced it as "an outrage on American Girlhood" for its frank treatment of Daisy's moral naivete, the novella was first published in England

and later pirated in the United States, where it gained wide renown.

During his most productive period, from 1898 to 1904, James wrote several volumes of stories, which included such important works as *The Turn of the Screw, In the Cage,* and "The Beast in the Jungle." After 1904 James's health and creativity began to decline, although he still wrote prolifically, producing mainly autobiographies, essays, and criticism. In 1906 he began extensively revising his fiction and writing the prodigious critical prefaces for the New York edition of his collected works. With the outbreak of the First World War, James devoted much of his energy to serving the Allied cause, and when the United States did not immediately back the Allies, he assumed British citizenship in protest. James died in 1916 after receiving the British Order of Merit.

In his early works James drew from personal experience and observation to focus on perhaps his most celebrated theme: the conflict between European and American culture. "Madame de Mauves," for example, juxtaposes the antithetical attitudes of a puritanical American woman with those of her sexually promiscuous husband, a French duke who commits suicide when his wife refuses to forgive his infidelities. The inability of the couple to understand personal differences arising from their cultural backgrounds is characteristic of James's international stories. In James's best-known story in this vein, *Daisy Miller,* the title character is a young American woman oblivious to the social codes of the Old World. Daisy befriends Frederick Winterbourne, a Europeanized American who misinterprets her youthful naivete as cunning flirtation and realizes only after her death that he could not understand her manners—he had "lived in foreign parts too long." As with much of James's work, critical estimation of *Daisy Miller* has fluctuated. While early discussion focused on the accuracy of James's depiction of the generic "American girl," later critics have suggested that Winterbourne is the pivotal character of the story. According to these critics, by presenting Winterbourne's disapproval of Daisy's essentially innocent activities, James subtly admonished the narrow attitudes adopted by many Americans abroad.

Another hallmark of James's fiction is his use of a viewpoint character or unreliable narrator. With this technique the reader often witnesses events through the eyes of a character whose perception may be clouded by personal jealousy, misunderstanding, or self-deception. This perspective provides unique insight into the minds of James's characters, while obscuring the distinction between objective truth and fabrication. The unreliable narrator, who appears in many of James's stories, provides much of the ambiguity surrounding *The Turn of the Screw.* Rivaling *Daisy Miller* in popularity, *The Turn of the Screw* continues to be James's most disputed work. The story is narrated by a governess who is confronted by a pair of ghosts and suspects them of corrupting the two young children in her charge. In 1934 Edmund Wison challenged the traditional view of this novella as a conventional ghost story with the contention that *The Turn of the Screw* is instead a psychological case study of the narrator as an emotionally unstable young woman. Wilson's essay initiated a critical debate that has continued for over fifty years. Although most critics now agree that James intended his work to remain ambiguous, speculation concerning the objective truth of the events in *The Turn of the Screw* depends upon the reader's acceptance or rejection of the governess's reliability as a narrator.

The conflict of the artist in society was a recurring subject throughout James's career, providing the central theme of such works as *The Aspern Papers* and "The Real Thing." Many of these stories place the artist at a crossroads at which he must decide between complete devotion to his work or to his personal and social life. Although some critics deny that these works are autobiographical, many view them as documentation of James's personal struggle as an artist. Perhaps the most intriguing of James's artist stories is "The Figure in the Carpet," in which rival literary critics search for the embedded meaning—the "figure in the carpet"—that author Hugh Vereker suggests is present throughout his works. This story is often considered to be James's plea for serious critical attention. While several commentators have taken Vereker's challenge as James's own and have attempted to discover the ultimate meaning that pervades his fiction, others claim that James was mocking the pretentious artist who sends admirers on a quest for nonexistant significance.

James was often faulted by his contemporaries for writing dull, esoteric, and "snobbish" fiction. Referring to his stories in which "nothing happened," Mrs. Henry Adams, a personal acquaintance, remarked that her difficulty with James was not that he "bites off more than he can chaw, . . . but he chaws more than he bites off." Although interest in James's work waned in the early twentieth century, renewed critical attention, led by F. O. Matthiessen, F. W. Dupee, and Leon Edel, followed the 1943 centennial of James's birth. Clifton Fadiman explained that "here is an author who is subtler than he seems, that there is hardly any end to his complexity, that underneath the surface veins are riches still to be mined. He is a writer with whom one does not easily finish." The myriad interpretations arising from the ambiguity of James's work have sustained interest in his fiction. His originality, stylistic distinction, and psychologically complex characters have led many modern critics to regard him as a subtle craftsman who contributed greatly to the development of both the novel and short fiction genres.

(For further information on James's life and career, see *Twentieth-Century Literary Criticism,* Vols. 2, 11, 24, 40; *Dictionary of Literary Biography,* Vols. 12, 71, 74; *Concise Dictionary of American Literary Biography, 1865-1917;* and *Contemporary Authors,* Vols. 104, 132.)

PRINCIPAL WORKS

SHORT FICTION

A Passionate Pilgrim, and Other Tales 1875
Daisy Miller: A Study 1879
An International Episode 1879
The Madonna of the Future, and Other Tales 1879

The Diary of a Man of Fifty, and A Bundle of Letters 1880
The Siege of London. The Pension Beaurepas. and The Point of View 1883
Tales of Three Cities 1884
The Author of Beltraffio. Pandora. Georgina's Reasons. The Path of Duty. Four Meetings 1885
Stories Revived. 3 vols. 1885
The Aspern Papers. Louisa Pallant. The Modern Warning 1888
A London Life. The Patagonia. The Liar. Mrs. Temperley 1889
The Lesson of the Master. The Marriages. The Pupil. Brooksmith. The Solution. Sir Edmund Orme 1892
The Private Life. Lord Beaupré. The Visits 1893
The Wheel of Time. Collaboration. Owen Wingrave 1893
The Real Thing, and Other Tales 1893
Terminations: The Death of the Lion. The Coxon Fund. The Middle Years. The Altar of the Dead 1895
Embarrassments 1896
In the Cage 1898
The Two Magics: The Turn of the Screw. Covering End 1898
The Soft Side 1900
The Better Sort 1903
The Finer Grain 1910

OTHER MAJOR WORKS

Roderick Hudson (novel) 1876
The American (novel) 1877
The Europeans (novel) 1878
French Poets and Novelists (criticism) 1878
Watch and Ward (novel) 1878
Confidence (novel) 1880
The Portrait of a Lady (novel) 1881
Washington Square (novel) 1881
A Little Tour in France (travel essays) 1885
The Bostonians (novel) 1886
The Princess Casamassima (novel) 1886
The Tragic Muse (novel) 1890
Guy Domville (drama) 1895
The Spoils of Poynton (novel) 1897
What Maisie Knew (novel) 1897
The Awkward Age (novel) 1899
The Sacred Fount (novel) 1901
The Wings of a Dove (novel) 1902
The Ambassadors (novel) 1903
The Golden Bowl (novel) 1904
The American Scene (travel essays) 1907
A Small Boy and Others (autobiography) 1913
Notes of a Son and Brother (autobiography) 1914
The Letters of Henry James. 2 vols. (letters) 1920

William Dean Howells (essay date 1879)

[*Howells, James's editor and literary agent for much of the author's career, was the chief progenitor of American Realism and one of the most influential American literary critics of the late nineteenth century. Through realism, a theory central to his fiction and criticism, he aimed to disperse "the conventional acceptations by which men live on easy terms with themselves" so that they might "examine the grounds of their social and moral opinions." In the following essay, originally published in the* Atlantic Monthly *in 1879, Howells responds to critics who had dubbed* Daisy Miller *"an outrage on American Girlhood."*]

—To read the silly criticisms which have been printed, and the far sillier ones which are every day uttered in regard to Mr. James's ***Daisy Miller*** would almost convince us that we are as provincial as ever in our sensitiveness to foreign opinion. It is actually regarded as a species of unpardonable incivism for Mr. James, because he lives in London, to describe an under-bred American family traveling in Europe. The fact that he has done so with a touch of marvelous delicacy and truth, that he has produced not so much a picture as a photograph, is held by many to be an aggravating circumstance. Only the most shiveringly sensitive of our shoddy population are bold enough to deny the truth of this wonderful little sketch. To those best acquainted with Mr. James's manner (and I believe I have read every word he has printed) ***Daisy Miller*** was positively startling in its straightforward simplicity and what I can only call *authenticity.* It could not have been written—I am almost ready to say it cannot be appreciated—except by one who has lived so long abroad as to be able to look at his own people with the eyes of a foreigner. All poor Daisy's crimes are purely conventional. She is innocent and good at heart, susceptible of praise and blame; she does not wish even to surprise, much less outrage, the stiffest of her censors. In short, the things she does with such dire effect at Vevay and at Rome would never for an instant be remarked or criticised in Schenectady. They would provoke no comment in Buffalo or Cleveland; they would be a matter of course in Richmond and Louisville. One of the most successful touches in the story is that where Daisy, astonished at being cut by American ladies, honestly avows her disbelief in their disapproval. "I should not think you would let them be so unkind!" she cries to Winterbourne, conscious of her innocence, and bewildered at the cruelty of a sophisticated world. Yet with such exquisite art is this study managed that the innocence and loveliness of Miss Miller are hardly admitted as extenuating circumstances in her reprehensible course of conduct. She is represented, by a chronicler who loves and admires her, as bringing ruin upon herself and a certain degree of discredit upon her countrywomen, through eccentricities of behavior for which she cannot justly be held responsible. Her conduct is without blemish, according to the rural American standard, and she knows no other. It is the merest ignorance or affectation, on the part of the anglicized Americans of Boston or New York, to deny this. A few dozens, perhaps a few hundreds, of families in America have accepted the European theory of the necessity of surveillance for young ladies, but it is idle to say it has ever been accepted by the country at large. In every city of the nation young girls of good family, good breeding, and perfect innocence of heart and mind, receive their male acquaintances *en tête-à-tête,* and go to parties and concerts with them, unchaperoned. Of course, I do not mean that Daisy Miller belongs to that category; her astonishing mother at once designates her as pertaining to one distinctly inferior. Who has not met them abroad? From the first word uttered by Miss Daisy to her rampant young brother in the garden at Vevay, "Well, I guess you'd better be quiet," you recognize her, and recall her under a dozen different names and forms. She went to dine with you one day at Sceaux, and climbed, with the fearless innocence of a bird, into the great chestnut-tree. She challenged you to take her to Schönbrunn, and amazed your Austrian acquaintances whom you met there, and who knew you were not married. At Naples, one evening—*Eheu, fugaces labuntur anni;* it is not worth while to continue the enumeration. It makes you feel melancholy to think she is doing the same acts of innocent recklessness with men as young and as happy, and what the French call as unenterprising, as you were once.

As to the usefulness of this little book, it seems to me as indubitable as its literary excellence. It is too long a question to discuss in this place, whether the freedom of American girls at home is beneficial or sinister in its results. But there is no question whatever as to the effect of their ignorance or defiance of conventionalities abroad. An innocent flirtation with a Frenchman or Italian tarnishes a reputation forever. All the waters of the Mediterranean cannot wash clean the name of a young lady who makes a rendezvous and takes a walk with a fascinating chance acquaintance. We need only refer to the darker miseries which often result from these reckless intimacies. A charming young girl, traveling with a simple-minded mother, a few years ago, in a European capital, married a branded convict who had introduced himself to them, calling himself, of course, a count. In short, an American girl, like Daisy Miller, accompanied by a woman like Daisy's mother, brought up in the simplicity of provincial life in the United States, has no more chance of going through Europe unscathed in her feelings and her character than an idiot millionaire has of amusing himself economically in Wall Street. This lesson is taught in Mr. James's story,—and never was necessary medicine administered in a form more delightful and unobtrusive.

The intimacy with the courier is a fact of daily observation on the Continent. A gentleman of my acquaintance, inquiring the other day for a courier he had employed some years before, was told that he was spoiled for any reasonable service by having been so much with American families, and that one family, after their tour in Europe was ended, had taken him home to South Boston as their guest, and had given a party for him! (pp. 88-91)

William Dean Howells, "Defense of Daisy Miller," in Discovery of a Genius: William Dean Howells and Henry James, *edited by Albert Mordell, Twayne Publishers, 1961, pp. 88-91.*

Joseph Warren Beach (essay date 1918)

[*Beach was an American critic and educator who specialized in American literature and English literature of the Romantic and Victorian eras. His* The Method of Henry James, *originally published in 1918, is one of the earliest book-length critiques of James's narrative technique. In the excerpt below from that work, Beach examines what he perceives to be the overall authorial scheme in James's fiction.*]

There is one group among the shorter stories of James that has a peculiar interest for anyone seeking hints and revelations of the personal experience, the temper and ideals of their author. It comprises nearly a dozen tales dealing with writers of fiction. It is of course a hazardous business making inferences in regard to James from any of these stories. The information we may suppose ourselves to derive from them is neither so substantial, so technical, nor so authoritative as what he offers us in the Prefaces. But it is not the less precious on that account. If, with tact and discretion, we do learn something from these stories about his attitude towards his art, it will be something of an intimacy nowhere else to be felt. It will be something, say, which modesty and pride forbade him to let us have straight from himself; but something he might be willing for us to learn by sympathetic inference, laying upon us the whole responsibility of assertion.

Most fascinating of all these tales, and the one which constitutes the greatest temptation for the interpreter of James, is **"The Figure in the Carpet."** For here he shows us a novelist of rare distinction flinging down to the eager critic the challenge of his secret. The critic is a clever fellow, a "demon of subtlety"; but he has failed, like everyone else, to discover the "little point" the novelist most wishes to make. In fact he has to be informed that there is any such little point to be discovered, that there is a "particular thing" the novelist has "written his books most *for.*" "Isn't there for every writer," asks Hugh Vereker, in their momentous midnight talk, "isn't there a particular thing of that sort, the thing that most makes him apply himself, the thing without the effort to achieve which he wouldn't write at all, the very passion of his passion, the part of the business in which, for him, the flame of art burns most intensely? Well, it's *that!*" And on a demand for more particularity he adds,

> There's an idea in my work without which I wouldn't have given a straw for the whole job. It's the finest fullest intention of the lot, and the application of it has been, I think, a triumph of patience, of ingenuity. . . . It stretches, this little trick of mine, from book to book, and everything else, comparatively, plays over the surface of it. The order, the form, the texture of my books will perhaps some day constitute for the initiated a complete representation of it. So it's naturally the thing for the critic to look for. It strikes me . . . even as the thing for the critic to find.

To the other's query, "You call it a little trick?" the novelist replies, "That's only my little modesty. It's really an exquisite scheme." It is later that the critic hits on the figure of speech by which this "little trick" is best to be described. "It was something, I guessed, in the primal plan; something like a complex figure in a Persian carpet. He [Vereker] highly approved of this image when I used it, and he used another himself. 'It's the very string,' he said, 'that my pearls are strung on.' "

"It's naturally the thing for the critic to look for," said Hugh Vereker of his "little trick." "It strikes me even as the thing for the critic to find." What head is cool enough to resist the suggestion that James had here in mind his own well-nigh desperate case? Was there not some "intention" of his own which had been regularly overlooked by reviewers in their hasty mention of his work? It was not that he *wished* to be difficult and esoteric. It was not so at least with Hugh Vereker.

> If my great affair's a secret, that's only because it's a secret in spite of itself—the amazing event has made it one. I not only never took the smallest precaution to keep it so, but never dreamed of any such accident. If I had I shouldn't in advance have had the heart to go on. As it was, I only became aware little by little, and meanwhile I had done my work.

But now his secret had become for him the great amusement of life. " 'I live almost to see if it will ever be detected.' He looked at me for a jesting challenge; something far within his eyes seemed to peep out. 'But I needn't worry—it won't!' " One cannot but wonder if Henry James, like Hugh Vereker, did pass away without ever having his secret put adequately into words.

We need not take this tale too gravely as a revelation of the artistic soul of Henry James. We need not set ourselves, with confident assumption, to solve the hinted riddle of his work. But we should be missing a rare occasion if we did not take up this metaphor and let it guide us in our summary of his art. Perhaps we should say there is not one, there are many figures in the carpet,—as many figures as there are fond, discerning readers. For me the figure in the carpet is that which gives life to the whole work. It must be implied in all that we have found to be true of it; it must be the inner meaning and the motive of all that is included in his method. This too is suggested by what Hugh Vereker says of his "secret." It is not a "kind of esoteric message": at least it cannot be adequately described "in cheap journalese." He will not limit it by saying it is "something in the style or something in the thought, an element of form or an element of feeling." "Well," says Hugh Vereker, "you've got a heart in your body. Is that an element of form or an element of feeling? What I contend that nobody has ever mentioned in my work is the organ of life."

"Esoteric message" is "cheap journalese." The same red lantern warns off from any statement of James's "philosophy of life." It may be James has no philosophy of life. But he has something which will serve the purpose as well. He has a scale of values, a preference in human experience, an absorbing preoccupation. From first to last he is preoccupied not with men's lives but with the quality of their experience; not with the pattern but with the texture of life. Most novelists seem by comparison all taken up with the pattern. In Fielding and Scott, in Balzac and Zola, in Thackeray and Tolstoi, it is the adventures of the characters that we are bidden to follow. The contrast is the more remarkable when it is the English contemporaries of James that are brought into comparison. In Meredith and George Eliot, a matter of prime importance is what the characters bring to pass in a practical way. These authors may indeed reconcile themselves to the littleness of accomplishment on the part of their heroes; but it is accomplishment of some sort on which heroes and authors alike are determined. Meredith and George Eliot had both a philosophy of life. They were both strongly imbued with perfectionist and utilitarian ideals. They staked their all on the progress and improvement of humanity. A better world was the cry they had taken up from the lips of Rousseau and Voltaire, Bentham and Mill. The fact is deeply hidden under romance and sentiment of the later day; but George Eliot and Meredith are still in the practical and materialist tradition, of, say, Benjamin Franklin. It is another tradition, as we have seen, to which James owes allegiance; an idealist tradition deriving ultimately from romantic Germany and reaching its finest expression in Wordsworth, Emerson and Hawthorne. Writing in the time of Gladstone and Bernard Shaw, James seems hardly to have given a thought to the political destinies of men or to the practical consequences and bearings of personal conduct. It is not in the relative terms of cause and effect that he considers human action. He is content, like some visionary Platonist, to refer each item of conduct to an absolute standard of the good and the beautiful. This is one reason why he is so strange a figure in our world all bent on getting results. We have, mostly, no such absolute standards. We know nothing of any Ideas in the mind of God.

In the stories of other writers, men and women are shown us obsessed with desires and ambitions and opposed by material difficulties. And our interest is absorbed in the process by which they overcome their difficulties and realize their desires. The characters of James too have ambitions and desires. But that is not the thing that strikes us most about them. What strikes us most about them is their capacity for renunciation—for giving up any particular gratification in favor of some fine ideal of conduct with which it proves incompatible. Common men and women have a more desperate grip on material values. There are things they insist on having. It may be money, or professional success, or social position, or some person indispensable to their happiness. And there is for them no immaterial substitute for these substantial goods. There is nothing in thought or feeling that can reconcile the lover to the loss of his mistress, nothing he will prefer to the woman he has set his heart upon. But the characters of James are not common men and women; and for the finest of them there is always something of more account than the substance of their experience,—namely, its quality. They may, like other mortals, long for the realization of some particular desire; but they long still more fervently for the supreme comfort of being right with themselves. We know what a capacity for happiness was Isabel Archer's; but we know that happiness was far from being the thing she most sought, and we know with what deliberation she chose to embrace her fate, when she was once made aware of "what most people know and suffer." We are gratified and appalled by the meekness with which these people accept their dole of misery and deprivation,—this Mitchy and Nanda, this Christopher Newman and Fleda Vetch. It seems that we must not use words of unhappy connotation to describe such exalted fervency of renunciation. It is only because we ourselves require the objective realization of our desires that we so misrepresent them. They seem in point of fact to take some higher ground inaccessible to our feet. They seem to say: Lo, we have in not having. We were denied the shadow, but we have always possessed the real substance. One fantastic creature even ventures to contend that, in the realm of art, realization—concrete achievement—is inimical to the true life of the soul. Gabriel Nash is actually afraid Nick Dormer will prove a successful painter and so spoil the beauty of his testimony to the artistic faith. He prefers to "work in life" himself. Nick is so practical: he wishes Gabriel "had more to show" for his "little system." "Oh," says Gabriel, "having something to show's such a poor business. It's a kind of confession of failure." One does not need to measure one's acts by their consequences. "One is one's self a fine consequence." This is the very inner citadel of intransigent idealism. On this system we may interpret the story of Fleda Vetch as the triumph of Fleda. Let her cover her face in sorrow as she will. Her vulgar rival may have her lover, and the flames may have devoured the Spoils. But somehow we are given to understand that, of all the people in her world, she remains the wealthiest. She remains in substantial possession of beauty and of love.

What counts in the world of James is not the facts themselves,—what one does or what happens to one, but the interpretation put upon the facts. James has a great fondness, especially in his tales, for subjects very slight and off the common track of observation. There is little in the circumstances themselves to attract attention, and the people are, on the surface, entirely wanting in romantic interest. The challenge is all the greater to an author who prides himself on seeing below the surface of human nature, who is like a naturalist delighted to bring home flowers of rare and neglected beauty from spots unnoted by vulgar eyes. Such a flower was the homely American kinswoman of Lady Beldonald, who was intended by that handsome woman to be her foil, her dull and unremarked companion, and who was declared by the portrait-painter to be as distinguished and "beautiful" as a Holbein. It is himself that James describes in the words of the painter. "It's not my fault," he says, "if I am so put together as often to find more life in situations obscure and subject to interpretation than in the gross rattle of the foreground." This note is forever recurring both in the stories themselves and in the author's comment on them. We hear it in Miriam Rooth's naïve explanation to the great French actress that "there were two kinds of scenes and speeches: those which acted themselves, of which the treatment was plain, the only way, so that you had just to take it; and those open to interpretation, with which you had to fight every step, rendering, arranging, doing the thing according to your idea." The note is sounded more delicately and modestly in the case of Mrs. Blessingbourne and her romantic and at the same time Platonic feeling for Colonel Voyt. That gentleman, who is in full enjoyment of the love of another woman, is inclined to regard such merely Platonic love as but thin material for romance. But in his discussion of the matter with his own mistress, he agrees that the pathetic lady's very *consciousness "was,* in the last analysis, a kind of shy romance. Not a romance like their own, a thing to make the fortune of any author up to the mark. . . . but a small scared starved subjective satisfaction that would do her no harm and nobody else any good." We may be sure it was not the creator of Fleda Vetch and Milly Theale who is applying to Mrs. Blessingbourne's experience this supercilious description. As he says himself in the preface, "The thing is, all beautifully, a matter of interpretation and of the particular conditions; without a view of which latter some of the most prodigious adventures, as one has often had occasion to say, may vulgarly show for nothing."

The same point is made still more significantly in reference to the "adventures" of Isabel Archer, which he seems to think are but mild ones by the ordinary romantic measure. "Without her sense of them, her sense *for* them, as one may say, they are next to nothing at all; but isn't the beauty and the difficulty just in showing their mystic conversion by that sense, conversion into the stuff of drama or, even more delightful word still, of 'story'?" He vouchsafes two "very good instances of this effect of conversion." One of them is

> . . . in the long statement, just beyond the middle of the book, of my young woman's extraordinary meditative vigil on the occasion that was to become for her such a landmark. Reduced to its essence, it is but the vigil of searching criticism; but it throws the action further forward than twenty "incidents" might have done. It was designed to have all the vivacity of incident and all the economy of picture. She sits up, by her dying fire, far into the night, under the spell of recognitions on which she finds the last sharpness suddenly wait. It is a representation simply of her motionlessly *seeing,* and an attempt withal to make the mere still lucidity of her act as "interesting" as the surprise of a caravan or the identification of a pirate. It represents, for that matter, one of the identifications dear to the novelist, and even indispensable to him; but it all goes on without her being approaced by another person and without her leaving her chair. It is obviously the best thing in the book, but it is only a supreme illustration of the general plan.

If Mr. James ever did trace out for us the Figure in the Carpet, it was in this passage, in which, concluding his review of the first book which really shows up the figure with any distinctness, he lets us know what is "obviously" the best thing in the book, and offers it to us as "only a supreme illustration of the general plan." We are reminded of the terms in which Hugh Vereker adumbrates for his young friend the "exquisite scheme," the "primal plan," not merely of his latest work, but of the whole series of his novels. We are further reminded of Hugh Vereker's attitude towards his public by Mr. James's apologetic and somewhat exasperated remark—it is in connection with his other instance of "the rare chemistry" of the character's sense for her adventures—"It is dreadful to have too much, for any artistic demonstration, to dot one's i's and insist on one's intentions, and I am not eager to do it now."

But however reluctant, he felt obliged on this one occasion to insist on his intentions. "The question here was that of producing the maximum of intensity with the minimum of strain. The interest was to be raised to its pitch and yet the elements to be kept in their key; so that, should the whole thing duly impress, I might show what an 'exciting' inward life may do for the person leading it even while it remains perfectly normal."

The Portrait of a Lady was the first book in which James plainly showed his "little trick," which he went on showing more and more plainly from that time out. His little trick was simply not to tell the "story" at all as the story is told by the Scotts and the Maupassants, but to give us instead the subjective accompaniment of the story. His "exquisite scheme" was to confine himself as nearly as possible to the "inward life" of his characters, and yet to make it as "exciting" for his readers as it was for the author, as exciting—were that possible—as it was for the characters themselves.

Such an interpretation of his "scheme" would conform very well, at any rate, to Hugh Vereker's comprehensive description of his own: "It's the finest fullest intention of the lot, and the application of it has been, I think, a triumph of patience, of ingenuity. . . . It stretches, this little trick of mine, from book to book, and everything else, comparatively, plays over the surface of it. The order, the form, the texture of my books will perhaps some day constitute for the initiated a complete representation of it." I don't know how the scheme I have indicated would be represented in the *order* of the books of James. But it might serve as an explanation of their form and texture, and of all the peculiarities of his method as we have made them out. Naturally a book devoted to the inward life of a group of people would be nothing without its "idea." But the strict limitation of the action to the consciousness of these people would insure against undue abstractness in the idea, would transform idea into "picture." The succession of incidents in an ordinary story would in such a narrative be represented by the process of "revelation" of the picture. Suspense would have reference not to what might happen but to the subjective reverberation of what happens. In a record of inward life it is obvious how important must be the choice and maintenance of a point of view. It is almost absolutely essential that the center of interest should be a person of penetrating intelligence. It is plain how this subjective bias would affect the nature of the dialogue, making it less picturesque, more fine-drawn and close-knit, being the record of mental exploration carried on by several persons in concert. This is true of the dialogue even in those more dramatic situations involving tense oppositions of will, and gives its peculiar character to the "drama" of James. The exclusive interest in mental exploration explains to a large extent the wholesale "eliminations," which in turn relate themselves to the "neutral tone" of James's writing. And the almost complete abstraction from the world of common accident and circumstance, the confinement of attention to the realm of spiritual reactions, gives to the work of James its insubstantial, its romantic, even fantastic, character, which makes it the scorn of the "general," the despair of the conscientious, and the supreme entertainment of those who like it.

Above all does the exclusive concern with the inward life of his people explain the dominance of ethical considerations and at the same time perhaps the peculiar character of those involved. For the characters of James the faculty of supreme importance is the intelligence, or insight, the faculty of perceiving "values" beyond those utilities upon which everyone agrees. Of such immaterial values there are two general groups, both of great importance and of unfailing concern to the people of James. The first group includes social and esthetic values, which I class together because of their close association in the characters' minds, and because of their being on a common level as contrasted with the other group of values,—the spiritual.

Minor classifications we must here ignore. We must ignore those contrasts in social ideals which play so large a part in the earlier stories of James, but which in the long run prove to be of secondary importance. Social ideals may appear on the surface to be relative; but at bottom they show themselves, for this conservative philosopher, as absolute as any Platonic Ideas. Tact and discernment, fairness and modesty, the preference of the fine to the vulgar, the instinct for the nice and the proper, are after all traits in which practically all his favored characters agree, whether they be of Albany or London, Paris or "Woollett," "Flickerbridge" or Rome. . . . So that, on the whole, we should be justified in employing the hyphenated term of social-esthetic to distinguish that type of intelligence which is shared by practically all the important characters of James. Or we might serve our purpose with the simpler, and equally comprehensive, term, good taste.

There is at least one important character who is lacking in good taste so understood. I mean Daisy Miller, whose peculiarity lies in her possession of a rare spiritual beauty quite unaccompanied by social tact and artistic discernment. But Mr. James has expressed doubts himself as to the reality of this charming poetic creation; and the one romantic exception will but make more notable the almost universal prevalence of good taste as a qualification for admittance into the gallery of Henry James. This is the first qualification,—that is, the one first to be considered: one must successfully stand this test before being advanced to the higher one reserved for heroes and heroines. It is good taste which unites in one great shining company the otherwise so various Gilbert Osmond and Isabel Archer, Mrs. Brookenham and Nanda, Kate Croy and Milly Theale, Chad Newsome and Lambert Strether.

The *ideal* of James is clearly a combination, or rather a *fusion,* of good taste with spiritual discernment, and perhaps the most complete, if not the most dramatic, instance of this fusion is the last named, Lambert Strether. For him there seems to be no such distinction between esthetic and ethical as perplexes most of us mortals. Madame de Vionnet has a claim upon Chad, he thinks, because she has worked upon him so fine a transformation; and this character of Chad's, of her creation, is all described in terms of esthetic and social connotation. No doubt the idea of an *obligation* is a moral idea at bottom; but this obligation is in direct opposition to the legal and religious code, and never were greater pains taken to translate moral concept into the language of simple good taste. In the mind of Lambert Strether there seems to be no clear dividing line between the categories of beauty and goodness.

Somewhat the same condition prevails in the psychology of *The Awkward Age;* and the tendency is always in this direction in the stories of James. But in many cases the distinction is much sharper between good taste and the moral sense. And whenever the distinction appears, the moral sense is clearly preferred as the higher and rarer, and as something added to the other or built upon it. (pp. 145-58)

So it is that Milly Theale is preferred to the superb and socially incomparable Kate Croy; that Mitchy and Nanda are preferred to the infinitely clever and subtle mother of Nanda; that Isabel Archer is preferred to the charming and accomplished Madame Merle and to Osmond, who had both so long a start of her in social and esthetic cultivation. In each case the one preferred has, in addition to the common good taste, the wit to distinguish moral beauty.

It is all, as we have seen, a matter of insight. The less favored characters, the false and the shady people, are morally color-blind. It is always the same story throughout the whole series of novels. It is so in *Roderick Hudson* at the beginning and in *The Golden Bowl* at the end. In *The Golden Bowl,* it is a question of whether the Prince Amerigo has enough discernment to perceive the superiority of his wife to his accomplished mistress. The "style" of Charlotte has indeed been "great" in the closing scenes of the drama, but great in a way far below the spiritual fineness of Maggie. Maggie is "great" enough to perceive the greatness of Charlotte. "Isn't she too splendid?" she asks her husband. "That's our help, you see." . . . "See?" says Amerigo, triumphantly meeting his final test, "I see nothing but *you.*" Roderick Hudson is an artist of genius, with endowments infinitely superior to those of his friend and benefactor in every respect except this of spiritual discernment. It is only at the end of his life that he has a glimpse of what he has missed. It is in his last conversation with Rowland, in which the latter has finally told him of his own love for Mary. Roderick comes to see how "hideous" is the appearance he has made. "Do you really care," Rowland is prompted to ask, "for what you may have appeared?" "Certainly. I've been damnably stupid. Isn't an artist supposed to be a man of fine perceptions? I haven't, as it turns out, had *one.*"

The stories of James are a continuous record of such "fine perceptions" had or missed. The stuff is as airy as gossamer: not at all

> Things done, that took the eye and had the price.

Hence the notorious difficulty and inaccessibility of James. And hence the romantic exhilaration of his work for so many denizens of a world in which the realization of ideals is so rare and hard of accomplishment. May this be the secret of his great following among women? His greatest appeal is perhaps to those whose lives have yielded the minimum of realization, to those who have the least control over the gross materials of life. (pp. 159-61)

Joseph Warren Beach, in his The Method of Henry James, *Albert Saifer, 1954, 289 p.*

Virginia Woolf (essay date 1921)

[An English novelist, essayist, and critic, Woolf was one of the most prominent literary figures of the twentieth century, forming part of the famous literary coterie the "Bloomsbury Group." Her critical essays, which cover almost the entire range of English literature, contain some of her finest prose and are widely praised for their insight. Woolf's father, Leslie Stephen, was a friend of James and the first publisher of Daisy Miller. *In the essay below, originally published in the* Times Literary Supplement *in 1921, Woolf reviews James's ghost stories.]*

It is plain that Henry James was a good deal attracted by the ghost story, or, to speak more accurately, by the story of the supernatural. He wrote at least eight of them, and if we wish to see what led him to do so, and what opinion he had of his success, nothing is simpler than to read his own account in the preface to the volume containing **"The Altar of the Dead."** Yet perhaps we shall keep our own view more distinct if we neglect the preface. As the years go by certain qualities appear, and others disappear. We shall only muddle our own estimate if we try, dutifully, to make it square with the verdict which the author at the time passed on his own work. For example, what did Henry James say of **"The Great Good Place"**?

> There remains **"The Great Good Place"** (1900)—to the spirit of which, however, it strikes me, any gloss or comment would be a tactless challenge. It embodies a calculated effect, and to plunge into it, I find, even for a beguiled glance—a course I indeed recommend—is to have left all else outside.

And to us, in 1921, **"The Great Good Place"** is a failure. It is another example of the fact that when a writer is completely and even ecstatically conscious of success he has, as likely as not, written his worst. We ought, we feel, to be inside, and we remain coldly outside. Something has failed to work, and we are inclined to accuse the supernatural. The challenge may be tactless, but challenge it we must.

That **"The Great Good Place"** begins admirably, no one will deny. Without the waste of a word we find ourselves at once in the heart of a situation. The harassed celebrity, George Dane, is surrounded by unopened letters and unread books; telegrams arrive; invitations accumulate; and the things of value lie hopelessly buried beneath the litter. Meanwhile, Brown the manservant announces that a strange young man has arrived to breakfast. Dane touches the young man's hand, and, at this culminating point of annoyance, lapses into a trance or wakes up in another world. He finds himself in a celestial rest cure establishment. Far bells toll; flowers are fragrant; and after a time the inner life revives. But directly the change is accomplished we are aware that something is wrong with the story. The movement flags; the emotion is monotonous. The enchanter waves his wand and the cows go on grazing. All the characteristic phrases are there in waiting—the silver bowls, the melted hours—but there is no work for them to do. The story dwindles to a sweet soliloquy. Dane and the Brothers become angelic allegorical figures pacing a world that is like ours but smoother and emptier. As if he felt the need of something hard and objective the author invokes the name of the city of Bradford; but it is vain. **"The Great Good Place"** is an example of the sentimental use of the supernatural and for that reason no doubt Henry James would be likely to feel that he had been more than usually intimate and expressive.

The other stories will presently prove that the supernatural offers great prizes as well as great risks; but let us for a moment dwell upon the risks. The first is undoubtedly that it removes the shocks and buffetings of experience. In the breakfast room with Brown and the telegram Henry James was forced to keep moving by the pressure of reality; the door must open; the hour must strike. Directly he sank through the solid ground he gained possession of a world which he could fashion to his liking. In the dream world the door need not open; the clock need not strike; beauty is to be had for the asking. But beauty is the most perverse of spirits; it seems as if she must pass through ugliness or lie down with disorder before she can rise in her own person. The ready-made beauty of the dream world produces only an anemic and conventionalized version of the world we know. And Henry James was much too fond of the world we know to create one that we do not know. The visionary imagination was by no means his. His genius was dramatic, not lyric. Even his characters wilt in the thin atmosphere he provides for them, and we are presented with a Brother when we would much rather grasp the substantial person of Brown.

We have been piling the risks, rather unfairly, upon one story in particular. The truth is perhaps that we have become fundamentally skeptical. Mrs. Radcliffe amused our ancestors because they were our ancestors; because they lived with very few books, an occasional post, a newspaper superannuated before it reached them, in the depths of the country or in a town which resembled the more modest of our villages, with long hours to spend sitting over the fire drinking wine by the light of half a dozen candles. Nowadays we breakfast upon a richer feast of horror than served them for a twelvemonth. We are tired of violence; we suspect mystery. Surely, we might say to a writer set upon the supernatural, there are facts enough in the world to go round; surely it is safer to stay in the breakfast room with Brown. Moreover, we are impervious to fear. Your ghosts will only make us laugh, and if you try to express some tender and intimate vision of a world stripped of its hide we shall be forced (and there is nothing more uncomfortable) to look the other way. But writers, if they are worth their salt, never take advice. They always run risks. To admit that the supernatural was used for the last time by Mrs. Radcliffe and that modern nerves are immune from the wonder and terror which ghosts have always inspired would be to throw up the sponge too easily. If the old methods are obsolete, it is the business of a writer to discover new ones. The public can feel again what it has once felt—there can be no doubt about that; only from time to time the point of attack must be changed.

How consciously Henry James set himself to look for the weak place in our armor of insensibility it is not necessary to decide. Let us turn to another story, **"The Friends of the Friends,"** and judge whether he succeeded. This is the story of a man and woman who have been trying for years to meet but only accomplish their meeting on the night of the woman's death. After her death the meetings are continued, and when this is divined by the woman he is engaged to marry she refuses to go on with the marriage. The relationship is altered. Another person, she says, has come between them. "You see her—you see her; you see her every night!" It is what we have come to call a typically Henry James situation. It is the same theme that was treated with enormous elaboration in *The Wings of the Dove.* Only there, when Milly has come between Kate and Densher and altered their relationship forever she has ceased to exist; here the anonymous lady goes on with her work after death. And yet—does it make very much difference? Henry James has only to take the smallest of steps and he is over the border. His characters with their extreme fineness of perception are already half-way out of the body. There is nothing violent in their release. They seem rather to have achieved at last what they have long been attempting—communication without obstacle. But Henry James, after all, kept his ghosts for his ghost stories. Obstacles are essential to *The Wings of the Dove.* When he removed them by supernatural means as he did in **"The Friends of the Friends"** he did so in order to produce a particular effect. The story is very short; there is no time to elaborate the relationship; but the point can be pressed home by a shock. The supernatural is brought in to provide that shock. It is the queerest of shocks—tranquil, beautiful, like the closing of chords in harmony; and yet, somehow obscene. The living and the dead by virtue of their superior sensibility have reached across the gulf; that is beautiful. The live man and the dead woman have met alone at night. They have their relationship. The spiritual and the carnal meeting together produce a strange emotion—not exactly fear, nor yet excitement. It is a feeling that we do not immediately recognize. There is a weak spot in our armor somewhere. Perhaps Henry James will penetrate by methods such as these.

Next, however, we turn to **"Owen Wingrave,"** and the enticing game of pinning your author to the board by detecting once more traces of his fineness, his subtlety, whatever his prevailing characteristics may be, is rudely interrupted. Pinioned, tied down, to all appearance lifeless, up he jumps and walks away. Somehow one has forgotten to account for the genius, for the driving power which is so incalculable and, so essential. With Henry James in particular we tend, in wonder at his prodigious dexterity, to forget that he had a crude and simple passion for telling stories. The preface to Owen Wingrave throws light upon that fact, and incidentally suggests why it is that Owen Wingrave as a ghost story misses its mark. One summer's afternoon, many years ago, he tells us, he sat on a penny chair under a great tree in Kensington Gardens. A slim young man sat down upon another chair near by and began to read a book.

> Did the young man then, on the spot, just *become* Owen Wingrave, establishing by the mere magic of type the situation, creating at a stroke all the implications and filling out all the picture? . . . my poor point is only that at the beginning of my session in the penny chair the seedless fable hadn't a claim to make or an excuse to give, and that, the very next thing, the pennyworth still partly unconsumed, it was fairly bristling with pretexts. "Dramatise it, drama-

> tise it!" would seem to have rung with sudden intensity in my ears.

So the theory of a conscious artist taking out his little grain of matter and working it into the finished fabric is another of our critical fables. The truth appears to be that he sat on a chair, saw a young man, and fell asleep. At any rate, once the group, the man, or perhaps only the sky and the trees become significant, the rest is there inevitably. Given Owen Wingrave, then Spencer Coyle, Mrs. Coyle, Kate Julian, the old house, the season, the atmosphere must be in existence. Owen Wingrave implies all that. The artist has simply to see that the relations between these places and people are the right ones. When we say that Henry James had a passion for storytelling we mean that when his significant moment came to him the accessories were ready to flock in.

In this instance they flocked in almost too readily. There they are on the spot with all the stir and importance that belong to living people. Miss Wingrave seated in her Baker-street lodging with "a fat catalogue of the Army and Navy Stores, which reposed on a vast desolate table-cover of false blue"; Mrs. Coyle, "a fair fresh slow woman," who admitted and indeed gloried in the fact that she was in love with her husband's pupils, "which shows that the subject between them was treated in a liberal spirit"; Spencer Coyle himself, and the boy Lechmere—all bear of course upon the question of Owen's temperament and situation, and yet they bear on so many other things besides. We seem to be settling in for a long absorbing narrative; and then, rudely, incongruously, a shriek rings out; poor Owen is found stretched on the threshold of the haunted room; the supernatural has cut the book in two. It is violent; it is sensational; but if Henry James himself were to ask us, "Now, have I frightened you?" we should be forced to reply, "Not a bit." The catastrophe has not the right relations to what has gone before. The vision in Kensington Gardens did not, perhaps, embrace the whole. Out of sheer bounty the author has given us a scene rich in possibilities—a young man whose problem (he detests war and is condemned to be a soldier) has a deep psychological interest; a girl whose subtlety and oddity are purposely defined as if in readiness for future use. Yet what use is made of them? Kate Julian has merely to dare a young man to sleep in a haunted room; a plump Miss from a parsonage would have done as well. What use is made of the supernatural? Poor Owen Wingrave is knocked on the head by the ghost of an ancestor; a stable bucket in a dark passage would have done it better.

The stories in which Henry James uses the supernatural effectively are, then, those where some quality in a character or in a situation can only be given its fullest meaning by being cut free from facts. Its progress in the unseen world must be closely related to what goes on in this. We must be made to feel that the apparition fits the crisis of passion or of conscience which sent it forth so exactly that the ghost story, besides its virtues as a ghost story, has the additional charm of being also symbolical. Thus the ghost of Sir Edmund Orme appears to the lady who jilted him long ago whenever her daughter shows signs of becoming engaged. The apparition is the result of her guilty conscience, but it is more than that. It is the guardian of the rights of lovers. It fits what has gone before; it completes. The use of the supernatural draws out a harmony which would otherwise be inaudible. We hear the first note close at hand, and then, a moment after, the second chimes far away.

Henry James's ghosts have nothing in common with the violent old ghosts—the blood-stained sea captains, the white horses, the headless ladies of dark lanes and windy commons. They have their origin within us. They are present whenever the significant overflows our powers of expressing it; whenever the ordinary appears ringed by the strange. The baffling things that are left over, the frightening ones that persist—these are the emotions that he takes, embodies, makes consoling and companionable. But how can we be afraid? As the gentleman says when he has seen the ghost of Sir Edmund Orme for the first time: "I am ready to answer for it to all and sundry that ghosts are much less alarming and much more amusing than was commonly supposed." The beautiful urbane spirits are only not of this world because they are too fine for it. They have taken with them across the border their clothes, their manners, their breeding, their band-boxes, and valets and ladies' maids. They remain always a little worldly. We may feel clumsy in their presence, but we cannot feel afraid. What does it matter, then, if we do pick up ***The Turn of the Screw*** an hour or so before bedtime? After an exquisite entertainment we shall, if the other stories are to be trusted, end with this fine music in our ears, and sleep the sounder.

Perhaps it is the silence that first impresses us. Everything at Bly is so profoundly quiet. The twitter of birds at dawn, the far-away cries of children, faint footsteps in the distance stir it but leave it unbroken. It accumulates; it weighs us down; it makes us strangely apprehensive of noise. At last the house and garden die out beneath it. "I can hear again, as I write, the intense hush in which the sounds of evening dropped. The rooks stopped cawing in the golden sky, and the friendly hour lost for the unspeakable minute all its voice." It is unspeakable. We know that the man who stands on the tower staring down at the governess beneath is evil. Some unutterable obscenity has come to the surface. It tries to get in; it tries to get at something. The exquisite little beings who lie innocently asleep must at all costs be protected. But the horror grows. Is it possible that the little girl, as she turns back from the window, has seen the woman outside? Has she been with Miss Jessel? Has Quint visited the boy? It is Quint who hangs about us in the dark; who is there in that corner and again there in that. It is Quint who must be reasoned away, and for all our reasoning returns. Can it be that we are afraid? But it is not a man with red hair and a white face whom we fear. We are afraid of something unnamed, of something, perhaps, in ourselves. In short, we turn on the light. If by its beams we examine the story in safety, note how masterly the telling is, how each sentence is stretched, each image filled, how the inner world gains from the robustness of the outer, how beauty and obscenity twined together worm their way to the depths—still we must own that something remains unaccounted for. We must admit that Henry James has conquered. That courtly, worldly, sentimental old gentleman can still make us afraid of the dark. (pp. 47-54)

> *Virginia Woolf, "The Ghost Stories," in* Henry James: A Collection of Critical Essays, *edited by Leon Edel, Prentice-Hall, Inc., 1963, pp. 47-54.*

Edna Kenton (essay date 1924)

[*In the following excerpt, Kenton asserts that James deluded his readers into believing in the ghosts of Peter Quint and Miss Jessel in* The Turn of the Screw, *while providing evidence that the ghosts were only hallucinations. For an opposing view, see Evans excerpt dated 1949.*]

In the submerged and disregarded foreword to the tale, in which the young governess and the children's uncle are set brightly before us—few readers of ***The Turn of the Screw*** remember this at all—lies a little painted portrait of the exquisite young creature who undertook the portentous task at Bly. The children and the ghosts have crowded forward to hide the only light thrown on her except for the irrepressible unconscious lights she casts on herself. It is never to be forgotten that it is she—not Henry James—who tells the story of Bly and its inhabitants, bound within confines of understanding as narrowly drawn as the circle which limited and defined, for instance, *What Maisie Knew.* But her freedom to tell her story, with no omniscient author at her elbow, is the "long rope, for acting herself out," that her creator, so fondly participating in her reality, tied so lightly to his foreword and then played out to her. The foreword is the only light we have on her present or her past—her whole concern is with the children and the ghosts. But of these we have only her story, and we have got nowhere near the "story of the story" until, pressing resolutely through her irresistibly credible recounting of the horrors at Bly, we come into closer quarters with the secret causes of her admirable *flair* for the evil she finds there.

She was twenty, so the submerged foreword tells us, a clergyman's daughter seeking her first position when she came up to London to answer an advertisement of the children's uncle. She found him "such a figure as had never risen, save in a dream or an old novel, before a fluttered, anxious girl out of a Hampstead vicarage." He was handsome and bold and pleasant, offhand and gay and kind, gallant and splendid. It was a difficult situation offered her, and it was put to her fairly; the condition of her taking it was that she should assume full responsibility for house, children and servants and leave him free to live his life in peace. She hesitated, but she was under a spell. "She succumbed to it . . . she saw him only twice . . . but that was the beauty of her passion . . . she never saw him again."

But she went to Bly. The master had come into her house and had gone out of it; she had only the house. She found it at first full of brightness, greatness, beauty and dignity and she began to enjoy it almost with a sense of property. Days passed, filled with dreams and dreamings. But there came a change which broke the hush of the first beautiful week at Bly; and the change, "actually like the spring of a beast," came at the close of a beautiful afternoon, at the end of a lonely stroll in which she walked, wrapped in day dreams.

> One of the thoughts (wrote the little governess in her desperate diary), that, as I don't in the least shrink from noting now, used to be with me in these wanderings was that it would be as charming as a charming story suddenly to meet some one. Some one would appear there at the turn of a path, and would stand before me and smile and approve. I didn't ask more than that—I only asked that he should know.

And that evening, as she came within sight of the house, "he did stand there"—the figure that her dreamings had invoked. (pp. 251-52)

This, no more, no less, is the first visitation of Peter Quint. There came another, as unexpectedly as the first, on a rainy Sunday afternoon.

> He appeared thus again with I won't say greater distinctness, for that was impossible, but with a nearness that represented a foreward stride in our intercourse and made me, as I met him, catch my breath and turn cold. . . . On the spot there came to me the added shock of a certitude that it was not for me he had come there. He had come for some one else.

So the little governess says, and upon it she acts—both so convincingly as to sweep the reader, wary or unwary, headlong with her into her nightmare of horrors. Her way of escape is the reader's. And so subtlely does she build up the ring of fire about her house of life—as frightened women, in pioneer forests with their men away, lighted circles of flames about their homes to ward off the prowling beasts of night—that it is desperately difficult to catch her in the act.

The children hounded by the prowling ghosts—this is the hard and shining surface story of ***The Turn of the Screw;*** or, to put it more accurately, it is the traditional and accepted interpretation of the story as it has come down through a quarter of a century of readers' reactions resulting from "a cold, artistic calculation" on the part of its highly entertained author. As a tiny matter of literal fact, no reader has more to go on than the young governess's word for this rather momentous and sidetracking allegation. As a rather large matter of literal fact, we may know, with but a modicum of attention paid to her recital of these nerve-shattering affairs at Bly, that it is she—always she herself—who sees the lurking shapes and heralds them to her little world. Not to the charming little Flora, but, behind Flora and facing the governess, the apparitional Miss Jessel first appeared. There are traps and lures in plenty, but just a little wariness will suffice to disprove, with a single survey of the ground, the traditional, we might almost call it lazy version of this tale. Not the children, but the little governess was hounded by the ghosts who, as James confides with such suave frankness in his Preface, merely "helped me to express my subject all directly and intensely." After her startling materializations of Peter Quint and Miss Jessel, Bly became a nest of lurking shapes, and she walked softly, in terror, expectantly. She came to know the moods that brought them:

> There were states of the air, conditions of sound and stillness, unspeakable impressions of the *kind* of ministering moment, that brought back to me, long enough to catch it, the medium in which, that June evening out of doors, I had had my first sight of Quint. . . . I recognized the signs, the portents—I recognized the moment, the spot.

So she made the shades of her recurring fevers dummy figures for the delirious terrifying of others, pathetically trying to harmonize her own disharmonies by creating discords outside herself.

"I meant to scare the whole world with that story," James has been quoted as saying—seemingly with serious solemnity. And indeed, in its exquisitely ironic Preface, he took up at length with its readers the turning, precisely, of just this little trick that has worked so well. He is more than confidential—he is explicit as to just how the screw was tightened, revelatory as to calculated causes of his calculated effects.

His problem here, he says gaily, was how *best* to convey that sense of the depths of the sinister which was essential for illusion. Portentous evil—how was that to be invoked;

Henry James, circa 1863.

or, invoked, how saved from the comparative vulgarity of "the cited act, the limited, deplorable, presentable instance."

> One had seen (he mused) in fiction, some grand form of wrong-doing or, better still, of wrong being, imputed, seen it promised and announced as by the hot breath of the Pit—and then, all lamentably, shrink to the compass of some particular brutality, some particular immorality, some particular infamy portrayed; with the result, alas, of the demonstration's falling sadly short.

So, from the heap of aesthetic failures lying along fiction's path, he evolved, for the novel of evil, an aesthetic moral. Its sinister agent, he concluded, be it man or ghost, must be, in the last analysis, capable of *anything,* the very worst conceivable action. So far, very good; he had his sinister agent—his pair of them—in his two "ghosts." But still the question remained, of how best to convey to the reader the sense of this utmost capability without the author himself falling into the deadly trap of the "cited act." And this is his answer:

> Only make the reader's general vision of evil intense enough, I said to myself—and that already is a charming job—and his own experience, his own imagination, his own sympathy (with the children) and horror (of their false friends) will supply him quite sufficiently with all the particulars. Make him *think* the evil, make him think it for himself, and you are released from weak specifications. This ingenuity I took pains—as indeed great pains were required—to apply; and with a success apparently beyond my liveliest hopes.

A success all the greater, incidentally, because he permitted his innocent young governess to write herself his novel of evil. She could not "specify," and readers of her tender, moving tale have of necessity had to think the evil for themselves. "Droll enough," adds James,

> some of the evidence—even when most convincing—of this success. How can I feel my calculation to have failed, my wrought suggestion not to have worked, that is, on my being assailed, as has befallen me, with the charge of a monstrous emphasis, the charge of all indecently expatiating. There is not only from beginning to end of the matter not an inch of expatiation, but my values are positively all blanks save only so far as an excited horror, a promoted pity, a created expertness—on which punctual effects of strong causes no writer can ever fail to plume himself—proceed to read into them more or less fantastic figures.

And the fantastic figures have been read into ***The Turn of the Screw;*** for once at least James succeeded in forcing his reader, however unconsciously, to do a share of the work left for him to do. Not all of it, however; the ironic beauty of his subtle device for best expressing the depths of evil is that it was at the same time the calculated trap of traps for the guarding of his heroine. The eager, thrilled, horrified reader, joined with her in her vivid hunt after hidden sins, has failed to think sufficiently of her; and has, all oddly, contrived to protect her quite as romantically as her creator permitted her to protect herself in her charming recital of the happenings at Bly. Her own story, so naively sympathetic, of the ghosts and children, has been her simple bulwark—even the cunning reader has been credulous.

So, on ***The Turn of the Screw,*** Henry James has won, hands down, all round; has won most of all when the reader, persistently baffled, but persistently wondering, comes face to face at last with the little governess, and realizes, with a conscious thrill greater than that of merely automatic nerve shudders before "horror," that the guarding ghosts and children—what they are and what they do—are only exquisite dramatizations of her little personal mystery, figures for the ebb and flow of troubled thought within her mind, acting out her story. If the reader has won for himself a blest sense of an extension of experience and consciousness in the recognition that her case, so delicate, so complicated, so critical and yet so transparent, has never in its whole treatment been cheapened or betrayed; if he has had, in the high modern sense, all of his "fun," he has none the less paid; he has worked for it all, and by that fruitful labor has verified James's earliest contention that there was a discoverable way to establish a relation of work shared between the writer and the reader sufficiently curious to follow through. (pp. 254-55)

Edna Kenton, "Henry James to the Ruminant Reader: The Turn of the Screw," in The Arts, *New York, Vol. VI, No. 5, November, 1924, pp. 245-55.*

Edmund Wilson (essay date 1934)

[*Wilson, considered America's foremost man of letters in the twentieth century, wrote widely on cultural, historical, and literary matters. He is often credited with bringing an international perspective to American letters through his widely read discussions of European literature. A central concern throughout Wilson's career was discussion of a literary work as a revelation of its author's personality. In* Axels's Castle *(1931), a seminal study of literary symbolism, Wilson wrote: "The real elements, of course, of any work of fiction are the elements of the author's personality: his imagination embodies in the images of characters, situations and scenes the fundamental conflicts of his nature." In the following excerpt from his essay "The Ambiguity of Henry James," Wilson presents a psychoanalytical interpretation of* The Turn of the Screw *in which he regards the ghosts of the story as illusions seen only by the governess. For an opposing view see Evans excerpt dated 1949.*]

A discussion of Henry James's ambiguity may appropriately begin with ***The Turn of the Screw.*** This story, which seems to have proved more fascinating to the general reading public than anything else of James's except ***Daisy Miller,*** apparently conceals another mystery behind the ostensible one. I do not know who first propounded the theory; but Miss Edna Kenton [see excerpt dated 1924], whose insight into James is profound, has been one of its principal elucidators, and Mr. Charles Demuth has done a set of illustrations based on it.

According to this interpretation, the young governess who tells the story is a neurotic case of sex repression, and the ghosts are not real ghosts at all but merely the governess's hallucinations.

Let us go through the story from the beginning. It opens with an introduction. The man who is presenting the governess's manuscript tells us first who she is. She is the youngest daughter of a poor country parson, who had come up to London and answered an advertisement and found a man who wanted a governess for his orphaned nephew and niece. "This prospective patron proved a gentleman, a bachelor in the prime of life, such a figure as had never risen, save in a dream or an old novel, before a fluttered, anxious girl out of a Hampshire vicarage." It is made clear that the young woman has become thoroughly infatuated with her employer. He is charming to her and lets her have the job on condition that she will never bother him about the children; and she goes down to the house in the country where they are staying with a housekeeper and some other servants.

The boy, she finds, has been sent home from school for reasons into which she does not inquire but which she colors, on no evidence at all so far as one can see, with a significance somehow sinister; she learns that the former governess left, and that she has since died, under circumstances which are not explained but which are made to seem ominous in the same way. She is alone with the illiterate housekeeper, a good and simple soul, and the children, who seem innocent and charming. As she wanders about the estate, she often thinks how delightful it would be to come suddenly round the corner and find that the master had arrived: he would be smiling, approving, handsome.

She is never to meet her employer again, but what she does meet are the apparitions. One day when his face has been in her mind, she comes out in sight of the house and sees the figure of a man on the tower, a figure which is not the master's. Not long afterwards, the figure appears again, toward the end of a rainy Sunday. She sees him at closer range and more clearly: he is wearing smart clothes but is not a gentleman. The housekeeper, meeting the governess immediately afterwards, behaves as if the governess herself were a ghost: "I wondered why she should be scared." The governess tells her about the apparition and learns that it answers the description of one of the master's valets who had stayed down there and used to wear his clothes. The valet had been a bad character, who used "to play with the boy . . . to spoil him"; he had been found dead, having slipped on the ice coming out of a public house: it is impossible to say that he was not murdered. The governess believes that he has come back to haunt the children.

Not long afterwards, she and the little girl are out on the shore of a lake, the little girl playing, the governess sewing. The latter becomes aware of a third person on the opposite side of the lake. But she looks first at the little girl, who is turning her back in that direction, and who, she notes, has "picked up a small flat piece of wood, which happened to have in it a little hole that had evidently suggested to her the idea of sticking in another fragment that might figure as a mast and make the thing a boat. This second morsel, as I watched her, she was very markedly and intently attempting to tighten in its place." This somehow "sustains" the governess so that she is able to raise her eyes: she sees a woman "in black, pale and dreadful". She concludes that it is the former governess. Her predecessor, the housekeeper intimates, though a lady, had had an affair with the valet. The boy had used to go away with the valet and then lie about it afterwards. The governess concludes that the boy must have known about the valet and the woman—the children have been corrupted by them.

Observe that there is never any evidence that anybody but the governess sees the ghosts. She believes that the children see them but there is never any proof that they do. The housekeeper insists that she does not see them; it is apparently the governess who frightens her. The children, too, become hysterical; but this is evidently the governess's doing, too. Observe, also, from the Freudian point of view, the significance of the governess's interest in the little girl's pieces of wood and of the fact that the male apparition first appears on a tower and the female apparition on a lake. There seems to be only a single circumstance which does not fit into the hypothesis that the ghosts are hallucinations of the governess: the fact that the governess's description of the first ghost at a time when she has never heard of the valet should be identifiable by the housekeeper. But when we look back, we see that even this has been left open to a double interpretation. The governess has never heard of the valet, but it has been suggested to her in a conversation with the housekeeper that there has been some other male somewhere about who "liked every one young and pretty", and the idea of this other person has been ambiguously confused with the master and with the master's interest in her, the present governess. The master has never been described; we have merely been told that he was "handsome." Of the ghost, who is described in detail, we are told that he has "straight, good features," and he is wearing the master's clothes.

The governess continues to see the spirits, and the atmosphere becomes more and more hysterical. She believes that the children get up at night to meet them, though they are able to give plausible explanations of their behavior. The children become obviously uncomfortable; they begin to resent the governess. The boy begs to be sent to another school and threatens to write to his uncle, and the girl, under the governess's pressure to make her admit that Miss Jessel is haunting her, breaks down and demands to be sent away.

The governess is now left alone with the boy. A gruesome scene ensues. "We continued silent while the maid was with us—as silent, it whimsically occurred to me, as some young couple who, on their wedding-journey, at the inn, feel shy in the presence of the waiter." When the maid has gone, and she presses him to tell her why he was expelled from school, the boy seems suddenly afraid of her. He finally confesses that he "said things"—to "a few", to "those he liked". It all sounds very harmless: there comes to her out of her "very pity the appalling alarm of his being perhaps innocent. It was for the instant confounding and bottomless, for if he *were* innocent, what then on earth was *I?*" The valet appears at the window—it is "the white face of damnation". (But is the governess condemning the spirits to damnation or is she becoming damned herself?) She is aware that the boy does not see it. "No more, no more, no more!" she shrieks to the apparition. "Is she *here*?" asks the boy in panic (he has heard from his sister the incident of the governess's trying to make her admit she has seen Miss Jessel). No, she says, it is not the woman; "But it's at the window—straight before us. It's *there*!" . . . "It's *he*?" then. Whom does he mean by "he"? " 'Peter Quint—you devil!' His face gave again, round the room, its convulsed supplication. 'Where?' " "What does he matter now, my own?" she cries. "What will he *ever* matter? *I* have you, but he has lost you forever!" Then she shows him that the figure has vanished: "There, *there*!" she says, pointing toward the window. He looks and gives a cry; she feels that he is dead in her arms. From her point of view, the disappearance of the spirit has proved too terrible a shock for him and "his little heart, dispossessed, has stopped"; but if we study the dialogue from the other point of view, we see that he must have taken her "There, *there*!" as an answer to his own "*Where?*" She has finally made him believe either that he has actually seen something or that he is on the point of seeing something. He gives "the cry of a creature hurled over an abyss". She has literally frightened him to death.

When one has once been given this clue to ***The Turn of the Screw,*** one wonders how one could ever have missed it. There is a very good reason, however, in the fact that nowhere does James unequivocally give the thing away: everything from beginning to end can be taken equally well in either of two senses. In the preface to the collected edition, however, as Miss Kenton has pointed out, James does seem to want to put himself on record. He asserts here that ***The Turn of the Screw*** is "a fairy-tale pure and simple"—but adds that the apparitions are of the order of those involved in witchcraft cases rather than of those in cases of psychic research. And he goes on to tell of his reply to one of his readers who had complained that he had not characterized the governess sufficiently. At this criticism, he says, "One's artistic, one's *ironic* heart shook for the instant almost to breaking"; and he answered: "It was 'déjà très-joli' . . . please believe, the general proposition of our young woman's keeping crystalline her record of so many intense anomalies and obscurities—*by which I don't of course mean her explanation of them, a different matter*. . . . She has 'authority', which is a good deal to have given her" . . . The italics above are mine: these words seem impossible to explain except on the hypothesis I have suggested. And note, too, in the collected edition that James has not included ***The Turn of the Screw*** in the volume with the other ghost stories but in another volume between ***The Aspern Papers*** and **"The Liar"**—this last the story of a pathological liar whose wife protects his lies against the world, behaving with the same sort of deceptive "authority" as the governess in ***The Turn of the Screw.*** When we look back at the story in the light of these hints, we can conceive that the whole thing has been primarily and completely a characterization of the governess: her visions and the way she behaves about them become as soon as we look at them from the obverse side, a solid and unmistakable picture of the poor country parson's daughter, with her English middle-class class-consciousness, her inability to admit to herself her sexual impulses and the relentless English "authority" which enables her to put over on inferiors even purposes which are totally mistaken and not at all to the other people's best interests.

The Turn of the Screw, then, on this theory, would be a masterpiece—not as a ghost story, there are a great many better ones of the ordinary kind—but as a study in morbid psychology. It is to this psychological value of the ghosts, I believe, that the story owes its fascination: it belongs with *Moby Dick* and the *Alice* books to a small group of fairy tales whose symbols exert a peculiar power by reason of the fact that they have behind them, whether or not the authors are aware of it, a profound grasp of subconscious processes. (pp. 385-91)

Edmund Wilson, "The Ambiguity of Henry James," in The Hound & Horn *Vol. VII, No. 3, April-May, 1934, pp. 385-406.*

R. P. Blackmur (essay date 1943)

[*Blackmur was a leading American critic of the twentieth century. Early in his career he was linked to the New Critics, who believed that literature was not a manifestation of sociology, psychology, or morality, and could not be evaluated in the terms of any nonliterary discipline. Blackmur distinguished himself from this group of critics, however, by broadening his analyses through discussions that explored a given work's relevance to society. Inspired by the moral thought of the American autobiographer Henry Adams, Blackmur conceived the critic's role as that of a crucial intermediary between artist and reader, for the dual purpose of offering literary insight as well as social commentary. In the essay below, he analyzes the theme of the artist's struggle in society as portrayed in James's short fiction.*]

We are now about to assay the deep bias, the controlling, characteristic tension in the fiction of Henry James as it erupts in those tales where the theme is that of the artist in conflict with society. To erupt is to break out irresistibly from some deep compulsion, whether of disease or disorder, into a major reaction; and that is exactly what happens to James when in the first full maturity of his fifties he began to meditate, to feel borne in upon him, the actual predicament of the artist as a man of integrity in a democratic society. He broke out, he erupted from the very center of his being, and with such violence that to save himself he had need of both that imagination which represents the actual and that which shapes the possible. James made of the theme of the artist a focus for the ultimate theme of human integrity, how it is conceived, how it is destroyed, and how, ideally, it may be regained. For James, imagination was the will of things, and as the will was inescapably moral, so the imagination could not help creating—could not fail rather to re-create—out of the evil of the artist's actual predicament the good of his possible invoked vision. As the artist is only a special case of the man, so his vision is only an emphatic image of the general human vision; that James could make so much of the special case and the emphatic image of the artist comes about because, more than any other novelist of his scope, he was himself completely the artist. By which I mean that he was free to dramatize the artist precisely because he was himself so utterly given up to his profession that he was free of the predicament of the artist the moment he began to write. He felt none of that difficulty about conviction or principle or aim in his work which troubles a lesser writer; both his experience and his values came straight and clear and unquestionable, so much so that he seems to inhabit another world, that other world which has as substance what for us is merely hoped for. James, as an artist, was above all a man of faith. As he said of one of his characters in another connection, he was copious with faith.

But there is a disadvantage in too complete a faith, as well for an artist as for a saint. Complete faith runs to fanaticism or narrowness. The act of faith tends to substitute for understanding of the thing believed in. If your values come to you unquestioned, you risk taking them on principle and of course. Only the steady supplication of doubt, the constant resolution of infirmity, can exercise your values and your principles enough to give them, together, that stretch and scope which is their life. If you dismiss doubt and ignore infirmity, you will restrict the scope that goes with the equivocal and reduce the vitality that goes with richness of texture. So it was with Henry James. His very faith in his powers kept him from using them to their utmost and caused him to emphasize only his chosen, his convicted view. That is why he is not of the very greatest writers, though he is one of the indubitably great artists, and especially in our present focus, the portrait of the artist. That is why, too, as his faith increased he came less and less to make *fictions* of people and more and more to make *fables,* to draw parables, for the ulterior purposes of his faith. He came less and less to tell and more and more to merely say. But—and this is what saves him to us for reading—the habit of the novelist was so pervasive in him that he could no more than breathing help dramatizing his fables or actualizing, to the possible limit of his frame, the story of his parables. Indeed, in his old age, which for him constituted a continuing rebirth, he made of the frame of his fables a new frame for the novel or tale only less than the greatest frames. I refer to *The Ambassadors, The Wings of the Dove, The Golden Bowl,* perhaps to *The Sense of the Past* and *The Ivory Tower,* and certainly to the tales in ***The Finer Grain;*** for in these works the form of the fable, the point of the parable, are brought to extreme use precisely by being embedded in the sensibility of fiction. These take rise I think in *The Sacred Fount,* which, not a novel at all but a vast shadowy disintegrating parable, disturbing distressing distrait, indeed distraught, remains in the degree of its fascination quite ineluctable. It is the nightmare nexus, in James's literary life, between the struggle to portray the integrity of the artist and the struggle to portray, to discover, the integrity of the self.

This is another way of saying that the tales which exhibit the artist occupy an intermediate position in James's work; and we shall see that they look both ways, to the social novels that preceded them and to the fiction of fate that came after them. They look back to the conditions of life in general and forward to the prophecy of life beyond and under, or at any rate in spite of, the mutilating conditions. I think of Isabelle Archer, in *The Portrait of a Lady,* how the conditions of life, particularly the conditions of money and marriage and their miring in manners, slowly dawned on her. You feel that if Isabelle can only acknowledge the conditions, if she can see for once what life is like, she will be free to go on, where to go on means to meet more and more conditions. We know that in the process of going on she will lose—indeed she has already lost them—the freshness and promise and candor of youth, which are taken as the ordinary expenses laid out for the general look, whether dimmed or sharpened always somehow maimed and marked, of maturity. So for Isabelle Archer and most of the early fiction. On the other hand I think of Milly Theale in *The Wings of the Dove,* whom we see actually killed by the conditions of life, acknowledge them how she will, but who yet so transcends them that her image—the image of the lost dead—brings to Kate Croy and Merton Densher, who had betrayed her in life, and unalterable unutterable knowledge of what life is under its mutilated likeness. Things could, as Kate told Merton at the end, never again be the same between them; all because of the freshness and candor which had not perished but been discovered in the death of Milly Theale, and the unbroken, unbreakable promise of life which merely for *them,* as they had failed Milly, could not be kept but was to hover over them unavailingly ever afterwards. Milly had her triumph in death; but in *The Ambassadors,* Lambert Strether had his triumph in life, and so Maggie Verver in *The Golden Bowl,* both triumphing precisely over the most mutilating conditions of life that could well have come their way. So again, perhaps with the most beautiful lucidity of all, there is the shabby little bookseller Herbert Dodd in **"The Bench of Desolation,"** whom we see deprived of the last resource of outward dignity—as a character he is all scar-tissue—till he has nothing left but his lonely hours upon his seaside bench of desolation. The bench of desolation is where you sit still with your fate—that of which you cannot be deprived. For Herbert Dodd that bench has these many years turned out to be enough, when the return of the lost love of his youth, who he thought had betrayed him, makes it a bench of triumph as well. The triumph consists for him, as for the others, in the gradual inward mastery of the outward experience, a poetic mastery which makes of the experience conviction.

Between the earlier persons who master life by submitting to its conditions and the later persons who master what lies under the conditions by achieving a conviction of the self—for surely a man's convictions may be said to be the very shape of his self—comes the little, the slightly anomalous race of artists. Why they come between rather than either as a culmination or a beginning is plain when we look at their characteristic fate. The man who is completely an artist is incompletely a man, though in his art he may envisage man completely. The meaning of the artist in history, that is in life as he lives it, in the conditions under which he works, is like the meaning of history itself. History, as Niebuhr says, is meaningful, but the meaning is not yet. The history of the artist is prophetic, but the meaning of the prophecy cannot now be known. What happens to the artist apart from his meaning, is common enough knowledge. If we look at the fables Henry James offers us, we see at once that all these artists are doomed men, as doomed as the characters in Hemingway, but not as in Hemingway by the coming common death. They are doomed either because they cannot meet the conditions of life imposed upon them by society or because society will have none of them no matter how hard they try. That, for James, was the drama of the artist, and he put it in the simple white and black terms of the fable and the fairy story. The artist either gave in to the evil and corruption of society, or society refused a living to the good and incorruptible artist. But let us ask why James chose the artist for the living focus of his drama, when it might as well have been the queen or the kitchen maid as in the fairy tales, or the men and women next door who provide us, unadulterated with any self-interest, such excellent views of our selves. Why, that is, did not James begin with the persons he came to?

We may say that he did not know enough, that he had not matured enough, and perhaps it would be better so to beg the question. But there is a kind of logic which we can apply after the event, which is where logic works best. The artist is *given* as in death-struggle with society, as much so as the thief or the murderer but with the advantage of heroism and nobility as a luminous character in the mere murk of the struggle. That every man and woman, and perhaps more so every child, is also engaged in a death-struggle with society, or at least with his neighbor's society, is not so clear; you would not think of *yourself* as struggling with society, but the artist and his critics have I regret to say vied with each other at every opportunity to see which could say so louder, especially since the spread of literacy and education has multiplied artists of all sorts at the same time that changing institutions took away the function of the artist in society. The artist became thus a natural puppet, ready-made, completely understandable, to represent the great central struggle of man as an individual, which is not often, when you consider the stakes, an understandable struggle at all, and to make a drama of which the novelist has to work from the ground up. It is no wonder then that James should consider the struggle of the artist as one of the great primary themes, especially when you add to the picture that he might incidentally dramatize himself a little—a temptation not beyond the purest artist—and do his trade a good turn.

But the evidence is not limited to the writings of artists and critics. There comes particularly pat to the kind of artist of whom James wrote a passage in de Tocqueville's classic work on The Republic of The United States of America. It was not quite going to be, he forsaw long before Henry James began writing novels, a model republic of letters. There is a little chapter in the first book of the second part called "The Trade of Literature" from which I extract the following passage. "Democracy not only infuses a taste for letters among the trading classes, but introduces a trading spirit into literature. . . . Among democratic nations, a writer may flatter himself that he will obtain at a cheap rate a meager reputation and a large fortune. For this purpose he need not be admired, it is enough that he is liked. . . . In democratic periods the public frequently treat authors as kings do their courtiers; they enrich and they despise them. . . . Democratic literature is always infested by a tribe of writers who look upon letters as a mere trade; and for some few great authors who adorn it, you may reckon thousands of idea-mongers." The picture is fresh enough for our own day, and we take it with the more authority because it was frankly prophetic on the part of a man more than generously disposed towards democracy. It is a description that James could have made for himself, and which in fact he did largely make, both in his life of Hawthorne and in the fiction which we are about to engage. De Tocqueville only reminds us of what James well knew, that an author can expect his readers to know that the race of literary artists is itself composed of good and bad, of very black and very white practitioners; so that the nobility of the good writer will go as granted once it is mentioned, as will the flunkeyism of the bad writer. Thus the author of a fiction about an artist has all the advantages of coarse melodrama without losing any of the advantages of high tragedy. He can merely impute unto his chosen character what virtues or vices he likes without being under any necessity to show them. In fiction, the stated intent of goodness, of high seriousness, is worthless in every realm of life except that of artist; elsewhere the character must be shown as actual, in the artist the stated intention is enough. We shall see that James fully availed himself of this freedom, redeeming himself only by the eloquence of his statement and the lesson of his parable. These, the eloquence and the lesson, will be what we bring away with us. For it goes without saying that James was never taken in, in his created characters, by the meretricious, and was always deliberately sold by the high serious. In this respect, as perhaps nowhere else in James, the reader always knows exactly where he is at. What happens to the literary personages will vary with the incident and the conditions recorded; but nothing can happen to their characters once they are stated, for their characters are articulated ready made as soon after their first appearance as possible, like puppets or like gods as you may choose to think.

This is no accident nor any part of James's idiosyncrasy; it is a limiting condition of the artist as a character in fiction to the extent that he is represented in the rôle of artist. If he drops the rôle, anything within the power of the author to represent may happen to him as a person; as artist he is only a shrunken and empty simulacrum of himself in his other rôles; he may know the meaning, but he cannot share the motion.

This is one of the lessons that if James's fables are taken literally they best attest; and literally is very near how James meant his lessons to be taken. But we do not need to stick to James. The character of Stephen Dedalus, both in *The Portrait of the Artist as a Young Man* and in *Ulysses,* certainly works of the greatest richness and scope, comes to us very fully as a young man, but as an artist he comes to us only by the eloquence of Joyce's mere statement. The poem he writes and the diary he keeps, the lecture he gives on Hamlet, come to us quite independent of the created figure of Stephen. Even the great declaration that ends the earlier book, where Stephen resolves that he will "forge in the smithy of his soul the uncreated conscience of his race," must be taken either as a free lyric spoken by an actor, where something else might have done as well, or as an image in which the whole boy shrinks suddenly into an agonized intention that can never be realized in life or act but only in art itself. It is much the same thing with Herr Aschenbach, the old novelist in Thomas Mann's *Death in Venice,* who is never given to us as a novelist except by imputation. The rôle of artist is indeed called on for other purposes, to give quickly a background against which the reader will find credible and dramatic the image of old Ashenbach, the famous and dignified novelist, as an outsider, a figure so isolated by his profession of artist that he fairly aches to corrupt himself, to debase himself, both as a man and as an artist. It might almost be put that to the degree that he had become an artist he had ceased existing—as it were, ceased living—so that the desire for life becomes identified with the temptation to corruption. And so it turns out. The only possible resumption of life for him is tainted with corruption, with effeminate infatuation, with deliberate indignity and self-humiliation. But it is too late in the season, the season of his life and the season in Venice, both of which are struck down by pestilence. His adored and beautiful Tadzio is taken away to safety, and Herr Aschenbach resumes his profession, in the act of dying, by in his delirium reenacting the Phaedo of Plato. Aschenbach the artist could have no life except in that terrible privation of life which is art.

It is only the obverse of the same coin that André Gide shows us in *The Counterfeiters* where the novelist reaches life only by a driven and deliberate corruption, a personal disintegration as great as the formal disintegration of the work of art in which it is represented. That Mann and Gide show us corruption as the necessary predilection of the artist, where James and Joyce show us art—that is, integrity of spirit—as the redemption of life, is perhaps due to the seeming fact that neither the German nor the Frenchman have as full and fanatic a conviction of their profession of artists as that suffered at an equal maximum by both James and Joyce.

To get back a little nearer to our particular problem of the portrait of the artist in Henry James—though indeed we have never been far from it—there is another way of expressing the predicament of the artist as a character in fiction. He comes to life only as he ceases to be an artist; he comes to life, in a word, only as he *fails* to be an artist, and he fails when the conditions of life overcome him at the expense of his art. This becomes a very pretty problem indeed when the novelist reflects that all this amounts to saying that the actual source of art, the life of which it is the meaning, is the artist's undoing. Gide solves the problem, and so does Mann, by disintegrating the art as well as the life. Joyce, with no greater honesty but with greater moral insight, represents the struggle of the man *in society,* not as an outsider but as one very much at the heart of things, to become an artist. It was not for nothing that Joyce defined the sentimentalist as him who "is unwilling to incur the enormous responsibility for a thing done." Stephen Dedalus is shown to us in the very process of realizing, for the sake of his art, responsibility for every deed of his life. In Joyce, the artist, like God, dies every day. He dies into man and is reborn; the death is necessary to the birth. Henry James had neither the catholicism of Joyce, the bitter protestantism of Gide, nor the faustian spirit of Mann at his back; he had rather—and only—his unquestioned faith in the adequacy of the free intelligence in life and the freed imagination in art. He had thus less equipment, or at any rate a less articulated philosophy, than the others, and it is perhaps for that reason that he produced his ideal artists who failed only in life and succeeded only in art, and his other artists, equally ideal, who failed in art only because they insisted on success, financial or social success, in life. The realm of the ideal is often nearest to those who have nearest to no philosophy; but so is the realm of the actual, which is the artist's realm, and James may have been nearer right in what he did with his facts than the others.

At least we have James's own abundantly eloquent answer to the charge that he ought never to have exhibited in art creatures who never existed in life. I give part of the answer as he made it in the preface to **"The Lesson of the Master."**

> What does your contention of non-existent conscious *exposures,* in the midst of all the stupidity and vulgarity and hypocrisy, imply but that we have been, nationally, so to speak, graced with no instance of recorded sensibility fine enough to react against these things?—an admission too distressing. What one would accordingly fain do is to baffle any such calamity, to *create* the record, in default of any other enjoyment of it; to imagine, in a word, the honourable, the producible case. What better example than this of the high and helpful public and, as it were, civic use of the imagination?—a faculty for the possible fine employments of which in the interest of morality my esteem grows every hour that I live. How can one consent to make a picture of the preponderant futilities and vulgarities and miseries of life without the impulse to exhibit as well from time to time, in its place, some fine example of the reaction, the opposition or the escape?

In this passage, and in the whole preface from which it is taken, I think James reaches the pinnacle of principle to which he was able to expose the idealism with which he worked; and I have planted my quotations here in the center of this discussion of the portrait of the artist because they raise—especially just after our references to the practice of Joyce and Gide and Mann—considerations of great importance not only to the criticism, the appreciation, of James's fictions but also to the whole general theory of fiction itself—if you like to the whole theory of art. There are several theories of the value of art which are tenable until you begin to apply them in the interpretation of particular works of art, when as a rule the value of the art shrinks at once to nothing and there is *nothing but* moral value left. No artist and hardly any user of art whose eyes are open can take the slightest interest in any *nothing but* theory of art's value. James's theory is very tempting because, if adopted, it shows how moral value gets into a work of art without leaving you to shudder for the fate of the art. The artist, he says with all the rush and eloquence of immediate experience, the artist *creates* the moral value out of the same material and by the same means with which he creates his other values—out of the actual and by means of imagination. The values are, though distinguishable, inextricable. Some works may show aesthetic values without moral values, and other works very clearly have no aesthetic values and yet shriek to heaven with their moral values, but where you have both orders of value as they are created, together, so they must be felt together, at least so long as the work being enjoyed is enjoyed as art.

Among the consequences which flow from James's statement, if I understand it right, there are two which deserve emphasis for the freedom and the privation they impose on the artist. One has to do with the inclusive nature of moral value in art. As the experience in art must be somehow of the actual and as the record must be somehow of the imaginative, then the artist is free to create evil as well as good without risk of police interference. It is not that his vision of evil may overcome his vision of good, but that, if he is to be an artist of any scope, he must create both, and if the emphasis is on the one in a given work it must have the other as its under or supporting side. It is truly the devil who minds God's business as it is God who gives the devil something to do. But, and this is the second consequence kept for emphasis from James's statement, to have validity whether moral or aesthetic, whatever the artist *creates* (though not what he merely puts in by the way) must show its source in the actual; for it is otherwise either immoral or vapid, and likely both. If the architecture of even the noblest cathedral were not based on the actual it would fall apart, but without a vision beyond the actual it could have never been built at all. Art, on this view, tends toward the ideal but without ever quite transcending the actual from which it sprang. The ideal, in fact, in this restricted sense of the word, is what the artist creates; but the ideal, to have any significant worth, must approach the actual, with the striking effect which needs every meditation we can give it, that the nearer it approaches the actual the more greatly ideal the creation will seem. There is the force of Dante's ideal hell, that it approaches so close to the actual of this life; and there is the relative weakness of James's tales of the literary life, and despite his plea of moral necessity, that though they spring from hints in the actual world the "super-subtle fry" of his authors do not approach near enough to the actual. The fable is always frailer than the image, however more cogent. Thus Joyce's Dubliners who translated the initials IHS of *In Hoc Signo* over the cross, as I Have Suffered, were not blasphemers but better believers for so doing.

The examples are endless; but to our present interest it is the principle that counts, and its relation to the artist, and if we turn to our chosen tales of Henry James we shall find that though as dramas they do not show us very much of the actual, as fables they illuminate the principles by which James was later to anchor his most difficult and precarious ideals safe and firm—poetically valid—in flesh and blood. That is, as these tales occupy an intermediate position in the general devolopement of James as works of art, so they represent for us an intermediate state of knowledge, that critical and fascinating state when principles fairly itch for action but have not yet run down into the skill of the hand that acts, that in this case writes. As stories they are stories about stories, and the most fascinating kind of stories, those that for both aesthetic and moral reasons can never quite be written. All the moral value is in the possibility not lived up to, and all the aesthetic value is in the possibility not lived down to. It is the same possibility, looking either way, the possibility of the really superior artist triumphing over society by cutting himself off from every aspect of it except the expressive, or the possibility of this same superior fellow—and I hardly know which version is more tragic—coming to failure and ruin, expressive failure and personal ruin, by hands whose caresses are their most brutalizing blows, the hands of society itself, the society that, in de Tocqueville's phrases, would like an author rather than admire him, or, worse, would enrich and despise him.

The possibilities are indeed wonderful, and furnish half the conversation at literary parties, where the most enriched authors always turn out the most despised, very often justly. James does not deal with the literary party, whether because the institution had not grown much in his day or because it was open only to satire, which was not his purpose. He deals rather with the English house party and the English dinner party where there is a reputable author present for demolition. The effect is not too different, and affords the advantages of an outwardly more decorous set of conventions and even for a welcome shift of scenes from lawn to church, dinner-table to parlor, or parlor to smoking room, smoking room to bedroom; which taken together, as even a novice at fiction should know, makes the problem of moving people from place to place and so of setting up new relations or modifying old ones, relatively easy. So it is that all but one of the fables we are dealing with make use of the machinery of entertainment for the mechanics of the plot. That is, the artifices that in actual society do most to prevent communication and obscure situations, James uses to promote intimacy and to clarify situations. He mastered the means which because of his life—in one London year he dined out three hundred times—were almost alone at his disposal; the lesson of which may be that it explains why so many of James's people are never able to meet each other openly and yet contrive to put everything between them that is necessary.

That is exactly the situation in **"The Figure in the Carpet"** where I think we may put it that we know what the puzzle is precisely to the extent we realize it is insoluble, like the breath of life. The narrator who is himself a writer and nameless (the narrators of all these tales are writers and most of them are nameless) reviews the latest novel of Hugh Vereker in a magazine called *The Middle,* and shortly afterwards attends a houseparty where Vereker is a guest, as is his book, both unopened by any of the company, though both are the principal subjects of attention. Some one shows Vereker the review and Vereker says it is very bad; he has not realized the reviewer is present. When he does so, he apologises to the narrator but insists that, nevertheless, like everybody else, he has missed the Figure in the Carpet: the general intention, the string to his pearls, the passion of his passion. The narrator tries his best to make up, both by reading Vereker's works and by tackling him personally. On his failure he passes the puzzle along to his friend George Corvick, who shares the problem with his fiancée. They in their turn grow futile and frenzied—so frenzied that their marriage comes to hang upon their success. Corvick goes off to Bombay as a correspondent, and while there wires: Eureka. The narrator and Corvick's fiancée, Gwendolyn Erme, try to guess what it must be. Corvick stops off on Vereker at Rapallo during his return journey, and writes that Vereker has verified his discovery. Gwendolyn marries George on condition that he reveal his secret; he dies on his honeymoon before writing it down. Gwen refuses to tell the narrator what it is, because, says she, it is her life. Vereker dies. Then Gwen, who has re-married to Drayton Deane a critic, herself dies on the birth of a second child. After a decent but excruciated interval—for in James decency most of all is subject to excruciation—the narrator does his best to discover from Deane what the secret of Vereker's work had been. But Gwendolyn had never told him; and the figure in the carpet is safe. Nobody knows or can know what it can be. What then was the puzzle? It may be that there was none, or none except to those who wrote—or read—for the passion of the passion; which was certainly not how the narrator, nor any of his friends, either wrote or read. A frenzied curiosity is not passion. Or it may be that the figure in the carpet is necessarily ineluctable. Perhaps it only ought to be there; that much, acuteness can discover. In his prefatory remarks, James does nothing to help; but says only that "the question that accordingly comes up, the issue of the affair, can be but whether the very secret of perception hasn't been lost. That is the situation, and **'The Figure in the Carpet'** exhibits a small group of well-meaning persons engaged in a test." We can only note that well-meaning persons are notoriously unperceptive, and add that the secret of perception in readers comes very near the secret of creation in artists.

"The Figure in the Carpet" is perhaps a tea-time and tepid whiskey fable, for it is over these beverages that it largely occurs; and so represents, I think, no more than at most can be made out of obsessed gossip. James may have meant more for it—his preface suggests that he did—but it would seem actually, as written, to mean no more than that there is a figure in the carpet if you can imagine it for yourself; it is not there to discover. It is rather like Kafka, manqué, the exasperation of the mystery without the presence of the mystery, or a troubled conscience without any evidence of guilt.

Rather similar but carried further, further for actuality, by the very conventionality of its fantasy—its *glaring* incredibility—is the fable of **"The Private Life."** Here again the narrator is a writer unnamed, this time on vacation in the Alps in a house full of people connected with the arts. Among the guests are Clare Vawdrey, a writer of genius but a second-rate man; Lord Mellfont, a magnificent public figure but nothing much when not in public; and Blanche Adney, a great actress, for whom Vawdrey is writing a play, and who is quite friendly with the narrator. The second-rateness of Vawdrey and the magnificent public presence of Mellfont gradually become suspect to Blanche and the narrator. Pursuing their curiosity, the narrator sneaks into Vawdrey's room in the evening, while Vawdrey is outside talking to Blanche; there the narrator discovers Vawdrey's other self writing industriously in the dark. Later, by plan, Blanche gets her chance, and while the narrator keeps Vawdrey outside herself makes the acquaintance of the other or "ghost" self and falls in love with him. Meantime the narrator finds the outer self even duller than he had thought: "the world," he reflects, "was vulgar and stupid, and the real man would have been a fool to come out for it when he could gossip and dine by deputy." Lord Mellfont, on the other hand, must be himself an apparition, called into being by a public relation only; by himself he must be nothing, literally nothing. Blanche and the narrator go looking for him on that assumption, and of necessity he appears in front of them; if they had not looked for him, he would have been unable to materialize. "He was all public and had no corresponding private life, just as Clare Vawdrey was all private and had no corresponding public." Of this little piece what does one say but that the ghost story is the most plausible form of the fairy tale; it makes psychological penetration ominous because not verifiable. Who would care to verify a ghost, especially two ghosts who have the unity only of opposites? Life, the actuality, lies somewhere between; and it is a relief to think that your dull man of genius keeps a brilliant ghost in his work-room, just as it is a malicious delight to figure that your brilliant public man is utterly resourceless without a public.

"The Private Life" is a fantastic statement, so far as it has a serious side, of the inviolable privacy of the man of genius. **"The Death of the Lion"** makes a plea for the protection of that privacy, and for much more, on the ground that if you successfully violate it your genius, if he have no deputy self to gossip and dine, perishes from exposure. The narrator is again a young, detached writer and journalist with a strong sense of allegiance to the great, is sent to write up Neil Paraday at the moment he achieves, at the age of fifty, after a long illness, with his new book, the public success of being made a subject of a leader in *The Empire.* An interviewer for 37 syndicated papers arrives just after Paraday has read the narrator the manuscript plan—a plan finished and perfect in itself—of his next and greatest book. The narrator takes over the interviewer, and goes on to take over as much protective custody of Paraday as possible. But Paraday, with his success, is nevertheless taken up by the unreading, by those who hate literature in the guise of adoring writers, especially by a Mrs. Wimbush who has the fortune of a great brewery. Paraday a little excuses his not throwing Mrs. Wimbush out of doors on the ground that he can get material for his writing out of her. The narrator, however, has a single success in keeping off an American girl with an autograph album to fill, but who really loves Paraday's work, understands that reading is greater than personality, and agrees to seek the author, as the narrator tells her to, "in his works even as God in Nature." Neil Paraday had been made, as the narrator says, a contemporary. "That was what had happened: the poor man was to be squeezed into his horrible age. I felt as if he had been overtaken on the crest of the hill and brought back to the city. A little more and he would have dipped down the short cut to posterity and escaped." To be a contemporary was to be a lion and lions of the contemporary necessarily die soon. Thus Paraday soon *wants* to become ill again; he knew what was happening to him, but he could not help surrendering to it. "He filled his lungs, for the most part, with the comedy of his queer fate: the tragedy was in the spectacles through which I chose to look. He was conscious of inconvenience, and above all of a great renouncement; but how could he have heard a mere dirge in the bells of his accession?"

What happens is inevitable from the title and from what has already been said. Paraday is seduced into going to a house-party at Mrs. Wimbush's country place which is called Prestidge—a surface quality obtained, if you remember your etymology, by sleight of hand. There is to be a great foreign Princess there, and many others, all to hear him read his precious manuscript plan. He falls sick and, dying, instructs the narrator to print it as his last work, small but perfect. However, Mrs. Wimbush has lent it to a guest who in turn has lent it to another, and so on, none of them by any chance reading it; so that it is lost. Before our Lion actually dies he has become a burden, for the next two in Mrs. Wimbush's series of Lions come before he is out of the way; and it is in the identity of the new beasts that we see the true estimation in which Mrs. Wimbush—in which society—holds literature. The new beasts are two popular successes, Guy Walsingham, who is a woman, and Dora Forbes, who is a man with red moustaches. Their publishers think it necessary that they take opposite sexes in their pen names. But the narrator says rather that they are writers of some third sex: the success-sex, no doubt, which can alone cope with the assaults of an adulating society.

Here we see the figure of a great writer preyed upon; the Lion is brought down by the brutality of a society which could have no use for him except as quarry. In **"The Next Time"** we have the contrary fable, that of the writer who struggles desperately to make society his prey, but fails because he cannot help remaining the harmless, the isolated monarch of his extreme imaginative ardent self. Society, seen as his prey, has no trouble at all in keeping out of his way. Ray Limbert's only successful step was the initial step of a "bad" marriage to a good wife, who has a mother and bears children who require support. He has a sister-in-law who is a successful popular novelist, where he himself is incontestably a great writer. He gave the narrator (again a literary man) "one of the rarest emotions of the literary life, the sense of an activity in which I could critically rest." However, it was necessary for him to earn his living, and after failing at journalism, the narrator gets him the post of editor with a year's contract at complete liberty. As an editor, Ray Limbert resolves to contribute serially a deliberately bad novel in the hope of achieving success, and requires of his friends that they do not read the instalments for shame. His difficulty there was that he was one of those "people who can't be vulgar for trying." He loses his post as editor, partly because of the authors whom he had printed but mostly because of his own novel, which so far from being popular or obvious was "charming with all his charm and powerful with all his power: it was an unscrupulous, an unsparing, a shameless merciless masterpiece. . . . The perversity of the effort, even though heroic, had been frustrated by the purity of the gift." As the narrator finished his reading he looked out the window for a sight of the summer dawn, his eyes "compassionately and admiringly filled. The eastern sky, over the London housetops, had a wonderful tragic crimson. That was the colour of his magnificent mistake." It was a mistake which Ray Limbert—by the terms of the fable—repeated, always believing that the next time he would do the trick. All the narrator could say was "that genius was a fatal disturber or that the unhappy man had no effectual *flair.* When he went abroad to gather garlic he came home with heliotrope." Finally he forgot "the next time." "He had merely waked up one morning again in the country of the blue and had stayed there with a good conscience and a great idea," and died, writing.

"In the country of the blue" is a very lonely place to be, for it is very nearly empty except for the self, and is gained only by something like a religious retreat, by an approximation of birth or death or birth-in-death. James tried for it in fiction I think but once, in **"The Great Good Place,"** here mentioned but in passing, where there is an adumbration rather than an account given of the retreat of the author George Doane, made for the recovery of genius, "which he had been in danger of losing"; he had returned to himself after eight hours to find his room "disencumbered, different, twice as large. It was all right." Yet there was some constant recourse for James to the country of the blue; it was where he would have had his projected great authors live, and it was where, as we shall see he reported, he sometimes lived himself.

But before we look at that sight, let us look at the tale which of all that James wrote best prepares us for it, **"The Lesson of the Master."** This is probably the finest, surely the clearest, most brilliant, and most eloquent of all James's pleading fables of the literary life. It has greater scope than the others, itself rings with greatness, and is more nearly dramatic in character, more nearly joins the issue of the ideal and the actual. Unlike the other tales in our present list it is related in the third person from the point of view of the most implicated person in it, Paul Overt. The relations between that distinguished young talent and the Master, Henry St. George, who has for years done less than his best work, are exhibited in terms of Marian Fancourt, of an interest and an intelligence in the arts hardly less than her beauty, as a nexus for the conflict of loyalties between the master and the disciple. All three meet for the first time on a country weekend at Summersoft. Both men are taken with Marian Fancourt. Overt respects St. George vastly, and when St. George tells him that he is good and must be better, referring to his own inadequacy, he responds by a kind of preliminary submission. In London Overt falls in love with Marian, St. George more or less making way for him. For each the two others are the poles of attraction. Overt visits St. George in his study after a party, and for most of thirteen pages St. George exhorts him magnificently to give up everything, marriage, money, children, social position—all the things to which St. George himself had succumbed—for the sake of his art. Overt takes the master pretty much at his word and goes abroad for two years writing his best thing yet under great privation of all personal life. While he is abroad St. George's wife dies, and Overt returns to find St. George and Marian on the verge of marriage, and so feels brutally cheated. It turns out that St. George has married Marian partly to save Overt from succumbing to the false gods, to save him from having everything but the great thing.

The great thing is "The sense of having done the best—the sense which is the real life of the artist and the absence of which is his death, of having drawn from his intellectual instrument the finest music that nature had hidden in it, of having played it as it should be played." When Overt complains that he is not to be allowed the common passions and affections of men, St. George answers that art is passion enough. When the whole ascetic position—for it is no less than ascetic in that it draws the artist as mostly not a man—Overt sums it up for him by crying that it leaves the artist condemned to be "a mere disfranchised monk" who "can produce his effect only by giving up personal happiness. What an arraignment of art!" And St. George takes him up: "Ah you don't imagine that I'm defending art? 'Arraignment'—I should think so! Happy the societies in which it hasn't made its appearance, for from the moment it comes they have a consuming ache, they have an uncurable corruption, in their breast. Most assuredly is the artist in a false position! But I thought we were taking him for granted." It was when Overt found Marian married to St. George that he realized *what* he had been taking for granted. One *hardly* knows whether society or the artist is worse flayed here; but one knows, and there is only the need one feels for a grace note in James's concluding remark that "the Master was essentially right and that Nature had dedicated him to intellectual, not to personal passion."

The portrait of the artist in Henry James is now almost complete: the man fully an artist is the man, short of the saint, most wholly deprived. This is the picture natural to the man still in revolt, to the man who still identifies the central struggle of life in society as the mere struggle of that aspect of his life of which he makes his profession, and who has not yet realized, but is on the verge of doing so, that all the professions possible in life are mutually inclusive. One's own profession is but the looking glass and the image of the others; and the artist is he who being by nature best fitted to see the image clear is damned only if he does not. If he sees, his vision disappears in his work, which is the country of the blue. That is why the only possible portrait to paint of the artist will be a portrait of him as a failure. Otherwise there will be only the portrait of the man. That is why James portrayed the artist chiefly during his intermediate dubious period, and why in his full maturity, like St. George, but in a different richer sense, took the artist for granted and portrayed men and women bent, not on a privation but a fullness of being.

There remains still to record only James's portrait of himself as the artist in the man mature, and for that there are two passages to quote, of which one is from a letter written at the age of seventy to Henry Adams urging him to cultivate the interest of his consciousness. "You see I still, in presence of life (or of what you deny to be such,) have reactions—as many as possible—and the book I sent you is proof of them. It's, I suppose, because I am that queer monster, the artist, an obstinate finality, an inexhaustible sensibility. Hence the reactions—appearances, memories, many things, go on playing upon it with consequences that

I note and 'enjoy' (grim word!) noting. It all takes doing—and I *do*. I believe I shall do yet again—it is still an act of life."

That is the man in life as artist. The other passage, with which we end the chapter, is taken from some pencilled notes written some time in his last years on a New Year's eve, near midnight, during a time of inspiration. Lubbock prints the whole of the notes in the Introduction to his edition of the Letters, saying that "There is no moment of all his days in which it is now possible to approach him more clearly." I quote only the last paragraph. The shape, the life, the being of a novel having shown itself clear, the exaltation is so great that James is left once again with just the story of a story to tell, this time of himself.

> Thus just these first little wavings of the oh so tremulously passionate little old wand (now!) make for me, I feel, a sort of promise of richness and beauty and variety; a sort of portent of the happy presence of the elements. The good days of last August and even my broken September and my better October come back to me with their gage of divine possibilities, and I welcome these to my arms, I press them with unutterable tenderness. I seem to emerge from these recent bad days—the fruit of blind accident—and the prospect clears and flushes, and my poor blest old Genius pats me so admirably and lovingly on the back that I turn, I screw round, and bend my lips to passionately, in my gratitude, kiss its hands.

The feeling in this passage is not uncommon; most of us have been terrified at its counterpart; but the ability to surrender to the expression of it is rare, and is what brought James himself, for the moment of expression, into the blue. (pp. 595-617)

R. P. Blackmur, "In the Country of the Blue," in The Kenyon Review, *Vol. V, No. 4, Autumn, 1943, pp. 595-617.*

Robert Heilman (essay date 1948)

[Heilman is an American educator, poet, and critic. In the following excerpt, he disputes Freudian interpretations of The Turn of the Screw.*]*

It is probably safe to say that the Freudian interpretation of [***The Turn of the Screw***], of which the best known exponent is Edmund Wilson [see excerpt dated 1934], no longer enjoys wide critical acceptance. [Heilman adds in a footnote: Philip Rahv calls attempts to explain away the ghosts "a fallacy of rationalism," and asserts, I think correctly, that the Freudian view narrows and conventionalizes the story in a way that contradicts both James's intentions and artistic habits, and, I might add, our own sense that large matters are at stake. In their symposium in *Invitation to Learning,* Katherine Anne Porter, Mark Van Doren, and Allen Tate have all specifically denied the validity of the Freudian reading of the story. I have attempted, in some detail, to show how Wilson's account of ***The Turn*** runs afoul of both the story and James's preface.] If, then, we cannot account for the evil by treating the governess as pathological, we must seek elsewhere an explanation of the story's hold. I am convinced that, at the level of action, the story means exactly what it says: that at Bly there are apparitions which the governess sees, which Mrs. Grose does not see but comes to believe in because they are consistent with her own independent experience, and of which the children have a knowledge which they endeavor to conceal. These dramatic circumstances have a symbolic import which seems not too difficult to get hold of: the ghosts are evil, evil which comes subtly, conquering before it is wholly seen; the governess, Cassandra-like in the intuitions which are inaccessible to others, is the guardian whose function it is to detect and attempt to ward off evil; Mrs. Grose—whose name, like the narrator's title, has virtually allegorical significance—is the commonplace mortal, well intentioned, but perceiving only the obvious; the children are the victims of evil, victims who, ironically, practice concealment—who doubtless must conceal—when not to conceal is essential to salvation. If this reading of the symbolism be tenable, we can understand in part the imaginative power of the story, for, beneath the strange and startling action-surface, we have the oldest of themes—the struggle of evil to possess the human soul. And if this struggle appears to resolve itself into a Christian form, that impulse, as it were, of the materials need not be surprising.

But the compelling theme and the extraordinarily vivid plot-form are not the entirety of ***The Turn of the Screw;*** there are other methods by which James extends and intensifies his meaning and strikes more deeply into the reader's consciousness. Chief of these is a highly suggestive and even symbolic language which permeates the entire story. After I had become aware of and begun to investigate this phenomenon, I found Mr. Matthiessen, in quite fortuitous corroboration of my own critical method, commenting on the same technical aspect of James's later works—his ability to "bind together his imaginative effects by subtly recurrent images of a thematic kind" and to "extend a metaphor into a symbol," and the fact that later in his career "realistic details had become merely the covering for a content that was far from realistic." In ***The Turn*** there is a great deal of recurrent imagery which powerfully influences the tone and the meaning of the story; the story becomes, indeed, a dramatic poem, and to read it properly one must assess the role of the language precisely as one would if public form of the work were poetic. For by his iterative imagery and by the very unobtrusive management of symbols, which in the organic work cofunction with the language, James has severely qualified the bare narrative; and, if he has not defined the evil which, as he specified, was to come to the reader as something monstrous and unidentified, he has at least set forth the mode and the terms of its operation with unrecognized fullness.

For a mature reader it is hardly necessary to insist that the center of horror is not the apparitions themselves, though their appearances are worked out with fine uniqueness, but is the children, and our sense of what is happening to them. What is happening to them is Quint and Jessel; the governess's awareness of the apparitions is her awareness of a change within the children; the shock of ghostly appearances is the shock of evil perceived unexpectedly, suddenly, after it has secretly made inroads. Matthiessen [in *Henry James: The Major Phase*] and R. P. Blackmur [in the introduction to James's *The Art of the Novel*] both refer, as a matter of course, to the corruption of the children; E.M.W. Tillyard, in a volume on Shakespeare, remarks incidentally that James "owes so much of the power with which evil is conveyed to showing it in the minds of children; where it should least be found." Perhaps two modern phenomena, the sentimentalizing of children and the disinclination to concede to evil any status more profound than the melodramatic, account for a frequent unwillingness to accept what the story says. James is not disposed to make things easier; he emphasizes that it is the incorruptible who have taken on corruption. He introduces no mere pathos of childhood catastrophe; his are not ordinary children. He is at pains to give them a special quality—by repetition which in so careful an artist can hardly have been a clumsy accident. As the repeated words achieve a cumulative tonal force, we can see the working of the poetic imagination.

Flora has "extraordinary charm," is "most beautiful." Miles is "incredibly beautiful." Both have "the bloom of health and happiness." Miles is "too fine and fair" for the world; he is a "beautiful little boy." The governess is "dazzled by their loveliness." They are "most loveable" in their "helplessness." Touching their "fragrant faces" one could believe only "their incapacity and their beauty." Miles is a "prodigy of delightful, loveable goodness." In midstory Flora still emerges from concealment "rosily," and one is caught by "the golden glow of her curls," by her "loveliest, eagerest simplicity," by "the excess of something beautiful that shone out of the blue" of her eyes, by "the lovely little lighted face." In both, "beauty and amiability, happiness and cleverness" are still paramount. Miles has still the "wonderful smile" and the "beautiful eye" of "a little fairy prince." Both write letters "too beautiful to be posted." On the final Sunday the governess sees still Miles's "beautiful face" and talks of him as "beautiful and perfect"; he smiles at her "with the same loveliness" and spars verbally with "serenity" and "unimpeachable gaiety." Even after Flora is gone, Miles is "the beautiful little presence" as yet with "neither stain nor shadow"; his expression is "the most beautiful" the governess has ever known.

James devotes an almost prodigal care to creating an impression of special beauty in the children, an impression upon which depends the extraordinary effectiveness of the change which takes place in them. In such children the appearance of any imperfection is a shock. The shock is emphasized when the governess wonders whether she must "pronounce their loveliness a trick of premature cunning" and reflects upon the possibility that "the immediate charm . . . was studied"; when Miles's "sweet face" must be described as a "sweet ironic face"; when his "happy laugh" goes off into "incoherent, extravagant song"; and when, above all, the governess must declare with conviction that their "more than earthly beauty, their absolutely unnatural goodness [is] a game, . . . a policy and a fraud."

Is James, then, laboriously overusing the principle of contrast, clothing the children with an astonishing fascination merely to accentuate the shock of their being stripped bare? Obviously not. Beneath the superficial clash we can already sense a deeper paradox. When James speaks of Miles's "beautiful fevered face" and says that he "lives in a setting of beauty and misery," he puts into words what the reader has already come to feel—that his real subject is the dual nature of man, who is a little lower than the angels, and who yet can become a slave in the realm of evil. The children's beauty, we have come to feel, is a symbol of the spiritual perfection of which man is capable. Thus the battle between the governess and the demons becomes the old struggle of the morality play in new dress.

But that statement of the struggle is much more general and abstract than the formulation of it made by the story itself. When James speaks of "any clouding of their innocence," he reminds us again of a special quality in their beauty which he has quietly stressed with almost thematic fullness. The *clouding* suggests a *change* in a characteristic brightness of theirs, a brightness of which we are made aware by a recurrent imagery of light. Flora, at the start, "brightly" faces the new governess; hers is a "radiant" image; the children "dazzle" the governess; Flora has "a lovely little lighted face," and she considers "luminously"; in his "brightness" Miles "fairly glittered"; he speaks "radiantly"; at his "revolution" he speaks with "extraordinary brightness." This light-giving quality of theirs is more than a mere amplification of a charm shockingly to be destroyed; it is difficult not to read it as a symbol of their being, as it were, at the dawn of existence. For they are children, and their radiance suggests the primal and the universal. This provisional interpretation is supported by another verbal pattern which James uses to describe the children. Miles has a "great glow of freshness," a "positive fragrance of purity," a "sweetness of innocence"; the governess comments again on the "rose-flush of his innocence"; in him she finds something "extraordinarily happy, that, . . . struck me as beginning anew each day"; he could draw upon "reserves of goodness." Then, as things change, the governess remarks, on one occasion, that "He couldn't play any longer at innocence," and mentions, on another, his pathetic struggles to "play . . . a part of innocence." To the emphasis upon beauty, then, is added this emphasis upon brightness and freshness and innocence. What must come across to us, from such a context, is echoes of the Garden of Eden; we have the morality play story, as we have said, but altered, complemented, and given unique poignance by being told of mankind at its first radical crisis, in consequence of which all other morality stories are; Miles and Flora become the childhood of the race. They are symbolic children as the ghosts are symbolic ghosts. Even the names themselves have a representative quality as those of James's characters often do: Miles—the soldier, the archetypal male; Flora—the flower, the essential female. Man and woman are caught even before the first hint of maturity, dissected, and shown to have within them all the seeds—possible of full growth even now—of their own destruction.

James's management of the setting and of other ingredients in the drama deepens one's sense of a story at once primeval and eternal, lurking beneath the surface of the action. Bly itself is almost an Eden with its "lawn and bright flowers"; the governess comments, "The scene had a greatness. . . . " Three times James writes of the "golden" sky, and one unconsciously recalls that Flora was a "rosy sprite" with "hair of gold." Miss Jessel first appears "in the garden," where "the old trees, the thick shrubbery, made a great and pleasant shade. . . . " Here, for a time, the three "lived in a cloud of music and love . . . "; the children are "extraordinarily at one" in "their quality of sweetness." Now it is significant that James uses even the seasons to heighten his drama: the pastoral idyl begins in June, when spring is at the full, and then is gradually altered until we reach the dark ending of a November whose coldness and deadness are unobtrusively but unmistakably stressed: " . . . the autumn had dropped . . . and blown out half our lights" (a variation of the light-pattern); the governess now notices "grey sky and withered garlands," "bared spaces and scattered dead leaves." What might elsewhere be Gothic trimming is here disciplined by the pattern. When, on the final Sunday night, the governess tries hard to "reach" Miles, there is "a great wind"; she hears "the lash of the rain and the batter of the gusts"; at the climax there is "an extraordinary blast and chill," and then darkness. The next afternoon is "damp and grey." After Flora's final escapade at the pond, James stresses the governess's feelings at the end of the day; the evening is "portentous" without precedent; she blows out the candles and feels a "mortal coldness." On the final day with Miles she notices "the stupid shrubs," "the dull things of November," "the dim day." So it is not merely the end of a year but the end of a cycle: the spring of gay, bright human innocence has given way to the dark autumn—or rather, as we might pun, to the dark *fall.*

And in the darkness of the latter end of things we might note the special development of the light which, to the sensitive governess, the children seem actually to give off. It is, I think, more than a coincidence that, when the governess mentions Miss Jessel, Flora's face shows a "quick, smitten glare," and that, in the final scene, Miles is twice said to be "glaring"—the same verb which has been used to describe Quint's look. All three characters, of course, look with malevolence; yet *glare* must suggest, also, a hard, powerful, ugly light—an especially effective transformation of the apparently benign luminousness of the spring.

The same movement of human experience James portrays in still another symbolic form. As the light changes and the season changes and the children's beauty becomes ambiguous, another alteration takes place in them. Their youth, of course, is the prime datum of the story, and of it we are ever conscious; and at the same time we are aware of a strange maturity in them—in, for instance, their poise, their controlled utilization of their unusual talents to give pleasure. Our sense of something that transcends their youth is first defined overtly late in the story when the governess speaks of her feeling that Miles is "accessible as an older person." Though she does not speak of change, there is subtly called forth in us a conviction that years have been added to Miles. So we are not surprised when the governess assures Mrs. Grose, and goes out of her way, a little later, to remind her of the assurance, that, at meetings with Miss Jessel, Flora is "not a child" but "an old, old woman"—an insight that receives a measure of authentication, perhaps, by its reminiscence of the Duessa motif. The suggestion that Flora has become older is skillfully conveyed, in the pond scene, by her silence (and silence itself has an almost symbolic value throughout the story), by her quick recovery of her poised gaiety, and especially by the picture of her peeping at the governess over the shoulder of Mrs. Grose, who is embracing her—the first intimation of a cold adult calculatingness which appears in all her remaining actions. The governess says, " . . . her incomparable childish beauty had suddenly failed, had quite vanished . . . she was literally . . . hideously, hard; she had turned common and almost ugly." Mrs. Grose sums up, "It has made her, every inch of her, quite old." More effective, however, than any of this direct presentation of vital change is a delicate symbol which may pass almost unnoticed: when she is discovered at the pond, Flora picks up, and drops a moment later, "a big, ugly spray of withered fern"—a quiet commentary on the passage of symbolic spring, on the spiritual withering that is the story's center. When, at the end of the scene, the governess looks "at the grey pool and its blank, haunted edge," we automatically recall, "The sedge has withered from the lake"—the imagery used by Keats in his account of an ailing knight-at-arms in another bitter autumn.

Besides the drying of foliage and the coming of storms and darkness there is one other set of elements, loosely working together and heavy with implications, which suggest that this is a story of the decay of Eden. At Quint's first appearance Bly "had been stricken with death." After Miles's nocturnal exploit the governess utters a cliché that, under the influence of the context, becomes vigorously meaningful: " . . . you . . . caught your death in the night air!" There are, further, some arresting details in the description of Quint: "His eyes are sharp, strange—awfully; . . . rather small and very fixed. His mouth's wide, and his lips are thin, . . . " These are unmistakably the characteristics of a snake. James is too fine an artist to allegorize the point, but, as he has shaped the story, the coming of Quint is the coming of the serpent into the little Eden that is Bly (both Miss Porter and Mr. Tate have noted other physical characteristics of Quint which traditionally belong to the devil). Quint's handsomeness and his borrowed finery, by which he apes the gentleman, suggest, perhaps, the specious plausibleness of the visitor in the Garden. As for the "fixed eyes": later we learn that Miss Jessel "only fixed the child" and that the apparition of Quint "fixed me exactly as it had fixed me from the tower and from the garden." Of Quint's position at Bly Mrs. Grose says, "The master believed in him and placed him here because he was supposed not to be well and the country air so good for him." The master, in other words, has nourished a viper in his bosom. The secret influence upon Miles the governess describes as "poison," and at the very end she says that the demonic presence "filled the room like the taste of poison." In the first passage the governess equates "poison" with "secret precocity"; toward the end she emphasizes Miles's freedom and sorrowfully gives up "the fiction that I had anything more to teach him." Why is it a fiction? Because he already knew too much, because he had eaten of the fruit of the tree of knowledge? We have already been told of the "dark prodigy" by which "the imagination of all evil *had* been opened up to him," and of his being "under some influence operating in his small intellectual life as a tremendous incitement."

We should not press such analogies too hard, or construct inflexible parables. Our business is rather to trace all the imaginative emanations that enrich the narrative, the associations and intimations by which it transcends the mere horror story and achieves its own kind of greatness. But by now it must be clear from the antipodal emphases of the story that James has an almost religious sense of the duality of man, and, as if to manifest an intention, he makes that sense explicit in terms broadly religious and even Christian. The image of Flora's "angelic beauty" is "beatific"; she has "the deep, sweet serenity . . . of one of Raphael's holy infants"; she has "placid heavenly eyes." In Miles there is "something divine that I have never found to the same degree in any child." In a mildly humorous context the children are called "cherubs." Seeing no signs of suffering from his school experience, the governess regards Miles as an "angel." Mrs. Grose imputes to Flora a "blessed innocence," and the governess surrenders to the children's "extraordinary childish grace"—a noun which in this patterned structure can hardly help being ambivalent. In midstory Flora has still a "divine smile"; both children remain "adorable." This verbal pattern, which is too consistent to be coincidental, irresistibly makes us think of the divine in man, of his capability of salvation. Now what is tragic and terrifying in man is that to be capable of salvation is to be capable also of damnation—an equivocal potentiality suggested early by the alternation of moods in the newly arrived governess, who senses immediately a kind of wavering, a waiting for determination, at Bly. And James, to present the spiritual decline of the children, finds terms which exactly balance those that connote their spiritual capabilities.

We are never permitted to see the apparitions except as moral realities. Miss Jessel is a figure of "unmistakeable horror and evil . . . in black, pale and dreadful." She is a "horror of horrors," with "awful eyes," "with a kind of fury of intention," and yet "with extraordinary beauty." Again she is described as "Dark as midnight in her black dress, her haggard beauty, and her unutterable woe. . . . " It is brilliant to give her beauty, which not only identifies her with Flora and thus underscores the dual possibilities that lie ahead of Flora, but also enriches the theme with its reminder of Milton's fallen angels who retain something of their original splendor—"the excess / Of glory obscured." So, with the repeated stress upon her woe, we almost expect the passage which tells us that she "suffers the torments . . . of the damned": she is both damned and an agent of damnation—another reminiscence of the Miltonic myth. She is called later a "pale and ravenous demon," not "an inch of whose evil . . . fell short"—which reminds us of James's prefatory insistence that the apparitions were to be thought of as demons. Again, she is "our infernal witness"; she and Quint are "those fiends"; "they were not angels," and they could be bringing "some yet more infernal message." "And to ply them with that evil still, to keep up the work of demons, is what brings the others back." They are "tempters," who work subtly by holding out fascinating "suggestions of danger." In the last scene Quint presents—the phrase is used twice—"his white face of damnation."

By this series of words, dispersed throughout the story yet combining in a general statement, James defines as diabolic the forces attacking the children of whose angelic part we are often reminded. Now these attacking forces, as often in Elizabethan drama, are seen in two aspects. Dr. Faustus has to meet an enemy which has an inner and an outer reality—his own thoughts, and Mephistopheles; James presents evil both as agent (the demons) and as effect (the transformation in the once fresh and beautiful and innocent children). The dualistic concept of reality appears most explicitly when Mrs. Grose asks, "And if he was so bad there as that comes to, how is he such an angel now?" and the governess replies, "Yes, indeed—and if he was a fiend at school!" By the *angel-fiend* antithesis James underscores what he sees as a central human contradiction, which he emphasizes throughout the book by his chosen verbal pattern. The governess speaks of the children's "love of evil" gained from Quint and Miss Jessel, of Miles's "wickedness" at school. In such a context the use of the word *revolution* to describe Miles's final taking matters up with the governess—a move by which, we should remember, he becomes completely "free"—cannot help calling to mind the Paradise and Eden revolutions of Judaeo-Christian mythology. The revolutionary change in character is nicely set forth by the verbal counterpoint in one passage. "He found the most divine little way," the governess says, "to keep me quiet while she went off." " 'Divine'?" Mrs. Grose asks, and the governess replies, "Infernal then!" The divine has paradoxically passed into the infernal. Then we see rapidly the completed transition in Flora: she turns upon the governess an expression of "hard, fixed gravity" and ignores the "hideous plain presence" of Miss Jessel—"a stroke that somehow converted the little girl herself into the very presence that could make me quail." In Miles, by contrast, we see a protracted struggle, poignantly conveyed by a recurrent metaphor of illness. Early in the story Miles is in "the bloom of health and happiness," but near the end he seems like a "wistful patient in a children's hospital," "like a convalescent slightly fatigued." At the end he shows "bravery" while "flushing with pain"; he gives "a sick little headshake"; his is a "beautiful fevered face." But the beauty goes, the fever gains; Miles gives "a frantic little shake for air and light"; he is in a "white rage." The climax of his disease, the binding together of all the strands we have been tracing, is his malevolent cry to the governess—"you devil!" It is his final transvaluation of values: she who would be his savior has become for him a demon. His face gives a "convulsive supplication"—that is, actually, a prayer, for and to Quint, the demon who has become his total deity. But the god isn't there, and Miles despairs and dies. We need not labor the dependence of this brilliant climax upon the host of associations and evocations by which, as this outline endeavors to show, James prepares us for the ultimate resolution of the children's being.

There are glimmerings of other imaginative kinships, such as that already mentioned, the Faustian. Miles's "You devil" is in one way almost identical with Faustus's savage attack, in Marlowe's play, upon the Old Man who has been trying to save him; indeed James's story, in its central combat, is not unlike the Faustus story as it might be told by the Good Angel. But whereas Dr. Faustus is a late intellectualist version of Everyman, James, as we have said, weaves in persuasive hints, one after another, of mankind undergoing, in his Golden Age, an elemental conflict: thus we have the morality play, but in a complicated, enriched, and intensified version. When the governess first sees Quint, she is aware of "some challenge between us"; the next time it seems "as if I had been looking at him for years and had known him always"; near the end she says, "I *was* . . . face to face with the elements," and, of the final scene, "It was like fighting with a demon for a human soul."

What, then, does the story say about the role of the governess, and how does this contribute to the complex of the impressions built up in part by James's language? From the start the words used by the governess suggest that James is attaching to her the quality of savoir, not only in a general sense, but with certain Christian associations. She uses words like "atonement"; she speaks of herself as an "expiatory victim," of her "pure suffering," and at various times—twice in the final scene—of her "torment." Very early she plans to "shelter my pupils," to "absolutely save" them; she speaks variously of her "service," "to protect and defend the little creatures . . . bereaved . . . loveable." When she fears that she cannot "save or shield them" and that "they're lost," she is a "poor protectress." At another time she is a "sister of Charity" attempting to "cure" Miles. But by now what we cannot mistake is the relation of pastor and flock, a relationship which becomes overt when the governess tells Miles, "I just want you to help me to save you." It is in this sense that the governess "loves" Miles—a loving which must not be confused, as it is confused by some critics, with "making love to" or "being in love with" him. Without such pastoral love no guardian would consider his flock worth the sacrifice. The governess's priestly function is made still more explicit by the fact that she comes ultimately to act as confessor and to use every possible means to bring Miles to confession; the long final scene really takes place in the confessional, with the governess as priest endeavoring, by both word and gesture, to protect her charge against the evil force whose invasion has, with consummate irony, carried even there. In one sense the governess must elicit confession because, in her need for objective reassurance, she will not take the lead as accuser; but securing the confession is, more importantly, a mitigation of Miles's own pride, his self-will; it could soften him, make him accessible to grace. The experience has a clear sacramental quality: the governess says that Miles senses "the need of confession . . . he'll confess. If he confesses, he's saved." It is when he begins to break and confess that "the white face of damnation" becomes baffled and at a vital moment retreats; but it returns "as if to blight his confession," and it is in part through the ineptitude of the governess-confessor-savior, we are led to understand, that Miles is lost.

It is possible that there are even faint traces of theological speculation to give additional substance to the theme of salvation and damnation which finally achieves specific form in the sacramentalism of the closing scenes. Less than halfway through the story the governess refers to the children thus: "blameless and foredoomed as they were." By *blameless* she can only mean that she does not have direct, tangible evidence of voluntary evil-doing on their part; they still look charming and beautiful; she does not have grounds for a positive placing of blame. Why, then, "foredoomed"? May this not be a suggestion of original sin (which Miss Porter has already seen as an ingredient in the story), an interpretation consistent with the view of Bly as a kind of Eden? Three-quarters of the way through the story the governess again turns to speculation: " . . . I constantly both attacked and renounced the enigma of what such a little gentleman could have done that deserved a penalty." *Enigma* is perhaps just the word to be applied to a situation, of which one technical explication is the doctrine of original sin, by an inquiring lay mind with a religious sense but without precise theological tools. What is significant is that the governess does not revolt against the penalty as if it betokened a cosmic injustice. And original sin, whether it be natural depravity or a revolt in a heavenly or earthly paradise, fits exactly into the machinery of this story of two beautiful children who in a lovely springtime of existence already suffer, not unwillingly, hidden injuries which will eventually destroy them. (pp. 277-86)

Robert Heilman, " 'The Turn of the Screw' as Poem," in The University of Kansas City Review, *Vol. XIV, No. 4, Summer, 1948, pp. 277-89.*

Osborn Andreas (essay date 1948)

[*Andreas is the author of* Henry James and the Expanding Horizon, *a study of fundamental themes in James's fiction. In this book Andreas asserts that the single most prominent concern in James's work is the expansion of individual consciousness. It is toward this increased awareness that, for Andreas, all James's protagonists strive. In the excerpt below from his preface to this book, Andreas delineates several themes that he considers central in James's work.*]

Henry James was the novelist of consciousness, not the historian of consciences. Levels of awareness and qualities of consciousness were his subject; good and evil entered his theme only as they contributed to a clearing or a clouding, to a dulling or a sharpening, of the consciousness and the sensibilities. (p. 1)

It is this interest of James in the experience of consciousness itself that entitles us to define James as a great humanist, that exonerates him from the charge of pure and unprincipled aestheticism, and that furnishes the clue for his manner of deep and passionate participation in life. James was no cold, unmoved and dispassionate spectator of the human world. There were certain things in human nature that he cared for, deeply and fiercely, and certain things that he hated; his art was consecrated to humanistic ends and consequently is charged with humanistic meanings and implications.

He deplored certain styles of human behavior because

they deadened the sensibilities of both the actor and him acted upon, and he esteemed others because they enhanced the power of the individual to rise to greater heights of awareness. He considered the cultivation of consciousness to be the most rewarding activity of man, the greatest privilege of life, and the supreme affirmation of man's essential nature.

The fiction of Henry James is an attempt to define the most conscious man. James believed that, since the contents of consciousness are the behavior of man, certain kinds of behavior enhance the vividness of consciousness and the richness of life while others depress the action and impair the limpidity of mind. His novels and stories are a search for and an exposure of the kind of behavior which muddies that limpidity and an analytic but embodied presentation of the kind of behavior that promotes it. (pp. 1-2)

James saw what is in human beings that smothers their minds and reduces their clarity of vision; he saw too what is required of him who would be mentally awake, commanding the power and exercising the gift of consciousness. James was the implacable analyst who pursued into its myriads of incarnations, exposing the oneness of identity under its many guises, that propensity in human beings to which he attributed all blunting of sensibility: the propensity to acts of intervention in the lives of other people. It was for the destruction of this propensity—and for the augmenting of its opposite: the impulse to tender and sympathetic carefulness with the expansive potentialities of other people—that James strove, creating a body of fiction as diligently wrought as Flaubert's and as large in quantity as Balzac's.

An 1886 drawing of James by John Singer Sargent.

I want to leave a multitude of pictures of my time, projecting my small circular frame upon as many different spots as possible and going in for number as well as quality, so that the number may constitute a total having a certain value as observation and testimony.

Henry James in a letter to Robert Louis Stevenson (1888).

What James principally saw in life was the harm which people inflict—not only on others but on themselves—by deeds of emotional cannibalism. The almost ubiquitous, vicious and deep-rooted illusion that one's own life can get sustenance from an emotional feeding on the lives of others was the object of his lifelong attack. Not only does intervention in the lives of others fail to allay the appetite of the intervener, it also—and this is its chief deadlines—poisons the sources of feeling. It deprives the assaulter of sensitive power and it paralyzes the sensory activity of the assaulted. Intervention was, in James's conception, a means to an unworthy end which reacts to the damage of its user.

James isolated several different modes of intervention which are identical in essence and variant only in degree. They possess in common a violence directed against the autonomy of the individual, an intent to manipulate the lives of others and a purposive interference with their behavior.

The mildest-seeming and yet one of the most vicious of these modes of intervention is opinion, opinion itself, about the private lives of other people. James felt that not only opinion publicly expressed but also opinion privately held about the conduct, particularly the moral conduct, of others is an affront to the right of every individual to base his conduct on the needs of his nature. Opinion about the private conduct of other people is by its very nature based on evidence insufficient to any definitive conclusion and is therefore invariably epistemologically unsound, undermining the sense of truth by violating the grounds of knowledge. That person, therefore, who consents to the lodgment in his mind of an opinion about the private conduct of his neighbor is more damaged by that consent than is the person about whom the opinion is held. This penumbra knowledge to which people give credence, sometimes in the form of mob opinion and sometimes in the form of secret moral snobbery, is in James's view an intolerable indignity and one to be mercilessly expunged from the face of the earth.

Another and more overt mode of intervention that James

identified and scorned is that of outright meddling in others' lives. This kind of interference is sometimes well-intentioned, sometimes merely heedless, but more often maliciously and acquisitively officious. In James's stories meddlers range from the nuisance category through the pest type to that of the predacious well-wisher. They possess in common the offensive trait of assuming that they know better than their victims what kind of life the latter should lead. The error of the busybody is germane to that of the disciplinarian: blindness to the fact that people are like plants that can only be watered, not touched.

Another form of aggression a shade more severe than meddling is parasitism. James conceived of parasitism, whether it be financial or emotional, as a total loss for the human parasite, since his resort to this means of escape from his natural destiny cheats him of the fruits of self-expansion in the terms of his internal nature, and as a mitigated loss for the host, since his consent to the presence of the parasite derives from a considerateness worthy in itself but unfortunate in its object. The helplessness of the host, his paralysis before the aggressive parasite, baffled and annoyed James because the power to support the parasite indicated the presence of reserves of sensibility, immobilized and made sterile, the creative exercise of which would have so enlarged the consciousness of its possessor. Pathos, however, rather than tragedy, is the dominant note of James's stories of parasitism.

The next more violent form of intervention is coercion. James's feeling of revulsion for any coercive act is almost mystical. He often traces a chain of tragic events back to one original act of coercion, a fateful deed as immutably tragic in its remotest consequences as a Greek sin. James always permits the blight to fall on so many additional and innocent people as well as on the person coerced, and he does not spare us one turn in tracing the path of the evil deed. He accents the intrinsic evilness of coercion by usually giving the coercer himself a creditable motive, thereby lifting the narrative from the villain-victim category to the true tragic level. James brooked no compromise on this issue: coercion was to him always and forever and in whatever guise an unmitigated bitterness.

The final and purest form of emotional cannibalism is exploitation. The disrespect for human individuality, even his own, in that person who makes a base and illegitimate use of other people for his own advantage and profit was, in James's scheme of values, the supreme source of evil. The evil itself was loss of consciousness, and since consciousness was the fruit of free development in the line of one's own idiosyncrasy, interference in that free development to such a degree as to amount to exploitation was the seed of evil. Indulgence in looting, James insisted, was not confined to the savage tribes who waged aggressive war; it is extensively practiced today in personal and emotional relationships between presumably civilized human beings, and it is the cardinal sin which people commit against one another.

A variant of the exploitation theme in James's fiction is that of revenge. Revenge is that form of exploitation which fancies that retaliation serves the cause of justice, whereas, in fact, it merely serves the cause of self-aggrandizement at the expense of someone who deserves to pay. Revenge and exploitation are essentially identical in that each seeks emotional satisfaction in the bending of another being to one's own purposes. The false assumption at the heart of these two forms of behavior, as well as of all other variants of emotional cannibalism, is that there is profit of any kind to be derived from intervention in the lives of other people.

The observe of this theme, the positive statement of which emotional cannibalism is the negative counterpart, asserts the supreme value for consciousness of a constant, unremitting, and sympathetic consideration of the feelings of others. One's own capacity for awareness, one's own sensibility, is increased by a study of, a respect for, and a nurturing of the sensibilities and awarenesses of other people. We grow, not by tearing other people down, but by building them up.

One of the approaches to acquaintance with this law of conduct is encountered by people who suddenly see that the revenge which they are about to accomplish will really avail them nothing. Revenge forsworn appears in James's fiction as a phenomenon of enlightenment, forbearance unexpectedly presenting itself to the vengeance seeker as more desirable than the sight of the opponent's humiliation. The suddenness of the revelation gives it a mystical character, but James always bases it on experience: long-plotted revenge, upon reaching the threshold of its goal, stays its hand. The longed-for and long striven-for act inexplicably loses its anticipated savor. This event is a first intimation of a truth deeply bedded in the logic of behavior.

Another approach to this principle of conduct which James uses in his fiction is that of regret and repentance for an act of intervention in the life of another, after longer life and reflection have yielded understanding. People severely schooled by the consequences of their actions sometimes do learn, James contends, the true nature of the damage they have inflicted on themselves. James shows, these people achieving awareness, but at a costly rate—often too costly for survival.

The truly superior persons, however, according to James's test for quality, are those whose native disposition impels them to maintain a scrupulous respect for the personal rights and sensibilities of all people, even those foreign in kind. People whose sensibilities we do not share, people who have predilections for strange classes or levels of phenomena and who may or may not respond to the values we ourselves cherish, are as entitled to our careful regard as are people of our own kind. Their humanity—not their class or race or even their personal quality—is what we are beholden to. Kindness to and noninterference with others is a principle of behavior which applies to all individuals, not just to some kindred spirits, and violation of the principle, even with reference to persons we do not understand or like, will make callous the soul and harden the sensibility.

In fact, the ideal person, in James's scheme of human values, is the one who knows—and acts in accordance with his knowledge—that compassion is the clue to conduct. It is to this theme that he devoted his greatest novel. The way of life which will enrich the consciousness, swiftly make one aware of and vibrant to more and more facets of the experience of living, is the one which subordinates all other emotions and desires and purposes to the emotion of compassion. Tenderness towards other people is the true grace, and its greatest fruit is the power to fathom, with pellucid clarity of mind, the world we live in.

This is not to be confused with humanitarianism. James was certainly no humanitarian. James was looking for a way of behavior which would enable him, or anyone, to see and understand the world the way it really is. His basic search was for truth, and the reason he wanted truth was that it, and it only, fills the mind. Error shrinks the mind, while truth enlarges it. Compassion was the device, the methodology, by means of which one purified one's sensibility and perfected it as one's instrument of perception.

Skepticism as to the value of personal love, romantic and sexual, in galvanizing the consciousness was, however, a characteristic Jamesian theme, and one which undoubtedly accounts for the cool reception bestowed on many of his novels by the general public. In his earliest stories, as well as in his very latest, love is presented as a mysterious malady, as a rival to the self-discipline required for the achievement of a career, and as a stimulus to the acquisitive rather than to the generous impulses in men and women. Furthermore, love miscarried is deadly; the risks of and the penalties for defeat are so great and the benefits of success so doubtful that the emotion is too dangerous to merit a commitment that is not wrenched from one. And the difficulty of disentangling the economic aspect of marriage from the emotional aggravated James's distrust.

James's principal objection, however, to the emotion of personal love was that it dulled the sense of truth. A man in love is not a completely self-reliant person, looking at the world through his own eyes: he is necessarily conditioned by the hostage which he has given to happiness. In a manner of speaking, every lover is a liar, simply because his every thought and emotion is oriented with reference, not primarily to accurate and just appraisal of the external world, but to the safety and exaltation of the loved object. James did not minimize the power of love and he did not deny that it filled the consciousness. His complaint was rather that it transfixed the attention of its victim, circumscribed and restricted his field of observation, and rendered his testimony invalid on any subject but that of his own feelings and those of his loved object. And even on these two subjects his testimony is untrustworthy because his allegiance goes primarily, not to objective truth, but to the state of his relation at the moment to the loved one. The solipsism, the anti-social character of love offended James because it removed each pair of lovers into a charmed circle wherein all activity other than preoccupation with themselves was arrested and immobilized.

James's final comment on love was that it usually turns into some form of emotional cannibalism, vicious in its rapacity and possessiveness. Both the lover and the beloved prey on each other's emotions—and to what end? Everything stands still while the lovers fight it out, and exhaustion and depletion are the only outcome. The lovers may think that they have lived—but James does not (or does any other observer?) think so. James conceives of living as an accumulation of consciousness and as a continually accelerating power to use one's consciousness; since personal love, romantic and sexual, does not further this process, James regards it as more of a deterrent than a help to the full life.

One of the positive helps to a quickened consciousness is a sense of the past, and of this enduring agency of enlightenment James was very fond. An intensified awareness of the present moment can be gained, he often demonstrates, by attempting to reach back imaginatively and relive past time. Substance is added to the present by awareness of the past, one's personal past as well as that of one's generation and its progenitors. It is not the historians' past, the past of recorded history, of which James was enamoured; it is the past yet tangibly present here in our midst in the form of architecture and furnishings of domestic use and traditional ways of living. The continuity of the present with the past, the perspective interrelation between the present and the immediate and the remoter past, observable to the senses, is a resource ready for the uses of an expanding capacity for life. The extension of consciousness to include what we are apt to think of as dead and gone, instead of diverting attention from today's real world, fertilizes the current day by, paradoxically, emphasizing its durability in time.

James was acutely aware, however, of the danger of romanticizing the past. The past was for one's present use, but it was not to be employed as a substitute for present living. His ideal—complete consciousness—was of course, necessarily, a matter of the immediate present, the current instant in time; the presence of the past, to enrich the present moment, was what he wanted: not a translation into the past, to evade the present. Many of his stories were written to expose the misuse of the past, to show that the past must be exorcized before it can be effectively put to present uses. To place oneself in relation to as large a segment of time as possible was not, for James, a looking backward to or a nostalgia for the past; it was one of the ways by means of which one enhanced the intensity of, and gained a more complete perception of, the present. (pp. 3-12)

Some of James's short stories are like pools quarried near the banks of the channel he dredged to carry the main stream of his themes. They are thoughts allied to, and consistent with, his principal thought, but they are not an integral part of his structure of meaning. These stories examine false values and endeavor to destroy them. If the development of one's consciousness is the supreme value, then other values which men have made supreme in their lives must be shown to be inferior or false.

Fame, social position, cosmopolitanism, moral appearances, nationalistic patriotism, the preservation of personal beauty, and pretense to talent: these are the false values he examines. (p. 17)

All of the false values depend in some degree on the repression of other people; therefore, like the forms of emotional cannibalism, they are potent and hostile forces counterposed to those which nourish man's capacity for greater awareness.

In three of James's stories—very short ones—the international theme provides the subject. The source of dramatic tension in this small group of stories lies in characteristic differences between national schools of opinion, notions common to a nation regarding the proper relation between society and the individual. Clashes between individuals traceable to differences in national character are, of course, necessarily shallower and less lasting in time than clashes due to differences in human character, since the qualities that pertain to a human being cover a far wider range than those which pertain to an American or an Englishman; therefore they are given but scant direct treatment in the body of James's fiction. (p. 18)

One considerable group of James's stories has no tributary connection whatever with either his main or his supplementary themes. Apart from this group, and from the small group dealing with international contrasts, all of James's stories and novels have some bearing on, and exist in some relation to, the central subject of his work: accession or depletion of consciousness.

The principal characters in these residual stories, which are so separate in kind from the bulk of his writing, are creative artists. These are the people, in James's view, who have solved the problem of consciousness. It is the very nature of their characteristic activity to carry on a continual exploration of consciousness, and therefore there is no need to teach them that more and more consciousness is the aim of existence, that the sympathetic study of others' consciousness will enhance their own, or that behavior has its adverse and its favorable bearings on consciousness. On the other hand, to have used the artist as a fictional character to illustrate his central theme would have lessened the force of that theme's impact on the nonartist public, as does any definition of the simpler in terms of the more complex.

James's stories of creative artists are, then, keyed in a much lower tone and possess a much slighter structure of meaning than that greater group of stories which carry his deepest thought. What these stories say is merely that it is the responsibility of the reading public to give the artist the attention he needs, that it is the responsibility of the literary critic to give the artist a thoughtful rather than a cursory perusal, that the created work instead of the artist's private life is the deserving object of attention, that the critic's business is to examine what the creative artist has done rather than to speculate on what he might have done had he been a different sort of man. These stories are in essence admonitory epistles addressed by a practicing creative artist to the critical reading public, and as such they are of the nature of prologues to his important work. (pp. 19-20)

Osborn Andreas, in his Henry James and the Expanding Horizon: A Study of the Meaning and Basic Themes of James's Fiction, *University of Washington Press, 1948, 179 p.*

Oliver Evans (essay date 1949)

[*Evans was an American critic, educator, translator, and poet. The following excerpt, which was originally published in the* Partisan Review *in 1949, responds to "nonapparitionist" interpretations of* The Turn of the Screw *(see excerpts dated 1924 and 1934) and interprets the ghosts in terms of their potential evil.*]

It is exactly half a century since ***The Turn of the Screw*** first appeared on the literary scene. Its commercial success, which it is very likely that James himself did not foresee, was instantaneous; it soon proved, after ***Daisy Miller,*** to be his most popular book. Reading contemporary reviews of the new Jamesian "thriller," one becomes convinced that it was the sensational character of the subject which, more than anything else, appealed to most readers, and that this sensationalism, in turn, derived from the two most immediately obvious elements in the story: the author's preoccupation, first, with the theme of the supernatural; and, second, with that of perverse sexuality. The first of these themes was new with James; the second had previously (in such stories as **"The Pupil"** and **"The Middle Years"**) only been obliquely hinted at.

If the popular success of ***The Turn of the Screw*** is thus easily to be accounted for, the reasons for its *aesthetic* success are by no means so immediately obvious, yet nothing can be plainer than the fact that the story is eminently successful in this sense also. Had its success been merely of one kind, critics would have let it go at that; they have not, however, been content to do so, and there are now almost as many interpretations of the story as there have been critics willing to venture them. On one point alone are they all (with the very prominent exception of Mr. T. S. Eliot, who does not definitely commit himself) in substantial agreement, and that is that ***The Turn of the Screw*** is one of James's finest novels. The disagreement, in other words, does not concern the fact, but the reason therefor.

I have little hope, in the face of so much distinguished discord, of settling once and for all a problem so delicate and so complex. I should like, however, to contribute to the general controversy by suggesting an interpretation which (all miraculously) has thus far, to my knowledge, never been put forth. And there is one thing which, before doing this, I *should* like to settle once and for all, and that is the question of the reality of the apparitions in the story.

It is commonly supposed that Miss Edna Kenton [see excerpt dated 1924] was the first to consider the possibility that the ghosts of Peter Quint and Miss Jessel do not really appear to the governess who tells the story, but are instead mere hallucinations, the creatures of her own disordered imagination. As a matter of fact, this possibility appears to have occurred previously to several readers, none of whom, however, was willing to entertain it very seriously or for very long. Only a few weeks after the book was published *The Critic* observed that "the heroine had nothing in the least substantial upon which to base her deep and startling cognitions. She perceives what is beyond all perception, and the reader who begins by questioning whether she is supposed to be sane ends by accepting her conditions and thrilling over the horrors they involve."

So far as I know, however, Miss Kenton was the first to go on record as *not* accepting the governess's conditions, and to state positively that the ghosts are nothing more than "exquisite dramatizations of her little personal mystery, figures for the ebb and flow of troubled thought within her mind." In her opinion James quite deliberately planned the story as a test of that attentiveness which he felt every author had a right to expect of his readers, and she offers in support of this theory James's reference to the story (in the definitive edition preface) as "a piece of ingenuity pure and simple, of cold, artistic calculation, an *amusette* to catch those not easily caught." She also stresses the fact that James nowhere *states* that the ghosts appear to anyone but the governess. On the strength, chiefly, of these two pieces of "evidence," she rather largely concludes: "Just a little wariness will suffice to disprove, with a single survey of the ground, the traditional, we might almost call it a *lazy* version of the tale. Not the children, but the little governess was hounded by the ghosts." It will be seen that, thus viewed, ***The Turn of the Screw*** becomes a sort of elaborate hoax, a trap for readers lazier and less wary than Miss Kenton.

This ingenious interpretation, which, as I shall later attempt to show, does so little justice to James's intention in writing the story and so narrowly delimits the reader's appreciation of it, attracted almost no attention when, in 1924, it appeared in *Arts* accompanied by an interesting set of illustrations by Charles Demuth. But ten years later Mr. Edmund Wilson published in *Hound and Horn* his now famous essay. "The Ambiguity of Henry James" [see essay dated 1934], in which he popularized and expanded this theory. In his opinion ***The Turn of the Screw*** is "simply a variation on one of James's familiar themes: the frustrated Anglo-Saxon spinster." He professes to discover specific Freudian meanings in the facts that the male ghost first appears on a tower, the female beside a lake; and that, on the occasion of the latter visitation, the child Flora is carrying (I quote from the story) "a small flat piece of wood, which happened to have in it a little hole that had evidently suggested to her the idea of sticking in another fragment that might figure as a mast and make the thing a boat."

Beyond pointing out such circumstances as these, Mr. Wilson did not really add substantially to Miss Kenton's interpretation. The Kenton-Wilson theory, at any rate, is now familiar to most Jamesians, and although it has elicited considerable random disapproval, I have nowhere seen it attacked point by point. An exception is Philip Rahv, but even he concedes, "Of course there is no doubt that the story may be read that way."

Both Miss Kenton and Mr. Wilson have conveniently ignored the letters, in which James made it perfectly clear that in ***The Turn of the Screw*** he was writing a tale of the *supernatural.* Its origin, as he declared in a letter to A. C. Benson (March 11, 1898) was a "small and gruesome *spectral* story" (italics mine) related to him by Archbishop Benson, grandfather of the educator. A few months later James wrote to Dr. Louis Waldstein that it was merely a "wanton little Tale" unworthy of such praise as the doctor had apparently given it. He added, however, that "the poet is always justified when he is not a humbug; always grateful to the justifying commentator," and continued: "My *bogey-tale* [italics mine] dealt with things so hideous that I felt that to save it at all I needed some infusion of beauty or prettiness, and the beauty of the pathetic was the only attainable—was indeed inevitable. But ah, the exposure indeed, the helpless plasticity of childhood that isn't dear or sacred to *somebody!* That *was* my little tragedy!" That was, indeed, the tragedy: the corruption of the two children by the living servants, and the possession (in the supernatural sense) of them afterwards by the ghosts of those same servants. In the light of this avowal, what happens to the "tragedy" if we think of the story simply as a careful trap, or as a mere case history of a governess subject to hallucinations?

In a letter to H. G. Wells (December 9, 1898), who had apparently objected that the governess's character did not receive sufficient delineation, James defended himself as follows:

> Of course I had, about my young woman, to take a very sharp line. The grotesque business I had to make her trace and present were, for me at least, a very difficult job, in which absolute lucidity and logic, a singleness of effect, were imperative. Therefore I had to rule out subjective complications of her own—play of tone, etc., and keep her impersonal save for the most obvious and indispensable little note of neatness, firmness and courage—without which she wouldn't have had her data.

Witness the phrase, "I had to rule out subjective complications of her own," and observe how incompatible it is with the notion that she is merely exposing her private neurosis in the story. Witness, too, how little this picture of the governess coincides with Wilson's conception of her as a pronounced hysteric.

Writing to F. W. H. Myers (December 19, 1898) he is even more specific:

> The thing that, as I recall it, I most wanted not to fail of doing, under penalty of extreme platitude, was to give the impression of the communication to the children of the most infernal imaginable evil and danger—the condition, on their part, of being as *exposed* as we can humanly conceive children to be. This was my artistic knot to untie, to put any sense or logic into the thing, and if I had known any way of producing *more* the image of their contact and condition I should have been proportionately eager to resort to it.

Here James specifically states his conscious ambition, and I hope I do not need to point out that without the apparitions there is no evil, no danger, and no *exposure.* Finally there is the letter to his French translator, August Monod (July 17, 1907). If James's intention had been as devious as the hoaxists and the nonapparitionists (if I may term them this) would have us believe, surely he would have hinted as much to his translator; instead, he unambiguously refers to his book as a *"fantaisie absolue dans le genre de recherche du frisson."*

There is some evidence that James's opinion of the merits of ***The Turn of the Screw*** altered between the date of its first publication in 1898 and its appearance ten years later in the definitive edition: thus, in the above-mentioned letter to F. W. H. Myers, he refers to it as "a very mechanical matter, I honestly think—an inferior, a merely *pictorial* subject and rather a shameless potboiler," but in the preface, as Philip Rahv has commented, he gives it serious and lengthy treatment. It is possible, of course, that James was merely being overmodest in the Myers letter (the tone of many of his letters is self-deprecatory in this way, betraying their author's concern for "good taste"), but again it is possible that he did not immediately realize how consummately successful he had been in his attempt to communicate to the reader a sense of "most infernal imaginable evil and danger"—the poet, as he himself so well put it, being always grateful to the justifying commentator. Neither explanation supports the Kenton-Wilson view: as we have seen, there is no evil or danger without the apparitions; and if James had intended to conceal the point of the narrative as carefully as they claim—if, in other words, it was to be the subtlest of his stories in this sense—he would scarcely have referred to it as a potboiler.

The changes which James made for the definitive edition were of a purely verbal character and do not affect the plot in any way. However, the preface which he composed for the new edition is invaluable for the light which it throws on his intentions. Miss Kenton has not ignored this preface; she has done what is far worse: she has lifted one of its sentences out of its context, interpreted it in a very special kind of way, and then, claiming it as "evidence," has proceeded to construct upon it her very largest argument. In the case of a writer such as James, where context is almost all-important, this is particularly reprehensible. The sentence in question reads as follows: "I need scarcely add after this that it [***The Turn of the Screw***] is a piece of ingenuity pure and simple, of cold artistic calculation, an *amusette* to catch those not easily caught (the fun of the capture of the merely witless being ever but small), the jaded, the disillusioned, the fastidious." Miss Kenton focuses on the first part of this sentence—very shrewdly for her purpose, for the adjectives "jaded," "disillusioned," and "fastidious" support a context she has deliberately chosen not to recognize. James has been speaking of the many difficulties which beset the writer of the fantastic, of how unsuccessful, in this age of sophistication, modern ghost stories have been in their attempt to "rouse the dear old sacred terror." The meaning of the sentence is simply that in ***The Turn of the Screw*** James believed he had hit upon the perfect formula for rousing this type of terror—rousing it, moreover, in those the least susceptible, "the jaded, the disillusioned, the fastidious." What this formula is we shall see in a moment.

Mr. Wilson is guilty of much the same sort of thing. He interprets James's statement in the preface, that "She [the governess] has 'authority,' which is a good deal to have given her," as meaning that the governess, by reason of her "neurosis," was a dubious person to exert authority over children. But James is not using "authority" in this sense at all; he does not mean that the governess has authority where the *children* are concerned, but where the *reader* is, as will be obvious when one views the statement in its context. James has been defending himself against the accusation that the governess is insufficiently characterized (H. G. Wells, as we have noted, made the same charge) and concludes: "It constitutes no little of a character indeed, in such conditions, for a young person, as she says, 'privately bred,' that she is able to make her particular credible [*sic*] statement of such strange matters. She has 'authority,' which is a deal to have given her, and I couldn't have arrived at so much had I clumsily tried for more." This last sentence, which we have seen the nonapparitionists quote (without benefit of context) to their own purpose, really offers the most convincing proof that they are mistaken; in it James is simply saying that we are to accept as authoritative the governess's account of what happens in ***The Turn of the Screw.***

James goes on to tell exactly what his motives were in writing his "bogey-tale": "Good ghosts, speaking by book, make poor subjects, and it was clear that from the first my hovering prowling blighting presences, my pair of abnormal agents, would have to depart altogether from the rules. They would be agents in fact; there would be laid in them the dire duty of causing the situation to reek with the air of Evil." Finally he defines his formula for making the situation reek to capacity with the "air of Evil." Alive, the servants had performed sufficient *specific* harm in corrupting their little charges; what additional outrage could they now perform that would not be anticlimactic? The problem, as James was perfectly aware, was a difficult one; he solved it, and solved it successfully, by deliberate refuse to the general, the nonspecific—solved it, in other words, by simple *omission:* "Only make the reader's general vision of evil intense enough, I said to myself . . . and his own experience, his own sympathy (with the children) and horror (of their false friends) will supply him quite sufficiently with all the particulars. Make him *think* the evil, make him think it for himself, and you are released from weak specifications." One may well wonder how it is possible to read all this and believe that James intended the ghosts to be nothing more than mere hallucinations.

The prologue is equally unambiguous. A group of house guests are gathered about a fire on Christmas Eve. Someone has just told a story in which a small child is visited by an apparition. One of the guests, Douglas, then remarks that he knows of a similar case involving *two* children; "Nobody but me, till now, has ever heard. It's quite too horrible. It's beyond everything. Nothing at all that I know touches it." The others are naturally curious, and he tells them he will send at once to London for the story, which it appears has already been written down by the governess of the haunted children, who was an actual witness.

Observe that Douglas himself never implies for a moment that he doubts the governess's account. On the contrary, one of James's motives in writing the prologue is to provide her with a "character reference" so that we may listen to her with respect. Douglas, who knew her intimately, certainly did not think that she was emotionally unstable: " 'She was my sister's governess,' he quietly said. 'She was the most agreeable woman I've ever known in her position; she would have been worthy of any whatever.' " Had James's intention been to characterize her as an irresponsible neurotic, what could have been his motive in having *the only person who knew her,* and was therefore able to vouch for her character, speak in this fashion?

I come now to the story itself. Miss Kenton and Mr. Wilson make much of the fact that, in the second scene by the lake, Miss Jessel's ghost is visible to the governess but not to the housekeeper. This power (of appearing only to certain individuals) has been the privilege of ghosts throughout all literature; it is, indeed, one of their most traditional attributes. And James has his own reasons for making use of it in ***The Turn of the Screw:*** it constitutes a definite victory for the ghosts, thus sharpening the conflict between them and the governess for the "possession" of the children; and it adds an almost unbearable tension to the story. One could not, incidentally, wish for stronger evidence of the stability of the governess's personality than the fact that, although the housekeeper herself has seen nothing, she does not doubt that her friend has—a point which James, who certainly sees the necessity for it, drives home again and again.

The nonapparitionists have never satisfactorily explained the coincidence between the governess's description of the ghosts and the impression which the housekeeper has retained of the living servants; and they have been forced to account for the death of little Miles at the end by saying that the governess herself, in attempting to make him see what is not there, simply scares the life out of him—this in spite of James's last sentence, "We were alone with the quiet day, and his little heart, *dispossessed* [italics mine], had stopped."

They also have not accounted for the fact that the housekeeper testifies toward the end that little Flora is, indeed, bewitched. For not only does Mrs. Grose believe that the governess has seen what she herself was unable to see, but her subsequent session with the little girl convinces her that the latter is definitely possessed. Referring to the last dreadful scene by the lake, Mrs. Grose observes: "It has made her, every inch of her, quite old." (Previously the governess has told the housekeeper, "At such times she's not a child: she's an old, old woman.") I reproduce the following conversation between the two servants:

> "You mean that, since yesterday, you *have* seen—?"
>
> She shook her head with dignity. "I've *heard*—!"
>
> "Heard?"
>
> "From that child—horrors! There!" she sighed with tragic relief. "On my honour, Miss, she says things—!" But at this evocation she broke down; she dropped, with a sudden sob, upon my sofa and, as I had seen her do before, gave way to all the grief of it.
>
> It was in quite another manner that I, for my part, let myself go.
>
> "Oh, thank God!"
>
> She sprang up at this, drying her eyes with a groan. "Thank God?"
>
> "It so justifies me!"
>
> "It does that, Miss."

Mrs. Grose then goes on to say that the child has been abusing the governess in language which she "can't think wherever she must have picked up." But immediately she adds, "Well, perhaps I ought to also—since I've heard some of it before." She has heard it "before," of course, from Miss Jessel herself. Finally the governess asks her:

> "Then, in spite of yesterday, you *believe?*"
>
> "In such doings?" Her simple description of them required, in the light of her expression, to be carried no further, and she gave me the whole thing as she had never done:
>
> "I believe."

Should there, after all this, remain any doubt in the reader's mind as to the reality of the apparitions, let him now glance back at the beginning of the story, *before* Peter Quint's ghost first appears. The governess has just arrived at Bly, knowing nothing of her unhappy predecessors. Immediately she senses that Mrs. Grose is strangely glad to see her: "I perceived within half an hour that she was so glad—stout, simple, plain, clean, wholesome woman—as to be positively on her guard against showing it too much. I wondered even then a little why she should not wish to show it . . . " It is several times hinted, at the first of the story, that the housekeeper is uneasy, that she is trying to conceal a suspicion that everything is not as it should be—a suspicion which she could only have arrived at independently, since the governess has barely arrived.

The governess, who has not even met the children yet, spends a rather uneasy first night: "There had been moments when I believed I recognized, faint and far, the cry of a child; there had been another when I found myself just consciously starting as at the passage, before the door, of a light footstep." From the very beginning James spares no pains in informing us that supernatural forces are at work within the house: the housekeeper is already aware of them, and the governess becomes aware long before she could have any reason to invent them.

I hope I have not overlabored my point here. I thought the risk worth running, at any rate, since I am convinced that it is impossible to fully appreciate ***The Turn of the Screw*** unless one accepts the reality of the apparitions.

Mr. Wilson remarks that ***The Turn of the Screw,*** on any other hypothesis than the one he proposes, would be "the only thing James ever wrote which did not have some more or less serious point." But to view the novel as an implied case history, a mere clinical record, is to deprive the reader of the peculiar sense of horror which it was James's ambition to arouse in him. Take, for example, the scene where little Miles, exerting all his charms, distracts the governess with his precocity at the piano, while his sister steals off to consort with Miss Jessel's evil shade. Suddenly the governess remembers: "Where, all this time, was little Flora? When I put the question to Miles he played on a minute without answering, and then could only say,

James on his objectives in writing *The Turn of the Screw*:

Nothing is so easy as improvisation, the running on and on of invention; it is sadly compromised, however, from the moment its stream breaks bounds and gets into flood. Then the waters may spread indeed, gathering houses and herds and crops and cities into their arms and wrenching off, for our amusement, the whole face of the land—only violating by the same stroke our sense of the course and the channel, which is our sense of the uses of a stream and the virtue of a story. Improvisation, as in the Arabian Nights, may keep on terms with encountered objects by sweeping them in and floating them on its breast; but the great effect it so loses—that of keeping on terms with itself. This is ever, I intimate, the hard thing for the fairy-tale; but by just so much as it struck me as hard did it in ***The Turn of the Screw*** affect me as irresistibly prescribed. To improvise with extreme freedom and yet at the same time without the possibility of ravage, without the hint of flood; to keep the stream, in a word, on something like ideal terms with itself: that was here my definite business. The thing was to aim at absolute singleness, clearness and roundness, and yet to depend on an imagination working freely, working (call it) with extravagance; by which law it wouldn't be thinkable except as free and wouldn't be amusing except as controlled. The merit of the tale, as it stands, is accordingly, I judge, that it has struggled successfully with its dangers. It is an excursion into chaos while remaining, like Blue-Beard and Cinderella, but an anecdote—though an anecdote amplified and highly emphasised and returning upon itself; as, for that matter, Cinderella and Blue-Beard return. I need scarcely add after this that it is a piece of ingenuity pure and simple, of cold artistic calculation, an *amusette* to catch those not easily caught (the "fun" of the capture of the merely witless being ever but small), the jaded, the disillusioned, the fastidious. Otherwise expressed, the study is of a conceived "tone," the tone of suspected and felt trouble, of an inordinate and incalculable sort—the tone of tragic, yet of exquisite, mystification. To knead the subject of my young friend's, the supposititious narrator's, mystification thick, and yet strain the expression of it so clear and fine that beauty would result: no side of the matter so revives for me as that endeavour.

Henry James in volume twelve of his collected works, The Novels and Tales of Henry James *(1908).*

'Why, my dear, how do *I* know?'—breaking moreover into a happy laugh which, immediately after, as if it were a vocal accompaniment, he prolonged into incoherent, extravagant song." The whole infernal effectiveness of this scene (and it is immensely effective) resides in the fact that the little concert has been nothing more than a careful ruse on the children's part to lure the governess into temporarily forgetting her responsibility and relaxing her vigilance.

Or take the eerie scene just before this, in which the governess is pleading with Miles to confess his domination by the evil ghost of Peter Quint: " 'Dear little Miles, I just want you to help me to save you!' But I knew in a moment after this that I had gone too far. The answer to my appeal was instantaneous, but it came in the form of an extraordinary blast and chill, a gust of frozen air and a shake of the room as great as if, in the wild wind, the casement had crashed in." The child shrieks ("a note either of jubilation or of terror") and the candle goes out:

> "Why, the candle's out!" I cried.
>
> "It was I who blew it, dear!" said little Miles.

Observe how immeasurably the effect of horror here is heightened by our conviction that the child is in league with those supernatural forces which, momentarily, and doubtless of his own volition, have become translated into natural ones.

I tend to agree with the late Ford Madox Ford when he says: "If you will take ***The Turn of the Screw,*** with its apparent digressions, its speculations, its twists and its turns, you will see that the real interest centres round the proposition: 'Is the narrator right or wrong in thinking that if the little boy can only disburden himself of a full confession, he will be saved for ever from the evil ascendency of Peter Quint?' " By "real" interest Ford here means narrative interest, and on the subject of James's narrative technique Ford was particularly well informed. Without the possession theme, which necessitates the reality of the ghosts, there is simply no conflict, no drama, no *story.* That James was thoroughly conscious of this is proved by the artistry with which he focuses on those details which sharpen the conflict and thus intensify the drama of the situation. Take for example the above-mentioned bedroom scene, and note how skillfully it is suggested to the reader (always through the medium of the governess, to whom the impressions occur in appropriate images) that little Miles is *sick,* spiritually sick: "His clear, listening face, framed in its smooth whiteness, made him for the moment as appealing as some wistful patient in a children's hospital; and I would have given, as the resemblance came to me, all I possessed on earth to be the nurse or the sister of charity who might have helped to cure him."

I agree also with Mr. Philip Rahv in his opinion that the sense of *evil* which James sought to communicate is to be conceived of largely in sexual terms. The horror of the situation is heightened, moreover, by the fact that the boy has been corrupted by the male servant; the girl, by the female. Peter Quint's abnormality is hinted at ("There had been matters in his life . . . secret disorders, vices more than half suspected"), and Mrs. Grose says in so many words that he had been "much too free" with little Miles, who had "gone off with the fellow, and spent hours with him." Then there is the unambiguous dialogue between the governess and Mrs. Grose:

> "At all events, while he was with the man—"

"Miss Flora was with the woman. It suited them all!"

Neither Ford's interpretation nor Mr. Rahv's is sufficient, however, to account for the really uncanny effectiveness of ***The Turn of the Screw.*** I feel that both are valid, and that they perhaps sufficiently explain the book's contemporary popularity; but it seems to me that these two elements (supernatural possession and sexual impropriety) are really secondary reasons, surface involvements of a theme at once more comprehensive, more fundamental, and more profound: the theme, that is, of appearance versus reality.

This theme, apparently not sufficiently serious for Mr. Wilson, is as old as philosophy itself. An extension of it, on the ethical plane, is the theme of good versus evil, and in fact some of the more perceptive contemporary reviewers of the book discovered this meaning in it. But in James the ethical conflict is not presented in a straightforward manner, as it is, say, in Blake (where a child is always a child, a lamb always a lamb, and both are always innocent), but with complication and irony. In ***The Turn of the Screw,*** with devastating effect, the lambs are not lambs at all, but tigers; the children are not really children, but, as Mrs. Grose perceives in the end, are as old as evil itself.

The problem of appearance versus reality, which to my mind constitutes the primary theme of the story, James logically expresses in the form of a paradox. Whether consciously or intuitively, he realized the artistic importance of selecting a situation wherein the *apparent* should be innocuous, and the *real* overwhelming in its horror. The horror of the real would, indeed, be in exact proportion to the charm of the apparent—which is why James makes his children the very personification of youthful beauty and innocence, and provides for them such an idyllic setting. Hawthorne was preoccupied with the same paradox; Wilde expressed it, though with infinitely less ingenuity than James, in *The Picture of Dorian Gray;* and it was to become almost an obsession with Pirandello. James himself had treated it earlier, and much less grimly, in **"The Liar";** and it is interesting to note that in the definitive edition he included ***The Turn of the Screw,*** not in the same volume with ***Covering End*** (as these two had first been issued under the title of ***The Two Magics***) or **"The Jolly Corner"** (another "ghost" story), but with **"The Liar."**

If one accepts this interpretation of the story, it is interesting to observe how skillfully James goes about the process of constructing his paradox. Again and again it is emphasized to the reader that the beauty of these children (like that of Dorian Gray) is a *lie.* At the very beginning it is suggested that Miles's appearance belies the suspicion which the governess (who has not yet seen him) is beginning to form concerning the reasons for his expulsion from school. "See him, Miss, first," Mrs. Grose tells her. "*Then* believe it!" When the governess does see him, it is "in the great glow of freshness, the same positive fragrance of purity, in which I had, from the first moment, seen his little sister." She is struck, not only by his beauty, but by something else too: "something divine that I have never found to the same degree in any child—his indescribable little air of knowing nothing in the world but love." This initial impression, terrible in its irony, is confirmed and reinforced by many later ones. And somehow the "rose flush of his innocence" is never so intense as when he is most actively engaged in positive evil.

I have no illusions that this interpretation of ***The Turn of the Screw*** exhausts the story's meanings. It does not exclude other interpretations; it has the virtue of extreme inclusiveness, though I fear there is no room in it for either Miss Kenton or Mr. Wilson. I think it does better justice to James's intention than certain narrower notions and that it permits a wider and deeper appreciation of the novel than any of these. As Mr. Rahv says, in James we are always justified in assuming a maximum of intention: the task of the "justifying commentator," in the case of a book like ***The Turn of the Screw,*** is indeed endless. (pp. 200-11)

Oliver Evans, "James's Air of Evil: 'The Turn of the Screw'," in A Casebook on Henry James's "The Turn of the Screw", *edited by Gerald Willen, Thomas Y. Crowell Company, 1959, pp. 200-11.*

Gorham Munson (essay date 1950)

[*Munson was an American educator and literary critic. In the essay below, he analyzes "The Real Thing" as a parable for the fiction writer's craft.*]

Henry James's short story, **"The Real Thing,"** is not, of course, a true parable. Its surface is not simple enough; James generally used too elaborate machinery to bring off his short stories. Nor is the meaning of **"The Real Thing"** seemingly inexhaustible, which is the parable's mark. Yet this short story does have a parabolic meaning for a select class of readers, namely, those who have a professional interest in the technique of fiction.

If we reduce James's short story to a simple parabolic form, it might be put like this:

The Parable of the Models

Because of straitened circumstances, a Gentleman and a Lady were constrained to offer themselves as Models to an Artist who did illustrations in black and white. In the drawing-room they were a distinguished couple, and they persuaded the Artist to try them on the ground that they were "the real thing." But the Artist had trouble in doing them. The illustrations he made were too photographic. A vital element was lacking, and those who ordered his illustrations began to complain of something deadening in his work.

The Artist did better work when he used for a model of a princess a little cockney woman who could represent the role. One day he engaged a young Italian street-vendor and the young man proved to be gifted for posing as an aristocrat. The cockney woman and the Italian man were not "the real thing" but they proved to be the ideal thing. The Artist was obliged to dismiss the Gentleman and the Lady, but before they left, they went into the kitchen and prepared tea for

> the Artist and his two Models. As servants, the Lady and the Gentleman were the ideal thing.

What is this parable about? Plainly, it is about the preference that graphic artists and literary artists have for inventing characters rather than copying characters from actual life. James's narrating artist in **"The Real Thing"** speaks of his "innate preference for the represented subject over the real one: the defect of the real one was so apt to be a lack of representation." James has made a little story out of the truth that art does not copy life but grows from suggestions offered by life. A close reading of **"The Real Thing"** will show that woven into it is "a figure in the carpet" that James intended his fellows in the writing of fiction to decipher.

To many readers of **"The Real Thing"** this "figure in the carpet" will appear only as substantiating detail, stuff put in to increase verisimilitude and to authenticate the studio atmosphere of the tale. And indeed the Irish novelist Sean O'Faolain, acting on the belief that Henry James tells too much, has offered a cut version of **"The Real Thing"** which leaves out most of the "figure." What O'Faolain's cut version does is to throw into relief the amusing anecdote that is the "storyable core" of James's story, but it robs this core of the parabolic significance James has been at pains to insert. I propose to do the opposite of O'Faolain's concentration on plot and to expatiate on the material he would remove from James's text. This will show that what attracted James to his anecdote was the chance it gave for clarifying what might be called the "medium-test" for characters.

"The Real Thing" is narrated by an artist who receives a call from a Major Monarch and his wife, both tall, middle-aged, well-mannered, "smart" in the social sense, but now dreadfully poor. They want to sit for hire. The narrator reflects that they would make a drawing-room look well, and then he reflects further that a drawing-room itself always ought to be a picture. It also strikes the artist that Mrs. Monarch would make a good model for jackets in a fashionable shop and that the Major could be what today we would call "a man of distinction" in an advertisement. He observes to himself that both look too distinguished to be celebrities, since celebrities rarely look distinguished. They would photograph extremely well, and in fact the photographers have been after them.

The most interesting observation he makes is this one: "in the pictorial sense I had immediately *seen* them. I had seized their type—I had already settled what I would do with it. Something that wouldn't absolutely have pleased them, I afterwards reflected." To sum up the artist's impressions: the couple applying for work as models for the romances of society which he illustrated look exactly the part they play in real life, whereas the pictorial thing they *suggest* is something else, undefined except as a treatment they wouldn't like. "Somehow," the narrator says, "with all their perfections I didn't easily believe in them" and yet, despite his misgivings, he takes them on. That is, he does what the novelist, usually the immature novelist, does when he tries to put a real person into a book.

James tells us a good deal about his artist's troubles with the real thing. Mrs. Monarch sat almost as motionless as if she were before a camera. "After a few times," says the artist-narrator, "I began to find her too insurmountably stiff; do what I would with it my drawing looked like a photograph or a copy of a photograph." She kept coming out too tall in his drawings. Moreover, there was no variety. "I placed her in every conceivable position . . . She was always a lady certainly, and into the bargain was always the same lady. She was the real thing, but always the same thing."

The case was worse with Major Monarch. "He became useful only for the representation of brawny giants . . . and the thing in the world I most hated was the danger of being ridden by a type."

At this point an artist friend back from Italy calls on the narrator and looks at his recent work.

> "I don't know—I don't like your types," he says.
>
> "I've had a couple of new models."
>
> "I see you have. *They* won't do."

Soon after this visit, the publisher for whom the narrator is illustrating on trial the first volume of a de luxe edition gives a warning: many of the illustrations are not what he has been looking for. The narrator is forced to abandon his models or risk losing the contract to illustrate the entire set of volumes.

In contrast to the Monarchs, there are in this story two professional models, a Miss Churm and a young Italian named Oronte. When she is not posing, Miss Churm is a small, poorly educated cockney woman, but when she was posing, well—"She was a meagre little Miss Churm, but she was an ample heroine of romance." She had a knack, and a mother-wit, and whimsical sensibility, and a love of the theatre. Costume her as a Russian princess, pose her, and she looked "distinguished and charming, foreign and dangerous." "The value of such a model," the narrator notes, "resided precisely in the fact that she had no positive stamp, combined of course with the other fact that what she did have was a curious and inexplicable talent for imitation. Her usual appearance was like a curtain which she could draw up at request for a capital performance. This performance was simply suggestive; but it was a word to the wise—it was vivid and pretty."

Oronte had been a pushcart vendor of ices before he became a combination servant and model for the narrator. In an uncultivated way, his attitudes and expressions are constantly making pictures; he "had in a wonderful degree the *sentiment de la pose.*" Oronte and Miss Churm posing together as Rutland Ramsay saying extraordinary things to Artemisia at the piano while she fingers out a difficult piece of music were exactly right, whereas the trouble with the drawings of the Monarchs was that they looked exactly like them. "When I drew the Monarchs I couldn't, somehow, get away from them—get into the character I wanted to represent."

And so the narrator has to resolve his crisis with his publisher by sending the real thing away and by choosing the ideal thing for his drawings.

The Monarchs take their failure gallantly. In the comraderie of the studio Mrs. Monarch improves the hair-dress of Miss Churm, and the Major, looking for something useful to do, cleans up the breakfast things in the little kitchen. "If my servants were my models, my models might be my servants. They would reverse the parts—the others could sit for the ladies and gentlemen, and *they* would do the work. They would still be in the studio—it was an intense dumb appeal to me not to turn them out." This ending has been prefigured by James when he has the fleeting thought visit his artist that he might use Major Monarch as a footman in a scene in which Oronte was playing the gentleman.

We have now traced in detail the "figure in the carpet" as a writer of fiction intently scanning the texture of James's story would make it out. The "figure" would convey something like this. There is for each art-medium a special suitability of characters. In the art of the motion picture this is discovered by a screen-test. In the medium of prose fiction, short or long, there is a fiction-test, and most real people can't pass it. Real people as a rule supply hints only for fictive people, just as Major Monarch supplies a hint for the footman he isn't and Oronte supplies hints for the gentleman he isn't. The copying of life-models for fiction is bad business; it's hard to scale them down, it's hard to avoid a sit-still photographic quality, it's hard to make them magnetic. The upshot is that you have to cast your characters especially for the short story, novelette or novel. Your invented characters must be ideal for the parts they have to play in the fictions you are inventing.

That is the parabolic substance of James's story. That I am not reading too much into Henry James's intention can, I think, be ascertained by anyone who will consult the prefaces to *The Wings of the Dove* and *The Ambassadors*, included in the collection, *The Art of the Novel.* In one James describes the casting of Milly Threale, over whom the sword of a fatal sickness visibly hangs by a thread but who has so many advantages apart from the disadvantage of precarious health. In the other he casts Strether, a man of mature character and of strong but not predominant imagination. James was so meticulous in describing his own fiction-tests for characters that it is impossible to think he did not have in mind the fiction writer's problems as well as the problems of the illustrative artist when he composed **"The Real Thing."** (pp. 261-64)

Gorham Munson, "The Real Thing: A Parable for Writers of Fiction," in The University of Kansas City Review, *Vol. XVI, No. 4, Summer, 1950, pp. 261-64.*

F. W. Dupee (essay date 1951)

[*Dupee was an American editor, educator, and critic. The following excerpt from Dupee's critical biography* Henry James *presents* Daisy Miller *as a tribute to the American girl and to American innocence.*]

In the summer of 1878, while *The Europeans* was failing to amuse the readers of the *Atlantic,* ***Daisy Miller: A Study*** was coming out with great success in the English *Cornhill.* It had been refused by an American publisher but was soon so famous that it was widely pirated in the United States before James could arrange for its legitimate publication. Described in the newspapers as "an outrage on American girlhood," the story was a success of scandal with the large American public; although the better critics, including Higginson, promptly recognized its justice and delicacy. In the long run the fame of ***Daisy Miller*** was to be a vexation to James. Reviewers were constantly to cite it as a touchstone; and none of his stories, except perhaps ***The Turn of the Screw,*** was to equal it in popularity. Meanwhile the excitement was gratifying, especially because it spread to the English public; and henceforth James's books were to be issued more or less simultaneously in both countries. On a small scale, then, ***Daisy Miller*** was an international event, and it established the importance of the international subject. It also vindicated, for the moment, his methods of economy and suggestion in the telling of a story—methods which appealed so little to a public accustomed to the Victorian abundance that he took the precaution of calling *The Europeans* "a sketch" and ***Daisy Miller*** "a study." Today the precaution seems unnecessary. ***Daisy Miller,*** a mere ninety pages of finely observed incident, has become part of the American experience.

It is both a love story and a story of comparative manners. Projected through a single mind in a stricter way than James has yet attempted, it is also a story of reality and appearance. The mind is that of Frederick Winterbourne, a young American long resident in Europe, whose doubts concerning Daisy's innocence in an equivocal situation influence the reader's sense of her worth and modify her own behavior. Daisy is lightly sketched, but in one thing she is more formidable than any figure James has yet drawn. This is her effect on the reader, which, thanks to Winterbourne's mediumship, is teasingly uncertain, admitting of ironic as well as lyric overtones. The latter are the more obvious. A kind of admiration of the misguided girl comes through strongly at last; and it is all the more poignant because it has come in spite of odds, because it has been so long in coming, because it has not come fully till she is dead. Surely it is her death that puts the final seal on her charm, and quite apart from anything heroic in the manner of it. She is dead in her youth and wealth and prettiness and *nil nisi bonum*. . . . So interpreted, Daisy is a tribute to the American girl, whose radical innocence is shown to triumph over the evil-mindedness of the old world as well as over her own rash conduct and indifferent manners. She is a champion, however unconscious, of the assumptions and immunities of her kind, a forerunner of Carol Kennicott. And in this light the great question of the story is whether she is innocent in the "technical" sense, for her ways are deceptively free and flirtatious, and she runs about Rome with a dubious native in defiance of the system of curfews and chaperons which the American colony holds dear. Even Winterbourne, who is half in love with her, as she is entirely in love with him, comes at last to suppose she is really bad. But after her death Giovanelli, her shady Italian friend, resolves the mystery in her favor. She has been guilty of nothing worse than "doing what she liked." In her instinctive way she has demonstrated—almost with her life—a point of morality, vindicated the individual against the group, the spirit against the letter. She has established the doctrine, so intrinsic to native Americanism, that human nature is guiltless till proved otherwise. The Europeanized Americans of her acquaintance, as Roman as the Romans if not more so, assume the contrary theory of human nature, the more astringent one on which traditional morals and manners rest. Judging her morals by her manners, they imagine the worst and they ostracize her. They are wrong. Winterbourne most of all is wrong. "I was booked to make a mistake," he says when it is too late. "I have lived too long in foreign parts." He has not only misjudged Daisy, he has made the mistake of judging where he should have loved.

For certain readers the very setting of the major incidents gives weight to this construction of the tale. Italy, Rome, the Colosseum where Daisy, like a new martyr to the Spirit, contracts her fatal fever—such scenes had of course deadly associations for the American libertarian mind, in whose processes James was able to share at least imaginatively. Yet within ***Daisy Miller*** as within *The Europeans* there are unmistakable though never insistent ironies, ironies that swim there like small gleams of welcome light to clarify, rather than annihilate, the more apparent meanings. And one of these is precisely the manner of Daisy's death, which, looked at closely, is no martyrdom. All Rome knows the Colosseum to be unwholesome by night. Daisy's death, if it proves anything, proves that not every superstition is a fraud. And Daisy herself clearly suffers as a person from the absence in her life of those very traditions for which she cares so little and of which the American colony undoubtedly makes too much. She fails to "compose," as James would say, because as a social being she is without a form and a frame. She has no sense of the inevitable—which was what traditions and taboos, conventions and manners finally signified to James when we discount his merely temperamental conservatism—and without this feeling for the limits of life she can scarcely be said to be fully alive. Her forerunner Newman is one of "nature's noblemen," as someone remarks in *The American;* and he is presented as almost entirely admirable. Even his terrible taste in paintings somehow recommends him; and his manners, rough Californian though he is, conform by some magic to those of the best Parisian society. Daisy Miller is Nature construed in a more sceptical mood. Like that of the field flower she is named for, her very prettiness is more generic than individual. Extremely imprudent and somewhat callow, even on occasion rude by any standard, she has within her a strange little will, which, when it is thwarted by Winterbourne's defection, turns rather easily into a will to die. "She did what she liked!" her two lovers agree when they meet beside her grave; and the words are not all eulogy. She does what she likes because she hardly knows what else to do. Her will is at once strong and weak by reason of the very indistinctness of her general aims. Her love for Winterbourne, the one clear impulse of her nature, is itself perfectly helpless. He says ruefully at the end that "she would have appreciated one's esteem"; to which his tough-minded aunt replies: "She took an odd way to gain it!" Like her sassy and not very amusing younger brother, like her mother who has no resource in life except to be always ill, like her father who is out of the picture somewhere making more money, Daisy inhabits a human vacuum created equally by a large fortune and no commitments, much freedom and little use for it.

The story is not, then, altogether a tribute to the American girl. It is also addressed critically to the *sentiment* of the American girl, and of American "innocence" generally—the kind of sentiment which, as James was aware, frequently did duty for realism in the native mind. The legend of American innocence is not denied by the story; it is only shown to be possibly irrelevant or obsolescent from any larger point of view. As the simple probity of the Wentworths is defined by the charmed enclosure of their provincial existence; so that of Daisy is incompatible with her survival and is in fact certified only by her death.

It should be noted, however, that Daisy is a product neither of Boston nor of old New York, both of which places contributed very different types of heroine to James's work. A daughter of the provincial plutocracy—Schenectady in process of taking over New York—she is the American girl of the future. The American girl was as various as Minny Temple herself had been, and James was to follow up ***Daisy Miller*** with a long series of such heroines, ingeniously altering their traits and implications from tale to tale. **"An International Episode," "The Pension Beaurepas," "A Bundle of Letters," "The Patagonia,"** *The Reverberator*—all tell of American girls whose free spirits bring them into some sort of trouble with the world of fact, which world is usually represented by Europe or Europeans. (pp. 107-12)

F. W. Dupee, in his Henry James, *William Sloane Associates, 1951, 301 p.*

Perry D. Westbrook (essay date 1953)

[*Westbrook is an American educator, critic, and fiction writer. In the essay below, he perceives a satiric intent in the stories "The Middle Years" and "The Figure in the Carpet" that counters the common critical view that James saw himself as an unappreciated artist, like those artists he depicted in many of his short stories.*]

This is not an attempt to trace even a minor whorl in the figure in Henry James's carpet. The risk of choking in the dust and perhaps getting rolled up in the carpet and smothering is too formidable. All I wish to do is to suggest for two stories, **"The Figure in the Carpet"** and **"The Middle Years,"** a different satirical intention from that accepted by those critics who are more impressed by James's Notebooks and Prefaces than by the stories themselves.

There has been no satisfactory interpretation of **"The Middle Years."** Comments made by editors in the various anthologies and in books like F. O. Matthiessen's edition of the Notebooks are to the effect that the story is simply another statement of its author's own doctrine of artistic perfectionism. No attempt has been made to underline the irony of the tale. Yet when aware of this irony, one realizes that James had in mind satire against the perfectionist's egotism rather than a maudlin presentation of "the plight of the artist in an ununderstanding world." Furthermore, James himself appears as less of a prig. Rather than the somewhat pompous self-pitier that his so-called admirers would have us believe him to be, he emerges, for the moment at least, as a man big enough to make fun of his own foibles as they are projected into the novelist Dencombe and in the other "supersubtle fry," as he calls them, of his tales of authors.

The meaning of **"The Middle Years"** hinges upon whether we take Dencombe's view of events as objective truth or as his egotistical distortion of what actually happened. Everything in the story points to the latter alternative as the only rational one. What has happened is not that Dencombe's book has at least been enthusiastically reviewed and that an intelligent young doctor has given up a fortune merely to be with the dying author whose style he idolizes. What has actually happened is that Dr. Hugh—a staunch admirer of Dencombe, to be sure—has written a laudatory review himself and has got it published in a newspaper with whose editors he has influence, and that he has pretended to have forgone the fortune, since this idealistic author rather ironically can appreciate no token of esteem except a monetary one.

Once one has accepted this basic fact about the story—the colossal hoodwinking that Dencombe's ego is so willing to submit to—the rest of the story unravels without a snarl. Miss Vernham in collusion with Dr. Hugh easily brings about Dencombe's refusal to see the admiring physician. In a manner fitting her character as an *intrigante,* to use James's word for her, she simply plays upon Dencombe's sense of decency by telling him that his relation with Dr. Hugh may well result in the latter's losing the fortune that the jealous countess is thinking of bequeathing to him. After this Dencombe naturally refuses to see Dr. Hugh for a day or two and thus unwittingly gives him the time to write the review and get it published in the London newspaper. Later, when the review fails to comfort Dencombe, it is easy to make up the story of the countess's outraged flight to London, her subsequent death, and the doctor's loss of the inheritance. Now notice James's ironical treatment of Dencombe's reaction.

> The incident was extraordinary as evidence, and it shed an intenser light. At last he signed to Dr. Hugh to listen, and, when he was down on his knees by the pillow, brought him very near.
>
> "You've made me think it all a delusion."
>
> "Not your glory, my dear friend," stammered the young man.
>
> "Not my glory—what there is of it! It *is* glory—to have been tested, to have had our little quality, and cast our little spell. The thing is to have made somebody care. You happen to be crazy, of course, but that doesn't affect the law."
>
> "You're a great success!" said Dr. Hugh, putting into his young voice the ring of a marriage bell.

What James has done is to show us a series of events as they appeared to the mind of a dying man. The strength of the story lies in the contrast between the dying man's distortion of events and the actual happenings as indicated by the somewhat subtle but unmistakable clues that James provides.

In the Notebooks James recorded at some length the conception of the story.

> The idea of an old artist, or man of letters, who, at the end, feels a kind of anguish of desire for a respite, a prolongation—another period of life to do the *real* thing that he has in him—the things for which all others have been but a slow preparation. He is the man who has developed late, obstructedly, with difficulty, has needed all life to learn, to see his way, to collect material, and now feels that if he can only have another life to make use of this clear start, he can show what he is really capable of. Some incident, then, to show that what he *has* done *is* that of which he is capable—that he has done all he can, that he has put into his things the love of perfection and that they will live by that. Or else an incident acting just the other way—showing him what he might do, just when he must give up forever. The *1*st idea the best. A young doctor, a young pilgrim who admires him. A deep sleep in which he dreams he *has* had his respite. Then his waking to find that what he has dreamed of is only what he has *done.*

The first idea or theme is, of course, the one James adopts. Through the doctor's ruse—a labor of love and pity—Dencombe has indeed been deluded into believing "that what he *has* done *is* that of which he is capable." And perhaps it is not delusion. Perhaps he is actually capable of nothing more; nor can one deny that the doctor's play acting is a handsome token of esteem. It is not the overwhelming sacrifice, however, that the forfeiture of the fortune would have been, and seemed to be, in Dencombe's eyes. As the entry in the Notebooks suggests, James was in no way certain just how he was to treat whatever theme he chose. The first page or so of the Preface to the New York edition of ***The Author of Beltraffio*** states **"The Middle Years"** in the writing itself gave even greater difficulty in choice of technique. Matthiessen is only partly right in saying in his comments in his edition of the Notebooks that the dream device was discarded. In its place was substituted the doctor's subterfuge. And this subterfuge—to repeat—succeeded only because Dencombe wished to believe what the doctor's feigned acts implied. As all dreams are wish fulfillments, so in Dencombe's disease-clouded fancy the reading of reality became a wish fulfillment. A superlatively clever manipulation of point of view has given us a perfect example of irony—a character, because of his own blindness or weakness, seeing exterior things and events as the reader knows they are not. Insofar as this point of view is determined by sickness, one can pity Dencombe, as did the doctor. But insofar as the point of view is determined by solipsism, one can only disapprove.

Now pity and disapproval are not complimentary attitudes, especially when directed toward artists. Yet these are two attitudes that James often rather masochistically assumes toward those literary men and other sensitive souls—like the heroes of ***The Aspern Papers*** and *The Ambassadors*—who supposedly resemble himself. But masochism in the eyes of the world is less objectionable than the priggishness with which one could charge James if one accepted Dencombe at face value, that is, as the "unappreciated genius" of the sort that so many recent critics have wanted us to believe James himself to be. As a matter of fact in another story, **"The Tree of Knowledge,"** James opens to us possibility that the "unappreciated genius" may deserve to be unappreciated.

An even more ironical treatment of novelists is contained in **"The Figure in the Carpet,"** though here the meaning of the story has been beclouded by the statements in the Preface in the New York Edition. James there implies that **"The Figure in the Carpet"** is a fable for the critics—a plea for more intelligent analysis and understanding of serious novels. If this actually was his intention, then he has failed wretchedly. For if one reads the story without the benefit of the Preface and the entries in his Notebooks, one is much more likely to take the story as a fable for the novelists—would-be supersubtle novelists—showing the results of pretense and pomposity. Both on the surface and in its implications the fable is a warning to the critics not to take a self-important author too seriously. The too-solemn, too-intense variety of critic is also satirized, of course, but so is the novelist and much more damningly. The critics in the story are mere dupes; the novelist is a poseur, a fraud.

The direction of the plot seems unmistakable. The narrator, a young book reviewer, meets his idol, the novelist Hugh Vereker, at a house party. During dinner Vereker refers to a review the young man has just written of one of his books as "the same old twaddle." Learning later that the author of the unsigned review was present when he had made the comment, Vereker apologizes, adding pretentiously that he meant that the review, like most others, had failed to recognize the over-all intention, the single dominant idea, in short, the figure in the carpet, of Vereker's work.

Fired with the purpose of revealing the figure in the carpet, the narrator rereads Vereker's voluminous output, in the meanwhile disclosing his project to another eager litterateur, George Corvick, who with the aid of his sweetheart, the even more intense Gwendolen Erme, plunges frantically into the search himself. Soon Vereker summons the narrator and exhorts him to tell no one of even the existence of the figure in the carpet. This strange request can be interpreted in various ways, one of the more feasible being that no such figure exists, but was merely a spur-of-the-moment idea Vereker had thought of to impress the reviewer he had previously insulted. The notion that the figure does not exist is, as a matter of fact, supported by James's own reference, in the Preface, to the secret as being "undiscovered, not to say undiscoverable." Why undiscoverable unless nonexistent?

Thus far, then, it is the novelist Vereker who has appeared in an unfavorable light, not the critics, who are earnest youngsters hoodwinked by a celebrity. The best thing we can say about Vereker is that he belatedly regrets his boastful loose talk.

The sequel proves the critics to be greater dupes and the secret to be more conclusively nonexistent. The narrator who has always had some doubts, becomes thoroughly skeptical, but the other two plunge onward with no success. Finally, Corvick sails for India on a newspaper assignment, announcing to the narrator that he has given up all thought of marrying Gwendolen and that, indeed, he had never definitely intended to marry her. Soon Corvick telegraphs exultantly from the East that he has found the secret. The fantastically literary Gwendolen now informs the narrator that she and Corvick *are* to be married. The impression, which James's entry in the Notebooks fortifies, is that Gwendolen, after having rejected the young man because of his inability to find the secret, has now decided to take him on again so that she will be made privy to his discovery. The inevitable further impression is that Corvick has only pretended to find the figure in the carpet in order to win the girl. This surmise is substantiated further when Corvick refuses to divulge any of the details by mail. Instead he visits Vereker in Italy to get his imprimateur. The postal report from Italy is, of course, again favorable, but still no details. Then Vereker dies, a device which in conjunction with the other sudden deaths in the story an artist like James would not have stooped to except for the all-important purpose of underlining the irony of the tale. On his return to England Corvick marries Gwendolen and is almost immediately killed in an accident, leaving only a completely uninformative fragment of his critique of Vereker.

From here on the irony is fortified by fantasy. Gwendolen refuses to tell the narrator whatever she knew about Corvick's findings because, the reader feels, she knows nothing and there is nothing to know. In a very short time she is married again to another critic, Drayton Deane. When the narrator eventually asks this second husband whether Gwendolen has told him anything concerning Vereker, Deane is amazed by the question and asserts he has never heard anything about any figure in any carpet. When the narrator and Deane, who is at once infected by the monomania, rush off to renew the fatal search, James supplies his readers with one of the few belly laughs afforded by the whole shelf of his collected works. Here we truly have the "ironic and fantastic stroke" James refers to in his Preface.

This interpretation need not be rejected because it goes counter to much of what James seems to say—for his expression is muddy—in his Preface. The story was published in 1896, the Preface in 1909. Half a generation of readers had to take the story without the Preface; and two generations, without the Notebooks, which are so fragmentary in connection with this piece that they prove nothing. I do not know the answer to the riddle: the story clearly says one thing, the Preface implies the opposite but says nothing definite. In the story, the critics are the victims of a pretentious novelist. In the Preface, the novelist has become a martyr to the stupidity of the critics, though the secret is referred to as "undiscoverable" and the story is "ironic and fantastic." As James says, "The reader is left on the evidence to conclude." (pp. 134-40)

Perry D. Westbrook, "The Supersubtle Fry," in Nineteenth-Century Fiction, *Vol. VIII, No. 2, September, 1953, pp. 134-40.*

Morton Dauwen Zabel (essay date 1958)

[*Zabel was an American poet, critic, and prominent scholar. He was influential in increasing the study of North American literature in South America and wrote two widely used American literary studies in Portugese and Spanish. In the following excerpt from his introduction to* In the Cage, and Other Tales, *Zabel examines James's theme of "captive consciousness" as realized in his later stories.*]

James, it perhaps goes without saying, achieved his greatest strength and powers as an artist in fiction in the twenty-one novels of varying length and success he wrote during his lifetime, from the crude beginnings of *Watch and Ward* in 1871 and the awkward but unmistakable force of *Roderick Hudson* in 1875, to the unfinished drafts of *The Sense of the Past* and *The Ivory Tower* that appeared in 1917 after his death. But during almost five decades he continuously exercised his skill and vision, in their fullest range of insight and invention, in the shorter narrative forms. Between the first of his stories thus far recovered, **"A Tragedy of Error"** in 1864, and the five tales of his last collection, ***The Finer Grain*** in 1910, he wrote some hundred and eleven of these—short stories, long stories, short novels, *nouvelles.* If we refer his larger powers to his novels, there is no necessity of limiting his subtlety or richness of art to these, for they are fully as evident in his shorter works. And it is in the tales perhaps even more than in his novels that the scope and diversity of his moral drama are apparent, as well as his developing resources as a craftsman and inventor. They give us not only the ground and reach of his imagination; they serve equally as matrix or seedbed of the major novels themselves. All his themes appear in them—his "international subject," his drama of the rival worlds of Europe and America, his studies of writers and artists, his criticism of manners and society, his essays in fantasy and the "ghostly," his exploration of character and morality, his analysis of the present and his sense of the past. The reader of James soon discovers one of his most engrossing pursuits to be the tracing and threading of these themes, in all their complex ramifications and relationships, as they appear in this great body of tales. And one of the discoveries he soon makes is that repeatedly, throughout his half century of fiction writing, James brought to concise or crystallized expression the problems that taxed his mind—gave focal or epigrammatic form to the moral themes and dramatic motifs that most deeply engaged his imagination. (pp. 3-4)

Certain of his novels have given classic terms or clues to the evaluation of modern experience, revealed in titles which, like proverbs, epitomize a historic situation or moral challenge: *The American, The Awkward Age, The Ambassadors, The Sense of the Past,* and notably the four of biblical origin—*The Sacred Fount, The Wings of the Dove, The Golden Bowl, The Ivory Tower.* His shorter tales show the same motif-stating instinct. He made the name of Daisy Miller a figure of speech for the generation that first puzzled over the problem of American innocence; the adjective of **"An International Episode"** pointed explicitly to a central test in modern culture. But with even greater ingenuity James frequently hit upon themes and titles that were to become part of the vocabulary of social, moral, or aesthetic criticism: thus **"The Passionate Pilgrim," "The Lesson of the Master," "The Real Thing," "The Figure in the Carpet," "The Altar of the Dead,"** ***The Turn of the Screw,*** **"The Great Good Place," "The Beast in the Jungle."** ***In the Cage*** is a notable case of such clue-defining precision. Once we have read the story it names, once we seize the key the phrase puts in our hands, we realize how here again James defined one of the focal ideas of his lifework. It is a theme that ramifies his social and moral drama in many directions. (pp. 5-6)

The "germ" that gave James his story—for here we find him putting into characteristic practice one of his cardinal axioms: that "odd law" which "somehow always makes the minimum of valid suggestion serve the man of imagination better than the maximum"—was gathered, like that of *The Princess Casamassima,* during his "attentive exploration of London" and from "the habit and the interest of walking the streets." There, his "eyes greatly open" and his "mind curious," he responded to the "mystic solicitation, the urgent appeal," of the "meanings and revelations" in "the thick jungle" of "the great grey Babylon." In those days of the 1890s before the spread of the telephone system, the telegram was a means of quick communication in large cities, and a common feature of the London streets was the local postal-telegraph office, usually installed in a convenient grocer's shop—"the small local office of one's immediate neighborhood, scene of the transaction of so much of one's daily business, haunt of one's needs and one's duties, of one's labours and one's patiences, almost of one's rewards and one's disappointments, one's joys and one's sorrows." Such shops had for an explorer like James "so much of London to give out, so much of its huge perpetual story to tell, that any momentary wait there seemed to take place in a strong social draught, the stiffest possible breeze of the human comedy." It was in such a shop, "in Mayfair or in Kensington"—so he tells us in his preface to Volume XI of the New York Edition—that the "spark" of his tale was kindled by the "wonderment" of his "speculation" about the "confined and cramped and yet considerably tutored young officials of either sex" who were "made so free, intellectually, of a range of experience otherwise quite closed to them." His inveterate speculation became "an amusement, or an obsession," in "that deepest abyss of all the wonderments that break out for the student of great cities." And it was thus that his "young woman," the "caged telegraphist," assumed the character of "a proper little monument" in the vast and complex social scene surrounding her obscure citadel—became one more opportunity for James to put into operation his insatiable "critical impulse." ("To criticise is to appreciate, to appropriate, to take intellectual possession, to establish in fine a relation with the criticised thing and make it one's own.") She struck him as a "focus of divination" and the key to her secret drama as "simply the girl's 'subjective' adventure—that of her quite definitely winged intelligence; just as the catastrophe, just as the solution, depend[ed] on her winged wit."

How accurately James's clue fastened itself on his mind is immediately evident in the aphoristic concision of the brilliant opening sentences with which his tale begins and by which he establishes at a stroke his scene and subject:

> It had occurred to her early that in her position—that of a young person spending, in framed and wired confinement, the life of a guinea-pig or a magpie—she should know a great many persons without their recognising the acquaintance. That made it an emotion the more lively—though singularly rare and always, even then, with opportunity still very much smothered—to see any one come in whom she knew outside, as she called it, any one who could add anything to the meanness of her function. Her function was to sit there with two young men—the other telegraphist and the counter-clerk; to mind the "sounder," which was always going, to dole out stamps and postal-orders, weigh letters, answer stupid questions, give difficult change and, more than anything else, count words as numberless as the sands of the sea, the words of the telegrams thrust, from morning to night, through the gap left in the high lattice, across the encumbered shelf that her forearm ached with rubbing.

Thus he situates the humblest heroine of all his tales—there in her "frail structure of wood and wire," in "the duskiest corner of a shop pervaded not a little, in winter, by the poison of perpetual gas, and at all times by the presence of hams, cheese, dried fish, soap, varnish, paraffin, and other solids and fluids that she came to know perfectly by their smells without consenting to know them by their names." Yet obscure though her life and work are in the vast scene of London, she is granted her shy fragment of destiny. She too is to become one of those "frail vessels"—to apply to her a phrase of George Eliot's that James always admired—in whom is "borne onward through the ages the treasure of human affection." She will join James's more splendid heroines in having her "inadequacy eked out with comic relief and underplots . . . when not with murders and battles and the great mutations of the world," and thus in "figuring as the main props of [his] theme."

"*Elle avait eu, comme une autre, son histoire d'amour.*" Like Flaubert's household drudge Félicité in "Un Coeur simple," of whom one seems to catch an echo here, James's telegraphist has her suitor. He is Mr. Mudge, once her co-worker in the Mayfair shop but now removed "to a higher sphere—to a more commanding position, that is, though to a much lower neighbourhood," to which he wants her transferred so that, "dangled before her every minute of the day, he should see her, as he called it, 'hourly.' " And behind her lies the harsh tragedy of her impoverished family—"the worries of the early times of their great misery, her own, her mother's and her elder sister's—the last of whom had succumbed to all but absolute want when, as conscious and incredulous ladies, suddenly bereft, betrayed, overwhelmed, they had slipped faster and faster down the steep slope at the bottom of which she alone had rebounded." The girl has thus far resisted Mr. Mudge's importunities. She is not ready to quit her cage in Mayfair, where the rumor of a great social world surrounds her and in whose stir she senses a summons. And it is out of that world that the one moment of thrilling adventure in her deprived life comes to her.

"The amusements of captives are full of a desperate contrivance." Early in Chapter III we are given this hint of the girl's plight. And as in higher and nobler instances of classic drama, her moment of fate, when it reaches her, proves to combine a stroke of chance with a prepared intention. Into the shop to send their telegrams come two persons who belong to the high aristocratic life of London—Lady Bradeen and Captain Everard. Some half-guessed, discreetly masked relationship exists between them—illicit love apparently, though it may be a more desperate collusion, some conspiracy of passion that presently threatens social disgrace and scandalous consequences.

What the danger is we never know, any more than the girl does—any more than James himself professes to know. (One of his friends in the '90s, André Raffalovich, remembered "once teasing" James "to know what the Olympian young man in ***In the Cage*** had done wrong. He swore he did not know, he would rather not know." Captain Everard's peril, whatever ingenuity we may give to deciphering it, is one of the many secrets that remain masked in James's fictions.) From her cage the girl projects her hungry curiosity, her covert desire to identify her obscure fate with the lovers' brilliant but hazardous lives. Gradually she feels something more. Like so many of James's captives she finds herself caught in an obsession. Everard's reckless gallantry appears to touch her own bleak plight. He too, she sees, "almost under peril of life," is also "clenched in a situation." It becomes "more and more between them that if he might convey to her he was free, with all the impossible locked away into a closed chapter, her own case might become different for her, she might understand him and meet him and listen." But—"he could convey nothing of the sort, and he only fidgeted and floundered in his want of power." The handsome cavalier is as helpless in the snare of his intrigue as she is in her caged and baffled yearning. Her desire to share or relieve his danger, her mute hope of coming to his rescue, possesses her days. And at length her chance is given her.

A telegram, apparently incriminating, has gone astray. She alone, with her tenacious memory of every word the lovers have exchanged in their messages, can recover the words that will save them from disaster. When crisis comes she recalls the words infallibly. She delivers the pair from danger—delivers them, at the same time, from her sharing of their secret and so prepares the day when Lady Bradeen, her husband dying, will claim her reluctant lover in marriage. The girl remembers his "supplicating eyes and a fever in his blood"; remembers the moment when danger almost brought him to a point of intimate communication with her; treasures her triumph of "having on her side, hard and pedantic, helped by some miracle," and "with her impossible condition, only answered him, yet supplicating back, through the bars of the cage." But once she has rescued him from his desperation, Everard simply walks out of the shop and out of her life. "And without another look, without a word of thanks, without time for anything or anybody, he turned on them the broad back of his great stature, straightened his triumphant shoulders and strode out of the place."

At the end, hearing from her friend Mrs. Jordan that the Captain will soon marry the widowed Lady Bradeen, "our young lady" goes off into the London fog. "Presently, after a few sightless turns," she comes out on the Paddington canal. "Distinguishing vaguely what the low parapet enclosed she stopped close to it and stood a while very intently, but perhaps still sightlessly, looking down on it. A policeman, while she remained, strolled past her; then, going his way a little further and half lost in the atmosphere, paused and watched her. But she was quite unaware—she was full of her thoughts. . . ."

What are they? Knowing her as we now do, we know they turn to the bleakness her life must resume, to the dull marriage with Mr. Mudge that awaits her, to the future to which poverty and privation condemn her—"the vivid reflexion of her own dreams and delusions and her own return to reality." Like Catherine Sloper at the end of *Washington Square* she too must sit down to her fate"—for life, as it were." Like Isabel Archer at the end of *The Portrait of a Lady,* though she may look "all about her" and listen "a little," she now knows "where to turn": "there [is] a very straight path." Like Maggie Verver at the end of *The Golden Bowl* she stands "in the cool twilight and [takes] in, all about her, where it lurked, her reason for what she had done" and "how, to her soul, all the while, it had been for the sake of this end."

She stands, like these other heroines of James in their hours of defeat or secret triumph, face to face with a recognition. It is, true enough, a recognition of her obscurity and surrender, of what bleak disillusionment has overtaken her "dreams and delusions"; yet it is something more. Her cruel experience of reality, whatever it brings of sacrifice or a diminishment of her faith in life, also brings what the foredoomed *peripeteia* must always compel—what one of the perceptive students of this subject in James has called "the extension and refinement of consciousness, of that intelligence which, in Santayana's words, is 'the highest form of vitality' " [L. C. Knights, "Henry James and the Trapped Spectator," in *Explorations* (1946)]. Of that illumination, the ultimate goal in James's moral faith, the little telegraphist can finally boast her share. She joins the other heroes and heroines of the Jamesian drama—Christopher Newman, Catherine Sloper, Isabel Archer, Hyacinth Robinson, Maisie, Fleda Vetch, Strether, Milly Theale, Maggie Verver—who, caught, caged, or pinioned in situations that bring them to defeat, tragedy, or a liberating disillusionment, snatch from the baffling odds or denials of experience the only reward which the life condemned to limitation and reality permits. It is to this final comfort—a strength or access of character—that the "sense of exclusion from experience" must come at last: to a capture of the trophy of the spirit's "vitality" and self-knowledge, the "qualities making for life."

In the Cage thus provides an essential key to the reading of James, even if it must at once be conceded that no single clue—whether it be the international theme, the American fate, the antagonisms of life and art, appearance and reality, privilege and privation, innocence and experience—suffices of itself in the full experience of his art, where ideas or conflicts so intricately intermesh and the moral debate is so complex and continuous. The story was written out of James's observation of the humble life of hardship and privation; it joins with *The Princess Casamassima* and **"The Bench of Desolation"** in showing his study of a realm of life he is usually charged with leaving unexplored. **"The Altar of the Dead"** also touches that way of experience in the obscure destiny of its heroine; so does **"Brooksmith"**; and they touch it with searching compassion. The other stories in [***In the Cage***] treat of more familiar Jamesian territory. Four of them—**"The Author of Beltraffio," "The Figure in the Carpet," "Broken Wings," "The Great Good Place"**—concern the vocation and claims of art that were James's most intimate experience and to which, early and late, he turned repeatedly in his novels and tales. Another, **"The Jolly Corner,"** the next to last story James published, is his culminating treatment of the conflict which Europe and America had imposed on the Americans of his generation and whose test he felt to be a moral imperative in his own career. But whatever the ostensible subject of these tales; however for convenience we may define, classify, or categorize them, they are all stories that hinge on the test of spiritual or moral truth and the inescapable proof it imposes on character. That test is basic to whatever external or superficial drama the tales may show. The clue provided by ***In the Cage*** helps to bring it into focus, under whatever guise or conditions it may manifest itself.

The men or women the tales present all arrive at a point of life when the reality to which, consciously or not, their fate or nature has committed them closes down—makes clear or final their responsibility to its demands; seizes or cages them in a destiny that at last declares itself as the body of their fate, the truth from which there is neither release nor reprieve. For it is a fundamental condition of James's drama—one, it may be said, that has often figured mistakenly or under distortion in the popular conception of his work—that it hinges on a contradiction, an implicit paradox. That drama appears to deal with the life of privilege or luxury, with the ardors of liberty and possibility, with freedom of choice or will and the social or personal amenity which makes such freedom operative: with, in other words, the great nineteenth-century aspiration toward self-reliance, self-fulfillment, moral emancipation. This is the larger *donnée* of James's lifework. It came to him as part of his personal inheritance: the wealth and station of his family in America, his father's moral and religious liberalism, the response and access to opportunity in his American generation, the sense of capacity that was fully as native to the air of James's world as it was to that of Emerson, Thoreau, and Whitman. Yet against these privileges there works, secretly or unsuspected, an opposing law—a law of limitation, of necessity and sacrifice; a law, as he himself defined it, of exclusion.

The great spectacle that presented itself to James's generation when they looked out, in America or Europe, on "history as a still-felt past and a complacently personal future, at society, manners, types, characters, possibilities and prodigies and mysteries of fifty sorts"; when they felt the "sense of glory" to offer "ever so many things at once, not only beauty and art and supreme design, but history and fame and power, the world in fine raised to the richest and noblest expression," was to be subjected, when the demands of moral realism began to assert themselves, to the check of a severe reproof, a chastening denial. To what curtailment of confidence in his own nature James's sense of this law may be referred can never be certain. To what refusals his character compelled him must perhaps always remain a matter for speculation. How far his instinct of estrangement or otherness dictated his recognition becomes only occasionally apparent in his utterances—as when, on one occasion late in life, he asserted that he was possessed by "the imagination of disaster" and saw "life indeed as ferocious and sinister." But there is no mistaking the workings of the rule in his tales.

It operates as the discipline of art in *Roderick Hudson* and all the tales of artists and writers that followed it. It asserts itself as a reversal of pride or expectation in *The American, The Portrait of a Lady,* and thus onward to *The Ambassadors, The Golden Bowl,* and *The Ivory Tower.* It acts repeatedly as a reproof to moral arrogance or as a corrective to the assumptions of an untested optimism. It acts continuously in certain forms of experience that James applied insistently to the characters of his drama—the experience of treachery for one, which stalks his people intently and seems to single out those who have given most of generous expectancy and confidence to life; the tragedy of failure in love or of responding to love which comes of the deceiving workings of an idealized conception of the self or the personal fate; the experience of a self-deception that is rooted in the cautions of egotism or selfishness; the pathos of innocence preyed upon by corruption or depravity. It appears at its most implacable in the discovery that one's fate is finally wholly one's own; that it is determined less by outward circumstance or delusion than by character; that neither wealth nor art nor even intelligence can be taken as refuges from its claims; and that liberation of spirit can be achieved only at the cost of acceptance, recognition, and the expiation which reality imposes on those who have challenged or denied its authority.

These are, to be sure, ancient modes of tragedy or tragic affirmation. But the force they assume in James's work comes of the unstinted ardor of his sensitivity to life, his excited response to its promises, his faith in the creative capacities of will and mind, the aspiration to "glory" he confers on his men and women. Few Americans of his time surpassed him in this sense of enthusiasm. It never deserted him personally: he could boast to the end of his "inexhaustible sensibility." And it is the very reach of their opportunities, the zeal of their expectation, that gives the measure of tragic and moral validity to his characters when reality descends on them. Then, from the trap or commitment of their personal fate, they become agents of the value life assumes when its limits declare themselves. The consequences vary. They do not necessarily insure a triumph, however secret or elusive. They do not always bring acceptance or vindication. What they bring inevitably is a vision, if perhaps only a glimpse, of the truth that liberates: the sense that while such truth, like sorrow, "wears us, uses us," we "wear it and use it in return; and it is blind, whereas we after a manner see."

It is not to be argued here that the stories in [***In the Cage***] are tales of caged characters, captive consciences, trapped spectators, and nothing else. Each has its "subject," social, moral, psychological, as the case may be; each refers to principles of conduct, choice, and responsibility which bring it into relationship with James's larger judgment of experience and values. But none of them would be seriously misread if the clue or criterion of ***In the Cage*** were applied. For it soon becomes evident that James's central moral situation appears in one form or another in each of them; that they are all, in fact, tales of the crisis of dilemma, isolation, or decision to which the necessity of moral choice brings a man, so defining the restrictive necessity in his personal fate and imposing on him the test of recognition or acceptance.

"The fictive hero successfully appeals to us only as an eminent instance," James said in opening the prefaces to his lifework, "of our own conscious kind." And in another preface he defined "the most general state of one's most exposed and assaulted figures" as a "state of bewilderment . . . the condition of a humble heart, a bowed head, a patient wonder, a suspended judgment, before the 'awful will' and the mysterious decrees of Providence." He laid emphasis on the fact that "the whole thing comes to depend on the *quality* of bewilderment characteristic of one's creature." The "exhibitional charm" he ascribes to his "salient characters" derives from their exposure or vulnerability to that bewilderment: from what they show of a "great capacity for life" doomed to "fall somehow into some abysmal trap" or into those "sad places at which the hand of generosity has been cautioned and stayed." Though the fate that brings them to "such straits" is of a kind to "*stifle* the sacred spark" and bring on the "shrinking hour"; though it repeatedly betrays "so much spent intensity" and "so much baffled calculation" to "negative adventure" or to "an absolutely blank reverse or starved residuum" of what life once promised, it is through the disappointment which enforces in "the weak agent," "blinded seeker," or "captured spirit" an enhancement of his "sense of experience" that he must seize the reward his "shrunken or blighted fortunes" offer him. Only then will his drama show what increasingly became a major issue with James: the "operative irony" which "implies and projects the possible other case, the case rich and edifying where the actuality is pretentious and vain."

James's prefaces, letters, and journals are continuous in these hints of a central preoccupation. The irony he postulates as constitutional to experience may work now as comedy, now as tragedy. The point is that it works persistently; and that it almost invariably hinges on the conflict of capacity with deprivation, privilege with denial, freedom with restriction, which forms the axis or leverage of his essential drama.

Thus Mark Ambient, the author of **"Beltraffio."** His genius has brought him to greatness in his art. The passionate young pilgrim who comes to pay him homage from America sees in his achievement a supreme "example of beauty of execution and 'intimate' importance of theme."

His art is complete, "triumphant," "the most complete presentation that had yet been made of the gospel of art," a "kind of aesthetic warcry." He evidently embodies an ideal James wrote down for himself in his notebooks: "To live *in* the world of creation—to get into it and stay in it—to frequent it and haunt it—to *think* intensely and fruitfully—to woo combinations and inspirations into being by a depth and continuity of attention and meditation—this is the only thing." His life appears to be an equivalent triumph of charm and amenity: "there was genius in his house too"—it is "a palace of art, on a slightly reduced scale," it is "the dearest haunt of the old English *genius loci.*" His wife, his child, his garden, pictures, books, all carry the stamp of an achieved perfection: "it was not the picture, the poem, the fictive page, that seemed to me a copy; these things were the originals, and the life of a happy and distinguished people was fashioned in their image." But it soon becomes apparent that Ambient's triumph is severely hedged.

His "love of beauty, of art, the aesthetic view of life," is despised by his "narrow, cold, Calvinistic wife, a rigid moralist." The issue between the pair is their child, whom she determines to save for "morality and religion, in order to expiate, as it were, the countenance that the family have given to godless ideas in the literary career of the father." The contest is deadly and it is closed. When he formulated the tale in his notebooks, James feared it would prove "very probably too gruesome—the catastrophe too unnatural." Yet he drives the catastrophe to its logical limits. It is not only an agent of expiation that the child becomes; it becomes a sacrifice. When its mother has allowed it to die rather than expose it to the "well of corruption" she believes her husband's mind and art to be, Ambient finds that his art has cost him his dearest possession; that his tragedy exemplifies what Rilke was to express in a bitter aphorism that employs the image of a prison: "In fortune art is an embellishment of life; in misfortune it becomes an iron door."

It proves to be such also in **"Brooksmith,"** where the issue is tragic, in **"Broken Wings,"** where it is bitter with disillusionment, in **"The Figure in the Carpet,"** where it produces a parable of enigma, and in **"The Great Good Place,"** where it ends in surrender and conciliation. Brooksmith, the immaculate butler, has made himself a kind of artist during his long service to Oliver Offord, and "in recall of Stendhal's inveterate motto, [has] caught a glimpse, all untimely, of 'la beauté parfaite,' " as embodied in the house and life of his master—the "delightful society," rare talk, perfection of comfort and order. When his master dies and the house with him, the servant, "formed by nature, as unluckily happened, to enjoy this privilege to the utmost," suffers a "deprivation of everything." His loss becomes a "bitterness in [his] cup"; he enacts what the editors of the *Notebooks* call "a dilemma that constantly fascinated James—the dilemma of the highly sensitive intelligence frustrated and starved by the lack of fit material and a proper environment for its development." A "poor lost spirit," he succumbs to "the measured maximum of the fatal experience." "He had indeed been spoiled," says the narrator; "he knew I really couldn't help him, and that I knew he knew I couldn't." He sinks in station; disappears; dies at last, apparently a suicide.

Here the outcome is unrelieved. In **"Broken Wings"** it is lit with fortitude and resolution. Stuart Straith and Mrs. Harvey, both artists, have had their years of success; have been taken on as ornaments of rich houses where, like Neil Paraday in **"The Death of the Lion,"** they have become "gallant victims" of social condescension and vanity. But when they fall from public favor it is "the grim realities of shrunken 'custom' " they must face, "the felt chill of a lower professional temperature." Then they must at last share a recognition of what has formerly kept them apart. "Sad companions," they must look "each other, with their identities of pluck and despair, a little hard in the face"; must "confess each to the other, relievingly, what they kept from every one else"; must acknowledge themselves in "confessions, *aveux,* tragic surrenders to the truth," and know themselves brought, "for some consolatory purpose, together." "Everything costs that one does for the rich," says Mrs. Harvey. "Let us at least be beaten together!" says Straith. "And now to work!" they both conclude "in sweetness as well as sadness."

They are permitted at length to share the secret that finally faces them, where Brooksmith took his into silence and Ambient was condemned to live with his in the solitude of his art. All four of the stories thus far considered have dealt with secret or barely communicable destinies: compacts with fate that impose a solitary commitment. Going on to the remaining four, we get an increasing sense of James's own share in such a commitment, his own pact with the fate to which his art and vocation compelled him, until at last, in **"The Jolly Corner,"** his avowal becomes all but explicit. That the life in art enforces such a dedication, that it pledges its votary to a secret that eludes his powers of communication, was clearly a living—and an increasingly urgent—presentiment to him. The "bewilderment" he specified as "characteristic" of "one's creature" became a cognate of the consciousness he set up as an imperative of the active, self-realizing mind.

"The Figure in the Carpet" is perhaps his most celebrated parable of the dilemma. James's notes on the tale insist on "secrecy" as its central clue. Hugh Vereker's art contains a "very beautiful and valuable, very interesting and remunerative *secret.*" "They don't *know* his work who don't know, who haven't felt, or guessed, or perceived, this interior thought—this special *beauty.*" His devotees, while "admiring," are driven almost to desperation—"inquisitive, sympathetic, mystified, sceptical"—in the clutch of their curiosity, "worriment," "wonderment," "torment." They are almost led to supposing Vereker "mad" in his concealment of the essential thread of his work—not its "esoteric meaning," as the newspapers say, but its "*only* meaning," the "very soul and core of the work." They become "quite possessed with their search," "devoured with curiosity," enslaved to "a strange mystifying uncomfortable delicacy." The fable becomes one of the most sheerly ingenious James ever devised, "spent intensity" and "baffled calculation" working at an extravagant pitch, and with the obsession of "the intended sense" ending in bafflement and "the issue of the affair" becoming "whether the very secret of perception hasn't been lost." James admitted that he was concerned here to exhibit "a small group of well-meaning persons engaged in a test." The test becomes the crux of the tale. It produces the ultimate case of the "caged consciousness" caught not only in a human riddle but in an aesthetic one—a virtual paradigm of James's notion of the creative mystery. It also becomes one of his ironic parables of the critical necessity—of that "responsive reach of critical perception" which Vereker "is destined never to waylay with success" in a public prone to an "odd numbness of the general sensibility," a "marked collective mistrust of anything like close or analytic appreciation."

In **"The Altar of the Dead"** the ground of obsession shifts from art to personal emotion, from an aesthetic secret to a human secret or prepossession become ingrown, all-consuming, morbid. The first paragraph of the story emphasizes pointedly the grip on Stransom of his lost love Mary Antrim's death, whose anniversary he keeps every year. "It would be more to the point perhaps to say that this occasion kept *him:* it kept him at least effectually from doing anything else. It took hold of him again and again with a hand of which time had softened but never loosened the touch." His dedication grows and deepens in him until it becomes a dedication to all the dead Stransom has ever lost. It becomes, as James phrased it in his notebook, a "worship of the Dead"—"the only religion he has," his private mode of expiating the oblivion of the "forgotten," the "unhonoured, neglected, shoved out of sight," and the "rudeness, the coldness, that surrounds their memory—the want of place made for them in the life of the survivors." It is because "the essence of his religion is really to make and to keep such a place" that Stransom, otherwise an unbeliever, engages to dedicate and maintain an altar for his dead in "a temple of the old persuasion," a Catholic church in a "great grey suburb of London" where candles are set, increasing in numbers as the years take toll, to the memory of every friend and person he has lost. To all, that is, but one. For Acton Hague, the hero of his youth, "the only man with whom he had ever been intimate, the friend, almost adored, of his University years, the subject, later, of his passionate loyalty," at whose hands Stransom had suffered a betrayal which had cut his soul to the quick and apparently maimed his faith in life, "no flame could ever rise on any altar of his."

James said in his preface to **"The Altar of the Dead"** that "the idea embodied in this composition must . . . have never been so absent from [his] view as to call for an organised search." "It was 'there'—it had always, or from ever so far back, been there." It "went back for its full intensity, no doubt, neither to a definite moment nor to a particular shock" but to an "old, deep-seated conception that had long awaited its opportunity," "amusedly biding its time." The idea derives, of course, from one of the deepest prepossessions of James's emotional and aesthetic life—that "sense of the past" in which he sensed not only a luxury of the spirit but a profound peril. And while he argues that "the sense of the state of the dead is but part of the sense of the state of the living," it is significant that in the New York Edition he paired **"The Altar of the Dead"** with **"The Beast in the Jungle,"** that other tale of a "poor sensitive gentleman" who becomes the victim of a "conviction, lodged in his brain, part and parcel of his imagination from far back," which estranges him from life, and who meets his doom in a horrified recognition that he is "the man of his time, *the* man, to whom nothing on earth was to have happened." John Marcher becomes the victim of his idealized conception of his personal fate. Stransom falls prey to his idealized conception of the dead. Both of them are victims of a fear, contempt, or distrust of life that deprives them of the will to affirm or engage themselves in it. As Marcher misses the love that May Bartram offers him, so Stransom finds himself baffled and confounded in his effort to respond to the appeal of the woman he discovers to be a fellow worshiper at his private altar—the woman Acton Hague had wronged by a greater betrayal than Stransom suffered but who has learned to pardon Hague and honor the memory of what he once gave her life. The missing of life through pride, the fear of life through a deceiving vanity, the desperate effort to come to terms with life when will or energy is spent or rendered impotent by self-delusion: this was the theme—tragic obverse in James's work of the companion theme of the passion for experience, consciousness, "the sense of having lived"—which by his own admission had engaged his mind "from ever so far back," and which gave him, in these two tales, two of his subtlest parables of the "blinded seeker" whose blindness, however nobly inflicted, is the darkest prison to which the spirit may be condemned.

George Dane, in **"The Great Good Place,"** is trapped not by privation, ignorance, or failure, but by success. James, we are bound to feel, was himself deeply involved in the subjects of **"The Figure in the Carpet"** and **"The Altar of the Dead."** In **"The Great Good Place"** his participation asserts itself as even more intimate—so intimate, apparently, that it led him to refrain from comment on the story in his prefaces. Though he admits that the tale "embodies a calculated effect," he says no more than that "any gloss or comment would be a tactless challenge."

Its hero is an author so beset by the claims, demands, and distractions of his calling; so beset, further, by his incurable avidity for life and art, his sense of unachieved purpose and unrecognized intention, that his ruling passion becomes a desire for "respite," "escape." The tale soon resorts to an imagery of imprisonment, of Gulliver-like impotence in captivity:

> There was no footing on which a man who had ever liked life—liked it at any rate as he had—could now escape it. He must reap as he had sown. It was a thing of meshes; he had simply gone to sleep under the net and had simply waked up there. The net was too fine; the cords crossed each other at spots too near together, making at each a little tight hard knot that tired fingers were this morning too limp and too tender to touch.

To this image James, in a brief foreshadowing of the story in an early notebook, adds another: the image of a releasing dream—"a deep sleep in which he dreams he *has* had his respite." We are moving now toward the realm of hallucination, and toward James's most elaborate excursion into it in *The Sense of the Past,* with **"The Altar of the**

Dead," "The Beast in the Jungle," and **"The Jolly Corner"** marking three of many stations on the way. We soon enter Dane's dream.

What Dane finds himself transported to is not a mindless freedom from the career that is baffling him, but an asylum—"some great abode of an Order, some mild Monte Cassino, some Grande Chartreuse more accessible." He knows "he had really never anywhere beheld anything at once so calculated and so generous." He has achieved a haven where the will is at last in abeyance, the clamor of achievement arrested, the claims of distraction silenced. And what James himself has arrived at is of course not "the vulgar daydream of a rich bourgeois intellectual" which some critics have accused him of writing here but—W. H. Auden's comment is undoubtedly the sound one—a kind of "religious parable" [in his introduction to James's *The American Scene* (1946)]. It is less a "social utopia" he depicts than "a spiritual state which is achievable by the individual": where, as the Brother says to Dane in the story, "every man must arrive by himself and on his own feet." "We must have first got here as we can, and we meet after long journeys by complicated ways." When Dane asks "Where is it?" the Brother replies "I shouldn't be surprised if it were much nearer than one ever suspected." "Nearer 'town,' do you mean?" "Nearer everything—nearer every one." Nearer, that is, to reality: to "life with all its rage," to "the vague unrest of the need for action," to distraction, vulgarity, frustration, without all of which, as Auden puts it, the dedicated spirit "would never understand by contrast the nature of the Good Place nor desire it with sufficient desperation to stand a chance of arriving." Success and ambition can bring their own kind of deprivation. Dane's vision of abnegation has permitted the withdrawal from rage that ensures sanity, and the only return to reality that enables the spirit to recover itself "refreshed and reconsecrated."

Of **"The Jolly Corner"** James said no more in his preface than that his motive was to produce "an analysis of some one of the conceivably rarest and intensest grounds for an 'unnatural' anxiety, a *malaise* so incongruous and discordant, in the given prosaic prosperous conditions, as almost to be compromising." And in his *Notebooks,* drafting his plan for *The Sense of the Past,* he allowed that **"The Jolly Corner"** was likewise the story of a "secret"—"that is within the hero's breast"—and that its "most intimate idea" hinged on "his turning the tables on a 'ghost,' " a "visiting or haunting apparition otherwise qualified to appall *him;* and thereby winning a sort of victory by the appearance, and the evidence, that this personage or presence was more overwhelmingly affected by him than he by *it.*" The story became, however, something more complex than this hint allows.

Spencer Brydon is another man beset—like Dane, like Stransom—by a "particular wanton bewilderment." He has lived for himself—lived for years in a Europe that has spared him the tumult of American life and given him, as he thinks, freedom for pleasure and self-fulfillment. He now returns after more than thirty years to the New York of his youth, where everything he encounters has the aspect of "so many set traps for displeasure." The trap most expressly laid for him is his old childhood home on lower Fifth Avenue. Around that house his "exasperated consciousness" revolves; the life he rejected insists on being appeased; "a real test for him" lurks in it. What he had put behind him is his old unmastered self, the past he has believed fully rejected, the "American fate" with which he has never come to terms. They have haunted him for years and now he determines to stalk them down. Yet when he tries to do so he finds his other self turning on him and challenging him—"the fanged or the antlered animal brought at last to bay." In Brydon's contest with "his *alter ego*" the pursued becomes the pursuer, the haunter the haunted. The trap has narrowed down to something even more intimate than Dane's baffled distraction. It has become the snare of Brydon's personal obsession, uneasy memory, unresolved conscience, unconfronted fate. His "concentrated conscious combat" thus engages him at the closest possible quarters. He stiffens his will against evading it. "The *question* springs" at him like another beast in the jungle: "wasn't he now in *most* intimate presence of some inconceivable occult activity?"

On the night Brydon returns to the empty house to lay his ghost at last, he finds himself in turn stalked by the specter. "It gloomed, it loomed, it was something, it was somebody, the prodigy of a personal presence." But when it finally faces him he is less shocked by its ravaged ugliness, "evil, odious, blatant, vulgar," than by "an irony." "Such an identity fitted his at *no* point, made its alternative monstrous": "that meaning at least, while he gaped, it offered him; for he could but gape at his other self in this other anguish, gape as a proof that *he,* standing there for the achieved, the enjoyed, the triumphant life, couldn't be faced in his triumph." Yet he faints on seeing it. Was the ghost that eluded him in the upper rooms of the house the ghost of the unlived and irrecoverable life he might have had at home, and the mutilated specter he confronts on descending to the street door a revelation of his actual self, maimed by evasion and selfishness, a stalking vision of the existence he has never fulfilled? [Zabel adds in a footnote: The maimed ghost in **"The Jolly Corner"** has been taken by almost all interpreters to be the specter of the mutilation Brydon's life would have suffered had he remained in America. But this view has never fully accounted for the complicated ambiguity of the haunter and haunted, pursued and pursuer, in the story, or for the apparent and puzzling presence of *two* ghosts—the one that eludes Brydon in the upper rooms of the house and the one that finally confronts him below near the street door. Floyd Stovall, in his recent analysis of the tale ("Henry James's **'The Jolly Corner,'** " Nineteenth-Century Fiction, June, 1957), argues that the mutilated specter is the apparition of Brydon's selfish life "as he lived during his European years," not the self he missed becoming by leaving America.]

When Brydon recovers from his shock it is with the sensation of having been brought back from "the uttermost end of an interminable grey passage," of feeling that his confrontation has "brought him to knowledge"—"to knowledge—yes, this was the beauty of his state." But that knowledge remains illusory until he hears from Alice Staverton, the woman who has known him from youth and who has waited patiently for his return (her role com-

Henry James in Rome, 1899.

pares closely with that of the woman in **"The Altar of the Dead"** or of May Bartram in **"The Beast in the Jungle"**), that she has known the other self, the "awful beast," all the time; that she "*could* have liked him": "he was no horror. I had accepted him." She has been, throughout the years, prepared to love Brydon not only for what he could have been but for what he is. His reconciliation comes less from what he has learned of himself than from what he discovers Alice never needed to learn. He is released from self-regard for life and love at last. **"The Jolly Corner"**—whose key words have from the first emphasized the "alter ego" "confronted" and "brought at last to bay"—ends with a confrontation Brydon's most desperate needs and ruses had never been able to anticipate. His recognition has broken open the cell of his self-deception and delivered him from "his poor ruined sight" into the light of a knowledge Alice can now share with him.

The issue here has been to define a central subject in James's art as eight of his most finished tales in the last twenty-five years of his career as a writer of fiction present it. That it was a subject profoundly involved in his moral vision, his sense of the claims of experience and knowledge, his lifelong concern with the tests of consciousness and selfhood, becomes apparent as soon as we pass from these particular tales to the many others that surround and connect with them, and notably to the novels in which the theme of the captive consciousness takes on the larger proportions of social and moral drama. And it is obvious that this theme is intimately allied with what is perhaps James's major concern as a dramatic artist—the "point of view" which he saw as an imperative of his craft and by means of which the structure and informing intelligence of a tale becomes focused in a center of consciousness—a center never so assertive as when some condition of isolation, moral captivity, or psychic obsession defines and imposes it on mind or emotion. The subject will not, of course, always appear with equal emphasis in James's work. It will often relax into comedy, satire, studies of manners and morals, of a different sort. But that it is focal and essential, a lifelong preoccupation and an almost obsessional claim in his drama, is beyond mistaking. (pp. 6-27)

Morton Dauwen Zabel, in an introduction to In the Cage & Other Tales *by Henry James, edited by Morton Dauwen Zabel, Doubleday, 1958, pp. 1-28.*

Peter Buitenhuis (essay date 1959)

[*An English educator, critic, and editor, Buitenhuis has written and edited several books on James. In the essay below, he traces the development of James's depiction of the American girl from* Daisy Miller *to the more critical* Julia Bride.]

In his preface to ***Daisy Miller,*** James recalled a summer's day toward the end of the last century when he was sitting sociably afloat in a gondola with his hostess, an American with a house in Venice, and another friend. The gondola was waiting at the water-steps of one of the hotels on the Grand Canal. Its three occupants were watching two young American girls who were shamelessly using the hotel terrace for what James ironically termed "certain demonstrations." One of James's companions commented that there were a couple of *real* Daisy Millers.

The hostess rounded on the speaker immediately: "How can you liken *those* creatures to a figure of which the only fault is touchingly to have transmuted so sorry a type and to have, by a poetic artifice, not only led our judgement of it astray, but made *any* judgment quite impossible?"

This formidable critic then turned on Henry James himself and accused him of falsifying the thing that had first been in his mind by the turn he had given his story. He had wasted his romance once again, she said, and yielded to his incurable prejudice in favor of grace. "Those awful young women capering at the hotel door," she wound up, "*they* are the real little Daisy Millers that were; whereas yours in the tale is such a one, more's the pity, as—for the pitch of the ingenuous, for quality of the artless—couldn't possibly have been at all."

Henry James's reply to this attack "bristled" with all sorts of professions, but the chief one was that his supposedly typical little figure was, of course, "pure poetry, and had never been anything else."

In this manner, James took note of one of the minor ironies of his career. ***Daisy Miller*** had first been submitted in manuscript to an editor of a magazine in Philadelphia. This worthy had turned it down because, according to the guess of a friend whom James consulted on the matter, he must have thought it to be "an outrage on American girlhood." The story had then been accepted and published by an English editor in 1878. It was promptly pirated in Boston. Very soon it had become what was to be in James's lifetime his only famous story. The American editor's supposed moral indignation and the fame of the story were both beside the point, for both were based on a misunderstanding of Daisy herself. The "real little Daisy Millers" capered about all over Europe in James's time, and have done so since, but none of them, as James's friend in Venice pointed out, have borne much resemblance to the graceful figure of the fictional Daisy.

The fact that she was "pure poetry," however, by no means detracts from the essential truth of the portrait of this particular lady. She has been truly called by one writer an "archetype of American innocence." Her natural manner, as this critic noted, "stood for a principle not easily formulated: inviolable innocence compounded with instinctive moral judgment" [Annette Kar, "Archetypes of American Innocence," *American Quarterly,* Spring 1953]. This protects her with a shield almost as strong as the chastity of the Lady in Milton's *Comus.*

Even Rome itself, with all its corruption and its evil tongues, cannot sully Daisy. Her only fault, as she herself points out, lies in not doing what the Romans do. "The young ladies of this country," she says, "have a dreadfully pokey time of it, by what I can discover; I don't see why I should change my habits for *such* stupids." As Winterbourne's aunt observes, she romps on from day to day just as they did in the Golden Age. The aunt, however, along with the rest of the American colony does not believe that Daisy shares the innocence of those who lived in that fabled era.

All the chattering tongues of Rome do not bother Daisy. She knows that Winterbourne, the one person whose opinion she values, believes in her innocence and chastity. But he too gullibly heeds the warning of his aunt that he has lived too long out of America. He begins to wonder. Are her eccentricities generic and national or are they merely personal? He cannot be sure. Yet he clings to his belief in her innocence up to the moment when he sees her alone with her Italian *cavaliere,* Giovanelli, in the Coliseum at the malarious hour of midnight.

At this point, Winterbourne not only expresses his concern for her health so recklessly exposed, but he also lets her see that he has lost his faith in her purity. As her carriage rolls away, she cries out to him, in a strange tone, that she doesn't care whether she has caught Roman fever or not. Winterbourne's change of heart hurts her deeply, perhaps even contributes to her death. A week later she succumbs to the fever. At her burial, Winterbourne encounters Giovanelli, who tells him that she was not only the most beautiful and most amiable lady that he had ever known, but also that she was the most innocent.

A year later, Winterbourne meets his aunt again at Vevey and tells her that it is on his conscience that he has done Daisy an injustice. He admits that his aunt had been right in predicting his mistake, and says, "I've lived too long in foreign parts." His aunt had meant that he no longer was aware of the social and moral climate of America. Winterbourne, however, is referring to something quite different. He has realized that without an understanding of Daisy's background he had been unable to perceive Daisy's inviolable innocence. He has realized too late that he could have loved Daisy, and that Daisy could have loved him.

Daisy's fate, as Henry James takes care to underline, is the result not only of her innocence, but also of her ignorance. Her mother is a whining hypochondriac with no more influence over Daisy than she has over that little monster Randolph, Daisy's brother. None of them sees anything anomalous in their undisciplined family situation. It is only a continuation of the way they live their lives in Schenectady—lives which are assumed by all of them to be, if not the only ones possible, at least the only ones desirable. The note of Schenectady is struck by Daisy when she says to the shocked Winterbourne: "I've always had a great deal of gentlemen's society."

So long as Daisy remained in America, she risked nothing by her behavior. When, however, her innocent attitude toward the relationships between the sexes is confronted by the complexities and rigidities of European life, a dangerous tension is created. Her stubbornness in the face of good advice makes disgrace inevitable. Her inflexibility, indeed, is of a piece with her lack of awareness and self-knowledge. As a result, she is a flat character, as James himself pointed out in his preface: "flatness indeed," he added, "was the very sum of her story." Yet he went on to claim that this flatness made for concentration. His claim is surely justified. ***Daisy Miller*** approaches the concentration of a short lyric poem. The image of Daisy seems to linger charmingly and gracefully in the mind like the image of, say, Robert Herrick's Julia.

James recorded the success of the American girl on her home ground in a later story, **"Pandora"** (1884). He admitted in his preface that a good deal of Daisy's element of poetry had also sneaked into this story. All the same he claimed that **"Pandora"** had grown out of an incident recorded in New York when at a pleasure party he had observed a young lady present in a "rather perceptibly unsupported and unguaranteed fashion." He had been told that she was a representative of a new social type, the self-made, or self-making girl, who had come on the social scene like one of the charges of Little Bo-Peep, leaving her "tail" of relatives, who were beyond the social pale, behind her.

In **"Pandora,"** such a girl's attributes are tested in the political arena. Pandora goes to Washington, meets the President at the house of the Bonnycastles and dazzles the chief executive into appointing her absent fiancé to a consular post. All this is done before the amazed eyes of Count Vogelstein, a highly intelligent and highly obtuse young German diplomat appointed to Washington. Mr. Bonnycastle (a thinly disguised Henry Adams) tries to explain to him how she does it: "She was possible doubtless only in America; American life has smoothed the way for her. She was not fast, nor emancipated, nor crude, nor loud . . . She hadn't been born with the silver spoon of social opportunity; she had grasped it by honest exertion." Bonnycastle was also voicing James's sentiments. The American girl, in America, could achieve almost anything.

"Pandora" was one of the fruits of James's two visits to America between 1881 and 1883 as were his other studies, **"Miss Gunton of Poughkeepsie"** and **"The Patagonia."** He did not return to his native land for over twenty years. One of the reasons for his return was to refresh his imagination and open up new resources for his fiction. Naturally, the American girl, so long the object of his scrutiny and reflection, came in for keenly renewed study. How had she fared on her native ground in the long interim?

In both ***Daisy Miller*** and **"Pandora,"** James had taken for granted the absence of the male members of the families of his two heroines. He found to his consternation on his return to America in 1904 that the absence of the male had practically become the law of social life. The American girl was now left in a completely uncorrected and unrelated state. She was expected to supply, as he put it in *The American Scene,* all the grace and all the interest that wasn't the mere interest on the money. She had been abandoned and betrayed by the absence of parents and brothers and male cousins until she was, James thought, practically lost.

What was to be done about this situation? James was no man to start a reform movement, but he felt that some protest should be made. Accordingly, in a series of splendid articles that ran in *Harper's Bazaar* from November, 1906 to July, 1907, he made a frontal attack on the manners and speech of American women. He intended to gather these essays in *The Sense of the West,* the projected second volume of his American impressions. When he gave up work on this volume, he did not trouble to collect the essays independently. Unfortunately, they remain today buried almost unknown among what he called "the ruins of the language" of the other contributions to the magazine.

It was James's conclusion that no witness who had been able to compare the manners and speech of American women as they were at this point early in the twentieth century with what they had been twenty years before could fail to notice the deterioration. Looking for causes for this falling-off, he took particular note of women "with hard faces and harsh accents" whom he had observed in force in American hotels. It seemed to him that they bore out some statistics he had seen on the rising rate of divorce. These women were the natural results of a system that made divorce cheap and easy. He speculated uneasily about the type of training that they would be giving to their "terrific bedizened little girls" ["The Manners of American Women, Part III," *Harper's Bazaar,* June 1907].

Partly in order to chronicle his sense of the change in a characteristic type of American girl, he wrote, in 1908, ***Julia Bride,*** the "companion study," as he called it, to ***Daisy Miller.*** There is no doubt that he intended his readers to compare the two stories in order that they should see the nature of the change, as well as realize the nature of James's advance in technical proficiency as a short-story writer.

Julia Bride has received very little scholarly attention, but James himself thought highly of his latter-day Daisy. He published the story twice in the short time before it appeared in the New York Edition. It was first printed in *Harper's Magazine* in 1908, then in a separate edition as a complete book in 1909. Julia is invoked for the third and last time int he preface to the tale in the New York Edition:

> 'Here we are again!' she seemed, with a chalked grimace, to call out to me, even as the clown at the circus launches the familiar greeting; and it was quite as if, while she understood all I asked of her. I confessed to her the oddity of my predicament. This was but a way, no doubt, of confessing it to myself—except indeed that she might be able to bear it. Her plea was—well, anything she would; but mine, in return, was that I really didn't take her for particularly important in herself, and would in fact have had no heart for her without the note, attaching to her as not in the least to poor little dim and archaic Daisy Miller, say; the note, so to call it, of multitudinous reference.

Julia's note had been struck again and again by the American girls he had seen during his visit. "What if she were," he wondered, "the silver key, tiny in itself, that would unlock a treasure?—the treasure of a whole view of manners and morals, a whole range of American social aspects?"

Julia, then, is no idealization. She has nothing to do with "pure poetry." She is instead a symbolic figure who embodies many of James's ideas about social change in America in the twenty years he had been absent from it. Julia was designed to be, for the attentive reader, a focus for a criticism of the new society. She was for James an archetype of American experience.

The story opens in the marble halls of the new Metropolitan Museum through which the lovely Julia has been walking with Basil French, the enormously rich young man whom she is seeking to make her seventh fiancé. There is no hint of Daisy's idleness and impulsiveness in her behavior. Julia is determinedly on the make. Basil is leaving the Museum when the story begins, but Julia turns back into one of the "pictured rooms" to meet Mr. Pitman, the second of her mother's two divorced husbands. He tells her, almost at once, that he too is after a rich prize—Mrs. Drack, a wealthy widow, who is soon to meet him in the Museum. They commiserate each other on the difficulties of their task, admitting their sadly compromised pasts.

At this point begins the intrigue which makes up the balance of the story. Mr. Pitman proposes a course of action which will "clear" their names. If Julia will vouch to Mrs. Drack for his innocence in his divorce from Julia's mother, then he in turn will vouch to Basil French for Julia's mother's innocence in that same divorce.

Julia is reluctant to agree, but when Mrs. Drack turns up,

she magnificently performs her part. She realizes, however, that Mr. Pitman's testimony would not count with Basil French and that she must get one of her former fiancés to vouch for her innocence. With this in mind she meets by appointment the most plausible and most intimate of them, Murray Brush, in "the devious paths and favouring shades" of Central Park. She asks him to assure Basil French that there had never been "anything the least bit serious" between them.

Brush gladly volunteers to "lie like a gentleman," but then he demands his own *quid pro quo.* He has just become engaged again, and he wants Julia, should his part of the bargain be fulfilled, to help him and the girl, Mary Lindeck, to rise to the level of the society to which Julia would be elevated by her marriage to Basil French. He suggests that she invite the two of them to have tea with Basil French and herself.

Julia has by this time realized the uselessness of her plan, but she fatalistically agrees to the arrangement and then hurries away to her room in "the horrible flat which was so much too far up and too near the East side." Once there she gives way to the "long lonely moan" of her conviction that Basil French would not for a moment be deceived and that her design is doomed to failure.

Most of the characters in ***Julia Bride*** are the natural products of a society that takes a system of "cheap and easy divorce" for granted. One exception is Basil French, who is a glamorous symbol to the rest of them of wealth, respectability and social prestige. Julia, having a mother with one impending and two past divorces to her credit, had naturally gone in for "the young *speculative* exchange of intimate vows," as James called it. Her plight, like that of Daisy Miller, was the result of ignorance. Julia's half-dozen engagements and disengagements were of no more account to her than Daisy's numerous trysts with Giovanelli in Rome. Julia sees that there might be something shabby in six broken engagements and some value in concealing them only after she has come to know Basil French, who is "cultivated, earnest, public-spirited, brought up in Germany, infinitely travelled, awfully like a high-caste Englishman." Murray Brush disposes of French by putting him in the category of those "who are not in sympathy," as he puts it, "with the old American freedom." Daisy, brought up like Julia in an extremely haphazard manner, simply takes for granted "the old American freedom" of association with the opposite sex. She can never seriously consider any alternative method of behavior and retains her outlook to her death. Julia, in contrast, comes to the conclusion that "the disgusting, the humiliating thing" was that her mother had allowed her to assume that "her own incredibly allowed, her own insanely fostered frivolity" had been the natural career for a young girl. She has to struggle to cut herself off from this career by means of deceit and intrigue.

Julia, by realizing that she has been caught irrevocably in the tangle of her own false upbringing, at least reaches a degree of self-knowledge. The other characters in the story, however, remain enmeshed in their own snobbery and, to use James's term, "money-passion." Mr. Pitman, seeking the hand of the bland, elephantine Mrs. Drack, tells his former stepdaughter, simply, "Julia, she has millions." Murray Brush, too, has taken the precaution this time of getting engaged to a girl who is "not, thank goodness, at all badly off." Mr. Pitman is also seeking respectability. He proudly observes that Mrs. Drack "disapproves of divorce quite as much as Mr. French." The calculated snobbery of Murray Brush in his efforts to climb socially makes the snobbery of Winterbourne's aunt look almost charitable by comparison. The theme of ***Julia Bride*** is similar to that of **"Pandora,"** of course. Julia, Murray and Mr. Pitman are all trying to raise themselves socially and financially. But the circumstances of each tale make directly opposing impressions on the mind of the reader. Pandora's method of self-advancement, though bold, is honest and admirable. The methods of Julia and company are devious and sordid.

No paraphrase of ***Julia Bride*** can encompass James's achievement in the story. It can take no account of what he called in the preface "the note of multitudinous reference." This note is quite lacking in the simple and poetic ***Daisy Miller.*** James sought to explain the difference between the two tales by saying: "A whole passage of intellectual history, if the term be not too pompous, occupies in fact, to my present sense, the waiting, the so fondly speculative interval." In that interval, James had been hanging around, as he whimsically termed it, like an "irrepressibly hopeful artistic Micawber," on the chance that something would turn up out of this repeatedly presented fictional situation.

In ***Julia Bride,*** as he explains in the preface, something did turn up. In this strictly "foreshortened" story, he was seeking to make "a full-fed statement . . .—the imaged résumé of as many of the vivifying elements as may be coherently packed into an image at once." James felt the necessity for such a statement because he believed that one whole area of American experience was closed to him. This was "the world downtown," the major key, as he called it, of American life. He felt himself to be disbarred from any attempt at representing it in his fiction by his sheer ignorance of any detail of business operations.

He was confined therefore, for subject, to "the minor key" of the uptown world. "To ride the *nouvelle* down-town," he wrote, "to prance and curvet and caracole with it there—that would have been the true ecstasy." But he knew that one spill, such as he might easily have had in Wall Street, or wherever, would have prevented him, for very shame, from ever mounting again.

The only way, then, that James could portray what he considered to be the most important aspect of American life was by implication. In ***Julia Bride,*** he sought to denote the major key by playing the minor, to image the downtown world in the smaller mirror of the up. He did this by the extensive, the almost exclusive, use of the imagery of money and the market.

All the characters have their appropriate correlative in the terms of the market place. Mrs. Drack, when she appears in the Museum, conveys her value as a commodity by the "whole metallic corruscation" of her brocade dress with enhancements that represent to Julia "the large figure of her income, largest of her attributes." Poor Mr. Pitman on the other hand has written all over him his "business slackness."

Julia herself exults in the items of her beauty, like a stockbroker in a rising market. "*Le compte y était,*" she thinks, "a sum of thumping little figures." She also has the stockbroker's caution:

> nobody knew better than Julia that inexpressible charm and quoteable 'charms' (quotable like prices, rates, shares, or whatever, the things they dealt in downtown) are two distinct categories; the safest thing for the latter being, on the whole, that it might include the former, and the great strength of the former being that it might perfectly dispense with the latter.

Julia plays the marriage market by attempting to realize on her quoteable charms. She finds out, however, that they won't include the inexpressible charms (the charms "not vulgar"), and realizes that the buyer, when he finds out about their inflated value, will back away. In the end, she looks forward, like any overreaching speculator, to "certain ruin."

The shadier aspects of the story are emphasized by another series of monetary images. Mr. Pitman and Julia, meeting in the Museum, are like "a pair of pickpockets comparing . . . their day's booty." Murray Brush and Julia in Central Park are like "Nancy and the Artful Dodger . . . talking things over in the manner of *Oliver Twist*" Julia realizes how little Murray Brush "was of metal without alloy." His charity towards her, all bogus as it is, is "like a subscription of a half a million."

Even the opening scene of the story is an ironic image of financial success. The Metropolitan Museum represents for Julia all the things she is vainly after, "with its mockery of art and 'style' and security." The ambiguity of the word "mockery" in this context is enriched by a knowledge of James's comments on the Museum in *The American Scene.* It signified for him "acquisition," and the word implies, of course, as much about the acquisition of money as it does about the architecture and the art that the money made possible. "There was money in the air," he wrote, "ever so much money—that was, grossly expressed, the sense of the whole intimation. And the money was to be all for the most exquisite things—for all the most exquisite except creation, which was to be off the scene altogether; for art, selection, criticism, for knowledge, piety, taste."

The imagery of ***Julia Bride*** is one of the devices with which James unlocks a treasure of American social aspects. The uptown world and by reflection the downtown are revealed in the language common to both—that of money. The "imaged résumé" thus presented is not a pleasant one, but it accurately reflects the harsh view that James took of New York financial and social life after his return visit. James believed that in this rapacious society the old American values of individualism and self-reliance had been corrupted into selfishness and self-aggrandizement.

In *The American Scene,* James made the skyscrapers the fitting symbols of a restless and all-devouring money-passion. The businessmen needed these towers of glass, he thought, in order that they might have the more light by which to outwit their competitors, and to see that their competitors did not outwit *them.* Uptown the women were left to run the social game unaided. Some of them took their cue from the financial game played downtown. Manners, grace, stability, all could be sacrificed in order to gain the best prize in the marriage market. Some regarded a marriage as but a steppingstone toward a better one, as Julia Bride's mother demonstrated. She cast off the unsuccessful Mr. Pitman in order that she might secure a better-equipped husband. Children, such as Julia, brought up in this kind of environment naturally accepted its rules without question.

Julia Bride thus has a dimension entirely missing from ***Daisy Miller.*** Mr. Miller, supplying the cash that makes the action possible, remains behind in Schenectady and is a cipher in the tale. Julia's real father doesn't appear either, yet so rich are the implications of the story that there is no sense of missing connections or motivations. Julia's life has a "full fusion," as James himself pointed out, "with other lives that remain undepicted, not lost." The other lives are a part of Julia's consciousness: her numerous ex-fiancés, her mother's ex-husbands, the "serried Frenches," and the spiteful Mrs. Maule, mother of four eligible "kittens," who is seeking to turn Basil's mind against Julia. The flat quality that James ascribed to Daisy thus disappears in ***Julia Bride*** under the pressure of the "other lives . . . [that] press in, squeeze forward, to the best of their ability." Daisy is a pathetic figure, for she dies innocent and wronged, but she can hardly arouse deep feelings of sympathy since she has very little comprehension of the causes of her fate. Julia Bride as the story progresses sees more and more that she is the victim of her own training, the unfortunate scapegoat for her own reckless career. She views the society around her from a new perspective and comes to judge it.

The "old American freedom" of the relations between the sexes that James had treated quite uncritically in ***Daisy Miller*** came in for critical appraisal in ***Julia Bride.*** Julia's generation had played fast and loose with the idea, stretched it so that it covered all kinds of free behavior. It needed evaluation and, above all, criticism from those who stood to lose most by its laxness. Julia's failure is thus both highly pathetic and highly illustrative. In the depths of her misery she has full knowledge of the causes of her defeat. "The whole passage of intellectual history" between ***Daisy Miller*** and ***Julia Bride*** thus records both Henry James's achieved mastery of the foreshortened and tightly-packed *nouvelle* and the transition of the consciousness of a certain type of American girl from innocence to experience and from ignorance to knowledge. (pp. 136-46)

Peter Buitenhuis, "From Daisy Miller to Julia Bride: 'A Whole Passage of Intellectual History'," in American Quarterly, *Vol. XI, No. 2, Summer, 1959, pp. 136-46.*

James W. Gargano (essay date 1960)

[*In the following essay, Gargano proposes that contrary to the common interpretation of* Daisy Miller *as a story about Daisy, the novella insightfully reflects narrator Frederick Winterbourne's quest for innocence.*]

When John Foster Kirk rejected ***Daisy Miller*** as "an outrage on American girlhood," he unhappily misled critics of Henry James's novel into an obsessive preoccupation with its heroine. In his preface to the New York edition, James himself, perhaps still smarting from his rebuff, waives consideration of other aspects of the novel in his excessive concern with justifying his portrait of the maligned Daisy. Howells, too, because of the nature of his subject in *Heroines of Fiction,* focuses discussion of the novel on the appealing heroine.

Critical preoccupation with Daisy has fostered the view that the theme of the novel is the peril of a good but naïve American girl in a stiffly conventional society. This simplification ignores the fact that Frederick Winterbourne, as the central intelligence, represents the consciousness upon which the events and characters of the novel have the greatest impact. Since he is always on the scene, observing, discriminating, and seeking to unravel the mystery of the enigmatic Daisy, the drama must, if James's art can be said to have any intention, structurally center in him. He, I believe, is the subject of the novel and not merely the lens through which Daisy's career is seen. His story has a richness that makes ***Daisy Miller*** more than a thin commentary on the lawless innocence of the American girl.

Winterbourne's visit to Vevey begins an experience which can be described, in one of James' favorite words, as an "initiation." In other words, Winterbourne leaves a world of fixed values, and adventures into a foreign one where only innate sensibility and large sympathy can guide him and where commitment to a restrictive code will surely hurt him. His attraction to Daisy, by wrenching him out of his moral and social insularity, offers him an opportunity to enlarge his consciousness and gain the psychic fulfillment that James's characters constantly seek and very rarely find in love. Thus, for all her independent charm, Daisy exists to test Winterbourne's ability to grow beyond his hitherto narrow and one-sided state into a fully realized human being.

Considered as Winterbourne's story, ***Daisy Miller*** is essentially the study of a young man's quest for innocence, a virtue from which his society has alienated itself. It is by no means accidental that Winterbourne meets Daisy in a garden—commonly associated with innocence—or that the severe Mrs. Costello describes the girl as romping "on from day to day, from hour to hour, as they did in the Golden Age." Indeed, the *mis-en scène* of the first section of the novel cleverly foreshadows the later conflict between innocence (here related to freedom) and the dark assumptions with which Winterbourne faces life. Winterbourne is visiting Vevey, which, because it resembles "an American watering-place," exhibits a more relaxed social life than is to be found elsewhere in Europe. Vevey is further identified with freedom by its proximity to the Castle of Chillon, unmistakably associated with Bonivard, a famous foe of tyranny. With typical finesse, James immediately emphasizes the spiritual distance between Vevey and Winterbourne, who "had an old attachment for the little capital of Calvinism." Certainly Geneva, later referred to "as the dark old city at the other end of the lake," symbolizes a rigidly conventional way of life whose forms mask a Puritan distrust of spontaneous and natural behavior. Winterbourne, who significantly attended school in Geneva and has many friends there, constantly assesses his new experiences by the standards of his spiritual home.

Vevey is the appropriate scene for Winterbourne's rencounter with a bewildering girl who "looked extremely innocent." But since innocence is the very thing in which Geneva has lost faith, Winterbourne consistently misreads Daisy's character and seeks to ferret out the *arrière pensée,* the dubious motive behind her artless conversation. Still, his admiration of her constitutes a self-betrayal, a persistent belief in innocence perhaps rooted in his American origin and fortified by the romantic idealism of youth. Lacking as yet a fatal rigidity, he is offered an opportunity to discover innocence and escape the propriety that menaces the full flowering of his nature.

Winterbourne's initiation begins in a comic manner calculated to show his inability to appreciate instinctively the innocence of Daisy's character. When, contrary to the code of Geneva, he speaks to the unmarried Daisy, he wonders whether "he has gone too far." He risks "an observation on the beauty of the scene" and wrongly assumes that an excursion to Chillon with the girl must perforce include her mother as chaperone. When he attempts to classify her, she undermines all of his stuffy and inapplicable generalizations. He decides that she may be "cold," "austere," and "prim" only to find her spontaneous and as "decently limpid as the very cleanest water."

Winterbourne's perplexity in the presence of innocence indicates the extent to which he is "morally muddled." Unable to believe in natural goodness, which usurps freedoms of speech and action, he must analyze it with the suspicious rationalism of Geneva and thus miss its essential luster. Distrusting the authority of his feeling for Daisy's "natural elegance," he complacently pronounces her a flirt:

> Winterbourne was almost grateful for having found the formula that applied to Miss Daisy Miller. He leaned back in his seat; . . . he wondered what were the regular conditions and limitations of one's intercourse with a pretty American flirt.

Winterbourne's comic ineptness demonstrates how poorly Geneva's formulas have prepared him to understand innocence.

His self-assurance is so halfhearted, however, that he takes his problem to his aunt, Mrs. Costello, the most reliable social authority he knows. Going to her with "a desire for trustworthy information," he suddenly betrays an inchoate perception of Daisy's nature. Though he uncritically allows Mrs. Costello's reference to the girl's "intimacy" with Eugenio to "make up his mind about Miss Daisy," he generously declares, "Ah you're cruel! . . . She's a very innocent girl!" In spite of his aunt's innuendoes, he holds to his purpose of taking Daisy to Chillon. Indeed, his momentary defection from Geneva appears so extreme that Mrs. Costello is confirmed in her refusal to be presented to his new acquaintance.

Winterbourne's recognition of Daisy's innocence may represent impatience with the stringent code of Geneva, but it can by no means be interpreted as thoroughgoing disillusionment. He sees only enough to be less blind than Mrs. Costello; if he departs from the dictates of propriety, he does so with customary prudence. Lacking the ardor and recklessness of a rebel, he is temperamentally doomed to swing in permanent vacillation between opposing claims. He has sensibility enough to be "touched, mortified, shocked" when he perceives Daisy's hurt at Mrs. Costello's refusal to see her; yet he is too tepid to do anything more than think of sacrificing "his aunt—conversationally." Even his trip to Chillon—perhaps his most daring action—is followed by his symbolical return to the bleak city of conformity. In his paralyzing introspection and most of his behavior, he is a morbid, though superficially cultivated, latter-day Puritan.

Nevertheless, before his visit to Rome, Winterbourne has found Daisy's innocence appealing enough to defend. On the free soil of Vevey, he has even dared to take an unchaperoned young lady on an excursion. He may cut a comic figure in his attempts to reduce Daisy's ingenuous license to formula, but his mind is open to impressions that the bigoted Mrs. Costello refuses to receive. Since Rome, however, is the city where one behaves as the Romans do, Winterbourne's capacity for freedom and conversely the extent of his commitment to Geneva are tested there.

The Roman phase of the novel ironically dramatizes the disintegration of Winterbourne's somewhat nebulous faith in innocence. In the presence of Daisy's critics, he defends her in a manner which reveals a desire to strengthen his own faltering belief in her. To Mrs. Costello's indictment of the Millers, he timidly responds: "They are very ignorant—very innocent only, and utterly uncivilized." When Mrs. Walker's carriage appears in the Pincian Gardens to rescue Daisy from her "tryst" with Giovanelli, Winterbourne again insists upon the girl's innocence, but as he does so he "reasoned in his own troubled interest." Indeed, before Mrs. Walker's intrusion, he had himself explored all manner of doubts about the "fineness" of Daisy's character. Obviously, then, in his debates with the girl's critics he is confronting, and only temporarily triumphing over, his own sinister suspicions. Basically, he never triumphs at all, for after his colloquy with Mrs. Costello he "checked his impulse to go straightway" to visit Daisy and after his bout with Mrs. Walker he confesses, "I suspect, Mrs. Walker, that you and I have lived too long at Geneva." His evaluation of himself is so accurate that when Mrs. Walker affords him a chance to return to Daisy, and thus to conquer his doubts, he permits mere appearance, "the couple united beneath the parasol," to undermine his insecure faith in innocence.

Winterbourne's desertion of Daisy in the Pincian Gardens (again the garden suggests innocence) characterizes him as incapable of embracing values larger than those of his parochial society. His acuteness in recognizing the cruelties of Mrs. Costello and Mrs. Walker is not vision, and his persistent defense of Daisy is hardly courage. With a finicky, formal taste, he wants his innocence wellbred and prudent, not realizing that innocence is by nature averse to calculation. When Daisy asks him if he thinks she should desert Giovanelli and enter Mrs. Walker's carriage, he advises her to "listen to the voice of civilized society." Sententiously, stiffly—Daisy describes him as having no more "give than a ramrod,"—he lectures her about the "custom of the country" and the "ineptitude of innocence."

His final incapacity to champion innocence is shown when, Mrs. Walker having turned her back on Daisy, he is "greatly touched" by the girl's "blighted grace" but characteristically does nothing more than accuse Mrs. Walker of cruelty. It is no wonder that he soon feels "that holding fast to a belief in [Daisy's] 'innocence' was more and more but a matter of gallantry too fine-spun for use." He admits that "he had helplessly missed her, and now it was too late." Yet, he cannot completely abandon his belief in an innocence that once charmed as well as bewildered him until he discovers Daisy and Giovanelli together in the Colosseum at night. Then, with "final horror" as well as "final relief," he capitulates to Geneva:

> It was as if a sudden clearance had taken place in the ambiguity of the poor girl's appearances and the whole riddle of her contradictions had grown easy to read. She was a young lady about the shades of whose perversity a foolish puzzled gentleman need no longer trouble his head or his heart. That once questionable quantity *had* no shades—it was a mere black little blot.

Winterbourne's quest has thus ended in a typically Puritan repudiation of innocence. Now, giving greater faith to his new discovery of Daisy's "evil nature" than he had ever given to his timid belief in her goodness, he spurns her with a severity as inhumane as Mrs. Costello's and Mrs. Walker's. His last conversation with the girl is a caustic revelation that his nature has shriveled rather than expanded. He counters her assurance that she is not engaged to Giovanelli with a confession of indifference made "with infinite point." "It was a wonder," says James, "how she didn't wince for it." Essentially the slave of a society that worships form and ignores humane considerations, he lifts his hat and leaves her while Daisy cries out, "I don't care . . . whether I have the Roman fever or not!" Even Daisy's death-bed message, reminding him of their trip to Chillon (freedom) and disavowing the rumors concerning Giovanelli and herself, leaves him intransigent and unaffected.

Winterbourne's harsh certainty about Daisy's character convicts him of a fatal coldness of heart fostered by the sin-obsessed society of Geneva. Having failed to respond to Daisy's need for affection, he can gain enlightenment only from without, never from within. Ultimately, he must be convinced of Daisy's purity by the impressionable fortune hunter, Giovanelli. Their short conversation after Daisy's burial brings home to Winterbourne how irremediably the dark old city has played him false. He has seen innocence—the only kind of innocence this complex world affords—and has conspired with Mrs. Costello and

Mrs. Walker to kill it. Listening to Giovanelli's elegy to Daisy, he is made to face his own incredible error:

> "She was the most beautiful young lady I ever saw, and the most amiable." To which he added in a moment: "Also—naturally!—the most innocent."
>
> Winterbourne sounded him with hard dry eyes, but presently repeated his words, "The most innocent?"
>
> It came somehow so much too late that our friend could only glare at its having come at all.

Months later Winterbourne reveals to Mrs. Costello that he has brooded over and measured the depth of his mistake. Nevertheless, though he locates the cause of his failure in his "foreign" education, his wisdom culminates in a retreat to Geneva. The quest for innocence has thus merely brought him experience of his own lugubrious inadequacy to transcend—even with the advantage of knowledge—the sham and cruel proprieties of the dark old city. (pp. 114-20)

James W. Gargano, "Daisy Miller: An Abortive Quest for Innocence," in South Atlantic Quarterly, *Vol. LIX, No. 1, Winter, 1960, pp. 114-20.*

Wayne C. Booth (essay date 1961)

[Booth is an American essayist and critic. In the following excerpt, he examines the ambiguous and unreliable viewpoints in "The Liar" and The Aspern Papers.*]*

If impersonal narration [in literature] had been limited to ambiguous heroes who narrate or reflect their own lives, our problems [as readers] would have been great enough. But as we see in ***The Turn of the Screw,*** the narrative situation is often far more complex. . . . Some of our greatest problems come when we are given another character as unreliable as the hero to tell his ambiguous story. [Complications of judgment] are compounded when the author, pursuing James's desire for "gradations and superpositions of effect" that will produce "a certain fulness of truth," seeks to give us one character's "troubled vision" as "reflected in the vision, also troubled enough," of an observer [R. P. Blackmur in his preface to **"The Pupil,"** in *The Art of the Novel* (1947)].

With few exceptions, James's effort in his maturity is to find for each story an observer, or group of observers, who because of their sensitivity can "reflect" the story to the reader. It is "in their minds" that the story really takes place; as they experience it, the reader experiences it. But James never formulates clearly the problem produced by the dramatic role of *inconscience* itself. He thus fails to provide any theory relevant to one large segment of his own work—those stories narrated, whether in the first or third person, by a profoundly confused, basically self-deceived, or even wrongheaded or vicious reflector.

Because we have his prefaces and notebooks, it is possible to trace in many of James's stories a process undoubtedly frequent in other modern authors but usually more deeply hidden: the transformation of a "subject," through the development of a "reflector" not important in the original conception, into something quite different. My interest here is in that surprisingly large body of works into which observers, and particularly unreliable observers, are imported *after* the original conception of the subject has been formulated.

In many of Jame's initial notebook entries about a story he includes a general description of how it is to be told. With such stories we can never be sure whether there was ever a prior version, unrecorded, existing in his mind as separated from any narrative manner, but it is clear that the manner has very early been seen as inseparable from the "subject." "And I suppose the observer, as usual, must tell the tale" (*The Golden Bowl*). "Can't I see my *biais* here, don't I see my solution, in my usual third person: the observer, the *knower,* the confidant of either the 2 women or the 2 men?" (**"The Given Case"**). "It comes to me that the thing might be related by the 3d person, according to my wont when I want something—as I always do want it—intensely objective" (**"The Friends of the Friends"**).

Sometimes his conception of this observer remains unchanged from original notebook entry to finished story. But often he gradually develops the reflector until the original subject is rivaled or even overshadowed. It is fascinating to watch James as he transforms a subject into a story of how it affects or is affected by an observer. One can see a new heroine emerging, for example, as he plans **"The Impressions of a Cousin."**

> The "Cousin" of the title is a young woman who relates the story (in the form of a journal), living with her kinswoman as a companion, observing these events [the original idea] and guessing the secret. It is only in her journal that the secret "transpires." She herself of course to be a "type." I thought of infusing a little American local colour into it by making the story take place in New York and representing the Cousin as a Bostonian, with the Boston moral tone, etc. But that would be pale.

He did finally make the cousin an American woman, and she becomes, like so many of James's narrators, the most vivid agent in the story. Instead of merely observing and recording, she acts. The original idea is completely transformed by having one of the key characters fall in love with the narrator who was originally conceived as a mere reflector.

A clearer instance of his conscious battle with the problem of the narrator who seems to take over a subject is shown in his comments on **"The Friends of the Friends."** At first his "I" is largely an observer. "I've spoken to them of each other—it's through me, mainly, that they know of each other. I mustn't be too much of an *entremetteur* or an *entremetteuse.*" He is clearly aware, then, of his temptations, but observe what happens: "I may even have been a little reluctant or suspicious, a little jealous, even, if the mediator is a woman. If a woman tells the story she may have this jealousy of her dead friend after the latter's death." But a reflector whose own jealousy affects the action is no longer a mere reflector. The story itself is changing under our eyes as the mode of narration is explored.

> Or if I don't have the "3d person" narrator, what effect would one get from the impersonal form—what peculiar and characteristic, what compensating, effect *might* one get from it? I should have in this case—shouldn't I?—to represent the *post-mortem* interview? Yes—but not necessarily. I might "impersonally" include the 3d person and his (or her) feelings—tell the thing even so from his, or her, point of view. Probably it would have to be longer so. . . .

And suddenly James begins to see his way and grows excited. "The LAST *empêchement* to the little meeting, the supreme one, the one that caps the climax and makes the thing 'past a joke,' *'trop fort,'* and all the rest of it, is the result of *my own act.*" His "lucid reflector" is becoming less lucid and less of a mere reflector by the moment. "I prevent it, because I become conscious of a burning jealousy. . . ." And from this point on, the true subject of what is by now a new tale is clear.

> [The young man] and the narrator became engaged. . . . What do I do? I write to my fiancé not to come [to meet her, the "friend," for the first time]—that *she* can't. . . . I don't tell *her* what I have done; but, that evening, I tell *him.* I'm ashamed of it—I'm ashamed and I make that reparation. . . . The effect of this view [of the death and subsequent visitations] upon *me.* From here to the end, the attitude, on the subject, is mine: the return of my jealousy . . . the final rupture that comes entirely from ME and from my imputations and suspicions. I am jealous of the dead; I feel, or imagine I feel, his detachment, his alienation, his coldness.

In the finished tale the first-person narrator is thus both self-deceived and deceiving. She never realizes her own perfidy, and the reader is left to infer it from her own almost unconscious admissions. There is no question but that the tale has become entirely "mine."

The notebook entries for **"The Next Time"** show that James was sometimes aware of the transforming effect of cracking his mirror's surface. He begins as usual.

> Mightn't one oppose to him [he says of his novelist who is trying to write a best seller by becoming vulgar], some contrasted figure of another type—the creature who, dimly conscious of deep-seated vulgarity, is always trying to be refined, which doesn't in the least prevent him—or her—from succeeding. Say it's a woman. *She* succeeds—and she *thinks* she's fine! Mightn't *she* be the narrator, with a fine grotesque *inconscience?* So that the whole thing becomes a masterpiece of close and finished irony?

One would expect an author to recognize that a misguided narrator would necessarily attract much of the reader's interest and thus transform the story, at least to some degree. James does not ordinarily take this effect into account. Here he does, though the discussion is brief and cryptic. "There *may* be a difficulty in that—I seem to see it: so that the necessity may be for the narrator to be *conscient,* OR SEMI-CONSCIENT, perhaps, to get the full force of certain effects. The narrator at any rate, a person in the little drama who is trying bewilderedly the opposite line—working helplessly for fineness."

Unable to resolve his problem, James puts the story aside, only to return to it later.

> In my former note of this I seemed to catch hold of the tail of a dim idea that my narrator might be made the ironic portrait of a deluded vulgarian (of letters too), some striving *confrère* who *has* all the success my hero hasn't, who *can* do exactly the thing he can't, and who, vaguely, mistily conscious that he hasn't the suffrages of the *raffinés,* the people who count, is trying to do something distinguished. . . . Is this person the narrator—and do I simplify and compress by making him so?

Precisely the point, but the answer would seem self-evident: if his real interests were in simplification and compression, he would not embark on this kind of pursuit in the first place. As he was later to write in the Preface to *The Princess Casamassima,* as soon as he pursues his main interest—his "appreciation" of his story—"simplification is imperilled."

Shifting to a different concept of irony in his pursuit of the proper way to tell **"The Next Time,"** James next decides that his narrator ought to be "fully and richly, must be ironically, *conscient*"—he must, that is, recognize the ironies of the whole story if he is to convey them to the reader with simplicity and compression. "That is, *musn't* he? Can I take such a person and make him—or her—narrate my little drama *naïvement?* I don't think so—especially with so *short* a chance: I risk wasting my material and missing my effect." He does, indeed. His tale requires, as he goes on to say, his "real ironic painter"—ironic not as victim of the ironies but as master of them. Since the vulgar, best-selling author will not do, the problem is to discover a more suitable observer.

"*I* become the narrator, either impersonally or in my unnamed, unspecified personality. Say I chose the latter line, as in the **'Death of the Lion,'** the **'Coxon Fund,'** etc." But as usual James cannot for a moment rest contented with a mere observer.

> I am a critic who doesn't sell, i.e., whose writing is too good—attracts no attention whatever. *My* distinguished writing fairly damages *his* [the original protagonist's] distinguished—by the good it tries to do for him. To keep me *quiet* about him becomes one of his needs—one of the features of his struggle, that struggle to manage to do once or twice, remuneratively, the thing that will be popular, the exhibition of which (pathetic little vain effort) is the essence of my subject. I try not to write about him—in order to help him. This attitude of mine is a part of the story.

A part of what story? Not, surely, a necessary part of the original "essence" he has just been talking about. The original hero's effort to write a potboiler recedes from the foreground just to the extent that this new narrator's effort "not to write about him" moves forward.

James embraces at this point what is in fact a new subject: "I seem to myself to want my denouement to be that in a final case I *do* speak—I uncontrollably break out (without his knowing I'm going to: I keep it secret, risk it); with the consequence that I just, after all, dish him." Who is the protagonist of *this* story? It becomes difficult to say, but it is not difficult to say that the narrator has become the primary agent, if it is his "breaking out" that "dishes" the novelist. The denouement is his; the interest is in his action and its effects, not primarily in those of the original hero.

Here we see, in short, the full force of James's drive for a realistic narrative technique. He creates and rejects one unreliable narrator, only to find himself creating another "I" who immediately becomes involved in the action so deeply that he produces the catastrophe. (pp. 339-44)

The use of narrators who run away, in effect, with the original subject, transmuting one idea into another very different though related idea, has been so common since James that we tend to take the results for granted. This is how a novelist works, we tell ourselves, and we can point to an unlimited number of novels to prove it. . . . [We] tell ourselves that the old-fashioned question, "Who is the protagonist?" is a meaningless one. The convincing texture of the whole, the impression of life as experienced by an observer, is in itself surely what the true artist seeks.

Yet the controversies over stories like ***The Turn of the Screw*** suggest that for most of us it is not enough. Though no one will deny to James his right to develop his original ideas as he discovers new complexities in his narrators, few of us feel happy with a situation in which we cannot decide whether the subject is two evil children as seen by a naïve but well-meaning governess or two innocent children as seen by a hysterical, destructive governess. Whatever James's final view of his subject in such stories, we can only conclude that the relationship between his developing narrators and the original subjects was often more complex than his own critical talk recognizes. Some of his stories present, in fact, a double focus that seems to spring from an incomplete fusion of original subject with the new subject that develops once a seriously flawed narrator has been created to reflect the original. We can never know how much of our difficulty James foresaw. But we can at least discover, in looking at two of his more troublesome stories, some of the sources of our perplexity in dealing with unreliable narrators since his time.

"The Liar" (1888) is a revealing instance of James's tendency to develop an observer far beyond his original function. It is not simply that "the story of one's story" has become more important than the original idea; that in itself would not necessarily cause trouble. But the reflector, in becoming *inconscient* about his own motives and about the reality around him, becomes a vicious agent in the story, and his viciousness and his unconscious distortions come to play a role far beyond anything James described in writing about observers.

In the original conception, as recorded in the *Notebooks,* the center of interest was the wife of an inveterate liar, Colonel Capadose. James's subject was the gradually corrupting effect upon the wife of having to pretend that her marriage is a success, that her husband's lying does not trouble her. "But there comes a day when he [the Colonel] tells a very big lie which she has . . . to adopt, to reinforce. To save him from exposure, in a word, she has to lie herself. The struggle, etc.; she lies—but after that she hates him." In James's subsequent discussion, in the Preface, he again centers on his initial vision of Capadose and his wife. There is never any mention of involving an observer as a prime agent in the action. The story is to be quite simply that of a woman corrupted into dishonesty by a lying husband. What James tells, however, is a story far more complex, the story of his observer's relationship with Mrs. Capadose. It is clear that as he developed his observer, his ironic bent gained control, transforming Lyon into a highly equivocal protagonist—indeed into something of a villain.

The kind of complex irony that results can best be seen by contrasting the two views of what takes place, Lyon's and the reader's. One is tempted, at a time like this, to fall into the pattern established by other recent explicators of Jamesian ironies: "A generation of readers has misread. . . . " But I am too much impressed by the difficulties to offer the following as anything more than a careful attempt at what may be an impossible task. Here is Lyon's view of the events (in the story it is given in the third person) followed by my own view as reader:

> After twelve years I meet again with the woman who once refused to marry me because she did not know then that one day I would be famous. She is even lovelier than ever, and I am horrified to discover that she has married an inveterate liar.

Actually she refused the narrator because she knew that happiness would be impossible with any man as self-centered as he. He is not so much horrified by the lying as jealous; he finds, in short, that he is still in love with her, and the discovery that her husband is a liar only contributes to his unconscious jealousy.

> How can she endure living with such a "monstrous foible"? And how can she avoid being herself morally destroyed by contact with such a contemptible man? I admit that Capadose is not—as yet—a "malignant liar," that he is strictly disinterested, that he has indeed a kind of code of honor in his lying. I also must admit that I, too, "lie," in a sense, when I lay on my colours as a painter. At the same time it seems to me a tragedy that a lovely creature like her should be tied to a man of no integrity.

He is really sure that she must regret having married a contemptible man, when she might have had someone like himself. His own lying is strictly "interested," and he has far less integrity than Capadose.

> I decide to force her to admit that she is distressed by her husband's lies.

He really decides to make her show signs of regret about having chosen wrongly.

> Using methods of a subtlety that almost makes me blush, I persuade them to allow me to paint Capadose's portrait, determined to paint it in such a way as to reveal the depths of his deceptive heart.

Lying to them about his motives, he persuades them to allow him to paint the husband's portrait, determined to paint it in such a way as to expunge all the good traits of the Colonel, whom everyone else in the story likes, and allow only the dishonesty to show, thus creating a monster out of what is actually, as James himself describes him in a letter, "a charming man, in spite of his little weakness."

> When she sees what I have revealed, surely she will give some sign that her basic integrity has not been shattered.

Surely she will show some sign that she regrets her marriage, that she could imagine her happiness with her husband "more unqualified."

> I paint the portrait as planned; it is a masterpiece of truth.

It is a masterpiece of the power of caricature.

> The Liar stands revealed upon my canvas in his true colours.

The Liar, stripped of all his redeeming human qualities, stands betrayed upon the canvas.

> But the Capadoses discover the portrait when they think I am away; actually I happen upon the scene and am forced to eavesdrop to protect my interests.

Having sneaked back without any announcement, he deliberately eavesdrops.

> Mrs. Capadose is shattered by the vision, seeing it truly; Capadose, somewhat more slowly seeing what I have revealed, slashes the portrait to bits.

Lyon is really delighted to see her horror when she discovers the cruel "truth" of the portrait, and even more delighted to see Capadose slash the portrait to bits.

> I do not try to stop him; rather I am glad that now, at last, I shall get her to admit regrets about her unfortunate marriage.

Now at last she is ashamed of her husband, and *Lyon* has made her so; but he has made her even more horrified by his own brutality.

> But instead she supports her husband in the falsehood he invents about how the portrait must have been destroyed, and she reveals unmistakably to me that she *has* been totally corrupted by her husband. The Liar has triumphed, and I have lost my vision of the incorruptible woman. "Her hypocrisy" is revolting.

In supporting her husband she reveals unmistakably that she still loves the better man and is willing to lie for him. The vicious Liar—Lyon—has been caught in his own trap.

One would hesitate to belabor what may seem obvious, if critics did not seem generally to take Lyon pretty much at his own word; since James never warns us in any of his own discussions that the story finally became Lyon-as-liar even more than Capadose-as-liar, they have read it as if it had been written according to plan. Ray B. West, Jr., and Robert W. Stallman [in *The Art of Modern Fiction* (1949)], for example, see Lyon as "inspired by the Muse of Truth," both as artist and as man. "It is *his* moral being, not hers [Mrs. Capadose's] that suffers the disillusioning shock. . . . He dares to pry beneath [the surface of her character] because his faith in her purity supports him. Call it the faith of a romantic, or call it the faith of an artist. She represents for Lyon, as artist, that Truth which is Beauty, that Beauty which is Truth." And though the authors think that he deserves his punishment at the end, he deserves it because he "has committed an offence against society [by insisting on the truth]. . . . His stripping of the social mask, we are made to feel, constitutes a breach of the mores, a betrayal of the social codes whose mechanism must be preserved even though it produces hypocrisies and grinds out falsities instead of truths." And his desire to wring a confession from her is a desire to redeem her: "Redemption begins in deep abasement."

It seems likely, to judge from the first notebook entry, that something not too far from this may have been James's original idea. But when we consider some of the lies inspired in Lyon by the Muse of Truth, we are forced to admit that James's conception changed. "Then he spoke to her of her husband, praised his appearance, his talent for conversation, professed to have felt a quick friendship for him, and asked, with an amount of 'cheek' for which he almost blushed, what manner of man he was." He pursues what he calls his "legitimate treachery" of Capadose with a relentlessness that makes him "almost wince" at his own success. He lies about his portrait of the Colonel's daughter, in order to pursue his unacknowledged courtship of the wife. It was a "matter of conscience with him sometimes to take his servants unawares." He lies to them whenever it is useful to do so, yet thinks of himself as a man who "cultivated frankness of intercourse with his domestics." But if one were to detail all of his lies, the whole story would be retold, because it consists largely of them.

What are we to make of the following signs of motive, if he is probing "because his faith in her purity supports him"? "Lyon guessed him [Capadose] capable on occasion of defending his position with violence. . . . Such moments as those would test his wife's philosophy—Lyon would have liked to see her there." "Oh to hear that woman's voice in that deep abasement. . . . He even imagined the hour when, with a burning face, she might ask *him* not to take the question up. Then he should be almost consoled—he would be magnanimous." When Mrs. Capadose cries, "It's cruel—oh it's too cruel!"—after first seeing the portrait—the man inspired by the Muse of Truth reacts characteristically: "The strangest part of all was . . . that Oliver Lyon lifted neither voice nor hand to save his picture [from Capadose's slashings]. The point is that he didn't feel as if he were losing it or didn't care if he were, so much more was he conscious of gaining a certitude. His old friend *was* ashamed of her husband, and he had made her so, and he had scored a great success, even at the sacrifice of his precious labour. . . . He trembled with his happy agitation."

In much of his lying there is an element of cruelty. Indeed, as the story progresses, Lyon's interest in his art is perverted more and more into an interest in the most blatant kind of attack upon the Colonel. In the service of this attack, his whole nature is coarsened. While at the beginning he seems interested in artistic subtlety, he later becomes troubled by the

> idea that when he should send his picture to the Academy he shouldn't be able to inscribe it in the catalogue under the simple rubric to which all propriety pointed. He couldn't in short send in the title as "The Liar"—more was the pity. However, this little mattered, for he had now determined to stamp that sense on it as legibly—and to the meanest intelligence—as it was stamped for his own vision on the living face. As he saw nothing else in the Colonel today, so he gave himself up to the joy of "rendering" nothing else.

It is impossible to reconcile this picture of the artist's task with any notion James ever espoused; it is, in fact, James's portrait of what happens to art when it is made to serve "interested," or practical ends. It is not for the sake of art that Lyon "lashed his victim on when he flagged."

Finally, one notes that all of the unequivocal intrusions by the reliable narrator—I count four and those very brief—are used to underline the difference between Lyon's picture of himself and the true picture; he acts not from artistic motives, nor from a mistaken commitment to an ideal, but rather from the motives of a disappointed lover. All the rest is rationalization, presented convincingly enough as Lyon "speaks" it or thinks it, but intended to be seen as rationalization by the discerning reader.

If this is an approximate picture of the ironies James intended to cluster about Lyon's picture of himself and his fellow liar, how do we account for the fact that only Marius Bewley [in *The Complex Fate: Hawthorne, Henry James and Some Other American Writers* (1952)], of those who have written about the story, has seen it from something like this point of view?

It is customary in critical controversy over James's meanings to attribute such differences to the stupidity or carelessness of all readers except those who see the "true" interpretation. But in dealing with such a story mutual accusations are likely to be pointless. No amount of care, no amount of intelligence, no amount of background reading, can yield the kind of security about **"The Liar"** that all readers can feel about **"The Beast in the Jungle."** Though the two strikingly disparate views of the events, the observer's and the author's, may seem unmistakable in my schematic presentation, in the story itself they are surrounded by complexities which make one feel unsure of any interpretation.

In the first place, the difference between Lyon's voice and James's voice, speaking behind and through the style, is usually not so great as in the passages I have quoted; sometimes, indeed, there is no discernible difference whatever. Much of what Lyon sees about Capadose is true. His opinion of himself as a great artist is justified; we have Mrs. Capadose's reluctant testimonial to that. And in the second place, to read the story properly we must combat our natural tendency to agree with the reflector. He wins our confidence simply by being the reflector, because in life the only mind we know as we know Lyon's is our own. Yet it is this very appeal which makes him dangerous: his touch will be fatal to certain effects.

Thus in **"The Liar,"** even when we have been alerted to Lyon's unreliability, we are still faced, after the most careful reading, with some inevitable ambiguities, ambiguities which James almost certainly did not intend. Granted that some of Lyon's opinions are unreliable and that some are not, what about the great middle group which are plausible from one point of view, implausible from another? He feels sorry for himself; he feels betrayed, lost. Does James intend us merely to scoff, or to sympathize? Are the final lies of Mrs. Capadose contemptible, as Lyon thinks, or noble, or a little of both? On the one hand, she is possibly endangering an innocent third party, but on the other she is defending a relatively harmless man from a predator. We are lost in wonder at the complexity of life—and this is part of what James undoubtedly intends. But it is at the same time clear that a story can hold together only if such perplexities are kept within certain boundaries—wide as those boundaries may be. Our very recognition of complexity depends upon the clarity of our vision of the elements which go to make it up. The mixture of good and evil in the characters of this story will be overlooked or misapprehended unless we grasp clearly which elements are good and which bad. If Lyon is read as the noble artist struggling for truth against a philistine culture, the story is a very weak one indeed; nine-tenths of the concentrated wit and irony is lost. Yet if he is not, it is still partially unrealized; the story of the liar, Lyon, is only half-developed.

If we had only the evidence I have given so far, I might be accused of doing to **"The Liar"** what I have accused other critics of doing to ***The Turn of the Screw:*** seeing more distance between author and narrator than the story justifies. But fortunately we have an unmistakable corroboration from James in the kind of revision he undertook when preparing this story for the New York edition of the collected works (1907-9). Much has been written about the complexities James introduced in revising his earlier stories, but in **"The Liar"** we find an attempt to *reduce* the moral complexity by heightening the interpretation I have given. Where the first version read, "Lyon put into practice that idea of drawing him [Capadose] out which he had been nursing for so many weeks," the revision says that "Lyon applied without mercy his own gift of provocation." Where the original says that "Lyon lashed him on," the revision says that he "lashed his victim on." [Booth adds in a footnote: There are many other changes working to the same effect: (1) The revision heightens the favorable features of Capadose. Instead of being a "thumping liar," he "pulls the long bow." We are told that in contrast to the selfish "interest" of Lyon, Capadose's lying is "quite disinterested." Instead of being "everything that's good and kind," he becomes "everything that's good and true and kind." (2) Similarly Lyon is worsened in our eyes;

"Lyon was too scrupulous" is changed to "Lyon was at once too discreet and too fond of his own intimate inductions"; "with an inward audacity at which he trembled a little" is changed to "an amount of cheek for which he almost blushed"; etc. Also we are alerted with at least one additional warning to the fact that Lyon is painting his own picture: "Don't you suppose Vandyke's things tell a lot about him?"] The many changes of this kind take us toward a clearer view of the artist caught by his own machinations. But even in the final version, after all of the changes, we are still left baffled at some points where James cannot profit from our bafflement. Regardless of where we choose to settle in our final interpretation, with the near-nobility seen by West and Stallman or the near-villainy which I see, the reader cannot be expected to infer with certainty whether a particular fact reported by Lyon has been distorted to reflect his own character or reported accurately to give what really happened to Mrs. Capadose.

The effect of an incompletely resolved double focus gives us even more difficulty in a better-known story, ***The Aspern Papers,*** published in the same year as **"The Liar"** (1888). In contrast with the other tales I have discussed, this one seems to have been conceived from the beginning as a story about the narrator. Though James's original notation of the possibilities of a story about his "publishing scoundrel" did not picture the full "immorality" which he finally portrays, from the beginning James clearly had in mind the comic and ironic excitement of the antiquarian's quest. "The interest would be in some price that the man has to pay—that the old woman—or the survivor—sets upon the papers. His hesitations—his struggle—for he really would give almost anything"—this is clearly moving in the direction of the narrator's statement in the finished story, "I'm sorry for it, but there's no baseness I wouldn't commit for Jeffrey Aspern's sake."

The astonishing thing is that in this first notebook entry there is only the barest suggestion of the "picture" of the romantic past that James described many years later as so important to the story. The closest James comes to it here is "the picture of the two faded, queer, poor and discredited old English women—living on into a strange generation, in their musty corner of a foreign town—with these illustrious letters their most precious possession." The primary interest is in the plotting "of the Shelley fanatic" against these two romantic figures.

When in the Preface he comes to remember his idea years later, however, the plot of the Shelley fanatic is passed over completely in favor of a discussion of his own effort to realize the "palpable imaginable *visitable* past." It is all talk about atmosphere and atmospheric contrasts, the delight in rendering "my old Venice" and "the still earlier one of Jeffrey Aspern"; it is all about the "romance" of his effort to evoke "a final scene of the rich dim Shelley drama played out in the very theatre of our own "modernity.' " Except to indicate that the original "Shelleyite" whose adventure suggested the story is not to the slightest extent reflected in the finished story, James does not even mention the protagonist.

We have here, then, two neatly distinct subjects. There is a plot, the narrator's unscrupulous quest for the papers and his ultimate frustration; it is a plot that requires an agent of a particularly insensitive kind. There is, secondly, a "picture," an air or an atmosphere, a past to be visited and recorded with all the poetic artistry at James's command. So far so good; there is nothing inherently incompatible about these two subjects. On the contrary, the notion of a "visitable past" being in effect violated by a modern antiquarian who hasn't the slightest idea of how the past can be effectively visited seems on the face of it a good one. But unfortunately there is a general principle in accordance with which James feels constrained to write his stories. "Picture" must not come from the author in his own voice. It should be pushed back into the consciousness of a large, *lucid* reflector. And who should that reflector be—who *can* it be in this case but the antiquarian himself? Unless Mrs. Prest—already rather shamelessly present as a mere *ficelle* to give him an excuse to tell of his plans—unless she is to be expanded into what would surely be a rather incredible observer, the only mind available with a sufficient grasp of what is going on is the mind of the antiquarian. He it is who must visit and evoke the past. And yet he must "pounce on" the possessions of the poet's aging mistress and violate the naïve spirit of the dying woman's niece.

The completed story is a good one, but to me it has paid a price for the mode of narration. Foolhardy as it may seem to tamper with the procedures of the great master, one cannot help concluding that the narrator as realized, though well-suited for the jilting of Tina Bordereau, was not adequate to the task of evoking the poetry of the visitable past.

All of the motive power, all of the sense of direction in the plot is concentrated on the narrator's efforts to get the Aspern papers, and particularly on the use he makes of Tina's affection. In his immorality, though not in the precise details of his quest, he is half-brother to other "publishing scoundrels" in James's fiction, like Mathias Pardon in *The Bostonians,* George Flack in *The Reverberator,* or the reporter in **"The Papers."** He is also half-brother to Morris Townsend, in *Washington Square,* who plays upon an innocent woman's affections for his own selfish ends. We have passed through a time when fidelity and honor have meant so little, in terms of literary convention, that it is easy to overlook what it meant still to James. But if one applies to the narrator of this tale the standards of integrity and honor that figure in, say, *The Spoils of Poynton,* if one judges the narrator, in short, by the standards of any one of James's really *lucid* reflectors, the antiquarian's immorality can only be seen as central to the effect. Our attention from first to last cannot help being centered on the comedy of the biter bit, the man of light character who manipulates others so cleverly that he "destroys" himself.

Again here, as in **"The Liar,"** the New York revision moves in the direction of our sharper awareness of the narrator's immorality. Anyone who doubts that James's final attention was primarily on the narrator should re-read the tale in the New York revision, checking against the original those passages that show him cheating, stealing, lying, or admitting to shame. In revising *The Portrait of a Lady,* as Matthiessen pointed out [in his *Henry James: The*

Major Phase (1944)], James tried to make Osmond's moral degeneracy clearer, so that "the mystification is only Isabel's the ambiguity is all in what Osmond concealed, not in any doubts that James entertained about him." James changed Osmond's view of Isabel, for example, from "as bright and soft as an April cloud" to "as smooth to his general need of her as handled ivory to the palm." The same kind of revision is performed in this story. The following examples are only some of the more extreme instances of James's efforts to prevent, in revision, the kind of identification with the narrator which, even in this "obvious" story, might easily result from the narrator's position of command. The italics have been added.

> [*Original*]: I'm sorry for it, but for Jeffrey Aspern's sake I would do *worse still.*
>
> [*Revised*]: I'm sorry for it, but there's no *baseness* I wouldn't commit for Jeffrey Aspern's sake.
>
> "You are very extravagant . . . ," said my companion. "Certainly you are prepared to *go far!*"
>
> [*Rev*]: "You're very extravagant—it adds to *your immorality.*"
>
> She would die next week, she would die tomorrow—then I could *seize her papers.*
>
> [*Rev*]: . . . then I could *pounce on her possessions and ransack her drawers.*
>
> . . . for the first, the last, the only time I beheld her extraordinary eyes. They glared at me, they made me horribly ashamed.
>
> [*Rev*]: . . . They glared at me; *they were like the sudden drench, for a caught burglar, of a flood of gaslight;* they made me horribly ashamed.
>
> I had said to Mrs. Prest that I would make love to her [the daughter]; but it had been a joke without consequence and I had never said it *to Tita Bordereau* [note that "Tita" is revised to the more attractive "Tina"].
>
> [*Rev*]: . . . I had never said it to *my victim.*
>
> How could she, since I had not come back before night to contradict, even as a simple form, such an idea [Miss Tina's idea that he has recoiled in horror from her offer of love]?
>
> [*Rev*]: . . . to contradict, even as a simple form, *even as an act of common humanity,* such an idea?

These isolated quotations give, of course, only a fraction of the emphasis one finds, in both versions, on the moral deterioration and ultimate baseness of James's narrator. [Booth adds in a footnote: For a clear-headed reading of the narrator's wide-ranging perfidies, see Sam S. Baskett, "The Sense of the Present in *The Aspern Papers,*" *Papers of the Michigan Academy of Science, Arts, and Letters,* XLIV (1959). Baskett recognizes that the narrator's vision of the past is far from a reliable one and that in fact the ironies of the story are based on an implied contrast between his "sense of the past" and the reader's and author's sense. He is willing to make use of the past for his present "base" ends. The past he evokes is tainted—though Baskett does not stress this point—by his mode of evocation. Another prosecution of the narrator is conducted by William Bysshe Stein in "The Aspern Papers: A Comedy of Masks," *Nineteenth-Century Fiction,* XIV (September 1959). Stein deals more fully with the narrator's aesthetic deficiencies; his view of the past is tainted, and the past he evokes is largely an absurd one—as we see in the absurdities of Juliana, the last living remnant of that past.] The effect of these and the other changes is in no case to make him worse in *fact;* his actions remain objectively the same in both versions. Rather they worsen only his picture of himself and thus increase our awareness that the drama is that of his unprincipled relationship with Miss Tina. They thus lessen the burden on the reader by making this aspect of the story less subtle and ambiguous than it originally was.

The story, then, consists simply of this unscrupulous man's quest for the Aspern papers, his discovery that his best way to get to them is to make love to the owner's unattractive niece, Tina, his further discovery that marriage is to be the price of full possession, his temporary withdrawal in the face of such a conflict and—but he should tell the climax in his own words. Observe how he betrays himself when he next encounters the undesirable woman he must learn to accept if he wants the papers. As he comes into the room, he recognizes that she has understood his involuntary recoil when she offered herself in exchange for the papers the day before.

> . . . I also saw something which had not been in my forecast. Poor Miss Tina's sense of her failure had produced a rare alteration in her, but I had been too full of stratagems and spoils to think of that. Now I took it in; I can scarcely tell how it startled me. She stood in the middle of the room with a face of mildness bent upon me, and her look of forgiveness, of absolution, made her angelic. It beautified her; she was younger; she was not a ridiculous old woman. This trick of her expression, this magic of her spirit, transfigured her, and while I still noted it I heard a whisper somewhere in the depths of my conscience: "Why not, after all—why not?" It seemed to me I *could* pay the price.

This is *his* idea of the voice of *conscience.* If he is so unreliable about that, what of his notion that her countenance has actually changed? Is the change simply his subjective interpretation? James increases our suspicions at once: "Still more distinctly however than the whisper I heard Miss Tina's own voice" saying that the papers have been destroyed and with them, of course, all reason for "paying the price."

"The room seemed to go round me as she said this and a real darkness for a moment descended on my eyes. When it passed, Miss Tina was there still, but the transfiguration was over and she had changed back to a plain dingy elderly person." Because of the narrative method, we are forever barred from knowing whether Miss Tina was, in fact, capable of forgiveness, whether she was, in fact, transformed, whether she was, in fact, a dingy elderly person in the first place. We are confined to the drama of the narrator's own scheming, and when he concludes by regretting his loss—"I mean of the precious papers"—we are left permanently in doubt as to whether he has any suspicion of suffering a more serious loss, whether we think of that loss as of his honor or as of Miss Tina herself. What we do know is, however, sufficient to make this aspect of the story highly successful: the schemer has shown himself as the chief victim of his own elaborate scheming.

But where has that other subject, as described in the Preface, been all this while? What has happened to the "visitable past"? Well, the poor blind narrator has been periodically struggling to bring himself back up to the level of sensitivity necessary to record, with the reader's unequivocal concurrence, the romantic atmosphere of Venice and particularly of this one corner of the past, the Bordereau's villa. Here is the comic schemer in his other role, as poetic celebrant: "There could be no Venetian business without patience, and since I adored the place I was much more in the spirit of it for having laid in a large provision. That spirit kept me perpetual company and seemed to look out at me from the revived immortal face—in which all his genius shone—of the great poet who was my prompter. I had invoked him and he had come." Surely this is no ridiculous schemer; this is the worthy disciple of the great poet, speaking in the voice that James himself uses in describing *his* feelings about Venice and his imagined Aspern. And the narrator carries on in this voice at some length. In the long passage concluding section four, which contains the narrator's opinions about Aspern, about America, and about American art, surely he is intended to be reliable as a spokesman for James's theme: "That was originally what I had prized him for: that at a period when our native land was nude and crude and provincial, when the famous 'atmosphere' it is supposed to lack was not even missed, when literature was lonely there and art and form almost impossible, he had found means to live and write like one of the first; to be free and general and not at all afraid; to feel, understand and express everything."

This can scarcely be considered as the same person at all. And there is a third tone of voice when the first two openly conflict.

> It was as if his [Aspern's] bright ghost had returned to earth to assure me he regarded the affair as his own no less than as mine and that we should see it fraternally and fondly to a conclusion. . . . My eccentric private errand became a part of the general romance and the general glory—I felt even a mystic companionship, a moral fraternity with all those who in the past had been in the service of art. They had worked for beauty, for a devotion; and what else was I doing? That element was in everything that Jeffrey Aspern had written, and I was only bringing it to light.

There can be little doubt that James has deliberately planted clues here to make us see that the narrator is rationalizing his conduct. In the service of art? *Only* bringing beauty to light? And what of Aspern's own conduct? "We were glad to think at least that in all our promulgations acquitting Aspern conscientiously of any grossness—some people now consider I believe that we have overdone them—we had only touched in passing and in the most discreet manner on Miss Bordereau's connexion. Oddly enough, even if we had had the material . . . this would have been the most difficult episode to handle." Aspern is, then, also tainted with the immorality shown by the narrator? Again, debating whether Aspern had "betrayed" Juliana in his works, "had given her away, as we say nowadays, to posterity," the antiquarian exonerates Aspern, in what must be another instance of his "overdone promulgations": "Moreover was not any fame fair enough that was so sure of duration and was associated with works immortal through their beauty?" Was James so naïve as to allow his narrator to get away with blurring the distinction between this kind of betrayal, without which romantic poetry could not exist at all, and the personal betrayals of the narrator in his antiquarian quest? Again and again in the story one is forced to throw up his hands and decide that James simply has provided insufficient clues for the judgments which he still quite clearly expects us to be able to make.

We have, then, three distinct narrative voices in this story: the narrator's self-betrayals, evident to any careful reader; his efforts at straightforward evocation of the past, which taken out of context might be indistinguishable from James's own voice; and the passages of mumbling, as it were, that lie between. There are so many good things in the story that it seems almost ungrateful of us to ask whether the three narrative voices are ever really harmonized. Critics have generally followed James himself in steering clear of such questions. It is so much easier to "dislike James" for his obscurities—without troubling very much to say what we mean—or to idolize him for his subtle ambiguities. Both positions are wholly safe, backed by troops in rank on rank, with traditions of honorable battle going back many decades. What is hard is to look squarely at the master and decide—without idolatry or iconoclasm—whether he has done, after all, as well as he might have.

It is time, then, to ask that final hard question about this story, even if we feel no great confidence about being able to answer it: Was James wrong to "give" the story to a single narrator, a narrator used on the one hand to reveal his own deficiencies with unconscious irony and on the other to praise praiseworthy things? There is no doubt that James showed himself to be experimental, advanced, sincere, objective, impersonal, difficult, but with all this said we still do not know whether his choice was the right one. To what extent did his choice of technique aid or hinder him in his effort to realize the inherent possibilities of this work?

This is not . . . a question that can be settled by constructing [a general rule]: "No narrator can be expected to do contradictory tasks." Huckleberry Finn performs contradictory tasks quite admirably, evoking the poetry of the Mississippi one minute and betraying abysmal ignorance the next. Nor is it inherently wrong to present a character who goes astray through his misunderstanding of values which are in themselves admirable. It is, in fact, one of the glories of fiction that it can encompass precisely the kind of complexity attempted here by James, without loss of clarity or intensity. But that complexity can be intense only if the elements that make it up are made to be intense, each one in its own way.

It seems clear that James always thought of this story as an effort to realize both of the elements he himself describes: the ironic comedy and the romantic evocation as background and contrast. He cannot have thought of either the publishing scoundrel or the evoked past as independent subjects with independent effects; the stronger the evocation of the true romance of Venice and its past, the greater the ironic comedy of the misled antiquarian who violates that past. And on the contrary, the more clearly his modern baseness is made to stand out, the more effective should be the contrasting genuine passion for beauty of the romantics. Far from being truly contradictory, the two effects could easily be seen as complementary; the deeper the ironic bite the sharper the contrast with what is not treated ironically. But it is evident from the published criticism of this story that most readers have fallen to one side or the other of this true complexity—not mere haze and muddlement—that the story implicitly seems to be striving for.

Some literary failures show themselves by producing the same result in all readers—boredom, disgust, or whatever. But from the nature of this story, it follows that the direction of the failure will show itself differently in different readers. Until recently most readers, to judge from printed commentary, apparently missed a good deal of the irony and comedy as a result of succumbing to the narrator's poetic talk about Venice. I find myself at the opposite extreme—unable to read the talk about Venice with anything like the effect James seems to have desired, because the narrator's voice rings false in my ears. And there must be a third group who, delighting in the very ambiguity which I am troubled by, overlook the clarities that James intended in both his condemnation of the narrator and his adulatory visitation of the past. But this is as serious a loss as the others: not the greatest ironic ambiguity but lucidity within complexity is James's goal; he always delights in "the comedy and the tragedy" fully as much as "the irony," and he would have been distressed to learn that anyone could read ***The Aspern Papers*** as a vague, realistic, unjudged blur.

We might, of course, imagine a reader so flexible and so thoroughly attuned to James's own values that he could shift nimbly from stance to stance, allowing the narrator to shift his character from moment to moment. But James has surrendered the very conventions which, in earlier fiction and drama, made such shifts easily acceptable. One has no difficulty when Shakespeare forces some of his characters, particularly in soliloquy, into narrative and evaluative statements that go far beyond any realistic assessment of their true capabilities within the world of the action. Shakespeare has made no claim that his *manner* will be realistically consistent. But James reminds us constantly, page by page, that he is attempting a new realistic intensity of narrative manner. How can I, then, excuse him when I find his narrator to be one kind of man in one paragraph and another kind of man in the next? Only by surrendering my responsibilities as a reader and saying that just because it is by James it is perfect. Good as it is, ***The Aspern Papers*** is not as good as James might have made it if he had preserved for a reliable voice the right to evoke the true visitable past and used the present narrator only on jobs for which he is qualified.

The attenuation of effect that must result for any reader who takes the work seriously as a whole can be seen by looking at any passage in which the narrator must do both of his jobs simultaneously. A good example is the concluding sentence: "When I look at it"—the portrait of Jeffrey Aspern—"I can scarcely bear my loss—I mean of the precious papers." In the original this read simply, "When I look at it may chagrin at the loss of the letters becomes almost intolerable." But it is not, as James well knew, really the letters that the narrator has lost, and he quite appropriately revised to introduce a shadow of doubt, a shadow of self-awareness of the price he has paid, in loss of human decency. But what happens, through this revision, to the evocation of the visitable past? Are the papers precious? Of course, one would say, of course they are precious. But they have been made to seem less so—indeed they become almost contemptible—as the result of a revision which beautifully reminds us of what the narrator has really lost.

In discussing what happens when Shakespeare's moral maxims come to us through an "unreliable spokesman," Alfred Harbage says [in *As They Liked It: An Essay on Shakespeare and Morality* (1947)] that the effect is to "throw the maxims a little out of focus, to blur them somewhat, to rob them of finality." The effect in James is similar: some—though by no means all—of the narrator's usefulness in evoking the romance of Shelley's Italy has been blurred and robbed of finality. (pp. 345-64)

Wayne C. Booth, "The Price of Impersonal Narration, II: Henry James and the Unreliable Narrator," in his The Rhetoric of Fiction, *The University of Chicago Press, 1961, pp. 339-74.*

Leon Edel (essay date 1963)

[*An American critic and biographer, Edel is a highly acclaimed authority on the life and work of Henry James. His five-volume biography* Henry James *(1953-73; see Further Reading list) is considered the definitive life and brought Edel critical praise for his research and interpretive skills. In the following excerpt, he describes how "by introducing the uncanny in bland settings," James created mystification in his ghost stories.*]

Ghostly tales cease to be ghostly if they require explaining—and criticism does them a favor when it leaves them alone. There is nevertheless valid reason for a brief introduction to Henry James's ghostly tales, if only to show his refinement of the form and the theory by which he worked. He wrote two kinds of ghost stories: those in which ghosts appear and do their haunting, and those in which no ghosts show themselves. But we see in both the inner-haunted individual in all his uneasiness and anxiety. (p. v)

This is not to say that "apparitional" ghosts are not psychological as well. Whether James showed us palpable ghosts or only those of the mind, his mastery of the form lay in his knowledge that man, brave though he is on earth and in space, can still be frightened by his own dreams. Upon this he based his fundamental theory of the ghostly tale. This theory was that the old-fashioned ghosts, those which walked at midnight emitting howling noises and clanking their chains, were, on the whole, pretty dull ghosts with an extremely limited repertoire of horror and of suggested evil. Once their monotonous little bag of tricks is exhausted, terror ceases and mystification is gone. We can best illustrate the difference between the old-time ghost and the Jamesian ghost by comparing Hamlet's father and Banquo. The apparition of Hamlet's father strikes terror when we see him in his ghostly pallor on the battlements of Elsinore walking restlessly at the chiming of the deathly hour: but by the time he is revealing the skeletons in Denmark's closet to his son he has become less a ghost than a lecturing father. Banquo is a ghost of a different order. He appears not in dark unearthly ambiance, but quietly seated in his place by flaring torchlight in the midst of a merry feast. He is visible only to Macbeth; and he is silent. In reality it is not the ghost of Banquo, but Macbeth's fear which offers the tension and the terror of this splendid scene. And it was the Banquo type of ghost, rather than the ghost of Hamlet's father, that appealed to James.

"The extraordinary," James wrote, "is most extraordinary in that it happens to you and me." James's ghosts accordingly walk by daylight; they appear in places where ghosts are least expected, lounging at their ease in a drawing-room, or quietly entering their pew in church and even politely proffering the hymn book to their neighbor. "A good ghost story," James wrote when he was a young man, "to be half as terrible as a good murder story, must be connected at a hundred different points with the common objects of life." In his maturity the novelist expressed this more characteristically—the ghostly tale called for "the strange and the sinister embroidered on the very type of the normal and the easy."

Henry James's ghostly tales, in a word, achieve their mystification by introducing the uncanny in bland settings. The terrors of life, he suggests, reside in the everyday event, and he invites us not to explain away ghosts but to reckon with them as that part of life which remains strange and queer and inexplicable, in which the irrational intrudes upon the rational, and logic yields to the illogical. We accept the mild-mannered gentleman in **"The Third Person,"** with his head on one side, because he brings a certain richness of experience into the lives of the spinsters, and affords them the chance of having a man around the house—even if it be a ghostly man. On the other hand, James's ghosts may appear casual and informal and still be conveyers of a sense of evil more potent than any we may know in real life. And this because the nature of that evil is not specified. James carefully explained his method in his preface to **"The Turn of the Screw."** It was all too easy, he said, to plant routine evil in a tale of terror. Bloodstains, a body, a crime, were matters clear to everyone, devoid of anything but the signs of violence and cruelty by which we know them. But what if there were no bloodstains, no body, no crime—only fear, a kind of chilling sense of the ominous, an extra-human foreboding of evil. His father had experienced such a fear in his "vastation," when he had conjured up a misshapen form and felt that it was radiating evil in the room: there was no hallucination—he saw nothing—he merely felt that some strange shape was somewhere at hand, a phantom of the mind, cutting him off from all security and ease. There had been day-nightmares in the family; and what James set himself to do in his ghostly stories was to create such nightmares for his reader. "Make him *think* evil, make him think it for himself, and you are released from weak specifications," James wrote. This was his formula for **"The Turn of the Screw,"** and the critics who have been explaining this story for more than half a century have, in reality, been telling us their own nightmares.

A good ghost story, to be half as terrible
as a good murder story, must be
connected at a hundred different points
with the common objects of life.

Henry James

His famous "ambiguity" in his ghostly tales was thus deliberate: but it was not as ambiguous as it seems. For always in the Jamesian tale there is not so much the haunting ghost as the haunted human—it is not Banquo but Macbeth who is the subject. His ghostly tale keeps its character best by being "the indispensable history of somebody's *normal* relation to something"—and that normal relation consists of the personal vision. Otherwise stated, James would have been interested, in the old trials for witchcraft, not in the accused but the accusers. He asked us to think of the ghostly tale as "the most possible form" of the fairy tale, hence the fruit of our imagination at its freest. To speak thus of ghost-tale and fairy-tale was to be at one with Hawthorne in describing the romance as a mingling of the marvellous with the real. The fairy tale celebrated a hero or heroine triumphing over ogres and witches; the ghostly tale recorded the battle with the ogres and witches of the mind. A ghost was a phantasmal correlative of an inner state of being. This recognized, Henry James could exercise his characteristic interest in personal relations, those between a man and his ghosts, and those between the bystanders and the haunted man. It was James himself who spoke of Peter Quint and Miss Jessel as being goblins, elves, imps, demons, "as loosely constructed as those of the old trials for witchcraft." And when we remember the testimony of the "bewitched" children at Salem, guided by the learned judges, and capturing with the discernment of childhood what was expected of them by their approving elders, we have a new clue to the meaning of **"The Turn of the Screw."** In the fairy tale, the improbable became the probable; in the ghostly tale man is in touch with things beyond his senses—mysteries that go back to the fables of time.

If we wish to attach James's ghosts to a tradition it would

be to the realism of Daniel Defoe's "True Relation of the Apparition of One Mrs. Veal" rather than the elaborate inventions of Mrs. Radcliffe and of *The Castle of Otranto.* One suspects however that James would have considered Defoe's story rather elementary—too documented and circumstantial, too much like a case history out of the records of the Society for Psychical Research. "Recorded and attested 'ghosts,' " he wrote, "are as little expressive, as little dramatic, as little continuous and conscious and responsive, as is consistent with their taking the trouble—and an immense trouble they find it, we gather—to appear at all." For the "certified" ghost, James preferred to substitute the agent of terror and of evil, save when he was creating a beneficent or constabulary ghost. Readers can find a twofold interest in these tales; they can read them simply as entertainments, which was their primary function, and experience the strange and the sinister within them. And then, if they wish, they can attempt to read the psychology residing in the stories. This was James's great discovery—that certain people who see ghosts—or witches, goblins, elves—become as it were contagious. They are not only haunted—they haunt. In this way James added a new dimension to the tale of terror: he showed the contagion of fear.

It was Henry James's ambition to write a ghost novel in which everyone haunts everyone else. He did not live to finish it, but the fragment, *The Sense of the Past,* suggests that it would have been the ghostliest of all novels. In this work a man from modern times walks into another age, like the Connecticut Yankee at the court of King Arthur. He begins gradually to haunt the people in the earlier time because he cannot help giving them uncanny glimpses into the future. And then he becomes haunted by them, for he fears he will give himself away. With this he experiences a chronic malaise that he is trapped in the past with its narrow vision and its bad drains, and may never return to the present. To read James's notes for this unfinished novel is to understand how in his ghostly tales anxiety begets anxiety, and how in the comfortable daylight of our lives we walk with ghosts, our own and those of others—and can encounter the demoniacal at the corner of a street. (pp. v-viii)

Leon Edel, in an introduction to Ghostly Tales of Henry James, *edited by Leon Edel, Grosset & Dunlap, 1963, pp. v-viii.*

Maxwell Geismar (essay date 1963)

[*Geismar is one of America's most prominent historical and social critics. Although he professes that literature is more than historical documentation, Geismar's critical method suggests that social patterns and the weight of history, more than any other phenomenon, affect the shape and content of all art. In the following excerpt from his* Henry James and the Jacobites, *he examines "The Jolly Corner" as a portrait of James's unconscious.*]

In effect [**"The Jolly Corner"**] was another of the Jamesian ghost tales in which one side of Henry James pursued—or was pursued by—another side of Henry James. Could anything be more complete—as a Jamesian id fancy—cozier, or more revealing? And in fact **"The Jolly Corner"** was a fascinating study of the Imperial Henry James tracking down his own ghost, his alter ego, or himself, in the upper floors of the deserted house which had once contained the "happy memories" of his childhood.

That was the central situation of the ghostly tale, which reverted in part to the psychological terror of ***The Turn of the Screw,*** and of a late tale which has been the subject of much critical speculation and interpretation. The hero is a man of fifty-six who, like the elderly exile of *The Ambassadors,* is too old to "live" any more, and has come back to New York, in this line of later Jamesian heroes, to rehearse his childhood experiences in a series of gossipy talks with a sympathetic confidante. (In this sense, now that the sexual barrier in James's work has been completely leveled by "old age," now when "good talk" is permissible as the *only* sexual link, these elderly, effeminate, gossipy Jamesian protagonists have just begun to live.) Spencer Brydon confides all this to Alice Staverton: that is, his speculations as to the financial titan he might have been if he had remained in America; and while, like the heroine of **"The Beast in the Jungle,"** she reassures him about any possible "selfishness," or even morbidity on his part, he pursues his new obsession. For he still thinks that all things come back "to the question of what he personally might have been, how he might have led his life and 'turned out,' if he had not so, at the outset, given it up"—

> Not to have followed my perverse young course—and almost in the teeth of my father's curse, as I may say; not to have kept it up so, "over there," from that day to this, without a doubt or a pang; not above all, to have liked it, to have loved it, so much, loved it, no doubt, with such an abysmal conceit of my own preference: some variation from that, I say, must have produced some different effect for my life and for my "form."

There is no doubt as to the personal, autobiographical reference to James's own career in this statement; the lingering consciousness of his own early conflict, choice, and exile. But this spokesman of **"The Jolly Corner"** is again careful to discriminate the purpose of his late obsession. "If I had waited . . . then I might have been, by staying here, something nearer to one of those types who have been hammered so hard and made so keen by their conditions." This was his reference, one assumes, to the new financial titans and monopolists; but—

> It isn't that I admire them so much—the question of any charm in them, or of any charm beyond that of the rank money-passion, exerted by their conditions *for* them, has nothing to do with the matter: it's only a question of what fantastic, yet perfectly possible, development of my own nature I mayn't have missed. It comes over me that I had then a strange *alter ego* deep down somewhere within me, as the full-blown flower is in the small tight bud, and that I just took the course, I just transferred him to the climate, that blighted him for once and for ever.

Thus, it was not a question of James (or his present hero) *preferring* America and New York life to the European existence which he had loved so much, without a doubt or pang. It was not a question, really, of choosing to have been one of the new robber barons whom he described so naïvely and in terms of floral growths. It was simply that he now felt capable of leading *both* lives; and this greedy ego could not forego any development of his own nature. In the story the sympathetic Miss Staverton agrees that this other flowering of the Jamesian temperament was possible, too. "I feel it would have been quite splendid, quite huge and monstrous." "Monstrous above all!" the hero echoes complacently, "and I imagine, by the same stroke, quite hideous and offensive." "Would you like me to have been a billionaire?" he asks her; to get her comforting reassurance, "How should I not have liked you?" And Spencer Brydon sets out to track down this Jamesian alter ego.

But note how often James himself now used the word "monstrous" himself, and how this insatiable fantasist is increasingly identified with the beastlike animals who figure in his own imagery of respectable, confined leisure-class life. Yet the ghostly atmosphere of **"The Jolly Corner"** is very well done; and high up in the house of childhood, in a series of connected rooms with the final room having no other outlet, the Jamesian ghost, tracked down, at bay, and bristling, makes its stand. "Brydon at this instant tasted probably of a sensation more complex than had ever before found itself consistent with sanity." He feels both pride and terror; pride that this other mask of himself is worthy of *him;* and terror indeed while, "softly panting, he felt his eyes almost leave their sockets." Those eyes—which have figured so largely throughout the voyeuristic pattern of James's work; and those high connecting "upper rooms" of the James family's house, which could very logically be the bedrooms about which a whole series of Jamesian "observers" have made their nocturnal tours.

Now what was *in* the locked room of the Jamesian unconscious? The conventional sociological interpretation, first expounded by Matthiessen [see Further Reading], is simply that James was writing a parable of what might have happened to his own character if he had stayed in the United States. For, desperately fleeing back down the long stairway, this once omnipotent ghost-tracker is not spared a final glimpse of a monstrous, alien countenance, not his own; but a hideous ghost whose ethereal hand is marked by mutilated fingers. The alter ego of the Jamesian billionaire has been corrupted and disfigured; he is a stranger.

The conventional Freudian interpretation of the story, however, as perhaps best expounded by Clifton Fadiman, explicitly following, as this critic acknowledged, "Dr. Saul Rosenzweig's remarkable monograph, 'The Ghost of Henry James: A Study in Thematic Apperception' [see Further Reading]," is on a much more personal level. It is based on Henry's mysterious wound or "obscure hurt" at the time of the Civil War, which prevented him "from joining in the masculine activity of making war," in Mr. Fadiman's words, and which also (probably) prevented him "from experiencing normal sex relations." Thus the early injury of James's is represented in the symbolically castrated fingers of the ghostly alter ego, and it symbolized a certain death in James, according to Mr. Fadiman, "the death of passion," while "The withdrawal to Europe, the most important outward event of his long life was another symbol of the retreat from the American experience that, in a sense, had been too much for him."

And, continuing with this theory of thematic apperception, these early wounds and repressions of Henry James's rose up to consciousness in later life (this is perhaps a Jungian touch) and his last visit to the United States was a compulsive act to relive this ancient trauma. (The orthodox Freudian repetition-compulsion.) "As Dr. Rosenzweig so persuasively puts it," added Mr. Fadiman glowingly, the visit " 'was largely actuated by an impulse to repair, if possible, the injury and to complete the unfinished experience of his youth.' " James wrote the story all unconsciously, we are told finally, and quite correctly; but it is obvious "that James's ghosts anticipate and dramatize many of the findings of psychoanalysis."

Here again, James is being hailed as the (unconscious) father of the Freudian thought which all of our findings tend utterly to disprove. He was indeed the sublime example of classical face-saving rationalization which completely avoided the least vestige of the Freudian truths. During the course of these speculations (in Mr. Fadiman's *Short Stories of Henry James*) [see Further Reading], we are also told that **"The Jolly Corner"** is one of the most difficult of James's last stories:

> Composed in his famous final manner, it serves as a fair example of the complexity of his mind, a complexity that forced him (as with Joyce and other innovators) virtually to invent a style.

Well, we have noticed that later Jamesian style whose "complexity" was often invented to cover a virtual absence of content. And this large statement represents an entire range of false, fatuous and grandiose claims which are recurrently made about James's work. His mind . . . was not so much "complex" as very often incredibly naïve. Once you have established the Jamesian hierarchy of values (strange as they are in any realistic appraisal of life), this famous mind becomes indeed almost conventional or trite—certainly clever or ingenious rather than profound. In one sense we can state categorically that Henry James *never had an idea.*

Mr. Fadiman has again joined the bewitched, bemused and Circe-ish circle of Jacobite commentators, at the loss, momentarily, one hopes, of his own normal intelligence. For there was no "death of passion" in James's life or career, simply because he had never reached the point of passion. His whole view of sex and love was on the oral, infantile, pre-oedipal and pre-sexual level. His own attitude is consistently that of the pubescent (at best) voyeur, "spying out" the hidden, mysterious, and ultimately sinful, area of "adult intimacy."

There was no "second death" in Henry James's withdrawal to Europe, simply because it was America which was always "death" to James. It was Europe which was, from his earliest literary fantasies of fame and the "good life," right down to the repeated affirmation of this theme by the divided hero in **"The Jolly Corner"** itself—it was Europe which was life, life, life to James. He could not possibly have returned to America to work out, to resolve these earlier traumas, because it is obvious throughout his career and his work that these traumas were buried deeply under layer upon layer of sublime rationalization. In his own life he possibly never even understood that there was a trauma—and in his work . . . every issue of depth psychology was always resolved by a sentimental, romantic kind of "psychomorality"—that is, when James was consciously aware of these issues at all. No, James returned to America simply to *confirm,* to expand, to applaud and to celebrate the whole purpose of his own European pilgrimage—as *The American Scene* shows without question; as the end of **"The Jolly Corner"** also proclaims. The only trouble with the Rosenzweig-Fadiman thesis is that, while fitting James into the conventional Freudian categories, it shows no knowledge of James's real motivation or temperament.

What was behind the locked door in the empty room of the Jamesian temperament—the room to which the omnipotent searcher of **"The Jolly Corner"** had pursued his psychological prey—was *the Jamesian unconscious.* (One should remember the early, recurrent dream of the young James during which he is chased down the long, empty corridors of an art museum by the hideous specter of his anxiety—only to turn upon, and to *defeat* this ogre by the sheer force of his will to power and to fame.) What lurked at bay in this empty, locked room was simply perhaps the real author of *The Sacred Fount;* or the artist who set down the curious oedipal-incestuous central situation in *The Golden Bowl*—and then refused to see it; or the writer-creator of a whole long series of neurotic, morbid, even hysterical "narrator-observers" in the Jamesian fiction who still persisted in denying the true nature of his own primary literary spokesmen. "Do you believe then—too dreadfully!—that I *am* as good as I might ever have been?" asks Spencer Brydon of **"The Jolly Corner"** in all the false modesty which covers his persistent, dominant concern with himself alone. But this monster egotist is still too clever, too self-protective, ever to stir—to *really* question—those hidden psychological depths lying deep down—not far up—within him.

The manner of this hero's "escape" from the repressed part of his own temperament is also interesting. For he surrenders abjectly. He is devoured by the necessity to "see" this hidden "monster"—to discover that in which "all the hunger of his prime need might have been met, his high curiosity crowned, his unrest assuaged." But he grasps at the idea of a saving, an inexorable and vital "discretion":

> Discretion—he jumped at that; and yet not, verily at such a pitch, because it saved his nerves or his skin, but because, much more valuably, it saved the situation. When I say he "jumped" at it I feel the consonance of this term with the fact that—at the end indeed of I know not how long—he did move again, he crossed straight to the door. He wouldn't touch it—it seemed now that he might *if* he would: he would only just wait there a little, to show, to prove, that he wouldn't. He had thus another station, close to the thin partition by which revelation was denied to him; but with his eyes bent and his hands held off in a mere intensity of stillness. He listened as if there had been something to hear, but this attitude while it lasted, was his own communication. "If you won't then—good: I spare you and I give up. You affect me as by the appeal positively to pity: you convince me that for reasons rigid and sublime—what do I know?—we both of us should have suffered. I respect them then, and, though moved and privileged as, I believe, it has never been given to man, I retire, I renounce—never, on my honour, to try again. So rest for ever—and let *me*!"

But wasn't this saving "discretion" the complete key to the Jamesian fiction throughout his long career: the discretion of a gentleman, say, though not of a major artist? What a fascinating passage this was indeed: since it was also the perfect self-projection of the Jamesian temperament and achievement alike. Wasn't the "saving of the situation" a key theme in James's work—the saving of "face," too, as in *The Golden Bowl,* by pretending in all one's respectable middle class American virtue that the situation, which was there, did not exist? (Not to mention the *other,* deeper situation, also so consistently there in the novel, and just as consistently denied by James, and described as filial or parental love.) Hovering by the closed door of the Jamesian unconscious, this hero—like so many other Jamesian figures back to the sensitive young Anglo-American observer in *The Portrait of a Lady*—"wouldn't touch it," though he might if he would! This hero, in the typically Jamesian vein, simply "waits," he listens, he "watches," though now with his eyes bent, and his hands held off, for the "revelation" which is there, and which is denied to him. He retires; he "renounces"—in the best Jamesian resolution of all the great problems and issues of life; I mean of living. And still he reasserts his own authority, his own ego, his own terrified but deeply covered, protected, and impenetrable self-image, by feeling that "appeal positively to pity." He is both moved and privileged, by what he has *not* seen, as no man before him. "I spare you and I give up." What a happy, face-saving and ego-saving solution; which still leaves the weight of the decision not upon the menacing Jamesian unconscious, but upon *him!* What then of "those reasons"—rigid indeed, if not possibly or entirely "sublime"—by which both halves of the divided Jamesian temperament might have suffered if they had become clear? "So rest for ever—and let *me!*"

Again the final accent was on the Jamesian "I," the "Omnipotent Me," who has come to the edge of his own darkness, and then has retreated frantically, even hysterically—but still with "dignity," and with immutable "self-possession." The hero of **"The Jolly Corner"** does think fleetingly of suicide, by escaping from his demon through the upper-floor window *without* a ladder. He yearns for "some comforting common fact, some vulgar human note, the passage of a scavenger or a thief, some night-bird however base." And why are these symbolic associations of dirt, crime and baseness linked so directly here with the "vulgar human note"? Did the Jamesian snobbery penetrate so deeply even into these unconscious areas of his temperament? Or was this the *true* imagery of his buried self? Retreating down the long stairway of his childhood, of his family's empty and haunted house, this hero also is forced to catch at least a fleeting glimpse (which is exactly what one does catch in James's best work) of "the monster with the mutilated fingers"—or of, shall we say, the inhibited Jamesian "id." He faints and falls upon the floor. "They were cold, these marble squares of his youth"—and where indeed is the **"Jolly Corner"** of James's younger American experience?

Yet even this brilliant self-portrait, perhaps the best and most accurate description of James's whole body of literary work—as compared with the apologetic, the evasive, the self-glorifying "Prefaces"—was muffled again by the "false" (that is to say, the *conscious*) ending of the story. The hidden self of the Jamesian hero is indeed "monstrous." It is "evil, odious, blatant, vulgar"—James's worst terms of abuse. But it is surely, this hero thinks, the "face of a stranger"—as indeed it was in James's work. And though the gentle, good, tactful Alice Staverton accepts the possible explanation that it *might have been* this hero's personality, if he had remained in America; and she accepts the maimed specter also because it is his, Spencer Brydon's—she comforts him with "the cool charity and virtue of her lips." That "charity and virtue," in truth, which is also a synonym, in James's work, for "discretion" or "pity" or "waiting" or "watching" or "retiring" or "renouncing"—for all these barely concealed modes of non-recognition, evasion, and flight as the "resolution" for the fleeting depth insights which appear indeed so hideous and so horrid to this neurotic and repressed late-Victorian artist who then rationalized and even glorified the obvious process of his literary sublimation. (pp. 355-64)

Maxwell Geismar, in his Henry James and the Jacobites, *Houghton Mifflin Company, 1963, 462 p.*

Stuart Hutchinson (essay date 1982)

[*In the excerpt below, Hutchinson disputes Morton Dauwen Zabel's interpretation of* In the Cage *(see excerpt dated 1958) and argues that "the cage" is a subjective symbol applicable to all James's characters in this story.*]

In the Cage is centred in the consciousness of an unnamed London telegraphist who, on the verge of marriage to Mr. Mudge, a grocer, becomes involved first in imagination but then in reality with Captain Everard. He frequently uses her services at the post-office to arrange his clandestine affair with Lady Bradeen. It is a story whose comparative neglect several critics have felt the need to alleviate. Their responses fall into two categories: those which are sympathetic to the telegraphist's experiences, and those which she herself might describe as being "cheaply sarcastic" at her expense. Both sets of responses, however, have one thing in common, and that is their rather straightforward application of the story's title to the telegraphist's life. This literalness, which I would like to redress, is evident in Morton Dauwen Zabel's representative conclusion [see excerpt dated 1958]. According to Zabel, the telegraphist "joins the other heroes and heroines of the Jamesian drama," whose condemnation to "limitation and reality" and "sense of exclusion from experience" bring them to "defeat, tragedy, or [as in the telegraphist's case] a liberating disillusionment." For Zabel, as for L. C. Knights [in "Henry James and the Trapped Spectator," *Explorations: Essays in Criticism Mainly on the Literature of the Seventeenth Century* (1946)], the telegraphist is another of James's "trapped spectators." Her only comfort derives from final acceptance of deprivation.

Admittedly, the story's first paragraph seems to offer support for this approach. There, the telegraphist conceives herself as a "young person spending, in framed and wired confinement, the life of a guineapig or a magpie." But there are other notes that soon reveal Zabel's polarisation of the story's themes (in the cage is "limitation and reality"; outside is the experience the telegraphist is denied) to be too simple. For though it is evident that like most of us the telegraphist intermittently sees her life in these stark terms, and has a sense of personal worth that reaches beyond Cocker's, it's equally clear she has a strong pride *in* her situation. Her job after all is the reward for her admirable resilience. At Cocker's too she is free from the oppressive claims of Mudge. From the beginning, therefore, the "caged" state is presented as a relative condition. Far from regarding themselves as less than human behind their wire-grill, her two male companions identify their customers as "animals." Who can say that these workers are any more caged than Everard, pursued and eventually "nailed" by Lady Bradeen; or than Lady Bradeen, "so compromised" by Captain Everard? When it comes to it, who isn't in some sort of cage?

James's story plays more variations on its title than Zabel allows. In an objective sense the telegraphist's lot *is* an example of social injustice: "the immense disparity." But James's interest draws its vitality from the individuality that transforms this state of affairs. The telegraphist lives as much in a cage of her own making (especially by her imagination) as in that her lot prescribes. When critics have seen this, however, they have not appreciated its true significance. As if few people but the telegraphist have the problem, E. Duncan Aswell announces that "the girl has trouble articulating the point at which imagination stops and reality begins" ["James's *In the Cage:* The Telegraphist As Artist," *Texas Studies in Literature and Language 8* (1966-67)]. This is so, but not as Aswell and others see it: not with respect to Everard. It's just because she is *consciously* imaginative about Everard and his class that she becomes perceptive about him. With respect to Everard, she *does* distinguish the real and imagined and, though she wants the thrill of letting them touch, she wants to keep them apart. Ironically, it's Mr. Mudge whom the cage of her imagination can cause her to misapprehend—Mr. Mudge, whose reality she feels so sure of.

No-one has done justice to James's wonderful presentation of Mudge. From the telegraphist's disparaging thoughts about her betrothed, it can seem her life with him will be unremittingly caged. Consider her reaction to the way Mudge plans their holiday: "When she thought of the danger in which another pair of lovers rapturously lived she enquired of him anew why he could leave nothing to chance. Then she got for answer that this profundity was just his pride, and he pitted Ramsgate against Bournemouth and even Boulogne against Jersey—for he had great ideas—with all the mastery of detail that was some day, professionally, to carry him far." Undoubtedly, James gives credit to the telegraphist's criticism of Mudge. But it must be recognized that this prose also qualifies her view, and not only by questioning the romanticism of "rapturously." More remarkable is the way James's enlivening mediation between the telegraphist and us creates an alternative response to hers. *We* see there is as much to be enjoyed, as lamented, about Mudge. Moreover, latent potential in the story resides in the fact that the telegraphist may grow into this more balanced view. She is anyway "subject . . . to sudden flickers of antipathy and sympathy." Her future with Mudge will never be the "ugliness and obscurity" which, at the end, she momentarily imagines it can only be. After all, nothing has happened to cast doubt on her earlier sense that Mudge "would build up a business to his chin, which he carried quite in the air." He is as ambitious as she. This is one reason for their attraction to each other.

In return for commitment to Mudge, the telegraphist gets nearly everything she needs and deserves, but when she recognises the benefits, she quarrels with them and wants more. She gets security vital to "a mere bruised fragment of wreckage" and in this cage, she gets freedom to carry on the "secret conversations" of her fantasies and even to live her fantasies with a gentleman. It's because she wants to hold herself superior to Mudge that she imagines him "the perfection of a type." James, however, always distrusting the temptation to see others as types, creates Mudge out of that very "interest in personal character" which inspired his creation of her. This is why Mudge, who to our joy believes *he* is inclined to see "too much in things," is endowed with "latent force." He is, the telegraphist feels, "somehow comparatively primitive." She remembers with pride his dealing with "a drunken soldier, a big, violent man." Such a primitive quality should not be demeaned as a "purely physical existence." On the contrary, the physical, and by implication sexual, reserves attributed to Mudge establish his superiority over, Everard, Cocker, Buckton and Drake who may never live up to the masculine prowess promised by their names. Mudge's latent force will always answer the telegraphist's protective need to feel superior to men. In fact, it's caused him to choose a wife who is certainly distinguished. He tells her, with reference to more than her pride in mind, "You're not inferior to anybody." To get her he will even arrange for her mother. His force makes for an order which will enhance, more than it will encage, the telegraphist's life. Even so, it would be a mistake to conclude that all her criticisms of Mudge have their edge blunted. Mudge *is* obtuse and, though it may be seen humorously, too encaged in obsessive planning. We applaud the telegraphist's conclusion that "her actual chance for a play of mind was worth any week the three shillings he desired to help her to save." Her play of mind, however, runs the risk of supplanting Mudge's cage by one of its own creating.

For much of the story her play of mind imagines a relationship between herself and Everard. What must be emphasised about this act is the degree of consciousness on her part. The telegraphist knows "if nothing was more impossible than the fact, nothing was more intense than the vision." By imagining an ideal relationship with Everard the girl finds refuge from her conviction that she is misunderstood, from her fear of vulgarity, and (perhaps most important of all) from the threat to her virginity which masculinity in the real world represents. She can experience what she is convinced are her best possibilities. Her problems with Everard arise not because she confuses, as with Mudge, the real world and the imagined, but because when the two worlds touch, the real threatens to break into the imagined. This possibility (and the sexual reality portends) is what frightens her during and after her scene with Everard in the park. This pivotal episode begins well within the control of her imagination. From her reading of those novels "in fine print and all about fine folks" she dreams of the possibility of Everard passing through town in August and of her accidentally meeting him. As she walks home one evening, reality enters her vision and Everard is there.

In the scene that follows it becomes fearfully clear to her that they are sitting together in the park for completely different reasons. At first she does not see this, and all the comedy, however painful, in the encounter arises from our earlier perception of their crossed purposes. Everard is aware she has taken "a particular interest" in his affairs. In so far as he interprets this as more than the special attention public servants may feel inclined to render people of his class, it's clear he has been wondering if it might not signal desire for more intimacy. This evening, he has been passing through town, bored and on the look out for female diversion. He has met a woman with whom he already has a relationship and, unbelievably, she appears with these words ready to meet him at least half way: "Anything you may have thought is perfectly true." To Everard, to sit together in the park in the evening, with other courting couples in view, is very "different" from meeting in the post-office. The telegraphist, however, insists "It's quite the same." She is attempting to keep the relationship on the ideal plane imagined in her cage at Cocker's. Only with his insistence on her "particular interest" does she get an intimation of the way Everard is seeing things. As she looks at the other couples in the darkness of the park, reality suddenly intrudes on idealization: "all that she had imagined . . . had only become more true, more dreadful and overwhelming." Aware as she now is about Everard's intentions, she is all the more troubled and very afraid.

It's typical of the ironic variations James plays on the title that the telegraphist now escapes from fear of Everard back into the safe cage of her imagination. This is how she habitually responds to Mudge. Because she cannot face the reality to which this meeting might lead, she makes a speech which gives climactic voice to their ideal relationship. By this stage Everard has lost all confidence that this young woman is what he had in mind for the evening. He goes through the motions, placing his hand "firmly enough" on her own, but he is finding himself out of his depth. He is after all, as James reveals with the detail of his pot-hat pushed back "in a boyish way," not very mature. Moreover, some of his motions take him further than he ever intended. Harried as he is by Lady Bradeen, he is perhaps momentarily attracted by the contrast of the telegraphist's ideal. Certainly, to keep himself in play, he is sufficiently carried away to be on the point of betraying his preference for the telegraphist as against Lady Bradeen. Yet, as she perceives, his capacity for sincerity is entirely circumscribed by manner. When he tells her, "I'd find you anywhere," the promise, which might have figured in her fondest imaginings, is no more than he would have said to any available and agreeable young woman. Furthermore, once conventions are set aside, Everard, unlike Mudge, is impotent, as becomes clear when the telegraphist sounds off about the "horrors" of his set. He may at this moment have an appalling vision of the telegraphist in that role of blackmailer, which earlier in the story she imagined for herself. Such an interpretation explains his subsequent attempts in the post-office to offer her money. By the end of the scene in the park, he is left inarticulately protesting against her accusations and the enfeeblement she has reduced him to. She is triumphant, not only over his masculinity, but also in her re-establishment of the saving gap between imagination and reality. This gap is maintained by her final peremptory command to Everard: "Stay where you are!"

Following the scene in the park, the telegraphist on holiday with Mudge becomes "conscious of an extraordinary collapse, a surrender to stillness and to retrospect." More clearly than ever she now perceives that Mr. Mudge is "distinctly her fate." But we should not be taken in by her decisiveness. Life for James's characters is never as conclusively transformed into knowledge as they convince themselves it might be. Continuing perplexity still awaits the telegraphist: she has tears now for her imminent reality with Mudge, just as earlier in the park she had tears for her imminent reality with Everard. Mudge and Everard, indeed, despite dissimilarity, embody an identical threat. In this respect, the title now more insistently takes on a meaning which has all along been implicit. One of the telegraphist's cages is her state of virginity, a sanctuary which all men threaten. Her deepest fear has to do with the imminence of sexual experience. When she returns from holiday, this fear becomes evident again in her recognition that her relationship with Everard is by no means finished: "Hadn't she precisely established on the part of each a consciousness that could only end with death?" To some extent the language of this recognition, and especially the romantic concept which necessitates the last word, derives from the novels the telegraphist reads. At the same time her words betray a fundamental fear which is a prime cause of her romanticism. Why must she see her relationship with Everard in terms of a mutual "consciousness" only to end "with death?" Her affair with Everard could end with, or could develop from, the kind of sexual relationship Everard continues to have in mind. The telegraphist continues to frustrate this relationship just because she is afraid of any life beyond the control of her consciousness; indeed, she is so afraid that she equates with death the sexual experience which might release life. As the baffled Everard persists, her cage of "safety" is indeed the case of virginity: "She was literally afraid of the alternate self who might be waiting outside. *He* might be waiting; it was he who was her alternate self, and of him she was afraid."

Not that Everard himself is without blame for the *impasse.* Although she is uncooperative, all his behaviour reveals him to be no more equipped than he was in the park with the "tremendous statement" he so wants to make. He remains incapable of managing any further intercourse with the telegraphist than his earlier plea and protest that she should "See here—see here!" Now we understand why the "h" is missing from the middle of his name. He can jokingly sign a telegram "Mudge," but so lacking is he in "latent force," he could never actually *be* a Mudge. For some time yet his women, as Lady Bradeen's first telegram ("Only understand and believe") establishes, will have to articulate and manage his life. It's putting it harshly, but he needs to be "nailed," just as the telegraphist will benefit from being intermittently awed and put in her place by Mudge's masculinity. This will save her from her defensive inclination to hold herself superior to the male point of view. It will liberate her sexual self. For too long, she has been taking the benefits of masculine stimulation without the compromise of reciprocation. In her last scene with Everard, when he is exploiting her as much as she is him, this onanistic trait is brought to another climax. More than ever Everard now wants her to be the impersonal, efficient public servant, who will pay special attention to his personal needs. She for her part is happy, at the expense of torturing him, to re-establish the separation of her real and ideal worlds, even while she has the thrill of letting them momentarily touch. For reality, she plays the girl from Paddington. But, in final tribute to her ideal, she gives Everard the numbers he so urgently needs, as the girl from Paddington never could from memory.

I have already indicated the qualifications to be made of the telegraphist's concluding sense of "her own return to reality." We should not respond too literally to her feeling that "Reality . . . could only be ugliness and obscurity." The words undoubtedly envisage too bleak a prospect, as is indicated a few lines later when the telegraphist is already beginning to conceive comforting differences between her own lot and Mrs. Jordan's. James's characters never put blindness and illusion behind them. They are, in Eliot's words from "East Coker": "only undeceived / Of that which, deceiving, could no longer harm. / In the middle, not only in the middle of the way / But all the way." No-one could draw a more appropriate general moral than the telegraphist's from her experience: "Where was one's pride and one's passion when the real way to judge of one's luck was by making not the wrong but the right comparison?" Her perception remains partial, however, to the extent that she does not understand that this conclusion is only another beginning in the middle. She *has* a more constant grasp of reality than the pitifully infatuated Mrs. Jordan. Even so, the problem of distinguishing the "wrong" from the "right" never ends and for her will never be simple. Her imagination will continue to make its complicating contributions, and Mudge too will forcefully play his part. It is indeed as true of ***In the Cage,*** as of anything James wrote that "the *whole* of anything is never told." In this work, which at its close leaves us with a heroine who is abandoning her cage at Cocker's, but who has yet to relinquish virginity, the end undeniably is potential. It is sustained, as is the entire piece, by the liberating energy of its creator's imagination—an energy that frees *us* to understand fully the telegraphist's life "in the cage" as an analogue of our own. (pp. 19-25)

Stuart Hutchinson, "James's 'In the Cage': A New Interpretation," in Studies in Short Fiction, *Vol. 19, No. 1, Winter, 1982, pp. 19-25.*

Joseph J. Waldmeir (essay date 1982)

[*Waldmeir is an American educator and critic. In the essay below, he proposes an Edenic interpretation of* The Aspern Papers *in which the narrator is innocent and Miss Tina is the tempting Eve.*]

The standard interpretation of Henry James' novella, ***The Aspern Papers,*** is based upon the assumption that the narrator-protagonist is the villain of the piece, that the two women, Juliana and Tina Bordereau, are his intended victims (though Tina far more than Juliana), and that the story has two objects: the exposure of the unscrupulous narrator, and the evocation, as James put it some twenty years later in the story's "Preface," of "a palpable imaginable *visitable past,*" reinforced by the passage which connects the story to the Shelley-Byron-Clairemont-Allegra hassle.

Unfortunately, a close reading of the text in terms of this interpretation uncovers certain problems with the story—particularly flaws in characterization, James' strong suit—which have caused many critics to shy away from discussing the story in any depth; or to attempt to rescue it from its flaws by appealing to James' penchant for and delight in dramatic irony; or, in at least one case, to openly attack it as a second-rate piece of work.

This essay will attempt to show, however, that the problems are in the interpretation, not the story; that given a very different interpretation based upon the exact same evidence, the flaws and the critical problems they cause either disappear or solve themselves.

On the literal level, the evidence overwhelmingly seems to support the standard interpretation, as well as exposing the troublesome flaws. The story clearly appears to be, in Wayne Booth's terms, "the comedy of the biter bit, the man of light character who manipulates others so cleverly that he 'destroys' himself" [see excerpt dated 1961]—though more commonly, the narrator is treated indignantly, as an unscrupulous scoundrel or at best as "the hollow man, the embodiment of death in life, unseared, uneducated by his experience" [Sam S. Baskett, "The Sense of the Present in *The Aspern Papers, PMASAL,* XLIV, 1959]. Certainly the narrator does come to Venice in order to avail himself by any means of anything of value concerning Jeffrey Aspern the ladies might possess. " 'I can arrive at my spoils only by putting her [Juliana] off her guard,' " he says to Mrs. Prest; " 'and I can put her off her guard only by ingratiating diplomatic airs. Hypocrisy, duplicity are my only chance. I'm sorry for it, but there's no baseness I wouldn't commit for Jeffrey Aspern's sake.' " When Mrs. Prest points out that the women may be suspicious of his motives, the narrator answers: " 'I see only one way to parry that. . . . To make love to the niece.' " And in the gondola scene, in a manner typically oblique though

Henry James, circa 1898.

untypically erotic, James makes certain that the reader understands exactly what his narrator means by "make love":

> We floated long and far, and though my friend gave no high-pitched voice to her glee I was sure of her full surrender. She was more than pleased, she was transported; the whole thing was an immense liberation. The gondola moved with slow strokes, to give her time to enjoy it, and she listened to the splash of the oars, which grew louder and more musically liquid as we passed into narrow canals, as if it were a revelation of Venice.

The scene, besides suggesting the true depth of the narrator's depravity, sets up and makes plausible his fantastic delusion of Miss Tina's beauty at the end of the novel—a delusion which would probably have seduced him into marriage had she possessed the papers.

But especially on the figurative level, upon which much of the argument of this paper will be based, but which, despite its strength, the critics generally have ignored, the evidence seems to reinforce their conclusion. The figurative level is an extended Edenic metaphor which pervades the story with remarkable consistency, operating contrapuntally to the literal level. On it, in the narrator's own words, Jeffrey Aspern becomes "the divine poet. . . . a part of the light by which we walk"; and when Mrs. Prest "pretended to make light of his genius," he "took no pains to defend him. One doesn't defend one's god; one's god is in himself a defence." Such references to Aspern's divinity recur throughout the story. Tina reports that Juliana " 'said he was a god' "; the narrator longs for " 'A portrait of the god. I don't know what I wouldn't give to see it.' "

In this context, Jeffrey Aspern's very name assumes a high significance, albeit in the nature of a rather low pun. And the asp whom Jeffrey spurns, in a 'typically Jamesian' ironic twist, has to be the narrator, who conceives of himself and John Cumnor, his collaborator, as "appointed ministers" of Aspern's "temple." He refers to himself as devilish or satanic here and there in the story; he practices subterfuge and deception, living under an assumed identity and pretending to a false occupation—though, since he admits to being a writer there is a certain amount of truth in the pretense, making it yet more devilish. He transforms the garden of the Bordereau palazzo, described by Mrs. Prest as " 'as negative . . . as a Protestant Sunday,' " into a virtual paradise of gorgeous flowers, saying to himself, " 'I must work the garden. I must work the garden.' "—then he lurks in it, waiting his chance at Miss Tina. When the chance comes he makes good use of it, inferring from Miss Tina's implications that Aspern relics are hidden somewhere in the palazzo. In addition to the garden, he uses the standard Satanic temptations to get what he wants: gold, with which commodity he pays his exorbitant rent; and sex, with which he persistently teases and tantalizes Miss Tina, hinting that his feelings toward her are more than simply friendly.

But it is just here, in the interpretation of the narrator as consummately evil, that we begin to run into difficulties with the story. For, as Wayne Booth points out, while such a narrator can help the story to fulfill its primary object, he is, by his very nature, incapable of helping it toward its secondary one. Booth argues that James cannot realize successfully both "his condemnation of the narrator and his adulatory visitation of the past" through the medium of such an unreliable narrative voice; that a narrator so unscrupulous could never possess the sensitivity to evoke convincingly "the romantic atmosphere of Venice and particularly of this one corner of the past." Booth takes to task those critics who tend to "idolize [James] for his subtle ambiguities" and thus explain away the difficulty instead of admitting that the story is simply not as good as it might be. "How can I . . . excuse him," Booth asks, "when I find his narrator to be one kind of man in one paragraph and another kind of man in the next? Only by surrendering my responsibilities as a reader and saying that just because it is by James it is perfect."

Within the context of the standard interpretation, Booth's criticism both of James and the critics is certainly justified. Indeed, it seems even more appropriate when applied to other more specifically internal problems which the story raises—problems particularly which have to do with the characterization of the two other principle characters, the Misses Bordereau.

For, despite the fact, as Baskett points out, that Juliana is imperiled by the narrator's lust for the papers (he prays for her death so that he may "ransack her drawers" and later, by ransacking, becomes a major cause of her death), she is at least as unscrupulous and guileful as the narrator. She is indeed "a diabolical incarnation" of the past, "greedy of its power to bargain with the present"; she is in fact, "a cunning, vicious, evil old lady who knows exactly what [the narrator] wants and outwits him at every turn"; indeed, she is "an evil old witch mother." All too true. Greed is at the root of her every action. Suspecting the narrator's true motives, she charges him exorbitantly for his lodgings, and, when it becomes apparent that he needs a little encouragement to keep his interest—and his rent—high, she produces the portrait of Jeffrey Aspern painted by her father.

Is this just another instance of James' delicious irony, to endow both villain and victim with the same reprehensible characteristics? Or is his intention somewhat more functional: to emphasize by unmistakable contrast the innocence of Miss Tina? But if the object of the story is to delineate the evil machinations of the narrator, machinations which lead to a deserved disappointment (the comedy of the biter bit, as Booth puts it), and if it is Juliana who suffers most at his hands, is not a good deal in terms both of logic and art sacrificed to this emphasis?

Again, consider the characterization of Miss Tina. Despite some rather disquieting observations by Mrs. Prest in which she links Tina to Juliana—" 'Perhaps the people are afraid of the Misses Bordereau. I dare say they have the reputation of witches,' " she says at one point; and again: " 'They'll lead you to your ruin. . . . They'll get all your money without showing you a scrap' "—we are led by the narrator to conclude that Miss Tina is an innocent, as different from Juliana as possible; to conclude along with Maxwell Geismar that she is "one of those modest small souls of English fiction," a true victim, caught between duty and love, corrupted then destroyed by the narrator. "Altogether," he thinks at one point, "her behaviour was such as would have been possible only to a perfectly artless and a considerably witless woman." He holds this attitude toward her throughout the story, even at the end, when he sees the manner of her proposal as "practical argumentative heroic . . . with the timidity, however, so much more striking than the boldness, that her reasons appeared to come first and her feelings afterward."

But be it noted, it is Miss Tina who writes the letter to John Cumnor denying the existence of the papers while hinting strongly that they do in fact exist; obviously in league with Juliana to milk the narrator of his money, it could only be she who reports to Juliana that he would give a great deal to see " 'a portrait of the god' " and it is she who puts temptation squarely in the narrator's way by suggesting where the papers might be and leaving the door unlocked, thus becoming at the very least an accessory before the fact to the death of Juliana. On what evidence may we conclude that such a character is an innocent? Only on the testimony of the narrator, that lying, conniving, dissembling scoundrel who, as Booth points out, is a totally unreliable observer, against that of Mrs. Prest, an objective, relatively disinterested, hence probably more reliable observer. Can this be yet another example of Jamesian irony—letting evil, the antithesis of good, identify the good most accurately? Or can it be that he has merely misled us, intentionally or not, into believing in her innocence? For, if the narrator is unreliable, his characterization of Miss Tina is necessarily false. In either case, in terms of the standard interpretation, we have uncovered a third major flaw in the story, each of them having to do with characterization.

These are serious charges to level against a writer whose strength admittedly is characterization coupled with careful craftsmanship. One can explain them away by an appeal to James' delight in ironic ambiguities, as we have seen; but Wayne Booth is right: such an argument is at best specious and at worst simply an excuse for failure.

But it is unnecessary to explain the charges away; they simply are invalid. The fault lies not with James, but with the interpretation and the assumptions upon which it is based. A vastly different interpretation, based on vastly different assumptions but employing the same evidence, can be arrived at by a careful examination of the story and especially of the characters *on their own terms,* that is, as James portrays them on both the literal and figurative levels—an interpretation within the framework of which most or all of the flaws and problems which have bothered Wayne Booth and many of the other critics either disappear or solve themselves.

Let us reconsider first of all the characterizations of Juliana and the narrator. Undeniably, he deeply desires the papers, and he testifies that he would do anything to get them including making love to Miss Tina. Undeniably he considers himself diabolical. But the fact is, that despite all his evil protestations, he does nothing truly evil in the story except to misrepresent his intentions for a time and yield to the temptation of an unlocked room. He does not make love to Tina; whether he'd have succumbed to the temptation to marry her is at best a moot question clearly to be answered in the negative should a reasonable alternative occur to him. He does pay exorbitantly for what he gets—the miniature portrait of Jeffrey Aspern. It would seem just as reasonable to assume, on the basis of the evidence of his "unreliable" testimony, that the narrator is not devilish as that he is. Indeed, he seems more to be a romantic, somewhat naive, all too fallible human Adam come to the home of the god in a blind and unsuccessful pursuit of knowledge and beauty. " 'That was what the old women represented,' " he says early on, " '—esoteric knowledge; and this was the idea with which my critical heart used to thrill.' " Thus, through the Edenic metaphor, the avowed minister-devil is identified as mere mortal, and the mortal women as devilish. Thus, also, Booth's protests that, because of his evil nature, the narrator is an unreliable evoker of the romantic past, begin to be muted. For, be it noted, the narrator *is* reliable in his perceptions and in his reporting them; he is *un*reliable in his understanding or interpretation of them. But that is due to innocence, not evil—a situation not uncommon in James' stories based on the confrontation of the New World Adam with the Old, or better, with the expatriate American Old—in ***Daisy Miller,*** for instance, or, most poignantly, in **"Four Meetings."**

But Juliana—whom Booth ignores completely, not even mentioning her name in his discussion of the story—is another matter entirely. Greedy as the narrator, but after gold rather than beauty; just as unscrupulous in fact as he is in intention, but more successful, she is portrayed as far more diabolical than he. It is she who insists on payment in gold; it is she who taunts the narrator with the portrait of Jeffrey Aspern; it is she who suggests the gondola ride as vividly described in sexual terms in that extraordinary passage cited earlier; and it is she who is described in these highly suggestive terms:

> . . .she had over her eyes a horrible green shade which served for her almost as a mask. . . . it created a presumption of some ghastly death's head lurking behind it. The divine Juliana as a grinning skull—the vision hung there until it passed. . . . She was dressed in black and her head was wrapped in a piece of old black lace which showed no hair.

The evocation of the hooded serpent and the death's head function on the figurative level as emphasis of Juliana's literal diabolism, recalling Mrs. Prest's reference to her probable reputation as a witch. The figures recur throughout the story, most tellingly at the climatic instant when Juliana catches the narrator searching her rooms for the first time—though she is presumed even by Tina to be blind—lifts the hood to expose her "extraordinary eyes. They glared at me; they were like the sudden drench . . . of a flood of gaslight; they made me horribly ashamed." The blind eyes of the death's head combined with the mesmeric eyes of the serpent as Juliana "hissed" her accusation: " 'Ah you publishing scoundrel!' "

The charge describes him perfectly. The motivation for this one overtly base act, ransacking Juliana's drawers, has been to gain knowledge of the god, Aspern, so that he might publish it. The irony is that he has sought his knowledge not so much in the wrong way as from the wrong source.

For it should be noted that there is no incontrovertible evidence—except the testimony of Miss Tina—that any Aspern papers exist at all. Indeed, it may be, as one critic argues, that a proud Juliana, having been jilted by Aspern, would have destroyed any mementoes of him—except perhaps for the portrait, which after all was painted by her father. [Waldmeir adds in a footnote: See Jacob Korg, 'What Aspern Papers? A Hypothesis,' *College English,* XXIII (February 1961). Unfortunately, Korg's argument is diluted by historical inaccuracy, by his misinterpretation of the Shelley-Byron-Clairmont-Allegra relationship and his application of this inaccurate external evidence to the argument. It is unnecessary to go into the errors here: Robert S. Phillips straightened it all out in 'A note on "What Aspern Papers?" ' *College English,* XXIV (November 1962).] Again, it may be that she never received any letters from Aspern, perhaps because of the something bad that happened " 'in other ages, in another world'. " On the Edenic metaphorical level, that something bad may easily be interpreted as the original Satanic fall from grace, making it reasonable to assume that it is Juliana not the narrator who is the asp that the divine Jeffrey spurned (or jilted), and it follows therefore that she possesses no knowledge while she leads the narrator to believe that she does.

Given an interpretation of the role and function of these two characters so different from the standard one, the problems with conflicting characterization and inconsistent motivation which we noted earlier start to solve themselves—and without an appeal to a possible ironic level of meaning which only serves to compound the conflicts and the inconsistencies.

It only remains now to consider Miss Tina, no insignificant task since it becomes increasingly clear as one digs at ***The Aspern Papers*** that upon her characterization, upon an identification of her role and function in it, rests any interpretation of the story. If she is the modest, humble, naive innocent that most critics have assumed her to be, then it follows that the narrator is villainous and she his most pitiable victim. [Waldmeir adds in a footnote: Indeed, Henry Seidel Canby, in *Turn West, Turn East* (1951) argues that "Tina, the credulous niece . . . becomes the heroine of the story. . . . Her tragedy, not the loss of the papers, is, or should be, its climax."] And again, unfortunately, we are faced with a great many inconsistencies resolvable only by an appeal to irony. If however she is not that enigmatic innocent victim, but an active accomplice of Juliana in milking the narrator of his substance as suggested earlier in this paper, then the inconsistencies begin to fade away. Further evidence on the metaphorical level of her lack of innocence will, I believe, dissipate them entirely.

Consider: the narrator builds the garden in order, Satan-like, to worm his way into the ladies' confidence; but it is Tina who lurks in it, trapping him there, and pumping all the information she desires from him while giving him nothing but hints in return. Consider: the narrator announces his dastardly intention to make love to Tina to effect his ends, but it is Tina who is sexually aggressive and manipulative—hers is the orgasm described in the gondola ride, not his; hers, not his, is the proposal to trade knowledge for marriage at the end. The situation is remindful of Satan's proposition to Eve, but it is even more strikingly similar, especially in its projected consequences, to Eve's proposition to Adam. For, consider once more that there is no tangible evidence of that "esoteric knowledge" which Tina bargains with, that there are any Aspern papers, and consider that Tina would know that there are none—and her unreliability has been sufficiently well established by the time that she says that there are and that she has them that we must have doubts of their existence—then her perpetuation of the myth of the papers to the very last possible moment as she bargains with them for marriage is clearly uninnocent, and suspiciously Eve-like.

Tina's posture of innocence is so convincing that the narrator rejects even his suspicions—suspicions which, were he truly evil he would surely have heeded—and he is therefore nearly ensnared by her temptations. But in rejecting the suspicions, he calls the reader's attention quite explicitly to the dubious quality of that innocence. At the discovery of Tina in the garden, he "asked myself if it might be a trap laid for me, the result of a design to make me show my hand," as indeed it turned out to be; but he continues: "before we parted for the night my mind was at rest as to what *she* might be. She was up to nothing at all." When she proposes marriage to him, her words "gave me an impression of a subtlety which at first I failed to follow," though immediately afterward he interprets the words as "practical argumentative heroic." And at the point where she offers the portrait to him either to keep or to sell, he is so shaken by his conflicting feelings about her that he appeals to the god for guidance: "I privately consulted Jeffrey Aspern's eyes with my own—they were so young and brilliant yet so wise and deep; I asked him what on earth was the matter with Miss Tina. He seemed to smile at me with mild mockery; he might have been amused at my case." But his naivete prevents him from interpreting even this mockery accurately; Aspern "was unsatisfactory for the only moment since I had known him."

Clearly, Tina's motivation is financial gain, the same as Juliana's; but her methods are far more drastic. Juliana is a sort of straightforward con-artist, luring the pigeon onward by subtle hints and sly disavowals until his own greed should trap him. But Tina forces the issue. When she entices the narrator to ransack her aunt's drawers, she becomes, as noted above, wittingly or unwittingly and accessory to the old lady's death. One would suppose that this would stir her conscience, but when the narrator returns to the palazzo after the funeral, he discovers her again in the garden ". . . she had clearly been crying, crying a great deal—simply, satisfyingly, refreshingly, with a primitive retarded sense of solitude and violence. *But she had none of the airs or graces of grief,* and I was almost surprised to see her stand there in the first dusk with her hands full of admirable roses and smile at me with reddened eyes." (emphasis supplied) After he has told her of his trip, she exclaimed "quite as if she had forgotten her aunt and her sorrow, 'Dear, dear, how much I should like to do such things—to take an amusing little journey!' " On the very next day, she proposes marriage with the promise of the papers as a dowry, knowing, one suspects, that her proposition will not be accepted hence she will never have to produce the papers—knowing too how to work for gold the narrator's romantic vulnerability. The ploy works. When she has him half suckered-in so that she seems transformed, beautified, younger, "not a ridiculous old woman," she tells him that she has destroyed the papers. Whereupon "the transfiguration was over and she had changed back to a plain dingy elderly person," and a complex sense of guilt is set up in the narrator motivating him to leap at the chance to salve his conscience by purchasing the portrait for far more gold than it was worth: "she kept it with thanks; she never sent it back."

If the interpretation of ***The Aspern Papers*** given here is correct—and I believe it is because it is based on a straight rather than ironic reading of the text—then it follows that the narrator is the true innocent in the story, unreliable only because of his innocence, another of James' Adamic Americans unsuccessfully playing at being unscrupulous. It follows too that he is unwittingly at the mercy of the unholy alliance of the truly unscrupulous, calculating females, Juliana and Tina—two of James' most notable fallen Americans, a sort of Satan and Eve who successfully devour the narrator's substance and return him nothing out of the "visitable past" save the portrait, a mocking image of the god, Jeffrey Aspern.

In the ambiguous last line of the story, the narrator voices his regrets: "When I look at [the portrait] I can scarcely bear my loss—I mean of the precious papers." The line may be taken literally, or ironically, as a reference to the excessive amount of money he paid for the portrait; or even as a reference to his loss of Miss Tina. But in any case, for all his regrets, in the context of this discussion he is very fortunate to have come away with his immortal soul. (pp. 256-67)

Joseph J. Waldmeir, "Miss Tina Did It: A Fresh Look at 'The Aspern Papers'," in The Centennial Review, *Vol. XXVI, No. 3, Summer, 1982, pp. 256-67.*

Elizabeth Allen (essay date 1984)

[*In the following excerpt, Allen argues that Daisy Miller relies upon Winterbourne's interpretation for her own definition of self and character.*]

The immense popularity of ***Daisy Miller*** when it was published, and the extent to which it was discussed and argued about, focussed on the nature of what Daisy was and how she was portrayed. As an American girl she was a recognisable figure, the question was the evaluation and composition of the American girl. Winterbourne is the consciousness through which the story is told, the onlooker within the text that *The American* lacks. He is an American himself, one who has lived in Europe and understands its conventions and language. In much of James's work involving the international element, it is the American who learns his or her way round the social world embodied in Europe, who is potentially most fully conscious of the interactions between individuals and the defining and limiting factors of social existence. The American individual, once fully aware of the world entered, is most free to 'pick and choose and assimilate'. Yet the Europeanised American may also be more corrupt, more consciously manipulative and condemnatory of fellow American innocents than the Europeans themselves. Desire to be socially functional and acceptable can lead to hostility to those who appear to be unconventional or independent. Thus the developing awareness of an Isabel Archer, Lambert Strether or Milly Theale is juxtaposed with the rigidity of the convert in the deeply conventional Gilbert Osmond, Madame Merle or Charlotte Stant.

Winterbourne is somewhere between the two, indeed ***Daisy Miller*** can be read as the dramatisation of his choice. P. J. Eakin sees the story as one of James's 'fables of redemptive courtship', a courtship which in this case is not brought to fruition. Eakin sees Daisy as Winterbourne's chance to embrace an American reality, its freshness and vitality along with its brashness and crudity. His failure to do so is a rejection of these national characteristics.

This is in accordance with Cristof Wegelin's more general statement that:

> It is a striking fact that while the promise of unencumbered American vitality is in James almost invariably symbolised by the young American girl, the questions which it raises and the threats which it contains are usually dramatised in American men.

Winterbourne is, however, not so much agonising over the relative attractions and merits of European and American values (as Roderick Hudson is, for instance, in his position between Christina Light and Mary Garland), nor is he simply weighing up the balance of good and bad in America, as represented in Daisy's prettiness, freshness, spontaneity, ignorance and crudity. He is faced with the problem of interpreting signs, of trying to decide *what* Daisy (or America) signifies, rather than simply the value of the signified. He attempts through Daisy both to decide what American girls are really signifying and, by referring Daisy back to this class, to place her as an American girl. Puzzled by Daisy's behaviour, he retreats again and again to generalisation, seeking to find a clue to her in a given social interpretation. Yet the very newness and lack of orthodoxy of the American girl presents its own problems:

> Some people had told him that, after all, American girls were exceedingly innocent; and others had told him that, after all, they were not.

The fact that Winterbourne bothers to expend energy on interpreting Daisy makes him active and conscious in relation to the rest of his society who 'read' Daisy simplistically, and condemn her against their own codes of womanhood and the ladylike. Mrs Costello can simply declare 'They are hopelessly vulgar,' but Winterbourne seeks to make out another layer of meaning in Daisy which will reconcile the fact that ' "Common", she was, as Mrs Costello had pronounced her; yet it was a wonder to Winterbourne that, with her commonness, she had a singularly delicate grace.'

We are given very few clues to Daisy's own response to events; we are given very little of her consciousness, and this is emphasised by the vision of her as socially unselfconscious, unaware of the potential response of others to her until she is brought face to face with it. As far as we are concerned, Daisy is presented as a surface to look at:

> Daisy stopped and looked at him, without a sign of troubled consciousness in her face; with nothing but the presence of her charming eyes and her happy dimples.

This surface being puzzling, Winterbourne, and by identification the reader, seeks for meaning 'behind' it, thus somehow bypassing the reality of Daisy herself. In *Decoding Advertisements,* Judith Williamson discusses how the use of jokes, puzzles, humour and understatement in advertisements directs the subjects' response to a channelled interpretation of the 'meaning' of the joke, etc., rather than to a questioning of the basic relationship of sign and the external reality it refers to:

> The motion of the mask . . . illustrates perfectly the overlooking of the materiality of the signifier in the hermeneutic pursuit of the signified, and apex 'behind' it . . . A crucial part of this is the advertisement's built in *concealment* of it, by re-

> ferring to a 'reality' or 'meaning' behind its surface: the 'mask' conceals nothing but itself.

Herself engaged in no conscious process of interpretation or self-presentation, Daisy is entirely an object of the experience of Winterbourne, and the reader. If she fails to provide an adequate correspondence between her 'appearance' and the meaning she is expected to point to, she has no adequate reality.

James deliberately isolates Daisy as a person, which serves both to intensify her social freedom as an American, and her vulnerability as sign. Daisy is unconstrained by her mother, her absent father, or her own sense of what is or is not socially acceptable or apposite. She does what she likes, responds to what she likes. To the world around her she is a young girl, an American girl, she represents a society and a sex. She is expected to be what she appears—whether that is an innocent girl or a fallen woman. The mechanisms of society simply expel Daisy when her behaviour no longer conforms—she is cut dead at a party, and no longer invited out in respectable society. Yet Winterbourne still attempts to correlate Daisy's behaviour with what she is, to read her as a sign and make sense of her. If he could succeed, Daisy would be saved, but his success, finally aided by another man, comes too late.

It is interesting that when Winterbourne comes upon Daisy at the Colosseum at night and thinks that he finally understands her, what he responds to instinctively is not the nature of that understanding but the fact that the process of interpretation can now cease:

> Winterbourne stopped, with a sort of horror; and, it must be added, with a sort of relief. It was as if a sudden illumination had been flashed upon the ambiguity of Daisy's behaviour and the riddle had become easy to read. She was a young lady whom a gentleman need no longer be at pains to respect . . . He felt angry with himself that he had bothered so much about the right way of regarding Miss Daisy Miller.

One of the significations of the American in Europe is the demand of the individual to be responded to individually. Conversance with social codes and conventions gives a shorthand for placing people, the arrival of the American disrupts this procedure, demanding a new approach to an individual who does not apparently fit the existing structures. Each new individual has both to take account of the society surrounding and responding to him or her, and to be taken account of by it. Existing values and correspondence may have to be adjusted accordingly. The juxtaposition of Europe and America continually shows up each in a new light. But this process is demanding and time consuming; what is more, it demands that the conscious subject attempting it risk his own, secure, social identity. So Winterbourne is glad to be spared the trouble, to retreat into the stiff formality of 'She was a young lady whom a gentleman need no longer be at pains to respect'.

That he is wrong in his judgement does not so much locate the questions raised by the tale in the final valuation of American qualities (in a sense, they are taken care of by Giovanelli), more it raises the question of Daisy's vulnerability to a wrong judgement, the implications of her subsequent death. Daisy is an inscrutable mixture of 'audacity and innocence', she appears wonderfully independent, subject to no restraints. Judith Fryer, in *The Faces of Eve,* identifies self-reliance as her major trait. But Daisy's final vulnerability and destruction go beyond the fictional realisation that each individual is in fact created through social existence, and cannot live in disregard of it. For Daisy does not die *only* through exposure to the fever-ridden air of the Colosseum, the sterility of a hostile, decaying society. She shrivels at the mis-interpretation of Winterbourne, his failure to validate her by continuing to see her and read her. Her other consistent value, as well as her independence, is, after all, her blankness, literalness, superficially, innocence—in short, her existence as observed other rather than a reflective self. As Winterbourne probes her chatter for nuance and import, he realises that 'in her bright, sweet, superficial little visage there was no mockery, no irony.' Daisy is what Winterbourne sees, it is up to him, the conscious subject, to accord Daisy some social place, some function as sign. Our attention is inevitably directed towards the tension between Daisy's signification as free and active, and her passive dependency on a subject, masculine response. Her freedom is not merely limited, like Newman's, it is denied by a society which decrees that young girls do not exist for themselves, and by a fictional presentation as a blank surface, a reflection for the consciousness of Winterbourne.

In *Communities of Honor and Love in Henry James,* Manfred Mackenzie describes Daisy's death as a kind of suicidal self-rejection in response to the shame of public condemnation—in the Colosseum itself—that Winterbourne exposes her to. I don't think Daisy's sense of self is really developed enough for this interpretation to be convincing. The dramatic picture of the American individual, and the individual *consciousness* of self, are divided between Daisy and Winterbourne, so that Winterbourne rejects Daisy as object at the same time as he ceases to bother about re-examining social assumptions. Daisy dies because she cannot be fitted into any European scheme of things, and because her very existence as American girl depends on her continuing to be seen within that scheme. Once she is cut dead by everyone, she ceases to exist. Paradoxically, the representative of unconventional individuality is thus totally dependent on external recognition—Daisy as self exists only as an objectification of selfhood for those already occupying a social position, and catalyses a re-examination of that position, from within.

Daisy's failure is thus not as an individual woman who may, or may not, be innocent, but in failing to be a satisfactory other to Winterbourne's subject meditation on experience. The fact that the process of ***Daisy Miller*** is the process of interpretation suggests that Daisy sinks under the pressure of study, of being an object of observation finally discarded as unsatisfactory.

The questions raised by the story are those of the confinement and ultimate destruction of the individual by the projected interpretations and objectifications of the external world. The process is, however, inevitable, Winterbourne occupies the middle position—both defined himself, and practising definition on Daisy. For Daisy herself there appears to be no reciprocal relation, she functions in the text only as the object of Winterbourne's experience. Winterbourne can attempt to define himself in relation to what Daisy signifies; can, as subject, make demands on the other to represent experience for him. In the same way Newman, though himself representative to the Bellegardes of the raw American, can demand to be 'interpreted to the world'. But as sign, and only sign, Daisy cannot be subject, she gets no reflection, makes no demands of European society. Endowed with freedom, she cannot use it for herself. Her only value is in her representative status, if that is unclear she is the passive prey to a host of misinterpretations.

As we are led to look at Daisy as self-reliant and individual, her death poses questions as to the possibility of the girl who signifies independence and freedom actually being free herself. Once discarded by her male interpreter, she sinks fast. Newman after all merely runs up against a wall of defiance and denial, he can't get what he wants from society, as an individual he has to recognise limitations. Daisy meets a negation of what she is—she is what Winterbourne might want to get, and as such she is rejected. If the social structures of power turn individuals into predators and prey, possessors and possessions, subjects and objects, then the possessor denied a possession has only to look elsewhere. The possession, on the other hand, if rejected as such, loses all value altogether. That the American girl can apparently never realise her freedom and independence for herself but must submit it to another, is intrinsic to the position of existence as sign, or other, functioning for an observing consciousness.

The problem of Daisy's death is still a problem for Winterbourne, or by implication for the reader. Her limitation as sign is not presented as a source of conflict for Daisy herself. Any real exploration of the conflict between the girl being defined through her sign status, and her own consciousness of her individual freedom, needs the presentation of the heroine as an 'object of study' to be balanced by the presentation of her attempts to be the subject of her own experience. In *The Portrait of a Lady,* the false nature of the freedom of the individual girl is confronted not simply by the observers for whom, as feminine, she is automatically confined, but by the girl herself. In ***Daisy Miller,*** the fictional presentation of Daisy is as 'one of them'. Daisy's existence within the text is limited to her feminine status as an American girl. With Isabel Archer, James attempted to go beyond this and present an American girl who is a person. (pp. 51-7)

Elizabeth Allen, in her A Woman's Place in the Novels of Henry James, *St. Martin's Press, 1984, 223 p.*

James W. Gargano (essay date 1986)

[In the essay below, Gargano examines imagery in "The Beast in the Jungle."]

In **"The Beast in the Jungle,"** Henry James attempts to make a formidable dramatic action out of what he calls in one of his most interesting prefaces "a great negative adventure." The point of the story is the pointlessness of John Marcher's subordination of reality to his belief that a unique and possibly terrible destiny awaits him. Marcher's special fate (to be "*the* man, to whom nothing on earth was to have happened") is made vivid by his involvement or noninvolvement with May Bartram, a devoted companion who represents the possibility of a more fruitful life. In essence, **"The Beast in the Jungle"** traces Marcher's tortuous route to total negation through a series of episodes in which he fails to perceive, or, as James puts it, "is afraid to recognise what he incidentally misses." Appropriately, Marcher's deathlike withdrawal from life reaches its climax at May's grave where his adventure is completed not in a traditional physical ordeal, but in his shrinking from a monster created by his own psychic urgencies and imagination.

James faced the technical problem inherent in dramatizing nonlife by shifting his artistic focus from narrative incidents to clusters of images that mark the stages of his protagonist's psychological evasions. By filling the void resulting from Marcher's inaction, imagery itself becomes a kind of dominant action, an adumbration of the subconscious energies of Marcher's inner life. The inventiveness that most fiction writers expend on plot James thus invests in interrelated images and symbols that tell a tense story of omissions and possibilities rather than accomplished deeds. What emerges is an engrossing tapestry or mosaic made up of roads not taken, wrong turns fearfully followed, and chances missed. Ultimately, all the the withdrawals, denials, and suppressions gather paradoxically into a symbol of startling emotional violence.

Both clear and suggestive, James's imagery possesses sharp immediacy and almost endless radiation. Even the most perfunctory reader will grasp the author's purport in naming his contrasting characters Marcher and May. More careful readers, however will see ramifications of meaning in other examples of seasonal imagery: the opening incident at Weatherend with its faint lure of October light; May and Marcher's comedy of terror in April; and the graveyard denouement in the fall that revives, with stunning variation, the April fiasco. The same mixture of obviousness and allusiveness controls most of the images in **"The Beast in the Jungle"** and keeps the novella from hardening into allegory or evaporating into supersubtle implications. Light, for instance, with all its elemental connotations and its association with seasonal change appears in the autumn sky, enters into the characters' language and shines in May's face. Light changes as seasons, moods, and human exigencies change, and its absence is as full of import as its many manifestations. Misleading, trustworthy, fierce, or positively revelatory, it is part of the labyrinth of images calculated to give readers a sense of mystery that cannot be fully rationalized away. The images, however, finally serve as the threads that conduct to understanding and awareness. Perhaps as convincingly as action in the traditional play or story, James's imagery quickens or retards narrative pace, provides ironic reversals, and creates climactic tensions.

An examination of James's imagery as the major vehicle of his thought in **"The Beast in the Jungle"** will reveal its pervasiveness, its closely woven texture, and its function in designating the phases of Marcher's fascinating psychological disintegration. Clearly, James's art depends most heavily on images associated with seasons, links or connections, light, and burial. With metaphysical subtlety, he also employs a complex of sibyl-seeress-sphinx images to elaborate May Bartram's role as a counterintelligence whose glimpses into Marcher's mind date many of the crises of his inner history. Finally, to achieve his almost surrealistic climax, James relies on violent beast imagery to conclude Marcher's negative, actionless adventure.

Of course, other image-symbol patterns wind intricately through James's novella, sometimes fusing with the dominant ones and sometimes modifying them. **"The Beast in the Jungle"** is, indeed, so fine a web of connotation that it may be described as a vision of life ultimately inseparable from its metaphorical expression.

Although my study will be concerned with James's imagery, I recognize that its dramatic impact is heightened by a style at once elliptical, tortuous, and full of qualifications, intensifications, and suspensefully delayed referents. As David Smit has recently written [in "The Leap of the Beast: The Dramatic Style of Henry James's "The Beast in the Jungle,' " *The Henry James Review* (Spring 1983)], the style of **"The Beast in the Jungle"** "is not chaotic and it is not dull. It is as dramatic as the leap of the beast in our mind's eye." In fact, James's involute style is the perfect vehicle for his all-informing and, at times, untranslatable imagery.

Because seasonal imagery pervades almost every facet and nuance of the six sections of **"The Beast in the Jungle,"** it deserves special attention. James employs it in naming and defining his characters, setting his scenes, stressing motivation, and giving poetic coloration and resonance to his theme of the unlived life. It is so sensitively stitched into the texture of the work that it might be called the figure in the carpet.

The overall purpose of the seasonal imagery is to contrast the unnatural "law" of Marcher's life with the law governing natural processes. James, of course, associates Marcher with the end of winter and the possibility of spring, but unlike the month of March, the protagonist possesses no new or creative energies. Time passes and he remains immovably constant. James allows him occasional stirrings of life, but these stirrings occur in the depths of his being and are—until the end of the novella—overruled by an emotional rigidity stemming from his view of himself as someone mysteriously placed outside the context of ordinary humanity. Whereas the seasons flow into one another and are part of a changing order, James's main character is first seen at Weatherend, an English country house where natural fluidity seems to end and a kind of stasis prevails. Even May Bartram, who should symbolize growth, typifies pallid possibilities and has little energizing power for Marcher. She affects him as a faded memory to which he can attach no importance: having fully blotted out his past life because in a real sense it has not happened, he cannot even recall that he had met her in his youth and confided his obsession to her. Indeed, James shows him as pathetically desiring "to invent something, to get her to make-believe with him that some passage of a romantic or critical kind *had* originally occurred. He was really reaching out in imagination—as against time."

As the interval between March and May, April has a sinister importance in James's novella. It looms as the cruelest month not because, as in T. S. Eliot's wasteland, it compels new growth, but because it acts as an unnatural, permanent barrier. For James, April does not serve as a bridge but as a lacuna, a gap never successfully spanned. It represents the germinal vigor almost entirely absent from Marcher's makeup. It represents the unruly and agitated time of the beast which in healthy lives must be lived through and thus accommodated to the procession of the months. To bypass it is to miss the initiating forces that stimulate and assure efflorescence and harvest. Predictably, then, what doesn't happen in **"The Beast in the Jungle"** actually does and does not take place in April: James shows that, though Marcher is physically present at his unique destiny, he witnesses no action as the beast springs. With his story beginning and ending in the fall, Marcher has more symbolic affinity with that season than with either April or May.

James places his climactic April scene with great care in the fourth section of **"The Beast in the Jungle."** It, therefore begins the second half of the novella with the tragic assurance that the protagonist will never discover in May Bartram the quickening force of the month for which she is named. This conclusion is reached, however, only after three preparatory sections in which highly dramatic images establish the characters' identities, their relations to each other, and their reactions to seasonal change and time.

In the first and least pessimistic section of the novella, the seasonal imagery is closely interwoven with images of linkage, light, and burial. In staging the meeting between Macher and May at Weatherend after a hiatus of ten years, James plays many imagistic changes on the themes of discontinuity and connection and opens up the slender possibility that his protagonist will end his self-inflicted isolation and enter life's mainstream. May's presence catches Marcher's attention and makes him feel in possession of the "sequel of something of which he had lost the beginning." He prods himself into imagining that the sound of May's voice furnishes him a "missing link," but for all his good will his memory draws a blank. With awkward earnestness, he fumbles toward knowledge as if it might forge a contact he apparently needs. Yet, James carefully shows that it is May and not Marcher who makes contact possible; her direct reminder that he had divulged his secret to her "cleared the air and supplied the link—the link it was so odd he should frivolously have managed to lose." A ray of hope appears when Marcher comforts himself that someone has shared his burden, "and lo he wasn't alone a bit." Indeed, May's agreement to "watch" with him as he awaits his fate awakens speculation as to whether Marcher has made a saving connection with a vital woman and entered into what is referred to, at the beginning of the second section, as a "goodly bond" that will enable him to meet April's incitement to union with May when it comes.

Ironically, however, since Marcher has not changed with

the years, his new meeting may become a mere reenactment of the earlier, forgotten one. He still practices detachment, entertains a "theory" that keeps him "lost in the crowd," and affects colorless manners that secure him anonymity. His guarded language and circumspect behavior constitute an elaborate series of defenses against comradeship and other distractions that may weaken his commitment to his idée fixe. If the "reunion" at Weatherend begins with "the feeling of an occasion missed" and a sense that "all the communities were wanting," it may already stamp Marcher as a hollow man to whom nothing can happen. Indeed, James does not encourage high hopes in his reader: when May stealthily leads up to her daring reminder of his confession, Marcher merely appraises her with "wonder" and stiffly gives "no sign" of support. The man who literally has no past to remember cannot be counted on to form a promising attachment. The question the whole novella will pose is, after all, what kind of link May can establish with someone so adept at dodges and expert in ego-preservation that he has, in a spiritual sense, converted life into an unalterable, arid autumn.

Light imagery, which James develops with a startling "jump" from images of links, affords a clue throughout the novella of the characters' clarity of perception and their fund of vitality. It is indicative of Marcher's original state of mind that he "recalls" the smallest detail of his earlier meeting with May and figuratively sees the dark past suddenly lit. In an artful use of light to give action and movement to his narrative, James compares Marcher's confidence in his memory to an "impression operating like the torch of a lamplighter who touches into flame . . . a long row of gas-jets." Imagery shapes the scene into a neat drama of Marcher's psychic ineptitude and his need to believe he shared a past with May. His brilliant illumination, which should prove a transforming acuteness, only proves to be a trick of his imagination as she refutes his version of their original encounter, leaving him comically in the dark. Imagery continues to function actively when May informs him of his earlier confession and "a light broke for him." Already preparing for later developments, James characterizes the light coming from Marcher's unaided sight as weak and misleading and that coming from May as genuine and revelatory. Her perceptions are, and continue to be, trustworthy and illuminating; before the end of the first section, Marcher himself comes to place implicit faith in "the light in her eyes."

Like his imagery of links and light, James's burial imagery offers a slight hint that Marcher may emerge from his privacy and adopt a creative interest in life. For example, Marcher's conjectures about his first encounter with May turn on the possibility that what happened then may be "too deeply buried—too deeply (didn't it seem?) to sprout after so many years." Yet, sprout it does as May attaches herself to a man whom she has a right to treat as a lunatic. It might not even be extravagant to propose, as some critics have, that James consciously staged one of the initial meetings between the ill-sorted pair "at Pompeii, on an occasion when they had been present there at an important find"—when the past came unexpectedly to light in the present. Marcher, with Mary's necessary assistance, unearths something precious—a past confidence, a spontaneous approach to a shared life—that had been buried, if not for centuries, at least for ten round years. The vexing question inherent in the burial imagery is, however, whether he will use his knowledge to foster a new relationship or to serve his old monomania. Obviously, May's freedom to attach herself to him derives from her roots in reality—her roots, if it is not too much of a conceit, in April. Will Marcher, James appears to tease his readers into asking, improve upon the one generous act of his early life and be worthy of May's proffered aid?

In summary, the general effect of the imagery in the opening section of **"The Beast in the Jungle"** is to highlight the novella's immanent problem: will Marcher achieve the light or warmth and perception to form a link or bond subversive of his estranging narcissism? Except for the ominous implications of Weatherend and the October setting, the images are neither conclusive nor heavily oppressive. Marcher's severance from his own past and his inability to generate "true" light do not augur well for him, but he does constructively desire to be less alone and he does link himself to the potentially regenerative and light-giving May. Rather than pronounce doom on his protagonist at the outset of his fiction, James guides him to the crossroads where the future appears to be "open" and character will determine fate.

The second section, however, moves from the emergence of opportunity to near fatalism as James dramatizes May's certainty that Marcher will never outgrow the fatuity that makes him incapable of change. The section is framed by the opening declaration of May's knowledge ("The fact that she 'knew' ") and her closing reliance on his inveterate blindness ("You'll never find out"). Unpromisingly, the goodly bond slackens into a loveless avoidance if not parody of marriage supported by the plausible argument, masking a fear of commitment, that a gentleman cannot ask a lady to accompany him on a "tiger-hunt." James's image patterns make it clear that as May desires the reality rather than the semblance of closeness, Marcher's sensibility narrows and his openness to the world's charm decreases; he retains his "dissimulation" toward the "people in London whose invitations he accepted and repaid," and, worst of all, he values his connection with May only because she supplies him with another pair of eyes with which to scrutinize his obsession. Link and bonding imagery paradoxically convicts Marcher of the cardinal Jamesian sin of exploiting a human being as if he or she were a means or tool to further egotistic ends.

In a little drama all its own, burial imagery also undergoes a radical change in the second section of **"The Beast in the Jungle."** James presents Marcher as at first buoyed up by the discovery that May is privy to his secret, which figures as "the buried treasure of her knowledge." Almost exuberantly, Marcher savors the good fortune of his new companionship: "He had with his own hands dug up this little hoard, brought to light . . . the object of value the hiding-place of which he had, after putting it into the ground himself, so strangely, so long forgotten." By the end of the section, however, James's imagery exposes Marcher's mismanagement of his excavated treasure. Moreover, in possibly the major twist of the second section, May now assumes importance as the possessor of a secret of her own, the closely guarded perception that by ceasing to respond to human vibrations Marcher is well on his way toward his destiny. This second secret, earned by shrewd observation and deeply hidden until the graveyard scene at the end of the novella, extends the burial imagery and serves as the dramatic center of Marcher's curiosity as he seeks to know what she knows. Still, he will pathologically fail to see that May and not any secret is the real treasure that might liberate him from his fate.

In perhaps the most audacious image in the second section, James begins to transform May into a Cassandra figure, one of the most penetrating of his uncommonly penetrating women. With a metaphysical élan worthy of John Donne, he ascribes to her an "indescribable" art which consists in the "feat of at once—or perhaps it was only alternately—meeting the [Marcher's] eyes from in front and mingling her own vision, as from over his shoulder, with their peep through the apertures." Obviously, May's vision has assumed an almost prophetesslike acuteness enabling her to formulate the law of Marcher's being: in possession of a light denied him, she penetrates his masks and hollow relationships and beholds him changeless and immovable in the flux of time. Indeed, as "they grew older together," her genuine attachment to him helps her to believe that he will never feel enough sympathy with another human being to "find out" what she has learned about him.

In the second section, James's skillful blurring of the time scheme of his novella emphasizes that for his protagonist the years accomplish nothing but their own passing. Though the beast crouches in "the twists and turns of the months and the years," Marcher exists physically *in* time while psychically *out* of it, sinking deeper and deeper into a temporal void, a constant autumn. No action takes place, but James's imagery invests his characters' inaction with developing drama. Unable to see that May comes to him like a new spring, Marcher is a striking example of what Henry Adams, in "The Dynamo and the Virgin," thought of as modern man's insensitivity to woman as a generative and dynamic force. By looking outside of time and beyond his own and May's innate energies, he perverts nature's laws instead of attuning himself to their rhythm. May, in contrast, achieves a kind of consummation through a life of effort and love even though she already assumes the burden of the sphinxlike intelligence who, in the fourth section, ponders the riddle of life and lost opportunities.

In the short third section, James's imagery pushes his vivid drama of consciousness toward its fatal turning point by intensifying the emptiness of the Marcher-May relationship and May's sibyllike clairvoyance. All is artful preparation for the April scene in which the "negative adventure" reaches its climax of inaction, imperceptiveness, and unfulfillment. With acuteness couched in a wry tone of social satire, James presents May and Marcher almost jesting about the meaning of their long-standing tie. With a levity with undercurrents of mordant irony, she states that in the eyes of the world she seems a woman who has had her man (which she hasn't) while he passes for a man like another (which he isn't). Still, May's secret knowledge makes her sensitive to the double entendre in their banter: her language implies the truth and yet guards her secret, salves his doubts, and still gives him enough encouragement to make a closer and more binding approach. With subtle indirection, she addresses her words to his inner ear or to some recess in him uncontaminated by his obsession. Nevertheless, despite the tactful ministry of her love, he clings to his mock link with her and maintains his separateness under the guise of nearness. There is little likelihood that he will be capable of making use of his approaching April opportunity.

The seasonal imagery in this section, however, indicates that Marcher's sensibility is not impermeable. Although he fails to pick up May's subliminal messages, he begins to heed the increasingly overt lesson of time. He worries that the fleeting months and years will leave him "no margin" for his adventure. He discovers time's predatoriness in May's illness and aging: "She looked older because, inevitably, after so many years, she *was* old, or almost; which was of course true in still greater measure of her companion." He is frightened by the bleak possibility that May will die unprivileged to see the enactment of his doom, and he is appalled that as a victim of time he may have been "sold." Indeed, he almost achieves real feeling and knowledge when he experiences the "dread of losing her by some catastrophe": ultimately, though, his brooding and fear are only new forms of his vast emotional expenditure on the road to inaction.

Nevertheless, the time imagery of the third section marks an important milestone on Marcher's journey. After the first chapter launches him on a fresh start and the second, with a countermovement, exposes that start as false, the third chapter reveals an incompatibility between his rationalizations about himself and his deeper, subconscious stresses. James ingeniously suspends Marcher in an inconclusive state of semiapprehension. May's subtle innuendos, the rapacity of the seasons, and the imminence of May's death have so upset his equilibrium that though his mind clings from habit to his own concerns, it is invaded by ambivalences and a new appreciation of May's humanity. He praises her for being "kind" and "beautiful"; he feels "sorry for her"; and he wonders before dismissing the thought, whether her death could be the fatality he has so long expected. He so identifies with her plight that as her health deteriorates, he imagines himself as suffering from "some disfigurement of his outer person." The train of surprises set in motion by her helplessness before time causes him to dread existence without her as an empty prospect.

Clearly, James complicates Marcher's psychological state by showing him as a man of divided sensibility who knows that he does not know what his subconscious is trying to reveal to him; he cannot convert into thought what May has begun to make him grope toward. Marcher thus acts according to earlier, fixed assumptions no longer relevant to his altered situation. He cannot quite grasp the idea that May embodies the primal creativity operating with inevitability in nature but capable of being rejected by narcissistic man. With a greater than usual emphasis, James makes his heroine suggest both a season and a woman, a natural and a human impulse: she affirms an eternal principle of growth and fruition, but as a mere woman, she can only urge by gesture and circumlocution that Marcher break out of himself and live to the fullest reaches of his humanity. Her physical breakdown signals that Marcher is approaching his last chance to "save" himself through her. At the conclusion of the third chapter, however, with her secret intact and her light fading, he appears an unlikely candidate to restore her and himself to health.

With a heavy reliance on light and linkage imagery, James places his climactic April scene in the fourth section of **"The Beast in the Jungle."** The strange couple meet on an April day whose "light" inauspiciously produces a "sadness sharper than the greyest hours of autumn." The fireplace in May's house has no fire or light, and James declares that "it would never see a fire again." The cold fireplace corresponds to the "cold light" in May's eyes and both prefigure a fundamental loss of spirit as Marcher imagines that "her light might at any instant go out." With little light at her disposal (and with the "perfect old French clock" ticking time away), May still sees April as a possible saving link between herself and Marcher. Insisting that "It's never too late," she makes a last effort toward union (as she had made the first) and walks toward him "with a gliding step" that "diminishes the distance between them." The reverberations which James's imagery has by this time achieved lend a special emotional power to her desperate effort at connection: her movement brings her "nearer" and "close" to Marcher and all but speaks, with a language all its own, with "some finer emphasis." Nevertheless, he remains frozen in self-concern and, wondering what she has to give him, maintains his separateness.

The ingenuity of the April scene consists in James's creation of an episode of simultaneous action and nonaction, tragic recognition and comic blindness, springtime possibilities and autumnal bleakness. Marcher, who keeps waiting for the answer to his question, seals his doom on that crucial April day. For May, with her "face shining at him, her contact imponderably pressing," the negative adventure has been all too positive. His climax has the chill of anticlimax, but as he "gape[s] . . . for her revelation," she closes her eyes as if she has seen too much and then gives way to "a slow fine shudder." Although James does not belabor his point, any reader responsive to the pressure of the novella's imagery can interpret the quiet melodrama of May's "slow fine shudder" and Marcher's "fear that she might die without giving him light." She has seen the beast leap while Marcher innocently and expectantly questions the vacancy. In her resultant collapse, she surrenders her function and all hope for him, and when he explicitly asks what has happened, she makes a sphinxlike pronouncement on his doom: "What *was* to." The light she brought to their affair has been extinguished and her bold experiment at linking him to life has been frustrated.

May's dual role as discerning intelligence and as the rejected spirit of spring culminates in two seemingly strained but entirely successful images. The first, May as sphinx, reveals her possession of the secret to the riddle that has puzzled Marcher since the end of the novella's opening pages; aged, and her face marked with innumerable "fine lines" that might have been "etched by a needle," she resembles "a serene and exquisite but impenetrable sphinx" who has attained ultimate wisdom. But the clue to her helpless sagacity is contained in the image almost implausibly intertwined with that of the sphinx. May's faded "green scarf, her wax-white face, and her soft white draperies" make her look like a lily: "She was a sphinx, yet with her white petals and green fronds she might have been a lily too—only an artificial lily, wonderfully imitated and constantly kept, without dust or stain, though not exempt from a slight droop and a complexity of faint creases, under some clear glass bell."

James's imagistic language resolves itself into a more compelling and intellectual drama than is usually conveyed by crude physical action. It leaves no doubt that Marcher has turned the natural woman into an artificial being preserved in an inviolate, inhuman state. Far from being the free germinal impulse she should naturally be, May is an object in a glass cage, a perfect victim of a monstrous egotist afraid to respond to her unspoken pleas.

The fifth section of **"The Beast in the Jungle"** begins with a variation on the sphinx motif and ends with Marcher's obsession with the buried secret (no longer likely to prove a treasure) that he must now exhume without May's help. James also weaves light imagery into his expanding psychological mosaic. However, the most moving motif in the special pathos of this section is that of the goodly bond established in the first section as Marcher's link to new possibilities is now permanently dissolved.

First, however, James refines upon the sphinx image and presents May, in her last conversation with Marcher, as a tender sibyl who speaks in riddles and mysteries. Although James describes her as communicating "with the perfect straightness of a sibyl," Marcher feels that her words are "all beyond him." The scene takes on structure, intellectual play, and emotional density from the energy of its controlling image. May tells Marcher strange and bewildering things that he believes without understanding: for instance, she convinces him that, despite his unawareness of it, he has met his fate; she assures him that he has crossed an unseen line and is now firmly established on "the other side" of his experience. She troubles him by warning him away from the knowledge of what has happened because "it's too much"; yet, she minimizes it by declaring it safely past. Her sibylline utterances leave him with the mournful sense of having had his ordeal and, at the same time, having been cheated of it. He suspects her of telling him that "his light has failed" but he ambivalently feels that as she speaks, "some light, hitherto hidden, had shimmered across his vision."

May's death functions as an ironic climax of the linking imagery by leaving Marcher stranded like some Hawthornian outcast of the universe. As if to emphasize the consequences of his mock hero's insensitivity to May's appeals, James shows him as having less claim to be one of her mourners than "the stupidest fourth cousin"; he is bereft, without the dignity of being able to claim any relationship with the woman who has been his mainstay. In terms of hard, practical reality, he and May had had no bond, no real intimacy. So Marcher deplores his outcast state, his banishment to the jungle that has grown more "spacious," stilled, and vacant. Even his visit to May's grave does not change his condition: it is as if the woman who offered him a link with life at Weatherend has broken all connection with him as "her two names [on the tombstone] became a pair of eyes that didn't know him."

The fifth section concludes with intermingled light and burial images that have the ring of a final verdict—Marcher beats "his forehead against the fact of the secret" kept in the grave and, in a bitter echo of May's Weatherend confession when a "light broke for him," now "no palest light broke." Nevertheless, James plants clues that these negative images will be replaced by unnaturally active ones: that his protagonist will see a lurid light, make an unexpected and catastrophic connection, and unearth a new and terrible "treasure." Before her death, May had been distressed that Marcher might be close to seeing his own folly and had put him off with kind ruses. But the accumulating data of his subconscious life will belatedly force him to see what she has seen. In fact, in his final colloquy with May, a "light . . . shimmered across his vision" only to be lost in darkness. Before it vanished, however, "the gleam had already become for him an idea" that would take the shape of a beastly nemesis.

In the last section, James arrives at his psychological climax by recapitulating the major motifs of his novella: The fall day of the concluding graveyard scene recalls the dim October light at Weatherend, where Marcher's alliance with May began; light, however, returns with phantasmagoric effect; the riddle of the buried, sphinxlike woman is spelled out with brutal distinctness; and the April horror Marcher had once failed to see weirdly returns in the deadness of the autumn.

James sets the scene of his protagonist's epiphany in a "garden of death," where Marcher rests "on the low stone table that bore May Bartram's name." Having severed all connection with the world and even with himself, Marcher revisits the cemetery to renew his tie with "the creature beneath the sod" and to get "back into his own presence"; he is ready for the shock given him by a grief-stricken man at a nearby grave, a man whose "ravaged" face expresses the full meaning of the goodly bond. What the sphinxlike woman had tried to tell Marcher becomes manifest: "The sight that had just met his eyes named to him, as in letters of quick flame, something he had utterly, insanely missed." Obviously an alter ego who is blest in spite of his affliction, the mourner conveys a message that Marcher might have learned from Pompeii, from May's constant movement toward him, and from her once bright and then failing light. Significantly, Marcher's enlightenment comes as images of light succeed one another with ghastly coruscations: James refers to "a train of fire," a meaning which "flared," a "smoky torch," an "illumination" that "blazed to the zenith."

As already noted, the opening scene at Weatherend, like the final episode, takes place in the fall of the year "when the leaves were thick in the alleys." The major difference between the two scenes, however, is the difference between a promising prospect and a bitter harvest. May, the original light-bringer and spirit of the "goodly bond," is dead, and the fate she could not save Marcher from has been realized. The last incident also resembles and contrasts with the earlier April scene in section four: April, the symbol of possible connection and actual separation, returns as a surrogate for May and functions as the law of retribution. Moreover, Marcher's imaginary re-creation of the April day ironically completes James's book of hours and seasons with the conversion of a negative adventure into charged sensation. In direct contrast to the earlier April scene, the concluding fall-April episode contains an outburst of melodramatic imagery. The hush becomes a rush, Marcher's avoidances end in confrontation, and his deferred expectations shape themselves into an abnormal reality. In describing the "horror of awakening," James does not sentimentally grant his protagonist a reprieve or allow the violated May to make a redemptive speech from the grave: sickened with self-knowledge, Marcher experiences the full measure of his fate, and the beast, thwarted once, makes his destined leap.

There may, initially, seem to be some imagistic incongruity in the leap of the beast as the culmination of Marcher's anxious, self-probing inactivity and negation. It is almost as if an introspective drama has flared into histrionics. Superficially viewed, James's imagistic drama may have seemed to point to a conclusion in which his protagonist would wither into bewildered nihilism. The failed light, the lost connection, the buried secret, and the sphinxian double entendre have, however, given birth to half-formed alarms and insights in Marcher's subconscious. The beast, in a sense, is the emergence of those alarms to the level of awareness. James's resolution of his nonhero's negative quest with a sensational hallucinatory "action" does not reverse the drift of his imagistic narrative. He undoubtedly designed his ending to show that Marcher, the skillful evader, cannot in the logic of events escape the consequences of his inaction. Concealed as long as Marcher is not ready to see him, the beast represents, as a metaphor of reality, the shocked recognition of self-devastation. It represents, too, the massed power of those primal energies Marcher had repressed in his offense against the spirit of May and time. In a sense, May, who in her human embodiment wished to protect him from knowledge, cannot shield him from his own nature, which had been slowly organizing a surge of energy in the covert lairs of his being. The beast, then, is only the active climactic image in a book of images remarkable for their intellectual content, emotional depth, and narrative accumulation of suspense and movement. (pp. 351-67)

James W. Gargano, "Imagery as Action in 'The Beast in the Jungle'," in Arizona Quarterly, *Vol. 42, No. 4, Winter, 1986, pp. 351-67.*

Lauren T. Cowdery (essay date 1986)

[*In the following essay, Cowdery explains James's technique of foreshortening in* Julia Bride.]

In the preface to ***Julia Bride*** in the New York Edition, James discusses this tale as an attempt to make "a majestic mass" of subject matter "turn round in a *nouvelle.*" First published in March-April 1908, ***Julia Bride*** was the most recently written of the nouvelles which James discussed in the prefaces as examples of their genre. While James did not have much distance from this tale, he did have his intention fresh in his mind. At best, this work is the product of his maturest conception of the possibilities of the nouvelle. ***Julia Bride*** is a good introductory example of the interrelation of structure and subject in James's nouvelle because only one "predominant artifice" of structure—foreshortening—is employed. In addition, the formal subject of the nouvelle is clearly identified in the preface: the social freedom of modern American girls to get engaged and "disengaged" without expecting to feel any effects. James sees this false freedom as a peril not because it savors of promiscuity; he fashions a main character who is winningly naive and sexually unscathed by her adventures in this line. Rather, the danger of making and breaking vows threatens personal integrity and mutual trust. In *The American Scene,* the same spectacle causes James to harangue bitterly. Here it evokes wonder: mingled pity and laughter at the verge of tears at the absurdity and waste to which this behavior can lead.

James's subject is deadly serious: a denial of continuity and responsibility in personal relationships results in social fragmentation and personal isolation. The comedy in the telling, however, minimizes the personal importance of the main character while it emphasizes the wider implications of the story. In addition, foreshortening as a technique of development mediates between the serious and the comic in this tale. According to James, foreshortening creates an aura of immediacy by making sequential, mimetic narrative into what he describes as soup or stew. Much of ***Julia Bride*** is most certainly narrative soup: the time scheme is violently disrupted and the action is blurred and distanced when chance remarks cause reverberations of feeling and reminiscence in the observer's mind. James claims in the preface that his goal is to imitate in literature the effect of romantic intuition of the things "we never *can* directly know," what he calls "achieved iridescence from within."

The plot of ***Julia Bride*** is ostensibly the machinations of a girl to get an admirer to propose. Julia Bride is the stunningly beautiful daughter of a mother who is also a famous beauty. Julia has won the admiration of Basil French, the modest and intelligent scion of the most wealthy and exclusive of New York families, and a man whose good qualities she truly values. Unfortunately, Julia and her mother come from the Wild West, where the mother has been divorced three times and the daughter has already broken six engagements, unaware that she was following a very poor example. Basil is honest and he is in love, but he has heard rumors and he hesitates. As the tale opens, Julia is about to be awakened to her true social position and to the enormity of the transgressions she childishly and thoughtlessly committed.

The action consists of two meetings which take place in the space of a few days. In the first scene, having just bid goodbye to Basil at the entrance to the Metropolitan Museum of Art (where they meet as if on neutral territory), Julia turns to chat with an old friend whom she has met by chance: her mother's second-to-last husband, Mr. Pitman. The sight of him triggers her memory, and she is filled with bitterness against her mother for undervaluing him, for treating him badly, and most of all for raising Julia herself so poorly. On the spur of the moment, she asks him for help: he is such a good-natured person and the closest thing she has to a father. Julia fears that her mother's divorces have hurt her own respectability: would Pitman lie and circulate a rumor that he treated her mother badly, so that the divorcé might receive some very useful sympathy? Unfortunately, Mr. Pitman needs social approval, too. He is about to propose to a wealthy widow who is also uncomfortable about that same divorce, and he asks Julia to exonerate him by telling the truth about the past. Julia is disappointed but she agrees, and her beauty and sweetness convince the widow immediately.

Determined to find masculine protection, Julia next asks her last fiancé to deny that they were ever associated. Floridly handsome Murray Brush had jilted Julia and left for Europe when it became clear that she had no dowry; he is recently returned. Now they arrange to meet in Central Park, and Julia is startled by Murray's enthusiasm for her plan to whitewash them both—and soon is sickened to discover the reason. Murray is about to marry rich but plain and unfashionable Mary Lindeck, a woman who would be glad to lie if that were the price to be introduced into the exclusive circle of the Frenches—a fact the women of the French family know quite well. Unable to find disinterested aid from reliable sources, Julia realizes that her cause is lost. She has imbibed enough of Basil's idealism and his family's fastidiousness to admire him for mistrusting her, and she gives him up with a sob of adoration.

Out of this slender farce James draws a complex of inferences and impressions through narrative technique. The key to James's management of his material is the tactic of foreshortening. In the preface he explains that foreshortening is not merely "harking back to make up," nor is it a way to leap over the passage of uneventful years. To resolve James's method into the "alternation between summary and scene," as does Kirshna Vaid in *Technique in the Tales of Henry James,* and then to conclude that in the more "compressed" tales, "James often resorts to summary more than scene," is to ignore James's search for "that effect of the distinctively rich presentation," what he calls "iridescence from within." He defines foreshortening by using the example of ***Julia Bride,*** which

> is "foreshortened" to within an inch of her life. . . . [The connections], the rest of the quantity of life, press in, . . . but, restricted as the whole thing is to implications and involutions only, they prevail at best by indirectness. . . . The effect presumably sought is by making us conceive and respond to them, making us feel, taste, smell and enjoy them, without our really knowing why or how. Full-fed statement here . . .—the imaged résumé of as many of the vivifying elements as may be coherently packed into an image at once—is the predominant artifice [of ***Julia Bride***].

This explanation echoes James's definition of the romantic

in the preface to *The American:* "The romantic stands, on the other hand, for the things that, with all the faculties in the world, all the wealth and all the courage and all the wit and all the adventure, we never *can* directly know; the things that can reach us only through the beautiful circuit and subterfuge of our thought and our desire." "Making us respond" to "the rest of the quantity of life" in an "imaged résumé," "making us feel, taste, smell and enjoy [the quantity and its implications], without our really knowing why or how" is using literature as a vehicle to disseminate romantic knowledge, or at least to imitate the process by which such knowledge is gained. While the anecdote tells the chain of causes, effects, and surprises which comprise "real" experience, "the things we cannot possibly *not* know, sooner or later in one way or another," the province of the nouvelle is the romantic, and its narrative device is foreshortening.

According to the preface, James felt that his choice of "predominant artifice" for ***Julia Bride*** held good and that the nouvelle was a success. As he recalls in the preface, the major problem of the composition of this tale was to devise a way to make the "developmental subject" and its ramifications, altogether a "majestic mass," "turn round in a nouvelle." "The dense thing to be clarified" in ***Julia Bride*** is an aspect of the American scene James observed when he returned to America in 1904.

> I had had, for any confidence, to make it out to myself that my little frisking haunter, under private stress, of the New York public scene, was related with a certain intensity to the world about her; so that her case might lose itself promptly enough in a complexus of larger and stranger cases—even in the very air. . . . What if she were the silver key, tiny in itself, that would unlock a treasure?—the treasure of a whole view of manners and morals, a whole range of American social aspects?

When he reread the tale, James listened for and believed he heard "the note of multitudinous reference," the "note" of the nouvelle he describes in the preface to **"The Author of Beltraffio,"** where he says that such "Connections . . . represent the whole sense of the matter" in nouvelles. It seemed to him that the implications overshadow the main character, who "is not particularly important in herself." Thus this tale differs in form from the anecdote, "the first of [whose] duties is to point directly to the person whom it so distinguishes [to whom an event 'oddly happened']." James is proud of this nouvelle because he believes it has "achieved irridescence" and because it successfully develops a subject with complex ramifications. In a tone of comic depreciation which runs throughout the prefatory comment, James addresses the problem of genre. He is well aware of the difficulty of writing in a form predicated on the intention to communicate indirectly many things which are never actually said. The writer may end up saying nothing, or at best telling a slight tale with none of the promised "multitudinous reference"—a failure as an anecdote also, since the plot is obscured and the main character undistinguished. James makes it clear in the preface that he knows just how silly he would look if ***Julia Bride*** failed him after all this fanfare. "What I have called, for ***Julia Bride,*** my predicament [is] . . . the consciousness, in that connexion, but of finding myself, after so many years astride the silver-shod, sober-paced, short-stepping but oh so hugely nosing, so tenderly and yearningly and ruefully sniffing, grey mule of the 'few thousand words,' ridiculously back where I had started." James humorously admits his fear: while he pretends to ride his high horse, to prance and curvet and caracole on a nouvelle, he might actually be riding the same old mule—a formless short tale with no genre, only a word count. For a moment he worries that he doesn't even have a mule to ride, ***Julia Bride*** being a complete debacle. Perhaps, he suggests, he is like "Moses Primrose welcomed home from the Fair," cozened out of his tired horse when he was bargaining for a new one. Goldsmith's Moses returned home on foot, as did the other idealistic failure who comes to James's mind, "limping Don Quixote assisted through his castle-gate and showing but thankless bruises for laurels." Even as he expresses all these comic misgivings, however, James reprints ***Julia Bride*** for the third time in two years. Like other writers whose prefaces are exaggerated apologies for offenses never committed—Goldsmith and Cervantes among them—James had confidence in his own craftsmanship. What he didn't trust was the inclination of his readership to accept the abstruser of his narrative experiments.

James's use of the nouvelle depended on his belief that he had an appropriately developmental subject—one with wide ramifications. In the preface, James identifies his theme as the American "social tone at large, the manners, habits and ideals" of the land of freedom, and the particular freedom whose "attendant signs and appreciable effects" concern him here is the freedom to "get engaged, disengaged and re-engaged."

As James develops his theme in ***Julia Bride,*** a society that condones breaking engagements on a large scale is a chaos, for it fails to encourage responsibility and continuity. Mrs. Connery cum Pitman cum Bride not only has made a travesty of marriage, she has ultimately sacrificed her identity to this energetic social climbing. Her failure of responsibility is shared by her shiftless mates, who are absent, apparently abdicating in favor of business or mere obscurity. As Julia looks backward in a fever of sudden shame, her education at the hands of her mother looks bad as well as "crazy." She remembers "all the folly and vanity and vulgarity, the lies, the perversities, the falsification of all life in the interest of who could say what wretched frivolity, what preposterous policy, amid which she [Julia] had been condemned so ignorantly, so pitifully to sit, to walk, to grope, to flounder, from the very dawn of her consciousness." Julia's mother has "incredibly allowed" and "insanely fostered" Julia's own "frivolity"—her tendency to make and break engagements in imitation of her mother's mobility. Ultimately, their frivolity has isolated them, has erected what Julia perceives as a social cage around them. Or is the frivolity not a cause but a result of the social cage? In her fever to place blame for her embarrassment on someone else, Julia not only blames her mother for being a sleek, showy animal with no sense of decency, but also blames everyone else, the spectators, for viewing the antics of the parent and child as if they were a circus

Henry James, about 1905.

attraction. For Julia and her mother have had a ready entrance into society—but only on the footing of planned entertainment.

> When you were as pretty as that you could, by the whole idiotic consensus, be nothing *but* pretty; and when you were nothing "but" pretty you could get into nothing but tight places, out of which you could then scramble by nothing but masses of fibs. . . . Every one had thrust upon them, had imposed upon them as by a great cruel conspiracy, their silliest possibilities; fencing them in to these, and so not only shutting them out from others, but mounting guard at the fence, walking round and round outside it to see they didn't escape, and admiring them, talking to them, through the rails, in mere terms of chaff, terms of chucked cakes and apples—as if they had been antelopes or zebras, or even some superior sort of performing, of dancing, bear.

Through Julia's indignation James heaps opprobrium on both the morally deficient mother *and* the "idiotic consensus" that can find such a woman and her predicaments entertaining or socially convenient. Furthermore, the whole society suffers from to say the least a lack of imagination if it can assign to such a bright spirit as Julia's the role of being "nothing but pretty." The imagery of the passage above is carefully developed. Julia remembers being maneuvered into "tight places"—that is, being pursued as an object of sexual desire. Somehow she didn't run in the right direction, or else the maze in which she found herself had no exit in the first place. By the end of the passage, the "tight places" become a cage—Julia's youth is spent living out her "silliest possibilities" while opportunities to expand and change are deliberately closed to her by people with the power to do so. James describes Julia as the victim of sexual discrimination, as her society limits her growth, treats her as entertainment, and condescends to her. In fact, much of the energy and drive of this tale, apparent especially in the imagery, has its source in James's exasperation with just this "great cruel conspiracy" which has caged a young woman while touting her American freedom. It is in ironies like this that Julia Bride is a representative American. Julia is beginning to realize that she has been cut off from genuine relations with people.

According to the mother's "graces and morals," everything is all right, but according to Julia's new value system, in which the highest good is to be a "decent girl," everything is all wrong. For Julia, decency means integrity, a quality which is so conspicuously absent from the mother's composition that she hardly has an identity at all. Her behavior is characterized as sudden and erratic, her motives are indecipherable, and she is a chronic liar. Not surprisingly, she remains nameless in the story, known only by the name of the establishment to which she is temporarily connected. Since litigation is about to begin again, she is only provisionally Mrs. Connery. Her child has been thrown out into the "public scene," and the orphan dreams of a home like the expensively stocked Metropolitan Museum of Art. But the Museum is only a "mockery of art and 'style' and security;" these, like charity, should begin at home, while the Museum collection is imported, and pirated, at that. Thus, Julia is a displaced person in more ways than one. She seems to need a father to defend her honor, since she has no parent to regulate her behavior—but in America, apparently, there aren't enough honorable men to go around. Should she find a defender, it is still obscure of what Julia's honor consists, considering how often she has forsworn herself. In any case, to defend Julia's honor would be to patronize the freeborn American girl, and in so doing compromise her yet more seriously. As the ironies mount, Julia's choices dwindle, and she seems more caged than ever.

Now Julia wants to be known as a "decent girl," and she refuses to lie about her past; she does, however, hope that someone else will lie for her and rewrite her history. The actors in the history are scattered, and each is intent on rewriting it in a different way. To tell Basil French the truth, Julia would have to admit, at the very least, that the events of her past lack continuity. The past of a person of integrity testifies to her good character; Julia's past suggests that she is a thoughtless jilt. Touched by her honest contrition, Mr. Pitman ingenuously advises Julia to swear by herself, like Shakespeare's Romeo.

> "And all the while, don't you see? There's no one to speak *for* me."

> It would have touched a harder heart than her loose friend's to note the final flush of clairvoyance witnessing this assertion and under which her eyes shone as with the rush of quick tears. He stared at her, and what this did for the deep charm of her prettiness. . . . "But can't you—lovely as you are, you beautiful thing!—speak for yourself?"

But Julia, unfortunately, has been inconstant as the moon, withdrawing promises and renouncing the past six times already; now she wants to renounce the past a seventh time. Thus, whether or not divorce and jilting are normal practices "all off in North Dakota" and how that will shape America are not topics pursued in detail in this tale. Like Daisy Miller, Julia Bride has left her native social circle and has entered another society where she is an exception. Julia does not represent a norm of American manners: the marriage market is a free-for-all in this tale, with every character convinced that his or her way is the best for America. Julia certainly doesn't set a trend for the social circle which seems to have the widest influence. The "American social aspects" of ***Julia Bride*** are the *causes* of Julia's problem—isolation—and not the results. Julia's problem is personal, and at the same time its implications are widespread, and therein lies its "multitudinous reference." Rather than following a line of development which would fill in details about the effect of divorce on the American family, James is interested in questions about the nature of the self, its relation to the past, and the way it makes discoveries about its limiting conditions.

Thus, despite James's deprecating comments which suggest that Julia Bride is out of place in the volume of the New York Edition which contains John Marcher and George Stransom, she is just as closely related to them as she is to Pandora Day and Francina Dosson. Like these men, Julia has not yet lived, and her story tells how, in the central experience of her life, she comes to understand her fate. I have indicated already how James dismisses her previous actions as morally and emotionally immature, the undisciplined exhuberance of American youth. Julia's engagements may have exercised her, but they did not educate her; she has learned nothing from each successive break. What awakens Julia to responsibility, social sensitivity, passion, and idealism—everything that is perception to Henry James—is a chance occurrence, her introduction to Basil French. Like Lambert Strether, Julia responds to an embodiment of culture because she has the seed of development in her character.

In the tale, the seed grows and bears fruit. As Julia begins to reflect on herself, she cannot help reflecting on those who molded her. We watch this process as it occurs:

> Something in the girl's vision of her quondam stepfather as still comparatively young—with *the confusion, the immense element of rectification, not to say of rank disproof* that it introduced into Mrs. Connery's favorite picture of her own injured past—all this worked, even at the moment, to quicken once more the clearness and harshness of judgement, the retrospective disgust, as she might have called it, that had of late grown up in her. (my emphasis)

Julia's eyes grow wider and wider as she discovers more reasons to break with her past. But Julia is maturing, not being reincarnated. She has had intimations of her present convictions; there is a thread of consistency: "It was she herself who, for so long, with her retained impression, had been right about him [Mr. Pitman]; and the rectification he represented had *all* shone out of him, ten minutes before . . . " James describes Julia's situation in a pun: she is both "right" and in need of "rectification." Thus the fledgling can be already familiar with Murray Brush's "whole charming coarse personality" and yet when she acts, still leave "gaps of connection" between her intimations and her convictions. The mistake from which Julia finally begins to learn is the mistake of applying to Brush for help in her desperation. The rudiments of "exquisite perceptions and proprieties" she learns from Basil French.

Basil erupts into Julia's life, bringing with him a standard of perfection which is both desirable and harmful: desirable because it has awakened her perception and revealed truth, but harmful because it completes the displacement her parents began. "It was a queer service Basil was going to have rendered her, this having made everything she had ever done impossible, if he wasn't going to give her a new chance." Julia's present habits and actions are "impossible"—certainly impossible to continue doing, and also apparently impossible to admit ever having done. New chances are rare in James, and they are only available to people who acknowledge and embrace their own past. Julia, still in transition between old standards and new, makes her bid for a new chance using old methods. Julia resists temptation long enough to tell the truth to help Mr. Pitman, but eventually she succumbs by asking Murray Brush to lie for her. She learns enough from the experience to understand her mistake, but she is not therefore transformed into the proper bride for Basil French. Julia at the end is still Julia, "haunter, under private stress, of the New York public scene." Her "jolly corner" is the Metropolitan Museum of Art, and Central Park is peopled with the ghosts of her past. First her family home was dissolved, and now she must "dodge" the "ghosts" that have taken possession of her refuge. Poor Julia has been dispossessed, it seems, of both time and space.

"Basil's queer service" has indeed been to deprive Julia of a conventional past and future. The fragmentary past must be rejected, and the cohesive, informed future holds no opportunity for action. Like Strether and Marcher, Julia is estranged from her time: she loves too late, and she learns to perceive at the moment when she can no longer act. In important ways and despite differences of tone, the thematic structure of ***Julia Bride*** is almost identical to that of **"The Beast in the Jungle."** Both Julia and Marcher are romantic egotists who have difficulties coping with the passage of time, the union of cause and consequence they create as well as suffer. Their defiance has an uncanny effect on their experience, and the forms in which their tales are told are experiments in narrative technique. Both tales concern awaited events, weddings, which never occur. What happens instead is endless preparation—preparation cut short by the sudden revelation of the truth that the event will not happen. The revelation, the "spring of the Beast," as James calls it, usurps the function of the event. The deluded activity of the main character does not contribute to, create, or prepare for the revelation; the truth breaks on the character like an equivocal gift of divine grace. The action of the past is at once explained and condemned in the light of the new truth; once rejected, the past is a mistake that does not even have the stature of salutary experience. The passing time brings no progress, only suspense, and the answer to the character's question finally comes in a flash of clairvoyance that reveals the barren future as well as the barren past. In these stories, the passage of time does not bring with it normal ripening and fruition, and so these tales might be termed "anti-anecdotes." What does not occur cannot distinguish a main character, exercise his or her powers, or fix his or her identity the way that events do in anecdotes. Thus, while all the other characters of ***Julia Bride*** have names which are as obvious as the names in *Pilgrim's Progress,* Julia alone has a name which doesn't fit, for she will never be a bride. To discover the powers and develop the identity of such a character in such a fix, James needed to experiment with narrative structure.

Carrying such a heavy burden of dark implication, ***Julia Bride*** could have been fashioned into a drama of human suffering and even seemed for a while to be the material of a novel. Both the comic tone and the form, however, result from James's choice to focus on the workings of Julia's mind: her right feeling, the muddle of her outrageous rationalizing, and her growing perception of truth. The resulting mixture of opposites, the mixture of existential crisis and slapstick farce, is characteristic of James, who claimed "the sense of an ampler comedy in human things" and admitted to a perversity that goaded him to fix on the most demanding narrative forms to develop his ideas. In the preface to the following volume, he dramatizes himself being teased for "misplaced drolling" in his account of the exploits and death of Daisy Miller. In his defense he claims that the drolling is a function of "helpful imagination" while he makes a cut at "the original grossness of readers." His overall intent, he explains, is to mystify the reader's judgment, and the humor functions to that end. In ***Julia Bride,*** James also uses humor to suspend instant, prejudiced judgment so that he can develop freely a complex of paradoxical implications. Humor distances the reader from the familiar subject and helps to create sympathy for the unlucky clown. By surprising and teasing readers out of their prejudices, comic treatment contributes to the development of the nouvelle.

In comparison to the comedy in the other three examples of James's nouvelle, the comedy of ***Julia Bride*** is broad slapstick. James's main resource is exaggeration: Julia has not one "disengagement" to live down but six, in addition to her mother's three divorces and one additional separation. The social causes and personal effects of Julia's situation would be the same should she have jilted only once. The outrageously high number, however, makes it clear from the start not only that the drama is farcical—not realistic—but also that Julia is doomed to failure: in other words, that the tale will be both funny and pathetic. In addition, as James explains in the preface, Julia is designed to be a clown. She has the clown's indefatigable resiliency, always bouncing back full of chatter and energy. What is her plan to establish a reputation as a decent girl? "If there had only been some one to (as it were) 'deny everything' the situation might yet be saved." Julia's plan to proliferate lies is morally unsound—but multiplied six times it becomes absurd, and the crazy logic of Julia's plotting takes on an interest of its own.

> "*Qui s'excuse s'accuse,* don't they say?—so that do you see me breaking out to him [Basil], unprovoked, with four or five what-do-you-call-'ems, the things mother used to have to prove in Court, a set of neat little 'alibis' in a row? How can I get hold of so *many* precious gentlemen, to turn them on? How can *they* want everything fished up?"
>
> She paused for her climax, in the intensity of these considerations. . . .

When Mr. Pitman affirms that the young men would be glad to help, he somehow offends the honor Julia is trying to rescue. "[They'd be] glad to swear they never had anything to do with such a creature? Then I'd be glad to swear they had lots!" Mr. Pitman is bewildered: "Why, my love, they've got to swear either one thing or the other." Julia's reasoning careens onward, however: " 'He knows about Murray Brush. The others'—and her pretty white-gloved hands and charming pink shoulders gave them up—'may go hang!' " Julia's gloved hands and pretty shoulders might take in an entranced Basil—they already have, to a certain extent—but pink and white are no defense against a counterattack by Mrs. George Maule, the "cat" capable of "fishing up" as much evidence as she needs to blacken Julia's reputation. James's real accomplishment is the way he keeps us hoping for this Francina Dosson's success when the odds against her are overwhelming and her strategy is patently absurd. Ultimately, like so many other of James's heroines, Julia may lose her campaign, but she has gained something precious in what she has come to understand. She is refreshingly different in that there is nothing blighted about her; we come to rely on her vitality and her ability to bounce back.

Unlike **"The Coxon Fund,"** whose narrator serves as a guide among paradoxes of humor and pathos, ***Julia Bride*** relies on immediate effects. Much of the drolling manifests itself in the imagery, as when James first introduces Julia's problem to the reader:

> The crazy divorces only, or the half-dozen successive and still crazier engagements only—gathered fruit, bitter fruit, of her own incredibly allowed, her own insanely fostered frivolity—either of these two groups of skeletons at the banquet might singly be dealt with; but the combination, the fact of each party's having been so mixed-up with whatever was least presentable for the other, the fact of their having so shockingly amused themselves together, made all present steering resemble the classic middle course between Scylla and Charybdis.

While the passage makes the serious point that Julia's portion is "bitter fruit," it goes on to liken her family secrets to nine jolly skeletons who crowd into the proverbial banquet uninvited and then present a seating problem. Thus the comic mode is the means by which James introduces elements of the bizarre into the tale. By incorporating ranks of skeletons, circus animals, and views from the air and underwater, he constantly keeps his reader in unfamiliar territory. His high-spirited, playful tone, used to describe a high-spirited, energetic heroine, helps to create confidence in the moral depth of this scatterbrained character, confidence which is crucially important to the success of the nouvelle. Julia fends off heavy blows, and the reader needs an assurance that she will survive.

As James discusses the theoretical underpinnings of this tale in the preface, however, the discussion of character takes an important twist. After he has created this engaging, zany heroine, he continues to insist that she is *not* the main interest of the story. She is a "very small reflector, which is of absolutely minimum size for its task," reflecting "a quite 'unlikely' amount . . . of the movement of life." Julia is not so much an example as a point of departure. For all its power to arouse frightening visions of American alienation, her plight must not be a distraction, as it would be if she were unable to bounce back. Thus, because of the comic treatment, "the case might lose itself promptly enough in a complexus of larger and stranger cases." Comedy is essential here in that it makes possible nouvellistic "development."

Thus, in ***Julia Bride,*** we see James treating his theme in a straightforward manner—straightforward insofar as he suits a devious method to a devious intent. In "The Story-Teller at Large: Mr. Henry Harland," an essay written in 1898, just three years before ***Julia Bride,*** James described the distinction between the anecdote and the nouvelle that served as a basis for his own work of this period.

> Are there not two quite distinct effects to be produced by this rigour of brevity? . . . The one with which we are most familiar is that of the detached incident, single and sharp, as clear as a pistol-shot; the other, of rarer performance, is that of the impression, comparatively generalized—simplified, foreshortened, reduced to a particular perspective—of a complexity or a continuity. The former is an adventure comparatively safe, in which you have, for the most part, but to put one foot after the other. It is just the risks of the latter, on the contrary, that make the best of the sport.

Julia Bride, so James says in the preface, is foreshortened "to within an inch of her life," and he is right. The time and action are so diffused that it is hard to locate the plot in the text. It is difficult to separate Julia's present from the memories and forebodings which intrude on it so often. The two conversations of the two days are events which occur in the present, but they are curiously underplayed and uninteresting, composed for the most part of reminiscence and explanation of background we already know. Our expectations concerning dialogue are flagrantly violated as potentially interesting scenes are suppressed and reported indirectly. Time itself does not proceed at a steady rate, but doubles back so that incidents seem to repeat, and the order in which they occur is obscured. Much of the story is told in the conditional voice, which is even used to express Julia's thoughts and impulses. Most of Julia's history and fate exists outside the boundaries of the narrative. What is left inside? "It is all a matter of odds and ends recovered and interpreted. The 'story' is nothing, the subject everything," James continues in the essay ostensibly on Harland. Such bravado needs to be backed by performance. "[The risks] are naturally—given the generally reduced scale—immense, for nothing is less intelligible than bad foreshortening, which, if it fails to mean everything intended, means less than nothing." In ***Julia Bride,*** James succeeded in making his subject expressive in that we know precisely how he feels about the American scene in many of its general aspects. The way he accomplished that subterfuge is one of the distinguishing techniques of the nouvelle.

Foreshortening is another way to create the impression of immediacy. An analogy may be helpful: foreshortening is to drama as free indirect discourse is to quotation in that each imitates the spirit and not the letter of an event. In fact, foreshortening, like free indirect discourse, is faithfully mimetic to reality in practically all aspects but one: they both make free with time. "Story" is suppressed so that theme and character may be emphasized; the "when" and the "where," accidence and contingency, are refined out of the textual passage in favor of the "how" and the "why." Strictly speaking, without the "when" and the "where," a passage of narrative cannot be dramatic, but that does not mean that it is therefore reduced to summary or to authorial explanation.

> [They had] been always so perfectly pink and white, so perfectly possessed of clothes, so perfectly splendid, so perfectly idiotic. . . . Such were the data Basil French's inquiry would elicit: her own six engagements and her mother's three nullified marriages—nine nice distinct little horrors in all. What on earth was to be done about them?

The passage describes Julia's condition and preoccupation, but it does not present her thoughts at any specific moment. "Such were the data" is a formula for simple authorial intrusion and explanation, yet there is no "narrative voice"—the idiom as well as the sentiment we hear is Julia's. There are no clear boundaries between narration and dialogue, and no temporal context at all for this passage. Here we have a sample of James's narrative soup. Once "the whole" has been "set . . . to simmer, to stew, or whatever," any ingredient, "exposed . . . to a new and richer saturation," has "its prime identity destroyed."

Foreshortening dramatizes thematic issues obliquely rather than directly. In Julia Bride's history, there is material for many episodes: the divorce of the Pitmans, the meeting of Julia and Basil, the fatal tea party at Julia's flat. In his preface, James makes much of the fact that the principal actors in these episodes of Julia's life are absent from the nouvelle. His point is not to quibble about how important a character must be to participate in truly dramatic anecdotal action. The obvious answer is that every relation has its own interest, and it is foolish to argue with a plot for failing to be another plot. Rather, ***Julia Bride*** is restricted "to implications and involutions only" because Julia must deal with signs, not with people. Julia is trying to make her way in a woman's world; every man she must deal with is only the representative of a woman. Mr. Pitman has been permanently affected by Julia's mother, and his plans are determined by Mrs. Drack; Mary Lindeck's shadow darkens Murray Brush's countenance; and even Basil French is not so problematic as his sisters and their friends. In fact, James shows Julia's cage being policed by women with an investment in the system as it is. The men Julia approaches are envoys of absent powers, envoys with messages, but not empowered to negotiate. Julia's fate depends on her relation to the powers; her personal relations with the envoys are interesting but unofficial. Thus, the theme and the subject of ***Julia Bride*** find themselves expressed in a plot of two days' duration involving characters who are intrinsically secondary. Julia is dispossessed once more, this time in literary terms: she acts out her dramatic hour at long distance from the main agents of her fate.

As James strives to make immediate his "subject," not his "story," the first items to be sacrificed are the claims that the envoys make to participation in the action: the two conversations in the precincts of the Museum and in Central Park.

> Though her friend, and though *his* friend, were both saying things, many things and perhaps quite wonderful things, she had no free attention for them and was only rising and soaring.

> At present, however, as everything was for her at first deadened and vague, true to the general effect of sounds and motions in water, she couldn't have said afterwards what words she spoke, what face she showed, what impression she made. . . .

Clearly, James is more interested in Julia's perception of her general condition than of any specific, immediate situation. Often the dialogue that is reported is strangely without interest because it has been undercut by previous passages of free indirect discourse. Julia's dialogues with Mr. Pitman and Murray Brush seem like background for passages of foreshortening—not, as one might expect, the reverse. The total effect is not temporally progressive, though "static" would be an unfortunate term to apply here. The foreshortened passage is active enough, but it is the activity of "development," not of "story."

In the preface to **"The Author of Beltraffio,"** James distinguishes between the anecdote and the nouvelle by stating that in order to develop the subject of the former, he must "follow it as much as possible from its outer edge in, rather than from its centre outward," that being the method of developing a nouvelle. Literally at the center of the first section of ***Julia Bride*** is a statement about Julia's condition that sends out a "swift wave" of resonance like a pebble thrown into a pool:

> "Why, you know, you've grown up so lovely—you're the prettiest girl I've ever seen!" Of course she was the prettiest girl he had ever seen; she was the prettiest girl people much more privileged than he had ever seen; since when hadn't she been passing for the prettiest girl anyone had ever seen? She had lived in that, from far back, from year to year, from day to day and from hour to hour—she had lived for it and literally *by* it, as who should say; but Mr. Pitman was somehow more illuminating than he knew.

The iteration of the sentences mimics the echoes in Julia's past. Julia's beauty is important; it is decisive. She says she had lived "in" it and "for" it and "by" it in a parody of the Declaration of Independence, and perhaps even of the Doxology. Her prettiness accounts for her history, for the social pressure which shaped her past and for the opportunity which shapes her present. The extended image of the cage makes it clear what kind of treatment Julia has received because of her feminine prettiness. Playing two games at once, James makes his criticism of society, pointing out the harmful mixture of license and repression which forms the lives of some American women, and at the same time he treats the conditions as a given in the limited experience of his central observer. What, after all, was the mark and sign of the middle-class American woman of the Gilded Age but her inexorable fashion and her much acclaimed beauty? Seen from Julia's point of view, her own beauty is somehow the cause of her problems. She feels, and we are invited to feel with her, that she has been cast out alone, and that her effect on others is somehow uncanny. More important than the quality of her character, Julia discovers, the quality of her appearance has determined her relations with those around her.

The articulation of this truth shapes the narrative form of section 1. It has such disruptive force that it stops time completely until the end of the section and causes the narration to double back twice. The immediate effect of the statement is to make Julia repeat an observation, one that she made when she first recognized Mr. Pitman across the gallery: she can see reflected in him how wrong her mother was in many ways. Suddenly the repetition becomes a flashback, and we are conveyed back to "ten minutes before" the tale started:

> the rectification he represented had *all* shone out of him, ten minutes before, on his catching her eye while she moved through the room with Mr. French. . . . It had been vague, yet it had been intense, the mute reflexion, "Yes, I'm going to like him, and he's going somehow to help me!" that had directed her steps so straight to him. . . . Perjury would have to come in somehow and somewhere—oh so quite certainly!

"It was present to her" that perjury was necessary, but when? When she first saw Mr. Pitman or when he remarked on her beauty? "—It had been present a hundred times," and therefore the question is irrelevant. Thus, the "flashback" leaves the past and becomes generalized before it returns conditionally to the present: "She might actually have wished in fact that he shouldn't now have seemed so tremendously struck with her." But the dialogue does not yet resume. Julia "could have worked it out at her leisure, to the last link of the chain, the way their prettiness . . . had foredoomed them . . . " Julia does not in fact have the leisure to work it out since she is involved in a conversation requiring some strategic maneuvering. But a leisurely explanation follows nevertheless which often echoes her idiom. When the conversation is resumed at the beginning of section 2, however, it starts all over again; Mr. Pitman's salutation might as well have never been recorded. "Mr. Pitman put it to her that, as soon as he had made her out 'for sure,' identified her there as old Julia grown-up and gallivanting with a new admirer, . . . he had had the inspiration of her being exactly the good girl to help him." Truths which had been present to Julia a hundred times are called forth by Mr. Pitman's greeting. He has done more than touch a spring of her memory; he has touched a spring of her imagination and has instantly put her in touch with truth.

Julia has the imagination to respond to Mr. Pitman's comment. She discovers what she needs to know about herself and her isolated condition by seeing through people to other people. By recognizing Mr. Pitman, she understands his relation to her mother and therefore her mother's relation to herself. Her vision of Mrs. Drack places Mr. Pitman, and the vision of Mary Lindeck in Murray Brush's face helps Julia finally to place herself. Julia's environment is a kind of chaos to be ordered by the imagination; it is a "flood, with . . . great lumps and masses of truth" floating in it. But at the same time, the personal imaginative order that Julia creates is not artificial; it lies concealed until the right connections are made to reveal it. The imagination uses the world as a key to unlock the treasure chest of multiudinous reference; this is the function of Julia's imagination, and also of the reader's. The "iridescence" of James's nouvelle, therefore, is complex: it is the play of Julia's consciousness as she perceives the play of symbolism that has an "iridescence" of its own, and it is the play of the reader's consciousness as he or she recombines the symbols to discover correspondences which "really, universally, stop nowhere."

In *Paul Bourget and the Nouvelle,* Walter Todd Secor suggests that one of "the artifices inherent in the genre" is "its suggestive power. . . . The novel . . . must inevitably reach conclusions. . . . [The *nouvelle* has the] ability to disturb one's thought, to call forth ideas and to elicit discussions." Without treating the novel reductively, we can agree that this effect of imitating and encouraging discovery is the effect James strove to create in ***Julia Bride.*** To proceed by "implications and involutions only," by "indirectedness," to express both the "quantity of life" of essential but absent characters as well as by extension "a whole view of manners and morals" of contemporary society—these are the claims of his preface. There is a point at which brevity ceases to be the mere compactness of the straightforward, the point at which a statement is so elliptical that its referential value is reduced to almost nothing while its symbolic meaning looms larger and larger. It is this point which fascinates Henry James. When he defines the romantic in the preface to *The American,* he discusses the problems caused when the development of a romantic idea seems to call for some falsification of the logic of the plot. This is not the only way romantic intuition may have an impact on plot. Instead of being falsified, plot may be trivialized, and even characters' responses to reported events may be suppressed in favor of an indirect exploration of theme. In all cases, the romantic mode, according to James, is an appeal to the other ways we perceive other truths. The romantic in art may represent a character's experience of perceiving indirectly, or it may operate as a vehicle for the readers' illumination, or, like ***Julia Bride,*** it may attempt to accomplish both kinds of imitation. Since this experience is art and not life, its "subterfuge" can be analyzed in terms of literary technique and effect. To recreate the romantic experience, "making us conceive and respond to [the quantity of life], making us feel, taste, smell and enjoy [it], without our really knowing why or how," is to strive for immediacy of vision. To James, this means imaginative vision mediated as little as possible by the conventional literary vehicles of character and action, the vehicles of realism. Therefore, in ***Julia Bride*** time schemes are disrupted to foster the illusion of simultaneity, free indirect discourse is used to obscure and complicate the narrative viewpoint, and paradox and humor upset all attempts to bind the text to a simple paraphrase. In order to force the tale to refer to varied and complex things outside itself, James tries to frustrate attempts to keep the tale enclosed and simplistic.

James offers ***Julia Bride*** as one model of "strong brevity." Its narrative structure helps to explain why James feels that brevity and lucidity are consummately difficult to achieve at the same time—that short fiction can be the least as well as the most simple of prose forms. Although "there is of course neither close nor fixed measure" of the potential for "development" in a chosen subject, the example of ***Julia Bride*** at least makes clear of what development consists. Development is the expansion of a point—a meeting, a chance remark, any fictional event—into an ever-widening circle of meaning, and developments are the implications which are opened to speculation. Furthermore, James is most pleased when the point of departure, the center of the circle, is very small. For James, writing the nouvelle can become a game of paradox and brinkmanship which he wins when he packs the greatest existential significance into statements, often clichés, of the least referential value. Foreshortening, and the nouvellistic method in general, are alternative methods of communication which presuppose, and even give priority to, alternative methods of perception. In the anecdote, according to James, only those narrative techniques are appropriate which conform to a conventional perception of time. Thus the nouvelle admits romantic modes of perception where the anecdote does not. To say that James's nouvelle is brief may be enough of a definition, provided that it is clearly understood how he goes about making this fiction brief. (pp. 35-51)

Lauren T. Cowdery, in her The Nouvelle of Henry James in Theory and Practice, *revised edition, UMI Research Press, 1986, 136 p.*

FURTHER READING

Barnett, Louise K. "Jamesian Feminism: Women in *Daisy Miller.*" *Studies in Short Fiction* 16, No. 4 (Fall 1979): 281-87.

Examines female characters in *Daisy Miller* and the life options James makes available to them.

Bell, Millicent. "*The Turn of the Screw* and the *recherche de l'absolu.*" *Delta* 15 (November 1982): 33-48.

Contends that the debate over the reality of the ghosts in *The Turn of the Screw* is unresolvable and that the story is inherently ambiguous.

Bouraoui, H. A. "Henry James and the French Mind: The International Theme in 'Madame de Mauves.'" *Novel: A Forum on Fiction* 4, No. 1 (Fall 1970): 69-76.

Examines the opposition of American and French cultures as presented in "Madame de Mauves."

Brooks, Van Wyck. *The Pilgrimage of Henry James.* New York: E. P. Dutton and Co., 1925, 170 p.

Critical biography emphasizing James's international travel and its effects on him and his work.

Brylowski, Anna Salne. "In Defense of the First Person Narrator in *The Aspern Papers.*" *The Centennial Review* XIII, No. 2 (Spring 1969): 215-40.

Responds to Wayne Booth's study of James's unreliable narrator (see excerpt dated 1961), arguing that *The Aspern Papers* is a dramatic monologue.

Chase, Dennis. "The Ambiguity of Innocence: *The Turn of the Screw.*" *Extrapolation* 27, No. 3 (Fall 1986): 197-202.

Discusses the ambiguity that arises in *The Turn of the Screw* from sexual innuendos surrounding the seemingly innocent governess and the boy Miles.

Crowley, John W. "The Wiles of a 'Witless' Woman: Tina in *The Aspern Papers.*" *ESQ* 22, No. 3 (1976): 159-68.

Argues that Miss Tina, whom critics often identify as an innocent victim, is in fact a clever manipulator.

Draper, R. P. "Death of a Hero? Winterbourne and Daisy Miller." *Studies in Short Fiction* VI, No. 1 (Fall 1968): 601-08.

Contends that Frederick Winterbourne in *Daisy Miller* is a tragic hero and his final loss of spirit is the novella's theme.

Edel, Leon. *Henry James.* 5 vols. Philadelphia and New York: J. B. Lippincott Co., 1953-73.

Definitive biography for which Edel was awarded the Pulitzer Prize.

Fadiman, Clifton, ed. Introduction to *The Short Stories of Henry James,* by Henry James, pp. ix-xx. New York: Random House, 1945.

Responds to negative criticism directed at James.

Geismar, Maxwell. "Henry James: 'The Beast in the Jungle.'" *Nineteenth-Century Fiction* 18, No. 1 (June 1963): 35-42.

Analyzes "The Beast in the Jungle" as a critical examination of James's own egotism.

Goetz, William R. *Henry James and the Darkest Abyss of Romance.* Baton Rouge: Louisiana State University Press, 1986, 215 p.

Studies how the self-conscious nature of James's works determines the author's various narrative techniques.

Hocks, Richard A. "*Daisy Miller,* Backward into the Past: A Centennial Essay." *The Henry James Review* I, No. 2 (Winter 1980): 164-78.

Comprehensive overview of *Daisy Miller*'s significance over the past hundred years.

Kennedy, Ian. "Frederick Winterbourne: The Good Bad Boy in *Daisy Miller.*" *Arizona Quarterly* 29, No. 2 (Summer 1973): 138-50.

Suggests that Winterbourne's Puritan ethics mask his true sexual nature.

Kirkham, E. Bruce. "A Study of Henry James' 'Mdme. de Mauves.'" *Ball State University Forum* XII, No. 2 (Spring 1971): 63-9.

Examines "Madame de Mauves" as a portrait of Longmore's personal struggle between realism, represented by Euphemia, and morality, represented by Monsieur de Mauves.

Kirschke, James J. *Henry James and Impressionism.* Troy, N.Y.: Whitson Publishing Co., 1981, 332 p.

Suggests that James was deeply influenced by Impressionist painters and adapted their techniques to his writing.

Levy, Leo B. "Consciousness in Three Early Tales of Henry James." *Studies in Short Fiction* 18, No. 4 (Fall 1981): 407-12.

Examines the "puzzling and wayward convolutions in which consciousness winds itself" in "A Landscape Painter," "My Friend Bingham," and "Osborne's Revenge."

Matthiessen, F. O. "Henry James' Portrait of the Artist." *Partisan Review* XI, No. 1 (Winter 1944): 71-87.

Discusses James's depiction of artists in his short fiction.

Mellard, James M. "Modal Counterpoint in James's *The Aspern Papers.*" *Papers on Language and Literature* IV, No. 3 (Summer 1968): 299-307.

Contends that *The Aspern Papers* is constructed on the opposition of realism and romance.

Miall, David S. "Designed Horror: James's Vision of Evil in *The Turn of the Screw.*" *Nineteenth-Century Fiction* 39, No. 3 (December 1984): 305-27.

Suggests that the ghosts in *The Turn of the Screw* embody "the state and condition of ultimate evil" and that the reader's awareness of this evil is James's concern in the story.

Mordell, Albert, ed. *Discovery of a Genius: William Dean Howells and Henry James.* New York: Twayne Publishers, 1961, 207 p.

Collection of articles and essays on James by his editor, admirer, and colleague, William Dean Howells.

Mottram, Eric. "'The Infected Air' and 'The Guilt of Interference': Henry James's Short Stories." In *The Nineteenth-Century American Short Story,* edited by A. Robert Ler, pp. 164-90. London: Vision Press, 1985.

Overview of dominant themes in James's short fiction.

Person, Leland S., Jr. "Eroticism and Creativity in *The Aspern Papers.*" *Literature and Psychology* XXXII, No. 2 (1986): 20-9.

Explores the failure of the narrator of *The Aspern Papers* "by analyzing his relationship to the deceased Jeffrey Aspern and to the letters that are the object of his plot."

Powers, Lyall H. "Henry James and the Ethics of the Artist: 'The Real Thing' and 'The Liar.'" *Texas Studies in Literature and Language* III, No. 3 (Autumn 1961): 360-68.

Examines the way in which James depicts and defines

the artist's use of people in "The Real Thing" and "The Liar."

———. "A Reperusal of James's 'The Figure in the Carpet.'" *American Literature* 33, No. 2 (May 1961): 224-28.

Suggests that the intent of "The Figure in the Carpet" lies not in the discovery of an artist's meaning, but in the process of perceiving and attempting to understand a work of art.

Purdy, Strother B. "Language As Art: The Ways of Knowing in Henry James's 'Crapy Cornelia.'" *Style* 1, No. 2 (Spring 1967): 139-49.

Detailed analysis of conversation and wordplay in "Crapy Cornelia."

Rozenzweig, Saul. "The Ghost of Henry James." *Partisan Review* XI, No. 4 (Fall 1944): 436-55.

Psychological analysis of James and his works, especially his ghost stories, the "ghosts" in which, according to Rosenzweig, "fail to represent the remnants of once-lived lives but point instead to the irrepressible unlived life."

Schneider, Daniel J. *The Crystal Cage: Adventures of the Imagination in the Fiction of Henry James.* Lawrence: Regents Press of Kansas, 1978, 189 p.

An important study attempting to determine "a single imaginative center" from which James's art unfolds.

Smith, F. E. "'The Beast in the Jungle': The Limits of Method." *Perspective* 1, No. 1 (Autumn 1947): 33-40.

Argues that the structure of "The Beast in the Jungle" hampers its theme.

Stone, Edward, ed. *Henry James: Seven Stories and Studies.* New York: Appleton-Century-Crofts, 1961, 310 p.

Includes texts of and critical essays about seven of James's stories: "The Marriages," "Europe," "The Liar," "The Real Thing," "The Pupil," "The Beast in the Jungle," and "The Jolly Corner."

Thorberg, Raymond. "Henry James and the Real Thing: 'The Beldonald Holbein.'" *Southern Humanities Review* 3, No. 1 (Winter 1969): 78-85.

Examines James's view of the relation of art to life as expressed in "The Beldonald Holbein."

Tompkins, Jane P., ed. *Twentieth Century Interpretations of "The Turn of the Screw" and Other Tales.* Englewood Cliffs, N.J.: Prentice Hall, 1970, 115 p.

Collection of critical essays on "The Pupil," "The Real Thing," "The Figure in the Carpet," "The Madonna of the Future," *The Turn of the Screw,* "The Beast in the Jungle," and "The Jolly Corner."

Toor, David. "Narrative Irony in Henry James' 'The Real Thing.'" *The University Review* XXXIV, No. 2 (Winter 1967): 95-9.

Examines James's use of the unreliable narrator device in "The Real Thing."

Tyler, Parker. "The Child as 'The Figure in the Carpet.'" *Chicago Review* 11, No. 4 (Winter 1958): 31-42.

Proposes a motif in James's works in which sexual passion can be controlled and converted into moral and creative passion.

Wagenknecht, Edward. *The Tales of Henry James.* New York: Frederick Ungar, 1984, 266 p.

Detailed survey of fifty-five of James's tales, including two appendices with summaries of fifty-two other tales and a list of the contents of James's collections of stories.

Ward, J. A. "Structural Irony in 'Madame de Mauves.'" *Studies in Short Fiction* II, No. 1 (Fall 1964): 170-82.

Examination of character interaction, narrative development, and setting in "Madame de Mauves" by which James explores "the delicate relationship between class and character, between cultural persuasion and private perception."

Wirth-Nesher, Hana. "The Thematics of Interpretation: James's Artist Tales." *The Henry James Review* V, No. 2 (Winter 1984): 117-27.

Suggests that in "The Author of Beltraffio," "The Figure in the Carpet," and "The Lesson of the Master," the creation and understanding of art is a metaphor for all human interaction.

W. Somerset Maugham

1874-1965

(Full name: William Somerset Maugham) English short story writer, novelist, dramatist, critic, and essayist.

Maugham is one of the most prolific and popular authors in world literature. During a career that spanned sixty-five years, he attained great renown, first as a dramatist, then as the author of entertaining and carefully crafted short stories and novels. Maugham's productivity has sometimes hindered his critical reception, leading commentators to assess him as a merely competent professional writer. A number of his works, however, most notably the novels *Of Human Bondage* and *Cakes and Ale; or, The Skeleton in the Cupboard,* and the short stories "The Letter" and "Rain," are acclaimed as masterpieces of twentieth-century literature.

Maugham was born to English parents at the British Embassy in Paris, where his father was employed as a lawyer. His mother died in 1882, and when his father died two years later Maugham was sent to live with a childless aunt and uncle in England. He attended King's School in Canterbury from 1885 to 1889, and although his guardians wanted him to go on to Oxford, Maugham persuaded them to allow him to study at the University of Heidelberg in Germany. By the time he returned to England in 1892 Maugham had privately decided to become a writer. Nevertheless, knowing that his guardians would disapprove of a literary career, he began medical training at St. Thomas's Hospital in London. Maugham earned a medical degree in 1897 but never practiced; that same year his first novel, *Liza of Lambeth,* was published. This work manifests many of the essential properties that characterize Maugham's fiction: he drew from personal experience and adhered to existing and successful literary traditions. The decade following the appearance of *Liza of Lambeth* is often termed the period of Maugham's literary apprenticeship. From 1897 until 1907 he published novels, short stories, a play, and a travel book, receiving increasingly favorable reviews in English literary periodicals. In 1907 his play *Lady Frederick* met with considerable success, and Maugham quickly attained celebrity as a dramatist. In 1908, four of his plays—*Lady Frederick, Jack Straw, Mrs Dot,* and *The Explorer*—ran simultaneously in London theaters. Over the next twenty-six years twenty-nine of Maugham's plays were produced, many of them among the most well-received of their time.

At the onset of World War I Maugham joined the Red Cross and went to France as an interpreter. There he met Gerald Haxton, and the two became lovers and remained close companions for the next thirty years. During the war the British government recruited Maugham as an intelligence agent and subsequently involved him in covert operations in Switzerland and Russia. Despite his ongoing relationship with Haxton, in 1917 Maugham married a woman with whom he had had a child two years earlier. The marriage was unsuccessful, however, and they divorced in 1929. During the years between the World Wars, Maugham lived lavishly and wrote prolifically. He bought an expansive villa in southeast France in 1926, which remained his home thereafter, although he traveled widely. His visits to Italy, the United States, the South Seas, and the Caribbean, provided the settings for the works that appeared between the World Wars, including the short story collections *The Trembling of a Leaf: Little Stories of the South Sea Islands, The Casuarina Tree,* and *Ashenden; or, The British Agent,* as well as the novels *The Moon and Sixpence* and *Cakes and Ale,* and the plays *Our Betters* and *The Circle.* Maugham fled France during the Nazi occupation, and went to the United States, where he lectured and oversaw the Hollywood production of several motion pictures based on his stories and novels. Haxton, who had accompanied Maugham, died in 1944. In 1948 Maugham returned to France. Although accounts of his later years portray Maugham as somewhat mentally unstable and given to irrational outbursts, he retained a sardonic wit. "Dying is a very dull, dreary affair," he told his nephew, Robin Maugham. "And my advice to you is to have nothing whatever to do with it." He died in 1965 at the age of ninety-one.

Despite his prolificacy, Maugham's renown rests chiefly on only a few works. Among his novels, critics cite as Maugham's best the semiautobiographical *Of Human Bondage,* with its penetrating psychological portrait of its protagonist, and *Cakes and Ale,* which satirizes aspects of London literary life. Maugham is most esteemed, however, for his short fiction. He emerged as a preeminent short story writer in the 1920s, and many commentators maintain that he consistently achieved excellence in this genre, concurring with Anthony Burgess that "the short story was Maugham's true *métier,* and some of the stories he wrote are among the best in the language." Maugham's most successful stories, which include "Before the Party," "The Book-Bag," "Mackintosh," "P. & O.," "The Pool," "Mr. Harrington's Washing," "The Letter," and "Rain," exploit the oppressive atmosphere of British colonies, featuring petty intrigue, marital infidelity, and sometimes violent death against a background of the rigidly stratified colonial communities in India and the Far East. In "The Letter," for example, the wife of an English plantation owner in Singapore shoots and kills a man she claims tried to rape her while her husband was absent. Her lawyer, however, discovers a letter she wrote to the murdered man arranging a meeting on the night of his death. She admits that she was the man's lover and killed him out of jealousy when he lost interest in her. In "Rain" a medical quarantine isolates a number of travelers, including Sadie Thompson, a prostitute; Dr. and Mrs. Macphail; and the Davidsons, a missionary couple, in a remote port of Pago Pago. Mr. Davidson soon becomes obsessed with reforming the flamboyant prostitute, and he bullies her into a cowed, terrified state by wielding the threat of a prison term. One night he is found dead, having cut his own throat. Sadie Thompson is angrily defiant, and the words she hurls at Dr. Macphail—"You men! You filthy, dirty pigs! You're all the same, all of you. Pigs! Pigs!"—suggest that what passed between her and the missionary was not entirely spiritual in nature. These two stories are among the most familiar and often-anthologized in world literature; both have undergone a number of stage and motion picture adaptations. Maugham's Ashenden stories, based on his experiences in the secret service, are credited with originating a style of sophisticated international espionage fiction that has remained popular for decades. His stories resemble his dramas in structure: plots hinge and pivot on some secret; suspense is heightened by the possibility of revelation; and tension builds on strategically timed entrances and exits, lost and found properties, and verbal combat. In fact, Maugham often transformed short stories into plays and rewrote unperformed dramas as novels or short stories, and this ease of adaptation attests to the unity of Maugham's literary construction.

Maugham himself stated that his place in literature was "in the very first row of the second-raters"; many critics concur with this assessment. Maugham's prolificacy, together with the generally even quality of his work, fosters the impression of an adept literary workman turning out competent but unremarkable fiction. While many commentators agree that this is a fair evaluation of much of Maugham's work, some have suggested that it required more than mere competence to sustain Maugham's long and successful career. They cite his consummate achievements in the short story form and suggest that Maugham's many works of fiction include a number of the finest English short stories of the twentieth century.

(For further information on Maugham's life and career, see *Contemporary Literary Criticism,* Vols. 1, 11, 15; *Contemporary Authors,* Vols. 5-8, rev. ed., 25-28, rev. ed.; and *Dictionary of Literary Biography,* Vols. 10, 36, 77, 100.)

PRINCIPAL WORKS

SHORT FICTION

Orientations 1899
The Merry-Go-Round 1904
The Trembling of a Leaf: Little Stories of the South Sea Islands 1921
The Casuarina Tree 1926
Ashenden; or, The British Agent 1928
Six Stories Written in the First Person Singular 1931
Ah King 1933
Altogether 1934; also published as *East and West,* 1934
Cosmopolitans: Very Short Stories 1936
The Mixture as Before 1940
Creatures of Circumstance 1947
The World Over 1952
The Complete Short Stories of W. Somerset Maugham 1953 [this collection includes *East and West* and *The World Over*]

OTHER MAJOR WORKS

Liza of Lambeth (novel) 1897
A Man of Honour (drama) 1903
The Land of the Blessed Virgin: Sketches and Impressions in Andalusia (travel book) 1905
Lady Frederick (drama) 1907
The Explorer (drama) 1908
Jack Straw (drama) 1908
Mrs Dot (drama) 1908
The Tenth Man (drama) 1910
Of Human Bondage (novel) 1915
Home and Beauty (Too Many Husbands) (drama) 1919
The Moon and Sixpence (novel) 1919
Our Betters (drama) 1919
The Circle (drama) 1921
East of Suez (drama) 1922
The Painted Veil (novel) 1925
The Letter (drama) 1927
Cakes and Ale; or, The Skeleton in the Cupboard (novel) 1930
The Narrow Corner (novel) 1932
Theatre (novel) 1937
The Summing Up (autobiographical sketch) 1938
Christmas Holiday (novel) 1939
The Razor's Edge (novel) 1944
A Writer's Notebook (journals) 1949
The Vagrant Mood (essays) 1952
Points of View (essays) 1958

Lee Wilson Dodd (essay date 1931)

[*Dodd is an American novelist and critic. In the following review of* Six Stories Written in the First Person Singular, *he commends Maugham's competence in matters of plotting, style, and execution.*]

Mr. Maugham is the most competent, the most professional of authors. Indeed, he is perhaps a little too publicly aware of his almost ruthless competence, his slightly hard-boiled professionalism. In his introduction to [***Six Stories Written In the First Person Singular***] there is a tone of uneasy truculence. "I have been accused of bad taste," he says:

> I have at one time or another been charged with portraying certain persons so exactly that it was impossible not to know them. This has disturbed me, not so much for my own sake (since I am used to the slings and arrows of outrageous fortune) as for the sake of criticism in general. We authors, of course, try to be gentlemen, but we often fail and we must console ourselves by reflecting that few writers of any consequence have been devoid of a certain streak of vulgarity. Life is vulgar. I have long known that journalists, in private free in their speech and fond enough of bawdry, are in print great sticklers for purity, and I have no doubt that this is as it should be; but I fear that if they become *too* refined there will be so few points of contact between them and the writers whom it is their pleasant duty to appraise that criticism will become almost impossible.

This passage is irony at its worst—that is, at its least convincing. Something is troubling Mr. Maugham, and he is trying to curl his lip contemptuously and shrug it away. "I have been accused of bad taste," he says. . . .

Nevertheless, as novelist, as playwright, as teller of tales, Mr. Maugham is always professionally competent, and from time to time he is a great deal better than that. From time to time he ceases to be merely slick, hard, and brilliant; he forgets himself in his material, his characters come alive, he illuminates the mind and touches the heart. There are two superb stories in the present volume—one a masterpiece of comedy, the other a tragedy of character and circumstance that is uncompromisingly seen and yet deeply and truly felt. The comedy, **"Jane,"** may be left to speak for itself; every line of it is right, and Jane herself is the sort of woman who would never insist upon being remembered, but whom discriminating readers will find it very difficult (and unnecessary) to forget. The tragedy, **"The Alien Corn,"** is a different and more difficult accomplishment. In this story Mr. Maugham seems to me to pass far beyond the usual range of his distinguished talent.

"The Alien Corn" is a study of a Jewish family of great wealth who are trying to escape from all the tremendous implications of their racial inheritance and turn themselves into the perfect, the complete, English county family. All the passionate pride and hope of Sir Adolphus Bland (the name was originally Bleikogel) and of his wife, Lady Muriel, are centered in their eldest son, George.

> George was a scratch at golf, and though tennis was not his game he played much better than the average; the Blands had had him taught to shoot as soon as he was old enough to hold a gun, and he was a fine shot; they had put him on a pony when he was two, etc.—George was so tall and slim, his curly hair, of a palish brown, was so fine, his eyes were so blue, he was the perfect type of the young Englishman.

Harry, the second son, was

> stocky, broad-shouldered, and strong for his age, but his black eyes, shining with cleverness, his coarse dark hair, and his big nose revealed his race. Freddy (Sir Adolphus) was severe with him . . . but with George he was all indulgence. Harry would go into the business, he had brains and push, but George was the heir. George would be an English gentleman.

But, unhappily, George had other needs, another ambition. He wished to become a great concert pianist. He fled to Munich on five pounds a week, and the resulting tragedy is a deeper sounding of those strange, compelling mid-sea currents of race than you might easily suppose. The story takes on passion, heartbreak, and a certain grandeur—only marred, alas, by a touch of cynical smartness in its concluding sentence. "One reads of such accidents in the paper often." But the blemish, if it be a blemish, is slight.

The other four stories are well enough in their way. Mr. Maugham knows how to plan a story and carry it through. Competence is the word. His style is without a trace of imaginative beauty; one feels that like Stendhal he has been studying the *Code Civil.* "There entered a youth in a very well-cut dinner jacket." That is the tone of his writing, clear, cold, charmless, efficient; an occasional glitter of wit, or the salt taste of irony. No nonsense about him; he knows perfectly how to do what he desires to do. And then, from time to time, unexpectedly, as in **"Rain"** or **"The Alien Corn,"** he feels something, as if in spite of himself, intensely—and knows surprisingly more.

Lee Wilson Dodd, "Set of Six," in The Saturday Review of Literature, *Vol. VIII, No. 13, October 17, 1931, p. 206.*

Louis Kronenberger (essay date 1934)

[*A drama critic for* Time *from 1938 to 1961, Kronenberger was a distinguished historian, literary critic, and author highly regarded for his expertise in eighteenth-century English history and literature. Of his critical work, Kronenberger's* The Thread of Laughter: Chapters on English Stage Comedy from Jonson to Maugham *(1952) and* The Republic of Letters *(1955) contain some of his best literary commentaries. In the following excerpt, Kronenberger provides a mixed review of Maugham's short story collection* East and West *(published in England as* Altogether*), commending the stories for their interest but charging that Maugham's extraordinary narrative skill is spent on unimaginative plots and commonplace, often sordid, subject matter.*]

[***East and West: The Complete Short Stories of W. Somerset Maugham***] makes very interesting and very disappointing reading. One finds one's self in the presence of an astounding story-teller and passes from each of these stories to the next with the impatient zest that only expert story-telling can foster. It is not conceivable that anybody should be bored reading Mr. Maugham; he is the sort of writer who can choose a subject in which you have no interest, who can indeed choose a subject that you definitely dislike, and yet by his gift for narrative compel you to read on to the end. He is perhaps the least dull writer, for the largest body of readers, of his generation: both the man who reads Tolstoy and the man who reads Sabatini can read Maugham with understanding and relish. Among living writers in English only Kipling and Tarkington, it seems to me, can equally share that honor.

Nor is this kinship with Kipling and Tarkington in any sense fortuitous; there is a very marked reason why all three men can attract everybody from the man in the street up to the genuine highbrow. All three are men of great natural talent with an astonishing power of story-telling, and all three are men whose sense of values lags far behind their ability. The picture they give us of life plainly has nothing in common with the skill they display in painting it. For those who are content with the picture the skill shown in painting it is of course an extraordinary boon. But for those who are not content with the picture the skilled brushwork becomes, sooner or later, an object of dissatisfaction. It seems more than wasteful; it seems almost immoral. For to see talent glorifying shoddiness, particularly when in the same hands you have seen it glorify truth, is a pretty unpleasant business. But certainly in most of Kipling's work one looks in vain for the light that shines through his half dozen best stories; in most of Tarkington's work one looks in vain for the conviction carried by *Alice Adams;* and in all of Maugham's later writing one looks in vain for the realistic promise of the early novels and the unchallenged reality of *Of Human Bondage.*

These thirty stories, most of them quite long as short stories go, are the products of the past fifteen years. The first of them, **"Rain,"** was written in the same year that Maugham published his last satisfactory book, *The Moon and Sixpence;* and they very definitely represent the arrived and mature man. Since it took him almost no time at all to master the short-story medium, we can at once dismiss from our inquiry any considerations of technique. Maugham started off writing short stories with a great deal of skill and gradually acquired a great deal more; on the technical side there is nothing further to say. But in all the years he has spent in writing these stories he has acquired nothing beyond additional skill; he began with a catchpenny and spectacular tale that lies all on the surface, and nothing he did afterward can be regarded as really more important or substantial. His themes, when you come to think about them, are remarkably varied, his locales are diversified, his story-telling is flexible; and yet for all their variety these tales seem altogether alike and produce an altogether like effect. The curse of a common point of view, and a very unsatisfying point of view, lies heavily upon them. The curse of a solved, tabloid outlook on life disfigures, belittles, desiccates them. It is not quite the outlook or point of view of the fairly well educated reader who may be described as Maugham's most enthusiastic audience; Maugham himself is on the one hand too superior, on the other hand too clever, to succumb to that outlook. But it *is* that outlook fortified by an immense worldliness—a worldliness so cynical, so adaptable, so penetrable that it lends to the provincial mind its own cosmopolitan eyes; and with those eyes one can see a great deal further than usual without seeing the least bit deeper. Maugham has dowered these stories with all his sophistication and wit and social presence, but he has made his gifts ornamental, not useful: nowhere has brilliance served to uncover depth—it has been turned into a kaleidoscope, not into a light.

While damning Chekhov with faint praise in a preface that often sounds like an apologia, Maugham remarks that "the pleasure of recognition, which is the pleasure [Chekhov] thus aimed at, is the lowest of all esthetic pleasures." In that one statement I think he gives himself away as fully as he does in all the succeeding stories. And acting on such a belief, Mr. Maugham in most of these narratives has set to work to dazzle us with surprise; in one story after another we are cheated of recognizing life as we know it to enjoy the banal and meretricious surprises, the swift melodrama, the cynical paradoxes of a writer who wants to make us gasp; and that is all. We gasp at **"Rain"** but we are not convinced; the trick was far better done by Anatole France in "Thaïs." There is a momentary catch in our throats at the end of **"The Alien Corn"**; the next moment we feel emotionally duped. And once the spell is broken, it is broken forever; nothing in the world can make us believe Mr. Maugham's contrived illusion again.

It is because, in every respect, Maugham is so much the reverse of a fool that all 900 pages of this book have so insidious a quality. His shrewdness is staggering; his objectivity, his "tolerance" are faultless. He doesn't point a moral; he doesn't take sides. Both the parties to his drama may be wrongheaded or prejudiced or idiotic; he plays no favorites. There is a real worldliness in such stories of human deadlock as **"The Door of Opportunity," "The Human Element," "The Book-Bag," "The Outstation"**; the situations they evolve are the situations of real life, and Maugham has let them be played out in a credible and suitable fashion. Yet those stories uncover nothing for the reader, release nothing in him. He accepts without participating; it is mathematics Maugham is giving him, not humanity. And this seems all the more strange when one considers how much drama and suspense Maugham has put into such stories, until one realizes how much emotion, how much intimate reality he has left out.

Maugham points out in his preface that, though many of these stories are told in the first person, they are in no way to be thought of as his own experiences [see excerpt dated 1934]. Yet the constant play of the "I" throughout this book has a very disconcerting effect. For the "I" is always a well-off and poised novelist who moves in the smartest society—a tiresome sort of narrator who presently grows into a very snobbish symbol. It is a calculated snobbery which is doubtless not true of Mr. Maugham himself, but which adds a further touch of worldly glamour to the very clever story-teller who would rather impress magazine readers than add to his stature as a writer. The same touch, for me, often spoils the lighter stories, which—since they are written frankly to amuse—are the best things in the book. Some of them are much in the manner of Max Beerbohm, but for a number of reasons they fall short of Beerbohm's success. For Beerbohm is much wittier and much more delicate, and he uses the artistic scene in a subtler way. Also the snob in him is based on a temperament, and is revealed with disarming playfulness. At heart Maugham is perhaps less of a snob, but on paper he seems much more of one.

Here is, beyond doubt, one of the most readable books that have been published in a very long time. But here too is the wreck of a very considerable talent, and it is a wreck in no way splendid. In their poorer work most writers of merit offer less completely and satisfyingly some traces and signs of themselves at their best; but whoever can find in these brilliantly flashy pieces any evidence of the solid worth of Philip Carey's journey through life, or even of the honest grossness and humor of *Liza of Lambeth,* has much deeper insight than I have. The Maugham of these pages seems to me an entirely different person.

Louis Kronenberger, "The Story-Telling Art of Mr. Maugham," in The New York Times Book Review, *August 12, 1934, p. 2.*

Maugham on his critical reception:

In my twenties the critics said I was brutal, in my thirties they said I was flippant, in my forties they said I was cynical, in my fifties they said I was competent, and now in my sixties they say I am superficial. I have gone my way, following the course I had mapped out for myself, and trying with my works to fill out the pattern I looked for. I think authors are unwise who do not read criticisms. It is salutary to train oneself to be no more affected by censure than by praise; for of course it is easy to shrug one's shoulders when one finds oneself described as a genius, but not so easy to be unconcerned when one is treated as a nincompoop.

From his The Summing Up *(1938).*

Raymond Mortimer (essay date 1934)

[*Mortimer was an English critic who succeeded Desmond MacCarthy as literary editor of the* New Statesman and Nation *and later joined MacCarthy as a book reviewer for the* Sunday Times. *In the following excerpt, he reviews Maugham's collection of short stories* Altogether *(published in the United States as* East and West*). Mortimer finds Maugham particularly apt in his characterizations, but suggests that Maugham's fiction suffers from the author's lack of a poetic vision of the world.*]

Mr. Somerset Maugham thinks that the critics have not given him a square deal, so the thirty stories in [***Altogether: The Collected Stories of W. Somerset Maugham***] are sandwiched between a preface by the author and a reprinted article by Mr. Desmond MacCarthy. The reviewer will find in the preface a warning of what he ought not to say, and in the article, which is almost wholly laudatory, an example of what he ought. The stories themselves are most of them told by a disillusioned man of the world who remains superbly objective in face of cruelty, treachery and murder, but for whom the highbrow is something he resents even more than he does the missionary: something to be treated with not only detestation but contempt. (Indeed **"The Creative Instinct"** seems to me the weakest story in the volume, in spite of its charming plot, because the author's hatred of highbrows has goaded him into unconvincing caricature.) It is odd that Mr. Maugham, who is, I suppose, the most successful living writer, should let his calm be ruffled by the criticisms of persons he believes to be so petty, gullible and insincere.

> Is one mocked by an elf,
> Is one baffled by toad or by rat?
> The gravamen's in that!

But if one is a highbrow it is little use pretending not to be, even to escape Mr. Maugham's contempt; and so I shall parade the cloven hoof by trying to criticise his stories by the highest standard I know.

In his preface Mr. Maugham implies, I think justly, that the critics have been cold to him largely because his stories derive rather from Maupassant than from the more fashionable Tchehov. (His remarks on these writers reveal him as a most acute critic.) Actually the stories of Tchehov have been too indiscriminately praised: many of them are mere jottings, and both he and Maupassant wrote too much. Mr. Maugham lives much more conscientiously up to his own highest level. To illustrate his methods he transcribes in his preface the working notes, made from observation, on which the story **"Rain"** was constructed. "They are written in hackneyed and slipshod phrases without grace," he says, "for nature has not endowed me with the happy gift of hitting instinctively upon the perfect word to indicate an object and the unusual, but apt, adjective to describe It" [see excerpt dated 1934]. In view of this statement it is interesting to find that in the story itself most of these "hackneyed and slipshod phrases" are repeated without alteration. Mr. Maugham complains that reviewers call his work "competent," and supposes that he is damned with this faint praise because of the definiteness of form in his stories. Lord knows there has rarely been a less incompetent writer, but I think it is true to say that he does not hit, either instinctively or on reflection, the perfect word to indicate an object. It would be difficult to find examples of clumsy writing in Mr. Maugham's late work (though he sometimes trips into such surprising *clichés* as calling a woman "exquisitely gowned"), but it would be equally difficult to find passages in which the words had a life of their own. Possibly a fresher, less business-like style would slacken the pace of the stories by side-tracking the reader's attention from the design to the texture, but I do miss vividness in Mr. Maugham's descriptive passages. After reading many—too many—stories with a Malay setting, I have no clear impression of the atmosphere of Malaya: I have merely become bored with the sarongs and padangs and kampongs which serve for local colour. On the other hand, Mr. Maugham describes persons prodigiously well by the phrases he puts into their mouths. In a scrap of dialogue we have their social background, their pretensions, and the passions they seek to conceal. As a result, when re-reading these stories I have been surprised not by their excellence as stories (which I remembered) but by the suspense in which they held me, although I already knew how they would end. In this respect he beats Maupassant, whose stories depend too often on surprise. For in Maupassant the characters are created for the plot: in Maugham the plot is created by the characters. **"Honolulu"** is one of the very few stories which are just stories: and afterwards in **"P. & O.,"** where he uses a similar plot, the interest has shifted from the action to the reaction which it has upon the spectators' characters. Very often the point is the revelation of some wholly unexpected trait, a "degrading" passion in an ambassador or a society beauty, or the ability to murder in apparently commonplace persons, as in **"The Letter," "Before the Party,"** and **"Footprints in the Jungle."** Mr. Maugham delights in uncovering the heel of Achilles—that is why he is called a cynic—and there are no whole-hearted heroes or villains in his work. His extraordinary knowledge of human beings is like that of an experienced confessor, and as a result of it he is never shocked. This comprehension of the essential piebaldness of human character gives his stories a peculiar virtue. As examples of his method take **"Mackintosh"** and **"The Outstation"**: in each case two incompatible men are isolated, with the result that one becomes accessory to the other's murder. The murders, though their circumstances are arranged with admirable skill, are merely logical deductions from the confrontation of characters, and the interest of each story lies chiefly not in the violent conclusion but in the subtly stated premises. And in both of them the reader's sympathies are made to waver delicately in the balance by the calculated mixture of qualities in each of the antagonists. Mr. Maugham has developed in the narrow room of the short story a richness of characterisation hardly previously found except in the novel.

Ultimately these stories are the work of a comic writer. "Life is really very fantastic," he says in one of them, "and one has to have a peculiar sense of humour to see the fun of it." Mr. Maugham has this himself. Most of the stories "end unhappily," but they are devised to excite irony rather than pity. Almost the only character treated with tenderness is the scoundrelly old Walker at the end of **"Mackintosh,"** and here the tenderness seems to me just off the note—in fact, to be sentimentality. Yet Rosie in *Cakes and Ale* proves that Mr. Maugham can be tender. In fact, his last two novels show that he is a writer of promise. *Of Human Bondage* is so far his most solid achievement, because of the passion behind it; and I suspect it is a better book than *The Old Wives' Tale,* for instance, or any other of the realistic novels of the decade before the war. But in the meanwhile Mr. Maugham, who is not a natural writer, I think, in the sense of having a gift for handling language as a *matière,* has learnt a great deal about writing; and in *The Narrow Corner* he put his acquired skill to new uses, so that it is probably true to say that his last book was also his most perfect.

Mr. Maugham lacks the gift which is not necessary to immortality but which alone can make it certain: he does not possess a poetic vision of the world. But he has the good taste not to pretend to it, and does not offer us electroplate in lieu of silver. There are few purple passages in his work, and it would be better if there were none. Though the critics have praised him less than he deserves, the public have appreciated him more than he could reasonably expect, for he has done nothing to placate them: his irony and amorality are the qualities which usually they most dislike. He would wish the critic, I gather, to praise his stories for their shapeliness, and indeed each of these thirty is a model of construction. But I humbly recommend them for what seems to me rarer and more important than shapeliness, for the first and essential literary virtue, a virtue which they possess in the highest degree and the lack of which stamps some supposed masterpieces of form as fraudulent—the power to seize and hold the reader's attention. (pp. 243-44)

Raymond Mortimer, "Re-Reading Mr. Maugham," in The New Statesman & Nation, *Vol. 8, No. 183, August 25, 1934, pp. 243-44.*

W. Somerset Maugham (essay date 1934)

[In the following excerpt from his preface to his collected short stories (published in the United States as East and West *and in England as* Altogether*), Maugham discusses his principal literary influences, his methods of writing short stories, and some characteristics of his short fiction.]*

[***East and West***] contains thirty stories. They are all about the same length and on the same scale. The first was written in 1919 and the last in 1931. Though in early youth I had written a number of short stories, for a long time, twelve or fifteen years at least, occupied with the drama, I had ceased to do so; and when a journey to the South Seas unexpectedly provided me with themes that seemed to suit this medium, it was as a beginner of over forty that I wrote the story which is now called **"Rain."** Since it caused some little stir the reader of this preface will perhaps have patience with me if I transcribe the working notes, made at the time, on which it was constructed. They are written in hackneyed and slipshod phrases, without grace; for nature has not endowed me with the happy gift of hitting instinctively upon the perfect word to indicate an object and the unusual but apt adjective to describe it. I was travelling from Honolulu to Pago Pago and, hoping they might at some time be of service, I jotted down as usual my impressions of such of my fellow-passengers as attracted my attention. This is what I said of Miss Thompson: 'Plump, pretty in a coarse fashion, perhaps not more than twenty-seven. She wore a white dress and a large white hat, long white boots from which the calves bulged in cotton stockings.' There had been a raid on the Red Light district in Honolulu just before we sailed and the gossip of the ship spread the report that she was making the journey to escape arrest. My notes go on:

> *W. The Missionary.* He was a tall thin man, with long limbs loosely jointed, he had hollow cheeks and high cheek bones, his fine, large, dark eyes were deep in their sockets, he had full sensual lips, he wore his hair rather long. He had a cadaverous air and a look of suppressed fire. His

> hands were large, with long fingers, rather finely shaped. His naturally pale skin was deeply burned by the tropical sun. *Mrs W. His Wife.* She was a little woman with her hair very elaborately done, New England; not prominent blue eyes behind gold-rimmed pince-nez, her face was long like a sheep's, but she gave no impression of foolishness, rather of extreme alertness. She had the quick movements of a bird. The most noticeable thing about her was her voice, high, metallic, and without inflection; it fell on the ear with a hard monotony, irritating to the nerves like the ceaseless clamour of a pneumatic drill. She was dressed in black and wore round her neck a gold chain from which hung a small cross.

She told me that W. was a missionary on the Gilberts and his district consisting of widely separated islands he frequently had to go distances by canoe. During this time she remained at headquarters and managed the mission. Often the seas were very rough and the journeys were not without peril. He was a medical missionary. She spoke of the depravity of the natives in a voice which nothing could hush, but with a vehement, unctuous horror, telling me of their marriage customs which were obscene beyond description. She said, when first they went it was impossible to find a single good girl in any of the villages. She inveighed against dancing. I talked with the missionary and his wife but once, and with Miss Thompson not at all. Here is the note for the story:

> A prostitute, flying from Honolulu after a raid, lands at Pago Pago. There lands there also a missionary and his wife. Also the narrator. All are obliged to stay there owing to an outbreak of measles. The missionary finding out her profession persecutes her. He reduces her to misery, shame, and repentance, he has no mercy on her. He induces the governor to order her return to Honolulu. One morning he is found with his throat cut by his own hand and she is once more radiant and self-possessed. She looks at men and scornfully exclaims: 'dirty pigs'.

An intelligent critic, who combines wide reading and a sensitive taste with a knowledge of the world rare among those who follow his calling, has found in my stories the influence of Guy de Maupassant. That is not strange. When I was a boy he was considered the best short story writer in France and I read his works with avidity. From the age of fifteen whenever I went to Paris I spent most of my afternoons poring over the books in the galleries of the Odéon. I have never passed more enchanted hours. The attendants in their long smocks were indifferent to the people who sauntered about looking at the books and they would let you read for hours without bothering. There was a shelf filled with the works of Guy de Maupassant, but they cost three francs fifty a volume and that was not a sum I was prepared to spend. I had to read as best I could standing up and peering between the uncut pages. Sometimes when no attendant was looking I would hastily cut a page and thus read more conveniently. Fortunately some of them were issued in a cheap edition at seventy-five centimes and I seldom came away without one of these. In this manner, before I was eighteen, I had read all the best stories. It is natural enough that when at that age I began writing stories myself I should unconsciously have chosen those little masterpieces as a model. I might very well have hit upon a worse. (pp. 42-5)

So far as I could remember it I have placed the stories in [***The Complete Short Stories***] in the order in which they were written. I thought it might possibly interest the reader to see how I had progressed from the tentativeness of the first ones, when I was very much at the mercy of my anecdote, to the relative certainty of the later ones when I had learnt so to arrange my material as to attain the result I wanted. Though all but two have been published in a magazine these stories were not written with that end in view. When I began to write them I was fortunately in a position of decent independence and I wrote them as a relief from work which I thought I had been too long concerned with. It is often said that stories are no better than they are because the editors of magazines insist on their being written to a certain pattern. This has not been my experience. All but **"Rain"** and **"The Book-Bag"** were published in the *Cosmopolitan Magazine* and Ray Long, the Editor, never put pressure on me to write other than as I wished. Sometimes the stories were cut and this is reasonable since no editor can affort one contributor more than a certain amount of space; but I was never asked to make the smallest alteration to suit what might be supposed to be the taste of the readers. Ray Long paid me for them not only with good money, but with generous appreciation. I did not value this less. We authors are simple, childish creatures and we treasure a word of praise from those who buy our wares. Most of them were written in groups from notes made as they occurred to me, and in each group I left naturally enough to the last those that seemed most difficult to write. A story is difficult to write when you do not know *all* about it from the beginning, but for part of it must trust to your imagination and experience. Sometimes the curve does not intuitively present itself and you have to resort to this method and that to get the appropriate line.

I beg the reader not to be deceived by the fact that a good many of these stories are told in the first person into thinking that they are experiences of my own. This is merely a device to gain verisimilitude. It is one that has its defects, for it may strike the reader that the narrator could not know all the events he sets forth; and when he tells a story in the first person at one remove, when he reports, I mean, a story that someone tells him, it may very well seem that the speaker, a police officer, for example, or a sea-captain, could never have expressed himself with such facility and with such elaboration. Every convention has its disadvantages. These must be as far as possible disguised and what cannot be disguised must be accepted. The advantage of this one is its directness. It makes it possible for the writer to tell no more than he knows. Making no claim to omniscience, he can frankly say when a motive or an occurrence is unknown to him, and thus often give his story a plausibility that it might otherwise lack. It tends also to put the reader on intimate terms with the author. Since Maupassant and Chekhov, who tried so hard to be objective, nevertheless are so nakedly personal, it has sometimes seemed to me that if the author can in no way keep himself out of his work it might be better if he put in as much of himself as possible. The danger is that he may put in too much and thus be as boring as a talker who insists on monopolizing the conversation. Like all conventions this one must be used with discretion. The reader may have observed that in the original note of **"Rain"** the narrator was introduced, but in the story as written omitted.

Three of the stories in this volume were told me and I had nothing to do but make them probable, coherent and dramatic. They are **"The Letter," "Footprints in the Jungle"** and **"The Book-Bag."** The rest were invented, as I have shown **"Rain"** was, by the accident of my happening upon persons here and there, who in themselves or from something I heard about them suggested a theme that seemed suitable for a short story. This brings me to a topic that has always concerned writers and that has at times given the public, the writer's raw material, some uneasiness. There are authors who state that they never have a living model in mind when they create a character. I think they are mistaken. They are of this opinion because they have not scrutinized with sufficient care the recollections and impressions upon which they have constructed the person who, they fondly imagine, is of their invention. If they did they would discover that, unless he was taken from some book they had read, a practice by no means uncommon, he was suggested by one or more persons they had at one time known or seen. The great writers of the past made no secret of the fact that their characters were founded on living people. We know that the good Sir Walter Scott, a man of the highest principles, portrayed his father, with sharpness first and then, when the passage of years had changed his temper, with tolerance; Henri Beyle, in the manuscript of at least one of his novels, has written in at the side the names of the real persons who were his models; and this is what Turgenev himself says: 'For my part, I ought to confess that I never attempted to create a type without having, not an idea, but a living person, in whom the various elements were harmonized together, to work from. I have always needed some groundwork on which I could tread firmly.' With Flaubert it is the same story; that Dickens used his friends and relations freely is notorious; and if you read the *Journal* of Jules Renard, a most instructive book to anyone who wishes to know how a writer works, you will see the care with which he set down every little detail about the habits, ways of speech and appearance of the persons he knew. When he came to write a novel he made use of this storehouse of carefully collected information. In Chekhov's diary you will find notes which were obviously made for use at some future time, and in the recollections of his friends there are frequent references to the persons who were the originals of certain of his characters. It looks as though the practice were very common. I should have said it was necessary and inevitable. Its convenience is obvious. You are much more likely to depict a character who is a recognizable human being, with his own individuality, if you have a living model. The imagination can create nothing out of the void. It needs the stimulus of sensation. The writer whose creative faculty has been moved by something peculiar in a person (peculiar perhaps only to the writer) falsifies his idea if he attempts to describe that person other than as he sees him. Character hangs together and if you try to throw people off the scent, by making a short man tall for example (as though stature had no effect on character) or by making him choleric when he has the concomitant traits of an equable temper, you will destroy the plausible harmony (to use the beautiful phrase of Baltasar Gracian) of which it consists. The whole affair would be plain sailing if it were not for the feelings of the persons concerned. The writer has to consider the vanity of the human race and the Schadenfreude which is one of its commonest and most detestable failings. A man's friends will find pleasure in recognizing him in a book and though the author may never even have seen him will point out to him, especially if it is unflattering, what they consider his living image. Often someone will recognize a trait he knows in himself or a description of the place he lives in and in his conceit jumps to the conclusion that the character described is a portrait of himself. Thus in the story called **"The Outstation"** the Resident was suggested by a British Consul I had once known in Spain and it was written ten years after his death, but I have heard that the Resident of a district in Sarawak, which I described in the story, was much affronted because he thought I had had him in mind. The two men had not a trait in common. I do not suppose any writer attempts to draw an exact portrait. Nothing, indeed, is so unwise as to put into a work of fiction a person drawn line by line from life. His values are all wrong, and, strangely enough, he does not make the other characters in the story seem false, but himself. He never convinces. That is why the many writers who have been attracted by the singular and powerful figure of the late Lord Northcliffe have never succeeded in presenting a credible personage. The model a writer chooses is seen through his own temperament and if he is a writer of any originality what he sees need have little relation with the facts. He may see a tall man short or a generous one avaricious; but, I repeat, if he sees him tall, tall he must remain. He takes only what he wants of the living man. He uses him as a peg on which to hang his own fancies. To achieve his end (the plausible harmony that nature so seldom provides) he gives him traits that the model does not possess. He makes him coherent and substantial. The created character, the result of imagination founded on fact, is art, and life in the raw, as we know, is of this only the material. The odd thing is that when the charge is made that an author has copied this person or the other from life, emphasis is laid only on his less praiseworthy characteristics. If you say of a character that he is kind to his mother, but beats his wife, everyone will cry: Ah, that's Brown, how beastly to say he beats his wife; and no one thinks for a moment of Jones and Robinson who are notoriously kind to their mothers. I draw from this the somewhat surprising conclusion that we know our friends by their vices and not by their virtues. I have stated that I never even spoke to Miss Thompson in **"Rain."** This is a character that the world has not found wanting in vividness. Though but one of a multitude of writers my practice is doubtless common to most, so that I may be permitted to give another instance of it. I was once asked to meet at dinner two persons, a husband and wife, of whom I was told only what the reader will shortly read. I think I never knew their names. I should certainly not recognize them if I met them in the street. Here are the notes I made at the time.

> A stout, rather pompous man of fifty, with pince-nez, grey-haired, a florid complexion, blue eyes, a neat grey moustache. He talks with assurance. He is resident of an outlying district and is somewhat impressed with the importance of his position. He despises the men who have let themselves go under the influence of the climate and the surroundings. He has travelled extensively during his short leaves in the East and knows Java, the Philippines, the coast of China and the Malay Peninsula. He is very British, very patriotic; he takes a great deal of exercise. He has been a very heavy drinker and always took a bottle of whisky to bed with him. His wife has entirely cured him and now he drinks nothing but water. She is a little insignificant woman, with sharp features, thin, with a sallow skin and a flat chest. She is very badly dressed. She has all the prejudices of an Englishwoman. All her family for generations have been in second-rate regiments. Except that you know that she has caused her husband to cease drinking entirely you would think her quite colourless and unimportant.

On these materials, I invented the story which is called **"Before the Party."** I do not believe that any candid person could think that these two people had cause for complaint because they had been made use of. It is true that I should never have thought of the story if I had not met them, but anyone who takes the trouble to read it will see how insignificant was the incident (the taking of the bottle to bed) that suggested it and how differently the two chief characters have in the course of writing developed from the brief sketch which was their foundation.

'Critics are like horse-flies which prevent the horse from ploughing,' said Chekhov. 'For over twenty years I have read criticisms of my stories, and I do not remember a single remark of any value or one word of valuable advice. Only once Skabichevsky wrote something which made an impression on me. He said I would die in a ditch, drunk.' He was writing for twenty-five years and during that time his writing was constantly attacked. I do not know whether the critics of the present day are naturally of a less ferocious temper; I must allow that on the whole the judgment that has been passed on the stories in this volume when from time to time a collection has been published in book form has been favourable. One epithet, however, has been much applied to them, which has puzzled me; they have been described with disconcerting frequency as 'competent' [see in particular the excerpt dated 1931]. Now on the face of it I might have thought this laudatory, for to do a thing competently is certainly more deserving of praise than to do it incompetently, but the adjective has been used in a disparaging sense and, anxious to learn and if possible to improve, I have asked myself what was in the mind of the critics who thus employed it. Of course none of us is liked by everybody and it is necessary that a man's writing, which is so intimate a revelation of himself, should be repulsive to persons who are naturally antagonistic to the creature he is. This should leave him unperturbed. But when an author's work is somewhat commonly found to have a quality that is unattractive to many it is sensible of him to give the matter his attention. There is evidently something that a number of people do not like in my stories and it is this they try to express when they damn them with the faint praise of competence. I have a notion that it is the definiteness of their form. I hazard the suggestion (perhaps unduly flattering to myself) because this particular criticism has never been made in France where my stories have had with the critics and the public much greater success than they have had in England. The French, with their classical sense and their orderly minds, demand a precise form and are exasperated by a work in which the ends are left lying about, themes are propounded and not resolved and a climax is foreseen and then eluded. This precision on the other hand has always been slightly antipathetic to the English. Our great novels have been shapeless and this, far from disconcerting their readers, has given them a sense of security. This is the life we know, they have thought, with its arbitrariness and inconsequence; we can put out of our minds the irritating thought that two and two make four. If I am right in this surmise I can do nothing about it and I must resign myself to being called competent for the rest of my days. My prepossessions in the arts are on the side of law and order. I like a story that fits. I did not take to writing stories seriously till I had had much experience as a dramatist, and this experience taught me to leave out everything that did not serve the dramatic value of my story. It taught me to make incident follow incident in such a manner as to lead up to the climax I had in mind. I am not unaware of the disadvantages of this method. It gives a tightness of effect that is sometimes disconcerting. You feel that life does not dovetail into its various parts with such neatness. In life stories straggle, they begin nowhere and tail off without a point. That is probably what Chekhov meant when he said that stories should have neither a beginning nor an end. It is certain that sometimes it gives you a sensation of airlessness when you see persons who behave so exactly according to character, and incidents that fall into place with such perfect convenience. The story-teller of this kind aims not only at giving his own feelings about life, but at a formal decoration. He arranges life to suit his purposes. He follows a design in his mind, leaving out this and changing that; he distorts facts to his advantage, according to his plan; and when he attains his object produces a work of art. It may be that life slips through his fingers; then he has failed; it may be that he seems sometimes so artificial that you cannot believe him, and when you do not believe a story-teller he is done. When he succeeds he has forced you for a time to accept his view of the universe and has given you the pleasure of following out the pattern he has drawn on the surface of chaos. But he seeks to prove nothing. He paints a picture and sets it before you. You can take it or leave it. (pp. 53-61)

W. Somerset Maugham, in a preface to "The Complete Short Stories: East and West, Vol. I," in his Selected Prefaces and Introductions of W. Somerset Maugham, *William Heinemann Ltd., 1963, pp. 42-61.*

H. E. Bates (essay date 1941)

[*Bates was a respected English short story writer, novel-*

Maugham in the 1940s.

ist, and critic. His The Modern Short Story *is considered an excellent introduction to the twentieth-century short story form. In the following excerpt from that work, Bates discusses Maugham's principal influences and pronounces him a proficient but excessively traditional and therefore not influential short story writer.*]

Maugham is at once an attractive and a rather disconcerting figure. Beginning as a writer with, as it were, no ear for words, Maugham had very early to choose a stylistic model which his own limitations would permit him to follow without embarrassment. To have chosen a pretentious, poetical, highly coloured writer would have been fatal. Maugham chose Maupassant, and throughout his career has stuck to Maupassant. It is interesting to recall here that Maupassant has been described as "the born popular writer, battered by Flaubert into austerity," and perhaps Maugham is an example of the sort of writer, popular, cosmopolitan, commercial and yet in some way distinguished, that Maupassant might have been if left alone. Maugham is now, at his best, as in *Cakes and Ale,* a master of cultivated acidity. The spare sere detachment of his prose may, with the exception of recurrent lapses into appalling sentimentality, be safely offered as a sound foundation course in commercial-literary craftsmanship.

One other influence, not I believe admitted by Maugham, seems to have shaped his craft. Repeatedly throughout his work, speaking both for himself and through his characters, Maugham reveals an ironic impatience with the stuffiness of literary and moral conventions (see the delicious dissection of the pompous social-climbing novelist in *Cakes and Ale*), and is constantly administering the acid corrective. The parallel for this side of Maugham's method is not Maupassant, but *The Way of All Flesh,* a book for which Maugham is admirably fitted to write a modern counterpart. Here are two quotations:

> Like other rich men at the beginning of this century he ate and drank a good deal more than was enough to keep him in health. Even his excellent constitution was not proof against a prolonged course of overfeeding and what we should now consider overdrinking. His liver would not unfrequently get out of order, and he would come down to breakfast looking yellow about the eyes.
>
> I fancy that life is more amusing now than it was forty years ago and I have a notion that people are more amiable. They may have been worthier then, possessed of more substantial knowledge; I do not know. I know they were more cantankerous; they ate too much, many of them drank too much, and they took too little exercise. Their livers were out of order and their digestions often impaired.

The account of the first paragraph, which is Butler, is pitched in a key identical with that of the second, which is Maugham. The effect in both is gained by a series of apparently matter-of-fact statements, made almost offhand, with a sort of casual formality, qualified by a sort of airy, "Of course I don't really know. Don't go and take my word for it," which in reality injects the note of irony. Maugham and Butler again and again use this trick of creating ironic effect by disclaiming all trustworthy knowledge of what they are talking about, and by pitching their remarks in a negative key. The effect is delicious; butter won't melt in these acid mouths. *The Way of All Flesh* and *Cakes and Ale* will, in fact, repay some pretty close comparative study, and will show, I think, that Maugham found a far more profitable and compatible influence in Butler than in Maupassant.

It is my contention in fact that if Maugham had, as a writer of stories, rejected Maupassant as a model and kept more closely to Butler, we should have been presented with the first full-length English short-story writer worthy of comparison with the best continental figures. Unfortunately Maugham, in spite of an excellent eye, a dispassionate steadiness, a genius for the diagnosis of human frailty, and a cosmopolitan temperament, lacks one very great and supremely important quality. Unlike Tchehov and Maupassant, in whom he professes to see great differences but who were much alike at least in this respect, Maugham lacks compassion. He has no heart, and in place of that heart one has the impression that he uses a piece of clockwork. It is this, I think, that gives Maugham's work the frequent impression of cheapness. This effect is heightened by something else. Maugham, having mastered the art of irony, mistakenly supposed himself to be a cynic. But throughout Maugham's work, and notably in the stories, there exists a pile of evidence to show that Maugham the cynic is in reality a tin-foil wrapping for Maugham the sentimentalist. Maugham's cynicism indeed peels off under too-close examination, thin, extraneous, tinny, revealing underneath a man who is afraid of trusting and finally of revealing his true emotions.

There would be little point, here, in doing more than summarize the quality of Maugham's stories. They are easily available, pleasantly readable; they tell a story—in the sense, that is, that what they have to say can be expressed anecdotally; they deal largely with romantic places, for Maugham, like Kipling and Conrad, loves the East, and to his talent for painting its scenery and people he owes, as they do, much of his popular success. He delights in exposing human frailty, particularly amorous and marital frailty, and the humbug of convention; he is suave and urbane; he has the keenest sense of dramatic situations and delights in leaving the reader, as Maupassant and O. Henry did, with the point of the story neatly sharpened and vinegared in his hands. His natural sense of poetry is nil; his methods are as objective as the newspaper report of a court case, and sometimes as bad; he wisely refrains, except on rare occasions, from the purple passage, yet he has apparently never discovered any conscious and simple method of detecting himself in the act of using a cliché. When he is good, like the little girl, he is very good; and similarly when he is bad he is horrid.

Maugham indeed, though presenting the interesting case of a man who (on his own confession) evolved an attractively individual style without the help of a natural ear for words, has nothing new to offer. He simply perpetuates a tradition of straightforward, objective story-telling, largely derived from French naturalism, that is already well known. Thus Maugham's influence is not, and never has been, wide or important. (pp. 142-46)

H. E. Bates, "Katherine Mansfield and A. E. Coppard," in his The Modern Short Story: A Critical Survey, *T. Nelson and Sons Ltd., 1941, pp. 122-47.*

John Pollock (essay date 1966)

[In the following excerpt, Pollock assesses what he considers Maugham's principal methods of characterization, drawing examples from several of Maugham's short stories.]

Somerset Maugham's place in literature will be fixed in years to come. At least a generation must go by before anything like certainty can be achieved about a writer of eminence. Often the favourite of to-day is the outcast of to-morrow, and by no means seldom does the pendulum of critical judgement swing back later from unjust depreciation. There are even now signs that George Meredith is coming again into his own. My view about Somerset Maugham is that he will be set among writers at the top of the first class, both as novelist and as playwright, really great authors being apart and above. I do not think he can be classed with Fielding, Thackeray, Voltaire, Balzac, Tolstoy, or Gogol; still less with Shakespeare, Goethe, Marlowe, Sophocles, Euripides, Racine, and Molière. As a short-story writer he comes certainly very close to those three masters Kipling, most tremendous of all, Guy de Maupassant, and Henry James, but it may be questioned whether, as a branch of art, the short story permits of development enough to enable true greatness to show itself.

This is by the way. I wish merely to show that Somerset Maugham is worthy to have his methods carefully considered, which might not be the case with an author, however good, of the second class like, say, George Eliot, Joseph Conrad, or Alphonse Daudet. It must always be of interest to see how a first-class writer, Anthony Trollope or Anatole France for instance, works. It is Somerset Maugham's method, or at least one part of his method, that I propose to study here, because it is the part that can best be studied with as little delay as possible after his death.

In the second half of his preface to ***First Person Singular*** Somerset Maugham deals with the question of how does an author come by his characters, and describes in a few incisive pages how traits from real persons among his acquaintance are used to create imaginary portraits. He refers to the notes of Henri Beyle, the letters of Flaubert, and the journal of Jules Renard as evidence that this is the general practice of authors. 'I think, indeed,' he writes, 'that most novelists, and surely the best, have worked from life. But though they have had in mind a particular person this is not to say that they have copied him nor that the character they have devised is to be taken for a portrait.' And he goes on to assert that to present an exact copy would be to defeat the author's aim, which is verisimilitude. 'Nothing,' he says, 'is so unsafe as to put into a novel a person drawn line by line from life. His values are all wrong and, strangely enough, he does not make the other characters of the book seem false, but himself. He never convinces.' Somerset Maugham's purpose in so discussing a novelist's method was to rebut the charge made against him of 'portraying certain persons so exactly that it was impossible not to know them,' in other words of painting word-portraits of real people. His method, he implies, was the method he has just praised, which was, as he might have said to strengthen his case had he thought it worth while, a method employed among others by Thackeray. The Marquis of Steyne is a famous example; George Warrington in *Pendennis* was in some respects drawn from Tennyson's great friend, George Venables, Wenham from J. W. Croker, Sir Pitt Crawley from Lord Rolle, and traits in Dorington, my father's godfather, went to make up the character of Major Pendennis. Meredith drew for Beauchamp on Admiral Maxse, and for *Diana of the Crossways* on Mrs Norton.

Somerset Maugham's own account of the manner in which he built up his characters from observation may be accepted without question. It is borne out by internal evidence. Only, as in Somerset Maugham the power of observation was developed to an unusually acute degree, so do his studies of character in which strokes are drawn from living models tend to resemble those models more than is usually the case with other novelists and more perhaps than Somerset Maugham himself intended or, when challenged, would concede. In one case, he tells us, he did paint a deliberately literal portrait. That is the character of Mortimer Ellis, the 'celebrated' bigamist, in that enchanting story called **"The Round Dozen."** He suggests that we ought all to know who the original was, but I confess that I do not; neither do the few knowledgeable people I have asked. Mortimer Ellis is so vivid and so plausible a character that Somerset Maugham may be supposed, without realizing it, to have added certain features from his imagination, otherwise he would be offering a flat contradiction of his own thesis that 'a person drawn line by line from life . . . never convinces.' In reality his imagination was so keen, if perhaps more keen than wide, that he could hardly have avoided doing so. It is only because his faculty of observation was so uncommonly prominent that he has sometimes been thought deficient in imagination.

Without a powerful imagination, working almost always in the sphere of psychological analysis, Somerset Maugham could never have created the gallery of life-like characters we have from his pen. It is evident that in constructing them he worked as a rule on the lines he described. The method closely resembles that of a painter working from models on an imaginative subject. The degree in which imagination is blended with observation may vary *ad infinitum;* but, however important may be the former in the resultant mixture, it is rare that the model is not recognizable. (pp. 365-67)

Somerset Maugham used two lines of approach to his subjects. In one, he took what may be called the outer psychological values of a real person and wrought them into an imaginary portrait by embodying them in a series of incidents which had no relation, or only a very slight relation, to those of his model's actual life. In the other, he took the fundamental values and put them into fictitious persons who had otherwise no relation at all to his models. This again he would vary by taking real incidents and putting fictitious persons among them, so that his characters took upon themselves a strong colour of being observed from life. An instance of this is his story called **"The Letter,"** which he turned into a still more famous play. Here he took an incident from real life that had, years before, been the subject of a *cause célèbre* in the Far East. It had happened long before Somerset Maugham's visit to the spot, therefore he could not have known any of the persons concerned. But he fitted characters of his imagination to the facts with such skill and force as to create astonishment and no little pain in the minds of those who had been personally acquainted with the protagonists in the real drama. In general, however, he so mixed his variations of method and so embroidered his characters with imaginary touches that readers, unless possessed of special knowledge, might not realize the personages in the story to have been drawn from life. It is therefore a matter of literary and historical interest to track down some of the models from which Somerset Maugham worked. The list that I can give is doubtless far from complete. Nevertheless it contains some striking figures.

A very good specimen of a canvas containing such an admixture of traits observed in real men and women and of imaginary characters and events is to be found in ***Ashenden; or, The British Agent.*** Here we are at once confronted with a figure drawn from a living model: that of Ashenden himself, the narrator, who is clearly a self-portrait of the author. In the war of 1914-18, Somerset Maugham was engaged in our Intelligence Service in Switzerland and his note-book served as a basis for the stories. He says so openly. Events are seen through the eyes of the narrator, that is, his own. Apart from the fact that the key is given by Ashenden being a novelist, delicious little touches here and there produce an intimate note that surely reveals a bit of Maugham's own mind. Take this passage: Ashenden is in his bath. He 'sighed, for the water was no longer quite so hot, he could not reach the tap with his hand nor could he turn it with his toes (as every properly regulated tap should turn), and if he got up to add more hot water he might just as well get out altogether.' This is a reflexion so personal that no imagination however vivid could invent it. Ashenden is doubtless not wholly Somerset Maugham, but Somerset Maugham sat as his own model for 'the British Agent.' To clinch the matter, Ashenden reappears later as the narrator and unfashionable novelist in *Cakes and Ale,* with the Christian name of Willie, which was Maugham's own, and gives us therein much interesting insight into Maugham's mind. Later again Maugham explicitly admitted his identity with Ashenden.

The entire book, ***Ashenden,*** gives the impression of being studded with similar scraps of reality, jotted down here and there from Maugham's actual experiences. It is a fairly safe wager that R., the enigmatic colonel who is Ashenden's chief, would be recognized by others in the same service. On the other hand many of the characters, the hairless Mexican, for instance, Miss King, the Hindu conspirator and his cabaret love, and Mr Hamilton, that priceless American, seem to bear the hallmark of invention: they are far more types than living individuals, however cunningly the types are individualized. It is not till late in the book that two of its personages other than Ashenden himself stand out with startling actuality. In the story called **"His Excellency"** there can be no question to those who knew him but that the model for the ambassador was Sir George Buchanan. Somerset Maugham does not directly mention Petrograd as the scene of the story, though he implicitly admits it in his preface to be so, but even were this not the case the portrait of Sir George Buchanan would be unmistakable. Here we have a striking example of Somerset Maugham's more usual manner of dealing with his models. All the facts narrated in the career of his ambassador are invented: the strange romance that his Excellency reveals in his life had plainly no counterpart whatever in that of Sir George Buchanan, although the minor romance which interrupts the career of the diplomat in the story called Byring had with equal certainty a basis in fact. But this apart, the psychological portrait of Buchanan, as he appeared at all events to visitors like Ashenden, is a masterpiece. That of his Excellency's wife, on the other hand, is totally unlike Lady Georgina Buchanan, who was so impressive a personality that the neglect of her by Somerset Maugham as a model clearly shows his intention not to copy reality, but merely to borrow traits from it. (pp. 367-69)

Somerset Maugham's second line of approach to his models, namely by taking their fundamental values and putting them into fictitious persons, is perfectly illustrated by his treatment of himself in *Of Human Bondage.* No one could ever doubt that the hero of his book, Philip, represents Maugham himself; and this is admitted in the preface to the volume in the collected edition of 1937. It is a spiritual autobiography. But the spiritual truth is set in trappings of slender verisimilitude. Philip's experiences at school must be reminiscences of Somerset Maugham's own youth; those at the hospital are evidently drawn from life; but the master thread on which this long chaplet of pearls is strung is not a bit of reporting. This is Philip's club foot. Somerset Maugham was not a cripple. Then how does this dominant motive, absent from the author's life, fit into an autobiographical novel? Very simply. Philip's crippled leg in the book is Somerset Maugham's stammer in real life. The author's infirmity was transmuted by him into a totally different sort of infirmity, graver physically, but morally perhaps not more galling than his. From Philip we know of the dreadful mental pain suffered by Somerset Maugham as the result of his infirmity, just as in Philip's torment in the linen-draper's shop we can read Maugham's detestation of the drudgery entailed by his medical practice in Lambeth. (pp. 373-74)

Another glimpse of Somerset Maugham's soul comes to us, I submit, in that brilliant short story, **"The Human Element."** Here, unless my shot is off the mark, Maugham projected something of his own feelings into the character of Lady Betty Welldon-Burns, daughter of a duke and electric leader of the bright young people in London, who retires to the Isle of Rhodes to live maritally with Albert, formerly 'the second footman at Aunt Louise's.' This drama is kept on the plane of high comedy and we are allowed to feel its deeper repercussions only in the despair of Humphrey Carruthers, the cultured Foreign Office clerk who vainly tries first to win, then to save, Lady Betty. 'What destroys me,' says Carruthers, 'what makes me so frightfully unhappy, is to think of her unspeakable degradation. . . . I admired her courage and her frankness, her intelligence and her love of beauty. She's just a sham and she's never been anything else.' In his rôle as narrator Somerset Maugham makes answer.

> I wonder if that's true. Do you think any of us are all of a piece? Do you know what strikes me? I should have said that Albert was only the instrument, her toll to the solid earth, so to speak, that left her soul at liberty to range the empyrean. Perhaps the mere fact that he was so far below her gave her a sense of freedom in her relations with him that she would have lacked with a man of her own class. The spirit is very strange, it never soars so high as when the body has wallowed for a period in the gutter.

It is difficult not to see here an apologia for Maugham's own way of life that cut him off for some years and in some degree from regular intercourse with men of his own station and from completely normal society. This partial and self-imposed ostracism, accentuated by Maugham's firm refusal ever to attach himself to a literary clique, seems to be reflected in Lady Betty's withdrawal from the great world, to live with her own thoughts and her own tastes on a far-off Greek island. Maugham was too big a man to fall in with the artifices of London literary snobs. They distrusted and envied his success; they feared his biting pen. His place was achieved by himself alone, against all adventitious aids. But to achieve it he had to withdraw within himself, and his professional aloofness was redoubled not only by his infirmity but by the ordering of his life that was in no way flaunting or tinged with proselytism but, though discreet and purely personal, none the less put him at odds with received British ethical standards. (pp. 374-75)

John Pollock, "Somerset Maugham and His Work," in The Quarterly Review, *Vol. 304, No. 650, October, 1966, pp. 365-78.*

Anthony Curtis (essay date 1982)

[*Curtis, an English critic, has written several studies of Maugham and coedited* W. Somerset Maugham: The Critical Heritage *(1987) with John Whitehead. In the following excerpt from his* Somerset Maugham, *he discusses the importance of short story writing in Maugham's career and notes the journalistic origins and traits of most of Maugham's short stories.*]

The kinship that exists between the art of play-writing and short-story-writing has often been noted; consider Chekhov or Pirandello; or, for that matter, Noël Coward. In both forms the writer has to put across a vast amount of information in a minimum number of words; the signals are often multiple while seeming to be simple. You can be a born novelist, but lack the ability required to execute either the play or the short story successfully. By contrast you can be a novelist who escapes occasionally into the short-story like a man snatching a weekend's break away from home; and you can be by vocation a short-story-writer who occasionally attempts the novel. On this question Graham Greene in the introduction to his *Collected Stories* (1972) writes:

> I remain in this field a novelist who has happened to write short stories, just as there are certain short story writers (Maupassant and V. S. Pritchett come to mind) who have happened to write novels. This is not a superficial distinction—or even a technical distinction as between an artist who paints in oil or watercolour; it is certainly not a distinction in value. It is a distinction between two different ways of life.

Maugham happened, like Maupassant, to write novels; one or two of them have become famous, but he was born a short-story writer, one of the most skilful and fertile ever to have practised the art. He appeared to be able to conjure stories out of the air. His *Notebook* abounds in excellent ideas for stories he never bothered to write up, and so, according to those closest to him, did his table talk. He destroyed one unpublished group relating to his espionage activities, for security reasons. Many of the earliest he never bothered to reprint after their magazine appearances. Nevertheless there remain readily accessible in different editions about ninety stories. They range from the very short ones collected in ***Cosmopolitans*** (1936), written originally to be printed on opposite pages of *Cosmopolitan Magazine,* such as **"Mr Know-All"** and **"Salvatore"**, to those occupying some forty to fifty printed pages, the bulk of them including such famous tales as **"Before the Party"**, **"The Outstation"**, **"P & O"**, **"The Alien Corn"**, **"Gigolo and Gigolette"**, **"The Colonel's Lady"** and many more.

The magazine origin of these stories is not fortuitous. The Maugham short story is a form of journalism; the point at which journalism becomes literary art. Let us pick one to look at closely. I have selected **"P & O"** from ***The Casuarina Tree*** (1926), almost at random. The whole of the action occurs on board one of the elegant Peninsular and Orient liners which is carrying an assorted group of British passengers back home after their tour of duty as planters or members of the administration of the Federated

Malay States. Maugham fixes on one of the passengers, a Mrs Hamlyn, as the mediating consciousness for his tale. In her early forties she is returning to England without her husband from whom, it soon emerges, she is estranged. He has fallen in love with the wife of a business colleague who, to Mrs Hamlyn's mortification, is considerably older than her. At the start, Mrs Hamlyn sits in her deckchair in the early morning, while the ship is tied up in Singapore. Like the good journalist he is, Maugham rapidly establishes the multi-racial background, the structure of ethnic strains, that is so relevant to his story:

> Singapore is the meeting place of many races. The Malays, though natives of the soil, dwell uneasily in towns, and are few; and it is the Chinese, supple, alert and industrious, who throng the streets; the dark-skinned Tamils walk on their silent naked feet, as though they were but brief sojourners in a strange land, but the Bengalis sleek and prosperous, are easy in their surroundings, and self-assured; the sly and obsequious Japanese seem busy with pressing and secret affairs; and the English in their topees and white ducks, speeding past in motor-cars or at leisure in their rickshaws, wear a nonchalant careless air. The rulers of these teeming peoples take their authority with smiling unconcern. And now, tired and hot, Mrs Hamlyn waited for the ship to set out again on her long journey across the Indian Ocean.

It is that long journey which provides Maugham with the natural linear progression for his story. By the time the ship comes into the sight of land at Aden, Mrs Hamlyn will have come to terms with her life of separation, and a fellow passenger will have died a mysterious death. He is an Irishman named Gallagher who has made his money out of the rubber boom, and is on his way back home for an early retirement. Mrs Hamlyn learns from his Cockney foreman, one of the second-class passengers on the ship, that while working up-country Gallagher had lived for some ten or twelve years with a Malay girl who, on being abandoned, has put a curse on him. Here, as in the play *The Circle,* we have a neat symmetry of construction: the situation of Mrs Hamlyn and Mr Gallagher mirrors each other.

The material of first-hand observation in this story has been arranged with precision to make a number of dramatic points. As soon as the ship leaves port Mr Gallagher begins to suffer from uncontrollable attacks of hiccups. At first this is treated as a joke by the other passengers, but his condition becomes so serious that he has to retire to the sick-bay under the care of the ship's doctor (who, incidentally, is having a flirtation with the wife of one of the other passengers). The curse has started to take effect. Gallagher's life may be in danger. One senses that the germ of the story lay in some traveller's tale that Maugham (or Haxton) overheard. By showing us the impact of Gallagher's mortal sickness on the whole shipboard community, passengers and crew, Maugham gives us a portrait of British society in the last days of the colonial era. The irony in his initial statement, 'The rulers of these teeming peoples take their authority with smiling unconcern', reverberates as the ship ploughs its way home. The class divisions ruling on board between the first-class passengers, the second-class passengers, and the lower decks, containing the humble members of the crew, Lascars and others, correspond neatly to those within the British Empire. The first-class passengers are planning a Fancy Dress Ball over Christmas and the great question is, should they drop the protocol for once and invite the second-class passengers? Some argue in favour, but the majority are against. All are concerned lest the death of Mr Gallagher, if it occurs, will cause the Ball to be cancelled. It is only a second-class citizen, Gallagher's Cockney assistant, who goes out of his way to do something practical which might help him. He takes the unprecedented step of applying to the third- and fourth-class citizens in the form of the native members of the crew to perform a magical ceremony to exorcise the curse Gallagher's mistress has cast over him. They agree to his request and slit the throat of a cockerel intoning curious chants. 'We're no match for them, us white men, and that's a fact,' he tells Mrs Hamlyn in explanation. But the exorcism does not work and Gallagher continues to languish.

As his death approaches, 'a definite malaise' overcomes the entire ship, and the reader senses a deeper malaise still: it is as if Maugham had sensed the collapse of the whole paternalist imperial system some thirty years before it happened. Mrs Hamlyn observes two Japanese passengers playing deck-quoits:

> They were trim and neat in their tennis shirts, white trousers and buckram shoes. They looked very European, they even called the score to one another in English, and yet somehow to look at them filled Mrs Hamlyn with a vague disquiet.

Maugham's stories had a huge readership. They seemed to appeal to all classes throughout the world save one, the professional literary critics. Turning through the pages of the pre-war *New Statesman* we can find plenty of critical attacks on Maugham's tales by people such as Rebecca West; but let us turn instead to the view taken by Cyril Connolly in his *The Modern Movement: 100 Key Books from England, France and America* (1965):

> In these Far Eastern stories . . . and in the secret service tales of ***Ashenden*** (1928), Maugham achieves an unspoken ferocity, a controlled ruthlessness before returning to sentimentality with Rosie in *Cakes and Ale.* He tells us—and it had not been said before—exactly what the British in the Far East were like, the judges and planters and civil servants and their womenfolk at home, even as ***Ashenden*** exposes what secret service work is really like. That would not be enough without his mastery of form, if not of language. His bloodless annexation of the Far East pays off in ***The Casuarina Tree*** which includes **"The Yellow Streak", "The Outstation", "Before the Party"** and **"The Letter"**—about a coward, a snob, a murderess and a blackmailer.

Nor was it only the Far East, and Europe on the eve of the Bolshevik revolution, to which Maugham applied his 'controlled ruthlessness' in short-story form. He viewed the exiled aristocracy and the nightclub entertainers of the French Riviera, the smart world of [his wife] Syrie's friends, the inmates of a French penal colony and a dozen other milieux across the world in the same manner. As far back as his medical student days he had been a great traveller, and now, as a rich man, he toured the world at will. His travel books have the same easy readability, the same journalist's flair for an arresting incident as his best stories, but involving less rigorous manipulation of the material. No one who wishes to know Maugham should neglect books like *On a Chinese Screen, The Gentleman in the Parlour* or *Don Fernando.*

Maugham found a statement of the aims of the short-story writer in Edgar Allan Poe's review of Nathaniel Hawthorne's *Twice-Told Tales.* 'In the whole composition,' Poe said, 'there should be no word written, of which the tendency, direct or indirect, is not to the pre-established design.' After quoting that, Maugham gives his own formulation of a good short story:

> It is a piece of fiction, dealing with a single incident, material or spiritual, that can be read at a sitting; it is original, it must sparkle, excite or impress; and it must have unity of effect or impression. It should move in an even line from its exposition to its close.
>
> (Introduction to *Tellers of Tales,* 1939)

(pp. 21-5)

Anthony Curtis, in his Somerset Maugham, *Profile Books Ltd., 1982, 47 p.*

Maugham on Short Story Writing:

I have written now nearly a hundred stories and one thing I have discovered is that whether you hit upon a story or not, whether it comes off or not, is very much a matter of luck. Stories are lying about at every street corner, but the writer may not be there at the moment they are waiting to be picked up or he may be looking at a shop window and pass them unnoticed. He may write them before he has seen all there is to see in them or he may turn them over in his mind so long that they have lost their freshness. He may not have seen them from the exact standpoint at which they can be written to their best advantage. It is a rare and happy event when he conceives the idea of a story, writes it at the precise moment when it is ripe, and treats it in such a way as to get out of it all that it implicitly contains. Then it will be within its limitations perfect. But perfection is seldom achieved. I think a volume of modest dimensions would contain all the short stories which even closely approach it. The reader should be satisfied if in any collection of these short pieces of fiction he finds a general level of competence and on closing the book feels that he has been amused, interested and moved.

From his preface to his Complete Short Stories of W. Somerset Maugham *(1952).*

Joseph Epstein (essay date 1985)

[*Epstein is an American educator and critic. In the following excerpt, he assesses Maugham's career and briefly surveys the chief characteristics of his short fiction.*]

> The critic I am waiting for is the one who will explain why, with all my faults, I have been read for so many years by so many people.
>
> —W. Somerset Maugham

"Four powers govern men: avarice, lust, fear, and snobbishness." Somerset Maugham didn't write that; Hilaire Belloc did. But Somerset Maugham, I think it fair to say, believed it. Avarice, lust, fear, and snobbishness are Maugham's great subjects; they are everywhere in his work, as theme, as motive, as background. Small wonder that they would be, for the same dark quartet—avarice, lust, fear, and snobbishness—were also the four reigning qualities in Somerset Maugham's own triumphant, lengthy, and finally rather sad life.

Cyril Connolly once called Somerset Maugham the "last of the great professional writers." He meant it as an honorific. It has not always been taken that way. One small step down from the professional writer is the hack; one large step up is the artist. A great many more critics have been willing to drop Maugham a step than have been willing to raise him a step. Maugham was always highly conscious of this; and one could string together a quite long necklace composed of the BB's he shot over his lifetime at highbrow critics, small-public writers, intellectual-magazine editors, and others who accorded his work less respect than he thought it deserved. "But you must remember the intelligentsia despise me," Maugham in late life told his nephew Robin Maugham. "Take that magazine that's indoors. What's it called? *Encounter*? Well, all the writers on *Encounter* despise me completely. I read it just to find out what's going on and what people are interested in. But I must confess I find it terribly boring." Not the least interesting item in that snippet of conversation is that, whatever his professed views of *Encounter,* Maugham nevertheless subscribed to and read it. He was a man who didn't miss much. (p. 1)

Maugham thought of himself, interestingly, as a professional humorist, which in his stories he calls himself more than a few times, and in one of his Ashenden stories, **"The Traitor,"** he speaks of "the pleasant comedy of life." He meant this, I believe, in the sense in which one speaks of the human comedy. He put his case in *The Summing Up,* where he wrote: "A sense of humour leads you to take pleasure in the discrepancies of human nature; it leads you to mistrust great professions and look for the unworthy motive that they conceal; the disparity between appearance and reality diverts you and you are apt when you cannot find it to create it." If the humorist sometimes misses truth, beauty, and goodness, he is nonetheless tolerant, for he has no interest in moralizing but is "content to understand; and it is true that to understand is to pity and forgive."

While there was nothing of the aesthete about Maugham, nor any aesthetic difficulty about his work, few modern writers have been clearer about their own aesthetic program and, with the exceptions of Paul Valéry and Henry James, perhaps none has thought more trenchantly about the aesthetic questions raised by literary creation. Maugham thought, for example, that the artist is not justified in wishing to be judged by his intention; for him the crucial moment in the aesthetic transaction is that of communication—that moment when the work of art addresses the viewer or listener or reader. He thought talent to be made up of a natural aptitude for creation combined with a strong outlook on life shorn of the prejudices of the current day. "Sometimes," he wrote in *Don Fernando,* "there will be found a man who has this facility for writing to an extraordinary degree and to this joins an outlook on life which is not only peculiar to himself, but appeals to all men, and then he will be called a genius." Once, when asked the secrets of his own craft by a Chinese professor, he replied: "I know only two. One is to have common sense and the other is to stick to the point." (pp. 6-7)

Maugham remains intensely, immensely readable. Why? One recalls his revealing the secrets of his craft to the Chinese professor: "One is to have common sense and the other is to stick to the point." The point Maugham stuck to throughout his long career was the investigation of that magnificent, comic, admirable, outrageous, depressing, impressive, grim, gracious, grudging, great, and elusive thing called human nature. Human nature was Maugham's enduring subject, and for fiction there is none greater. If you are interested in it, you have to be interested in the writing of Somerset Maugham. As for his common sense, it was pervasive; the test is that he was an artist who knew that there are things in life greater than art. "I think," he wrote in *A Writer's Notebook,* "there is in the heroic courage with which man confronts the irrationality of the world a beauty greater than the beauty of art." Because he was able to insinuate such sentiments, subtly, dramatically, into his work—see, for an example, the story entitled **"Sanatorium"**—Maugham shall always be a writer for readers who care for more than writing alone. (p. 10)

One is unlikely to encounter Maugham's books in a university curriculum. In my youth his work, because he was an international bestseller, was ubiquitous, and if one was at all bookish one was likely, when young, to have read *The Razor's Edge* and *Of Human Bondage;* or if one thought of oneself as artistic to have found self-justification in reading *The Moon and Sixpence,* his not very good novel modeled on the life of Paul Gauguin. Today I think the best introduction—or re-introduction—to Maugham is through his short stories. So many of these seem so good that it may be unjust to single out a few. But among the four volumes of stories now available in Penguin editions, **"Mr. Harrington's Washing"** is a work of comic genius; **"The Pool"** may be the best story ever written on the subject of going native; **"The Hairless Mexican"** is spy fiction raised to the highest power; and **"Lord Montdrago"** is but one of his many stories that provide a cunning anatomy of snobbery. Maugham's nonfiction also bears looking into. At the top of his form he was a very capable essayist—see the volumes entitled *The Vagrant Mood* and *Points of View*—and *Don Fernando,* the book on Spanish culture, contains many clever and wise things. My sense is that it is best to read Maugham's stories and nonfiction first, and let them lead one back to the novels, where one is likely to discover that Maugham is one of those novelists who can be profitably read when young but who get better as one gets older.

Maugham would probably be best served by a single volume on the order of the "Viking Portable" series, except that, in his case, the volume, to suit his ample talent, would have to be of a thickness beyond portability. Such a volume, if I were its editor, would include all of *Cakes and Ale,* the better part of *The Summing Up,* the portrait of Elliott Templeton from *The Razor's Edge,* the essays on El Greco, Burke's prose, and Kant's aesthetics, and nearly everything he wrote on prose style. What would make the volume bulge, proving a severe test of the binder's art, would be the number of short stories that would have to be included. The short story really was Maugham's best form, and he published more than a hundred of them—among serious writers, perhaps only Chekhov wrote more. Some of his stories are thin, especially those that attempt to point an easy moral or have a trick ending, but the vast majority are very sturdily made. Those set in the Malay States, taken together, conduce to give as complete a picture of the British abroad as do Kipling's stories of India. Maugham's stories about the artistic life—**"The Alien Corn," "The Creative Impulse"** chief among them—are also too good not to be included.

Often Maugham's stories seem akin to reading La Rochefoucauld with illustrations—not drawings of course but illustrations from life. Maugham resembles La Rochefoucauld in taking avarice, lust, fear, and snobbishness for his subjects. Yet unlike La Rochefoucauld, Maugham's dark views about human nature are often stood on their head by evidence of courage, honesty, and integrity, almost always of an unexpected and complicated kind. Maugham is that odd phenomenon: a moralist who is never surprised by immorality. As he puts it in **"The Pool,"** "I held my breath, for to me there is nothing more awe-inspiring than when a man discovers to you the nakedness of his soul. Then you see that no one is so trivial or debased but that in him is a spark of something to excite compassion." (pp. 11-12)

Joseph Epstein, "Is It All Right to Read Somerset Maugham?" in The New Criterion, *Vol. IV, No. 3, November, 1985, pp. 1-13.*

John Whitehead (essay date 1987)

[*Whitehead, an English critic, is the editor of* W. Somerset Maugham, a Traveller in Romance: Uncollected Writings, 1901-1964 *(1984), and coeditor, with Anthony Curtis, of* W. Somerset Maugham: The Critical Heritage *(1987). In the following excerpt, Whitehead surveys Maugham's principal short stories.*]

In the notebooks Maugham brought back from his wartime voyaging in the South Seas were entries relating to other places besides Tahiti, in particular Honolulu and islands in the Samoan group, and these he came to recognize as providing raw material for short stories, a *genre* he had abandoned along with the novel ten years previously on making his breakthrough in the theatre. But the stories suggested by this material would be of a different kind and on an ampler scale than any he had previously attempted. There were eventually six of them, each of between 12,000 and 15,000 words in length, which together made a book about the size of the average novel. ***The Trembling of a Leaf*** was the first of five volumes published between 1921 and 1932, each containing six short stories of roughly that length. All thirty were issued in one volume in 1934 as Maugham's collected short stories [published as ***Altogether*** in England and as ***East and West*** in the United States], and they have been included in his subsequent collections; but it is worth stressing at this point how much the reader gains by reading the stories in their original volumes. The six stories in each by supplementing and illuminating one another form a distinct artistic whole, giving a unity of effect which is lost when a particular story is read out of context. In the case of ***The Trembling of a Leaf*** this effect is enhanced by the stories being prefaced by a sketch of the Pacific and rounded off by an 'Envoi', which do not appear in any of the collected editions. The irony in its sub-title 'Little Stories of the South Sea Islands', which suggests a series of improving tales issued by some missionary society, is only fully borne in on the reader when he has finished the last story.

For Maugham's purpose in these six stories (as well as in those which were to follow) was to explore the extremes of human emotion and behaviour, so that as a matter of course they deal with sex in its less domestic aspects, suicide, and murder. Each has for its skeleton an anecdote with—as Maugham so often insisted—a beginning, a middle and an end; and these bony structures he fleshed out by presenting his main characters in the round against authentically described backgrounds. For equally with Hardy's Wessex fiction they may properly be termed stories of character and environment. There is a further preliminary point to be made. The very readability of Maugham's stories carries with it the inherent risk that the reader will rest content with the superficial pleasures they offer and fail to appreciate their wider points of reference and deeper resonances. **"Mackintosh"**, the first story in ***The Trembling of a Leaf,*** furnishes a convenient example of this.

It is set in the fictitious island of Talua in the western part of the Samoan group which, having fallen to Germany's share when Germany and America divided the islands between themselves, was occupied by the British in 1914. It can be inferred that the events described took place two years later, about the time of Maugham's visit to the islands. Despite the story's title its central character is Walker, the 60-year-old, self-made administrator who for a quarter of a century has administered the island with a rough but benevolent paternalism. Under his coarse banter his assistant Mackintosh, a dour Aberdeen Scot, comes to hate him to such an extent that, though he manages to keep himself under control, his hatred grows into monomania. Walker overreaches himself by his high-handed response to the natives' demand for a fair wage for carrying out a road-making scheme dear to his heart, thereby incurring their enmity as well. Mackintosh, appalled at what he is doing, connives at the theft of his revolver by the chief's son who had instigated the natives' demand and is horrified when Walker is later brought in, dying from bullet wounds. Lying on his bed, Walker calls for whisky and tells Mackintosh he has advised the government in Apia that he is the right man to succeed him in the job of administrator. He asks him to treat the natives fairly: they are children, he says; be firm, kind and just to them. He will not have the crowd round his bed turned out and will not allow anyone to be punished for shooting him; Mackintosh is to say it was an accident.

> 'You're a religious chap, Mac. What's that about forgiving them? You know.'
>
> 'Forgive them, for they know not what they do.'
>
> 'That's right. Forgive them. . . .'

When Walker dies Mackintosh goes out, gets his revolver (which has been silently returned to him), walks down to the sea and, wading out into the lagoon where he had been swimming when the story begins, shoots himself.

The authenticity of background, on which the effectiveness of this and later Eastern stories depends, is achieved by the process of restraint Maugham imposed on himself. He did not attempt to give more than an intelligent traveller's account of the places in which they are set, nor give the natives parts to play in them that would have demanded a greater knowledge of their customs and language than he possessed—in this avoiding the blunder that falsifies much of Conrad's early work. Maugham's principal characters are European or white American about whom he could write with the authority conferred by sharing a common culture with them; and during his travels he learnt just enough about the places where his stories are located and of their inhabitants to provide the exotic context in which the principal characters could give rein to their idiosyncrasies. As to wider points of reference and deeper resonances, the analogy of the theme of **"Mackintosh"**, of which sufficient hints are given and which underpins the drama enacted on the island of Talua, is Christ's betrayal by Judas Iscariot. Much of the story's impact is missed if the reader fails to detect this.

No sacred parallel need be sought to the theme of **"The Fall of Edward Barnard"** which, in strong contrast to the previous story, is pure comedy. It tells how the beautiful Isabel Longstaffe, a member of a Chicago brahmin family, finding herself rejected by her fiancé Barnard who opts for a lotus life in Tahiti with Eva a half-caste girl—a goddess of the Polynesian spring, expert in mixing cocktails—settles for his best friend Bateman Hunter, a substantial dollar-bringing male virgin. The story with its edge of good-humoured satire is deftly constructed by means of unobtrusive flashbacks and has the additional interest that, twenty years after it was written, its three principal characters were to be reincarnated in Isobel Bradley, Larry Darrell and Gray Maturin in Maugham's last major novel *The Razor's Edge.* It is not until the reader has read a later story in ***The Trembling of a Leaf*** called **"The Pool"** that a doubt as to the permanence of Barnard's idyll with Eva enters his mind, as it is likely Maugham intended it should.

The third story in the volume **"Red"** is put together like a Chinese nest of boxes. All that 'happens' in it—the outer box—is that on the arrival of a shabby schooner smelling of paraffin and copra at an unnamed island in the Samoan group, off its usual run between Apia and Pago-Pago, the skipper, elderly and gross, goes ashore and calls on Neilson, a Swede living in a bungalow there, who tells him the story of the people who had lived there before. The skipper leaves to go about his business, and Neilson decides to return to Europe. The next box enclosed by the outer one is an account of Neilson's earlier history, how he had come to the island twenty-five years before for the sake of his health, having been told he had only a year to live, and been so overwhelmed by the beauty of the island that he determined to spend it there. Eying the repellent obesity of the skipper, he asks him if he had known a man called Red but gives him no chance to reply. The third box inside the other two is the story Neilson tells him of Red, 22 years old and a deserter from an American man-of-war, a comely youth who arrives on the island in a dugout from the native cutter in which he had escaped from Apia and is sheltered by Sally, a beautiful native girl. They fall in love and go to live in a hut on the creek where Neilson's bungalow stands. After an idyllic year together Red is shanghai'd aboard a British whaling-ship. Broken-hearted, Sally waits month after month for his return and four months after his disappearance bears his stillborn child. Neilson's thoughts wander back to his own part in the story—the next in smallness of the boxes—for two years afterwards he had fallen in love with Sally and married her, only to learn with anguish that she was still in love with Red and waited only for his return. For many years now they had lived in mutual indifference, she having aged prematurely as native women do. Red should be grateful, he tells the skipper, that fate had separated him from Sally while their love was still at its height. Suddenly suspicious, he asks him his name, and just as the skipper has admitted that for thirty years he has been known in the islands as Red, a stout, grey-haired native woman comes in, makes a commonplace remark to Neilson, glances indifferently at the skipper and goes out. The smallest box at the centre of the story is this moment of truth when Red and Sally are brought face to face and do not know each other.

"The Pool" is Maugham's first attempt to describe what happens when a European—in this case Lawson the manager of an English bank in Apia—marries a half-caste girl. Ethel, one of several children by native women begotten by a Norwegian adventurer, though able to wear European clothes with elegance prefers putting on a mother hubbard and swimming in a pool of the river a mile or two out of town. When Lawson takes her and their dismayingly dark-coloured son to Scotland she soon begins to pine and unable to bear it returns home with the child. Lawson follows, and while Ethel relapses more and more into her native background, he takes to drink, descending from job to job until he is glad to work for a half-caste store-keeper. On hearing she has taken a fat, elderly German-American as her lover, he drowns himself in the pool where she is accustomed to swim. In writing the story Maugham moved from first-person-singular to third-person-singular narration and back again, a proceeding so unobtrusively accomplished that it is not until he has reached the end that the reader finds himself wondering how certain incidents could have been known to the narrator.

Maugham took a chance of a different kind when constructing **"Honolulu"**, about the bewitching of the English skipper of a small Chinese-owned schooner plying between Honolulu and the islands. It is the first of his stories to open with a leisurely introduction written in the first person singular as if he were embarking on an essay. There follows an account of his being taken on a tour of the city by an American friend who in the Union Saloon (where Stevenson used to drink with King Kalakaua) introduces him to Captain Butler. Having been presented at length with what amounts to a factual travelogue, the reader is the more ready to swallow the tall story of black magic told to the narrator by Butler after dinner that evening aboard his schooner. The story has an effective surprise ending, though the reader who cares to look back to see how Maugham laid the trap will find that he permitted himself to play a trick which in a detective story would be considered against the rules.

The last of the six stories in ***The Trembling of a Leaf*** (though the first to be written) is **"Rain"**, which by way of stage and four film adaptations has become one of the best known of all Maugham's stories. In wartime a ship bound for Apia is detained at Pago-Pago because a crew member had contracted measles, a disease often fatal to Kanakas. Among the passengers are Sadie Thompson an American prostitute, who had joined the ship at Honolulu where she had been plying her trade in Iwelei, its Red Light district, and the high-minded missionary Davidson and his wife. Putting up in inadequately furnished rooms in a two-story frame house belonging to a half-caste, the respectable passengers—their nerves already frayed by the incessant rattling of the rain on the iron roof—are outraged by the wheezy strains of a gramophone playing ragtime and the sounds of dancing and popping corks coming from Miss Thompson's room, indicating that she is in business again. The story moves to its climax as Davidson attempts to bring her to repentance, using as his ultimate weapon the threat of having her deported to San Francisco where a three-year gaol sentence awaits her. The last stage of their duel so strongly resembles the inquisitor's struggle for the soul of the Maid in *St. Joan* (written in 1923) that it is difficult to resist the inference either that Shaw was influenced by Maugham's story or that Maugham had some earlier account of St. Joan's trial in mind when he devised **"Rain"**. However that may be, an awareness of the parallel gives the story an added depth. (pp. 83-9)

In February 1921 Maugham accompanied by [his secretary-companion Gerald] Haxton embarked at San Francisco for Honolulu and Sydney, where they took ship for Singapore, the starting-point for extensive travels in the Malay States, Borneo, New Guinea and the Dutch East Indies lasting several months, from which the travellers retired in August to a sanatorium in Java to recuperate. From the raw material acquired on the journey Maugham first composed six short stories, of similar length to those set in the South Seas, which were published in 1926 under the title ***The Casuarina Tree.*** The setting of four of them is the fictitious sultanate of Sembulu in Borneo having Kuala Solor as its chief town, probably a stand-in for Sarawak with its capital Kuching. The action of the other two takes place respectively on board a homeward-bound P. & O. passenger ship and in Malaya. Like the earlier ones they are stories of character and environment which explore the extremes of human emotion and behaviour, but written with greater assurance and less resort to poster-paint colours and strident melodrama.

His purpose in **"Before the Party"** was not to tell a murder story, but to describe ironically the reactions of the members of a respectable family to the knowledge that one of them is a murderess. One afternoon in early summer somewhere in England the Skinners are getting ready to leave home for a garden-party given by Canon Heywood in honour of an old college friend, now Bishop of Hong Kong. Mr. Skinner is a family solicitor with a silly wife and two daughters, the younger one Kathleen unmarried at 35, snobbish and forthright, the elder one Millicent, a year older and putting on weight, home with her daughter after eight years in Sembulu where eight months before her husband Harold, resident of a district there, had died. A rumour emanating from the bishop having got about that Harold had not died of fever as reported, but had cut his own throat in a fit of *delirium tremens,* Millicent's family demand to know the truth. The middle section of the story contains the account she gives them of her married life in Sembulu, in which she had fought a losing battle with Harold's alcoholism, culminating in her killing him with a parang in a fit of rage and making it appear to have been suicide. Each member of her family reacts in character to what, showing no sign of remorse or guilt, she has revealed, before they are all driven off to the canon's garden-party.

Although the anecdote round which he constructed **"P & O"** is a great deal more far-fetched than that of a woman killing her drunken husband, the story is more convincing because it is given a moral framework. It forms a pair with **"Honolulu"** in ***The Trembling of a Leaf,*** both being concerned with voodoo on shipboard, but whereas **"Honolulu"** leads to nothing more profound than a trick ending, there is a touch of Conrad in the account of the voyage of the unnamed liner on passage during December from Yokohama to England with its complement of home-bound expatriates. At Singapore the big Irish rubber-planter Gallaher comes aboard, retiring to Galway after twenty-five years in the F.M.S. [Federated Malay States]. Among the other passengers is Mrs. Hamlyn, on her way to England to divorce her husband, a silk-merchant in Japan, after twenty years of marriage, because at the age of 52 he has fallen passionately in love with a woman eight years older than himself. In the Indian Ocean the ship's surgeon becomes worried about Gallaher, who is in the hospital unable to keep food down or sleep, suffering from hiccups. Only Pryce the Cockney engineer from Gallaher's rubber estate knows what is wrong with him: the Malay girl whom he has abandoned after living with her for a dozen years has cast a spell on him, ensuring his death at sea. The notion that he is bewitched spreads among the passengers, distracting them from their preparations for a fancy-dress ball on Christmas Eve, and they become morose and resentful, wishing he would hurry up and peg out. The effect of Gallaher's decline on Mrs. Hamlyn is to make her regret not having turned a blind eye to her husband's infatuation; by leaving him she has given up a happy, comfortable life and now faces a bleak and lonely one.

> She was as lonely as the ship that throbbed her hasting way through an unpeopled sea, and lonely as the friendless man who lay dying in the ship's lazaret.

Despite a ceremony involving the killing of a cock performed by one of the Lascars who is a witch-doctor, Gallaher dies just as the ship makes its landfall at Aden. That evening, unable to bear the merriment of the ball any longer, Mrs. Hamlyn slips away and, finding no longer any anger and jealousy in her heart, writes her husband a letter glowing with forgiveness and affection.

In **"The Outstation"**, a reworking of the theme of **"Mackintosh"**, two British officials stationed in the back of beyond develop such a hatred of each other that the situation can only resolve itself through catastrophe. In contrast to the coarse and vulgar Walker, Mr. Warburton is an English gentleman who had been forced to seek a job in the Colonies when at the age of 34 he had come to the end of the substantial fortune he had inherited. For twenty years he has been in the service of the Sultan of Sembulu and is now resident of a district. Even in the remote area he administers he strictly follows the code of his class, insisting on dressing for dinner, especially when dining alone. Courageous and just, devoted to the Malays, his one failing is that he is an arch-snob. It is inevitable that he and Cooper, the uncouth ex-ranker who is sent out as his assistant after the War, should antagonize one another, and after a while they cease to be on speaking terms though living only 200 yards apart. Cooper is competent but treats the Malays as he had done the 'niggers' in Africa during the War, and it is only because Warburton instructs them to stay that he can keep any servants at all. Warburton warns him officially that, if he continues to withhold his boy's Abas's wages so as to prevent him running away, there is a great risk that Abas will kill him, and, when Cooper replies aggressively, decides with a shrug to let events take their course.

A little outstation in Sembulu is also the scene of **"The Force of Circumstance"**, to which the cheerful young assistant Guy brings his English wife. At first they are happy; then it comes to Doris's notice that there is often a Malay girl with a baby in her arms hanging round the bungalow and making scenes, and once walking through the kampong she comes on two half-caste children. Eventually Guy is forced to confess that the girl had lived with him in the bungalow for ten years and that the children are his. 'It's quite a family you've got', she says. Needing time to think about this unexpected news, she makes him sleep in his dressing-room, herself exchanging the double bed in which the Malay girl had had her family for a camp bed; but she has developed such a physical repulsion for Guy that she asks him to let her go home. Having seen her off on the coasting steamer, he takes back the Malay girl and his half-caste family.

In the fourth story set in Sembulu **"The Yellow Streak"** Maugham makes use of the hazardous experience he and Haxton underwent when the boat in which they were travelling upriver in Sarawak was caught in the bore (or tidal-

At the Villa Mauresque in 1951.

wave) and overturned. In the story the experience is transferred to the rough diamond Campion, a mining engineer prospecting for minerals in the interior, and the representative of the resident at Kuala Solor, Izzart, who carries the secret stigma that his mother is a half-caste. The knowledge undermines his self-confidence, since he has come to accept the general view that a Eurasian will always let you down in a crisis. When that moment occurs and the two are thrown into the turbulent river Izzart makes for the shore with the assistance of his Malay boy, leaving Campion (whose cry for help he has heard) to drown. But Campion also manages to escape, and Izzart, racked with guilt at having deserted him, contrives to suggest, when back in Kuala Solor he makes his report to the resident, that it is Campion who had got the wind up. Later he learns that Campion had been under the impression that he it was who had been the first to strike for the shore; he has no intention of accusing Izzart of cowardice, but hopes Izzart will not make out that he has behaved badly. The ending in fact is ambiguous owing to an apparent confusion in Maugham's mind between the yellow streak, meaning cowardice, and the touch of the tarbrush, the admixture of native blood of which Izzart is so bitterly conscious.

"The Letter" with which he concludes the volume, based on an actual *cause célèbre* Maugham heard about during his stay in Singapore, has, by way of the stage and film adaptations, become as well known as **"Rain".** Unlike the dramatization of **"Rain",** which was made by [John Colton in 1922], Maugham wrote the play of *The Letter* himself, and it is interesting to note that in writing the play he was able to take over whole chunks of dialogue from the story almost *verbatim,* and that most of the alterations from the story were occasioned by the practical necessity of reducing the number of scene changes; for the story itself has a three-act structure which facilitated its conversion into a play.

The story is written entirely from the viewpoint of Mr. Joyce the Singapore lawyer. Ong Chi Seng his westernized Cantonese clerk shows into his office Robert Crosbie a gentle giant of a rubber-planter, now haggard and unkempt, whose wife Leslie is in prison awaiting trial for murder. She had shot in self-defence a man called Hammond, who Crosbie maintains had thoroughly deserved it; but what worries Joyce is that she had fired six times. After Crosbie has left, Joyce turns over the papers of his brief and reflects on the account Leslie, a shy and unassuming woman, had given of the affair: how one evening when Robert was away in Singapore on business Hammond, the manager of a rubber estate eight miles away, a popular playboy with a good war record, had come in and tried to rape her, and she snatching a revolver from the desk must have shot him, for she now remembers nothing. The head boy had sent the seis in the car to fetch the Assistant Police Officer Withers who lived thirty-five miles away, and Leslie leaving Hammond's body lying on the veranda locked herself in her bedroom. (These events correspond with the action in Act I, Scenes 1 and 2, of the play.)

Chi Seng approaches Joyce, still sitting in his office, wanting to speak to him on a delicate and confidential matter concerning the case R. v. Crosbie. There is in existence a letter, of which he produces a copy, from the defendant to the victim, written on the day of his death, beseeching him to come at eleven, she is desperate. It is in the possession of the Chinese woman who for several months had been living with Hammond. In the visitors' room at the gaol, replying to Joyce's questioning, Leslie is positive she had had no communication with Hammond for several weeks before the catastrophe; they had heard he was living with a Chinese woman, and Robert would not have him in the house. Faced with the copy of her letter she goes to pieces, first swearing she had not written it, then explaining she had asked Hammond to call because she wanted him to order a gun as a birthday present for Robert. Joyce, sceptical, warns her that unless the court concludes that she had shot Hammond in self-defence, she would be found guilty of murder and sentenced to death. Recovering from a faint, she pleads with him to buy the letter; Robert has some shares that could be sold to provide the money. Back in his office Chi Seng tells him the price is $10,000; he will arrange for them to call on the Chinese woman in the house of a friend of his that night. In the card-room of their club after lunch Joyce tackles Crosbie, repeating Leslie's story about the birthday present and pointing out how awkward it would be if the letter found its way into the hands of the prosecution. If Leslie is to be acquitted, they must get hold of it, otherwise it could mean two or three years' imprisonment. Appalled at the price, which is about all the money he has got, Crosbie argues but, realization beginning to dawn, insists on accompanying Joyce when he calls on the Chinese woman. (This is covered by Act II of the play.)

Chi Seng leads Joyce and Crosbie to a Chinese shop in Victoria Street, up a flight of stairs to a small room where opium has been smoked, where they are joined by a fat Chinaman. The woman comes in, looking much as Leslie describes her in the play, and through Chi Seng banknotes pass in exchange for the letter, which Crosbie intercepts and having read puts in his pocket. When the others have left, Chi Seng remains behind to collect his share of the money, and Crosbie before leaving Joyce to drive back, preferring to walk, tells him that on the night of Hammond's death he had gone to Singapore partly to buy a gun, implying that he knows Leslie's story is false. Up to this point the story has covered a single day in Joyce's life. (Act III, Scene 1.)

After the trial, at which Leslie is acquitted to an outburst of applause, there is a celebratory lunch at the Joyces', after which Crosbie returns to his rubber-estate, wanting Leslie to stay with them until they have decided what to do. Leslie coming into the drawing-room with the letter, which Joyce burns, tells him that Robert knows Hammond had been her lover, and her confession follows. They had been lovers for years, ever since Hammond came back from the War; then he had begun to cool, and she had learned about his Chinese mistress. She had written the letter—madness, they had always been so careful—there had been a quarrel during which he had told her that only the Chinese woman, whom he had known since before the War, meant anything to him. Her face a mask of passion, she describes how she had emptied the revolver into him, then her features recompose themselves and she is once more herself. (Act III, Scene 2.)

In adapting this classic story for the stage Maugham felt it necessary, besides providing an unconvincing 'happy ending', to vulgarize it by crudely emphasizing what in the story is merely suggested. The main structural change he made was to postpone Crosbie's learning how much the letter had cost, so as to provide a theatrical *coup* in the third act; for which reason also Crosbie does not accompany the others to the Chinese shop when the banknotes are handed over. And throughout the play sufficient padding is introduced so that the playing-time will be of the required length. (pp. 96-102)

[***Ah King*** is Maugham's] third and last volume of Eastern short stories, which marks the summit of his achievement in this *genre.* Four of them are set in Malaya; one in the fictitious Alas Islands, a chain located somewhere between Macassar in Celebes and Merauke in New Guinea; the last in the fictitious sultanate in Borneo having Kuala Solor as its chief town, which (though unnamed) can be recognized as the Sembulu of some of the stories in ***The Casuarina Tree.***

"Footprints in the Jungle" opens with a leisurely description of the pleasant seaside town of Tanah Merah in Malaya, where the narrator is staying with the head of police Major Gaze, who arranges a bridge foursome in the club with the Cartwrights, an unremarkable middle-aged couple. They drive in from their rubber estate on Wednesdays so that their daughter can dance. Back in his bungalow Gaze tells the narrator, in a protracted flashback, how twenty years before in another part of Malaya he had been called upon to investigate the murder of Mrs. Cartwright's previous husband Bronson, at a time when Cartwright, out of a job, had been staying with them. Towards the end of the story Maugham expresses regret that he has not the skill to write a detective story, of which he had read a good many; but that is precisely what **"Footprints in the Jungle"** is, and a very skilfully told one, too. Like **"The Letter"** it is based on a true story which was told Maugham while he was on his travels.

The three-act structure is present in **"The Door of Opportunity",** its main narrative in the form of a flashback set in the isolated (and fictitious) district of Sondurah in Malaya being placed between two shorter 'acts' set in London whose action is continuous. The device is simple and effective. A married couple, Alban and Anne Tovel, arrive home from Singapore having left Sondurah for good, travel by train from Tilbury to London and take a taxi to a hotel in Jermyn Street. He goes to his club for mail, leaving her to unpack, but instead she tells the porter to put his baggage in the hall and remains in a chair dreading the scene she has planned when he returns. The main narrative describes the dramatic events that have led to her decision. When Alban returns to their hotel room, Anne who has not moved from her chair tells him in a theatrical outburst that she is leaving him; the cowardice he had shown has killed her love for him and he has become physically repulsive to her. He is sobbing into her empty chair as she runs out, blinded by tears. The decisive events which are the true subject of the story centre on the rising of the Chinese labour force at an upcountry rubber estate in which the European manager is killed. Alban the district officer, despite the pleas of Anne who is thinking of the manager's native wife and half-caste children, refuses to act until police reinforcements arrive. When they do and a dawn attack is made on the coolie lines, there is no resistance, the riot having been quelled by the resolute action of the Dutch manager of a timber camp twenty miles away. Even when later the governor of the colony dismisses him from the service for cowardice Alban believes he had been right not to intervene with only eight constables to back him, and when having embarked at Singapore on his journey home he receives an anonymous parcel containing, in reference to his nickname in the colony Powder-Puff Percy, an enormous powder-puff he thinks it must have been meant for Anne.

In **"The Vessel of Wrath"—**a reference to the proverb 'A woman scorned is a vessel of wrath'—Gruyter the Dutch Contrôleur of the Alas Islands (their name is ironic) sentences to six months' imprisonment for causing a drunken disturbance in a Chinese shop the 30-year-old remittance man known as Ginger Ted, a man reticent about his background but who had had some education and likes the natives, especially the women. The Christian headman of an outlying island fifty miles away having been stricken with acute appendicitis, Martha the sister of the medical missionary Mr. Jones who is down with malaria—a woman hard on 40, flat-chested, shrewish and indomitable—sets out in the prahu which has brought the news and under great difficulty successfully performs an operation on the headman. A passenger with her on the return launch is Ginger Ted in a prison sarong, his luggage a jar of native spirit, who had been with a work gang of prisoners on the island and has now completed his sentence. When they are forced by a broken propeller to spend the night on an uninhabited island, her terror that he is going to rape her turns (when he neglects to do so) into disappointment, which generates in her an implacable resolve to reform him. Her opportunity occurs when cholera breaks out on another island, and she shames Ginger Ted into accompanying her when she sets out, trusting in God, to enforce the necessary prophylactic measures on the outlying islands, on some of which the natives are treacherous. She succeeds in containing the epidemic and in reforming Ginger Ted, who returns, to Gruyter's incredulous disgust, determined to become a missionary and engaged to Martha. They will spend their honeymoon on the island where they had been marooned. The parallels between this cautionary tale and **"Rain"** are for the reader to work out for himself.

The leisurely opening of **"The Book-Bag"**, a story written in the first person singular, resembles that of **"Footprints in the Jungle"**, while its theme mirrors that of **"The Force of Circumstance"** with the substitution of incest for miscegenation. The first two paragraphs describe the narrator's addiction to reading and his practice of taking on his travels a sack of books to suit every occasion and mood. While wandering in Malaya he is invited to spend a few days with Featherstone, acting resident of Tenggarah (a fictitious district) to observe the water festival. He takes the narrator to the club where two others join them for bridge, one of them Tim Hardy, and after dinner in the residency, Featherstone—who the evening before had borrowed from him a life of Byron from his book-bag—tells the narrator what had occurred, years before, when Hardy had been living with his sister Olive on his rubber estate up north near Siam. Tim had gone home for three months to see about re-letting their old family house in Dorset, to which they had hoped to retire, and Featherstone calling on Olive, with whom he was in love, finds her in tears at the news that Tim had married. She remains distraught and though agreeing to become secretly engaged to Featherstone clearly half-hopes Tim is not really married. The evening before his arrival with Sally his bride Olive breaks her engagement to Featherstone: 'I can't marry anyone. It was absurd of me ever to think I could.' The disclosure that explains the tragedy of Olive's suicide and Sally's horror-stricken departure has been so discreetly prepared for—as when Featherstone and the narrator at the beginning of the story discuss Byron's love for his sister, and later when Olive refers to herself as 'a presumably maiden lady'—that the reader is prepared for the undeniable shock it gives.

Although their subject matter is widely dissimilar, **"The Back of Beyond"** forms a pair with **"P & O"** because the theme of both is forgiveness. In it Maugham once more uses with considerable craftsmanship the three-act structure, and tackles his favourite subject, marital infidelity. The entire action covers a single morning in the office of George Moon, shortly to retire as the resident of Timbang Belud, a fictitious district in Malaya. Tom Saffary, manager of the largest rubber estate in the district, calls on him, and they discuss the recent death at sea, while on his way home on leave with his pregnant wife, of his best friend, a neighbouring planter Knobby Clarke. The main narrative takes the form of a long flashback taking up half the story's length, in which Saffary, wanting his advice, tells him how his wife Violet on hearing the news of Knobby's death had broken down and, on being asked what Knobby had been to her, had confessed that they had been lovers. In a rage he had beaten her up until she was unconscious, after which she had insisted on making a full confession. The details of the affair Maugham imparts to the reader are more elaborate than Saffary could plausibly have given to Moon, a difficulty he smoothly pastes over with the aside: 'While George Moon was listening to as much of this story as Tom Saffary was able to tell him . . .'. Before giving his advice to Saffary, who feels he has no option but to divorce Violet, Moon tells him of the break-up of his own marriage twenty-five years before, when catching his wife hopping into bed with another man, he had—like a damned fool—divorced her, a decision he now bitterly regretted. Foolishly he had thrown away what he wanted most because he could not have exclusive possession of it; he should have shut his eyes or, like Saffary had done, given her a good hiding and let it go at that. Brushing aside Saffary's maunderings about Violet's ingratitude and the need for himself to 'behave like a tuan' and his broken heart, Moon advises him to let bygones be bygones: Knobby is dead. Charged with being a cynic, Moon—whose attitudes clearly mirror those of the author—defends himself in words which seem intended to refute the same charge which had often been brought against Maugham's work:

> . . . if to look truth in the face and not resent it when it's unpalatable, and [to] take human nature as you find it, smiling when it's absurd and grieved without exaggeration when it's painful, is to be cynical, then I suppose I'm a cynic. Mostly human nature is both absurd and pitiful, but if life has taught you tolerance you find in it more to smile at than to weep [at].

The central character in **"Neil MacAdam"** is Darya the sexually voracious Russian wife of Angus Munroe, curator of the museum at Kuala Solor. Neil is the young Scot, priggish and prudish, who arrives as assistant curator and—taken round the brothels of Singapore by the captain of the ship which would take him to Borneo—refuses the various girls he is offered, confessing himself to be a virgin. While a guest in the Munroes' bungalow, Darya shocks him by her outspokenness and extravagant behaviour, but when in the club Neil is chaffed by one of the members as not being the first to have had a romp with her, he hits him. She insists, untypically because she is afraid of the jungle, on accompanying Munroe and Neil on an expedition to collect insects and birds upriver towards Mount Hitam. Relentlessly pursuing her objective of seducing the reluctant Neil, she strips and joins him when he is bathing naked in a pool of the river. 'Don't be so Scotch', she says when he hesitates to help her get out. She finds further opportunities for forcing her attentions on him while nursing him through an attack of malaria, but when she makes vehement love to him he upbraids her, calling her a wicked woman, for he cannot bring himself to tell her that the idea of the sexual act horrifies him, that he takes a mystical joy in his purity. Seizing the opportunity when Munroe sends a message that he has found such a good collecting place that he will not be back that night, she makes a desperate attempt to rape him, in the course of which he strikes her when she bites his hand. Blind with rage he flees headlong into the jungle, pursued by Darya, now possessed by ravening desire, who catching up with him in a clearing threatens, if he will not do what she wants, to tell Munroe he had tried to rape her, showing her bruise and his tooth-marked hand as evidence. 'Now will you be good?' Taking to his heels, he leaves her to die in the jungle. (pp. 107-12)

[Maugham's short spy fiction], having appeared in American magazines between September 1927 and February 1928, was published in book form as ***Ashenden; or, The British Agent*** in March 1928. The dedication to the portrait-painter Gerald Kelly, a friend of Maugham's since their residence in Paris in 1905 who had also served in Intelligence, describes the book as the 'narrative of some experiences during the Great War of a very insignificant member of the Intelligence Department'. In the Preface written when it was included in 1934 in the Collected Edition of Maugham's works (where the dedication was dropped) he emphasized that, though founded on his own experiences, they had been rearranged for the purposes of fiction. He had chosen Ashenden as the name of his *alter ego* 'because like Gann and Driffield it is a common surname in the neighbourhood of Canterbury, where I spent many years of my youth. The first syllable had to me a peculiar connotation which I found suggestive'—suggestive, presumably, of the character's wry world-weariness. Although the episodes first appeared in magazines as six short stories, each of between 12,000 and 15,000 words in length, which have been reprinted as such in the various collected editions of Maugham's stories, the work gains considerably if it is read in the original separate volume because, though each episode is self-contained, together they form a connected narrative which should be read as an episodic novel. In the separate volume the narrative is divided into sixteen titled sections, two or three of which constitute one episode. In the case of Section XII **"The Flip of a Coin"**, this was dropped when the work was rearranged as stories, and so can only be read in the separate volume.

His object being, as he stated in the Preface, to tell the truth about the work of an intelligence agent, which on the whole is extremely monotonous, much of it being uncommonly useless, Maugham adopted a leisurely, conversational prose leavened by many touches of humour, which has the effect of de-sensationalizing the melodramatic climaxes in which most of the episodes culminate. Though not written in the first person, everything is presented exclusively from Ashenden's point of view, and there is such a profusion of realistic detail that it is impossible for the reader to tell where autobiography ends and fiction begins. Its low-keyed opening, in which Ashenden is enrolled in the secret service by a colonel, known as 'R', whom he met at a party, sets the tone. His qualifications are an acquaintance with several European languages and the fact that his profession of writer provides excellent cover for his presence in a neutral country. Posted to Geneva where he lives in a comfortable hotel, writing a comedy in his ample spare time, he surmounts such routine hazards as a police search and interrogation, and the threats of one of his agents, a German-Swiss, who demands extra money from him at pistol-point. His work takes him across the lake to Berne to pass information to headquarters, and he receives his instructions by the hand of an old woman in the market who comes over early each morning from French Savoy to sell butter and eggs and passes him notes with his change. Among the cosmopolitan guests in the hotel are several agents in the pay of one or other of the belligerents, including the Baronne de Higgins, now in the German secret service, whose grandfather had been a Yorkshire stable-boy who had risen to become Austrian ambassador to an Italian court. She asks Ashenden to play bridge in her sitting-room, also inviting a disaffected Egyptian prince and his secretary to make up the four; and Ashenden senses that they are discreetly sounding him on the possibility of his selling himself. In Prince Ali's entourage is Miss King (whose name provides the story's title), a little old raddled English lady who is governess to his fat, high-stepping daughters. That night Ashenden is woken by a maid with the message that Miss King, who had previously ignored his civilities, is dying and wanted to see him; but though he sits long by her bedside, the stroke she has suffered prevents her from uttering what he reads in her eyes she desperately wants him to hear.

"The Hairless Mexican" is about the failure of a mission.

In an old-fashioned hotel in Lyons 'R' gives Ashenden his next assignment, which is under the assumed name of Somerville to accompany Manuel Carmona, a self-styled Mexican general, whom 'R' had engaged to intercept a Greek passing through Brindisi in order to prevent him from delivering certain documents to the German ambassador in Rome. Ashenden was to hand over to the general a large sum in American thousand-dollar notes in exchange for the documents. Carmona proves to be a fantastic creature—'a purple patch on two legs'—who comes in wearing a fur coat, wafting perfume; his finger-nails are painted red, and his hairless face is surmounted by a wig with disordered locks. Ashenden warms to his baroque personality. "The Dark Woman" is a story within the story, told by the Mexican to Ashenden as they travel by train to Rome, of how having persuaded a beautiful girl from a brothel in Mexico City to go to bed with him he had allowed her to cajole out of him the secrets of the revolution he and others were plotting and then had cut her throat. Waiting for the Mexican in Naples, Ashenden nostalgically visits its sights including the statute of Agrippina the Younger in the museum 'which he had particular reasons for remembering with affection', the same statue that had suggested to Maugham the character of Miss Ley in his Edwardian fiction. Despite 'R''s admonition to the Mexican not to compromise Ashenden, he is introduced to the seamy side of espionage when together they search for the papers in the hotel room where the Greek lies dead.

Ashenden needed to keep a tight rein on his compassion in the next episode, the story **"Giulia Lazzari".** In Paris 'R' had given him instructions to supervise the betrayal of a dangerous Indian agitator by his Italian mistress, a dancer-cum-prostitute. Chandra Lal had been fomenting rebellion in India with the aid of German money, thereby preventing the transfer of troops to the front, and had found asylum in Berlin. Giulia had been arrested in England for spying and, while in Holloway Prison awaiting trial with the prospect of a ten-year sentence ahead of her, had been induced to agree to decoy Lal across the Swiss frontier to France in exchange for her freedom. Ashenden accompanies her by train to Thonou on the French side of the Lake of Geneva and, having thwarted her inept efforts to escape to Switzerland, forces her despite her hysterical protests to write letters to Lal inveigling him across the border. Their scenes together are reminiscent of those between Mr. Davidson and Sadie Thompson in **"Rain".** When she finally refuses to do any more, Ashenden sends for two policemen to take her back to England, and they casually watch her dress; but the sight of a pair of handcuffs is enough to break her will. Lal eventually comes over in response to another letter, which she writes at Ashenden's dictation, then realizing he has been betrayed takes poison in the station waiting-room. In **"The Traitor"** the Englishman Grantly Caypor, a German agent who had been responsible for a British agent in Germany being caught and shot, is living in a hotel in Lucerne with his rabid German wife and their pampered bull-terrier Fritzi. Ashenden, still as Mr. Somerville, is sent to assess whether he could be 'turned' and persuaded to work for the British; if not, to induce him to cross the frontier on his way to England. After Caypor has gone, his wife divines from Fritzi's howling that he has been arrested.

Like Maugham, Ashenden is finally sent to Russia, where a large party is antagonistic to the war and a revolution is possible, with orders to keep in touch with the dissidents without embarrassing the British and American ambassadors whose governments supported the present régime. His first task is to effect a reconciliation between the two ambassadors, the stuffed shirt Sir Herbert Witherspoon and his opposite number William Shafer, a loquacious and stupid ex-politician, who have barely been on speaking terms. In **"His Excellency"** Ashenden dines tête-à-tête with Sir Herbert in the enormous dining-room at the British Embassy—

> . . . . on the other side of the wall was a restless, turbulent population that might at any moment break into bloody revolution, while not two hundred miles away men in the trenches were sheltering in their dug-outs from the bitter cold and the pitiless bombardment—

and they discuss a common acquaintance, Byring in the embassy in Paris who was about to throw up a promising career and marry Rose Auburn, once a dancer at the Moulin Rouge and now the best-known courtesan in France. This leads Sir Herbert to reminisce about an incident in his own life thirty years before when he had been a junior clerk in the Foreign Office with a promising career before him. He had fallen in love with Alix, the female member of a trio of acrobats, a vivacious whisky-voiced guttersnipe who had supplemented her income by selective prostitution. He had been under no illusions about her but could not help himself, and when his well-connected fiancée had gone with her parents to stay in South Africa for the summer before their wedding, he had abjectly accepted Alix's invitation to accompany the troupe on a provincial tour, on condition he did not make scenes when she slept with someone else. Tears were falling down Sir Herbert's cheeks as he described their last night together before he left to join his fiancée and resume his career, for he knew he had wasted his life and should have done what Byring is doing, whatever the cost.

"The Flip of a Coin", which Maugham discarded when rearranging the ***Ashenden*** material into six short stories, presents Ashenden faced with the decision whether or not to authorize one of his agents, a Galician Pole, to organize the blowing up of certain munition factories in Austria, thereby killing or maiming a number of Polish workers.

The first of the three sections comprising the story **"Mr. Harrington's Washing"** describes Ashenden's journey from New York to San Francisco, across the Pacific to Japan, up the Sea of Japan to Vladivostok, and thence by train—in the company of an American businessman from Philadelphia—to Petrograd. He is on the same mission to Russia as forms the background to Sir Herbert's reminiscence. Mr. Harrington, small and neat and bald, is a compulsive, monotonous talker, a New England snob who when he is not boring Ashenden with an account of himself, his family and his employers, reads aloud to him interminably as the train makes its leisurely way through the steppes of Siberia. He is a crashing bore for whom Ashenden yet manages to kindle an affection, for Mr. Harrington is kindly and generous. There is a humorous interlude

"Love and Russian Literature" describing Ashenden's pre-war love-affair with Anastasia, daughter and wife of Russian revolutionaries exiled in London, which founders during an experimental weekend in Paris on her insistence that he have scrambled eggs for breakfast every day. Their affair had flourished at a time when enthusiasm for everything Russian—art, ballet, music, literature—was sweeping London, which had somewhat clouded Ashenden's judgement.

> In her eyes Ashenden saw the boundless steppes of Russia, and the Kremlin with its pealing bells, and the solemn ceremonies of Easter at St. Isaacs, and forests of silver beeches and the Nevsky Prospekt; it was astonishing how much he saw in her eyes. They were round and shining and slightly protuberant like those of a Pekinese.

Now, five years later in Petrograd, he seeks her help, and though she shows no spark of her former sentiment for Ashenden, a strange friendship develops between Anastasia and Mr. Harrington, who calls her Delilah. It is his mixture of innocence and determination as he pursues his business negotiations while revolution is erupting all round him that touches her heart; and his insistence on collecting his washing from the laundry before he will consent to leave for Sweden that leads to his undoing.

What distinguishes ***Ashenden*** is its unobtrusive blending of humour and melodrama, its sharp evocations of the places—Geneva, Naples, Thonou, Lucerne, Paris, Petrograd—in which the episodes are set, and the authenticity of the autobiographical, wartime background. Besides being the prototype for an entire *genre* of spy fiction which has not yet run its course, the book makes as valid a contribution to the literature of the Great War as Hemingway's *A Farewell to Arms* published a year later.

Of the six stories with a European setting (of similar length to the Far Eastern and Ashenden stories) which were published under the title ***First Person Singular*** in 1931, three—**"Jane"** (1923), **"The Round Dozen"** (1924) and **"The Creative Impulse"** (1926)—predate ***Ashenden,*** while the rest—**"The Human Element"**, **"Virtue"** and **"The Alien Corn"** (all 1931)—postdate both ***Ashenden*** and *Cakes and Ale*. . . . (pp. 138-44)

As with **"The Vessel of Wrath"** and **"The Book-Bag"** in ***Ah King,*** Maugham winds himself into **"Virtue"** by means of a mock-essay, the purpose of which is to introduce the (unnamed) narrator as an urbane, easy-going character, fond of the good things of life and given to humorously odd philosophical speculations. Imperceptibly the story gets started as he is strolling down Bond Street one spring morning in 1922 or thereabouts, on his way to Sotheby's, and by chance encounters Morton, a young District Officer who had once put him up in his bungalow when he had been travelling in Borneo. Wanting to return his hospitality—the situation foreshadows that of Coward's one-act play *Hands Across the Sea* (1936)—he takes him to supper at Ciro's to meet some friends, Charlie Bishop a middle-aged pathologist who thirty years before had been a fellow medical student, and his wife Margery, a woman of 45. The introduction has tragic consequences, as the narrator learns some time later from another friend, Janet Marsh, who had been abetting Margery in her (unconsummated) affair with Morton during his leave. Having fallen in love with him, Margery had found when he returned to Borneo that she could no longer tolerate living with Charlie. When she leaves him, he takes an overdose of veronal. Morton on learning the news writes Margery a letter of sympathy, making clear that he does not want her to join him; and the narrator reflects that, if she had only had the courage to go to bed with him and get him out of her system, the tragedy would never have occurred.

If **"Virtue"** leaves the reader uneasy at Maugham's light-hearted treatment of human unhappiness, the faultlessly written humorous story that follows it, **"The Round Dozen"**, restores his sense of well-being.

One November two or three years after the War, that is in 1920 or 1921, the narrator is staying in an old-fashioned hotel at Elsom, a fictitious town near Brighton, where he becomes distantly acquainted with Mr. and Mrs. Edwin St. Clair, survivals from the 1880s with genteel literary tastes, and their niece Miss Porchester, a maiden of 50. On the sea-front he is accosted by a shabby little man in a battered bowler hat who at their second meeting tells him proudly—producing creased newspaper cuttings to substantiate his claim—that he is the celebrated bigamist Mortimer Ellis. Having achieved eleven wives—('Most people', observes the narrator, 'find one about as much as they can manage')—he would like to bring the number up to the round dozen, undeterred by the five-year prison sentence his hobby has already earned him. Seaside resorts in winter are his hunting-ground, respectable widows and spinsters aged between 35 and 50 with modest fortunes his prey. He had made all his wives happy, he claims, given them Romance, a ray of sunshine in their drab lives. Miss Porchester, who had never cared for another man since breaking off her engagement to a barrister on learning of his intrigue with a laundress's daughter, was to prove putty in his hands, though the attentive reader will gather from the note prefixed to the book that his success with her eventually resulted in another spell of hard labour.

In **"The Human Element"** Maugham again winds himself into his subject by means of a mock-essay, on this occasion a discourse on Rome in the dead season. Having dinner in the almost empty dining-room of his hotel, he sees at a table opposite him someone he knows slightly, Humphrey Carruthers, who besides holding a senior position in the Foreign Office has written several books of stories which are not to the narrator's taste. In the lounge afterwards Carruthers opens his heart and tells him the unhappy story of his pursuit of Betty Weldon-Burns, a lady living in Rhodes whom the narrator had met in London. Daughter of the impoverished Duke of St. Erth, she had engaged in much publicized patriotic duties during the War and after it was over, still in her twenties, had become notorious for her extravagant behaviour, especially in night clubs. Carruthers had proposed to her a dozen times, but in 1921 when she was 25 she had married instead Jimmie Weldon-Burns, son of an aitchless manufacturer in the North who had bought a baronetcy and sent his son to Eton. Before long Jimmie had taken to drink and contracting tuberculosis had spent a couple of winters in Switzerland; it was the news of his death that had prompted Carruthers to visit Rhodes and renew his addresses to Betty. She lived there in solitary style, gathering materials for the history of the Knights of St. John she planned to write, looked after by the indispensable Albert, her chauffeur and handyman who had been second footman in the London house of her aunt Louise and later Jimmie's valet. It is Carruthers's at first gradual, then blindingly sudden, realization—for going to the beach for a midnight swim he comes upon them bathing together in the nude—of the nature of their relationship that has reduced him to a nervous wreck. When the narrator suggests to him that he could obtain relief from his unhappiness by putting it all in a story, he replies that to do so would be caddish, besides—echoing the end of Henry James's story 'The Story of It'—there was no story there.

The fourth and sixth stories in the collection, **"Jane"** and **"The Creative Impulse"**, may be treated briefly together because of their similarity, each consisting of the portrait of an eccentric woman, the point of which tends to elude the present-day reader. Jane is a dowdy, middle-aged spinster who blossoms, under the hand of the young architect she marries, into a flamboyant creature wearing outrageous clothes and an eyeglass, much in demand in society for her wit. Mrs. Albert Forrester in **"The Creative Impulse"** is a London hostess who has written many volumes of verse and precious prose which, though earning her a *succès d'estime,* have made no money. When her nondescript husband elopes with the cook she decides, on the cook's suggestion, to write a detective story. Both stories, though they have some amusing moments, give the impression of being *contes à clef* whose keys have been lost; and neither the blending of the themes of the Ugly Duckling and Pygmalion and Galatea in the one, nor the satirical picture of London literary life given in the other, are of sufficient interest to justify narratives of such length.

In **"The Alien Corn"**, which has the same theme as the Fanny Price incident in *Of Human Bondage,* Maugham attempted a not unfriendly satire on English Jewry. The reader is first introduced to the 70-year-old Ferdy Rabenstein—rich, elegant, a patron of the arts—whose biography the narrator regrets had not been undertaken by Max Beerbohm.

> There is no one else in this hard world of today who can look upon the trivial with such tender sympathy and wring such a delicate pathos from futility. I wonder that Max, who must have known Ferdy much better than I and long before, was never tempted to exercise his exquisite fancy on such a theme.

The narrator is surprised to learn that Sir Adolphus Bland, owner of an Elizabethan mansion in Sussex who wears plus-fours and likes to be called Freddy, is Ferdy's nephew, his sister Hannah having married Alphonse Bleikogel *alias* Sir Alfred Bland, the first baronet. Freddy dotes on his elder son George, loving him with a most un-English love, and is dismayed when, just down from Oxford, he announces that he does not want to be an English gentleman but to go to Munich to study music with a view to becoming a professional pianist. He is proud of being a Jew, wishes he knew Yiddish and is not only attracted to the synagogue but longs for the ghetto. There is a moving scene when father and son quarrel after dinner about George's future and Freddy breaks down—sobbing, pulling his beard, beating his chest and rocking to and fro; and soon the whole family, including Ferdy, are in tears. A deal is done: George's grandmother (Ferdy's sister), the family matriarch, will give him £5 a week so that he can study music in Germany for two years. If at the end of that time his playing is judged to be first rate, they will help him in his career; if not, he will accede to his father's wishes and stand for parliament. When the time comes he, like Fanny, is found wanting and kills himself.

The quotation from **"The Alien Corn"** given above provides the hint, if one were needed, as to the model Maugham had in mind when writing these stories, for the technique he employed is strongly reminiscent of the first-person-singular narratives of Max Beerbohm in *Seven Men* (1919). It is a measure of Maugham's success that his stories stand up to the comparison so well. If Max's gentle pen would have flinched from the unsparing realism of some of them, it is likely that **"The Round Dozen"** at least would have met with his full approval. (pp. 144-48)

The title Maugham gave to his last volume of pre-war short stories, ***The Mixture as Before*** (1940) . . . raises hopes which are not fulfilled. It comprises ten stories, all of which had appeared in American magazines between 1933 and 1939. Two of them, **"A Man with a Conscience"** and **"An Official Position"**, both concerned with wife-murderers, used up material Maugham had obtained in St. Laurent when he was collecting background material for *Christmas Holiday.* The theme of **"Three Fat Women of Antibes"** is the breakdown of the resolution of three middle-aged women—a divorcée, a widow and a Lesbian—to maintain their diet when faced with the daily sight of the cousin of one of them, who has been invited to stay in the house they had rented in Antibes after the rigours of a slimming-cure at Carlsbad, eating to her heart's content without her weight being affected. **"The Lotus-Eater"**, also about a failure in resolution, concerns an ex-bank manager who had sold up in order to settle on Capri, determined to commit suicide when his money ran out. Two others, set in the South of France, present examples of courage. In **"The Lion's Skin"** an ex-garage hand who has successfully masqueraded as an English gentleman, thereby acquiring a rich American wife, is shown behaving like a sahib when the moment of crisis comes. The Gigolette of **"Gigolo and Gigolette"** is an Australian girl whose act as a 'stunt' performer at the Casino consists of diving sixty feet into a flaming tank five feet deep. Although she has lost her nerve she gamely decides to continue with her act, because jobs are hard to come by. In **"The Voice of the Turtle"** the narrator invites to stay in his house on the Riviera a young writer, Peter Melrose, who is writing a novel about a love-affair between a young writer and a celebrated prima donna. Since he has never met one, the narrator invites to dinner La Falterona, a famous opera-singer of obscure parentage who has had many lovers and husbands. Despite her obvious stupidity and selfishness, Melrose chooses to see in her what he wants to see, regardless of reality, whereas the narrator, more clear-eyed, accepts that her incomparable artistry as a singer makes up for all her human faults. **"Lord Montdrago"** is a tale of the supernatural unusual in Maugham's work; and **"The Facts of Life"** about an English youth on holiday in France who inadvertently pockets a whore's savings is a variation of Charley Mason's situation in *Christmas Holiday.*

"The Treasure" is a sour little anecdote which, like Maugham's 1909 play *Smith,* toys with the notion of love across the class barriers. Richard Harenger is a Home Office official approaching 50, amicably separated from his wife, who is looked after in his flat near Whitehall by a cook and a new house-parlourmaid Pritchard, a comely widow of 35, a real treasure. One evening on the spur of the moment he asks her to go to the cinema with him, after which they dine and dance in a restaurant in Oxford Street, and finish up together in his bed. In the morning, waking alone, he is at first dismayed at the recollection of what had happened, for clearly Pritchard would have to go; but when she comes in to put out his clothes and behaves exactly as if nothing had happened he realizes with relief that all is well: she would never refer to the incident. (pp. 160-62)

[In 1947] Maugham published his last volume of short stories under the title ***Creatures of Circumstance.*** They are a mixed bag, a number of which have been discussed earlier in this study. These consist of **"The Happy Couple"** and three stories with a Spanish setting, being (in the case of **"A Romantic Young Lady"** conjecturally) revised versions of stories which had been written nearly forty years before; two substandard Eastern stories; and the propaganda piece **"The Unconquered".** For the rest, **"A Woman of Fifty"** is a routine melodrama set in Italy, containing several familiar ingredients. The narrator, having just given an informal chat at a mid-Western university (in 1944), is approached by the wife of one of the dons, a middle-aged woman who claims to have known him years before in Italy—an opening closely resembling that of **"A Romantic Young Lady".** That night he remembers her as Laura, a girl belonging to the English and American colony in Florence just after the Great War who had married Tito, a feckless Italian of noble family. Rightly suspecting that his father was having an affair with her, Tito shoots him, and Laura is persuaded to confess her adultery in order to save her husband from life imprisonment. Instead he is committed to an asylum. The opening of **"A Man from Glasgow"** closely resembles that of **"The Spanish Priest".** The narrator who is staying at an inn in Algeciras is accosted in the dining-room by a stranger, a Scot long resident in Spain as manager of some olive groves outside Ecija, who tells him a tale of a haunted house.

In **"Sanatorium"** the narrator (named Ashenden) describes his fellow-inmates at a TB sanatorium in the North of Scotland at the end of the Great War, a story which—because founded on Maugham's own experience—has been tacked on to the end of ***Ashenden*** in the Penguin edition; misguidedly, for its mood is entirely different from that of the secret service stories.

There are three rancid little anecdotes of the kind that have given Maugham a reputation for cheapness. **"Appearance and Reality"** aims to extract amusement from the situation of a rich French industrialist and senator who, discovering that Lisette the young mannequin he had set up in a flat in Paris as his mistress had taken a lover, saves his own honour by providing a dowry of a million francs to enable them to marry. In this way, instead of being the deceived one, the industrialist has the additional gratification, whenever he goes to bed with Lisette, of deceiving her husband. **"Winter Cruise"** leaves an equally sour taste and concerns a drab English spinster of forty, sole passenger in a German freighter on a cruise to South America by way of the West Indies. Worn out by her ceaseless chatter, the officers succeed in shutting her up by the expedient of ordering the radio-operator, a fine specimen of Teutonic manhood, to go to her cabin and provide his services as her lover. The only point of **"The Colonel's Lady",** about a middle-aged man who finds out when his wife publishes a book of poems that she has had a passionate affair with a younger man, is the husband's curtain-line: ' . . . what did the fellow ever see in her?'.

The two remaining stories, set in the East End of London, appear to be the surviving fragments of what Maugham had intended to be his last novel. Wishing to impose a 'pattern' on his life's work, he thought it would be appropriate for his last novel, like his first one, to have as its setting the slums of London; but on revisiting Bermondsey after World War II he found the attitudes of its inhabitants distasteful to him, and the idea was shelved. Both stories purport to be told by Ned Preston a prison visitor, said to have been modelled on Alan Searle, Maugham's secretary-companion during the post-war years, Haxton having died in America in 1944. In **"Episode"** a Brixton postman Fred, gaoled for stealing, has thought about his girl Gracie so obsessively while in prison that by the time he is released after eighteen months he is heartily sick of her; and she puts her head in a gas oven. **"The Kite"** presents the unusual domestic drama of a marriage breaking up because the wife, a typist, is jealous of her accountant husband's obsession with flying his kite on the common. When she smashes his kite with a hatchet he chooses to go to gaol rather than pay her maintenance. Judging by these two fragments, Maugham's decision to abandon his projected East End novel is little to be regretted. (pp. 186-88)

As a short-story writer Maugham did himself a great disservice when, towards the end of his life, he put together the collected editions in three and four volumes. His work in this *genre* undeniably includes a lot of third-rate stuff, written with the object of achieving an immediate cheap effect, which cannot stand up to serious critical scrutiny. In this class are several of his most 'popular' stories relying for their effect on sexual innuendo—**"The Treasure", "The Facts of Life", "The Colonel's Lady", "Appearance and Reality", "Winter Cruise"**—to which . . . has been applied the adjective 'rancid'. Also scattered throughout the collected volumes are the thumb-nail sketches published in ***Cosmopolitans*** most of which are of a trivial nature. In such company the major stories tend to lose caste.

These were the ones which appeared, six apiece, in five separate volumes published between 1921 and 1933 and were later collected under the title ***Altogether*** in England and ***East and West*** in America. They include the 'Ashenden' spy stories and those, influenced by Beerbohm's *Seven Men,* which appeared in ***First Person Singular.*** Above all they include the eighteen stories with an Eastern setting which, uniquely preserving a colonial world that has vanished, represent quintessential Maugham in this field. They well stand up to a comparison with Kipling's Indian stories; and if—as Maugham was not alone in believing—Kipling is England's greatest short-story writer, their permanence should be assured. (p. 212)

John Whitehead, in his Maugham: A Reappraisal, *Vision Press, 1987, 224 p.*

Archie K. Loss (essay date 1987)

[*In the following excerpt, Loss offers an extensive analysis of the short story "Rain," which he considers representative of Maugham's best short fiction. Loss also discusses aspects of Maugham's espionage stories and commends Maugham's short fiction as a notable literary achievement.*]

Very early in his career as a writer, Maugham published a volume of short fiction, but then, for nearly two decades, he abandoned the form, concentrating instead upon drama and longer fiction. In 1920, however, following a trip to the South Seas, he returned to it by writing a classic story—surely his most famous contribution to the genre—the often-anthologized **"Rain,"** which became the basis of a popular play (not by Maugham) and also of a number of films. **"Rain"** is in many respects a paradigm for what Maugham was to do in the short-story form for the next thirty years or so. The work of a mature writer who knew what he was aiming at, it deserves a close examination for what it can tell about his short-story technique and subject matter.

Of the latter, the first thing that strikes us in **"Rain"** is the exotic locale, a setting that Maugham staked out early as his own. Other authors in England had written of colonial types in similar settings—Rudyard Kipling and Joseph Conrad come first to mind—but Maugham in his short stories focuses especially on the effect of an exotic environment upon marital (or extramarital) relationships. In his plays (for the most part comedies) Maugham focuses similarly on personal relationships, but generally not in exotic settings. In the short stories, the subject of conjugal fidelity (or infidelity) is transferred from the drawing room to the tropical porch, with its bamboo furniture and ever-present native servants. E. M. Forster once said that Sinclair Lewis, with his American characters, had managed "to lodge a piece of a continent in our imagination"; Maugham, with characters who are predominantly English colonials, manages to do almost the same in his short fiction, set primarily in the East. The key element of the characters in **"Rain"** and elsewhere in the early stories is less their Englishness, however, than the sense of exile that they convey. Three of the major characters in **"Rain"** are in fact American, but all of the characters, whether American, English, or European, are in some way exiled from their native land.

For the Davidsons, as well as for the MacPhails, exile is a matter of choice. For Miss Sadie Thompson, it is a matter of necessity. In no case, however, is anyone in his or her native environment. Maugham writes many stories with an English setting, and many of them are among his finest achievements in the form. However, it is for the exotic setting that he is best known, and it is on the whole in stories like these that he had his greatest success as a writer of short fiction. If we consider Maugham's personal relationship to the English environment, his interest in the exiled is not difficult to understand.

In **"Rain,"** there is on the one hand the grimly puritanical Reverend Davidson and his wife, for only the latter of whom one might feel the slightest degree of sympathy by the end of the story. On the other, there is the slatternly Sadie Thompson, whose attempt at greater moral perfection leads to an even greater imperfection of personal appearance and who ends up no more appealing a character than she was at the beginning, in spite of the unpleasant experience to which she has been subjected and the sympathy it creates for her in the reader. In the final analysis, Sadie is not the whore with a golden heart of popular fiction, nor is she a type of the adulteress Christ encounters at the well and to whom the reverend refers in the story. She is exactly what she is, and what she learns is that the Reverend Davidson is exactly like all the other men she has ever known.

Between these characters (both in the physical and the moral sense) comes the important character of Doctor MacPhail. MacPhail serves as the buffer between the Reverend Davidson's overbearing self-righteousness and Sadie Thompson's crumbling, highly vulnerable sense of self. He is described more than once in the story as "timid" or unable to take a firm stand, but when push comes to shove he goes to the governor's office on the behalf of Sadie Thompson. His sympathies go increasingly to her as Reverend Davidson's attempts at her reformation persist. "Live and let live," is Doctor MacPhail's motto; he does not like to be put in the position of having to judge the behavior, moral or otherwise, of other people, but, all the same, he clearly does not side with Reverend Davidson and what he represents.

It is significant in regard to this prevailingly neutral attitude that MacPhail is a physician, for his attitude toward human behavior is much the same as a physician's attitude toward his patients: he notes their behavior, for the most part without passing judgment on it. In other words, he takes the same attitude [espoused by] Maugham as an author and in the first-person narrators who serve as Maugham's personae in his longer fiction. Doctor MacPhail corresponds to these dispassionate commentators on the human condition. Like them, MacPhail serves to bring the other characters of the story into focus for the reader. It is *through* him that one finds out what Reverend Davidson is hoping to accomplish with Sadie Thompson—or, more properly, through his conversations with Horn or with Davidson or with Sadie herself—not by direct access to the prayer sessions they hold. No major incident of the story is rendered directly for the reader.

This indirect approach, one might argue, is essential to the point of Maugham's story. If one knew precisely what was going on between Sadie and Davidson—in particular what emotions Davidson felt—there would be no surprise at the end. As it is, the reader is given more than a sufficient number of clues that the story will end as it does, beginning with the reference early on to the reverend's "suppressed fire" and "full" and "sensual lips," but these clues come primarily from what others say about the principals and from how Doctor MacPhail reacts to what they say, not from the principals themselves.

Doctor MacPhail thus serves an essential purpose as the character who, by what he observes more than by what he says, brings the behavior of the other characters into focus, both in terms of the plot and of the theme. His place in other Maugham stories may be taken by the narrator through whom characters and events are seen, but, whatever the person, it is more typical of Maugham to tell a story indirectly than to tell it through the unmediated actions of its main characters. In this, **"Rain"** conforms to the narrative strategy typical of most of Maugham's short stories.

It also conforms to the structure of the typical Maugham story. In his novels Maugham tends at times toward a loose structure, but in his short stories, as in his work for the theater, he follows the classic pattern of the short tale that tends toward a single effect, defined so well in the nineteenth century by Edgar Allan Poe. Without too much distortion, the elements of the classic tale, including turning point and climax, can be perceived in **"Rain,"** though the result of applying such terms to it is to tell only what is already known: that the author builds his story toward Sadie Thompson's final line and the suicide that immediately precedes it. The plot structure of the story thus consists of a series of items of withheld information that can be rendered as questions—why does Sadie not want to return to San Francisco? why is Reverend Davidson so eager to reform her?—and the curve of the plot begins its inevitable descent at that point in the story when Reverend Davidson resolves to break Sadie's will. All else follows in the wake of that ominous decision.

At its best, as in **"Rain,"** this sort of action has a sense of inevitability to it; at its worst, it is merely slick. Seldom, however, is Maugham content simply to sketch a character and not provide a plot by which that character can demonstrate his or her potential for good or evil. Even the most trivial of his stories builds toward some final line or action. The stories end emphatically, and the sense of character they convey is fixed: our initial impression of a character is usually borne out by his or her subsequent behavior. If bad, they may grow slightly worse, but they seldom become better; if good—though their goodness may lead them to folly—they are likely not to turn evil. Good may come of evil actions, or evil of good, but the moral nature of the characters tends to be of a piece.

The cynic always tends to view human nature as fixed, and this perhaps accounts for the feeling one gets in Maugham's best short fiction (as in his long) that his characters are simply fulfilling our expectations of them. In the course of his long career as a writer of short fiction, Maugham varies his subject matter, but seldom his themes, his technique, or his fundamental sense of human nature. The ground might shift to England or to the south of France, but with great consistency the themes remain the selfishness of human motives and the frailty of human will.

For all this consistency of theme, Maugham's stories derive from a variety of sources. The main purpose of most of his travels was to find material to write about. The stories about British colonials in the Far East began after Maugham's first trip there, and all of his subsequent journeys throughout the world produced their own material. Some stories show almost a reportorial approach to their subject matter, as, for instance, **"The Letter,"** which appeared in a collection of 1926 and which sticks very close to the details of a celebrated murder trial in Kuala Lumpur of some twenty-five years earlier.

If the real-life sources of Maugham's subject matter lay in various and sundry places, his literary sources are easier to trace. For his technique of telling a story, Maugham's great model from beginning to end is Guy de Maupassant, [as he stated in his preface to ***The Complete Short Stories,*** Vol. 1 (see excerpt dated 1934)]:

> From the age of fifteen whenever I went to Paris I spent most of my afternoons poring over the books in the galleries of the Odeon. I have never passed more enchanted hours. The attendants in their long smocks were indifferent to the people who sauntered about looking at the books and they would let you read for hours without bothering. There was a shelf filled with the works of Guy de Maupassant, but they cost three francs fifty a volume and that was not a sum I was prepared to spend. I had to read as best I could standing up and peering between the uncut pages. Sometimes when no attendant was looking I would hastily cut a page and thus read more conveniently. Fortunately some of them were issued in a cheap edition at seventy-five centimes and I seldom came away without one of these. In this manner, before I was eighteen, I had read all the best stories. It is natural enough that when at that age I began writing stories myself I should unconsciously have chosen those little masterpieces as a model. I might very well have hit upon a worse.

Thus Maugham wrote of his first encounter with the work of the nineteenth-century French master. In contrast with Maupassant, he goes on in the same preface, is the work of Anton Chekhov (and one might add, by extension, many masters of the early twentieth-century short story). Such work emphasizes not action, but character or atmosphere; in contrast with Maugham's ideal short story, little happens in it. Maugham clearly favors the technique of Maupassant, in spite of his clear admiration for Chekhov's gifts.

A second important literary source for Maugham's short fiction is Poe. In one of his last literary essays Maugham described what Poe's concept of the short story meant to him:

> It is a piece of fiction, dealing with a single incident, material or spiritual, that can be read at a sitting; it is original, it must sparkle, excite or impress; and it must have unity of effect or im-

> pression. It should move in an even line from its exposition to its close. To write a story on the principles he laid down is not so easy as some think.

If the effect of some of Maugham's tales is less concentrated than some of his pronouncements suggest, one cannot impugn his intention to achieve the desired single effect.

In short fiction as in long, Maugham's technique—especially in the first person—is that of teller of tales. This approach allows him a high degree of narrative flexibility. He can move at will from character to character, shifting viewpoint as he pleases. He can even make use of one or more tellers before getting to the heart of his story. Furthermore, he can do all of this without shifting narrative tone except as the conversation of his characters dictates. If he does not provide a story made aesthetically consistent by its portrayal of the consciousness of a single character (in the manner of Henry James or James Joyce), he does achieve unity through the *tone* in which each story is told. The voice of the narrator, whether in first person or third (or occasionally second, as in one paragraph in **"Rain"**), thus becomes the most important single unifying element in a Maugham short story.

Atmosphere is another important unifying element. I noted earlier the exotic locale of **"Rain."** In virtually all of the stories set in the East, descriptive details are important in establishing both mood and character. **"Rain"** itself provides an obvious example with the physical circumstance suggested by the title. The repeated references to the rain pouring down in the steamy tropical climate add to the sense of imminence created by the small events of the story. Like the celebrated drums constantly in the background in Eugene O'Neill's play *The Emperor Jones* (1920), Maugham's rain suggests the lack of will and obsessiveness often associated with the tropical environment.

Among modern British short stories, Maugham's work stands in the conservative side of a generally conservative lot. Authors like Katherine Mansfield or Virginia Woolf or D. H. Lawrence, whose work was considered innovative when it first appeared, were innovative chiefly in terms of their subject matter or themes. In comparison, continental authors were abandoning traditional forms of short fiction altogether in favor of new, polygeneric forms that fused fiction, poetry, and drama into one. Mainstream twentieth-century British short fiction, as practiced by later writers such as L. P. Hartley, H. E. Bates, or V. S. Pritchett, was neither experimental nor innovative; it is well-crafted work that deals with closely observed patterns of human behavior, with occasional insights gleaned from psychology or myth. Maugham's work, which was essentially nineteenth-century in form, lay somewhat to the right of this solid center. In the end, Maugham's work is closer to that of earlier authors like Rudyard Kipling or Poe—not to mention Maupassant—than it is to the work of most of his contemporaries.

One group of stories in the Maugham canon deserves particular mention—the group, including the celebrated **"Mr. Harrington's Washing,"** collected under the title ***Ashenden; or, The British Agent*** (1928). In this volume Maugham brought to fictional life his experiences as a British agent during World War I. Together, these stories achieve sufficient unity of tone and purpose to amount nearly to a novel.

Their central character is the precise opposite of the conventional image of the spy. That image—nurtured in fiction of this period and before by such popular authors as E. Phillips Oppenheim, Anthony Hope, and Ouida—required the spy to be a dashing, romantic figure: handsome, cosmopolitan, ready to do service to the ladies as readily as to his country, native or chosen. Such spies and adventurers were latter-day versions of the Count of Monte Cristo and predecessors to Ian Fleming's popular James Bond.

The Ashenden of Maugham's stories, on the other hand, is reserved, stoic, unromantic; his work is dull, repetitive, even meaningless. He seems to have been chosen for his task because, whatever talent he may have as a writer, he does not know much about espionage and is not likely to wish to distinguish himself by unusually courageous and possibly foolish behavior. He is, in short, more acted upon than active; he lets events (or superiors) dictate his moves rather than attempt to dictate events for himself; and he deliberately avoids romantic contacts the result of which might be the vitiation of his responsibilities. He is the unheroic hero—not a hero at all, but an observer, chosen for his task because of his powers of observation and his distance from others. He is soon to reappear in fiction in the spy novels of Graham Greene and, much later, in the novels of John le Carré.

In Maugham's body of work, Ashenden is remarkable for his contribution to the development of the persona that I have already noted in the longer fiction and that I have suggested came partly as a result of Maugham's desire to distance himself from his alter ego in *Of Human Bondage.* Unheroic or unromantic though he may be, Ashenden is at least not the victim of a self-willed persecution, the slave of emotions that lead him to increasingly neurotic behavior. He is, if anything, above emotions, so that one tends (as with Doctor MacPhail in **"Rain"**) to see events through him. He suggests a dimension of character distinctly different from Philip Carey's, and his next major manifestation—in *Cakes and Ale*—sees him broadened further still.

One of the best features of ***Ashenden*** (as in much of the short fiction) is its understated style, and one of the best examples of that style comes in the final story of the group, as Anastasia Alexandrovna leads Ashenden to Mr. Harrington's body in revolutionary Russia:

> Anastasia Alexandrovna touched Ashenden's arm to draw his attention: sitting on the pavement, her head bent right down to her lap, was a woman and she was dead. A little way on two men had fallen together. They were dead too. The wounded, one supposed, had managed to drag themselves away or their friends had carried them. Then they found Mr. Harrington. His derby had rolled in the gutter. He lay on his face, in a pool of blood, his bald head, with its prominent bones, very white; his neat black coat smeared and muddy. But his hand was clenched tight on the parcel that contained four shirts,

> two union suits, a pair of pyjamas and four collars. Mr. Harrington had not let his washing go.

The prose in this passage has both tautness and immediacy, and the final line (typical of a Maugham story) provides a satisfying touch. If one is fond of this kind of fiction, one ends by wishing that Maugham had decided to come back to it again.

In the end, the Ashenden stories notwithstanding, one probably remembers best the Maugham short stories that, like **"Rain,"** have exotic settings. These stories continue the account of the British imperial experience begun by Kipling, carrying it into its decadence and ultimate corruption, the last to be memorialized in fiction much later on by writers like Paul Scott (in his *Raj Quartet*). Maugham's short stories also continue the tradition of the nineteenth-century tale. "No author," Angus Wilson observed of Maugham in a preface to a selection of his short stories [***Cakes and Ale and Twelve Stories*** (1967)]:

> has more cleverly converted his defects into assets, not only by his assumption of the classic and stoic framework of life (through which the lost romantic is only occasionally allowed yearningly to peer), but far more by the perfection of his craft, imposing upon his carefully limited material an even more rigorous form, and then becoming so completely master of this highly artificial technique that his stories appear to flow with the ease and simplicity of ordinary, everyday muddled life.

In the best of the short fiction, through such means, Maugham achieved a vision and tone uniquely his. If he had written nothing else, his best short stories would guarantee him a place of note in English literary history. (pp. 72-82)

Archie K. Loss, in his W. Somerset Maugham, *Ungar, 1987, 139 p.*

FURTHER READING

Aldington, Richard. *W. Somerset Maugham: An Appreciation.* New York: Doubleday, Doran & Co., 1939, 34 p.

Includes the title essay by Aldington; "Sixty-Five," an essay by Maugham; a primary bibliography; reprinted excerpts from favorable reviews of Maugham's books; and an index of short stories.

Auden, W. H. "Notebooks of Somerset Maugham." *The New York Times Book Review* (23 October 1949): 1, 22.

Review of *A Writer's Notebook* in which Auden comments on Maugham's self-assessments.

Burgess, Anthony. "Somerset Maugham, 1874-1965." *The Listener* LXXIV, No. 1917 (23 December 1965): 1033.

Obituary tribute in which Burgess declares that "the short story was Maugham's true *métier,* and some of the stories he wrote are among the best in the language."

Burt, Forrest D. *W. Somerset Maugham.* Boston: Twayne Publishers, 1985, 157 p.

Chronologically arranged survey of Maugham's life and career.

Calder, Robert. *Willie: The Life of W. Somerset Maugham.* London: Heinemann, 1989, 429 p.

Scholarly biography prepared with the assistance of Maugham's companion-secretary Alan Searle.

Connolly, Cyril. "The Art of Being Good." *The New Statesman and Nation* XXVIII, No. 705 (26 August 1944): 140.

Review of *The Razor's Edge* that includes the assessment: "Maugham is the greatest living short-story writer, and so one expects his handling of plot to force one into a breathless, non-stop reading from the first page to the last, and his character-drawing and observation to be in the fine tradition—but one would not expect to be so captivated by the brilliant fluency of the writing. Here at last is a great writer, on the threshold of old age, determined to tell the truth in a form which releases all the possibilities of his art."

Costa, Richard Hauer. "Maugham's 'Partial Self': The 'Unexpected View' on the Way to 'The Death of Ivan Ilych'." *The CEA Critic* 43, No. 4 (May 1981): 3-7.

Compares Maugham's short story "Sanatorium" with Tolstoy's "Ivan Ilych."

Curtis, Anthony, and Whitehead, John, eds. *W. Somerset Maugham: The Critical Heritage.* London: Routledge & Kegan Paul, 1987, 470 p.

Reprints important first reviews of Maugham's plays and books. The editors provide an insightful introduction that surveys Maugham's life and career.

Greene, Graham. Review of *Cosmopolitans: Very Short Stories,* by W. Somerset Maugham. *The Spectator* 156, No. 5625 (17 April 1936): 720.

Suggests that while the stories in the collection are not among Maugham's best, they reflect Maugham's "supreme competence, the dry amusing reserve of a man who has the highest admiration for the interest, rather than the goodness, of human nature."

Kanin, Garson. *Remembering Mr. Maugham.* New York: Atheneum, 1966, 313 p.

Reminiscence by the screenwriter, novelist, and short story writer who, together with his wife, actress Ruth Gordon, maintained a friendship with Maugham for the last twenty years of Maugham's life.

MacKay, L. A. "Somerset Maugham." *The Canadian Forum* XVI, No. 184 (May 1936): 23-4.

Commends the stylistic "purity" of Maugham's prose.

Maugham, Robin. *Somerset and All the Maughams.* London: Longmans, 1966, 274 p.

Reminiscences by Maugham's nephew providing genealogical information and insights into Maugham's character.

Moore, Harry T. Review of *Seventeen Lost Stories,* by W. Somerset Maugham. *The Saturday Review* 52, No. 47 (22 November 1969): 87.

Considers these early stories, originally published between 1898 and 1908 and not previously collected, revelatory about Maugham's development as a fiction writer.

Morley, Christopher. "Gin and Quinine Tonic." *The New York Times Book Review* (8 October 1950): 3, 24.

Review praising *The Maugham Reader,* comprising novels, short stories, plays, essays, and an autobiographical sketch, as "a generous load of the most continuously readable storyteller of our lifetime."

Mortimer, Armine Kotin. "Second Stories: The Example of 'Mr. Know-All'." *Studies in Short Fiction* 25, No. 3 (Summer 1988): 307-14.

Examines the technique whereby Maugham embedded a "hidden" or "second" story in the narrative of "Mr. Know-All."

Nicholas, Beverley. *A Case of Human Bondage.* London: Secker & Warburg, 1966, 153 p.

Account of the Maughams' marriage by a longtime acquaintance of both Maugham and his wife, written to refute Maugham's vilification of Syrie Wellcome Maugham in *Looking Back.*

Pritchett, V. S. Review of *The Mixture as Before,* by W. Somerset Maugham. *The New Statesman and Nation* XIX, No. 486 (15 June 1940): 750.

Assesses some essential characteristics of Maugham's fiction, noting in particular his cynicism, moralism, and class-consciousness.

———. Review of *A Writer's Notebook,* by W. Somerset Maugham. *The New Statesman and Nation* XXXVIII, No. 970 (8 October 1949): 401.

Commends the interest and readability of Maugham's published notebooks.

Sunne, Richard. "Current Literature: Books in General." *The New Statesman and Nation* 2, No. 35 (24 October 1931): 516.

Asserts that Maugham's inability to effectively portray character has prevented him from receiving wide critical regard.

Sykes, Gerald. "An Author in Evening Dress." *The Nation,* New York 133, No. 3464 (25 November 1931): 576.

Charges that the short story collection *First Person Singular* demonstrates Maugham's preference for writing purely commercial popular fiction rather than striving to recapture the excellence displayed in *Of Human Bondage.*

Vidal, Gore. "Maugham's Half and Half." *The New York Times Review of Books* XXXVII, No. 1 (1 February 1990): 39-44.

Acerbic account of Maugham's life and works occasioned by the publication of Robert Calder's *Willie: The Life of W. Somerset Maugham* and the republication of several of Maugham's works.

Wilson, Edmund. "The Apotheosis of Somerset Maugham." In his *Classics and Commercials: A Literary Chronicle of the Forties,* pp. 319-26. New York: Farrar, Straus and Co., 1950.

Negative assessment of Maugham's career.

Grace Paley

1922-

(Born Grace Goodside) American short story writer, poet, and essayist.

Considered one of the most innovative contemporary American short fiction writers, Paley combines traditional subject matter with postmodern fictional techniques to depict modern urban life in the United States. A feminist and political activist, Paley addresses many social concerns in her stories, often focusing on female or Jewish protagonists who contend with issues of oppression, community, and cultural heritage and their personal and social impact. Marked by lively, colloquial prose and a combination of humor and poignancy, Paley's stories are also characterized by narrative ambiguities and inconclusive endings that defy such literary conventions as linear plot and closure—the indication that a story's conflict has been finally resolved. Admired for the clarity with which she portrays the sounds and textures of urban life as well as for the seriousness of her commitment to social change, Paley has been praised by author Donald Barthelme as "a wonderful writer and troublemaker."

Paley was born in 1922 in New York City, where she has lived most of her life and which provides the setting for many of her short stories. Her parents were Jewish immigrants from Europe who supported leftist and Zionist movements, and Paley has cited them as influences on her lifelong political activism. Her father, Isaac Goodside, also inspired the father figures in her stories, as she has acknowledged in a prefatory note to her collection *Enormous Changes at the Last Minute:* "Everyone in this book is imagined into life except the father. No matter what story he has to live in, he's my father, I. Goodside, M.D., artist, and storyteller." Paley enrolled at Hunter College in New York at age sixteen, but dropped out before receiving a degree. In 1942 she married Jess Paley, a motion-picture cameraman. They separated three years later, although they were not divorced for twenty years, and many critics believe Jess provided the model for the absent husbands of many of Paley's characters. In the early 1940s she studied poetry under W. H. Auden at New York's New School for Social Research and wrote poetry exclusively until the age of thirty-three, when she began writing the stories that would comprise her collection *The Little Disturbances of Man.* In the 1960s Paley became increasingly active in a number of political movements, including feminism and the opposition to the war in Vietnam, and was arrested during antiwar demonstrations. During this period she also began writing a novel, an abortive attempt to satisfy others' expectations that she later called "the wrongest thing I ever did." Her commitment to political activism and to raising her children has limited her literary activity, and she has released only two collections of short stories since 1959, *Enormous Changes at the Last Minute* and *Later the Same Day,* and the poetry collection *Leaning Forward.* Paley currently teaches creative writing at Sarah Lawrence College.

With *The Little Disturbances of Man* Paley established a reputation as a masterful stylist, able to vividly capture the idiomatic speech of native New Yorkers of various ethnicities in a manner that critics have compared to William Faulkner's renderings of Southern dialects. Her protagonists in this and later collections are characterized by their vivaciousness and indomitability of spirit, which they maintain in spite of economic difficulties and painful personal relationships. In "Goodbye and Good Luck" Rose Lieber recounts her longtime affair with the matinee idol Volodya Vlashkin, a married man who has also been unfaithful to Rose. Now fifty and unmarried, she prefers her independent life to that of her married sister, whose pity Rose spurns: "[My sister] waits in a spotless kitchen for a kind word and thinks—poor Rosie. . . . Poor Rosie! If there was more life in my little sister, she would know my heart is a regular college of feelings and there is such information between my corset and me that her whole married life is a kindergarten." In other works, Paley explores the aftermath of failed relationships, and several stories examine the search for cultural identity among Jewish Americans.

In her two later collections, *Enormous Changes at the Last Minute* and *Later the Same Day,* Paley focused increasingly on the political and social themes which she included only briefly in *The Little Disturbances of Man* and began to experiment with different forms of narrative. These collections, which feature a number of extremely short stories and vignettes, enhanced her reputation as a major postmodernist writer through their use of metafictional devices and nonlinear, often surrealistic plots, as in "At That Time; or, The History of a Joke," a satiric story of a modern-day virgin birth. Paley's characters in these stories are more highly politically conscious than those in *Little Disturbances,* paralleling her own increasing political activity. The status of women in American society is a predominant theme as well: Paley's female protagonists rebel against authority by protesting government actions or asserting their independence in romantic relationships. Frequently, these women are single mothers—abandoned or "unmarried on principle"—who develop informal, independent communities of support.

Several of Paley's stories feature one such independent woman, Faith Darwin, a writer who shares a number of biographical characteristics with Paley, and who many critics perceive as Paley's alter ego. Faith, like other Paley heroines, maintains an awareness of the relationship between politics and personal life. She also expresses many of Paley's principles on the nature of art and the role of the writer in society. In one of Paley's most critically discussed stories, "A Conversation with My Father," Faith's father, hospitalized with heart illness, reproaches her for not writing simple, tragic stories in the vein of Anton Chekhov or Guy de Maupassant. Faith attempts to improvise such a story for him, but leaves open the possibility that her drug-addicted protagonist might overcome her difficulties. To her father's accusation that she is unable to cope with tragedy—artistically or personally—Faith responds by calling traditional plot "the absolute line between two points which I've always despised. . . . [It] takes all hope away. Everyone, real or invented, deserves the open destiny of life." Paley has maintained that this rejection of finality more accurately presents reality in the modern world, in which "enormous changes at the last minute" cannot be ruled out.

The majority of Paley's characters are either Jewish immigrants or their descendants who must come to terms with the past oppressions of their race as well as with contemporary prejudices encountered by cultural and racial minority groups in the United States. The burden of Jewish history is a recurrent theme in Paley's stories: in the story "In Time Which Made A Monkey of Us All" victims of the Holocaust are described with bitter humor as those who "died in the epidemics of Jewishness," and in "Zagrowsky Tells" a Jewish immigrant charges that an "American-born girl has some nerve to mention history." Paley faithfully reproduces the cadences of Yiddish speech in a manner critics have compared to that of Isaac Babel, and Paley herself acknowledges the influence of the Jewish oral tradition on her prose style. In "Debts" the narrator, a writer, says that her work is like the oral storytelling of the past—an act necessary to the preservation of the culture and dignity of one's people and family.

While much of Paley's work is informed by her politics, her stories are rarely constructed around a specific political or moral message. Rather, many concern characters who are themselves politically conscious and who attempt to integrate their worldviews into their personal lives, most frequently in their familial and romantic relationships. In "The Expensive Moment," Faith, visiting China as part of an artist's delegation, commiserates with a Chinese woman on the demands that historical and political exigencies can make on a family. Some critics have noted that Paley's direct linking of personal life to political issues mirrors the approach to politics taken by feminist theorists, and indeed much of her fiction compares the value systems of male and female characters. Whereas women in Paley's stories are generally concerned with establishing communal bonds and finding peace, men pursue wealth and individual honor and frequently abandon their families in order to do so. In "An Interest in Life," the female protagonist speculates on the differences between a woman's idea of happiness and a man's, noting that a woman "could lie down, nuzzling a regiment of men and little kids, she could just die of the pleasure. But men are different, they have to own money, or they have to be famous, or everybody on the block has to look up to them from the cellar stairs."

Paley's combination of traditional oral storytelling aesthetics with a postmodern narrative self-awareness and approach to plot has led critics to hail her as a major renovator of the short story. Critics generally consider the stories featuring Faith Darwin her most successful, and some have speculated that, taken together, these works might comprise a novel. However, Paley has repeatedly disavowed such an approach, commenting that she prefers writing short stories because "art is too long and life is too short. There is a lot more to do in life than just writing." Some critics charge that Paley's politics overwhelms her later stories; but others argue that while she writes about politically engaged characters, she never writes polemically or didactically. Novelist Anne Tyler has commented that Paley's characters "avoid self-righteousness; they're not offensive. The reason . . . is that Grace Paley never loses sight of the personal." While critics sometimes fault Paley for incompletely rendering her subject matter, particularly in her shorter stories, the emotional intensity of her narratives and the fullness of her characters have earned her widespread respect.

(For further information on Paley's life and career, see *Contemporary Literary Criticism,* Vols. 4, 6, 37; *Contemporary Authors,* Vols. 25-28, rev. ed.; *Contemporary Authors New Revision Series,* Vol. 13; and *Dictionary of Literary Biography,* Vol. 28.)

PRINCIPAL WORKS

SHORT FICTION

The Little Disturbances of Man 1959

Enormous Changes at the Last Minute 1974
Later the Same Day 1985

OTHER MAJOR WORKS

Leaning Forward (poetry) 1985

Patricia MacManus (essay date 1959)

[*In the following essay, MacManus favorably reviews* The Little Disturbances of Man.]

The glad tidings from this reviewer's corner are of the appearance of a newcomer possessed of an all-too-infrequent literary virtue—the comic vision. Grace Paley is the writer, and heretofore, apparently, her light has been confined to some of the smaller quarterlies. Now, however, ***The Little Disturbances of Man*** brings together ten of her short stories, and a welcome event it is. While they may not, to be sure, fully satisfy confirmed plot-watchers, they are by no means simply "mood" stories—rather, they are marked throughout by a well-defined and artfully guileless form of narrative progression. But the heart of the matter in these tales is their serio-comic stance: character revealed through the wry devices that man contrives, consciously and unconsciously, to shore up his uncertain existence and, sometimes, to salvage laughter from lamentation.

In **"The Loudest Voice,"** for example, the Paley approach is glimpsed in the reaction of a Jewish immigrant to his wife's horrified announcement that their child is to be in a Christmas—a *Christian*—play. "You're in America," the husband retorts. "In Palestine the Arabs would be eating you alive. Europe you had pogroms. Argentina is full of Indians. Here you got Christmas." Or in the lyrically risible opening of **"The Contest"**—"Up early or late, it never matters, the day gets away from me. Summer or winter, the shade of trees or their hard shadow, I never get into my Rice Krispies till noon."

The people in these tales exist on the far periphery of the Important world; and the themes are as the title states: the little disturbances of man—"little" vis-à-vis cosmic catastrophes, but major to the personal business of daily living. A middle-aging, sanguine-spirited "bachelor girl" recollects an amorous past on the eve of her marriage to a long-ago beau; a determined teen-ager cons a bemused young soldier into a thoroughly entangling alliance; a husband-abandoned wife and mother wait out the idolized prodigal's return, imperturbably confident; a pixilated youth who lives in a philodendron-decorated automobile and functions as a kind of curb-service problem consultant; a girl's long, frustrated need for love is examined from her own viewpoint—and from the viewpoint of the man she wants. These are a few of the characters who move through the oblique human comedy of Mrs. Paley's stories. Small-time people, in terms of the world worldly, they none the less reflect the perdurable instinct of most people everywhere to improvise ways and means of accepting the indifferent universe. (pp. 28-9)

Patricia MacManus, "Laughter from Tears," in The New York Times Book Review, *April 19, 1959, pp. 28-9.*

Irving Malin (essay date 1963)

[*Malin is an American educator and critic. In the following excerpt, he discusses Paley's affirmation of the physical in* The Little Disturbances of Man.]

Although she may refer now and then to such big problems as the Bomb or the Population Explosion, Mrs. Paley is more interested in those "little disturbances" we meet daily. Gestures of love and hate dominate her stories. She refuses to offer psychological motivation, the underlying causes for these gestures—by no means is she a Happy Freudian, as we can see from her nasty remark about a "world just bristling with goddamn phallic symbols." Mrs. Paley simply affirms that the body lusts for warmth and liveliness (even directing the psyche). But she doesn't sentimentalize golden, Vic Tanny-like health. She is obsessed by malevolent time which hits out at us, hampering our natural, bodily wishes.

Thus in an exciting way Mrs. Paley gives us an old theme: Time versus Love. We can never say whether or not her characters *win.* When they forget, if only for an instant, the attack of time, they are happy; when their bodies ache, they remember that they are in "time which (makes) a monkey of us all." Perhaps Mrs. Paley possesses Jewish vision. The Jews accept the joyous *substantiality* of this world, the verve of life. But they also know toughly that such joys cannot last, that there is Something More. So does Mrs. Paley.

Once we perceive this basic opposition, we are startled that we did not see it before. In the very first story [in ***The Little Disturbances of Man***], **"Goodbye and Good Luck,"** Aunt Rose mourns the fact that "change is a fact of God. From this no one is excused." She reminds Lillie that her mother (Rose's sister) doesn't notice "how big her behind is getting . . ." Then she proceeds to recount the story of her past affair with Vlashkin, the "Yiddish Valentino." She wants to recapture the joys of the body, to fight change. Once she was beautiful, with circulation "fore and aft." Vlashkin adored her. Both were "driven by love"—propelled instinctively. But time intervened: Vlashkin left on tour; when they met again they saw how much they had lost. Aunt Rose tells Lillie that she "noticed it first on my mother's face, the rotten handwriting of time, scribbled up and down her cheeks, across her forehead back and forth—a child could read—it said, old, old, old." Then she saw Vlashkin "creep," like her story, to the end; she saw herself unwillingly become "fat and fifty." Suddenly Rose pauses and announces the unexpected: only yesterday Vlashkin invited her to go out with him; they are, in fact, contemplating marriage after all these years. *Goodbye and good luck to the past. Present and future love count.*

In another comic story, **"A Woman, Young and Old,"** remarkable body-lusts reappear. Again the body defies age, convention, and order: it "wills itself to power." Instead of presenting one woman musing about past and present,

Mrs. Paley gives us women of different generations—the mother, the grandmother, the narrator (Josephine) and others. All agree that "a man, a real one," is more important than abstract symbols or empty conventions. They are incomplete without friendly masculinity.

We whirl from jauntiness to violence to sadness to joy. After Josephine and her mother discuss cozy pleasure, the mother reads a newspaper story "about a farmer in Provence who had raped his niece and killed his mother and lived happily for thirty-eight years into respected old age before the nosy prefect caught up with him." When Corporal Brownstar, A Man, appears, the women treat him with respect; the newspaper story is forgotten. But we get the same message: the body disregards Morality. Young Josephine and the Corporal, separated by age and convention, talk and play after the others retire. Josephine is "really surprised the way a man is transformed by his feelings. He loved me all over myself . . . " Of course, hungry Mother and Lizzy are unhappy about this "funny" relationship. Mother complains about the Corporal's responsibility, Josephine's craziness; Lizzy doesn't want to lose her fiance. Things do work out well. The Corporal flunks his Wasserman; Mother latches on to someone else; Liz needs no help in finding many men; and Josephine sleeps next to her sister.

Mrs. Paley has not only given us Josephine's pleasure in "hugging with Browny's body," but she insists that such hugging will go on despite injunctions of family, morality, or disease. Only time will kill it.

"The Pale Pink Roast" begins with great vitality: Peter strides into the park, grinning grandly to two "young girls." Anna, his divorced wife, and their daughter see him. There is a "collusion of charm," fun-talk. Peter speaks to Anna about Health, as the "sunshiny spring afternoon seeped through his fingers." He is a liberating god.

After Anna and Peter go to her new apartment (leaving Judy with a babysitter), they continue discussing health. Both compliment each other. Is it "vegetables, high proteins" which make Peter "look just—well—healthy"? He claims that he has a philosophical basis for his new life. When he delivers his "sermon," he echoes the underlying reasons for Mrs. Paley's fascination with the body. Peter says:

> "You know what you see? A structure of flesh. You know when it hit me? About two years ago, around the time we were breaking up, you and me. I took my grandpa to the bathroom one time when I was over there visiting—you remember him, Anna, that old jerk, the one that was so mad, he didn't want to die . . . I was leaning on the door; he was sitting on the pot concentrating on his guts. Just to make conversation—I thought it'd help him relax—I said, 'Pop? Pop, if you had to do it all over again, what would you do different? Any real hot tips?'
>
> "He came up with an answer right away. 'Peter,' he said, 'I'd go to a gym every goddamn day of my life; the hell with the job, the hell with the women. Peter, I'd build my body up till God hisself wouldn't know how to tear it apart.' "

Such health is more important than "itsy-bitsy motivations."

Finally Peter and Anna flop onto the bed. He takes her "at once without a word." We don't get any lengthy romantic scene, any mystical statements, but we sense the "good time," the "reward, strength, and beauty" of health. Then we are shocked: Anna reveals that she is married; Peter feels guilty. Mrs. Paley insists, however, that "this is the way things are"—the body, "this me" must be maintained, no matter what convention or loyalty dictates. We believe Anna when she says that their act was love, not meanness, revenge, or illness. We accept their swift leave-taking as Peter prances into the street; "easy and impervious, in full control, he cartwheels into the source of night."

Perhaps Philip Roth is right in thinking that **"An Interest in Life"** is the best story in Mrs. Paley's collection. The three stories already discussed are wonderfully done, except for the fact that Mrs. Paley doesn't give the other side real power. Morality doesn't really fight the body; Time is vanquished somewhat easily. But here she develops those dense inhibitions which elude a Peter or Josephine. The struggle between Time and Love, the Law and Humanity, is greater.

The narrator begins with bitterness. She is alone; her husband has just left her. The man who "got onto [her] all the time, drunk or sober, even when everybody had to get up early in the morning . . . " cannot accept the conventional family. She is tearful: sadness is "stretched world-wide across [her] face." Her neighbor, Mrs. Raftery, tells her to "look around for comfort." Thus the first few pages immediately convey the "awful" rebelliousness of men, and the need of women to live within the family. Virginia is trapped. The realities of money, aging, and frustrated desire cramp her health.

John Raftery, unlike most of Mrs. Paley's male characters, is a family man, not a pleasure-seeking bachelor. He has sacrificed body-lusts to Stability. John is devout, believing that "children come from God." To which Virginia answers: "You're still great on holy subjects, aren't you. You know damn well where children come from." I take this exchange as the thematic center of the story. Does the body assert its needs against Holiness? Is the body itself—ugly, frantic, and tense—still holy? Can it defeat the eternal forces?

The rest of the story answers these questions. Although John is married, "a leader of the Fathers' Club at his church," he cannot control his body. Virginia knows "that if he stayed late to love with me, he would not do it lightly but would in the end pay terrible penance and ruin his long life." A man "must do well in the world;" a woman "invents" life. At last Virginia allows John to yield to his body; he is warm and youthful, relinquishing his "married" coldness. As she says: "It is still hard to believe that a man who sends out the Ten Commandments every year for a Christmas card can be so easy buttoning and unbuttoning." But Virginia dreams about the return of her wild husband, perhaps realizing that she cannot, after all, share John with his family and Lord. Her "interest in life," keeps her going, not any belief that Orthodoxy or Convention can wholly satisfy her. The last sentence presents her true happiness—"before I can even make myself half comfortable on that polka-dotted linoleum, he got onto me where we were, and the truth is, we were so happy, we forgot the precautions." This is Mrs. Paley's tough verve: the body achieves happiness, forgetting precaution; but the Enemies—Time, Responsibility, and Morality—constantly wait.

I have probably made these stories seem dreary or simple-minded. They are vitally complex because of their style. If I correctly view Mrs. Paley's basic theme, then the appropriateness of her style—her imagery, her syntax—becomes clear.

The most obvious aspect of her style is the choice of narrator. Mrs. Paley assumes that we must meet a *lively* person, usually a woman, whose words ramble, pause, turn, and stride as her body-feelings change. There is no artificial, straight entrapment in plot. Plot is an "eternal" restriction; conversation, however, is a series of free-swinging gestures.

The conversation flashes with fitting imagery. Aunt Rose, for example, says: "Others are like grass, the north wind of time has cut out their heart." (Actually she repeats Vlashkin here.) Time is viewed as human; it too is active, even when it defeats *our* liveliness. Rose always talks about abstractions in terms of personal gestures: Lillie grows up "from a plain seed;" Time writes realities on Vlashkin's face; her life is "a regular college of feelings."

The "Spiritual" becomes Physical in Mrs. Paley's fiction. Josephine's "lonesome soul" is bare when she is nude. Judy and her friendly babysitter flutter lashes "like kissing angels do." The body is the *"dwelling place of the soul."* Girls, "slim and tender or really stacked, dark brown at their centers" are "smeared by time." A girl hopes to "breathe eternity into a mortal matter, love." Life "sits." Truth "floats."

And the inanimate becomes animate. Phallic symbols "bristle;" a doorbell is "full of initiative;" a bra is "wall-eyed;" acorns are "disappointed;" "every window is a mother's mouth bidding the street shut up, go skate somewhere else, come home . . . ;" good looks "wink" and the consistency of a girl is "cozy."

Because the non-physical becomes physical, there is no rigid demarcation of worlds. There is *one* world in which body-presences move quickly, energetically, or violently: "Change is a fact of God." Blood is "so busy warming the toes and the finger tips, it don't have time to circulate where it's most required." Vlashkin ages "a half century" in one play. From a bed Rose will "finally fall to a bed not so lonesome." Moral turpitude takes a "lively turn." Discouragement is a "turnpike." Girls skip around a Maypole. Peter "cartwheels," Shirley says: "if a girl is within ten feet of you, you have her stripped and on the spit." A young man hops on his scooter and moves forward "on spectacular errands of mercy." Thus Mrs. Paley emphasises present participles. On only four pages of **"An Interest in Life"** we find the following participles: "seeing," "ringing," "looking," "putting," "raining," "paying," "parting," "kneeling," "gawking," "doing," "dumping," "standing," "telling," "kidding," "telling," "kidding," "fainting," "deserting," "pulling," "leaving," "expecting," "leaning," "living."

Harvey Swados has suggested that Mrs. Paley's language "takes off into a realm that borders on the surrealist" [see Further Reading]. Can't we say that it does this because it fuses the spiritual and the physical? Her imagery asserts that Reality is *fluid* and *dreamlike*—the Body cannot be tamed; there is quirky Spirit in it. But the imagery also asserts that imaginative vision is more exhilarating, more full of verve, than Fixity. We "think with the body."

In a recent essay on Jewish stories Saul Bellow has written: "In them, laughter and trembling are so curiously mingled that it is not easy to determine the relations of the two. At times the laughter seems simply to restore the equilibrium of sanity; at times the figures of the story, or parable, appear to invite or encourage trembling with the secret aim of overcoming it by means of laughter." Mrs. Paley's style implies that there is comedy in turning things upside down. Because the body defies morality (creating its own "style of life"), it makes us sense the deceptive stability of such institutions as the Church or Marriage or Business. The body and these institutions should "marry," but they *cannot* because any marriage would destroy one or the other. Mrs. Paley views the situation with humor which is unsettling at the same time it is full of verve. (Is there any difference between verve and unbalance?) It is comic for men to fall in love with young girls (as in **"A Woman, Young and Old"** or **"An Irrevocable Diameter"**) or devout Catholics to submit to their bodies, but the crazy power of the body cannot be stopped. The body becomes divine, creating and destroying at once. Mrs. Paley's fictional world is so lively that it bounces irrationally.

Perhaps there is a way out of the problem. Saul Bellow claims that when we laugh, "our minds refer us to God's existence. Chaos is exposed." Mrs. Paley's verve upsets Reality, showing us Chaos. But this very vision thrills us because we recognize *Chaos* as *Chaos.* We sense that there is a Higher Force, one which made our liberating, joyous, and destroying flesh. In a sacred, paradoxical way Grace Paley presents a Hassidic dance. (pp. 73-8)

Irving Malin, "The Verve of Grace Paley," in Genesis West, *Vol. 2, No. 5, Fall, 1963, pp. 73-8.*

Granville Hicks (essay date 1968)

[*Hicks was an American literary critic whose study* The Great Tradition: An Interpretation of American Literature since the Civil War *(1933) established him as the foremost advocate of Marxist critical thought in Depression-era America. After 1939 Hicks sharply denounced Marxist criticism as a "hopelessly narrow way of judging literature," and in his later years adopted a less ideological position in criticism. In the following excerpt, Hicks praises Paley's perceptiveness and narrative style in* The Little Disturbances of Man.]

The case of Grace Paley is unique. She published a first book of short stories, ***The Little Disturbances of Man,*** in 1959. It caused no great stir, but it so impressed a certain number of people that its reputation has steadily grown. Out of print for some time, it has now been reissued. . . .

The book's contents are described as "eleven stories of men and women at love." This is not exactly a novel subject, but Miss Paley has brought to it depth of feeling, fresh powers of observation, and a personal, vigorous style. Look at the first paragraph of the first story, **"Goodbye and Good Luck":**

> I was popular in certain circles, says Aunt Rosie. I wasn't no thinner then, only more stationary in the flesh. In time to come, Lillie, don't be surprised—change is a fact of God. From this no one is excused. Only a person like your mama stands on one foot, she don't notice how big her behind is getting and sings in the canary's ear for thirty years. Who's listening? Papa's in the shop. You and Seymour thinking about yourself. So she waits in a spotless kitchen for a kind word and thinks—poor Rosie. . . .

Rosie goes on to make it clear to her niece that she is not to be pitied. When she was a girl, she fell in love with a popular actor in the Yiddish theater, and became his mistress. He was a charmer, a matinee idol: "On the opening night, in the middle of the first scene, one missus—a widow or maybe her husband worked too long hours—began to clap and sing out, 'Oi, oi, Vlashkin.' " The affair followed a strange course over many years, and now, as she wants the niece to understand, it has reached a strange but to her satisfying climax.

It is Miss Paley's masterly use of the vernacular that makes us feel Rosie's vitality. In this, as in several other stories, the language is that of persons who have been influenced by Yiddish, and Miss Paley knows how to get the most out of the colorful idioms of that speech; but the voice is always unmistakably her own—alive, eager, fearless, a little tough, a little tender.

There are extraordinary characters: Josephine, the thirteen-year-old who goes after and nearly gets her man; Shirley Abramovitch, who plays the leading part in the public school Christmas play because she has the loudest voice; Eddie Teitelbaum, an inventive boy whose ingeniousness gets him into serious trouble. Most of the stories are told in the first person, and in most of these the narrator is a woman. One or two of the characters are grotesques, and their stories could be described as far-out, but Miss Paley's great gift is for making something remarkable out of the commonplace. (p. 29)

Granville Hicks, "Some Stopped Short and Sold," in Saturday Review, *Vol. LI, No. 17, April 27, 1968, pp. 29-30.*

Marianne DeKoven (essay date 1981)

[*In the following essay, DeKoven examines the reconciliation of postmodern form with traditional subjects in Paley's works, particularly in "A Conversation with My Father" and "Faith in the Afternoon."*]

In contemporary fiction, the impulse to recreate form is at loggerheads with the impulse to tell about everyday life. Grace Paley is a rare contemporary who feels both impulses, and in her work they cohere. It would be easy to read her stories without recognizing that they give two very different kinds of pleasure—the intellectual, aesthetic pleasure of inventive language and form, and the emotional, moral pleasure of deftly handled, poignant theme—without realizing that one was having the best of two historically sundered fictional modes.

Though Paley has published only two collections of stories, ***The Little Disturbances of Man*** and ***Enormous Changes at the Last Minute,*** she is nonetheless an important writer—important in the significance of the fictional possibilities she realizes rather than in the uniform merit of her published work. She is not always at her best. But when she is, Paley reconciles the demands of avant-garde or postmodern form for structural openness and the primacy of the surface with the seemingly incompatible demands of traditional realist material for orchestrated meaning and cathartic emotion.

"A Conversation with My Father," in ***Enormous Changes,*** makes of this seeming incompatibility an argument between father and daughter, from which emerges the statement, crucial to Paley's work, that traditional themes can no longer be treated *truthfully* by formally traditional fiction: formal inventiveness and structural open-endedness not only make fiction interesting, they make it "true-to-life." Paley's concern is not mimesis or verisimilitude, but rather the problem of creating a literary form which does not strike one as artificial; which is adequate to the complexity of what we know. Her narrator in **"A Conversation with My Father"** calls traditional plot "the absolute line between two points which I've always despised. Not for literary reasons, but because it takes away all hope. Everyone, real or invented, deserves the open destiny of life." Her father, arguing that plot is the truth of tragedy, wants her to write like Chekhov or Maupassant: "Tragedy! Plain tragedy! Historical tragedy! No hope. The end." Paley's narrator-surrogate, arguing for open-ended hope and change, clearly bests her father in the conversation. But in the story, Paley gives him the last word: the setting is his hospital room, and he speaks from what we may assume is his deathbed. His lecture on writing is "last-minute advice," and the closing speech, from father's pain to daughter's guilt, is his: " 'How long will it be?' he asked. 'Tragedy! You too. When will you look it in the face?' "

The assertion of hope through change and open-endedness is therefore neither easy nor unambiguous. As the literary father sees, an inevitable component of optimistic belief in saving the situation through "enormous changes at the last minute" is evasion of genuine and unavoidable horror, the father's tragedy. As Faith herself says in **"Living"** (***Enormous Changes***), "You have to be cockeyed to love, and blind in order to look out the window at your own ice-cold street."

Paley herself, though endorsing in the structure of her fiction the narrator's point of view, is increasingly ambivalent about traditional storytelling. (pp. 217-18)

Though linear storytelling is attractive to Paley's moral-political sensibility, and she feels guilty that she doesn't write that way, the marrow of her fictions remains "enormous changes at the last minute." (p. 218)

Paley places the tragic material which interests and moves her within an anti-tragic structure of sudden, abrupt transformations, "enormous changes," but the tragic material is nonetheless left intact. There is none of the hollow laughter, the mocking, alienated distance from pathos that is characteristic of serious modern fiction. But transformation undercuts tragic inevitability—fictional structure becomes tragedy's antidote rather than either its vehicle or its negation—and, equally important, as we will see, transformation undercuts the sentimentality that so easily trivializes pathos.

The people Paley's narrator in **"A Conversation with My Father"** would accuse of having merely "literary reasons" for rejecting traditional plot might explain the "enormous change" as an interesting substitute for outworn, tedious literary convention (linear plots are stale and boring), infusing new life into fiction. But Paley's structures are more than that. They are rooted not only in an assertion of open-endedness and possibility, and in a nonlinear vision of life's events, but also, ultimately, in a profound commitment to freedom as a primary value (nonlinearity is not as alien to Paley's politics as it might appear). For many postmodernists, that freedom is problematic; tangled with fear of chaos on one hand and of authority on the other. . . . But the freedom implied for Paley by "enormous changes," the freedom from inevitability or plot, is synonymous with hope; hence her larger assertion that open-endedness in fiction is the locus of "the open destiny of life," to which everyone is "*entitled*"—a strongly political statement. . . . Tentatively and comically, Paley offers fiction's "enormous changes" as a warbling counternote to the tragic gong, even in twentieth century political life, that notoriously unredeemed domain.

The tragic subject matter of Paley's work reaches the reader emotionally as pathos, a tricky entity because it so easily becomes sentimental. However, pathos remains pathos in Paley's work: she jerks no tears but neither does she freeze them. Instead, she distracts the reader from pathos at dangerous moments, when sentimentality threatens, by calling attention to her wildly inventive, comic language and imagery. In those moments when her language takes on the burden of simultaneously communicating and distracting from pathos, Paley creates a unique and fascinating literary object.

In **"Faith in the Afternoon"** (***Enormous Changes***), Faith, recently abandoned by her husband, is visiting her parents in their old people's home, "The Children of Judea." Faith's mother belongs to the "Grandmothers' Wool Socks Association," governed by the formidable Mrs. Hegel-Shtein, who rolls noiselessly in and out of everyone's privacy "on oiled wheelchair wheels." Mrs. Hegel-Shtein is an ineluctable and pitiless purveyor of sad stories. She forces Faith's mother, who wants to spare her daughter more unhappiness, to discuss the tragic fates of various of Faith's childhood friends, beginning with Tess Slovinsky, whose first child was a "real monster," and:

> "[The second] was born full of allergies. It had rashes from orange juice. It choked from milk. Its eyes swoll up from going to the country. All right. Then her husband, Arnold Lever, a very pleasant boy, got a cancer. They chopped off a finger. It got worse. They chopped off a hand. It didn't help. Faithy, that was the end of a lovely boy. That's the letter I got this morning just before you came."
>
> Mrs. Darwin stopped. Then she looked up at Mrs. Hegel-Shtein and Faith. "He was an only son," she said. Mrs. Hegel-Shtein gasped. "You said an only son!"

Mrs. Hegel-Shtein is vulnerable to Arnold Lever's gruesome fate through her love of her own "only son," Archie. Faith's mother tells Arnold Lever's story from the great distance of the comic grotesque. He does not represent the kind of pathos Paley is interested in: his is sensational horror, not the unostentatious, commonplace pain of everyday life. Because she feels deeply Mrs. Hegel-Shtein's commonplace pain, Paley reaches a moment of potential sentimentality, her cue for magnificent writing: "On deep tracks, the tears rolled down her old cheeks. But she had smiled so peculiarly for seventy-seven years that they suddenly swerved wildly toward her ears and hung like glass from each lobe." The image of Mrs. Hegel-Shtein's tears swerving along deep tracks, formed by seventy-seven years of peculiar smiling, to hang from her ear lobes like crystals, is so striking that it appropriates most of our attention as we read, preventing us from noticing particularly the pathos which we nonetheless feel. The fate of Mrs. Hegel-Shtein's tears is exactly the fate of our own. They fall, but they are "wildly" diverted along literally comic tracks to become something other than tears, something not at all commonplace; in fact, something transcendent: they crystallize into literary epiphany.

Pathos is neither transformed nor displaced by language: it remains intact, registered at a more or less subliminal level. But it combines with the startling, comic-bizarre language and imagery to make a profound literary moment which we experience simultaneously as a unity beyond both pathos and language, and also as a concatenation of the two separate elements, each maintaining its integrity.

For Paley, "life" need not be rescued from sordid insignificance by "literature." She does not translate or transform one into the other, but rather allows them to coexist in her work, partly separate, partly clashing, partly fused. We do not look *through* her images to find the meanings behind them; instead, the arresting, startling language and imagery comprise one element of the fiction, the feelings and meanings they communicate another. We receive them with different kinds of attention. . . . (pp. 219-21)

But just as often as they function separately in Paley's work, prose surface and story come together in the peculiar way of Mrs. Hegel-Shtein's tears, in those moments when language must suddenly distract the reader from pathos, misleading us about the primary emotion of the fictional material. Again, in the best of those moments, surface and feeling register on the one hand separately, as strangely irreconcilable, and on the other harmoniously, as an irreducible literary epiphany. (p. 222)

At the heart of Paley's engagement with everyday life is her deep empathy with her characters. Even the deserters and betrayers she allows their "reasons," as she might say, and the rest she actively likes—a stance even more unusual in serious postmodern fiction than her assertions of hope in the face of our despair. It is not surprising that this uncommon empathy, which is really the condition of adherence to subjects of everyday life, is the province of a woman. Empathy and compassion are legacies of sexism that women do well to assert as privileged values rather than reject as stigmata of oppression. Uncomfortable as it makes her to write in such a predominantly male tradition, as a woman in the avant-garde, Paley is in an especially propitious position to unite interesting forms with important themes. She uses innovative form much as she uses innovative activism, to make new the endlessly dreary and shameful moral-political world we inhabit. (pp. 222-23)

Marianne DeKoven, "Mrs. Hegel-Shtein's Tears," in Partisan Review, *Vol. XLVIII, No. 2, 1981, pp. 217-23.*

Grace Paley (interview with Joan Lidoff) (interview date 1981)

[Lidoff was an American educator and critic who wrote extensively on women writers. The interview excerpted below is a composite of private conversations and classroom discussions held while Paley visited the University of Texas in 1981. In the interview, Paley discusses her literary origins, influences, and priorities.]

[Lidoff]: *At your reading last night, you said that all story tellers are story hearers. Would you tell us some more about that?*

[Paley]: If you're a person who doesn't pay attention, and who isn't listening, you won't be a writer, you won't even be a story teller. Those of you who are writers from the very beginning of your lives were probably unusually attentive children. You heard things that the other kids on the block really weren't listening to. You may not have known it; you didn't go around when you were six years old saying "Oh, what I heard today!" but you probably did tend to come home from school with more stories for your mother or for whoever your afternoon-listener was. If they were there, if there were people to listen, you tended to be a very talkative child. You were an extremely good listener also, which everybody doubted, always saying to you, "Will you listen?" when you knew that you heard four times as much as anybody. If there was no one to listen to you, you probably heard anyway. You were a listener and you felt crummy because you were storing up all this information all the time. There's an example in that really wonderful story in Chekhov where the son dies and the father is a coachman and he keeps going around looking for people to tell "My son, my boy died" to, to tell them what happened. And nobody is listening to him at all. Finally he just takes his horse and tells the story to the horse. I think there are a lot of story hearers that nobody listens to. I think the world is full of people that nobody listens to who have a lot to say. And then I think there are people who aren't saying anything, who are storing it all up for some moment.

Is there anyone in particular in your family who was a story teller who influenced you?

When I say a story hearer, that doesn't mean that you just listen to people tell stories. Sometimes you really are extracting them from people. You say, "Well, what happened?" And they say "Nothing." That happens in a lot of families. And it takes you years sometimes to extract stories from people in your family. But no, my father was a very good talker. And my mother as a result was somewhat more quiet. But he really was a good talker, and he spoke well about lots of things. A lot of people told stories: my grandmother, aunts, mother, sister. I don't think they thought of themselves as storytellers, but neither do most people. But almost everybody in this room, in this school, is a story teller. You tell stories all the time. So it's really one of the things that almost anybody can do. It's something that's natural. I have a little grandchild and I just know that from the first time she can put half a sentence together she's going to tell me some little story. She's already telling jokes. People tell stories everywhere in the world. When you and I were sitting around having coffee we must have told each other fourteen stories.

There does seem to be a quality in your writing voice of people sitting around a kitchen table telling stories.

Well, that's nice. I'm glad. We had a kind of family life with people around tables telling and speaking. My father talked an awful lot, when he had time, and my aunts told stories. Mostly people, as they get older, begin to defend their lives in some way. They say, I did this and this and this and why I did it. My aunt especially lived in constant defense of her life. Those are the stories people tell: what happened, and why and how.

Those are the stories I heard, and then the stories on the street. We had a very lively street life at that time in the Bronx. The descendants of those families don't realize the extent to which we lived on the street, played on the street, and the way the older people, the parents of my friends, would sit out on the street all the time. Everyone would sit out on boxes and folding chairs and talk, and that to me is also terribly interesting and quite-different: they would be talking about in-laws, children, husbands, wives, what it was all about. That's what you listen for and what you expect when you are a kid: the next conversation will tell you what it's all about, if you only listen to it.

If we think about the particular qualities of your own story telling, isn't there a Yiddish cadence in your writing voice?

Yes, I do write with an accent. I did have three languages spoken around me when I was a kid: English and Russian and Yiddish. Those were my languages. That's what's in my ear, so it got through my Eustachian tubes or whatever into my throat, with several diseases that also came along. (pp. 3-5)

How did you start to write?

I was a good kid writer in school and in junior high and so forth. I really wrote all the time. But I didn't write stories until after I was thirty, about thirty-three or so.

What got you started on stories instead of poems?

Well, just the things we were talking about. First of all, my husband did encourage me, I have to say that. He did. But mostly, it was that I was really terribly upset and concerned about women, and men and kids and all of that. I became terribly interested in the life of women and children, how they were living apart from men. It just bugged me a lot. I had lived in Army camps with the guys during the second World War. . . .

Was your husband in the Army?

Yes, he was a soldier. Everybody's husband was a soldier. I mean, that was a big war. But that really troubled me. Not so much troubles between the two of us, but more troubles among my friends and also a sudden consciousness—I won't say feminist consciousness, because I didn't know enough, but a certain female or feminine or woman's consciousness. . . .

From the lives of people around you?

Just feeling that I as a part of this bunch of women, that our lives were common and important. A lot of that came from working with women in PTAs and organizations like that, things that the early women's movement mocked and laughed at.

When I wrote poems, there was a lot of "I feel," so I made this a kind of generalized, slightly inaccurate definition for myself that when I was writing poems, it was really me speaking to the world, and when I was writing stories, it was really me getting the world to speak to me. But a lot of people do that in poetry now, as we get out of that big "I-I-I-I"—that's been the meaning of this whole country for a long time. As we got out of that, I think the poems changed also. But for a long, long time in poetry, as poetry's area, place of living, got narrower and narrower, it was very hard to do anything but that. Because every other mode of expression was doing all the other things. Films were being epics and novels were taking over whole narrative areas. So the poem really was just left with this person, alone. When I was younger, I couldn't have made a story for anything.

How did you learn to?

It was sudden. You hear the expression "breakthrough," and it really was a breaking through. I had just been so distressed about—well, about the things I'm writing about: all these friendships and the guys upstairs and the women friends I was getting closer and closer to. And all of these problems: the way people live in this world and the relationships and . . . what it was all about—I just couldn't deal with it in poetry. I really had an awful lot of pressure. The first story I wrote, actually, was **"The Contest."** Because I was trying to figure out what made all these guys tick—this guy who was upstairs was the one really; I did my best, I got into his head and I just sorta sat there and I said, "I've gotta write this story." And then the second one was **"Goodbye and Good Luck."**

Throughout her adult life, Paley has been actively involved in social and political causes; above, she is arrested at an antiwar demonstration.

And before I wrote those stories, I was just stuck in my own voice. Until I was able to use other people's voices, until I was able to hear other people's voices, that I'd been hearing all my life, you know, I was just talking me-me-me. While I was doing that, I couldn't write these stories. And when I was able to get into other voices consciously, or use what I was hearing, and become the story hearer—when I could do that, I just suddenly wrote them. It was a true breakthrough. I'd written one story about eight years before and another one when I was about sixteen and that was it. I often think of how it could happen so suddenly. So I'm waiting for something else to happen suddenly. I don't know what, but something. Maybe we only get one sudden thing per life. (pp. 6-8)

In a number of your short stories, and some of the best, you have continuing characters, especially the narrator, Faith. Do you ever consider putting them into a novel?

I could, but I wouldn't like that. Those Faith stories are part of the book they're in. You could play hopscotch, and take the book and make another book if you wanted to, but I would hate to break the integrity of those books.

Is Faith someone you identify with strongly?

Well, I do, somewhat. But when I first used her, she was absolutely not me at all. She really is my friend, up to whose house I went. I went up to see my friend Sybil, and I saw she was sitting there, and there were "two husbands disappointed by eggs." I mean that really was true, a present husband and a former husband and they were both sitting there complaining about the breakfast. And that was the first line of the story I wrote: "There were two husbands disappointed by eggs." And that was really the beginning of Faith too. Actually, from then on, it wasn't Sybil either. She began to just take on characteristics of at least four friends. She's somewhat different from me, but she's all of us, she's a collective us really, but she began with my friend Syb. I mean, Syb had one child and I had two. I have a girl and a boy, and there are two boys. Faith sort of became my women friends more than anything else . . . not a composite really, because you can't take four people and make a person. It's very hard to do. It's like cooking, I guess. But she became an invented person who lived in circumstances similar to most of the women I knew—which were not my circumstances, but which were the lives of women I knew pretty well during those years when my kids were small, and when I was very close mostly to lots of women with little kids. (p. 10)

In your story **"A Conversation with My Father,"** *the characters discuss the problem of plot. People are sometimes critical of your stories, and say nothing happens in them, there is no plot. I wonder if perhaps that's a peculiarly woman's form of story, where a lot happens, but it's not always what's called plot.*

Well, I think by writing that story I sort of screwed myself up, because people really don't read. I mean, a great deal happens in almost any one of those stories, really sometimes more than in lots of other peoples', enough to make a novel or something. When people say, well, she really doesn't care much about plot, all they're doing is repeating what I said in my story. Plot is nothing. Plot is only movement in time. If you move in time you have a plot, if you don't move in time, you don't have a plot, you just have a stand-still, a painting maybe, or you have something else. But if you move in time you have a plot.

Your stories move around in time—almost Einsteinian time; there's long time and short time. Do you intentionally compress time and spread it out?

That's the way I think. I say it has to move in time but that doesn't mean it moves dead ahead in time. It can curl around on itself, it can just fall down and slip out through one of the spirals and go back again. That's the way I see. I see us all in a great big bathtub of time just swimming around; everything's in this ocean called time and it's a place. (pp. 18-19)

Going back to **"A Conversation with My Father"** . . .

Well, actually the story's about a couple of things. It's about story telling, but it's also really about generational attitudes towards life, and it's about history. I tend not to look at things psychologically so much, but historically, I think. And for him, he was quite right, from his point of view. He came from a world where there *was* no choice, where you couldn't really decide to change careers when you were forty-one years old, you know. You couldn't decide to do things like that. Once you were a junkie, that was the end of everything. Once you were anything, that was it. Who you were was what you were. And she was speaking really from her own particular historical moment, and in another country besides, where things were more open. So it wasn't that she was giving some philosophical attitude, or some attitude close to her own optimistic disposition, although both of those things were true. That's also true, but she was also really (although neither of them knew it, only the writer knew this), they were really speaking from their own latitude and longitude, and from their own time in history when they spoke about these things. So that's really, I think, what was happening there. And her feeling which she talked about in terms of stories was pretty much exactly the same. I mean she really lives at a time when things have more open possibility, and for a group or a class that had more possibilities and a generation in that line, because he was an immigrant and he just about got here and did all right by the skin of his teeth. So she was really speaking for people who had more open chances. And so she brought that into literature, because we just don't hop out of our time so easy. (pp. 19-20)

Did you ever look for women writers, in particular, or look to find your own experience in your reading?

No, not when I was very young. It's not so much that I looked for women writers, but I had sense enough to know that, like Henry Miller, he wasn't writing for me. That's as far as I went. I knew that these guys, even the Beats—I thought they were nice, nice to see all those boys, and nice to see all the sexual feelings, but I knew it really wasn't written for me at all. It's not so much that I looked for women writers, as that I understood certain much admired writers, like Burroughs, weren't talking to me. There was nothing to get from them. Though at the same time I did get stuff from Proust. That talked to me, but all those ballsy American heroes had nothing to say to me, though my friends thought they were just hot shit, excuse me.

When did you start getting a sense of a female voice in literature?

Well, late really, after I was writing. My book was called ***The Little Disturbances of Man.*** And the subtitle was *Women and Men at Love.* And the very second edition, they wrote it "Men and Women at Love." They meant no harm by it, but you look at the first edition, the Doubleday edition; it says "Women and Men." It just got normally changed, because of the guy's ear. I didn't even see it myself, although I had been very strict and said, No, the "women" goes first.

Do you consider yourself a feminist writer?

I'm a feminist and a writer. Whatever is in here comes

from the facts of my life. To leave them out would be false. I do write a lot about women and the men they know. That's who the people are and what they think about. (pp. 22-3)

You're not really interested in the kind of theoretical speculations the French like, are you?

I went to a lot of those meetings at MLA, to try to see what's going on. I think a lot of that's interesting, but, see, first of all, for me the story exists really off the page in a way that for them, it's all lying around there on the table. And for a lot of Americans too it does. And I don't think that's the direction for literature to go. I see it getting deeper and deeper into the page, until it disappears out the back end of the book. So that's the direction it's going to take. It's not that I don't love the page. I mean I love the books. But we really have to think of the throat it comes out of. I feel it's too great a movement away from the people, if you want to put it that way, and certainly away from female life.

When you say it exists off the page, is that the kind of thing you mean?

I'm really speaking about speaking the story, or being able to say it and to tell it and to talk it. And I don't mean you can sit down and read a whole novel out loud. (Though I don't see why not. I mean I just think that there's no reason not to.) As for the story, it's not so much that you don't read it on the page, it's just that in the story itself there has to be some memory, some human memory of where it came from. Of course, most stories that the person writes are much more complicated than the story you tell at the supper table. It's much more complicated, and it has to be attended to. But I think very complicated stories used to be heard all the time, and people really heard them. Sometimes because they heard them twice. At the same time, I love the privacy of the book and the privacy of your chair and your room and your book. That has got to not go. But that memory for me has to be somewhere in the story—that a person knew it and lived it and told it.

Are you thinking about tales from the oral tradition?

When you write them down they are different. It's not the same story. One is wrong to say that that's what the written story is; it's much more. What's changed is the time in which to tell the story. Still look how long—they had a lot of time cooking up the *Iliad,* right? They told it one way, then another way, then it got stuck in that particular way. And so we have time. We have time. (pp. 25-6)

Grace Paley and Joan Lidoff in an interview in Shenandoah, *Vol. XXXII, No. 3, 1981, pp. 3-26.*

Diane Cousineau (essay date 1982)

[*In the following excerpt, taken from an issue of the periodical* Delta *devoted to Paley (see Further Reading), Cousineau examines the incompatibility of the desires expressed by Paley's female characters and those of her male characters.*]

"What is man that woman lies down to adore him?" asks Faith in Grace Paley's story **"A Subject of Childhood."** One might rephrase the question and ask: What is woman that she lies down to adore man? Or, to echo Freud, what does woman want?

Grace Paley's stories of "men and women at love" lead to a reflection on the nature of feminine desire. The following remarks are an attempt to understand the general design of this desire as it appears in Paley's fiction and to indicate the coincidence of this pattern with certain psychoanalytical insights.

Paley's stories begin in the awareness of sexual difference. In **"A Woman, Young and Old"** the precocious fourteen-year-old allows her younger sibling one line in her narrative: " 'Men are different than women,' said Joanna, and it's the only thing she says in the entire story." In **"Goodbye and Good Luck"** the commonplace is returned to its original mystery when Aunt Rose gently but insistently asks her lover about his married life: " 'What is this lady like? It hurts me to ask, but tell me, Vlashkin . . . a man's life is something I don't clearly see'." The simplicity and directness of her words open up the ineradicable difference at the center of life. The degree to which this difference exists in nature is not really the question here. What is crucial, as Jacques Lacan has emphasized, is that sexual difference is taken up symbolically on the level of language by men and women as they assume their distinct identities in the world of ordered relations. Aunt Rose speaks without self-pity or hostility in her acknowledgement of the difference upon which her own identity rests.

In Paley's fiction the consciousness of difference is central to the question of feminine desire. This consciousness is two-fold. Woman's sensitivity to the line of partition separating the two sexes is intensified by the experience of division that is inscribed within her own body. Eugénie Lemoine-Luccioni in her book *Partage des femmes* suggests that woman's central experience is that of division and loss, most dramatically felt in the act of childbirth yet already present in the law of feminine identity, the menstrual cycle. Very early, woman is forced into physical knowledge of the otherness of her body. This heightened awareness of difference surrounds Paley's women, creating an intense desire for unity at the same time that their bodies speak the impossibility of this desire.

In **"An Interest in Life"** the unsophisticated narrator's musings underscore the ironic dimension of male-female relations. Virginia, like Paley's other women, is certain that men are essentially different from women: "men are different, they have to own money, or they have to be famous, or everybody on the block has to look up to them from the cellar stairs." Her husband has just left her with four children, without money or support, but she is neither bitter nor man-despising, for she realizes that her own idea of happiness is inimical to man:

> I was happy, but I am now in possession of knowledge that this is wrong. Happiness isn't so bad for a woman. She gets fatter, she gets older, she could just die of the pleasure. . . .
>
> A woman counts her children and acts snotty,

like she invented life, but men *must* do well in the world. I know that men are not fooled by being happy.

Virginia's words suggest that if women can be fulfilled and contained by their participation in the creation of life, men are driven frantic by those "noisy signs of life that are so much trouble." The knowledge that passion spent has entrapped him in a life rooted in domestic repetition, a life that can only mean "more of the same thing" is unbearable to Virginia's husband. The relation of the sexes is steeped in irony, as psychoanalytic thought has underlined. Man, insatiable for the knowledge of origins that he lacks, draws close to woman, the maternal presence, as the source of this knowledge. The cyclical rhythm of her body holds the promise of revelation, the forbidden knowledge of birth and death. But if woman represents the other for man, she cannot fulfill the longing for absolute otherness that he seeks. Approaching woman as the mythical embodiment of truth that she, as an individualized woman, cannot be, man must inevitably be disappointed. Often, like Virginia's husband, he leaves her, threatened by suffocation, once again in pursuit of the elusive objects of his imagination.

Individual woman cannot fulfill man's desire, as Virginia recognizes. She can meet his demands, but she cannot stay his restlessness. Although Virginia is filled with rage and hatred at her husband's action, she does not entirely blame him, for she knows that she cannot impose her vision on his life. Her forbearance is not a matter of weakness, however. The strength of Paley's women lies in the combination of their generosity of vision and their lack of self-deception. They do not delude themselves as to man's intent or his sentiments. Virginia looks starkly at her husband's cruelty and nastiness. She unflinchingly faces the fact that the claustrophobic domesticity of their lives has made him hate her and the children. But she also knows that she must allow for this difference. "Men are not fooled by being happy," she concludes. The line is filled with innocence and humor, but it is painful in its implications. Are we to conclude that woman is fooled by being happy? An implicit answer to this question is found in **"Wants,"** the first story in Paley's second collection, ***Enormous Changes at the Last Minute.***

In **"Wants"** the ex-husband of the narrator bitterly accuses her of desiring nothing: " 'But as for you, it's too late, you'll always want nothing.' " Accused, judged, and found guilty of the ultimate transgression, the narrator is left, for the moment, speechless. The force of his words, emphatically affirming her nothingness, leaves her choking, for their implicit meaning is overpowering: to want nothing is the equivalent of a denial of life. But this interpretation (his reading of her life) is inadequate, as she realizes almost immediately. True, she desires no particular object, no sailboat as he does, but her body lives in want:

> I want, for instance, to be a different person.
>
> I want to be the woman who brings these two books back in two weeks. . . .
>
> I *had* promised my children to end the war before they grew up.
>
> I wanted to have been married forever to one person, my ex-husband or my present one. Either has enough character for a whole life, which as it turns out is really not such a long time. . . .

These wants reveal a desire that is radical, that demands no less than the utter transformation of the world and the self. They ask for the impossible while knowing it is impossible. The sequence of tenses in the last statement ("I wanted to have been married forever"), from the past to past perfect, poignantly emphasizes this impossibility, underlining the division and otherness at the foundation of human desire.

To want nothing, that is, no thing, as the narrator does, is not to be without desire but to understand the incommensurability of human desire. To want nothing is to know that no thing of this world will ever meet the intention of one's desire, for desire is rooted in impossibility, in a lack which cannot be filled or desire (and life itself) would cease to exist. One always feels inadequate to desire, as the long-distance runner of the final story in the volume [**"The Long-Distance Runner"**] acknowledges: "One day, before or after forty-two, I became a long-distance runner. Though I was stout and in many ways inadequate to this desire, I wanted to go far and fast. . . ."

The narrator of **"Wants,"** like the long-distance runner, recognizes the gap at the heart of desire. Her statement of wants, however, is not spoken in anger or despair. If the words are painful in their knowledge of irreparable loss, they are also tinged with humor as if this feminine desire, knowing that its deepest longings will never be realized, is liberated from an obsessive attachment to desire. It is thus freed from the quest for difference, the restless search for objects and substitute objects that characterizes male desire, leading man through a succession of women. The narrator knows that another material possession will not make the difference in her life; she knows that even two husbands are in excess of what she most profoundly wants. But she will be happy just the same, not out of self-deception which she, like Virginia, staunchly refuses, but because happiness comes without pursuit:

> Just this morning I looked out the window to watch the street for a while and saw that the little sycamores the city had dreamily planted a couple of years before the kids were born had come that day to the prime of their lives.

The ending of the story suggests that the acceptance of the otherness at the heart of desire not only ripens woman for happiness, but also allows her privileged access to the sphere of creation. (pp. 55-9)

Paley's women learn early that the presence of man and his gifts are transient: "Afterward, having established tenancy, he rewarded her with kisses. But he dressed quickly because he was obligated by the stories of his life to remind her of transience" **("The Pale Pink Roast")**. In Paley's stories the presence of man and his gifts are most forcibly known through absence. **"An Interest in Life"** begins with a man offering his wife a Christmas gift as he tells her that he is going off to join the army: "My husband gave me a broom one Christmas. This wasn't right. No one can tell me it was meant kindly." The irony is painful; it is an unconsciously mean present, a present that simultaneously speaks his absence and affirms his presence in the same way his act of leave-taking does: "He took hold of me with his two arms as though in love and pressed his body hard against mine so that I could feel him for the last time and suffer my loss." Sexual experience fails to provide Paley's women with that experience of unity which will belie their deep sense of fragmentation and loss. They know that man's gift will not fulfill their longings for wholeness, for it is rooted in irony and ambiguity. Paley's women do not reject this gift, but neither do they delude themselves as to its worth: "White or black, I said, returning to men, they did think they were bringing a rare gift, whereas it was just sex, which is common like bread, though essential" (**"The Long-Distance Runner"**).

Disappointed in her attempt to achieve unity and totality of being through sexual experience, woman often seeks compensation in pregnancy and childbirth. In the act of creating life, she is tempted to a belief in her plenitude and self-sufficiency. In her new strength she is tempted to feel that she no longer needs man; she has her child who symbolically fulfills her longing for the phallus. She responds to her original sense of loss and fragmentation with the fantasy of encompassing all (both sexes) within herself. . . . Imaginatively she lives as both man and woman, and for the moment her dream of totality supplants the anxiety of division.

In Paley's stories the mother-child relationship presents a seductive retreat from the emotional storm of man-woman relations:

> I held him so and rocked him. I cradled him. I closed my eyes and leaned on his dark head. But the sun in its course emerged from among the water towers of downtown office buildings and suddenly shone white and bright on me. Then through the short fat fingers of my son, interred forever, like a black and white barred king in Alcatraz, my heart lit up in stripes.
>
> (**"A Subject of Childhood"**)

After a shattering quarrel with her lover, Faith takes comfort in her young son's unquestioning love and promise of eternal fidelity: " 'I don't care if Richard goes away, or Clifford. They can go do whatever they wanna do. I don't even care. I'm never gonna go away. I'm gonna stay right next to you forever, Faith.' " This relation, too however, is fraught with illusion. Finally, as the grandmother in **"A Woman, Young and Old"** tells us, sons are no more reliable than lovers: " 'Everyone's sons are like that . . . First grouchy, then gone.' " More seriously, the fantasy of totality and self-sufficiency that can accompany motherhood is psychically dangerous; if woman continues to refuse man, she is denied access to the other whose presence constitutes the difference which is essential to her being.

The lure of totality that motherhood brings is dangerous and illusory, and Paley's women return to their desire for the other, to man who represents that ideal of unity (of oneness) which they are not. Divided by nature, denied the promise of unity within her own body, woman invokes man as an idealization of unified being and posits her own love as the integral force which will sustain their lives. In spite of their knowledge that man's gifts are unreliable, Paley's heroines again and again choose to live for love. " 'I am driven by love,' " Aunt Rose tells her mother in **"Goodbye and Good Luck"** as she prepares to leave the house of her family. Years later elaborating on her decision to her niece, she says:

> "I thought to myself, poor Mama . . . it is true she got more of an idea of life than me. She married who she didn't like, a sick man, his spirit already swallowed up by God. He never washed. He had an unhappy smell. His teeth fell out, his hair disappeared, he got smaller, shriveled up little by little, till goodbye and good luck he was gone and only came to Mama's mind when she went to the mailbox under the stairs to get the electric bill. In memory of him and out of respect for mankind, I decide to live for love."

The choice is made deliberately, passionately in a moment of self-assertion that is neither easy nor secure. It is made with the knowledge that her man is not one who can easily be exchanged among many. After her husband has turned against her in hatred and left her with fourteen dollars and four children, Virginia (**"An Interest in Life"**) will still say: " 'Once I met my husband with his winking looks, he was my only interest. Wild as I had been with John and others, I turned all my wildness over to him and then there was no question in my mind.' " Faith, another abandoned wife, is willing to tell anyone of her feelings toward her husband: "she loved Ricardo. She began indeed to love herself, to love the properties which, for a couple of years anyway, extracted such heart-warming activity from him" (**"Faith in the Afternoon"**). Again and again Paley's women try to "breathe eternity into a mortal matter, love" (**"The Contest"**), while deep within they know "life don't stop. It only sits a minute and dreams a dream" (**"Goodbye and Good Luck"**). They choose to dwell in the insecurity and instability of love, but this instability is a mark of their independence at the same time as it marks the fragility of that independence. As Aunt Rose, initiating her niece into womanhood across generations, tells her: "This was my independence, Lillie dear, blooming, but it didn't have no roots and its face was paper." The image of a flower blooming with vitality without either the substance (roots) of life or the means of viable expression (paper face) underlines the ironic setting of woman's independence.

Insecure in their independence, subjects of abandonment, Paley's women are nevertheless triumphant in their moments of self-assertion. However powerfully they are drawn to their men, they never sacrifice their integrity to them. The moment of decisiveness in which Aunt Rose announces her commitment to love is later echoed (through the repetition of the title phrase, goodbye and good luck) when she ends her affair with her adored Vlashkin:

> "No more. This isn't for me. I am sick from it all.
>
> I am no home breaker."
>
> "Girlie," he said, "don't be foolish."

> "No, no, goodbye, good luck," I said. I am sincere.

The firmness of Aunt Rose's decision has its parallel in **"Enormous Changes at the Last Minute"** when Alexandra refuses to let her young lover, the father of the child she is carrying, move in with her. Divided between the generation of her father who urges marriage and the generation of her young man who wants Alexandra and the child to join his commune, she refuses to capitulate to their versions of her life and makes her own resolve:

> This is what Alexandra did in order to make good use of the events of her life. She invited three pregnant clients who were fifteen and sixteen years old to live with her. She visited each one and explained to them that she was pregnant too, and that her apartment was very large.

Committed to a life that is unstable and insecure, Paley's women never abdicate their independence of judgment or sense of personal responsibility. Their sensitivity to the line of difference passing between men and women forces them to recognize that they cannot depend on men for either their security or the direction of their lives.

The consciousness of difference, the recognition of the inaccessible otherness that each sex holds for the other and the division which woman finds within her own body, is the distinguishing mark of Paley's fiction. In the stories this awareness issues in a generosity of vision, an openness towards other human beings and the other within the self. The stories are thus free to delight in the unexpectedness of human response and the contradictions and inconsistencies that abound in personal relations. In **"Wants,"** for example, an ex-husband and wife meet unexpectedly in the street. Their shared history, however, a marriage of twenty-seven years, justifies no assumptions, no common vision of their past:

> I saw my ex-husband in the street. I was sitting on the steps of the new library.
>
> Hello, my life, I said. We had once been married for twenty-seven years, so I felt justified.
>
> He said, what? What life? No life of mine.
>
> I said, O.K. I don't argue when there's real disagreement.
>
> **("Wants")**

The voice of Paley's fiction luxuriates in the irreconcilable and illogical and assumes its freedom to create its own laws and logic through play:

> In many ways, he said, as I look back, I attribute the dissolution of our marriage to the fact that you never invited the Bertrams to dinner.
>
> That's possible, I said. But really if you remember: first, my father was sick that Friday, then the children were born, then the war began. Then we didn't seem to know them any more. But you're right. I should have had them to dinner.

The man's smug explanation of the failure of his marriage is striking in its absurdity. But his ex-wife takes up his words seriously and offers her own equally absurd interpretation of events, couched in the form of a logical argument. While this form accentuates the inadequacy of her use of logic, it also points up the impossibility of imposing logic on material which cannot be contained within the laws of logic, for exammple, the dissolution of a marriage.

Paley's refusal to dwell within the restraints of a narrow logic is an aspect of her desire to give speech to the voice of the other which hovers at the edge of thought. Breaking out of the silence of restraint, this voice approaches the unutterable, what is not usually said. Faith's unexpected outburst on the State of Israel in **"The Used-Boy Raisers"** astounds her listeners, her present and former husbands:

> I believe in the Diaspora, not only as a fact but a tenet. I'm against Israel on technical grounds. I'm very disappointed that they decided to become a nation in my lifetime. I believe in the Diaspora. After all, they *are* the chosen people. Don't laugh. They really are. But once they're huddled in one little corner of a desert, they're like anyone else; Frenchies, Italians, temporal nationalities. Jews have one hope only—to remain a remnant in the basement of world affairs—, no, I mean something else—a splinter in the toe of civilizations, a victim to aggravate the conscience.
>
> Livid and Pallid were astonished at my outburst, since I rarely express my opinion on any serious matter but only live out my destiny, which is to be, until my expiration date, laughingly the servant of man.

Faith's words suggest that if woman submits to the laws and desires of men, she does it laughingly, with a sense of irony that never allows man's vision to eradicate her own. When she speaks in her own voice, she refuses to be bound by the laws of men or convention. This same resistance is voiced by the writer-narrator in **"Conversation with My Father."** She speaks of her hatred of traditional plot, "the absolute line between two points which I've always despised." Paley refuses linearity, for it cannot suggest the complexity and ironic possibilities of human existence. Her aim is to embody the totality that a life is, in its irrationality and contradictions, in order, as the narrator of **"Debts"** says: "to save a few lives." Paley's attempt to give voice to the otherness of human life issues in an epigrammatic style which reveals her talent for swiftly and deftly embodying the complexity of a person or a relation:

> Then he peed. He did not pee like a boy who expects to span a continent, but like a man—in a puddle.
>
> **("The Floating Truth")**
>
> He is my first child, and if he thinks he is ugly, I think I am ugly.
>
> **("An Interest in Life")**

Paley's humour, her lightness and sureness of tone enable her to deal with the most crucial of human matters without undue solemnity or sentimentality. Through this mastery of tone, she can suggest the implicit incompatibility of the desires of women and the presence of men at the same time that she affirms the enigmatic dance of difference at the center of being. (pp. 59-65)

Diane Cousineau, "The Desires of Women, the Presence of Men," in Delta, *France, May, 1982, pp. 55-66.*

Paley illustrates the principle of open-ended fiction:

[*In Paley's story, "A Conversation with My Father," the narrator's dying father asks her to tell him a simple story in the style of Anton Chekhov. She responds with a story of a heroin addict's mother who becomes addicted herself. The narrator has just finished her story.*]

"Poor woman. Poor girl, to be born in a time of fools, to live among fools. The end. The end. You were right to put that down. The end."

I didn't want to argue, but I had to say, "Well, it is not necessarily the end, Pa."

"Yes," he said, "what a tragedy. The end of a person." . . .

I had promised the family to always let him have the last word when arguing, but in this case I had a different responsibility. That woman lives across the street. She's my knowledge and my invention. I'm sorry for her. I'm not going to leave her there in that house crying. (Actually neither would Life, which unlike me has no pity.)

Therefore: She did change. Of course her son never came home again. But right now, she's the receptionist in a storefront community clinic in the East Village. Most of the customers are young people, some old friends. The head doctor has said to her, "If we only had three people in this clinic with your experiences . . . "

"The doctor said that?" My father took the oxygen tubes out of his nostrils and said, "Jokes. Jokes again."

"No, Pa, it could really happen that way, it's a funny world nowadays."

"No," he said. "Truth first. She will slide back. A person must have character. She does not."

"No, Pa," I said. "That's it. She's got a job. Forget it. She's in that storefront working."

"How long will it be?" he asked. "Tragedy! You too. When will you look it in the face?"

Grace Paley, from "A Conversation with My Father," in Enormous Changes at the Last Minute.

Nicholas Peter Humy (essay date 1982)

[*In the following essay, taken from an issue of the periodical* Delta *devoted to Paley (see Further Reading), Humy analyzes Paley's eschewal of traditional short story form and Aristotelian aesthetics in "A Conversation with My Father."*]

"I would like you to write a simple story just once more. . . ."

It seems a straightforward request to the narrator's aging father, although he does ask specific qualities of his story: "the kind de Maupassant wrote, or Chekhov, the kind you used to write. Just recognizable people and then write down what happened to them next."

This request is made in the second paragraph of **"A Conversation with My Father,"** but we are already aware of the difference between the sort of story the father wants to hear and that which the narrator is in the process of telling. The father, like all aging fathers, is concerned with the past. His request is for a story like those of the past, like those the narrator "used to write." His story is to be peopled with "recognizable" characters, those he is familiar with, and is to tell "what happened to them next." The narrator's story, **"A Conversation with My Father,"** [exists] not in the past, but in the present. Its events and characters do not exist prior to the writing of their story.

> My father is eighty-six years old and in bed. His heart, that bloody motor, is equally old and will not do certain jobs any more. It still floods his head with brainy light. But it won't carry the weight of his body around the house. Despite my metaphors, this muscle failure is not due to his old heart, he says, but to a potassium shortage.

In these first five sentences we are shown how the narrator wishes to tell her father's story. He and his condition are not described with language, but created in it. The metaphors which the narrator uses do not help to make her father "recognizable" to the reader, rather, they call attention to the language and testify that the act of writing will intrude upon the tale. The father protests. It is a description of him, after all, and, "despite [her] metaphors," he and his "potassium shortage," would like to be found within it. It would seem to the father that his daughter has forgotten the responsibilities of the writer.

These responsibilities seem to be derived from Aristotle's theory of tragedy as it appears in *Poetics,* which is to say that, whether or not the father has read *Poetics,* he is one of those who have been made to expect, by the various wrappings which are used to package art in our culture, that literature will provide a purgative arousal of fear and pity brought about by the description or imitation of an action, culminating in the demise of the flawed hero. The father also asks that the story be neatly contained within its bounds consisting of beginning, middle, and end, and, in order to ensure its status as bearer of truth, that the protagonist be faceless enough to be universal ("recognizable"), while maintaining consistent enough character to go from one action to the next according to the laws of probable cause.

When she agrees to tell her father his story, one "that begins: 'There was a woman . . . ' followed by plot, the absolute line between two points," the narrator agrees to repress those intrusions which her writing makes on the tale, to take "all hope away," denying her own beliefs that "everyone, real or invented, deserves the open destiny of life." At this point, as though to close the lid on the matter, **"A Conversation with My Father"** switches from the present to the past tense.

But the lid is not quite closed, for the narrator has "misunderstood [her father] on purpose." She chooses as the center figure of her story a woman, who cannot properly be a "tragic" character, and, while claiming to simply write down the story she has thought of, implying that the roles of writer and writing are no more than the chroniclers of the action, she "lays bare" the arbitrary nature of the elements of a causal progression in any fiction.

Her "unadorned and miserable tale" does seem to move in "an absolute line between two points," and yet the narrator demonstrates that the line exists only as her creation, and that, as William Gass points out, "its telling is a record of the choices, inadvertent or deliberate, the author has made from all possibilities of language " [*Fiction and the Figures of Life,* (1971)].

It is precisely those choices to which she makes her father attend. By maintaining her claim on the tale ("Once in my time . . . "), by failing to give it a proper end, allowing it to seep into the present ("We all visit her"), by describing neither compelling causes ("which is not unusual," "for a number of reasons"), nor "recognizable" characters, she forces her father to ask her to fill in what he feels is absent. "You know there's a lot more to it. You know that. You left everything out."

His main concern is for a more complete knowledge of the woman's character, for he knows, as do all Aristotelians, that character is the servant of dramatic action, that without it the action will not reveal the moral purpose of its agents, and hence, the meaning of the tale.

The greater part of any character in a given fiction is always left unstated. The reader of **"A Conversation with My Father"** is comfortable in attributing to the character of the father a certain life-in-words, though he has almost none of the necessary organs for life-on-earth, as it were, with only his legs, heart/motor, and brain somewhat resembling a lightbulb. What of his bowels? to say nothing of his nose, throat and ears. In the narrator's "unadorned and miserable tale" the mother and her son are not described physically, historically, or emotionally at all. When the father asks for details of the woman's hair and heritage, he is making choices, his choices, of what is "of consequence." His choices happen to be the traditional ones, those that are usually made inadvertently by writers of fiction, and so seem to him not to be choices at all, but necessary to the form which will convey what the work is about.

Harold Bloom, in "The Breaking of Form," reminds us that the word 'about' means 'to be on the outside of' something. "All that a poem can be about, or what a poem *is* other than trope, is the skill or faculty of invention or discovery, the heuristic gift." The narrator shares this sense of her work, and does not see herself as relating to her father his story, history, but as *telling* a story. She wants him to see the process of storytelling anew, to see how, in the telling, the story becomes defamiliarized, becomes, not what it is about, but what it *is.* And what it is is a form which, according to Shklovsky, reveals the experience of its making.

What the father sees as unmotivated events in the narrator's first attempt are unmotivated only in the referential sense of what the story is about. They are perfectly motivated in the technical sense of calling attention to the telling of the tale.

But the telling of the tale is not of primary interest to the father, for the creation of 'telling' subverts the disclosure of 'told.' The daughter is aware that a story is no more and no less than the language in which it is created, and the desire by which it is formed. The father's demands for disclosure of what went before the telling of the tale are attempts to halt the free flow of desire, to reentangle his daughter in the incestuous net of Oedipus, where her telling would become told, would become the law of the father. And the narrator's father invokes law when he demands disclosure of what was not spoken of the woman:

> "For Godsakes, doesn't anyone in your stories get married? Doesn't anyone have the time to run down to City Hall before they jump into bed?"
>
> "No," I said. "In real life, yes. But in my stories, no."
>
> "Why do you answer me like that?"

In order to explain her choices the narrator, in exasperation, steps outside of the tale and tells her father what her fiction is 'about,' and in so doing, undercuts to a certain extent, the very freedom, the very hope and desire, she had maintained in its telling.

> "Oh, Pa, this is a simple story about a smart woman who came to N.Y.C. full of interest love trust excitement very up to date, and about her son, what a hard time she had in this world. Married or not, it's of small consequence."

But to the father, it is "of great consequence," for he senses the woman in the story as though she were flesh, as though he has somehow reached through the artifice of fiction to shake the hand of this person "with heavy braids, as though she were a girl or a foreigner," and wants better to understand her, understand the character, not the artifice: " . . . but listen. I believe you that she's good-looking, but I don't think she was so smart." Character and action do not correspond as the rules state they should. Intelligence would have prevented her from acting as she did.

And, in a sense, the narrator agrees with her father that the woman she has created has a life, though not one of flesh. As an invention in language the woman is alive and responsive to language, to its intrusions, to its metaphors. The narrator has already expressed her dislike for any portion of a fiction which is predetermined, outside of language, for such predetermination "takes all hope away," and, in agreeing with her father that her explanation of what the story was 'about' may have precluded a portion of her character's 'life,' she reiterates her sense of the relation between character and language in fiction.

> Actually that's the trouble with stories. People start out fantastic.
>
> You think they're extraordinary, but it turns out as the work goes along, they're just average with a good education. Sometimes the other way around, the person's a kind of dumb innocent,

> but he outwits you and you can't even think of an ending good enough.

The father, "still interested in details, craft and technique," accuses his daughter of "talking silly" when she explains that sometimes the end is not predetermined by traits attributed to the character and wholly controlled by the author. She suggests that sometimes it is reached in "some agreement" between the writer and the invention, mediated by the language.

In the second attempt to please her father, the narrator begins her story as though to include her father. Instead of "Once in my time . . . " the new story opens, "Once, across the street from us . . . " She has also kept the story entirely in the past tense and given it an end ("The End"), in capital letters, closing the tale from any reverberation into the present. It is at this point that we are presented with the most marked contrast between written text and speech. It is here that we see the tension in the concessions the narrator makes in this text within a conversation. The narrator has provided her father with an end, has filled out the causal relationships between one event and the next, has even given her character a hint of a tragic flaw ("She would rather be with the young, it was an honor, than with her own generation"), and yet her father is not entirely satisfied. He has three comments.

"Number One: You have a nice sense of humor." Here he is referring to the way in which his daughter chose to explain the juxtaposition of various events. The story exposes probable cause for what it is—a convention—by using irony to systematically undo our understanding and belief in causality. The mother becomes a junkie like her son "in order to keep him from feeling guilty." She wants to prevent him from feeling guilty "because guilt is the stony heart of nine tenths of all clinically diagnosed cancers in America today." And in double irony, she explains that the mother loved her son "because she'd known him since birth (in helpless chubby infancy and in the wrestling, hugging ages, seven to ten, as well as earlier and later). "The father, by insisting on determining factors for all events in the fiction, is given an explanation for drug addiction and mother love which seems to him to be a joke.

"Number Two: I see you can't tell a plain story. So don't waste time." This comment echoes the conclusion of the second story, ("she would cry out, My baby! My baby! and burst into terrible face-scarring, time-consuming tears"), and comments upon the different demands father and daughter make on a story. The daughter wishes her father to *hear* her story. Instead he discounts the tale as unrecognizable, unwilling to listen to that which is new. The narrator shares with Shklovsky the belief that "the purpose of art is to impart the sensation of things as they are perceived and not as they are known" ["Art as Technique" in *Russian Formalist Criticism,* edited by Paul A. Olson, (1965)]. She does not feel that failure to arrive at an anticipated end is a waste of time, but that it is rather an exercise in the process of perception, which "is an aesthetic end in itself and must be prolonged."

But the father still desires an end to the story, both in the sense of conclusion and purpose. A "plain story" would provide this but his daughter's tale, while seeming to come to a proper end, has already undermined, through irony, the means she has used to arrive there. Nonetheless, the father will try to salvage that which he so desires.

> "Number Three: I suppose that means she was left like that, his mother. Alone. Probably sick?"
>
> I said, "Yes."
>
> "Poor woman. Poor girl, to be born in a time of fools, to live among fools. The end. The end. You were right to put that down. The end."

But the narrator knows that the telling of a story is the creating of a story is the creating of a form, and she will not let her father impose the end which the tragic form dictates.

> I didn't want to argue, but I had to say, "Well, it is not necessarily the end, Pa."

Her father is insistent. "You don't want to recognize it. Tragedy! Plain tragedy! Historical tragedy! No hope. The end." He feels that the form of tragedy is a given truth, just as he feels his eventual death to be. He urges his daughter to face the dictates of form just as we are told to brave death. His daughter's life, like his, will teach the lesson of death. "In your own life, too, you have to look it in the face." And, in speaking those words, he demonstrates his own desire to delay that end, while still entrenching himself in the conviction of its meaning.

> He took a couple of nitroglycerin. "Turn to five," he said, pointing to the dial on the oxygen tank. He inserted the tubes into his nostrils and breathed deep. He closed his eyes and said, "No."

Though the narrator "had promised the family to always let him have the last word when arguing," she recognizes "a different responsibility" towards him. She will demonstrate to him that it is not in the end that meaning is found by changing the ending of the woman's story. Believing that form dictates the limits of perception, the father is convinced that meaning resides in the end, in death, in the summing up of life. His daughter, believing that perception gives rise to the possibilities of form, and knowing that all stories and lives must eventually come to an end of some kind, at some point, plays Scheherazade to her father, dislocating the end from the tale, trying to save her father's death from meaning. Life might have no pity; it does not commute the sentence of death, but that sentence is only the last of the tale, and its connection to the body of the story is no more secure than that between the creation and its conception. The woman in the story exists for the telling, fathers for the living. The daughter knows this, and, as she moves her tale out of the stasis of the end, as she shifts the story of the woman out of the past and into the present tense, she reminds us that she has also played Scheherazade to the reader. She begins her new ending as she did the second version of the story, with a colon. But the addition has the same spacing as the body of **"A Conversation with My Father"** has had and is not indented. The father has closed his eyes; the narrator is addressing the reader. The doctor's speech is presented in quotation marks, which have appeared before only in dialogue between the father and his daughter, so that the two stories merge into one. When the father breaks in, "The doctor said that?" we are made aware of the play between past and present tense, made aware of the weaving together of the two stories. The intrusion of the father's voice at this point lays bare the device of the contrasting forms of the stories within a story, and transfers our perception of the father's story "into the sphere of a new perception," where, ironically, written text becomes speech, speech a written text. This piece is the story of a conversation and it traces for us the struggle that we all encounter when we acquire language, the tool of the father, and use it with, for, or against him. Grace Paley is perfectly aware of the relationship she is entering into with the father when she is telling a story. On the page facing the table of contents of the collection in which the story appears, she informs us: "Everyone in this book is imagined into life except the father." The father cannot be imagined into life in words for he dwells in them already. The narrator, by telling the stories within the father's story, has demonstrated what the responsibility of the storyteller is not. She has not formed the lives of her inventions to *his* given end and meaning, to *his* law. And, in the telling of her father's story, she has commuted the sentence, and, like the narrator of **"Debts,"** fulfilled her true responsibility: "That is, to tell their stories as simply as possible in order, you might say, to save a few lives." (pp. 87-95)

Nicholas Peter Humy, "A Different Responsibility: Form and Technique in G. Paley's 'A Conversation with Father'," in Delta, *France, May, 1982, pp. 87-95.*

Adam J. Sorkin (essay date 1982)

[*Sorkin is an American critic and educator. In the following excerpt, Sorkin discusses Paley's use of humor to demonstrate human triumph over tragedy in "In Time Which Made a Monkey of Us All."*]

The events of **"In Time Which Made a Monkey of Us All"** focus on one of the most vivacious characters in Paley's cityscape, Eddie Teitelbaum. Eddie, "a dark-jawed, bossy youth in need of repair," is a teenage "journeyman in knowledge" whose idealistic efforts— "a great act of love"—to perfect his War Attenuator fail abysmally when, as a result of his experiments, he inadvertently destroys his father's business and consolation in life. He therefore falls "headfirst into the black heart of a deep depression" that "required all his personal attention for years." First he imposes upon himself the penitence of two years of silence; then, after being told by Jim Sunn, his good-natured attendant at the institution to which he was remanded, that "you're acquiring back your identity," an externally imposed self he could not accept, he once again retreats from life in what we must see as a desperate accommodation to his moral sense. Because of his twisted idealism, he sees himself not as humanity's potential messiah but fatalistically as life's destroyer. In the end Eddie chooses as it were to resign his humanity into renewed silence, "making the decision to go out of his mind as soon as possible. . . . " In the same breath Eddie relinquishes both talk and life, hope and love, as he elects silence and time's oblivion, which are synonymous.

When we first meet him, however, Eddie is lord of the stoop in his "bricklined Utrillo" world with the little kids coming "to buzz at his feet . . . rumbling at the knee of his glowering personality" while he makes pipe cleaner animals, wise-ass remarks, bubble-gum offerings, warnings of neighborhood "spies" like Mrs. Goredinsky, and talk "of the ineluctable future." His dour optimism is hard won. His life since childhood has been one of shoveling "dog shit and birdseed, watching the goldfish float and feed and die" in the Teitelbaum Zoo, his father's pet shop. Nonetheless at the beginning of the story's rendition of his summer's activities, Eddie is innocent, "only knee-deep so far in man's inhumanity"; Paley's allusion significantly excises the conclusion of Robert Burns' poetic chestnut for as much as man, it is animals, from his pipe cleaner toys to his father's shop to his experiment to his final disavowal of life in A Home For Boys, that haunt Eddie's experiences. Moreover, despite his "bitterness for his cramped style and secondhand pants," he is also "reconciled to his father's hair-shirted Jacob, Itzik Halbfunt," a monkey which "looked like Mr. Teitelbaum's uncle who," the narrator's barbed humor tells us, "had died of Jewishness in the epidemics of '40, '41." with the same "lonely patience" Eddie evidences in pursuing his inventions, his sorrowful father "had turned away forever from his neighbor, man, and for life, then, he squinted like a cat and hopped like a bird and drooped like a dog," repeating himself "like a parrot."

Itzik the monkey plays an important symbolic role in the story's development, figuring as both dependent and victim, dumb animal and fellow being, close relative and, to Eddie, usurping foe. To Eddie's father, Itzik Halbfunt, Itzikel Halfpound, is as it were Eddie's half-brother, a closeness about which Eddie jokes obscenely when he explains that Itzik is indeed his "big brother," sired just before his marriage when his father "rammed it up a chimpanzee" in the Bronx Zoo. Fittingly, it is his father's monkey, both *memento mori* and "little friend," with whom Eddie shares the room where he conjures up the dismal futurology of his political lectures and also where, one supposes, he gains his wildly hopeful insights into the "prostheses" which he "approved of " and which, an "immanent" "progress" in "durable plastics," would make both "the race problem" and, by extension, human infirmity "kaput." In any case, Itzik is truly the hairshirted usurper of Eddie's birthright, his father's tenderness. It is ironically appropriate, although the antithesis of Eddie's purposes, that his War Attenuator trials eventually not only decimate the pet shop, suffocating the puppies, birds, turtles, fish, and "even the worms that were the fishes' Sunday dinner," but also kill Itzik, with whom Eddie "gently" shared his only "peaceful and happy" moment in the story as he cleaned the bird cages a few days before the monkey's death. In death as in life, the monkey supplants Eddie: "He lay in Eddie's bed on Eddie's new mattress, between Eddie's sheets. 'Let him die at home,' said Mr. Teitelbaum, 'not with a bunch of poodles at Speyer's.' " Beyond the joke of the veterinarian's name, his father's gruffness hides his grief, just as Eddie's later speechlessness conceals the nature of his feeling even while betraying its strength. It is Eddie's sense of responsibility for his father's despair and Itzik's death, which is as if the murder of his own brother, that closes "the door to Eddie's mind." Henceforth the often brash, sometimes bickering, and always sardonic Eddie, whose frequently morbid wit is shared with the rather more ingratiating and elegant voice of the narrator, pursues his destiny shut up in wordlessness, as speechless and helpless as Itzik, a self-made monkey cared for like the animals in his father's "stinking zoo." By this gesture Eddie cancels simultaneously his human potentiality and his conscious commitment to the active moral life that the intent of his inventions suggested.

Eddie's discovery of a gas which he claims is, "no matter how concentrated, non-toxic," turns out to be not only a dismaying mistake but, significantly, also a bitter historical irony. During his development of the War Attenuator, Eddie insists to his friends that, "if there is any danger involved at any point, I will handle it and be responsible"; later the police find "an outline of a paper Eddie had planned for the anti-vivisectionist press, describing his adventures as a self-prepared subject for the gas tolerance experiments." His fine scruples about involving others, either human or inhuman, are finally misdirected, however. Thus although Eddie complains about his defeated, apathetic father that "that lousy sonofabitch. . . . used to be a whole expert on world history," he himself similarly misreads time's teachings. "The lesson of the cockroach segregator," he declares to his cohorts, is that "the peaceful guy who listens to the warning of his senses will survive generations of defeat. . . . I haven't worked out the political strategy altogether, but our job here, anyway, is just to figure out the technology." This is a strange passivity as well as a piece of uncharacteristically amoral reasoning from the humane and sensitive, if crass and aggressive, Eddie who, even with "the clients" for his segregator, took a "philosophic approach" and "pointed out a human duty to interfere with nature as little as possible except for food-getting (survival), a seminal tragedy. . . . "

Eddie's youthful American idealism is very much the counterpart of his Yankee ingenuity, his skill at tinkering which makes available the technology for the inverted results of his attempts to do good. On the other hand, it is his disaster-haunted urban imagination which stimulates Eddie's efforts to improve "the peculiar conditions of his environment." A sense of catastrophe seems inherent in Eddie. Eddie's politics are summarized as based on a future of dire events: "From the four-by-six room which Eddie shared with Itzik Halbfunt, . . . he saw configurations of disaster revise the sky before anyone even smelled smoke." His most important inventions aim to control vermin and war. After two years of silence, the third thing he says is to ask sarcastically about the latest cataclysm: "What's the news? Long Island sink yet?" Moreover the past, as hinted in Itzik's family resemblance, sharpens both his expectations for calamity and the bitterness of his failure. Although gas is a recurrent vulgarism throughout the story—when the initial test takes place, the building superintendent, Mr. Clop, first "howled, 'Jesus, who farted?' " and when Eddie finally talks, his second pronouncement, after growling "where the hell's my father?" is "I'm sick of peppers, Jim. They give me gas"—what finally happens is not funny at all: in small, Eddie recapitulates the murderous efficiency of the holocaust. Unintentionally, with the help of the super's light-hearted son Carl's joke of connecting the rubber tubing to the pet store, he makes a gas chamber of his father's shop. The lesson of the War Attenuator, as is partially the lesson of Hitler's machinery of death, is not the naive and politically impractical Eddie's illusory hope that the peaceful will survive passively on the wisdom of their senses. Indeed, the lethal gas of the German extermination camps was specially manufactured without its indicator, its warning odor. Thus it is not so much his failure itself or his choice of wordlessness or even Carl's trick but time's recapitulation, history's horror, that most of all makes a monkey out of Eddie and his values and plans, just as in a cruel joke past events made a monkey out of Mr. Teitelbaum's uncle Itzik. The crowning irony is that Eddie's "War Attenuator has been bottled weak under pressure" for the same function as Zyklon B, the insect and uncle killer of I. G. Farben's death empire: "It is sometimes called Teitelbaum's Mixture, and . . . is one of the greatest bug killers of all time." Far from lacking toxicity, the pesticide is so potent that, even in dilute formulation, "it is sometimes hard on philodendrons and old family rubber plants."

In the end Eddie faces up to the results of his mechanical genius by turning, like his father, forever away from man. As in his anti-vivisectionist tract, "NO GUINEA PIG FRONTS FOR ME," Eddie takes full responsibility and unflinchingly defines his identity in his letter to the director of A Home For Boys when he resigns his position in charge of the popular snake and its feedings of, not the long-tailed pipe cleaner mice from the beginning of the story, but little, live, squeaking white mice. Eddie writes, "Thank you, Dr. Tully. I know who I am. I am no mouse killer. I am Eddie Teitelbaum, the Father of the Stink Bomb, and I am known for my Dedication to Cause and my Fearlessness in the Face of Effect. Do not bother me any more. I have nothing to say, Sincerely." Soon after Eddie's second leavetaking from life, his enormous, last-minute change, his father likewise makes a parallel but perhaps less voluntary choice when he "decided to die of grief and old age—which frequently overlap," and this is "the final decision for all Teitelbaums." Others, however, seem more resilient than Teitelbaums, tough philodendrons, and rubber trees. Dr. Scott Tully, proud of his "consistent pessimism" in Eddie's case that is "remarkable, in the face of so much hope," writes a report that is "remembered by his peers." Eddie's friends in the Saturday night club, whose neighborhood escapades counterpoint Eddie's idealism and form a modest subplot in the story, go on to their own destinies. In contrast to the wordless protagonist, Shmul Klein, "a journalist of life" who ends up playing scrivener to Eddie's preferred wall of Bartleby-like refusal, chronicles the story's events in notebooks and two memoirs cited by the author in footnotes, thus animating the characters and rescuing them from the past's lostness for both the internal narrator and the reader. And Carl Clop, in a sense having "tasted with Eddie's tongue," fulfills unidealistically the promise of Eddie's renounced potentiality by becoming "an atomic physicist for the Navy": "He has retained his cheerful disposition and for this service to the world has just received a wife who was washed out of the Rockettes for being too beautiful." Through the deadpan narrative sarcasm we hear a suggestion that perhaps it is Eddie's intent seriousness, deriving from his history and informing his future by transforming his hopeful political idealism into nay-saying passivity and desolation, that most of all determines his silent fate as a casualty of time and good intentions. Ah, humanity!

Nonetheless, Paley's fiction never fixes blame or finds fault. Thus it is a bleak cheerfulness, characteristic of the writer's world (her optimism, remember, is more a hopeful flattery of life than a confirmed trust), with which her story ends as Eddie's "head spy the consistency of fresh putty," Mrs. Goredinsky, "an old-fashioned lady, . . . drops in bulk to her knees to scrub the floor." Seeing a cockroach on the wire of the segregator, "she smiles and praises Eddie." The final note is that of ongoing life. The detached but sympathetic narrative voice and the story's sometimes antic but always humane comedy fundamentally respect Eddie's steadfastness—his self-proclaimed fearlessness and dedication—at the same time as implicitly decrying (in the words of the writer's aged father quoted earlier) his "plain. . . . historical tragedy." If ultimately Eddie remains behind a wall of silence just as the peaceful cockroach "which could take a hint" survives behind the baseboards of kitchens protected by his segregator, his is a moral choice and act of devotion, despite the fact that his final decision imitates the obstinacy of those cockroaches who were "stubborn fools not meant by Darwin anyway to survive" and "emigrated . . . into the corn flakes of people." In any event, in Eddie's beginning was the word and in his end, silence: "I am the vena cava and the aorta," Eddie paraphrases in engineering his gas experiments, in pursuit of which, he "bitterly" tells his friends, "I promise you . . . a lot of fun." But the story's end is far from silent. Eddie's moral action, both before and after the defeat of his good intentions, signifies an answer to the question muttered by Clop early in the story, "What are we, animals?" as much as so the story's kindly fun in its comic celebration of Eddie and its deep fascination with and dismay at time's pitiless making monkey of us all. (pp. 148-53)

Adam J. Sorkin, " 'What Are We, Animals?': Grace Paley's World of Talk and Laughter," in Studies in American Jewish Literature, *Vol. 2, 1982, pp. 144-54.*

Dena Mandel (essay date 1983)

[In the following excerpt, Mandel analyzes the indomitability and optimism of Paley's recurring character Faith Darwin from a perspective of Jewish-American culture and history.]

Unsuccessful daughter, twice-abandoned wife, struggling single mother, Faith Darwin embosses Grace Paley's fiction as an emblem of hope in a hopeless world. Despite hardships, both real and self-perpetuated, Faith Darwin, the protagonist of eight of Paley's short stories collected in two volumes and in the *New Yorker,* has willfully chosen her crusty life and is sustained by a rosy, secular creed. Faith's averred bohemianism, her marginal existence, her commitment to urban life, her adoration of her children, her love of her family, her devotion to friends and neighbors, comprise the ever-expanding nucleus of her alternative faith. Paley does more than yearn for a time when her heroine's heart will find its "ultimate need." For Faith envisions a redeeming and happier future as naturally evolving out of historical process which improves upon the past. For most of Paley's other characters who cohabit Faith's imaginative world, such faith in the future is often questioned, and more often rejected. But Faith, sturdy American Jewess, is a persistent optimist.

Paley's optimism survives on a ready supply of hope. In **"A Conversation with My Father"** Paley enunciates her conviction that such hope assures "Everyone, real or imagined, deserves the open destiny of life." While endurance over oppression may in some sense justify the Jew's claim to hope as an ethnic characteristic, other qualities have been similarly extolled as constituting a uniquely Jewish world view. Josephine Knopp in *The Trial of Judaism in Contemporary Jewish Writing* asserts that those values "embodied in the [Jewish] moral code: the belief that man has a right to fulfillment, affirmation of gentleness and repudiation of violence, the assumption of responsibility of man for his fellow man" comprise a notion of humanity which is "uniquely Jewish." While the values that Faith Darwin espouses in Paley's stories remain inherently the same as those to which Knopp alludes, the sources for Faith's own *"mentshlekhkayt,"* or notion of humanity, are derived from typically Jewish American foundations.

Faith Darwin, like her creator, is a product of a dual heritage and Faith's altruistic creed has been enriched by the plurality of her Jewish American upbringing. Robert Alter wisely cautions that in seeking a definition of Jewish American literature, "There has been a tacit conspiracy in recent years to foist upon the American public as particularly Jewish various admired characteristics which in fact belong to the common humanity of us all." This admonition when registered against the list of laudatory Jewish traits outlined by Josephine Knopp and others leaves readers to decipher just what attributes distinguish Grace Paley as a Jewish American writer and just what it is that makes Faith Darwin's benevolent beliefs peculiarly Jewish. Again, Alter advises that "If we are to discover any clue to the connection between a writer's origins in a particular group and the nature of his work, we must begin in *time,* and we must take *history* seriously into account. . . ." By applying Alter's guidelines to Knopp's roster of Jewish values we find that Faith Darwin, like Paley herself, is the product of an urban environment and the offspring of Jewish immigrant parents, who raised their daughter upon the liberalism and Zionism of the 1920s, the inspirational socialism of the 1930s, and the dreams of American prosperity and happiness in the 1940s.

Faith's sense of her Jewish American identity modulates her blithesome view of the world. Unlike her parents and grandparents, she identifies herself as an American and

Cover of Paley's second short story collection, Enormous Changes at the Last Minute.

disavows any allegiance to the Jewish homeland. In **"The Used-Boy Raisers"** Faith testily complains to her husband and former husband:

> What do I know about Kaddish. Who's dead? You know my opinions perfectly well. I believe in the Diaspora, not only as a fact but as a tenet. I'm against Israel on technical grounds. I'm very disappointed that they decided to become a nation in my lifetime. I believe in the Diaspora. After all, they *are* the chosen people. Don't laugh. They really are. But once they're huddled in one little corner of the desert, they're like anyone else: Frenchies, Italians, temporal nationalities. Jews have one hope only—to remain a remnant in the basement of world affairs—no, I mean something else—a splinter in the toe of civilizations, a victim to aggravate the conscience.

Despite Faith's two intermarriages, her lack of familiarity with Jewish law and custom, and the Dubnowism of her diaspora nationalism, she remains in her own consciousness very much a Jewish American. In **"The Immigrant Story"** Faith tells her childhood friend and current lover, Jack, that "I grew up in the summer sunlight of upward mobility. This leached out a lot of that dark ancestral grief." Although not unmoved by the genocide of the past, Faith as the more acculturated Jewish American does not share as intensely as Jack does the feelings of survivor's guilt. Faith identifies herself not solely in relation to her Jewish past, but within the context of the Jewish American present. Raised in Brooklyn's Coney Island, along with siblings, Hope and Charles, an auspiciously sanguine trio, Faith's parents, Gittle and Gersh, instilled in their children the ethnic liberal politics which typified many Jewish homes in the 1930s. Not unmindful of their Jewish heritage, Faith's father welded his secular socialism to a commitment to Judaism as Faith recalls her father distributing pamphlets which "cried out in Yiddish: "Parents! A little child's voice calls to you, 'Papa, Mama, what does it mean to be a Jew in the world today?' " Faith, reared on this blend of Jewish singularity and social responsibility is more likely to ask, "What is it like to be a human in the world today?"

Faith's Jewish American identity is the curious consequence of a process of reversed assimilation. Visiting her parents who have prematurely retired to the Daughters of Judea nursing home in **"Faith in the Afternoon,"** Paley elucidates Faith's tangled heritage.

> Her [Faith's] grandmother pretended she was German in just the same way that Faith pretends she is an American. Faith's mother flew in the fat face of all that and once safely among her own kind in Coney Island, learned real Yiddish, and . . . she took an oath to expostulate in Yiddish and grieve only in Yiddish, and she has kept that oath to this day.

Unlike her immigrant parents Faith "really is an American" and ". . . was raised up like everyone else to the true assumption of happiness." Nurtured on this American dream which has been so appealing, Faith in maturity finds that her private world frequently crumbles when this happy myth goes unfulfilled. Nevertheless, the American belief in endless possibilities still fuels Faith's social commitment and her personal life.

The blend of conventional American expectations, Jewish consciousness, and social responsibility on which Faith was nurtured inform the heartening precepts by which Faith Darwin confronts the obligations of her unorthodox life. The mixture of values she inherits from her parents is evident as Faith reluctantly visits them in the Daughters of Judea after the failure of her first marriage. Faith's mother tries in her inflected English, which Paley masterfully captures, to console her daughter with conventional wisdom.

> He'll be back in a couple of days. After all, the children . . . just say you're sorry. . . . Clean up the house, put in a steak. Tell the children to be a little quiet, send them next door for the television. He'll be home before you know it. . . . Do up your hair something special. Papa would be more than glad to give you a little cash. We're not poverty-stricken, you know. You only have to tell us you want help.

Gersh Darwin, lovingly turns to his broken-hearted, disappointed daughter and draws her attention outward to the social transformations he has witnessed. He instructs Faith.

> Learn from life. Mine. I was going to organize the help. You know, the guards, elevator boys—colored fellows, mostly. You notice, they're coming up in the world. Regardless of hopes, I never expected it in my lifetime. The war, I suppose, did it. . . . The war made Jews Americans and Negroes Jews.

It is precisely this kind of conversion by her own immigrant parents that has impelled Faith to adopt an active social creed. For Faith, as for many other real life New York City Jews, "Democracy appeared to be the real religion of America and second generation Jews embraced the new faith." The new beliefs which Faith affirms in Paley's stories take shape as Faith changes from harrowed housewife in ***The Little Disturbances*** to a busy social activist in ***Enormous Changes at the Last Minute.***

Guiding much of Faith's transformation and her developing trust in a better future is Paley's own aesthetic principles. In interviews as well as in stories such as **"Debts"** and **"A Conversation with My Father,"** Paley's artistic goals are underlined by a commitment to social change. In a *Ms Magazine* interview Paley mentions that "it may come from my political feelings, but I think art, literature, fiction, poetry, whatever it is, makes justice in the world. That's why it almost always has to be on the side of the underdog." Questioned about the intervention of her own political activism into her creative work Paley responded that "There isn't a story written that isn't about blood and money, . . . People and their relationship to each other is the blood, the family. And how they live, the money of it. That's the way it is when you write about people and believe that their lives are about certain economic and political facts. " (pp. 85-8)

In ***The Little Disturbances of Man*** Faith is introduced in two stories which bear the collective title, "Two Short Sad Stories from a Long and Happy Life." The first of these stories, **"The Used-Boy Raisers"** depicts Faith as oppressed by the men in her life, depressed by circumstances, and domesticated by children. In this early portrait Paley confines Faith to the apartment in which she serves an unsatisfying breakfast to her visiting ex-husband and her present husband. As Faith listens to the men converse, she embroiders, "God Bless Our Home," thereby uttering an ironic, inaudible comment upon her limited life. Unable to remain completely self-effacing, Faith is drawn into the conversation as she corrects the mens' misunderstanding of her feelings concerning the role of Jews in the twentieth century. Faith's concepts of diaspora nationalism essentially concur with those of Simon Dubnow who maintained that:

> . . . a people held together mainly by race was at the lowest stage of national development; a people held together mainly by territory was at the intermediate stage, and a people held together by culture—like the Jews of the Diaspora—was 'the very archetype of a nation, a nation in the purest and loftiest sense'. . . .

Having registered her views, Faith retreats once more into the domestic routine: "I did the dishes and organized the greedy day; dinosaurs in the morning, park in the afternoon, peanut butter inbetween. . . . " The contrast between Faith's small sphere and that of the men who have "the grand affairs of the day ahead of them" completes the predictable scenario of the plight of the unliberated woman in the 1950s. However, Paley must be commended as Faith's awareness of her feminist predicament predates much of the women's fiction and rhetoric that was churned out in the succeeding decade.

The second story in which Faith commands attention is **"A Subject of Childhood."** Again, the themes revolve around motherhood, child rearing, disappointing love affairs, and self-definition. In this story Faith's boyfriend, Clifford, accuses Faith of being a lousy mother following an episode of rough housing with Faith's children, Richard and Tonto, in which the play unpredictably turned to violence. Faith, hurt by Clifford's unjust accusations defends herself:

> . . . I have raised these kids, with one hand typing behind my back to earn a living. I have raised them all alone without a father to identify themselves with in the bathroom like all the other little boys in the playground. Laugh. I was forced by inclement management into a yellow-dog contract with Bohemia, . . . I have stuck by it despite the encroachments of kind relatives who offer ski pants, piano lessons, tickets to the rodeo. Meanwhile I have serviced Richard and Tonto, taught them to keep clean and hold an open heart on the subjects of childhood.

Here is the rudimentary vocalization of Faith's creed, not only as it pertains to child rearing, but upon those precepts which she will base her actions in ensuing stories.

The seriousness with which Paley regards the values enunciated in **"A Subject of Childhood"** is demonstrated by her return to the same issues in her essay, "Mom." In this nonbelligerent confutation of material such as Roth's *Portnoy's Complaint,* Paley reaffirms the lessons she has learned from her German grandmother and immigrant mother. In the same way as the "Mom" essay salutes motherhood, Paley champions adolescence in **"A Subject of Childhood."** After the day's upsetting events—the physical turmoil and the emotional strain of Clifford's accusations and desertion—Faith begs her youngest son, Tonto, for "ten minutes all alone." This plea recalls the predicament of thousands of tired mothers who have little time for themselves. But Tonto, in typically childish fashion, refuses to leave his mother to herself and curls up in Faith's lap. Imprisoned by Tonto's love, Faith simultaneously enjoys and resents her captivity, but the consolation of being loved ultimately supercedes the limitations that such love imposes. The story concludes with these dichotomous emotions as Faith rocks her son in her lap and feels "through the short fat fingers of my son, interred forever, like a black and white barred king in Alcatraz, my heart lit up in stripes."

In ***The Little Disturbances of Man*** Faith is depicted primarily as a woman in search of a self-awareness which will grant her some satisfaction for the unpaid work she performs—raising children, keeping house, and caring for the men in her life. The issues of Paley's first volume revolve around what has been derogatively designated as the themes of "women's fiction." But in Paley's second collection, ***Enormous Changes at the Last Minute,*** which appeared after an interval of fifteen years, Faith's quest for self-assertion is no longer the motivating force behind her actions. In this second collection of stories Faith displays a surer sense of herself and her values. She appears to know both what she is as well as what she might have been. She concedes her mistakes, and given her idealism, will probably have to concede a few more. But in ***Enormous Changes at the Last Minute*** Faith is not preoccupied with who she is, but with how to live. In stories such as **"Faith in a Tree"** and **"The Long Distance Runner"** Faith commits herself to a world which she wishes to change in some manner. Her identity is no longer portrayed in terms of opposing choices—between Jew or American, between domesticated wife or lonely single mother, between dedicated mother or career activist. No longer interested in seeking such a mutually exclusive definition of herself, Faith finds satisfaction within the parameters of each of these designations.

Personal maturity precedes social and political activism in ***Enormous Changes at the Last Minute.*** In **"Faith in the Afternoon,"** the myth of American happiness has to be dispelled before Faith can recognize that her own personal sorrows can be alleviated to some degree by registering them against the greater suffering of those close to her heart. Faith, visiting her parents after the dissolution of her marriage, sits hurt, unhappy, and ashamed as her mother tries to comfort her. Their tête-á-tête is interrupted by the intrusion of Mrs. Hegel Shtein, a stereotypic, interfering yente, from whom Faith inadvertently learns that many former friends and neighbors have met greater adversity than her own. Their losses—premature deaths and serious illnesses, blacklisting and bankruptcy, adultery and scandal—overshadow her own disappointments. Even with this knowledge, Faith does not succeed in bearing her own unhappiness resolutely. Her self-absorption in her own misery is at last undercut by the gentle inquiries of her father. Gersh Darwin makes few demands upon Faith and hopes only that his daughter reorder her life and bring his grandchildren to the Daughters of Judea to visit him. When Faith's personal grief prevents her from responding to her father's unassuming needs, it is his ultimate disgust that most effectively awakens Faith to her own selfishness.

The movement from self-preoccupation to a recognition of the pain that others endure is again the theme of **"Living"** in which Faith's concern with her own sickness prevents her from adequately responding to the more serious illness and eventual death of her close friend, Ellen. But the progression from personal to social awareness is best exemplified in **"Faith in a Tree"** in which Faith, for the first time, pledges herself to a world which lies beyond that of her immediate family, intimate friends, and neighborhood companions.

In **"Faith in a Tree"** Faith observes from her perch above the Washington Square Park playground the microcosmic replica of the social stratification and social interaction of the greater urban scene. With equal parts of humor and seriousness Faith reaffirms her commitment to the utility that inner city life holds for her children. She explains to Richard, her eldest son, that "I could be living in the country, which I love, but I know how hard that is on children—I stay here in this creepy slum. I dwell in soot and slime just so you can meet kids like Arnold Lee and live on this wonderful block with all the Irish and Puerto Ricans. . . . "

Throughout **"Faith in a Tree"** the blighted urban scene unfolds beneath Faith's dangling feet. As the male passers-by ogle or ignore the women seated on park benches watching their children at play, Faith reflects with perverse urban pride upon her city life. She sees advantages in her stifled upward mobility, the deteriorating public school system from which the wealthy children are unfortunately excluded, the diversity of people who lounge, scrounge, and parade through her neighborhood park.

Tempted by the arrival of an eligible male, Philip Mazzano, Faith descends from her twelve-foot-high sycamore branch. But realizing that Philip's attention is directed at Anna Kraat, "whose character is terrible, but she's beautiful," Faith is about to return to her branch-like balcony when a group of war protestors arrest her climb. Clanging pots and pans the group carried three posters:

> The first showed a prime-living, prime earning, well-dressed man about thirty-five years old next to a small girl. A question was asked: WOULD YOU BURN A CHILD? In the next poster he placed a burning cigarette on the child's arm. The cool answer was given: WHEN NECESSARY. The third poster carried no words, only a napalmed Vietnamese baby, seared, scarred, with twisted hands.

The policeman on the beat makes this small band of protestors disperse. In a fit of idealistic fury, Richard unleashes his anger at his mother's silence and the adult world's cowardice in resisting unethical authority. Enraged, Richard writes, "in pink flamingo chalk—in letters fifteen feet high, so the entire Saturday walking world could see—WOULD YOU BURN A CHILD? and under it, a little taller, the red reply, WHEN NECESSARY." Faith relates that "I think that is exactly when events turned me around."

From this awakening into political consciousness by her son Faith alters her entire life by "changing my hairdo, my job uptown, my style of living and telling." And, as a consequence of her "children's heartfelt brains," Faith "thought more and more and everyday about the world." As an adult who has been well-educated by her children, Faith descends from her perch in the tree to enter the battle for peace. And in her newly donned activism, Faith moves away from the playground politics of her immediate community to the battleground of world wide protest against the war in Viet Nam.

Faith has learned from her encounter in **"Faith in a Tree"** that for her an ethical life demands an active participation in current social issues. In **"The Long Distance Runner"**

Faith who is now stout and forty-two, jogs out to explore the urban streets beyond her Greenwich Village neighborhood before "old age and urban renewal ended them and me." Faith seeks in this story, as she does on a more intimate level in **"Friends"** and **"Living"** that key which will unlock the past in order to better understand the present and foretell the future. In **"The Long Distance Runner"** Faith sprints through the city streets to her former neighborhood in Coney Island, once Jewish, now black. By revisiting these scenes from her childhood, Faith witnesses those physical and social transformations which foreshadow "What in the world is coming next."

As Faith scuffles through the littered streets of New York she confesses an admiration for the city despite its decay. "I wanted to stop and admire the long beach. . . . There aren't many rotting cities so tan and sandy and speckled with citizens at their salty edges." Faith's excursion ends at the tenement building in which she was raised. She is escorted through the dwelling by a Girl Scout with whom she reminisces about the inhabitants of each apartment. Time past interlocks with the present as Faith's adolescent black guide updates the history of each family unit. As Faith progresses through her former building it seemed "as though remembering was in charge of the existence of the past. This was not so." In actuality it is not memory that enlivens the past for Faith, but the contrast with the present that reawakens her recollections of childhood.

Faith improbably entrenches herself for three weeks as an uninvited guest in her former apartment, now the residence of a black family headed by Mrs. Luddy who lives with her son, Donald and three baby girls. Paley benignly ridicules her heroine as Faith, the rosy tempered white idealist, encounters the ravaged black neighborhood with gushing sympathy. To offset Faith's do-goodism the Luddy family counterbalances Faith's Polyannaism with cynical realism. As Donald looks out at the men lounging on the stoops he scowls, "Look at them. They ain't got self-respect. They got Afros *on* their heads, but they don't know they black *in* their heads." Faith predictably thinks Donald "ought to learn to be more sympathetic . . . " because "There are reasons that people are that way." In a similarly charitable mode Faith comments as she looks out the window upon the urban ruins, "Someone ought to clean that up, . . . " to which Mrs. Luddy replies, "Who you got in mind, Mrs. Kennedy?—. . . . " Donald's disgust and Faith's overwrought concern are wisely undercut by Mrs. Luddy's practical wisdom.

Immersing herself in the Luddys's affairs, Faith cannot resist the role of social missionary. She decides that Donald, though brilliant, needs to be brought up to reading level at once, and undertakes this task with lessons in fiction, poetry, and social history. She notices that two-year old Eloise is undersized for her age and purchases the requisite nutritional food-stuffs to promote proper growth. Faith is equally concerned with Mrs. Luddy's lot and imagines Mrs. Luddy to be yet another abandoned woman waiting for the return of her man. After three weeks Mrs. Luddy has had enough and tells Faith, "Time to go, lady. This ain't Free Vacation Farm." Teary-eyed, Faith kisses Donald goodbye and jogs home, on the way proffering unsolicited advice to the dozen young mothers she passes in the northeast playground. Faith warns them, "In fifteen years, you girls will be like me, wrong in everything."

Paley's mild mockery of her stocky, white heroine jogging through the street-wise black ghetto does not diminish Paley's obvious respect for the beliefs to which Faith has committed herself in story after story. It seems that while Paley acknowledges that Faith's values may appear to be too optimistic to be acted upon in a harsh world, they are still the only values worth retaining and striving to fulfill. (pp. 89-95)

In [**"Friends"**] Paley records the journey Faith undertakes in order to visit her dying friend, Selena. In turn, Selena mourns the earlier death of her daughter, Abby, from a drug overdose. Although saddened by the deaths of these two women, Faith, in spite of her grief renews her belief in human connections. Once again, it is Faith's child who berates her for her unabashed optimism. A skeptical Anthony wonders how his mother as well as Selena could have been deceived by the destructiveness of Abby's misspent life. Faith argues that Tonto is too young to "know yet what their times can do to a person." But Anthony persists in his attack by chiding his mother, "Here she goes with her goody-goodies—everything is so groovy wonderful far-out terrific. Next thing you'll say people are darling and the world is so nice and round that Union Carbide will never blow it up." While Faith concedes that Anthony was "right to harass my responsible nature," she will not relinquish her view that life, even in its tragic moments, can inform the future with hope and consolation. Faith therefore insists, as she reflects upon the deaths of her friends that "I was right to invent for my friends and our children a report on these private deaths and the condition of our lifelong attachments."

The optimism which Faith Darwin Asbury inherits from Paley is most evident in **"The Immigrant Story."** Here, Faith defends her "rotten rosy temperament" against the grim view of the world held by her childhood companion and present lover, Jack, who sees Faith's cheerfulness as a betrayal of the tragic past. Essentially, **"The Immigrant Story"** centers upon a debate about the connection between second generation Jewish Americans and their common Jewish past. Perhaps it is because Faith has inherited from her immigrant parents a more secularized vision that she is able to see the world more brightly than Jack. Like many children of Jewish immigrants Jack has grown "up in the shadow of another person's sorrow." The Holocaust has inflicted such loss upon Jack's parents that Jack finds that he cannot unburden himself from the guilt which he feels for having survived. Faith, although enraged by the "cruel history of Europe" which she acknowledges as "one of my own themes" was raised in the heartening American tradition of happiness and freedom for all. Her optimism, it appears, is rooted in the Americanness of her Jewish upbringing.

Recollecting their mutual heritage, Jack perceives, "Misery, misery, misery. Grayness. I see it all very gray." But Faith interprets the same "cruel history of Europe" as a thousand year history lesson from which we "may have learned some sense." Although Jack and Faith are both children of Jewish immigrants, they observe their past from different sides of the same street. Faith proclaims, "I thank God I'm American-born and live on East 172nd Street where there is a grocery store, a candy store, and a drugstore on one corner and on the same block a shul and two doctors's offices." Jack responds, "One hundred and Seventy-second Street was a pile of shit. . . . Everyone was on relief except you."

These two second generation American Jews were raised on the same block and each has inherited a portion of the same "cruel history." Yet Jack and Faith regard their lives from opposing perspectives. Neither character will convince the other of the validity of his own position. Faith, trying to be objective and rational in this debate argues, "I believe I see the world as clearly as you do. . . . Rosiness is not a worse windowpane than gloomy gray when viewing the world." Maybe not. But Paley knows that her compassionate heroine will not always convince those like Jack who, with equal justification, see the world in hues of "gloomy gray."

Like the title of Paley's first book, Faith Darwin comes to regard her personal disappointments as nothing more than the "little disturbances of man." Because this sturdy American Jewess with her staunch set of values remains adamantly optimistic, she can always envision the possibility of "enormous changes at the last minute." Faith believes in the simple, yet seldom respected, and less seldomly extolled values of motherhood, childhood, and social good. In the course of those stories in which Faith figures prominently, she graduates from rosy optimist to committed activist. If some are disturbed by the optimism and spunk of this sturdy woman, then perhaps Faith should be regarded metaphorically as the Jewess who endures because her "capacity for survival has not been overwhelmed by her susceptibility to abuse—. . . . " (pp. 96-7)

Dena Mandel, "Keeping Up with Faith: Grace Paley's Sturdy American Jewess," in Studies in American Jewish Literature, *No. 3, 1983, pp. 85-98.*

Anne Tyler (essay date 1985)

[*Tyler is an American novelist, short story writer, and critic acclaimed for her depictions of eccentric characters and family relationships in such novels as* Dinner at the Homesick Restaurant *(1982) and* The Accidental Tourist *(1985). Critics contend that Tyler has refined the southern literary tradition of William Faulkner and Flannery O'Connor by writing works that emphasize the effects of history on individuals, but which are considered more restrained in action and personal in scope than the works of these other southern writers. In the following review, Tyler praises Paley's delineation of urban mothers in* Later the Same Day.]

American short-story writers are a tough breed in any event—standing firm in a country where the average reader prefers a novel—but Grace Paley must be one of the toughest. Not only does she continue to produce stories, and usually very brief ones; she continues to speak in a voice so absolutely her own that a single line, one suspects, could be identified as hers among a hundred other lines. She is resolute, stalwart, vigorous. She is urban to an unusual degree, cataloging both the horrors and the surprising pockets of green in her native New York City. And she is unique, or very nearly unique, in her ability to fit large-scale political concerns both seamlessly and effectively onto very small canvases.

The stories collected in ***The Little Disturbances of Man*** (1959) and ***Enormous Changes at the Last Minute*** (1974) brought to our attention a particular kind of heroine: the gritty, embattled urban mother. Sometimes on welfare, sometimes not, generally between husbands, fiercely protective of her children but often a little sloppy with her housekeeping, this woman had different names but always the same amused, ironic voice—a sort of "Oh, well" tone, accompanied by a shrug of the shoulders. In the case of Faith, the most endearing of these women, the shrug was meant solely for her own messy life, never for the messy state of the world, which she was constantly hoping (and picketing, and petitioning) to alter.

Faith is the character who emerges most clearly from this new collection, and she's the one who gives special meaning to the title. It is, indeed, later the same day: the woman we observed rearing her two little boys alone and dealing with the middle age of her parents is now middle-aged herself. Now she is coping with her parents' old age and with the eventual death of her mother. She is facing the fact that even though romantic love continues to interest her, it will have to be weighted with a history of past loves. And when she worries about her sons, it is because they are beyond her reach, out in that very world she's been trying to change all these years.

In **"Friends"** a woman who is Faith's contemporary is dying of cancer. They've known each other since the day they met in the park with their babies. ("I think a bond was sealed then," Faith tells us, "at least as useful as the vow we'd all sworn with husbands to whom we're no longer married.") The talk at Selena's deathbed is of children grown and lost. "You know the night [my daughter] died," Selena says, "when the police called me and told me? That was my first night's sleep in two years. I *knew* where she was." And Faith—in one of those trade-offs by which the lucky mothers appease the unlucky mothers—responds by claiming she has no idea where her son is, although in fact he keeps in touch admirably.

"Dreamer in a Dead Language" takes us to Children of Judea, Home for the Golden Ages, Coney Island Branch, where Faith's parents live—still her parents no matter what, still capable of wounding and distressing her. Faith's mother has settled in but her father is itching to leave, protesting, writing love poems, unresigned. He doesn't feel old at all, he says:

> Trotsky pointed out, the biggest surprise that comes to a man is old age. O.K. That's what I mean, I don't feel it. Surprise. Isn't that interesting that he had so much to say on every subject. Years ago I didn't have the right appreciation of him. Thrown out the front door of history, sneaks in the window to sit in the living room,

> excuse me, I mean I do not feel old. Do NOT. In any respect. You understand me, Faith?

Faith has hung on to her political fervor, as have the other characters in this collection. In **"Anxiety"** a woman leans out her apartment window to harangue a young father. "Son," she says, "I must tell you that madmen intend to destroy this beautifully made planet. That the murder of our children by these men has got to become a terror and a sorrow to you, and starting now, it had better interfere with any daily pleasure." In the old days, she reflects, these windows were full of various women issuing their orders and instructions. It's a thought that calls up an instant image of the Paley heroine: arms akimbo, jaw set pugnaciously, but her head now grayer and body thicker.

When characters meet on these pages, it's at the National Meeting of Town Meetings or the League for Revolutionary Youth. When they travel, it's to observe socialist societies. When they start a conversation with an attractive man, their subject is the ecological damage in Vietnam. Yet they avoid self-righteousness; they're not offensive. The reason, I believe, is that Grace Paley never loses sight of the personal. She is in touch with those individual lives affected by the larger issues; she can tally the cost of what she calls the "expensive moment," the private sacrifice that historical considerations may demand.

> We were speaking, the Chinese woman said. About the children, how to raise them. My youngest sister is permitted to have a child this year, so we often talk thoughtfully. This is what we think: Shall we teach them to be straightforward, honorable, kind, brave, maybe shrewd, selfserving a little? What is the best way to help them in the real world? We don't know the best way. You don't want them to be cruel, but you want them to take care of themselves wisely. Now my own children are nearly grown. Perhaps it's too late. Was I foolish? I didn't know in those years how to do it.
>
> Yes, yes, said Faith. I know what you mean. Ruthy?
>
> Ruthy remained quiet.
>
> Faith waited a couple of seconds. Then she turned to the Chinese woman. Oh, Xie Feng, she said. Neither did I.

There is humor, too; that always helps—a kind of running thread of humor underlying nearly every passage. And there's an earthy, angular style of speech. If I had to summarize this book's best feature, though, I would quote a single sentence. It's a line referring to Faith and her friends, but it describes Grace Paley's stories equally well: "They were all, even Edie, ideologically, spiritually, and on puritanical principle against despair." (pp. 38-9)

Anne Tyler, "Mothers in the City," in The New Republic, *Vol. 192, No. 17, April 29, 1985, pp. 38-9.*

Adam Mars-Jones (essay date 1985)

[*Mars-Jones is a British short story writer, editor, and critic. In the following review, he focuses on ideological inconsistencies within the stories of* Later the Same Day.]

It is stories featuring Faith as a character . . . which have done most to win Paley her following, and which show her rhetoric at its most characteristic. The name "Faith" has a somehow ominous similarity to "Grace"; Faith's father, as Paley admits in a note in ***Enormous Changes at the Last Minute,*** is unmistakably Paley's own. But there is no consistency of approach; sometimes Faith narrates, sometimes she is described from outside. Sometimes she is the subject of the picture, sometimes only the frame.

One result of such shifts is a problem of tone. What is the expected reaction to a sentence like this: "Then we talked over the way the SALT treaty looked more like a floor than a ceiling, read a poem written by one of his daughters, looked at a TV show telling the destruction of the European textile industry, and then made love"? Is this an ironic portrait of a pair of armchair politicos casting themselves as observers of history? Or is there perceived to be a unity to the acts of attention described here?

The second version is the true one. Grace Paley seems to be what Americans call "a red-diaper baby", that is, someone brought up in a politicized household. Certainly Faith's father, even in the Children of Judea Home, lectures his fellow-residents about the "regular germinating seeds of Stalinist anti-Semitism". Paley, in other words, inherited dissent. For her there is no conflict between radicalism and family values, since for her they are the same thing (the Faith-figure in one story, at an unspecified young age, issues a domestic manifesto attacking the family's position on the Soviet Union). Her oppositional politics have the emotional structure of an orthodoxy.

Faith and similar figures in Paley's fiction continue to inhabit a world of congruent theory and practice. There is Margaret, with whom there were "many years of political agreement before some matters relating to the Soviet Union separated us". There is the neighbourhood grocer, with whom Faith fights over Chilean plums (she is forced to resort to a supermarket). A misleading whisper of Woody Allen's voice seems to hang about these scenes of anguished ideological shopping; misleading because these stories are as free of irony as modern fiction can be and still be called modern.

One consequence of Paley's oddly undivided sensibility is a general disinclination to recognize barriers. This shows up even on the level of punctuation: she rejects the use of inverted commas to indicate dialogue, not even compromising with a continental or Joycean dash. This economy is sometimes costly for the reader, who must separate out the different registers for himself, but well expresses a sensibility that assumes the continuity of inside and outside. The same tendency on the level of form marks some of the stories, which may for instance have Faith as a character but end up (like **"Ruthy and Edie"**) in someone else's mind.

But the problems lie deeper. Politics and writing offer different orders of access to reality. How may they be reconciled? Feminism proposes a solution, with the notion that the personal is political: women's lives contain great issues. By this criterion, **"Lavinia: An Old Story"** is political, though the issues it contains are of wastage and defeat.

Feminism, once invoked, brings consequences in its train. It presents a critique of traditional politics, branding them as inherently male and evasive. But conversation between Faith and her intimates, her lover Jack and son Richard for instance, regularly rebounds from the doctrinaire to the sentimental:

> But Jack said, Don't you dare talk to your mother like that, Richard! Don't you dare! Ma, Richard said, get his brains out of the pickle jar, it's no insult. Everyone knows, the intelligentsia strikes the spark, so that they'll be relevant for a long time, striking sparks here and there. Of course, he explained, the fire of revolution would only be advanced, contained and put to productive use by the working class. . . .

There is something nightmarish about this yoking of cant and cuteness, all seemingly endorsed by the narrator Faith:

> Then Jack asked, Richard, tell me, do you forgive your father for having run out on you kids years ago?
>
> I don't forgive him and I don't not forgive him. I can't spend my life on personal animosities. The way imperialism's leaning on the Third World the way it does. . . .
>
> Jack said, Ah . . . He blinked his eyes a couple of times, which a person who can't cry too well often does.

Faith's attitude throughout is indulgently maternal. When in another story Richard challenges her: "Mother, he said, have you ever read any political theory? No. All those dumb peace meetings you go to. Don't they ever talk about anything but melting up a couple of really great swords?", her response is to speak as mother to child, not as one person to another: "Richard, she said. You're absolutely white. You seem to have quit drinking orange juice." This simple remark, we are told, made him leave home for three days.

Paley's women characters aspire to a maternal relation with the world. In **"Anxiety"** an unnamed woman, "an older person who feels free because of that to ask questions and give advice", leans out of her window and resolves a conflict between a young father and his little daughter. "Then I sit in the nice light and wonder how to make sure that they gallop safely home . . . I wish I could see just how they sit down at their kitchen tables for a healthy snack (orange juice or milk and cookies) before going out into the new spring afternoon to play." In maternity, and specifically in childbirth, the inside becomes the outside, the body speaking unchallengeably in the first person. This dream of intervention seeks to generalize it.

Grace Paley's Faith is always concerned with community, but the community that claims her allegiance subtly modulates: community of radicals, community of women, community of parents, community of neighbours. These communities have incompatible interests, but Paley tries to keep them reconciled.

A single story, **"Zagrowsky Tells"**, makes an attempt to examine the conflicts between different definitions of community, instead of hushing them up. Faith meets Zagrowsky, who used to be the neighbourhood pharmacist, in the park; the story is told from his point of view. He asks her a question: "Is it true, no matter what time you called, even if I was closing up, I came to your house with the penicillin or the tetracycline later?" Faith, moved, thanks him. But it turns out that she and her friends picketed the pharmacy because Zagrowsky was slow to serve blacks.

Zagrowsky has some poor excuses: "a stranger comes into the store, naturally you have to serve the old customers first". But he also has some strong lines ("An American-born girl has some nerve to mention history") and a sense of economics far in advance of Faith's: "my pharmacy, what a beautiful place it was . . . it sent three children to college, saved a couple lives—imagine: one store!"

He has also suffered real damage through Faith's actions: his unstable daughter Cissy is inspired to picket the pharmacy herself, shouting "Racist!", shouting "He sells poison chemicals!", shouting "He's a terrible dancer, he got three left legs!". She is sent to a home.

By picketing Zagrowsky's pharmacy, Faith turns her back on a community of neighbours, although it has fulfilled its obligations towards her, in favour of a community of radicals committed to social change. She refuses to consider that community is about exclusion just as surely as about inclusion (the radical notion of community excludes Zagrowsky, just as his excludes blacks). The story **"Zagrowsky Tells"** would dramatize the shifts in her position, except that throughout the story Zagrowsky is playing with his much-loved grandson, fathered on Cissy by the home's black gardener, and so Faith can claim not only moral right but all's well that ends well. Conflict is only examined retrospectively, after the fact of reconciliation.

Other acts of exclusion are not so easily made good. In the last two pages of ***Later The Same Day*** a lesbian friend of Faith's confronts her:

> You've told everybody's story but mine. I don't even mean my whole story, that's my job. You probably can't. But I mean you've just omitted me from the other stories and I was there. . . . Where is *my* life? It's been women and men, women and men, fucking fucking. Goddamnit, where the hell is my woman and woman, woman-loving life in all this?

Any answer to this would mean exploring the conflicting claims of feminism and old-fashioned radicalism, and in Paley the "prism of isms" is always kept spinning. These last two pages of the book amount to a session of public self-criticism rather than an undertaking to change.

"Faith in what?" asks a Chinese woman when introduced to Paley's central character. The answer seems to be, faith in meetings. Faith is old enough to remember "the silk-stocking boycott which coincided with the Japanese devastation of Manchuria", but not old enough to consider

Paley near the time of the publication of Later the Same Day.

that her lifelong style of politics is not actually effective. She has a hardened innocence which attracts many readers, but is hard to share when the text is read closely.

Faith tells the Chinese woman that one of Jack's two employees (Jack has a discount furniture store) once led a strike against him and won. "Jack says that they were right." There's something dotty about this satisfaction taken in the political process, in the proof that radicalism gets results. If "they were right", how come they needed to strike before Jack saw it (strikes in any case being displays of power, and not teaching aids)?

Radical politics was the religion in which Faith was brought up, and she continues to make her devotions; but she is working out her own salvation rather than advancing a cause. Meetings take up a lot of time: "Of course, because of this planet, which is dropping away from us in poisonous disgust, I'm hardly ever home." The suppressed logic of this sentence is startling. Because the planet is dropping away from us in poisonous disgust, Faith must go to more meetings than ever before. The planet insists. It's as if Candide was to propose that by cultivating your own garden you could re-stock the Earth with oxygen.

Sometimes the problem is acknowledged to be distance, separation, irrelevance (though thanks to the first person plural, shared distance, shared separation, shared irrelevance), before the cosmic perspective reasserts itself:

> I am stuck here among my own ripples and tides. Don't you wish you could rise powerfully above your time and name? I'm sure we all try, but here we are, always slipping and falling down into them, speaking their narrow language, though the subject, which is how to save the world—and quickly—is immense.

But the world which Grace Paley in most of these stories puts all her energy into saving is not a shared and vulnerable planet, but her private world of unified emotions and assumed politics, which she must perpetually repair without ever actually admitting that it has been exposed to damage.

Adam Mars-Jones, "From Red-Diaper Baby to Mother of the Planet," in The Times Literary Supplement, *No. 4312, November 22, 1985, p. 1311.*

Ronald Schleifer (essay date 1985)

[*Schleifer is an American critic and educator. In the following excerpt, he examines storytelling technique and the rendering of daily life in Paley's stories.*]

In a recent interview Grace Paley discussed the relation between her storytelling and the fact that she is a woman. "For a long time," she said, "I thought women's lives . . . I didn't really think I was shit, but I really thought my life as a woman was shit. Who could be interested in this crap? I was very interested in it, but I didn't have enough social ego to put it down. . . . Women who have thought their lives were boring have found they're interesting to one another." Paley is speaking of the difficult discovery of what Jonathan Culler, following Elaine Showalter, has recently called the possibility of "reading as a woman," the discovery, that is, that the *position* of a woman—what Culler calls "the experience of being watched, seen as a 'girl,' restricted, marginalized" and what Paley calls simply the experience of the ordinary boredom of a woman's life—can offer articulations of experience that can "show," as Paley goes on to say, "how mysterious ordinary life is." Reading as a woman, then, is not only reading from the margin—what Gayatri Spivak calls a "feminization" of reading that problematizes the subject of discourse—but also a reading that articulates another version of experience altogether. It is, as Peggy Kamuf has written, to read a text as if it were written by a woman: "reading it *as if* it had no (determined) father, *as if,* in other words, it were illegitimate, recognized by its mother who can only give it a borrowed name." Reading as a woman transforms the form and authority of fiction so that the boring quotidian concerns Paley could not imagine as the legitimate subject of art are transformed into concern for the ordinary ongoingness of the surface of things—not only their comic agitations, but, as I will argue, their chaste compactness without depths—that characterizes Paley's short stories.

Paley has also said that the subject of her writing—"life, death, desertion, loss, divorce, failure, love"—is "daily life. I wouldn't call it ordinary, just daily life. . . . And I'm very anti-symbolical. . . . I don't write anything but what I'm writing about. I'm not writing about meaning beyond meaning." Paley uses her situation as a woman, and especially her situation as a mother, to eschew the appropriation and totalization of "meaning"—its authority and form—for a more spacious conception of life. The appropriation of meaning is a species of will to power; it is an attempt, as Kamuf says, to "contain an unlimited textual system, install a measure of protection between this boundlessness and one's own power to know, to be this power and to know that one is this power." In contrast to a plural voice, the appropriating voice is what Mary Jacobus calls "the unified 'I' which falls as a dominating phallic shadow across the male page, like Casaubon's monumental egotism."

Against this power of subject and form Julia Kristeva posits the spaciousness Paley attempts to narrate as "a nexus of life and language (of species and society)—the child." In the writings of Rousseau and Freud, Kristeva explains,

> it was as if Reason were suddenly neither satisfied simply to test its restraining bond by confronting texts, nor to strain meaning by writing the speaking being's identity as fiction; it was forced, instead, to face reproduction of the species (the boundary between "nature" and "culture") and the varied attitudes toward it. Reason was thus transcended by a *heterogeneous element* (biology: life) and by a *third party* (*I/you* communication is displaced by *it:* the child). These challenge the speaker with the fact that he is not whole, but they do so in a manner altogether different from that in which the obsessed person's wretched consciousness ceaselessly signifies his bondage to death. For if death is the Other, life is a third party; and as this signification, asserted by the child, is disquieting, it might well unsettle the speaker's paranoid enclosure.

The position between species and society, nature and culture, transforms the Other of death into the "third party" of life: an other figured by Kristeva as a child. This, she argues, is best comprehended from the *position* of woman, and thus she sees the artist as someone who "gives birth," just as Paley describes the subject of her art simply as "daily life." In this situation, "sublation here is both eroticizing without residue and a disappearance of eroticism as it returns to its source." "The speaker reaches this limit," Kristeva continues, "this requisite of sociality, only by virtue of a particular, discursive practice called "art." A woman also attains it (and in our society, *especially*) through the strange form of split symbolization (threshold of language and instinctual drive, of the "symbolic" and the "semiotic") of which the act of giving birth consists.

This is the *position* of a woman that Paley articulates in her stories. Paley's woman is marginalized without "interest," excluded from power, illegitimate. She is the mother who recognizes a world of life beyond herself in her children; an artist who recognizes voices besides her own in her "work"; and a citizen who recognizes a world—"tornadoes," "flood," "catastrophes of God"—beyond her own concerns. As she says, her stories deal with ordinary relations between men and women—life, death, desertion, loss, divorce, failure, love—and her stories aim, as I shall argue, at reconceiving the form of storytelling by reconceiving their endings and at discovering a different authority of telling by articulating a new sense of their subject's relation to voice. At her best, Paley achieves the chaste compact spaciousness of short stories in which authority does not come from deathbed pronouncements and summings up, but can best be figured in terms of birthbeds, listening, and calling forth voices. (pp. 31-3)

The goal of Paley's storytelling can be seen in one of her best early stories, **"The Pale Pink Roast,"** in ***The Little Disturbances of Man.*** Anna and her daughter accidentally meet Peter, Anna's former husband and Judy's father, as they walk through the park. They have not seen each other in several years, and when Peter learns that Anna is moving back to New York, he finds a sitter for Judy and goes to help Anna move in. In her new and expensive apartment "Peter put up the Venetian blinds, followed by the curtains. He distributed books among the available bookcases. He glued the second drawer of Judy's bureau. . . . He whistled while he worked." Afterwards, they kiss: "She was faint and leaden, a sure sign in Anna, if he remembered correctly, of passion. 'Shall we dance?' he asked softly, a family joke. With great care, a patient lover, he undid the sixteen tiny buttons of her pretty dress and in Judy's room on Judy's bed he took her at once without a word. Afterwards, having established tenancy, he rewarded her with kisses. He dressed quickly because he was obliged by the stories of his life to remind her of transience."

Over coffee in the next room, Peter asks Anna how she can afford her new apartment, and she answers that her new husband, who will be following her from Rochester in a few days, is quite successful in business. Peter is dumbfounded: "You're great, Anna. Man, you're great. You wiggle your ass. You make a donkey out of me and him both. You could've said no. . . . Why'd you do it? Revenge? Meanness? Why?" "Wait a minute, Peter," she says; "Honest to God, listen to me, I did it for love." In this interchange, virtually at the end of the story, Paley offers a sense of their whole married life together: how Peter is not able to notice what is happening right before him, but seeks instead to find the meaning and explanation of his experience. There is no symbolic significance in this ordinary conversation after lovemaking—Paley offers us no psychological analysis—the conversation is simply there, calling for interpretation rather than providing explanation.

Such a call is intrinsic in all stories, according to Paley: a story is embedded in life. A story does not show life from the vantage point of the ending. A story eschews the egotism of meaning—Peter's understanding of Anna's behavior solely as a *symbolic* gesture in relation to himself—in favor (like life, like children) of possibilities. A story, for Paley, in Walter Benjamin's expression, is an "exchange of experiences"; its value lies in the possible readings it provokes, the necessity of its repetition, and in the fact that, as Benjamin continues, it "sinks the thing into the life of the storyteller, in order to bring it out of him again. Thus traces of the storyteller cling to the story the way the handprints of the potter cling to the clay vessel."

Here we can see why many reviewers of Paley's work have

noted the extraordinary power of her stories to articulate different voices, and we can see why she herself emphasizes storytelling as a form of listening.

Speaking of her first stories, Paley has said [See Lidoff excerpt dated 1981] "And before I wrote those stories, I was just stuck in my own voice. Until I was able to use other people's voices . . . , that I'd been hearing all my life, you know, I was just talking me-me-me. While I was doing that, I couldn't write these stories. And when I was able to get into other voices consciously, or use what I was hearing, and become the story hearer—when I could do that, I just suddenly wrote them. It was a true breakthrough." What Peter cannot do is tell the story in Anna's voice; he cannot see her love when it is right before him. Other characters in Paley also cannot listen and retell stories: Mrs. Raftery has only her own voice, "distanced" from others, while the narrator of **"A Conversation with My Father,"** in ***Enormous Changes at the Last Minute,*** has learned the patience to wait and listen. "Well," she tells her father, "you just have to let the story lie around till some agreement can be reached between you and the stubborn hero." "Aren't you talking silly, now?" her father answers.

Her father thinks she is talking silly because, like Peter, he wants to discover the meaning of her stories: he wants her characters to have backgrounds, stock, character, direction, truth, meaning ("Tragedy! Plain tragedy! Historical tragedy! No hope. The end"). That is, he wants a plot like a line—in his dying he *sees* that plot is inexorably like a line. Against this notion the daughter says, it is "plot, the absolute line between two points, which I've always despised. Not for literary reasons, but because it takes all hope away. Everyone, real or invented, deserves the open destiny of life."

What the daughter is interested in—what the story embedded in **"A Conversation with My Father"** offers—is a sense of the surface of things, the ordinary disturbances of everyday life, not their depths. As John tells Ginny in **"An Interest in Life,"** her list of troubles would never get her on "Strike It Rich": " 'No question in my mind at all,' said John. 'Have you ever seen that program? I mean, in addition to all of this—the little disturbances of man'—he waved a scornful hand at my list—'they *suffer.* They live in the forefront of tornadoes, their lives are washed off by flood—catastrophes of God. Oh, Virginia.' " What Ginny hopes for—what, after all, "Strike It Rich" or "Queen for a Day" offers—is enormous changes at the last minute. These changes, embodied in the titles of Paley's books, are part of her project as a storyteller: "Everyone would sit out on boxes and folding chairs and talk," Paley remembers of her childhood, "about in-laws, children, husbands, wives, what it was all about. That's what you listen for and expect when you're a kid: the next conversation will tell you what it's all about, if you only listen to it." Telling stories means listening to the real life of people—"everyone can tell one"—articulating and discovering the possibility of change and freedom in the end.

As a woman, Paley is in a position to make such discoveries in stories. In Benjamin's study, entitled "The Storyteller," of the works of Nikolai Leskov, Benjamin argues that the story, as opposed to the novel, focuses on the most *ordinary* of things. While the novel, like Peter in **"The Pale Pink Roast,"** attempts to fathom the "meaning of life," stories are both focused and based upon the ordinary: the ability to exchange experiences, the reality of boredom, and both the usualness and the authority of death. "There used to be no house," Benjamin writes,

> hardly a room, in which someone had not once died. . . . Today people live in rooms that have never been touched by death. . . . It is, however, characteristic that not only a man's knowledge or wisdom, but above all his real life—and this is the stuff stories are made of—first assumes transmissible form at the moment of his death. . . . Suddenly in his expressions and looks the unforgettable emerges and imparts to everything that concerned him that authority which even the poorest wretch in dying possesses for the living around him. This authority is the very source of the story.

What Benjamin leaves out in defining the authority of the story is the fact that people used to be born as well as die in those houses and rooms—a fact that the position and experience of being a woman makes more readily discernible. For Paley, stories concern themselves with real life and with things as ordinary (and as powerful and mysterious in their ordinariness) as birth and death. The concern for ordinary relations—transmissions—is central to Benjamin, yet he focuses on the authority of possession—*his* knowledge, *his* wisdom, the traces of the storyteller—rather than on that other authority of beginnings that Paley offers. Ongoingness is important to Benjamin—"actually," he says, "there is no story for which the questions as to how it continued could not be legitimate. The novelist, on the other hand, cannot take the smallest step beyond that limit at which he invites the reader to a divinatory realization of the meaning of life by writing 'Finis.' " But ongoingness is accomplished in bequeathing possessions, not in the strange and complicated relations between generations living together.

Thus Benjamin's emphasis on possibility does not imply the resources of articulation that Paley, as a mother as well as a storyteller, possesses. At the end of **"The Long-Distance Runner"**—also the end of ***Enormous Changes at the Last Minute***—Faith tells her story to her family:

> I repeated the story. They all said, what?
>
> Because it isn't usually so simple. Have you known it to happen much nowadays? A woman inside the steamy energy of middle age runs and runs. She finds the houses and streets where her childhood happened. She lives in them. She learns as though she was still a child what in the world is coming next.

At the end of her collection Paley presents a story that combines beginning and ending, the imagined child as well as the middle-aged woman. Such a combination defines her storytelling, in which both the ordinary pain of a fact as commonplace as time making a monkey of us all and the possibility of some hoped-for change can be heard. That is, stories possess the authority of a living voice—even the disturbing authority of the last words of the suffering of living—yet they also possess that other authority (this is what makes them living) of transmission without possession; such transmission creates at least the illusion of enormous changes and new beginnings. Both kinds of authority are clearly seen in **"A Conversation with My Father,"** where approaching death makes the father want to hear only his own story, a story that ends, and where also sympathy and love make the narrator conceive of her other story, which depicts an enormous change at the last minute for the addict, as a narrative of new beginnings.

This combination defines the characteristic endings of Paley's stories. Both little disturbances and enormous changes are brought together at the close of her stories to create a sense of ordinary ongoingness that eschews that melodrama of closure. Instead of articulating the meaning of life, her stories attempt to address ongoing life, to illuminate the play of closure and openness in "lives that haven't been seen." At the end of **"Wants"** the heroine articulates her desire for both ending and not ending—"I want, for instance, to be a different person"; "I wanted to have been married forever to one person, my ex-husband or my present one." Mrs. Raftery ends **"Distance"** by asking "What the devil is it all about, the noisiness and the speediness, when it's no distance at all? How come John had to put all the courtesy calls in to [his wife] Margaret on his lifelong trip to Ginny?" **"An Interest in Life"** ends with John and Ginny on the kitchen floor making love, "and the truth is, we were so happy, we forgot the precautions". **"Living"** ends with the placement of dying amid all the ordinary hubbub of life, and as we have seen, **"The Pale Pink Roast"** ends with the ordinary articulation of love. All Paley's endings are marked by a sense that life goes on.

But perhaps the most enormous of changes is the death of Samuel at the end of his story—a death Paley portrays, without melodrama, in the ordinariness of ongoing life:

> Oh, oh, she hopelessly cried. She did not know how she could ever find another boy like that one. However, she was a young woman and she became pregnant. Then for a few months she was hopeful. The child born to her was a boy. They brought him to be seen and nursed. She smiled. But immediately she saw that this baby wasn't Samuel. She and her husband together have had other children, but never again will a boy exactly like Samuel be known.

Faced with the enormity of the changes she portrays, Paley eschews melodrama for the quotidian, the articulation of the ordinary. Rather than the melodrama of conclusion—whether it is the "Finis" of the novel or Peter's authoritative interpretation—she presents endings that project ongoing love, the authority of possibilities.

Thus the love articulated at the end of **"The Pale Pink Roast"** plays on the surface of life, a kind of fiction, an exchange of experience, a signifier of desire (which is also a surface experience). And even the title of this story suggests that experience can play rather than signify—so that alterity becomes nuance, contradiction a variant, tension a passage—and that experience can be valued in its activity, on the surface, rather than in its meaning:

> "Peter, you're the one who really looks wonderful. You look just—well—healthy."
>
> "I take care of myself, Anna. That's why. . . . "
>
> "You always did take care of yourself, Peter."
>
> "No, Anna, this is different." He stopped and settled on a box of curtains. "I mean it's not egocentric and selfish, the way I used to be. Now it has a real philosophical basis. Don't mix me up with biology. Look at me, what do you see?"
>
> Anna had read that cannibals, tasting man, saw him thereafter as the great pig, the pale pink roast.
>
> "Peter, Peter, pumpkin eater," Anna said.

The title of the story does not suggest (if we use the terms of Peter Brooks) a "metaphorical and expressionistic quest," but a kind of metonymy, a "true mannerism, a love of surfaces for their own sake." Anna recognizes Peter in his otherness and so, unlike Peter in his need to understand and explain her, she does not have to refer all his actions symbolically back to herself. Peter learned to take care of himself, he tells Anna, when he asked his grandfather—"that old jerk, the one that was so mad, he didn't want to die"—if he had any "real hot tips" about life:

> "He came up with an answer right away. 'Peter,' he said, 'I'd go to a gym every goddamn day of my life; the hell with the job, the hell with the women. Peter, I'd build my body up till God hisself wouldn't know how to tear it apart. . . . This structure, this . . . thing'—he pinched himself across his stomach and his knees—'this me'—he cracked himself sidewise across his jaw—'this is got to be maintained. The reason is, Peter, *It is the dwelling place of the soul.*' " In the end, long life is the reward, strength, and beauty."

For Peter, his body represents himself—metaphorically it is his dwelling place, its condition a kind of reward—whereas for Anna, no such signification exists.

Here, just as Benjamin suggests, it is a story of dying that occasions another story—Peter's story about his grandfather. The story is as authoritative as any Peter tells. It certainly carries more authority than Peter's assertion that he is no longer egocentric and selfish, yet it still betrays his repeated gesture to *explain* things. So, of his grandfather, Peter finally says, "Bad or good, Anna, he got his time in, he lived long enough to teach the next generation." Peter understands his grandfather's story as an explanation, nothing more; he dismisses his grandfather in the same way he dismisses Anna when he learns she is married. Peter reads to get the point—a point that always refers back to himself—and once he thinks that he gets the point, the subject of discourse is no longer of any interest—good, bad, or peculiar—to him.

When I spoke of the **"The Pale Pink Roast"** earlier, I said that the interchange between Anna and Peter came virtually at the end of the story. In fact, there is a little more, as if Paley legitimately wanted to question the continuation of the story, to know "what's gonna happen next."

> Anna was crying. "I really mean it, Peter, I did it for love."
>
> "Love?" he asked. "Really?" He smiled. He was embarrassed but happy. . . .
>
> In no time at all his cheerful face appeared at the door of the spring dusk. In the street among peaceable strangers he did a handstand. Then easy and impervious, in full control, he cartwheeled eastward into the source of night.

At the end Peter regains control and dances off. Paley, then, combines endings: Peter's understanding that he is loved, that love itself is a commodity, a thing to be possessed, and that he will continue to be sure and full of himself; and a second ending showing us—asking us to hear—the marriage of Anna and Peter, the play of love between people, the possibility of happiness beyond the comedy of social relations. Anna did indeed give him a gift of love, one that is repeated throughout Paley's stories; yet it is a gift that Peter, full of himself, cannot see as something other than what he is to himself, a sign for his meaning. Lacking the generosity of spirit most of Paley's women exhibit, Peter cannot see that love is an exchange of experiences.

> Every animal, including *la bête philosophe,* strives instinctively for the optimum conditions under which it may release its powers. Every animal, instinctively, and with a subtle flair that leaves reason far behind, abhors all interference that might conceivably block its path to that optimum. (The path I am speaking of does not lead to "happiness" but to power, to the most energetic activity, and in a majority of cases to actual unhappiness.) Thus the philosopher abhors marriage and all that would persuade him to marriage, for he sees the married state as an obstacle to fulfillment. What great philosopher has ever been married?
>
> —Friedrich Nietzsche
>
> All that is really necessary for the survival of the fittest, it seems, is an interest in life, good, bad, or peculiar.
>
> —Grace Paley

If, as I have been arguing, Paley describes a source of authority in her authorship, her storytelling, that is different from the authority of dying described by Benjamin, then some important questions still remain: What difference does this make for her narratives? How does this difference arise? What—to ask the novelist's question—does it mean? Benjamin begins his essay by lamenting the fact that "the art of storytelling is coming to an end":

> Less and less frequently do we encounter people with the ability to tell a tale properly. More and more often there is embarrassment all around when the wish to hear a story is expressed. It is as if something that seemed inalienable to us, the securest among our possessions, were taken from us: the ability to exchange experiences.
>
> One reason for this phenomenon is obvious: experience has fallen in value. And it looks as if it is continuing to fall into bottomlessness.

For Benjamin the loss of the value of experience is directly related to the need to explain experience that I have already discussed. Although Benjamin does not say so, this loss is directly related to the will to power articulated by Nietzsche in the [above epigraph]. . . . Paley is trying to achieve something other than power and explanation; she is "trying," as she says, "to show how mysterious ordinary life is." To this end her stories have to reconceive experience beyond (or before) a sense of power and closure. They are her attempt, in a way richer than Benjamin's deathbed scene suggests, to exchange experiences.

For Paley such exchanges are ongoing—stories go on and it is legitimate to ask how they continue. Thus **"An Interest in Life"**—told in Ginny's voice—is repeated in the voice of Mrs. Raftery in a later story, **"Distance."** In the earlier story Ginny's husband has left her with three children and she begins to have an affair, as we have seen, with Mrs. Raftery's married son, John. At one point, speaking of her husband, she articulates the problem we are addressing here, the problem of the ordinary, the difference between the experience of men and women:

> But for his own comfort, he should have done better lifewise and moneywise. I was happy, but I am now in possession of knowledge that this is wrong. Happiness isn't so bad for a woman. She gets fatter, she gets older, she could lie down, nuzzling a regiment of men and little kids, she could just die of the pleasure. But men are different, they have to own money, or they have to be famous, or everybody on the block has to look up to them from the cellar stairs.
>
> A woman counts her children and acts snotty, like she invented life, but men *must* do well in the world. I know that men are not fooled by being happy.

Articulating the ordinary is altogether different from explaining the world; it is a way, if it is possible, of articulating happiness. Such happiness, as Ginny expresses it, has to do with *others*—with men and kids here—and the recognition that they are, in fact, here. Rather than the egotism of being looked up to—and the supreme egotism of meaning and truth—there is something else; nuzzling, pleasure, the invention of life.

Yet why should woman be distinguished from man in relation to happiness? The difference, as I have suggested, has to do with the recognition of others. Anna and Ginny *recognize* the existence of others in ways that Peter, Mrs. Raftery, and Benjamin's novelists do not. They recognize that their experience is not necessarily *all* experience, that the "truth" cannot be *one*. . . . When asked whether writing is aggressive, Paley said that telling a story is "bringing lives together and speaking for groups of people, not for one person. . . . But mostly, when you're doing something worthwhile . . . you're really illuminating a dark object, or person, or fact." Illumination rather than explanation is her aim, and it produces a kind of invention of life.

This invention is not possession. After John fails to visit,

Ginny thinks, "I had to give him up after two weeks' absence and no word. I didn't know how to tell the children; something about right and wrong, goodness and meanness, men and women. I had it all at my finger tips, ready to hand over. But I didn't think I ought to take mistakes and truth away from them. Who knows? They might make a truer friend in this world somewhere than I have ever made. So I just put them to bed and sat in the kitchen and cried." Ginny can explain her experience, but she knows, or hopes, that there are other explanations, different experiences. That is, she hopes for the play of voices, for the possibility—fulfilled in **"An Interest in Life"**—of an enormous change.

The play of voices in Paley's stories offers what could be called, following Socrates and Kierkegaard, the maieutic function of discourse, the role of the midwife in the dialectic of (in Paley's words) "two events or two characters or two winds or two different weathers or two ideas or whatever bumping into each other" in stories. Such a maieutic function has the authority of transmission, but its aim, as Kierkegaard says, is ("*without authority* to call attention") to be an occasion for "upbringing and development." Such storytelling radically depends on the listener. "I think what you're forgetting," Paley answered William Gass [in *Shenandoah* XXVII, 1976; see Further Reading],

> what you're underestimating, are the readers. It's true to write one part of that town but they bring something to it and they hear and they understand and they make that whole town and that's what happens when you write. . . .
>
> GASS: What I mean by this is that I don't want the reader filling in anything behind the language.
>
> PALEY: Right, that's what's wrong with you. You don't leave him enough space to move around.

It is room that Ginny wants for her children, room for play, for happiness beyond (or within) the plottedness of the world; she prefers a sense of time—pleasure, nuzzling, happiness, or simply interest—as a kind of radiation outside of plottedness. She is fooled by an interest in the surface of life because she recognizes others, because, perhaps, she possesses that authority (which Benjamin overlooks) inherent in giving birth. Pertinently, Jane Gallop has recently written of "the mother's dilemma": "the experience of an internal heterogeneity which she cannot command." "The experience of motherhood," Gallop continues, "is not the phallic experience that the child supposes it to be. Rather it is an experience of vulnerability—'in a body there is grafted, unmasterable, an other.' . . . 'In a body' that the woman is accustomed to think of as her own, there is an other which cannot be hers. The mother calls herself as totality, as self, into question because within 'her' is something she does not encompass that goes beyond her, is other. This experience, Kristeva thinks, might prepare her for a general, 'permanent calling into question.' "

This embedded otherness, this calling into question, is achieved in Paley's storytelling through its ability to be retold again and again and repeatedly made meaningful for both its teller and its future teller, its listener. Ginny does not want to explain the world to her children because hers might not be the only world, and to explain it is to close "the open destiny of life." In retelling the same story, Mrs. Raftery is faced with things—the noisiness of love, the speediness of life—that she cannot explain.

Such a conception of storytelling necessarily involves a reconception of narrative economy and narrative temporality. As Kathleen Hulley has written of Paley's stories,

> Now, there are a number of interesting technical strategies occurring here: If on the surface her text seems ordinary, unthreatening, untheoretical, it is nevertheless true that she "leaves everything out." The world evoked is so fully conceived, so solidly physical that we hardly notice that the text is without narrative center, that time and space float to us not from hidden depths, but upon surfaces which disturb our conventions of solidity and reflection. . . .
>
> By leaving no behind or underneath to her telling, Paley performs the scene of writing. Truth is not veiled, yet it is a woman.

What Paley leaves out is the symbolical self-reference of the novelist, the psychological analysis that is precluded by the chaste compactness of storytelling. In its stead is the surface of the world, the play of happiness. Consider Nietzsche's remark that "all people who have depth find happiness in being for once like flying fish, playing on the peaks of waves; what they consider best in things is that they have surface: their skin-coveredness." The world is solid because it is "other"—because Ginny can conceive of another, because beneath her skin has been another. The people of Paley's fiction are born into a world separate from themselves, even when, like Mrs. Raftery or Peter, they take themselves as the sole measure of their experience.

And more importantly, they are born into time. Time is not a line, as the father in **"A Conversation with My Father"** wants; it is not a thing to be manipulated, or saved, or, as Peter suggests, "rewarded." Rather, time, like happiness, is lived, as Ginny says, "good, bad or peculiar" by a particular individual and contains a particular value. "I tend not to look at things psychologically, but historically," Paley has said, and by this she means she has eschewed the symbol for the surface relationships, the meaning for the person. The time of her stories is the time of voices—digressive, nonlinear, recognizing a listener as an other as well as *evaluating* time. Pertinently, Kierkegaard too attempts to conceive of time, not as a "spatializing model" that reifies and commodifies time, but in a sense of "lived-time." This spatialized model "allows for the 'placing' of events in spatial relation but does not allow for judgment of their value". . . . To follow a linear plot is to assume that all time is equal—points on a line in the "spatialized" model. It assumes the necessity of putting "Finis," or the "The End," of which the narrator's father so approves in **"A Conversation with My Father,"** in a narrative because no ongoing authority marks the ending.

Because Paley attempts to narrate lived-time, because in her stories she attempts to exchange experiences, she marks their endings, as we have seen, with little disturbances that are also enormous changes, both of which catch in her throat. Both can register in a voice because her time is the lived coherence of past, present, and future—of generations—rather than the plotted differences of homogenized time. Thus **"Enormous Changes at the Last Minute,"** a story that places Alexandra between her dying father and her young, hippy lover, ends with the birth of Alexandra's illegitimate son and her lover's song of praise that "was responsible for a statistical increase in visitors to old-age homes by the apprehensive middle-aged and the astonished young." This story brings the times of these generations together with a sleight of hand that saves Alexandra's father from a "novelistic" ruination of "his interesting life at the very end of it when ruin is absolutely retroactive." Paley saves the situation and at the same time narrates the kind of lived-time of which Kierkegaard speaks by substituting a birth for the dying implied by the temporal logic of the story. In doing so she also defines, I think, the kind of "happiness" that Ginny describes: "Alexandra's father's life was not ruined, nor did he have to die. Shortly before the baby's birth, he fell hard on the bathroom tiles, cracked his skull, dipped the wires of his brain into his heart's blood. Short circuit! He lost twenty, thirty years in the flood, the faces of nephews, in-laws, the names of two Presidents, and a war. His eyes were rounder, he was often awestruck, but he was smart as ever, and able to begin again with fewer scruples to notice and appreciate."

When Mrs. Raftery notices how much younger than she Ginny is, she thinks "all of a sudden they look at you, and then it comes to them, young people, they are bound to outlast you, so they temper up their icy steel and stare into about an inch away from you a lot." Here Mrs. Raftery's conception of time is the same as that of Peter, for whom the crises of linear time—marriage, divorce, remarriage—define and explain experience, even love. In the end Alexandra's father's accident short-circuits the linear circuit of time and allows him to understand and live—in a way Mrs. Raftery cannot—the coherence of generations; he seems a newborn playing and bearing children. The accident allows him to realize that real life is transmissible in a way different from Benjamin's notion of bequeathment. If deathbeds provide the authoritative legacies that are sources of stories, real life also provides the different authority of that other ordinary, yet mysterious event of giving birth to and conceiving—and conceiving of—another, which Paley recovers and articulates in her work. The generosity of Paley's storytelling goes further than the legacy of wisdom and knowledge Benjamin describes by transforming the authority and form of stories and offering possibilities—articulations—of change and love and happiness in the ordinary goings-on of life. (pp. 33-46)

Ronald Schleifer, "Grace Paley: Chaste Compactness," in Contemporary American Women Writers: Narrative Strategies, *edited by Catherine Rainwater and William J. Scheick, The University Press of Kentucky, 1985, pp. 31-48.*

Laura Tracy (essay date 1988)

[In the following excerpt, Tracy discusses the authority of the narrator and the role of the reader in "Love" and "Somewhere Else."]

Although Paley . . . works with narrative structures denying closure and emphasizing ambiguity, she includes technical changes which explicitly function to deauthorize the narrator and almost demand the reader's collaboration in constructing the textual world. That is, Paley . . . explicitly defines life as the art of fiction, finding in that conjunction the affirmation of continuous creation.

Paley has published three collections of short stories, each of which functions in some way as a unified text. I chose for critical interpretation her most recent collection, ***Later the Same Day*** (although, as its title implies, this last group of stories is connected through character and narrative design to both of the earlier books). It is extraordinarily difficult to summarize the plot structures of any of the stories in Paley's work. This difficulty is itself evidence of Paley's emphatic lack of closure. For example, the first story in the collection is titled **"Love."** Only five pages long, it moves from the interior meditation of an unnamed female narrator; through exterior dialogue, not defined by quotation marks, between the narrator and her husband; back into interior reflection; through a limited third-person perspective; and concludes with a sentence spoken by the narrator's husband.

The plot, then, is not a movement from event to event but a movement among and between narrating perspectives that wander freely in past, present, future, and "fictional" time, the latter as the narrator and her husband create stories to represent their emotional reality. Although **"Love"** focuses on the female narrative voice, her perspective is one among several, constantly undermined by her own willingness to suspend narrative authority, freely conceding that her "plot" is dialogue. The reader addressed by this story is given no formal place to lodge; the reader, like the narrator, finds a traditionally fixed position made fluid, transformed into the process of recognition. For example, returning home after a brief shopping trip, the narrator describes her encounter with an old friend, more recently a new enemy. Her husband responds: "Well of course, he said. Don't you know? The smile was for Margaret but really you do miss Louise a lot and the kiss was for Louise. We both said, 'Ah!' Then we talked over the way the SALT treaty looked more like a floor than a ceiling, read a poem written by one of his daughters, looked at a TV show telling the destruction of the European textile industry, and then made love." In this short paragraph the reader is located at the conjunction between the fluid conversation and the moment of emotional revelation—"Ah!"—invited both to participate in epiphany and to rest in the mundane events of "real" time that are always the aftermath of illumination, the real life which supports and is supported by revelation. The paragraph enables the reader to participate in art *and* in life.

"Love" is a love story because it describes the way a loving relationship is lived. With its title, it also acts as an implied corrective to cultural fantasies which define love stories as tales of romance. Because **"Love"** is so unromantic, it permits its reader both to make visible cultural structures that authorize literary traditions of the romantic and to draw an interesting analogy between cultural suppression of women and narrative suppression of the reader. In both suppressions, free use of the imagination to create alternative fictions representing an experiential reality is severely curtailed. In seeking to restore and revalue female imagination, Paley's work offers her reader an opportunity for creative free play, for her text can be unified only with the addition of the reader who will respond to textual strategies that subvert traditional literary patterns; Paley's reader must grapple with the real, rather than the ideal, object.

Although two of Paley's subversive techniques are relatively facile—the absence of quotation marks to separate speaking characters and the use of titles that refer the reader forward and back in the collection—in Paley's work these devices are used as first-level teaching codes for her reader. Paley does not use an experimental technique to defamiliarize the reader; instead, her effort is to give the reader creative confidence which she will, at another textual level, call upon as a resource for a larger, more significant collaboration between reader and writer.

The absence of quotation marks is general throughout her volume. By omitting textual signifiers noting separation, Paley emphasizes fluid boundaries between characters, and that fluidity requires the reader to pay close attention to the text at its simplest level. Who said what becomes a process of reader collaboration, reflecting the collaborative quality of the conversations in which no particular speaker is empowered, where each statement is vital only because it engenders response. With this technique, of course, Paley alludes to the structure of a cooperative female culture existing subversively within the larger patriarchal social order. The fluid conversations reflect Chodorow's work on the psychodynamic development of the female ego; because of gender coincidence, the little girl's ego structures never entirely separate from the mother identification. Thus women find most comfortable relationships that emphasize connection and cooperation, whereas men, whose ego development depends on separation, are generally more at ease in relationships structured to emphasize hierarchy and distance.

If Paley's work merely valorized the feminine against the masculine model, however, it would retain didactic importance but lose psychological significance for the reader, who would be requested to accept another sort of subordinate position, that of the student of an ideology enforced in an old authoritarian way. Such an assertion of feminist ideas would deny its own effort. Instead, Paley undermines ideology by scrutinizing the act of interpretation, which she implies is the act of distorting fiction according to personal and cultural needs and desires: "In this simple way the lifelong past is invented, which, as we know, thickens the present and gives all kinds of advice to the future." That is, "in this simple way," Paley ironically comments on the reader's effort to interpret the text, to make a fiction out of another fiction. Defining the act of reading as an act of fiction making makes visible, and therefore simultaneously undermines as it affirms, both the writer's and the reader's unconscious transference. Given that transference *is* the unconscious act of making fictions, explicitly defining interpretation as fiction denies the content of transference while paradoxically validating its process. Moreover, Paley almost demands that her readers interpret her elusive stories—two of which are titled **"The Story Hearer"** and **"Listening,"** titles literally directing the reader's activity—but emphasizes that the reader's interpretations must be as fluid as the conversations shared by her characters. In particular, the story titled **"Somewhere Else"** makes this effort to explore the rigid content of unconscious transference by insisting that it is a distorting lens. At the same time, the story affirms the continuous necessity for the process of fiction by juxtaposing two central images.

Like several of her other stories, **"Somewhere Else"** is a two-part story, designed so that each section comments on the other. In the first section, twenty-two Americans are touring China. They all are devoted to Chinese culture and politics, all in their forties and fifties, all experiencing the trip as the culmination of a life-long fantasy. Their intention is to love the Chinese people, on whom they have transferred all their aspirations, ideals, and desires for radical change in their own country. Paley, of course, is well aware of the fiction-making process her Americans bring to China, a realization she signals to the reader when the tourists find they have violated a crucial Chinese precept: "We took too many photographs. We had learned how to say hello, goodbye, may I take your photograph? Frequently the people did not wish to be photographed." Taking photographs, as both the Chinese and the Americans understand, is an act of interpretation. The frozen images will be used in a larger process of making political interpretations, just as their memories, frozen internal portraits, will be used to construct the fiction of China they will bring back to America when the trip concludes.

The Chinese tour guide and political counselor accuses the group of taking, without permission, the picture of a "lower middle peasant lugging a two wheel cart full of country produce into the city. A boy had been sleeping on top." According to Paley's American narrator: "Ah, what a picture! China! The heavy cart, the toiling man, the narrow street. . . . In the foreground the photographed man labored—probably bringing early spring vegetables to some distant neighborhood in order to carry back to his commune honey buckets of the city's stinking gold." By juxtaposing the Chinese guide's straightforward language with the narrator's ironically romantic interpretation of the picture, Paley subtly undermines the content of the photograph, implying that the camera lens inevitably distorts because omitted from the photograph is the context of its taking. Where is the photographer? What were his or her intentions when the picture was snapped? What is the nature of the relationship between photographer and subject? The fixed photograph transforms the subject of the picture into an object represented *by* the picture, and in so doing, it denies dialogue. The peasant has become an object of interpretation, an object of fictional transference.

In the second section of the story, however, Paley affirms the process of making fiction, which she here translates into the process of taking photographs. Although unconsciously transferred needs, desires, and conflicts inevitably distort connections between and among human subjects, transference as an emotional metaphor signals the human desire for connection and community. Seeking to enter the world as a human subject, the self uses transference needs to make the world like itself. Ironically, the content of transferred fantasies, like the finished photograph, omits to scrutinize the relationship. Acting on the content of transference inevitably transforms the other into an object to be interpreted according to individually transferred needs. But just as the desire to take the picture of another subject—to transfer fantasies—is the desire for connection, so the process of making fiction, for Paley, becomes the desire—inevitably distorted—to make connection, to return the other to the status of human subject relating to the self as another human subject. In this effort Paley alludes to what Keller has defined as dynamic objectivity, "a form of knowledge that grants to the world around us its independent integrity but does so in a way that remains cognizant of, indeed relies on, our connectivity with that world. In this, dynamic objectivity is not unlike empathy, a form of knowledge of other persons that draws explicitly on the commonality of feelings and experience in order to enrich one's understanding of another in his or her own right."

In the second section of the story, Paley uses the image of a photograph *not* taken to illuminate dynamic objectivity. Joe Larson, one of the group of former tourists, now all returned to America, is on his way to a reunion at which the Chinese photographs will be shown. Joe has been working with a youth group, reclaiming devastated buildings in the South Bronx ghetto. He has also been filming the work—"Maybe just to keep a record." Walking back to the subway, a detail indicating that he is just as much a foreign presence in the South Bronx as he was in China, Joe pauses for one last long pan shot of the building he and his group have spent the day reconstructing. The shot unintentionally takes in "a group of guys on one of the stoops." Joe feels uncomfortable enough about including human subjects in the photograph to move with increased speed toward his subway entrance. Suddenly, he hears a running thud. "A human form flew past me, ripping the musette bag [with the film inside] off my shoulder."

Unable to accept the loss of his film, but perhaps even more unable to leave the area without attempting to explain and apologize, Joe approaches the group of Puerto Rican men to which the thief has retreated. There, he sees the film taken out of the camera, unraveled, and destroyed. At this point, the thieves demonstrate that their action was a political gesture. They return the empty camera. Joe protests: "Here, you take the camera. No, no, said the leader. Take it, I said. No, no—you crazy, man? Listen, take it, use it. We'll come over and help you out. You can make a movie. . . . I shoved the camera into their hands. I walked away fast. And here I am—that's all there is. What do you think?"

Although Joe's final question is delivered to his friends, the former Chinese tourists, it also functions as a direct address to Paley's reader. "What do you think?" invites her reader to project an interpretation, a photograph, onto an image inviting such projection precisely because Joe's photograph has been destroyed. In its absence, the photograph Joe attempted to take provides the open creative arena for character and reader to converse, to create together a visibly fictional conclusion to Joe's adventure. Juxtaposed to the earlier photograph of the Chinese laborer and coupled with the latter's ironic interpretation by Paley's narrator, Joe's absent photograph affirms the process of fiction making in contrast to the interpreted story. In so doing, the two images affirm the desire for human connection inherent in the transference phenomenon; the interpreted photograph of the Chinese laborer bears witness to the distorted uses fantasy makes of reality, while the absent photograph denies distortion by insisting on dialogue. As with her technical decision to abandon quotation marks, the two images emphasize Paley's determination to collaborate with her reader. Implying that the point of her text is its function as a ground upon which she and her real reader can meet, Paley also implies that such a meeting is possible only when interpretation is understood to close off the process of fiction, a process which, finally, grants to both reader and writer the possibility of empathy, the potential to recognize the other as other because the self, by denying the interpreted photograph, has become visible to itself by making transference conscious. (pp. 200-06)

Laura Tracy, in a conclusion to her "Catching the Drift": Authority, Gender, and Narrative Strategy in Fiction, *Rutgers University Press, 1988, pp. 188-206.*

FURTHER READING

Baba, Minako. "Faith Darwin as Writer-Heroine: A Study of Grace Paley's Short Stories." *Studies in American Jewish Literature* 7, No. 1 (Spring 1988): 40-54.

Analyzes Paley's recurring protagonist Faith Darwin and evaluates "the achievement of Paley's artistic vision . . . , that rare combination of humanistic concerns and novelistic attention."

Delta 14 (May 1982).

Issue devoted to Paley containing critical essays, an interview, and her story "Lavinia: An Old Story." Among the critical pieces are Kathleen Hulley's introductory essay "Grace Paley's Resistant Forms," Harry Blake's "Grace Paley: A Plea for English Writing," and Joyce Meier's "The Subversion of the Father in the Tales of Grace Paley."

Gelfant, Blanche. "Grace Paley: Fragments for a Portrait in Collage." *New England Review* 3, No. 2 (Winter 1980): 276-93.

Reminisces about encounters with Paley, as well as offering a critical overview of her works and a fragment of an interview.

Gold, Ivan. "On Having Grace Paley Once More among

Us." *Commonweal* LXXXIX, No. 4 (25 October 1968): 111-12.

Discusses the reissue of *The Little Disturbances of Man.*

Harris, Robert R. "Pacifists with Their Dukes Up." *The New York Times Book Review* (14 April 1985): 7.

Review of *Later the Same Day* and brief interview with Paley.

Iannone, Carol. "A Dissent on Grace Paley." *Commentary* 80, No. 2 (August 1985): 54-8.

Criticizes Paley's prose style and political stances, arguing that her stories are vague and her characters are weakly drawn.

Kamel, Rose. "To Aggravate the Conscience: Grace Paley's Loud Voice." *The Journal of Ethnic Studies* 11, No. 3 (Fall 1983): 29-49.

Discusses Paley's female narrators and their rejection of traditional gender roles and morality.

Klinkowitz, Jerome. "Grace Paley: The Sociology of Metafiction." In his *Literary Subversions: New American Fiction and the Practice of Criticism,* pp. 70-7. Carbondale and Edwardsville: Southern Illinois University Press, 1985.

Explores Paley's use of metafictional techniques and unusual narrative styles, concluding that she uses these devices to rejuvenate traditional subject matter.

Mickelson, Anne Z. "Piecemeal Liberation: Marge Piercy, Sara Davidson, Marilyn French, Grace Paley." In her *Reaching Out: Sensitivity and Order in Recent American Fiction by Women,* pp. 175-234. Metuchen, N.J.: The Scarecrow Press, 1979.

Analyzes Paley's female characters and feminist viewpoints in her fiction.

Midwood, Barton. "Short Visits with Five Writers and One Friend." *Esquire* LXXIV, No. 5 (November 1970): 150-53.

Brief character sketch of Paley noting her anti-Vietnam War protests and including her comments on the writing of Donald Barthelme.

Neff, D. S. " 'Extraordinary Means': Healers and Healing in 'A Conversation with My Father.' " In *Images of Healers.* Literature and Medicine, edited by Anne Hudson Jones, Vol. 2, pp. 118-24. Albany: State University of New York Press, 1983.

Examines the treatment of death in Paley's story "A Conversation with My Father," concluding that "the living and the dying in 'A Conversation with My Father' never fully understand each other, but it is the initiative shown by both parties that matters."

Paley, Grace. "A Conversation." *ACM: Another Chicago Magazine* 14 (1985): 100-14.

Discusses a variety of social and literary topics with Barry Sileski, Robin Hemley, and Sharon Solwitz.

"A Symposium on Fiction." *Shenandoah* XXVII, No. 2 (Winter 1976): 3-31.

Transcript of a symposium on contemporary fiction featuring Paley, Donald Barthelme, William Gass, and Walker Percy.

"Grace Paley." *South Dakota Review* 13, No. 2 (Autumn 1975): 10-11.

Paley's response to a questionnaire on the significance of regionality in writing, in which she says that her work is influenced by New York to a "large extent."

Suárez-Lafuente, Maria. "The Contemporary Disruption in Grace Paley's Narrative." In *Cross-Cultural Studies: American, Canadian, and European Literatures: 1945-1985,* edited by Mirko Jurak, pp. 171-76. Ljubljana, Yugoslavia: The English Department, Filozofska fakulteta, Edvard Kardelj University of Ljubljana, 1988.

Discusses attempts to combat suffering through communality in stories by Paley.

Swados, Harvey. "Good and Short." *The Hudson Review* XII, No. 3 (Autumn 1959): 454-59.

Favorable review of *The Little Disturbances of Man.*

Taylor, Jacqueline. "Grace Paley on Storytelling and Story Hearing." *Literature in Performance* 7, No. 2 (April 1987): 46-58.

Interview with Paley in which she discusses her work in the context of oral storytelling traditions.

Kurt Vonnegut, Jr.

1922-

American novelist, short story writer, dramatist, scriptwriter, and essayist.

An important figure in contemporary literature, Vonnegut uses satire, irony, and iconoclastic humor to raise philosophic questions about the validity of modern institutions, ideals, and values. Although his novels, which include *Cat's Cradle* and *Slaughterhouse-Five,* have gained wider recognition than his short fiction, Vonnegut's stories are valued for their insights into his longer fiction and for their use of recurring settings and characters from his novels. Although characterized at various stages in his career as a science fiction writer, a black humorist, a fantasist, and a postmodernist, Vonnegut commonly uses elements from all these modes in his writing. He is particularly noted for his deadpan narrative style, which typically features puns, aphorisms, slapstick, running gags, and self-effacing humor. His themes include lovelessness and the human need for compassion, the importance of declining middle-class values in modern society, and the dangers inherent in conformism, institutional control, and simplistic solutions to complex problems.

Vonnegut grew up during the Depression as a member of a large middle-class family in Indianapolis. His relatively secure lifestyle was drastically altered following his experience as a soldier in the United States armed forces in World War II. Like the protagonist of his novel *Slaughterhouse-Five,* Vonnegut was captured by German forces and interned as a prisoner of war in Dresden, Germany. Ensconced in a meat storage shelter below a slaughterhouse, Vonnegut survived the Allied firebombing of Dresden, a city that proved to be of dubious military and strategic value. After the bombing Vonnegut was forced to dig corpses out of the rubble, and as a result of the entire affair he suffered guilt and mental anguish. Describing himself as a "total pessimist," Vonnegut later asserted in his fiction that humanity is inherently self-destructive and existence is a "higgledy-piggledy cultural smorgasbord" that ends only in death. Despite his caustic message, however, Vonnegut tempers his commentary with compassion for his characters, suggesting that humanity's ability to love may partially compensate for its destructive tendencies.

Following World War II, Vonnegut moved to Schenectady, New York, where he worked briefly as a public relations representative for General Electric; he quit this job in the late 1940s, determined to become a writer. Vonnegut's stories appeared in such diverse publications as *Collier's, Redbook,* the *New Yorker, Playboy,* and the *Saturday Evening Post,* and during the 1960s his underground popularity, particularly among college students enchanted by his novels, prompted the republication of approximately half of his short stories in *Canary in a Cat House.* This collection was later expanded as *Welcome to the Monkey House,* a volume containing what Vonnegut described in his preface as "samples of work I sold in order to finance the writing of the novels." Vonnegut virtually stopped writing short stories after the 1960s, devoting himself instead to his novels.

Many of Vonnegut's stories feature contemporary settings and affirm middle-class values by focusing on unexceptional characters whose claims of wealth and respectability prove unsatisfying or illusory. In "Bagombo Snuff Box," for example, a man attempts to impress a former lover by presenting her with a purportedly valuable trinket that is revealed to be counterfeit; in "A Night for Love," a man of limited resources worries that his wife might have been happier with a previous, more wealthy suitor until he learns that his would-be rival is solely concerned with his career. The superiority of middle-class values pervades many of Vonnegut's contemporary stories, which often center upon narrators who deal with emotional problems by adopting roles. In "The Foster Portfolio," a bookkeeper refuses to cash in an extensive stock portfolio he inherited from his profligate father, a musician who abandoned his wife and son, on the grounds that the money is tainted. He instead moonlights as a musician to support his own family, thereby satisfying his domestic responsibilities and paying penance for his father's irresponsibility. Among Vonnegut's pieces are also several sentimental yet gently satirical love stories, including "Who Am I This Time," a story originally published as "My Name Is Everyone." In this piece, a shy clerk who expresses himself only when portraying characters in a local drama group finds his perfect mate, a young actress who is also lacking in personality.

Another group of Vonnegut's stories superficially utilize such science fiction elements as time travel and futuristic situations and discoveries to comment upon trends in contemporary society, both liberal and conservative. These stories are generally among the most frequently discussed works in Vonnegut's short fiction oeuvre. "Harrison Bergeron," for example, is set in an unspecified future in which the "United States Handicapper General" strictly enforces the liberal ideal of human equality by forcing attractive people to wear masks, the graceful or strong to wear weights, and the intelligent to be periodically disoriented by devices implanted in their heads that broadcast cannon shots and other alarming noises. While Vonnegut seems to be overtly denouncing conservative government control, Larry L. King pointed out an alternate interpretation: "I know nothing of Mr. Vonnegut's personal politics, but extant Goldwaterites or Dixiecrats might read into this the ultimate horrors of any further extension of civil-rights or equal opportunity laws."

Many critics have asserted that Vonnegut's uncollected short stories as well as those collected in *Welcome to the Monkey House* reveal customary weaknesses of writing for commercial markets—slick, often facile prose, underdeveloped story lines, and an irregularity caused by tailoring pieces to the audiences of different magazines. Some scholars, however, have defended these pieces as consistent with Vonnegut's novels, maintaining that they make similarly effective use of iconoclastic humor and science fiction elements to comment on contemporary society.

(For further information on Vonnegut's life and career, see *Contemporary Literary Criticism,* Vols. 1, 2, 3, 4, 5, 8, 12, 22, 40, 60; *Contemporary Authors,* Vols. 1-4, rev. ed.; *Contemporary Authors New Revision Series,* Vols. 1, 25; *Dictionary of Literary Biography,* Vols. 2, 8; *Dictionary of Literary Biography Yearbook: 1980; Dictionary of Literary Biography Documentary Series,* Vol. 3; and *Concise Dictionary of American Literary Biography: 1968-1988.*)

PRINCIPAL WORKS

SHORT FICTION

Canary in a Cat House 1963; also published as *Welcome to the Monkey House: A Collection of Short Works* [enlarged edition], 1968

OTHER MAJOR WORKS

Player Piano (novel) 1952; republished as *Utopia 14,* 1954
Mother Night (novel) 1962
Cat's Cradle (novel) 1963
God Bless You, Mr. Rosewater; or, Pearls before Swine (novel) 1965
Slaughterhouse-Five; or, The Children's Crusade: A Duty-Dance with Death (novel) 1969
Breakfast of Champions; or, Goodbye Blue Monday (novel) 1973
Wampeters, Foma & Granfalloons: Opinions (essays) 1974
Slapstick; or, Lonesome No More (novel) 1976
Palm Sunday: An Autobiographical Collage (reviews, essays, interview, speeches, and reflections) 1981
Galápagos (novel) 1985
Bluebeard (novel) 1987
Hocus Pocus (novel) 1990

Mitchel Levitas (essay date 1968)

[*In the following review of* Welcome to the Monkey House, *Levitas separates Vonnegut's stories into two categories: those that make use of contemporary settings and those that belong to the genre of science fiction.*]

[In 1967], when *The New York Times Book Review* asked a pride of distinguished novelists which of their works they would most like to reread while lolling among the sand castles, Kurt Vonnegut Jr. replied, disarmingly: "I can't stand to read what I write. I make my wife do that, then ask her to keep her opinions to herself." Diogenes would have shucked his barrel for honesty such as that. Nor was the remark a momentary lapse of candor. In his preface to ***Welcome to the Monkey House*** . . . [(see Further Reading), Vonnegut] again smiles and tells it straight.

"The contents of this book," he says with good-natured detachment, "are samples of work I sold in order to finance the writing of the novels. Here one finds the fruits of Free Enterprise." Well, to paraphrase Lamont Cranston, "the seeds of Free Enterprise bear bitter fruit."

From *Collier's,* a conspicuous failure of our capitalist magazine economy, comes the largest harvest of stories (seven) and the earliest. The oldest saw print in the faraway year of 1950. From *Playboy,* a heart-warming success story of competition in the marketplace, comes the title story, published this year. Between these dead and thriving examples of what turns a freelancer's heart to pulp, readers will also find represented *Esquire,* the *Saturday Evening Post, Cosmopolitan, Venture, Galaxy,* and *Fantasy and Science Fiction Magazine.* Plus, as a bonus,

> In honor of the marriage that worked I include in this collection [**"The Long Walk to Forever"**], a sickeningly slick love story from *The Ladies Home Journal,* God help us. . . . It describes an afternoon I spent with my wife-to-be. Shame, shame, to have lived scenes from a woman's magazine.

This Vonnegut is obviously a lovable fellow. Moreover, he's right about the story, which is indeed a sickening and slick little nothing about a soldier who goes A.W.O.L. in order—How to say it?—to sweep his girl from the steps of the altar into his strong and loving arms.

When not in love, Vonnegut's stories fall into two general classifications. One uses contemporary settings, smoothly and mechanically plotted down to the obligatory twist near the finale and featuring easily recognizable types: the rich, stuffy benefactor of a prep school who tries to wangle the admission of his nice-but-not-too-bright son; a neighbor obsessed with the exciting idea of home decoration and furnishing; a vicious juvenile delinquent saved by a high school band teacher's therapy ("Love yourself, and make your instrument sing about it."). A subcategory of this group, if you're still interested, often takes place on Cape Cod—Vonnegut lives in Barnstable—and describes the encounters of simple folk in unlikely circumstances. A shy clerk comes commandingly alive only as an actor in amateur theatricals. A salesman of storm windows and bathtub enclosures tells tales of a few high and mighty who have been his customers.

Vonnegut's other favorite bag is science fiction, a genre usually marked by a weakness of real characters and the pronouncement of human messages. Here, the message is crisply transmitted and often with humor in stories about a world without war, achieved by a single scientist's powers of concentration; life without fear, won by freeing the spirit from the body; and the realization of instant, synthetic happiness by tuning in on the radio waves of distant stars with a "euphoriaphone." In one of the liveliest sci-fi stories. **"Tomorrow and Tomorrow and Tomorrow,"** the discovery of an anti-aging potion has pushed the world of 2158 to a population of 12 billion, which largely exists on a diet of processed seaweed and sawdust. In the three-room apartment of a housing development that covers what once was southern Connecticut live the children, grandchildren and great-grandchildren of Harold Schwartz, 172. Gramps, a crochety tyrant who is glued to television, barks, "Hell, we did that 100 years ago," and regularly disinherits family grumblers who are restlessly waiting—vainly, it seems—for him to die and vacate the only private bedroom in the place.

[**"Welcome to the Monkey House"**] takes up the same theme, overpopulation, but treats it sententiously. World Government is waging a two-front war on the problem by encouraging "ethical" suicide and by making sex joyless; the latter is accomplished with mandatory pills that numb the body from the waist down. Our hero is Billy the Poet, whose special pleasure is deflowering the Junoesque virgins administering the program and who heads a coeducational underground whose members favor birth control, of course, and aim to revive the hearty sex of their ancestors. Among these forefathers, presumably, is Hugh Hefner of *Playboy,* author of a relentlessly documented "philosophy" that rests on pillars of thought similar to Billy's. With this in mind, how uncharacteristically unkind of Vonnegut to have written on another, earlier, occasion: ". . . the science fiction magazine that pays the most and seems to have the poorest judgment is *Playboy.*"

Mitchel Levitas, "A Slight Case of Candor," in The New York Times, *August 19, 1968, p. 35.*

Charles Nicol (essay date 1968)

[In the following review, Nicol compares Vonnegut's technique in Welcome to the Monkey House *to that of his novels.]*

[In his preface to ***Welcome to the Monkey House*** (see Further Reading), Vonnegut] announces that one of the themes of his novels is "No pain." Kurt Vonnegut, Jr., probably our finest Black Humorist, is offering us comfort.

He is the little Dutch boy stopping the hole in the dike: while he conscientiously aids us, he reminds us that we live in the shadow of deep waters. Or, to use the idea that appears frequently in his work as a main character, a minor figure, part of the background, or the tail of a metaphor, he is the volunteer fireman, unselfishly and innocently rushing to put out the random blazes of civilization. His comforts frighten us with their inadequacy, and we laugh in self-defense.

Vonnegut's special enemies are science, morality, free enterprise, socialism, fascism, Communism, all government—any force in our lives which regards human beings as ciphers. His villains are simple egotists, indifferent to other people, his protagonists men who adapt events to their own discontent with the system, rolling with the times to create change, which is rarely, in Vonnegut's world, an improvement. His third group of characters, his saints, his volunteer firemen, are content to aid others in their own small world, unaware of the larger actions that swirl around them. Failing to participate in events, they nevertheless become the focus of all activity, their relevance being the undeniable fact that they exist.

Vonnegut is a pessimist. But he is also an idealist; his irony is not cynicism. His writing has a disarming directness, and his few statements about style reinforce this simplicity, yet the apparent slickness of his short, tight paragraphs—almost a paradigm of the popular magazine—fails to conceal the size of his concepts. And what appears at first to be gratuitous satire is always integral to the tale.

For instance, [**"Welcome to the Monkey House"**] occurs in an overcrowded world of the future where even Howard Johnson's is nationalized, where, to reverse the population trend, all citizens are required to take pills which make them numb from the waist down. "The pills were ethical because they didn't interfere with a person's ability to reproduce, which would have been unnatural and immoral. All the pills did was take every bit of pleasure out of sex." Curiously, in *God Bless You, Mr. Rosewater,* a novel that Vonnegut wrote several years before the story, this setting is attributed to the inventiveness of an old science-fiction writer named Kilgore Trout, whose "favorite formula was to describe a perfectly hideous society, not unlike his own, and then, toward the end, to suggest ways in which it could be improved."

The story, which first appeared in *Playboy,* climaxes with a rape in the "ancient Kennedy Compound" in Hyannis Port: "On the green cement, in front of the ancient frame houses, were statues representing the fourteen Kennedys who had been Presidents of the United States of the World. They were playing touch football." While recent events have made this scene poignant, its original intention was not so much satire as explanation of the future's quite-acceptable-to-Catholics method of birth control.

Further, that Billy the Poet, the hedonist rebel against the social order, after raping a girl to restore her sensuality, reads her Elizabeth Barrett's "How Do I Love Thee?" sonnet seems a put-on, a cheap irony, or worse, until one realizes that the whole situation of the story comments on the fabled Browning romance. It is not only of interest to psychologists that Elizabeth had been thrown from a horse at puberty and remained an invalid until she married Robert Browning. Freed from her domineering father, she rapidly regained her health on her honeymoon. "What you've been through," says Billy the Poet to his rapee, "is a typical wedding night for a strait-laced girl of a hundred years ago." The poem is functional to the story, for this whole society, numb from the waist down, is more sexually repressed than any Victorian lady poet.

Like the settings of the novels, those of the stories remain close to Vonnegut's own experience. The Kennedys at Hyannis Port, who appear in several stories, are not gratuitous in *that* respect either, for Vonnegut lives on Cape Cod; a nouveau Yankee, he resents the tourists, hot on the Kennedy trail, who despoil his haven. His boyhood home in Indianapolis, the General Electric plant where he was a public relations man, and his new home on Cape Cod—these settings are common to almost all his novels and short stories.

The style may bring to mind another Black Humorist, Terry Southern. But only Southern's filmscript for *Dr. Strangelove* approaches Vonnegut's brilliance. Both authors use the cliché for effect, but where the sardonic Mr. Southern uses the commonplace to reinforce our own complacency, Vonnegut uses it to throw new light on those thoughts which we hoped were *not* ordinary. A cliché is dead language, as when an author deliberately inserts one into the unresisting mouth of a character, he is registering contempt for that character, labeling him dead. In *Cat's Cradle,* a nihilist strangles a cat and hangs a "Meow" sign around its neck. Vonnegut does not find that funny.

Roughly half of Vonnegut's published short stories are included in this collection. It is a good selection, although an unimpressive review of the big Random House dictionary has unaccountably crept in. Vonnegut's writing has only recently brought him a fair amount of success, and these stories occasionally bear the scars of their commercial birth. His predilection for science-fiction modes has limited his acceptability as far as the upper-class journals are concerned. Respectability has its own limitations.

The reader should not expect full-fledged apocalypse from these pleasant tales, only brush fires of varying intensity that a good fireman can handle. "The contents of this book are samples of work I sold in order to finance the writing of the novels." It is a modest and unnecessary disclaimer. (pp. 123-24)

Charles Nicol, "The Volunteer Fireman," in The Atlantic Monthly, *Vol. 222, No. 3, September, 1968, pp. 123-24.*

Larry L. King (essay date 1968)

[*King is an American critic, nonfiction writer, playwright, and novelist. In the following review, King negatively appraises* Welcome to the Monkey House.]

Most collections are little more than old soup warmed over. Possibly a few bridging pages or paragraphs will be added in an effort to spark new flame under the kettle. The literary gourmet will not be fooled, however. Old soup is old soup no matter how you ladle it.

Welcome to the Monkey House fails to enhance Kurt Vonnegut's reputation. There are only brief glimpses of the hilarious, uproarious Vonnegut whose black-logic extensions of today's absurdities into an imagined society of tomorrow at once gives us something to laugh at and much to fear. At his wildest best (as in his earlier *God Bless You, Mr. Rosewater* or in *Cat's Cradle* Kurt Vonnegut is a laughing prophet of doom. Too much of this book—Vonnegut's seventh—is slick, slapdash prose lifted from the pages of magazines of limited distinction. "When I write," the author's preface instructs, "I simply become what I seemingly must become." Those of us living the shoddy life of the freelancer—as Mr. Vonnegut has since 1949—appreciate his message.

For as reluctant as the writer may be to cater to the prejudices of this editor or that magazine, he almost invariably makes certain midnight compromises. Though magazine editors may encourage the writer to "be himself" they usually will bounce his prose back for endless patches or rewrites should he have the audacity to stray too far from certain rigid house concepts. Thus the writer of limited financial means, whose family table depends for meat on his prolific production, can ill afford excessive seizures of artistic integrity. He soon finds himself writing one way for *Harper's,* another way for *Cosmopolitan,* a third way for *Playboy*—becoming, to repeat Mr. Vonnegut, "What I . . . must become." Such literary fluctuations invariably make for uneven reading when bound together between hard covers. (pp. 4-5)

Not all the tender editing, disciplined rewriting or careful planning in the world goes into the average collection. The publisher may have originally opposed the project because he figures to be lucky to get his investment back. Perhaps he consented only to keep his writer reasonably content and in the house stable. His attitude will therefore be tepid. (p. 5)

In such circumstances the writer is largely left to his own devices in pulling the thing together with whatever small effort he is willing to give in the way of selections and new material. In Mr. Vonnegut's case, he was content to write a three-page preface and then, apparently willy-nilly, toss together whatever materials appeared handiest.

Kurt Vonnegut is honest enough not to tell us a sow's ear is a silk purse. "The contents of this book," he writes, "are samples of work I sold in order to finance the writing of the novels. Here one finds the fruits of Free Enterprise." And he quite accurately labels one selection, lifted from one of the more horrid of the "women's magazines," "a sickeningly slick love story."

Some few of the selections are worthwhile. There's a pleasant little essay on the Cape Cod village where the author lives, a funny review of The Random House Dictionary, and some three or four stories dealing competently and wildly with improbable tomorrows. My favorites are these: **"Harrison Bergeron,"** which is set in 2081 when

> everybody was finally equal. They weren't only equal before God and the law, they were equal in every which way. Nobody was smarter than anybody else. Nobody was better looking than anybody else. Nobody was stronger or quicker than anybody else.

To achieve this imperfect perfection, the "United States Handicapper General" decrees each citizen's handicap: beautiful people wear masks; the more intelligent have their thought waves periodically broken by piped-in sirens, cannon shots or other unsettling noises; the strong or the quick wear bags of stones. I know nothing of Mr. Vonnegut's personal politics, but extant Goldwaterites or Dixiecrats might read into this the ultimate horrors of any further extension of civil-rights or equal-opportunity laws. (pp. 5, 19)

[**"Welcome to the Monkey House"**] takes place at a time when the earth is so densely populated as to have inspired "Federal Ethical Suicide Parlors" where world government encourages citizens to report to suicide "Barcaloungers." "Compulsory ethical birth control" is in effect; birth-control pills numb people

> from the waist down. . . . The pills were ethical because they didn't interfere with a person's ability to reproduce, which would be unnatural and immoral. All the pills did was take every bit of pleasure out of sex.

Marvelous! Those who refuse the pills ("nothingheads") are fair game to be shot on sight. The most notorious of these, Billy the Poet, specializes in deflowering cold suicide-parlor hostesses once the numbing effect of their pills wears off. This story should give scant comfort either to puritans or to defenders of Pope Paul's most recent encyclical.

Unhappily, such touches are rare. The rather pitiful state of magazine fiction is what one most remembers about this book. (p. 19)

Larry L. King, "Old Soup," in The New York Times Book Review, *September 1, 1968, pp. 4-5, 19.*

Vonnegut around the time he resigned his position at General Electric and began writing fiction.

Gerard Reedy (essay date 1968)

[In the following review, Reedy praises Vonnegut's stories in Welcome to the Monkey House *for the insights they afford into his novels.]*

Addicts of the slick fiction of Kurt Vonnegut Jr. can find out from [***Welcome to the Monkey House***] how circuitous is the writer's route to his proper *métier.* And this potpourri of early Vonnegut shows a new side to the black humorist—blatant sentimentality. The ultra-cool author of *Cat's Cradle* and *Player Piano* has, one finds, a heart. He blushes this out in the preface to ***Monkey House*** [see Further Reading]: "I include in this collection a sickeningly slick love story from the *Ladies Home Journal,* God help us . . . " He might have said the same about other stories in the collection; for every mad scientist in the volume, there seems to be an ever faithful spouse. The Vonnegut fan is surprised yet pleased by these uncharacteristic exhibitions of emotion. It is like discovering that Dean Rusk sends friendship cards to Uncle Ho.

Vonnegut is at his best in drawing future horrors that have resulted from contemporary liberalisms. Thus in **"Harrison Bergeron"** he conjures up the year 2081, when "everybody was finally equal." One way of establishing this has been that those unequally intelligent, handsome or athletic are ordered to wear a "handicap bag" around the throat; the weight of this, proportionate to the respective talent, is set by the Handicapper General, ruler of the era. It is revealing to contrast his brief treatment of Harrison Bergeron, all-American boy, with other contemporary treatments of the type, like John Updike's and Philip Roth's. Vonnegut does not get as involved as they in extended satire of American types. He is certainly not as serious. A social critic only by indirection, he humorously draws our present idolodulia of technology, progress and equality to the frighteningly logical extreme.

Indicative of the literary experimentation going on in ***Monkey House*** is the variety of first person narrators employed. These are not points of view in the technical sense; they serve as functions of the setting rather than limitations on it. The result, however, makes for fresh reading. The narrator of two stories, a storm window salesman and installer on Cape Cod, manages to get into the house of a Goldwater supporter who lives next door to Kennedys—wherein certainly hangs a tale. Another narrator is a scientist about to inherit the "Barnhouse effect" from his mentor; this will enable him to destroy the armaments of the world. A third, a sociology professor, fights a machine that will tranquilize the neighborhood at the flick of a switch. In these and other stories, one sees Vonnegut's predilection for the mechanical and technological as the symbol for contemporary men, as well as his zany facility in mixing comedy and comment. (pp. 190-91)

[**"Welcome to the Monkey House"**] is something of a letdown. Although the futuristic nightmare is cleverly drawn—one scene takes place in the paved-over Kennedy compound in some future over-populated Hyannis Port—the story, written for *Playboy,* succumbs to Hefneresque special pleading for more relish in sex. Taking on the liberal nostrums he elsewhere derides, Vonnegut destroys with cant his promising *mis-en-scène.*

Vonnegut seems most creatively himself in inventing a situation in which to work. There are no depths of character in these stories; even the plots take second place to the elaborate stage built by the author. He is, of course, tremendously successful at this; the stories are gems, vivid and clear even in their fantasy. In much of ***Monkey House,*** as in his longer fiction, this power of inventing worlds is at its best. (p. 191)

Gerard Reedy, in a review of "Welcome to the Monkey House," in America, *Vol. 119, No. 7, September 14, 1968, pp. 190-91.*

Stanley Schatt (essay date 1976)

[*A distinguished scholar in the fields of contemporary American literature and ethnic studies, Schatt often explores in his writings a self-confessed interest "in the relationship between science and the humanities." In the following excerpt, Schatt examines themes, settings, and characters in Vonnegut's early short stories that recur in his later novels.*]

Kurt Vonnegut, Jr., will probably be remembered for his novels and not for his short stories though some are certainly memorable. He published his first collection of short fiction in ***Canary in a Cat House*** which appeared in 1961. Though the book is now long out of print, Vonnegut incorporated most of the stories in ***Welcome to the Monkey House*** which appeared in 1968. Vonnegut has confessed that the

> short stories in ***Welcome to the Monkey House*** supported me through the lean years. They are sunny because the magazines (paying up to $3000 a shot) wanted them to be that way. Stories were often rejected with the comment that they were "too downbeat." I learned how to be more upbeat. Business is business.

While these stories were written expressly for the popular market, many of them are somewhat superior to the usual stories found during the 1950's in such periodicals as *Saturday Evening Post, Colliers,* and *Ladies' Home Journal.* Vonnegut has pointed out that, when he quit General Electric in 1951, there was a flourishing short-story industry in the United States. [In a letter to Stanley Schatt, Vonnegut] admitted that from this experience he did "learn how to tell a story, how to make a story work, so that the thing has a certain flow and suspense and so forth. It is mechanical and it's somewhat worth knowing. Because I went through that apprenticeship I did learn how to tell a story." While Vonnegut has denied even contemplating the creation of a fictional Rosewater County with a consistent history and a set of characters much like those of William Faulkner's Yoknapatawpha County, he does use in his short fiction many of the same characters and settings that are found in his novels. Moreover, he focuses in his short stories on many of the same themes that dominate his fiction: the dangers of unchecked technology, the evils of egotism, and the need for love and compassion.

Vonnegut's scientists frequently discover that they have unwittingly opened a modern version of Pandora's box, and the question becomes whether or not mankind has the emotional, spiritual, and moral strength to match its technological progress. **"Thanasphere"** (1950) deals with the relationship between science and religion in much the same way as *Cat's Cradle.* In this story American military officials send a secret rocket ship orbiting around the earth; and the stoic pilot aboard is assigned the job of observing weather conditions over enemy territory and the accuracy of guided atomic missiles in the event of war. Doctor Bernard Groszinger, the youthful rocket consultant for the Air Force, cares nothing about the military purpose of the mission. Like Felix Hoenikker (*Cat's Cradle*), Groszinger cares nothing about politics and muses to himself that the "threat of war was an incident, the military men about him an irritating condition of work—the experiment was the heart of the matter."

The pilot discovers that the dead space, the thanasphere, is not empty but filled with ghosts who keep whispering messages to him that vary from a murder victim's indictment of his own brother to an invitation from his own deceased wife to join her. The pilot crashes the rocket ship into the ocean, and young Groszinger is left to ponder the implications of a world

> in constant touch with the spirits, the living inseparable from the dead . . . Would it make life heaven or hell? Every bum and genius, criminal and hero, average man and madman, now and forever part of humanity—advising, squabbling, conniving, placating. . . .

"Report on the Barnhouse Effect" (1950) describes the pressures applied to a scientist who courageously chooses to face real problems rather than to accept the comforting illusions that military men offer him. He dares to question the morality of using an invention with potentially enormous beneficial humanitarian effect as a strictly destructive military weapon. When Professor Barnhouse first discovers the power of dynamopschism, he looks upon it as only a toy, as a way to amuse himself by causing dice to produce the combinations he requests. Gradually the absent-minded psychology professor practices and perfects this power to the point where he can destroy individuals, houses, even mountains. While he would have preferred to use this power to run generators "where there isn't any coal or waterpower" and to irrigate deserts, the United States Army feels that this priceless gift should be used as a weapon since "Eternal vigilance is the price of freedom." Since this time-worn cliché is so much patriotic bilge as far as Vonnegut is concerned, it becomes clear that Barnhouse eventually must oppose the military establishment.

When Barnhouse turns to his graduate research assistant for advice, he repeatedly asks him such questions as "Think we should have dropped the atomic bomb on Hiroshima?" and "Think every new piece of scientific information is a good thing for humanity?" When Paul Proteus is asked in *Player Piano* to tell a lie during his trial so that his lie detector can be calibrated, he replies that "every new piece of scientific knowledge is a good thing for humanity." The turning point for Barnhouse comes when military officials request him to prove how powerful his gift is by destroying a number of missiles and ships during "Operation Barnhouse," for the scientist reacts by declaring that he finds the idea "childish and insanely expensive." While the military officials are exulting over Barnhouse's successful destruction of the weapons, he quietly makes his escape. The scientist, from his secluded sanctuary, spends the next few years destroying all military stockpiles despite the outraged cries of "stouthearted patriots." Vonnegut concludes his story by revealing that the narrator, Barnhouse's former research assistant, is planning to flee and assume his former mentor's antiwar activities so that the elderly scientist's death will not result in the resumption of hostilities.

"Report on the Barnhouse Effect" provides a rather unsatisfactory answer to the question of how man is to control his scientific and technological advances. Barnhouse is a godlike figure who, when asked by the military establishment to do what he feels is morally wrong, personally guarantees the safety of the world by destroying all weapons; Barnhouse, a scientist who values human life over research in pure science, does not appear either in *Cat's Cradle* or in *Player Piano* to help Paul Proteus or John. If Vonnegut means to imply that the world is in such dire straits that no mere mortal, but only a man with superhuman power like Barnhouse, can solve its problems, then his cosmic view is a pessimistic one indeed. He seems to modify this view, however, in his short story **"EPICAC"** (1950).

In *Player Piano* EPICAC is the giant computer that helps to govern men in an automated society. Its decisions result in the elimination of Bud Calhoun's job classification and in his subsequent relegation to the rank virtually of a nonperson. EPICAC is the heart of such a society, and perhaps it does represent the progressive decline of man, the epic of man since Christ's crucifixion. It is little wonder in *Player Piano* that when the Shah of Bratpuhr, the religious potentate of millions, visits the computer center, he addresses the machine directly, not bothering to deal with the humans who are obviously merely middle men. In his short story **"EPICAC"** Vonnegut shifts the emphasis from the omnipotence of EPICAC to the relationship between it and its human operator.

EPICAC was designed to be a "super computing machine that [who] could plot the course of a rocket from anywhere on earth to the second button from the bottom of Joe Stalin's overcoat." For some reason, the computer appears to be sluggish, almost reluctant to do its job. One day, when its operator playfully feeds a simple code that will enable it to converse with him, the result is a dialogue of sorts. The technician describes his girl friend Pat Kilgallen in such attractive terms that the computer quite logically falls in love with her; it writes beautiful love poems for the girl; and the human shamelessly pirates these as his own. When the machine questions the justice of its operator's contention that "Machines are built to serve men," the technician replies that men are superior since they are composed of protoplasm which is indestructible. He also points out that "Women can't love machines" because of fate which is "Predetermined and inevitable destiny." EPICAC responds by destroying itself, and it leaves a final suicide note saying that it does not "want to be a machine and think about war"; it wants to "be made out of protoplasm and last forever" so Pat can love it. The human victor in this struggle between man and machine declares that "Epicac loved and lost, but he bore me no grudge. I shall always remember him as a sportsman and a gentleman. Before he departed this vale of tears, he did all he could to make our marriage a happy one. Epicac gave me anniversary poems for Pat—enough for 500 years."

"EPICAC" is the only Vonnegut tale in which a man manages successfully to outwit a machine, and even here a certain amount of ambivalence is evident. The computer professes the very values that Vonnegut himself seems to hold sacred—a dislike for war and a strong feeling for the importance of love. The human technician manages to outwit EPICAC by deceit, something it obviously was not programmed to handle. The computer operator manages to redeem himself in his readers' estimation by candidly confessing to EPICAC and by admitting that he is ashamed of his actions. The story contains an additional twist that distinguishes it from Vonnegut's other tales; for instead of illustrating the dehumanizing effect that machines have on man, **"EPICAC"** illustrates the humanizing effect man can have on machines.

Unlike the bemused tone of EPICAC's operator, both **"Welcome to the Monkey House"** (1968), the title story of Vonnegut's collection of short stories, and **"Tomorrow and Tomorrow and Tomorrow"** (1954), its concluding selection, demonstrate on a more somber note how the irresponsibility of the scientific community and the American government, combined with a lack of respect for man's individuality and personal dignity, can create an intolerable situation. In **"Welcome to the Monkey House,"** Vonnegut describes a future America in which a scientist has invented an ethical birth-control pill that removes all pleasure from the sexual act, and in which the government requires all men and women to take them. The narrator points out that

> The pills are ethical because they didn't interfere with a person's ability to reproduce, which would have been unnatural and immoral. All the pills did was take every bit of pleasure out of sex.
>
> Thus did science and morals go hand in hand.

The hero who works to alter this situation is not a Barnhouse with superhuman power, but a very short, funny looking man named Billy the Poet. He spends his time seducing Suicide Parlor Hostesses at gun point and then forcing them to abandon their ethical birth-control pills. The young poet also repudiates the scientist who invented the pills and rebels against a government that forces its citizens to use them.

Billy describes how after a scientist had brought his family to a zoo and had been shocked because a monkey was playing with his private parts, he had gone home and invented an ethical birth-control pill that would make monkeys insensible below their waists. Vonnegut describes the results of this scientist's actions quite succinctly: "When he got through with the monkey house, you couldn't tell it from the Michigan Supreme Court. Meanwhile there was this crisis going on in the United Nations. The people who understood science said people had to quit reproducing so much, and the people who understood morals said society would collapse if people used sex for nothing but pleasure." Billy's avowed purpose is to "restore a certain amount of innocent pleasure to the world which is poorer in pleasure than it needs to be." He appears to find absolutely no pleasure in his role as a human rape machine, but he is driven by his altruistic desire to bring sexual pleasure back to the American people.

While this story is not so pessimistic as many of Vonnegut's novels, it certainly is not optimistic and it has an ambivalent note. The government obviously felt that something had to be done to prevent Americans from overpopulating themselves out of existence, especially since it is quite clear that citizens have a strong desire to live. Yet, does this fact make the government and the scientific community villains for marketing ethical birth-control pills and for requiring citizens to take them—and does it make Billy the Poet a hero for rebelling against such an edict and for trying to spread his philosophy of pleasure through sexual intercourse? Since the story was written for *Playboy,* it is easy to assume that the sympathy of the reader will probably be with Billy the Poet rather than with J. Edgar Nation, the scientist who invented the pill, or with the government that required it.

Vonnegut's tone is ambivalent, however, particularly in the story's final lines. After Billy rapes Nancy and removes her ethical birth-control pills, he leaves her with a poem and with a bottle of birth-control pills that has a label on it. The poem, Elizabeth Barrett Browning's "How Do I Love Thee? Let Me Count the Ways," is ironic since Billy has shown no love for Nancy, only a certain degree of missionary zeal to convert her to a "nothinghead." Yet, the now trite lines are also appropriate because Nancy's feelings about sex were shared by many Victorian ladies and because her numbness below her hips is much like that experienced by Elizabeth Barrett Browning after she fell from her horse. Many scholars now believe her injuries were psychosomatic, the result of her domineering father; for, during her honeymoon, her injury miraculously healed. The label on Nancy's birth-control pills reads "Welcome to the Monkey House." Billy the Poet points out that the legislation for ethical birth-control pills was forced upon the people by misguided moralists who did not realize that the world can afford sex, but that what "it can't afford anymore is reproduction." His birth-control pills provide a possible answer to this problem: Nancy can now be herself, another monkey in the human zoo that Vonnegut both satirizes and loves.

In **"Tomorrow and Tomorrow and Tomorrow"** (1954), Vonnegut once again deals with the major themes of **"Welcome to the Monkey House"**—the problem of overpopulation and the irresponsibility of the scientific community which constantly produces new inventions but which fails to deal with the moral problems that each new product brings. These sentiments are well expressed by a college president who is quoted by a newscaster as saying that "most of the world's ills can be traced to the fact that Man's knowledge of himself has not kept pace with his knowledge of the physical world." In the story, the example of such views is the Schwartz clan, all eleven couples, which lives in a four-room apartment in New York in 2158 A.D. Medical science has invented anti-gerasone which prevents humans from aging; unfortunately, it has ignored the question of how the ever-increasing population could live together in cramped conditions without any privacy.

Perhaps the resulting loss of human dignity is best illustrated in the indignant complaint of the newest member of the Schwartz clan, a great grand-nephew Mortimer, and his new wife who have arrived for a honeymoon. Mortimer advises anybody who thinks he has it rough to "try honeymooning in the hall for a real kick." The conclusion of the story finds Vonnegut again refusing to provide a workable solution to the problems he recognizes. Grandfather Schwartz gains suitable revenge on his clan for what he feels is an attempt to dilute his anti-gerasone by disappearing after leaving a will which requests that his apartment and fortune be divided equally among all his family. As a result of the subsequent riot among the Schwartzes, the police arrest all of them and place them in jail cells. The tale ends with the contentment of Lou and Emerald Schwartz who are amazed about how wonderful it is to have a jail cell of their own. A turnkey admonishes them to "pipe down . . . or I'll toss the whole kit and caboodle of you right out. And first one who lets on to anybody outside how good jail is ain't never getting back in!"

Since obviously all humans cannot crowd themselves into their nations' prisons, the Schwartzes' solution is amusing but impractical. The story concludes with a television advertisement for the new super anti-gerasone which will make all senior citizens look years younger. Gramps

Schwartz writes his name on a postcard; sends for a free sample; and, looking like a man in his early thirties, apparently no longer has any reason to contemplate suicide. Vonnegut is astute enough to realize, however, that the desire for longevity is a very human wish; it is not merely a goal of the scientific community. What science has achieved in **"Tomorrow and Tomorrow and Tomorrow"** is, therefore, the fulfillment of one of man's most basic desires, his will to live.

Ironically, the price man must pay for longevity is the loss of his dignity and his privacy, without which long life becomes a mere prison sentence rather than a blessing. Perhaps this price is too high to pay, as Vonnegut implies by the bleak despair associated with Macbeth's "Tomorrow and Tomorrow and Tomorrow" speech. The Schwartz clan feels as trapped and as resigned to its collective fate as Shakespeare's tragic hero. Just as Macbeth must shoulder responsibility for his actions, so too must the members of the Schwartz clan because they cannot blame science for their plight since scientific institutions are man-made and are mere reflections of man's ever-increasing knowledge and curiosity. This Faust-like quality of mankind is what Vonnegut blames for the creation of Ilium, New York; ice-nine; ethical birth-control pills; and anti-gerasone. Perhaps because of his anthropological training, Vonnegut appears to believe that man may be fatally flawed, an idea developed more fully in such popular anthropological studies as Arthur Koestler's *The Ghost in the Machine* and Robin Fox and Lionel Tiger's *The Imperial Animal.* If Frank Hoenikker in *Cat's Cradle* learns anything at all from the ants that survived ice-nine, it is that, although man might survive even that holocaust by clinging at all costs to the will to live, he will eventually reach a state of development where he will once again attempt annihilation of the entire human race.

The answer to man's dilemma, however, is not to seek a separate peace. There is no place for Paul Proteus (*Player Piano*) or John (*Cat's Cradle*) to flee. On the other hand, it is impractical for man to await the arrival of a superman figure such as Professor Barnhouse to save him. What man can do, Vonnegut suggests in his fiction, is to realize his own limitations. He should consciously shun anything, no matter how appealing, if it will dehumanize him. Scientists as men, rather than machines, should be morally responsible for their inventions. Any invention that would treat men as mere numbers, rather than as individuals, or that would at all limit their personal dignity and privacy should be discarded since the human animal's proclivity for destruction is enhanced when he is able to think of his carnage in terms of abstract casualty lists rather than in terms of flesh and blood people he has destroyed. The alternative to such measures is either total annihilation or the world of **"Tomorrow and Tomorrow and Tomorrow"** in which life becomes "a tale / told by an idiot, full of sound and fury, / signifying nothing."

Several Vonnegut stories written for *Saturday Evening Post* feature George M. Helmholtz, the fat, jovial head of the music department and the director of the Lincoln High School Band. Good-hearted, sincere, and completely devoted to his band, Helmholtz dreams of winning first place every year in the state's high-school-band competition. His obsessive devotion to this dream makes him a comical yet strangely moving character. Helmholtz has much in common with the traditional Jewish *Das Kleine Menschele* figure, the little man of Eastern European Jewish folklore who is physically helpless to control his own destiny and who constantly lives in fear of the outside world entering his *shtetl* community. The band director lives in his own private world of music, and he dreads the frequent invasions by the Principal who is constantly shaken by Helmholtz's budget requests. In virtually every Helmholtz story Vonnegut focuses on the relationship between the harassed band director and a very unhappy boy with whom he frequently tries to share his dream about music in order to open a new world for him.

"The No-Talent Kid" (1952) is the story of Helmholtz's confrontation with Plummer, a boy who has no musical talent but who has an all-consuming desire to make the "A" band. Each challenge day Plummer challenges the first clarinetist in the elite "A" band even though he barely holds down the last chair in the remedial "C" band. He is convinced that he loses each week only because Helmholtz is prejudiced. Meanwhile, Helmholtz has serious problems of his own. His band was defeated the previous spring because the enemy band had a seven-foot drum, and he longs for a bigger drum. Plummer buys the biggest drum in town, demands to be made the first drummer in the "A" band, and then wounds Helmholtz by informing him that he will give the drum to his mother to use as a coffee table. The compromise Vonnegut conceives to obtain the instrument is a typical *Saturday Evening Post* formula ending: Plummer agrees to provide his drum and to contribute to the band by carrying the drum during parades. Thus the boy becomes part of the band he loves, and the music teacher gets the drum he needs without having to compromise his ideals.

"The Ambitious Sophomore" (1954) is the story of Helmholtz's efforts to understand why his brilliant piccoloist LeRoi Duggan suddenly forgets how to march and stumbles whenever people watch. Helmholtz buys a special and incredibly ornate uniform that is specially padded to make LeRoi look like a professional football player. The uniform gives LeRoi confidence in himself; and, when a rival suitor rips the uniform to shreds, he floors the bully and then performs a magnificent piccolo solo that wins the band first place in the competition. Helmholtz sells his spare tire to help pay for the uniform and then has to take a streetcar home when he has a flat tire, but these seem minor inconveniences compared to the trophy awarded his band for first place.

"The Boy Who Hated Girls" (1956) reveals Helmholtz's naïveté. He is so devoted to his boys and to his band that he does not realize that the fatherless boy Bert feels rejected when Helmholtz sends him to a different music teacher for final polishing. Bert has limited musical ability but apparently practices constantly to please Helmholtz. Bert does not really hate girls, but he does ignore them. The story ends with Bert's returning a beautiful coed's interest in him. A school nurse scolds Helmholtz for playing with human life and then ignoring the results. Unlike Vonnegut's cold father figures who tend to ignore their sons because of their own egotism, Helmholtz is so shocked by the nurse's revelation that he presumably reforms and assumes his responsibility.

In **"The Kid Nobody Could Handle"** (1955), the most revealing of the George Helmholtz stories, Helmholtz echoes some of the despair that years later permeates *Breakfast of Champions.* The music teacher is appalled to discover that Jim Donnini, a juvenile delinquent from the streets of Chicago, has been vandalizing Lincoln High School. Filled with compassion and desperation, Helmholtz offers him his most precious possession, John Philip Sousa's trumpet. When the boy initially shows no interest, Helmholtz hammers the instrument against a coat tree and mutters that "Life is no damn good". and only then does Donnini show any interest in Helmholtz. With the start of the new school semester, Jim Donnini takes his seat in the last seat of the worst trumpet section of the "C" band. As Helmholtz tells him and the rest of the band, "Our aim is to make the world more beautiful than it was when we came into it. . . . Love yourself . . . and make your instrument sing about it." Without a sense of self-worth, Vonnegut thinks it is impossible for anyone to achieve anything.

One of Vonnegut's major subjects has always been the relationship between fathers and sons, and his fathers are often driven men who either are indifferent to their sons or seek actively to transform their children into carbon copies of themselves. **"This Son of Mine"** (1956) is a very early short story that deals with the conflict between a father's expectations for his son and his child's responsibilities both to his father and to himself. Merle Waggoner, a fifty-one-year-old widower, owns a centrifugal pump factory and longs for his son Franklin to inherit the business. When he observes the relationship between his lathe operator Rudy Linbert and his son Karl, he wonders why Franklin could even think of becoming an actor instead of following in his footsteps.

Franklin sees that his career decision has wounded his father deeply, and he does not feel like attending a country club dance where he would see his friends who also had rejected their fathers' business and thus become "the killers of their fathers' dreams." The Waggoners and Linberts take a short hunting trip together, and Franklin is shocked when Karl tells him "get out from under your old man . . . that's the thing to do." He then goes on to point out "Your father doesn't just have you. He's got his big success . . . All my old man's got is me." Listening to Rudy and Karl play a duet, the two Waggoner men feel very close; and Franklin listens to the music and realizes that

> It was speaking of all fathers and sons. It was saying hauntingly what they had all been saying haltingly, what they had all been saying, sometimes with pain and sometimes with love—that fathers and sons were one.
>
> It was saying too, that a time for a parting in spirit was near—no matter how close anyone held anyone, no matter what anyone tried.

Rarely has Vonnegut come closer to articulating the complex relationship he sees between fathers and sons—the bond between Paul Proteus and his father (*Player Piano*) and between Eliot Rosewater and Senator Rosewater (*God Bless You, Mr. Rosewater*). The son must rebel against his father despite his subsequent guilt feelings because, if he does not, he will not be an individual but only a carbon copy of his parent.

In **"The Foster Portfolio"** (1951), another Vonnegut story about the relationship between fathers and sons, Herbert Foster works as a bookkeeper to support his wife and child by moonlighting. He has inherited almost a million-dollar stock portfolio, but he feels the money is tainted because it came from his father, a man who abandoned wife and child to devote his life to playing music in dives and to drinking gin. Three nights a week Herbert goes to a cheap bar for, as Vonnegut points out, Herbert "had the respectability his mother had hammered into him. But just as priceless as that was an income not quite big enough to go around. It left him no alternative but—in the holy names of wife, child, and home—to play piano in a dive, and breathe smoke, and drink gin, to be Firehouse Harris, his father's son, three nights out of seven." Foster's split personality links him to many Vonnegut protagonists including Paul Proteus, Eliot Rosewater, and Billy Pilgrim; for all find it necessary to create roles that help them to cope with what appears to be unbearable problems.

Vonnegut's stories often focus on characters' attempts to play roles that appear to be more exciting than their real lives, but these roles are frequently linked to unrealistic dreams that tend to stultify the dreamers. **"Custom-Made Bride"** (1954) is the story of Otto Krummbein, an eccentric inventor who tries to redesign everything and everyone to fit his specifications. The story is narrated by an investment counselor who tries to straighten out Krummbein's tangled finances; for, brilliant as an inventor but incredibly naïve as a businessman, Krummbein has never paid income tax because he has never received a bill. He introduces his wife Falloleen whose hair is bleached silver with a touch of blue and who wears zebra-striped leotards and one large earring. Falloleen is really Otto's former secretary, Kitty Calhoun, who has allowed her husband to redesign her. Otto confesses though that, when Falloleen is not striking a pose or making a dramatic entrance or exit, she is a "crashing bore." The story concludes with her reassumption of her original identity. This conclusion is consistent with other Vonnegut stories and novels since his personal version of Nathaniel Hawthorne's "unpardonable sin" is the distortion or elimination of an individual's personality.

In **"The Powder Blue Dragon"** (1954) Vonnegut describes the plight of Higgins, a twenty-one-year-old boy who has worked at three jobs for four years in order to save the $5651 necessary to buy a Marittima Frascati. A native living in a seacoast resort city, he resents the way tourists seem to lord it over him. When he takes his new car for a trial run, he sees a beautiful girl driving a Cadillac. He follows her into the cocktail lobby of a resort hotel where he feels "he'd been dumped in a strange, hostile world." Lacking the sophistication or money of the girl's fiancé, he races him even though his car has not been properly broken in. The car's engine burns out, and young Higgins sobs "I'm glad it's dead . . . I'm glad I killed it." Like the poor creature in the song "Puff the Magic Dragon," Higgins' powder-blue dragon cannot survive in the adult world. The lesson he learns is a common Vonnegut bromide, for a kindly old druggist tells the boy that expensive cars are part of a "phony world, a toy world, full of useless trinkets. . . . " In Vonnegut's fictive universe, anyone who places a higher value on things than on people inevitably suffers.

In **"More Stately Mansions"** (1951), which is built around much the same theme as **"The Powder Blue Dragon,"** the dream is always more precious and satisfying than the reality. A couple moves into a suburban home and discovers that their neighbor Grace has an obsessive interest in home decoration. She collects dozens of home magazines and files the best ideas for the dream home she will have when she has enough money to redecorate her home. When she is stricken with virus and hospitalized, her husband inherits enough money to redecorate secretly according to her plans. He surprises her with the newly decorated home, but he destroys in the process the hobby that has given her so much pleasure for years. When he points out that a new *House Beautiful* has just arrived, Grace's response is "Read one and you've read them all."

In **"Bagombo Snuff Box"** (1954) Eddie Laird, a traveling salesman, decides to visit his ex-wife whom he has not seen in eleven years. Like so many Vonnegut characters, he feels compelled to play a role, that of the adventurous man of the world; and he gives a Bagombo snuff box to Amy and her husband that he says he purchased in Ceylon. As he describes his adventures in France, Ceylon, and the Klondike, his former wife and her department-store-manager husband begin to wince at the lack of adventure in their own lives. However, their nine-year-old-boy Stevie punctures Eddie's facade by revealing that the snuff box was actually made in Japan and that Eddie does not even know where Ceylon is. The story ends with Amy's family united in its common amusement while it watches Eddie flee; later, he calls his second wife long distance and discusses his son's reading problem and his daughter's need for braces. His adventurous tales are mere fantasies and are as unrealistic as Higgins' dream of owning a Marittima Frascati.

"Who Am I This Time?" (originally published in 1961 as **"My Name Is Everyone"**) is another example of Vonnegut's concern with role playing. The shy clerk Harry is only alive when he becomes the character he plays for the local drama group in North Crawford. When the director decides to do Tennessee Williams' *A Streetcar Named Desire* for the spring play, Harry is chosen to play the role Marlon Brando made famous. He becomes Marlon Brando, and a young girl named Helene who plays Stella falls in love with him. Because Harry was left at the doorstep of a church and never knew his real parents, he has no concept of self; and Helene has moved around so much as a child that she never has been able to develop a personality of her own. As a result, both are chameleons who yearn to blend into any environment so that they can feel that they have identity. They marry and make their marriage work by playing different roles each week that range from those of Romeo and Juliet to those of Othello and Desdemona.

When writing for magazines with essentially middle-class audiences, Vonnegut often twists the role-playing theme to imply that his readers should be content with their lives since the very wealthy are really unhappy role players who long for a middle-class life style. **"A Night for Love"** (1957), which first appeared in *Saturday Evening Post,* is a good example of just such a Vonnegut formula story. Turley Whitman and his wife lie in bed awaiting their daughter's return from a date with the son of the wealthy L. C. Reinbeck. Turley had once dreamed of being wealthy, but he is now merely working as a policeman in Reinbeck's factory. Because Turley's wife was once the town beauty who had dated Reinbeck, Turley has never really forgiven his wife for those dates because he is convinced that she constantly compares the two men and regrets her decision to marry him.

The tension between the Whitmans is matched by the Reinbecks; for, when Turley calls them to complain that his daughter is still not home, he mentions that surely Reinbeck must remember his wife. Both couples anguish over what might have been, both decide that their marriages have been the result of a lover's moon in the sky, and both learn that their children have just been married. Vonnegut concludes by pointing out that now there is a new household: "Whether everything was all right here, remained to be seen. The moon went down." The story is competently plotted but shallow. Reinbeck and his wife are conventionally rich; the Whitmans are conventionally middle class. Whitman is poor but capable of love; Reinbeck is shown to be married to his factory. As is made clear, in Vonnegut's personal hierarchy, love is valued far more than money or personal possessions as long as it is real love and not mere infatuation.

In **"Runaways"** (1961), a variation on **"A Night for Love,"** the daughter of the governor of Indiana flees with the son of a clerk. When the two families express common grief and outrage, both are convinced that mere children cannot really know what true love is. After the teenagers are captured, returned to their parents, and flee again, the parents decide this time that the two youngsters should be allowed to be married. Both now agree that they are too young—not too young to love, but too young "for about everything else there is that goes with love." Significantly, the boy and girl are merely role playing; they never really talk to each other; instead, they mouth platitudes they have heard expressed in the popular music of the time. If the two had really listened to each other's conversation, Vonnegut concludes that they would have bored each other. Years later, in *Breakfast of Champions,* Vonnegut once again expresses his feelings about an American culture composed almost entirely of commercials, sports, and popular music.

Perhaps Vonnegut's lightest treatment of role playing is **"Any Reasonable Offer"** (1952) in which a real-estate salesman learns that a Colonel and Mrs. Peckham wish to see an estate. After they have stayed for cocktails and have swum and walked in the gardens, the salesman eventually learns that the Colonel is really a draftsman who manages to enjoy free vacations each year by pretending he is interested in expensive homes and by enjoying the hospitality offered him by the anxious-to-sell owners. The salesman concludes that maybe such role playing is not a bad idea for other middle-class Americans—considering the price of vacations.

Many Vonnegut stories are political fables that satirize the American political system and this country's relationship with both China and the Soviet Union. **"Harrison Bergeron"** (1961) is a fable about what ultimately could happen in America if all people are forced to be equal. A Handicapper General, the same Diane Moon Glompers who appears in *God Bless You, Mr. Rosewater,* places weights on strong people and hideous masks on beautiful girls to insure that everyone is equally mediocre. When seven-foot Harrison Bergeron strips himself of his handicaps and dances with a beautiful ballerina over national television, he shows Americans how beautiful life could be with individual differences. Since such flagrant abuse of the law cannot be tolerated, Miss Glompers kills the two dancers. In any leveling process, what really is lost, according to Vonnegut, is beauty, grace, and wisdom.

"All the King's Horses" (1951) is a product of the Cold War of the early 1950's when Americans were becoming more and more suspicious of the Soviet Union and China, and the story describes the battle between Colonel Kelley and Pi Ying, a Chinese guerilla leader. Ying brings Kelley, his wife, his sons, and twelve American soldiers to a hideout where he offers the Colonel one chance to save their lives: he must use the Americans as chess pieces in a game against Pi Ying while the Russian advisor observes. If Kelley wins, the Americans will go free. Ying is described as inscrutable and evil, and his Russian advisor Barzov is presented as a military man eager for a confrontation between Russia and the United States as soon as the time is ripe. After Ying is assassinated by his mistress, Kelley wins; and the Russian is outraged. He lets the Americans go, but he indicates that he will look forward to the war that ultimately will come. While the story now seems very dated, it does reflect accurately American sentiment during the early Cold War period.

"Unready to Wear" (1953) is a Vonnegut story that suggests a way of eliminating wars between nations. A scientist with an ugly, highly ineffective body discovers how to leave his body and become "amphibious." He soon is joined by thousands of people, and one of them is a pay-toilet businessman who describes how enjoyable it is to be free of material goods. Amphibians choose among several bodies whenever they wish to march in parades or read books. The real reason nations fight each other, suggests the businessman, is a Darwinian drive toward self-preservation. With no bodies to preserve, the amphibians represent the ultimate in counterculture values since they have no desire for commercial products.

Because Vonnegut's short stories were written to meet the formulaic requirements of mass-circulation magazines, they tend to be rather conventional both technically and thematically. They do reveal, however, a good deal of information about Vonnegut himself, particularly that he is the product of an Indianapolis middle-class family. Since most of these short stories were written in the interval between *Player Piano* and *The Sirens of Titan,* they reflect the preoccupation of both Vonnegut and Middle America with the Cold War, love, status, and identity. In many ways they reflect a childhood during which Vonnegut was nurtured on an anthology of sentimental poetry "about love which would not die, about faithful dogs and humble cottages where happiness was, about people growing old, about visits to cemeteries, about babies who died." Vonnegut, remembering this anthology, confesses he wished he had a copy now since "it has so much to do with what I am." (pp. 119-35)

Stanley Schatt, in his Kurt Vonnegut, Jr., *Twayne Publishers, 1976, 174 p.*

Jerome Klinkowitz (essay date 1982)

[*A professor of English at the University of Northern Iowa, Klinkowitz is the author of such critical studies as* Literary Disruptions *(1975; revised, 1980) and* The Life of Fiction *(1977), as well as several books on Vonnegut. In the following essay, Klinkowitz closely examines sev-*

Vonnegut's 1961 collection of short fiction, later revised and expanded as Welcome to the Monkey House *(1968).*

eral of Vonnegut's short stories that comment upon his theme of the modern individual's "longing for a large permanent *family."*]

Kurt Vonnegut's family in Indianapolis was a large and comfortably situated one. His father and grandfather were successful architects, and their buildings were landmarks of the commerce and culture of this Midwestern capital. Aunts, uncles and cousins abounded, giving young Kurt the true sense of an extended family. It was a child's ideal world—before the Great Depression, before the Second World War—and it prompted no doubts in him about identity or the threat of the future. Vonnegut's first world was indeed the American dream of its time. But succeeding decades of the twentieth century destroyed that ideal community; and Kurt Vonnegut found himself at the center of that dissolution, experiencing it over his most formative years. Large and stable American families have in our own day become the exception rather than the rule. The typical family is now nuclear, stripped down to essentials for economic mobility—a mobility that disperses these units away from their ancestral homes and keeps them continually moving at a rate of once every four years. All this constitutes a great loss, one that invades the entire tone of his work. As Vonnegut explains:

> I think that most of the unhappiness—the indescribable malaise—that people are feeling these days is really a longing for a large *permanent* family. The ideal commune would be one in which the people have actually grown up together—that's the sort of commune humans have lived in for most of their history on earth. So it's better if you have bloodlines. But, if you can't, you can at least have a lot of people.

Throughout the seventies, when he was in great demand as a college commencement speaker, Vonnegut brought this same message to the students:

> Your class spokesperson mourned the collapse of the institution of marriage in this country. Marriage is collapsing because our families are too small. A man cannot be a whole society to a woman, and a woman cannot be a whole society to a man. We try, but it is scarcely surprising that so many of us go to pieces.

The imaginative reconstruction of such primitive ideals as the extended family and regional stability determine both theme and structure for Vonnegut's work of the sixties and seventies, but the essentials of this vision can be found in his earliest and more popular publications. Beginning on 11 February 1950, and continuing through October 1963, Kurt Vonnegut contributed fifty stories to such popular, family-oriented magazines as *Collier's, Redbook, Cosmopolitan* and *The Saturday Evening Post* (half were later collected in the volume ***Welcome to the Monkey House***). Such markets were, of course, hospitable to (and probably even demanding of) a middle-class perspective in their fiction, and Vonnegut's approach was solidly structured within his Indiana experience and ideals. By its very name, the American 'middle' class suggests it can be measured from two directions, above or below. Hence Vonnegut's short stories from these years often alternate between two types of narrators: this figure is either 'a contact man for an investment counseling firm' who will call on potential clients (who by his help may climb up out of the middle class), or a tradesman in 'aluminum combination storm windows and screens', an honest workman and solid representative of the American middle class whose job sometimes takes him into the homes of the rich and famous. Whether seen from the first angle or the second, each type of story has a similar plot. The world of bourgeois stability is threatened with a disruption confounding the principles Vonnegut and his narrator hold dear; the narrator, however, manages to reshape the experience according to his own values, maintaining order for himself and for the world depicted in each story. There are, of course, other variations—several stories about a high school bandmaster who solves a wide range of teenage problems, others about folks on American Main Streets who must deal with various disruptive intrusions—but these are simply more direct exercises in the meliorating process given dynamic play in the stockbroker/storm-window salesman tales.

So in **"The Foster Portfolio"** Vonnegut's narrator is careful to remind readers that he is not one of the very rich himself. 'Since *I* don't have a portfolio, my job is a little like being a hungry delivery boy for a candy store,' he begins; however, he does represent the expertise that can transform middle-class hopes into the reality of wealth. Hence, when he answers the humble Mr Foster's call, the narrator carefully notes the telltale signs of a family just barely scraping its way into the middle class: jerry-built home with expansion attic, bargain-store living-room suite (complete with pictures and ashtrays), even the soap on the washstand, 'mottled and dingy—a dozen little chips moistened and pressed together to make a new bar.' Such enforced frugality creates a lifestyle the narrator, who has his own dreams of riches, can only pity:

> My client, Herbert Foster, hadn't had a new suit in three years; he had never owned more than one pair of shoes at a time. He worried about payments on his second-hand car, and ate tuna and cheese instead of meat, because meat was too expensive. His wife made her own clothes, and those of Herbert, Jr., and the curtains and slipcovers—all cut from the same bargain bolt. The Fosters were going through hell, trying to choose between new tires or retreads for the car; and television was something they had to go two doors down the street to watch. Determinedly, they kept within the small salary Herbert made as a bookkeeper for a wholesale grocery house.

'God knows it's no disgrace to live that way, which is better than the way I live,' the narrator is quick to admit; yet he is dumbfounded when he learns Herbert Foster is holding nearly a million dollars in bonds and securities, an inheritance from his grandfather with which he'd prefer not to be bothered. Simply drawing on his dividends would change his life—for the better, our narrator presumes—but Herbert is unwilling to interfere. Material goods? He would rather save up or buy them on time, for they mean more that way; moreover, he takes pride earning every penny that he spends. Freedom from his boring and humiliating job? That is indeed a temptation. 'Got bawled out at work again,' a dejected Herbert tells his financial counselor, who in turn suggests that he 'Buy the place and burn it down'. For a moment Herbert realizes he could, and 'A wild look came into his eyes, then disappeared.' The investment income will remain untouched. But why? Because as a bona fide member of the American middle class Herbert Foster has effected his own little personal self-transformation: in the fully responsible name of extra income, he practices three nights each week as a *demimonde* jazz pianist, a separate identity he cherishes because he has created it himself. The narrator at once understands, sympathizes, and vows to help him guard his precious poverty—an ideal that will return often in Vonnegut's work.

"Unpaid Consultant" and **"Custom-Made Bride"** are similar excursions into the American middle class, a class under fire by virtue of the optimistic economic times. In the former, Vonnegut's investment counselor visits an old girlfriend, who is now a highly paid TV star, yet is still happily married to her high school beau, a garage mechanic. The husband, it turns out, has developed a protective camouflage. He is supposedly the world's expert on catsup and pretends he works as a highly sought-after industry consultant; in fact, he has continued in secret as a humble yet proficient repairman ('Not half an hour ago,' he confesses to the narrator, 'a man with a broken fuel pump thanked God for me'). **"Custom-Made Bride"** celebrates the return-to-reason of a fantastically successful high-tech designer who has recrafted to perfection every aspect of his mundane, middle-class wife, while neglecting the integrity of what is inside. As we might expect, the narrator (who is able to bridge the best in both worlds) helps put things straight. As the middle-class community of **"Poor Little Rich Town"** replies to the efficiency expert about to introduce it to undreamed-of wealth, "What is a village profited, if it shall gain a real-estate boom and lose its own soul?' That soul of integrity is still to be found, in these stories, within the middle-class virtues of ordinariness, honesty, hard work and fair play, tempered with healthy suspicion of success and new glamorous ideas, especially those promising quick solutions and rewards. The storm-window salesman stories are similar. In **"Go Back To Your Precious Wife and Son,"** the salesman becomes involved in the marital fights of a glamorous Hollywood star and her husband. His estrangement turns to sympathy when the husband tells a sentimental tale of being seduced by a *femme fatale,* and gives his own homely advice on family life.

Perhaps the story that most concentrates this attitude is **"The Hyannis Port Story"** Vonnegut's testament to John F. Kennedy's popular sway over middle-class America and the power of the Camelot myth. The story was the last Vonnegut wrote for the family magazines and was to appear in *The Saturday Evening Post;* ironically, it never ran because, just before it was scheduled to appear, President Kennedy was assassinated on 22 November 1963. Included in the collection ***Welcome to the Monkey House*** (1968), it now can serve as Vonnegut's most explicit statement of how middle-class stability can stand up to anything, even the hysteria of a glamorous presidency. It is his reflection on the tension between normal life and politics and history, another theme that would last in his work. The story sets off firmly in the normative middle-class world, from which every future deviation will be measured: 'The farthest away from home I ever sold a storm window was in Hyannis Port, Massachusetts, practically in the front yard of President Kennedy's summer home,' it begins. Even the narrator's journey out of New Hampshire is a disruption of convention; he usually sells only within an hour's drive of his home town, North Crawford, New Hampshire. The sale too is a product of confusion. A young man from Hyannis named Robert Taft Rumfoord addresses the North Crawford Lions Club supporting Barry Goldwater's conservative presidential campaign, and is heckled by a Kennedy liberal who then quarrels with the narrator about a leaky bathtub. 'Commodore' Rumfoord of Hyannis, the speaker's father, imagines the narrator is defending his son's speech and gives him an order for windows for his Hyannis Port mansion. And thus the Vonnegut narrator acquires the task of carrying the values of middle-class America into the world of Camelot itself.

So the story proceeds, with social norms established which are exceeded step by step, as the narrator moves into the world of political heroes and brings them toward his own measurement. Approaching Hyannis, he finds the route clogged with sightseers, but stalls in traffic next to Ambassador Adlai Stevenson: 'He wasn't moving any faster than I was,' the narrator notes, 'and his radiator was boiling, too.' He quickly adjusts Stevenson to back-fence level:

> One place there, we got stuck so long that Mr Stevenson and I got out and walked around a little. I took the opportunity to ask him how the United Nations were getting along. He told me they were getting along about as well as could be expected. That wasn't anything I didn't know.

He equally adapts the absurdities of Hyannis Port, where almost everything is renamed to capitalize on Kennedy fame: the predictable Presidential Motor Inn, the improbable PT-109 Cocktail Lounge, the absurd New Frontier miniature golf course. In the First Family Waffle Shop he finds similar items on the menu:

> All the different kinds of waffles were named after the Kennedys and their friends and relatives. A waffle with strawberries and cream was a *Jackie*. A waffle with a scoop of ice cream was a *Caroline*. They even had a waffle named *Arthur Schlesinger, Jr.*

The narrator maintains middle-class dignity by ordering a *'Teddy',* thankfully undescribed, 'and a cup of *Joe*.') Finally, at Commodore Rumfoord's home he finds on the balcony a rival claim: a gigantic billboard portrait of Goldwater, with flashing lights and bicycle reflectors for eyes, stares straight into the Kennedy compound next door. The troubles of the Rumfoord wealth are explored; Rumfoord's wife draws the lesson, which is that inherited wealth is inferior to meaningful work: 'I would love you, no matter what. But I can't tell you now, darling—it's awfully hard for a woman to *admire* a man who doesn't actually do anything.' Which justifies the only worker in the bunch, the narrator himself, who has been judging things by these standards all along. And in the political world the same old good sense comes to rule. The President of the United States appears at last, asking why Rumford has not switched on his Goldwater sign: ' "That way," said the President, "I can find my way home".' Political opposition is another quarrel between neighbors to be resolved in lively good humor; the norms of North Crawford can be elevated to match or surpass the most ridiculous challenges life can present.

Nearly all of Vonnegut's early stories are written in this same spirit, expressing a skeptical, home-centered view of life, a sensible notion of community and the value of the extended family. The *Collier's* story **"The Package"** is about a rich retired businessman trying to impress a friend with his excessively luxurious home; the ploy backfires as he becomes ashamed by the other's admirable life of, again, poverty and sacrifice. **"Bagombo Snuff Box,"** published two years later in *Cosmopolitan,* a monthly magazine slanted toward the woman's angle, describes how an unexpected guest tries to show off in front of a humbly married former girlfriend; this violator of hearth and home is of course promptly humiliated himself and revealed as an utter phony. Vonnegut combines his two beliefs—in the extended family aspect of a community and the roles it offers people to play—in **"Who Am I This Time?"** a story *The Saturday Evening Post* [originally published under the title] **"My Name Is Everyone."** Here he is again, Vonnegut's perennial storm-window salesman, now directing a play for the North Crawford community theater; as always, his role is therapeutic. Harry Nash is a young man virtually without identity, until he assumes one on stage, when he always becomes the company's best actor. Helene Shaw is a young woman whose employment takes her from place to place at eight-week intervals; as a child, she moved just as frequently, her father being a construction worker who followed work from town to town. Each is an isolated soul—until Vonnegut's narrator helps them convert their parts in the play to more permanent roles within the company's repertoire.

Vonnegut's ideal of the extended family is so functionally convincing, perhaps, because his own biography has seen both its disruption (in natural form) and its re-establishment (as artifice). The same is true for another important element in his fiction: its demonstration that reality is not absolute but is instead an arbitrary convention. As a child just turning nine years old, and continuing through his teens, Kurt Vonnegut saw the social and economic 'reality' of his family changed quite radically, from financially secure respectability to a decade of unemployment for his father, loss of social standing and of elegant possessions by his mother, and hard times in general for the rest of his relatives in Indianapolis—all because of abstract financial events happening 700 miles away on Wall Street in New York. As an architect, Kurt Vonnegut, Sr, had no clients during the Great Depression; and, as heiress of a now depleted fortune, Edith Lieber Vonnegut could no longer plan the exclusive private schooling she had anticipated for her younger son. The older children, Bernard and Alice, had attended Park School and Tudor Hall School respectively; Kurt's fortune was to be enrolled at Public School No. 43 and later Shortridge High. The country's economic collapse had changed the terms of his present life and his education for the future.

'Everything I believe,' Vonnegut once told an interviewer who questioned him on his social norms and politics, 'I was taught in junior civics during the Great Depression—at School 43 in Indianapolis.' As for his mother's hopes to regain sufficient funds to transfer him to the Park School, 'She could not understand that to give up my friends at Pubic School No. 43, "The James Whitcomb Riley School", by the way, would be for me to give up *everything.*' The restructuring of young Kurt Vonnegut's life which the Great Depression provoked may have been a disguised blessing. In his fiction, at least, Vonnegut has been emphatic about this point. In the early *Cosmopolitan* story, **"Hal Irwin's Magic Lamp,"** he describes how a frugal middle-class husband, with some luck and in strict secrecy, amasses a great deal of money, which he then reveals to his wife in a charming little charade of 'making wishes' while 'rubbing a magic lamp'. Her every wish is fulfilled, yet the wealth does not make her happy. Instead, it destroys the humble happiness she and her husband had earlier shared. And so she makes one last innocent wish, that the lamp take back everything it has given and just return the simpler life they'd once enjoyed. It does—by means of the Great Depression.

At college Vonnegut found many of his earliest experiences repeated and socially confirmed. Half a continent away from his home, at Cornell University in upstate New York, he discovered that the fraternity and sorority system could offer him not only a place to hang his hat but also an extended family with scores of artificially construed but none the less helpful brothers and sisters, and even a housemother. He pledged the fraternity Delta Upsilon, is to this day an interested alumnus, and uses it as a frequent metaphor in his novels and essays. He also found a family of sorts on the student newspaper, which he joined as managing editor (having held similar rank on his high school daily); here he continued writing not as an isolated literary figure but as a working journalist delivering essential news to a community of which he could feel a part. During his three years at Cornell, Vonnegut had been told to study 'something useful'—the aesthetically gifted Kurt, Sr, had no wish for his son to become a similarly unemployed artist—and so he took courses in chemistry and biology for a career as a biochemist, much as his older brother Bernard had earned a doctorate at the Massachusetts Institute of Technology and was on his way to becoming an internationally renowned atmospheric physicist. These were the years of science and technology triumphant, of popular slogans such as 'Better Living Through Chemistry' and 'Progress is our Most Important Product'. Of these times Vonnegut recalls:

> I thought scientists were going to find out exactly how everything worked, and then make it work better. I fully expected by the time I was twenty-one, some scientist, maybe my brother, would have taken a color photograph of God Almighty—and sold it to *Popular Mechanics* magazine.

By the time Kurt Vonnegut was twenty-one, however, a different reality had intervened. Midway through his junior year he contracted pneumonia and was forced to drop his classes; losing his student standing made him subject to military service. He enlisted in the US Army, which sent him to the Carnegie Institute of Technology and then the University of Tennessee for training as a mechanical engineer. He was sent overseas, however, as an advance infantry scout, and was captured by the Wehrmacht on 22 December 1944, during the Battle of the Bulge. He was interned as a prisoner of war in the supposedly open city of Dresden, which was nevertheless destroyed in a fire-bombing by the Allies on 13 February 1945. Few of the city's quarter-million inhabitants survived. One of the fortunate was young Vonnegut, the German-American infantryman from Indianapolis and recent student of modern science, who had now seen scientific truth (in the form of a carefully engineered firestorm) destroy one of the artistic and architectural treasure houses of European culture.

Following his repatriation by the Red Army and a summer of convalescence back home in Indianapolis, Vonnegut married his childhood sweetheart, Jane Cox, and enrolled in the University of Chicago's graduate program in anthropology (though he still lacked a college degree). As he recalls from these years, 'A first-grader should understand his culture isn't a rational invention; that there are thousands of other cultures and they all work pretty well; that all cultures function on faith rather than truth; that there are lots of alternatives to our own society.' Vonnegut had, of course, been taught similar notions of cultural relativism and transformation by his family's experience in the Depression, but it was at Chicago that he found these beliefs codified and explained. Another childhood notion now confirmed by the brightest minds in anthropology was the ideal of extended families; the department chairman, Robert Redfield, was presently at work on his theory of 'The Folk Society'. Vonnegut's thesis adviser, Sydney Slotkin, was even more ahead of the times—too far, in fact, for his method of studying primitive groups and industrialized societies in parallel made him disreputable in a field that did not adopt this approach until years later. Between 1945 and 1947 Vonnegut proposed, drafted and had rejected three theses of this nature, including a comparison of the Cubist painters and the American Indian Ghost Dance movement (to determine the criterion for a revolutionary group) and a scheme called 'Fluctuations Between Good and Evil in Simple Tales', which identified characteristic stories (whether primitive folktales or contemporary magazine pieces) by their narrative structures.

In 1947 Vonnegut left Chicago without a degree and signed on as a publicist for the Research Laboratory of the General Electric Corporation in Schenectady, New York, where his brother worked as a scientist. Hundreds of thousands of ex-soldiers like him attended college on the GI Bill; even more were moving into white-collar jobs within another post-war phenomenon, the conglomeration of American businesses into the giant corporations so conveniently known by their initials: GMC, AT & T, IBM and GE. At GE Vonnegut wrote press releases and mixed socially with the young scientists and their wives. From this post-war corporate experience he was to draw themes and structures for his early fiction, such as **"Deer in the Works"** and **"This Son of Mine"**. But he was also becoming restless, rebellious and deeply skeptical of the good life promised by such corporate ideals. As anyone might, and as countless self-taught writers do, he began work on a novel venting these frustrations. He also began writing and submitting stories to the popular family magazines which at the time welcomed such unsolicited work. In 1950 three of these short stories were published by *Collier's.* By 1951 they had accepted six others and were offering better rates for more, and a major New York publisher had signed a contract for Vonnegut's 'get even' novel, *Player Piano;* with much relief Kurt Vonnegut quit GE and left dreary Schenectady for the attractive environs of Cape Cod, Massachusetts, and his own short-story business.

But in no sense can Vonnegut's decision to support himself and his family by writing be regarded as a departure from the commercial middle class. The magazines he wrote for—*Collier's, The Saturday Evening Post, Redbook, Cosmopolitan, The Ladies' Home Journal*—were themselves staples of average American life, scorned by intellectuals and 'serious' writers as decidedly lowbrow affairs. Some of his stories appeared in science-fiction magazines, but only after being rejected by the better-paying family markets. Settling in West Barnstable among the tradesmen and small businessmen he came to feature in his stories, Vonnegut worked his own cottage industry while they plied theirs. Writers, critics and intellectuals were not part of Kurt Vonnegut's community. Salesmen and tradesmen were, and it was their families he lived among and for whom he wrote.

The magazine market was strong enough throughout the 1950s for Vonnegut to earn a modest living, about as much as 'being in charge of a cafeteria at a pretty good junior high school', he reports. His first novel, *Player Piano,* was not a financial success, and he probably would never have written another had not the family magazines begun to falter, change staffs (costing Vonnegut his editorial contacts) and eventually cease publication, as did his two best customers, *Collier's* and the *Post.* Ever the enterprising salesman, Kurt Vonnegut found a new form for his middle-class fictions and fantasies—the pulp-paperback market, which demanded a steady supply of novels that unsophisticated readers could comfortably enjoy: science fiction; spy novels; apocalyptic, end-of-the-world adventures in exotic realms; formulaic narratives like the prince-and-the-pauper story, revealing the hidden riches of poverty and the poverty of wealth. As his short-story business petered out, Kurt Vonnegut quickly retooled for a heavier industry: the production of paperback originals to fill the book racks in drugstores, airports and newsstands across America. Ten years of this would make him neither rich nor famous, but he was still the reliable tradesman of his own stories, crafting middle-class artifacts on Scudder's Lane in West Barnstable, Massachusetts. The basic elements of larger literary innovation (and so of acclaim) might be there, but they were only to emerge from a decade's slow experiments with the novel's more familiar forms and possibilities. (pp. 21-33)

Jerome Klinkowitz, in his Kurt Vonnegut, *Methuen, 1982, 96 p.*

FURTHER READING

Klinkowitz, Jerome. "Why They Read Vonnegut." In *The Vonnegut Statement,* edited by Jerome Klinkowitz and John Somer, pp. 18-30. New York: Delacorte Press/Seymour Lawrence, 1973.

Briefly assesses Vonnegut's popular status through analysis of his early short stories and novels.

———. "The Self-Effacing Word." In his *The Self-Apparent Word: Fiction as Language/Language as Fiction,* pp. 17-29. Carbondale and Edwardsville: Southern Illinois University Press, 1977.

Comparative study of Vonnegut's "The Hyannis Port Story" and Philip Roth's *Goodbye, Columbus.*

———. "A Do-It-Yourself Story Collection by Kurt Vonnegut." In *Vonnegut in America: An Introduction to the Life and Work of Kurt Vonnegut,* edited by Jerome Klinkowitz and Donald L. Lawler, pp. 53-60. New York: Delacorte Press, 1977.

Provides instructions for readers to create a "do-it-yourself" collection of Vonnegut's uncollected short fiction.

Pieratt, Asa B., Jr.; Huffman-klinkowitz, Julie; and Klinkowitz, Jerome. *Kurt Vonnegut: A Comprehensive Bibliography.* Hamden, Conn.: Archon Books, 1987, 283 p.

An exhaustive guide to Vonnegut's works, including foreign collections of his short fiction and a listing of his uncollected stories. Also features indexes of secondary criticism and doctoral dissertations on Vonnegut.

Vonnegut, Kurt, Jr. Preface to his *Welcome to the Monkey House: A Collection of Short Works,* pp. xiii-xv. New York: Delacorte Press, 1968.

Vonnegut comments in characteristic, self-effacing fashion upon his themes and commercial motivations behind stories in *Welcome to the Monkey House.*

Appendix:

Select Bibliography of General Sources on Short Fiction

BOOKS OF CRITICISM

Allen, Walter. *The Short Story in English.* New York: Oxford University Press, 1981, 413 p.

Aycock, Wendell M., ed. *The Teller and the Tale: Aspects of the Short Story* (Proceedings of the Comparative Literature Symposium, Texas Tech University, Volume XIII). Lubbock: Texas Tech Press, 1982, 156 p.

Averill, Deborah. *The Irish Short Story from George Moore to Frank O'Connor.* Washington, D.C.: University Press of America, 1982, 328 p.

Bates, H. E. *The Modern Short Story: A Critical Survey.* Boston: Writer, 1941, 231 p.

Bayley, John. *The Short Story: Henry James to Elizabeth Bowen.* Great Britain: The Harvester Press Limited, 1988, 197 p.

Bennett, E. K. *A History of the German Novelle: From Goethe to Thomas Mann.* Cambridge: At the University Press, 1934, 296 p.

Bone, Robert. *Down Home: A History of Afro-American Short Fiction from Its Beginning to the End of the Harlem Renaissance.* Rev. ed. New York: Columbia University Press, 1988, 350 p.

Bruck, Peter. *The Black American Short Story in the Twentieth Century: A Collection of Critical Essays.* Amsterdam: B. R. Grüner Publishing Co., 1977, 209 p.

Burnett, Whit, and Burnett, Hallie. *The Modern Short Story in the Making.* New York: Hawthorn Books, 1964, 405 p.

Canby, Henry Seidel. *The Short Story in English.* New York: Henry Holt and Co., 1909, 386 p.

Current-García, Eugene. *The American Short Story before 1850: A Critical History.* Twayne's Critical History of the Short Story, edited by William Peden. Boston: Twayne Publishers, 1985, 168 p.

Flora, Joseph M., ed. *The English Short Story, 1880-1945: A Critical History.* Twayne's Critical History of the Short Story, edited by William Peden. Boston: Twayne Publishers, 1985, 215 p.

Foster, David William. *Studies in the Contemporary Spanish-American Short Story.* Columbia, Mo.: University of Missouri Press, 1979, 126 p.

George, Albert J. *Short Fiction in France, 1800-1850.* Syracuse, N.Y.: Syracuse University Press, 1964, 245 p.

Gerlach, John. *Toward an End: Closure and Structure in the American Short Story.* University, Ala.: The University of Alabama Press, 1985, 193 p.

Hankin, Cherry, ed. *Critical Essays on the New Zealand Short Story.* Auckland: Heinemann Publishers, 1982, 186 p.

Hanson, Clare, ed. *Re-Reading the Short Story.* London: MacMillan Press, 1989, 137 p.

Harris, Wendell V. *British Short Fiction in the Nineteenth Century.* Detroit: Wayne State University Press, 1979, 209 p.

Huntington, John. *Rationalizing Genius: Idealogical Strategies in the Classic American Science Fiction Short Story.* New Brunswick: Rutgers University Press, 1989, 216 p.

Kilroy, James F., ed. *The Irish Short Story: A Critical History.* Twayne's Critical History of the Short Story, edited by William Peden. Boston: Twayne Publishers, 1984, 251 p.

Lee, A. Robert. *The Nineteenth-Century American Short Story.* Totowa, N. J.: Vision / Barnes & Noble, 1986, 196 p.

Leibowitz, Judith. *Narrative Purpose in the Novella.* The Hague: Mouton, 1974, 137 p.

Lohafer, Susan. *Coming to Terms with the Short Story.* Baton Rouge: Louisiana State University Press, 1983, 171 p.

Lohafer, Susan, and Clarey, Jo Ellyn. *Short Story Theory at a Crossroads.* Baton Rouge: Louisiana State University Press, 1989, 352 p.

Mann, Susan Garland. *The Short Story Cycle: A Genre Companion and Reference Guide.* New York: Greenwood Press, 1989, 228 p.

Matthews, Brander. *The Philosophy of the Short Story.* New York: Longmans, Green and Co., 1901, 83 p.

May, Charles E., ed. *Short Story Theories.* Athens, Oh.: Ohio University Press, 1976, 251 p.

McClave, Heather, ed. *Women Writers of the Short Story: A Collection of Critical Essays.* Englewood Cliffs, N. J.: Prentice-Hall, 1980, 171 p.

Moser, Charles, ed. *The Russian Short Story: A Critical History.* Twayne's Critical History of the Short Story, edited by William Peden. Boston: Twayne Publishers, 1986, 232 p.

New, W. H. *Dreams of Speech and Violence: The Art of the Short Story in Canada and New Zealand.* Toronto: The University of Toronto Press, 1987, 302 p.

Newman, Frances. *The Short Story's Mutations: From Petronius to Paul Morand.* New York: B. W. Huebsch, 1925, 332 p.

O'Connor, Frank. *The Lonely Voice: A Study of the Short Story.* Cleveland: World Publishing Co., 1963, 220 p.

O'Faolain, Sean. *The Short Story.* New York: Devin-Adair Co., 1951, 370 p.

Orel, Harold. *The Victorian Short Story: Development and Triumph of a Literary Genre.* Cambridge: Cambridge University Press, 1986, 213 p.

O'Toole, L. Michael. *Structure, Style and Interpretation in the Russian Short Story.* New Haven: Yale University Press, 1982, 272 p.

Pattee, Fred Lewis. *The Development of the American Short Story: An Historical Survey.* New York: Harper and Brothers Publishers, 1923, 388 p.

Peden, Margaret Sayers, ed. *The Latin American Short Story: A Critical History.* Twayne's Critical History of the Short Story, edited by William Peden. Boston: Twayne Publishers, 1983, 160 p.

Peden, William. *The American Short Story: Continuity and Change, 1940-1975.* Rev. ed. Boston: Houghton Mifflin Co., 1975, 215 p.

Reid, Ian. *The Short Story.* The Critical Idiom, edited by John D. Jump. London: Methuen and Co., 1977, 76 p.

Rhode, Robert D. *Setting in the American Short Story of Local Color, 1865-1900.* The Hague: Mouton, 1975, 189 p.

Rohrberger, Mary. *Hawthorne and the Modern Short Story: A Study in Genre.* The Hague: Mouton and Co., 1966, 148 p.

Shaw, Valerie, *The Short Story: A Critical Introduction.* London: Longman, 1983, 294 p.

Stephens, Michael. *The Dramaturgy of Style: Voice in Short Fiction.* Carbondale, Ill.: Southern Illinois University Press, 1986, 281 p.

Stevick, Philip, ed. *The American Short Story, 1900-1945: A Critical History.* Twayne's Critical History of the Short Story, edited by William Peden, Boston: Twayne Publishers, 1984, 209 p.

Summers, Hollis, ed. *Discussion of the Short Story.* Boston: D. C. Heath and Co., 1963, 118 p.

Vannatta, Dennis, ed. *The English Short Story, 1945-1980: A Critical History.* Twayne's Critical History of the Short Story, edited by William Peden. Boston: Twayne Publishers, 1985, 206 p.

Voss, Arthur. *The American Short Story: A Critical Survey.* Norman, Okla.: University of Oklahoma Press, 1973, 399 p.

Ward, Alfred C. *Aspects of the Modern Short Story: English and American.* London: University of London Press, 1924, 307 p.

Weaver, Gordon, ed. *The American Short Story, 1945-1980: A Critical History.* Twayne's Critical History of the Short Story, edited by William Peden. Boston: Twayne Publishers, 1983, 150 p.

West, Ray B., Jr. *The Short Story in America, 1900-1950.* Chicago: Henry Regnery Co., 1952, 147 p.

Williams, Blanche Colton. *Our Short Story Writers.* New York: Moffat, Yard and Co., 1920, 357 p.

Wright, Austin McGiffert. *The American Short Story in the Twenties.* Chicago: University of Chicago Press, 1961, 425 p.

CRITICAL ANTHOLOGIES

Atkinson, W. Patterson, ed. *The Short-Story.* Boston: Allyn and Bacon, 1923, 317 p.

Baldwin, Charles Sears, ed. *American Short Stories.* New York: Longmans, Green and Co., 1904, 333 p.

Charters, Ann, ed. *The Story and Its Writer: An Introduction to Short Fiction.* New York: St. Martin's Press, 1983, 1239 p.

Current-García, Eugene, and Patrick, Walton R., eds. *American Short Stories: 1820 to the Present.* Key Editions, edited by John C. Gerber. Chicago: Scott, Foresman and Co., 1952, 633 p.

Fagin, N. Bryllion, ed. *America through the Short Story.* Boston: Little, Brown, and Co., 1936, 508 p.

Frakes, James R., and Traschen, Isadore, eds. *Short Fiction: A Critical Collection.* Prentice-Hall English Literature Series, edited by Maynard Mack. Englewood Cliffs, N.J.: Prentice-Hall, 1959, 459 p.

Gifford, Douglas, ed. *Scottish Short Stories, 1800-1900.* The Scottish Library, edited by Alexander Scott. London: Calder and Boyars, 1971, 350 p.

Gordon, Caroline, and Tate, Allen, eds. *The House of Fiction: An Anthology of the Short Story with Commentary.* Rev. ed. New York: Charles Scribner's Sons, 1960, 469 p.

Greet, T. Y., et. al. *The Worlds of Fiction: Stories in Context.* Boston: Houghton Mifflin Co., 1964, 429 p.

Gullason, Thomas A., and Caspar, Leonard, eds. *The World of Short Fiction: An International Collection.* New York: Harper and Row, 1962, 548 p.

Havighurst, Walter, ed. *Masters of the Modern Short Story.* New York: Harcourt, Brace and Co., 1945, 538 p.

Litz, A. Walton, ed. *Major American Short Stories.* New York: Oxford University Press, 1975, 823 p.

Matthews, Brander, ed. *The Short-Story: Specimens Illustrating Its Development.* New York: American Book Co., 1907, 399 p.

Menton, Seymour, ed. *The Spanish American Short Story: A Critical Anthology.* Berkeley and Los Angeles: University of California Press, 1980, 496 p.

Mzamane, Mbulelo Vizikhungo, ed. *Hungry Flames, and Other Black South African Short Stories.* Longman African Classics. Essex: Longman, 1986, 162 p.

Schorer, Mark, ed. *The Short Story: A Critical Anthology.* Rev. ed. Prentice-Hall English Literature Series, edited by Maynard Mack. Englewood Cliffs, N. J.: Prentice-Hall, 1967, 459 p.

Simpson, Claude M., ed. *The Local Colorists: American Short Stories, 1857-1900.* New York: Harper and Brothers Publishers, 1960, 340 p.

Stanton, Robert, ed. *The Short Story and the Reader.* New York: Henry Holt and Co., 1960, 557 p.

West, Ray B., Jr., ed. *American Short Stories.* New York: Thomas Y. Crowell Co., 1959, 267 p.

Short Story Criticism Indexes

Literary Criticism Series
Cumulative Author Index

SSC Cumulative Nationality Index

SSC Cumulative Title Index

This Index Includes References to Entries in These Gale Series

Contemporary Literary Criticism presents excerpts of criticism on the works of novelists, poets, dramatists, short story writers, scriptwriters, and other creative writers who are now living or who have died since 1960.

Twentieth-Century Literary Criticism contains critical excerpts by the most significant commentators on poets, novelists, short story writers, dramatists, and philosophers who died between 1900 and 1960.

Nineteenth-Century Literature Criticism offers significant passages from criticism on authors who died between 1800 and 1899.

Literature Criticism from 1400 to 1800 compiles significant passages from the most noteworthy criticism on authors of the fifteenth through eighteenth centuries.

Classical and Medieval Literature Criticism offers excerpts of criticism on the works of world authors from classical antiquity through the fourteenth century.

Short Story Criticism compiles excerpts of criticism on short fiction by writers of all eras and nationalities.

Poetry Criticism presents excerpts of criticism on the works of poets from all eras, movements, and nationalities.

Drama Criticism contains excerpts of criticism on dramatists of all nationalities and periods of literary history.

Children's Literature Review includes excerpts from reviews, criticism, and commentary on works of authors and illustrators who create books for children.

***Contemporary Authors* Series** encompasses five related series. *Contemporary Authors* provides biographical and bibliographical information on more than 97,000 writers of fiction and nonfiction. *Contemporary Authors New Revision Series* provides completely updated information on authors covered in *CA. Contemporary Authors Permanent Series* consists of listings for deceased and inactive authors. *Contemporary Authors Autobiography Series* presents specially commissioned autobiographies by leading contemporary writers. *Contemporary Authors Bibliographical Series* contains primary and secondary bibliographies as well as analytical bibliographical essays by authorities on major modern authors.

Dictionary of Literary Biography encompasses four related series. *Dictionary of Literary Biography* furnishes illustrated overviews of authors' lives and works. *Dictionary of Literary Biography Documentary Series* illuminates the careers of major figures through a selection of literary documents, including letters, interviews, and photographs. *Dictionary of Literary Biography Yearbook* summarizes the past year's literary activity and includes updated entries on individual authors. *Concise Dictionary of American Literary Biography* comprises six volumes of revised and updated sketches on major American authors that were originally presented in *Dictionary of Literary Biography.*

***Something about the Author* Series** encompasses three related series. *Something about the Author* contains well-illustrated biographical sketches on juvenile and young adult authors and illustrators from all eras. *Something about the Author Autobiography Series* presents specially commissioned autobiographies by prominent authors and illustrators of books for children and young adults. *Authors & Artists for Young Adults* provides high school and junior high school students with profiles of their favorite creative artists.

Yesterday's Authors of Books for Children contains heavily illustrated entries on children's writers who died before 1961. Complete in two volumes.

Literary Criticism Series Cumulative Author Index

This index lists all author entries in the Gale Literary Criticism Series and includes cross-references to other Gale sources. References in the index are identified as follows:

AAYA: *Authors & Artists for Young Adults,* Volumes 1-6
CAAS: *Contemporary Authors Autobiography Series,* Volumes 1-13
CA: *Contemporary Authors* (original series), Volumes 1-132
CABS: *Contemporary Authors Bibliographical Series,* Volumes 1-3
CANR: *Contemporary Authors New Revision Series,* Volumes 1-33
CAP: *Contemporary Authors Permanent Series,* Volumes 1-2
CA-R: *Contemporary Authors* (revised editions), Volumes 1-44
CDALB: *Concise Dictionary of American Literary Biography,* Volumes 1-6
CLC: *Contemporary Literary Criticism,* Volumes 1-65
CLR: *Children's Literature Review,* Volumes 1-24
CMLC: *Classical and Medieval Literature Criticism,* Volumes 1-7
DC: *Drama Criticism,* Volume 1
DLB: *Dictionary of Literary Biography,* Volumes 1-104
DLB-DS: *Dictionary of Literary Biography Documentary Series,* Volumes 1-8
DLB-Y: *Dictionary of Literary Biography Yearbook,* Volumes 1980-1988
LC: *Literature Criticism from 1400 to 1800,* Volumes 1-16
NCLC: *Nineteenth-Century Literature Criticism,* Volumes 1-31
PC: *Poetry Criticism,* Volumes 1-2
SAAS: *Something about the Author Autobiography Series,* Volumes 1-12
SATA: *Something about the Author,* Volumes 1-64
SSC: *Short Story Criticism,* Volumes 1-8
TCLC: *Twentieth-Century Literary Criticism,* Volumes 1-41
YABC: *Yesterday's Authors of Books for Children,* Volumes 1-2

A. E. 1867-1935 .... **TCLC 3, 10**
See also Russell, George William
See also DLB 19

Abbey, Edward 1927-1989 ...... **CLC 36, 59**
See also CANR 2; CA 45-48; obituary CA 128

Abbott, Lee K., Jr. 19??- .... **CLC 48**

Abe, Kobo 1924- .... **CLC 8, 22, 53**
See also CANR 24; CA 65-68

Abell, Kjeld 1901-1961 .... **CLC 15**
See also obituary CA 111

Abish, Walter 1931- .... **CLC 22**
See also CA 101

Abrahams, Peter (Henry) 1919- ..... **CLC 4**
See also CA 57-60

Abrams, M(eyer) H(oward) 1912- ... **CLC 24**
See also CANR 13; CA 57-60; DLB 67

Abse, Dannie 1923- .... **CLC 7, 29**
See also CAAS 1; CANR 4; CA 53-56; DLB 27

Achebe, (Albert) Chinua(lumogu) 1930- .... **CLC 1, 3, 5, 7, 11, 26, 51**
See also CLR 20; CANR 6, 26; CA 1-4R; SATA 38, 40

Acker, Kathy 1948- .... **CLC 45**
See also CA 117, 122

Ackroyd, Peter 1949- .... **CLC 34, 52**
See also CA 123, 127

Acorn, Milton 1923- .... **CLC 15**
See also CA 103; DLB 53

Adamov, Arthur 1908-1970 ...... **CLC 4, 25**
See also CAP 2; CA 17-18; obituary CA 25-28R

Adams, Alice (Boyd) 1926- ... **CLC 6, 13, 46**
See also CANR 26; CA 81-84; DLB-Y 86

Adams, Douglas (Noel) 1952- ... **CLC 27, 60**
See also CA 106; DLB-Y 83

Adams, Henry (Brooks) 1838-1918 .... **TCLC 4**
See also CA 104; DLB 12, 47

Adams, Richard (George) 1920- .... **CLC 4, 5, 18**
See also CLR 20; CANR 3; CA 49-52; SATA 7

Adamson, Joy(-Friederike Victoria) 1910-1980 .... **CLC 17**
See also CANR 22; CA 69-72; obituary CA 93-96; SATA 11; obituary SATA 22

Adcock, (Kareen) Fleur 1934- ..... **CLC 41**
See also CANR 11; CA 25-28R; DLB 40

Addams, Charles (Samuel) 1912-1988 .... **CLC 30**
See also CANR 12; CA 61-64; obituary CA 126

Adler, C(arole) S(chwerdtfeger) 1932- .... **CLC 35**
See also CANR 19; CA 89-92; SATA 26

Adler, Renata 1938- .... **CLC 8, 31**
See also CANR 5, 22; CA 49-52

Ady, Endre 1877-1919 .... **TCLC 11**
See also CA 107

Agee, James 1909-1955 .... **TCLC 1, 19**
See also CA 108; DLB 2, 26; CDALB 1941-1968

Agnon, S(hmuel) Y(osef Halevi) 1888-1970 .... **CLC 4, 8, 14**
See also CAP 2; CA 17-18; obituary CA 25-28R

Ai 1947- .... **CLC 4, 14**
See also CA 85-88

Aickman, Robert (Fordyce) 1914-1981 .... **CLC 57**
See also CANR 3; CA 7-8R

Aiken, Conrad (Potter) 1889-1973 .... **CLC 1, 3, 5, 10, 52**
See also CANR 4; CA 5-8R; obituary CA 45-48; SATA 3, 30; DLB 9, 45

Aiken, Joan (Delano) 1924- .... **CLC 35**
See also CLR 1, 19; CANR 4; CA 9-12R; SAAS 1; SATA 2, 30

Ainsworth, William Harrison 1805-1882 .... **NCLC 13**
See also SATA 24; DLB 21

Ajar, Emile 1914-1980
See Gary, Romain

Akhmadulina, Bella (Akhatovna) 1937- .... **CLC 53**
See also CA 65-68

Akhmatova, Anna 1888-1966 .... **CLC 11, 25, 64; PC 2**
See also CAP 1; CA 19-20; obituary CA 25-28R

Aksakov, Sergei Timofeyvich 1791-1859 .... **NCLC 2**

Aksenov, Vassily (Pavlovich) 1932-
See Aksyonov, Vasily (Pavlovich)

Aksyonov, Vasily (Pavlovich) 1932- .... **CLC 22, 37**
See also CANR 12; CA 53-56

Akutagawa Ryunosuke 1892-1927 .... **TCLC 16**
See also CA 117

Alain 1868-1951 .... **TCLC 41**
See also Chartier, Emile-Auguste

Alain-Fournier 1886-1914 .... **TCLC 6**
See also Fournier, Henri Alban
See also DLB 65

Alarcon, Pedro Antonio de 1833-1891 .... **NCLC 1**

Alas (y Urena), Leopoldo (Enrique Garcia) 1852-1901 .... **TCLC 29**
See also CA 113

Albee, Edward (Franklin III) 1928- ... **CLC 1, 2, 3, 5, 9, 11, 13, 25, 53**
See also CANR 8; CA 5-8R; DLB 7; CDALB 1941-1968

Alberti, Rafael 1902- .... **CLC 7**
See also CA 85-88

Alcott, Amos Bronson 1799-1888 .. **NCLC 1**
See also DLB 1

Alcott, Louisa May 1832-1888 .... **NCLC 6**
See also CLR 1; YABC 1; DLB 1, 42, 79; CDALB 1865-1917

Aldanov, Mark 1887-1957 .... **TCLC 23**
See also CA 118

Aldington, Richard 1892-1962 ...... **CLC 49**
See also CA 85-88; DLB 20, 36

Aldiss, Brian W(ilson) 1925- .... **CLC 5, 14, 40**
See also CAAS 2; CANR 5; CA 5-8R; SATA 34; DLB 14

Alegria, Fernando 1918- .... **CLC 57**
See also CANR 5; CA 11-12R

Aleixandre, Vicente 1898-1984 ... **CLC 9, 36**
See also CANR 26; CA 85-88; obituary CA 114

Alepoudelis, Odysseus 1911-
See Elytis, Odysseus

Aleshkovsky, Yuz 1929- .... **CLC 44**
See also CA 121, 128

Alexander, Lloyd (Chudley) 1924- .. **CLC 35**
See also CLR 1, 5; CANR 1; CA 1-4R; SATA 3, 49; DLB 52

Alger, Horatio, Jr. 1832-1899 ..... **NCLC 8**
See also SATA 16; DLB 42

Algren, Nelson 1909-1981 .... **CLC 4, 10, 33**
See also CANR 20; CA 13-16R; obituary CA 103; DLB 9; DLB-Y 81, 82; CDALB 1941-1968

Alighieri, Dante 1265-1321 .... **CMLC 3**

Allard, Janet 1975- .... **CLC 59**

Allen, Edward 1948- .... **CLC 59**

Allen, Roland 1939-
See Ayckbourn, Alan

Allen, Woody 1935- .... **CLC 16, 52**
See also CANR 27; CA 33-36R; DLB 44

Allende, Isabel 1942- .... **CLC 39, 57**
See also CA 125

Alleyne, Carla D. 1975?- .... **CLC 65**

Allingham, Margery (Louise) 1904-1966 .... **CLC 19**
See also CANR 4; CA 5-8R; obituary CA 25-28R; DLB 77

Allingham, William 1824-1889 ... **NCLC 25**
See also DLB 35

Allston, Washington 1779-1843 .... **NCLC 2**
See also DLB 1

Almedingen, E. M. 1898-1971 ...... **CLC 12**
See also Almedingen, Martha Edith von
See also SATA 3

Almedingen, Martha Edith von 1898-1971
See Almedingen, E. M.
See also CANR 1; CA 1-4R

Alonso, Damaso 1898- .... **CLC 14**
See also CA 110; obituary CA 130

Alta 1942- .... **CLC 19**
See also CA 57-60

Alter, Robert B(ernard) 1935- ...... **CLC 34**
See also CANR 1; CA 49-52

Alther, Lisa 1944- .... **CLC 7, 41**
See also CANR 12; CA 65-68

Altman, Robert 1925- .... **CLC 16**
See also CA 73-76

Alvarez, A(lfred) 1929- .... **CLC 5, 13**
See also CANR 3; CA 1-4R; DLB 14, 40

Alvarez, Alejandro Rodriguez 1903-1965
See Casona, Alejandro
See also obituary CA 93-96

Amado, Jorge 1912- .... **CLC 13, 40**
See also CA 77-80

Ambler, Eric 1909- .... **CLC 4, 6, 9**
See also CANR 7; CA 9-12R; DLB 77

Amichai, Yehuda 1924- ...... **CLC 9, 22, 57**
See also CA 85-88

Amiel, Henri Frederic 1821-1881 .. **NCLC 4**

Amis, Kingsley (William) 1922- ...... **CLC 1, 2, 3, 5, 8, 13, 40, 44**
See also CANR 8; CA 9-12R; DLB 15, 27

Amis, Martin 1949- .... **CLC 4, 9, 38, 62**
See also CANR 8, 27; CA 65-68; DLB 14

Ammons, A(rchie) R(andolph) 1926- .... **CLC 2, 3, 5, 8, 9, 25, 57**
See also CANR 6; CA 9-12R; DLB 5

Anand, Mulk Raj 1905- .... **CLC 23**
See also CA 65-68

Anaya, Rudolfo A(lfonso) 1937- .... **CLC 23**
See also CAAS 4; CANR 1; CA 45-48; DLB 82

Andersen, Hans Christian 1805-1875 .... **NCLC 7; SSC 6**
See also CLR 6; YABC 1, 1

Anderson, Jessica (Margaret Queale) 19??- .... **CLC 37**
See also CANR 4; CA 9-12R

Anderson, Jon (Victor) 1940- .... **CLC 9**
See also CANR 20; CA 25-28R

Anderson, Lindsay 1923- .... **CLC 20**
See also CA 125

Anderson, Maxwell 1888-1959 ..... **TCLC 2**
See also CA 105; DLB 7

Anderson, Poul (William) 1926- .... **CLC 15**
See also CAAS 2; CANR 2, 15; CA 1-4R; SATA 39; DLB 8

Anderson, Robert (Woodruff) 1917- .... **CLC 23**
See also CA 21-24R; DLB 7

Anderson, Roberta Joan 1943-
See Mitchell, Joni

Anderson, Sherwood 1876-1941 ..... **TCLC 1, 10, 24; SSC 1**
See also CAAS 3; CA 104, 121; DLB 4, 9; DLB-DS 1

Andrade, Carlos Drummond de 1902-1987 .... **CLC 18**
See also CA 123

Andrewes, Lancelot 1555-1626 .... **LC 5**

Andrews, Cicily Fairfield 1892-1983
See West, Rebecca

Andreyev, Leonid (Nikolaevich) 1871-1919 .... **TCLC 3**
See also CA 104

Andrezel, Pierre 1885-1962
See Dinesen, Isak; Blixen, Karen (Christentze Dinesen)

Andric, Ivo 1892-1975 .... **CLC 8**
See also CA 81-84; obituary CA 57-60

Angelique, Pierre 1897-1962
See Bataille, Georges

Angell, Roger 1920- .... **CLC 26**
See also CANR 13; CA 57-60

Angelou, Maya 1928- .... **CLC 12, 35, 64**
See also CANR 19; CA 65-68; SATA 49; DLB 38

Annensky, Innokenty 1856-1909 ... **TCLC 14**
See also CA 110

Anouilh, Jean (Marie Lucien Pierre) 1910-1987 ..... **CLC 1, 3, 8, 13, 40, 50**
See also CA 17-20R; obituary CA 123

Anthony, Florence 1947-
See Ai

Anthony (Jacob), Piers 1934- ...... **CLC 35**
See also Jacob, Piers A(nthony) D(illingham)
See also DLB 8

Antoninus, Brother 1912-
See Everson, William (Oliver)

Antonioni, Michelangelo 1912- ..... **CLC 20**
See also CA 73-76

Antschel, Paul 1920-1970....... **CLC 10, 19**
See also Celan, Paul
See also CA 85-88

Anwar, Chairil 1922-1949 .... **TCLC 22**
See also CA 121

Apollinaire, Guillaume
1880-1918 .... **TCLC 3, 8**
See also Kostrowitzki, Wilhelm Apollinaris de

Appelfeld, Aharon 1932- .... **CLC 23, 47**
See also CA 112

Apple, Max (Isaac) 1941-........ **CLC 9, 33**
See also CANR 19; CA 81-84

Appleman, Philip (Dean) 1926-..... **CLC 51**
See also CANR 6; CA 13-16R

Apuleius, (Lucius) (Madaurensis)
125?-175?.................... **CMLC 1**

Aquin, Hubert 1929-1977.......... **CLC 15**
See also CA 105; DLB 53

Aragon, Louis 1897-1982........ **CLC 3, 22**
See also CA 69-72; obituary CA 108; DLB 72

Arbuthnot, John 1667-1735.......... **LC 1**

Archer, Jeffrey (Howard) 1940- .... **CLC 28**
See also CANR 22; CA 77-80

Archer, Jules 1915- .... **CLC 12**
See also CANR 6; CA 9-12R; SAAS 5; SATA 4

Arden, John 1930- .... **CLC 6, 13, 15**
See also CAAS 4; CA 13-16R; DLB 13

Arenas, Reinaldo 1943-........... **CLC 41**
See also CA 124, 128

Aretino, Pietro 1492-1556.......... **LC 12**

Arguedas, Jose Maria
1911-1969 .... **CLC 10, 18**
See also CA 89-92

Argueta, Manlio 1936-............ **CLC 31**

Ariosto, Ludovico 1474-1533.......... **LC 6**

Aristophanes
c. 450 B. C.-c. 385 B. C. .... **CMLC 4**

Arlt, Roberto 1900-1942 .... **TCLC 29**
See also CA 123

Armah, Ayi Kwei 1939-......... **CLC 5, 33**
See also CANR 21; CA 61-64

Armatrading, Joan 1950-.......... **CLC 17**
See also CA 114

Arnim, Achim von (Ludwig Joachim von Arnim) 1781-1831 .... **NCLC 5**
See also DLB 90

Arnold, Matthew 1822-1888 ... **NCLC 6, 29**
See also DLB 32, 57

Arnold, Thomas 1795-1842 ...... **NCLC 18**
See also DLB 55

Arnow, Harriette (Louisa Simpson)
1908-1986 .... **CLC 2, 7, 18**
See also CANR 14; CA 9-12R; obituary CA 118; SATA 42, 47; DLB 6

Arp, Jean 1887-1966.............. **CLC 5**
See also CA 81-84; obituary CA 25-28R

Arquette, Lois S(teinmetz) 1934-
See Duncan (Steinmetz Arquette), Lois
See also SATA 1

Arrabal, Fernando 1932- ... **CLC 2, 9, 18, 58**
See also CANR 15; CA 9-12R

Arrick, Fran 19??- .... **CLC 30**

Artaud, Antonin 1896-1948 ..... **TCLC 3, 36**
See also CA 104

Arthur, Ruth M(abel) 1905-1979.... **CLC 12**
See also CANR 4; CA 9-12R; obituary CA 85-88; SATA 7; obituary SATA 26

Artsybashev, Mikhail Petrarch
1878-1927 .... **TCLC 31**

Arundel, Honor (Morfydd)
1919-1973 .... **CLC 17**
See also CAP 2; CA 21-22; obituary CA 41-44R; SATA 4; obituary SATA 24

Asch, Sholem 1880-1957 .... **TCLC 3**
See also CA 105

Ashbery, John (Lawrence)
1927- ... **CLC 2, 3, 4, 6, 9, 13, 15, 25, 41**
See also CANR 9; CA 5-8R; DLB 5; DLB-Y 81

Ashton-Warner, Sylvia (Constance)
1908-1984 .... **CLC 19**
See also CA 69-72; obituary CA 112

Asimov, Isaac 1920- .... **CLC 1, 3, 9, 19, 26**
See also CLR 12; CANR 2, 19; CA 1-4R; SATA 1, 26; DLB 8

Astley, Thea (Beatrice May)
1925- .... **CLC 41**
See also CANR 11; CA 65-68

Aston, James 1906-1964
See White, T(erence) H(anbury)

Asturias, Miguel Angel
1899-1974 .... **CLC 3, 8, 13**
See also CAP 2; CA 25-28; obituary CA 49-52

Atheling, William, Jr. 1921-1975
See Blish, James (Benjamin)

Atherton, Gertrude (Franklin Horn)
1857-1948 .... **TCLC 2**
See also CA 104; DLB 9, 78

Atwood, Margaret (Eleanor)
1939- .... **CLC 2, 3, 4, 8, 13, 15, 25, 44; SSC 2**
See also CANR 3, 24; CA 49-52; SATA 50; DLB 53

Aubin, Penelope 1685-1731? .... **LC 9**
See also DLB 39

Auchincloss, Louis (Stanton)
1917- .... **CLC 4, 6, 9, 18, 45**
See also CANR 6; CA 1-4R; DLB 2; DLB-Y 80

Auden, W(ystan) H(ugh)
1907-1973 ..... **CLC 1, 2, 3, 4, 6, 9, 11, 14, 43; PC 1**
See also CANR 5; CA 9-12R; obituary CA 45-48; DLB 10, 20

Audiberti, Jacques 1899-1965 ...... **CLC 38**
See also obituary CA 25-28R

Auel, Jean M(arie) 1936-.......... **CLC 31**
See also CANR 21; CA 103

Augier, Emile 1820-1889 .... **NCLC 31**

Augustine, St. 354-430.......... **CMLC 6**

Austen, Jane 1775-1817.... **NCLC 1, 13, 19**

Auster, Paul 1947-............... **CLC 47**
See also CANR 23; CA 69-72

Austin, Mary (Hunter)
1868-1934 .... **TCLC 25**
See also CA 109; DLB 9

Averroes 1126-1198 .... **CMLC 7**

Avison, Margaret 1918-.......... **CLC 2, 4**
See also CA 17-20R; DLB 53

Ayckbourn, Alan 1939- .... **CLC 5, 8, 18, 33**
See also CA 21-24R; DLB 13

Aydy, Catherine 1937-
See Tennant, Emma

Ayme, Marcel (Andre) 1902-1967... **CLC 11**
See also CA 89-92; DLB 72

Ayrton, Michael 1921-1975......... **CLC 7**
See also CANR 9, 21; CA 5-8R; obituary CA 61-64

Azorin 1874-1967 .... **CLC 11**
See also Martinez Ruiz, Jose

Azuela, Mariano 1873-1952........ **TCLC 3**
See also CA 104

"Bab" 1836-1911
See Gilbert, (Sir) W(illiam) S(chwenck)

Babel, Isaak (Emmanuilovich)
1894-1941 .... **TCLC 2, 13**
See also CA 104

Babits, Mihaly 1883-1941 .... **TCLC 14**
See also CA 114

Bacchelli, Riccardo 1891-1985 ..... **CLC 19**
See also CA 29-32R; obituary CA 117

Bach, Richard (David) 1936-....... **CLC 14**
See also CANR 18; CA 9-12R; SATA 13

Bachman, Richard 1947-
See King, Stephen (Edwin)

Bacovia, George 1881-1957 .... **TCLC 24**

Bagehot, Walter 1826-1877 ...... **NCLC 10**
See also DLB 55

Bagnold, Enid 1889-1981.......... **CLC 25**
See also CANR 5; CA 5-8R; obituary CA 103; SATA 1, 25; DLB 13

Bagryana, Elisaveta 1893-.......... **CLC 10**

Bailey, Paul 1937- .... **CLC 45**
See also CANR 16; CA 21-24R; DLB 14

Baillie, Joanna 1762-1851 .... **NCLC 2**

Bainbridge, Beryl
1933- .... **CLC 4, 5, 8, 10, 14, 18, 22, 62**
See also CANR 24; CA 21-24R; DLB 14

Baker, Elliott 1922-............ **CLC 8, 61**
See also CANR 2; CA 45-48

Baker, Nicholson 1957-........... **CLC 61**

Author Index

Baker, Russell (Wayne) 1925- ...... **CLC 31**
See also CANR 11; CA 57-60

Bakshi, Ralph 1938- .... **CLC 26**
See also CA 112

Bakunin, Mikhail (Alexandrovich)
1814-1876 .... **NCLC 25**

Baldwin, James (Arthur)
1924-1987 ..... **CLC 1, 2, 3, 4, 5, 8, 13, 15, 17, 42, 50; DC 1**
See also CANR 3,24; CA 1-4R; obituary CA 124; CABS 1; SATA 9, 54; DLB 2, 7, 33; DLB-Y 87; CDALB 1941-1968; AAYA 4

Ballard, J(ames) G(raham)
1930- .... **CLC 3, 6, 14, 36; SSC 1**
See also CANR 15; CA 5-8R; DLB 14

Balmont, Konstantin Dmitriyevich
1867-1943 .... **TCLC 11**
See also CA 109

Balzac, Honore de
1799-1850 .... **NCLC 5; SSC 5**

Bambara, Toni Cade 1939- .... **CLC 19**
See also CA 29-32R; DLB 38

Bandanes, Jerome 1937- .... **CLC 59**

Banim, John 1798-1842 .... **NCLC 13**

Banim, Michael 1796-1874 ...... **NCLC 13**

Banks, Iain 1954- .... **CLC 34**
See also CA 123

Banks, Lynne Reid 1929- .... **CLC 23**
See also Reid Banks, Lynne

Banks, Russell 1940- .... **CLC 37**
See also CANR 19; CA 65-68

Banville, John 1945- .... **CLC 46**
See also CA 117, 128; DLB 14

Banville, Theodore (Faullain) de
1832-1891 .... **NCLC 9**

Baraka, Imamu Amiri
1934- .... **CLC 1, 2, 3, 5, 10, 14, 33**
See also Jones, (Everett) LeRoi
See also DLB 5, 7, 16, 38; CDALB 1941-1968

Barbellion, W. N. P. 1889-1919 ... **TCLC 24**

Barbera, Jack 1945- .... **CLC 44**
See also CA 110

Barbey d'Aurevilly, Jules Amedee
1808-1889 .... **NCLC 1**

Barbusse, Henri 1873-1935 .... **TCLC 5**
See also CA 105; DLB 65

Barea, Arturo 1897-1957 .... **TCLC 14**
See also CA 111

Barfoot, Joan 1946- .... **CLC 18**
See also CA 105

Baring, Maurice 1874-1945 .... **TCLC 8**
See also CA 105; DLB 34

Barker, Clive 1952- .... **CLC 52**
See also CA 121

Barker, George (Granville)
1913- .... **CLC 8, 48**
See also CANR 7; CA 9-12R; DLB 20

Barker, Howard 1946- .... **CLC 37**
See also CA 102; DLB 13

Barker, Pat 1943- .... **CLC 32**
See also CA 117, 122

Barlow, Joel 1754-1812 .... **NCLC 23**
See also DLB 37

Barnard, Mary (Ethel) 1909- .... **CLC 48**
See also CAP 2; CA 21-22

Barnes, Djuna (Chappell)
1892-1982 ... **CLC 3, 4, 8, 11, 29; SSC 3**
See also CANR 16; CA 9-12R; obituary CA 107; DLB 4, 9, 45

Barnes, Julian 1946- .... **CLC 42**
See also CANR 19; CA 102

Barnes, Peter 1931- .... **CLC 5, 56**
See also CA 65-68; DLB 13

Baroja (y Nessi), Pio 1872-1956 .... **TCLC 8**
See also CA 104

Barondess, Sue K(aufman) 1926-1977
See Kaufman, Sue
See also CANR 1; CA 1-4R; obituary CA 69-72

Barrett, (Roger) Syd 1946-
See Pink Floyd

Barrett, William (Christopher)
1913- .... **CLC 27**
See also CANR 11; CA 13-16R

Barrie, (Sir) J(ames) M(atthew)
1860-1937 .... **TCLC 2**
See also CLR 16; YABC 1; CA 104; DLB 10

Barrol, Grady 1953-
See Bograd, Larry

Barry, Philip (James Quinn)
1896-1949 .... **TCLC 11**
See also CA 109; DLB 7

Barth, John (Simmons)
1930- ...... **CLC 1, 2, 3, 5, 7, 9, 10, 14, 27, 51**
See also CANR 5, 23; CA 1-4R; CABS 1; DLB 2

Barthelme, Donald
1931-1989 ..... **CLC 1, 2, 3, 5, 6, 8, 13, 23, 46, 59; SSC 2**
See also CANR 20; CA 21-24R, 129; SATA 7; DLB 2; DLB-Y 80

Barthelme, Frederick 1943- .... **CLC 36**
See also CA 114, 122; DLB-Y 85

Barthes, Roland 1915-1980 .... **CLC 24**
See also obituary CA 97-100

Barzun, Jacques (Martin) 1907- .... **CLC 51**
See also CANR 22; CA 61-64

Bashkirtseff, Marie 1859-1884 ... **NCLC 27**

Bassani, Giorgio 1916- .... **CLC 9**
See also CA 65-68

Bataille, Georges 1897-1962 .... **CLC 29**
See also CA 101; obituary CA 89-92

Bates, H(erbert) E(rnest)
1905-1974 .... **CLC 46**
See also CA 93-96; obituary CA 45-48

Baudelaire, Charles
1821-1867 .... **NCLC 6, 29; PC 1**

Baudrillard, Jean 1929- .... **CLC 60**

Baum, L(yman) Frank 1856-1919 ... **TCLC 7**
See also CLR 15; CA 108; SATA 18; DLB 22

Baumbach, Jonathan 1933- ...... **CLC 6, 23**
See also CAAS 5; CANR 12; CA 13-16R; DLB-Y 80

Bausch, Richard (Carl) 1945- ...... **CLC 51**
See also CA 101

Baxter, Charles 1947- .... **CLC 45**
See also CA 57-60

Baxter, James K(eir) 1926-1972 .... **CLC 14**
See also CA 77-80

Bayer, Sylvia 1909-1981
See Glassco, John

Beagle, Peter S(oyer) 1939- .... **CLC 7**
See also CANR 4; CA 9-12R; DLB-Y 80

Beard, Charles A(ustin)
1874-1948 .... **TCLC 15**
See also CA 115; SATA 18; DLB 17

Beardsley, Aubrey 1872-1898 ..... **NCLC 6**

Beattie, Ann 1947- ... **CLC 8, 13, 18, 40, 63**
See also CA 81-84; DLB-Y 82

Beattie, James 1735-1803 .... **NCLC 25**

Beauvoir, Simone (Lucie Ernestine Marie Bertrand) de
1908-1986 ... **CLC 1, 2, 4, 8, 14, 31, 44, 50**
See also CANR 28; CA 9-12R; obituary CA 118; DLB 72; DLB-Y 86

Becker, Jurek 1937- .... **CLC 7, 19**
See also CA 85-88; DLB 75

Becker, Walter 1950- .... **CLC 26**

Beckett, Samuel (Barclay)
1906-1989 ..... **CLC 1, 2, 3, 4, 6, 9, 10, 11, 14, 18, 29, 57, 59**
See also CA 5-8R; DLB 13, 15

Beckford, William 1760-1844 .... **NCLC 16**
See also DLB 39

Beckman, Gunnel 1910- .... **CLC 26**
See also CANR 15; CA 33-36R; SATA 6

Becque, Henri 1837-1899 .... **NCLC 3**

Beddoes, Thomas Lovell
1803-1849 .... **NCLC 3**

Beecher, Catharine Esther
1800-1878 .... **NCLC 30**
See also DLB 1

Beecher, John 1904-1980 .... **CLC 6**
See also CANR 8; CA 5-8R; obituary CA 105

Beer, Johann 1655-1700 .... **LC 5**

Beer, Patricia 1919?- .... **CLC 58**
See also CANR 13; CA 61-64; DLB 40

Beerbohm, (Sir Henry) Max(imilian)
1872-1956 .... **TCLC 1, 24**
See also CA 104; DLB 34

Behan, Brendan
1923-1964 .... **CLC 1, 8, 11, 15**
See also CA 73-76; DLB 13

Behn, Aphra 1640?-1689 .... **LC 1**
See also DLB 39, 80

Behrman, S(amuel) N(athaniel)
1893-1973 .... **CLC 40**
See also CAP 1; CA 15-16; obituary CA 45-48; DLB 7, 44

Beiswanger, George Edwin 1931-
See Starbuck, George (Edwin)

Belasco, David 1853-1931 .... **TCLC 3**
See also CA 104; DLB 7

Belcheva, Elisaveta 1893-
See Bagryana, Elisaveta

Belinski, Vissarion Grigoryevich
1811-1848 .... **NCLC 5**

Belitt, Ben 1911-................ **CLC 22**
See also CAAS 4; CANR 7; CA 13-16R; DLB 5

Bell, Acton 1820-1849
See Bronte, Anne

Bell, Currer 1816-1855
See Bronte, Charlotte

Bell, Madison Smartt 1957-........ **CLC 41**
See also CA 111

Bell, Marvin (Hartley) 1937-..... **CLC 8, 31**
See also CA 21-24R; DLB 5

Bellamy, Edward 1850-1898 ...... **NCLC 4**
See also DLB 12

Belloc, (Joseph) Hilaire (Pierre Sebastien Rene Swanton)
1870-1953 .... **TCLC 7, 18**
See also YABC 1; CA 106; DLB 19

Bellow, Saul
1915- ..... **CLC 1, 2, 3, 6, 8, 10, 13, 15, 25, 33, 34, 63**
See also CA 5-8R; CABS 1; DLB 2, 28; DLB-Y 82; DLB-DS 3; CDALB 1941-1968

Belser, Reimond Karel Maria de 1929-
See Ruyslinck, Ward

Bely, Andrey 1880-1934........... **TCLC 7**
See also CA 104

Benary-Isbert, Margot 1889-1979... **CLC 12**
See also CLR 12; CANR 4; CA 5-8R; obituary CA 89-92; SATA 2; obituary SATA 21

Benavente (y Martinez), Jacinto
1866-1954 .... **TCLC 3**
See also CA 106

Benchley, Peter (Bradford)
1940- .... **CLC 4, 8**
See also CANR 12; CA 17-20R; SATA 3

Benchley, Robert 1889-1945 .... **TCLC 1**
See also CA 105; DLB 11

Benedikt, Michael 1935- .... **CLC 4, 14**
See also CANR 7; CA 13-16R; DLB 5

Benet, Juan 1927-............... **CLC 28**

Benet, Stephen Vincent
1898-1943 .... **TCLC 7**
See also YABC 1; CA 104; DLB 4, 48

Benet, William Rose 1886-1950 ... **TCLC 28**
See also CA 118; DLB 45

Benford, Gregory (Albert) 1941-.... **CLC 52**
See also CANR 12, 24; CA 69-72; DLB-Y 82

Benjamin, Walter 1892-1940...... **TCLC 39**

Benn, Gottfried 1886-1956......... **TCLC 3**
See also CA 106; DLB 56

Bennett, Alan 1934- .... **CLC 45**
See also CA 103

Bennett, (Enoch) Arnold
1867-1931 .... **TCLC 5, 20**
See also CA 106; DLB 10, 34

Bennett, George Harold 1930-
See Bennett, Hal
See also CA 97-100

Bennett, Hal 1930-................ **CLC 5**
See also Bennett, George Harold
See also DLB 33

Bennett, Jay 1912-............... **CLC 35**
See also CANR 11; CA 69-72; SAAS 4; SATA 27, 41

Bennett, Louise (Simone) 1919-..... **CLC 28**
See also Bennett-Coverly, Louise Simone

Bennett-Coverly, Louise Simone 1919-
See Bennett, Louise (Simone)
See also CA 97-100

Benson, E(dward) F(rederic)
1867-1940 .... **TCLC 27**
See also CA 114

Benson, Jackson J. 1930-......... **CLC 34**
See also CA 25-28R

Benson, Sally 1900-1972 .... **CLC 17**
See also CAP 1; CA 19-20; obituary CA 37-40R; SATA 1, 35; obituary SATA 27

Benson, Stella 1892-1933......... **TCLC 17**
See also CA 117; DLB 36

Bentley, E(dmund) C(lerihew)
1875-1956 .... **TCLC 12**
See also CA 108; DLB 70

Bentley, Eric (Russell) 1916-....... **CLC 24**
See also CANR 6; CA 5-8R

Berger, John (Peter) 1926- ...... **CLC 2, 19**
See also CA 81-84; DLB 14

Berger, Melvin (H.) 1927-......... **CLC 12**
See also CANR 4; CA 5-8R; SAAS 2; SATA 5

Berger, Thomas (Louis)
1924- .... **CLC 3, 5, 8, 11, 18, 38**
See also CANR 5; CA 1-4R; DLB 2; DLB-Y 80

Bergman, (Ernst) Ingmar 1918-..... **CLC 16**
See also CA 81-84

Bergson, Henri 1859-1941........ **TCLC 32**

Bergstein, Eleanor 1938- .... **CLC 4**
See also CANR 5; CA 53-56

Berkoff, Steven 1937-............. **CLC 56**
See also CA 104

Bermant, Chaim 1929-............ **CLC 40**
See also CANR 6; CA 57-60

Bernanos, (Paul Louis) Georges
1888-1948 .... **TCLC 3**
See also CA 104; DLB 72

Bernard, April 19??-............. **CLC 59**

Bernhard, Thomas
1931-1989 .... **CLC 3, 32, 61**
See also CA 85-88,; obituary CA 127; DLB 85

Berriault, Gina 1926-............ **CLC 54**
See also CA 116

Berrigan, Daniel J. 1921-.......... **CLC 4**
See also CAAS 1; CANR 11; CA 33-36R; DLB 5

Berrigan, Edmund Joseph Michael, Jr.
1934-1983
See Berrigan, Ted
See also CANR 14; CA 61-64; obituary CA 110

Berrigan, Ted 1934-1983 .... **CLC 37**
See also Berrigan, Edmund Joseph Michael, Jr.
See also DLB 5

Berry, Chuck 1926- .... **CLC 17**

Berry, Wendell (Erdman)
1934- .... **CLC 4, 6, 8, 27, 46**
See also CA 73-76; DLB 5, 6

Berryman, John
1914-1972 ..... **CLC 1, 2, 3, 4, 6, 8, 10, 13, 25, 62**
See also CAP 1; CA 15-16; obituary CA 33-36R; CABS 2; DLB 48; CDALB 1941-1968

Bertolucci, Bernardo 1940- .... **CLC 16**
See also CA 106

Bertrand, Aloysius 1807-1841 .... **NCLC 31**

Bertran de Born c. 1140-1215..... **CMLC 5**

Besant, Annie (Wood) 1847-1933 ... **TCLC 9**
See also CA 105

Bessie, Alvah 1904-1985........... **CLC 23**
See also CANR 2; CA 5-8R; obituary CA 116; DLB 26

Beti, Mongo 1932- .... **CLC 27**
See also Beyidi, Alexandre

Betjeman, (Sir) John
1906-1984 .... **CLC 2, 6, 10, 34, 43**
See also CA 9-12R; obituary CA 112; DLB 20; DLB-Y 84

Betti, Ugo 1892-1953 .... **TCLC 5**
See also CA 104

Betts, Doris (Waugh) 1932-.... **CLC 3, 6, 28**
See also CANR 9; CA 13-16R; DLB-Y 82

Bialik, Chaim Nachman
1873-1934 .... **TCLC 25**

Bidart, Frank 19??-............... **CLC 33**

Bienek, Horst 1930-............ **CLC 7, 11**
See also CA 73-76; DLB 75

Bierce, Ambrose (Gwinett)
1842-1914?................ **TCLC 1, 7**
See also CA 104; DLB 11, 12, 23, 71, 74; CDALB 1865-1917

Billington, Rachel 1942-........... **CLC 43**
See also CA 33-36R

Binyon, T(imothy) J(ohn) 1936- .... **CLC 34**
See also CA 111

Bioy Casares, Adolfo 1914-.... **CLC 4, 8, 13**
See also CANR 19; CA 29-32R

Birch, Allison 1974?- .... **CLC 65**

Bird, Robert Montgomery
1806-1854 .... **NCLC 1**

Birdwell, Cleo 1936-
See DeLillo, Don

Birney (Alfred) Earle
1904- .... **CLC 1, 4, 6, 11**
See also CANR 5, 20; CA 1-4R

Bishop, Elizabeth 1911-1979 ...... **CLC 1, 4, 9, 13, 15, 32**
See also CANR 26; CA 5-8R; obituary CA 89-92; CABS 2; obituary SATA 24; DLB 5

Bishop, John 1935- .... **CLC 10**
See also CA 105

Bissett, Bill 1939- .... **CLC 18**
See also CANR 15; CA 69-72; DLB 53

Bitov, Andrei (Georgievich) 1937- ... **CLC 57**

Biyidi, Alexandre 1932-
See Beti, Mongo
See also CA 114, 124

Bjornson, Bjornstjerne (Martinius) 1832-1910 .... **TCLC 7, 37**
See also CA 104

Blackburn, Paul 1926-1971 ...... **CLC 9, 43**
See also CA 81-84; obituary CA 33-36R; DLB 16; DLB-Y 81

Black Elk 1863-1950 .... **TCLC 33**

Blackmore, R(ichard) D(oddridge) 1825-1900 .... **TCLC 27**
See also CA 120; DLB 18

Blackmur, R(ichard) P(almer) 1904-1965 .... **CLC 2, 24**
See also CAP 1; CA 11-12; obituary CA 25-28R; DLB 63

Blackwood, Algernon (Henry) 1869-1951 .... **TCLC 5**
See also CA 105

Blackwood, Caroline 1931- .... **CLC 6, 9**
See also CA 85-88; DLB 14

Blair, Eric Arthur 1903-1950
See Orwell, George
See also CA 104; SATA 29

Blais, Marie-Claire 1939- .... **CLC 2, 4, 6, 13, 22**
See also CAAS 4; CA 21-24R; DLB 53

Blaise, Clark 1940- .... **CLC 29**
See also CAAS 3; CANR 5; CA 53-56R; DLB 53

Blake, Nicholas 1904-1972
See Day Lewis, C(ecil)

Blake, William 1757-1827 .... **NCLC 13**
See also SATA 30

Blasco Ibanez, Vicente 1867-1928 .... **TCLC 12**
See also CA 110

Blatty, William Peter 1928- .... **CLC 2**
See also CANR 9; CA 5-8R

Blessing, Lee 1949- .... **CLC 54**

Blish, James (Benjamin) 1921-1975 .... **CLC 14**
See also CANR 3; CA 1-4R; obituary CA 57-60; DLB 8

Blixen, Karen (Christentze Dinesen) 1885-1962
See Dinesen, Isak
See also CAP 2; CA 25-28; SATA 44

Bloch, Robert (Albert) 1917- .... **CLC 33**
See also CANR 5; CA 5-8R; SATA 12; DLB 44

Blok, Aleksandr (Aleksandrovich) 1880-1921 .... **TCLC 5**
See also CA 104

Bloom, Harold 1930- .... **CLC 24, 65**
See also CA 13-16R; DLB 67

Blount, Roy (Alton), Jr. 1941- ..... **CLC 38**
See also CANR 10; CA 53-56

Bloy, Leon 1846-1917 .... **TCLC 22**
See also CA 121

Blume, Judy (Sussman Kitchens) 1938- .... **CLC 12, 30**
See also CLR 2, 15; CANR 13; CA 29-32R; SATA 2, 31; DLB 52

Blunden, Edmund (Charles) 1896-1974 .... **CLC 2, 56**
See also CAP 2; CA 17-18; obituary CA 45-48; DLB 20

Bly, Robert (Elwood) 1926- .... **CLC 1, 2, 5, 10, 15, 38**
See also CA 5-8R; DLB 5

Bochco, Steven 1944?- .... **CLC 35**

Bodker, Cecil 1927- .... **CLC 21**
See also CLR 23; CANR 13; CA 73-76; SATA 14

Boell, Heinrich (Theodor) 1917-1985
See Boll, Heinrich
See also CANR 24; CA 21-24R; obituary CA 116

Bogan, Louise 1897-1970 ..... **CLC 4, 39, 46**
See also CA 73-76; obituary CA 25-28R; DLB 45

Bogarde, Dirk 1921- .... **CLC 19**
See also Van Den Bogarde, Derek (Jules Gaspard Ulric) Niven
See also DLB 14

Bogosian, Eric 1953- .... **CLC 45**

Bograd, Larry 1953- .... **CLC 35**
See also CA 93-96; SATA 33

Bohl de Faber, Cecilia 1796-1877
See Caballero, Fernan

Boiardo, Matteo Maria 1441-1494 .... **LC 6**

Boileau-Despreaux, Nicolas 1636-1711 .... **LC 3**

Boland, Eavan (Aisling) 1944- ...... **CLC 40**
See also DLB 40

Boll, Heinrich (Theodor) 1917-1985 ... **CLC 2, 3, 6, 9, 11, 15, 27, 39**
See also Boell, Heinrich (Theodor)
See also DLB 69; DLB-Y 85

Bolt, Robert (Oxton) 1924- .... **CLC 14**
See also CA 17-20R; DLB 13

Bond, Edward 1934- .... **CLC 4, 6, 13, 23**
See also CA 25-28R; DLB 13

Bonham, Frank 1914- .... **CLC 12**
See also CANR 4; CA 9-12R; SAAS 3; SATA 1, 49

Bonnefoy, Yves 1923- .... **CLC 9, 15, 58**
See also CA 85-88

Bontemps, Arna (Wendell) 1902-1973 .... **CLC 1, 18**
See also CLR 6; CANR 4; CA 1-4R; obituary CA 41-44R; SATA 2, 44; obituary SATA 24; DLB 48, 51

Booth, Martin 1944- .... **CLC 13**
See also CAAS 2; CA 93-96

Booth, Philip 1925- .... **CLC 23**
See also CANR 5; CA 5-8R; DLB-Y 82

Booth, Wayne C(layson) 1921- ..... **CLC 24**
See also CAAS 5; CANR 3; CA 1-4R; DLB 67

Borchert, Wolfgang 1921-1947 ..... **TCLC 5**
See also CA 104; DLB 69

Borges, Jorge Luis 1899-1986 ... **CLC 1, 2, 3, 4, 6, 8, 9, 10, 13, 19, 44, 48; SSC 4**
See also CANR 19; CA 21-24R; DLB-Y 86

Borowski, Tadeusz 1922-1951 ...... **TCLC 9**
See also CA 106

Borrow, George (Henry) 1803-1881 .... **NCLC 9**
See also DLB 21, 55

Bosschere, Jean de 1878-1953 ..... **TCLC 19**
See also CA 115

Boswell, James 1740-1795 .... **LC 4**

Bottoms, David 1949- .... **CLC 53**
See also CANR 22; CA 105; DLB-Y 83

Boucolon, Maryse 1937-
See Conde, Maryse
See also CA 110

Bourget, Paul (Charles Joseph) 1852-1935 .... **TCLC 12**
See also CA 107

Bourjaily, Vance (Nye) 1922- .... **CLC 8, 62**
See also CAAS 1; CANR 2; CA 1-4R; DLB 2

Bourne, Randolph S(illiman) 1886-1918 .... **TCLC 16**
See also CA 117; DLB 63

Bova, Ben(jamin William) 1932- .... **CLC 45**
See also CLR 3; CANR 11; CA 5-8R; SATA 6; DLB-Y 81

Bowen, Elizabeth (Dorothea Cole) 1899-1973 ..... **CLC 1, 3, 6, 11, 15, 22; SSC 3**
See also CAP 2; CA 17-18; obituary CA 41-44R; DLB 15

Bowering, George 1935- .... **CLC 15, 47**
See also CANR 10; CA 21-24R; DLB 53

Bowering, Marilyn R(uthe) 1949- ... **CLC 32**
See also CA 101

Bowers, Edgar 1924- .... **CLC 9**
See also CANR 24; CA 5-8R; DLB 5

Bowie, David 1947- .... **CLC 17**
See also Jones, David Robert

Bowles, Jane (Sydney) 1917-1973 .... **CLC 3**
See also CAP 2; CA 19-20; obituary CA 41-44R

Bowles, Paul (Frederick) 1910- .... **CLC 1, 2, 19, 53; SSC 3**
See also CAAS 1; CANR 1, 19; CA 1-4R; DLB 5, 6

Box, Edgar 1925-
See Vidal, Gore

Boyd, William 1952- .... **CLC 28, 53**
See also CA 114, 120

Boyle, Kay 1903- .. **CLC 1, 5, 19, 58; SSC 5**
See also CAAS 1; CA 13-16R; DLB 4, 9, 48

Boyle, Patrick 19??- .... **CLC 19**

Boyle, Thomas Coraghessan 1948- .... **CLC 36, 55**
See also CA 120; DLB-Y 86

Brackenridge, Hugh Henry 1748-1816 .... **NCLC 7**
See also DLB 11, 37

Bradbury, Edward P. 1939-
See Moorcock, Michael

Bradbury, Malcolm (Stanley) 1932- .... **CLC 32, 61**
See also CANR 1; CA 1-4R; DLB 14

Bradbury, Ray(mond Douglas) 1920- .... **CLC 1, 3, 10, 15, 42**
See also CANR 2; CA 1-4R; SATA 11; DLB 2, 8

Bradford, Gamaliel 1863-1932..... **TCLC 36**
See also DLB 17

Bradley, David (Henry), Jr. 1950- .. **CLC 23**
See also CANR 26; CA 104; DLB 33

Bradley, John Ed 1959-........... **CLC 55**

Bradley, Marion Zimmer 1930-..... **CLC 30**
See also CANR 7; CA 57-60; DLB 8

Bradstreet, Anne 1612-1672.......... **LC 4**
See also DLB 24; CDALB 1640-1865

Bragg, Melvyn 1939- .... **CLC 10**
See also CANR 10; CA 57-60; DLB 14

Braine, John (Gerard) 1922-1986 .... **CLC 1, 3, 41**
See also CANR 1; CA 1-4R; obituary CA 120; DLB 15; DLB-Y 86

Brammer, Billy Lee 1930?-1978
See Brammer, William

Brammer, William 1930?-1978 ..... **CLC 31**
See also obituary CA 77-80

Brancati, Vitaliano 1907-1954..... **TCLC 12**
See also CA 109

Brancato, Robin F(idler) 1936- ..... **CLC 35**
See also CANR 11; CA 69-72; SATA 23

Brand, Millen 1906-1980 .... **CLC 7**
See also CA 21-24R; obituary CA 97-100

Branden, Barbara 19??- .... **CLC 44**

Brandes, Georg (Morris Cohen) 1842-1927 .... **TCLC 10**
See also CA 105

Brandys, Kazimierz 1916- .... **CLC 62**

Branley, Franklyn M(ansfield) 1915- .... **CLC 21**
See also CLR 13; CANR 14; CA 33-36R; SATA 4

Brathwaite, Edward 1930- .... **CLC 11**
See also CANR 11; CA 25-28R; DLB 53

Brautigan, Richard (Gary) 1935-1984 .... **CLC 1, 3, 5, 9, 12, 34, 42**
See also CA 53-56; obituary CA 113; SATA 56; DLB 2, 5; DLB-Y 80, 84

Brecht, (Eugen) Bertolt (Friedrich) 1898-1956 .... **TCLC 1, 6, 13, 35**
See also CA 104; DLB 56

Bremer, Fredrika 1801-1865 ..... **NCLC 11**

Brennan, Christopher John 1870-1932 .... **TCLC 17**
See also CA 117

Brennan, Maeve 1917-............. **CLC 5**
See also CA 81-84

Brentano, Clemens (Maria) 1778-1842 .... **NCLC 1**
See also DLB 90

Brenton, Howard 1942- .... **CLC 31**
See also CA 69-72; DLB 13

Breslin, James 1930-
See Breslin, Jimmy
See also CA 73-76

Breslin, Jimmy 1930- .... **CLC 4, 43**
See also Breslin, James

Bresson, Robert 1907- .... **CLC 16**
See also CA 110

Breton, Andre 1896-1966... **CLC 2, 9, 15, 54**
See also CAP 2; CA 19-20; obituary CA 25-28R; DLB 65

Breytenbach, Breyten 1939-..... **CLC 23, 37**
See also CA 113, 129

Bridgers, Sue Ellen 1942- .... **CLC 26**
See also CANR 11; CA 65-68; SAAS 1; SATA 22; DLB 52

Bridges, Robert 1844-1930......... **TCLC 1**
See also CA 104; DLB 19

Bridie, James 1888-1951 .... **TCLC 3**
See also Mavor, Osborne Henry
See also DLB 10

Brin, David 1950-................ **CLC 34**
See also CANR 24; CA 102

Brink, Andre (Philippus) 1935- .... **CLC 18, 36**
See also CA 104

Brinsmead, H(esba) F(ay) 1922- .... **CLC 21**
See also CANR 10; CA 21-24R; SAAS 5; SATA 18

Brittain, Vera (Mary) 1893?-1970... **CLC 23**
See also CAP 1; CA 15-16; obituary CA 25-28R

Broch, Hermann 1886-1951....... **TCLC 20**
See also CA 117; DLB 85

Brock, Rose 1923-
See Hansen, Joseph

Brodkey, Harold 1930-........... **CLC 56**
See also CA 111

Brodsky, Iosif Alexandrovich 1940-
See Brodsky, Joseph (Alexandrovich)
See also CA 41-44R

Brodsky, Joseph (Alexandrovich) 1940- .... **CLC 4, 6, 13, 36, 50**
See also Brodsky, Iosif Alexandrovich

Brodsky, Michael (Mark) 1948- .... **CLC 19**
See also CANR 18; CA 102

Bromell, Henry 1947-............. **CLC 5**
See also CANR 9; CA 53-56

Bromfield, Louis (Brucker) 1896-1956 .... **TCLC 11**
See also CA 107; DLB 4, 9

Broner, E(sther) M(asserman) 1930- .... **CLC 19**
See also CANR 8, 25; CA 17-20R; DLB 28

Bronk, William 1918-............. **CLC 10**
See also CANR 23; CA 89-92

Bronte, Anne 1820-1849.......... **NCLC 4**
See also DLB 21

Bronte, Charlotte 1816-1855 .... **NCLC 3, 8**
See also DLB 21

Bronte, (Jane) Emily 1818-1848 .. **NCLC 16**
See also DLB 21, 32

Brooke, Frances 1724-1789 .... **LC 6**
See also DLB 39

Brooke, Henry 1703?-1783 .... **LC 1**
See also DLB 39

Brooke, Rupert (Chawner) 1887-1915 .... **TCLC 2, 7**
See also CA 104; DLB 19

Brooke-Rose, Christine 1926- ...... **CLC 40**
See also CA 13-16R; DLB 14

Brookner, Anita 1928- ...... **CLC 32, 34, 51**
See also CA 114, 120; DLB-Y 87

Brooks, Cleanth 1906- .... **CLC 24**
See also CA 17-20R; DLB 63

Brooks, Gwendolyn 1917- .... **CLC 1, 2, 4, 5, 15, 49**
See also CANR 1; CA 1-4R; SATA 6; DLB 5, 76; CDALB 1941-1968

Brooks, Mel 1926- .... **CLC 12**
See also Kaminsky, Melvin
See also CA 65-68; DLB 26

Brooks, Peter 1938- .... **CLC 34**
See also CANR 1; CA 45-48

Brooks, Van Wyck 1886-1963...... **CLC 29**
See also CANR 6; CA 1-4R; DLB 45, 63

Brophy, Brigid (Antonia) 1929- .... **CLC 6, 11, 29**
See also CAAS 4; CANR 25; CA 5-8R; DLB 14

Brosman, Catharine Savage 1934-.... **CLC 9**
See also CANR 21; CA 61-64

Broughton, T(homas) Alan 1936- ... **CLC 19**
See also CANR 2, 23; CA 45-48

Broumas, Olga 1949- .... **CLC 10**
See also CANR 20; CA 85-88

Brown, Charles Brockden 1771-1810 .... **NCLC 22**
See also DLB 37, 59, 73; CDALB 1640-1865

Brown, Christy 1932-1981 .... **CLC 63**
See also CA 105; obituary CA 104

Brown, Claude 1937- .... **CLC 30**
See also CA 73-76

Brown, Dee (Alexander) 1908- .. **CLC 18, 47**
See also CAAS 6; CANR 11; CA 13-16R; SATA 5; DLB-Y 80

Brown, George Douglas 1869-1902
See Douglas, George

Brown, George Mackay 1921-.... **CLC 5, 28**
See also CAAS 6; CANR 12; CA 21-24R; SATA 35; DLB 14, 27

Brown, Rita Mae 1944- .... **CLC 18, 43**
See also CANR 2, 11; CA 45-48

Brown, Rosellen 1939- .... **CLC 32**
See also CANR 14; CA 77-80

Brown, Sterling A(llen) 1901-1989 .... **CLC 1, 23, 59**
See also CANR 26; CA 85-88; obituary CA 27; DLB 48, 51, 63

Brown, William Wells 1816?-1884............ **NCLC 2; DC 1**
See also DLB 3, 50

Author Index

Browne, Jackson 1950- . . . . **CLC 21**
See also CA 120

Browning, Elizabeth Barrett 1806-1861 . . . . **NCLC 1, 16**
See also DLB 32

Browning, Robert 1812-1889 . . . . **NCLC 19; PC 2**
See also YABC 1; DLB 32

Browning, Tod 1882-1962 . . . . **CLC 16**
See also obituary CA 117

Bruccoli, Matthew J(oseph) 1931- . . **CLC 34**
See also CANR 7; CA 9-12R

Bruce, Lenny 1925-1966 . . . . **CLC 21**
See also Schneider, Leonard Alfred

Brunner, John (Kilian Houston) 1934- . . . . **CLC 8, 10**
See also CAAS 8; CANR 2; CA 1-4R

Brutus, Dennis 1924- . . . . **CLC 43**
See also CANR 2; CA 49-52

Bryan, C(ourtlandt) D(ixon) B(arnes) 1936- . . . . **CLC 29**
See also CANR 13; CA 73-76

Bryant, William Cullen 1794-1878 . . . . **NCLC 6**
See also DLB 3, 43, 59; CDALB 1640-1865

Bryusov, Valery (Yakovlevich) 1873-1924 . . . . **TCLC 10**
See also CA 107

Buchan, Sir John 1875-1940 . . . . . . **TCLC 41**
See also YABC 2; brief entry CA 108; DLB 34, 70

Buchanan, George 1506-1582 . . . . **LC 4**

Buchheim, Lothar-Gunther 1918- . . . . **CLC 6**
See also CA 85-88

Buchner, (Karl) Georg 1813-1837 . . . . **NCLC 26**

Buchwald, Art(hur) 1925-. . . . . **CLC 33**
See also CANR 21; CA 5-8R; SATA 10

Buck, Pearl S(ydenstricker) 1892-1973 . . . . **CLC 7, 11, 18**
See also CANR 1; CA 1-4R; obituary CA 41-44R; SATA 1, 25; DLB 9

Buckler, Ernest 1908-1984. . . . . **CLC 13**
See also CAP 1; CA 11-12; obituary CA 114; SATA 47

Buckley, Vincent (Thomas) 1925-1988 . . . . **CLC 57**
See also CA 101

Buckley, William F(rank), Jr. 1925- . . . . **CLC 7, 18, 37**
See also CANR 1, 24; CA 1-4R; DLB-Y 80

Buechner, (Carl) Frederick 1926- . . . . **CLC 2, 4, 6, 9**
See also CANR 11; CA 13-16R; DLB-Y 80

Buell, John (Edward) 1927-. . . . . **CLC 10**
See also CA 1-4R; DLB 53

Buero Vallejo, Antonio 1916- . . . **CLC 15, 46**
See also CANR 24; CA 106

Bukowski, Charles 1920- . . . . **CLC 2, 5, 9, 41**
See also CA 17-20R; DLB 5

Bulgakov, Mikhail (Afanas'evich) 1891-1940 . . . . **TCLC 2, 16**
See also CA 105

Bullins, Ed 1935- . . . . **CLC 1, 5, 7**
See also CANR 24; CA 49-52; DLB 7, 38

Bulwer-Lytton, (Lord) Edward (George Earle Lytton) 1803-1873 . . . . **NCLC 1**
See also Lytton, Edward Bulwer
See also DLB 21

Bunin, Ivan (Alexeyevich) 1870-1953 . . . . **TCLC 6; SSC 5**
See also CA 104

Bunting, Basil 1900-1985 . . . . **CLC 10, 39, 47**
See also CANR 7; CA 53-56; obituary CA 115; DLB 20

Bunuel, Luis 1900-1983 . . . . **CLC 16**
See also CA 101; obituary CA 110

Bunyan, John 1628-1688 . . . . **LC 4**
See also DLB 39

Burgess (Wilson, John) Anthony 1917- . . . . . **CLC 1, 2, 4, 5, 8, 10, 13, 15, 22, 40, 62**
See also Wilson, John (Anthony) Burgess
See also DLB 14

Burke, Edmund 1729-1797. . . . . **LC 7**

Burke, Kenneth (Duva) 1897- . . . . **CLC 2, 24**
See also CA 5-8R; DLB 45, 63

Burney, Fanny 1752-1840 . . . . **NCLC 12**
See also DLB 39

Burns, Robert 1759-1796 . . . . **LC 3**

Burns, Tex 1908?-
See L'Amour, Louis (Dearborn)

Burnshaw, Stanley 1906- . . . . . **CLC 3, 13, 44**
See also CA 9-12R; DLB 48

Burr, Anne 1937- . . . . **CLC 6**
See also CA 25-28R

Burroughs, Edgar Rice 1875-1950 . . . . **TCLC 2, 32**
See also CA 104; SATA 41; DLB 8

Burroughs, William S(eward) 1914- . . . . **CLC 1, 2, 5, 15, 22, 42**
See also CANR 20; CA 9-12R; DLB 2, 8, 16; DLB-Y 81

Busch, Frederick 1941- . . . **CLC 7, 10, 18, 47**
See also CAAS 1; CA 33-36R; DLB 6

Bush, Ronald 19??-. . . . . **CLC 34**

Butler, Octavia E(stelle) 1947- . . . . . **CLC 38**
See also CANR 12, 24; CA 73-76; DLB 33

Butler, Samuel 1612-1680 . . . . **LC 16**
See also DLB 101

Butler, Samuel 1835-1902 . . . . . . **TCLC 1, 33**
See also CA 104; DLB 18, 57

Butor, Michel (Marie Francois) 1926- . . . . **CLC 1, 3, 8, 11, 15**
See also CA 9-12R

Buzo, Alexander 1944-. . . . . **CLC 61**
See also CANR 17; CA 97-100

Buzzati, Dino 1906-1972 . . . . **CLC 36**
See also obituary CA 33-36R

Byars, Betsy 1928-. . . . . **CLC 35**
See also CLR 1, 16; CANR 18; CA 33-36R; SAAS 1; SATA 4, 46; DLB 52

Byatt, A(ntonia) S(usan Drabble) 1936- . . . . **CLC 19, 65**
See also CANR 13, 33; CA 13-16R; DLB 14

Byrne, David 1953?-. . . . . **CLC 26**

Byrne, John Keyes 1926-
See Leonard, Hugh
See also CA 102

Byron, George Gordon (Noel), Lord Byron 1788-1824 . . . . **NCLC 2, 12**

Caballero, Fernan 1796-1877. . . . . **NCLC 10**

Cabell, James Branch 1879-1958 . . . **TCLC 6**
See also CA 105; DLB 9, 78

Cable, George Washington 1844-1925 . . . . **TCLC 4; SSC 4**
See also CA 104; DLB 12, 74

Cabrera Infante, G(uillermo) 1929- . . . . **CLC 5, 25, 45**
See also CANR 29; CA 85-88

CAEdmon fl. 658-680 . . . . **CMLC 7**

Cage, John (Milton, Jr.) 1912- . . . . . **CLC 41**
See also CANR 9; CA 13-16R

Cain, G. 1929-
See Cabrera Infante, G(uillermo)

Cain, James M(allahan) 1892-1977 . . . . **CLC 3, 11, 28**
See also CANR 8; CA 17-20R; obituary CA 73-76

Caldwell, Erskine (Preston) 1903-1987 . . . . **CLC 1, 8, 14, 50, 60**
See also CAAS 1; CANR 2; CA 1-4R; obituary CA 121; DLB 9, 86

Caldwell, (Janet Miriam) Taylor (Holland) 1900-1985 . . . . **CLC 2, 28, 39**
See also CANR 5; CA 5-8R; obituary CA 116

Calhoun, John Caldwell 1782-1850 . . . . **NCLC 15**
See also DLB 3

Calisher, Hortense 1911- . . . . **CLC 2, 4, 8, 38**
See also CANR 1, 22; CA 1-4R; DLB 2

Callaghan, Morley (Edward) 1903-1990 . . . . **CLC 3, 14, 41, 65**
See also CANR 33; CA 9-12R; obituary CA 132; DLB 68

Calvino, Italo 1923-1985 . . . . **CLC 5, 8, 11, 22, 33, 39; SSC 3**
See also CANR 23; CA 85-88; obituary CA 116

Cameron, Carey 1952- . . . . **CLC 59**

Cameron, Peter 1959-. . . . . **CLC 44**
See also CA 125

Campana, Dino 1885-1932. . . . . **TCLC 20**
See also CA 117

Campbell, John W(ood), Jr. 1910-1971 . . . . **CLC 32**
See also CAP 2; CA 21-22; obituary CA 29-32R; DLB 8

Campbell, (John) Ramsey 1946- . . . . **CLC 42**
See also CANR 7; CA 57-60

Campbell, (Ignatius) Roy (Dunnachie) 1901-1957 . . . . **TCLC 5**
See also CA 104; DLB 20

Campbell, Thomas 1777-1844 . . . . **NCLC 19**

Campbell, (William) Wilfred 1861-1918 . . . . **TCLC 9**
See also CA 106

Camus, Albert
1913-1960 ... **CLC 1, 2, 4, 9, 11, 14, 32, 63**
See also CA 89-92; DLB 72

Canby, Vincent 1924- .... **CLC 13**
See also CA 81-84

Canetti, Elias 1905- .... **CLC 3, 14, 25**
See also CANR 23; CA 21-24R; DLB 85

Canin, Ethan 1960- .... **CLC 55**

Cape, Judith 1916-
See Page, P(atricia) K(athleen)

Capek, Karel
1890-1938 .... **TCLC 6, 37; DC 1**
See also CA 104

Capote, Truman
1924-1984 ..... **CLC 1, 3, 8, 13, 19, 34, 38, 58; SSC 2**
See also CANR 18; CA 5-8R; obituary CA 113; DLB 2; DLB-Y 80, 84; CDALB 1941-1968

Capra, Frank 1897- .... **CLC 16**
See also CA 61-64

Caputo, Philip 1941- .... **CLC 32**
See also CA 73-76

Card, Orson Scott 1951- .... **CLC 44, 47, 50**
See also CA 102

Cardenal, Ernesto 1925- .... **CLC 31**
See also CANR 2; CA 49-52

Carducci, Giosue 1835-1907 .... **TCLC 32**

Carew, Thomas 1595?-1640 .... **LC 13**

Carey, Ernestine Gilbreth 1908- .... **CLC 17**
See also CA 5-8R; SATA 2

Carey, Peter 1943- .... **CLC 40, 55**
See also CA 123, 127

Carleton, William 1794-1869 ...... **NCLC 3**

Carlisle, Henry (Coffin) 1926- ...... **CLC 33**
See also CANR 15; CA 13-16R

Carlson, Ron(ald F.) 1947- .... **CLC 54**
See also CA 105

Carlyle, Thomas 1795-1881 ...... **NCLC 22**
See also DLB 55

Carman, (William) Bliss
1861-1929 .... **TCLC 7**
See also CA 104

Carpenter, Don(ald Richard)
1931- .... **CLC 41**
See also CANR 1; CA 45-48

Carpentier (y Valmont), Alejo
1904-1980 .... **CLC 8, 11, 38**
See also CANR 11; CA 65-68; obituary CA 97-100

Carr, Emily 1871-1945 .... **TCLC 32**
See also DLB 68

Carr, John Dickson 1906-1977 ...... **CLC 3**
See also CANR 3; CA 49-52; obituary CA 69-72

Carr, Virginia Spencer 1929- .... **CLC 34**
See also CA 61-64

Carrier, Roch 1937- .... **CLC 13**
See also DLB 53

Carroll, James (P.) 1943- .... **CLC 38**
See also CA 81-84

Carroll, Jim 1951- .... **CLC 35**
See also CA 45-48

Carroll, Lewis 1832-1898 .... **NCLC 2**
See also Dodgson, Charles Lutwidge
See also CLR 2; DLB 18

Carroll, Paul Vincent 1900-1968 .... **CLC 10**
See also CA 9-12R; obituary CA 25-28R; DLB 10

Carruth, Hayden 1921- .... **CLC 4, 7, 10, 18**
See also CANR 4; CA 9-12R; SATA 47; DLB 5

Carter, Angela (Olive) 1940- ..... **CLC 5, 41**
See also CANR 12; CA 53-56; DLB 14

Carver, Raymond
1938-1988 ... **CLC 22, 36, 53, 55; SSC 8**
See also CANR 17; CA 33-36R; obituary CA 126; DLB-Y 84, 88

Cary, (Arthur) Joyce (Lunel)
1888-1957 .... **TCLC 1, 29**
See also CA 104; DLB 15

Casanova de Seingalt, Giovanni Jacopo
1725-1798 .... **LC 13**

Casares, Adolfo Bioy 1914-
See Bioy Casares, Adolfo

Casely-Hayford, J(oseph) E(phraim)
1866-1930 .... **TCLC 24**
See also CA 123

Casey, John 1880-1964
See O'Casey, Sean

Casey, John 1939- .... **CLC 59**
See also CANR 23; CA 69-72

Casey, Michael 1947- .... **CLC 2**
See also CA 65-68; DLB 5

Casey, Warren 1935- .... **CLC 12**
See also Jacobs, Jim and Casey, Warren
See also CA 101

Casona, Alejandro 1903-1965 ...... **CLC 49**
See also Alvarez, Alejandro Rodriguez

Cassavetes, John 1929- .... **CLC 20**
See also CA 85-88, 127

Cassill, R(onald) V(erlin) 1919- ... **CLC 4, 23**
See also CAAS 1; CANR 7; CA 9-12R; DLB 6

Cassity, (Allen) Turner 1929- .... **CLC 6, 42**
See also CANR 11; CA 17-20R

Castaneda, Carlos 1935?- .... **CLC 12**
See also CA 25-28R

Castedo, Elena 1937- .... **CLC 65**
See also CA 132

Castelvetro, Lodovico 1505-1571 ..... **LC 12**

Castiglione, Baldassare 1478-1529 ... **LC 12**

Castro, Rosalia de 1837-1885 ..... **NCLC 3**

Cather, Willa (Sibert)
1873-1947 ...... **TCLC 1, 11, 31; SSC 2**
See also CA 104; SATA 30; DLB 9, 54; DLB-DS 1; CDALB 1865-1917

Catton, (Charles) Bruce
1899-1978 .... **CLC 35**
See also CANR 7; CA 5-8R; obituary CA 81-84; SATA 2; obituary SATA 24; DLB 17

Cauldwell, Frank 1923-
See King, Francis (Henry)

Caunitz, William 1935- .... **CLC 34**

Causley, Charles (Stanley) 1917- ..... **CLC 7**
See also CANR 5; CA 9-12R; SATA 3; DLB 27

Caute, (John) David 1936- .... **CLC 29**
See also CAAS 4; CANR 1; CA 1-4R; DLB 14

Cavafy, C(onstantine) P(eter)
1863-1933 .... **TCLC 2, 7**
See also CA 104

Cavanna, Betty 1909- .... **CLC 12**
See also CANR 6; CA 9-12R; SATA 1, 30

Cayrol, Jean 1911- .... **CLC 11**
See also CA 89-92; DLB 83

Cela, Camilo Jose 1916- ...... **CLC 4, 13, 59**
See also CAAS 10; CANR 21; CA 21-24R

Celan, Paul 1920-1970 ...... **CLC 10, 19, 53**
See also Antschel, Paul
See also DLB 69

Celine, Louis-Ferdinand
1894-1961 ..... **CLC 1, 3, 4, 7, 9, 15, 47**
See also Destouches, Louis-Ferdinand-Auguste
See also DLB 72

Cellini, Benvenuto 1500-1571 .... **LC 7**

Cendrars, Blaise 1887-1961 .... **CLC 18**
See also Sauser-Hall, Frederic

Cernuda, Luis (y Bidon)
1902-1963 .... **CLC 54**
See also CA 89-92

Cervantes (Saavedra), Miguel de
1547-1616 .... **LC 6**

Cesaire, Aime (Fernand) 1913- .. **CLC 19, 32**
See also CANR 24; CA 65-68

Chabon, Michael 1965?- .... **CLC 55**

Chabrol, Claude 1930- .... **CLC 16**
See also CA 110

Challans, Mary 1905-1983
See Renault, Mary
See also CA 81-84; obituary CA 111; SATA 23; obituary SATA 36

Chambers, Aidan 1934- .... **CLC 35**
See also CANR 12; CA 25-28R; SATA 1

Chambers, James 1948-
See Cliff, Jimmy

Chambers, Robert W. 1865-1933 ... **TCLC 41**

Chandler, Raymond 1888-1959 ... **TCLC 1, 7**
See also CA 104

Channing, William Ellery
1780-1842 .... **NCLC 17**
See also DLB 1, 59

Chaplin, Charles (Spencer)
1889-1977 .... **CLC 16**
See also CA 81-84; obituary CA 73-76; DLB 44

Chapman, Graham 1941?- .... **CLC 21**
See also Monty Python
See also CA 116; obituary CA 169

Chapman, John Jay 1862-1933 ..... **TCLC 7**
See also CA 104

Chappell, Fred 1936- .... **CLC 40**
See also CAAS 4; CANR 8; CA 5-8R; DLB 6

Char, Rene (Emile) 1907-1988 .... **CLC 9, 11, 14, 55**
See also CA 13-16R; obituary CA 124

Charles I 1600-1649 .... **LC 13**

Chartier, Emile-Auguste 1868-1951
See Alain

Charyn, Jerome 1937- .... **CLC 5, 8, 18**
See also CAAS 1; CANR 7; CA 5-8R; DLB-Y 83

Chase, Mary (Coyle) 1907-1981 ...... **DC 1**
See also CA 77-80, 105; SATA 17, 29

Chase, Mary Ellen 1887-1973 .... **CLC 2**
See also CAP 1; CA 15-16; obituary CA 41-44R; SATA 10

Chateaubriand, Francois Rene de 1768-1848 .... **NCLC 3**

Chatier, Emile-Auguste 1868-1951
See Alain

Chatterji, Bankim Chandra 1838-1894 .... **NCLC 19**

Chatterji, Saratchandra 1876-1938 .... **TCLC 13**
See also CA 109

Chatterton, Thomas 1752-1770 .... **LC 3**

Chatwin, (Charles) Bruce 1940-1989 .... **CLC 28, 57, 59**
See also CA 85-88,; obituary CA 127

Chayefsky, Paddy 1923-1981....... **CLC 23**
See also CA 9-12R; obituary CA 104; DLB 7, 44; DLB-Y 81

Chayefsky, Sidney 1923-1981
See Chayefsky, Paddy
See also CANR 18

Chedid, Andree 1920-............. **CLC 47**

Cheever, John 1912-1982 ..... **CLC 3, 7, 8, 11, 15, 25, 64; SSC 1**
See also CANR 5, 27; CA 5-8R; obituary CA 106; CABS 1; DLB 2; DLB-Y 80, 82; CDALB 1941-1968

Cheever, Susan 1943-.......... **CLC 18, 48**
See also CA 103; DLB-Y 82

Chekhov, Anton (Pavlovich) 1860-1904 ...... **TCLC 3, 10, 31; SSC 2**
See also CA 104, 124

Chernyshevsky, Nikolay Gavrilovich 1828-1889 .... **NCLC 1**

Cherry, Caroline Janice 1942-
See Cherryh, C. J.

Cherryh, C. J. 1942-.............. **CLC 35**
See also CANR 10; CA 65-68; DLB-Y 80

Chesnutt, Charles Waddell 1858-1932 .... **TCLC 5, 39; SSC 7**
See also CA 106, 125; DLB 12, 50, 78

Chester, Alfred 1929?-1971 .... **CLC 49**
See also obituary CA 33-36R

Chesterton, G(ilbert) K(eith) 1874-1936 .... **TCLC 1, 6; SSC 1**
See also CA 104; SATA 27; DLB 10, 19, 34, 70

Ch'ien Chung-shu 1910-........... **CLC 22**

Child, Lydia Maria 1802-1880 .... **NCLC 6**
See also DLB 1, 74

Child, Philip 1898-1978 .... **CLC 19**
See also CAP 1; CA 13-14; SATA 47

Childress, Alice 1920-.......... **CLC 12, 15**
See also CLR 14; CANR 3; CA 45-48; SATA 7, 48; DLB 7, 38

Chislett, (Margaret) Anne 1943?- ... **CLC 34**

Chitty, (Sir) Thomas Willes 1926- .. **CLC 11**
See also Hinde, Thomas
See also CA 5-8R

Chomette, Rene 1898-1981
See Clair, Rene
See also obituary CA 103

Chopin, Kate (O'Flaherty) 1851-1904 .... **TCLC 5, 14; SSC 8**
See also CA 122; brief entry CA 104; DLB 12, 78; CDALB 1865-1917

Christie, (Dame) Agatha (Mary Clarissa) 1890-1976 ...... **CLC 1, 6, 8, 12, 39, 48**
See also CANR 10; CA 17-20R; obituary CA 61-64; SATA 36; DLB 13

Christie, (Ann) Philippa 1920-
See Pearce, (Ann) Philippa
See also CANR 4; CA 7-8

Christine de Pizan 1365?-1431?....... **LC 9**

Chulkov, Mikhail Dmitrievich 1743-1792 .... **LC 2**

Churchill, Caryl 1938- .... **CLC 31, 55**
See also CANR 22; CA 102; DLB 13

Churchill, Charles 1731?-1764........ **LC 3**

Chute, Carolyn 1947-............. **CLC 39**
See also CA 123

Ciardi, John (Anthony) 1916-1986 .... **CLC 10, 40, 44**
See also CAAS 2; CANR 5; CA 5-8R; obituary CA 118; SATA 1, 46; DLB 5; DLB-Y 86

Cicero, Marcus Tullius 106 B.C.-43 B.C............... **CMLC 3**

Cimino, Michael 1943?-........... **CLC 16**
See also CA 105

Cioran, E. M. 1911-.............. **CLC 64**
See also CA 25-28R

Clair, Rene 1898-1981 .... **CLC 20**
See also Chomette, Rene

Clampitt, Amy 19??-.............. **CLC 32**
See also CA 110

Clancy, Tom 1947-............... **CLC 45**
See also CA 125

Clare, John 1793-1864 .... **NCLC 9**
See also DLB 55

Clark, (Robert) Brian 1932-........ **CLC 29**
See also CA 41-44R

Clark, Eleanor 1913- .... **CLC 5, 19**
See also CA 9-12R; DLB 6

Clark, John Pepper 1935- .... **CLC 38**
See also CANR 16; CA 65-68

Clark, Mavis Thorpe 1912?- .... **CLC 12**
See also CANR 8; CA 57-60; SAAS 5; SATA 8

Clark, Walter Van Tilburg 1909-1971 .... **CLC 28**
See also CA 9-12R; obituary CA 33-36R; SATA 8; DLB 9

Clarke, Arthur C(harles) 1917- ...... **CLC 1, 4, 13, 18, 35; SSC 3**
See also CANR 2; CA 1-4R; SATA 13

Clarke, Austin 1896-1974......... **CLC 6, 9**
See also CANR 14; CAP 2; CA 29-32; obituary CA 49-52; DLB 10, 20, 53

Clarke, Austin (Ardinel) C(hesterfield) 1934- .... **CLC 8, 53**
See also CANR 14; CA 25-28R; DLB 53

Clarke, Gillian 1937- .... **CLC 61**
See also CA 106; DLB 40

Clarke, Marcus (Andrew Hislop) 1846-1881 .... **NCLC 19**

Clarke, Shirley 1925-............. **CLC 16**

Clash, The .... **CLC 30**

Claudel, Paul (Louis Charles Marie) 1868-1955 .... **TCLC 2, 10**
See also CA 104

Clavell, James (duMaresq) 1924- .... **CLC 6, 25**
See also CANR 26; CA 25-28R

Clayman. Gregory 1974?-.......... **CLC 65**

Cleaver, (Leroy) Eldridge 1935- .... **CLC 30**
See also CANR 16; CA 21-24R

Cleese, John 1939- .... **CLC 21**
See also Monty Python
See also CA 112, 116

Cleland, John 1709-1789 .... **LC 2**
See also DLB 39

Clemens, Samuel Langhorne 1835-1910 ...... **TCLC 6, 12, 19; SSC 6**
See also Twain, Mark
See also YABC 2; CA 104; DLB 11, 12, 23, 64, 74; CDALB 1865-1917

Cliff, Jimmy 1948- .... **CLC 21**

Clifton, Lucille 1936-............. **CLC 19**
See also CLR 5; CANR 2, 24; CA 49-52; SATA 20; DLB 5, 41

Clough, Arthur Hugh 1819-1861.. **NCLC 27**
See also DLB 32

Clutha, Janet Paterson Frame 1924-
See Frame (Clutha), Janet (Paterson)
See also CANR 2; CA 1-4R

Coburn, D(onald) L(ee) 1938- ...... **CLC 10**
See also CA 89-92

Cocteau, Jean (Maurice Eugene Clement) 1889-1963 .... **CLC 1, 8, 15, 16, 43**
See also CAP 2; CA 25-28; DLB 65

Codrescu, Andrei 1946- .... **CLC 46**
See also CANR 13; CA 33-36R

Coetzee, J(ohn) M. 1940-....... **CLC 23, 33**
See also CA 77-80

Cohen, Arthur A(llen) 1928-1986 .... **CLC 7, 31**
See also CANR 1, 17; CA 1-4R; obituary CA 120; DLB 28

Cohen, Leonard (Norman) 1934- .... **CLC 3, 38**
See also CANR 14; CA 21-24R; DLB 53

Cohen, Matt 1942-................ **CLC 19**
See also CA 61-64; DLB 53

Cohen-Solal, Annie 19??-.......... **CLC 50**

Colegate, Isabel 1931- .... **CLC 36**
See also CANR 8, 22; CA 17-20R; DLB 14

Coleridge, Samuel Taylor 1772-1834 .... **NCLC 9**

Coleridge, Sara 1802-1852....... **NCLC 31**

Coles, Don 1928- .... **CLC 46**
See also CA 115

Colette (Sidonie-Gabrielle) 1873-1954 .... **TCLC 1, 5, 16**
See also CA 104; DLB 65

Collett, (Jacobine) Camilla (Wergeland) 1813-1895 .... **NCLC 22**

Collier, Christopher 1930-......... **CLC 30**
See also CANR 13; CA 33-36R; SATA 16

Collier, James L(incoln) 1928- ..... **CLC 30**
See also CLR 3; CANR 4; CA 9-12R; SATA 8

Collier, Jeremy 1650-1726........... **LC 6**

Collins, Hunt 1926-
See Hunter, Evan

Collins, Linda 19??- .... **CLC 44**
See also CA 125

Collins, Tom 1843-1912
See Furphy, Joseph

Collins, (William) Wilkie 1824-1889 .... **NCLC 1, 18**
See also DLB 18, 70

Collins, William 1721-1759 .... **LC 4**

Colman, George 1909-1981
See Glassco, John

Colter, Cyrus 1910- .... **CLC 58**
See also CANR 10; CA 65-68; DLB 33

Colton, James 1923-
See Hansen, Joseph

Colum, Padraic 1881-1972......... **CLC 28**
See also CA 73-76; obituary CA 33-36R; SATA 15; DLB 19

Colvin, James 1939-
See Moorcock, Michael

Colwin, Laurie 1945- .... **CLC 5, 13, 23**
See also CANR 20; CA 89-92; DLB-Y 80

Comfort, Alex(ander) 1920-......... **CLC 7**
See also CANR 1; CA 1-4R

Compton-Burnett, Ivy 1892-1969 .... **CLC 1, 3, 10, 15, 34**
See also CANR 4; CA 1-4R; obituary CA 25-28R; DLB 36

Comstock, Anthony 1844-1915 .... **TCLC 13**
See also CA 110

Conde, Maryse 1937-............. **CLC 52**
See also Boucolon, Maryse

Condon, Richard (Thomas) 1915- .... **CLC 4, 6, 8, 10, 45**
See also CAAS 1; CANR 2, 23; CA 1-4R

Congreve, William 1670-1729 .... **LC 5**
See also DLB 39

Connell, Evan S(helby), Jr. 1924- .... **CLC 4, 6, 45**
See also CAAS 2; CANR 2; CA 1-4R; DLB 2; DLB-Y 81

Connelly, Marc(us Cook) 1890-1980 .... **CLC 7**
See also CA 85-88; obituary CA 102; obituary SATA 25; DLB 7; DLB-Y 80

Conner, Ralph 1860-1937......... **TCLC 31**

Conrad, Joseph 1857-1924 .... **TCLC 1, 6, 13, 25**
See also CA 104; SATA 27; DLB 10, 34

Conroy, Pat 1945-................ **CLC 30**
See also CANR 24; CA 85-88; DLB 6

Constant (de Rebecque), (Henri) Benjamin 1767-1830 .... **NCLC 6**

Cook, Michael 1933- .... **CLC 58**
See also CA 93-96; DLB 53

Cook, Robin 1940- .... **CLC 14**
See also CA 108, 111

Cooke, Elizabeth 1948- .... **CLC 55**

Cooke, John Esten 1830-1886..... **NCLC 5**
See also DLB 3

Cooney, Ray 19??- .... **CLC 62**

Cooper, J. California 19??- .... **CLC 56**
See also CA 125

Cooper, James Fenimore 1789-1851 .... **NCLC 1, 27**
See also SATA 19; DLB 3; CDALB 1640-1865

Coover, Robert (Lowell) 1932- .... **CLC 3, 7, 15, 32, 46**
See also CANR 3; CA 45-48; DLB 2; DLB-Y 81

Copeland, Stewart (Armstrong) 1952- .... **CLC 26**
See also The Police

Coppard, A(lfred) E(dgar) 1878-1957 .... **TCLC 5**
See also YABC 1; CA 114

Coppee, Francois 1842-1908 ...... **TCLC 25**

Coppola, Francis Ford 1939-....... **CLC 16**
See also CA 77-80; DLB 44

Corcoran, Barbara 1911-........... **CLC 17**
See also CAAS 2; CANR 11; CA 21-24R; SATA 3; DLB 52

Corman, Cid 1924-................ **CLC 9**
See also Corman, Sidney
See also CAAS 2; DLB 5

Corman, Sidney 1924-
See Corman, Cid
See also CA 85-88

Cormier, Robert (Edmund) 1925-..................... **CLC 12, 30**
See also CLR 12; CANR 5, 23; CA 1-4R; SATA 10, 45; DLB 52

Corn, Alfred (Dewitt III) 1943-..... **CLC 33**
See also CA 104; DLB-Y 80

Cornwell, David (John Moore) 1931- .... **CLC 9, 15**
See also le Carre, John
See also CANR 13; CA 5-8R

Corso, (Nunzio) Gregory 1930-... **CLC 1, 11**
See also CA 5-8R; DLB 5, 16

Cortazar, Julio 1914-1984 ..... **CLC 2, 3, 5, 10, 13, 15, 33, 34; SSC 7**
See also CANR 12; CA 21-24R

Corvo, Baron 1860-1913
See Rolfe, Frederick (William Serafino Austin Lewis Mary)

Cosic, Dobrica 1921- .... **CLC 14**
See also CA 122

Costain, Thomas B(ertram) 1885-1965 .... **CLC 30**
See also CA 5-8R; obituary CA 25-28R; DLB 9

Costantini, Humberto 1924?-1987... **CLC 49**
See also obituary CA 122

Costello, Elvis 1955-.............. **CLC 21**

Cotter, Joseph Seamon, Sr. 1861-1949 .... **TCLC 28**
See also CA 124; DLB 50

Couperus, Louis (Marie Anne) 1863-1923 .... **TCLC 15**
See also CA 115

Courtenay, Bryce 1933-........... **CLC 59**

Cousteau, Jacques-Yves 1910-...... **CLC 30**
See also CANR 15; CA 65-68; SATA 38

Coward, (Sir) Noel (Pierce) 1899-1973 .... **CLC 1, 9, 29, 51**
See also CAP 2; CA 17-18; obituary CA 41-44R; DLB 10

Cowley, Malcolm 1898-1989 .... **CLC 39**
See also CANR 3; CA 5-6R; obituary CA 128; DLB 4, 48; DLB-Y 81

Cowper, William 1731-1800....... **NCLC 8**

Cox, William Trevor 1928- ...... **CLC 9, 14**
See also Trevor, William
See also CANR 4; CA 9-12R

Cozzens, James Gould 1903-1978 .... **CLC 1, 4, 11**
See also CANR 19; CA 9-12R; obituary CA 81-84; DLB 9; DLB-Y 84; DLB-DS 2; CDALB 1941-1968

Crabbe, George 1754-1832....... **NCLC 26**

Crace, Douglas 1944-............. **CLC 58**

Crane, (Harold) Hart 1899-1932 .... **TCLC 2, 5**
See also CA 104; DLB 4, 48

Crane, R(onald) S(almon) 1886-1967 .... **CLC 27**
See also CA 85-88; DLB 63

Crane, Stephen 1871-1900 ..... **TCLC 11, 17, 32; SSC 7**
See also YABC 2; CA 109; DLB 12, 54, 78; CDALB 1865-1917

Craven, Margaret 1901-1980....... **CLC 17**
See also CA 103

Crawford, F(rancis) Marion 1854-1909 .... **TCLC 10**
See also CA 107; DLB 71

Crawford, Isabella Valancy 1850-1887 .... **NCLC 12**
See also DLB 92

Crayencour, Marguerite de 1903-1987
See Yourcenar, Marguerite

Creasey, John 1908-1973.......... **CLC 11**
See also CANR 8; CA 5-8R; obituary CA 41-44R; DLB 77

Crebillon, Claude Prosper Jolyot de (fils) 1707-1777 .... **LC 1**

Creeley, Robert (White) 1926- .... **CLC 1, 2, 4, 8, 11, 15, 36**
See also CANR 23; CA 1-4R; DLB 5, 16

Crews, Harry (Eugene) 1935- . . . . **CLC 6, 23, 49**
See also CANR 20; CA 25-28R; DLB 6

Crichton, (John) Michael 1942- . . . . **CLC 2, 6, 54**
See also CANR 13; CA 25-28R; SATA 9; DLB-Y 81

Crispin, Edmund 1921-1978 . . . . **CLC 22**
See also Montgomery, Robert Bruce
See also DLB 87

Cristofer, Michael 1946- . . . . **CLC 28**
See also CA 110; DLB 7

Croce, Benedetto 1866-1952 . . . . . . **TCLC 37**
See also CA 120

Crockett, David (Davy) 1786-1836 . . . . **NCLC 8**
See also DLB 3, 11

Croker, John Wilson 1780-1857 . . **NCLC 10**

Cronin, A(rchibald) J(oseph) 1896-1981 . . . . **CLC 32**
See also CANR 5; CA 1-4R; obituary CA 102; obituary SATA 25, 47

Cross, Amanda 1926-
See Heilbrun, Carolyn G(old)

Crothers, Rachel 1878-1953 . . . . **TCLC 19**
See also CA 113; DLB 7

Crowley, Aleister 1875-1947 . . . . **TCLC 7**
See also CA 104

Crowley, John 1942-
See also CA 61-64; DLB-Y 82

Crumb, Robert 1943- . . . . **CLC 17**
See also CA 106

Cryer, Gretchen 1936?- . . . . **CLC 21**
See also CA 114, 123

Csath, Geza 1887-1919 . . . . **TCLC 13**
See also CA 111

Cudlip, David 1933- . . . . **CLC 34**

Cullen, Countee 1903-1946 . . . . . **TCLC 4, 37**
See also CA 108, 124; SATA 18; DLB 4, 48, 51; CDALB 1917-1929

Cummings, E(dward) E(stlin) 1894-1962 . . . . **CLC 1, 3, 8, 12, 15**
See also CA 73-76; DLB 4, 48

Cunha, Euclides (Rodrigues) da 1866-1909 . . . . **TCLC 24**
See also CA 123

Cunningham, J(ames) V(incent) 1911-1985 . . . . **CLC 3, 31**
See also CANR 1; CA 1-4R; obituary CA 115; DLB 5

Cunningham, Julia (Woolfolk) 1916- . . . . **CLC 12**
See also CANR 4, 19; CA 9-12R; SAAS 2; SATA 1, 26

Cunningham, Michael 1952- . . . . **CLC 34**

Currie, Ellen 19??- . . . . **CLC 44**

Dabrowska, Maria (Szumska) 1889-1965 . . . . **CLC 15**
See also CA 106

Dabydeen, David 1956?- . . . . **CLC 34**
See also CA 106

Dacey, Philip 1939- . . . . **CLC 51**
See also CANR 14; CA 37-40R

Dagerman, Stig (Halvard) 1923-1954 . . . . **TCLC 17**
See also CA 117

Dahl, Roald 1916- . . . . **CLC 1, 6, 18**
See also CLR 1, 7; CANR 6; CA 1-4R; SATA 1, 26

Dahlberg, Edward 1900-1977 . . . **CLC 1, 7, 14**
See also CA 9-12R; obituary CA 69-72; DLB 48

Daly, Elizabeth 1878-1967 . . . . **CLC 52**
See also CAP 2; CA 23-24; obituary CA 25-28R

Daly, Maureen 1921- . . . . **CLC 17**
See also McGivern, Maureen Daly
See also SAAS 1; SATA 2

Daniken, Erich von 1935-
See Von Daniken, Erich

Dannay, Frederic 1905-1982
See Queen, Ellery
See also CANR 1; CA 1-4R; obituary CA 107

D'Annunzio, Gabriele 1863-1938 . . . . **TCLC 6, 40**
See also CA 104

Dante (Alighieri)
See Alighieri, Dante

Danziger, Paula 1944- . . . . **CLC 21**
See also CLR 20; CA 112, 115; SATA 30, 36

Dario, Ruben 1867-1916 . . . . **TCLC 4**
See also Sarmiento, Felix Ruben Garcia
See also CA 104

Darley, George 1795-1846 . . . . **NCLC 2**

Daryush, Elizabeth 1887-1977 . . . . **CLC 6, 19**
See also CANR 3; CA 49-52; DLB 20

Daudet, (Louis Marie) Alphonse 1840-1897 . . . . **NCLC 1**

Daumal, Rene 1908-1944 . . . . **TCLC 14**
See also CA 114

Davenport, Guy (Mattison, Jr.) 1927- . . . . **CLC 6, 14, 38**
See also CANR 23; CA 33-36R

Davidson, Donald (Grady) 1893-1968 . . . . **CLC 2, 13, 19**
See also CANR 4; CA 5-8R; obituary CA 25-28R; DLB 45

Davidson, John 1857-1909 . . . . **TCLC 24**
See also CA 118; DLB 19

Davidson, Sara 1943- . . . . **CLC 9**
See also CA 81-84

Davie, Donald (Alfred) 1922- . . . . **CLC 5, 8, 10, 31**
See also CAAS 3; CANR 1; CA 1-4R; DLB 27

Davies, Ray(mond Douglas) 1944- . . **CLC 21**
See also CA 116

Davies, Rhys 1903-1978 . . . . **CLC 23**
See also CANR 4; CA 9-12R; obituary CA 81-84

Davies, (William) Robertson 1913- . . . . **CLC 2, 7, 13, 25, 42**
See also CANR 17; CA 33-36R; DLB 68

Davies, W(illiam) H(enry) 1871-1940 . . . . **TCLC 5**
See also CA 104; DLB 19

Davis, H(arold) L(enoir) 1896-1960 . . . . **CLC 49**
See also obituary CA 89-92; DLB 9

Davis, Rebecca (Blaine) Harding 1831-1910 . . . . **TCLC 6**
See also CA 104; DLB 74

Davis, Richard Harding 1864-1916 . . . . **TCLC 24**
See also CA 114; DLB 12, 23, 78, 79

Davison, Frank Dalby 1893-1970 . . . **CLC 15**
See also obituary CA 116

Davison, Peter 1928- . . . . **CLC 28**
See also CAAS 4; CANR 3; CA 9-12R; DLB 5

Davys, Mary 1674-1732 . . . . **LC 1**
See also DLB 39

Dawson, Fielding 1930- . . . . **CLC 6**
See also CA 85-88

Day, Clarence (Shepard, Jr.) 1874-1935 . . . . **TCLC 25**
See also CA 108; DLB 11

Day, Thomas 1748-1789 . . . . **LC 1**
See also YABC 1; DLB 39

Day Lewis, C(ecil) 1904-1972 . . . . **CLC 1, 6, 10**
See also CAP 1; CA 15-16; obituary CA 33-36R; DLB 15, 20

Dazai Osamu 1909-1948 . . . . **TCLC 11**
See also Tsushima Shuji

De Crayencour, Marguerite 1903-1987
See Yourcenar, Marguerite

Deer, Sandra 1940- . . . . **CLC 45**

De Ferrari, Gabriella 19??- . . . . **CLC 65**

Defoe, Daniel 1660?-1731 . . . . **LC 1**
See also SATA 22; DLB 39

De Hartog, Jan 1914- . . . . **CLC 19**
See also CANR 1; CA 1-4R

Deighton, Len 1929- . . . . . . **CLC 4, 7, 22, 46**
See also Deighton, Leonard Cyril
See also DLB 87

Deighton, Leonard Cyril 1929-
See Deighton, Len
See also CANR 19; CA 9-12R

De la Mare, Walter (John) 1873-1956 . . . . **TCLC 4**
See also CLR 23; CA 110; SATA 16; DLB 19

Delaney, Shelagh 1939- . . . . **CLC 29**
See also CA 17-20R; DLB 13

Delany, Mary (Granville Pendarves) 1700-1788 . . . . **LC 12**

Delany, Samuel R(ay, Jr.) 1942- . . . . **CLC 8, 14, 38**
See also CA 81-84; DLB 8, 33

De la Roche, Mazo 1885-1961 . . . . . **CLC 14**
See also CA 85-88; DLB 68

Delbanco, Nicholas (Franklin) 1942- . . . . **CLC 6, 13**
See also CAAS 2; CA 17-20R; DLB 6

del Castillo, Michel 1933- . . . . **CLC 38**
See also CA 109

Deledda, Grazia 1871-1936 . . . . **TCLC 23**
See also CA 123

Delibes (Setien), Miguel 1920- . . . . **CLC 8, 18**
See also CANR 1; CA 45-48

DeLillo, Don
1936- . . . . **CLC 8, 10, 13, 27, 39, 54**
See also CANR 21; CA 81-84; DLB 6

De Lisser, H(erbert) G(eorge)
1878-1944 . . . . **TCLC 12**
See also CA 109

Deloria, Vine (Victor), Jr. 1933- . . . . **CLC 21**
See also CANR 5, 20; CA 53-56; SATA 21

Del Vecchio, John M(ichael)
1947- . . . . **CLC 29**
See also CA 110

de Man, Paul 1919-1983 . . . . **CLC 55**
See also obituary CA 111; DLB 67

De Marinis, Rick 1934- . . . . **CLC 54**
See also CANR 9, 25; CA 57-60

Demby, William 1922- . . . . **CLC 53**
See also CA 81-84; DLB 33

Denby, Edwin (Orr) 1903-1983 . . . . . **CLC 48**
See also obituary CA 110

Dennis, John 1657-1734 . . . . **LC 11**

Dennis, Nigel (Forbes) 1912- . . . . **CLC 8**
See also CA 25-28R; obituary CA 129; DLB 13, 15

De Palma, Brian 1940- . . . . **CLC 20**
See also CA 109

De Quincey, Thomas 1785-1859 . . . **NCLC 4**

Deren, Eleanora 1908-1961
See Deren, Maya
See also obituary CA 111

Deren, Maya 1908-1961 . . . . **CLC 16**
See also Deren, Eleanora

Derleth, August (William)
1909-1971 . . . . **CLC 31**
See also CANR 4; CA 1-4R; obituary CA 29-32R; SATA 5; DLB 9

Derrida, Jacques 1930- . . . . **CLC 24**
See also CA 124, 127

Desai, Anita 1937- . . . . **CLC 19, 37**
See also CA 81-84

De Saint-Luc, Jean 1909-1981
See Glassco, John

De Sica, Vittorio 1902-1974 . . . . **CLC 20**
See also obituary CA 117

Desnos, Robert 1900-1945 . . . . **TCLC 22**
See also CA 121

Destouches, Louis-Ferdinand-Auguste
1894-1961
See Celine, Louis-Ferdinand
See also CA 85-88

Deutsch, Babette 1895-1982 . . . . **CLC 18**
See also CANR 4; CA 1-4R; obituary CA 108; SATA 1; obituary SATA 33; DLB 45

Devenant, William 1606-1649 . . . . **LC 13**

Devkota, Laxmiprasad
1909-1959 . . . . **TCLC 23**
See also CA 123

DeVoto, Bernard (Augustine)
1897-1955 . . . . **TCLC 29**
See also CA 113; DLB 9

De Vries, Peter
1910- . . . . **CLC 1, 2, 3, 7, 10, 28, 46**
See also CA 17-20R; DLB 6; DLB-Y 82

Dexter, Pete 1943- . . . . **CLC 34, 55**
See also CA 127

Diamond, Neil (Leslie) 1941- . . . . **CLC 30**
See also CA 108

Dick, Philip K(indred)
1928-1982 . . . . **CLC 10, 30**
See also CANR 2, 16; CA 49-52; obituary CA 106; DLB 8

Dickens, Charles
1812-1870 . . . . **NCLC 3, 8, 18, 26**
See also SATA 15; DLB 21, 55, 70

Dickey, James (Lafayette)
1923- . . . . **CLC 1, 2, 4, 7, 10, 15, 47**
See also CANR 10; CA 9-12R; CABS 2; DLB 5; DLB-Y 82; DLB-DS 7

Dickey, William 1928- . . . . **CLC 3, 28**
See also CANR 24; CA 9-12R; DLB 5

Dickinson, Charles 1952- . . . . **CLC 49**

Dickinson, Emily (Elizabeth)
1830-1886 . . . . **NCLC 21; PC 1**
See also SATA 29; DLB 1; CDALB 1865-1917

Dickinson, Peter (Malcolm de Brissac)
1927- . . . . **CLC 12, 35**
See also CA 41-44R; SATA 5; DLB 87

Didion, Joan 1934- . . . . . **CLC 1, 3, 8, 14, 32**
See also CANR 14; CA 5-8R; DLB 2; DLB-Y 81, 86; CDALB 1968-1987

Dillard, Annie 1945- . . . . **CLC 9, 60**
See also CANR 3; CA 49-52; SATA 10; DLB-Y 80

Dillard, R(ichard) H(enry) W(ilde)
1937- . . . . **CLC 5**
See also CAAS 7; CANR 10; CA 21-24R; DLB 5

Dillon, Eilis 1920- . . . . **CLC 17**
See also CAAS 3; CANR 4; CA 9-12R; SATA 2

Dinesen, Isak
1885-1962 . . . . **CLC 10, 29; SSC 7**
See also Blixen, Karen (Christentze Dinesen)
See also CANR 22

Disch, Thomas M(ichael) 1940- . . . **CLC 7, 36**
See also CAAS 4; CANR 17; CA 21-24R; SATA 54; DLB 8

Disraeli, Benjamin 1804-1881 . . . . . **NCLC 2**
See also DLB 21, 55

Dixon, Paige 1911-
See Corcoran, Barbara

Dixon, Stephen 1936- . . . . **CLC 52**
See also CANR 17; CA 89-92

Doblin, Alfred 1878-1957 . . . . **TCLC 13**
See also Doeblin, Alfred

Dobrolyubov, Nikolai Alexandrovich
1836-1861 . . . . **NCLC 5**

Dobyns, Stephen 1941- . . . . **CLC 37**
See also CANR 2, 18; CA 45-48

Doctorow, E(dgar) L(aurence)
1931- . . . . . **CLC 6, 11, 15, 18, 37, 44, 65**
See also CANR 2, 33; CA 45-48; DLB 2, 28; DLB-Y 80; CDALB 1968-1987

Dodgson, Charles Lutwidge 1832-1898
See Carroll, Lewis
See also YABC 2

Doeblin, Alfred 1878-1957 . . . . **TCLC 13**
See also CA 110; DLB 66

Doerr, Harriet 1910- . . . . **CLC 34**
See also CA 117, 122

Donaldson, Stephen R. 1947- . . . . **CLC 46**
See also CANR 13; CA 89-92

Donleavy, J(ames) P(atrick)
1926- . . . . **CLC 1, 4, 6, 10, 45**
See also CANR 24; CA 9-12R; DLB 6

Donnadieu, Marguerite 1914-
See Duras, Marguerite

Donne, John 1572?-1631 . . . . . . **LC 10; PC 1**

Donnell, David 1939?- . . . . **CLC 34**

Donoso, Jose 1924- . . . . **CLC 4, 8, 11, 32**
See also CA 81-84

Donovan, John 1928- . . . . **CLC 35**
See also CLR 3; CA 97-100; SATA 29

Doolittle, Hilda 1886-1961
See H(ilda) D(oolittle)
See also CA 97-100; DLB 4, 45

Dorfman, Ariel 1942- . . . . **CLC 48**
See also CA 124

Dorn, Ed(ward Merton) 1929- . . . **CLC 10, 18**
See also CA 93-96; DLB 5

Dos Passos, John (Roderigo)
1896-1970 . . . **CLC 1, 4, 8, 11, 15, 25, 34**
See also CANR 3; CA 1-4R; obituary CA 29-32R; DLB 4, 9; DLB-DS 1

Dostoevski, Fedor Mikhailovich
1821-1881 . . . . **NCLC 2, 7, 21; SSC 2**

Doughty, Charles (Montagu)
1843-1926 . . . . **TCLC 27**
See also CA 115; DLB 19, 57

Douglas, George 1869-1902 . . . . **TCLC 28**

Douglas, Keith 1920-1944 . . . . **TCLC 40**
See also DLB 27

Douglass, Frederick 1817-1895 . . . . **NCLC 7**
See also SATA 29; DLB 1, 43, 50; CDALB 1640-1865

Dourado, (Waldomiro Freitas) Autran
1926- . . . . **CLC 23, 60**
See also CA 25-28R

Dove, Rita 1952- . . . . **CLC 50**
See also CA 109

Dowson, Ernest (Christopher)
1867-1900 . . . . **TCLC 4**
See also CA 105; DLB 19

Doyle, (Sir) Arthur Conan
1859-1930 . . . . **TCLC 7, 26**
See also CA 104, 122; SATA 24; DLB 18, 70

Dr. A 1933-
See Silverstein, Alvin and Virginia B(arbara Opshelor) Silverstein

Drabble, Margaret
1939- . . . . **CLC 2, 3, 5, 8, 10, 22, 53**
See also CANR 18; CA 13-16R; SATA 48; DLB 14

Drayton, Michael 1563-1631 . . . . **LC 8**

Dreiser, Theodore (Herman Albert) 1871-1945 .... **TCLC 10, 18, 35**
See also CA 106; SATA 48; DLB 9, 12; DLB-DS 1; CDALB 1865-1917

Drexler, Rosalyn 1926- .... **CLC 2, 6**
See also CA 81-84

Dreyer, Carl Theodor 1889-1968.... **CLC 16**
See also obituary CA 116

Drieu La Rochelle, Pierre 1893-1945 .... **TCLC 21**
See also CA 117; DLB 72

Droste-Hulshoff, Annette Freiin von 1797-1848 .... **NCLC 3**

Drummond, William Henry 1854-1907 .... **TCLC 25**
See also DLB 92

Drummond de Andrade, Carlos 1902-1987
See Andrade, Carlos Drummond de

Drury, Allen (Stuart) 1918-........ **CLC 37**
See also CANR 18; CA 57-60

Dryden, John 1631-1700 .... **LC 3**

Duberman, Martin 1930-........... **CLC 8**
See also CANR 2; CA 1-4R

Dubie, Norman (Evans, Jr.) 1945- .. **CLC 36**
See also CANR 12; CA 69-72

Du Bois, W(illiam) E(dward) B(urghardt) 1868-1963 .... **CLC 1, 2, 13, 64**
See also CA 85-88; SATA 42; DLB 47, 50, 91; CDALB 1865-1917

Dubus, Andre 1936-........... **CLC 13, 36**
See also CANR 17; CA 21-24R

Ducasse, Isidore Lucien 1846-1870
See Lautreamont, Comte de

Duclos, Charles Pinot 1704-1772 ..... **LC 1**

Dudek, Louis 1918- .... **CLC 11, 19**
See also CANR 1; CA 45-48; DLB 88

Dudevant, Amandine Aurore Lucile Dupin 1804-1876
See Sand, George

Duerrenmatt, Friedrich 1921- .... **CLC 1, 4, 8, 11, 15, 43**
See also CA 17-20R; DLB 69

Duffy, Bruce 19??- .... **CLC 50**

Duffy, Maureen 1933-............ **CLC 37**
See also CA 25-28R; DLB 14

Dugan, Alan 1923-.............. **CLC 2, 6**
See also CA 81-84; DLB 5

Duhamel, Georges 1884-1966 .... **CLC 8**
See also CA 81-84; obituary CA 25-28R; DLB 65

Dujardin, Edouard (Emile Louis) 1861-1949 .... **TCLC 13**
See also CA 109

Duke, Raoul 1939-
See Thompson, Hunter S(tockton)

Dumas, Alexandre (Davy de la Pailleterie) (pere) 1802-1870........... **NCLC 11**
See also SATA 18

Dumas, Alexandre (fils) 1824-1895 .... **NCLC 9; DC 1**

Dumas, Henry 1918-1968 .... **CLC 62**

Dumas, Henry (L.) 1934-1968....... **CLC 6**
See also CA 85-88; DLB 41

Du Maurier, Daphne 1907- ... **CLC 6, 11, 59**
See also CANR 6; CA 5-8R; obituary CA 128; SATA 27

Dunbar, Paul Laurence 1872-1906 .... **TCLC 2, 12; SSC 8**
See also CA 124; brief entry CA 104; SATA 34; DLB 50, 54, 78; CDALB 1865-1917

Duncan (Steinmetz Arquette), Lois 1934- .... **CLC 26**
See also Arquette, Lois S(teinmetz)
See also CANR 2; CA 1-4R; SAAS 2; SATA 1, 36

Duncan, Robert (Edward) 1919-1988 ... **CLC 1, 2, 4, 7, 15, 41, 55; PC 2**
See also CANR 28; CA 9-12R; obituary CA 124; DLB 5, 16

Dunlap, William 1766-1839....... **NCLC 2**
See also DLB 30, 37, 59

Dunn, Douglas (Eaglesham) 1942- .... **CLC 6, 40**
See also CANR 2; CA 45-48; DLB 40

Dunn, Elsie 1893-1963
See Scott, Evelyn

Dunn, Stephen 1939- .... **CLC 36**
See also CANR 12; CA 33-36R

Dunne, Finley Peter 1867-1936.... **TCLC 28**
See also CA 108; DLB 11, 23

Dunne, John Gregory 1932-....... **CLC 28**
See also CANR 14; CA 25-28R; DLB-Y 80

Dunsany, Lord (Edward John Moreton Drax Plunkett) 1878-1957.......... **TCLC 2**
See also CA 104; DLB 10

Durang, Christopher (Ferdinand) 1949- .... **CLC 27, 38**
See also CA 105

Duras, Marguerite 1914- .... **CLC 3, 6, 11, 20, 34, 40**
See also CA 25-28R; DLB 83

Durban, Pam 1947-.............. **CLC 39**
See also CA 123

Durcan, Paul 1944-.............. **CLC 43**

Durrell, Lawrence (George) 1912-1990 .... **CLC 1, 4, 6, 8, 13, 27, 41**
See also CA 9-12R; DLB 15, 27

Durrenmatt, Friedrich 1921- .... **CLC 1, 4, 8, 11, 15, 43**
See also Duerrenmatt, Friedrich
See also DLB 69

Dutt, Toru 1856-1877........... **NCLC 29**

Dwight, Timothy 1752-1817...... **NCLC 13**
See also DLB 37

Dworkin, Andrea 1946- .... **CLC 43**
See also CANR 16; CA 77-80

Dylan, Bob 1941-.......... **CLC 3, 4, 6, 12**
See also CA 41-44R; DLB 16

Eagleton, Terry 1943-............ **CLC 63**

East, Michael 1916-
See West, Morris L.

Eastlake, William (Derry) 1917-..... **CLC 8**
See also CAAS 1; CANR 5; CA 5-8R; DLB 6

Eberhart, Richard 1904-... **CLC 3, 11, 19, 56**
See also CANR 2; CA 1-4R; DLB 48; CDALB 1941-1968

Eberstadt, Fernanda 1960-......... **CLC 39**

Echegaray (y Eizaguirre), Jose (Maria Waldo) 1832-1916 .... **TCLC 4**
See also CA 104

Echeverria, (Jose) Esteban (Antonino) 1805-1851 .... **NCLC 18**

Eckert, Allan W. 1931- .... **CLC 17**
See also CANR 14; CA 13-16R; SATA 27, 29

Eco, Umberto 1932-........... **CLC 28, 60**
See also CANR 12; CA 77-80

Eddison, E(ric) R(ucker) 1882-1945 .... **TCLC 15**
See also CA 109

Edel, Leon (Joseph) 1907-...... **CLC 29, 34**
See also CANR 1, 22; CA 1-4R

Eden, Emily 1797-1869 .... **NCLC 10**

Edgar, David 1948-.............. **CLC 42**
See also CANR 12; CA 57-60; DLB 13

Edgerton, Clyde 1944-............ **CLC 39**
See also CA 118

Edgeworth, Maria 1767-1849...... **NCLC 1**
See also SATA 21

Edmonds, Helen (Woods) 1904-1968
See Kavan, Anna
See also CA 5-8R; obituary CA 25-28R

Edmonds, Walter D(umaux) 1903- .. **CLC 35**
See also CANR 2; CA 5-8R; SAAS 4; SATA 1, 27; DLB 9

Edson, Russell 1905- .... **CLC 13**
See also CA 33-36R

Edwards, G(erald) B(asil) 1899-1976 .... **CLC 25**
See also obituary CA 110

Edwards, Gus 1939-.............. **CLC 43**
See also CA 108

Edwards, Jonathan 1703-1758........ **LC 7**
See also DLB 24

Ehle, John (Marsden, Jr.) 1925-..... **CLC 27**
See also CA 9-12R

Ehrenburg, Ilya (Grigoryevich) 1891-1967 .... **CLC 18, 34, 62**
See also CA 102; obituary CA 25-28R

Eich, Guenter 1907-1971
See also CA 111; obituary CA 93-96

Eich, Gunter 1907-1971 .... **CLC 15**
See also Eich, Guenter
See also DLB 69

Eichendorff, Joseph Freiherr von 1788-1857 .... **NCLC 8**
See also DLB 90

Eigner, Larry 1927- .... **CLC 9**
See also Eigner, Laurence (Joel)
See also DLB 5

Eigner, Laurence (Joel) 1927-
See Eigner, Larry
See also CANR 6; CA 9-12R

Eiseley, Loren (Corey) 1907-1977.... **CLC 7**
See also CANR 6; CA 1-4R; obituary CA 73-76

Eisenstadt, Jill 1963- .... **CLC 50**

Ekeloef, Gunnar (Bengt) 1907-1968
See Ekelof, Gunnar (Bengt)
See also obituary CA 25-28R

Ekelof, Gunnar (Bengt) 1907-1968 .. **CLC 27**
See also Ekeloef, Gunnar (Bengt)

Ekwensi, Cyprian (Odiatu Duaka) 1921- .... **CLC 4**
See also CANR 18; CA 29-32R

Eliade, Mircea 1907-1986 .... **CLC 19**
See also CA 65-68; obituary CA 119

Eliot, George 1819-1880.... **NCLC 4, 13, 23**
See also DLB 21, 35, 55

Eliot, John 1604-1690 .... **LC 5**
See also DLB 24

Eliot, T(homas) S(tearns) 1888-1965 .... **CLC 1, 2, 3, 6, 9, 10, 13, 15, 24, 34, 41, 55, 57**
See also CA 5-8R; obituary CA 25-28R; DLB 7, 10, 45, 63; DLB-Y 88

Elizabeth 1866-1941 .... **TCLC 41**
See also Russell, Mary Annette Beauchamp

Elkin, Stanley (Lawrence) 1930- .... **CLC 4, 6, 9, 14, 27, 51**
See also CANR 8; CA 9-12R; DLB 2, 28; DLB-Y 80

Elledge, Scott 19??- .... **CLC 34**

Elliott, George P(aul) 1918-1980..... **CLC 2**
See also CANR 2; CA 1-4R; obituary CA 97-100

Elliott, Janice 1931-.............. **CLC 47**
See also CANR 8; CA 13-16R; DLB 14

Elliott, Sumner Locke 1917-....... **CLC 38**
See also CANR 2, 21; CA 5-8R

Ellis, A. E. 19??-.................. **CLC 7**

Ellis, Alice Thomas 19??-.......... **CLC 40**

Ellis, Bret Easton 1964-........... **CLC 39**
See also CA 118, 123

Ellis, (Henry) Havelock 1859-1939 .... **TCLC 14**
See also CA 109

Ellis, Trey 1964-.................. **CLC 55**

Ellison, Harlan (Jay) 1934-... **CLC 1, 13, 42**
See also CANR 5; CA 5-8R; DLB 8

Ellison, Ralph (Waldo) 1914- .... **CLC 1, 3, 11, 54**
See also CANR 24; CA 9-12R; DLB 2, 76; CDALB 1941-1968

Ellmann, Lucy 1956- .... **CLC 61**
See also CA 128

Ellmann, Richard (David) 1918-1987 .... **CLC 50**
See also CANR 2; CA 1-4R; obituary CA 122; DLB-Y 87

Elman, Richard 1934-............ **CLC 19**
See also CAAS 3; CA 17-20R

Eluard, Paul 1895-1952 .... **TCLC 7, 41**
See also Grindel, Eugene

Elyot, (Sir) Thomas 1490?-1546 ..... **LC 11**

Elytis, Odysseus 1911-......... **CLC 15, 49**
See also CA 102

Emecheta, (Florence Onye) Buchi 1944- .... **CLC 14, 48**
See also CA 81-84

Emerson, Ralph Waldo 1803-1882 .... **NCLC 1**
See also DLB 1, 59, 73; CDALB 1640-1865

Empson, William 1906-1984 .... **CLC 3, 8, 19, 33, 34**
See also CA 17-20R; obituary CA 112; DLB 20

Enchi, Fumiko (Veda) 1905-1986 ... **CLC 31**
See also obituary CA 121

Ende, Michael 1930-............. **CLC 31**
See also CLR 14; CA 118, 124; SATA 42; DLB 75

Endo, Shusaku 1923- ..... **CLC 7, 14, 19, 54**
See also CANR 21; CA 29-32R

Engel, Marian 1933-1985.......... **CLC 36**
See also CANR 12; CA 25-28R; DLB 53

Engelhardt, Frederick 1911-1986
See Hubbard, L(afayette) Ron(ald)

Enright, D(ennis) J(oseph) 1920- .... **CLC 4, 8, 31**
See also CANR 1; CA 1-4R; SATA 25; DLB 27

Enzensberger, Hans Magnus 1929- .... **CLC 43**
See also CA 116, 119

Ephron, Nora 1941- .... **CLC 17, 31**
See also CANR 12; CA 65-68

Epstein, Daniel Mark 1948- .... **CLC 7**
See also CANR 2; CA 49-52

Epstein, Jacob 1956- .... **CLC 19**
See also CA 114

Epstein, Joseph 1937-............. **CLC 39**
See also CA 112, 119

Epstein, Leslie 1938- .... **CLC 27**
See also CANR 23; CA 73-76

Equiano, Olaudah 1745?-1797 .... **LC 16**
See also DLB 37, 50

Erasmus, Desiderius 1469?-1536..... **LC 16**

Erdman, Paul E(mil) 1932- .... **CLC 25**
See also CANR 13; CA 61-64

Erdrich, Louise 1954-.......... **CLC 39, 54**
See also CA 114

Erenburg, Ilya (Grigoryevich) 1891-1967
See Ehrenburg, Ilya (Grigoryevich)

Erickson, Steve 1950-............ **CLC 64**
See also CA 129

Eseki, Bruno 1919-
See Mphahlele, Ezekiel

Esenin, Sergei (Aleksandrovich) 1895-1925 .... **TCLC 4**
See also CA 104

Eshleman, Clayton 1935-............ **CLC 7**
See also CAAS 6; CA 33-36R; DLB 5

Espriu, Salvador 1913-1985......... **CLC 9**
See also obituary CA 115

Estleman, Loren D. 1952- .... **CLC 48**
See also CA 85-88

Evans, Marian 1819-1880
See Eliot, George

Evans, Mary Ann 1819-1880
See Eliot, George

Evarts, Esther 1900-1972
See Benson, Sally

Everett, Percival L. 1957?- .... **CLC 57**
See also CA 129

Everson, Ronald G(ilmour) 1903- ... **CLC 27**
See also CA 17-20R; DLB 88

Everson, William (Oliver) 1912- .... **CLC 1, 5, 14**
See also CANR 20; CA 9-12R; DLB 5, 16

Evtushenko, Evgenii (Aleksandrovich) 1933-
See Yevtushenko, Yevgeny

Ewart, Gavin (Buchanan) 1916- .... **CLC 13, 46**
See also CANR 17; CA 89-92; DLB 40

Ewers, Hanns Heinz 1871-1943 ... **TCLC 12**
See also CA 109

Ewing, Frederick R. 1918-
See Sturgeon, Theodore (Hamilton)

Exley, Frederick (Earl) 1929- .... **CLC 6, 11**
See also CA 81-84; DLB-Y 81

Ezekiel, Nissim 1924-............ **CLC 61**
See also CA 61-64

Ezekiel, Tish O'Dowd 1943- .... **CLC 34**

Fagen, Donald 1948-............. **CLC 26**

Fair, Ronald L. 1932-............. **CLC 18**
See also CANR 25; CA 69-72; DLB 33

Fairbairns, Zoe (Ann) 1948- .... **CLC 32**
See also CANR 21; CA 103

Fairfield, Cicily Isabel 1892-1983
See West, Rebecca

Fallaci, Oriana 1930-............. **CLC 11**
See also CANR 15; CA 77-80

Faludy, George 1913-............. **CLC 42**
See also CA 21-24R

Fante, John 1909-1983............ **CLC 60**
See also CANR 23; CA 69-72; obituary CA 109; DLB-Y 83

Farah, Nuruddin 1945-............ **CLC 53**
See also CA 106

Fargue, Leon-Paul 1876-1947 ..... **TCLC 11**
See also CA 109

Farigoule, Louis 1885-1972
See Romains, Jules

Farina, Richard 1937?-1966.......... **CLC 9**
See also CA 81-84; obituary CA 25-28R

Farley, Walter 1920- .... **CLC 17**
See also CANR 8; CA 17-20R; SATA 2, 43; DLB 22

Farmer, Philip Jose 1918-....... **CLC 1, 19**
See also CANR 4; CA 1-4R; DLB 8

Farrell, J(ames) G(ordon) 1935-1979 .... **CLC 6**
See also CA 73-76; obituary CA 89-92; DLB 14

Farrell, James T(homas) 1904-1979 .... **CLC 1, 4, 8, 11**
See also CANR 9; CA 5-8R; obituary CA 89-92; DLB 4, 9, 86; DLB-DS 2

Farrell, M. J. 1904-
See Keane, Molly

Fassbinder, Rainer Werner 1946-1982 .... **CLC 20**
See also CA 93-96; obituary CA 106

Fast, Howard (Melvin) 1914- ...... **CLC 23**
See also CANR 1; CA 1-4R; SATA 7; DLB 9

Faulkner, William (Cuthbert) 1897-1962 .... **CLC 1, 3, 6, 8, 9, 11, 14, 18, 28, 52; SSC 1**
See also CA 81-84; DLB 9, 11, 44; DLB-Y 86; DLB-DS 2

Fauset, Jessie Redmon 1884?-1961................ **CLC 19, 54**
See also CA 109; DLB 51

Faust, Irvin 1924-................. **CLC 8**
See also CA 33-36R; DLB 2, 28; DLB-Y 80

Fearing, Kenneth (Flexner) 1902-1961 .... **CLC 51**
See also CA 93-96; DLB 9

Federman, Raymond 1928- ...... **CLC 6, 47**
See also CANR 10; CA 17-20R; DLB-Y 80

Federspiel, J(urg) F. 1931-........ **CLC 42**

Feiffer, Jules 1929-........... **CLC 2, 8, 64**
See also CANR 30; CA 17-20R; SATA 8, 61; DLB 7, 44; AAYA 3

Feinberg, David B. 1956-.......... **CLC 59**

Feinstein, Elaine 1930-............ **CLC 36**
See also CAAS 1; CA 69-72; DLB 14, 40

Feke, Gilbert David 1976?-........ **CLC 65**

Feldman, Irving (Mordecai) 1928-.... **CLC 7**
See also CANR 1; CA 1-4R

Fellini, Federico 1920-............ **CLC 16**
See also CA 65-68

Felsen, Gregor 1916-
See Felsen, Henry Gregor

Felsen, Henry Gregor 1916- .... **CLC 17**
See also CANR 1; CA 1-4R; SAAS 2; SATA 1

Fenton, James (Martin) 1949-...... **CLC 32**
See also CA 102; DLB 40

Ferber, Edna 1887-1968.......... **CLC 18**
See also CA 5-8R; obituary CA 25-28R; SATA 7; DLB 9, 28, 86

Ferlinghetti, Lawrence (Monsanto) 1919?- .... **CLC 2, 6, 10, 27; PC 1**
See also CANR 3; CA 5-8R; DLB 5, 16; CDALB 1941-1968

Ferrier, Susan (Edmonstone) 1782-1854 .... **NCLC 8**

Ferrigno, Robert 19??-............ **CLC 65**

Feuchtwanger, Lion 1884-1958 ..... **TCLC 3**
See also CA 104; DLB 66

Feydeau, Georges 1862-1921...... **TCLC 22**
See also CA 113

Ficino, Marsilio 1433-1499 .... **LC 12**

Fiedler, Leslie A(aron) 1917- .... **CLC 4, 13, 24**
See also CANR 7; CA 9-12R; DLB 28, 67

Field, Andrew 1938-.............. **CLC 44**
See also CANR 25; CA 97-100

Field, Eugene 1850-1895 .... **NCLC 3**
See also SATA 16; DLB 21, 23, 42

Fielding, Henry 1707-1754 .... **LC 1**
See also DLB 39, 84

Fielding, Sarah 1710-1768 .... **LC 1**
See also DLB 39

Fierstein, Harvey 1954-........... **CLC 33**
See also CA 123, 129

Figes, Eva 1932-................ **CLC 31**
See also CANR 4; CA 53-56; DLB 14

Finch, Robert (Duer Claydon) 1900- .... **CLC 18**
See also CANR 9, 24; CA 57-60; DLB 88

Findley, Timothy 1930- .... **CLC 27**
See also CANR 12; CA 25-28R; DLB 53

Fink, Janis 1951-
See Ian, Janis

Firbank, Louis 1944-
See Reed, Lou
See also CA 117

Firbank, (Arthur Annesley) Ronald 1886-1926 .... **TCLC 1**
See also CA 104; DLB 36

Fisher, Roy 1930-................ **CLC 25**
See also CANR 16; CA 81-84; DLB 40

Fisher, Rudolph 1897-1934 .... **TCLC 11**
See also CA 107; DLB 51

Fisher, Vardis (Alvero) 1895-1968.... **CLC 7**
See also CA 5-8R; obituary CA 25-28R; DLB 9

FitzGerald, Edward 1809-1883 .... **NCLC 9**
See also DLB 32

Fitzgerald, F(rancis) Scott (Key) 1896-1940 .... **TCLC 1, 6, 14, 28; SSC 6**
See also CA 110, 123; DLB 4, 9, 86; DLB-Y 81; DLB-DS 1; CDALB 1917-1929

Fitzgerald, Penelope 1916-... **CLC 19, 51, 61**
See also CAAS 10; CA 85-88,; DLB 14

Fitzgerald, Robert (Stuart) 1910-1985 .... **CLC 39**
See also CANR 1; CA 2R; obituary CA 114; DLB-Y 80

FitzGerald, Robert D(avid) 1902-... **CLC 19**
See also CA 17-20R

Flanagan, Thomas (James Bonner) 1923- .... **CLC 25, 52**
See also CA 108; DLB-Y 80

Flaubert, Gustave 1821-1880 .... **NCLC 2, 10, 19**

Fleming, Ian (Lancaster) 1908-1964 .... **CLC 3, 30**
See also CA 5-8R; SATA 9; DLB 87

Fleming, Thomas J(ames) 1927- .... **CLC 37**
See also CANR 10; CA 5-8R; SATA 8

Fletcher, John Gould 1886-1950... **TCLC 35**
See also CA 107; DLB 4, 45

Flieg, Hellmuth
See Heym, Stefan

Flying Officer X 1905-1974
See Bates, H(erbert) E(rnest)

Fo, Dario 1929-................. **CLC 32**
See also CA 116

Follett, Ken(neth Martin) 1949- .... **CLC 18**
See also CANR 13; CA 81-84; DLB-Y 81

Fontane, Theodor 1819-1898..... **NCLC 26**

Foote, Horton 1916-............. **CLC 51**
See also CA 73-76; DLB 26

Forbes, Esther 1891-1967.......... **CLC 12**
See also CAP 1; CA 13-14; obituary CA 25-28R; SATA 2; DLB 22

Forche, Carolyn 1950-............ **CLC 25**
See also CA 109, 117; DLB 5

Ford, Ford Madox 1873-1939 .... **TCLC 1, 15, 39**
See also CA 104; DLB 34

Ford, John 1895-1973............. **CLC 16**
See also obituary CA 45-48

Ford, Richard 1944-.............. **CLC 46**
See also CANR 11; CA 69-72

Foreman, Richard 1937-.......... **CLC 50**
See also CA 65-68

Forester, C(ecil) S(cott) 1899-1966 .... **CLC 35**
See also CA 73-76; obituary CA 25-28R; SATA 13

Forman, James D(ouglas) 1932- .... **CLC 21**
See also CANR 4, 19; CA 9-12R; SATA 8, 21

Fornes, Maria Irene 1930-..... **CLC 39, 61**
See also CANR 28; CA 25-28R; DLB 7

Forrest, Leon 1937- .... **CLC 4**
See also CAAS 7; CA 89-92; DLB 33

Forster, E(dward) M(organ) 1879-1970 .... **CLC 1, 2, 3, 4, 9, 10, 13, 15, 22, 45**
See also CAP 1; CA 13-14; obituary CA 25-28R; SATA 57; DLB 34

Forster, John 1812-1876 .... **NCLC 11**

Forsyth, Frederick 1938-...... **CLC 2, 5, 36**
See also CA 85-88; DLB 87

Forten (Grimke), Charlotte L(ottie) 1837-1914 .... **TCLC 16**
See also Grimke, Charlotte L(ottie) Forten
See also DLB 50

Foscolo, Ugo 1778-1827.......... **NCLC 8**

Fosse, Bob 1925-1987............. **CLC 20**
See also Fosse, Robert Louis

Fosse, Robert Louis 1925-1987
See Bob Fosse
See also CA 110, 123

Foster, Stephen Collins 1826-1864 .... **NCLC 26**

Foucault, Michel 1926-1984 .... **CLC 31, 34**
See also CANR 23; CA 105; obituary CA 113

Fouque, Friedrich (Heinrich Karl) de La Motte 1777-1843 .... **NCLC 2**

Fournier, Henri Alban 1886-1914
See Alain-Fournier
See also CA 104

Fournier, Pierre 1916-............ **CLC 11**
See also Gascar, Pierre
See also CANR 16; CA 89-92

Fowles, John (Robert) 1926- .... **CLC 1, 2, 3, 4, 6, 9, 10, 15, 33**
See also CANR 25; CA 5-8R; SATA 22; DLB 14

Fox, Paula 1923-............... **CLC 2, 8**
See also CLR 1; CANR 20; CA 73-76; SATA 17; DLB 52

Fox, William Price (Jr.) 1926- ..... **CLC 22**
See also CANR 11; CA 17-20R; DLB 2; DLB-Y 81

Foxe, John 1516?-1587 .... **LC 14**

Frame (Clutha), Janet (Paterson) 1924- .... **CLC 2, 3, 6, 22**
See also Clutha, Janet Paterson Frame

France, Anatole 1844-1924 .... **TCLC 9**
See also Thibault, Jacques Anatole Francois

Francis, Claude 19??- .... **CLC 50**

Francis, Dick 1920- .... **CLC 2, 22, 42**
See also CANR 9; CA 5-8R; DLB 87

Francis, Robert (Churchill) 1901-1987 .... **CLC 15**
See also CANR 1; CA 1-4R; obituary CA 123

Frank, Anne 1929-1945 .... **TCLC 17**
See also CA 113; SATA 42

Frank, Elizabeth 1945- .... **CLC 39**
See also CA 121, 126

Franklin, (Stella Maria Sarah) Miles 1879-1954 .... **TCLC 7**
See also CA 104

Fraser, Antonia (Pakenham) 1932- .... **CLC 32**
See also CA 85-88; SATA 32

Fraser, George MacDonald 1925- .... **CLC 7**
See also CANR 2; CA 45-48

Fraser, Sylvia 1935- .... **CLC 64**
See also CANR 1, 16; CA 45-48

Frayn, Michael 1933- ...... **CLC 3, 7, 31, 47**
See also CA 5-8R; DLB 13, 14

Fraze, Candida 19??- .... **CLC 50**
See also CA 125

Frazer, Sir James George 1854-1941 .... **TCLC 32**
See also CA 118

Frazier, Ian 1951- .... **CLC 46**
See also CA 130

Frederic, Harold 1856-1898 ...... **NCLC 10**
See also DLB 12, 23

Frederick the Great 1712-1786 ...... **LC 14**

Fredman, Russell (Bruce) 1929-
See also CLR 20

Fredro, Aleksander 1793-1876 ..... **NCLC 8**

Freeling, Nicolas 1927- .... **CLC 38**
See also CANR 1, 17; CA 49-52; DLB 87

Freeman, Douglas Southall 1886-1953 .... **TCLC 11**
See also CA 109; DLB 17

Freeman, Judith 1946- .... **CLC 55**

Freeman, Mary (Eleanor) Wilkins 1852-1930 .... **TCLC 9; SSC 1**
See also CA 106; DLB 12, 78

Freeman, R(ichard) Austin 1862-1943 .... **TCLC 21**
See also CA 113; DLB 70

French, Marilyn 1929- ...... **CLC 10, 18, 60**
See also CANR 3; CA 69-72

Freneau, Philip Morin 1752-1832 .. **NCLC 1**
See also DLB 37, 43

Friedman, B(ernard) H(arper) 1926- .... **CLC 7**
See also CANR 3; CA 1-4R

Friedman, Bruce Jay 1930- .... **CLC 3, 5, 56**
See also CANR 25; CA 9-12R; DLB 2, 28

Friel, Brian 1929- .... **CLC 5, 42, 59**
See also CA 21-24R; DLB 13

Friis-Baastad, Babbis (Ellinor) 1921-1970 .... **CLC 12**
See also CA 17-20R; SATA 7

Frisch, Max (Rudolf) 1911- .... **CLC 3, 9, 14, 18, 32, 44**
See also CA 85-88; DLB 69

Fromentin, Eugene (Samuel Auguste) 1820-1876 .... **NCLC 10**

Frost, Robert (Lee) 1874-1963 ... **CLC 1, 3, 4, 9, 10, 13, 15, 26, 34, 44; PC 1**
See also CA 89-92; SATA 14; DLB 54; DLB-DS 7; CDALB 1917-1929

Fry, Christopher 1907- .... **CLC 2, 10, 14**
See also CANR 9; CA 17-20R; DLB 13

Frye, (Herman) Northrop 1912- .... **CLC 24**
See also CANR 8; CA 5-8R; DLB 67, 68

Fuchs, Daniel 1909- .... **CLC 8, 22**
See also CAAS 5; CA 81-84; DLB 9, 26, 28

Fuchs, Daniel 1934- .... **CLC 34**
See also CANR 14; CA 37-40R

Fuentes, Carlos 1928- ...... **CLC 3, 8, 10, 13, 22, 41, 60**
See also CANR 10; CA 69-72

Fugard, Athol 1932- ... **CLC 5, 9, 14, 25, 40**
See also CA 85-88

Fugard, Sheila 1932- .... **CLC 48**
See also CA 125

Fuller, Charles (H., Jr.) 1939- .... **CLC 25; DC 1**
See also CA 108, 112; DLB 38

Fuller, John (Leopold) 1937- .... **CLC 62**
See also CANR 9; CA 21-22R; DLB 40

Fuller, (Sarah) Margaret 1810-1850 .... **NCLC 5**
See also Ossoli, Sarah Margaret (Fuller marchesa d')
See also DLB 1, 59, 73; CDALB 1640-1865

Fuller, Roy (Broadbent) 1912- .... **CLC 4, 28**
See also CA 5-8R; DLB 15, 20

Fulton, Alice 1952- .... **CLC 52**
See also CA 116

Furphy, Joseph 1843-1912 .... **TCLC 25**

Futrelle, Jacques 1875-1912 ...... **TCLC 19**
See also CA 113

Gaboriau, Emile 1835-1873 ...... **NCLC 14**

Gadda, Carlo Emilio 1893-1973 .... **CLC 11**
See also CA 89-92

Gaddis, William 1922- .... **CLC 1, 3, 6, 8, 10, 19, 43**
See also CAAS 4; CANR 21; CA 17-20R; DLB 2

Gaines, Ernest J. 1933- ...... **CLC 3, 11, 18**
See also CANR 6, 24; CA 9-12R; DLB 2, 33; DLB-Y 80

Gale, Zona 1874-1938 .... **TCLC 7**
See also CA 105; DLB 9, 78

Gallagher, Tess 1943- .... **CLC 18, 63**
See also CA 106

Gallant, Mavis 1922- .... **CLC 7, 18, 38; SSC 5**
See also CA 69-72; DLB 53

Gallant, Roy A(rthur) 1924- .... **CLC 17**
See also CANR 4; CA 5-8R; SATA 4

Gallico, Paul (William) 1897-1976 ... **CLC 2**
See also CA 5-8R; obituary CA 69-72; SATA 13; DLB 9

Galsworthy, John 1867-1933 .... **TCLC 1**
See also CA 104; DLB 10, 34

Galt, John 1779-1839 .... **NCLC 1**

Galvin, James 1951- .... **CLC 38**
See also CANR 26; CA 108

Gamboa, Frederico 1864-1939 ..... **TCLC 36**

Gann, Ernest K(ellogg) 1910- ...... **CLC 23**
See also CANR 1; CA 1-4R

Garcia Lorca, Federico 1899-1936 .... **TCLC 1, 7**
See also CA 104

Garcia Marquez, Gabriel (Jose) 1928- ... **CLC 2, 3, 8, 10, 15, 27, 47, 55; SSC 8**
See also CANR 10, 28; CA 33-36R; AAYA 3

Gardam, Jane 1928- .... **CLC 43**
See also CLR 12; CANR 2, 18; CA 49-52; SATA 28, 39; DLB 14

Gardner, Herb 1934- .... **CLC 44**

Gardner, John (Champlin, Jr.) 1933-1982 .... **CLC 2, 3, 5, 7, 8, 10, 18, 28, 34; SSC 7**
See also CA 65-68; obituary CA 107; obituary SATA 31, 40; DLB 2; DLB-Y 82

Gardner, John (Edmund) 1926- ..... **CLC 30**
See also CANR 15; CA 103

Garfield, Leon 1921- .... **CLC 12**
See also CA 17-20R; SATA 1, 32

Garland, (Hannibal) Hamlin 1860-1940 .... **TCLC 3**
See also CA 104; DLB 12, 71, 78

Garneau, Hector (de) Saint Denys 1912-1943 .... **TCLC 13**
See also CA 111; DLB 88

Garner, Alan 1935- .... **CLC 17**
See also CLR 20; CANR 15; CA 73-76; SATA 18

Garner, Hugh 1913-1979 .... **CLC 13**
See also CA 69-72; DLB 68

Garnett, David 1892-1981 .... **CLC 3**
See also CANR 17; CA 5-8R; obituary CA 103; DLB 34

Garrett, George (Palmer, Jr.) 1929- .... **CLC 3, 11, 51**
See also CAAS 5; CANR 1; CA 1-4R; DLB 2, 5; DLB-Y 83

Garrick, David 1717-1779 .... **LC 15**
See also DLB 84

Garrigue, Jean 1914-1972 .... **CLC 2, 8**
See also CANR 20; CA 5-8R; obituary CA 37-40R

Garvey, Marcus 1887-1940 ...... **TCLC 41**
See also CA 124; brief entry CA 120

Gary, Romain 1914-1980 .... CLC 25
See also Kacew, Romain

Gascar, Pierre 1916- .... CLC 11
See also Fournier, Pierre

Gascoyne, David (Emery) 1916- .... CLC 45
See also CANR 10; CA 65-68; DLB 20

Gaskell, Elizabeth Cleghorn 1810-1865 .... NCLC 5
See also DLB 21

Gass, William H(oward) 1924- .... CLC 1, 2, 8, 11, 15, 39
See also CA 17-20R; DLB 2

Gates, Henry Louis, Jr. 1950- ...... CLC 65
See also CANR 25; CA 109; DLB 67

Gautier, Theophile 1811-1872 ..... NCLC 1

Gaye, Marvin (Pentz) 1939-1984 ... CLC 26
See also obituary CA 112

Gebler, Carlo (Ernest) 1954- .... CLC 39
See also CA 119

Gee, Maggie 19??- .... CLC 57

Gee, Maurice (Gough) 1931- .... CLC 29
See also CA 97-100; SATA 46

Gelbart, Larry 1923?- .... CLC 21, 61
See also CA 73-76

Gelber, Jack 1932- .... CLC 1, 6, 14, 60
See also CANR 2; CA 1-4R; DLB 7

Gellhorn, Martha (Ellis) 1908- .. CLC 14, 60
See also CA 77-80; DLB-Y 82

Genet, Jean 1910-1986 ... CLC 1, 2, 5, 10, 14, 44, 46
See also CANR 18; CA 13-16R; DLB 72; DLB-Y 86

Gent, Peter 1942- .... CLC 29
See also CA 89-92; DLB 72; DLB-Y 82

George, Jean Craighead 1919- ...... CLC 35
See also CLR 1; CA 5-8R; SATA 2; DLB 52

George, Stefan (Anton) 1868-1933 .... TCLC 2, 14
See also CA 104

Gerhardi, William (Alexander) 1895-1977
See Gerhardie, William (Alexander)

Gerhardie, William (Alexander) 1895-1977 .... CLC 5
See also CANR 18; CA 25-28R; obituary CA 73-76; DLB 36

Gertler, T(rudy) 1946?- .... CLC 34
See also CA 116

Gessner, Friedrike Victoria 1910-1980
See Adamson, Joy(-Friederike Victoria)

Ghelderode, Michel de 1898-1962 .... CLC 6, 11
See also CA 85-88

Ghiselin, Brewster 1903- .... CLC 23
See also CANR 13; CA 13-16R

Ghose, Zulfikar 1935- .... CLC 42
See also CA 65-68

Ghosh, Amitav 1943- .... CLC 44

Giacosa, Giuseppe 1847-1906 ...... TCLC 7
See also CA 104

Gibbon, Lewis Grassic 1901-1935 ... TCLC 4
See also Mitchell, James Leslie

Gibbons, Kaye 1960- .... CLC 50

Gibran, (Gibran) Kahlil 1883-1931 .... TCLC 1, 9
See also CA 104

Gibson, William 1914- .... CLC 23
See also CANR 9; CA 9-12R; DLB 7

Gibson, William 1948- .... CLC 39, 63
See also CA 126

Gide, Andre (Paul Guillaume) 1869-1951 .... TCLC 5, 12, 36
See also CA 104, 124; DLB 65

Gifford, Barry (Colby) 1946- ...... CLC 34
See also CANR 9; CA 65-68

Gilbert, (Sir) W(illiam) S(chwenck) 1836-1911 .... TCLC 3
See also CA 104; SATA 36

Gilbreth, Ernestine 1908-
See Carey, Ernestine Gilbreth

Gilbreth, Frank B(unker), Jr. 1911- .... CLC 17
See also CA 9-12R; SATA 2

Gilchrist, Ellen 1935- .... CLC 34, 48
See also CA 113, 116

Giles, Molly 1942- .... CLC 39
See also CA 126

Gilliam, Terry (Vance) 1940-
See Monty Python
See also CA 108, 113

Gilliatt, Penelope (Ann Douglass) 1932- .... CLC 2, 10, 13, 53
See also CA 13-16R; DLB 14

Gilman, Charlotte (Anna) Perkins (Stetson) 1860-1935 .... TCLC 9, 37
See also CA 106

Gilmour, David 1944-
See Pink Floyd

Gilpin, William 1724-1804 .... NCLC 30

Gilroy, Frank D(aniel) 1925- .... CLC 2
See also CA 81-84; DLB 7

Ginsberg, Allen 1926- .... CLC 1, 2, 3, 4, 6, 13, 36
See also CANR 2; CA 1-4R; DLB 5, 16; CDALB 1941-1968

Ginzburg, Natalia 1916- ...... CLC 5, 11, 54
See also CA 85-88

Giono, Jean 1895-1970 .... CLC 4, 11
See also CANR 2; CA 45-48; obituary CA 29-32R; DLB 72

Giovanni, Nikki 1943- ..... CLC 2, 4, 19, 64
See also CLR 6; CAAS 6; CANR 18; CA 29-32R; SATA 24; DLB 5, 41

Giovene, Andrea 1904- .... CLC 7
See also CA 85-88

Gippius, Zinaida (Nikolayevna) 1869-1945
See Hippius, Zinaida
See also CA 106

Giraudoux, (Hippolyte) Jean 1882-1944 .... TCLC 2, 7
See also CA 104; DLB 65

Gironella, Jose Maria 1917- .... CLC 11
See also CA 101

Gissing, George (Robert) 1857-1903 .... TCLC 3, 24
See also CA 105; DLB 18

Gladkov, Fyodor (Vasilyevich) 1883-1958 .... TCLC 27

Glanville, Brian (Lester) 1931- ...... CLC 6
See also CANR 3; CA 5-8R; SATA 42; DLB 15

Glasgow, Ellen (Anderson Gholson) 1873?-1945 .... TCLC 2, 7
See also CA 104; DLB 9, 12

Glassco, John 1909-1981 .... CLC 9
See also CANR 15; CA 13-16R; obituary CA 102; DLB 68

Glasser, Ronald J. 1940?- .... CLC 37

Glendinning, Victoria 1937- .... CLC 50
See also CA 120

Glissant, Edouard 1928- .... CLC 10

Gloag, Julian 1930- .... CLC 40
See also CANR 10; CA 65-68

Gluck, Louise (Elisabeth) 1943- .... CLC 7, 22, 44
See also CA 33-36R; DLB 5

Gobineau, Joseph Arthur (Comte) de 1816-1882 .... NCLC 17

Godard, Jean-Luc 1930- .... CLC 20
See also CA 93-96

Godden, (Margaret) Rumer 1907- ... CLC 53
See also CLR 20; CANR 4, 27; CA 7-8R; SATA 3, 36

Godwin, Gail 1937- .... CLC 5, 8, 22, 31
See also CANR 15; CA 29-32R; DLB 6

Godwin, William 1756-1836 ...... NCLC 14
See also DLB 39

Goethe, Johann Wolfgang von 1749-1832 .... NCLC 4, 22

Gogarty, Oliver St. John 1878-1957 .... TCLC 15
See also CA 109; DLB 15, 19

Gogol, Nikolai (Vasilyevich) 1809-1852 ..... NCLC 5, 15, 31; DC 1; SSC 4
See also CAAS 1, 4

Gokceli, Yasar Kemal 1923-
See Kemal, Yashar

Gold, Herbert 1924- .... CLC 4, 7, 14, 42
See also CANR 17; CA 9-12R; DLB 2; DLB-Y 81

Goldbarth, Albert 1948- .... CLC 5, 38
See also CANR 6; CA 53-56

Goldberg, Anatol 1910-1982 .... CLC 34
See also obituary CA 117

Goldemberg, Isaac 1945- .... CLC 52
See also CANR 11; CA 69-72

Golding, William (Gerald) 1911- ..... CLC 1, 2, 3, 8, 10, 17, 27, 58
See also CANR 13; CA 5-8R; DLB 15

Goldman, Emma 1869-1940 .... TCLC 13
See also CA 110

Goldman, William (W.) 1931- .... CLC 1, 48
See also CA 9-12R; DLB 44

Goldmann, Lucien 1913-1970 ...... CLC 24
See also CAP 2; CA 25-28

Goldoni, Carlo 1707-1793 .... LC 4

Goldsberry, Steven 1949- .... CLC 34

Goldsmith, Oliver 1728?-1774 . . . . **LC 2**
See also SATA 26; DLB 39

Gombrowicz, Witold
1904-1969 . . . . **CLC 4, 7, 11, 49**
See also CAP 2; CA 19-20;
obituary CA 25-28R

Gomez de la Serna, Ramon
1888-1963 . . . . **CLC 9**
See also obituary CA 116

Goncharov, Ivan Alexandrovich
1812-1891 . . . . **NCLC 1**

Goncourt, Edmond (Louis Antoine Huot) de
1822-1896 . . . . **NCLC 7**

Goncourt, Jules (Alfred Huot) de
1830-1870 . . . . **NCLC 7**

Gontier, Fernande 19??- . . . . **CLC 50**

Goodman, Paul 1911-1972 . . . . **CLC 1, 2, 4, 7**
See also CAP 2; CA 19-20;
obituary CA 37-40R

Gordimer, Nadine
1923- . . . . **CLC 3, 5, 7, 10, 18, 33, 51**
See also CANR 3; CA 5-8R

Gordon, Adam Lindsay
1833-1870 . . . . **NCLC 21**

Gordon, Caroline
1895-1981 . . . . **CLC 6, 13, 29**
See also CAP 1; CA 11-12;
obituary CA 103; DLB 4, 9; DLB-Y 81

Gordon, Charles William 1860-1937
See Conner, Ralph
See also CA 109

Gordon, Mary (Catherine)
1949- . . . . **CLC 13, 22**
See also CA 102; DLB 6; DLB-Y 81

Gordon, Sol 1923- . . . . **CLC 26**
See also CANR 4; CA 53-56; SATA 11

Gordone, Charles 1925- . . . . **CLC 1, 4**
See also CA 93-96; DLB 7

Gorenko, Anna Andreyevna 1889?-1966
See Akhmatova, Anna

Gorky, Maxim 1868-1936 . . . . **TCLC 8**
See also Peshkov, Alexei Maximovich

Goryan, Sirak 1908-1981
See Saroyan, William

Gosse, Edmund (William)
1849-1928 . . . . **TCLC 28**
See also CA 117; DLB 57

Gotlieb, Phyllis (Fay Bloom)
1926- . . . . **CLC 18**
See also CANR 7; CA 13-16R; DLB 88

Gould, Lois 1938?- . . . . **CLC 4, 10**
See also CA 77-80

Gourmont, Remy de 1858-1915 . . . . **TCLC 17**
See also CA 109

Govier, Katherine 1948- . . . . **CLC 51**
See also CANR 18; CA 101

Goyen, (Charles) William
1915-1983 . . . . **CLC 5, 8, 14, 40**
See also CANR 6; CA 5-8R;
obituary CA 110; DLB 2; DLB-Y 83

Goytisolo, Juan 1931- . . . . **CLC 5, 10, 23**
See also CA 85-88

Gozzi, (Conte) Carlo 1720-1806 . . **NCLC 23**

Grabbe, Christian Dietrich
1801-1836 . . . . **NCLC 2**

Grace, Patricia 1937- . . . . **CLC 56**

Gracian y Morales, Baltasar
1601-1658 . . . . **LC 15**

Gracq, Julien 1910- . . . . **CLC 11, 48**
See also Poirier, Louis
See also DLB 83

Grade, Chaim 1910-1982 . . . . **CLC 10**
See also CA 93-96; obituary CA 107

Graham, Jorie 1951- . . . . **CLC 48**
See also CA 111

Graham, R(obert) B(ontine) Cunninghame
1852-1936 . . . . **TCLC 19**

Graham, W(illiam) S(ydney)
1918-1986 . . . . **CLC 29**
See also CA 73-76; obituary CA 118;
DLB 20

Graham, Winston (Mawdsley)
1910- . . . . **CLC 23**
See also CANR 2, 22; CA 49-52;
obituary CA 118

Granville-Barker, Harley
1877-1946 . . . . **TCLC 2**
See also CA 104

Grass, Gunter (Wilhelm)
1927- . . **CLC 1, 2, 4, 6, 11, 15, 22, 32, 49**
See also CANR 20; CA 13-16R; DLB 75

Grau, Shirley Ann 1929- . . . . **CLC 4, 9**
See also CANR 22; CA 89-92; DLB 2

Graves, Richard Perceval 1945- . . . . **CLC 44**
See also CANR 9, 26; CA 65-68

Graves, Robert (von Ranke)
1895-1985 . . . **CLC 1, 2, 6, 11, 39, 44, 45**
See also CANR 5; CA 5-8R;
obituary CA 117; SATA 45; DLB 20;
DLB-Y 85

Gray, Alasdair 1934- . . . . **CLC 41**
See also CA 123

Gray, Amlin 1946- . . . . **CLC 29**

Gray, Francine du Plessix 1930- . . . . **CLC 22**
See also CAAS 2; CANR 11; CA 61-64

Gray, John (Henry) 1866-1934 . . . . **TCLC 19**
See also CA 119

Gray, Simon (James Holliday)
1936- . . . . **CLC 9, 14, 36**
See also CAAS 3; CA 21-24R; DLB 13

Gray, Spalding 1941- . . . . **CLC 49**

Gray, Thomas 1716-1771 . . . . **LC 4; PC 2**

Grayson, Richard (A.) 1951- . . . . **CLC 38**
See also CANR 14; CA 85-88

Greeley, Andrew M(oran) 1928- . . . . **CLC 28**
See also CAAS 7; CANR 7; CA 5-8R

Green, Hannah 1932- . . . . **CLC 3, 7, 30**
See also Greenberg, Joanne
See also CA 73-76

Green, Henry 1905-1974 . . . . **CLC 2, 13**
See also Yorke, Henry Vincent
See also DLB 15

Green, Julien (Hartridge) 1900- . . **CLC 3, 11**
See also CA 21-24R; DLB 4, 72

Green, Paul (Eliot) 1894-1981 . . . . . . **CLC 25**
See also CANR 3; CA 5-8R;
obituary CA 103; DLB 7, 9; DLB-Y 81

Greenberg, Ivan 1908-1973
See Rahv, Philip
See also CA 85-88

Greenberg, Joanne (Goldenberg)
1932- . . . . **CLC 3, 7, 30**
See also Green, Hannah
See also CANR 14; CA 5-8R; SATA 25

Greenberg, Richard 1959?- . . . . **CLC 57**

Greene, Bette 1934- . . . . **CLC 30**
See also CLR 2; CANR 4; CA 53-56;
SATA 8

Greene, Gael 19??- . . . . **CLC 8**
See also CANR 10; CA 13-16R

Greene, Graham (Henry)
1904- . . . . . **CLC 1, 3, 6, 9, 14, 18, 27, 37**
See also CA 13-16R; SATA 20; DLB 13, 15;
DLB-Y 85

Gregor, Arthur 1923- . . . . **CLC 9**
See also CANR 11; CA 25-28R; SATA 36

Gregory, Lady (Isabella Augusta Persse)
1852-1932 . . . . **TCLC 1**
See also CA 104; DLB 10

Grendon, Stephen 1909-1971
See Derleth, August (William)

Grenville, Kate 1950- . . . . **CLC 61**
See also CA 118

Greve, Felix Paul Berthold Friedrich
1879-1948
See Grove, Frederick Philip
See also CA 104

Grey, (Pearl) Zane 1872?-1939 . . . . . **TCLC 6**
See also CA 104; DLB 9

Grieg, (Johan) Nordahl (Brun)
1902-1943 . . . . **TCLC 10**
See also CA 107

Grieve, C(hristopher) M(urray) 1892-1978
See MacDiarmid, Hugh
See also CA 5-8R; obituary CA 85-88

Griffin, Gerald 1803-1840 . . . . **NCLC 7**

Griffin, Peter 1942- . . . . **CLC 39**

Griffiths, Trevor 1935- . . . . **CLC 13, 52**
See also CA 97-100; DLB 13

Grigson, Geoffrey (Edward Harvey)
1905-1985 . . . . **CLC 7, 39**
See also CANR 20; CA 25-28R;
obituary CA 118; DLB 27

Grillparzer, Franz 1791-1872 . . . . . . **NCLC 1**

Grimke, Charlotte L(ottie) Forten 1837-1914
See Forten (Grimke), Charlotte L(ottie)
See also CA 117, 124

Grimm, Jakob (Ludwig) Karl
1785-1863 . . . . **NCLC 3**
See also SATA 22; DLB 90

Grimm, Wilhelm Karl 1786-1859 . . **NCLC 3**
See also SATA 22; DLB 90

Grimmelshausen, Johann Jakob Christoffel von 1621-1676 . . . . **LC 6**

Grindel, Eugene 1895-1952
See also brief entry CA 104

Grossman, Vasily (Semenovich)
1905-1964 . . . . **CLC 41**
See also CA 124, 130

Grove, Frederick Philip 1879-1948 .... **TCLC 4**
See also Greve, Felix Paul Berthold Friedrich

Grumbach, Doris (Isaac) 1918- .... **CLC 13, 22, 64**
See also CAAS 2; CANR 9; CA 5-8R

Grundtvig, Nicolai Frederik Severin 1783-1872 .... **NCLC 1**

Grunwald, Lisa 1959- .... **CLC 44**
See also CA 120

Guare, John 1938- .... **CLC 8, 14, 29**
See also CANR 21; CA 73-76; DLB 7

Gudjonsson, Halldor Kiljan 1902-
See Laxness, Halldor (Kiljan)
See also CA 103

Guest, Barbara 1920- .... **CLC 34**
See also CANR 11; CA 25-28R; DLB 5

Guest, Judith (Ann) 1936- .... **CLC 8, 30**
See also CANR 15; CA 77-80

Guild, Nicholas M. 1944- .... **CLC 33**
See also CA 93-96

Guillen, Jorge 1893-1984 .... **CLC 11**
See also CA 89-92; obituary CA 112

Guillen, Nicolas 1902-1989 .... **CLC 48**
See also CA 116, 125; obituary CA 129

Guillevic, (Eugene) 1907- .... **CLC 33**
See also CA 93-96

Guiney, Louise Imogen 1861-1920 .... **TCLC 41**
See also DLB 54

Guiraldes, Ricardo 1886-1927 ..... **TCLC 39**

Gunn, Bill 1934-1989 .... **CLC 5**
See also Gunn, William Harrison
See also DLB 38

Gunn, Thom(son William) 1929- .... **CLC 3, 6, 18, 32**
See also CANR 9; CA 17-20R; DLB 27

Gunn, William Harrison 1934-1989
See Gunn, Bill
See also CANR 12, 25; CA 13-16R; obituary CA 128

Gurney, A(lbert) R(amsdell), Jr. 1930- .... **CLC 32, 50, 54**
See also CA 77-80

Gurney, Ivor (Bertie) 1890-1937 ... **TCLC 33**

Gustafson, Ralph (Barker) 1909- .... **CLC 36**
See also CANR 8; CA 21-24R; DLB 88

Guthrie, A(lfred) B(ertram), Jr. 1901- .... **CLC 23**
See also CA 57-60; DLB 6

Guthrie, Woodrow Wilson 1912-1967
See Guthrie, Woody
See also CA 113; obituary CA 93-96

Guthrie, Woody 1912-1967 .... **CLC 35**
See also Guthrie, Woodrow Wilson

Guy, Rosa (Cuthbert) 1928- .... **CLC 26**
See also CLR 13; CANR 14; CA 17-20R; SATA 14; DLB 33

Haavikko, Paavo (Juhani) 1931- .... **CLC 18, 34**
See also CA 106

Hacker, Marilyn 1942- .... **CLC 5, 9, 23**
See also CA 77-80

Haggard, (Sir) H(enry) Rider 1856-1925 .... **TCLC 11**
See also CA 108; SATA 16; DLB 70

Haig-Brown, Roderick L(angmere) 1908-1976 .... **CLC 21**
See also CANR 4; CA 5-8R; obituary CA 69-72; SATA 12; DLB 88

Hailey, Arthur 1920- .... **CLC 5**
See also CANR 2; CA 1-4R; DLB-Y 82

Hailey, Elizabeth Forsythe 1938- ... **CLC 40**
See also CAAS 1; CANR 15; CA 93-96

Haines, John 1924- .... **CLC 58**
See also CANR 13; CA 19-20R; DLB 5

Haldeman, Joe 1943- .... **CLC 61**
See also CA 53-56; DLB 8

Haley, Alex (Palmer) 1921- ...... **CLC 8, 12**
See also CA 77-80; DLB 38

Haliburton, Thomas Chandler 1796-1865 .... **NCLC 15**
See also DLB 11

Hall, Donald (Andrew, Jr.) 1928- .... **CLC 1, 13, 37, 59**
See also CAAS 7; CANR 2; CA 5-8R; SATA 23; DLB 5

Hall, James Norman 1887-1951 ... **TCLC 23**
See also CA 123; SATA 21

Hall, (Marguerite) Radclyffe 1886-1943 .... **TCLC 12**
See also CA 110

Hall, Rodney 1935- .... **CLC 51**
See also CA 109

Halpern, Daniel 1945- .... **CLC 14**
See also CA 33-36R

Hamburger, Michael (Peter Leopold) 1924- .... **CLC 5, 14**
See also CAAS 4; CANR 2; CA 5-8R; DLB 27

Hamill, Pete 1935- .... **CLC 10**
See also CANR 18; CA 25-28R

Hamilton, Edmond 1904-1977 .... **CLC 1**
See also CANR 3; CA 1-4R; DLB 8

Hamilton, Gail 1911-
See Corcoran, Barbara

Hamilton, Ian 1938- .... **CLC 55**
See also CA 106; DLB 40

Hamilton, Mollie 1909?-
See Kaye, M(ary) M(argaret)

Hamilton, (Anthony Walter) Patrick 1904-1962 .... **CLC 51**
See also obituary CA 113; DLB 10

Hamilton, Virginia (Esther) 1936- .. **CLC 26**
See also CLR 1, 11; CANR 20; CA 25-28R; SATA 4; DLB 33, 52

Hammett, (Samuel) Dashiell 1894-1961 .... **CLC 3, 5, 10, 19, 47**
See also CA 81-84; DLB-DS 6

Hammon, Jupiter 1711?-1800? .... **NCLC 5**
See also DLB 31, 50

Hamner, Earl (Henry), Jr. 1923- ... **CLC 12**
See also CA 73-76; DLB 6

Hampton, Christopher (James) 1946- .... **CLC 4**
See also CA 25-28R; DLB 13

Hamsun, Knut 1859-1952 .... **TCLC 2, 14**
See also Pedersen, Knut

Handke, Peter 1942- .. **CLC 5, 8, 10, 15, 38**
See also CA 77-80; DLB 85

Hanley, James 1901-1985 ... **CLC 3, 5, 8, 13**
See also CA 73-76; obituary CA 117

Hannah, Barry 1942- .... **CLC 23, 38**
See also CA 108, 110; DLB 6

Hansberry, Lorraine (Vivian) 1930-1965 .... **CLC 17, 62**
See also CA 109; obituary CA 25-28R; CABS 3; DLB 7, 38; CDALB 1941-1968

Hansen, Joseph 1923- .... **CLC 38**
See also CANR 16; CA 29-32R

Hansen, Martin 1909-1955 .... **TCLC 32**

Hanson, Kenneth O(stlin) 1922- .... **CLC 13**
See also CANR 7; CA 53-56

Hardenberg, Friedrich (Leopold Freiherr) von 1772-1801
See Novalis

Hardwick, Elizabeth 1916- .... **CLC 13**
See also CANR 3; CA 5-8R; DLB 6

Hardy, Thomas 1840-1928 ... **TCLC 4, 10, 18, 32; SSC 2**
See also CA 104, 123; SATA 25; DLB 18, 19

Hare, David 1947- .... **CLC 29, 58**
See also CA 97-100; DLB 13

Harlan, Louis R(udolph) 1922- ..... **CLC 34**
See also CANR 25; CA 21-24R

Harling, Robert 1951?- .... **CLC 53**

Harmon, William (Ruth) 1938- ..... **CLC 38**
See also CANR 14; CA 33-36R

Harper, Frances Ellen Watkins 1825-1911 .... **TCLC 14**
See also CA 111, 125; DLB 50

Harper, Michael S(teven) 1938- .. **CLC 7, 22**
See also CANR 24; CA 33-36R; DLB 41

Harris, Christie (Lucy Irwin) 1907- .... **CLC 12**
See also CANR 6; CA 5-8R; SATA 6; DLB 88

Harris, Frank 1856-1931 .... **TCLC 24**
See also CAAS 1; CA 109

Harris, George Washington 1814-1869 .... **NCLC 23**
See also DLB 3, 11

Harris, Joel Chandler 1848-1908 ... **TCLC 2**
See also YABC 1; CA 104; DLB 11, 23, 42, 78, 91

Harris, John (Wyndham Parkes Lucas) Beynon 1903-1969 .... **CLC 19**
See also Wyndham, John
See also CA 102; obituary CA 89-92

Harris, MacDonald 1921- .... **CLC 9**
See also Heiney, Donald (William)

Harris, Mark 1922- .... **CLC 19**
See also CAAS 3; CANR 2; CA 5-8R; DLB 2; DLB-Y 80

Harris, (Theodore) Wilson 1921- .... **CLC 25**
See also CANR 11, 27; CA 65-68

Harrison, Harry (Max) 1925- ...... **CLC 42**
See also CANR 5, 21; CA 1-4R; SATA 4; DLB 8

Harrison, James (Thomas) 1937-
See Harrison, Jim
See also CANR 8; CA 13-16R

Harrison, Jim 1937- .... **CLC 6, 14, 33**
See also Harrison, James (Thomas)
See also DLB-Y 82

Harrison, Tony 1937- .... **CLC 43**
See also CA 65-68; DLB 40

Harriss, Will(ard Irvin) 1922- ...... **CLC 34**
See also CA 111

Harte, (Francis) Bret(t)
1836?-1902 .... **TCLC 1, 25; SSC 8**
See also brief entry CA 104; SATA 26; DLB 12, 64, 74, 79; CDALB 1865-1917

Hartley, L(eslie) P(oles)
1895-1972 .... **CLC 2, 22**
See also CA 45-48; obituary CA 37-40R; DLB 15

Hartman, Geoffrey H. 1929- .... **CLC 27**
See also CA 117, 125; DLB 67

Haruf, Kent 19??- .... **CLC 34**

Harwood, Ronald 1934- .... **CLC 32**
See also CANR 4; CA 1-4R; DLB 13

Hasek, Jaroslav (Matej Frantisek)
1883-1923 .... **TCLC 4**
See also CA 104, 129

Hass, Robert 1941- .... **CLC 18, 39**
See also CANR 30; CA 111

Hastings, Selina 19??- .... **CLC 44**

Hauptmann, Gerhart (Johann Robert)
1862-1946 .... **TCLC 4**
See also CA 104; DLB 66

Havel, Vaclav 1936- .... **CLC 25, 58, 65**
See also CA 104

Haviaras, Stratis 1935- .... **CLC 33**
See also CA 105

Hawkes, John (Clendennin Burne, Jr.)
1925- ...... **CLC 1, 2, 3, 4, 7, 9, 14, 15, 27, 49**
See also CANR 2; CA 1-4R; DLB 2, 7; DLB-Y 80

Hawking, Stephen (William)
1948- .... **CLC 63**
See also CA 126, 129

Hawthorne, Julian 1846-1934 ..... **TCLC 25**

Hawthorne, Nathaniel
1804-1864 ... **NCLC 2, 10, 17, 23; SSC 3**
See also YABC 2; DLB 1, 74; CDALB 1640-1865

Hayashi Fumiko 1904-1951 .... **TCLC 27**

Haycraft, Anna 19??-
See Ellis, Alice Thomas
See also CA 122

Hayden, Robert (Earl)
1913-1980 .... **CLC 5, 9, 14, 37**
See also CANR 24; CA 69-72; obituary CA 97-100; CABS 2; SATA 19; obituary SATA 26; DLB 5, 76; CDALB 1941-1968

Hayman, Ronald 1932- .... **CLC 44**
See also CANR 18; CA 25-28R

Haywood, Eliza (Fowler) 1693?-1756 .. **LC 1**
See also DLB 39

Hazlitt, William 1778-1830 ...... **NCLC 29**

Hazzard, Shirley 1931- .... **CLC 18**
See also CANR 4; CA 9-12R; DLB-Y 82

H(ilda) D(oolittle)
1886-1961 .... **CLC 3, 8, 14, 31, 34**
See also Doolittle, Hilda

Head, Bessie 1937-1986 .... **CLC 25**
See also CANR 25; CA 29-32R; obituary CA 119

Headon, (Nicky) Topper 1956?- .... **CLC 30**
See also The Clash

Heaney, Seamus (Justin)
1939- .... **CLC 5, 7, 14, 25, 37**
See also CANR 25; CA 85-88; DLB 40

Hearn, (Patricio) Lafcadio (Tessima Carlos)
1850-1904 .... **TCLC 9**
See also CA 105; DLB 12, 78

Hearne, Vicki 1946- .... **CLC 56**

Hearon, Shelby 1931- .... **CLC 63**
See also CANR 18; CA 25-28

Heat Moon, William Least 1939- ... **CLC 29**

Hebert, Anne 1916- .... **CLC 4, 13, 29**
See also CA 85-88; DLB 68

Hecht, Anthony (Evan)
1923- .... **CLC 8, 13, 19**
See also CANR 6; CA 9-12R; DLB 5

Hecht, Ben 1894-1964 .... **CLC 8**
See also CA 85-88; DLB 7, 9, 25, 26, 28, 86

Hedayat, Sadeq 1903-1951 .... **TCLC 21**
See also CA 120

Heidegger, Martin 1889-1976 ...... **CLC 24**
See also CA 81-84; obituary CA 65-68

Heidenstam, (Karl Gustaf) Verner von
1859-1940 .... **TCLC 5**
See also CA 104

Heifner, Jack 1946- .... **CLC 11**
See also CA 105

Heijermans, Herman 1864-1924 ... **TCLC 24**
See also CA 123

Heilbrun, Carolyn G(old) 1926- ..... **CLC 25**
See also CANR 1, 28; CA 45-48

Heine, Harry 1797-1856
See Heine, Heinrich

Heine, Heinrich 1797-1856 .... **NCLC 4**
See also DLB 90

Heinemann, Larry C(urtiss) 1944- .. **CLC 50**
See also CA 110

Heiney, Donald (William) 1921- ..... **CLC 9**
See also Harris, MacDonald
See also CANR 3; CA 1-4R

Heinlein, Robert A(nson)
1907-1988 ...... **CLC 1, 3, 8, 14, 26, 55**
See also CANR 1, 20; CA 1-4R; obituary CA 125; SATA 9, 56; DLB 8

Heller, Joseph
1923- .... **CLC 1, 3, 5, 8, 11, 36, 63**
See also CANR 8; CA 5-8R; CABS 1; DLB 2, 28; DLB-Y 80

Hellman, Lillian (Florence)
1905?-1984 ..... **CLC 2, 4, 8, 14, 18, 34, 44, 52; DC 1**
See also CA 13-16R; obituary CA 112; DLB 7; DLB-Y 84

Helprin, Mark 1947- ..... **CLC 7, 10, 22, 32**
See also CA 81-84; DLB-Y 85

Hemans, Felicia 1793-1835 ...... **NCLC 29**

Hemingway, Ernest (Miller)
1899-1961 ... **CLC 1, 3, 6, 8, 10, 13, 19, 30, 34, 39, 41, 44, 50, 61; SSC 1**
See also CA 77-80; DLB 4, 9; DLB-Y 81, 87; DLB-DS 1; CDALB 1917-1929

Hempel, Amy 1951- .... **CLC 39**
See also CA 118

Henley, Beth 1952- .... **CLC 23**
See also Henley, Elizabeth Becker
See also CABS 3; DLB-Y 86

Henley, Elizabeth Becker 1952-
See Henley, Beth
See also CA 107

Henley, William Ernest
1849-1903 .... **TCLC 8**
See also CA 105; DLB 19

Hennissart, Martha
See Lathen, Emma
See also CA 85-88

Henry, O. 1862-1910 ... **TCLC 1, 19; SSC 5**
See also Porter, William Sydney
See also YABC 2; CA 104; DLB 12, 78, 79; CDALB 1865-1917

Henry VIII 1491-1547 .... **LC 10**

Hentoff, Nat(han Irving) 1925- ..... **CLC 26**
See also CLR 1; CAAS 6; CANR 5, 25; CA 1-4R; SATA 27, 42; AAYA 4

Heppenstall, (John) Rayner
1911-1981 .... **CLC 10**
See also CANR 29; CA 1-4R; obituary CA 103

Herbert, Frank (Patrick)
1920-1986 .... **CLC 12, 23, 35, 44**
See also CANR 5; CA 53-56; obituary CA 118; SATA 9, 37, 47; DLB 8

Herbert, Zbigniew 1924- .... **CLC 9, 43**
See also CA 89-92

Herbst, Josephine 1897-1969 ...... **CLC 34**
See also CA 5-8R; obituary CA 25-28R; DLB 9

Herder, Johann Gottfried von
1744-1803 .... **NCLC 8**

Hergesheimer, Joseph
1880-1954 .... **TCLC 11**
See also CA 109; DLB 9

Herlagnez, Pablo de 1844-1896
See Verlaine, Paul (Marie)

Herlihy, James Leo 1927- .... **CLC 6**
See also CANR 2; CA 1-4R

Hermogenes fl.c. 175- .... **CMLC 6**

Hernandez, Jose 1834-1886 ...... **NCLC 17**

Herrick, Robert 1591-1674 .... **LC 13**

Herriot, James 1916- .... **CLC 12**
See also Wight, James Alfred
See also AAYA 1

Herrmann, Dorothy 1941- .... **CLC 44**
See also CA 107

Hersey, John (Richard)
1914- .... **CLC 1, 2, 7, 9, 40**
See also CA 17-20R; SATA 25; DLB 6

Herzen, Aleksandr Ivanovich
1812-1870 .... **NCLC 10**

Herzl, Theodor 1860-1904 .... **TCLC 36**

Herzog, Werner 1942- . . . . **CLC 16**
See also CA 89-92

Hesiod c. 8th Century B.C.- . . . . . . **CMLC 5**

Hesse, Hermann
1877-1962 . . . . **CLC 1, 2, 3, 6, 11, 17, 25**
See also CAP 2; CA 17-18; SATA 50; DLB 66

Heyen, William 1940- . . . . **CLC 13, 18**
See also CAAS 9; CA 33-36R; DLB 5

Heyerdahl, Thor 1914- . . . . **CLC 26**
See also CANR 5, 22; CA 5-8R; SATA 2, 52

Heym, Georg (Theodor Franz Arthur)
1887-1912 . . . . **TCLC 9**
See also CA 106

Heym, Stefan 1913- . . . . **CLC 41**
See also CANR 4; CA 9-12R; DLB 69

Heyse, Paul (Johann Ludwig von)
1830-1914 . . . . **TCLC 8**
See also CA 104

Hibbert, Eleanor (Burford) 1906- . . . . **CLC 7**
See also CANR 9, 28; CA 17-20R; SATA 2

Higgins, George V(incent)
1939- . . . . **CLC 4, 7, 10, 18**
See also CAAS 5; CANR 17; CA 77-80; DLB 2; DLB-Y 81

Higginson, Thomas Wentworth
1823-1911 . . . . **TCLC 36**
See also DLB 1, 64

Highsmith, (Mary) Patricia
1921- . . . . **CLC 2, 4, 14, 42**
See also CANR 1, 20; CA 1-4R

Highwater, Jamake 1942- . . . . **CLC 12**
See also CLR 17; CAAS 7; CANR 10; CA 65-68; SATA 30, 32; DLB 52; DLB-Y 85

Hijuelos, Oscar 1951- . . . . **CLC 65**
See also CA 123

Hikmet (Ran), Nazim 1902-1963. . . . **CLC 40**
See also obituary CA 93-96

Hildesheimer, Wolfgang 1916- . . . . . **CLC 49**
See also CA 101; DLB 69

Hill, Geoffrey (William)
1932- . . . . **CLC 5, 8, 18, 45**
See also CANR 21; CA 81-84; DLB 40

Hill, George Roy 1922- . . . . **CLC 26**
See also CA 110, 122

Hill, Susan B. 1942- . . . . **CLC 4**
See also CANR 29; CA 33-36R; DLB 14

Hillerman, Tony 1925- . . . . **CLC 62**
See also CANR 21; CA 29-32R; SATA 6

Hilliard, Noel (Harvey) 1929- . . . . . . **CLC 15**
See also CANR 7; CA 9-12R

Hilton, James 1900-1954 . . . . **TCLC 21**
See also CA 108; SATA 34; DLB 34, 77

Himes, Chester (Bomar)
1909-1984 . . . . **CLC 2, 4, 7, 18, 58**
See also CANR 22; CA 25-28R; obituary CA 114; DLB 2, 76

Hinde, Thomas 1926- . . . . **CLC 6, 11**
See also Chitty, (Sir) Thomas Willes

Hine, (William) Daryl 1936- . . . . **CLC 15**
See also CANR 1, 20; CA 1-4R; DLB 60

Hinton, S(usan) E(loise) 1950- . . . . . **CLC 30**
See also CLR 3, 23; CA 81-84; SATA 19, 58; AAYA 2

Hippius (Merezhkovsky), Zinaida (Nikolayevna) 1869-1945 . . . . . . **TCLC 9**
See also Gippius, Zinaida (Nikolayevna)

Hiraoka, Kimitake 1925-1970
See Mishima, Yukio
See also CA 97-100; obituary CA 29-32R

Hirsch, Edward (Mark) 1950- . . . **CLC 31, 50**
See also CANR 20; CA 104

Hitchcock, (Sir) Alfred (Joseph)
1899-1980 . . . . **CLC 16**
See also obituary CA 97-100; SATA 27; obituary SATA 24

Hoagland, Edward 1932- . . . . **CLC 28**
See also CANR 2; CA 1-4R; SATA 51; DLB 6

Hoban, Russell C(onwell) 1925- . . **CLC 7, 25**
See also CLR 3; CANR 23; CA 5-8R; SATA 1, 40; DLB 52

Hobson, Laura Z(ametkin)
1900-1986 . . . . **CLC 7, 25**
See also CA 17-20R; obituary CA 118; SATA 52; DLB 28

Hochhuth, Rolf 1931- . . . . **CLC 4, 11, 18**
See also CA 5-8R

Hochman, Sandra 1936- . . . . **CLC 3, 8**
See also CA 5-8R; DLB 5

Hochwalder, Fritz 1911-1986 . . . . . . **CLC 36**
See also CA 29-32R; obituary CA 120

Hocking, Mary (Eunice) 1921- . . . . . **CLC 13**
See also CANR 18; CA 101

Hodgins, Jack 1938- . . . . **CLC 23**
See also CA 93-96; DLB 60

Hodgson, William Hope
1877-1918 . . . . **TCLC 13**
See also CA 111; DLB 70

Hoffman, Alice 1952- . . . . **CLC 51**
See also CA 77-80

Hoffman, Daniel (Gerard)
1923- . . . . **CLC 6, 13, 23**
See also CANR 4; CA 1-4R; DLB 5

Hoffman, Stanley 1944- . . . . **CLC 5**
See also CA 77-80

Hoffman, William M(oses) 1939- . . . **CLC 40**
See also CANR 11; CA 57-60

Hoffmann, Ernst Theodor Amadeus
1776-1822 . . . . **NCLC 2**
See also SATA 27; DLB 90

Hoffmann, Gert 1932- . . . . **CLC 54**

Hofmannsthal, Hugo (Laurenz August Hofmann Edler) von
1874-1929 . . . . **TCLC 11**
See also CA 106; DLB 81

Hogg, James 1770-1835 . . . . **NCLC 4**

Holbach, Paul Henri Thiry, Baron d'
1723-1789 . . . . **LC 14**

Holberg, Ludvig 1684-1754 . . . . **LC 6**

Holden, Ursula 1921- . . . . **CLC 18**
See also CAAS 8; CANR 22; CA 101

Holderlin, (Johann Christian) Friedrich
1770-1843 . . . . **NCLC 16**

Holdstock, Robert (P.) 1948- . . . . **CLC 39**

Holland, Isabelle 1920- . . . . **CLC 21**
See also CANR 10, 25; CA 21-24R; SATA 8

Holland, Marcus 1900-1985
See Caldwell, (Janet Miriam) Taylor (Holland)

Hollander, John 1929- . . . . . . **CLC 2, 5, 8, 14**
See also CANR 1; CA 1-4R; SATA 13; DLB 5

Holleran, Andrew 1943?- . . . . **CLC 38**

Hollinghurst, Alan 1954- . . . . **CLC 55**
See also CA 114

Hollis, Jim 1916-
See Summers, Hollis (Spurgeon, Jr.)

Holmes, John Clellon 1926-1988. . . . **CLC 56**
See also CANR 4; CA 9-10R; obituary CA 125; DLB 16

Holmes, Oliver Wendell
1809-1894 . . . . **NCLC 14**
See also SATA 34; DLB 1; CDALB 1640-1865

Holt, Victoria 1906-
See Hibbert, Eleanor (Burford)

Holub, Miroslav 1923- . . . . **CLC 4**
See also CANR 10; CA 21-24R

Homer c. 8th century B.C.- . . . . **CMLC 1**

Honig, Edwin 1919- . . . . **CLC 33**
See also CAAS 8; CANR 4; CA 5-8R; DLB 5

Hood, Hugh (John Blagdon)
1928- . . . . **CLC 15, 28**
See also CANR 1; CA 49-52; DLB 53

Hood, Thomas 1799-1845. . . . . **NCLC 16**

Hooker, (Peter) Jeremy 1941- . . . . . . **CLC 43**
See also CANR 22; CA 77-80; DLB 40

Hope, A(lec) D(erwent) 1907- . . . . **CLC 3, 51**
See also CA 21-24R

Hope, Christopher (David Tully)
1944- . . . . **CLC 52**
See also CA 106

Hopkins, Gerard Manley
1844-1889 . . . . **NCLC 17**
See also DLB 35, 57

Hopkins, John (Richard) 1931- . . . . . . **CLC 4**
See also CA 85-88

Hopkins, Pauline Elizabeth
1859-1930 . . . . **TCLC 28**
See also DLB 50

Horgan, Paul 1903- . . . . **CLC 9, 53**
See also CANR 9; CA 13-16R; SATA 13; DLB-Y 85

Horovitz, Israel 1939- . . . . **CLC 56**
See also CA 33-36R; DLB 7

Horwitz, Julius 1920-1986 . . . . **CLC 14**
See also CANR 12; CA 9-12R; obituary CA 119

Hospital, Janette Turner 1942- . . . . . **CLC 42**
See also CA 108

Hostos (y Bonilla), Eugenio Maria de
1893-1903 . . . . **TCLC 24**
See also CA 123

Hougan, Carolyn 19??- . . . . **CLC 34**

Household, Geoffrey (Edward West) 1900-1988 .... **CLC 11**
See also CA 77-80; obituary CA 126; SATA 14, 59; DLB 87

Housman, A(lfred) E(dward) 1859-1936 .... **TCLC 1, 10; PC 2**
See also CA 104, 125; DLB 19

Housman, Laurence 1865-1959 ..... **TCLC 7**
See also CA 106; SATA 25; DLB 10

Howard, Elizabeth Jane 1923- ... **CLC 7, 29**
See also CANR 8; CA 5-8R

Howard, Maureen 1930- ..... **CLC 5, 14, 46**
See also CA 53-56; DLB-Y 83

Howard, Richard 1929- ...... **CLC 7, 10, 47**
See also CANR 25; CA 85-88; DLB 5

Howard, Robert E(rvin) 1906-1936 .... **TCLC 8**
See also CA 105

Howe, Fanny 1940- .... **CLC 47**
See also CA 117; SATA 52

Howe, Julia Ward 1819-1910 ..... **TCLC 21**
See also CA 117; DLB 1

Howe, Tina 1937-................ **CLC 48**
See also CA 109

Howell, James 1594?-1666.......... **LC 13**

Howells, William Dean 1837-1920 .... **TCLC 7, 17, 41**
See also brief entry CA 104; DLB 12, 64, 74, 79; CDALB 1865-1917

Howes, Barbara 1914- .... **CLC 15**
See also CAAS 3; CA 9-12R; SATA 5

Hrabal, Bohumil 1914-............ **CLC 13**
See also CA 106

Hubbard, L(afayette) Ron(ald) 1911-1986 .... **CLC 43**
See also CANR 22; CA 77-80; obituary CA 118

Huch, Ricarda (Octavia) 1864-1947 .... **TCLC 13**
See also CA 111; DLB 66

Huddle, David 1942- .... **CLC 49**
See also CA 57-60

Hudson, W(illiam) H(enry) 1841-1922 .... **TCLC 29**
See also CA 115; SATA 35

Hueffer, Ford Madox 1873-1939
See Ford, Ford Madox

Hughart, Barry 1934-............. **CLC 39**

Hughes, David (John) 1930- .... **CLC 48**
See also CA 116, 129; DLB 14

Hughes, Edward James 1930-
See Hughes, Ted

Hughes, (James) Langston 1902-1967 .... **CLC 1, 5, 10, 15, 35, 44; PC 1; SSC 6**
See also CLR 17; CANR 1; CA 1-4R; obituary CA 25-28R; SATA 4, 33; DLB 4, 7, 48, 51, 86; CDALB 1929-1941

Hughes, Richard (Arthur Warren) 1900-1976 .... **CLC 1, 11**
See also CANR 4; CA 5-8R; obituary CA 65-68; SATA 8; obituary SATA 25; DLB 15

Hughes, Ted 1930- ..... **CLC 2, 4, 9, 14, 37**
See also CLR 3; CANR 1; CA 1-4R; SATA 27, 49; DLB 40

Hugo, Richard F(ranklin) 1923-1982 .... **CLC 6, 18, 32**
See also CANR 3; CA 49-52; obituary CA 108; DLB 5

Hugo, Victor Marie 1802-1885 .... **NCLC 3, 10, 21**
See also SATA 47

Huidobro, Vicente 1893-1948 ..... **TCLC 31**

Hulme, Keri 1947- .... **CLC 39**
See also CA 125

Hulme, T(homas) E(rnest) 1883-1917 .... **TCLC 21**
See also CA 117; DLB 19

Hume, David 1711-1776............. **LC 7**

Humphrey, William 1924- .... **CLC 45**
See also CA 77-80; DLB 6

Humphreys, Emyr (Owen) 1919-.... **CLC 47**
See also CANR 3, 24; CA 5-8R; DLB 15

Humphreys, Josephine 1945-.... **CLC 34, 57**
See also CA 121, 127

Hunt, E(verette) Howard (Jr.) 1918- .... **CLC 3**
See also CANR 2; CA 45-48

Hunt, (James Henry) Leigh 1784-1859 .... **NCLC 1**

Hunter, Evan 1926- .... **CLC 11, 31**
See also CANR 5; CA 5-8R; SATA 25; DLB-Y 82

Hunter, Kristin (Eggleston) 1931-... **CLC 35**
See also CLR 3; CANR 13; CA 13-16R; SATA 12; DLB 33

Hunter, Mollie (Maureen McIlwraith) 1922- .... **CLC 21**
See also McIlwraith, Maureen Mollie Hunter

Hunter, Robert ?-1734 .... **LC 7**

Hurston, Zora Neale 1891-1960 .... **CLC 7, 30, 61; SSC 4**
See also CA 85-88; DLB 51, 86

Huston, John (Marcellus) 1906-1987 .... **CLC 20**
See also CA 73-76; obituary CA 123; DLB 26

Hutten, Ulrich von 1488-1523....... **LC 16**

Huxley, Aldous (Leonard) 1894-1963 .. **CLC 1, 3, 4, 5, 8, 11, 18, 35**
See also CA 85-88; DLB 36

Huysmans, Charles Marie Georges 1848-1907
See Huysmans, Joris-Karl
See also CA 104

Huysmans, Joris-Karl 1848-1907 ... **TCLC 7**
See also Huysmans, Charles Marie Georges

Hwang, David Henry 1957-........ **CLC 55**
See also CA 127

Hyde, Anthony 1946?- .... **CLC 42**

Hyde, Margaret O(ldroyd) 1917- ... **CLC 21**
See also CLR 23; CANR 1; CA 1-4R; SAAS 8; SATA 1, 42

Hynes, James 1956?- .... **CLC 65**

Ian, Janis 1951- .... **CLC 21**
See also CA 105

Ibarguengoitia, Jorge 1928-1983.... **CLC 37**
See also obituary CA 113, 124

Ibsen, Henrik (Johan) 1828-1906 .... **TCLC 2, 8, 16, 37**
See also CA 104

Ibuse, Masuji 1898- .... **CLC 22**
See also CA 127

Ichikawa, Kon 1915-.............. **CLC 20**
See also CA 121

Idle, Eric 1943-.................. **CLC 21**
See also Monty Python
See also CA 116

Ignatow, David 1914-...... **CLC 4, 7, 14, 40**
See also CAAS 3; CA 9-12R; DLB 5

Ihimaera, Witi (Tame) 1944-....... **CLC 46**
See also CA 77-80

Ilf, Ilya 1897-1937 .... **TCLC 21**

Immermann, Karl (Lebrecht) 1796-1840 .... **NCLC 4**

Ingalls, Rachel 19??-.............. **CLC 42**
See also CA 123, 127

Ingamells, Rex 1913-1955 .... **TCLC 35**

Inge, William (Motter) 1913-1973 .... **CLC 1, 8, 19**
See also CA 9-12R; DLB 7; CDALB 1941-1968

Innaurato, Albert 1948-........ **CLC 21, 60**
See also CA 115, 122

Innes, Michael 1906-
See Stewart, J(ohn) I(nnes) M(ackintosh)

Ionesco, Eugene 1912- .... **CLC 1, 4, 6, 9, 11, 15, 41**
See also CA 9-12R; SATA 7

Iqbal, Muhammad 1877-1938 ..... **TCLC 28**

Irving, John (Winslow) 1942- .... **CLC 13, 23, 38**
See also CANR 28; CA 25-28R; DLB 6; DLB-Y 82

Irving, Washington 1783-1859 .... **NCLC 2, 19; SSC 2**
See also YABC 2; DLB 3, 11, 30, 59, 73, 74; CDALB 1640-1865

Isaacs, Susan 1943- .... **CLC 32**
See also CANR 20; CA 89-92

Isherwood, Christopher (William Bradshaw) 1904-1986 .... **CLC 1, 9, 11, 14, 44**
See also CA 13-16R; obituary CA 117; DLB 15; DLB-Y 86

Ishiguro, Kazuo 1954- ...... **CLC 27, 56, 59**
See also CA 120

Ishikawa Takuboku 1885-1912 .... **TCLC 15**
See also CA 113

Iskander, Fazil (Abdulovich) 1929- .... **CLC 47**
See also CA 102

Ivanov, Vyacheslav (Ivanovich) 1866-1949 .... **TCLC 33**
See also CA 122

Ivask, Ivar (Vidrik) 1927- .... **CLC 14**
See also CANR 24; CA 37-40R

Jackson, Jesse 1908-1983 .... **CLC 12**
See also CANR 27; CA 25-28R; obituary CA 109; SATA 2, 29, 48

Jackson, Laura (Riding) 1901- ...... **CLC 7**
See also Riding, Laura
See also CANR 28; CA 65-68; DLB 48

Jackson, Shirley 1919-1965 ..... **CLC 11, 60**
See also CANR 4; CA 1-4R; obituary CA 25-28R; SATA 2; DLB 6; CDALB 1941-1968

Jacob, (Cyprien) Max 1876-1944 ... **TCLC 6**
See also CA 104

Jacob, Piers A(nthony) D(illingham) 1934-
See Anthony (Jacob), Piers
See also CA 21-24R

Jacobs, Jim 1942- and **Casey, Warren** 1942- .... **CLC 12**
See also CA 97-100

Jacobs, Jim 1942-
See Jacobs, Jim and Casey, Warren
See also CA 97-100

Jacobs, W(illiam) W(ymark) 1863-1943 .... **TCLC 22**
See also CA 121

Jacobsen, Josephine 1908- .... **CLC 48**
See also CANR 23; CA 33-36R

Jacobson, Dan 1929- .... **CLC 4, 14**
See also CANR 2, 25; CA 1-4R; DLB 14

Jagger, Mick 1944- .... **CLC 17**

Jakes, John (William) 1932- .... **CLC 29**
See also CANR 10; CA 57-60; DLB-Y 83

James, C(yril) L(ionel) R(obert) 1901-1989 .... **CLC 33**
See also CA 117, 125; obituary CA 128

James, Daniel 1911-1988
See Santiago, Danny
See also obituary CA 125

James, Henry (Jr.) 1843-1916 ... **TCLC 2, 11, 24, 40; SSC 8**
See also CA 132; brief entry CA 104; DLB 12, 71, 74; CDALB 1865-1917

James, M(ontague) R(hodes) 1862-1936 .... **TCLC 6**
See also CA 104

James, P(hyllis) D(orothy) 1920- .... **CLC 18, 46**
See also CANR 17; CA 21-24R

James, William 1842-1910 ..... **TCLC 15, 32**
See also CA 109

Jami, Nur al-Din 'Abd al-Rahman 1414-1492 .... **LC 9**

Jandl, Ernst 1925- .... **CLC 34**

Janowitz, Tama 1957- .... **CLC 43**
See also CA 106

Jarrell, Randall 1914-1965 .... **CLC 1, 2, 6, 9, 13, 49**
See also CLR 6; CANR 6; CA 5-8R; obituary CA 25-28R; CABS 2; SATA 7; DLB 48, 52; CDALB 1941-1968

Jarry, Alfred 1873-1907 .... **TCLC 2, 14**
See also CA 104

Jeake, Samuel, Jr. 1889-1973
See Aiken, Conrad

Jean Paul 1763-1825 .... **NCLC 7**

Jeffers, (John) Robinson 1887-1962 .... **CLC 2, 3, 11, 15, 54**
See also CA 85-88; DLB 45; CDALB 1917-1929

Jefferson, Thomas 1743-1826 .... **NCLC 11**
See also DLB 31; CDALB 1640-1865

Jellicoe, (Patricia) Ann 1927- ...... **CLC 27**
See also CA 85-88; DLB 13

Jenkins, (John) Robin 1912- .... **CLC 52**
See also CANR 1; CA 4R; DLB 14

Jennings, Elizabeth (Joan) 1926- .... **CLC 5, 14**
See also CAAS 5; CANR 8; CA 61-64; DLB 27

Jennings, Waylon 1937- .... **CLC 21**

Jensen, Johannes 1873-1950 ...... **TCLC 41**

Jensen, Laura (Linnea) 1948- ...... **CLC 37**
See also CA 103

Jerome, Jerome K. 1859-1927 ..... **TCLC 23**
See also CA 119; DLB 10, 34

Jerrold, Douglas William 1803-1857 .... **NCLC 2**

Jewett, (Theodora) Sarah Orne 1849-1909 .... **TCLC 1, 22; SSC 6**
See also CA 108, 127; SATA 15; DLB 12, 74

Jewsbury, Geraldine (Endsor) 1812-1880 .... **NCLC 22**
See also DLB 21

Jhabvala, Ruth Prawer 1927- .... **CLC 4, 8, 29**
See also CANR 2, 29; CA 1-4R

Jiles, Paulette 1943- .... **CLC 13, 58**
See also CA 101

Jimenez (Mantecon), Juan Ramon 1881-1958 .... **TCLC 4**
See also CA 104

Joel, Billy 1949- .... **CLC 26**
See also Joel, William Martin

Joel, William Martin 1949-
See Joel, Billy
See also CA 108

Johnson, B(ryan) S(tanley William) 1933-1973 .... **CLC 6, 9**
See also CANR 9; CA 9-12R; obituary CA 53-56; DLB 14, 40

Johnson, Charles (Richard) 1948- .... **CLC 7, 51, 65**
See also CA 116; DLB 33

Johnson, Denis 1949- .... **CLC 52**
See also CA 117, 121

Johnson, Diane 1934- .... **CLC 5, 13, 48**
See also CANR 17; CA 41-44R; DLB-Y 80

Johnson, Eyvind (Olof Verner) 1900-1976 .... **CLC 14**
See also CA 73-76; obituary CA 69-72

Johnson, James Weldon 1871-1938 .... **TCLC 3, 19**
See also Johnson, James William
See also CA 104, 125; SATA 31; DLB 51; CDALB 1917-1929

Johnson, James William 1871-1938
See Johnson, James Weldon
See also SATA 31

Johnson, Joyce 1935- .... **CLC 58**
See also CA 125, 129

Johnson, Lionel (Pigot) 1867-1902 .... **TCLC 19**
See also CA 117; DLB 19

Johnson, Marguerita 1928-
See Angelou, Maya

Johnson, Pamela Hansford 1912-1981 .... **CLC 1, 7, 27**
See also CANR 2, 28; CA 1-4R; obituary CA 104; DLB 15

Johnson, Samuel 1709-1784 .... **LC 15**
See also DLB 39, 95

Johnson, Uwe 1934-1984 .... **CLC 5, 10, 15, 40**
See also CANR 1; CA 1-4R; obituary CA 112; DLB 75

Johnston, George (Benson) 1913- ... **CLC 51**
See also CANR 5, 20; CA 1-4R; DLB 88

Johnston, Jennifer 1930- .... **CLC 7**
See also CA 85-88; DLB 14

Jolley, Elizabeth 1923- .... **CLC 46**
See also CA 127

Jones, D(ouglas) G(ordon) 1929- .... **CLC 10**
See also CANR 13; CA 29-32R, 113; DLB 53

Jones, David 1895-1974 .... **CLC 2, 4, 7, 13, 42**
See also CANR 28; CA 9-12R; obituary CA 53-56; DLB 20

Jones, David Robert 1947-
See Bowie, David
See also CA 103

Jones, Diana Wynne 1934- .... **CLC 26**
See also CLR 23; CANR 4, 26; CA 49-52; SAAS 7; SATA 9

Jones, Gayl 1949- .... **CLC 6, 9**
See also CANR 27; CA 77-80; DLB 33

Jones, James 1921-1977 .... **CLC 1, 3, 10, 39**
See also CANR 6; CA 1-4R; obituary CA 69-72; DLB 2

Jones, (Everett) LeRoi 1934- .... **CLC 1, 2, 3, 5, 10, 14, 33**
See also Baraka, Amiri; Baraka, Imamu Amiri
See also CA 21-24R

Jones, Louis B. 19??- .... **CLC 65**

Jones, Madison (Percy, Jr.) 1925- ... **CLC 4**
See also CAAS 11; CANR 7; CA 13-16R

Jones, Mervyn 1922- .... **CLC 10, 52**
See also CAAS 5; CANR 1; CA 45-48

Jones, Mick 1956?- .... **CLC 30**
See also The Clash

Jones, Nettie 19??- .... **CLC 34**

Jones, Preston 1936-1979 .... **CLC 10**
See also CA 73-76; obituary CA 89-92; DLB 7

Jones, Robert F(rancis) 1934- .... **CLC 7**
See also CANR 2; CA 49-52

Jones, Rod 1953- .... **CLC 50**
See also CA 128

Jones, Terry 1942?- .... **CLC 21**
See also Monty Python
See also CA 112, 116; SATA 51

Jong, Erica 1942- .... **CLC 4, 6, 8, 18**
See also CANR 26; CA 73-76; DLB 2, 5, 28

Jonson, Ben(jamin) 1572-1637 .... **LC 6**
See also DLB 62

Jordan, June 1936- .... **CLC 5, 11, 23**
See also CLR 10; CANR 25; CA 33-36R; SATA 4; DLB 38; AAYA 2

Jordan, Pat(rick M.) 1941- .... **CLC 37**
See also CANR 25; CA 33-36R

Josipovici, Gabriel (David) 1940- .... **CLC 6, 43**
See also CAAS 8; CA 37-40R; DLB 14

Joubert, Joseph 1754-1824 .... **NCLC 9**

Jouve, Pierre Jean 1887-1976 ...... **CLC 47**
See also obituary CA 65-68

Joyce, James (Augustine Aloysius) 1882-1941 ...... **TCLC 3, 8, 16, 26, 35; SSC 3**
See also CA 104, 126; DLB 10, 19, 36

Jozsef, Attila 1905-1937 .... **TCLC 22**
See also CA 116

Juana Ines de la Cruz 1651?-1695 .... **LC 5**

Julian of Norwich 1342?-1416? .... **LC 6**

Just, Ward S(wift) 1935- .... **CLC 4, 27**
See also CA 25-28R

Justice, Donald (Rodney) 1925- .. **CLC 6, 19**
See also CANR 26; CA 5-8R; DLB-Y 83

Kacew, Romain 1914-1980
See Gary, Romain
See also CA 108; obituary CA 102

Kacewgary, Romain 1914-1980
See Gary, Romain

Kadare, Ismail 1936- .... **CLC 52**

Kadohata, Cynthia 19??- .... **CLC 59**

Kafka, Franz 1883-1924 .... **TCLC 2, 6, 13, 29; SSC 5**
See also CA 105, 126; DLB 81

Kahn, Roger 1927- .... **CLC 30**
See also CA 25-28R; SATA 37

Kaiser, (Friedrich Karl) Georg 1878-1945 .... **TCLC 9**
See also CA 106

Kaletski, Alexander 1946- .... **CLC 39**
See also CA 118

Kallman, Chester (Simon) 1921-1975 .... **CLC 2**
See also CANR 3; CA 45-48; obituary CA 53-56

Kaminsky, Melvin 1926-
See Brooks, Mel
See also CANR 16; CA 65-68

Kaminsky, Stuart 1934- .... **CLC 59**
See also CANR 29; CA 73-76

Kane, Paul 1941-
See Simon, Paul

Kanin, Garson 1912- .... **CLC 22**
See also CANR 7; CA 5-8R; DLB 7

Kaniuk, Yoram 1930- .... **CLC 19**

Kant, Immanuel 1724-1804 ...... **NCLC 27**

Kantor, MacKinlay 1904-1977 ...... **CLC 7**
See also CA 61-64; obituary CA 73-76; DLB 9

Kaplan, David Michael 1946- ...... **CLC 50**

Kaplan, James 19??- .... **CLC 59**

Karamzin, Nikolai Mikhailovich 1766-1826 .... **NCLC 3**

Karapanou, Margarita 1946- .... **CLC 13**
See also CA 101

Karl, Frederick R(obert) 1927- ..... **CLC 34**
See also CANR 3; CA 5-8R

Kassef, Romain 1914-1980
See Gary, Romain

Katz, Steve 1935- .... **CLC 47**
See also CANR 12; CA 25-28R; DLB-Y 83

Kauffman, Janet 1945- .... **CLC 42**
See also CA 117; DLB-Y 86

Kaufman, Bob (Garnell) 1925-1986 .... **CLC 49**
See also CANR 22; CA 41-44R; obituary CA 118; DLB 16, 41

Kaufman, George S(imon) 1889-1961 .... **CLC 38**
See also CA 108; obituary CA 93-96; DLB 7

Kaufman, Sue 1926-1977 .... **CLC 3, 8**
See also Barondess, Sue K(aufman)

Kavan, Anna 1904-1968 .... **CLC 5, 13**
See also Edmonds, Helen (Woods)
See also CANR 6; CA 5-8R

Kavanagh, Patrick (Joseph Gregory) 1905-1967 .... **CLC 22**
See also CA 123; obituary CA 25-28R; DLB 15, 20

Kawabata, Yasunari 1899-1972 .... **CLC 2, 5, 9, 18**
See also CA 93-96; obituary CA 33-36R

Kaye, M(ary) M(argaret) 1909?- .... **CLC 28**
See also CANR 24; CA 89-92

Kaye, Mollie 1909?-
See Kaye, M(ary) M(argaret)

Kaye-Smith, Sheila 1887-1956 ..... **TCLC 20**
See also CA 118; DLB 36

Kazan, Elia 1909- .... **CLC 6, 16, 63**
See also CA 21-24R

Kazantzakis, Nikos 1885?-1957 .... **TCLC 2, 5, 33**
See also CA 105

Kazin, Alfred 1915- .... **CLC 34, 38**
See also CAAS 7; CANR 1; CA 1-4R; DLB 67

Keane, Mary Nesta (Skrine) 1904-
See Keane, Molly
See also CA 108, 114

Keane, Molly 1904- .... **CLC 31**
See also Keane, Mary Nesta (Skrine)

Keates, Jonathan 19??- .... **CLC 34**

Keaton, Buster 1895-1966 .... **CLC 20**

Keaton, Joseph Francis 1895-1966
See Keaton, Buster

Keats, John 1795-1821 ...... **NCLC 8; PC 1**

Keene, Donald 1922- .... **CLC 34**
See also CANR 5; CA 1-4R

Keillor, Garrison 1942- .... **CLC 40**
See also Keillor, Gary (Edward)
See also CA 111; SATA 58; DLB-Y 87; AAYA 2

Keillor, Gary (Edward)
See Keillor, Garrison
See also CA 111, 117

Kell, Joseph 1917-
See Burgess (Wilson, John) Anthony

Keller, Gottfried 1819-1890 .... **NCLC 2**

Kellerman, Jonathan (S.) 1949- ..... **CLC 44**
See also CANR 29; CA 106

Kelley, William Melvin 1937- ...... **CLC 22**
See also CANR 27; CA 77-80; DLB 33

Kellogg, Marjorie 1922- .... **CLC 2**
See also CA 81-84

Kelly, M. T. 1947- .... **CLC 55**
See also CANR 19; CA 97-100

Kelman, James 1946- .... **CLC 58**

Kemal, Yashar 1922- .... **CLC 14, 29**
See also CA 89-92

Kemble, Fanny 1809-1893 .... **NCLC 18**
See also DLB 32

Kemelman, Harry 1908- .... **CLC 2**
See also CANR 6; CA 9-12R; DLB 28

Kempe, Margery 1373?-1440? .... **LC 6**

Kempis, Thomas á 1380-1471 .... **LC 11**

Kendall, Henry 1839-1882 .... **NCLC 12**

Keneally, Thomas (Michael) 1935- ...... **CLC 5, 8, 10, 14, 19, 27, 43**
See also CANR 10; CA 85-88

Kennedy, John Pendleton 1795-1870 .... **NCLC 2**
See also DLB 3

Kennedy, Joseph Charles 1929- ...... **CLC 8**
See also Kennedy, X. J.
See also CANR 4, 30; CA 1-4R; SATA 14

Kennedy, William (Joseph) 1928- .... **CLC 6, 28, 34, 53**
See also CANR 14; CA 85-88; SATA 57; DLB-Y 85; AAYA 1

Kennedy, X. J. 1929- .... **CLC 8, 42**
See also Kennedy, Joseph Charles
See also CAAS 9; DLB 5

Kerouac, Jack 1922-1969 .... **CLC 1, 2, 3, 5, 14, 29, 61**
See also Kerouac, Jean-Louis Lebris de
See also DLB 2, 16; DLB-DS 3; CDALB 1941-1968

Kerouac, Jean-Louis Lebris de 1922-1969
See Kerouac, Jack
See also CANR 26; CA 5-8R; obituary CA 25-28R; CDALB 1941-1968

Kerr, Jean 1923- .... **CLC 22**
See also CANR 7; CA 5-8R

Kerr, M. E. 1927- .... **CLC 12, 35**
See also Meaker, Marijane
See also SAAS 1; AAYA 2

Kerr, Robert 1970?- .... **CLC 55, 59**

Kerrigan, (Thomas) Anthony 1918- .... **CLC 4, 6**
See also CAAS 11; CANR 4; CA 49-52

Kesey, Ken (Elton) 1935- .... **CLC 1, 3, 6, 11, 46, 64**
See also CANR 22; CA 1-4R; DLB 2, 16; CDALB 1968-1987

Kesselring, Joseph (Otto) 1902-1967 .... **CLC 45**

Kessler, Jascha (Frederick) 1929-.... **CLC 4**
See also CANR 8; CA 17-20R

Kettelkamp, Larry 1933-.......... **CLC 12**
See also CANR 16; CA 29-32R; SAAS 3; SATA 2

Kherdian, David 1931-........... **CLC 6, 9**
See also CLR 24; CAAS 2; CA 21-24R; SATA 16

Khlebnikov, Velimir (Vladimirovich)
1885-1922 .... **TCLC 20**
See also CA 117

Khodasevich, Vladislav (Felitsianovich)
1886-1939 .... **TCLC 15**
See also CA 115

Kielland, Alexander (Lange)
1849-1906 .... **TCLC 5**
See also CA 104

Kiely, Benedict 1919-.......... **CLC 23, 43**
See also CANR 2; CA 1-4R; DLB 15

Kienzle, William X(avier) 1928- .... **CLC 25**
See also CAAS 1; CANR 9; CA 93-96

Killens, John Oliver 1916-......... **CLC 10**
See also CAAS 2; CANR 26; CA 77-80, 123; DLB 33

Killigrew, Anne 1660-1685........... **LC 4**

Kincaid, Jamaica 1949?- .... **CLC 43**
See also CA 125

King, Francis (Henry) 1923-..... **CLC 8, 53**
See also CANR 1; CA 1-4R; DLB 15

King, Stephen (Edwin)
1947- .... **CLC 12, 26, 37, 61**
See also CANR 1, 30; CA 61-64; SATA 9, 55; DLB-Y 80; AAYA 1

Kingman, (Mary) Lee 1919-........ **CLC 17**
See also Natti, (Mary) Lee
See also CA 5-8R; SAAS 3; SATA 1

Kingsley, Sidney 1906-........... **CLC 44**
See also CA 85-88; DLB 7

Kingsolver, Barbara 1955-......... **CLC 55**
See also CA 129

Kingston, Maxine Hong
1940- .... **CLC 12, 19, 58**
See also CANR 13; CA 69-72; SATA 53; DLB-Y 80

Kinnell, Galway
1927- .... **CLC 1, 2, 3, 5, 13, 29**
See also CANR 10; CA 9-12R; DLB 5; DLB-Y 87

Kinsella, Thomas 1928- ...... **CLC 4, 19, 43**
See also CANR 15; CA 17-20R; DLB 27

Kinsella, W(illiam) P(atrick)
1935- .... **CLC 27, 43**
See also CAAS 7; CANR 21; CA 97-100

Kipling, (Joseph) Rudyard
1865-1936 .... **TCLC 8, 17; SSC 5**
See also YABC 2; CA 105, 120; DLB 19, 34

Kirkup, James 1918- .... **CLC 1**
See also CAAS 4; CANR 2; CA 1-4R; SATA 12; DLB 27

Kirkwood, James 1930-1989 .... **CLC 9**
See also CANR 6; CA 1-4R; obituary CA 128

Kis, Danilo 1935-1989 .... **CLC 57**
See also CA 118, 129; brief entry CA 109

Kivi, Aleksis 1834-1872 .... **NCLC 30**

Kizer, Carolyn (Ashley) 1925-... **CLC 15, 39**
See also CAAS 5; CANR 24; CA 65-68; DLB 5

Klappert, Peter 1942-............ **CLC 57**
See also CA 33-36R; DLB 5

Klausner, Amos 1939-
See Oz, Amos

Klein, A(braham) M(oses)
1909-1972 .... **CLC 19**
See also CA 101; obituary CA 37-40R; DLB 68

Klein, Norma 1938-1989 .... **CLC 30**
See also CLR 2, 19; CANR 15; CA 41-44R; obituary CA 128; SAAS 1; SATA 7, 57; AAYA 2

Klein, T.E.D. 19??-............... **CLC 34**
See also CA 119

Kleist, Heinrich von 1777-1811.... **NCLC 2**
See also DLB 90

Klima, Ivan 1931-................ **CLC 56**
See also CANR 17; CA 25-28R

Klimentev, Andrei Platonovich 1899-1951
See Platonov, Andrei (Platonovich)
See also CA 108

Klinger, Friedrich Maximilian von
1752-1831 .... **NCLC 1**

Klopstock, Friedrich Gottlieb
1724-1803 .... **NCLC 11**

Knebel, Fletcher 1911-............ **CLC 14**
See also CAAS 3; CANR 1; CA 1-4R; SATA 36

Knight, Etheridge 1931-........... **CLC 40**
See also CANR 23; CA 21-24R; DLB 41

Knight, Sarah Kemble 1666-1727 ..... **LC 7**
See also DLB 24

Knowles, John 1926- ...... **CLC 1, 4, 10, 26**
See also CA 17-20R; SATA 8; DLB 6; CDALB 1968-1987

Koch, C(hristopher) J(ohn) 1932- ... **CLC 42**
See also CA 127

Koch, Kenneth 1925- .... **CLC 5, 8, 44**
See also CANR 6; CA 1-4R; DLB 5

Kochanowski, Jan 1530-1584........ **LC 10**

Kock, Charles Paul de
1794-1871 .... **NCLC 16**

Koestler, Arthur
1905-1983 .... **CLC 1, 3, 6, 8, 15, 33**
See also CANR 1; CA 1-4R; obituary CA 109; DLB-Y 83

Kohout, Pavel 1928-.............. **CLC 13**
See also CANR 3; CA 45-48

Kolmar, Gertrud 1894-1943....... **TCLC 40**

Konigsberg, Allen Stewart 1935-
See Allen, Woody

Konrad, Gyorgy 1933- .... **CLC 4, 10**
See also CA 85-88

Konwicki, Tadeusz 1926-..... **CLC 8, 28, 54**
See also CAAS 9; CA 101

Kopit, Arthur (Lee) 1937- .... **CLC 1, 18, 33**
See also CA 81-84; CABS 3; DLB 7

Kops, Bernard 1926-.............. **CLC 4**
See also CA 5-8R; DLB 13

Kornbluth, C(yril) M. 1923-1958.... **TCLC 8**
See also CA 105; DLB 8

Korolenko, Vladimir (Galaktionovich)
1853-1921 .... **TCLC 22**
See also CA 121

Kosinski, Jerzy (Nikodem)
1933- .... **CLC 1, 2, 3, 6, 10, 15, 53**
See also CANR 9; CA 17-20R; DLB 2; DLB-Y 82

Kostelanetz, Richard (Cory) 1940- .. **CLC 28**
See also CAAS 8; CA 13-16R

Kostrowitzki, Wilhelm Apollinaris de
1880-1918
See Apollinaire, Guillaume
See also CA 104

Kotlowitz, Robert 1924-............ **CLC 4**
See also CA 33-36R

Kotzebue, August (Friedrich Ferdinand) von
1761-1819 .... **NCLC 25**

Kotzwinkle, William 1938- ... **CLC 5, 14, 35**
See also CLR 6; CANR 3; CA 45-48; SATA 24

Kozol, Jonathan 1936-............ **CLC 17**
See also CANR 16; CA 61-64

Kozoll, Michael 1940?-............ **CLC 35**

Kramer, Kathryn 19??-............ **CLC 34**

Kramer, Larry 1935- .... **CLC 42**
See also CA 124, 126

Krasicki, Ignacy 1735-1801 .... **NCLC 8**

Krasinski, Zygmunt 1812-1859 .... **NCLC 4**

Kraus, Karl 1874-1936........... **TCLC 5**
See also CA 104

Kreve, Vincas 1882-1954 .... **TCLC 27**

Kristofferson, Kris 1936-.......... **CLC 26**
See also CA 104

Krizanc, John 1956-.............. **CLC 57**

Krleza, Miroslav 1893-1981......... **CLC 8**
See also CA 97-100; obituary CA 105

Kroetsch, Robert (Paul)
1927- .... **CLC 5, 23, 57**
See also CANR 8; CA 17-20R; DLB 53

Kroetz, Franz Xaver 1946- .... **CLC 41**
See also CA 130

Kropotkin, Peter 1842-1921....... **TCLC 36**
See also CA 119

Krotkov, Yuri 1917-.............. **CLC 19**
See also CA 102

Krumgold, Joseph (Quincy)
1908-1980 .... **CLC 12**
See also CANR 7; CA 9-12R; obituary CA 101; SATA 1, 48; obituary SATA 23

Krutch, Joseph Wood 1893-1970.... **CLC 24**
See also CANR 4; CA 1-4R; obituary CA 25-28R; DLB 63

Krylov, Ivan Andreevich
1768?-1844................. **NCLC 1**

Kubin, Alfred 1877-1959 .... **TCLC 23**
See also CA 112; DLB 81

Kubrick, Stanley 1928-............ **CLC 16**
See also CA 81-84; DLB 26

Kumin, Maxine (Winokur) 1925- .... **CLC 5, 13, 28**
See also CAAS 8; CANR 1, 21; CA 1-4R; SATA 12; DLB 5

Kundera, Milan 1929- ..... **CLC 4, 9, 19, 32**
See also CANR 19; CA 85-88; AAYA 2

Kunitz, Stanley J(asspon) 1905- .... **CLC 6, 11, 14**
See also CANR 26; CA 41-44R; DLB 48

Kunze, Reiner 1933- .... **CLC 10**
See also CA 93-96; DLB 75

Kuprin, Aleksandr (Ivanovich) 1870-1938 .... **TCLC 5**
See also CA 104

Kureishi, Hanif 1954- .... **CLC 64**

Kurosawa, Akira 1910- .... **CLC 16**
See also CA 101

Kuttner, Henry 1915-1958 .... **TCLC 10**
See also CA 107; DLB 8

Kuzma, Greg 1944- .... **CLC 7**
See also CA 33-36R

Kuzmin, Mikhail 1872?-1936 ...... **TCLC 40**

Labrunie, Gerard 1808-1855
See Nerval, Gerard de

Laclos, Pierre Ambroise Francois Choderlos de 1741-1803 .... **NCLC 4**

La Fayette, Marie (Madelaine Pioche de la Vergne, Comtesse) de 1634-1693 .... **LC 2**

Lafayette, Rene
See Hubbard, L(afayette) Ron(ald)

Laforgue, Jules 1860-1887 .... **NCLC 5**

Lagerkvist, Par (Fabian) 1891-1974 .... **CLC 7, 10, 13, 54**
See also CA 85-88; obituary CA 49-52

Lagerlof, Selma (Ottiliana Lovisa) 1858-1940 .... **TCLC 4, 36**
See also CLR 7; CA 108; SATA 15

La Guma, (Justin) Alex(ander) 1925-1985 .... **CLC 19**
See also CANR 25; CA 49-52; obituary CA 118

Lamartine, Alphonse (Marie Louis Prat) de 1790-1869 .... **NCLC 11**

Lamb, Charles 1775-1834 .... **NCLC 10**
See also SATA 17

Lamming, George (William) 1927- .... **CLC 2, 4**
See also CANR 26; CA 85-88

LaMoore, Louis Dearborn 1908?-
See L'Amour, Louis (Dearborn)

L'Amour, Louis (Dearborn) 1908-1988 .... **CLC 25, 55**
See also CANR 3, 25; CA 1-4R; obituary CA 125; DLB-Y 80

Lampedusa, (Prince) Giuseppe (Maria Fabrizio) Tomasi di 1896-1957 .... **TCLC 13**
See also CA 111

Lampman, Archibald 1861-1899 .. **NCLC 25**
See also DLB 92

Lancaster, Bruce 1896-1963 .... **CLC 36**
See also CAP 1; CA 9-12; SATA 9

Landis, John (David) 1950- .... **CLC 26**
See also CA 112, 122

Landolfi, Tommaso 1908-1979 ... **CLC 11, 49**
See also CA 127; obituary CA 117

Landon, Letitia Elizabeth 1802-1838 .... **NCLC 15**

Landor, Walter Savage 1775-1864 .... **NCLC 14**

Landwirth, Heinz 1927-
See Lind, Jakov
See also CANR 7; CA 11-12R

Lane, Patrick 1939- .... **CLC 25**
See also CA 97-100; DLB 53

Lang, Andrew 1844-1912 .... **TCLC 16**
See also CA 114; SATA 16

Lang, Fritz 1890-1976 .... **CLC 20**
See also CANR 30; CA 77-80; obituary CA 69-72

Langer, Elinor 1939- .... **CLC 34**
See also CA 121

Lanier, Sidney 1842-1881 .... **NCLC 6**
See also SATA 18; DLB 64

Lanyer, Aemilia 1569-1645 .... **LC 10**

Lao Tzu c. 6th-3rd century B.C. ... **CMLC 7**

Lapine, James 1949- .... **CLC 39**
See also CA 123, 130

Larbaud, Valery 1881-1957 .... **TCLC 9**
See also CA 106

Lardner, Ring(gold Wilmer) 1885-1933 .... **TCLC 2, 14**
See also CA 104; DLB 11, 25, 86; CDALB 1917-1929

Larkin, Philip (Arthur) 1922-1985 ... **CLC 3, 5, 8, 9, 13, 18, 33, 39, 64**
See also CANR 24; CA 5-8R; obituary CA 117; DLB 27

Larra (y Sanchez de Castro), Mariano Jose de 1809-1837 .... **NCLC 17**

Larsen, Eric 1941- .... **CLC 55**

Larsen, Nella 1891-1964 .... **CLC 37**
See also CA 125; DLB 51

Larson, Charles R(aymond) 1938- ... **CLC 31**
See also CANR 4; CA 53-56

Latham, Jean Lee 1902- .... **CLC 12**
See also CANR 7; CA 5-8R; SATA 2

Lathen, Emma .... **CLC 2**
See also Hennissart, Martha; Latsis, Mary J(ane)

Latsis, Mary J(ane) .... **CLC 2**
See also Lathen, Emma
See also CA 85-88

Lattimore, Richmond (Alexander) 1906-1984 .... **CLC 3**
See also CANR 1; CA 1-4R; obituary CA 112

Laughlin, James 1914- .... **CLC 49**
See also CANR 9; CA 21-24R; DLB 48

Laurence, (Jean) Margaret (Wemyss) 1926-1987 .. **CLC 3, 6, 13, 50, 62; SSC 7**
See also CA 5-8R; obituary CA 121; SATA 50; DLB 53

Laurent, Antoine 1952- .... **CLC 50**

Lautreamont, Comte de 1846-1870 .... **NCLC 12**

Lavin, Mary 1912- ...... **CLC 4, 18; SSC 4**
See also CA 9-12R; DLB 15

Lawler, Raymond (Evenor) 1922- ... **CLC 58**
See also CA 103

Lawrence, D(avid) H(erbert) 1885-1930 .... **TCLC 2, 9, 16, 33; SSC 4**
See also CA 104, 121; DLB 10, 19, 36

Lawrence, T(homas) E(dward) 1888-1935 .... **TCLC 18**
See also CA 115

Lawson, Henry (Archibald Hertzberg) 1867-1922 .... **TCLC 27**
See also CA 120

Laxness, Halldor (Kiljan) 1902- .... **CLC 25**
See also Gudjonsson, Halldor Kiljan

Laye, Camara 1928-1980 .... **CLC 4, 38**
See also CANR 25; CA 85-88; obituary CA 97-100

Layton, Irving (Peter) 1912- ..... **CLC 2, 15**
See also CANR 2; CA 1-4R; DLB 88

Lazarus, Emma 1849-1887 .... **NCLC 8**

Leacock, Stephen (Butler) 1869-1944 .... **TCLC 2**
See also CA 104; DLB 92

Lear, Edward 1812-1888 .... **NCLC 3**
See also CLR 1; SATA 18; DLB 32

Lear, Norman (Milton) 1922- ...... **CLC 12**
See also CA 73-76

Leavis, F(rank) R(aymond) 1895-1978 .... **CLC 24**
See also CA 21-24R; obituary CA 77-80

Leavitt, David 1961?- .... **CLC 34**
See also CA 116, 122

Lebowitz, Fran(ces Ann) 1951?- .... **CLC 11, 36**
See also CANR 14; CA 81-84

Le Carre, John 1931- ... **CLC 3, 5, 9, 15, 28**
See also Cornwell, David (John Moore)
See also DLB 87

Le Clezio, J(ean) M(arie) G(ustave) 1940- .... **CLC 31**
See also CA 116, 128; DLB 83

Leconte de Lisle, Charles-Marie-Rene 1818-1894 .... **NCLC 29**

Leduc, Violette 1907-1972 .... **CLC 22**
See also CAP 1; CA 13-14; obituary CA 33-36R

Ledwidge, Francis 1887-1917 ...... **TCLC 23**
See also CA 123; DLB 20

Lee, Andrea 1953- .... **CLC 36**
See also CA 125

Lee, Andrew 1917-
See Auchincloss, Louis (Stanton)

Lee, Don L. 1942- .... **CLC 2**
See also Madhubuti, Haki R.
See also CA 73-76

Lee, George Washington 1894-1976 .... **CLC 52**
See also CA 125; DLB 51

Lee, (Nelle) Harper 1926- ...... **CLC 12, 60**
See also CA 13-16R; SATA 11; DLB 6; CDALB 1941-1968

Lee, Lawrence 1903- .... CLC 34
See also CA 25-28R

Lee, Manfred B(ennington)
1905-1971 .... CLC 11
See also Queen, Ellery
See also CANR 2; CA 1-4R;
obituary CA 29-32R

Lee, Stan 1922- .... CLC 17
See also CA 108, 111

Lee, Tanith 1947- .... CLC 46
See also CA 37-40R; SATA 8

Lee, Vernon 1856-1935 .... TCLC 5
See also Paget, Violet
See also DLB 57

Lee-Hamilton, Eugene (Jacob)
1845-1907 .... TCLC 22
See also CA 117

Leet, Judith 1935- .... CLC 11

Le Fanu, Joseph Sheridan
1814-1873 .... NCLC 9
See also DLB 21, 70

Leffland, Ella 1931- .... CLC 19
See also CA 29-32R; DLB-Y 84

Leger, (Marie-Rene) Alexis Saint-Leger
1887-1975 .... CLC 11
See also Perse, St.-John
See also CA 13-16R; obituary CA 61-64

Le Guin, Ursula K(roeber)
1929- .... CLC 8, 13, 22, 45
See also CLR 3; CANR 9; CA 21-24R;
SATA 4, 52; DLB 8, 52;
CDALB 1968-1987

Lehmann, Rosamond (Nina) 1901- ... CLC 5
See also CANR 8; CA 77-80; DLB 15

Leiber, Fritz (Reuter, Jr.) 1910- .... CLC 25
See also CANR 2; CA 45-48; SATA 45;
DLB 8

Leimbach, Marti 1963- .... CLC 65

Leino, Eino 1878-1926 .... TCLC 24

Leiris, Michel 1901- .... CLC 61
See also CA 119, 128

Leithauser, Brad 1953- .... CLC 27
See also CANR 27; CA 107

Lelchuk, Alan 1938- .... CLC 5
See also CANR 1; CA 45-48

Lem, Stanislaw 1921- .... CLC 8, 15, 40
See also CAAS 1; CA 105

Lemann, Nancy 1956- .... CLC 39
See also CA 118

Lemonnier, (Antoine Louis) Camille
1844-1913 .... TCLC 22
See also CA 121

Lenau, Nikolaus 1802-1850 ...... NCLC 16

L'Engle, Madeleine 1918- .... CLC 12
See also CLR 1, 14; CANR 3, 21; CA 1-4R;
SATA 1, 27; DLB 52; AAYA 1

Lengyel, Jozsef 1896-1975 .... CLC 7
See also CA 85-88; obituary CA 57-60

Lennon, John (Ono)
1940-1980 .... CLC 12, 35
See also CA 102

Lennon, John Winston 1940-1980
See Lennon, John (Ono)

Lennox, Charlotte Ramsay
1729?-1804 .... NCLC 23
See also DLB 39

Lentricchia, Frank (Jr.) 1940- ...... CLC 34
See also CANR 19; CA 25-28R

Lenz, Siegfried 1926- .... CLC 27
See also CA 89-92; DLB 75

Leonard, Elmore 1925- .... CLC 28, 34
See also CANR 12, 28; CA 81-84

Leonard, Hugh 1926- .... CLC 19
See also Byrne, John Keyes
See also DLB 13

Leopardi, (Conte) Giacomo (Talegardo Francesco di Sales Saverio Pietro)
1798-1837 .... NCLC 22

Lerman, Eleanor 1952- .... CLC 9
See also CA 85-88

Lerman, Rhoda 1936- .... CLC 56
See also CA 49-52

Lermontov, Mikhail Yuryevich
1814-1841 .... NCLC 5

Leroux, Gaston 1868-1927 .... TCLC 25
See also CA 108

Lesage, Alain-Rene 1668-1747 .... LC 2

Leskov, Nikolai (Semyonovich)
1831-1895 .... NCLC 25

Lessing, Doris (May)
1919- .... CLC 1, 2, 3, 6, 10, 15, 22, 40;
SSC 6
See also CA 9-12R; DLB 15; DLB-Y 85

Lessing, Gotthold Ephraim
1729-1781 .... LC 8

Lester, Richard 1932- .... CLC 20

Lever, Charles (James)
1806-1872 .... NCLC 23
See also DLB 21

Leverson, Ada 1865-1936 .... TCLC 18
See also CA 117

Levertov, Denise
1923- .... CLC 1, 2, 3, 5, 8, 15, 28
See also CANR 3, 29; CA 1-4R; DLB 5

Levi, Peter (Chad Tiger) 1931- ..... CLC 41
See also CA 5-8R; DLB 40

Levi, Primo 1919-1987 .... CLC 37, 50
See also CANR 12; CA 13-16R;
obituary CA 122

Levin, Ira 1929- .... CLC 3, 6
See also CANR 17; CA 21-24R

Levin, Meyer 1905-1981 .... CLC 7
See also CANR 15; CA 9-12R;
obituary CA 104; SATA 21;
obituary SATA 27; DLB 9, 28; DLB-Y 81

Levine, Norman 1924- .... CLC 54
See also CANR 14; CA 73-76; DLB 88

Levine, Philip 1928- .. CLC 2, 4, 5, 9, 14, 33
See also CANR 9; CA 9-12R; DLB 5

Levinson, Deirdre 1931- .... CLC 49
See also CA 73-76

Levi-Strauss, Claude 1908- .... CLC 38
See also CANR 6; CA 1-4R

Levitin, Sonia 1934- .... CLC 17
See also CANR 14; CA 29-32R; SAAS 2;
SATA 4

Lewes, George Henry
1817-1878 .... NCLC 25
See also DLB 55

Lewis, Alun 1915-1944 .... TCLC 3
See also CA 104; DLB 20

Lewis, C(ecil) Day 1904-1972
See Day Lewis, C(ecil)

Lewis, C(live) S(taples)
1898-1963 .... CLC 1, 3, 6, 14, 27
See also CLR 3; CA 81-84; SATA 13;
DLB 15

Lewis (Winters), Janet 1899- .... CLC 41
See also Winters, Janet Lewis
See also CANR 29; CAP 1; CA 9-10R;
DLB-Y 87

Lewis, Matthew Gregory
1775-1818 .... NCLC 11
See also DLB 39

Lewis, (Harry) Sinclair
1885-1951 .... TCLC 4, 13, 23, 39
See also CA 104; DLB 9; DLB-DS 1;
CDALB 1917-1929

Lewis, (Percy) Wyndham
1882?-1957 .... TCLC 2, 9
See also CA 104; DLB 15

Lewisohn, Ludwig 1883-1955 ...... TCLC 19
See also CA 73-76, 107;
obituary CA 29-32R; DLB 4, 9, 28

L'Heureux, John (Clarke) 1934- .... CLC 52
See also CANR 23; CA 15-16R

Lieber, Stanley Martin 1922-
See Lee, Stan

Lieberman, Laurence (James)
1935- .... CLC 4, 36
See also CANR 8; CA 17-20R

Li Fei-kan 1904- .... CLC 18
See also Pa Chin
See also CA 105

Lightfoot, Gordon (Meredith)
1938- .... CLC 26
See also CA 109

Ligotti, Thomas 1953- .... CLC 44
See also CA 123

Liliencron, Detlev von
1844-1909 .... TCLC 18
See also CA 117

Lima, Jose Lezama 1910-1976
See Lezama Lima, Jose

Lima Barreto, (Alfonso Henriques de)
1881-1922 .... TCLC 23
See also CA 117

Lincoln, Abraham 1809-1865 ..... NCLC 18

Lind, Jakov 1927- .... CLC 1, 2, 4, 27
See also Landwirth, Heinz
See also CAAS 4; CA 9-12R

Lindsay, David 1876-1945 .... TCLC 15
See also CA 113

Lindsay, (Nicholas) Vachel
1879-1931 .... TCLC 17
See also CA 114; SATA 40; DLB 54;
CDALB 1865-1917

Linney, Romulus 1930- .... CLC 51
See also CA 1-4R

Li Po 701-763 .... CMLC 2

Lipsius, Justus 1547-1606 .... **LC 16**

Lipsyte, Robert (Michael) 1938- .... **CLC 21**
See also CLR 23; CANR 8; CA 17-20R; SATA 5

Lish, Gordon (Jay) 1934- .... **CLC 45**
See also CA 113, 117

Lispector, Clarice 1925-1977 .... **CLC 43**
See also obituary CA 116

Littell, Robert 1935?- .... **CLC 42**
See also CA 109, 112

Liu E 1857-1909 .... **TCLC 15**
See also CA 115

Lively, Penelope 1933- .... **CLC 32, 50**
See also CLR 7; CANR 29; CA 41-44R; SATA 7; DLB 14

Livesay, Dorothy 1909- .... **CLC 4, 15**
See also CAAS 8; CA 25-28R; DLB 68

Lizardi, Jose Joaquin Fernandez de 1776-1827 .... **NCLC 30**

Llewellyn, Richard 1906-1983 .... **CLC 7**
See also Llewellyn Lloyd, Richard (Dafydd Vyvyan)
See also DLB 15

Llewellyn Lloyd, Richard (Dafydd Vyvyan) 1906-1983
See Llewellyn, Richard
See also CANR 7; CA 53-56; obituary CA 111; SATA 11, 37

Llosa, Mario Vargas 1936-
See Vargas Llosa, Mario

Lloyd, Richard Llewellyn 1906-
See Llewellyn, Richard

Locke, John 1632-1704 .... **LC 7**
See also DLB 31

Lockhart, John Gibson 1794-1854 .... **NCLC 6**

Lodge, David (John) 1935- .... **CLC 36**
See also CANR 19; CA 17-20R; DLB 14

Loewinsohn, Ron(ald William) 1937- .... **CLC 52**
See also CA 25-28R

Logan, John 1923- .... **CLC 5**
See also CA 77-80; obituary CA 124; DLB 5

Lo Kuan-chung 1330?-1400? .... **LC 12**

Lombino, S. A. 1926-
See Hunter, Evan

London, Jack 1876-1916 ...... **TCLC 9, 15, 39; SSC 4**
See also London, John Griffith
See also SATA 18; DLB 8, 12, 78; CDALB 1865-1917

London, John Griffith 1876-1916
See London, Jack
See also CA 110, 119

Long, Emmett 1925-
See Leonard, Elmore

Longbaugh, Harry 1931-
See Goldman, William (W.)

Longfellow, Henry Wadsworth 1807-1882 .... **NCLC 2**
See also SATA 19; DLB 1, 59; CDALB 1640-1865

Longley, Michael 1939- .... **CLC 29**
See also CA 102; DLB 40

Longus fl. c. 2nd century- .... **CMLC 7**

Lopate, Phillip 1943- .... **CLC 29**
See also CA 97-100; DLB-Y 80

Lopez Portillo (y Pacheco), Jose 1920- .... **CLC 46**
See also CA 129

Lopez y Fuentes, Gregorio 1897-1966 .... **CLC 32**

Lord, Bette Bao 1938- .... **CLC 23**
See also CA 107; SATA 58

Lorde, Audre (Geraldine) 1934- ..... **CLC 18**
See also CANR 16, 26; CA 25-28R; DLB 41

Loti, Pierre 1850-1923 .... **TCLC 11**
See also Viaud, (Louis Marie) Julien

Lovecraft, H(oward) P(hillips) 1890-1937 .... **TCLC 4, 22; SSC 3**
See also CA 104

Lovelace, Earl 1935- .... **CLC 51**
See also CA 77-80

Lowell, Amy 1874-1925 .... **TCLC 1, 8**
See also CA 104; DLB 54

Lowell, James Russell 1819-1891 .. **NCLC 2**
See also DLB 1, 11, 64, 79; CDALB 1640-1865

Lowell, Robert (Traill Spence, Jr.) 1917-1977 ... **CLC 1, 2, 3, 4, 5, 8, 9, 11, 15, 37**
See also CANR 26; CA 9-12R; obituary CA 73-76; CABS 2; DLB 5

Lowndes, Marie (Adelaide) Belloc 1868-1947 .... **TCLC 12**
See also CA 107; DLB 70

Lowry, (Clarence) Malcolm 1909-1957 .... **TCLC 6, 40**
See also CA 105, 131; DLB 15

Loy, Mina 1882-1966 .... **CLC 28**
See also CA 113; DLB 4, 54

Lucas, Craig .... **CLC 64**

Lucas, George 1944- .... **CLC 16**
See also CANR 30; CA 77-80; SATA 56; AAYA 1

Lucas, Victoria 1932-1963
See Plath, Sylvia

Ludlam, Charles 1943-1987 ..... **CLC 46, 50**
See also CA 85-88; obituary CA 122

Ludlum, Robert 1927- .... **CLC 22, 43**
See also CANR 25; CA 33-36R; DLB-Y 82

Ludwig, Ken 19??- .... **CLC 60**

Ludwig, Otto 1813-1865 .... **NCLC 4**

Lugones, Leopoldo 1874-1938 ..... **TCLC 15**
See also CA 116

Lu Hsun 1881-1936 .... **TCLC 3**

Lukacs, Georg 1885-1971 .... **CLC 24**
See also Lukacs, Gyorgy

Lukacs, Gyorgy 1885-1971
See Lukacs, Georg
See also CA 101; obituary CA 29-32R

Luke, Peter (Ambrose Cyprian) 1919- .... **CLC 38**
See also CA 81-84; DLB 13

Lurie (Bishop), Alison 1926- .... **CLC 4, 5, 18, 39**
See also CANR 2, 17; CA 1-4R; SATA 46; DLB 2

Lustig, Arnost 1926- .... **CLC 56**
See also CA 69-72; SATA 56; AAYA 3

Luther, Martin 1483-1546 .... **LC 9**

Luzi, Mario 1914- .... **CLC 13**
See also CANR 9; CA 61-64

Lynn, Kenneth S(chuyler) 1923- .... **CLC 50**
See also CANR 3, 27; CA 1-4R

Lytle, Andrew (Nelson) 1902- ...... **CLC 22**
See also CA 9-12R; DLB 6

Lyttelton, George 1709-1773 .... **LC 10**

Lytton, Edward Bulwer 1803-1873
See Bulwer-Lytton, (Lord) Edward (George Earle Lytton)
See also SATA 23

Maas, Peter 1929- .... **CLC 29**
See also CA 93-96

Macaulay, (Dame Emile) Rose 1881-1958 .... **TCLC 7**
See also CA 104; DLB 36

MacBeth, George (Mann) 1932- .... **CLC 2, 5, 9**
See also CA 25-28R; SATA 4; DLB 40

MacCaig, Norman (Alexander) 1910- .... **CLC 36**
See also CANR 3; CA 9-12R; DLB 27

MacCarthy, Desmond 1877-1952 .. **TCLC 36**

MacDermot, Thomas H. 1870-1933
See Redcam, Tom

MacDiarmid, Hugh 1892-1978 .... **CLC 2, 4, 11, 19, 63**
See also Grieve, C(hristopher) M(urray)
See also DLB 20

Macdonald, Cynthia 1928- ...... **CLC 13, 19**
See also CANR 4; CA 49-52

MacDonald, George 1824-1905 ..... **TCLC 9**
See also CA 106; SATA 33; DLB 18

MacDonald, John D(ann) 1916-1986 .... **CLC 3, 27, 44**
See also CANR 1, 19; CA 1-4R; obituary CA 121; DLB 8; DLB-Y 86

Macdonald, (John) Ross 1915-1983 ...... **CLC 1, 2, 3, 14, 34, 41**
See also Millar, Kenneth
See also DLB-DS 6

MacEwen, Gwendolyn (Margaret) 1941-1987 .... **CLC 13, 55**
See also CANR 7, 22; CA 9-12R; obituary CA 124; SATA 50, 55; DLB 53

Machado (y Ruiz), Antonio 1875-1939 .... **TCLC 3**
See also CA 104

Machado de Assis, (Joaquim Maria) 1839-1908 .... **TCLC 10**
See also CA 107

Machen, Arthur (Llewellyn Jones) 1863-1947 .... **TCLC 4**
See also CA 104; DLB 36

Machiavelli, Niccolo 1469-1527 ...... **LC 8**

Author Index

MacInnes, Colin 1914-1976...... **CLC 4, 23**
See also CANR 21; CA 69-72; obituary CA 65-68; DLB 14

MacInnes, Helen (Clark) 1907-1985................ **CLC 27, 39**
See also CANR 1, 28; CA 1-4R; obituary CA 65-68, 117; SATA 22, 44; DLB 87

Macintosh, Elizabeth 1897-1952
See Tey, Josephine
See also CA 110

Mackenzie, (Edward Montague) Compton 1883-1972.................... **CLC 18**
See also CAP 2; CA 21-22; obituary CA 37-40R; DLB 34

Mac Laverty, Bernard 1942-....... **CLC 31**
See also CA 116, 118

MacLean, Alistair (Stuart) 1922-1987........... **CLC 3, 13, 50, 63**
See also CANR 28; CA 57-60; obituary CA 121; SATA 23, 50

MacLeish, Archibald 1892-1982............... **CLC 3, 8, 14**
See also CA 9-12R; obituary CA 106; DLB 4, 7, 45; DLB-Y 82

MacLennan, (John) Hugh 1907-..................... **CLC 2, 14**
See also CA 5-8R; DLB 68

MacLeod, Alistair 1936-.......... **CLC 56**
See also CA 123; DLB 60

Macleod, Fiona 1855-1905
See Sharp, William

MacNeice, (Frederick) Louis 1907-1963............ **CLC 1, 4, 10, 53**
See also CA 85-88; DLB 10, 20

Macpherson, (Jean) Jay 1931-...... **CLC 14**
See also CA 5-8R; DLB 53

MacShane, Frank 1927-........... **CLC 39**
See also CANR 3; CA 11-12R

Macumber, Mari 1896-1966
See Sandoz, Mari (Susette)

Madach, Imre 1823-1864........ **NCLC 19**

Madden, (Jerry) David 1933-.... **CLC 5, 15**
See also CAAS 3; CANR 4; CA 1-4R; DLB 6

Madhubuti, Haki R. 1942-.......... **CLC 6**
See also Lee, Don L.
See also CANR 24; CA 73-76; DLB 5, 41

Maeterlinck, Maurice 1862-1949... **TCLC 3**
See also CA 104

Mafouz, Naguib 1912-
See Mahfuz, Najib

Maginn, William 1794-1842....... **NCLC 8**

Mahapatra, Jayanta 1928-......... **CLC 33**
See also CAAS 9; CANR 15; CA 73-76

Mahfuz Najib 1912-........... **CLC 52, 55**
See also DLB-Y 88

Mahon, Derek 1941-............. **CLC 27**
See also CA 113, 128; DLB 40

Mailer, Norman 1923-...... **CLC 1, 2, 3, 4, 5, 8, 11, 14, 28, 39**
See also CANR 28; CA 9-12R; CABS 1; DLB 2, 16, 28; DLB-Y 80, 83; DLB-DS 3; CDALB 1968-1987

Maillet, Antonine 1929-........... **CLC 54**
See also CA 115, 120; DLB 60

Mais, Roger 1905-1955........... **TCLC 8**
See also CA 105, 124

Maitland, Sara (Louise) 1950-...... **CLC 49**
See also CANR 13; CA 69-72

Major, Clarence 1936-....... **CLC 3, 19, 48**
See also CAAS 6; CANR 13, 25; CA 21-24R; DLB 33

Major, Kevin 1949-.............. **CLC 26**
See also CLR 11; CANR 21; CA 97-100; SATA 32; DLB 60

Malamud, Bernard 1914-1986..... **CLC 1, 2, 3, 5, 8, 9, 11, 18, 27, 44**
See also CANR 28; CA 5-8R; obituary CA 118; CABS 1; DLB 2, 28; DLB-Y 80, 86; CDALB 1941-1968

Malherbe, Francois de 1555-1628..... **LC 5**

Mallarme, Stephane 1842-1898.... **NCLC 4**

Mallet-Joris, Francoise 1930-...... **CLC 11**
See also CANR 17; CA 65-68; DLB 83

Maloff, Saul 1922-................ **CLC 5**
See also CA 33-36R

Malone, Louis 1907-1963
See MacNeice, (Frederick) Louis

Malone, Michael (Christopher) 1942-....................... **CLC 43**
See also CANR 14; CA 77-80

Malory, (Sir) Thomas ?-1471........ **LC 11**
See also SATA 33, 59

Malouf, David 1934-............. **CLC 28**

Malraux, (Georges-) Andre 1901-1976...... **CLC 1, 4, 9, 13, 15, 57**
See also CAP 2; CA 21-24; obituary CA 69-72; DLB 72

Malzberg, Barry N. 1939-.......... **CLC 7**
See also CAAS 4; CANR 16; CA 61-64; DLB 8

Mamet, David (Alan) 1947-1987.......... **CLC 9, 15, 34, 46**
See also CANR 15; CA 81-84, 124; CABS 3; DLB 7; AAYA 3

Mamoulian, Rouben 1898-......... **CLC 16**
See also CA 25-28R; obituary CA 124

Mandelstam, Osip (Emilievich) 1891?-1938?................ **TCLC 2, 6**
See also CA 104

Mander, Jane 1877-1949......... **TCLC 31**

Mandiargues, Andre Pieyre de 1909-...................... **CLC 41**
See also CA 103; DLB 83

Mangan, James Clarence 1803-1849................. **NCLC 27**

Manley, (Mary) Delariviere 1672?-1724..................... **LC 1**
See also DLB 39, 80

Mann, (Luiz) Heinrich 1871-1950... **TCLC 9**
See also CA 106; DLB 66

Mann, Thomas 1875-1955...... **TCLC 2, 8, 14, 21, 35; SSC 5**
See also CA 104, 128; DLB 66

Manning, Frederic 1882-1935..... **TCLC 25**
See also CA 124

Manning, Olivia 1915-1980...... **CLC 5, 19**
See also CANR 29; CA 5-8R; obituary CA 101

Mano, D. Keith 1942-.......... **CLC 2, 10**
See also CAAS 6; CANR 26; CA 25-28R; DLB 6

Mansfield, Katherine 1888-1923............. **TCLC 2, 8, 39**
See also CA 104

Manso, Peter 1940-.............. **CLC 39**
See also CA 29-32R

Manzoni, Alessandro 1785-1873.. **NCLC 29**

Mapu, Abraham (ben Jekutiel) 1808-1867................. **NCLC 18**

Marat, Jean Paul 1743-1793........ **LC 10**

Marcel, Gabriel (Honore) 1889-1973.................. **CLC 15**
See also CA 102; obituary CA 45-48

Marchbanks, Samuel 1913-
See Davies, (William) Robertson

Marie de l'Incarnation 1599-1672.... **LC 10**

Marinetti, F(ilippo) T(ommaso) 1876-1944................. **TCLC 10**
See also CA 107

Marivaux, Pierre Carlet de Chamblain de (1688-1763).................... **LC 4**

Markandaya, Kamala 1924-...... **CLC 8, 38**
See also Taylor, Kamala (Purnaiya)

Markfield, Wallace (Arthur) 1926-... **CLC 8**
See also CAAS 3; CA 69-72; DLB 2, 28

Markham, Robert 1922-
See Amis, Kingsley (William)

Marks, J. 1942-
See Highwater, Jamake

Marley, Bob 1945-1981........... **CLC 17**
See also Marley, Robert Nesta

Marley, Robert Nesta 1945-1981
See Marley, Bob
See also CA 107; obituary CA 103

Marlowe, Christopher 1564-1593..... **DC 1**
See also DLB 62

Marmontel, Jean-Francois 1723-1799..................... **LC 2**

Marquand, John P(hillips) 1893-1960................. **CLC 2, 10**
See also CA 85-88; DLB 9

Marquez, Gabriel Garcia 1928-
See Garcia Marquez, Gabriel

Marquis, Don(ald Robert Perry) 1878-1937.................. **TCLC 7**
See also CA 104; DLB 11, 25

Marryat, Frederick 1792-1848.... **NCLC 3**
See also DLB 21

Marsh, (Dame Edith) Ngaio 1899-1982................ **CLC 7, 53**
See also CANR 6; CA 9-12R; DLB 77

Marshall, Garry 1935?-........... **CLC 17**
See also CA 111; AAYA 3

Marshall, Paule 1929-..... **CLC 27; SSC 3**
See also CANR 25; CA 77-80; DLB 33

Marsten, Richard 1926-
See Hunter, Evan

Martin, Steve 1945?- .... **CLC 30**
See also CANR 30; CA 97-100

Martin du Gard, Roger
1881-1958 .... **TCLC 24**
See also CA 118; DLB 65

Martineau, Harriet 1802-1876.... **NCLC 26**
See also YABC 2; DLB 21, 55

Martinez Ruiz, Jose 1874-1967
See Azorin
See also CA 93-96

Martinez Sierra, Gregorio
1881-1947 .... **TCLC 6**
See also CA 104, 115

Martinez Sierra, Maria (de la O'LeJarraga)
1880?-1974.................... **TCLC 6**
See also obituary CA 115

Martinson, Harry (Edmund)
1904-1978 .... **CLC 14**
See also CA 77-80

Marvell, Andrew 1621-1678........... **LC 4**

Marx, Karl (Heinrich)
1818-1883 .... **NCLC 17**

Masaoka Shiki 1867-1902 .... **TCLC 18**

Masefield, John (Edward)
1878-1967 .... **CLC 11, 47**
See also CAP 2; CA 19-20; obituary CA 25-28R; SATA 19; DLB 10, 19

Maso, Carole 19??-............... **CLC 44**

Mason, Bobbie Ann
1940- .... **CLC 28, 43; SSC 4**
See also CANR 11; CA 53-56; SAAS 1; DLB-Y 87

Mason, Nick 1945-............... **CLC 35**
See also Pink Floyd

Mason, Tally 1909-1971
See Derleth, August (William)

Masters, Edgar Lee
1868?-1950.......... **TCLC 2, 25; PC 1**
See also CA 104; DLB 54; CDALB 1865-1917

Masters, Hilary 1928-............ **CLC 48**
See also CANR 13; CA 25-28R

Mastrosimone, William 19??- ...... **CLC 36**

Matheson, Richard (Burton)
1926- .... **CLC 37**
See also CA 97-100; DLB 8, 44

Mathews, Harry 1930-.......... **CLC 6, 52**
See also CAAS 6; CANR 18; CA 21-24R

Mathias, Roland (Glyn) 1915-...... **CLC 45**
See also CANR 19; CA 97-100; DLB 27

Matthews, Greg 1949- .... **CLC 45**

Matthews, William 1942-.......... **CLC 40**
See also CANR 12; CA 29-32R; DLB 5

Matthias, John (Edward) 1941-...... **CLC 9**
See also CA 33-36R

Matthiessen, Peter
1927- .... **CLC 5, 7, 11, 32, 64**
See also CANR 21; CA 9-12R; SATA 27; DLB 6

Maturin, Charles Robert
1780?-1824.................. **NCLC 6**

Matute, Ana Maria 1925- .... **CLC 11**
See also CA 89-92

Maugham, W(illiam) Somerset
1874-1965 .... **CLC 1, 11, 15; SSC 8**
See also CA 5-8R; obituary CA 25-28R; SATA 54; DLB 10, 36, 77, 100

Maupassant, (Henri Rene Albert) Guy de
1850-1893 .... **NCLC 1; SSC 1**

Mauriac, Claude 1914-............. **CLC 9**
See also CA 89-92; DLB 83

Mauriac, Francois (Charles)
1885-1970 .... **CLC 4, 9, 56**
See also CAP 2; CA 25-28; DLB 65

Mavor, Osborne Henry 1888-1951
See Bridie, James
See also CA 104

Maxwell, William (Keepers, Jr.)
1908- .... **CLC 19**
See also CA 93-96; DLB-Y 80

May, Elaine 1932- .... **CLC 16**
See also CA 124; DLB 44

Mayakovsky, Vladimir (Vladimirovich)
1893-1930 .... **TCLC 4, 18**
See also CA 104

Mayhew, Henry 1812-1887 ...... **NCLC 31**
See also DLB 18, 55

Maynard, Joyce 1953-............ **CLC 23**
See also CA 111, 129

Mayne, William (James Carter)
1928- .... **CLC 12**
See also CA 9-12R; SATA 6

Mayo, Jim 1908?-
See L'Amour, Louis (Dearborn)

Maysles, Albert 1926- and **Maysles, David**
1926- .... **CLC 16**
See also CA 29-32R

Maysles, Albert 1926- .... **CLC 16**
See also Maysles, Albert and Maysles, David
See also CA 29-32R

Maysles, David 1932-............. **CLC 16**
See also Maysles, Albert and Maysles, David

Mazer, Norma Fox 1931- .... **CLC 26**
See also CLR 23; CANR 12; CA 69-72; SAAS 1; SATA 24

McAuley, James (Phillip)
1917-1976 .... **CLC 45**
See also CA 97-100

McBain, Ed 1926-
See Hunter, Evan

McBrien, William 1930- .... **CLC 44**
See also CA 107

McCaffrey, Anne 1926-........... **CLC 17**
See also CANR 15; CA 25-28R; SATA 8; DLB 8

McCarthy, Cormac 1933-........ **CLC 4, 57**
See also CANR 10; CA 13-16R; DLB 6

McCarthy, Mary (Therese)
1912-1989-... **CLC 1, 3, 5, 14, 24, 39, 59**
See also CANR 16; CA 5-8R; obituary CA 129; DLB 2; DLB-Y 81

McCartney, (James) Paul
1942- .... **CLC 12, 35**

McCauley, Stephen 19??-.......... **CLC 50**

McClure, Michael 1932- .... **CLC 6, 10**
See also CANR 17; CA 21-24R; DLB 16

McCorkle, Jill (Collins) 1958-..... **CLC 51**
See also CA 121; DLB-Y 87

McCourt, James 1941-............. **CLC 5**
See also CA 57-60

McCoy, Horace 1897-1955 .... **TCLC 28**
See also CA 108; DLB 9

McCrae, John 1872-1918......... **TCLC 12**
See also CA 109; DLB 92

McCullers, (Lula) Carson (Smith)
1917-1967 .... **CLC 1, 4, 10, 12, 48**
See also CANR 18; CA 5-8R; obituary CA 25-28R; CABS 1; SATA 27; DLB 2, 7; CDALB 1941-1968

McCullough, Colleen 1938?- .... **CLC 27**
See also CANR 17; CA 81-84

McElroy, Joseph (Prince)
1930- .... **CLC 5, 47**
See also CA 17-20R

McEwan, Ian (Russell) 1948- ...... **CLC 13**
See also CANR 14; CA 61-64; DLB 14

McFadden, David 1940-........... **CLC 48**
See also CA 104; DLB 60

McFarland, Dennis 1956- .... **CLC 65**

McGahern, John 1934-........ **CLC 5, 9, 48**
See also CANR 29; CA 17-20R; DLB 14

McGinley, Patrick 1937-.......... **CLC 41**
See also CA 120, 127

McGinley, Phyllis 1905-1978 ...... **CLC 14**
See also CANR 19; CA 9-12R; obituary CA 77-80; SATA 2, 44; obituary SATA 24; DLB 11, 48

McGinniss, Joe 1942-............. **CLC 32**
See also CANR 26; CA 25-28R

McGivern, Maureen Daly 1921-
See Daly, Maureen
See also CA 9-12R

McGrath, Patrick 1950-........... **CLC 55**

McGrath, Thomas 1916- .... **CLC 28, 59**
See also CANR 6; CA 9-12R, 130; SATA 41

McGuane, Thomas (Francis III)
1939- .... **CLC 3, 7, 18, 45**
See also CANR 5, 24; CA 49-52; DLB 2; DLB-Y 80

McGuckian, Medbh 1950-.......... **CLC 48**
See also DLB 40

McHale, Tom 1941-1982 .... **CLC 3, 5**
See also CA 77-80; obituary CA 106

McIlvanney, William 1936-........ **CLC 42**
See also CA 25-28R; DLB 14

McIlwraith, Maureen Mollie Hunter 1922-
See Hunter, Mollie
See also CA 29-32R; SATA 2

McInerney, Jay 1955- .... **CLC 34**
See also CA 116, 123

McIntyre, Vonda N(eel) 1948- ..... **CLC 18**
See also CANR 17; CA 81-84

McKay, Claude
1889-1948 .... **TCLC 7, 41; PC 2**
See also CA 104, 124; DLB 4, 45, 51

McKuen, Rod 1933- . . . . **CLC 1, 3**
See also CA 41-44R

McLuhan, (Herbert) Marshall
1911-1980 . . . . **CLC 37**
See also CANR 12; CA 9-12R; obituary CA 102; DLB 88

McManus, Declan Patrick 1955-
See Costello, Elvis

McMillan, Terry 1951- . . . . **CLC 50, 61**

McMurtry, Larry (Jeff)
1936- . . . . **CLC 2, 3, 7, 11, 27, 44**
See also CANR 19; CA 5-8R; DLB 2; DLB-Y 80, 87; CDALB 1968-1987

McNally, Terrence 1939- . . . . . . **CLC 4, 7, 41**
See also CANR 2; CA 45-48; DLB 7

McPhee, John 1931- . . . . **CLC 36**
See also CANR 20; CA 65-68

McPherson, James Alan 1943- . . . . . **CLC 19**
See also CANR 24; CA 25-28R; DLB 38

McPherson, William 1939- . . . . **CLC 34**
See also CA 57-60

McSweeney, Kerry 19??- . . . . **CLC 34**

Mead, Margaret 1901-1978 . . . . **CLC 37**
See also CANR 4; CA 1-4R; obituary CA 81-84; SATA 20

Meaker, M. J. 1927-
See Kerr, M. E.; Meaker, Marijane

Meaker, Marijane 1927-
See Kerr, M. E.
See also CA 107; SATA 20

Medoff, Mark (Howard) 1940- . . . **CLC 6, 23**
See also CANR 5; CA 53-56; DLB 7

Megged, Aharon 1920- . . . . **CLC 9**
See also CANR 1; CA 49-52

Mehta, Ved (Parkash) 1934- . . . . **CLC 37**
See also CANR 2, 23; CA 1-4R

Mellor, John 1953?-
See The Clash

Meltzer, Milton 1915- . . . . **CLC 26**
See also CLR 13; CA 13-16R; SAAS 1; SATA 1, 50; DLB 61

Melville, Herman
1819-1891 . . . . . . **NCLC 3, 12, 29; SSC 1**
See also SATA 59; DLB 3, 74; CDALB 1640-1865

Membreno, Alejandro 1972- . . . . **CLC 59**

Mencken, H(enry) L(ouis)
1880-1956 . . . . **TCLC 13**
See also CA 105, 125; DLB 11, 29, 63; CDALB 1917-1929

Mercer, David 1928-1980 . . . . **CLC 5**
See also CANR 23; CA 9-12R; obituary CA 102; DLB 13

Meredith, George 1828-1909 . . . . . . **TCLC 17**
See also CA 117; DLB 18, 35, 57

Meredith, William (Morris)
1919- . . . . **CLC 4, 13, 22, 55**
See also CANR 6; CA 9-12R; DLB 5

Merezhkovsky, Dmitri
1865-1941 . . . . **TCLC 29**

Merimee, Prosper
1803-1870 . . . . **NCLC 6; SSC 7**

Merkin, Daphne 1954- . . . . **CLC 44**
See also CANR 123

Merrill, James (Ingram)
1926- . . . . **CLC 2, 3, 6, 8, 13, 18, 34**
See also CANR 10; CA 13-16R; DLB 5; DLB-Y 85

Merton, Thomas (James)
1915-1968 . . . . **CLC 1, 3, 11, 34**
See also CANR 22; CA 5-8R; obituary CA 25-28R; DLB 48; DLB-Y 81

Merwin, W(illiam) S(tanley)
1927- . . . . . . **CLC 1, 2, 3, 5, 8, 13, 18, 45**
See also CANR 15; CA 13-16R; DLB 5

Metcalf, John 1938- . . . . **CLC 37**
See also CA 113; DLB 60

Mew, Charlotte (Mary)
1870-1928 . . . . **TCLC 8**
See also CA 105; DLB 19

Mewshaw, Michael 1943- . . . . **CLC 9**
See also CANR 7; CA 53-56; DLB-Y 80

Meyer-Meyrink, Gustav 1868-1932
See Meyrink, Gustav
See also CA 117

Meyers, Jeffrey 1939- . . . . **CLC 39**
See also CA 73-76

Meynell, Alice (Christiana Gertrude Thompson) 1847-1922 . . . . **TCLC 6**
See also CA 104; DLB 19

Meyrink, Gustav 1868-1932 . . . . **TCLC 21**
See also Meyer-Meyrink, Gustav

Michaels, Leonard 1933- . . . . **CLC 6, 25**
See also CANR 21; CA 61-64

Michaux, Henri 1899-1984 . . . . **CLC 8, 19**
See also CA 85-88; obituary CA 114

Michelangelo 1475-1564 . . . . **LC 12**

Michelet, Jules 1798-1874 . . . . **NCLC 31**

Michener, James A(lbert)
1907- . . . . **CLC 1, 5, 11, 29, 60**
See also CANR 21; CA 5-8R; DLB 6

Mickiewicz, Adam 1798-1855 . . . . . **NCLC 3**

Middleton, Christopher 1926- . . . . . . **CLC 13**
See also CANR 29; CA 13-16R; DLB 40

Middleton, Stanley 1919- . . . . **CLC 7, 38**
See also CANR 21; CA 25-28R; DLB 14

Migueis, Jose Rodrigues 1901- . . . . . **CLC 10**

Mikszath, Kalman 1847-1910 . . . . . **TCLC 31**

Miles, Josephine (Louise)
1911-1985 . . . . **CLC 1, 2, 14, 34, 39**
See also CANR 2; CA 1-4R; obituary CA 116; DLB 48

Mill, John Stuart 1806-1873 . . . . . **NCLC 11**
See also DLB 55

Millar, Kenneth 1915-1983 . . . . **CLC 14**
See also Macdonald, Ross
See also CANR 16; CA 9-12R; obituary CA 110; DLB 2; DLB-Y 83; DLB-DS 6

Millay, Edna St. Vincent
1892-1950 . . . . **TCLC 4**
See also CA 103; DLB 45; CDALB 1917-1929

Miller, Arthur
1915- . . . . . . **CLC 1, 2, 6, 10, 15, 26, 47; DC 1**
See also CANR 2, 30; CA 1-4R; CABS 3; DLB 7; CDALB 1941-1968

Miller, Henry (Valentine)
1891-1980 . . . . **CLC 1, 2, 4, 9, 14, 43**
See also CA 9-12R; obituary CA 97-100; DLB 4, 9; DLB-Y 80; CDALB 1929-1941

Miller, Jason 1939?- . . . . **CLC 2**
See also CA 73-76; DLB 7

Miller, Sue 19??- . . . . **CLC 44**

Miller, Walter M(ichael), Jr.
1923- . . . . **CLC 4, 30**
See also CA 85-88; DLB 8

Millhauser, Steven 1943- . . . . **CLC 21, 54**
See also CA 108, 110, 111; DLB 2

Millin, Sarah Gertrude 1889-1968 . . **CLC 49**
See also CA 102; obituary CA 93-96

Milne, A(lan) A(lexander)
1882-1956 . . . . **TCLC 6**
See also CLR 1; YABC 1; CA 104; DLB 10, 77

Milner, Ron(ald) 1938- . . . . **CLC 56**
See also CANR 24; CA 73-76; DLB 38

Milosz Czeslaw
1911- . . . . **CLC 5, 11, 22, 31, 56**
See also CANR 23; CA 81-84

Milton, John 1608-1674 . . . . **LC 9**

Miner, Valerie (Jane) 1947- . . . . **CLC 40**
See also CA 97-100

Minot, Susan 1956- . . . . **CLC 44**

Minus, Ed 1938- . . . . **CLC 39**

Miro (Ferrer), Gabriel (Francisco Victor)
1879-1930 . . . . **TCLC 5**
See also CA 104

Mishima, Yukio
1925-1970 . . . . **CLC 2, 4, 6, 9, 27; DC 1; SSC 4**
See also Hiraoka, Kimitake

Mistral, Gabriela 1889-1957 . . . . **TCLC 2**
See also CA 104

Mitchell, James Leslie 1901-1935
See Gibbon, Lewis Grassic
See also CA 104; DLB 15

Mitchell, Joni 1943- . . . . **CLC 12**
See also CA 112

Mitchell (Marsh), Margaret (Munnerlyn)
1900-1949 . . . . **TCLC 11**
See also CA 109, 125; DLB 9

Mitchell, S. Weir 1829-1914 . . . . . . **TCLC 36**

Mitchell, W(illiam) O(rmond)
1914- . . . . **CLC 25**
See also CANR 15; CA 77-80; DLB 88

Mitford, Mary Russell 1787-1855 . . **NCLC 4**

Mitford, Nancy 1904-1973 . . . . **CLC 44**
See also CA 9-12R

Miyamoto Yuriko 1899-1951 . . . . . . **TCLC 37**

Mo, Timothy 1950- . . . . **CLC 46**
See also CA 117

Modarressi, Taghi 1931- . . . . **CLC 44**
See also CA 121

Modiano, Patrick (Jean) 1945- . . . . . **CLC 18**
See also CANR 17; CA 85-88; DLB 83

Mofolo, Thomas (Mokopu)
1876-1948 . . . . **TCLC 22**
See also CA 121

Mohr, Nicholasa 1935- . . . . **CLC 12**
See also CLR 22; CANR 1; CA 49-52; SAAS 8; SATA 8

Mojtabai, A(nn) G(race) 1938- . . . . **CLC 5, 9, 15, 29**
See also CA 85-88

Moliere 1622-1673 . . . . **LC 10**

Molnar, Ferenc 1878-1952 . . . . **TCLC 20**
See also CA 109

Momaday, N(avarre) Scott 1934- . . . . **CLC 2, 19**
See also CANR 14; CA 25-28R; SATA 30, 48

Monroe, Harriet 1860-1936 . . . . **TCLC 12**
See also CA 109; DLB 54, 91

Montagu, Elizabeth 1720-1800 . . . . **NCLC 7**

Montagu, Lady Mary (Pierrepont) Wortley 1689-1762 . . . . **LC 9**

Montague, John (Patrick) 1929- . . . . **CLC 13, 46**
See also CANR 9; CA 9-12R; DLB 40

Montaigne, Michel (Eyquem) de 1533-1592 . . . . **LC 8**

Montale, Eugenio 1896-1981 . . . **CLC 7, 9, 18**
See also CANR 30; CA 17-20R; obituary CA 104

Montgomery, Marion (H., Jr.) 1925- . . . . **CLC 7**
See also CANR 3; CA 1-4R; DLB 6

Montgomery, Robert Bruce 1921-1978
See Crispin, Edmund
See also CA 104

Montherlant, Henri (Milon) de 1896-1972 . . . . **CLC 8, 19**
See also CA 85-88; obituary CA 37-40R; DLB 72

Montisquieu, Charles-Louis de Secondat 1689-1755 . . . . **LC 7**

Monty Python . . . . **CLC 21**

Moodie, Susanna (Strickland) 1803-1885 . . . . **NCLC 14**

Mooney, Ted 1951- . . . . **CLC 25**

Moorcock, Michael (John) 1939- . . . . **CLC 5, 27, 58**
See also CAAS 5; CANR 2, 17; CA 45-48; DLB 14

Moore, Brian 1921- . . . . **CLC 1, 3, 5, 7, 8, 19, 32**
See also CANR 1, 25; CA 1-4R

Moore, George (Augustus) 1852-1933 . . . . **TCLC 7**
See also CA 104; DLB 10, 18, 57

Moore, Lorrie 1957- . . . . **CLC 39, 45**
See also Moore, Marie Lorena

Moore, Marianne (Craig) 1887-1972 . . . **CLC 1, 2, 4, 8, 10, 13, 19, 47**
See also CANR 3; CA 1-4R; obituary CA 33-36R; SATA 20; DLB 45; CDALB 1929-1941

Moore, Marie Lorena 1957-
See Moore, Lorrie
See also CA 116

Moore, Thomas 1779-1852 . . . . **NCLC 6**

Morand, Paul 1888-1976 . . . . **CLC 41**
See also obituary CA 69-72; DLB 65

Morante, Elsa 1918-1985 . . . . **CLC 8, 47**
See also CA 85-88; obituary CA 117

Moravia, Alberto 1907- . . . . **CLC 2, 7, 11, 18, 27, 46**
See also Pincherle, Alberto

More, Hannah 1745-1833 . . . . **NCLC 27**

More, Henry 1614-1687 . . . . **LC 9**

More, (Sir) Thomas 1478-1535 . . . . . . **LC 10**

Moreas, Jean 1856-1910 . . . . **TCLC 18**

Morgan, Berry 1919- . . . . **CLC 6**
See also CA 49-52; DLB 6

Morgan, Edwin (George) 1920- . . . . . **CLC 31**
See also CANR 3; CA 7-8R; DLB 27

Morgan, (George) Frederick 1922- . . . . **CLC 23**
See also CANR 21; CA 17-20R

Morgan, Janet 1945- . . . . **CLC 39**
See also CA 65-68

Morgan, Lady 1776?-1859 . . . . **NCLC 29**

Morgan, Robin 1941- . . . . **CLC 2**
See also CA 69-72

Morgan, Seth 1949-1990 . . . . **CLC 65**
See also CA 132

Morgenstern, Christian (Otto Josef Wolfgang) 1871-1914 . . . . **TCLC 8**
See also CA 105

Moricz, Zsigmond 1879-1942 . . . . . **TCLC 33**

Morike, Eduard (Friedrich) 1804-1875 . . . . **NCLC 10**

Mori Ogai 1862-1922 . . . . **TCLC 14**
See also Mori Rintaro

Mori Rintaro 1862-1922
See Mori Ogai
See also CA 110

Moritz, Karl Philipp 1756-1793 . . . . . . **LC 2**

Morris, Julian 1916-
See West, Morris L.

Morris, Steveland Judkins 1950-
See Wonder, Stevie
See also CA 111

Morris, William 1834-1896 . . . . **NCLC 4**
See also DLB 18, 35, 57

Morris, Wright (Marion) 1910- . . . . **CLC 1, 3, 7, 18, 37**
See also CANR 21; CA 9-12R; DLB 2; DLB-Y 81

Morrison, James Douglas 1943-1971
See Morrison, Jim
See also CA 73-76

Morrison, Jim 1943-1971 . . . . **CLC 17**
See also Morrison, James Douglas

Morrison, Toni 1931- . . . . . **CLC 4, 10, 22, 55**
See also CANR 27; CA 29-32R; DLB 6, 33; DLB-Y 81; CDALB 1968-1987; AAYA 1

Morrison, Van 1945- . . . . **CLC 21**
See also CA 116

Mortimer, John (Clifford) 1923- . . . . **CLC 28, 43**
See also CANR 21; CA 13-16R; DLB 13

Mortimer, Penelope (Ruth) 1918- . . . . **CLC 5**
See also CA 57-60

Mosher, Howard Frank 19??- . . . . . . **CLC 62**

Mosley, Nicholas 1923- . . . . **CLC 43**
See also CA 69-72; DLB 14

Moss, Howard 1922-1987 . . . . **CLC 7, 14, 45, 50**
See also CANR 1; CA 1-4R; obituary CA 123; DLB 5

Motion, Andrew (Peter) 1952- . . . . . **CLC 47**
See also DLB 40

Motley, Willard (Francis) 1912-1965 . . . . **CLC 18**
See also CA 117; obituary CA 106; DLB 76

Mott, Michael (Charles Alston) 1930- . . . . **CLC 15, 34**
See also CAAS 7; CANR 7, 29; CA 5-8R

Mowat, Farley (McGill) 1921- . . . . . **CLC 26**
See also CLR 20; CANR 4, 24; CA 1-4R; SATA 3, 55; DLB 68; AAYA 1

Mphahlele, Es'kia 1919-
See Mphahlele, Ezekiel

Mphahlele, Ezekiel 1919- . . . . **CLC 25**
See also CA 81-84

Mqhayi, S(amuel) E(dward) K(rune Loliwe) 1875-1945 . . . . **TCLC 25**

Mrozek, Slawomir 1930- . . . . **CLC 3, 13**
See also CAAS 10; CANR 29; CA 13-16R

Mtwa, Percy 19??- . . . . **CLC 47**

Mueller, Lisel 1924- . . . . **CLC 13, 51**
See also CA 93-96

Muir, Edwin 1887-1959 . . . . **TCLC 2**
See also CA 104; DLB 20

Muir, John 1838-1914 . . . . **TCLC 28**

Mujica Lainez, Manuel 1910-1984 . . . . **CLC 31**
See also CA 81-84; obituary CA 112

Mukherjee, Bharati 1940- . . . . **CLC 53**
See also CA 107; DLB 60

Muldoon, Paul 1951- . . . . **CLC 32**
See also CA 113, 129; DLB 40

Mulisch, Harry (Kurt Victor) 1927- . . . . **CLC 42**
See also CANR 6, 26; CA 9-12R

Mull, Martin 1943- . . . . **CLC 17**
See also CA 105

Munford, Robert 1737?-1783 . . . . **LC 5**
See also DLB 31

Munro, Alice (Laidlaw) 1931- . . . . **CLC 6, 10, 19, 50; SSC 3**
See also CA 33-36R; SATA 29; DLB 53

Munro, H(ector) H(ugh) 1870-1916
See Saki
See also CA 104; DLB 34

Murasaki, Lady c. 11th century- . . . **CMLC 1**

Murdoch, (Jean) Iris 1919- . . . . . . **CLC 1, 2, 3, 4, 6, 8, 11, 15, 22, 31, 51**
See also CANR 8; CA 13-16R; DLB 14

Murphy, Richard 1927- . . . . **CLC 41**
See also CA 29-32R; DLB 40

Murphy, Sylvia 19??- . . . . **CLC 34**

Murphy, Thomas (Bernard) 1935- . . . **CLC 51**
See also CA 101

Author Index

Murray, Les(lie) A(llan) 1938- ..... **CLC 40**
See also CANR 11, 27; CA 21-24R

Murry, John Middleton 1889-1957 .... **TCLC 16**
See also CA 118

Musgrave, Susan 1951- .... **CLC 13, 54**
See also CA 69-72

Musil, Robert (Edler von) 1880-1942 .... **TCLC 12**
See also CA 109; DLB 81

Musset, (Louis Charles) Alfred de 1810-1857 .... **NCLC 7**

Myers, Walter Dean 1937- .... **CLC 35**
See also CLR 4, 16; CANR 20; CA 33-36R; SAAS 2; SATA 27, 41; DLB 33; AAYA 4

Nabokov, Vladimir (Vladimirovich) 1899-1977 .... **CLC 1, 2, 3, 6, 8, 11, 15, 23, 44, 46, 64**
See also CANR 20; CA 5-8R; obituary CA 69-72; DLB 2; DLB-Y 80; DLB-DS 3; CDALB 1941-1968

Nagy, Laszlo 1925-1978............ **CLC 7**
See also CA 129; obituary CA 112

Naipaul, Shiva(dhar Srinivasa) 1945-1985 .... **CLC 32, 39**
See also CA 110, 112; obituary CA 116; DLB-Y 85

Naipaul, V(idiadhar) S(urajprasad) 1932- .... **CLC 4, 7, 9, 13, 18, 37**
See also CANR 1; CA 1-4R; DLB-Y 85

Nakos, Ioulia 1899?-
See Nakos, Lilika

Nakos, Lilika 1899?- .... **CLC 29**

Nakou, Lilika 1899?-
See Nakos, Lilika

Narayan, R(asipuram) K(rishnaswami) 1906- .... **CLC 7, 28, 47**
See also CA 81-84

Nash, (Frediric) Ogden 1902-1971 .. **CLC 23**
See also CAP 1; CA 13-14; obituary CA 29-32R; SATA 2, 46; DLB 11

Nathan, George Jean 1882-1958 ... **TCLC 18**
See also CA 114

Natsume, Kinnosuke 1867-1916
See Natsume, Soseki
See also CA 104

Natsume, Soseki 1867-1916..... **TCLC 2, 10**
See also Natsume, Kinnosuke

Natti, (Mary) Lee 1919-
See Kingman, (Mary) Lee
See also CANR 2; CA 7-8R

Naylor, Gloria 1950- .... **CLC 28, 52**
See also CANR 27; CA 107

Neff, Debra 1972-................ **CLC 59**

Neihardt, John G(neisenau) 1881-1973 .... **CLC 32**
See also CAP 1; CA 13-14; DLB 9, 54

Nekrasov, Nikolai Alekseevich 1821-1878 .... **NCLC 11**

Nelligan, Emile 1879-1941........ **TCLC 14**
See also CA 114; DLB 92

Nelson, Willie 1933-.............. **CLC 17**
See also CA 107

Nemerov, Howard 1920- .... **CLC 2, 6, 9, 36**
See also CANR 1, 27; CA 1-4R; CABS 2; DLB 5, 6; DLB-Y 83

Neruda, Pablo 1904-1973 ..... **CLC 1, 2, 5, 7, 9, 28, 62**
See also CAP 2; CA 19-20; obituary CA 45-48

Nerval, Gerard de 1808-1855...... **NCLC 1**

Nervo, (Jose) Amado (Ruiz de) 1870-1919 .... **TCLC 11**
See also CA 109

Neufeld, John (Arthur) 1938- ...... **CLC 17**
See also CANR 11; CA 25-28R; SAAS 3; SATA 6

Neville, Emily Cheney 1919-....... **CLC 12**
See also CANR 3; CA 5-8R; SAAS 2; SATA 1

Newbound, Bernard Slade 1930-
See Slade, Bernard
See also CA 81-84

Newby, P(ercy) H(oward) 1918- .... **CLC 2, 13**
See also CA 5-8R; DLB 15

Newlove, Donald 1928- .... **CLC 6**
See also CANR 25; CA 29-32R

Newlove, John (Herbert) 1938-..... **CLC 14**
See also CANR 9, 25; CA 21-24R

Newman, Charles 1938-.......... **CLC 2, 8**
See also CA 21-24R

Newman, Edwin (Harold) 1919- .... **CLC 14**
See also CANR 5; CA 69-72

Newton, Suzanne 1936- .... **CLC 35**
See also CANR 14; CA 41-44R; SATA 5

Ngema, Mbongeni 1955- .... **CLC 57**

Ngugi, James (Thiong'o) 1938- .... **CLC 3, 7, 13, 36**
See also Ngugi wa Thiong'o; Wa Thiong'o, Ngugi
See also CANR 27; CA 81-84

Ngugi wa Thiong'o 1938-... **CLC 3, 7, 13, 36**
See also Ngugi, James (Thiong'o); Wa Thiong'o, Ngugi

Nichol, B(arrie) P(hillip) 1944-..... **CLC 18**
See also CA 53-56; DLB 53

Nichols, John (Treadwell) 1940-.... **CLC 38**
See also CAAS 2; CANR 6; CA 9-12R; DLB-Y 82

Nichols, Peter (Richard) 1927- .... **CLC 5, 36, 65**
See also CANR 33; CA 104; DLB 13

Nicolas, F.R.E. 1927-
See Freeling, Nicolas

Niedecker, Lorine 1903-1970.... **CLC 10, 42**
See also CAP 2; CA 25-28; DLB 48

Nietzsche, Friedrich (Wilhelm) 1844-1900 .... **TCLC 10, 18**
See also CA 107, 121

Nievo, Ippolito 1831-1861 .... **NCLC 22**

Nightingale, Anne Redmon 1943-
See Redmon (Nightingale), Anne
See also CA 103

Nin, Anais 1903-1977 ...... **CLC 1, 4, 8, 11, 14, 60**
See also CANR 22; CA 13-16R; obituary CA 69-72; DLB 2, 4

Nissenson, Hugh 1933-........... **CLC 4, 9**
See also CANR 27; CA 17-20R; DLB 28

Niven, Larry 1938-................ **CLC 8**
See also Niven, Laurence Van Cott
See also DLB 8

Niven, Laurence Van Cott 1938-
See Niven, Larry
See also CANR 14; CA 21-24R

Nixon, Agnes Eckhardt 1927-...... **CLC 21**
See also CA 110

Nizan, Paul 1905-1940........... **TCLC 40**
See also DLB 72

Nkosi, Lewis 1936-............... **CLC 45**
See also CANR 27; CA 65-68

Nodier, (Jean) Charles (Emmanuel) 1780-1844 .... **NCLC 19**

Nolan, Christopher 1965-.......... **CLC 58**
See also CA 111

Nordhoff, Charles 1887-1947...... **TCLC 23**
See also CA 108; SATA 23; DLB 9

Norman, Marsha 1947- .... **CLC 28**
See also CA 105; CABS 3; DLB-Y 84

Norris, (Benjamin) Frank(lin) 1870-1902 .... **TCLC 24**
See also CA 110; DLB 12, 71; CDALB 1865-1917

Norris, Leslie 1921- .... **CLC 14**
See also CANR 14; CAP 1; CA 11-12; DLB 27

North, Andrew 1912-
See Norton, Andre

North, Christopher 1785-1854
See Wilson, John

Norton, Alice Mary 1912-
See Norton, Andre
See also CANR 2; CA 1-4R; SATA 1, 43

Norton, Andre 1912- .... **CLC 12**
See also Norton, Mary Alice
See also DLB 8, 52

Norway, Nevil Shute 1899-1960
See Shute (Norway), Nevil
See also CA 102; obituary CA 93-96

Norwid, Cyprian Kamil 1821-1883 .... **NCLC 17**

Nossack, Hans Erich 1901-1978 ..... **CLC 6**
See also CA 93-96; obituary CA 85-88; DLB 69

Nova, Craig 1945-.............. **CLC 7, 31**
See also CANR 2; CA 45-48

Novak, Joseph 1933-
See Kosinski, Jerzy (Nikodem)

Novalis 1772-1801 .... **NCLC 13**

Nowlan, Alden (Albert) 1933-...... **CLC 15**
See also CANR 5; CA 9-12R; DLB 53

Noyes, Alfred 1880-1958 .... **TCLC 7**
See also CA 104; DLB 20

Nunn, Kem 19??-................. **CLC 34**

Nye, Robert 1939- .... **CLC 13, 42**
See also CANR 29; CA 33-36R; SATA 6; DLB 14

Nyro, Laura 1947- . . . . **CLC 17**

Oates, Joyce Carol
1938- . . . . . **CLC 1, 2, 3, 6, 9, 11, 15, 19, 33, 52; SSC 6**
See also CANR 25; CA 5-8R; DLB 2, 5; DLB-Y 81; CDALB 1968-1987

O'Brien, Darcy 1939- . . . . **CLC 11**
See also CANR 8; CA 21-24R

O'Brien, Edna
1936- . . . . **CLC 3, 5, 8, 13, 36, 65**
See also CANR 6; CA 1-4R; DLB 14

O'Brien, Fitz-James 1828?-1862 . . **NCLC 21**
See also DLB 74

O'Brien, Flann
1911-1966 . . . . **CLC 1, 4, 5, 7, 10, 47**
See also O Nuallain, Brian

O'Brien, Richard 19??- . . . . **CLC 17**
See also CA 124

O'Brien, (William) Tim(othy)
1946- . . . . **CLC 7, 19, 40**
See also CA 85-88; DLB-Y 80

Obstfelder, Sigbjorn 1866-1900 . . . . **TCLC 23**
See also CA 123

O'Casey, Sean
1880-1964 . . . . **CLC 1, 5, 9, 11, 15**
See also CA 89-92; DLB 10

Ochs, Phil 1940-1976 . . . . **CLC 17**
See also obituary CA 65-68

O'Connor, Edwin (Greene)
1918-1968 . . . . **CLC 14**
See also CA 93-96; obituary CA 25-28R

O'Connor, (Mary) Flannery
1925-1964 . . . **CLC 1, 2, 3, 6, 10, 13, 15, 21; SSC 1**
See also CANR 3; CA 1-4R; DLB 2; DLB-Y 80; CDALB 1941-1968

O'Connor, Frank
1903-1966 . . . . **CLC 14, 23; SSC 5**
See also O'Donovan, Michael (John)
See also CA 93-96

O'Dell, Scott 1903- . . . . **CLC 30**
See also CLR 1, 16; CANR 12; CA 61-64; SATA 12; DLB 52

Odets, Clifford 1906-1963 . . . . **CLC 2, 28**
See also CA 85-88; DLB 7, 26

O'Donovan, Michael (John)
1903-1966 . . . . **CLC 14**
See also O'Connor, Frank
See also CA 93-96

Oe, Kenzaburo 1935- . . . . **CLC 10, 36**
See also CA 97-100

O'Faolain, Julia 1932- . . . . **CLC 6, 19, 47**
See also CAAS 2; CANR 12; CA 81-84; DLB 14

O'Faolain, Sean 1900- . . . . . **CLC 1, 7, 14, 32**
See also CANR 12; CA 61-64; DLB 15

O'Flaherty, Liam
1896-1984 . . . . **CLC 5, 34; SSC 6**
See also CA 101; obituary CA 113; DLB 36; DLB-Y 84

O'Grady, Standish (James)
1846-1928 . . . . **TCLC 5**
See also CA 104

O'Grady, Timothy 1951- . . . . **CLC 59**

O'Hara, Frank 1926-1966 . . . . . **CLC 2, 5, 13**
See also CA 9-12R; obituary CA 25-28R; DLB 5, 16; CDALB 1929-1941

O'Hara, John (Henry)
1905-1970 . . . . **CLC 1, 2, 3, 6, 11, 42**
See also CA 5-8R; obituary CA 25-28R; DLB 9; DLB-DS 2; CDALB 1929-1941

O'Hara Family
See Banim, John and Banim, Michael

O'Hehir, Diana 1922- . . . . **CLC 41**
See also CA 93-96

Okigbo, Christopher (Ifenayichukwu)
1932-1967 . . . . **CLC 25**
See also CA 77-80

Olds, Sharon 1942- . . . . **CLC 32, 39**
See also CANR 18; CA 101

Olesha, Yuri (Karlovich)
1899-1960 . . . . **CLC 8**
See also CA 85-88

Oliphant, Margaret (Oliphant Wilson)
1828-1897 . . . . **NCLC 11**
See also DLB 18

Oliver, Mary 1935- . . . . **CLC 19, 34**
See also CANR 9; CA 21-24R; DLB 5

Olivier, (Baron) Laurence (Kerr)
1907- . . . . **CLC 20**
See also CA 111, 129

Olsen, Tillie 1913- . . . . **CLC 4, 13**
See also CANR 1; CA 1-4R; DLB 28; DLB-Y 80

Olson, Charles (John)
1910-1970 . . . . . **CLC 1, 2, 5, 6, 9, 11, 29**
See also CAP 1; CA 15-16; obituary CA 25-28R; CABS 2; DLB 5, 16

Olson, Theodore 1937-
See Olson, Toby

Olson, Toby 1937- . . . . **CLC 28**
See also CANR 9; CA 65-68

Ondaatje, (Philip) Michael
1943- . . . . **CLC 14, 29, 51**
See also CA 77-80; DLB 60

Oneal, Elizabeth 1934- . . . . **CLC 30**
See also Oneal, Zibby
See also CLR 13; CA 106; SATA 30

Oneal, Zibby 1934- . . . . **CLC 30**
See also Oneal, Elizabeth

O'Neill, Eugene (Gladstone)
1888-1953 . . . . **TCLC 1, 6, 27**
See also CA 110; DLB 7; CDALB 1929-1941

Onetti, Juan Carlos 1909- . . . . **CLC 7, 10**
See also CA 85-88

O'Nolan, Brian 1911-1966
See O'Brien, Flann

O Nuallain, Brian 1911-1966
See O'Brien, Flann
See also CAP 2; CA 21-22; obituary CA 25-28R

Oppen, George 1908-1984 . . . . **CLC 7, 13, 34**
See also CANR 8; CA 13-16R; obituary CA 113; DLB 5

Orlovitz, Gil 1918-1973 . . . . **CLC 22**
See also CA 77-80; obituary CA 45-48; DLB 2, 5

Ortega y Gasset, Jose 1883-1955 . . . **TCLC 9**
See also CA 106, 130

Ortiz, Simon J. 1941- . . . . **CLC 45**

Orton, Joe 1933?-1967 . . . . **CLC 4, 13, 43**
See also Orton, John Kingsley
See also DLB 13

Orton, John Kingsley 1933?-1967
See Orton, Joe
See also CA 85-88

Orwell, George
1903-1950 . . . . **TCLC 2, 6, 15, 31**
See also Blair, Eric Arthur
See also DLB 15

Osborne, John (James)
1929- . . . . **CLC 1, 2, 5, 11, 45**
See also CANR 21; CA 13-16R; DLB 13

Osborne, Lawrence 1958- . . . . **CLC 50**

Osceola 1885-1962
See Dinesen, Isak; Blixen, Karen (Christentze Dinesen)

Oshima, Nagisa 1932- . . . . **CLC 20**
See also CA 116

Oskison, John M. 1874-1947 . . . . . . **TCLC 35**

Ossoli, Sarah Margaret (Fuller marchesa d')
1810-1850
See Fuller, (Sarah) Margaret
See also SATA 25

Ostrovsky, Alexander
1823-1886 . . . . **NCLC 30**

Otero, Blas de 1916- . . . . **CLC 11**
See also CA 89-92

Ovid 43 B.C.-c. 18 A.D. . . . . **CMLC 7; PC 2**

Owen, Wilfred (Edward Salter)
1893-1918 . . . . **TCLC 5, 27**
See also CA 104; DLB 20

Owens, Rochelle 1936- . . . . **CLC 8**
See also CAAS 2; CA 17-20R

Owl, Sebastian 1939-
See Thompson, Hunter S(tockton)

Oz, Amos 1939- . . . **CLC 5, 8, 11, 27, 33, 54**
See also CANR 27; CA 53-56

Ozick, Cynthia 1928- . . . . . . **CLC 3, 7, 28, 62**
See also CANR 23; CA 17-20R; DLB 28; DLB-Y 82

Ozu, Yasujiro 1903-1963 . . . . **CLC 16**
See also CA 112

Pa Chin 1904- . . . . **CLC 18**
See also Li Fei-kan

Pack, Robert 1929- . . . . **CLC 13**
See also CANR 3; CA 1-4R; DLB 5

Padgett, Lewis 1915-1958
See Kuttner, Henry

Padilla, Heberto 1932- . . . . **CLC 38**
See also CA 123

Page, Jimmy 1944- . . . . **CLC 12**

Page, Louise 1955- . . . . **CLC 40**

Page, P(atricia) K(athleen)
1916- . . . . **CLC 7, 18**
See also CANR 4, 22; CA 53-56; DLB 68

Paget, Violet 1856-1935
See Lee, Vernon
See also CA 104

Palamas, Kostes 1859-1943 .... **TCLC 5**
See also CA 105

Palazzeschi, Aldo 1885-1974 .... **CLC 11**
See also CA 89-92; obituary CA 53-56

Paley, Grace 1922-.... **CLC 4, 6, 37; SSC 8**
See also CANR 13; CA 25-28R; DLB 28

Palin, Michael 1943- .... **CLC 21**
See also Monty Python
See also CA 107

Palliser, Charles 1948?- .... **CLC 65**

Palma, Ricardo 1833-1919 .... **TCLC 29**
See also CANR 123

Pancake, Breece Dexter 1952-1979
See Pancake, Breece D'J

Pancake, Breece D'J 1952-1979 .... **CLC 29**
See also obituary CA 109

Papadiamantis, Alexandros
1851-1911 .... **TCLC 29**

Papini, Giovanni 1881-1956....... **TCLC 22**
See also CA 121

Paracelsus 1493-1541 .... **LC 14**

Parini, Jay (Lee) 1948- .... **CLC 54**
See also CA 97-100

Parker, Dorothy (Rothschild)
1893-1967 .... **CLC 15; SSC 2**
See also CAP 2; CA 19-20;
obituary CA 25-28R; DLB 11, 45. 86

Parker, Robert B(rown) 1932-...... **CLC 27**
See also CANR 1, 26; CA 49-52

Parkin, Frank 1940-.............. **CLC 43**

Parkman, Francis 1823-1893..... **NCLC 12**
See also DLB 1, 30

Parks, Gordon (Alexander Buchanan)
1912- .... **CLC 1, 16**
See also CANR 26; CA 41-44R; SATA 8;
DLB 33

Parnell, Thomas 1679-1718 .... **LC 3**

Parra, Nicanor 1914- .... **CLC 2**
See also CA 85-88

Pasolini, Pier Paolo
1922-1975 .... **CLC 20, 37**
See also CA 93-96; obituary CA 61-64

Pastan, Linda (Olenik) 1932- ...... **CLC 27**
See also CANR 18; CA 61-64; DLB 5

Pasternak, Boris
1890-1960 .... **CLC 7, 10, 18, 63**
See also CA 127; obituary CA 116

Patchen, Kenneth 1911-1972 ... **CLC 1, 2, 18**
See also CANR 3; CA 1-4R;
obituary CA 33-36R; DLB 16, 48

Pater, Walter (Horatio)
1839-1894 .... **NCLC 7**
See also DLB 57

Paterson, Andrew Barton
1864-1941 .... **TCLC 32**

Paterson, Katherine (Womeldorf)
1932- .... **CLC 12, 30**
See also CLR 7; CANR 28; CA 21-24R;
SATA 13, 53; DLB 52; AAYA 1

Patmore, Coventry Kersey Dighton
1823-1896 .... **NCLC 9**
See also DLB 35

Paton, Alan (Stewart)
1903-1988 .... **CLC 4, 10, 25, 55**
See also CANR 22; CAP 1; CA 15-16;
obituary CA 125; SATA 11

Paulding, James Kirke 1778-1860.. **NCLC 2**
See also DLB 3, 59, 74

Paulin, Tom 1949- .... **CLC 37**
See also CA 123; DLB 40

Paustovsky, Konstantin (Georgievich)
1892-1968 .... **CLC 40**
See also CA 93-96; obituary CA 25-28R

Paustowsky, Konstantin (Georgievich)
1892-1968
See Paustovsky, Konstantin (Georgievich)

Pavese, Cesare 1908-1950 .... **TCLC 3**
See also CA 104

Pavic, Milorad 1929- .... **CLC 60**

Payne, Alan 1932-
See Jakes, John (William)

Paz, Octavio
1914- ...... **CLC 3, 4, 6, 10, 19, 51, 65; PC 1**
See also CANR 32; CA 73-76

Peacock, Molly 1947-............. **CLC 60**
See also CA 103

Peacock, Thomas Love
1785-1886 .... **NCLC 22**

Peake, Mervyn 1911-1968 .... **CLC 7, 54**
See also CANR 3; CA 5-8R;
obituary CA 25-28R; SATA 23; DLB 15

Pearce, (Ann) Philippa 1920-....... **CLC 21**
See also Christie, (Ann) Philippa
See also CLR 9; CA 5-8R; SATA 1

Pearl, Eric 1934-
See Elman, Richard

Pearson, T(homas) R(eid) 1956- .... **CLC 39**
See also CA 120, 130

Peck, John 1941- .... **CLC 3**
See also CANR 3; CA 49-52

Peck, Richard 1934-.............. **CLC 21**
See also CLR 15; CANR 19; CA 85-88;
SAAS 2; SATA 18; AAYA 1

Peck, Robert Newton 1928-........ **CLC 17**
See also CA 81-84; SAAS 1; SATA 21;
AAYA 3

Peckinpah, (David) Sam(uel)
1925-1984 .... **CLC 20**
See also CA 109; obituary CA 114

Pedersen, Knut 1859-1952
See Hamsun, Knut
See also CA 104, 109, 119

Peguy, Charles (Pierre)
1873-1914 .... **TCLC 10**
See also CA 107

Pepys, Samuel 1633-1703.......... **LC 11**

Percy, Walker
1916-1990 ... **CLC 2, 3, 6, 8, 14, 18, 47, 65**
See also CANR 1, 23; CA 1-4R;
obituary CA 131; DLB 2; DLB-Y 80

Perec, Georges 1936-1982 .... **CLC 56**
See also DLB 83

Pereda, Jose Maria de
1833-1906 .... **TCLC 16**

Perelman, S(idney) J(oseph)
1904-1979 ... **CLC 3, 5, 9, 15, 23, 44, 49**
See also CANR 18; CA 73-76;
obituary CA 89-92; DLB 11, 44

Peret, Benjamin 1899-1959 .... **TCLC 20**
See also CA 117

Peretz, Isaac Leib 1852?-1915..... **TCLC 16**
See also CA 109

Perez, Galdos Benito 1853-1920... **TCLC 27**
See also CA 125

Perrault, Charles 1628-1703 .... **LC 2**
See also SATA 25

Perse, St.-John 1887-1975.... **CLC 4, 11, 46**
See also Leger, (Marie-Rene) Alexis
Saint-Leger

Pesetsky, Bette 1932-............. **CLC 28**

Peshkov, Alexei Maximovich 1868-1936
See Gorky, Maxim
See also CA 105

Pessoa, Fernando (Antonio Nogueira)
1888-1935 .... **TCLC 27**
See also CA 125

Peterkin, Julia (Mood) 1880-1961... **CLC 31**
See also CA 102; DLB 9

Peters, Joan K. 1945-............. **CLC 39**

Peters, Robert L(ouis) 1924-........ **CLC 7**
See also CAAS 8; CA 13-16R

Petofi, Sandor 1823-1849........ **NCLC 21**

Petrakis, Harry Mark 1923-........ **CLC 3**
See also CANR 4, 30; CA 9-12R

Petrov, Evgeny 1902-1942 .... **TCLC 21**

Petry, Ann (Lane) 1908- ...... **CLC 1, 7, 18**
See also CLR 12; CAAS 6; CANR 4;
CA 5-8R; SATA 5; DLB 76

Petursson, Halligrimur 1614-1674 .... **LC 8**

Philipson, Morris (H.) 1926-....... **CLC 53**
See also CANR 4; CA 1-4R

Phillips, Jayne Anne 1952- ..... **CLC 15, 33**
See also CANR 24; CA 101; DLB-Y 80

Phillips, Robert (Schaeffer) 1938-... **CLC 28**
See also CANR 8; CA 17-20R

Pica, Peter 1925-
See Aldiss, Brian W(ilson)

Piccolo, Lucio 1901-1969.......... **CLC 13**
See also CA 97-100

Pickthall, Marjorie (Lowry Christie)
1883-1922 .... **TCLC 21**
See also CA 107; DLB 92

Pico della Mirandola, Giovanni
1463-1494 .... **LC 15**

Piercy, Marge
1936- .... **CLC 3, 6, 14, 18, 27, 62**
See also CAAS 1; CANR 13; CA 21-24R

Pilnyak, Boris 1894-1937?........ **TCLC 23**

Pincherle, Alberto 1907- .... **CLC 11, 18**
See also Moravia, Alberto
See also CA 25-28R

Pineda, Cecile 1942-.............. **CLC 39**
See also CA 118

Pinero, Miguel (Gomez)
1946-1988 .... **CLC 4, 55**
See also CANR 29; CA 61-64;
obituary CA 125

Pinero, Sir Arthur Wing 1855-1934 .... **TCLC 32**
See also CA 110; DLB 10

Pinget, Robert 1919- .... **CLC 7, 13, 37**
See also CA 85-88; DLB 83

Pink Floyd .... **CLC 35**

Pinkney, Edward 1802-1828 ..... **NCLC 31**

Pinkwater, D(aniel) M(anus) 1941- .... **CLC 35**
See also Pinkwater, Manus
See also CLR 4; CANR 12; CA 29-32R; SAAS 3; SATA 46; AAYA 1

Pinkwater, Manus 1941-
See Pinkwater, D(aniel) M(anus)
See also SATA 8

Pinsky, Robert 1940- .... **CLC 9, 19, 38**
See also CAAS 4; CA 29-32R; DLB-Y 82

Pinter, Harold 1930- ..... **CLC 1, 3, 6, 9, 11, 15, 27, 58**
See also CA 5-8R; DLB 13

Pirandello, Luigi 1867-1936..... **TCLC 4, 29**
See also CA 104

Pirsig, Robert M(aynard) 1928- ... **CLC 4, 6**
See also CA 53-56; SATA 39

Pisarev, Dmitry Ivanovich 1840-1868 .... **NCLC 25**

Pix, Mary (Griffith) 1666-1709....... **LC 8**
See also DLB 80

Plaidy, Jean 1906-
See Hibbert, Eleanor (Burford)

Plant, Robert 1948- .... **CLC 12**

Plante, David (Robert) 1940- .... **CLC 7, 23, 38**
See also CANR 12; CA 37-40R; DLB-Y 83

Plath, Sylvia 1932-1963 .... **CLC 1, 2, 3, 5, 9, 11, 14, 17, 50, 51, 62; PC 1**
See also CAP 2; CA 19-20; DLB 5, 6; CDALB 1941-1968

Platonov, Andrei (Platonovich) 1899-1951 .... **TCLC 14**
See also Klimentov, Andrei Platonovich
See also CA 108

Platt, Kin 1911- .... **CLC 26**
See also CANR 11; CA 17-20R; SATA 21

Plimpton, George (Ames) 1927-..... **CLC 36**
See also CA 21-24R; SATA 10

Plomer, William (Charles Franklin) 1903-1973 .... **CLC 4, 8**
See also CAP 2; CA 21-22; SATA 24; DLB 20

Plumly, Stanley (Ross) 1939- ...... **CLC 33**
See also CA 108, 110; DLB 5

Poe, Edgar Allan 1809-1849 ... **NCLC 1, 16; PC 1; SSC 1**
See also SATA 23; DLB 3, 59, 73, 74; CDALB 1640-1865

Pohl, Frederik 1919- .... **CLC 18**
See also CAAS 1; CANR 11; CA 61-64; SATA 24; DLB 8

Poirier, Louis 1910-
See Gracq, Julien
See also CA 122, 126

Poitier, Sidney 1924?- .... **CLC 26**
See also CA 117

Polanski, Roman 1933- .... **CLC 16**
See also CA 77-80

Poliakoff, Stephen 1952- .... **CLC 38**
See also CA 106; DLB 13

Police, The .... **CLC 26**

Pollitt, Katha 1949- .... **CLC 28**
See also CA 120, 122

Pollock, Sharon 19??-............. **CLC 50**
See also DLB 60

Pomerance, Bernard 1940-......... **CLC 13**
See also CA 101

Ponge, Francis (Jean Gaston Alfred) 1899- .... **CLC 6, 18**
See also CA 85-88; obituary CA 126

Pontoppidan, Henrik 1857-1943 ... **TCLC 29**
See also obituary CA 126

Poole, Josephine 1933-............ **CLC 17**
See also CANR 10; CA 21-24R; SAAS 2; SATA 5

Popa, Vasko 1922- .... **CLC 19**
See also CA 112

Pope, Alexander 1688-1744.......... **LC 3**

Porter, Gene Stratton 1863-1924 .. **TCLC 21**
See also CA 112

Porter, Katherine Anne 1890-1980 ..... **CLC 1, 3, 7, 10, 13, 15, 27; SSC 4**
See also CANR 1; CA 1-4R; obituary CA 101; obituary SATA 23, 39; DLB 4, 9; DLB-Y 80

Porter, Peter (Neville Frederick) 1929- .... **CLC 5, 13, 33**
See also CA 85-88; DLB 40

Porter, William Sydney 1862-1910
See Henry, O.
See also YABC 2; CA 104; DLB 12, 78, 79; CDALB 1865-1917

Post, Melville D. 1871-1930 ...... **TCLC 39**
See also brief entry CA 110

Potok, Chaim 1929- .... **CLC 2, 7, 14, 26**
See also CANR 19; CA 17-20R; SATA 33; DLB 28

Potter, Dennis (Christopher George) 1935- .... **CLC 58**
See also CA 107

Pound, Ezra (Loomis) 1885-1972 ..... **CLC 1, 2, 3, 4, 5, 7, 10, 13, 18, 34, 48, 50**
See also CA 5-8R; obituary CA 37-40R; DLB 4, 45, 63; CDALB 1917-1929

Povod, Reinaldo 1959-............ **CLC 44**

Powell, Anthony (Dymoke) 1905- .... **CLC 1, 3, 7, 9, 10, 31**
See also CANR 1; CA 1-4R; DLB 15

Powell, Padgett 1952-............. **CLC 34**
See also CA 126

Powers, J(ames) F(arl) 1917- .... **CLC 1, 4, 8, 57; SSC 4**
See also CANR 2; CA 1-4R

Pownall, David 1938-............. **CLC 10**
See also CA 89-92; DLB 14

Powys, John Cowper 1872-1963 .... **CLC 7, 9, 15, 46**
See also CA 85-88; DLB 15

Powys, T(heodore) F(rancis) 1875-1953 .... **TCLC 9**
See also CA 106; DLB 36

Prager, Emily 1952-.............. **CLC 56**

Pratt, E(dwin) J(ohn) 1883-1964.... **CLC 19**
See also obituary CA 93-96; DLB 92

Premchand 1880-1936 .... **TCLC 21**

Preussler, Otfried 1923-........... **CLC 17**
See also CA 77-80; SATA 24

Prevert, Jacques (Henri Marie) 1900-1977 .... **CLC 15**
See also CANR 29; CA 77-80; obituary CA 69-72; obituary SATA 30

Prevost, Abbe (Antoine Francois) 1697-1763 .... **LC 1**

Price, (Edward) Reynolds 1933- .... **CLC 3, 6, 13, 43, 50, 63**
See also CANR 1; CA 1-4R; DLB 2

Price, Richard 1949- .... **CLC 6, 12**
See also CANR 3; CA 49-52; DLB-Y 81

Prichard, Katharine Susannah 1883-1969 .... **CLC 46**
See also CAP 1; CA 11-12

Priestley, J(ohn) B(oynton) 1894-1984 .... **CLC 2, 5, 9, 34**
See also CA 9-12R; obituary CA 113; DLB 10, 34, 77; DLB-Y 84

Prince (Rogers Nelson) 1958?- ..... **CLC 35**

Prince, F(rank) T(empleton) 1912- .. **CLC 22**
See also CA 101; DLB 20

Prior, Matthew 1664-1721........... **LC 4**

Pritchard, William H(arrison) 1932- .... **CLC 34**
See also CANR 23; CA 65-68

Pritchett, V(ictor) S(awdon) 1900- .... **CLC 5, 13, 15, 41**
See also CA 61-64; DLB 15

Probst, Mark 1925- .... **CLC 59**
See also CA 130

Procaccino, Michael 1946-
See Cristofer, Michael

Prokosch, Frederic 1908-1989.... **CLC 4, 48**
See also CA 73-76; obituary CA 128; DLB 48

Prose, Francine 1947-............. **CLC 45**
See also CA 109, 112

Proust, Marcel 1871-1922.. **TCLC 7, 13, 33**
See also CA 104, 120; DLB 65

Pryor, Richard 1940- .... **CLC 26**
See also CA 122

Przybyszewski, Stanislaw 1868-1927 .... **TCLC 36**
See also DLB 66

Puig, Manuel 1932-1990 .... **CLC 3, 5, 10, 28, 65**
See also CANR 2, 32; CA 45-48

Purdy, A(lfred) W(ellington) 1918- .... **CLC 3, 6, 14, 50**
See also CA 81-84

Author Index

Purdy, James (Amos) 1923- .... **CLC 2, 4, 10, 28, 52**
See also CAAS 1; CANR 19; CA 33-36R; DLB 2

Pushkin, Alexander (Sergeyevich) 1799-1837 .... **NCLC 3, 27**

P'u Sung-ling 1640-1715 .... **LC 3**

Puzo, Mario 1920- .... **CLC 1, 2, 6, 36**
See also CANR 4; CA 65-68; DLB 6

Pym, Barbara (Mary Crampton) 1913-1980 .... **CLC 13, 19, 37**
See also CANR 13; CAP 1; CA 13-14; obituary CA 97-100; DLB 14; DLB-Y 87

Pynchon, Thomas (Ruggles, Jr.) 1937- ..... **CLC 2, 3, 6, 9, 11, 18, 33, 62**
See also CANR 22; CA 17-20R; DLB 2

Quarrington, Paul 1954?- .... **CLC 65**
See also CA 129

Quasimodo, Salvatore 1901-1968 ... **CLC 10**
See also CAP 1; CA 15-16; obituary CA 25-28R

Queen, Ellery 1905-1982 .... **CLC 3, 11**
See also Dannay, Frederic; Lee, Manfred B(ennington)

Queneau, Raymond 1903-1976 .... **CLC 2, 5, 10, 42**
See also CA 77-80; obituary CA 69-72; DLB 72

Quin, Ann (Marie) 1936-1973 .... **CLC 6**
See also CA 9-12R; obituary CA 45-48; DLB 14

Quinn, Simon 1942-
See Smith, Martin Cruz
See also CANR 6, 23; CA 85-88

Quiroga, Horacio (Sylvestre) 1878-1937 .... **TCLC 20**
See also CA 117

Quoirez, Francoise 1935-
See Sagan, Francoise
See also CANR 6; CA 49-52

Rabe, David (William) 1940- ... **CLC 4, 8, 33**
See also CA 85-88; CABS 3; DLB 7

Rabelais, Francois 1494?-1553 .... **LC 5**

Rabinovitch, Sholem 1859-1916
See Aleichem, Sholom
See also CA 104

Rachen, Kurt von 1911-1986
See Hubbard, L(afayette) Ron(ald)

Radcliffe, Ann (Ward) 1764-1823 .. **NCLC 6**
See also DLB 39

Radiguet, Raymond 1903-1923 .... **TCLC 29**
See also DLB 65

Radnoti, Miklos 1909-1944 .... **TCLC 16**
See also CA 118

Rado, James 1939- .... **CLC 17**
See also CA 105

Radomski, James 1932-
See Rado, James

Radvanyi, Netty Reiling 1900-1983
See Seghers, Anna
See also CA 85-88; obituary CA 110

Rae, Ben 1935-
See Griffiths, Trevor

Raeburn, John 1941- .... **CLC 34**
See also CA 57-60

Ragni, Gerome 1942- .... **CLC 17**
See also CA 105

Rahv, Philip 1908-1973 .... **CLC 24**
See also Greenberg, Ivan

Raine, Craig 1944- .... **CLC 32**
See also CANR 29; CA 108; DLB 40

Raine, Kathleen (Jessie) 1908- ... **CLC 7, 45**
See also CA 85-88; DLB 20

Rainis, Janis 1865-1929 .... **TCLC 29**

Rakosi, Carl 1903- .... **CLC 47**
See also Rawley, Callman
See also CAAS 5

Ramos, Graciliano 1892-1953 ..... **TCLC 32**

Rampersad, Arnold 19??- .... **CLC 44**

Ramuz, Charles-Ferdinand 1878-1947 .... **TCLC 33**

Rand, Ayn 1905-1982 .... **CLC 3, 30, 44**
See also CANR 27; CA 13-16R; obituary CA 105

Randall, Dudley (Felker) 1914- ...... **CLC 1**
See also CANR 23; CA 25-28R; DLB 41

Ransom, John Crowe 1888-1974 .... **CLC 2, 4, 5, 11, 24**
See also CANR 6; CA 5-8R; obituary CA 49-52; DLB 45, 63

Rao, Raja 1909- .... **CLC 25, 56**
See also CA 73-76

Raphael, Frederic (Michael) 1931- .... **CLC 2, 14**
See also CANR 1; CA 1-4R; DLB 14

Rathbone, Julian 1935- .... **CLC 41**
See also CA 101

Rattigan, Terence (Mervyn) 1911-1977 .... **CLC 7**
See also CA 85-88; obituary CA 73-76; DLB 13

Ratushinskaya, Irina 1954- .... **CLC 54**
See also CA 129

Raven, Simon (Arthur Noel) 1927- .... **CLC 14**
See also CA 81-84

Rawley, Callman 1903-
See Rakosi, Carl
See also CANR 12; CA 21-24R

Rawlings, Marjorie Kinnan 1896-1953 .... **TCLC 4**
See also YABC 1; CA 104; DLB 9, 22

Ray, Satyajit 1921- .... **CLC 16**
See also CA 114

Read, Herbert (Edward) 1893-1968 .. **CLC 4**
See also CA 85-88; obituary CA 25-28R; DLB 20

Read, Piers Paul 1941- ...... **CLC 4, 10, 25**
See also CA 21-24R; SATA 21; DLB 14

Reade, Charles 1814-1884 .... **NCLC 2**
See also DLB 21

Reade, Hamish 1936-
See Gray, Simon (James Holliday)

Reading, Peter 1946- .... **CLC 47**
See also CA 103; DLB 40

Reaney, James 1926- .... **CLC 13**
See also CA 41-44R; SATA 43; DLB 68

Rebreanu, Liviu 1885-1944 .... **TCLC 28**

Rechy, John (Francisco) 1934- .... **CLC 1, 7, 14, 18**
See also CAAS 4; CANR 6; CA 5-8R; DLB-Y 82

Redcam, Tom 1870-1933 .... **TCLC 25**

Redgrove, Peter (William) 1932- .... **CLC 6, 41**
See also CANR 3; CA 1-4R; DLB 40

Redmon (Nightingale), Anne 1943- .... **CLC 22**
See also Nightingale, Anne Redmon
See also DLB-Y 86

Reed, Ishmael 1938- .... **CLC 2, 3, 5, 6, 13, 32, 60**
See also CANR 25; CA 21-24R; DLB 2, 5, 33

Reed, John (Silas) 1887-1920 ...... **TCLC 9**
See also CA 106

Reed, Lou 1944- .... **CLC 21**

Reeve, Clara 1729-1807 .... **NCLC 19**
See also DLB 39

Reid, Christopher 1949- .... **CLC 33**
See also DLB 40

Reid Banks, Lynne 1929-
See Banks, Lynne Reid
See also CANR 6, 22; CA 1-4R; SATA 22

Reiner, Max 1900-
See Caldwell, (Janet Miriam) Taylor (Holland)

Reizenstein, Elmer Leopold 1892-1967
See Rice, Elmer

Remark, Erich Paul 1898-1970
See Remarque, Erich Maria

Remarque, Erich Maria 1898-1970 .... **CLC 21**
See also CA 77-80; obituary CA 29-32R; DLB 56

Remizov, Alexey (Mikhailovich) 1877-1957 .... **TCLC 27**
See also CA 125

Renan, Joseph Ernest 1823-1892 .... **NCLC 26**

Renard, Jules 1864-1910 .... **TCLC 17**
See also CA 117

Renault, Mary 1905-1983 .... **CLC 3, 11, 17**
See also Challans, Mary
See also DLB-Y 83

Rendell, Ruth 1930- .... **CLC 28, 48**
See also Vine, Barbara
See also CA 109; DLB 87

Renoir, Jean 1894-1979 .... **CLC 20**
See also CA 129; obituary CA 85-88

Resnais, Alain 1922- .... **CLC 16**

Reverdy, Pierre 1899-1960 .... **CLC 53**
See also CA 97-100; obituary CA 89-92

Rexroth, Kenneth 1905-1982 ...... **CLC 1, 2, 6, 11, 22, 49**
See also CANR 14; CA 5-8R; obituary CA 107; DLB 16, 48; DLB-Y 82; CDALB 1941-1968

Reyes, Alfonso 1889-1959 .... **TCLC 33**

Reyes y Basoalto, Ricardo Eliecer Neftali 1904-1973
See Neruda, Pablo

Reymont, Wladyslaw Stanislaw 1867-1925 .... **TCLC 5**
See also CA 104

Reynolds, Jonathan 1942?- ...... **CLC 6, 38**
See also CANR 28; CA 65-68

Reynolds, (Sir) Joshua 1723-1792.... **LC 15**

Reynolds, Michael (Shane) 1937- ... **CLC 44**
See also CANR 9; CA 65-68

Reznikoff, Charles 1894-1976 .... **CLC 9**
See also CAP 2; CA 33-36; obituary CA 61-64; DLB 28, 45

Rezzori, Gregor von 1914-......... **CLC 25**
See also CA 122

Rhys, Jean 1890-1979 ...... **CLC 2, 4, 6, 14, 19, 51**
See also CA 25-28R; obituary CA 85-88; DLB 36

Ribeiro, Darcy 1922- .... **CLC 34**
See also CA 33-36R

Ribeiro, Joao Ubaldo (Osorio Pimentel) 1941- .... **CLC 10**
See also CA 81-84

Ribman, Ronald (Burt) 1932- .... **CLC 7**
See also CA 21-24R

Rice, Anne 1941- .... **CLC 41**
See also CANR 12; CA 65-68

Rice, Elmer 1892-1967.......... **CLC 7, 49**
See also CAP 2; CA 21-22; obituary CA 25-28R; DLB 4, 7

Rice, Tim 1944- .... **CLC 21**
See also CA 103

Rich, Adrienne (Cecile) 1929- .... **CLC 3, 6, 7, 11, 18, 36**
See also CANR 20; CA 9-12R; DLB 5, 67

Richard, Keith 1943- .... **CLC 17**
See also CA 107

Richards, David Adam 1950-....... **CLC 59**
See also CA 93-96; DLB 53

Richards, I(vor) A(rmstrong) 1893-1979 .... **CLC 14, 24**
See also CA 41-44R; obituary CA 89-92; DLB 27

Richards, Keith 1943-
See Richard, Keith
See also CA 107

Richardson, Dorothy (Miller) 1873-1957 .... **TCLC 3**
See also CA 104; DLB 36

Richardson, Ethel 1870-1946
See Richardson, Henry Handel
See also CA 105

Richardson, Henry Handel 1870-1946 .... **TCLC 4**
See also Richardson, Ethel

Richardson, Samuel 1689-1761 .... **LC 1**
See also DLB 39

Richler, Mordecai 1931- .... **CLC 3, 5, 9, 13, 18, 46**
See also CLR 17; CA 65-68; SATA 27, 44; DLB 53

Richter, Conrad (Michael) 1890-1968 .... **CLC 30**
See also CANR 23; CA 5-8R; obituary CA 25-28R; SATA 3; DLB 9

Richter, Johann Paul Friedrich 1763-1825
See Jean Paul

Riddell, Mrs. J. H. 1832-1906..... **TCLC 40**

Riding, Laura 1901- .... **CLC 3, 7**
See also Jackson, Laura (Riding)

Riefenstahl, Berta Helene Amalia 1902- .... **CLC 16**
See also Riefenstahl, Leni
See also CA 108

Riefenstahl, Leni 1902- .... **CLC 16**
See also Riefenstahl, Berta Helene Amalia
See also CA 108

Rilke, Rainer Maria 1875-1926 .... **TCLC 1, 6, 19; PC 2**
See also CA 104, 132; DLB 81

Rimbaud, (Jean Nicolas) Arthur 1854-1891 .... **NCLC 4**

Ringwood, Gwen(dolyn Margaret) Pharis 1910-1984 .... **CLC 48**
See also obituary CA 112

Rio, Michel 19??- .... **CLC 43**

Ritsos, Yannis 1909-......... **CLC 6, 13, 31**
See also CA 77-80

Ritter, Erika 1948?- .... **CLC 52**

Rivera, Jose Eustasio 1889-1928... **TCLC 35**

Rivers, Conrad Kent 1933-1968...... **CLC 1**
See also CA 85-88; DLB 41

Rizal, Jose 1861-1896........... **NCLC 27**

Roa Bastos, Augusto 1917- .... **CLC 45**

Robbe-Grillet, Alain 1922- ...... **CLC 1, 2, 4, 6, 8, 10, 14, 43**
See also CA 9-12R; DLB 83

Robbins, Harold 1916-............. **CLC 5**
See also CANR 26; CA 73-76

Robbins, Thomas Eugene 1936-
See Robbins, Tom
See also CA 81-84

Robbins, Tom 1936- .... **CLC 9, 32, 64**
See also Robbins, Thomas Eugene
See also CANR 29; CA 81-84; DLB-Y 80

Robbins, Trina 1938- .... **CLC 21**

Roberts, (Sir) Charles G(eorge) D(ouglas) 1860-1943 .... **TCLC 8**
See also CA 105; SATA 29; DLB 92

Roberts, Kate 1891-1985 .... **CLC 15**
See also CA 107; obituary CA 116

Roberts, Keith (John Kingston) 1935- .... **CLC 14**
See also CA 25-28R

Roberts, Kenneth 1885-1957 ...... **TCLC 23**
See also CA 109; DLB 9

Roberts, Michele (B.) 1949-........ **CLC 48**
See also CA 115

Robinson, Edwin Arlington 1869-1935 .... **TCLC 5; PC 1**
See also CA 104; DLB 54; CDALB 1865-1917

Robinson, Henry Crabb 1775-1867 .... **NCLC 15**

Robinson, Jill 1936-.............. **CLC 10**
See also CA 102

Robinson, Kim Stanley 19??-....... **CLC 34**
See also CA 126

Robinson, Marilynne 1944- .... **CLC 25**
See also CA 116

Robinson, Smokey 1940- .... **CLC 21**

Robinson, William 1940-
See Robinson, Smokey
See also CA 116

Robison, Mary 1949- .... **CLC 42**
See also CA 113, 116

Roddenberry, Gene 1921-.......... **CLC 17**
See also CANR 110; SATA 45

Rodgers, Mary 1931- .... **CLC 12**
See also CLR 20; CANR 8; CA 49-52; SATA 8

Rodgers, W(illiam) R(obert) 1909-1969 .... **CLC 7**
See also CA 85-88; DLB 20

Rodman, Howard 19??- .... **CLC 65**

Rodriguez, Claudio 1934-.......... **CLC 10**

Roethke, Theodore (Huebner) 1908-1963 ...... **CLC 1, 3, 8, 11, 19, 46**
See also CA 81-84; CABS 2; SAAS 1; DLB 5; CDALB 1941-1968

Rogers, Sam 1943-
See Shepard, Sam

Rogers, Thomas (Hunton) 1931- .... **CLC 57**
See also CA 89-92

Rogers, Will(iam Penn Adair) 1879-1935 .... **TCLC 8**
See also CA 105; DLB 11

Rogin, Gilbert 1929-.............. **CLC 18**
See also CANR 15; CA 65-68

Rohan, Koda 1867-1947.......... **TCLC 22**
See also CA 121

Rohmer, Eric 1920- .... **CLC 16**
See also Scherer, Jean-Marie Maurice

Rohmer, Sax 1883-1959.......... **TCLC 28**
See also Ward, Arthur Henry Sarsfield
See also CA 108; DLB 70

Roiphe, Anne (Richardson) 1935- .... **CLC 3, 9**
See also CA 89-92; DLB-Y 80

Rolfe, Frederick (William Serafino Austin Lewis Mary) 1860-1913...... **TCLC 12**
See also CA 107; DLB 34

Rolland, Romain 1866-1944....... **TCLC 23**
See also CA 118; DLB 65

Rolvaag, O(le) E(dvart) 1876-1931 .... **TCLC 17**
See also CA 117; DLB 9

Romains, Jules 1885-1972 .... **CLC 7**
See also CA 85-88

Romero, Jose Ruben 1890-1952 ... **TCLC 14**
See also CA 114

Ronsard, Pierre de 1524-1585........ **LC 6**

Rooke, Leon 1934- .... **CLC 25, 34**
See also CANR 23; CA 25-28R

Roper, William 1498-1578.......... **LC 10**

Rosa, Joao Guimaraes 1908-1967... **CLC 23**
See also obituary CA 89-92

Author Index

Rosen, Richard (Dean) 1949- . . . . **CLC 39**
See also CA 77-80

Rosenberg, Isaac 1890-1918 . . . . . . **TCLC 12**
See also CA 107; DLB 20

Rosenblatt, Joe 1933- . . . . **CLC 15**
See also Rosenblatt, Joseph

Rosenblatt, Joseph 1933-
See Rosenblatt, Joe
See also CA 89-92

Rosenfeld, Samuel 1896-1963
See Tzara, Tristan
See also obituary CA 89-92

Rosenthal, M(acha) L(ouis) 1917- . . . **CLC 28**
See also CAAS 6; CANR 4; CA 1-4R; SATA 59; DLB 5

Ross, (James) Sinclair 1908- . . . . **CLC 13**
See also CA 73-76; DLB 88

Rossetti, Christina Georgina 1830-1894 . . . . **NCLC 2**
See also SATA 20; DLB 35

Rossetti, Dante Gabriel 1828-1882 . . . . **NCLC 4**
See also DLB 35

Rossetti, Gabriel Charles Dante 1828-1882
See Rossetti, Dante Gabriel

Rossner, Judith (Perelman) 1935- . . . . **CLC 6, 9, 29**
See also CANR 18; CA 17-20R; DLB 6

Rostand, Edmond (Eugene Alexis) 1868-1918 . . . . **TCLC 6, 37**
See also CA 104, 126

Roth, Henry 1906- . . . . **CLC 2, 6, 11**
See also CAP 1; CA 11-12; DLB 28

Roth, Joseph 1894-1939 . . . . **TCLC 33**
See also DLB 85

Roth, Philip (Milton) 1933- . . . . . . **CLC 1, 2, 3, 4, 6, 9, 15, 22, 31, 47**
See also CANR 1, 22; CA 1-4R; DLB 2, 28; DLB-Y 82

Rothenberg, James 1931- . . . . **CLC 57**

Rothenberg, Jerome 1931- . . . . **CLC 6, 57**
See also CANR 1; CA 45-48; DLB 5

Roumain, Jacques 1907-1944 . . . . . . **TCLC 19**
See also CA 117

Rourke, Constance (Mayfield) 1885-1941 . . . . **TCLC 12**
See also YABC 1; CA 107

Rousseau, Jean-Baptiste 1671-1741 . . . **LC 9**

Rousseau, Jean-Jacques 1712-1778 . . . **LC 14**

Roussel, Raymond 1877-1933 . . . . . **TCLC 20**
See also CA 117

Rovit, Earl (Herbert) 1927- . . . . **CLC 7**
See also CANR 12; CA 5-8R

Rowe, Nicholas 1674-1718 . . . . **LC 8**

Rowson, Susanna Haswell 1762-1824 . . . . **NCLC 5**
See also DLB 37

Roy, Gabrielle 1909-1983 . . . . **CLC 10, 14**
See also CANR 5; CA 53-56; obituary CA 110; DLB 68

Rozewicz, Tadeusz 1921- . . . . **CLC 9, 23**
See also CA 108

Ruark, Gibbons 1941- . . . . **CLC 3**
See also CANR 14; CA 33-36R

Rubens, Bernice 192?- . . . . **CLC 19, 31**
See also CA 25-28R; DLB 14

Rudkin, (James) David 1936- . . . . . . **CLC 14**
See also CA 89-92; DLB 13

Rudnik, Raphael 1933- . . . . **CLC 7**
See also CA 29-32R

Ruiz, Jose Martinez 1874-1967
See Azorin

Rukeyser, Muriel 1913-1980 . . . . **CLC 6, 10, 15, 27**
See also CANR 26; CA 5-8R; obituary CA 93-96; obituary SATA 22; DLB 48

Rule, Jane (Vance) 1931- . . . . **CLC 27**
See also CANR 12; CA 25-28R; DLB 60

Rulfo, Juan 1918-1986 . . . . **CLC 8**
See also CANR 26; CA 85-88; obituary CA 118

Runyon, (Alfred) Damon 1880-1946 . . . . **TCLC 10**
See also CA 107; DLB 11

Rush, Norman 1933- . . . . **CLC 44**
See also CA 121, 126

Rushdie, (Ahmed) Salman 1947- . . . . **CLC 23, 31, 55, 59**
See also CA 108, 111

Rushforth, Peter (Scott) 1945- . . . . . **CLC 19**
See also CA 101

Ruskin, John 1819-1900 . . . . **TCLC 20**
See also CA 114; SATA 24; DLB 55

Russ, Joanna 1937- . . . . **CLC 15**
See also CANR 11; CA 25-28R; DLB 8

Russell, George William 1867-1935
See A. E.
See also CA 104

Russell, (Henry) Ken(neth Alfred) 1927- . . . . **CLC 16**
See also CA 105

Russell, Mary Annette Beauchamp 1866-1941
See Elizabeth

Russell, Willy 1947- . . . . **CLC 60**

Rutherford, Mark 1831-1913 . . . . . . **TCLC 25**
See also CA 121; DLB 18

Ruyslinck, Ward 1929- . . . . **CLC 14**

Ryan, Cornelius (John) 1920-1974 . . . **CLC 7**
See also CA 69-72; obituary CA 53-56

Ryan, Michael 1946- . . . . **CLC 65**
See also CA 49-52; DLB-Y 82

Rybakov, Anatoli 1911?- . . . . **CLC 23, 53**
See also CA 126

Ryder, Jonathan 1927-
See Ludlum, Robert

Ryga, George 1932- . . . . **CLC 14**
See also CA 101; obituary CA 124; DLB 60

Sévigné, Marquise de Marie de Rabutin-Chantal 1626-1696 . . . . . **LC 11**

Saba, Umberto 1883-1957 . . . . **TCLC 33**

Sabato, Ernesto 1911- . . . . **CLC 10, 23**
See also CA 97-100

Sacher-Masoch, Leopold von 1836?-1895 . . . . **NCLC 31**

Sachs, Marilyn (Stickle) 1927- . . . . . **CLC 35**
See also CLR 2; CANR 13; CA 17-20R; SAAS 2; SATA 3, 52

Sachs, Nelly 1891-1970 . . . . **CLC 14**
See also CAP 2; CA 17-18; obituary CA 25-28R

Sackler, Howard (Oliver) 1929-1982 . . . . **CLC 14**
See also CA 61-64; obituary CA 108; DLB 7

Sade, Donatien Alphonse Francois, Comte de 1740-1814 . . . . **NCLC 3**

Sadoff, Ira 1945- . . . . **CLC 9**
See also CANR 5, 21; CA 53-56

Safire, William 1929- . . . . **CLC 10**
See also CA 17-20R

Sagan, Carl (Edward) 1934- . . . . **CLC 30**
See also CANR 11; CA 25-28R; SATA 58

Sagan, Francoise 1935- . . . . **CLC 3, 6, 9, 17, 36**
See also Quoirez, Francoise
See also CANR 6; DLB 83

Sahgal, Nayantara (Pandit) 1927- . . . **CLC 41**
See also CANR 11; CA 9-12R

Saint, H(arry) F. 1941- . . . . **CLC 50**

Sainte-Beuve, Charles Augustin 1804-1869 . . . . **NCLC 5**

Sainte-Marie, Beverly 1941-1972?
See Sainte-Marie, Buffy
See also CA 107

Sainte-Marie, Buffy 1941- . . . . **CLC 17**
See also Sainte-Marie, Beverly

Saint-Exupery, Antoine (Jean Baptiste Marie Roger) de 1900-1944 . . . . **TCLC 2**
See also CLR 10; CA 108; SATA 20; DLB 72

Saintsbury, George 1845-1933 . . . . . **TCLC 31**
See also DLB 57

Sait Faik (Abasiyanik) 1906-1954 . . . . **TCLC 23**

Saki 1870-1916 . . . . **TCLC 3**
See also Munro, H(ector) H(ugh)
See also CA 104

Salama, Hannu 1936- . . . . **CLC 18**

Salamanca, J(ack) R(ichard) 1922- . . . . **CLC 4, 15**
See also CA 25-28R

Salinas, Pedro 1891-1951 . . . . **TCLC 17**
See also CA 117

Salinger, J(erome) D(avid) 1919- . . . . **CLC 1, 3, 8, 12, 56; SSC 2**
See also CA 5-8R; DLB 2; CDALB 1941-1968

Salter, James 1925- . . . . **CLC 7, 52, 59**
See also CA 73-76

Saltus, Edgar (Evertson) 1855-1921 . . . . **TCLC 8**
See also CA 105

Saltykov, Mikhail Evgrafovich 1826-1889 . . . . **NCLC 16**

Samarakis, Antonis 1919- . . . . **CLC 5**
See also CA 25-28R

Sanchez, Florencio 1875-1910 . . . . . **TCLC 37**

Sanchez, Luis Rafael 1936- . . . . **CLC 23**

Sanchez, Sonia 1934- .... **CLC 5**
See also CANR 24; CA 33-36R; SATA 22; DLB 41

Sand, George 1804-1876.......... **NCLC 2**

Sandburg, Carl (August) 1878-1967 ... **CLC 1, 4, 10, 15, 35; PC 2**
See also CA 5-8R; obituary CA 25-28R; SATA 8; DLB 17, 54; CDALB 1865-1917

Sandburg, Charles August 1878-1967
See Sandburg, Carl (August)

Sanders, (James) Ed(ward) 1939- ... **CLC 53**
See also CANR 13; CA 15-16R, 103; DLB 16

Sanders, Lawrence 1920-.......... **CLC 41**
See also CA 81-84

Sandoz, Mari (Susette) 1896-1966 .. **CLC 28**
See also CANR 17; CA 1-4R; obituary CA 25-28R; SATA 5; DLB 9

Saner, Reg(inald Anthony) 1931- .... **CLC 9**
See also CA 65-68

Sannazaro, Jacopo 1456?-1530 .... **LC 8**

Sansom, William 1912-1976....... **CLC 2, 6**
See also CA 5-8R; obituary CA 65-68

Santayana, George 1863-1952..... **TCLC 40**
See also CA 115; DLB 54, 71

Santiago, Danny 1911-............ **CLC 33**
See also CA 125

Santmyer, Helen Hooven 1895-1986 .... **CLC 33**
See also CANR 15; CA 1-4R; obituary CA 118; DLB-Y 84

Santos, Bienvenido N(uqui) 1911-... **CLC 22**
See also CANR 19; CA 101

Sappho c. 6th-century B.C.-....... **CMLC 3**

Sarduy, Severo 1937-............. **CLC 6**
See also CA 89-92

Sargeson, Frank 1903-1982 .... **CLC 31**
See also CA 106, 25-28R; obituary CA 106

Sarmiento, Felix Ruben Garcia 1867-1916
See Dario, Ruben
See also CA 104

Saroyan, William 1908-1981 ..... **CLC 1, 8, 10, 29, 34, 56**
See also CA 5-8R; obituary CA 103; SATA 23; obituary SATA 24; DLB 7, 9; DLB-Y 81

Sarraute, Nathalie 1902- .... **CLC 1, 2, 4, 8, 10, 31**
See also CANR 23; CA 9-12R; DLB 83

Sarton, Eleanore Marie 1912-
See Sarton, (Eleanor) May

Sarton, (Eleanor) May 1912-............... **CLC 4, 14, 49**
See also CANR 1; CA 1-4R; SATA 36; DLB 48; DLB-Y 81

Sartre, Jean-Paul (Charles Aymard) 1905-1980 ... **CLC 1, 4, 7, 9, 13, 18, 24, 44, 50, 52**
See also CANR 21; CA 9-12R; obituary CA 97-100; DLB 72

Sassoon, Siegfried (Lorraine) 1886-1967 .... **CLC 36**
See also CA 104; obituary CA 25-28R; DLB 20

Saul, John (W. III) 1942- .... **CLC 46**
See also CANR 16; CA 81-84

Saura, Carlos 1932- .... **CLC 20**
See also CA 114

Sauser-Hall, Frederic-Louis 1887-1961 .... **CLC 18**
See also Cendrars, Blaise
See also CA 102; obituary CA 93-96

Savage, Thomas 1915- .... **CLC 40**
See also CA 126

Savan, Glenn 19??-............... **CLC 50**

Sayers, Dorothy L(eigh) 1893-1957 .... **TCLC 2, 15**
See also CA 104, 119; DLB 10, 36, 77

Sayers, Valerie 19??- .... **CLC 50**

Sayles, John (Thomas) 1950- .... **CLC 7, 10, 14**
See also CA 57-60; DLB 44

Scammell, Michael 19??- .... **CLC 34**

Scannell, Vernon 1922- .... **CLC 49**
See also CANR 8; CA 5-8R; DLB 27

Schaeffer, Susan Fromberg 1941- .... **CLC 6, 11, 22**
See also CANR 18; CA 49-52; SATA 22; DLB 28

Schell, Jonathan 1943-........... **CLC 35**
See also CANR 12; CA 73-76

Schelling, Friedrich Wilhelm Joseph von 1775-1854 .... **NCLC 30**
See also DLB 90

Scherer, Jean-Marie Maurice 1920-
See Rohmer, Eric
See also CA 110

Schevill, James (Erwin) 1920-....... **CLC 7**
See also CA 5-8R

Schisgal, Murray (Joseph) 1926-..... **CLC 6**
See also CA 21-24R

Schlee, Ann 1934-................ **CLC 35**
See also CA 101; SATA 36, 44

Schlegel, August Wilhelm von 1767-1845 .... **NCLC 15**

Schlegel, Johann Elias (von) 1719?-1749..................... **LC 5**

Schmidt, Arno 1914-1979.......... **CLC 56**
See also obituary CA 109; DLB 69

Schmitz, Ettore 1861-1928
See Svevo, Italo
See also CA 104, 122

Schnackenberg, Gjertrud 1953-..... **CLC 40**
See also CA 116

Schneider, Leonard Alfred 1925-1966
See Bruce, Lenny
See also CA 89-92

Schnitzler, Arthur 1862-1931 ..... **TCLC 4**
See also CA 104; DLB 81

Schor, Sandra 1932?-1990 .... **CLC 65**
See also CA 132

Schorer, Mark 1908-1977 .... **CLC 9**
See also CANR 7; CA 5-8R; obituary CA 73-76

Schrader, Paul (Joseph) 1946-...... **CLC 26**
See also CA 37-40R; DLB 44

Schreiner (Cronwright), Olive (Emilie Albertina) 1855-1920......... **TCLC 9**
See also CA 105; DLB 18

Schulberg, Budd (Wilson) 1914- .... **CLC 7, 48**
See also CANR 19; CA 25-28R; DLB 6, 26, 28; DLB-Y 81

Schulz, Bruno 1892-1942.......... **TCLC 5**
See also CA 115, 123

Schulz, Charles M(onroe) 1922- .... **CLC 12**
See also CANR 6; CA 9-12R; SATA 10

Schuyler, James (Marcus) 1923-..................... **CLC 5, 23**
See also CA 101; DLB 5

Schwartz, Delmore 1913-1966 .... **CLC 2, 4, 10, 45**
See also CAP 2; CA 17-18; obituary CA 25-28R; DLB 28, 48

Schwartz, John Burnham 1925- .... **CLC 59**

Schwartz, Lynne Sharon 1939-..... **CLC 31**
See also CA 103

Schwarz-Bart, Andre 1928-....... **CLC 2, 4**
See also CA 89-92

Schwarz-Bart, Simone 1938-........ **CLC 7**
See also CA 97-100

Schwob, (Mayer Andre) Marcel 1867-1905 .... **TCLC 20**
See also CA 117

Sciascia, Leonardo 1921-1989 .... **CLC 8, 9, 41**
See also CA 85-88

Scoppettone, Sandra 1936-......... **CLC 26**
See also CA 5-8R; SATA 9

Scorsese, Martin 1942- .... **CLC 20**
See also CA 110, 114

Scotland, Jay 1932-
See Jakes, John (William)

Scott, Duncan Campbell 1862-1947 .... **TCLC 6**
See also CA 104; DLB 92

Scott, Evelyn 1893-1963........... **CLC 43**
See also CA 104; obituary CA 112; DLB 9, 48

Scott, F(rancis) R(eginald) 1899-1985 .... **CLC 22**
See also CA 101; obituary CA 114; DLB 88

Scott, Joanna 19??-............... **CLC 50**
See also CA 126

Scott, Paul (Mark) 1920-1978.... **CLC 9, 60**
See also CA 81-84; obituary CA 77-80; DLB 14

Scott, Sir Walter 1771-1832 ..... **NCLC 15**
See also YABC 2

Scribe, (Augustin) Eugene 1791-1861 .... **NCLC 16**

Scudery, Madeleine de 1607-1701..... **LC 2**

Sealy, I. Allan 1951- .... **CLC 55**

Seare, Nicholas 1925-
See Trevanian; Whitaker, Rodney

Sebestyen, Igen 1924-
See Sebestyen, Ouida

Sebestyen, Ouida 1924-.......... **CLC 30**
See also CLR 17; CA 107; SATA 39

Sedgwick, Catharine Maria 1789-1867 .... **NCLC 19**
See also DLB 1, 74

Seelye, John 1931- .... **CLC 7**
See also CA 97-100

Seferiades, Giorgos Stylianou 1900-1971
See Seferis, George
See also CANR 5; CA 5-8R; obituary CA 33-36R

Seferis, George 1900-1971 .... **CLC 5, 11**
See also Seferiades, Giorgos Stylianou

Segal, Erich (Wolf) 1937- .... **CLC 3, 10**
See also CANR 20; CA 25-28R; DLB-Y 86

Seger, Bob 1945- .... **CLC 35**

Seger, Robert Clark 1945-
See Seger, Bob

Seghers, Anna 1900-1983 .... **CLC 7, 110**
See also Radvanyi, Netty Reiling
See also DLB 69

Seidel, Frederick (Lewis) 1936- ..... **CLC 18**
See also CANR 8; CA 13-16R; DLB-Y 84

Seifert, Jaroslav 1901-1986 ..... **CLC 34, 44**
See also CA 127

Sei Shonagon c. 966-1017? .... **CMLC 6**

Selby, Hubert, Jr. 1928- ..... **CLC 1, 2, 4, 8**
See also CA 13-16R; DLB 2

Senacour, Etienne Pivert de 1770-1846 .... **NCLC 16**

Sender, Ramon (Jose) 1902-1982 .... **CLC 8**
See also CANR 8; CA 5-8R; obituary CA 105

Seneca, Lucius Annaeus 4 B.C.-65 A.D. .... **CMLC 6**

Senghor, Léopold Sédar 1906- ...... **CLC 54**
See also CA 116

Serling, (Edward) Rod(man) 1924-1975 .... **CLC 30**
See also CA 65-68; obituary CA 57-60; DLB 26

Serpieres 1907-
See Guillevic, (Eugene)

Service, Robert W(illiam) 1874-1958 .... **TCLC 15**
See also CA 115; SATA 20

Seth, Vikram 1952- .... **CLC 43**
See also CA 121, 127

Seton, Cynthia Propper 1926-1982 .... **CLC 27**
See also CANR 7; CA 5-8R; obituary CA 108

Seton, Ernest (Evan) Thompson 1860-1946 .... **TCLC 31**
See also CA 109; SATA 18; DLB 92

Settle, Mary Lee 1918- .... **CLC 19, 61**
See also CAAS 1; CA 89-92; DLB 6

Sevigne, Marquise de Marie de Rabutin-Chantal 1626-1696 ..... **LC 11**

Sexton, Anne (Harvey) 1928-1974 ... **CLC 2, 4, 6, 8, 10, 15, 53; PC 2**
See also CANR 3; CA 1-4R; obituary CA 53-56; CABS 2; SATA 10; DLB 5; CDALB 1941-1968

Shaara, Michael (Joseph) 1929- .... **CLC 15**
See also CA 102; obituary CA 125; DLB-Y 83

Shackleton, C. C. 1925-
See Aldiss, Brian W(ilson)

Shacochis, Bob 1951- .... **CLC 39**
See also CA 119, 124

Shaffer, Anthony 1926- .... **CLC 19**
See also CA 110, 116; DLB 13

Shaffer, Peter (Levin) 1926- .... **CLC 5, 14, 18, 37, 60**
See also CANR 25; CA 25-28R; DLB 13

Shalamov, Varlam (Tikhonovich) 1907?-1982 .... **CLC 18**
See also obituary CA 105

Shamlu, Ahmad 1925- .... **CLC 10**

Shammas, Anton 1951- .... **CLC 55**

Shange, Ntozake 1948- .... **CLC 8, 25, 38**
See also CA 85-88; DLB 38

Shapcott, Thomas W(illiam) 1935- .. **CLC 38**
See also CA 69-72

Shapiro, Karl (Jay) 1913- .. **CLC 4, 8, 15, 53**
See also CAAS 6; CANR 1; CA 1-4R; DLB 48

Sharp, William 1855-1905 .... **TCLC 39**

Sharpe, Tom 1928- .... **CLC 36**
See also CA 114; DLB 14

Shaw, (George) Bernard 1856-1950 .... **TCLC 3, 9, 21**
See also CA 104, 109, 119; DLB 10, 57

Shaw, Henry Wheeler 1818-1885 .... **NCLC 15**
See also DLB 11

Shaw, Irwin 1913-1984 .... **CLC 7, 23, 34**
See also CANR 21; CA 13-16R; obituary CA 112; DLB 6; DLB-Y 84; CDALB 1941-1968

Shaw, Robert 1927-1978 .... **CLC 5**
See also CANR 4; CA 1-4R; obituary CA 81-84; DLB 13, 14

Shawn, Wallace 1943- .... **CLC 41**
See also CA 112

Sheed, Wilfrid (John Joseph) 1930- .... **CLC 2, 4, 10, 53**
See also CA 65-68; DLB 6

Sheffey, Asa 1913-1980
See Hayden, Robert (Earl)

Sheldon, Alice (Hastings) B(radley) 1915-1987
See Tiptree, James, Jr.
See also CA 108; obituary CA 122

Shelley, Mary Wollstonecraft Godwin 1797-1851 .... **NCLC 14**
See also SATA 29

Shelley, Percy Bysshe 1792-1822 .... **NCLC 18**

Shepard, Jim 19??- .... **CLC 36**

Shepard, Lucius 19??- .... **CLC 34**
See also CA 128

Shepard, Sam 1943- .... **CLC 4, 6, 17, 34, 41, 44**
See also CANR 22; CA 69-72; DLB 7

Shepherd, Michael 1927-
See Ludlum, Robert

Sherburne, Zoa (Morin) 1912- ...... **CLC 30**
See also CANR 3; CA 1-4R; SATA 3

Sheridan, Frances 1724-1766 .... **LC 7**
See also DLB 39, 84

Sheridan, Richard Brinsley 1751-1816 .... **NCLC 5; DC 1**
See also DLB 89

Sherman, Jonathan Marc 1970?- .... **CLC 55**

Sherman, Martin 19??- .... **CLC 19**
See also CA 116

Sherwin, Judith Johnson 1936- ... **CLC 7, 15**
See also CA 25-28R

Sherwood, Robert E(mmet) 1896-1955 .... **TCLC 3**
See also CA 104; DLB 7, 26

Shiel, M(atthew) P(hipps) 1865-1947 .... **TCLC 8**
See also CA 106

Shiga, Naoya 1883-1971 .... **CLC 33**
See also CA 101; obituary CA 33-36R

Shimazaki, Haruki 1872-1943
See Shimazaki, Toson
See also CA 105

Shimazaki, Toson 1872-1943 .... **TCLC 5**
See also Shimazaki, Haruki

Sholokhov, Mikhail (Aleksandrovich) 1905-1984 .... **CLC 7, 15**
See also CA 101; obituary CA 112; SATA 36

Sholom Aleichem 1859-1916 .... **TCLC 1, 35**
See also Rabinovitch, Sholem

Shreve, Susan Richards 1939- ...... **CLC 23**
See also CAAS 5; CANR 5; CA 49-52; SATA 41, 46

Shue, Larry 1946-1985 .... **CLC 52**
See also obituary CA 117

Shulman, Alix Kates 1932- ...... **CLC 2, 10**
See also CA 29-32R; SATA 7

Shuster, Joe 1914- .... **CLC 21**

Shute (Norway), Nevil 1899-1960 ... **CLC 30**
See also Norway, Nevil Shute
See also CA 102; obituary CA 93-96

Shuttle, Penelope (Diane) 1947- ..... **CLC 7**
See also CA 93-96; DLB 14, 40

Siegel, Jerome 1914- .... **CLC 21**
See also CA 116

Sienkiewicz, Henryk (Adam Aleksander Pius) 1846-1916 .... **TCLC 3**
See also CA 104

Sigal, Clancy 1926- .... **CLC 7**
See also CA 1-4R

Sigourney, Lydia (Howard Huntley) 1791-1865 .... **NCLC 21**
See also DLB 1, 42, 73

Siguenza y Gongora, Carlos de 1645-1700 .... **LC 8**

Sigurjonsson, Johann 1880-1919 ... **TCLC 27**

Sikelianos, Angeles 1884-1951 ..... **TCLC 39**

Silkin, Jon 1930- .... **CLC 2, 6, 43**
See also CAAS 5; CA 5-8R; DLB 27

Silko, Leslie Marmon 1948- .... **CLC 23**
See also CA 115, 122

Sillanpaa, Franz Eemil 1888-1964... **CLC 19**
See also CA 129; obituary CA 93-96

Sillitoe, Alan
1928- .... **CLC 1, 3, 6, 10, 19, 57**
See also CAAS 2; CANR 8, 26; CA 9-12R; DLB 14

Silone, Ignazio 1900-1978 .... **CLC 4**
See also CAAS 2; CANR 26; CAP 2; CA 25-28, 11-12R,; obituary CA 81-84

Silver, Joan Micklin 1935- .... **CLC 20**
See also CA 114, 121

Silverberg, Robert 1935- .... **CLC 7**
See also CAAS 3; CANR 1, 20; CA 1-4R; SATA 13; DLB 8

Silverstein, Alvin 1933- .... **CLC 17**
See also CANR 2; CA 49-52; SATA 8

Silverstein, Virginia B(arbara Opshelor)
1937- .... **CLC 17**
See also CANR 2; CA 49-52; SATA 8

Simak, Clifford D(onald)
1904-1988 .... **CLC 1, 55**
See also CANR 1; CA 1-4R; obituary CA 125; DLB 8

Simenon, Georges (Jacques Christian)
1903-1989 .... **CLC 1, 2, 3, 8, 18, 47**
See also CA 85-88; obituary CA 129; DLB 72

Simenon, Paul 1956?-
See The Clash

Simic, Charles 1938-....... **CLC 6, 9, 22, 49**
See also CAAS 4; CANR 12; CA 29-32R

Simmons, Charles (Paul) 1924-..... **CLC 57**
See also CA 89-92

Simmons, Dan 1948-............. **CLC 44**

Simmons, James (Stewart Alexander)
1933- .... **CLC 43**
See also CA 105; DLB 40

Simms, William Gilmore
1806-1870 .... **NCLC 3**
See also DLB 3, 30, 59, 73

Simon, Carly 1945-.............. **CLC 26**
See also CA 105

Simon, Claude (Henri Eugene)
1913- .... **CLC 4, 9, 15, 39**
See also CA 89-92; DLB 83

Simon, (Marvin) Neil
1927- .... **CLC 6, 11, 31, 39**
See also CA 21-24R; DLB 7

Simon, Paul 1941- .... **CLC 17**
See also CA 116

Simonon, Paul 1956?-
See The Clash

Simpson, Louis (Aston Marantz)
1923- .... **CLC 4, 7, 9, 32**
See also CAAS 4; CANR 1; CA 1-4R; DLB 5

Simpson, Mona (Elizabeth) 1957-... **CLC 44**
See also CA 122

Simpson, N(orman) F(rederick)
1919- .... **CLC 29**
See also CA 11-14R; DLB 13

Sinclair, Andrew (Annandale)
1935- .... **CLC 2, 14**
See also CAAS 5; CANR 14; CA 9-12R; DLB 14

Sinclair, Mary Amelia St. Clair 1865?-1946
See Sinclair, May
See also CA 104

Sinclair, May 1865?-1946 ...... **TCLC 3, 11**
See also Sinclair, Mary Amelia St. Clair
See also DLB 36

Sinclair, Upton (Beall)
1878-1968 .... **CLC 1, 11, 15, 63**
See also CANR 7; CA 5-8R; obituary CA 25-28R; SATA 9; DLB 9

Singer, Isaac Bashevis
1904- .... **CLC 1, 3, 6, 9, 11, 15, 23, 38; SSC 3**
See also CLR 1; CANR 1; CA 1-4R; SATA 3, 27; DLB 6, 28, 52; CDALB 1941-1968

Singer, Israel Joshua 1893-1944 ... **TCLC 33**

Singh, Khushwant 1915-........... **CLC 11**
See also CANR 6; CA 9-12R

Sinyavsky, Andrei (Donatevich)
1925- .... **CLC 8**
See also CA 85-88

Sirin, V.
See Nabokov, Vladimir (Vladimirovich)

Sissman, L(ouis) E(dward)
1928-1976 .... **CLC 9, 18**
See also CANR 13; CA 21-24R; obituary CA 65-68; DLB 5

Sisson, C(harles) H(ubert) 1914-..... **CLC 8**
See also CAAS 3; CANR 3; CA 1-4R; DLB 27

Sitwell, (Dame) Edith 1887-1964... **CLC 2, 9**
See also CA 9-12R; DLB 20

Sjoewall, Maj 1935-
See Wahloo, Per
See also CA 61-64, 65-68

Sjowall, Maj 1935-
See Wahloo, Per

Skelton, Robin 1925- .... **CLC 13**
See also CAAS 5; CA 5-8R; DLB 27, 53

Skolimowski, Jerzy 1938- .... **CLC 20**

Skolimowski, Yurek 1938-
See Skolimowski, Jerzy

Skram, Amalie (Bertha)
1847-1905 .... **TCLC 25**

Skrine, Mary Nesta 1904-
See Keane, Molly

Skvorecky, Josef (Vaclav)
1924- .... **CLC 15, 39**
See also CAAS 1; CANR 10; CA 61-64

Slade, Bernard 1930- .... **CLC 11, 46**
See also Newbound, Bernard Slade
See also DLB 53

Slaughter, Carolyn 1946-.......... **CLC 56**
See also CA 85-88

Slaughter, Frank G(ill) 1908- ...... **CLC 29**
See also CANR 5; CA 5-8R

Slavitt, David (R.) 1935- .... **CLC 5, 14**
See also CAAS 3; CA 21-24R; DLB 5, 6

Slesinger, Tess 1905-1945 .... **TCLC 10**
See also CA 107

Slessor, Kenneth 1901-1971....... **CLC 14**
See also CA 102; obituary CA 89-92

Slowacki, Juliusz 1809-1849 ..... **NCLC 15**

Smart, Christopher 1722-1771........ **LC 3**

Smart, Elizabeth 1913-1986........ **CLC 54**
See also CA 81-84; obituary CA 118; DLB 88

Smiley, Jane (Graves) 1949-....... **CLC 53**
See also CA 104

Smith, A(rthur) J(ames) M(arshall)
1902-1980 .... **CLC 15**
See also CANR 4; CA 1-4R; obituary CA 102; DLB 88

Smith, Betty (Wehner) 1896-1972... **CLC 19**
See also CA 5-8R; obituary CA 33-36R; SATA 6; DLB-Y 82

Smith, Cecil Lewis Troughton 1899-1966
See Forester, C(ecil) S(cott)

Smith, Charlotte (Turner)
1749-1806 .... **NCLC 23**
See also DLB 39

Smith, Clark Ashton 1893-1961 .... **CLC 43**

Smith, Dave 1942- .... **CLC 22, 42**
See also Smith, David (Jeddie)
See also CAAS 7; CANR 1; DLB 5

Smith, David (Jeddie) 1942-
See Smith, Dave
See also CANR 1; CA 49-52

Smith, Florence Margaret 1902-1971
See Smith, Stevie
See also CAP 2; CA 17-18; obituary CA 29-32R

Smith, Iain Crichton 1928- .... **CLC 64**
See also DLB 40

Smith, John 1580?-1631............. **LC 9**
See also DLB 24, 30

Smith, Lee 1944-................. **CLC 25**
See also CA 114, 119; DLB-Y 83

Smith, Martin Cruz 1942-......... **CLC 25**
See also CANR 6; CA 85-88

Smith, Martin William 1942-
See Smith, Martin Cruz

Smith, Mary-Ann Tirone 1944-..... **CLC 39**
See also CA 118

Smith, Patti 1946- .... **CLC 12**
See also CA 93-96

Smith, Pauline (Urmson)
1882-1959 .... **TCLC 25**
See also CA 29-32R; SATA 27

Smith, Rosamond 1938-
See Oates, Joyce Carol

Smith, Sara Mahala Redway 1900-1972
See Benson, Sally

Smith, Stevie 1902-1971.... **CLC 3, 8, 25, 44**
See also Smith, Florence Margaret
See also DLB 20

Smith, Wilbur (Addison) 1933-..... **CLC 33**
See also CANR 7; CA 13-16R

Smith, William Jay 1918- .... **CLC 6**
See also CA 5-8R; SATA 2; DLB 5

Smolenskin, Peretz 1842-1885.... **NCLC 30**

Smollett, Tobias (George) 1721-1771 .. **LC 2**
See also DLB 39

Snodgrass, W(illiam) D(e Witt)
1926- .... **CLC 2, 6, 10, 18**
See also CANR 6; CA 1-4R; DLB 5

Author Index

Snow, C(harles) P(ercy) 1905-1980 .... **CLC 1, 4, 6, 9, 13, 19**
See also CA 5-8R; obituary CA 101; DLB 15, 77

Snyder, Gary (Sherman) 1930- .... **CLC 1, 2, 5, 9, 32**
See also CANR 30; CA 17-20R; DLB 5, 16

Snyder, Zilpha Keatley 1927- ...... **CLC 17**
See also CA 9-12R; SAAS 2; SATA 1, 28

Sobol, Joshua 19??- .... **CLC 60**

Soderberg. Hjalmar 1869-1941 .... **TCLC 39**

Sodergran, Edith 1892-1923....... **TCLC 31**

Sokolov, Raymond 1941- .... **CLC 7**
See also CA 85-88

Sologub, Fyodor 1863-1927 .... **TCLC 9**
See also Teternikov, Fyodor Kuzmich
See also CA 104

Solomos, Dionysios 1798-1857 ... **NCLC 15**

Solwoska, Mara 1929-
See French, Marilyn
See also CANR 3; CA 69-72

Solzhenitsyn, Aleksandr I(sayevich) 1918- ... **CLC 1, 2, 4, 7, 9, 10, 18, 26, 34**
See also CA 69-72

Somers, Jane 1919-
See Lessing, Doris (May)

Sommer, Scott 1951- .... **CLC 25**
See also CA 106

Sondheim, Stephen (Joshua) 1930- .... **CLC 30, 39**
See also CA 103

Sontag, Susan 1933- ... **CLC 1, 2, 10, 13, 31**
See also CA 17-20R; DLB 2, 67

Sophocles c. 496? B.C.-c. 406? B.C. ..... **CMLC 2; DC 1**

Sorrentino, Gilbert 1929- .... **CLC 3, 7, 14, 22, 40**
See also CANR 14; CA 77-80; DLB 5; DLB-Y 80

Soto, Gary 1952-................. **CLC 32**
See also CA 119, 125; DLB 82

Souster, (Holmes) Raymond 1921- .... **CLC 5, 14**
See also CANR 13; CA 13-16R; DLB 88

Southern, Terry 1926- .... **CLC 7**
See also CANR 1; CA 1-4R; DLB 2

Southey, Robert 1774-1843 .... **NCLC 8**
See also SATA 54

Southworth, Emma Dorothy Eliza Nevitte 1819-1899 .... **NCLC 26**

Soyinka, Akinwande Oluwole 1934-
See Soyinka, Wole

Soyinka, Wole 1934- .. **CLC 3, 5, 14, 36, 44**
See also CA 13-16R; DLB-Y 86

Spackman, W(illiam) M(ode) 1905- .... **CLC 46**
See also CA 81-84

Spacks, Barry 1931-............. **CLC 14**
See also CA 29-32R

Spanidou, Irini 1946- .... **CLC 44**

Spark, Muriel (Sarah) 1918- .... **CLC 2, 3, 5, 8, 13, 18, 40**
See also CANR 12; CA 5-8R; DLB 15

Spencer, Elizabeth 1921- .... **CLC 22**
See also CA 13-16R; SATA 14; DLB 6

Spencer, Scott 1945-............. **CLC 30**
See also CA 113; DLB-Y 86

Spender, Stephen (Harold) 1909- .... **CLC 1, 2, 5, 10, 41**
See also CA 9-12R; DLB 20

Spengler, Oswald 1880-1936 ...... **TCLC 25**
See also CA 118

Spenser, Edmund 1552?-1599 .... **LC 5**

Spicer, Jack 1925-1965 .... **CLC 8, 18**
See also CA 85-88; DLB 5, 16

Spielberg, Peter 1929- .... **CLC 6**
See also CANR 4; CA 5-8R; DLB-Y 81

Spielberg, Steven 1947- .... **CLC 20**
See also CA 77-80; SATA 32

Spillane, Frank Morrison 1918-
See Spillane, Mickey
See also CA 25-28R

Spillane, Mickey 1918- .... **CLC 3, 13**
See also Spillane, Frank Morrison

Spinoza, Benedictus de 1632-1677 .... **LC 9**

Spinrad, Norman (Richard) 1940- ... **CLC 46**
See also CANR 20; CA 37-40R; DLB 8

Spitteler, Carl (Friedrich Georg) 1845-1924 .... **TCLC 12**
See also CA 109

Spivack, Kathleen (Romola Drucker) 1938- .... **CLC 6**
See also CA 49-52

Spoto, Donald 1941-............. **CLC 39**
See also CANR 11; CA 65-68

Springsteen, Bruce 1949- .... **CLC 17**
See also CA 111

Spurling, Hilary 1940- .... **CLC 34**
See also CANR 25; CA 104

Squires, (James) Radcliffe 1917-.... **CLC 51**
See also CANR 6, 21; CA 1-4R

Stael-Holstein, Anne Louise Germaine Necker, Baronne de 1766-1817....... **NCLC 3**

Stafford, Jean 1915-1979 ...... **CLC 4, 7, 19**
See also CANR 3; CA 1-4R; obituary CA 85-88; obituary SATA 22; DLB 2

Stafford, William (Edgar) 1914- .... **CLC 4, 7, 29**
See also CAAS 3; CANR 5, 22; CA 5-8R; DLB 5

Stannard, Martin 1947- .... **CLC 44**

Stanton, Maura 1946- .... **CLC 9**
See also CANR 15; CA 89-92

Stapledon, (William) Olaf 1886-1950 .... **TCLC 22**
See also CA 111; DLB 15

Starbuck, George (Edwin) 1931- .... **CLC 53**
See also CANR 23; CA 21-22R

Stark, Richard 1933-
See Westlake, Donald E(dwin)

Stead, Christina (Ellen) 1902-1983 .... **CLC 2, 5, 8, 32**
See also CA 13-16R; obituary CA 109

Steele, Timothy (Reid) 1948-....... **CLC 45**
See also CANR 16; CA 93-96

Steffens, (Joseph) Lincoln 1866-1936 .... **TCLC 20**
See also CA 117; SAAS 1

Stegner, Wallace (Earle) 1909- ... **CLC 9, 49**
See also CANR 1, 21; CA 1-4R; DLB 9

Stein, Gertrude 1874-1946... **TCLC 1, 6, 28**
See also CA 104; DLB 4, 54, 86; CDALB 1917-1929

Steinbeck, John (Ernst) 1902-1968 ..... **CLC 1, 5, 9, 13, 21, 34, 45, 59**
See also CANR 1; CA 1-4R; obituary CA 25-28R; SATA 9; DLB 7, 9; DLB-DS 2; CDALB 1929-1941

Steinem, Gloria 1934-............ **CLC 63**
See also CANR 28; CA 53-56

Steiner, George 1929-............ **CLC 24**
See also CA 73-76; DLB 67

Steiner, Rudolf(us Josephus Laurentius) 1861-1925 .... **TCLC 13**
See also CA 107

Stendhal 1783-1842............ **NCLC 23**

Stephen, Leslie 1832-1904 .... **TCLC 23**
See also CANR 9; CA 21-24R, 123; DLB 57

Stephens, James 1882?-1950 .... **TCLC 4**
See also CA 104; DLB 19

Stephens, Reed
See Donaldson, Stephen R.

Steptoe, Lydia 1892-1982
See Barnes, Djuna

Sterchi, Beat 1949-.............. **CLC 65**

Sterling, George 1869-1926 .... **TCLC 20**
See also CA 117; DLB 54

Stern, Gerald 1925- .... **CLC 40**
See also CA 81-84

Stern, Richard G(ustave) 1928- ... **CLC 4, 39**
See also CANR 1, 25; CA 1-4R; DLB 87

Sternberg, Jonas 1894-1969
See Sternberg, Josef von

Sternberg, Josef von 1894-1969..... **CLC 20**
See also CA 81-84

Sterne, Laurence 1713-1768.......... **LC 2**
See also DLB 39

Sternheim, (William Adolf) Carl 1878-1942 .... **TCLC 8**
See also CA 105

Stevens, Mark 19??-............. **CLC 34**

Stevens, Wallace 1879-1955..... **TCLC 3, 12**
See also CA 104, 124; DLB 54

Stevenson, Anne (Katharine) 1933- .... **CLC 7, 33**
See also Elvin, Anne Katharine Stevenson
See also CANR 9; CA 17-18R; DLB 40

Stevenson, Robert Louis 1850-1894 .... **NCLC 5, 14**
See also CLR 10, 11; YABC 2; DLB 18, 57

Stewart, J(ohn) I(nnes) M(ackintosh) 1906- .... **CLC 7, 14, 32**
See also CAAS 3; CA 85-88

Stewart, Mary (Florence Elinor) 1916- .... **CLC 7, 35**
See also CANR 1; CA 1-4R; SATA 12

Stewart, Will 1908-
See Williamson, Jack
See also CANR 23; CA 17-18R

Still, James 1906-................ **CLC 49**
See also CANR 10, 26; CA 65-68; SATA 29; DLB 9

Sting 1951-
See The Police

Stitt, Milan 1941-................ **CLC 29**
See also CA 69-72

Stoker, Abraham
See Stoker, Bram
See also CA 105; SATA 29

Stoker, Bram 1847-1912 .... **TCLC 8**
See also Stoker, Abraham
See also SATA 29; DLB 36, 70

Stolz, Mary (Slattery) 1920-....... **CLC 12**
See also CANR 13; CA 5-8R; SAAS 3; SATA 10

Stone, Irving 1903-1989........... **CLC 7**
See also CAAS 3; CANR 1; CA 1-4R, 129; SATA 3

Stone, Robert (Anthony) 1937?- .... **CLC 5, 23, 42**
See also CANR 23; CA 85-88

Stoppard, Tom 1937- ... **CLC 1, 3, 4, 5, 8, 15, 29, 34, 63**
See also CA 81-84; DLB 13; DLB-Y 85

Storey, David (Malcolm) 1933- .... **CLC 2, 4, 5, 8**
See also CA 81-84; DLB 13, 14

Storm, Hyemeyohsts 1935- .... **CLC 3**
See also CA 81-84

Storm, (Hans) Theodor (Woldsen) 1817-1888 .... **NCLC 1**

Storni, Alfonsina 1892-1938 .... **TCLC 5**
See also CA 104

Stout, Rex (Todhunter) 1886-1975 ... **CLC 3**
See also CA 61-64

Stow, (Julian) Randolph 1935- .. **CLC 23, 48**
See also CA 13-16R

Stowe, Harriet (Elizabeth) Beecher 1811-1896 .... **NCLC 3**
See also YABC 1; DLB 1, 12, 42, 74; CDALB 1865-1917

Strachey, (Giles) Lytton 1880-1932 .... **TCLC 12**
See also CA 110

Strand, Mark 1934- .... **CLC 6, 18, 41**
See also CA 21-24R; SATA 41; DLB 5

Straub, Peter (Francis) 1943- ...... **CLC 28**
See also CA 85-88; DLB-Y 84

Strauss, Botho 1944- .... **CLC 22**

Straussler, Tomas 1937-
See Stoppard, Tom

Streatfeild, (Mary) Noel 1897- ..... **CLC 21**
See also CA 81-84; obituary CA 120; SATA 20, 48

Stribling, T(homas) S(igismund) 1881-1965 .... **CLC 23**
See also obituary CA 107; DLB 9

Strindberg, (Johan) August 1849-1912 .... **TCLC 1, 8, 21**
See also CA 104

Stringer, Arthur 1874-1950 .... **TCLC 37**
See also DLB 92

Strugatskii, Arkadii (Natanovich) 1925- .... **CLC 27**
See also CA 106

Strugatskii, Boris (Natanovich) 1933- .... **CLC 27**
See also CA 106

Strummer, Joe 1953?-
See The Clash

Stuart, (Hilton) Jesse 1906-1984 .... **CLC 1, 8, 11, 14, 34**
See also CA 5-8R; obituary CA 112; SATA 2; obituary SATA 36; DLB 9, 48; DLB-Y 84

Sturgeon, Theodore (Hamilton) 1918-1985 .... **CLC 22, 39**
See also CA 81-84; obituary CA 116; DLB 8; DLB-Y 85

Styron, William 1925- .... **CLC 1, 3, 5, 11, 15, 60**
See also CANR 6; CA 5-8R; DLB 2; DLB-Y 80; CDALB 1968-1987

Sudermann, Hermann 1857-1928 .. **TCLC 15**
See also CA 107

Sue, Eugene 1804-1857 .... **NCLC 1**

Sukenick, Ronald 1932-..... **CLC 3, 4, 6, 48**
See also CAAS 8; CA 25-28R; DLB-Y 81

Suknaski, Andrew 1942- .... **CLC 19**
See also CA 101; DLB 53

Sully Prudhomme, Rene 1839-1907 .... **TCLC 31**

Su Man-shu 1884-1918........... **TCLC 24**
See also CA 123

Summers, Andrew James 1942-
See The Police

Summers, Andy 1942-
See The Police

Summers, Hollis (Spurgeon, Jr.) 1916- .... **CLC 10**
See also CANR 3; CA 5-8R; DLB 6

Summers, (Alphonsus Joseph-Mary Augustus) Montague 1880-1948 .... **TCLC 16**
See also CA 118

Sumner, Gordon Matthew 1951-
See The Police

Surtees, Robert Smith 1805-1864 .... **NCLC 14**
See also DLB 21

Susann, Jacqueline 1921-1974....... **CLC 3**
See also CA 65-68; obituary CA 53-56

Suskind, Patrick 1949-........... **CLC 44**

Sutcliff, Rosemary 1920- .... **CLC 26**
See also CLR 1; CA 5-8R; SATA 6, 44

Sutro, Alfred 1863-1933.......... **TCLC 6**
See also CA 105; DLB 10

Sutton, Henry 1935-
See Slavitt, David (R.)

Svevo, Italo 1861-1928......... **TCLC 2, 35**
See also Schmitz, Ettore

Swados, Elizabeth 1951- .... **CLC 12**
See also CA 97-100

Swados, Harvey 1920-1972 .... **CLC 5**
See also CANR 6; CA 5-8R; obituary CA 37-40R; DLB 2

Swarthout, Glendon (Fred) 1918- ... **CLC 35**
See also CANR 1; CA 1-4R; SATA 26

Swenson, May 1919-1989..... **CLC 4, 14, 61**
See also CA 5-8R; obituary CA 130; SATA 15; DLB 5

Swift, Graham 1949- .... **CLC 41**
See also CA 117, 122

Swift, Jonathan 1667-1745........... **LC 1**
See also SATA 19; DLB 39

Swinburne, Algernon Charles 1837-1909 .... **TCLC 8, 36**
See also CA 105; DLB 35, 57

Swinfen, Ann 19??-............... **CLC 34**

Swinnerton, Frank (Arthur) 1884-1982 .... **CLC 31**
See also obituary CA 108; DLB 34

Symons, Arthur (William) 1865-1945 .... **TCLC 11**
See also CA 107; DLB 19, 57

Symons, Julian (Gustave) 1912- .... **CLC 2, 14, 32**
See also CAAS 3; CANR 3; CA 49-52; DLB 87

Synge, (Edmund) John Millington 1871-1909 .... **TCLC 6, 37**
See also CA 104; DLB 10, 19

Syruc, J. 1911-
See Milosz, Czeslaw

Szirtes, George 1948-............ **CLC 46**
See also CANR 27; CA 109

Tabori, George 1914- .... **CLC 19**
See also CANR 4; CA 49-52

Tagore, (Sir) Rabindranath 1861-1941 .... **TCLC 3**
See also Thakura, Ravindranatha
See also CA 120

Taine, Hippolyte Adolphe 1828-1893 .... **NCLC 15**

Talese, Gaetano 1932-
See Talese, Gay

Talese, Gay 1932-............... **CLC 37**
See also CANR 9; CA 1-4R

Tallent, Elizabeth (Ann) 1954- ..... **CLC 45**
See also CA 117

Tally, Ted 1952-................. **CLC 42**
See also CA 120, 124

Tamayo y Baus, Manuel 1829-1898 .... **NCLC 1**

Tammsaare, A(nton) H(ansen) 1878-1940 .... **TCLC 27**

Tan, Amy 1952- .... **CLC 59**

Tanizaki, Jun'ichiro 1886-1965 .... **CLC 8, 14, 28**
See also CA 93-96; obituary CA 25-28R

Tarbell, Ida 1857-1944........... **TCLC 40**
See also CA 122; DLB 47

Author Index

Tarkington, (Newton) Booth 1869-1946 .... **TCLC 9**
See also CA 110; SATA 17; DLB 9

Tasso, Torquato 1544-1595 .... **LC 5**

Tate, (John Orley) Allen 1899-1979 .... **CLC 2, 4, 6, 9, 11, 14, 24**
See also CA 5-8R; obituary CA 85-88; DLB 4, 45, 63

Tate, James 1943-........... **CLC 2, 6, 25**
See also CA 21-24R; DLB 5

Tavel, Ronald 1940-............... **CLC 6**
See also CA 21-24R

Taylor, C(ecil) P(hillip) 1929-1981 .. **CLC 27**
See also CA 25-28R; obituary CA 105

Taylor, Edward 1644?-1729......... **LC 11**
See also DLB 24

Taylor, Eleanor Ross 1920-......... **CLC 5**
See also CA 81-84

Taylor, Elizabeth 1912-1975 ... **CLC 2, 4, 29**
See also CANR 9; CA 13-16R; SATA 13

Taylor, Henry (Splawn) 1917-...... **CLC 44**
See also CAAS 7; CA 33-36R; DLB 5

Taylor, Kamala (Purnaiya) 1924-
See Markandaya, Kamala
See also CA 77-80

Taylor, Mildred D(elois) 1943-..... **CLC 21**
See also CLR 9; CANR 25; CA 85-88; SAAS 5; SATA 15; DLB 52

Taylor, Peter (Hillsman) 1917-......... **CLC 1, 4, 18, 37, 44, 50**
See also CANR 9; CA 13-16R; DLB-Y 81

Taylor, Robert Lewis 1912-........ **CLC 14**
See also CANR 3; CA 1-4R; SATA 10

Teasdale, Sara 1884-1933......... **TCLC 4**
See also CA 104; SATA 32; DLB 45

Tegner, Esaias 1782-1846......... **NCLC 2**

Teilhard de Chardin, (Marie Joseph) Pierre 1881-1955 .... **TCLC 9**
See also CA 105

Tennant, Emma 1937- .... **CLC 13, 52**
See also CAAS 9; CANR 10; CA 65-68; DLB 14

Tennyson, Alfred 1809-1892 ..... **NCLC 30**
See also DLB 32

Teran, Lisa St. Aubin de 19??- ..... **CLC 36**

Terkel, Louis 1912-
See Terkel, Studs
See also CANR 18; CA 57-60

Terkel, Studs 1912- .... **CLC 38**
See also Terkel, Louis

Terry, Megan 1932-.............. **CLC 19**
See also CA 77-80; CABS 3; DLB 7

Tertz, Abram 1925-
See Sinyavsky, Andrei (Donatevich)

Tesich, Steve 1943?-............. **CLC 40**
See also CA 105; DLB-Y 83

Tesich, Stoyan 1943?-
See Tesich, Steve

Teternikov, Fyodor Kuzmich 1863-1927
See Sologub, Fyodor
See also CA 104

Tevis, Walter 1928-1984 .... **CLC 42**
See also CA 113

Tey, Josephine 1897-1952 .... **TCLC 14**
See also Mackintosh, Elizabeth

Thackeray, William Makepeace 1811-1863 .... **NCLC 5, 14, 22**
See also SATA 23; DLB 21, 55

Thakura, Ravindranatha 1861-1941
See Tagore, (Sir) Rabindranath
See also CA 104

Thelwell, Michael (Miles) 1939- .... **CLC 22**
See also CA 101

Theroux, Alexander (Louis) 1939- .... **CLC 2, 25**
See also CANR 20; CA 85-88

Theroux, Paul 1941- .... **CLC 5, 8, 11, 15, 28, 46**
See also CANR 20; CA 33-36R; SATA 44; DLB 2

Thesen, Sharon 1946-............. **CLC 56**

Thibault, Jacques Anatole Francois 1844-1924
See France, Anatole
See also CA 106

Thiele, Colin (Milton) 1920- .... **CLC 17**
See also CANR 12; CA 29-32R; SAAS 2; SATA 14

Thomas, Audrey (Grace) 1935-.................. **CLC 7, 13, 37**
See also CA 21-24R; DLB 60

Thomas, D(onald) M(ichael) 1935-................. **CLC 13, 22, 31**
See also CANR 17; CA 61-64; DLB 40

Thomas, Dylan (Marlais) 1914-1953 ..... **TCLC 1, 8; PC 2; SSC 3**
See also CA 104, 120; SATA 60; DLB 13, 20

Thomas, Edward (Philip) 1878-1917 .... **TCLC 10**
See also CA 106; DLB 19

Thomas, John Peter 1928-
See Thomas, Piri

Thomas, Joyce Carol 1938-........ **CLC 35**
See also CLR 19; CA 113, 116; SAAS 7; SATA 40; DLB 33

Thomas, Lewis 1913- .... **CLC 35**
See also CA 85-88

Thomas, Piri 1928-................ **CLC 17**
See also CA 73-76

Thomas, R(onald) S(tuart) 1913- .... **CLC 6, 13, 48**
See also CAAS 4; CA 89-92; DLB 27

Thomas, Ross (Elmore) 1926- ...... **CLC 39**
See also CANR 22; CA 33-36R

Thompson, Ernest 1860-1946
See Seton, Ernest (Evan) Thompson

Thompson, Francis (Joseph) 1859-1907 .... **TCLC 4**
See also CA 104; DLB 19

Thompson, Hunter S(tockton) 1939- .... **CLC 9, 17, 40**
See also CANR 23; CA 17-20R

Thompson, Judith 1954-.......... **CLC 39**

Thomson, James 1700-1748 .... **LC 16**
See also DLB 95

Thomson, James 1834-1882...... **NCLC 18**
See also DLB 35

Thoreau, Henry David 1817-1862.................. **NCLC 7, 21**
See also DLB 1; CDALB 1640-1865

Thurber, James (Grover) 1894-1961 .... **CLC 5, 11, 25; SSC 1**
See also CANR 17; CA 73-76; SATA 13; DLB 4, 11, 22

Thurman, Wallace 1902-1934 ...... **TCLC 6**
See also CA 104, 124; DLB 51

Tieck, (Johann) Ludwig 1773-1853 .... **NCLC 5**
See also DLB 90

Tilghman, Christopher 1948?- ...... **CLC 65**

Tillinghast, Richard 1940-......... **CLC 29**
See also CANR 26; CA 29-32R

Timrod, Henry 1828-1867 .... **NCLC 25**

Tindall, Gillian 1938-.............. **CLC 7**
See also CANR 11; CA 21-24R

Tiptree, James, Jr. 1915-1987 ... **CLC 48, 50**
See also Sheldon, Alice (Hastings) B(radley)
See also DLB 8

Tocqueville, Alexis (Charles Henri Maurice Clerel, Comte) de 1805-1859.. **NCLC 7**

Tolkien, J(ohn) R(onald) R(euel) 1892-1973 .... **CLC 1, 2, 3, 8, 12, 38**
See also CAP 2; CA 17-18; obituary CA 45-48; SATA 2, 24, 32; obituary SATA 24; DLB 15

Toller, Ernst 1893-1939 .... **TCLC 10**
See also CA 107

Tolson, Melvin B(eaunorus) 1900?-1966.................. **CLC 36**
See also CA 124; obituary CA 89-92; DLB 48, 124

Tolstoy, (Count) Alexey Nikolayevich 1883-1945 .... **TCLC 18**
See also CA 107

Tolstoy, (Count) Leo (Lev Nikolaevich) 1828-1910 .... **TCLC 4, 11, 17, 28**
See also CA 104, 123; SATA 26

Tomlin, Lily 1939- .... **CLC 17**

Tomlin, Mary Jean 1939-
See Tomlin, Lily
See also CA 117

Tomlinson, (Alfred) Charles 1927- .... **CLC 2, 4, 6, 13, 45**
See also CA 5-8R; DLB 40

Toole, John Kennedy 1937-1969 .... **CLC 19, 64**
See also CA 104; DLB-Y 81

Toomer, Jean 1894-1967 ..... **CLC 1, 4, 13, 22; SSC 1**
See also CA 85-88; DLB 45, 51

Torrey, E. Fuller 19??-........... **CLC 34**
See also CA 119

Tournier, Michel 1924- ...... **CLC 6, 23, 36**
See also CANR 3; CA 49-52; SATA 23; DLB 83

Townsend, Sue 1946- .... **CLC 61**
See also CA 119, 127; SATA 48, 55

Townshend, Peter (Dennis Blandford) 1945- .... **CLC 17, 42**
See also CA 107

Tozzi, Federigo 1883-1920........ **TCLC 31**

Traill, Catharine Parr 1802-1899 .... **NCLC 31**
See also DLB 99

Trakl, Georg 1887-1914........... **TCLC 5**
See also CA 104

Transtromer, Tomas (Gosta) 1931- .... **CLC 52, 65**
See also CA 129; brief entry CA 117

Traven, B. 1890-1969........... **CLC 8, 11**
See also CAP 2; CA 19-20; obituary CA 25-28R; DLB 9, 56

Tremain, Rose 1943-............. **CLC 42**
See also CA 97-100; DLB 14

Tremblay, Michel 1942-........... **CLC 29**
See also CA 116; DLB 60

Trevanian 1925- .... **CLC 29**
See also CA 108

Trevor, William 1928- ..... **CLC 7, 9, 14, 25**
See also Cox, William Trevor
See also DLB 14

Trifonov, Yuri (Valentinovich) 1925-1981 .... **CLC 45**
See also obituary CA 103, 126

Trilling, Lionel 1905-1975.... **CLC 9, 11, 24**
See also CANR 10; CA 9-12R; obituary CA 61-64; DLB 28, 63

Trogdon, William 1939-
See Heat Moon, William Least
See also CA 115, 119

Trollope, Anthony 1815-1882 ..... **NCLC 6**
See also SATA 22; DLB 21, 57

Trollope, Frances 1780-1863 ..... **NCLC 30**
See also DLB 21

Trotsky, Leon (Davidovich) 1879-1940 .... **TCLC 22**
See also CA 118

Trotter (Cockburn), Catharine 1679-1749 .... **LC 8**
See also DLB 84

Trow, George W. S. 1943-......... **CLC 52**
See also CA 126

Troyat, Henri 1911-.............. **CLC 23**
See also CANR 2; CA 45-48

Trudeau, G(arretson) B(eekman) 1948-
See Trudeau, Garry
See also CA 81-84; SATA 35

Trudeau, Garry 1948-............. **CLC 12**
See also Trudeau, G(arretson) B(eekman)

Truffaut, Francois 1932-1984....... **CLC 20**
See also CA 81-84; obituary CA 113

Trumbo, Dalton 1905-1976 .... **CLC 19**
See also CANR 10; CA 21-24R; obituary CA 69-72; DLB 26

Trumbull, John 1750-1831....... **NCLC 30**
See also DLB 31

Tryon, Thomas 1926-........... **CLC 3, 11**
See also CA 29-32R

Ts'ao Hsueh-ch'in 1715?-1763........ **LC 1**

Tsushima Shuji 1909-1948
See Dazai Osamu
See also CA 107

Tsvetaeva (Efron), Marina (Ivanovna) 1892-1941 .... **TCLC 7, 35**
See also CA 104, 128

Tunis, John R(oberts) 1889-1975 ... **CLC 12**
See also CA 61-64; SATA 30, 37; DLB 22

Tuohy, Frank 1925- .... **CLC 37**
See also DLB 14

Tuohy, John Francis 1925-
See Tuohy, Frank
See also CANR 3; CA 5-8R

Turco, Lewis (Putnam) 1934- ... **CLC 11, 63**
See also CANR 24; CA 13-16R; DLB-Y 84

Turgenev, Ivan 1818-1883 .... **NCLC 21; SSC 7**

Turner, Frederick 1943-.......... **CLC 48**
See also CANR 12; CA 73-76; DLB 40

Tutuola, Amos 1920- .... **CLC 5, 14, 29**
See also CA 9-12R

Twain, Mark 1835-1910 ... **TCLC 6, 12, 19, 36; SSC 6**
See also Clemens, Samuel Langhorne
See also YABC 2; DLB 11, 12, 23, 64, 74

Tyler, Anne 1941- .... **CLC 7, 11, 18, 28, 44, 59**
See also CANR 11; CA 9-12R; SATA 7; DLB 6; DLB-Y 82

Tyler, Royall 1757-1826.......... **NCLC 3**
See also DLB 37

Tynan (Hinkson), Katharine 1861-1931 .... **TCLC 3**
See also CA 104

Tytell, John 1939- .... **CLC 50**
See also CA 29-32R

Tzara, Tristan 1896-1963.......... **CLC 47**
See also Rosenfeld, Samuel

Uhry, Alfred 1947?- .... **CLC 55**
See also CA 127

Unamuno (y Jugo), Miguel de 1864-1936 .... **TCLC 2, 9**
See also CA 104

Underwood, Miles 1909-1981
See Glassco, John

Undset, Sigrid 1882-1949.......... **TCLC 3**
See also CA 104

Ungaretti, Giuseppe 1888-1970 .... **CLC 7, 11, 15**
See also CAP 2; CA 19-20; obituary CA 25-28R

Unger, Douglas 1952-............. **CLC 34**
See also CA 130

Unger, Eva 1932-
See Figes, Eva

Updike, John (Hoyer) 1932- ...... **CLC 1, 2, 3, 5, 7, 9, 13, 15, 23, 34, 43**
See also CANR 4; CA 1-4R; CABS 2; DLB 2, 5; DLB-Y 80, 82; DLB-DS 3

Urdang, Constance (Henriette) 1922- .... **CLC 47**
See also CANR 9, 24; CA 21-24R

Uris, Leon (Marcus) 1924-....... **CLC 7, 32**
See also CANR 1; CA 1-4R; SATA 49

Ustinov, Peter (Alexander) 1921- .... **CLC 1**
See also CANR 25; CA 13-16R; DLB 13

Vaculik, Ludvik 1926- .... **CLC 7**
See also CA 53-56

Valenzuela, Luisa 1938-........... **CLC 31**
See also CA 101

Valera (y Acala-Galiano), Juan 1824-1905 .... **TCLC 10**
See also CA 106

Valery, Paul (Ambroise Toussaint Jules) 1871-1945 .... **TCLC 4, 15**
See also CA 104, 122

Valle-Inclan (y Montenegro), Ramon (Maria) del 1866-1936............... **TCLC 5**
See also CA 106

Vallejo, Cesar (Abraham) 1892-1938 .... **TCLC 3**
See also CA 105

Van Ash, Cay 1918-.............. **CLC 34**

Vance, Jack 1916?-............... **CLC 35**
See also DLB 8

Vance, John Holbrook 1916?-
See Vance, Jack
See also CANR 17; CA 29-32R

Van Den Bogarde, Derek (Jules Gaspard Ulric) Niven 1921-
See Bogarde, Dirk
See also CA 77-80

Vandenburgh, Jane 19??-.......... **CLC 59**

Vanderhaeghe, Guy 1951- .... **CLC 41**
See also CA 113

Van der Post, Laurens (Jan) 1906-... **CLC 5**
See also CA 5-8R

Van de Wetering, Janwillem 1931- .... **CLC 47**
See also CANR 4; CA 49-52

Van Dine, S. S. 1888-1939........ **TCLC 23**

Van Doren, Carl (Clinton) 1885-1950 .... **TCLC 18**
See also CA 111

Van Doren, Mark 1894-1972..... **CLC 6, 10**
See also CANR 3; CA 1-4R; obituary CA 37-40R; DLB 45

Van Druten, John (William) 1901-1957 .... **TCLC 2**
See also CA 104; DLB 10

Van Duyn, Mona 1921-....... **CLC 3, 7, 63**
See also CANR 7; CA 9-12R; DLB 5

Van Itallie, Jean-Claude 1936- ...... **CLC 3**
See also CAAS 2; CANR 1; CA 45-48; DLB 7

Van Ostaijen, Paul 1896-1928..... **TCLC 33**

Van Peebles, Melvin 1932- ...... **CLC 2, 20**
See also CA 85-88

Vansittart, Peter 1920-........... **CLC 42**
See also CANR 3; CA 1-4R

Van Vechten, Carl 1880-1964 ...... **CLC 33**
See also obituary CA 89-92; DLB 4, 9, 51

Van Vogt, A(lfred) E(lton) 1912-...... **CLC 1**
See also CANR 28; CA 21-24R; SATA 14; DLB 8

Varda, Agnes 1928- .... **CLC 16**
See also CA 116, 122

Vargas Llosa, (Jorge) Mario (Pedro)
1936- .... **CLC 3, 6, 9, 10, 15, 31, 42**
See also CANR 18; CA 73-76

Vassilikos, Vassilis 1933- .... **CLC 4, 8**
See also CA 81-84

Vaughn, Stephanie 19??- .... **CLC 62**

Vazov, Ivan 1850-1921 .... **TCLC 25**
See also CA 121

Veblen, Thorstein Bunde
1857-1929 .... **TCLC 31**
See also CA 115

Verga, Giovanni 1840-1922 .... **TCLC 3**
See also CA 104, 123

Verhaeren, Emile (Adolphe Gustave)
1855-1916 .... **TCLC 12**
See also CA 109

Verlaine, Paul (Marie)
1844-1896 .... **NCLC 2; PC 2**

Verne, Jules (Gabriel) 1828-1905 ... **TCLC 6**
See also CA 110; SATA 21

Very, Jones 1813-1880 .... **NCLC 9**
See also DLB 1

Vesaas, Tarjei 1897-1970 .... **CLC 48**
See also obituary CA 29-32R

Vian, Boris 1920-1959 .... **TCLC 9**
See also CA 106; DLB 72

Viaud, (Louis Marie) Julien 1850-1923
See Loti, Pierre
See also CA 107

Vicker, Angus 1916-
See Felsen, Henry Gregor

Vidal, Eugene Luther, Jr. 1925-
See Vidal, Gore

Vidal, Gore
1925- .... **CLC 2, 4, 6, 8, 10, 22, 33**
See also CANR 13; CA 5-8R; DLB 6

Viereck, Peter (Robert Edwin)
1916- .... **CLC 4**
See also CANR 1; CA 1-4R; DLB 5

Vigny, Alfred (Victor) de
1797-1863 .... **NCLC 7**

Vilakazi, Benedict Wallet
1905-1947 .... **TCLC 37**

Villiers de l'Isle Adam, Jean Marie Mathias Philippe Auguste, Comte de
1838-1889 .... **NCLC 3**

Vinci, Leonardo da 1452-1519 .... **LC 12**

Vine, Barbara 1930- .... **CLC 50**
See also Rendell, Ruth

Vinge, Joan (Carol) D(ennison)
1948- .... **CLC 30**
See also CA 93-96; SATA 36

Visconti, Luchino 1906-1976 .... **CLC 16**
See also CA 81-84; obituary CA 65-68

Vittorini, Elio 1908-1966 ...... **CLC 6, 9, 14**
See also obituary CA 25-28R

Vizinczey, Stephen 1933- .... **CLC 40**

Vliet, R(ussell) G(ordon)
1929-1984 .... **CLC 22**
See also CANR 18; CA 37-40R; obituary CA 112

Voight, Ellen Bryant 1943- .... **CLC 54**
See also CANR 11; CA 69-72

Voigt, Cynthia 1942- .... **CLC 30**
See also CANR 18; CA 106; SATA 33, 48; AAYA 3

Voinovich, Vladimir (Nikolaevich)
1932- .... **CLC 10, 49**
See also CA 81-84

Voltaire 1694-1778 .... **LC 14**

Von Daeniken, Erich 1935-
See Von Daniken, Erich
See also CANR 17; CA 37-40R

Von Daniken, Erich 1935- .... **CLC 30**
See also Von Daeniken, Erich

Vonnegut, Kurt, Jr.
1922- ...... **CLC 1, 2, 3, 4, 5, 8, 12, 22, 40, 60; SSC 8**
See also CANR 1, 25; CA 1-4R; DLB 2, 8; DLB-Y 80; DLB-DS 3; CDALB 1968-1988; AAYA 6

Vorster, Gordon 1924- .... **CLC 34**

Voznesensky, Andrei 1933- ... **CLC 1, 15, 57**
See also CA 89-92

Waddington, Miriam 1917- .... **CLC 28**
See also CANR 12, 30; CA 21-24R; DLB 68

Wagman, Fredrica 1937- .... **CLC 7**
See also CA 97-100

Wagner, Richard 1813-1883 .... **NCLC 9**

Wagner-Martin, Linda 1936- .... **CLC 50**

Wagoner, David (Russell)
1926- .... **CLC 3, 5, 15**
See also CAAS 3; CANR 2; CA 1-4R; SATA 14; DLB 5

Wah, Fred(erick James) 1939- ...... **CLC 44**
See also CA 107; DLB 60

Wahloo, Per 1926-1975 .... **CLC 7**
See also CA 61-64

Wahloo, Peter 1926-1975
See Wahloo, Per

Wain, John (Barrington)
1925- .... **CLC 2, 11, 15, 46**
See also CAAS 4; CANR 23; CA 5-8R; DLB 15, 27

Wajda, Andrzej 1926- .... **CLC 16**
See also CA 102

Wakefield, Dan 1932- .... **CLC 7**
See also CAAS 7; CA 21-24R

Wakoski, Diane
1937- .... **CLC 2, 4, 7, 9, 11, 40**
See also CAAS 1; CANR 9; CA 13-16R; DLB 5

Walcott, Derek (Alton)
1930- .... **CLC 2, 4, 9, 14, 25, 42**
See also CANR 26; CA 89-92; DLB-Y 81

Waldman, Anne 1945- .... **CLC 7**
See also CA 37-40R; DLB 16

Waldo, Edward Hamilton 1918-
See Sturgeon, Theodore (Hamilton)

Walker, Alice
1944- ...... **CLC 5, 6, 9, 19, 27, 46, 58; SSC 5**
See also CANR 9, 27; CA 37-40R; SATA 31; DLB 6, 33; CDALB 1968-1988

Walker, David Harry 1911- .... **CLC 14**
See also CANR 1; CA 1-4R; SATA 8

Walker, Edward Joseph 1934-
See Walker, Ted
See also CANR 12; CA 21-24R

Walker, George F. 1947- .... **CLC 44, 61**
See also CANR 21; CA 103; DLB 60

Walker, Joseph A. 1935- .... **CLC 19**
See also CANR 26; CA 89-92; DLB 38

Walker, Margaret (Abigail)
1915- .... **CLC 1, 6**
See also CANR 26; CA 73-76; DLB 76

Walker, Ted 1934- .... **CLC 13**
See also Walker, Edward Joseph
See also DLB 40

Wallace, David Foster 1962- .... **CLC 50**

Wallace, Irving 1916- .... **CLC 7, 13**
See also CAAS 1; CANR 1; CA 1-4R

Wallant, Edward Lewis
1926-1962 .... **CLC 5, 10**
See also CANR 22; CA 1-4R; DLB 2, 28

Walpole, Horace 1717-1797 .... **LC 2**
See also DLB 39

Walpole, (Sir) Hugh (Seymour)
1884-1941 .... **TCLC 5**
See also CA 104; DLB 34

Walser, Martin 1927- .... **CLC 27**
See also CANR 8; CA 57-60; DLB 75

Walser, Robert 1878-1956 .... **TCLC 18**
See also CA 118; DLB 66

Walsh, Gillian Paton 1939-
See Walsh, Jill Paton
See also CA 37-40R; SATA 4

Walsh, Jill Paton 1939- .... **CLC 35**
See also CLR 2; SAAS 3

Wambaugh, Joseph (Aloysius, Jr.)
1937- .... **CLC 3, 18**
See also CA 33-36R; DLB 6; DLB-Y 83

Ward, Arthur Henry Sarsfield 1883-1959
See Rohmer, Sax
See also CA 108

Ward, Douglas Turner 1930- .... **CLC 19**
See also CA 81-84; DLB 7, 38

Warhol, Andy 1928-1987 .... **CLC 20**
See also CA 89-92; obituary CA 121

Warner, Francis (Robert le Plastrier)
1937- .... **CLC 14**
See also CANR 11; CA 53-56

Warner, Marina 1946- .... **CLC 59**
See also CANR 21; CA 65-68

Warner, Rex (Ernest) 1905-1986.... **CLC 45**
See also CA 89-92; obituary CA 119; DLB 15

Warner, Susan 1819-1885 .... **NCLC 31**
See also DLB 3, 42

Warner, Sylvia Townsend
1893-1978 .... **CLC 7, 19**
See also CANR 16; CA 61-64; obituary CA 77-80; DLB 34

Warren, Mercy Otis 1728-1814... **NCLC 13**
See also DLB 31

Warren, Robert Penn 1905-1989 ... **CLC 1, 4, 6, 8, 10, 13, 18, 39, 53, 59; SSC 4**
See also CANR 10; CA 13-16R. 129. 130; SATA 46; DLB 2, 48; DLB-Y 80; CDALB 1968-1987

Warton, Thomas 1728-1790 .... **LC 15**

Washington, Booker T(aliaferro) 1856-1915 .... **TCLC 10**
See also CA 114, 125; SATA 28

Wassermann, Jakob 1873-1934 ..... **TCLC 6**
See also CA 104; DLB 66

Wasserstein, Wendy 1950- ...... **CLC 32, 59**
See also CA 121; CABS 3

Waterhouse, Keith (Spencer) 1929- .... **CLC 47**
See also CA 5-8R; DLB 13, 15

Waters, Roger 1944-
See Pink Floyd

Wa Thiong'o, Ngugi 1938- .... **CLC 3, 7, 13, 36**
See also Ngugi, James (Thiong'o); Ngugi wa Thiong'o

Watkins, Paul 1964- .... **CLC 55**

Watkins, Vernon (Phillips) 1906-1967 .... **CLC 43**
See also CAP 1; CA 9-10; obituary CA 25-28R; DLB 20

Waugh, Auberon (Alexander) 1939- .. **CLC 7**
See also CANR 6, 22; CA 45-48; DLB 14

Waugh, Evelyn (Arthur St. John) 1903-1966 ... **CLC 1, 3, 8, 13, 19, 27, 44**
See also CANR 22; CA 85-88; obituary CA 25-28R; DLB 15

Waugh, Harriet 1944- .... **CLC 6**
See also CANR 22; CA 85-88

Webb, Beatrice (Potter) 1858-1943 .... **TCLC 22**
See also CA 117

Webb, Charles (Richard) 1939- ...... **CLC 7**
See also CA 25-28R

Webb, James H(enry), Jr. 1946- .... **CLC 22**
See also CA 81-84

Webb, Mary (Gladys Meredith) 1881-1927 .... **TCLC 24**
See also CA 123; DLB 34

Webb, Phyllis 1927- .... **CLC 18**
See also CANR 23; CA 104; DLB 53

Webb, Sidney (James) 1859-1947 .... **TCLC 22**
See also CA 117

Webber, Andrew Lloyd 1948- ...... **CLC 21**

Weber, Lenora Mattingly 1895-1971 .... **CLC 12**
See also CAP 1; CA 19-20; obituary CA 29-32R; SATA 2; obituary SATA 26

Webster, Noah 1758-1843 .... **NCLC 30**
See also DLB 1, 37, 42, 43, 73

Wedekind, (Benjamin) Frank(lin) 1864-1918 .... **TCLC 7**
See also CA 104

Weidman, Jerome 1913- .... **CLC 7**
See also CANR 1; CA 1-4R; DLB 28

Weil, Simone 1909-1943 .... **TCLC 23**
See also CA 117

Weinstein, Nathan Wallenstein 1903?-1940
See West, Nathanael
See also CA 104

Weir, Peter 1944- .... **CLC 20**
See also CA 113, 123

Weiss, Peter (Ulrich) 1916-1982 .... **CLC 3, 15, 51**
See also CANR 3; CA 45-48; obituary CA 106; DLB 69

Weiss, Theodore (Russell) 1916- .... **CLC 3, 8, 14**
See also CAAS 2; CA 9-12R; DLB 5

Welch, (Maurice) Denton 1915-1948 .... **TCLC 22**
See also CA 121

Welch, James 1940- .... **CLC 6, 14, 52**
See also CA 85-88

Weldon, Fay 1933- .... **CLC 6, 9, 11, 19, 36, 59**
See also CANR 16; CA 21-24R; DLB 14

Wellek, Rene 1903- .... **CLC 28**
See also CAAS 7; CANR 8; CA 5-8R; DLB 63

Weller, Michael 1942- .... **CLC 10, 53**
See also CA 85-88

Weller, Paul 1958- .... **CLC 26**

Wellershoff, Dieter 1925- .... **CLC 46**
See also CANR 16; CA 89-92

Welles, (George) Orson 1915-1985 .... **CLC 20**
See also CA 93-96; obituary CA 117

Wellman, Mac 1945- .... **CLC 65**

Wellman, Manly Wade 1903-1986 .. **CLC 49**
See also CANR 6, 16; CA 1-4R; obituary CA 118; SATA 6, 47

Wells, Carolyn 1862-1942 .... **TCLC 35**
See also CA 113; DLB 11

Wells, H(erbert) G(eorge) 1866-1946 ...... **TCLC 6, 12, 19; SSC 6**
See also CA 110, 121; SATA 20; DLB 34, 70

Wells, Rosemary 1943- .... **CLC 12**
See also CLR 16; CA 85-88; SAAS 1; SATA 18

Welty, Eudora (Alice) 1909- .... **CLC 1, 2, 5, 14, 22, 33; SSC 1**
See also CA 9-12R; CABS 1; DLB 2; DLB-Y 87; CDALB 1941-1968

Wen I-to 1899-1946 .... **TCLC 28**

Werfel, Franz (V.) 1890-1945 ...... **TCLC 8**
See also CA 104; DLB 81

Wergeland, Henrik Arnold 1808-1845 .... **NCLC 5**

Wersba, Barbara 1932- .... **CLC 30**
See also CLR 3; CANR 16; CA 29-32R; SAAS 2; SATA 1, 58; DLB 52

Wertmuller, Lina 1928- .... **CLC 16**
See also CA 97-100

Wescott, Glenway 1901-1987 .... **CLC 13**
See also CANR 23; CA 13-16R; obituary CA 121; DLB 4, 9

Wesker, Arnold 1932- .... **CLC 3, 5, 42**
See also CAAS 7; CANR 1; CA 1-4R; DLB 13

Wesley, Richard (Errol) 1945- .... **CLC 7**
See also CA 57-60; DLB 38

Wessel, Johan Herman 1742-1785 .... **LC 7**

West, Anthony (Panther) 1914-1987 .... **CLC 50**
See also CANR 3, 19; CA 45-48; DLB 15

West, Jessamyn 1907-1984 ...... **CLC 7, 17**
See also CA 9-12R; obituary CA 112; obituary SATA 37; DLB 6; DLB-Y 84

West, Morris L(anglo) 1916- ..... **CLC 6, 33**
See also CA 5-8R; obituary CA 124

West, Nathanael 1903?-1940 .... **TCLC 1, 14**
See also Weinstein, Nathan Wallenstein
See also CA 125, 140; DLB 4, 9, 28

West, Paul 1930- .... **CLC 7, 14**
See also CAAS 7; CANR 22; CA 13-16R; DLB 14

West, Rebecca 1892-1983 .. **CLC 7, 9, 31, 50**
See also CANR 19; CA 5-8R; obituary CA 109; DLB 36; DLB-Y 83

Westall, Robert (Atkinson) 1929- ... **CLC 17**
See also CLR 13; CANR 18; CA 69-72; SAAS 2; SATA 23

Westlake, Donald E(dwin) 1933- .... **CLC 7, 33**
See also CANR 16; CA 17-20R

Westmacott, Mary 1890-1976
See Christie, (Dame) Agatha (Mary Clarissa)

Whalen, Philip 1923- .... **CLC 6, 29**
See also CANR 5; CA 9-12R; DLB 16

Wharton, Edith (Newbold Jones) 1862-1937 .... **TCLC 3, 9, 27; SSC 6**
See also CA 104; DLB 4, 9, 12, 78; CDALB 1865-1917

Wharton, William 1925- .... **CLC 18, 37**
See also CA 93-96; DLB-Y 80

Wheatley (Peters), Phillis 1753?-1784 .... **LC 3**
See also DLB 31, 50; CDALB 1640-1865

Wheelock, John Hall 1886-1978 .... **CLC 14**
See also CANR 14; CA 13-16R; obituary CA 77-80; DLB 45

Whelan, John 1900-
See O'Faolain, Sean

Whitaker, Rodney 1925-
See Trevanian

White, E(lwyn) B(rooks) 1899-1985 .... **CLC 10, 34, 39**
See also CLR 1; CANR 16; CA 13-16R; obituary CA 116; SATA 2, 29, 44; obituary SATA 44; DLB 11, 22

White, Edmund III 1940- .... **CLC 27**
See also CANR 3, 19; CA 45-48

White, Patrick (Victor Martindale) 1912-1990 ..... **CLC 3, 4, 5, 7, 9, 18, 65**
See also CA 81-84; obituary CA 132

White, T(erence) H(anbury) 1906-1964 .... **CLC 30**
See also CA 73-76; SATA 12

White, Terence de Vere 1912- ...... **CLC 49**
See also CANR 3; CA 49-52

White, Walter (Francis) 1893-1955 .... **TCLC 15**
See also CA 115, 124; DLB 51

White, William Hale 1831-1913
See Rutherford, Mark
See also CA 121

Whitehead, E(dward) A(nthony) 1933- .... **CLC 5**
See also CA 65-68

Whitemore, Hugh 1936- .... **CLC 37**

Whitman, Sarah Helen 1803-1878 .... **NCLC 19**
See also DLB 1

Whitman, Walt 1819-1892 ..... **NCLC 4, 31**
See also SATA 20; DLB 3, 64; CDALB 1640-1865

Whitney, Phyllis A(yame) 1903- .... **CLC 42**
See also CANR 3, 25; CA 1-4R; SATA 1, 30

Whittemore, (Edward) Reed (Jr.) 1919- .... **CLC 4**
See also CAAS 8; CANR 4; CA 9-12R; DLB 5

Whittier, John Greenleaf 1807-1892 .... **NCLC 8**
See also DLB 1; CDALB 1640-1865

Wicker, Thomas Grey 1926-
See Wicker, Tom
See also CANR 21; CA 65-68

Wicker, Tom 1926- .... **CLC 7**
See also Wicker, Thomas Grey

Wideman, John Edgar 1941- .... **CLC 5, 34, 36**
See also CANR 14; CA 85-88; DLB 33

Wiebe, Rudy (H.) 1934- ...... **CLC 6, 11, 14**
See also CA 37-40R; DLB 60

Wieland, Christoph Martin 1733-1813 .... **NCLC 17**

Wieners, John 1934- .... **CLC 7**
See also CA 13-16R; DLB 16

Wiesel, Elie(zer) 1928- ..... **CLC 3, 5, 11, 37**
See also CAAS 4; CANR 8; CA 5-8R; SATA 56; DLB 83; DLB-Y 87

Wiggins, Marianne 1948- .... **CLC 57**

Wight, James Alfred 1916-
See Herriot, James
See also CA 77-80; SATA 44

Wilbur, Richard (Purdy) 1921- .... **CLC 3, 6, 9, 14, 53**
See also CANR 2; CA 1-4R; CABS 2; SATA 9; DLB 5

Wild, Peter 1940- .... **CLC 14**
See also CA 37-40R; DLB 5

Wilde, Oscar (Fingal O'Flahertie Wills) 1854-1900 .... **TCLC 1, 8, 23, 41**
See also CA 119; brief entry CA 104; SATA 24; DLB 10, 19, 34, 57

Wilder, Billy 1906- .... **CLC 20**
See also Wilder, Samuel
See also DLB 26

Wilder, Samuel 1906-
See Wilder, Billy
See also CA 89-92

Wilder, Thornton (Niven) 1897-1975 ..... **CLC 1, 5, 6, 10, 15, 35; DC 1**
See also CA 13-16R; obituary CA 61-64; DLB 4, 7, 9

Wiley, Richard 1944- .... **CLC 44**
See also CA 121, 129

Wilhelm, Kate 1928- .... **CLC 7**
See also CAAS 5; CANR 17; CA 37-40R; DLB 8

Willard, Nancy 1936- .... **CLC 7, 37**
See also CLR 5; CANR 10; CA 89-92; SATA 30, 37; DLB 5, 52

Williams, C(harles) K(enneth) 1936- .... **CLC 33, 56**
See also CA 37-40R; DLB 5

Williams, Charles (Walter Stansby) 1886-1945 .... **TCLC 1, 11**
See also CA 104

Williams, Ella Gwendolen Rees 1890-1979
See Rhys, Jean

Williams, (George) Emlyn 1905-1987 .... **CLC 15**
See also CA 104, 123; DLB 10, 77

Williams, Hugo 1942- .... **CLC 42**
See also CA 17-20R; DLB 40

Williams, John A(lfred) 1925- .... **CLC 5, 13**
See also CAAS 3; CANR 6, 26; CA 53-56; DLB 2, 33

Williams, Jonathan (Chamberlain) 1929- .... **CLC 13**
See also CANR 8; CA 9-12R; DLB 5

Williams, Joy 1944- .... **CLC 31**
See also CANR 22; CA 41-44R

Williams, Norman 1952- .... **CLC 39**
See also CA 118

Williams, Paulette 1948-
See Shange, Ntozake

Williams, Tennessee 1911-1983 .... **CLC 1, 2, 5, 7, 8, 11, 15, 19, 30, 39, 45**
See also CA 5-8R; obituary CA 108; DLB 7; DLB-Y 83; DLB-DS 4; CDALB 1941-1968

Williams, Thomas (Alonzo) 1926- ... **CLC 14**
See also CANR 2; CA 1-4R

Williams, Thomas Lanier 1911-1983
See Williams, Tennessee

Williams, William Carlos 1883-1963 .... **CLC 1, 2, 5, 9, 13, 22, 42**
See also CA 89-92; DLB 4, 16, 54, 86

Williamson, David 1932- .... **CLC 56**

Williamson, Jack 1908- .... **CLC 29**
See also Williamson, John Stewart
See also DLB 8

Williamson, John Stewart 1908-
See Williamson, Jack
See also CANR 123; CA 17-20R

Willingham, Calder (Baynard, Jr.) 1922- .... **CLC 5, 51**
See also CANR 3; CA 5-8R; DLB 2, 44

Wilson, A(ndrew) N(orman) 1950- .. **CLC 33**
See also CA 112, 122; DLB 14

Wilson, Andrew 1948-
See Wilson, Snoo

Wilson, Angus (Frank Johnstone) 1913- .... **CLC 2, 3, 5, 25, 34**
See also CANR 21; CA 5-8R; DLB 15

Wilson, August 1945- .... **CLC 39, 50, 63**
See also CA 115, 122

Wilson, Brian 1942- .... **CLC 12**

Wilson, Colin 1931- .... **CLC 3, 14**
See also CAAS 5; CANR 1, 122; CA 1-4R; DLB 14

Wilson, Edmund 1895-1972 .... **CLC 1, 2, 3, 8, 24**
See also CANR 1; CA 1-4R; obituary CA 37-40R; DLB 63

Wilson, Ethel Davis (Bryant) 1888-1980 .... **CLC 13**
See also CA 102; DLB 68

Wilson, John 1785-1854 .... **NCLC 5**

Wilson, John (Anthony) Burgess 1917-
See Burgess, Anthony
See also CANR 2; CA 1-4R

Wilson, Lanford 1937- .... **CLC 7, 14, 36**
See also CA 17-20R; DLB 7

Wilson, Robert (M.) 1944- .... **CLC 7, 9**
See also CANR 2; CA 49-52

Wilson, Sloan 1920- .... **CLC 32**
See also CANR 1; CA 1-4R

Wilson, Snoo 1948- .... **CLC 33**
See also CA 69-72

Wilson, William S(mith) 1932- ..... **CLC 49**
See also CA 81-84

Winchilsea, Anne (Kingsmill) Finch, Countess of 1661-1720 .... **LC 3**

Winters, Janet Lewis 1899-
See Lewis (Winters), Janet
See also CAP 1; CA 9-10

Winters, (Arthur) Yvor 1900-1968 .... **CLC 4, 8, 32**
See also CAP 1; CA 11-12; obituary CA 25-28R; DLB 48

Winterson, Jeannette 1959- .... **CLC 64**

Wiseman, Frederick 1930- .... **CLC 20**

Wister, Owen 1860-1938 .... **TCLC 21**
See also CA 108; DLB 9, 78

Witkiewicz, Stanislaw Ignacy 1885-1939 .... **TCLC 8**
See also CA 105; DLB 83

Wittig, Monique 1935?- .... **CLC 22**
See also CA 116; DLB 83

Wittlin, Joseph 1896-1976 .... **CLC 25**
See also Wittlin, Jozef

Wittlin, Jozef 1896-1976
See Wittlin, Joseph
See also CANR 3; CA 49-52; obituary CA 65-68

Wodehouse, (Sir) P(elham) G(renville) 1881-1975 ... **CLC 1, 2, 5, 10, 22; SSC 2**
See also CANR 3; CA 45-48; obituary CA 57-60; SATA 22; DLB 34

Woiwode, Larry (Alfred) 1941- ... **CLC 6, 10**
See also CANR 16; CA 73-76; DLB 6

Wojciechowska, Maia (Teresa) 1927- .... **CLC 26**
See also CLR 1; CANR 4; CA 9-12R; SAAS 1; SATA 1, 28

Wolf, Christa 1929- .... **CLC 14, 29, 58**
See also CA 85-88; DLB 75

Wolfe, Gene (Rodman) 1931-...... **CLC 25**
See also CAAS 9; CANR 6; CA 57-60; DLB 8

Wolfe, George C. 1954- .... **CLC 49**

Wolfe, Thomas (Clayton)
1900-1938 .... **TCLC 4, 13, 29**
See also CA 104; DLB 9; DLB-Y 85; DLB-DS 2

Wolfe, Thomas Kennerly, Jr. 1931-
See Wolfe, Tom
See also CANR 9; CA 13-16R

Wolfe, Tom 1931-... **CLC 1, 2, 9, 15, 35, 51**
See also Wolfe, Thomas Kennerly, Jr.

Wolff, Geoffrey (Ansell) 1937- ..... **CLC 41**
See also CA 29-32R

Wolff, Tobias (Jonathan Ansell)
1945- .... **CLC 39, 64**
See also CA 114, 117

Wolfram von Eschenbach
c. 1170-c. 1220 .... **CMLC 5**

Wolitzer, Hilma 1930- .... **CLC 17**
See also CANR 18; CA 65-68; SATA 31

Wollstonecraft (Godwin), Mary
1759-1797 .... **LC 5**
See also DLB 39

Wonder, Stevie 1950- .... **CLC 12**
See also Morris, Steveland Judkins

Wong, Jade Snow 1922- .... **CLC 17**
See also CA 109

Woodcott, Keith 1934-
See Brunner, John (Kilian Houston)

Woolf, (Adeline) Virginia
1882-1941 .... **TCLC 1, 5, 20; SSC 7**
See also CA 130; brief entry CA 104; DLB 36

Woollcott, Alexander (Humphreys)
1887-1943 .... **TCLC 5**
See also CA 105; DLB 29

Wordsworth, Dorothy
1771-1855 .... **NCLC 25**

Wordsworth, William 1770-1850.. **NCLC 12**

Wouk, Herman 1915- .... **CLC 1, 9, 38**
See also CANR 6; CA 5-8R; DLB-Y 82

Wright, Charles 1935- .... **CLC 6, 13, 28**
See also CAAS 7; CA 29-32R; DLB-Y 82

Wright, Charles (Stevenson) 1932- .. **CLC 49**
See also CA 9-12R; DLB 33

Wright, James (Arlington)
1927-1980 .... **CLC 3, 5, 10, 28**
See also CANR 4; CA 49-52; obituary CA 97-100; DLB 5

Wright, Judith 1915- .... **CLC 11, 53**
See also CA 13-16R; SATA 14

Wright, L(aurali) R. 1939- .... **CLC 44**

Wright, Richard (Nathaniel)
1908-1960 ... **CLC 1, 3, 4, 9, 14, 21, 48; SSC 2**
See also CA 108; DLB 76; DLB-DS 2

Wright, Richard B(ruce) 1937- ...... **CLC 6**
See also CA 85-88; DLB 53

Wright, Rick 1945-
See Pink Floyd

Wright, Stephen 1946- .... **CLC 33**

Wright, Willard Huntington 1888-1939
See Van Dine, S. S.
See also CA 115

Wright, William 1930- .... **CLC 44**
See also CANR 7, 23; CA 53-56

Wu Ch'eng-en 1500?-1582? .... **LC 7**

Wu Ching-tzu 1701-1754 .... **LC 2**

Wurlitzer, Rudolph 1938?- ..... **CLC 2, 4, 15**
See also CA 85-88

Wycherley, William 1640?-1716 ...... **LC 8**
See also DLB 80

Wylie (Benet), Elinor (Morton Hoyt)
1885-1928 .... **TCLC 8**
See also CA 105; DLB 9, 45

Wylie, Philip (Gordon) 1902-1971... **CLC 43**
See also CAP 2; CA 21-22; obituary CA 33-36R; DLB 9

Wyndham, John 1903-1969 .... **CLC 19**
See also Harris, John (Wyndham Parkes Lucas) Beynon

Wyss, Johann David 1743-1818 .. **NCLC 10**
See also SATA 27, 29

Yanovsky, Vassily S(emenovich)
1906-1989 .... **CLC 2, 18**
See also CA 97-100; obituary CA 129

Yates, Richard 1926- .... **CLC 7, 8, 23**
See also CANR 10; CA 5-8R; DLB 2; DLB-Y 81

Yeats, William Butler
1865-1939 .... **TCLC 1, 11, 18, 31**
See also CANR 10; CA 104; DLB 10, 19

Yehoshua, A(braham) B.
1936- .... **CLC 13, 31**
See also CA 33-36R

Yep, Laurence (Michael) 1948- ..... **CLC 35**
See also CLR 3, 17; CANR 1; CA 49-52; SATA 7; DLB 52

Yerby, Frank G(arvin) 1916- ... **CLC 1, 7, 22**
See also CANR 16; CA 9-12R; DLB 76

Yevtushenko, Yevgeny (Alexandrovich)
1933- .... **CLC 1, 3, 13, 26, 51**
See also CA 81-84

Yezierska, Anzia 1885?-1970 .... **CLC 46**
See also CA 126; obituary CA 89-92; DLB 28

Yglesias, Helen 1915- .... **CLC 7, 22**
See also CANR 15; CA 37-40R

Yorke, Henry Vincent 1905-1974
See Green, Henry
See also CA 85-88; obituary CA 49-52

Young, Al 1939- .... **CLC 19**
See also CANR 26; CA 29-32R; DLB 33

Young, Andrew 1885-1971 .... **CLC 5**
See also CANR 7; CA 5-8R

Young, Edward 1683-1765 .... **LC 3**

Young, Neil 1945- .... **CLC 17**
See also CA 110

Yourcenar, Marguerite
1903-1987 .... **CLC 19, 38, 50**
See also CANR 23; CA 69-72; DLB 72; DLB-Y 88

Yurick, Sol 1925- .... **CLC 6**
See also CANR 25; CA 13-16R

Zamyatin, Yevgeny Ivanovich
1884-1937 .... **TCLC 8, 37**
See also CA 105

Zangwill, Israel 1864-1926 .... **TCLC 16**
See also CA 109; DLB 10

Zappa, Francis Vincent, Jr. 1940-
See Zappa, Frank
See also CA 108

Zappa, Frank 1940- .... **CLC 17**
See also Zappa, Francis Vincent, Jr.

Zaturenska, Marya 1902-1982.... **CLC 6, 11**
See also CANR 22; CA 13-16R; obituary CA 105

Zelazny, Roger 1937- .... **CLC 21**
See also CANR 26; CA 21-24R; SATA 39, 59; DLB 8

Zhdanov, Andrei A(lexandrovich)
1896-1948 .... **TCLC 18**
See also CA 117

Ziegenhagen, Eric 1970- .... **CLC 55**

Zimmerman, Robert 1941-
See Dylan, Bob

Zindel, Paul 1936- .... **CLC 6, 26**
See also CLR 3; CA 73-76; SATA 16, 58; DLB 7, 52

Zinoviev, Alexander 1922- .... **CLC 19**
See also CAAS 10; CA 116

Zola, Emile 1840-1902 ... **TCLC 1, 6, 21, 41**
See also brief entry CA 104

Zoline, Pamela 1941- .... **CLC 62**

Zorrilla y Moral, Jose 1817-1893.. **NCLC 6**

Zoshchenko, Mikhail (Mikhailovich)
1895-1958 .... **TCLC 15**
See also CA 115

Zuckmayer, Carl 1896-1977 .... **CLC 18**
See also CA 69-72; DLB 56

Zukofsky, Louis
1904-1978 .... **CLC 1, 2, 4, 7, 11, 18**
See also CA 9-12R; obituary CA 77-80; DLB 5

Zweig, Paul 1935-1984 .... **CLC 34, 42**
See also CA 85-88; obituary CA 113

Zweig, Stefan 1881-1942 .... **TCLC 17**
See also CA 112; DLB 81

Author Index

SSC Cumulative Nationality Index

AMERICAN
Anderson, Sherwood **1**
Barnes, Djuna **3**
Barthelme, Donald **2**
Bowles, Paul **3**
Boyle, Kay **5**
Cable, George Washington **4**
Capote, Truman **2**
Carver, Raymond **8**
Cather, Willa **2**
Cheever, John **1**
Chesnutt, Charles Wadell **7**
Chopin, Kate **8**
Crane, Stephen **7**
Dunbar, Paul Laurence **8**
Faulkner, William **1**
Fitzgerald, F. Scott **6**
Freeman, Mary Wilkins **1**
Gardner, John **7**
Harte, Bret **8**
Hawthorne, Nathaniel **3**
Hemingway, Ernest **1**
Henry, O. **5**
Hughes, Langston **6**
Hurston, Zora Neale **4**
Irving, Washington **2**
James, Henry **8**
Jewett, Sarah Orne **6**
London, Jack **4**
Marshall, Paule **3**
Mason, Bobbie Ann **4**
Melville, Herman **1**
Oates, Joyce Carol **6**
O'Connor, Flannery **1**
Paley, Grace **8**
Parker, Dorothy **2**
Poe, Edgar Allan **1**
Porter, Katherine Anne **4**
Powers, J. F. **4**
Salinger, J. D. **2**
Singer, Isaac Bashevis **3**
Thurber, James **1**
Toomer, Jean **1**
Twain, Mark **6**
Vonnegut, Kurt, Jr. **8**
Walker, Alice **5**
Warren, Robert Penn **4**
Welty, Eudora **1**
Wharton, Edith **6**
Wright, Richard **2**

ARGENTINIAN
Borges, Jorge Luis **4**
Cortazar, Julio **7**

AUSTRIAN
Kafka, Franz **5**

CANADIAN
Atwood, Margaret **2**
Gallant, Mavis **5**
Laurence, Margaret **7**
Munro, Alice **3**

COLUMBIAN
García Márquez, Gabriel **8**

CUBAN
Calvino, Italo **3**

CZECHOSLOVAKIAN
Kafka, Franz **5**

DANISH
Andersen, Hans Christian **6**
Dinesen, Isak **7**

ENGLISH
Ballard, J. G. **1**
Bowen, Elizabeth **3**
Chesterton, G. K. **1**
Clarke, Arthur C. **3**
Hardy, Thomas **2**
Kipling, Rudyard **5**
Lawrence, D. H. **4**
Lessing, Doris (Newbold Jones) **6**
Lovecraft, H. P. **3**
Maugham, W. Somerset **8**
Wells, H. G. **6**
Wodehouse, P. G. **2**
Woolf, Virginia **7**

FRENCH
Balzac, Honore de **5**
Maupassant, Guy de **1**
Merimee, Prosper **7**

GERMAN
Kafka, Franz **5**
Mann, Thomas **5**

IRISH
Bowen, Elizabeth **3**
Joyce, James **3**
Lavin, Mary **4**
O'Connor, Frank **5**
O'Flaherty, Liam **6**

ITALIAN
Calvino, Italo **3**

JAPANESE
Mishima, Yukio **4**

RUSSIAN
Bunin, Ivan **5**

Chekhov, Anton 2
Dostoevski, Fedor 2
Gogol, Nikolai 4
Turgenev, Ivan 7

WELSH
Thomas, Dylan 3

SSC Cumulative Title Index

"À sale" (Maupassant) **1**:262
"L'abandonné" (Maupassant) **1**:259
"L'abbé Aubain" (Mérimée) **7**:290, 292, 295, 300
"The Abduction from the Seraglio" (Barthelme) **2**:46, 51-2
"The Abortion" (Walker) **5**:412, 414
"About How Ivan Ivanovič Quarreled with Ivan Nikiforovič" (Gogol)
See "The Tale of How Ivan Ivanovich Quarrelled with Ivan Nikiforovich"
"About Love" (Chekhov) **2**:139, 141, 143, 157
"The Absence of Mr. Glass" (Chesterton) **1**:131
"Absent-Mindedness in a Parish Choir" (Hardy) **2**:206, 215, 217
"Absolution" (Fitzgerald) **6**:46, 77, 81, 83-4, 86, 100, 102-03
"Acceptance of Their Ways" (Gallant) **5**:139-40
"El acercamiento a Almotásim" ("The Approach towards Al-Mu'tásim") (Borges) **4**:4, 16
"Achilles' Heel" (O'Connor) **5**:370, 372
Acia (Turgenev)
See *Asya*
Actions and Reactions (Kipling) **5**:272, 283-85
"The Actor and the Alibi" (Chesterton) **1**:138
"Ad Astra" (Faulkner) **1**:147
"Adam, One Afternoon" (Calvino) **3**:112
Adam, One Afternoon, and Other Stories (Calvino)
See *Ultimo viene il corvo*
"Adam's Death" (Boyle) **5**:57
"Adieu" (Balzac) **5**:17-18, 22, 24, 31, 33
"The Adjuster" (Fitzgerald) **6**:46
"The Admirer" (Singer) **3**:378, 384
"Advancing Luna—and Ida B. Wells" (Walker) **5**:412-13
"Adventure" (Anderson) **1**:18, 58
"An Adventure from a Work in Progress" (Thomas) **3**:402, 407
"The Adventure of a Clerk" (Calvino) **3**:116
"Adventure of a Photographer" (Calvino) **3**:111
"Adventure of a Poet" (Calvino) **3**:111, 116
"The Adventure of a Reader" (Calvino) **3**:112
"Adventure of a Traveller" (Calvino) **3**:111
"The Adventure of Lieutenant Jergounoff" (Turgenev)
See "Istoriya leytenanta Ergunova"
"The Adventure of the Black Fisherman" (Irving) **2**:241, 247
"The Adventure of the Englishman" (Irving) **2**:262
"The Adventure of the German Student" (Irving) **2**:241, 256-57, 261
"The Adventure of the Mason" (Irving) **2**:266
"Adventure of the Mysterious Picture" (Irving) **2**:261, 265
"Adventure of the Mysterious Stranger" (Irving) **2**:261
Adventures in the Skin Trade, and Other Stories (Thomas) **3**:396, 403-04
"The Adventures of Françoise and Suzanne" (Cable) **4**:49
"Advice to Young Men" (Chesnutt) **7**:14
"Aepyornis Island" (Wells) **6**:388, 399
"The Affair at Grover Station" (Cather) **2**:102
"The Aficionados" (Carver) **8**:50
"African Morning" (Hughes) **6**:116-17, 122
African Stories (Lessing) **6**:189-91, 196, 212, 214-15, 217-18
"After Dinner" (Cortázar) **7**:70
"After Fourteen Years" (O'Connor) **5**:381, 387, 392
"After Holbein" (Wharton) **6**:422-23
After-Hours (Cortázar)
See *Deshoras*
"After Lunch" (Cortázar) **7**:70
After Such Pleasures (Parker) **2**:273-74
"After the Denim" (Carver) **8**:14
"After the Fair" (Thomas) **3**:399
"After the Race" (Joyce) **3**:205, 208-09, 226, 231, 234, 247-48
"After the Storm" (Hemingway) **1**:216, 234
"After the Winter" (Chopin) **8**:93
"An Afternoon Miracle" (Henry) **5**:162, 181
"Afternoon of a Playwright" (Thurber) **1**:424
Afternoon of an Author (Fitzgerald) **6**:60
"Afterward" (Wharton) **6**:433
"Agafia" (Chekhov) **2**:155
Ah King (Maugham) **8**:374, 378
"Ahí, pero dónde, cómo" (Cortázar) **7**:61-2
Ahí y ahora (*There and Now*) (Cortázar) **7**:91
"An Akoulina of the Irish Midlands" (Lavin) **4**:182-83
"Al-Mamun" (Gogol) **4**:83
"Albert Savarus" (Balzac) **5**:27
"Alec" (O'Connor) **5**:371, 390
"The Aleph" (Borges) **4**:25, 28, 31-2, 34
El Aleph (*The Aleph, and Other Stories*) (Borges) **4**:15, 18-20, 34, 36, 39-41
The Aleph, and Other Stories (Borges)
See *El Aleph*
"Alguien desordena estas rosas" ("Someone Has Disturbed the Roses") (García Márquez) **8**:154, 158
The Alhambra (Irving) **2**:242-46, 251, 254, 265, 268
"Alicia's Diary" (Hardy) **2**:211, 214

"The Alien Corn" (Maugham) **8**:356-57, 366, 369, 378-79
"An Alien Flower" (Gallant) **5**:124, 132-33
"The Alien Skull" (O'Flaherty) **6**:262, 280
"Alix de Morainville" (Cable) **4**:60
"Alkmene" (Dinesen) **7**:165
"All at One Point" (Calvino) **3**:103, 108
All Fires Are Fire (Cortázar)
See *Todos los fuegos el fuego*
"All Fires the Fire" (Cortázar)
See "Todos los fuegos el fuego"
All Fires the Fire (Cortázar)
See *Todos los fuegos el fuego*
"All Saints" (Bowen) **3**:40, 42
"All Souls'" (Wharton) **6**:423, 426-27
"All That Glitters" (Clarke) **3**:134
"All the Dead Pilots" (Faulkner) **1**:147
"ALL the Good People I've Left Behind" (Oates) **6**:250, 252-53
All the Good People I've Left Behind (Oates) **6**:247-48, 250, 252-54
"All the King's Horses" (Vonnegut) **8**:434
"All the Other Stories" (Calvino) **3**:101
All the Sad Young Men (Fitzgerald) **6**:46, 94
"All the Time in the World" (Clarke) **3**:135
"Allal" (Bowles) **3**:69
"Aller et Retour" (Barnes) **3**:7-8, 10, 14-17, 24
"Aloha Oe" (London) **4**:269
"Alone" (Singer) **3**:360-61, 364
"Alpimalyan Dialogue" (Turgenev) **7**:335
"An Alpine Idyll" (Hemingway) **1**:210, 217
Alquien que anda por ahí (*Someone Walking Around*) (Cortázar) **7**:85-7, 90
"Alquien que anda por ahí" ("Someone Walking Around") (Cortázar) **7**:83, 90-1
"The Altar of the Dead" (James) **8**:269, 302, 304, 307-09
Altogether: The Collected Stories of W. Somerset Maugham (*East and West: The Complete Short Stories of W. Somerset Maugham*) (Maugham) **8**:356, 358, 360, 370, 380, 382
"Am I Not Your Rosalind?" (Thurber) **1**:420, 425
"Amargura para tres sonámbulos" ("Bitterness for Three Sleepwalkers") (García Márquez) **8**:154-55, 157-58, 182
"Amateurs" (Barthelme) **2**:47
"The Ambitious Guest" (Hawthorne) **3**:182, 186-87
"The Ambitious Sophomore" (Vonnegut) **8**:431
"Ambuscade" (Faulkner) **1**:170, 177
"The American Wife" (O'Connor) **5**:373
"Les âmes du purgatoire" ("The Souls in Purgatory") (Mérimée) **7**:283-84, 289-90, 292
"Los amigos" ("The Friends") (Cortázar) **7**:70, 88-9
"Among the Paths to Eden" (Capote) **2**:74-5
Gli amori difficili (*Difficult Loves*) (Calvino) **3**:111-13, 116-18
"Amour" (Maupassant) **1**:278, 280
Analytical Studies (Balzac)
See *Etudes analytiques*
"Ancestors" (Woolf) **7**:381, 389
"& Answers" (Oates) **6**:232
"And Then" (Barthelme) **2**:47
"Andrei Kolosov" ("Andrei Kolossov") (Turgenev) **7**:313, 320, 323-24, 335, 339-40, 359
"Andrei Kolossov" (Turgenev)
See "Andrei Kolosov"
"Andrey Satchel and the Parson and Clerk" (Hardy) **2**:215
"Androcles and the Army" (O'Connor) **5**:369, 374
"L'âne" (Maupassant) **1**:259
Anecdotes of Destiny (Dinesen) **7**:175
"The Angel" (Andersen) **6**:15
"The Angel at the Grave" (Wharton) **6**:414
"The Angel of the Bridge" (Cheever) **1**:96, 100, 110
"The Angel of the Odd" (Poe) **1**:407-08
"Angst" (Oates) **6**:241
"Ann Lee's" (Bowen) **3**:54
Ann Lee's (Bowen) **3**:37, 39-40, 55
"Anna on the Neck" (Chekhov) **2**:131, 157
"Anne Lisbeth" (Andersen) **6**:14-15
"Anner 'Lizer's Stumblin' Block" (Dunbar) **8**:120-21, 129, 136
"Annette Delarbre" (Irving) **2**:241, 251, 259
"Gli anni-lucci" (Calvino) **3**:92
"An Anonymous Story" ("A Story without a Title") (Chekhov) **2**:130-31, 157-58
"Another Man's Wife" (Anderson) **1**:39
"Another Story" (Cheever) **1**:112
"Another Wife" (Anderson) **1**:31, 50-1
"Answer to Prayer" (Wells) **6**:392
"The Antchar" (Turgenev) **7**:318-19
The Antheap (Lessing) **6**:189-91, 193-94, 196
"Antigona" ("Antigone") (Bunin) **5**:113
"Antigone" (Bunin)
See "Antigona"
"The Antique Ring" (Hawthorne) **3**:189, 191
"Antónov Apples" (Bunin) **5**:81, 100
"Antonovskie jabloki" (Bunin) **5**:98-9
"Anxiety" (Paley) **8**:411-12
"Any Reasonable Offer" (Vonnegut) **8**:433
"Apacalipsis de Solentiname" ("Apocalypse at Solentiname") (Cortázar) **7**:83, 86, 88, 90-1
"Apocalypse at Solentiname" (Cortázar)
See "Apacalipsis de Solentiname"
"The Apostate" (London) **4**:263, 291-92
"An Apostle of the Tulles" (Harte) **8**:247-49
"Apparition" (Maupassant) **1**:265, 281
"Appearance and Reality" (Maugham) **8**:380
"The Apple" (Wells) **6**:359, 383
"The Apple Tree" (Bowen) **3**:33, 41
"The Apple-Tree Table" (Melville) **1**:294-95, 298
"The Approach towards Al-Mu'tásim" (Borges)
See "El acercamiento a Almotásim"
"April Fish" (Gallant) **5**:151
"Apropos of the Wet Snow" ("Concerning Wet Snow") (Dostoevski) **2**:169, 187
"The Aquatic Uncle" (Calvino)
See "Lo zio acquativo"
Arabesques (Gogol) **4**:104
"Araby" (Joyce) **3**:202-03, 205, 208, 217-18, 225, 231, 234, 237, 242, 245-46, 249
"Ardessa" (Cather) **2**:99, 110-11
"Are These Actual Miles?" (Carver) **8**:47
"Are You a Doctor?" (Carver) **8**:9-10, 18, 32, 34, 47
The Argentine Ant (Calvino)
See *La formica argentina*
"The Argonauts of North Liberty" (Harte) **8**:214, 216-17, 223
"The Argonauts of the Air" (Wells) **6**:359, 367, 374, 380, 383, 388, 403
"Ariadna" (Chekhov)
See "Ariadne"
"Ariadne" ("Ariadna") (Chekhov) **2**:131-32, 157
"La armas secretas" ("Secret Weapons") (Cortázar) **7**:56-8, 81-3
Las Armas Secretas (*Secret Weapons*) (Cortázar) **7**:50, 53-4, 70-1
"Army of Occupation" (Boyle) **5**:64, 74-5
Around the Day in Eighty Worlds (Cortázar)
See *La vuelta al día en ochenta mundos*
"Arrangement in Black and White" (Parker) **2**:274-75, 278, 280, 283, 286
"The Arrest of Lieutenant Golightly" (Kipling) **5**:288, 290
"The Arrow of Heaven" (Chesterton) **1**:128
"Arsène Guillot" (Mérimée) **7**:279, 290-92, 300
"The Art of Bookmaking" (Irving) **2**:254
"The Art of Living" (Gardner) **7**:224-28, 235, 240
The Art of Living, and Other Stories (Gardner) **7**:223-28, 235
"Artemis, the Honest Well-Digger" (Cheever) **1**:107-08
"Arthur Jermyn" (Lovecraft) **3**:258, 264
"The Artificial Nigger" (O'Connor) **1**:343, 345, 347, 353
"Artificial Roses" (García Márquez) **8**:185
"The Artist of the Beautiful" (Hawthorne) **3**:169-71, 174, 183-84
"The Artistic Career of Corky" (Wodehouse) **2**:342
"An Artist's Story" ("The House with an Attic"; "The House with the Maisonette"; "The House with a Mezzanine") (Chekhov) **2**:131, 139, 157
"Ash-Cake Hannah and Her Ben" (Dunbar) **8**:122
Ashenden; or, The British Agent (Maugham) **8**:365, 367, 376-78, 380, 383
"Asigh" (Lavin) **4**:167-68, 181-83
Asja (Turgenev)
See *Asya*
The Aspern Papers (James) **8**:275, 300, 321-22, 324, 332, 335
"Asphodel" (Welty) **1**:467-69, 472
"The Assassination of John Fitzgerald Kennedy Considered as a Downhill Motor Race" (Ballard) **1**:70-1, 75
"Assault" (Oates) **6**:243
"The Assembly" (Borges)
See "El congreso"
"The Assembly" (Gallant) **5**:147
"The Assessor of Success" (Henry) **5**:187
"The Assignation" (Poe) **1**:394
Asya (*Acia*; *Asja*) (Turgenev) **7**:320, 323-24, 326-27, 334, 337, 339, 347-52, 360
"At Chênière Caminada" (Chopin) **8**:95, 99, 110
"At Christmas-Time" (Chekhov) **2**:130-31
"At Daybreak" (Calvino) **3**:109
"At Geisenheimer's" (Wodehouse) **2**:355
"At Home" (Chekhov) **2**:139, 142, 155, 157-58
"At Paso Rojo" (Bowles) **3**:59, 61-2, 66, 79
"At Sallygap" (Lavin) **4**:169, 171-72, 175, 178-79, 182
"At Shaft 11" (Dunbar) **8**:120-21, 127, 129, 131, 136, 139-40, 143
"At the 'Cadian Ball" (Chopin) **8**:72, 91, 95, 99, 106-07

"At the End of the Mechanical Age" (Barthelme) **2**:47
"At the End of the Passage" ("The End of the Passage") (Kipling) **5**:264, 271-72, 274, 278, 280-81, 290-91
"At the Krungthep Plaza" (Bowles) **3**:80
"At the Landing" (Welty) **1**:468
"At the Prophet's" (Mann) **5**:323
"At the Rainbow's End" (London) **4**:286
"At the Seminary" (Oates) **6**:255-56
"At the Tolstoy Museum" (Barthelme) **2**:31, 35, 40, 48, 56
"Athénaïse" (Chopin) **8**:66, 72-3, 78, 86, 96, 99, 113-14
"The Atrocity Exhibition" (Ballard) **1**:75
The Atrocity Exhibition (*Love and Napalm: Export U.S.A.*) (Ballard) **1**:70-1, 76-8, 80-3
"Atrophy" (Wharton) **6**:424
"Attack" (O'Connor) **5**:371, 391
"An Attack of Nerves" ("A Nervous Breakdown") (Chekhov) **2**:153, 155-56
"Attalie Brouillard" (Cable) **4**:59
"Attractive Modern Homes" (Bowen) **3**:54
"Au large" (Cable) **4**:58-9
"Au Seabhac" (O'Flaherty) **6**:286-89
"L'auberge" (Maupassant) **1**:265
"L'auberge rouge" (Balzac) **5**:31, 33
"An Auction" (Crane) **7**:108, 110
"Aunt Lucy's Search" (Chesnutt) **7**:13
"Aunt Lympy's Interference" (Chopin) **8**:84
"Aunt Mandy's Investment" (Dunbar) **8**:121, 127, 137, 143, 147
"Aunt Mimy's Son" (Chesnutt) **7**:28
"Aunt Tempy's Revenge" (Dunbar) **8**:122
"Aunt Tempy's Triumph" (Dunbar) **8**:122
"Auprès d'un mort" (Maupassant) **1**:281
"The Author of Beltraffio" (James) **8**:304-05, 345, 350
The Author of Beltraffio (James) **8**:300
"The Author's Chamber" (Irving) **2**:265
"An Author's Confession" (Gogol) **4**:83
"Autobiography" (Atwood) **2**:15
"An Autobiography" (Gallant) **5**:133
"La autopista del sur" (Cortázar) **7**:54-5, 61
"Autre étude de femme" (Balzac) **5**:32-3, 35-6, 39
"Autre temps..." (Wharton) **6**:424-26, 436
"Gli avangnardisti a Mentone" (Calvino) **3**:97
"L'aventure de Walter Schnafs" (Maupassant) **1**:263
"Averroes's Search" (Borges) See "La busca de Averroes"
"L'aveu" (Maupassant) **1**:263, 274
"Avey" (Toomer) **1**:441, 443-45, 451, 453, 458-59
"An Awakening" (Anderson) **1**:34, 44-5
"The Awakening" (Clarke) **3**:143, 148
"The Awakening of Rollo Podmarsh" (Wodehouse) **2**:344
"The Awful Gladness of the Mate" (Wodehouse) **2**:356
"Axolotl" (Cortázar) **7**:58, 63-4, 66-7, 70-5, 81
"Azathoth" (Lovecraft) **3**:273
"Azélie" (Chopin) **8**:110
"Baa, Baa, Black Sheep" (Kipling) **5**:277-78, 283, 293
"Las babas del diablo" ("Blow-Up") (Cortázar) **7**:54, 65-6, 68-9, 86
"Babes in the Woods" (Henry) **5**:193
"The Babes in the Woods" (O'Connor) **5**:380
"Babette's Feast" (Dinesen) **7**:166, 195
"The Baby Party" (Fitzgerald) **6**:46, 94-5
"Babylon Revisted" (Fitzgerald) **6**:47, 51, 53, 60, 63-4, 72, 74, 76, 81, 85-6, 99-100, 104
"The Babylonian Lottery" (Borges) See "La lotería en Babilonia"
"The Back Drawing-Room" (Bowen) **3**:40, 54
"The Back of Beyond" (Maugham) **8**:375
"The Backwater" (Turgenev) **7**:320, 335
"Bagombo Snuff Box" (Vonnegut) **8**:433, 437
"Le bal de sceaux" (Balzac) **5**:4, 29
"The Balcony" (Irving) **2**:266
"A Ballad" (Bunin) See "Ballada"
"Ballada" ("A Ballad") (Bunin) **5**:115
"The Ballet of Central Park" (Boyle) **5**:66
"The Balloon" (Barthelme) **2**:31, 33, 36, 42
"The Balloon Hoax" (Poe) **1**:406
"Balthazar's Marvelous Afternoon" (García Márquez) See "La prodigiosa tarde de Baltazar"
"Banquet in Honor" (Hughes) **6**:122
"The Banquet of Crow" (Parker) **2**:280, 285
"Un baptême" (Maupassant) **1**:256, 259, 284
"Baptizing" (Munro) **3**:331, 339-40
"Barbados" (Marshall) **3**:299-300, 302-04, 306-08, 316-17
"Barbara of the House of Grebe" (Hardy) **2**:204, 209, 214-15, 221
"Barker's Luck" (Harte) **8**:222, 244
"Barn Burning" (Faulkner) **1**:163, 165
The Baron in the Trees (Calvino) See *Il barone rampante*
Il barone rampante (*The Baron in the Trees*) (Calvino) **3**:89-91, 93-5, 99, 117-18
"The Barrel" (Maupassant) **1**:269
"The Barricade" (Hemingway) **1**:208
"Bartleby, the Scrivener: A Story of Wall-Street" (Melville) **1**:293, 295, 297-98, 303-04, 311, 317, 322-23, 325, 328, 331
"Bás na Bó" (O'Flaherty) **6**:287-88
"Basil and Cleopatra" (Fitzgerald) **6**:50
"Batard" ("Diable—A Dog") (London) **4**:288-89
"The Bath" (Carver) **8**:15, 19-24, 26-7, 30, 39, 56-60
"The Battler" (Hemingway) **1**:242, 244-45, 247
"Baum Gabriel, 1935 - ( )" (Gallant) **5**:137-38
"Bavarian Gentians" (Lawrence) **4**:233
"Baxter's Procrustes" (Chesnutt) **7**:15
Bayou Folk (Chopin) **8**:65-8, 72, 77, 84, 88-9, 93, 97, 103-08, 110-11, 114
"The Beach Murders" (Ballard) **1**:72-4
"The Bear" (Faulkner) **1**:148, 152-58, 167, 172-74, 182
"A Bear Hunt" (Faulkner) **1**:177
"The Beard" (Singer) **3**:375
The Beast in Me, and Other Animals: A New Collection of Pieces and Drawings about Human Beings and Less Alarming Creatures (Thurber) **1**:425
"The Beast in the Jungle" (James) **8**:302, 307-09, 320, 326, 338-40, 342, 347
"The Beauties" (Chekhov) **2**:156
"A Beautiful Child" (Capote) **2**:81
"The Beautiful Suit" (Wells) **6**:361-62, 376, 391
"Beauty" (O'Flaherty) **6**:262, 285
"Beauty Spots" (Kipling) **5**:280
"The Becker Wives" (Lavin) **4**:166-67, 184-90, 192
"Becky" (Toomer) **1**:445, 456-58
"Before Breakfast" (Cather) **2**:93-4
"Before Eden" (Clarke) **3**:127
"Before the Law" (Kafka) See "Vor dem Gesetz"
"Before the Party" (Maugham) **8**:359, 362, 366-67, 372
"Before the War" (Atwood) **2**:16
The Beggar Maid: Stories of Flo and Rose (Munro) See *Who Do You Think You Are?*
"The Beggars" (O'Flaherty) **6**:276-78
"Behind the Singer Tower" (Cather) **2**:99, 103-04, 111
"Un bel gioco dura poco" (Calvino) **3**:97
"Belaja lošad'" (Bunin) **5**:98
"The Belated Travellers" (Irving) **2**:262
"The Bell" (Andersen) **6**:6-8, 15, 30, 33
"The Bell-Ringer of Angels" (Harte) **8**:214, 248-49
"The Bell-Tower" (Melville) **1**:298, 303
"The Bella Lingua" (Cheever) **1**:93, 106, 112
"La Belle Zoraïde" (Chopin) **8**:71, 87, 90-1, 106
"Belles Demoiselles Plantation" (Cable) **4**:48, 53, 62-4, 66-7, 73-4
"Below the Mill Dam" (Kipling) **5**:268, 283
"The Bench of Desolation" (James) **8**:277, 304
"Beneath the Willow-Tree" (Andersen) **6**:30
"Benediction" (Fitzgerald) **6**:45, 57-8
"The Benefit of the Doubt" (London) **4**:291
"Benito Cereno" (Melville) **1**:293, 295-300, 303-04, 310-12, 320-23, 328, 330
"The Bênitou's Slave" (Chopin) **8**:89
"Benjamin Button" (Fitzgerald) See "The Curious Case of Benjamin Button"
"An Beo" (O'Flaherty) **6**:286-88
"Berenice" (Poe) **1**:396, 398
"Bernadette" (Gallant) **5**:122, 125, 139
"Bernice Bobs Her Hair" (Fitzgerald) **6**:58, 96
"Berry" (Hughes) **6**:121, 142
"Bertie Changes His Mind" (Wodehouse) **2**:356
"Bertram and Bini" (Kipling) **5**:274
"The Best China Saucer" (Jewett) **6**:166
The Best of Arthur C. Clarke: 1937-1971 (Clarke) **3**:149
The Best of Simple (Hughes) **6**:137
"Best-Seller" (Henry) **5**:159
The Best Short Stories of J. G. Ballard (Ballard) **1**:74
"The Best Years" (Cather) **2**:93-4, 105
"Bestiario" (Cortázar) **7**:57-8, 77-8
Bestiario (*Bestiary*) (Cortázar) **7**:50-1, 53-4, 69-70
Bestiary (Cortázar) See *Bestiario*
"The Bet" (Chekhov) **2**:130
"La bête à Maître Belhomme" (Maupassant) **1**:259, 273, 281
"The Betrayer of Israel" (Singer) **3**:383
"Die Betrogene" ("The Black Swan"; "The Deceived") (Mann) **5**:313-16, 324-26, 340-42
"Betrothed" (Chekhov) **2**:131, 139, 143, 149, 151
"Betty" (Atwood) **2**:14, 22
"Between Men" (Lessing) **6**:197, 200, 207

Title Index

"Between the Devil and the Deep Sea" (Kipling) **5**:268
"Between Zero and One" (Gallant) **5**:134, 144
"Bewitched" (Wharton) **6**:422, 427
"The Bewitched Spot" (Gogol)
See "Zakoldovannoe mesto"
"Beyond" (Faulkner) **1**:162
"Beyond the Bayou" (Chopin) **8**:89, 104
"Beyond the End" (Barnes)
See "Spillway"
"Beyond the Pale" (Kipling) **5**:261-62, 273
"Beyond the Wall of Sleep" (Lovecraft) **3**:258, 268
"Bezhin Meadow" (Turgenev)
See "Byezhin Prairie"
"El biblioteca de Babel" ("The Library of Babel") (Borges) **4**:6-7, 18, 29
"Bicycles, Muscles, Cigarettes" (Carver) **8**:10, 20, 42
"Big Black Good Man" (Wright) **2**:364
"Big Blonde" (Parker) **2**:273-74, 276, 278-81, 284
"Big Boy Leaves Home" (Wright) **2**:360-61, 363, 365, 367-69, 371-76, 379-81, 386-90
"The Big Broadcast of 1938" (Barthelme) **2**:26
"Big Claus and Little Claus" (Andersen)
See "Little Claus and Big Claus"
"Big Fiddle" (Boyle) **5**:66-8
"Big Game Hunt" (Clarke) **3**:133-34
Big Mama's Funeral (*The Funeral of Mama Grand*; "Los funerale de la Mamá Grande") (García Márquez) **8**:169-70, 183, 185, 187, 189
"Big Meeting" (Hughes) **6**:119, 122, 132-33
"Big Two-Hearted River" (Hemingway) **1**:208, 214, 220, 231, 234, 240, 243-48
"Les bijoux" (Maupassant) **1**:273, 286, 288
"Bill" (Powers) **4**:375, 381-82
"Billenium" (Ballard) **1**:68-9, 75
Billy Budd, Sailor: An Inside Narrative (Melville) **1**:294-303, 305-16, 318, 321, 329
"Biography of Tadeo Isidoro Cruz" (Borges) **4**:9
"A Bird in the House" (Laurence) **7**:255, 257-58
A Bird in the House (Laurence) **7**:246-49, 251, 253-54, 256-57, 259-60, 262-64, 266-70, 270-72
"A Bird of Bagdad" (Henry) **5**:196
"The Birds and the Foxes" (Thurber) **1**:426, 431
"Birth" (O'Flaherty) **6**:262
"The Birthmark" (Hawthorne) **3**:159, 168-70, 178, 183-84, 189, 191-94
"The Bisara of Pooree" (Kipling) **5**:262, 265
"The Bishop" (Chekhov) **2**:131, 148-49, 157-58
"The Bishop of Børglum" (Andersen) **6**:18
"The Bishop's Robe" (Singer) **3**:374
"A Bit of Shore Life" (Jewett) **6**:166
"Bitterness for Three Sleepwalkers" (García Márquez)
See "Amargura para tres sonámbulos"
"Blacamán the Good, Vendor of Miracles" (García Márquez) **8**:167-69, 186
"The Black Bird's Mate" (O'Flaherty) **6**:280
"Black Boy" (Boyle) **5**:56
"The Black Cat" (Poe) **1**:389-90, 406, 408
"Black Death" (Hurston) **4**:142
"The Black Friar" (Chekhov)
See "The Black Monk"
"A Black Jack Bargainer" (Henry) **5**:162, 170
"The Black Madonna" (Lessing) **6**:189, 193, 196-97, 212, 214
"The Black Magic of Barney Haller" (Thurber) **1**:415
"The Black Mare" (O'Flaherty) **6**:264, 281
"The Black Monk" ("The Black Friar") (Chekhov) **2**:126, 131-32, 143, 147-48
"The Black Rabbit" (O'Flaherty) **6**:274, 281
"The Black Swan" (Mann)
See "Die Betrogene"
"The Black Wedding" (Singer) **3**:359, 375-76
"Blackberry Winter" (Warren) **4**:387-94, 396-99, 401-04
"The Blackbird" (O'Flaherty) **6**:268, 280
"Blackbird Pie" (Carver) **8**:51
Blandings Castle (Wodehouse) **2**:346-47, 353
"The Blank Page" (Dinesen) **7**:200
"The Blast of the Book" (Chesterton) **1**:131
"Blessed Assurance" (Hughes) **6**:123-24
"A Blessed Deceit" (Dunbar) **8**:122
"The Blessing" (Powers) **4**:368-70, 373
"The Blind Man" (Chopin) **8**:100
"The Blind Man" (Lawrence) **4**:231, 233-36, 242-46
"Blindfold" (Oates) **6**:231
"The Blizzard" (Singer) **3**:374
"The Blond Beast" (Wharton) **6**:435
"Blood" (Singer) **3**:356, 358, 364, 375
"Blood-Burning Moon" (Toomer) **1**:443, 445, 450, 452-53, 458
"Blood Lust" (O'Flaherty) **6**:261, 269, 277, 283
"The Blood of the Walsungs" (Mann) **5**:310-11, 321, 323, 344
"Blood, Sea" (Calvino) **3**:109-10
"Blood-Swollen Landscape" (Oates) **6**:250
"The Blow" (O'Flaherty) **6**:260, 282, 287
"Blow-Up" (Cortázar)
See "Las babas del diablo"
"Blue and Green" (Woolf) **7**:374-75, 398
"The Blue Cross" (Chesterton) **1**:119, 123, 133, 135, 138
"Blue-Dog Eyes" (García Márquez)
See "Ojos de perro azul"
"The Blue Hotel" (Crane) **7**:104-06, 108-16, 127, 129, 142-43, 145, 151-52, 154-55
"Blue Island" (Powers) **4**:368, 372
"The Blue Moccasins" (Lawrence) **4**:220
"The Blue Room" (Mérimée)
See "La chambre bleue"
"Bluebeard's Egg" (Atwood) **2**:17, 21
Bluebeard's Egg (Atwood) **2**:17-18, 20-2
"Bluejay Yarn" (Twain) **6**:310
"The Blues I'm Playing" (Hughes) **6**:121-22, 129, 134-36
"Blumfeld, an Elderly Bachelor" (Kafka) **5**:243-44
"The Boarding House" (Joyce) **3**:201, 205-07, 234, 237, 247-48
"Bodies in the Moonlight" (Hughes) **6**:117-18, 127
"The Bog King's Daughter" (Andersen)
See "The Marsh King's Daughter"
"The Bohemian Girl" (Cather) **2**:96-7, 101, 103-05, 108
"Boitelle" (Maupassant) **1**:263
"The Bold Dragoon" (Irving) **2**:256
"Bombard" (Maupassant) **1**:263
"Bona and Paul" (Toomer) **1**:444, 446, 450, 452-54, 458-62
"Bonaventure" (Gallant) **5**:144
Bonaventure: A Prose Pastoral of Acadian Louisiana (Cable) **4**:48, 50-1, 53, 58-60, 62, 73, 75
"The Bond" (Singer) **3**:385, 387
"Bone Bubbles" (Barthelme) **2**:31
"Bones of Contention" (O'Connor) **5**:371, 377
Bones of Contention, and Other Stories (O'Connor) **5**:364, 371, 377, 380, 382
A Book (Barnes) **3**:3-4, 14, 22, 26
"The Book-Bag" (Maugham) **8**:357, 360-61, 375, 378
"Book of Harlem" (Hurston) **4**:155
"The Book of the Grotesque" (Anderson) **1**:57
"The Bookkeeper's Wife" (Cather) **2**:99, 110
"The Border Line" (Lawrence) **4**:219, 238
"A Born Farmer" (Jewett) **6**:156, 158
"A Bottle of Perrier" (Wharton) **6**:423-24
"The Bottomless Well" (Chesterton) **1**:122
"Boule de suif" (Maupassant) **1**:255-57, 259, 263, 266, 269, 271-76, 281-83, 286-88, 290
"Boulôt and Boulotte" (Chopin) **8**:88, 102-03
"The Bouquet" (Chesnutt) **7**:3, 16, 22-3, 29-30, 33, 36
"La bourse" (Balzac) **5**:29
"Box Seat" (Toomer) **1**:440, 443, 445-48, 450-53, 458
"A Box to Hide In" (Thurber) **1**:414, 417
"Boxes" (Carver) **8**:43
"The Boy and the Bayonet" (Dunbar) **8**:122, 147
"A Boy Asks a Question of a Lady" (Barnes) **3**:10-11
"Boy in Rome" (Cheever) **1**:100
"The Boy Knows the Truth" (Singer) **3**:380
"The Boy Who Hated Girls" (Vonnegut) **8**:431
"Boys and Girls" (Munro) **3**:321, 343-44
Bracebridge Hall (Irving) **2**:240, 244-46, 251, 254-55, 258-59, 265
"Brain Damage" (Barthelme) **2**:32-3, 39-40, 42, 47, 55
"The Brandon House and the Lighthouse" (Jewett) **6**:154, 167
"Brazil" (Marshall) **3**:299, 300, 302-04, 306, 317
"Bread" (Atwood) **2**:19-20
"The Bread of Charity" (Turgenev) **7**:318
"Breakfast" (Bowen) **3**:54
"Breakfast" (Cortázar)
See "Desayuno"
Breakfast at Tiffany's (Capote) **2**:67-76, 78-9, 81
"Breaking Strain" (Clarke) **3**:144, 150
"The Breaking Up of the Winships" (Thurber) **1**:419, 435
"Brethren" ("Brothers") (Bunin) **5**:80-2, 87-8, 93-7, 106, 115
"The Bridal Night" (O'Connor) **5**:363-64, 371, 377, 380, 383, 390, 395, 398
"The Bridal Party" (Fitzgerald) **6**:48, 61
"Bridal Sheets" (Lavin) **4**:165, 167, 180-81
"The Bride Comes to Yellow Sky" (Crane) **7**:104-05, 108-09, 116-17, 126-27, 149, 151
"The Bride of the Innisfallen" (Welty) **1**:476, 479, 484, 495
"The Bridegroom's Body" (Boyle) **5**:58-63, 66, 68
"The Bridge-Builders" (Kipling) **5**:267, 283, 294

"The Brief Cure of Aunt Fanny" (Dunbar) **8**:122, 149
"The Brief Début of Tildy" (Henry) **5**:171
"The Brigadier" (Turgenev)
See "Brigadir"
The Brigadier and the Golf Widow (Cheever) **1**:94-5, 100
"Brigadir" ("The Brigadier") (Turgenev) **7**:316, 320-21, 324, 337, 358
"Bright and Morning Star" (Wright) **2**:363, 368, 373, 375, 377, 379-83, 387-88, 391-92
"Brigid" (Lavin) **4**:167
"British Guiana" (Marshall) **3**:299-300, 302, 305, 317
"The Broken Heart" (Irving) **2**:243, 245
"Broken Sword" (Chesterton)
See "The Sign of the Broken Sword"
"Broken Wings" (James) **8**:304, 306
"The Brooch" (Faulkner) **1**:165
"Brooklyn" (Marshall) **3**:300, 302, 304-05, 307-08, 314-17
"Brooksmith" (James) **8**:304, 306
"Brother Boniface" (Lavin) **4**:183
"Brother Death" (Anderson) **1**:32, 37, 39, 50-1, 56-7
"Brother Earl" (Anderson) **1**:52
"Brothers" (Anderson) **1**:52
"Brothers" (Bunin)
See "Brethren"
"Brown of Calavaras" (Harte) **8**:214, 236, 244, 246-48
"Brugglesmith" (Kipling) **5**:266
"The Brushwood Boy" (Kipling) **5**:266-67, 273-74, 283
"La bûche" (Maupassant) **1**:274
"Buckeye Hollow Inheritance" (Harte) **8**:218
"Buckthorne and His Friends" (Irving) **2**:241, 251, 261-62
"The Buckwheat" (Andersen) **6**:7, 12, 18, 34
"Build-Up" (Ballard) **1**:68, 76-7
"An Buille" (O'Flaherty) **6**:286-89
"The Bull That Thought" (Kipling) **5**:279, 286
"A Bundle of Letters" (James) **8**:299
"Bunner Sisters" (Wharton) **6**:418, 422, 433
"The Burglar's Christmas" (Cather) **2**:100
"The Burning" (Welty) **1**:476, 479, 484
"The Burning Baby" (Thomas) **3**:399, 407
"The Burrow" (Kafka) **5**:206, 209, 241
"Burutu Moon" (Hughes) **6**:118
"The Bus" (Singer) **3**:381-82
"The Bus to St. James's" (Cheever) **1**:100, 106
"La busca de Averroes" ("Averroes's Search") (Borges) **4**:26, 37, 41
"The Business Man" (Poe) **1**:407
"Busride" (Cortázar)
See "Omnibus"
"A Busy Day in a Lawyer's Office" (Chesnutt) **7**:14
"Butterball's Night" (Cortázar)
See "La noche de Mantequilla"
"The Butterfly" (Chekhov) **2**:126
By the North Gate (Oates) **6**:223
"By the People" (Faulkner) **1**:178
"By the Road" (Bunin) **5**:106
"By the Water" (Bowles) **3**:71-2
"Byezhin Prairie" ("Bezhin Meadow") (Turgenev) **7**:316, 345
"The Cabalist of East Broadway" (Singer) **3**:374, 383-84
"The Caballero's Way" (Henry) **5**:167
Cabbages and Kings (Henry) **5**:155, 160, 162-63, 167-69, 172
"The Cabin" (Carver) **8**:50
"Café des exilés" (Cable) **4**:58, 62, 68
"Cahoots" (Dunbar) **8**:122, 132, 145
Cakes and Ale and Twelve Stories (Maugham) **8**:384
"Caline" (Chopin) **8**:94
"The Caliph and the Cad" (Henry) **5**:158
"The Caliph, Cupid, and the Clock" (Henry) **5**:158
"Call at Corazón" (Bowles) **3**:59, 61-2, 66, 69, 77, 79
"The Call of Cthulhu" (Lovecraft) **3**:258, 261, 263-64, 269-70, 274, 278, 280, 283, 290
"The Call of the Tame" (Henry) **5**:191, 194
"A Call on Mrs. Forrester" (Thurber) **1**:431
"Calling Cards" (Bunin)
See "Vizitnye kartochki"
"Calling Jesus" (Toomer) **1**:445, 447, 450
"The Calm" (Carver) **8**:14, 42
"The Camel's Back" (Fitzgerald) **6**:45, 59, 96-7
"The Canals of Mars" (Boyle) **5**:55
"A Canary for One" (Hemingway) **1**:209, 217, 232, 237
Canary in a Cat House (Vonnegut) **8**:428
Cane (Toomer) **1**:439-55, 458-60, 462
"The Cane in the Corridor" (Thurber) **1**:420, 422
"The Canterbury Pilgrims" (Hawthorne) **3**:185-86
"The Capital of the World" (Hemingway) **1**:217, 232, 234, 245
"Captain Sands" (Jewett) **6**:167
Captain Stormfield's Visit to Heaven (Twain)
See *Extracts from Captain Stormfield's Visit to Heaven*
"The Captains" (Jewett) **6**:154, 167
"The Captain's Doll" (Lawrence) **4**:197, 204, 210-12, 223-26, 234-36, 239-40
"The Captive" (Kipling) **5**:283
"The Captive" (Singer) **3**:374, 384
"The Captured Shadow" (Fitzgerald) **6**:49
"The Captured Woman" (Barthelme) **2**:46
"The Car We Had to Push" (Thurber) **1**:431
"Carancro" (Cable) **4**:58
"Carcassonne" (Faulkner) **1**:181
"The Cardinal's First Tale" (Dinesen) **7**:162-63, 172, 186, 194, 198
"The Cardinal's Third Tale" (Dinesen) **7**:168, 200
"Careful" (Carver) **8**:26, 31, 35, 51
"Careless Talk" (Bowen) **3**:31
"Careless Talk" (Gallant) **5**:151
"The Caress" (O'Flaherty) **6**:267
"Caricature" (Singer) **3**:359, 375
"La caricia más profunda" ("The Most Profound Caress") (Cortázar) **7**:58, 61, 94
"Carma" (Toomer) **1**:456-57
Carmen (Mérimée) **7**:276, 280-82, 285-86, 290, 294-96, 305-06, 308
"Carnival" (Dinesen) **7**:190-91
"Carpe Noctem, If You Can" (Thurber) **1**:424
"The Carriage Lamps" (Crane) **7**:104
Carry On, Jeeves (Wodehouse) **2**:337, 346
"Carta a un Señorita en París" ("Carta a un srta. en París"; "Letter to a Young Lady in Paris") (Cortázar) **7**:56-7, 61, 70-1
"Carta a un srta. en París" (Cortázar)
See "Carta a un Señorita en París"
"The Caryatids" (Dinesen) **7**:167, 191-92, 203-04
"Un cas de divorce" (Maupassant) **1**:286
"Le cas de Madame Luneau" (Maupassant) **1**:259, 286
"La casa de Asterión" ("The House of Asterión") (Borges) **4**:7, 10, 25
"Casa tomada" ("House Taken Over") (Cortázar) **7**:53, 81
"The Case of 'Ca'line': A Kitchen Monologue" (Dunbar) **8**:122, 127, 147
"The Case of Lieutenant Yelaghin" (Bunin)
See "The Elaghin Affair"
"The Cask of Amontillado" (Poe) **1**:378, 394, 407-08
"Cassation" ("A Little Girl Tells a Story to a Lady") (Barnes) **3**:6, 10, 16, 24-5
"The Cassowary" (Bowen) **3**:33
"Castaway" (Clarke) **3**:125, 135-36, 149
"The Castle of Crossed Destinies" (Calvino) **3**:101-02
The Castle of Crossed Destinies (Calvino) **3**:99-102, 106, 114, 116, 118
The Casuarina Tree (Maugham) **8**:366-67, 371, 374
"Cat in the Rain" (Hemingway) **1**:244-45
"The Cat Jumps" (Bowen) **3**:41, 53
The Cat Jumps (Bowen) **3**:33, 41
"The Cat That Walked by Himself" (Kipling) **5**:284
"A Catastrophe" (Wells) **6**:389
"The Catbird Seat" (Thurber) **1**:422, 425, 431-32, 435
"The Catechist" (Barthelme) **2**:37, 39, 55
"Cathedral" (Carver) **8**:26, 30, 34-5, 40-1, 43-4, 48-9, 51
Cathedral (Carver) **8**:17, 20, 23, 26-8, 30-2, 34, 39-40, 46, 49, 55-61
"The Cats of Ulthar" (Lovecraft) **3**:262
"The Cattle Dealers" (Chekhov) **2**:128
Il cavaliere inesistente (*The Nonexistent Knight*; *The Invisible Knight*; *The Nonexistent Knight and the Cloven Viscount*) (Calvino) **3**:90-1, 99, 106-07, 117
"Cavenelle" (Chopin) **8**:94, 108, 111
"Cefalea" (Cortázar) **7**:58
"Celebrated Jumping Frog of Calaveras County" ("Jumping Frog"; "Notorious Jumping Frog of Calaveras County") (Twain) **6**:300, 309-12, 316-21
"The Celestial Railroad" (Hawthorne) **3**:178, 181, 183
"Les célibataires" (Balzac) **5**:5
Les célibataires (Balzac) **5**:9, 25
"The Cemetery in the Demesne" (Lavin) **4**:166, 176
"Centaur in Brass" (Faulkner) **1**:177
A Certain Lucas (Cortázar)
See *Un tal Lucas*
"Châli" (Maupassant) **1**:259
"The Challenge" (O'Flaherty) **6**:277-78
"La chambre 11" (Maupassant) **1**:288
"La chambre bleue" ("The Blue Room") (Mérimée) **7**:277, 296-97
"Le champ d'Oliviers" (Maupassant) **1**:273, 283
"The Champion of the Weather" (Henry) **5**:159
"A Change of Heart" (Jewett) **6**:156, 158
A Change of Light (Cortázar) **7**:62-3
"A Changed Man" (Hardy) **2**:211, 220

Title Index

A Changed Man, The Waiting Supper, and Other Tales (Hardy) **2**:210-11, 214-15, 221
"Charity" (O'Flaherty) **6**:264
"Charlie" (Chopin) **8**:84, 86
"A Charm" (Kipling) **5**:283
"An Charraig Dhubh" (O'Flaherty) **6**:287
"Chasy" ("The Watch") (Turgenev) **7**:324-25, 327, 358
"Le chat-qui-pelote" (Balzac)
See "La maison du chat-qui-pelote"
"Che ti dice la patria?" (Hemingway) **1**:232
"The Cheapjack" ("The New Teacher") (O'Connor) **5**:371, 389
"An Chearc Uisce" (O'Flaherty) **6**:287
"The Cheery Soul" (Bowen) **3**:32, 54
"Le chef d'oeuvre inconnu" ("The Unknown Masterpiece") (Balzac) **5**:12, 16, 23, 48-9
"À Cheval" (Maupassant) **1**:278, 280
"Chicken-Grethe" (Andersen) **6**:7
"The Chief Mourner of Marne" (Chesterton) **1**:128, 138
"Le chien" (Maupassant) **1**:259
"The Child in the Grave" ("The Dead Child") (Andersen) **6**:15, 26
"The Child of God" (O'Flaherty) **6**:262, 269-70, 281
"The Child Who Favored Daughter" (Walker) **5**:403, 409-11
"The Children" (Oates) **6**:225
Children of the Frost (London) **4**:258, 282, 285-88
"The Children of the Zodiac" (Kipling) **5**:283, 286
"Children on Their Birthdays" (Capote) **2**:61, 63-6, 70, 72-3, 75-8
"The Child's Evening Prayer" (Andersen) **6**:15
"The Chimera" (Cheever) **1**:97, 105
"The Chinago" (London) **4**:263
"Chistyi ponedel'nik" ("The First Monday in Lent") (Bunin) **5**:114
"The Choice" (Wharton) **6**:418
"The Chorus Girl" (Chekhov) **2**:130, 137, 139
"The Christening" (Lawrence) **4**:197, 202, 234
"A Christian Education" (Warren) **4**:390, 394, 396
"The Christmas Banquet" (Hawthorne) **3**:181, 183
"Christmas by Injunction" (Henry) **5**:162
"A Christmas Carol for Harold Ross" (Boyle) **5**:64
"Christmas Eve" (Gogol)
See "Noč pered roždestvom"
"Christmas Gift" (Warren) **4**:388-90, 394
"Christmas Is a Sad Season for the Poor" (Cheever) **1**:107
"Christmas Jenny" (Freeman) **1**:191
"A Christmas Memory" (Capote) **2**:67, 72-3, 75-6
"Christmas Morning" (O'Connor) **5**:378
"A Christmas Party and a Wedding" (Dostoevski)
See "A Christmas Tree and a Wedding"
"A Christmas Tree and a Wedding" ("A Christmas Party and a Wedding") (Dostoevski) **2**:171, 190, 193-95, 197
"The Chronic Argonauts" (Wells) **6**:388
Chronicle of a Death Foretold (García Márquez)
See *Crónica de una muerta anunciada*
Chronicle of an Unexpected Death (García Márquez)
See *Crónica de una muerta anunciada*
"Chronopolis" (Ballard) **1**:69, 84
Chronopolis, and Other Stories (Ballard) **1**:71
"Chu Chu, The Devotion of Enriquez" (Harte) **8**:228
"An Chulaith Nua" (O'Flaherty) **6**:287
"Chun Ah Chun" (London) **4**:269
"The Church That Was at Antioch" (Kipling) **5**:272
"The Church with an Overshot Wheel" (Henry) **5**:163, 180-81
"Cicadas" (Bunin) **5**:82
"Cicely's Dream" (Chesnutt) **7**:22-3, 33-4, 37
"Ciclismo en Gringnan" ("Cycling in Gringnan") (Cortázar) **7**:95
"The Cigarstore Robbery" (Hemingway) **1**:208
"A Circle in the Fire" (O'Connor) **1**:343-44, 347, 356
"Circle of Prayer" (Munro) **3**:348
The Circular Ruins (Borges)
See "La ruinas circulares"
"The Circular Valley" (Bowles) **3**:66, 69-71, 79
"The Circus" (Porter) **4**:331-34, 340, 353
"The Circus at Denby" (Jewett) **6**:150, 155, 167
"The Circus in the Attic" (Warren) **4**:387-89, 391, 395-98, 404
The Circus in the Attic, and Other Stories (Warren) **4**:387-90, 393, 396-97
"City Life" (Barthelme) **2**:40
City Life (Barthelme) **2**:30-5, 37-9
"A City of Churches" (Barthelme) **2**:37, 39, 41, 54
"The City of Dreadful Night" (Henry) **5**:188, 197
"Civil War" (O'Flaherty) **6**:262, 274
"Clancy in the Tower of Babel" (Cheever) **1**:107
"Clara Milich" (Turgenev)
See "Klara Milich"
"Clarence" (Harte) **8**:222, 251-52
"Clay" (Joyce) **3**:205, 209, 211, 221-22, 226, 233-34, 237, 247
"A Clean, Well-Lighted Place" (Hemingway) **1**:216, 230, 232, 237-38
"The Clemency of the Court" (Cather) **2**:96, 100, 103, 105
"Clementina" (Cheever) **1**:100, 107
The Clicking of Cuthbert (Wodehouse) **2**:344, 354
"The Cloak" (Gogol)
See "The Overcoat"
"Clone" (Cortázar) **7**:69-71
"Clothe the Naked" (Parker) **2**:275, 280-81, 286
The Cloven Viscount (Calvino)
See *Il visconte dimezzato*
The Club of Queer Trades (Chesterton) **1**:120, 122, 139
"Clytie" (Welty) **1**:466, 468, 471, 481, 495
"The Coach House" (Chekhov) **2**:128
"Cock-a-Doodle-Doo!" (Melville) **1**:295, 298, 303, 305, 322
"Cockadoodledoo" (Singer) **3**:358
"Coco" (Maupassant) **1**:275
"Un coeur simple" (Maupassant) **1**:286
"Cold Autumn" (Bunin) **5**:115-16
"Colic" (O'Flaherty) **6**:271
Collected Stories (García Márquez) **8**:182-84
Collected Stories (Lavin) **4**:174
Collected Stories (Lessing) **6**:196, 218-19
Collected Stories (O'Connor) **5**:398
Collected Stories: 1939-1976 (Bowles) **3**:65, 68-9
The Collected Stories of Isaac Bashevis Singer (Singer) **3**:383-84
The Collected Stories of Katherine Anne Porter (Porter) **4**:347, 351, 358, 361
Collected Stories of William Faulkner (Faulkner) **1**:151, 161-62, 177, 181
Collected Works (Bunin) **5**:99
"Collectors" (Carver) **8**:11, 19
"Le collier" (Maupassant) **1**:259
"The Colloquy of Monos and Una" (Poe) **1**:401-02
Colomba (Mérimée) **7**:276-77, 280-83, 290, 294-95, 300-05, 308
"Le Colonel Chabert" (Balzac) **5**:8, 18, 24-7
"Colonel Starbottle for the Plaintiff" (Harte) **8**:229
"Colonel Starbottle's Client" (Harte) **8**:216, 245
"The Colonel's Awakening" (Dunbar) **8**:121, 127, 131, 148
"The Colonel's Lady" (Maugham) **8**:366, 380
"The Colour Out of Space" (Lovecraft) **3**:261, 263, 267-69, 274, 281, 290-91
Come Back, Dr. Caligari (Barthelme) **2**:26-9, 31, 37-9, 46, 49, 51
"Come On Back" (Gardner) **7**:224-25, 227-28, 235, 240-41
Comédie humaine (*The Human Comedy; Comedy*) (Balzac) **5**:6-13, 16-17, 19-20, 26-33, 43, 48
"Les comédiens sans le savoir" (Balzac) **5**:31
Comedy (Balzac)
See *Comédie humaine*
"A Comedy in Rubber" (Henry) **5**:158
"The Comforts of Home" (O'Connor) **1**:343-44, 351, 353, 365
"Coming Apart" (Walker) **5**:412-14
"Coming, Aphrodite!" (Cather) **2**:91-2, 95, 104, 111-12
"Coming, Eden Bower!" (Cather) **2**:111-12, 114
"Coming Home" (Bowen) **3**:40
"The Coming Out of Maggie" (Henry) **5**:171, 197
"A Committee-Man of 'The Terror'" (Hardy) **2**:220
The Common Chord (O'Connor) **5**:364-65, 371, 378, 380, 383-84
"A Common Confusion" (Kafka) **5**:207
"Company for Gertrude" (Wodehouse) **2**:346
"The Compartment" (Carver) **8**:26, 32, 35
"A Compatriot" (Bunin) **5**:81
"The Complaint Ledger" (Chekhov) **2**:130
"The Complete Life of John Hopkins" (Henry) **5**:159, 188
"Con legítimo orgullo" ("With Justifiable Pride") (Cortázar) **7**:94
"Concerning the Bodyguard" (Barthelme) **2**:44
"Concerning Wet Snow" (Dostoevski)
See "Apropos of the Wet Snow"
"Condemned Door" (Cortázar) **7**:69
Condensed Novels, and Other Papers (Harte) **8**:225, 230, 249
"Conducta en los velorios" ("Our Demeanor at Wakes") (Cortázar) **7**:92

"The Cone" (Wells) **6**:361, 383
"The Conference" (Singer) **3**:385, 388
"A Conference of the Powers" (Kipling) **5**:259
"The Confession of Brother Grimes" (Warren) **4**:390, 394, 396
"A Conflict Ended" (Freeman) **1**:196-97, 199
"Confused" (Singer) **3**:384
"The Conger Eel" (O'Flaherty) **6**:269, 274
"El congreso" ("The Assembly") (Borges) **4**:27-8
The Conjure Woman (Chesnutt) **7**:2-5, 7-12, 14, 26, 30, 33, 38-40, 43
"The Conjurer's Revenge" (Chesnutt) **7**:6-7, 10, 18, 42
"The Conjuring Contest" (Dunbar) **8**:122, 149
"A Conquest of Humility" (Freeman) **1**:198
"The Conscript" (Balzac) **5**:12-13
"Consequences" (Cather) **2**:110-11, 115
"Conservatory" (Barthelme) **2**:51
"A Consolatory Tale" (Dinesen) **7**:164, 186, 193, 200
"The Constant Tin Soldier" (Andersen)
See "The Steadfast Tin Soldier"
Contes de la Bécasse (Maupassant) **1**:257
Contes drolatiques (*Droll Stories*) (Balzac) **5**:19-21
Contes philosophiques (Balzac)
See *Romans et contes philosophiques*
"The Contessina" (Bowen) **3**:40
"The Contest" (Paley) **8**:388, 394, 398
"Continuity of Parks" (Cortázar) **7**:54, 70, 83
"The Contract" (Anderson) **1**:52
"The Convalescence of Jack Hamlin" (Harte) **8**:247, 249
"A Conversation" (Turgenev) **7**:335
"Conversation at Night" (Bunin)
See "A Night Conversation"
"The Conversation of Eiron and Charmion" (Poe) **1**:402
"A Conversation with My Father" (Paley) **8**:390, 392, 395, 399-402, 405, 407, 415-16, 418
"Conversations with Goethe" (Barthelme) **2**:51
"Converse at Night" (Dinesen) **7**:168, 171, 186
"The Conversion of Aurelian McGoggin" (Kipling) **5**:261, 274
"The Conversion of Sum Loo" (Cather) **2**:102
"The Convert" (Lavin) **4**:165-68
"A Convert of the Mission" (Harte) **8**:216, 254
"Cool Air" (Lovecraft) **3**:258, 262, 274
"The Cop and the Anthem" (Henry) **5**:173, 187
"Copenhagen Season" (Dinesen) **7**:166, 169-71, 186, 190-91
"Un coq chanta" (Maupassant) **1**:272
"Cora Unashamed" (Hughes) **6**:109-10, 118-19, 121-23, 129
"The Corn Planting" (Anderson) **1**:37
"The Cornet Yelagin Affair" (Bunin)
See "The Elaghin Affair"
"A Correspondence" (Turgenev) **7**:317-18, 320, 324-26, 328, 361
"Cortísimo metraje" ("Short Feature") (Cortázar) **7**:95
"Cosmic Casanova" (Clarke) **3**:133
Le cosmicomiche (*Cosmicomics*) (Calvino) **3**:92-6, 98-100, 103-04, 106-07, 110, 112, 116-17
Cosmicomics (Calvino)
See *Le cosmicomiche*
Cosmopolitans (Maugham) **8**:366, 380
"The Cost of Living" (Gallant) **5**:130, 140-41, 149
"A Council of State" (Dunbar) **8**:122, 124-25, 128, 136, 141, 144, 150
"Counsel for Oedipus" (O'Connor) **5**:370
"The Count of Crow's Nest" (Cather) **2**:100, 102
"The Count of Monte Cristo" (Calvino) **3**:93, 95-6
"Counterparts" (Joyce) **3**:200-01, 205, 209, 226, 231, 234, 246, 249
"The Counting House" (Turgenev) **7**:313
"Country Church" (Irving) **2**:244
The Country Doctor (Kafka) **5**:216
"A Country Doctor" (Kafka)
See "Ein Landarzt"
"The Country Husband" (Cheever) **1**:90, 100-02
"The Country Inn" (Turgenev)
See "The Inn"
"The Country of the Blind" (Wells) **6**:361-62, 368-73, 376-79, 383-84, 391-92, 399-400, 405
The Country of the Blind, and Other Stories (Wells) **6**:359-61, 366, 380, 391-92
The Country of the Pointed Firs (*Pointed Firs*) (Jewett) **6**:152, 154-55, 157, 162-66, 168-69, 174-82
"A Country Tale" (Dinesen) **7**:168-69
"Le coup de pistolet" (Mérimée) **7**:277
"A Couple of Hamburgers" (Thurber) **1**:418-19
"The Courting of Dinah Shadd" (Kipling) **5**:260, 263-64, 274
"The Courting of Sister Wisby" (Jewett) **6**:152, 160, 162, 178
"A Courtship" (Faulkner) **1**:151, 178
"Cousin Larry" (Parker) **2**:280, 283
Covering End (James) **8**:296
"The Coward" (Barnes) **3**:18-22
"The Coward" (Wharton) **6**:414
"The Cow's Death" (O'Flaherty) **6**:274
"The Coxon Fund" (James) **8**:317, 348
Crab Apple Jelly (O'Connor) **5**:362, 364, 371, 377-78, 380, 383
"The Cracked Looking-Glass" (Porter) **4**:327, 329-30, 339-40, 342, 360
"Cracker Prayer" (Hughes) **6**:138
"The Crazy Hunter" (Boyle) **5**:58-9, 61-3, 66, 68-9
The Crazy Hunter: Three Short Novels (Boyle) **5**:66
"Crazy Sunday" (Fitzgerald) **6**:47, 52, 60-1, 77-9
"Created He Them" (London) **4**:253
"The Creative Impulse" (Maugham) **8**:369, 378-79
"The Creative Instinct" (Maugham) **8**:358
Creatures of Circumstance (Maugham) **8**:380
Credos and Curios (Thurber) **1**:424
"Cressy" (Harte) **8**:221
"Crevasse" (Faulkner) **1**:147
"Le crime au père Boniface" (Maupassant) **1**:274
"The Crime of Gabriel Gale" (Chesterton) **1**:124
"The Crime Wave at Blandings" (Wodehouse) **2**:344, 346, 349
"The Cripple" (Andersen) **6**:13
"Critical Mass" (Clarke) **3**:134
"Critique de la vie quotidienne" (Barthelme) **2**:39-40, 42, 55
Crónica de una muerta anunciada (*Chronicle of a Death Foretold; Chronicle of an Unexpected Death*) (García Márquez) **8**:167, 173-82, 186, 190, 200-04
Cronopios and Famas (Cortázar)
See *Historia de cronopios y de famas*
The Croquet Player (Wells) **6**:400-02
"Cross-Country Snow" (Hemingway) **1**:217, 244
"Crossing the Border" (Oates) **6**:248-49
Crossing the Border: Fifteen Tales (Oates) **6**:226-29, 231, 247-48, 250, 253-54
"A Crown of Feathers" (Singer) **3**:374
A Crown of Feathers, and Other Stories (Singer) **3**:374-76, 380, 382, 384
Crucial Instances (Wharton) **6**:413
"The Cruel Master" (Oates) **6**:237
The Crusade of the Excelsior (Harte) **8**:245
"The Crystal Egg" (Wells) **6**:383, 389-91, 393-94, 404-05
"Crystals" (Calvino) **3**:108-09
"The Cuckoo Spit" (Lavin) **4**:172, 176, 183, 185
"Cuello de gatito negro" ("Throat of a Black Cat") (Cortázar) **7**:61, 69
"Cunner-Fishing" (Jewett) **6**:155, 167
"A Cup of Cold Water" (Wharton) **6**:424
"The Cup of Life" (Bunin) **5**:90, 92, 109
The Cup of Life (Bunin) **5**:90
"Cupid's Arrows" (Kipling) **5**:261
"The Curb in the Sky" (Thurber) **1**:418, 425
"The Cure" (Cheever) **1**:89
"Le curé de Tours" ("The Curé of Tours") (Balzac) **5**:7-8, 18, 25-6
"The Curé of Tours" (Balzac)
See "Le curé de Tours"
"The Curious Case of Benjamin Button" ("Benjamin Button") (Fitzgerald) **6**:59, 79-80, 92
"The Curse" (Clarke) **3**:124, 143-44
"A Curtain of Green" (Welty) **1**:487
The Curtain of Green (Welty) **1**:465-67, 469, 471, 476, 481-82, 484, 496
"The Custard Heart" (Parker) **2**:275, 280-81, 286
"The Custody of the Pumpkin" (Wodehouse) **2**:346-47
"Custom-Made Bride" (Vonnegut) **8**:432, 436
"The Custom of the Country" (O'Connor) **5**:370-71, 384, 387, 389
"Customs" (Oates) **6**:227, 248-50
"The Cut-Glass Bowl" (Fitzgerald) **6**:57
"Cycling in Gringnan" (Cortázar)
See "Ciclismo en Gringnan"
"The Dagger with Wings" (Chesterton) **1**:130-31
"Dagon" (Lovecraft) **3**:258, 262, 268, 272-73, 282, 285, 289
"The Daisy" (Andersen) **6**:3, 7
Daisy Miller: A Study (James) **8**:264, 274, 291, 298-99, 309-14, 334, 336-38
"Dalyrimple Goes Wrong" (Fitzgerald) **6**:45, 57
"The Dance at Chevalier's" (Cather) **2**:101, 105, 107

Title Index

"Dance of the Happy Shades" (Munro) **3**:321, 328-30, 335, 346
Dance of the Happy Shades (Munro) **3**:320, 322, 328-29, 331, 335, 343-44, 347
"Dancing Girls" (Atwood) **2**:6-8, 10, 12
Dancing Girls, and Other Stories (Atwood) **2**:3-7, 10, 13-16, 20-2
"The Dancing Mistress" (Bowen) **3**:30, 43, 54
"The Dandy Frightening the Squatter" (Twain) **6**:300
"Dandy Jim's Conjure Scare" (Dunbar) **8**:122, 149
"The Danger in the House" (Thurber) **1**:429
"Les dangers de l'inconduite" (Balzac) **5**:4
"Danny" (Jewett) **6**:150, 167
"Daoine Bochta" (O'Flaherty) **6**:287, 289
"Darcy in the Land of Youth" (O'Connor) **5**:371
Dark Alleys (Bunin)
See *Dark Avenues*
"Dark Avenues" (Bunin) **5**:115
Dark Avenues (*Dark Alleys*) (Bunin) **5**:82, 90, 113-16
"A Dark Brown Dog" (Crane) **7**:
"The Darling" (Chekhov) **2**:131-32, 135
"The Darning Needle" (Andersen) **6**:20
"Datos para entender a los perqueos" ("Some Facts for Understanding the Perkians") (Cortázar) **7**:95
"Daughter of Albion" (Chekhov) **2**:126
"A Daughter of the Aurora" (London) **4**:286
"The Daughter of the Regiment" (Kipling) **5**:260
"Daughters" (Anderson) **1**:52
"Daughters of the Vicar" (Lawrence) **4**:197-98, 202, 204, 212, 233
"Daumier" (Barthelme) **2**:39, 42, 49, 55
"De Daumier-Smith's Blue Period" (Salinger) **2**:293, 301, 315
"The Daunt Diana" (Wharton) **6**:421, 428
"Dave's Neckliss" (Chesnutt) **7**:18
"David Swan" (Hawthorne) **3**:160
"Dawn" (Powers) **4**:370
"A Day in Coney Island" (Singer) **3**:374
"Day of the Butterfly" (Munro) **3**:329-30, 337
"The Day Resurgent" (Henry) **5**:188
"The Day the Dam Broke" (Thurber) **1**:426, 428, 432
"The Day the Pig Fell into the Well" (Cheever) **1**:100
Daylight and Nightmare (Chesterton) **1**:140
"A Day's Lodging" (London) **4**:253
"A Day's Work" (Capote) **2**:81
The Day's Work (Kipling) **5**:266-68, 273-74, 283, 294-95
"A Day's Work" (Porter) **4**:339-40, 342, 360
"Dayspring Mishandled" (Kipling) **5**:270, 278, 282-83, 299-303
"The De Wets Come to Kloof Grange" (Lessing) **6**:186, 189
"The Dead" (Joyce) **3**:202-06, 208, 210-11, 214-15, 217, 223-26, 228, 232-40, 242-45, 247, 249
"The Dead" (Oates) **6**:225, 234, 254
"The Dead Child" (Andersen)
See "The Child in the Grave"
"The Dead Fiddler" (Singer) **3**:369, 384
"Dead Mabelle" (Bowen) **3**:30, 44, 54
"The Dead Man" (Borges)
See "El muerto"
"Death" (Anderson) **1**:30, 42
"Death" (Calvino) **3**:110
"Death" (Mann) **5**:322
"Death and the Child" (Crane) **7**:100-01, 104-08
"Death and the Compass" (Borges)
See "La muerte y la brújula"
"Death and the Senator" (Clarke) **3**:147
"Death Constant beyond Love" (García Márquez) **8**:167, 169-72, 186
"Death in Midsummer" (Mishima) **4**:313-14, 318, 321-22
Death in Midsummer, and Other Stories (Mishima) **4**:313-18, 321-23
"A Death in the Desert" (Cather) **2**:90-1, 98, 103, 105, 113
"Death in the Woods" (Anderson) **1**:31, 37-8, 40, 50-2, 56, 58-62
Death in the Woods (Anderson) **1**:31, 37, 50-1, 56
"Death in Venice" (Mann)
See "Der Tod in Venedig"
"Death of a Traveling Salesman" (Welty) **1**:466, 472, 481, 493, 497
"The Death of Edward Lear" (Barthelme) **2**:49, 52
"The Death of Justina" (Cheever) **1**:100
"The Death of Ligoun" (London) **4**:287
"The Death of Methuselah" (Singer) **3**:389
The Death of Methuselah, and Other Stories (Singer) **3**:389
"The Death of Mrs. Sheer" (Oates) **6**:224
"The Death of the Lion" (James) **8**:281, 306, 317
Debits and Credits (Kipling) **5**:275, 279, 283, 296
"The Debt" (Wharton) **6**:421, 429
"Debts" (Paley) **8**:399, 403, 407
"Un début dans la vie" (Balzac) **5**:8-9
"The Deceived" (Mann)
See "Die Betrogene"
"Décoré" (Maupassant) **1**:256, 263
"Découverte" (Maupassant) **1**:259
"Deep End" (Ballard) **1**:69
Deephaven (Jewett) **6**:150, 154-57, 165-69
"Deephaven Cronies" (Jewett) **6**:150, 167
"Deephaven Excursions" (Jewett) **6**:150, 168
"Deephaven Society" (Jewett) **6**:154, 167
"Deer in the Works" (Vonnegut) **8**:438
"Defeat" (Boyle) **5**:66
"The Defeat of the City" (Henry) **5**:184
"The Defection of Mary Ann Gibbs" (Dunbar) **8**:122
"A Defender of the Faith" (Dunbar) **8**:122, 132
"The Defenestration of Ermintrude Inch" (Clarke) **3**:134
"The Deliberation of Mr. Dunkin" (Dunbar) **8**:119, 121, 131, 136, 143
"The Delicate Prey" (Bowles) **3**:59-63, 66, 72, 77
The Delicate Prey, and Other Stories (Bowles) **3**:58-65, 67, 70-2, 76-7, 79-80
"The Delta at Sunset" (Ballard) **1**:69
"Delta Autumn" (Faulkner) **1**:166
"The Deluge at Norderney" (Dinesen) **7**:163, 170, 174, 176, 179-80, 182-83, 186, 190, 195-98, 200, 204
"The Demon Lover" (Bowen) **3**:31-2, 41, 50-2, 54
The Demon Lover, and Other Stories (*Ivy Gripped the Steps, and Other Stories*) (Bowen) **3**:30-3, 41, 44, 48, 50-2
"The Demonstrators" (Welty) **1**:488
"Departure" (Anderson) **1**:31, 42, 45-6
"Derring-Do" (Capote) **2**:81
"Desayuno" ("Breakfast") (Cortázar) **7**:95
The Desborough Connections (Harte) **8**:220
"A Descent into the Maelström" (Poe) **1**:385, 400, 402
"The Descent of Man" (Wharton) **6**:428-29
The Descent of Man (Wharton) **6**:420-21
"A Desertion" (Crane) **7**:106
Deshoras (*After-Hours; Off-Hours*) (Cortázar) **7**:79
Desire (O'Flaherty)
See *Dúil*
"Desire in November" (Calvino) **3**:112
"Désirée's Baby" (Chopin) **8**:66, 68, 74-6, 81-4, 91-2, 99, 103, 105-06
"The Desperado" (Turgenev) **7**:324
"A Desperate Character" (Turgenev)
See "Otchayanny"
"The Destruction of Kreshev" (Singer) **3**:358-59, 368, 375, 383-84
"Deutsches requiem" (Borges) **4**:9, 18, 24-6, 30, 37, 40-2
"Deux amis" (Maupassant) **1**:275
"Les deux rêves" (Balzac) **5**:31
"The Devil and Tom Walker" (Irving) **2**:241, 247-48, 250-51, 254, 262
"The Devil in the Belfry" (Poe) **1**:407
The Devil's Race-Track: Mark Twain's Great Dark Writings (Twain) **6**:336
"Le diable" (Maupassant) **1**:270, 284
"Diable—A Dog" (London)
See "Batard"
"Diagnosis" (Wharton) **6**:424
"Dial F for Frankenstein" (Clarke) **3**:145
"Diálogo del espejo" ("Dialogue with a Mirror") (García Márquez) **8**:154-56, 182
"Dialogue" (Lessing) **6**:200-04
"Dialogue with a Mirror" (García Márquez)
See "Diálogo del espejo"
"The Diamond as Big as the Ritz" (Fitzgerald) **6**:46-7, 58-60, 88, 92, 100-02
"A Diamond Guitar" (Capote) **2**:67
"The Diamond Maker" (Wells) **6**:383, 388, 408
"The Diamond Mine" (Cather) **2**:91-2
"The Diamond of Kali" (Henry) **5**:184
"Diary of a Madman" ("A Madman's Diary"; "Notes of a Madman") (Gogol) **4**:82-3, 88, 91, 98, 100-01, 105-07, 122, 124, 126, 128-29
"The Diary of a Superfluous Man" ("The Journal of a Superfluous Man") (Turgenev) **7**:314, 318-20, 339
"The Diary of an African Nun" (Walker) **5**:402, 404
"Dick Boyle's Business Card" (Harte) **8**:216, 252
"Diddling Considered as One of the Exact Sciences" (Poe) **1**:407
"Dieu d'amour" (Wharton) **6**:428
Difficult Loves (Calvino)
See *Gli amori difficili*
"Difficult People" (Chekhov) **2**:155
"The Dilettante" (Mann) **5**:320, 323, 330, 335-37
"The Dilettante" (Wharton) **6**:424
"The Dinosaurs" (Calvino) **3**:103, 109
"Díoltas" (O'Flaherty) **6**:287-88
"The Discounters of Money" (Henry) **5**:159
"A Disgrace to the Family" (Boyle) **5**:64
"Disillusionment" (Mann) **5**:321, 330

"The Disinherited" (Bowen) **3**:33, 41, 45, 48-9, 51
"The Dismissal" (Bowles) **3**:75, 80
"Disorder and Early Sorrow" ("Early Sorrow") (Mann) **5**:310-12, 323, 350
"The Displaced Person" (O'Connor) **1**:335-36, 338, 343-45, 347, 359
"Distance" ("Everything Stuck to Him") (Carver) **8**:4-5, 29, 42, 59
"Distance" (Oates) **6**:236-37
"Distance" (Paley) **8**:416-17
"The Distance of the Moon" (Calvino) See "La distanza della luna"
"The Distances" (Cortázar) See "Lejana"
"A Distant Episode" (Bowles) **3**:59, 61-2, 66-9, 72, 78
"La distanza della luna" ("The Distance of the Moon") (Calvino) **3**:92, 103, 107, 109
"The Distracted Preacher" (Hardy) **2**:203, 205, 208, 213-15, 219-21
"The Disturber of Traffic" (Kipling) **5**:283
"The Ditch" (O'Flaherty) **6**:265
"The Diver" (Dinesen) **7**:163, 167-68, 171
A Diversity of Creatures (Kipling) **5**:275, 282-84
"The Division" (Turgenev) **7**:318
"Dizzy-Headed Dick" (Dunbar) **8**:122
"Djoûmane" (Mérimée) **7**:285, 296-98
"Do You Want to Make Something Out of It?" (Thurber) **1**:428
"Doc Marlowe" (Thurber) **1**:414
"The Doctor" (Gallant) **5**:135, 139
"The Doctor and the Doctor's Wife" (Hemingway) **1**:208, 217, 234, 241, 245
Doctor Brodie's Report (Borges) See *El informe de Brodie*
"Dr. Bullivant" (Hawthorne) **3**:164
"Dr. Chevalier's Lie" (Chopin) **8**:73
"Dr. Heidegger's Experiment" (Hawthorne) **3**:154, 178, 186-87
Doctor Martino, and Other Stories (Faulkner) **1**:180
"A Doctor of Medicine" (Kipling) **5**:285
"The Doctors" (Barnes) **3**:9-10
"A Doctor's Visit" (Chekhov) **2**:127, 156-58
"The Dog" (Turgenev) **7**:316, 321, 323-24, 326, 335-36, 338
"The Dog Hervey" (Kipling) **5**:275, 284-85
"A Dog Named Trilby" (Hughes) **6**:122
"The Doll" (Chesnutt) **7**:17
Dollari e vecchie mondane (*Dollars and the Demi-Mondaine*) (Calvino) **3**:91
Dollars and the Demi-Mondaine (Calvino) See *Dollari e vecchie mondane*
"Dolph Heyliger" (Irving) **2**:241, 247-48, 251, 254, 256, 259-60
"The Dolt" (Barthelme) **2**:38, 52
Domestic Relations: Short Stories (O'Connor) **5**:371, 375
"Don Joaquin" (Cable) **4**:58
"Don Juan (Retired)" (O'Connor) **5**:369, 371
"Don Juan's Temptation" (O'Connor) **5**:366, 371, 389
"Doña Faustina" (Bowles) **3**:64, 66, 80, 83
"Le donneur d'eau bénite" (Maupassant) **1**:281
"Don't Let Them" (Cortázar) See "No te dejes"
"The Doom of the Darnaways" (Chesterton) **1**:131, 138
"The Door in the Wall" (Wells) **6**:361-62, 368-70, 376, 381, 383-84, 391-92, 404, 406
"The Door of Opportunity" (Maugham) **8**:357, 374
"The Door of the Trap" (Anderson) **1**:27, 39, 52
"El Dorado: A Kansas Recessional" (Cather) **2**:101, 105
"Dos fantasías memorables" (Borges) **4**:16
A Double-Barrelled Detective Story (Twain) **6**:295
"Double Birthday" (Cather) **2**:99, 113-15
"A Double-Dyed Deceiver" (Henry) **5**:182
"Une double famille" (Balzac) **5**:22, 29-31
La double méprise (Mérimée) **7**:276, 281, 283, 286, 290-92, 304
".007" (Kipling) **5**:266, 268, 279
"Down at the Dinghy" (Salinger) **2**:290-91, 295-96, 298-300, 314
"Down by the Riverside" (Wright) **2**:360-61, 363, 365-69, 371, 374-75, 379-81, 387, 390-91
"The Downward Path to Wisdom" (Porter) **4**:339-40, 342, 359
"The Dragon at Hide and Seek" (Chesterton) **1**:140
"Un drame au bord de la mer" (Balzac) **5**:16, 26, 31
"The Dream" (Turgenev) See "Son"
"The Dream of a Queer Fellow" ("The Dream of a Ridiculous Man") (Dostoevski) **2**:166, 183, 185
"The Dream of a Ridiculous Man" (Dostoevski) See "The Dream of a Queer Fellow"
"The Dream of an Hour" (Chopin) See "The Story of an Hour"
"A Dream of Armageddon" (Wells) **6**:360, 383-84, 391, 404
"A Dream of Oblómov's Grandson" (Bunin) **5**:81, 90
"Dreamer in a Dead Language" (Paley) **8**:410
"The Dreamers" (Dinesen) **7**:167, 170, 174, 191, 195, 197-98, 200, 209
"The Dreaming Child" (Dinesen) **7**:165, 171
"Dreams" (Chekhov) **2**:156
"The Dreams in the Witch-House" (Lovecraft) **3**:258, 260, 263, 268, 272, 274-76, 282
"The Dreams of Chang" (Bunin) **5**:80-1, 83-4, 93
The Dreams of Chang (Bunin) **5**:80
"A Dreary Story" ("A Dull Story") (Chekhov) **2**:126, 131, 143, 150, 156
"Drenched in Light" (Hurston) **4**:136-38, 149-50
"A Dresden Lady in Dixie" (Chopin) **8**:94
"The Dress" (Thomas) **3**:399, 408
Droll Stories (Balzac) See *Contes drolatiques*
"The Drowned Giant" (Ballard) **1**:68, 74
"Drowne's Wooden Image" (Hawthorne) **3**:185
"The Drummer of All the World" (Laurence) **7**:245, 248-50, 256, 260-61, 272
"The Drums of the Fore and Aft" (Kipling) **5**:264-65, 269, 273
"The Drunkard" (O'Connor) **5**:369, 371, 378
"Dry September" (Faulkner) **1**:148, 180-81
Dry Valley (Bunin) **5**:82-3, 90, 100-01
"The Dryad" (Andersen) **6**:7
Dubliners (Joyce) **3**:201-03, 205-07, 210, 213-14, 216-18, 224-26, 228-30, 233-35, 237-39, 244-45, 247-49
"The Duchess" (Cheever) **1**:106
"The Duchess and the Bugs" (Thurber) **1**:430
"The Duchess and the Jeweller" (Woolf) **7**:377, 388
"The Duchess at Prayer" (Wharton) **6**:413, 415, 428
"The Duchess of Hamptonshire" (Hardy) **2**:204
La Duchesse de Langeais (Balzac) **5**:43-5, 47
"The Duckling" (Andersen) See "The Ugly Duckling"
"The Ducks" (Carver) **8**:10
"The Duel" (Borges) See "El duelo"
"The Duel" (Chekhov) **2**:131, 143, 145, 150-51, 155, 157
"The Duel" (Henry) **5**:191
"The Duel of Dr. Hirsch" (Chesterton) **1**:138
"A Duel without Seconds" (Barnes) **3**:13
"El duelo" ("The Duel") (Borges) **4**:20, 27
"Dúil" (O'Flaherty) **6**:286, 288-89
Dúil (*Desire*) (O'Flaherty) **6**:285-89
"The Duke's Reappearance" (Hardy) **2**:210
"The Dulham Ladies" (Jewett) **6**:160
"A Dull Story" (Chekhov) See "A Dreary Story"
"Dulse" (Munro) **3**:346
"Dummy" (Carver) **8**:5, 29, 34
"The Dunwich Horror" (Lovecraft) **3**:258-59, 263, 269-70, 274-76, 290-92, 294
"The Duplicity of Hargraves" (Henry) **5**:159, 171
"Dusie" (Barnes) **3**:10, 16
"Dusk before Fireworks" (Parker) **2**:273-74, 281, 284-85
"Dutch Courage" (Kipling) **5**:264
"Each Other" (Lessing) **6**:197, 200, 214, 218
"Early Sorrow" (Mann) See "Disorder and Early Sorrow"
Early Stories (Bowen) **3**:40
"Earth's Holocaust" (Hawthorne) **3**:162, 181-82, 189
East and West: The Complete Short Stories of W. Somerset Maugham (Maugham) See *Altogether: The Collected Stories of W. Somerset Maugham*
"The Easter Egg Party" (Bowen) **3**:43, 47
"Easter Eve" (Chekhov) **2**:130
"The Easter of the Soul" (Henry) **5**:188
"The Easter Wedding" (Dunbar) **8**:122, 136
"The Eccentric Seclusion of the Old Lady" (Chesterton) **1**:120
"The Echo" (Bowles) **3**:59, 61-2, 66, 72, 77, 79
"Echoes" (Dinesen) **7**:173-74
"The Edge of the Evening" (Kipling) **5**:269
"The Edge of the World" (Cheever) **1**:88
"The Educational Experience" (Barthelme) **2**:53
"Edward and Pia" (Barthelme) **2**:30
"Edward Randolph's Portrait" (Hawthorne) **3**:179, 182
"Effigy of War" (Boyle) **5**:63-4
"The Egg" (Anderson) See "The Triumph of the Egg"
"L'église" (Balzac) **5**:14, 23, 31
"Egotism; or, The Bosom Serpent" (Hawthorne) **3**:159, 178, 183, 189
"An Egyptian Cigarette" (Chopin) **8**:99

Eight Men (Wright) **2**:364, 366, 370, 386, 388
"The Elaghin Affair" ("The Case of Lieutenant Yelaghin"; "The Cornet Yelagin Affair"; "The Elaghin Case"; "The Yelagin Affair") (Bunin) **5**:82-3, 85, 87, 103, 108-09, 115, 119
The Elaghin Affair, and Other Stories (Bunin) **5**:82
"The Elaghin Case" (Bunin)
See "The Elaghin Affair"
"The Elder Lady" (Borges) **4**:19
"The Elder Mother" (Andersen)
See "The Elder-Tree Mother"
"The Elder-Tree Mother" ("The Elder Mother"; "The Elm-Tree Mother") (Andersen) **6**:3-4, 14, 24
Eldorado (Lessing) **6**:191, 194-95
"Eleanor's House" (Cather) **2**:99, 103
"Elements of True Manhood" (Jewett) **6**:167
"Elephant" (Carver) **8**:43
"Elethia" (Walker) **5**:413
"The Elfin Mound" (Andersen) **6**:7
"Elizabeth Stock's One Story" (Chopin) **8**:100
"The Elm-Tree Mother" (Andersen)
See "The Elder-Tree Mother"
"An Eloquence of Grief" (Crane) **7**:130
"Elsie in New York" (Henry) **5**:194
"The Embarkment for Cythera" (Cheever) **1**:93
"An Embarrassing Situation" (Chopin) **8**:72
"Emma Zunz" (Borges) **4**:16, 18-19, 23, 37, 39, 40
"Emotional Bankruptcy" (Fitzgerald) **6**:50
"The Emperor's New Clothes" (Andersen) **6**:10-11, 13, 16, 18, 26, 30
"The Empire of the Ants" (Wells) **6**:361, 365, 382, 391-92, 403
"The Empty Amulet" (Bowles) **3**:76
"An Empty Purse" (Jewett) **6**:156
"En famille" (Maupassant) **1**:259-60, 263, 272, 274, 278
"En voyage" (Maupassant) **1**:280
"En wagon" (Maupassant) **1**:263
"The Encantadas; or, The Enchanted Isles" ("Hood's Isle and the Hermit Oberlus"; "Two Sides to a Tortoise") (Melville) **1**:293, 297-99, 303-04, 308, 310-11, 321-22, 329
"The Enchanted Bluff" (Cather) **2**:97, 102, 104-05, 108
"An Enchanted Garden" (Calvino)
See "Un giardino incantato"
"The Enchanted Kiss" (Henry) **5**:159, 163
"The Enchanted Sea-Wilderness" (Twain) **6**:337
"An Encounter" (Joyce) **3**:201, 205, 208, 217-18, 225-26, 230, 232, 234, 237, 247
"Encounter at Dawn" (Clarke) **3**:127, 135, 143
"Encounter with Evil" (Cortázar)
See "Encuentro con el mal"
Encounters (Bowen) **3**:29, 40
"Encuentro con el mal" ("Encounter with Evil") (Cortázar) **7**:94
"The End" (Borges) **4**:10
"The End of Something" (Hemingway) **1**:208, 234, 244-45
"The End of the Duel" (Borges) **4**:20, 33-4
End of the Game (Cortázar)
See *Final del juego*
"The End of the Passage" (Kipling)
See "At the End of the Passage"
"The End of the Story" (London) **4**:256
"The End of the World" (Turgenev) **7**:335
The End of the World, and Other Stories (Gallant) **5**:130
"The End of Wisdom" (Chesterton) **1**:140
"Endicott and the Red Cross" (Hawthorne) **3**:175-76
"L'endormeuse" (Maupassant) **1**:284
"The Enduring Chill" (O'Connor) **1**:342-43, 356, 365
"Enemies" (Chekhov) **2**:158
"The Enemies" (Thomas) **3**:407-09
"The Enemies to Each Other" (Kipling) **5**:283
"Engineer-Private Paul Klee Misplaces an Aircraft between Milbertschofen and Cambrai, March 1916" (Barthelme) **2**:49, 54
"England, My England" (Lawrence) **4**:212-13, 229, 231-32, 235
England, My England, and Other Stories (Lawrence) **4**:202, 230-31, 233-37
"England versus England" (Lessing) **6**:199, 218
"English Writers on America" (Irving) **2**:244, 254
"L'enlèvement de la redoute" ("Taking of the Redoubt"; "The Storming of the Redoubt") (Mérimée) **7**:278, 280-81, 283, 287-89
"The Enlightenments of Pagett, M. P." (Kipling) **5**:261
"Enormous Changes at the Last Minute" (Paley) **8**:399, 419
Enormous Changes at the Last Minute (Paley) **8**:391-92, 397, 407-08, 410-11, 415
"The Enormous Radio" (Cheever) **1**:106, 109
The Enormous Radio, and Other Stories (Cheever) **1**:89, 92, 95, 98-100
"Enough" (Turgenev) **7**:323, 325, 336
"Enragée" (Maupassant) **1**:274
"Enter a Dragoon" (Hardy) **2**:215
"The Entomologist" (Cable) **4**:50
L'entrata in guerra (Calvino) **3**:97, 116
"EPICAC" (Vonnegut) **8**:429
"Epilogue: The Photographer" (Munro) **3**:332, 338, 340, 343
"Les epingles" (Maupassant) **1**:263, 286
"Episode" (Maugham) **8**:380
"Episode in the Life of an Ancestor" (Boyle) **5**:54, 70
"An Episode of War" (Crane) **7**:104, 109-10
"Episode under the Terror" (Balzac) **5**:11-12, 18
Eréndira (García Márquez)
See *La increíble y triste historia de la cándida Eréndira y de su abuela* desalmada
"Eric Hermannson's Soul" (Cather) **2**:96, 100-01, 105, 107
"Ermolai and the Miller's Wife" (Turgenev)
See "Yermolai and the Miller's Wife"
"Ernst in Civilian Clothes" (Gallant) **5**:133, 138
"Errand" (Carver) **8**:43
"Error" (Singer) **3**:377
"An Error in Chemistry" (Faulkner) **1**:179
"The Escaped Cock" (Lawrence)
See "The Man Who Died"
"Escapement" (Ballard) **1**:68
"La escritura del Dios" ("The God's Script") (Borges) **4**:7, 23, 28-9
"La escuela de noche" ("The School by Night") (Cortázar) **7**:91
"Eskimo" (Munro) **3**:347
"La espera" (Borges) **4**:16
"Estación de la mano" ("Season of the Hand") (Cortázar) **7**:94
"Esther" (Toomer) **1**:445, 450-51, 457, 459
"Esther Kreindel the Second" (Singer) **3**:363
"Eterna" (Lavin) **4**:184, 189
"The Eternal Husband" (Dostoevski) **2**:166-67, 175-77, 184-85
"The Eternity of Forms" (London) **4**:255-56, 295
"Ethan Brand" (Hawthorne) **3**:159, 179-80, 182
Ethan Frome (Wharton) **6**:415-17, 419, 422, 438-39
"The Ethics of Pig" (Henry) **5**:166
"Etude de femme" (Balzac) **5**:31
Etudes analytiques (*Analytical Studies*) (Balzac) **5**:8-9, 31
Etudes philosophiques (*Philosophic Studies*; *Philosophical Studies*) (Balzac) **5**:8-9, 12, 31, 48
Etudes sur les moeurs (Balzac) **5**:3
"Eugénie Grandet" (Barthelme) **2**:40
"Euphrasie" (Chopin) **8**:69-70
"Eva está dentro de su gato" ("Eve inside Her Cat") (García Márquez) **8**:154-55
"Eve inside Her Cat" (García Márquez)
See "Eva está dentro de su gato"
"Eveline" (Joyce) **3**:205, 226, 231, 234, 247-48
"Evening at Home" (Boyle) **5**:63-4
"The Evening's at Seven" (Thurber) **1**:417, 425
"Evenings on a Farm Near Dikanka" (Gogol)
See "Vechera no xutore bliz Dikan'ki"
"Events of That Easter" (Cheever) **1**:93
Eventyr, fortalte for bøorn (*Fairy Tales*; *New Stories*; *Stories*; *Stories Told for Children*; *Wonder Tales*; *Wonder Tales for Children*; *Wonder Stories Told for Children*) (Andersen) **6**:8, 12, 15, 22, 30
"An Every-Day Girl" (Jewett) **6**:156-59
"Everyday Use" (Walker) **5**:402-03, 406, 416-17
"Everything in Its Right Place" (Andersen) **6**:4, 22-3
"Everything Stuck to Him" (Carver)
See "Distance"
"Everything That Rises Must Converge" (O'Connor) **1**:341, 363
Everything That Rises Must Converge (O'Connor) **1**:341-43
"Eve's Diary" (Twain) **6**:295
"The Eviction" (O'Flaherty) **6**:277, 280
"Excellent People" (Chekhov) **2**:155
"Exile of Eons" (Clarke) **3**:144
"Expedition to Earth" (Clarke) **3**:150
Expedition to Earth (Clarke) **3**:124, 135, 149-50
"Experiment in Luxury" (Crane) **7**:136, 138
"An Experiment in Misery" (Crane) **7**:102, 108-09, 129, 136, 138, 145
"The Explanation" (Barthelme) **2**:35, 40-1, 55
Extracts from Captain Stormfield's Visit to Heaven (*Captain Stormfield's Visit to Heaven*) (Twain) **6**:295, 303, 339
"Extraordinary Little Cough" (Thomas) **3**:394, 403, 406, 411-12

"Extricating Young Gussie" (Wodehouse) **2**:342
"The Eye" (Bowles) **3**:75, 80
"The Eye" (Powers) **4**:368
"The Eye of Allah" (Kipling) **5**:283, 285
"The Eye of Apollo" (Chesterton) **1**:121, 136
"Eye-Witness" (Oates) **6**:251-52
"The Eyes" (Wharton) **6**:424, 426, 428, 430, 433
Eyes of a Blue Dog (García Márquez) **8**:182
"Eyes of a Blue Dog" (García Márquez) See "Ojos de perro azul"
"A Fable" (Lavin) **4**:183
Fables for Our Time and Famous Poems Illustrated (Thurber) **1**:415, 417, 422, 424, 426-27
"The Face in the Target" (Chesterton) **1**:122
"Faces of the Medal" (Cortázar) **7**:63
"Facino Cane" (Balzac) **5**:26, 31, 33
"The Facts in the Case of M. Valdemar" (Poe) **1**:379, 385, 400
"The Facts of Life" (Maugham) **8**:380
"The Fad of the Fisherman" (Chesterton) **1**:122
"The Failure of David Berry" (Jewett) **6**:151
"A Faint Heart" ("A Weak Heart") (Dostoevski) **2**:170-72, 191-92, 195
"The Fair at Sorotchintsy" (Gogol) See "Soročinskaja jamarka"
"The Fairy Goose" (O'Flaherty) **6**:261-62, 269-70, 272, 275, 281, 285
"Fairy-Kist" (Kipling) **5**:284
"Fairy Tale" (Chesterton) **1**:136
Fairy Tales (Andersen) See *Eventyr, fortalte for bøorn*
"The Faith Cure Man" (Dunbar) **8**:122, 128-29
"Faith in a Tree" (Paley) **8**:408
"Faith in the Afternoon" (Paley) **8**:392, 398, 406, 408
"The Faith of Men" (London) **4**:258
The Faith of Men (London) **4**:259, 282, 285, 287
"The Fall of Edward Barnard" (Maugham) **8**:370
"The Fall of Joseph Timmins" (O'Flaherty) **6**:262
"The Fall of the House of Usher" (Poe) **1**:377, 379-80, 383, 385-86, 391, 398-99, 403-07
"Fallen" (Mann) See "Gefallen"
"The Falling Dog" (Barthelme) **2**:55
"Falling in Love in Ashton, British Columbia" (Oates) **6**:230
"The Falling Sleet" (Dostoevski) **2**:165
"The False Collar" (Andersen) **6**:7
"False Dawn" (Kipling) **5**:261
False Dawn (The 'Forties) (Wharton) **6**:439-40
"Fame" (Walker) **5**:412
"A Family Affair" (Chopin) **8**:84, 86
"The Family de Cats" (Dinesen) **7**:177
"A Family Feud" (Dunbar) **8**:120-21, 131, 140, 148
"Family in the Wind" (Fitzgerald) **6**:47, 60, 62
"The Fanatic" (O'Flaherty) **6**:276, 288
"Fancy's Show Box" (Hawthorne) **3**:160, 190-91
"Fanny and Annie" (Lawrence) **4**:232, 234-35
Fantomas contra los vampiros mulinacionales (Cortázar) **7**:60
"A Far-Away Melody" (Freeman) **1**:191
"Faraway Image" (Cortázar) See "Lejana"
"Farce Normande" (Maupassant) **1**:272
"Farewell" (Barthelme) **2**:51
"Farewell" (Powers) **4**:381
"Farewell to Earth" (Clarke) **3**:128
"The Fascination of the Pool" (Woolf) **7**:408, 410-12
"The Fast" (Singer) **3**:355, 361
"Fat" (Carver) **8**:3, 29, 42-3, 54
"The Father" (Carver) **8**:9, 18, 50-1, 55
"Father Alexey's Story" (Turgenev) See "Rasskaz ottsa Aleksaya"
"Father and Son" (Hughes) **6**:109, 119, 121-22, 141-42
"Fathers and Sons" (Hemingway) **1**:212, 216, 230, 240-42
Faust (Turgenev) **7**:320, 323-25, 328, 334-35, 337
"The Fear That Walks by Noonday" (Cather) **2**:100
"The Feast of Crispian" (Ballard) **1**:72
"Feathers" (Carver) **8**:24, 31-2, 34-5, 44
"Feathertop" (Hawthorne) **3**:158, 179
"Federigo" (Mérimée) **7**:283, 287, 289, 299-300
"Fedora" (Chopin) **8**:87, 100
"Fellow-Townsmen" (Hardy) **2**:202-03, 207, 215-16, 228-31
"La femme abandonnée" (Balzac) **5**:8, 31
"La femme de Paul" (Maupassant) **1**:259, 261
"La femme vertueuse" (Balzac) **5**:4, 29
"Le fermier" (Maupassant) **1**:274, 285
"Fern" (Toomer) **1**:441, 444, 457-58, 460
"Ferragus" (Balzac) **5**:43-6
"The Ferry of Unfulfillment" (Henry) **5**:158, 186
"The Ferry, or Another Trip to Paris" (Cortázar) **7**:63
"The Festival" (Lovecraft) **3**:263, 269, 274, 292, 294-95
"Fever" (Carver) **8**:26-8, 30, 33-4, 40
"A Few Crusted Characters" (Hardy) **2**:206, 209, 214-15, 217, 219-20
"An Fiach" (O'Flaherty) **6**:287
Ficciones, 1935-1944 (Borges) **4**:15-16, 18-20, 41
"La ficelle" ("A Piece of String") (Maupassant) **1**:259, 262, 284, 286, 288
"The Fiddler" (Melville) **1**:304
"The Fiddler of the Reels" (Hardy) **2**:216-22, 224-25
"Fifty Grand" (Hemingway) **1**:209, 211, 218, 232, 234-35, 248
Fifty Stories (Boyle) **5**:65
"The Fig Tree" (Porter) **4**:340, 352-53
"The Fight" (Anderson) **1**:31, 50
"The Fight" (O'Flaherty) **6**:269
"The Fight" (Thomas) **3**:402, 406, 411-12
"The Figure in the Carpet" (James) **8**:265, 280, 299, 301-02, 304, 306-07
"La fille aux yeux d'or" (Balzac) **5**:44, 46-7
"Filmer" (Wells) **6**:403, 406
"Un fils" (Maupassant) **1**:275
Final del juego (*End of the Game*) (Cortázar) **7**:50-1, 53, 62-3, 69-70, 79
"A Final Note on Chanda Bell" (Thurber) **1**:421
"A Financial Failure" (Jewett) **6**:158
"The Finding of Martha" (Dunbar) **8**:122
"The Finding of Zach" (Dunbar) **8**:122, 128, 147
"Fine Accommodations" (Hughes) **6**:131, 133
"A Fine Beginning" (Thomas) **3**:403
The Finer Grain (James) **8**:276, 302
"The Finest Story in the World" (Kipling) **5**:273, 280
"Finis" (London) **4**:256
"The Finish of Patsy Barnes" (Dunbar) **8**:122, 125, 128, 137
"The Fir-Tree" ("The Little Fir Tree") (Andersen) **6**:6, 14, 18, 30, 40
"Fire and Cloud" (Wright) **2**:361, 363, 365, 368, 371, 373, 375, 379-81, 383-84, 387
"The Fire and the Hearth" (Faulkner) **1**:182
"Fire Worship" (Hawthorne) **3**:182
"The Fireman's Death" (O'Flaherty) **6**:284
Fires: Essays, Poems, Stories (Carver) **8**:18, 30, 32, 40-1, 45, 50, 57-60
"The Fires Within" (Clarke) **3**:125, 129, 135, 143, 149
"First Blood" (Fitzgerald) **6**:50
"The First-Class Passenger" (Chekhov) **2**:130
"First Confession" (O'Connor) **5**:364, 366, 386, 389
"The First Countess of Wessex" (Hardy) **2**:204, 208-09
"First Encounter" (Clarke) **3**:128
"A First Family of Tasajara" (Harte) **8**:216, 218
The First Forty-Nine Stories (Hemingway) **1**:230, 240
First Love (Turgenev) **7**:321, 323-24, 327-29, 332-34, 337-39, 341, 352
"First Love" (Welty) **1**:467-69, 482
"The First Monday in Lent" (Bunin) See "Chistyi ponedel'nik"
"The First of April" (Barnes) **3**:13
"The First Poet" (London) **4**:256
"First Sorrow" (Kafka) **5**:239
"The First Sunday in June" (Jewett) **6**:159
"Fish for Friday" (O'Connor) **5**:369
"Fits" (Munro) **3**:347
"The Five-Forty-Eight" (Cheever) **1**:100
"Five Peas from One Pod" (Andersen) **6**:35
"The Five White Mice" (Crane) **7**:104, 106, 126, 150
"Flanagan and His Short Filibustering Adventure" (Crane) **7**:100-01, 151
Flappers and Philosophers (Fitzgerald) **6**:45-6, 56-8
"The Flats Road" (Munro) **3**:331-32
"Flavia and Her Artists" (Cather) **2**:98, 103
"Flavours of Exile" (Lessing) **6**:191, 211
"The Flax" (Andersen) **6**:7
"Flight and Pursuit" (Fitzgerald) **6**:56
"The Flight of Pigeons from the Palace" (Barthelme) **2**:37, 40, 55-6
"The Flight of the Israelites" (Ballard) **1**:72
"The Fling" (Carver) **8**:4, 34
"Flip, a California Romance" (Harte) **8**:253, 255
"The Flip of a Coin" (Maugham) **8**:376-77
"The Floating Truth" (Paley) **8**:399
"The Flood" (Anderson) **1**:51
"Una flor amarilla" ("A Yellow Flower") (Cortázar) **7**:52
"Florence Green is 81" (Barthelme) **2**:27
"Flowering Judas" (Porter) **4**:329, 339-40, 342, 344, 346, 349-51, 356

Title Index

Flowering Judas, and Other Stories (Porter) **4**:326-28, 347, 351, 354, 365
"The Flowering of the Strange Orchid" (Wells) **6**:361, 365, 394-96, 404
"The Flowers" (Walker) **5**:402
"Flowers for Marjorie" (Welty) **1**:466, 487-88
"The Flute Player" (O'Flaherty) **6**:281
"The Flying Man" (Wells) **6**:397-98
"The Flying Stars" (Chesterton) **1**:119, 127, 129
"A Flying Start" (Gallant) **5**:147
"The Flying Trunk" (Andersen) **6**:7, 30
Folks from Dixie (Dunbar) **8**:118-21, 123, 127-29, 131, 140-41, 143, 145-46
"Foma, the Wolf" (Turgenev) **7**:316
"The Food of the Gods" (Clarke) **3**:133-34
"Fool about a Horse" (Faulkner) **1**:177
"The Foolish Butterfly" (O'Flaherty) **6**:264, 278-79
The Foot Journey to Amager (Andersen) **6**:4
"Foothold" (Bowen) **3**:40, 44
"Footprints in the Jungle" (Maugham) **8**:359, 361, 374-75
"Footsteps in the Footprints" (Cortázar) **7**:63
"For Conscience' Sake" (Hardy) **2**:207, 212, 214-15, 220
"For Esmé—With Love and Squalor" (Salinger) **2**:289, 293-97, 299-300, 303-05, 314, 316-18
"For Marse Chouchoute" (Chopin) **8**:89
"The Force of Circumstance" (Maugham) **8**:372, 375
"The Foreign Policy of Company 99" (Henry) **5**:197
"The Foreigner" (Jewett) **6**:156, 174-76
"Forging Ahead" (Fitzgerald) **6**:50
"Forgiveness in Families" (Munro) **3**:331
"The Forgotten Enemy" (Clarke) **3**:124
"The Forks" (Powers) **4**:374, 382
"The Form of Space" (Calvino)
See "La forma dello spazio"
"La forma de la espada" ("The Shape of the Sword") (Borges) **4**:10, 25, 42
"La forma dello spazio" ("The Form of Space") (Calvino) **3**:92, 109
La formica argentina (*The Argentine Ant*) (Calvino) **3**:91-2, 98, 117
"The Forsaken" (Turgenev) **7**:318-19
"Forty Stories" (Barthelme) **2**:56
"The Foster Portfolio" (Vonnegut) **8**:432, 435
"The Found Boat" (Munro) **3**:346
The Four-Dimensional Nightmare (Ballard) **1**:68
Four Faultless Felons (Chesterton) **1**:126, 132
"The Four Fists" (Fitzgerald) **6**:58
"Four Meetings" (James) **8**:334
The Four Million (Henry) **5**:155, 171-72, 192
"The Four Seasons" (Gallant) **5**:130, 135, 137-38
"The Fourth Alarm" (Cheever) **1**:101, 110
"The Fourth Day Out from Santa Cruz" (Bowles) **3**:61-2, 72
"The Fox" (Lawrence) **4**:197, 203-04, 210-12, 223-26, 229, 231, 235-36
"The Fqih" (Bowles) **3**:68
"A Fragment of Stained Glass" (Lawrence) **4**:202
"Frail Vessel" (Lavin) **4**:165, 167, 183-84
"The" *Francis Spaight* (London) **4**:262, 291
"Franny" (Salinger) **2**:291, 293, 297, 302-03, 305
Franny and Zooey (Salinger) **2**:297, 304, 318
"The Freeholder Ovsyanikov" ("Ovsianko the Freeholder") (Turgenev) **7**:313, 344
"French Harvest" (Boyle) **5**:64
"The Freshest Boy" (Fitzgerald) **6**:49, 58, 80-1, 84-6
"A Friend of Kafka" (Singer) **3**:384
A Friend of Kafka, and Other Stories (Singer) **3**:370, 373, 375
"A Friend of the Earth" (Thurber) **1**:422, 427
"Friend of the Family" (Boyle) **5**:55
"The Friend of the Family" (Dostoevski)
See "The Village of Stepanchikovo"
"A Friend of the World" (Bowles) **3**:64, 83
"Friendly Brook" (Kipling) **5**:275, 279
"The Friends" (Cortázar)
See "Los amigos"
"Friends" (Paley) **8**:409-10
"Friends of the Family" (O'Connor) **5**:371
"The Friends of the Friends" (James) **8**:270, 316
"From a Window in Vartou" (Andersen) **6**:4
"From Each According to His Ability" (Henry) **5**:159
"From the Cabby's Seat" (Henry) **5**:158
"From the Diary of a New York Lady" (Parker) **2**:278, 286
"From the Fifteenth District" (Gallant) **5**:136-37
From the Fifteenth District (Gallant) **5**:135-37
"The Frozen Fields" (Bowles) **3**:65-6, 79, 84
"The Fruitful Sleeping of the Rev. Elisha Edwards" (Dunbar) **8**:122, 127
"The Frying Pan" (O'Connor) **5**:371, 389
"The Fullness of Life" (Wharton) **6**:424
The Funeral of Mama Grand (García Márquez)
See *Big Mama's Funeral*
"Los funerale de la Mamá Grande" ("Big Mama's Funeral") (García Márquez) **8**:155, 162, 174, 185, 187, 191, 198
"Funes, el memorioso" ("Funes, the Memorious") (Borges) **4**:19-20, 30
"Funes, the Memorious" (Borges)
See "Funes, el memorioso"
"The Furious Seasons" (Carver) **8**:5, 50
Furious Seasons, and Other Stories (Carver) **8**:4, 30, 32, 34, 46, 50, 57-8
"The Furnished Room" (Henry) **5**:156, 171, 174, 180-81, 184, 187-89
Further Fables for Our Time (Thurber) **1**:426-28
"The Future, If Any, of Comedy; or, Where Do We Not-Go from Here?" (Thurber) **1**:424
G. K. Chesterton: Selected Short Stories (Chesterton) **1**:135
The Gadsbys (Kipling)
See *The Story of the Gadsbys*
"A Gala Dress" (Freeman) **1**:196, 201
"La gallina di reparto" (Calvino) **3**:98
"The Galoshes of Fortune" (Andersen)
See "The Goloshes of Fortune"
"Galway Bay" (O'Flaherty) **6**:265, 269, 282
"Galya Ganskaya" (Bunin) **5**:114
"Gambara" (Balzac) **5**:16, 26
"The Gambler, the Nun, and the Radio" (Hemingway) **1**:218, 234
"The Game" (Barthelme) **2**:40
"The Game of Backgammon" (Mérimée)
See "La partie de trictrac"
"Games without End" (Calvino) **3**:109
"The Garden" (Bowles) **3**:64, 68, 80
"The Garden at Mons" (Hemingway) **1**:208, 236
"The Garden Lodge" (Cather) **2**:90, 98, 103
"The Garden of Eden" (Andersen) **6**:30, 37
The Garden of Forking Paths (Borges)
See *El jardín de senderos que se bifurcan*
"The Garden of Forking Paths" (Borges)
See "El jardín de senderos que se bifurcan"
"Garden of Paradise" (Andersen) **6**:7
"The Garden of Time" (Ballard) **1**:71, 74, 77
"A Garden Story" (Jewett) **6**:156, 158-59
"The Gardener" (Kipling) **5**:276, 279, 282-83, 296-97
"The Gardener" (Lavin) **4**:181
"The Gardener and the Family" (Andersen) **6**:15
"The Gate of the Hundred Sorrows" (Kipling) **5**:262, 265
"Le gâteau" (Maupassant) **1**:274, 286
"Gaudissart" (Balzac)
See "L'illustre Gaudissart"
"Gazebo" (Carver) **8**:14-15, 19-20
"Gefallen" ("Fallen") (Mann) **5**:319, 323, 351-53
"The Generations of America" (Ballard) **1**:82
"The Genius" (O'Connor) **5**:376
"Gentian" (Freeman) **1**:197
"The Gentle Boy" (Hawthorne) **3**:164, 167, 181, 185-87
The Gentle Grafter (Henry) **5**:155, 162, 172, 182
"A Gentle Soul" (Lavin) **4**:165-66, 168
"The Gentleman from Cracow" (Singer) **3**:358, 368, 383-84
"The Gentleman from New Orleans" (Chopin) **8**:99
"The Gentleman from San Francisco" (Bunin) **5**:80-3, 85, 87-90, 92, 94-7, 117
The Gentleman from San Francisco (Bunin) **5**:90
"A Gentleman of Bayou Têche" (Chopin) **8**:88, 103
"A Gentleman's Friend" (Chekhov) **2**:137-39
"The Geometry of Love" (Cheever) **1**:97, 101
"Georgia's Ruling" (Henry) **5**:162, 164, 170
"The Geranium" (O'Connor) **1**:364
"A Germ Destroyer" (Kipling) **5**:290
"Get Thee to a Monastery" (Thurber) **1**:429
"Getting off the Altitude" (Lessing) **6**:190, 214
"Getzel the Monkey" (Singer) **3**:359
"The Ghost" (Andersen) **6**:30
"A Ghostly Chess Game" (London) **4**:294
Ghosts (Wharton) **6**:426-27, 430
"The Giant Mole" (Kafka) **5**:206
"Un giardino incantato" ("An Enchanted Garden") (Calvino) **3**:90, 97, 112
"Gift from the Stars" (Clarke) **3**:128
"The Gift of the Magi" (Henry) **5**:166, 171-72, 181-82, 184-85, 187-88
"Gifts" (Singer) **3**:389
"Gigolo and Gigolette" (Maugham) **8**:366, 379
"The Gilded Six-Bits" (Hurston) **4**:135-36, 138, 151-52
"Gimpel the Fool" (Singer) **3**:352, 355, 363, 365-68, 375, 382-84, 389
Gimpel the Fool, and Other Stories (Singer) **3**:370
"The Gioconda of the Twilight Noon" (Ballard) **1**:69

"La giornata d'uno scrutatore" ("The Watcher") (Calvino) **3**:98-9, 116-19
"Girl" (Henry) **5**:163, 182
"The Girl" (Oates) **6**:232
"The Girl and the Habit" (Henry) **5**:158, 164
"The Girl Who Trod on the Loaf" (Andersen) **6**:13
"The Girl with the Cannon Dresses" (Jewett) **6**:157
"The Girl with the Stoop" (Bowen) **3**:54
"Giulia Lazzari" (Maugham) **8**:377
"The Given Case" (James) **8**:316
"Giving Birth" (Atwood) **2**:3-4, 6-10, 12, 14, 16
"Glad Ghosts" (Lawrence) **4**:220, 230
"Gladius Dei" (Mann) **5**:310, 323, 329, 331
"The Glass Mountain" (Barthelme) **2**:34, 40
"A Gleam" (Mann) **5**:322-23
"Gloire et malheur" (Balzac) **5**:4, 29
Gloomy People (Chekhov) **2**:146
"Glory in the Daytime" (Parker) **2**:273-74, 280, 283
"Go Back to Your Precious Wife and Son" (Vonnegut) **8**:436
"Go Down, Moses" (Faulkner) **1**:182-83
Go Down Moses (Faulkner) **1**:148, 154, 165-67, 173, 180-83
"The Go-Getter" (Wodehouse) **2**:346
"A Goatherd at Luncheon" (Calvino) **3**:116
"The Goblin at the Grocer's" ("The Pixy and the Grocer") (Andersen) **6**:30, 34, 41
"Gobseck" (Balzac) **5**:18, 22, 24, 28, 31, 33
"The God of His Fathers" (London) **4**:258, 286-87
The God of His Fathers (London) **4**:264, 282, 285-87
"The God of the Gongs" (Chesterton) **1**:127
"God Rest You Merry, Gentlemen" (Hemingway) **1**:216
"The Goddess" (Oates) **6**:231
The Goddess and Other Women (Oates) **6**:231, 243
"Godliness" (Anderson) **1**:18, 42, 57
"Godman's Master" (Laurence) **7**:245-46, 249-50, 252-53, 261, 263
"The Godmother" (Chopin) **8**:100
"The God's Script" (Borges)
See "La escritura del Dios"
"The Going Away of Liza" (Chopin) **8**:71
"Going into Exile" (O'Flaherty) **6**:261, 269, 276-77, 281-82, 284
"Going to Naples" (Welty) **1**:476, 484
"The Gold Bug" (Poe) **1**:378, 390
"Gold Is Not Always" (Faulkner) **1**:177
"A Gold Slipper" (Cather) **2**:91
"The Gold That Glittered" (Henry) **5**:188
"The Golden Age" (Cheever) **1**:106
The Golden Apples (Welty) **1**:473-74, 479, 483-85, 492, 494, 497
"Golden Gate" (Hughes) **6**:138
"Golden Land" (Faulkner) **1**:167
"The Goloshes of Fortune" ("The Galoshes of Fortune") (Andersen) **6**:11, 18, 22, 24-5, 30, 36
"Gone Away" (Bowen) **3**:53
"Good-by, Jack" (London) **4**:269
"Good Country People" (O'Connor) **1**:335, 343-45, 350, 356, 359-60
"Good-for-Nothing" ("She Was Good for Nothing"; "She Was No Good") (Andersen) **6**:4, 14, 26, 30
"The Good Girl" (Bowen) **3**:33
"Good Humor" (Andersen) **6**:7
"A Good Job Gone" (Hughes) **6**:109, 121-22, 128, 140, 142
"A Good Man Is Hard to Find" (O'Connor) **1**:339, 344, 347-48, 356, 358, 360-63, 371
A Good Man Is Hard to Find (O'Connor) **1**:334-36, 348
"The Good Soldier" (London) **4**:291
"A Good Temper" (Andersen) **6**:30, 36
"Goodbye and Good Luck" (Paley) **8**:388, 391, 394, 396, 398
"Goodbye, My Brother" (Cheever) **1**:89, 99, 103-05, 108
"A Goodly Life" (Bunin) **5**:81, 90, 92
"Goodwood Comes Back" (Warren) **4**:387, 389-90, 394, 396
"The Goophered Grapevine" (Chesnutt) **7**:4-6, 9-10, 41
"Goose Fair" (Lawrence) **4**:197
"Gooseberries" (Chekhov) **2**:136-37, 139, 141-43, 155-57
"The Gospel according to Mark" (Borges) **4**:20, 28, 30
"A Gourdful of Glory" (Laurence) **7**:245-46, 248-50
"Grace" (Joyce) **3**:202, 205-06, 208, 210-11, 214-15, 225-26, 232-235, 237, 247-48
"Grafitti" (Cortázar) **7**:83, 85-6, 91
"Grammar of Love" (Bunin) **5**:89-90, 93, 106
"La grand bretèche" (Balzac) **5**:11-12, 14-15, 18-19, 31, 35-9
"The Grand Vizier's Daughter" (O'Connor) **5**:381
"The Grande Malade" ("The Little Girl Continues") (Barnes) **3**:5-6, 9-10, 16, 24-6
"Grandfather and Grandson" (Singer) **3**:374
"The Grasshopper" (Chekhov) **2**:155
"The Grave" (Porter) **4**:329-34, 340-42, 344, 352, 354, 365
"The Grave by the Handpost" (Hardy) **2**:210
"The Grave of the Famous Poet" (Atwood) **2**:3-5, 7, 10-11, 16
"The Gravedigger" (Singer) **3**:378
"The Gray Champion" (Hawthorne) **3**:164, 167, 171, 175-76, 178, 186-87
"The Gray Mills of Farley" (Jewett) **6**:156
"The Gray Wolf's Ha'nt" (Chesnutt) **7**:7, 10-11, 40
Great Battles of the World (Crane) **7**:104
"The Great Carbuncle" (Hawthorne) **3**:157, 159, 181-82, 184-85, 188
"The Great Dark" (Twain) **6**:331-42, 350-53
Great Days (Barthelme) **2**:44, 46
"The Great Good Place" (James) **8**:269, 282, 302, 304, 306-07
"The Great Interrogation" (London) **4**:265, 286
"The Great Road" (Bunin) **5**:87
"A Great Sorrow" (Andersen) **6**:4, 7
"The Great Stone Face" (Hawthorne) **3**:159, 178, 182, 184
"The Great Wall of China" (Kafka) **5**:206
The Great Wall of China: Stories and Reflections (Kafka) **5**:206
"The Great Wave" (Lavin) **4**:167-68, 174, 184
The Great Wave, and Other Stories (Lavin) **4**:166
The Greater Inclination (Wharton) **6**:413
"The Greatest Man in the World" (Thurber) **1**:420, 431
"The Greatest Television Show on Earth" (Ballard) **1**:71
"The Green Banana" (Powers) **4**:379
"The Green Door" (Henry) **5**:159, 190
"The Green Grave and the Black Grave" (Lavin) **4**:166-67, 174, 180, 184
"Green Holly" (Bowen) **3**:32, 54
"The Green Isle in the Sea" (Thurber) **1**:417
"The Green Man" (Chesterton) **1**:129
Green Water, Green Sky (Gallant) **5**:123, 144, 146
"Greenleaf" (O'Connor) **1**:343, 358, 360
"Gregory's Island" (Cable)
See "The Solitary"
"La grenadière" (Balzac) **5**:8, 16
"Gretchen's Forty Winks" (Fitzgerald) **6**:46
"Grey Seagull" (O'Flaherty) **6**:262
"A Grey Sleeve" (Crane) **7**:103, 106
"Grief" (Andersen) **6**:26
"Grippes and Poche" (Gallant) **5**:147
"The Grisly Folk" (Wells) **6**:382
"The Grit of Women" (London) **4**:286, 288
"Grjotgard Ålvesøon and Aud" (Dinesen)
See "Grjotgard Ålvesøon og Aud"
"Grjotgard Ålvesøon og Aud" ("Grjotgard Ålvesøon and Aud") (Dinesen) **7**:177
A Group of Noble Dames (Hardy) **2**:203-07, 209, 212-13, 220-21
"The Growtown 'Bugle'" (Jewett) **6**:156, 159
"Guardian Angel" (Clarke) **3**:149
"Guayaquil" (Borges) **4**:20, 27
"A Guest at Home" (Jewett) **6**:156, 158-59
"Guests from Gibbet Island" (Irving) **2**:241, 247-48
"Guests of the Nation" (O'Connor) **5**:369, 375-76, 379-82, 384, 388-89, 393
Guests of the Nation (O'Connor) **5**:363, 370, 375, 377-80, 382, 384, 387, 390-93
"The Guilty Party—An East Side Tragedy" (Henry) **5**:188, 198
Guilty Pleasures (Barthelme) **2**:39, 41
"Gumption" (Hughes) **6**:131, 133
"Gusev" (Chekhov) **2**:128-29, 143, 147
"The Habit of Loving" (Lessing) **6**:218
"An Habitation Enforced" (Kipling) **5**:283
"Hacienda" (Porter) **4**:327, 329-30, 346, 351
"The Hag" (Turgenev) **7**:335
"The Hair" (Carver) **8**:50-1
"Hair" (Faulkner) **1**:147, 151
"Hair Jewellery" (Atwood) **2**:3, 5-7, 10-11, 14, 16
"The Hair Shirt" (Powers) **4**:380
"The Hairless Mexican" (Maugham) **8**:369, 376
"Hal Irwin's Magic Lamp" (Vonnegut) **8**:437
"Halberdier of the Little Rheinschloss" (Henry) **5**:181, 196
"Half a Grapefruit" (Munro) **3**:334, 342
"The Half-Husky" (Laurence) **7**:253, 270
"The Hall of Fantasy" (Hawthorne) **3**:181
"The Hallucination" (Oates) **6**:250
"The Hamlet of Stepanchikovo" (Dostoevski)
See "The Village of Stepanchikovo"
"The Hammer of God" (Chesterton) **1**:124, 130, 136
"Hand" (Atwood) **2**:20
"Hand in Glove" (Bowen) **3**:54
"Hand upon the Waters" (Faulkner) **1**:179
"Handcarved Coffins: A Nonfiction Account of an American Crime" (Capote) **2**:80-2
"Hands" (Anderson) **1**:32-3, 42, 44, 57

Title Index

"The Handsomest Drowned Man in the World" (García Márquez) **8**:160, 167-70, 183, 186
"Hanka" (Singer) **3**:377
"Happiness" (Chekhov) **2**:130, 156
"Happiness" (Lavin) **4**:182, 185
"The Happy Autumn Fields" (Bowen) **3**:31-2, 50-1
"The Happy Couple" (Maugham) **8**:380
"A Happy Death" (Lavin) **4**:165, 167
"Happy Endings" (Atwood) **2**:15, 19-20
"The Happy Failure" (Melville) **1**:303
"The Happy Family" (Andersen) **6**:18
"Hapworth 16, 1924" (Salinger) **2**:308, 314
"A Harbinger" (Chopin) **8**:71
"The Harbinger" (Henry) **5**:158
"The Hardy Tin Soldier" (Andersen)
See "The Steadfast Tin Soldier"
"Harrison Bergeron" (Vonnegut) **8**:427, 434
"A Haunted House" (Woolf) **7**:369, 374-75, 389-90, 392, 399
A Haunted House, and Other Short Stories (Woolf) **7**:372, 374, 386, 388, 400
"The 'Haunted House' in Royal Street" (Cable) **4**:53, 59, 61, 75-6
"The Haunted Mind" (Hawthorne) **3**:181
"The Haunter of the Dark" (Lovecraft) **3**:259, 263, 273-75, 279, 284
"Hautot père et fils" (Maupassant) **1**:270, 280, 285, 288
"Having a Wonderful Time" (Ballard) **1**:79
"The Hawk" (O'Flaherty) 269, 274, 279
"The Haymaking" (Lavin) **4**:167
"He" (Lovecraft) **3**:259, 262, 283, 289
"He" (Porter) **4**:327-30, 339-40, 349-50, 354, 360
"He Don't Plant Cotton" (Powers) **4**:368
"He of the Assembly" (Bowles) **3**:68, 83-4
"He Thinks He's Wonderful" (Fitzgerald) **6**:47, 49
"Head and Shoulders" (Fitzgerald) **6**:45, 57, 96-7
"The Head-Hunter" (Henry) **5**:166
"The Head of Babylon" (Barnes) **3**:19-20
"The Head of the Family" (Chekhov) **2**:127
"The Headless Hawk" (Capote) **2**:61-3, 66, 69, 72, 75-6
The Heart o' the West (*Heart of the West*) (Henry) **5**:155, 172, 182
The Heart of a Goof (Wodehouse) **2**:329, 350
The Heart of Happy Hollow (Dunbar) **8**:120-22, 127-29, 131-32, 141, 145
Heart of the West (Henry)
See *The Heart o' the West*
"Heartbreak" (Andersen) **6**:30, 32, 35
"Hearts and Crosses" (Henry) **5**:155, 181
"Heimkehr" ("Homecoming") (Kafka) **5**:254
"Heinrich" (Bunin) **5**:114
"The Heir of the McHulisches" (Harte) **8**:217, 252
"An Heiress of Red Dog" (Harte) **8**:248
"Hello Fine Day Isn't It?" (Oates) **6**:248-50
"Henne Fire" (Singer) **3**:370, 383-84
"Her Boss" (Cather) **2**:111
"Her Ladyship's Private Office" (Turgenev) **7**:337
"Her Letters" (Chopin) **8**:92, 98-9, 112-13
"Her Own People" (Warren) **4**:389-90, 395, 399
"Her Son" (Wharton) **6**:423-24
"Her Sweet Jerome" (Walker) **5**:402, 405-06, 419
"Her Table Spread" (Bowen) **3**:34-6, 38, 41, 51
"Her Virginia Mammy" (Chesnutt) **7**:16, 23, 33-5, 37
"Herbert West--Reanimator" (Lovecraft) **3**:282, 293-94
Here and Beyond (Wharton) **6**:422
"Here Come the Tigers" (Thurber) **1**:429
Here Lies: The Collected Stories of Dorothy Parker (Parker) **2**:274-76
"Here to Learn" (Bowles) **3**:75, 79-80
"Here We Are" (Parker) **2**:273-74, 281, 283
"L'heritage" (Maupassant) **1**:256, 259-60, 263, 270, 276, 283
"The Heritage of Dedlow Marsh" (Harte) **8**:254
"The Hermit and the Wild Woman" (Wharton) **6**:428
The Hermit and the Wild Woman (Wharton) **6**:420, 435
"The Hermits" (Dinesen) **7**:177
"The Heroine" (Dinesen) **7**:165, 168, 195
"Hide and Seek" (Clarke) **3**:124-26, 133, 150
"Hiding Man" (Barthelme) **2**:26, 41-2, 54
"High" (Oates) **6**:252
"The High Constable's Wife" (Balzac) **5**:19
"High-Water Mark" (Harte) **8**:210, 232
"The Higher Abdication" (Henry) **5**:180-81
"The Higher Pragmatism" (Henry) **5**:187
"The Hill of the Elves" (Andersen) **6**:31
"Hills Like White Elephants" (Hemingway) **1**:210, 217, 232, 234
"The Hiltons' Holiday" (Jewett) **6**:152
"Him" (Atwood) **2**:20
"His Chest of Drawers" (Anderson) **1**:52
"His Excellency" (Maugham) **8**:365, 377
"His Father's Son" (Wharton) **6**:421, 424, 435
"His Mother" (Gallant) **5**:135, 137
Histoire de treize (*The Thirteen*; *Treize*) (Balzac) **5**:5, 45-7
"L'histoire d'une fille de ferme" (Maupassant) **1**:257, 259, 261, 272, 274-75
Historia de cronopios y de famas (*Cronopios and Famas*) (Cortázar) **7**:50, 53, 60, 91-2, 94
Historia universal de la infamia (*A Universal History of Infamy*) (Borges) **4**:4, 17
"History Lesson" (Clarke) **3**:124, 133, 143-44
"The History of Lieutenant Ergunov" (Turgenev)
See "Istoriya leytenanta Ergunova"
"The History of the Hardcomes" (Hardy) **2**:215
"The Hitch-Hikers" (Welty) **1**:466, 468, 481, 487-88, 494
"The Hobo and the Fairy" (London) **4**:255
"Hoboes That Pass in the Night" (London) **4**:291
"Hog Pawn" (Faulkner) **1**:178
La hojarasca (*Leaf Storm*) (García Márquez) **8**:154, 160, 162, 171
"Holding Her Down" (London) **4**:291
"The Hole in the Wall" (Chesterton) **1**:122
"Holiday" (Porter) **4**:347, 349-50, 355
"The Hollow of the Three Hills" (Hawthorne) **3**:154, 157, 180-81
"The Holy Door" (O'Connor) **5**:365, 367, 371, 384, 390
"The Holy Six" (Thomas) **3**:399, 407-08
"Homage to Isaac Babel" (Lessing) **6**:196-99, 214
"Homage to Switzerland" (Hemingway) **1**:211
"Hombre de la esquina rosada" ("Hombres de las orillas"; "Streetcorner Man"; "The Pink Corner Man") (Borges) **4**:10, 14-16
"El hombre en el umbral" ("The Man on the Threshold") (Borges) **4**:4, 40-1
"Hombres de las orillas" (Borges)
See "Hombre de la esquina rosada"
"Home" (Boyle) **5**:57
"Home" (Hughes) **6**:109, 118-19, 121-22, 133
"The Home-Coming of 'Rastus Smith" (Dunbar) **8**:122, 135
A Home for the Highland Cattle (Lessing) **6**:189-91, 195-96
Home Truths: Selected Canadian Stories (Gallant) **5**:138, 141, 143-44, 147
"Homecoming" (Kafka)
See "Heimkehr"
"Un homme d'affaires" (Balzac) **5**:32
"The Honest Quack" (Chesterton) **1**:133
"An Honest Soul" (Freeman) **1**:198, 201
"An Honest Thief" (Dostoevski) **2**:166, 171, 193
"The Honey Tree" (Jewett) **6**:156, 158
"Honolulu" (Maugham) **8**:359, 371-72
"Honorine" (Balzac) **5**:18, 31, 33
"The Honour of Israel Gow" (Chesterton) **1**:134, 137
"Hood's Isle and the Hermit Oberlus" (Melville)
See "The Encantadas; or, The Enchanted Isles"
"The Hook" (O'Flaherty) **6**:264, 269
"Hop-Frog" (Poe) **1**:408
"Hopeless" (Atwood) **2**:20
"Le horla" (Maupassant) **1**:259, 262, 265, 269, 273, 283-84, 286-88
"The Horror at Red Hook" (Lovecraft) **3**:258, 262, 289
"The Horror in the Museum" (Lovecraft) **3**:279
"The Horse-Dealer's Daughter" (Lawrence) **4**:202-03, 231-33, 235-36, 240
"The Horse-Stealers" (Chekhov) **2**:130
Horses and Men (Anderson) **1**:23, 25, 27, 30, 46, 50
"The Horse's Ha" (Thomas) **3**:409
"A Horse's Name" (Chekhov) **2**:130
"Horses of the Night" (Laurence) **7**:255, 259, 262-63, 270
"Horses—One Dash" ("One Dash—Horses") (Crane) **7**:104, 106, 108, 125-26, 149, 153-54
"A Horse's Tale" (Twain) **6**:303
"Horsie" (Parker) **2**:273-75, 280, 283-84
"A Host of Furious Fancies" (Ballard) **1**:79
"Hot and Cold Blood" (Fitzgerald) **6**:46
"Hot-Foot Hannibal" (Chesnutt) **7**:7, 10-11, 40
"Hotel behind the Lines" (Boyle) **5**:74
"The Hound" (Faulkner) **1**:177
"The Hound" (Lovecraft) **3**:258, 262, 274, 276, 282
"The Hours after Noon" (Bowles) **3**:64-6, 80, 82
"The House of Asterión" (Borges)
See "La casa de Asterión"
"House of Flowers" (Capote) **2**:67, 69, 72, 75
The House of Pride, and Other Tales of Hawaii (London) **4**:268-69, 283

"The House of the Dead Hand" (Wharton) 6:428
"The House Surgeon" (Kipling) 5:272, 275, 284-85
"House Taken Over" (Cortázar) See "Casa tomada"
"The House That Johnny Built" (O'Connor) 5:363, 371
"The House with a Mezzanine" (Chekhov) See "An Artist's Story"
"The House with an Attic" (Chekhov) See "An Artist's Story"
"The House with the Maisonette" (Chekhov) See "An Artist's Story"
"The Housebreaker of Shady Hill" (Cheever) 1:111
The Housebreaker of Shady Hill, and Other Stories (Cheever) 1:89-92, 95, 100
"The Household" (Irving) 2:265
"How a Good Man Went Wrong" (Chesnutt) 7:14
"How about This?" (Carver) 8:32
"How Brother Parker Fell from Grace" (Dunbar) 8:122
"How Dasdy Came Through" (Chesnutt) 7:13
"How I Finally Lost My Heart" (Lessing) 6:197, 200-01, 206, 220
"How I Write My Songs" (Barthelme) 2:52
"How Many Midnights" (Bowles) 3:60, 69, 72, 79
"How Much Shall We Bet?" (Calvino) 3:104
"How Santa Claus Came to Simpson's Bar" (Harte) 8:223-24, 227, 236, 244
"How to Write a *Blackwood* Article" (Poe) 1:405
"Howe's Masquerade" (Hawthorne) 3:154, 187
"The Human Being and the Dinosaur" (Thurber) 1:426, 430
The Human Comedy (Balzac) See *Comédie humaine*
"The Human Element" (Maugham) 8:357, 366, 378
"Human Habitation" (Bowen) 3:55
"A Humble Romance" (Freeman) 1:196
A Humble Romance, and Other Stories (Freeman) 1:191, 194-95, 197, 201
"A Humorous Southern Story" (Chesnutt) 7:13
"The Hunchback in the Park" (Thomas) 3:400
A Hundred Camels in the Courtyard (Bowles) 3:68
Hunger (Lessing) 6:190, 192-93, 195-97
"A Hunger-Artist" (Kafka) See "Ein Hungerkünstler"
Ein Hungerkünstler (Kafka) 5:237
"Ein Hungerkünstler" ("A Hunger-Artist") (Kafka) 5:207-09, 220, 225, 237-40
"The Hungry" (Mann) 5:319, 322-23, 330
The Hungry Ghosts (Oates) 6:241, 243
"The Hunter Gracchus" (Kafka) 5:210
"The Hunter's Waking Thoughts" (Gallant) 5:151
"The Huntsman" (Chekhov) 2:155
"Hurricane Hazel" (Atwood) 2:21-3
"The Husband" (Bowles) 3:80
"The Hyannis Port Story" (Vonnegut) 8:436
"The Hyena" (Bowles) 3:64-5, 68, 80
"Hygeia at the Solito" (Henry) 5:182
"The Hypothesis of Failure" (Henry) 5:184
"I and My Chimney" (Melville) 1:298, 304, 322, 326-27
"I Could See the Smallest Things" (Carver) 8:19, 34-5
"I Live on Your Visits" (Parker) 2:283
I nostri antenati (Our Ancestors) (Calvino) 3:91-2, 106, 117
I racconti (Calvino) 3:96-7, 116
"I Remember Babylon" (Clarke) 3:131
"I Want to Know Why" (Anderson) 1:20, 23, 27, 35, 37-8, 40, 48-9, 62
"Ib and Christine" (Andersen) 6:14
"Ibn Hakkan al-Bokhari, Dead in His Labryinth" (Borges) 4:30, 35
"The Ice Maiden" (Andersen) 6:12, 19, 26, 34-5, 37
"The Ice Palace" (Fitzgerald) 6:57-8, 88, 96-7, 100, 103
"The Ice Wagon Going Down the Street" (Gallant) 5:139, 144
"Iconography" (Atwood) 2:15, 20
"Ida" (Bunin) 5:106-07, 116-20
"The Idea" (Carver) 8:7
"An Idle Fellow" (Chopin) 8:73, 78, 98
"The Idol of the Cyclades" (Cortázar) See "Ídolo de las Cícladas"
"Ídolo de las Cícladas" ("The Idol of the Cyclades") (Cortázar) 7:57-8, 69-70, 76, 78
"The Idyl of Red Gulch" (Harte) 8:210, 217, 236-37, 246
"An Idyll of North Carolina Sand-Hill Life" (Chesnutt) 7:14
"Une idylle" (Maupassant) 1:256, 270
"'If I Forget Thee, O Earth'" (Clarke) 3:124, 126, 143
"If I Should Open My Mouth" (Bowles) 3:64, 68-9, 80, 83, 85
"Ignat" (Bunin) 5:100
"The Illuminated Man" (Ballard) 1:69
"An Illusion in Red and White" (Crane) 7:
"L'illustre Gaudissart" ("Gaudissart"; "The Illustrious Gaudissart") (Balzac) 5:18, 26
"The Illustrious Gaudissart" (Balzac) See "L'illustre Gaudissart"
"I'm a Fool" (Anderson) 1:23, 25, 27, 30, 37-8, 40, 48-50
The Image, and Other Stories (Singer) 3:384-86
"Images" (Munro) 3:326, 338, 343-44
"An Imaginative Woman" (Hardy) 2:215, 220, 223, 225
"The Immigrant Story" (Paley) 8:406, 409
"The Immortals" (Borges) See "El inmortal"
"Impertinent Daughters" (Lessing) 6:215
"The Impossible Man" (Ballard) 1:75-7
"The Impossible Marriage" (O'Connor) 5:372, 374
"The Impresario" (Singer) 3:389
"The Impressions of a Cousin" (James) 8:316
"In a Café" (Lavin) 4:183, 185, 189
"In a Far Country" (London) 4:264, 267-68, 279, 281-82, 284-86, 290
"In a Public Place" (Oates) 6:237
"In a Strange Town" (Anderson) 1:50
"In a Thousand Years' Time" (Andersen) 6:30
"In and Out of Old Nachitoches" (Chopin) 8:103, 105, 113
"In Another Country" (Hemingway) 1:209, 230-32, 234
"In Autumn" (Bunin) 5:114
"In der Strafkolonie" ("In the Penal Colony") (Kafka) 5:218, 223-224, 229-30, 235-36, 240, 249-52
"In Exile" (Chekhov) 2:157
In Love and Trouble: Stories of Black Women (Walker) 5:401-03, 405, 407, 411-12, 418-19, 422
In Old Plantation Days (Dunbar) 8:120-22, 127-29, 132, 134, 141, 145, 148
in our time (Hemingway) 1:206-07, 235, 241, 243
In Our Time (Hemingway) 1:207-08, 212, 214-15, 234, 236, 238, 243-45
"In Paris" (Bunin) 5:114
"In Sabine" (Chopin) 8:90, 99, 103
"In Shadow" (Jewett) 6:150, 168
"In the Abyss" (Wells) 6:366, 389, 403, 408-09
"In the Autumn of the Year" (Oates) 6:247
"In the Avu Observatory" (Wells) 6:361
In the Cage (James) 8:302-05, 329, 331
"In the Carquinez Woods" (Harte) 8:216, 223, 227, 233, 244, 251
"In the Cart" (Chekhov) 2:156-58
"In the Direction of the Beginning" (Thomas) 3:396, 402, 407, 409
"In the Forests of the North" (London) 4:265, 280
"In the House of Suddhu" (Kipling) 5:265
"In the Matter of a Private" (Kipling) 5:260
"In the Middle of the Fields" (Lavin) 4:183, 185
In the Middle of the Fields, and Other Stories (Lavin) 4:172
"In the Orchard" (Woolf) 7:411
"In the Penal Colony" (Kafka) See "In der Strafkolonie"
"In the Pride of His Youth" (Kipling) 5:274
"In the Ravine" ("In the River") (Chekhov) 2:128, 131-32, 145, 156-57
"In the River" (Chekhov) See "In the Ravine"
"In the Rukh" (Kipling) 5:287
"In the Same Boat" (Kipling) 5:284-85
"In the Square" (Bowen) 3:31
"In the Train" (O'Connor) 5:364, 371, 376-77, 381-82, 388, 395
"In the Tules" (Harte) 8:244
"In the Tunnel" (Gallant) 5:130-31, 144
"In the Vault" (Lovecraft) 3:262
"In the Warehouse" (Oates) 6:232
"In Time Which Made a Monkey of Us All" (Paley) 8:403
"In Transit" (Gallant) 5:150
In Transit: Twenty Stories (Gallant) 5:150
"In Youth Is Pleasure" (Gallant) 5:128-29, 134, 143, 148
"The Incarnation of Krishna Mulvaney" (Kipling) 5:259, 262
"An Incident in the Park" (Oates) 6:248-49
The Incredible and Sad Story of Innocent Eréndira and Her Heartless Grandmother (García Márquez) See *La increíble y triste historia de la cándida Eréndira y de su abuela desalmada*
The Incredulity of Father Brown (Chesterton) 1:128

La increíble y triste historia de la cándida Eréndira y de su abuela desalmada (*The Incredible and Sad Story of Innocent Eréndira and Her Heartless Grandmother; Eréndira*) (García Márquez) **8**:167, 169-72, 182, 186, 198-200
"The Independence of Silas Bollender" (Dunbar) **8**:127, 134
"An Independent Thinker" (Freeman) **1**:196
"Indian Camp" (Hemingway) **1**:214, 219, 234, 240-41, 244-45
"The Indian Sign" (Thurber) **1**:425
"Indian Summer" (Barnes) **3**:12, 22
"The Indian Summer of Dry Valley Johnson" (Henry) **5**:162
"The Indian Uprising" (Barthelme) **2**:35-6, 38, 42, 46, 53
"The Inevitable White Man" (London) **4**:266
"The Inexperienced Ghost" (Wells) **6**:400
"The Infant Prodigy" (Mann) **5**:324, 330-31
El informe de Brodie (*Doctor Brodie's Report*) (Borges) **4**:17-20, 26-7
"An Ingènue of the Sierra" (Harte) **8**:244, 252
"The Ingrate" (Dunbar) **8**:122-23, 128-29, 136, 142-43, 149
"The Inherited Clock" (Bowen) **3**:31-2
"La inmiscusión terrupta" ("Meddlance Tersplat") (Cortázar) **7**:95
"El inmortal" ("The Immortals") (Borges) **4**:7-8, 10-12, 14, 18-20, 26-7
"The Inn" ("The Wayside Inn"; "The Country Inn") (Turgenev) **7**:315, 320, 323, 325, 337, 359
The Innocence of Father Brown (Chesterton) **1**:119-21, 124-25
"The Inquisition" (O'Flaherty) **6**:264, 284
"The Insoluble Problem" (Chesterton) **1**:128
"Instrucciones para John Howell" (Cortázar) **7**:62
"Instructions for the Third Eye" (Atwood) **2**:16-17
"Instructions on How to Dissect a Ground Owl" (Cortázar) **7**:92
"Intensive Care Unit" (Ballard) **1**:79
"L'interdiction" (Balzac) **5**:8, 16, 26
"An Interest in Life" (Paley) **8**:389-90, 396-99, 415-18
"The Interference of Patsy Ann" (Dunbar) **8**:122, 132
"Interlopers at the Knap" (Hardy) **2**:203, 205, 207, 216, 229-31
"Interlude in a Book Shop" (Powers) **4**:368-69
"An International Episode" (James) **8**:299, 302
"The Intervention of Peter" (Dunbar) **8**:121, 127, 140
"The Interview" (Singer) **3**:387
"The Interview" (Thurber) **1**:420
"Interview with a Lemming" (Thurber) **1**:417
"Intimacy" (Carver) **8**:43
"Into the Comet" (Clarke) **3**:147
"Intoxication" (Oates) **6**:252
"The Introducers" (Wharton) **6**:424, 437-38
"The Introduction" (Woolf) **7**:381, 390-91, 393, 395, 397, 399
"The Intruder" (Borges)
See "La intrusa"
"La intrusa" ("The Intruder") (Borges) **4**:14-15, 20, 37, 40-1
"L'inutile beauté" (Maupassant) **1**:273, 275, 286-87
"The Inverted Forest" (Salinger) **2**:309
"Investigations of a Dog" (Kafka) **5**:206, 229, 238, 241
"The Invincible Slave-Owners" (Dinesen) **7**:177, 196
The Invisible Knight (Calvino)
See *Il cavaliere inesistente*
"The Invisible Man" (Chesterton) **1**:130, 134, 136, 142
"Ionitch" (Chekhov)
See "Ionych"
"Ionych" ("Ionitch") (Chekhov) **2**:128, 131-32, 155
Iounn the Weeper (Bunin) **5**:90
"Irina" (Gallant) **5**:128-32, 137
"An Irrevocable Diameter" (Paley) **8**:390
"La isla a mediodía" (Cortázar) **7**:55-6, 61
Island Tales (London)
See *On the Makaloa Mat*
"Istoriya leytenanta Ergunova" ("The Story of Lieutenant Ergunov"; "The Adventure of Lieutenant Jergounoff"; "Lieutenant Yergunov's Story"; "The History of Lieutenant Ergunov") (Turgenev) **7**:316, 321, 326, 337, 358-59
"It Was the Devil's Work" (O'Flaherty) **6**:259
"The Italian Banditti" (Irving) **2**:251, 261
Italian Folktales (Calvino) **3**:105, 119
"Italian Robber" (Irving) **2**:255
"Its Image on the Mirror" (Gallant) **5**:122-23, 135, 140, 148-49
"It's Perfectly True" (Andersen) **6**:30
"Ivan Federovič Špon'ka and His Aunt" (Gogol)
See "Ivan Federovič Špon'ka i ego tetsuška"
"Ivan Federovič Špon'ka i ego tetsuška" ("Ivan Federovič Špon'ka and His Aunt") (Gogol) **4**:105, 117, 121
"Ivory, Apes, and People" (Thurber) **1**:426
"L'ivrogne" (Maupassant) **1**:274
"Ivy Day in the Committee Room" (Joyce) **3**:201, 205-06, 210-11, 214, 218-21, 225-26, 228, 231, 234, 237, 240, 242, 248
"Ivy Gripped the Steps" (Bowen) **3**:31-2, 38, 41, 48, 51
Ivy Gripped the Steps, and Other Stories (Bowen)
See *The Demon Lover, and Other Stories*
"Jachid and Jechidah" (Singer) **3**:357, 363, 375
"Jack and Gill of the Sierras" (Harte) **8**:214
"Jack the Dullard" (Andersen) **6**:11
Jacob Pasinkov (Turgenev)
See *Yakov Pasynkov*
"Jamesie" (Powers) **4**:368, 371-72
"Jan the Unrepentant" (London) **4**:286
"Jane" (Maugham) **8**:356, 378-79
El jardín de senderos que se bifurcan (*The Garden of Forking Paths*) (Borges) **4**:4, 18
"El jardín de senderos que se bifurcan" ("The Garden of Forking Paths") (Borges) **4**:5, 8, 10-11, 13, 16, 18-19, 28
"Jazz, Jive and Jam" (Hughes) **6**:143-44, 146
"The Jealous Hens" (O'Flaherty) **6**:262, 280
"Jean-ah Poquelin" (Cable) **4**:67-70, 72-3
"Jeeves and the Dog MacIntosh" (Wodehouse) **2**:355-56
"Jeeves and the Greasy Bird" (Wodehouse) **2**:344
"Jeeves and the Yuletide Spirit" (Wodehouse) **2**:356
"Jeff Brigg's Love Story" (Harte) **8**:216
"The Jelly-Bean" (Fitzgerald) **6**:58-9
"Jemima, the Mountain Girl" (Fitzgerald) **6**:45, 58
"Jenny Garrow's Lovers" (Jewett) **6**:156-58, 166
"Jericho's Brick Battlements" (Laurence) **7**:252, 259, 267
"Jerry and Molly and Sam" (Carver) **8**:12
"Jesse and Meribeth" (Munro) **3**:347, 349
"The Jest of Jests" (Barnes) **3**:18
"Jésus-Christ en Flandre" (Balzac) **5**:14, 16-17, 23
"The Jew" (Turgenev) **7**:316, 320, 324, 359
"The Jew from Babylon" (Singer) **3**:389
"The Jewels of the Cabots" (Cheever) **1**:101
"The Jilting of Granny Weatherall" (Porter) **4**:327-28, 340, 348, 356-58
"The Jilting of Jane" (Wells) **6**:360, 392
"Jim Blaine and His Grandfather's Old Ram" (Twain) **6**:310
"Jimmy and the Desperate Woman" (Lawrence) **4**:219, 238
"Jimmy Goggles the God" (Wells) **6**:360
"Jimmy Rose" (Melville) **1**:303-04, 325-26
"Jim's Big Brother from California" (Harte) **8**:254
"Jim's Probation" (Dunbar) **8**:122, 127
"Jimsella" (Dunbar) **8**:119, 121, 127, 129, 143, 146
"Jo" (O'Connor) **5**:382
"John Bull" (Irving) **2**:244, 251, 253
"John Inglefield's Thanksgiving" (Hawthorne) **3**:189
"John Napper Sailing through the Universe" (Gardner) **7**:214, 216-17, 222, 233, 235, 238
"John Redding Goes to Sea" (Hurston) **4**:136-38, 149, 153
"Johnsonham, Jr." (Dunbar) **8**:135, 148
"Joining Charles" (Bowen) **3**:30, 47
Joining Charles (Bowen) **3**:30, 33, 40
"The Joker's Greatest Triumph" (Barthelme) **2**:28, 34
"The Jokers of New Gibbon" (London) **4**:266
"The Jolly Corner" (James) **8**:296, 304, 306, 308-09, 326-29
"Jorinda and Jorindel" (Gallant) **5**:138, 141-44
Josephine (Kafka)
See "Josephine the Singer, or the Mouse Folk"
"Josephine" (O'Flaherty) **6**:264
"Josephine the Singer, or the Mouse Folk" (Josephine) (Kafka) **5**:231, 240, 242
"The Journal of a Superfluous Man" (Turgenev)
See "The Diary of a Superfluous Man"
"The Journey" (Irving) **2**:244, 265
"The Journey" (Porter) **4**:352, 358, 363
"A Journey" (Wharton) **6**:423
"Journey to Polessie" (Turgenev) **7**:335
"Joy" (Singer) **3**:360, 363-64, 368
"The Joy of Nelly Deane" (Cather) **2**:98, 104
"The Joy of the Just" (Gardner) **7**:226-28
"Juana Muraña" (Borges) **4**:19-20
"Juanita" (Chopin) **8**:98, 110-11
"Judas" (O'Connor) **5**:368-69, 378, 381
"Judgement Day" (O'Connor) **1**:343, 365
"The Judgment" (Kafka)

See "Das Urteil"
"The Judgment of Dungara" (Kipling) **5**:262
"A Judgment of Paris" (Dunbar) **8**:122, 128, 136
"Jug of Silver" (Capote) **2**:63, 65-6, 70
Julia Bride (James) **8**:311-13, 343-45, 347-51
"Jumbo's Wife" (O'Connor) **5**:390
"Jumping Frog" (Twain)
See "Celebrated Jumping Frog of Calaveras County"
"June Recital" (Welty) **1**:474, 480, 483, 485, 495, 497
"The Jungle" (Bowen) **3**:30, 33, 49
The Jungle Book (Kipling) **5**:277, 287, 292
Jungle Books (Kipling) **5**:279, 282, 285, 287-88, 292-94
"Jupiter Five" (Clarke) **3**:124, 129, 134-35, 149
"A Jury Case" (Anderson) **1**:50
"Just a Little One" (Parker) **2**:281
"Just Before the War with the Eskimos" (Salinger) **2**:300
"Just Like Little Dogs" (Thomas) **3**:403, 406, 411-12
"Just Meat" (London) **4**:253-54, 262-63, 291
"Just One More Time" (Cheever) **1**:100
Just So Stories (Kipling) **5**:273, 279, 287, 293
"Just Tell Me Who It Was" (Cheever) **1**:90
"A Justice" (Faulkner) **1**:147, 177, 181
"Kabnis" (Toomer) **1**:440, 442-44, 446-48, 451-54, 457, 459-60
"Kacheli" ("The Swing") (Bunin) **5**:113
"The Kanaka Surf" (London) **4**:257, 266
"Karintha" (Toomer) **1**:441, 452, 455-56, 459
"Kashtánka" (Chekhov) **2**:130
"Kas'ian of the Beautiful Lands" (Turgenev) **7**:343-45
"Kate Lancaster's Plan" (Jewett) **6**:167
"Kazimír Stanislávovich" (Bunin) **5**:81
"Keela, the Outcast Indian Maiden" (Welty) **1**:468, 470, 497
"Keep Your Pity" (Boyle) **5**:55
"Keesh, Son of Keesh" (London) **4**:287-88
"Kerfol" (Wharton) **6**:426-28, 431-32
"Kew Gardens" (Woolf) **7**:368, 370-71, 374-76, 378, 382-83, 385, 387-88, 392, 398-99, 404-07
Kew Gardens (Woolf) **7**:382
"The Key" (Welty) **1**:468
"The Keystone" (Powers) **4**:376, 381
"Khor and Kalinych" (Turgenev) **7**:313, 342, 362
"The Kid Nobody Could Handle" (Vonnegut) **8**:432
"Kidnapped" (Kipling) **5**:274
"Kierkegaard Unfair to Schlegel" (Barthelme) **2**:31, 38-9, 54
"The Kill" (Boyle) **5**:64
"The Killers" (Hemingway) **1**:211, 218-19, 234-36, 242
"The Killing Ground" (Ballard) **1**:76
"Kin" (Welty) **1**:475-76, 487
"King Gregor and the Fool" (Gardner) **7**:234
"A King Lear of the Steppes" (Turgenev)
See "Stepnoy Korol 'Lir"
"A King Listens" (Calvino) **3**:119
"The King of Folly Island" (Jewett) **6**:154
The King of Folly Island and Other People (Jewett) **6**:154
"The King of Greece's Tea Party" (Hemingway) **1**:208
"King Pest" (Poe) **1**:406
"King's Ankus" (Kipling) **5**:293
The King's Indian: Stories and Tales (Gardner) **7**:213-21, 226, 228-29, 235
"The Kiss" (Chekhov) **2**:126, 156
"The Kiss" (Chopin) **8**:72, 111-12
"The Kite" (Maugham) **8**:380
"Kitty" (Bowles) **3**:76, 80
"Klara Milich" ("Clara Milich") (Turgenev) **7**:321, 324, 326-28, 334, 338, 362
"Kleine Fabel" ("Little Fable") (Kafka) **5**:254
"The Knife and the Naked Chalk" (Kipling) **5**:284, 292
"A Knight-Errant of the Foothills" (Harte) **8**:249
"Knight's Gambit" (Faulkner) **1**:178-81
Knight's Gambit (Faulkner) **1**:151, 178-79
"The Knock at the Manor Gate" (Kafka) **5**:206
"Knock...Knock...Knock" (Turgenev)
See "Stuk...stuk...stuk"
"Koolau the Leper" (London) **4**:269
"Kroy Wen" (Boyle) **5**:55
"De la grafología como ciencia aplicada" ("On Graphology As an Applied Science") (Cortázar) **7**:95
"Labour Day Dinner" (Munro) **3**:346
"Lady Eleanore's Mantle" (Hawthorne) **3**:184
"The Lady from the Land" (Thurber) **1**:424
"The Lady Icenway" (Hardy) **2**:205
"The Lady in the Looking-Glass: A Reflection" (Woolf) **7**:375-76, 378-80, 388, 392, 399, 407-12
"Lady Mottisfont" (Hardy) **2**:208
"A Lady of Bayou St. John" (Chopin) **8**:72, 84, 87, 91, 106, 110
"The Lady of the Sagas" (O'Connor) **5**:371
"The Lady Penelope" (Hardy) **2**:209
"A Lady Slipper" (Dunbar) **8**:122
"Lady with a Lamp" (Parker) **2**:273-74, 280, 285
"The Lady with the Dog" (Chekhov) **2**:127-28, 131-33, 135, 150, 155, 157
"The Lady with the Pet Dog" (Oates) **6**:234
"The Ladybird" (Lawrence) **4**:219, 230, 238-39
"The Lady's Maid's Bell" (Wharton) **6**:427
"The Lame Shall Enter First" (O'Connor) **1**:343-45, 356, 365
"The Lament" (O'Flaherty) **6**:276
"The Lamentable Comedy of Willow Wood" (Kipling) **5**:261
Laments for the Living (Parker) **2**:272, 274
"The Lamias" (Wells) **6**:380
"Lamp in a Window" (Capote) **2**:80
"The Lamp of Psyche" (Wharton) **6**:424, 427
"The Land Ironclads" (Wells) **6**:374, 380, 403
"Ein Landarzt" ("A Country Doctor") (Kafka) **5**:213-14, 230, 246
"The Landing" (O'Flaherty) **6**:264, 269, 273, 276-77
"Landing in Luck" (Faulkner) **1**:177
"The Landlady" (Dostoevski) **2**:163, 170-71, 173-74, 181, 191, 193
"A Landlocked Sailor" (Jewett) **6**:156
"The Landowner" (Turgenev) **7**:313
"The Landscape Chambers" (Jewett) **6**:154
The Langston Hughes Reader (Hughes) **6**:122-23
"Le lapin" (Maupassant) **1**:263, 274
"Lappin and Lapinova" (Woolf) **7**:376-77, 388, 393-94, 398
"L'Lapse" (Barthelme) **2**:40
"The Last Asset" (Wharton) **6**:424-25
Last Days (Oates) **6**:254
"Last Days in Deephaven" (Jewett) **6**:167
"The Last Demon" (Singer) **3**:383
"The Last Dream of the Old Oak" ("Old Oak Tree's Last Dream") (Andersen) **6**:18, 40
"The Last Fiddling of Mordaunt's Jim" (Dunbar) **8**:122, 149
"The Last Leaf" (Henry) **5**:185
"The Last Leaf" (Porter) **4**:339, 352-53, 358, 361
"The Last Night in the Old Home" (Bowen) **3**:41
"The Last of the Belles" (Fitzgerald) **6**:46-8, 100, 103
"The Last Pearl" (Andersen) **6**:36
Last Round (Cortázar)
See *Ultimo round*
Last Tales (Dinesen) **7**:162, 166, 171, 175-76, 180-81, 191, 198, 200
"The Last Tea" (Parker) **2**:274, 285
"The Last Voyage of the Ghost Ship" (García Márquez)
See "El último viaje del buque fantasma"
Last Words (Crane) **7**:103
"A Late Encounter with the Enemy" (O'Connor) **1**:356
"The Late Henry Conran" (O'Connor) **5**:369, 371, 398
"A Late Supper" (Jewett) **6**:166
"The Latehomecomer" (Gallant) **5**:130, 133, 136-37
Later the Same Day (Paley) **8**:412, 419
"The Laughing Man" (Salinger) **2**:293, 296, 299, 313-14, 316
Laughing to Keep from Crying (Hughes) **6**:111-12, 116, 119, 121-22, 127, 131, 133
"Laughter" (O'Connor) **5**:390-91
"Lavinia: An Old Story" (Paley) **8**:412
"The Law of Life" (London) **4**:287-89, 292
"The Law of the Jungle" (Cheever) **1**:99
"Lazy Sons" (Calvino) **3**:112
"A Leaf from the Sky" (Andersen) **6**:6
Leaf Storm (García Márquez)
See *La hojarasca*
Leaf Storm, and Other Stories (García Márquez) **8**:155, 158, 184, 193
"The League of Old Men" (London) **4**:265, 287
"The Leaning Tower" (Porter) **4**:331, 339-40
The Leaning Tower, and Other Stories (Porter) **4**:331, 347, 352
"The Leap" (Barthelme) **2**:45, 55
"The Leap" (Oates) **6**:250, 252
"The Leap Frog" (Andersen) **6**:7, 10
"A Lear of the Steppes" (Turgenev)
See "Stepnoy Korol 'Lir"
"Learning to Be Dead" (Calvino) **3**:113
"The Lees of Happiness" (Fitzgerald) **6**:45, 58-9
"The Legacy" (Woolf) **7**:376-77, 388, 393-95
"The Legend" (Wharton) **6**:429, 437
"Legend of Prince Ahmed Al Kemel, or The Pilgrim of Love" (Irving) **2**:267
"The Legend of Saamtsadt" (Harte) **8**:250
"The Legend of Sleepy Hollow" (Irving) **2**:239, 241, 243-51, 253, 255, 259-60
"Legend of the Arabian Astrologer" (Irving) **2**:267

Title Index

"The Legend of the Moor's Legacy" (Irving) **2**:246, 254, 268
"Legend of the Rose of Alhambra" (Irving) **2**:246, 268
"Legend of the Three Beautiful Princesses" (Irving) **2**:267
"La légende du Mont-Saint-Michel" (Maupassant) **1**:285, 288
"Lejana" ("Faraway Image"; "The Distances") (Cortázar) **7**:52, 56-7, 81
"The Lemon" (Thomas) **3**:396, 399, 407-08
"Lemonade" (Lavin) **4**:166
"Leopard George" (Lessing) **6**:186, 190
"The Lesson of the Master" (James) **8**:279, 282, 302
"Let There Be Honour" (Boyle) **5**:56
"Let There Be Light" (Clarke) **3**:130
Let Your Mind Alone! and Other More or Less Inspirational Pieces (Thurber) **1**:414, 422-23, 426
"The Letter" (Maugham) **8**:359, 361, 367, 373-74, 382
"The Letter" (Oates) **6**:236
"The Letter" (O'Flaherty) **6**:262, 265, 276, 280
"A Letter from Home" (Lessing) **6**:199
"The Letter That Was Never Mailed" (Barnes) **3**:13
"Letter to a Young Lady in Paris" (Cortázar) See "Carta a un Señorita en París"
"The Letter Writer" (Singer) **3**:360, 384
"The Letters" (Wharton) **6**:424-25, 427, 436
Letters from the Underworld (*Notes from the Underground*) (Dostoevski) **2**:164-65, 168, 172-73, 178-83, 186, 188-89
"Letters to the Editore" (Barthelme) **2**:40
"The Liar" (Faulkner) **1**:177
"The Liar" (James) **8**:275, 296, 318, 320-21
"The Liberation of Jake Hanley" (Oates) **6**:230
"The Library Horror" (Gardner) **7**:226
"The Library of Babel" (Borges) See "El biblioteca de Babel"
"Lichen" (Munro) **3**:347-49
"A Lickpenny Lover" (Henry) **5**:163, 171, 186
"The Lie" (Carver) **8**:34
"Lieutenant Yergunov's Story" (Turgenev) See "Istoriya leytenanta Ergunova"
"Life" (O'Flaherty) **6**:260, 269, 271, 277-78, 280
"The Life and Work of Professor Roy Millen" (Warren) **4**:387, 389-90, 395, 400
"Life Everlastin'" (Freeman) **1**:192, 195
"The Life of Nancy" (Jewett) **6**:152
"Life with Freddie" (Wodehouse) **2**:344
"The Life You Save May Be Your Own" (O'Connor) **1**:343-44, 348-49, 356, 359-60
Life's Handicap (Kipling) **5**:274, 291
Life's Little Ironies (Hardy) **2**:205-08, 210, 212, 214-16, 220, 222-23
"Ligeia" (Poe) **1**:377, 379-80, 385, 393-97, 399
"Light" (O'Flaherty) **6**:265, 280
"A Light Breath" (Bunin) See "Light Breathing"
"Light Breathing" ("A Light Breath") (Bunin) **5**:81, 93, 104
"The Light of the World" (Hemingway) **1**:242, 245
"The Light-Years" (Calvino) **3**:104
"Lightning" (Barthelme) **2**:51
"The Lightning-Rod Man" (Melville) **1**:298, 303-04
"Like a Queen" (Anderson) **1**:31, 52-3
"Liking Men" (Atwood) **2**:20
"Lilacs" (Chopin) **8**:72, 87, 108-10, 112
"Lilacs" (Lavin) **4**:171
"Liliana llorando" ("Liliana Weeping") (Cortázar) **7**:62-3
"Liliana Weeping" (Cortázar) See "Liliana llorando"
"The Lilies" (Chopin) **8**:93
"Lily Daw and the Three Ladies" (Welty) **1**:470, 482, 497
"The Lily's Quest" (Hawthorne) **3**:181
"Limbo" (Lavin) **4**:167
Limits and Renewals (Kipling) **5**:278, 283
"Lion" (Faulkner) **1**:182
"The Lion of Comarre" (Clarke) **3**:145, 148
"Lions, Harts, Leaping Does" (Powers) **4**:371, 377-78, 380, 384
"The Lion's Skin" (Maugham) **8**:379
"Lispeth" (Kipling) **5**:262
"Listening" (Paley) **8**:420
"Le lit 29" (Maupassant) **1**:274
"The Litigants" (Singer) **3**:385
"Little Bessie" (Twain) **6**:339
"Little Bull" (Cortázar) See "Torito"
"Little Claus and Big Claus" ("Little Klaus and Big Klaus"; "Big Claus and Little Claus") (Andersen) **6**:4, 11, 13, 16, 18, 26, 30, 37
"A Little Cloud" (Joyce) **3**:205, 209-10, 226, 231, 234, 245, 248
"Little Curtis" (Parker) **2**:274, 280-81, 283
The Little Disturbances of Man (Paley) **8**:388, 391, 395, 407, 410, 414
"Little Dog" (Hughes) **6**:109, 121-23, 129-30, 142
"Little Fable" (Kafka) See "Kleine Fabel"
"The Little Fir Tree" (Andersen) See "The Fir-Tree"
"A Little Free Mulatto" (Chopin) **8**:105
"Little French Mary" (Jewett) **6**:155
"The Little Girl Continues" (Barnes) See "The Grande Malade"
"A Little Girl Tells a Story to a Lady" (Barnes) See "Cassation"
"The Little Girl's Room" (Bowen) **3**:33, 43
"Little Her Friedemann" (Mann) **5**:319, 323, 327, 332, 334, 336
"The Little Hero" (Dostoevski) **2**:171, 189-90
"The Little Hours" (Parker) **2**:274, 281
"The Little House" (Bowles) **3**:76
"Little Ida's Flowers" (Andersen) **6**:3-4, 6, 23, 30
"Little Klaus and Big Klaus" (Andersen) See "Little Claus and Big Claus"
"Little Lizzy" (Mann) **5**:322-23, 327, 331, 334-36
"A Little Local Color" (Henry) **5**:191
"The Little Man in Black" (Irving) **2**:242
"The Little Match Girl" ("The Little Match Seller") (Andersen) **6**:18-9, 25-6, 30, 41
"The Little Match Seller" (Andersen) See "The Little Match Girl"
"The Little Mermaid" ("The Little Sea-Maid") (Andersen) **6**:6-7, 11-3, 18, 26-30, 36-7, 40-1
"The Little Mother" (O'Connor) **5**:371-72
"Little Old Spy" (Hughes) **6**:131
"The Little Prince" (Lavin) **4**:165-67, 183
"The Little Regiment" (Crane) **7**:102, 106
The Little Regiment and Other Episodes of the Civil War (Crane) **7**:102
"The Little Sea-Maid" (Andersen) See "The Little Mermaid"
"The Little Shoemakers" (Singer) **3**:356, 375, 378, 383-84
"Little Tembi" (Lessing) **6**:191, 197
"Little Tuk" (Andersen) **6**:3-4
"The Little Virgin" (Hughes) **6**:127
"The Little White Dog" (O'Flaherty) **6**:280
"A Little Woman" (Kafka) **5**:239
Lives of Girls and Women (Munro) **3**:323, 325-28, 330-33, 335-36, 338-46
"Lives of the Poets" (Atwood) **2**:3-4, 6, 10-11
"The Living" (Lavin) **4**:167
"Living" (Paley) **8**:391, 408-09, 416
"A Living Relic" ("Living Relics") (Turgenev) **7**:321-22, 326, 337
"Living Relics" (Turgenev) See "A Living Relic"
"Livvie" (Welty) **1**:467, 469, 471
"Lizards in Jamshyd's Courtyard" (Faulkner) **1**:177
"Lofty" (O'Connor) **5**:382
"Logarithms" (Singer) **3**:388
"Lokis" (Mérimée) **7**:276-77, 283, 285-86, 296-99
"The Lone Charge of Francis B. Perkins" (Crane) **7**:108
"Loneliness" (Anderson) **1**:30, 44
"A Lonely Ride" (Harte) **8**:210
"Lonely Rock" (O'Connor) **5**:371-72
"Long Black Song" (Wright) **2**:360-63, 365, 367, 369, 371, 374, 376, 379-81, 387
"The Long-Distance Runner" (Paley) **8**:397-98, 408-09, 415
"Long, Long Ago" (Bunin) **5**:82
"The Long Road to Ummera" (O'Connor) **5**:362-65, 378, 380, 383, 388-89, 397-98
"The Long Run" (Wharton) **6**:418, 424-25, 436
"The Long Walk to Forever" (Vonnegut) **8**:424
"The Longest Science Fiction Story Ever Told" (Clarke) **3**:133
"The Lonliest Man in the U.S. Army" (Boyle) **5**:55
"Look at All Those Roses" (Bowen) **3**:55
Look at All Those Roses (Bowen) **3**:33, 39, 41
"Look How the Fish Live" (Powers) **4**:368, 373-74, 376-77
Look How the Fish Live (Powers) **4**:375-76, 380-82
"The Loons" (Laurence) **7**:255, 259, 270
"Loophole" (Clarke) **3**:125, 148-50
"Loopy Ears" (Bunin) See "Petlistye ushi"
"Lord Emsworth Acts for the Best" (Wodehouse) **2**:346, 348
"Lord Emsworth and the Girl Friend" (Wodehouse) **2**:346-49
"Lord Mountdrago" (Maugham) **8**:369, 380
"The Lord of the Dynamos" (Wells) **6**:361, 365-67, 375-76, 381-82, 396-97
"The Lord's Day" (Powers) **4**:380-81
"A Losing Game" (Powers) **4**:370
"Loss" (Oates) **6**:236
"Loss of Breath" (Poe) **1**:407
"The Lost" (Boyle) **5**:57, 74-6

"The Lost Blend" (Henry) **5**:163
"Lost Face" (London) **4**:265, 289
Lost Face (London) **4**:265, 283, 288
"The Lost Legion" (Kipling) **5**:272-75, 285
"The Lost Letter" (Gogol)
See "Propavšaja gramotax"
"A Lost Lover" (Jewett) **6**:156, 159, 166
"The Lost Novel" (Anderson) **1**:31
"Lost on Dress Parade" (Henry) **5**:158, 189
"The Lost Turkey" (Jewett) **6**:156
"La lotería en Babilonia" ("The Babylonian Lottery") (Borges) **4**:5-7, 11-12, 14
"The Lotus-Eater" (Maugham) **8**:379
"Lou, the Prophet" (Cather) **2**:96, 100, 105
"The Loudest Voice" (Paley) **8**:388
"Louisa" (Freeman) **1**:196
"Loulou; or, The Domestic Life of the Language" (Atwood) **2**:18, 21, 23
"Love" (Bowen) **3**:33, 41
"Love" (Paley) **8**:419
"Love seventy-seven" (Cortázar) **7**:93
"Love among the Haystacks" (Lawrence) **4**:197
"Love and Death" (Oates) **6**:225, 254
Love and Napalm: Export U.S.A. (Ballard)
See *The Atrocity Exhibition*
"Love and Russian Literature" (Maugham) **8**:378
"Love. Friendship." (Oates) **6**:227-28
"Love is for Lovers" (Lavin) **4**:166
"Love o' Women" (Kipling) **5**:266, 276, 279
"The Love of Elsie Barton: A Chronicle" (Warren) **4**:389-91, 394
"Love of Life" (London) **4**:253, 265, 272-73, 278, 288-89, 291-92
Love of Life, and Other Stories (London) **4**:252, 264-65, 282, 285, 288-89
"Love on the Bon-Dieu" (Chopin) **8**:89
"The Love-Philtre of Ikey Schoenstein" (Henry) **5**:182
"A Love Story" (Bowen) **3**:41, 54
"The Lovely Lady" (Lawrence) **4**:220
The Lovely Lady, and Other Stories (Lawrence) **4**:230, 238
"The Lovely Leave" (Parker) **2**:277, 280, 285-86
"The Lover" (Bowen) **3**:40
"The Lover" (Walker) **5**:413-14
"The Lovers" (Andersen) **6**:7
"Lovers" (O'Flaherty) **6**:282
"Loving Memory" (Lavin) **4**:166, 168
"Low-Flying Aircraft" (Ballard) **1**:73-4, 83
Low-Flying Aircraft, and Other Stories (Ballard) **1**:71-3
"The Lowboy" (Cheever) **1**:112
"Luani of the Jungle" (Hughes) **6**:127
"Luc and His Father" (Gallant) **5**:147
"Lucas, His Modesty" (Cortázar)
See "Lucas, sus pudores"
"Lucas, His Partisan Arguments" (Cortázar)
See "Lucas, sus discusiones partidarias"
"Lucas, sus discusiones partidarias" ("Lucas, His Partisan Arguments") (Cortázar) **7**:94
"Lucas, sus pudores" ("Lucas, His Modesty") (Cortázar) **7**:94
"The Luceys" (O'Connor) **5**:371, 378, 381-83, 389
"An Luchóg" (O'Flaherty) **6**:287
"The Luck of Roaring Camp" (Harte) **8**:208, 210, 219, 225-26, 228, 231-32, 237-39, 241, 243-44, 245, 249, 251-52, 255, 257
The Luck of Roaring Camp, and Other Sketches (Harte) **8**:219, 229, 236, 238, 255-56
"The Lucky Pair" (Lavin) **4**:173, 183
"Lucy Grange" (Lessing) **6**:191
"Lui?" (Maupassant) **1**:265-66, 281
"Luna e G N A C" (Calvino) **3**:97
"Lunch" (Bowen) **3**:40
"The Lurking Fear" (Lovecraft) **3**:258, 260, 281
"The Lynching of Jube Benson" (Dunbar) **8**:121-22, 126, 128-30, 132, 136
"Lynx Hunting" (Crane) **7**:104
"Ma femme" (Maupassant) **1**:280
"Ma'ame Pélagie" (Chopin) **8**:87, 105
"The Macbeth Murder Mystery" (Thurber) **1**:426
"The Machine-Gun Corps in Action" (O'Connor) **5**:369, 371, 390-91
"Mackintosh" (Maugham) **8**:359, 370, 372
"The Mad Lomasneys" (O'Connor) **5**:363, 370-71, 378, 383, 389
"Madame Celestine's Divorce" (Chopin) **8**:72-3, 84, 91
"Madame Délicieuse" (Cable) **4**:48, 56, 67, 69-71
"Madame Delphine" (Cable) **4**:48, 51-2, 56-7, 67, 75-8
"Mademoiselle Fifi" (Maupassant) **1**:256, 259, 274, 287
"A Madman's Diary" (Gogol)
See "Diary of a Madman"
"The Madness of Ortheris" (Kipling) **5**:260
"A Madonna of the Trenches" (Kipling) **5**:271
"A Mæcenas of the Pacific Slope" (Harte) **8**:216, 255
"Maelstrom II" (Clarke) **3**:129, 147
"The Maenads" (Cortázar) **7**:69-70
"The Magazine" (Singer) **3**:374
"Magic" (Porter) **4**:327-30, 339-40, 360
"The Magician" (Singer) **3**:375
"Magna Mater" (Oates) **6**:232
"Magnetism" (Fitzgerald) **6**:61
"Magnolia Flower" (Hurston) **4**:136
"The Mahatma's Little Joke" (London) **4**:294
"The Maid of Saint Phillippe" (Chopin) **8**:71
"Maiden, Maiden" (Boyle) **5**:56, 65
"La main" (Maupassant) **1**:281
"La main d'ecorché" (Maupassant) **1**:281
"La maison du chat-qui-pelote" ("Le chat-qui-pelote") (Balzac) **5**:21-2, 29, 31-3
"La maison nucingen" (Balzac) **5**:31
"La maison Tellier" (Maupassant) **1**:271-72, 274, 287
La maison Tellier (Maupassant) **1**:256-61, 266, 272, 274, 276, 282-83
"Majesty" (Fitzgerald) **6**:47
"The Majesty of the Law" (O'Connor) **5**:364-66, 369, 371, 377, 381, 389, 395, 398
"Majskaja noč, ili Vtoplennica" ("A May Night; or, The Drowned Maiden") (Gogol) **4**:118-19
"Making Arrangements" (Bowen) **3**:54
"The Making of a New Yorker" (Henry) **5**:194
"Making Poison" (Atwood) **2**:17
"Making Westing" (London) **4**:263
"The Maltese Cat" (Kipling) **5**:279
"Mammon and the Archer" (Henry) **5**:195
"Mammy Peggy's Pride" (Dunbar) **8**:121, 128, 131
"Mamouche" (Chopin) **8**:93
"A Man and His Dog" (Mann) **5**:312
"A Man and Two Women" (Lessing) **6**:198, 205, 208, 218, 220
A Man and Two Women (Lessing) **6**:198, 200-01, 203, 208
"A Man from Glasgow" (Maugham) **8**:380
"The Man from Mars" (Atwood) **2**:3, 5-7, 10-11, 14, 21
"The Man Higher Up" (Henry) **5**:166, 193
"The Man in a Case" (Chekhov)
See "The Man in a Shell"
"The Man in a Shell" ("The Man in a Case") (Chekhov) **2**:139, 141, 143, 155, 157
"The Man in the Brown Coat" (Anderson) **1**:21, 27
"The Man in the Passage" (Chesterton) **1**:136
"The Man of Adamant" (Hawthorne) **3**:171, 185
"Man of All Work" (Wright) **2**:388
"The Man of No Account" (Harte) **8**:236
"The Man of the Crowd" (Poe) **1**:379
"The Man of the Family" (Bowen) **3**:45
"The Man of the House" (O'Connor) **5**:371
"The Man of the World" (O'Connor) **5**:386
"The Man on the Threshold" (Borges)
See "El hombre en el umbral"
"The Man That Corrupted Hadleyburg" (Twain) **6**:293-95, 301-03, 305-09, 325, 334-35, 345
"The Man That Stopped" (O'Connor) **5**:371
"The Man That Was Used Up" (Poe) **1**:407-08
The Man Upstairs, and Other Stories (Wodehouse) **2**:347
"The Man Who Became a Woman" (Anderson) **1**:30, 37, 48-50
"The Man Who Could Work Miracles: A Pantoum in Prose" (Wells) **6**:367, 375, 383, 389, 404-06
"The Man Who Died" ("The Escaped Cock") (Lawrence) **4**:212, 220-21, 226, 238
"The Man Who Killed a Shadow" (Wright) **2**:366, 385-86
The Man Who Knew Too Much (Chesterton) **1**:121-22, 125-26
"The Man Who Lived Underground" (Wright) **2**:364, 366, 370, 373-74, 377, 379, 387-88
"The Man Who Loved His Kind" (Woolf) **7**:373, 376, 381, 388
"The Man Who Loved Islands" (Lawrence) **4**:197, 212-17, 221, 230, 233, 238
"The Man Who Ploughed the Sea" (Clarke) **3**:134
"The Man Who Saw the Flood" (Wright) **2**:366
"The Man Who Turned into a Statue" (Oates) **6**:224
"The Man Who Was" (Kipling) **5**:293
"The Man Who Was Almost a Man" (Wright) **2**:366, 376, 388
"The Man Who Would Be King" (Kipling) **5**:262, 264, 273, 278, 282, 291, 299
"The Man Whom Women Adored" (Oates) **6**:255
"A Man with a Conscience" (Maugham) **8**:379
The Man with Two Left Feet (Wodehouse) **2**:327
"Manhole 69" (Ballard) **1**:68
"The Maniac" (Oates) **6**:243
"The Manor of Stepanchikovo" (Dostoevski)

See "The Village of Stepanchikovo"
"The Man's Story" (Anderson) 1:39, 52
"The Mantle of Whistler" (Parker) 2:273, 283
"Manuscript Found in a Pocket" (Cortázar) See "Manuscrito hallado en un bolsillo"
"Manuscrito hallado en un bolsillo" ("Manuscript Found in a Pocket") (Cortázar) 7:61-2, 69
Many Inventions (Kipling) 5:266, 273, 283, 287
"The Map of Love" (Thomas) 3:399, 402, 407
The Map of Love (Thomas) 3:410
"El mar del tiempo perdido" ("The Sea of Lost Time") (García Márquez) 8:155, 167-68, 172
"Les marana" (Balzac) 5:8, 26, 31
"Maravillosas ocupaciones" ("Marvelous Pursuits") (Cortázar) 7:92
"The March of Progress" (Chesnutt) 7:27-8, 37
"The Marchioness of Stonehenge" (Hardy) 2:204, 217
Marcovaldo; or, The Seasons in the City (Calvino) 3:106-07
"María Concepcíon" (Porter) 4:326, 328, 330, 339-40, 346, 349
"Marie, Marie, Hold on Tight" (Barthelme) 2:34, 40
"Mario and the Magician" (Mann) See "Mario und der Zauberer"
"Mario und der Zauberer" ("Mario and the Magician") (Mann) 5:310-12, 337, 340-41, 353-59
"The Mark of the Beast" (Kipling) 5:271, 273-74, 280, 299
"The Mark on the Wall" (Woolf) 7:368, 370-71, 378, 382-83, 385-88, 392, 397-98, 405, 409
The Mark on the Wall (Woolf) 7:382
Mark Twain's :Which Was the Dream?: and Other Symbolic Writings of the Later Years (Twain) 6:331
"Marklake Witches" (Kipling) 5:285
"Marrakesh" (Munro) 3:346
"The Marriage of Phaedra" (Cather) 2:98, 103
Marriages and Infidelities (Oates) 6:224, 234, 254
"The Married Couple" (Kafka) 5:206-07
"Marroca" (Maupassant) 1:257
"The Marry Month of May" (Henry) 5:163
"Mars Jeem's Nightmare" (Chesnutt) 7:7-8, 10, 40
"The Marsh King's Daughter" ("The Bog King's Daughter") (Andersen) 6:13-5, 35-7
"Marsh Rosemary" (Jewett) 6:150
"Maruja" (Harte) 8:216, 244, 251
"Marvelous Pursuits" (Cortázar) See "Maravillosas ocupaciones"
"Mary Postgate" (Kipling) 5:279, 281-83
"Mary Winosky" (Hughes) 6:117-19
"The Masculine Principle" (O'Connor) 5:366, 371-72, 381, 388-89
"Masculine Protest" (O'Connor) 5:387
"The Mask of the Bear" (Laurence) 7:254, 259, 263
"Le masque" (Maupassant) 1:274, 286
"The Masque of the Red Death" (Poe) 1:379, 389-90, 398, 406
"The Mass Island" (O'Connor) 5:372
"Massimilla doni" (Balzac) 5:16
"Master John Horseleigh, Knight" (Hardy) 2:210
"Master Misery" (Capote) 2:63-5, 72-3, 75, 78
"Mateo Falcone" (Mérimée) 7:278, 280-81, 283, 285, 287-89, 300-01
"A Matter of Doctrine" (Dunbar) 8:122
"A Matter of Prejudice" (Chopin) 8:93
"A Matter of Principle" (Chesnutt) 7:16, 23, 33-6
"May Day" (Fitzgerald) 6:45, 57-9, 74-6, 96-101
"A May Night; or, The Drowned Maiden" (Gogol) See "Majskaja noč, ili Vtoplennica"
"May you learn to open the door to go out to play" (Cortázar) See "que sepa abrir la puerta para ir a jugar"
"The Maypole of Merry Mount" (Hawthorne) 3:164-67, 180-81, 183-84, 187, 188
"Me and Miss Mandible" (Barthelme) 2:26-7, 35, 47, 49, 53
"Mearbhall" (O'Flaherty) 6:287-89
"Meddlance Tersplat" (Cortázar) See "La inmiscusión terrupta"
Meet Mr. Mulliner (Wodehouse) 2:325, 338
"The Meeting" (Borges) 4:20
"The Meeting" (Cortázar) See "Reunión"
"A Meeting South" (Anderson) 1:37, 52-3
"A Meeting with Medusa" (Clarke) 3:128, 130, 132, 135-36, 138-40, 146
"Meiosis" (Calvino) 3:109
"Mejdoub" (Bowles) 3:68
"The Melancholy Hussar of the German Legion" (Hardy) 2:214-15, 220
"Mellonta Tauta" (Poe) 1:401, 406
"Melmoth Converted" (Balzac) See "Melmoth réconcilié"
"Melmoth réconcilié" ("Melmoth Converted") (Balzac) 5:12, 31
"The Memento" (Henry) 5:185
"Memoirs" (Balzac) 5:11
The Memoirs of a Sportsman (Turgenev) See *Sportsman's Sketches*
"Memorial" (Munro) 3:331
"Memories of D. H. Lawrence" (Thurber) 1:414
"A Memory" (Lavin) 4:178-79, 182-83
"A Memory" (Welty) 1:466, 469-70, 472
"The Memory of Martha" (Dunbar) 8:122
"Men in the Storm" (Crane) 7:108, 110, 136-37, 145
"The Men of Forty-Mile" (London) 4:267, 282, 284, 286
Men without Women (Hemingway) 1:209-12, 214, 216-17
"A Mental Suggestion" (Chopin) 8:72, 100
"Menudo" (Carver) 8:43
"Menuet" (Maupassant) 1:278
"The Merchant of Heaven" (Laurence) 7:245-46, 249-50, 255, 260
"A Mercury of the Foothills" (Harte) 8:214, 249
"A Mere Interlude" (Hardy) 2:211, 215
"Mère Pochette" (Jewett) 6:156
"La mère sauvage" (Maupassant) 1:277-78
"Merle" (Marshall) 3:317
Merle: A Novella, and Other Stories (Marshall) See *Reena, and Other Stories*
"Mes vingt-cinq jours" (Maupassant) 1:274
"Mesmeric Revelation" (Poe) 1:401
"A Mess of Pottage" (Dunbar) 8:122, 124, 128
"Le message" (Balzac) 5:8, 31, 40-1, 43
"La messe de l'athée" (Balzac) 5:16, 26, 31
"Metamorphoses" (Cheever) 1:94, 100
"The Metamorphosis" (Kafka) See "Die Verwandlung"
"The Metamorphosis" (Oates) 6:225, 234
"Metzengerstein" (Poe) 1:379
"The Mexican" (London) 4:291
"Michael's Wife" (O'Connor) 5:377
The Middle-Aged Man on the Flying Trapeze: A Collection of Short Pieces (Thurber) 1:413, 420, 423
"A Middle-Class Education" (Oates) 6:246
"The Middle Years" (James) 8:291, 299-300
"Midnight at Tim's Place" (Thurber) 1:429
"Midnight Mass" (Bowles) 3:75, 80
Midnight Mass (Bowles) 3:75-6, 79-80
"A Midsummer Knight's Dream" (Henry) 5:184
"Miggles" (Harte) 8:209-10, 236, 254
"A Mild Attack of Locusts" (Lessing) 6:191
"Miles City, Montana" (Munro) 3:347-48
"Milking Time" (O'Flaherty) 6:262, 277
"A Millionaire of Rough and Ready" (Harte) 8:254
"Mine" (Carver) 8:30, 34
"The Minister's Black Veil" (Hawthorne) 3:154, 159-60, 164, 171, 177-78, 184, 186-87
"The Minority Committee" (Dunbar) 8:127
"The Miracle" (O'Connor) 5:388
"The Miracle of Purun Bhagat" ("Purun Bhagat") (Kipling) 5:295
"Miracles" (Singer) 3:385-86
Mirgorod (Gogol) 4:86-7, 117
"Miriam" (Capote) 2:61-2, 64, 66, 69, 73-5, 78-9, 83
"The Mirror" (O'Flaherty) 6:260, 265, 276-77, 279
"The Mirror" (Singer) 3:364, 368, 375
"A Miscellany of Characters That Will Not Appear" (Cheever) 1:93, 100
"The Miser" (O'Connor) 5:371
"Misery" (Chekhov) 2:128, 130, 155
"A Misfortunate Girl" (Turgenev) See "Neschastnaya"
"Miss Chauncey" (Jewett) 6:168
"Miss Gunton of Poughkeepsie" (James) 8:311
"Miss Harriet" (Maupassant) 1:259, 271, 274, 280, 285-87
"Miss Manning's Minister" (Jewett) 6:156, 159
"Miss Mary Pask" (Wharton) 6:431
"Miss Sydney's Flowers" (Jewett) 6:157, 166, 168
"Miss Tempy's Watchers" (Jewett) 6:151, 156
"Miss Winchelsea's Heart" (Wells) 6:391
"Miss Witherwell's Mistake" (Chopin) 8:84, 86
"The Missing Line" (Singer) 3:389
"The Mission of Jane" (Wharton) 6:424-25
"The Mission of Mr. Scatters" (Dunbar) 8:122, 132, 137, 147
"Mrs. Bullfrog" (Hawthorne) 3:180
"Mrs. Moysey" (Bowen) 3:30, 33, 40, 42
"Mrs. Windermere" (Bowen) 3:40, 54

"The Mistake of the Machine" (Chesterton) **1**:131
"Mr. and Mrs. Elliot" (Hemingway) **1**:208
"Mr. Bruce" (Jewett) **6**:157, 166
"Mr. Coffee and Mr. Fixit" (Carver) **8**:18-19, 32-3, 59-60
"Mr. Cornelius Johnson, Office-Seeker" (Dunbar) **8**:122, 125, 128, 131, 141, 144
"Mr. Durant" (Parker) **2**:274
"Mr. Foolfarm's Journal" (Barthelme) **2**:40
"Mr. Groby's Slippery Gift" (Dunbar) **8**:122
"Mr. Harrington's Washing" (Maugham) **8**:369, 377, 383
"Mr. Higginbotham's Catastrophe" (Hawthorne) **3**:154
"Mr. Icky" (Fitzgerald) **6**:58
"Mr. Jack Hamlin's Mediation" (Harte) **8**:248-49
"Mr. Jones" (Wharton) **6**:426-27
"Mr. Know-All" (Maugham) **8**:366
Mr. Mulliner Speaking (Wodehouse) **2**:338
Mister Palomar (Calvino) **3**:113-18
"Mister Palomar in the City" (Calvino) **3**:113, 115
"Mister Palomar's Vacation" (Calvino) **3**:113
"Mr. Potter Takes a Rest Cure" (Wodehouse) **2**:355-56
"Mr. Preble Gets Rid of His Wife" (Thurber) **1**:418
"Mr. Prokharchin" (Dostoevski) **2**:170, 191-94
"Mr. Skelmersdale in Fairyland" (Wells) **6**:391-92
"Mr. Taylor's Funeral" (Chesnutt) **7**:18
"Mrs. Bathurst" (Kipling) **5**:266, 278-79, 281
"Mrs. Bonny" (Jewett) **6**:150, 168
"Mrs. Dalloway in Bond Street" (Woolf) **7**:381-82
Mrs. Dalloway's Party: A Short Story Sequence (Woolf) **7**:381-82, 388, 392
"Mrs. Hofstadter on Josephine Street" (Parker) **2**:283
"Mrs. Mobry's Reason" (Chopin) **8**:71
"Mrs. Parkins's Christmas Eve" (Jewett) **6**:156, 159
"Mrs. Skagg's Husbands" (Harte) **8**:234, 244
"Mitosis" (Calvino) **3**:109-10
The Mixture as Before (Maugham) **8**:379
"M'liss" (Harte) **8**:210, 219, 222, 224-25, 231-32, 234
"Mobile" (Ballard) **1**:68
"The Mock Auction" (Lavin) **4**:183
"The Moderate Murderer" (Chesterton) **1**:132
A Modern Lover (Lawrence) **4**:230
"Moebius Strip" (Cortázar) **7**:69
"Mohammed Fripouille" (Maupassant) **1**:275
"Mojave" (Capote) **2**:79-80
"Moments of Being:"Slater's Pins Have No Points"' ("Slater's Pins Have No Points") (Woolf) **7**:375, 388-89, 391-92, 398, 408-10
"Mon oncle Jules" (Maupassant) **1**:277
"Mon oncle Sosthène" (Maupassant) **1**:263, 272
"Monday or Tuesday" (Woolf) **7**:371, 374-75, 390, 392, 397-98, 402
Monday or Tuesday (Woolf) **7**:367-69, 371, 374, 392, 398-401, 404
"The Money Diggers" (Irving) **2**:251, 261-62
"Monk" (Faulkner) **1**:165, 179
"The Monkey" (Dinesen) **7**:163, 167, 170, 173, 200-01, 203
"Monkey Nuts" (Lawrence) **4**:231, 234-35
"Monologue of Isabel Watching It Rain in Macondo" (García Márquez) **8**:194
"Monsieur les deux chapeux" (Munro) **3**:348
"Monsieur Parent" (Maupassant) **1**:259-60, 283
"The Monster" (Crane) **7**:103-05, 107, 114, 116, 131, 134, 138, 146-48
The Monster and Other Stories (Crane) **7**:104
"Moon-Face" (London) **4**:252, 258-59
Moon-Face, and Other Stories (London) **4**:252
"The Moon in the Orange Street Skating Rink" (Munro) **3**:348-49
"Moon Lake" (Welty) **1**:474, 486
"Moon-Watcher" (Clarke) **3**:127-28
"A Moonlight Fable" (Wells) **6**:376
"Moonlight in the Snow" (Crane) **7**:108
The Moons of Jupiter (Munro) **3**:346-47
"The Mordivinian Sarafin" (Bunin) See "Mordovskiy sarafan"
"Mordovskiy sarafan" ("The Mordivinian Sarafin") (Bunin) **5**:82, 106-08
"More Alarms at Night" (Thurber) **1**:428
"More Stately Mansions" (Vonnegut) **8**:433
More Stories by Frank O'Connor (O'Connor) **5**:371
"Morning" (Barthelme) **2**:45, 55
"A Morning Walk" (Chopin) **8**:98
"The Mortal Coil" (Lawrence) **4**:235
"The Mortification of the Flesh" (Dunbar) **8**:127
Mosaïque (Mérimée) **7**:287-88, 290, 300
"The Moslem Wife" (Gallant) **5**:135-38
Mosses from an Old Manse (Hawthorne) **3**:155, 160, 174, 180, 185
"The Most Extraordinary Thing" (Andersen) **6**:11
"The Most Profound Caress" (Cortázar) See "La caricia más profunda"
"Motel Architecture" (Ballard) **1**:79
"The Moth" (Wells) **6**:383
"Mother" (Anderson) **1**:33, 44
"Mother" (Barnes) **3**:22, 26
"A Mother" (Joyce) **3**:205, 210-11, 234, 237, 245, 247, 249
"Mother and Child" (Hughes) **6**:119, 142
"Mother and Daughter" (Lawrence) **4**:205, 220
"Mother and Son" (O'Flaherty) **6**:262
"The Mother Hive" (Kipling) **5**:279
"The Mother of a Queen" (Hemingway) **1**:211
"Motherhood" (Anderson) **1**:27
"The Motive" (Cortázar) **7**:69-70
"Mouche" (Maupassant) **1**:273, 284
"The Mound" (Lovecraft) **3**:270-71, 274, 279
"The Mountain Tavern" (O'Flaherty) **6**:277-78, 281, 284
The Mountain Tavern, and Other Stories (O'Flaherty) **6**:262-65, 278, 283
"Mountjoy" (Irving) **2**:242
"The Mouse" (Lavin) **4**:167, 182
"The Mouse and the Woman" (Thomas) **3**:399-402, 408
"La moustache" (Maupassant) **1**:274
"The Moving Finger" (Wharton) **6**:414
"Moving Spirit" (Clarke) **3**:134
"Mowgli's Brothers" (Kipling) **5**:293
"MS. Found in a Bottle" (Poe) **1**:379, 391-92, 398
"Mt. Pisgah's Christmas Possum" (Dunbar) **8**:121, 127, 131, 136
"La muerte y la brújula" ("Death and the Compass") (Borges) **4**:4, 10, 16, 19-24, 28-30, 35-6
"El muerto" ("The Dead Man") (Borges) **4**:4-5, 8-9, 23, 37-9
"Mule in the Yard" (Faulkner) **1**:177
Mules and Men (Hurston) **4**:133-36, 139-49, 153, 155-56, 158-59
Mulliner Nights (Wodehouse) **2**:338
"Mumu" (Turgenev) **7**:315, 320, 323, 326, 352-57, 363
"The Municipal Report" (Henry) **5**:156, 165, 171-72, 179, 182, 192
"The Murder" (Chekhov) **2**:150
"Murder in the Dark" (Atwood) **2**:15, 17, 19-20
The Murder in the Dark (Atwood) **2**:15, 17-20
"The Murders in the Rue Morgue" (Poe) **1**:378, 387, 389, 395, 406
"Muriel" (Gardner) **7**:234
"The Muse of the Coming Age" (Andersen) **6**:7
"The Muse's Tragedy" (Wharton) **6**:414, 428
"Music for Chameleons" (Capote) **2**:80
Music for Chameleons (Capote) **2**:79-81
"Music from Spain" (Welty) **1**:474, 495
"The Music Lesson" (Cheever) **1**:100
"The Music Lover" (Gardner) **7**:223, 225-26, 238
"The Music of Erich Zann" (Lovecraft) **3**:269
"The Music Teacher" (Cheever) **1**:106
"The Mutability of Literature" (Irving) **2**:251, 254
"Mute" (Atwood) **2**:16
"Muttsy" (Hurston) **4**:136, 138, 151
"Muza" (Bunin) **5**:114
"My Aunt" (Irving) **2**:242
"My Da" (O'Connor) **5**:388
"My First Protestant" (O'Connor) **5**:386-87
"My Heart Is Broken" (Gallant) **5**:141
My Heart Is Broken (Gallant) **5**:122-23, 130, 139-41
"My Kinsman, Major Molineux" (Hawthorne) **3**:164-65, 167, 171, 175-76, 179-80, 182-83, 186-87, 189
"My Lady Brandon and the Widow Jim" (Jewett) **6**:154
"My Life" (Chekhov) **2**:128, 130-32, 135-36, 145, 155, 157
My Life and Hard Times (Thurber) **1**:413-14, 419, 421-24, 426-28, 435
"My Metamorphosis" (Harte) **8**:254
"My Molly" (Lavin) **4**:167
"My Mother's Life" (Lessing) **6**:216
"My Name is Everyone" ("Who Am I This Time?") (Vonnegut) **8**:433, 437
"My Neighbor" (Kafka) **5**:206
"My Oedipus Complex" (O'Connor) **5**:368-69, 378, 386-87
"My Old Man" (Hemingway) **1**:208, 219, 234, 245
"My Own True Ghost-Story" (Kipling) **5**:272-73
"My Side of the Matter" (Capote) **2**:61-2, 65, 70, 83-5
"My Uncle John" (Irving) **2**:242
"My Vocation" (Lavin) **4**:167
"My Warszawa: 1980" (Oates) **6**:255
My World—And Welcome to It (Thurber) **1**:420

"Myra Meets His Family" (Fitzgerald) **6**:56, 96
"Mysterious Kôr" (Bowen) **3**:31-2, 39, 41-2, 44, 53
The Mysterious Stranger (Twain) **6**:294-99, 301-02, 305-06, 312-16, 322-25, 331, 334, 345-50, 353
"A Mystery of Heroism" (Crane) **7**:102, 106, 109
"The Mystery of Marie Rogêt" (Poe) **1**:386, 388, 400, 406
"Myths of the Near Future" (Ballard) **1**:78-9
Myths of the Near Future (Ballard) **1**:78-9, 82
"Na kraj sveta" (Bunin) **5**:98
"Na xutore" (Bunin) **5**:98
"Nabo: The Black Man Who Made the Angels Wait" (García Márquez) **8**:154-55, 157-58, 183, 185
"The Name-Day Party" ("The Party") (Chekhov) **2**:128, 130-31, 133, 149, 155-56
"The Name, the Nose" (Calvino) **3**:119
"The Nameless City" (Lovecraft) **3**:262-63, 269, 274, 276
"The Namesake" (Cather) **2**:97, 103-04, 113
"Namgay Doola" (Kipling) **5**:262
"Nanette: An Aside" (Cather) **2**:101
"Nathalie" (Bunin) **5**:87, 113, 115
"A Nation of Wheels" (Barthelme) **2**:40
"The National Pastime" (Cheever) **1**:100
"Native of Winby" (Jewett) **6**:155
"Natural Boundaries" (Oates) **6**:248-50
"A Natural History of the Dead" (Hemingway) **1**:211
"Nature" (Turgenev) **7**:335
"The Naughty Boy" (Andersen) **6**:30, 32
"The Necklace" (Maupassant)
See "La parure"
"The Needlecase" (Bowen) **3**:41
"The Negro in the Drawing Room" (Hughes) **6**:121-22
"The Neighboring Families" (Andersen) **6**:7
"Neighbors" (Carver) **8**:4-6, 9-10, 34, 42, 47, 54
"Neighbors" (Singer) **3**:384
"Neighbour Rosicky" (Cather) **2**:105, 115-17
"Neil MacAdam" (Maugham) **8**:376
"Nelse Hatton's Revenge" (Dunbar) **8**:119, 121, 127, 140, 143
"A Nervous Breakdown" (Chekhov)
See "An Attack of Nerves"
"Neschastnaya" ("An Unhappy Girl"; "A Misfortunate Girl") (Turgenev) **7**:321, 324, 326, 336-38, 358-59
"Neutron Tide" (Clarke) **3**:133
"Never Bet the Devil Your Head" (Poe) **1**:407
"Nevskij Avenue" (Gogol)
See "Nevsky Prospect"
"Nevsky Prospect" ("Nevskij Avenue") (Gogol) **4**:95, 122, 124-25, 128
"The New Accelerator" (Wells) **6**:367, 391, 393, 404, 406
"The New Country House" (Chekhov)
See "The New Villa"
"The New Dress" (Woolf) **7**:373, 376, 381-82, 387, 393, 395
"A New England Nun" (Freeman) **1**:192, 197, 199
A New England Nun, and Other Stories (Freeman) **1**:191, 194-95, 197
"A New England Prophet" (Freeman) **1**:197
"The New Englander" (Anderson) **1**:27, 30, 39, 46-7, 53, 55
"New Eve and Old Adam" (Lawrence) **4**:220
"The New House" (Bowen) **3**:40, 54
"The New Man" (Lessing) **6**:191, 198
"The New Music" (Barthelme) **2**:55
"A New Refutation of Time" (Borges) **4**:5
New Stories (Andersen)
See *Eventyr, fortalte for bøorn*
"The New Suit" (O'Flaherty) **6**:287
"The New Teacher" (O'Connor)
See "The Cheapjack"
"The New Villa" ("The New Country House") (Chekhov) **2**:131, 156
New Year's Eve (The 'Seventies) (Wharton) **6**:439-40, 442
"New York by Campfire Light" (Henry) **5**:159
New York Quartet (Wharton)
See *Old New York*
"New York to Detroit" (Parker) **2**:274, 280, 285
"News for the Church" (O'Connor) **5**:371, 383, 385, 389
"News from the Sun" (Ballard) **1**:78-9
"The Next Tenants" (Clarke) **3**:135
"The Next Time" (James) **8**:281, 317
"Nice Girl" (Anderson) **1**:52
"A Nice Quiet Place" (Fitzgerald) **6**:80
The Nick Adams Stories (Hemingway) **1**:240
"The Nigger" (Barnes) **3**:5, 10-11, 14, 22
"Night" (Bunin) **5**:100, 108, 114
"A Night among the Horses" (Barnes) **3**:5-7, 10, 14, 16, 22-4
"A Night at Greenway Court" (Cather) **2**:100
"A Night at the Fair" (Fitzgerald) **6**:49
"The Night-Born" (London) **4**:291
The Night-Born (London) **4**:266
"The Night Came Slowly" (Chopin) **8**:98, 110-11
"A Night Conversation" ("Conversation at Night") (Bunin) **5**:81, 90-1
"Night Driver" (Calvino) **3**:109
"Night Face Up" (Cortázar)
See "La noche boca arriba"
"A Night for Love" (Vonnegut) **8**:433
"A Night in Acadie" (Chopin) **8**:95
A Night in Acadie (Chopin) **8**:66-8, 77, 84, 93-4, 97, 110-14
"A Night in New Arabia" (Henry) **5**:184
"A Night in the Woods" (Barnes) **3**:18
"The Night of Denial" (Bunin) **5**:82
"The Night of the Curlews" (García Márquez)
See "La noche de los alcaravanes"
"A Night on the Divide" (Harte) **8**:216, 253
"Night Sketches" (Hawthorne) **3**:189, 191
"The Night the Bed Fell" (Thurber) **1**:428
"The Night the Ghost Got In" (Thurber) **1**:428, 432
"The Nightingale" (Andersen) **6**:7, 16, 27, 30, 32-4, 37, 40
"Nightmares" (Cortázar)
See "Pesadillas"
"Nightpiece with Figures" (O'Connor) **5**:382, 385, 391-92
"Nights in Europe's Ministeries" (Cortázar)
See "Noches en los ministerios de Europa"
"Nimram" (Gardner) **7**:223-27, 235, 238, 241
"The Nine Billion Names of God" (Clarke) **3**:134-35, 137, 145
Nine Stories (Salinger) **2**:289-91, 299, 312-13, 316, 318-19
"Nineteen Fifty-Five" (Walker) **5**:412, 414
"No. 44, The Mysterious Stranger" (Twain) **6**:331
"A No-Account Creole" (Chopin) **8**:90, 103
"No Harm Trying" (Fitzgerald) **6**:69-70
"No-Man's-Mare" (Barnes) **3**:11-2, 22
"No Morning After" (Clarke) **3**:149
No One Writes to the Colonel (García Márquez) **8**:162, 185, 192-97
"No Place for You, My Love" (Welty) **1**:476, 479, 484, 493
"The No-Talent Kid" (Vonnegut) **8**:431
"No te dejes" ("Don't Let Them") (Cortázar) **7**:95
"No Witchcraft for Sale" (Lessing) **6**:186, 190-91
"Nobody Knows" (Anderson) **1**:34, 45
"Nobody Said Anything" (Carver) **8**:54
"Noč pered roždestvom" ("Christmas Eve") (Gogol) **4**:86, 118
"La noche boca arriba" ("On His Back under the Night"; "Night Face Up") (Cortázar) **7**:52, 54, 57, 64, 69-71, 81
"La noche de los alcaravanes" ("The Night of the Curlews") (García Márquez) **8**:154-55, 159, 183
"La noche de Mantequilla" ("Butterball's Night") (Cortázar) **7**:89, 91
"Noches en los ministerios de Europa" ("Nights in Europe's Ministeries") (Cortázar) **7**:94
"None of That" (Lawrence) **4**:219, 230
The Nonexistent Knight (Calvino)
See *Il cavaliere inesistente*
The Nonexistent Knight and the Cloven Viscount (Calvino)
See *Il cavaliere inesistente*
The Nonexistent Knight and the Cloven Viscount (Calvino)
See *Il visconte dimezzato*
Noon Wine (Porter) **4**:327-30, 339-40, 347, 349-52, 355-56, 359-60
"Norman and the Killer" (Oates) **6**:224, 226
"Un normand" (Maupassant) **1**:288
"Nos Anglais" (Maupassant) **1**:263
"The Nose" (Gogol) **4**:82-4, 91-5, 97, 124-25, 127-29
"Not a Very Nice Story" (Lessing) **6**:188, 197, 220
"Not for the Sabbath" (Singer) **3**:381
"Not Sixteen" (Anderson) **1**:52
"Notes by Flood and Field" (Harte) **8**:210
"Notes for a Case History" (Lessing) **6**:198, 200, 208, 218
Notes from the Underground (Dostoevski)
See *Letters from the Underworld*
Notes of a Hunter (Turgenev)
See *Sportsman's Sketches*
"Notes of a Madman" (Gogol)
See "Diary of a Madman"
Nothing Ever Breaks except the Heart (Boyle) **5**:63
Nothing Serious (Wodehouse) **2**:345
"Notorious Jumping Frog of Calaveras County" (Twain)
See "Celebrated Jumping Frog of Calaveras County"
"A Novel in Nine Letters" (Dostoevski) **2**:170

"Now I Lay Me" (Hemingway) **1**:220, 241, 247
"Now: Zero" (Ballard) **1**:68
"The Nuisance" (Lessing) **6**:186, 217
"No. 16" (Bowen) **3**:41
La nuvola di smog (*Smog*) (Calvino) **3**:98, 111-12, 117
"Nyarlathotep" (Lovecraft) **3**:269, 273
"O City of Broken Dreams" (Cheever) **1**:89, 107
"O Lasting Peace" (Gallant) **5**:124, 133
"O Russet Witch!" (Fitzgerald) **6**:45, 59, 91-3
"O Youth and Beauty!" (Cheever) **1**:90, 110
"The Oar" (O'Flaherty) **6**:262, 265, 274, 276-77
Obscure Destinies (Cather) **2**:92, 115, 117-18
"L'occhio del padrone" (Calvino) **3**:97
"The Ocean" (Cheever) **1**:94, 111
Octaedro (Cortázar) **7**:60
"October and June" (Henry) **5**:182
"Odalie Misses Mass" (Chopin) **8**:93
"An Odor of Verbena" (Faulkner) **1**:171
"Odour of Chrysanthemums" (Lawrence) **4**:197-98, 202, 220, 230
"An Odyssey of the North" (London) **4**:251, 258, 278, 282-84, 289, 291
"Of Emelya, the Fool" (Bunin) **5**:82
"Of Love: A Testimony" (Cheever) **1**:88, 99
Off-Hours (Cortázar)
See *Deshoras*
"Offerings" (O'Flaherty) **6**:262, 264, 281
"The Office" (Munro) **3**:322, 325, 340, 343
"An Official Position" (Maugham) **8**:379
"The Offshore Pirate" (Fitzgerald) **6**:45, 56, 58-9, 96-7
Oh What a Paradise It Seems (Cheever) **1**:108, 113-15
"An Ohio Pagan" (Anderson) **1**:27, 30, 39
Ohio Pastorals (Dunbar) **8**:127, 134
"Oifig an Phoist" ("The Post Office") (O'Flaherty) **6**:280, 287, 289
"Ojos de perro azul" ("Blue-Dog Eyes"; "Eyes of a Blue Dog") (García Márquez) **8**:154, 157
"Ol' Bennet and the Indians" (Crane) **7**:103
"Old Abe's Conversion" (Dunbar) **8**:122, 146
"The Old Adam" (Lawrence) **4**:220
"Old-Age Pensioners" (O'Connor) **5**:369
"The Old Apple Dealer" (Hawthorne) **3**:189
"Old Aunt Peggy" (Chopin) **8**:89
"The Old Bachelor's Nightcap" (Andersen) **6**:12
"The Old Beauty" (Cather) **2**:93-4
The Old Beauty and Others (Cather) **2**:93
"The Old Bird, a Love Story" (Powers) **4**:368, 371, 373
"An Old Boot" (Lavin) **4**:165, 168
"The Old Chevalier" (Dinesen) **7**:163, 165-66, 169, 175
"The Old Chief Mshlanga" (Lessing) **6**:186, 189, 196-97, 213
Old Creole Days (Cable) **4**:47, 49-58, 60-2, 64-8, 75-6, 78
"Old Esther Dudley" (Hawthorne) **3**:186
"The Old Faith" (O'Connor) **5**:369, 372, 385, 398
"An Old-Fashioned Christmas" (Dunbar) **8**:125
"Old Fellows" (O'Connor) **5**:366, 389
"The Old Friends" (Gallant) **5**:124, 133
Old Friends and New (Jewett) **6**:165-66, 168
"Old Garbo" (Thomas) **3**:403-06, 410-12
"The Old House" (Andersen) **6**:4, 25
"The Old Hunter" (O'Flaherty) **6**:264, 280
"Old John's Place" (Lessing) **6**:186, 190, 211, 213-14, 217
"Old Love" (Singer) **3**:376, 384
Old Love (Singer) **3**:380-82
The Old Maid (The 'Fifties) (Wharton) **6**:439-41
"Old Man" (Faulkner) **1**:159-61, 167-68
"The Old Man" (Singer) **3**:355-56
The Old Man and the Sea (Hemingway) **1**:222-24, 226-28, 238-39, 247-50
"Old Man at the Bridge" (Hemingway) **1**:234
"The Old Manse" (Hawthorne) **3**:159, 174, 184
"Old Mr. Marblehall" (Welty) **1**:466, 471, 498
"Old Mrs. Harris" (Cather) **2**:97, 102, 115-17
Old Mortality (Porter) **4**:327, 329-34, 338, 340-42, 346-52, 361-65
Old New York (*New York Quartet*) (Wharton) **6**:439-40, 442
"Old News" (Hawthorne) **3**:174
"Old Oak Tree's Last Dream" (Andersen)
See "The Last Dream of the Old Oak"
"The Old Order" (Porter) **4**:339-40, 348, 350-54, 358, 361-62, 365
"Old Portraits" (Turgenev)
See "Starye portrety"
"The Old Street Lamp" (Andersen) **6**:4, 7
"Old Ticonderoga" (Hawthorne) **3**:174
"An Old Time Christmas" (Dunbar) **8**:122, 128, 133, 144
"The Old Woman" (O'Flaherty) **6**:277-78, 280
"An Old Woman and Her Cat" (Lessing) **6**:188
"Old-World Landowners" (Gogol)
See "Starosvetskie Pomeščiki"
"Ole Luköie" ("The Sandman") (Andersen) **6**:12
"Ole Shut Eye" (Andersen) **6**:3
"Omnibus" ("Busride") (Cortázar) **7**:50, 54, 56
"On A Wagon" (Singer) **3**:375
"On Angels" (Barthelme) **2**:32, 38
"On Graphology As an Applied Science" (Cortázar)
See "De la grafología como ciencia aplicada"
"On Greenhow Hill" (Kipling) **5**:260
"On His Back under the Night" (Cortázar)
See "La noche boca arriba"
"On Official Duty" (Chekhov) **2**:128
"On the City Wall" (Kipling) **5**:265
"On the Divide" (Cather) **2**:96-7, 100-01, 105-07
"On the Gate" (Kipling) **5**:271, 283
"On the Great Wall" (Kipling) **5**:292
"On the Gulls' Road" (Cather) **2**:99, 104
"On the Makaloa Mat" (London) **4**:266
On the Makaloa Mat (*Island Tales*) (London) **4**:256-57, 266, 270
"On the Quai at Smyrna" (Hemingway) **1**:244
"On the Road" (Hughes) **6**:122, 131-32
"On the Run" (Boyle) **5**:70, 72
"On the Walpole Road" (Freeman) **1**:201
"On the Way Home" (Hughes) **6**:119, 121-23, 132-33
"On the Western Circuit" (Hardy) **2**:206-07, 214, 220, 222-23
"On Writing" (Hemingway) **1**:240, 243
"One Christmas at Shiloh" (Dunbar) **8**:122, 138, 146
"One Christmas Eve" (Hughes) **6**:109
"One Dash—Horses" (Crane)
See "Horses—One Dash"
"One Day After Saturday" (García Márquez) **8**:185
"One Day of Happiness" (Singer) **3**:385-86
"One Friday Morning" (Hughes) **6**:111-12, 119, 121
"One Good Time" (Freeman) **1**:198
"One Interne" (Fitzgerald) **6**:47-8
"One is a Wanderer" (Thurber) **1**:417, 420, 425, 427, 435
"One Man's Fortune" (Dunbar) **8**:120, 122, 125, 128, 131, 136, 145, 150
"The £1,000,000 Bank-Note" (Twain) **6**:303, 328-30
"One More Thing" (Carver) **8**:17, 19, 38, 53
"One of Them" (Powers) **4**:375-76
"One Off the Short List" (Lessing) **6**:197, 199, 200, 203-08, 214, 218
"One Reader Writes" (Hemingway) **1**:211
"One Summer" (Lavin) **4**:173, 183
"One Sunday Morning" (Boyle) **5**:64
"One Thousand Dollars" (Henry) **5**:184
"One Trip Abroad" (Fitzgerald) **6**:61, 100, 104
"One Warm Saturday" (Thomas) **3**:394-95, 398, 403, 410-12
"Only a Subaltern" (Kipling) **5**:272
"The Only Rose" (Jewett) **6**:169
"An Only Son" (Jewett) **6**:152-53
"Onnagata" (Mishima) **4**:313, 315, 318, 322-23
"The Open Boat" (Crane) **7**:100-01, 103-04, 107-13, 116-18, 120, 140, 142-43, 145, 148-49, 151-53
The Open Boat and Other Tales of Adventure (Crane) **7**:102, 104
"The Oracle of the Dog" (Chesterton) **1**:133-34, 136
"The Orchards" (Thomas) **3**:396, 399-402, 407-08
"The Ordeal" (Fitzgerald) **6**:58
"The Ordeal at Mt. Hope" (Dunbar) **8**:118, 120-21, 127, 131, 146
"Orientation of Cats" (Cortázar) **7**:69, 71
"The Origin of the Birds" (Calvino) **3**:108-10
"The Origin of the Hatchet Story" (Chesnutt) **7**:14-15
"Orphan's Progress" (Gallant) **5**:138
"Orpheus and His Lute" (O'Connor) **5**:377, 382
"Oscar" (Barnes) **3**:2-4
"Otchayanny" ("A Desperate Character") (Turgenev) **7**:337, 362-63
"The Other Death" (Borges) **4**:35, 37, 42-4
"The Other Gods" (Lovecraft) **3**:274
"The Other Man" (Kipling) **5**:274
"The Other Paris" (Gallant) **5**:125-26, 148
"The Other Rib of Death" (García Márquez)
See "La otra costilla de la muerte"
The Other Side of the Sky (Clarke) **3**:125, 131-32
"The Other Two" (Wharton) **6**:421, 424-26
"The Other Woman" (Anderson) **1**:30
"Others' Dreams" (Oates) **6**:234
"La otra costilla de la muerte" ("The Other Rib of Death") (García Márquez) **8**:154-56, 182
"El otro cielo" (Cortázar) **7**:55, 57, 59, 61-2

Title Index

"The Ottawa Valley" (Munro) **3**:337
Our Ancestors (Calvino)
See *I nostri antenati*
"Our Demeanor at Wakes" (Cortázar)
See "Conducta en los velorios"
"Our Exploits at West Poley" (Hardy) **2**:214, 216, 221
"Our Friend Judith" (Lessing) **6**:201-02, 218-20
"Our Lady of the Easy Death of Alferce" (Oates) **6**:237
"Our Wall" (Oates) **6**:255
"Out of Nowhere into Nothing" (Anderson) **1**:21, 27, 30, 39, 46-7, 53
"Out of Season" (Hemingway) **1**:245
"Out of the Eons" (Lovecraft) **3**:279
"Out of the Sun" (Clarke) **3**:132, 135-36
"The Outcasts" (O'Flaherty) **6**:262, 264, 284
"The Outcasts of Poker Flat" (Harte) **8**:209-10, 219, 223, 226-27, 232-33, 236, 244, 250-51, 254-55, 257
"Outside the Cabinet-Maker's" (Fitzgerald) **6**:51
"Outside the Ministry" (Lessing) **6**:199
"The Outsider" (Lovecraft) **3**:258, 260, 262, 264, 274
"The Outstation" (Maugham) **8**:357, 359, 361, 366-67, 372
"The Oval Portrait" (Poe) **1**:392
"The Overcoat" ("The Cloak") (Gogol) **4**:82-3, 87-91, 93, 106-08, 110-11, 113-17, 127, 129-30
Overhead in a Balloon: Stories of Paris (Gallant) **5**:147
"The Overloaded Man" (Ballard) **1**:74-7
The Overloaded Man (Ballard) **1**:73
Overnight to Many Distant Cities (Barthelme) **2**:50-1, 56
"The Overtone" (Lawrence) **4**:238-39
"Ovsianko the Freeholder" (Turgenev)
See "The Freeholder Ovsyanikov"
"Owen Wingrave" (James) **8**:270
"Ozème's Holiday" (Chopin) **8**:94, 113
"P. & O." (Maugham) **8**:359, 366, 372, 375
"The Pace of Youth" (Crane) **7**:149
"The Package" (Vonnegut) **8**:437
"The Page" (Atwood) **2**:15, 17
"Pages from Cold Point" (Bowles) **3**:59, 61-2, 66, 69, 73, 76-7, 85
"Pain maudit" (Maupassant) **1**:263
"A Painful Case" (Joyce) **3**:203, 205, 209-11, 234-35, 246, 249
"The Painted Woman" (O'Flaherty) **6**:262, 264
"The Painter's Adventure" (Irving) **2**:262
"A Pair" (Singer) **3**:377, 384
"A Pair of Silk Stockings" (Chopin) **8**:72
"La paix du ménage" (Balzac) **5**:5, 29, 31
Pale Horse, Pale Rider (Porter) **4**:327, 329, 331-35, 339-41, 347, 349, 361, 364-65
Pale Horse, Pale Rider: Three Short Novels (Porter) **4**:327-28, 331, 339
"The Pale Pink Roast" (Paley) **8**:389, 397, 414-16
"La panchina" (Calvino) **3**:97
"Pandora" (James) **8**:310-12
"Pantaloon in Black" (Faulkner) **1**:148, 174, 183
"Le Papa de Simon" (Maupassant) **1**:261, 271
"The Papers" (James) **8**:321
"The Paradise of Bachelors and the Tartarus of Maids" ("The Tartarus of Maids") (Melville) **1**:298, 303-05, 323
The Paradoxes of Mr. Pond (Chesterton) **1**:125, 139
"The Paragon" (O'Connor) **5**:371-72
"Paraguay" (Barthelme) **2**:35, 38, 41
"Le parapluie" (Maupassant) **1**:286
"Parker's Back" (O'Connor) **1**:344-45, 357, 359, 368-70
"The Parrot" (Bowen) **3**:37, 55
"The Parrot" (Singer) **3**:358
"The Parshley Celebration" (Jewett) **6**:156
Parti-colored Stories (Chekhov) **2**:130
"Une partie de campagne" (Maupassant) **1**:260-61
"La partie de trictrac" ("The Game of Backgammon") (Mérimée) **7**:280, 283, 287-91
"The Parting" (O'Flaherty) **6**:265, 281, 286, 288
"The Partridge Festival" (O'Connor) **1**:356
"The Party" (Barthelme) **2**:39, 55
"The Party" (Chekhov)
See "The Name-Day Party"
"La parure" ("The Necklace") (Maupassant) **1**:273, 278, 280, 284, 286, 288
"Los paso en las huellas" (Cortázar) **7**:62
"A Passage in the Life of Mr. John Oakhurst" (Harte) **8**:233
"The Passenger's Story" (Twain) **6**:337
"Passer-By" (Clarke) **3**:134
"Passing" (Hughes)
See "Who's Passing for Who?"
"The Passing of Ambrose" (Wodehouse) **2**:356
"The Passing of Black Eagle" (Henry) **5**:158
"The Passing of Enriquez" (Harte) **8**:228
"The Passing of Grandison" (Chesnutt) **7**:16, 19, 22-3, 25-6
"The Passion" (Barnes) **3**:5, 24-7
"Une passion" (Maupassant) **1**:274
"Une passion dans le désert" ("A Passion in the Desert") (Balzac) **5**:12-14, 31
"A Passion in the Desert" (Balzac)
See "Une passion dans le désert"
"The Passionate Pilgrim" (James) **8**:302
"Passions" (Singer) **3**:378
Passions, and Other Stories (Singer) **3**:376-77, 381, 384
"Past One at Rooney's" (Henry) **5**:198
"Pastor Dowe at Tacaté" (Bowles) **3**:59, 61-3, 66-7, 69, 79
"The Pastor of Six Mile Bush" (Lavin) **4**:169
"Pastoral" (Anderson) **1**:52
"Pastoral" (Carver) **8**:5, 30, 50
"Pastoral Care" (Gardner) **7**:217, 219-22, 229, 232
"Pat Hobby's Christmas Wish" (Fitzgerald) **6**:69-70
"The Patagonia" (James) **8**:299, 311
"Patent Pending" (Clarke) **3**:133-34
"The Patented Gate and the Mean Hamburger" (Warren) **4**:387, 390, 394, 396, 399
"A Patient Waiter" (Freeman) **1**:201
"The Patriarch" (O'Connor) **5**:393-94
"Patricia, Edith, and Arnold" (Thomas) **3**:402, 405, 410, 412
"Patricide" (Oates) **6**:237
"The Patriot Son" (Lavin) **4**:167, 172, 183
The Patriot Son, and Other Stories (Lavin) **4**:165
"A Patriotic Short" (Fitzgerald) **6**:70-1
"Patriotism" (Mishima) **4**:313-15, 317-23
"La patronne" (Maupassant) **1**:256
"Paul's Case" (Cather) **2**:90-1, 94, 103, 113, 118, 121-22
"The Peace of Utrecht" (Munro) **3**:321, 326
"The Peacelike Mongoose" (Thurber) **1**:426
"The Peaches" (Thomas) **3**:394, 396, 402, 404-05, 410-12
"Peacock" (Carver) **8**:39
"The Pearl" (Dinesen) **7**:165, 167-68, 198
"The Pearl" (Mishima) **4**:313, 317-18, 322
"The Pearl of Love" (Wells) **6**:376
"The Peasant Marey" (Dostoevski) **2**:166
"Peasant Women" (Chekhov) **2**:155
"Peasants" (Chekhov) **2**:126, 131, 156
"Peasants" (O'Connor) **5**:371, 377-78, 389, 394-95, 398
"Pecheneg" (Chekhov) **2**:155
"Pedro Salvadores" (Borges) **4**:14-17
"The Pegnitz Junction" (Gallant) **5**:124, 127, 132-34, 143
The Pegnitz Junction (Gallant) **5**:124, 127, 130-32
"The Pelican" (Wharton) **6**:413, 423, 428-29
"Pen and Inkstand" (Andersen) **6**:7
"The Pendulum" (Henry) **5**:158-59, 163, 188
"The Pension Beaurepas" (James) **8**:299
"Un pequeño paraíso" ("A Small Paradise") (Cortázar) **7**:93
"Le père" (Maupassant) **1**:275
"Le père amable" (Maupassant) **1**:259, 284
"Père Raphaël" (Cable) **4**:51, 77-9
"Pereval" (Bunin) **5**:98
"A Perfect Day for Bananafish" (Salinger) **2**:290-93, 295, 297-99, 303, 305, 308, 312, 314, 318
"The Perfect Life" (Fitzgerald) **6**:47, 49
"The Perfect Murder" (Barnes) **3**:13
"The Perfume Sea" (Laurence) **7**:245. 248-50, 256
"The Peril in the Streets" (Cheever) **1**:99
"The Perishing of the Pendragons" (Chesterton) **1**:131, 138
"Perpetua" (Barthelme) **2**:55
"El Perseguidor" ("The Pursuer") (Cortázar) **7**:50-1, 58, 61, 67-8, 70
"Pesadillas" ("Nightmares") (Cortázar) **7**:91
"Pesci grossi, pesci piccoli" (Calvino) **3**:96
"Pesn' torzhestruyushchey lyubvi" ("The Song of the Triumphant Love") (Turgenev) **7**:321, 323, 337-38, 362
"Peter" (Cather) **2**:96-7, 100, 105
"Peter Atherley's Ancestors" (Harte) **8**:215
"Peter Goldthwaite's Treasure" (Hawthorne) **3**:183, 185
"Le petit fût" (Maupassant) **1**:259, 284
"Petit soldat" (Maupassant) **1**:259
"La petite rogue" (Maupassant) **1**:275, 283, 288
"Petlistye ushi" ("Loopy Ears"; "Thieves' Ears") (Bunin) **5**:81, 101-04, 110-13
Petlistye ushi i drugie rasskazy (Bunin) **5**:101
"Petrified Man" (Welty) **1**:465, 467, 469, 471, 482, 490, 493-95, 497
"Petunias" (Walker) **5**:413
"La peur" (Maupassant) **1**:265, 288
"The Phantom of the Opera's Friend" (Barthelme) **2**:31, 35, 52, 54

"The Phantom 'Rickshaw" (Kipling) **5**:261, 265, 271-75, 297-99
The Phantom 'Rickshaw (Kipling) **5**:272-73
"Phantoms" (Turgenev) **7**:321, 323, 325, 334-35, 338
"The Pheasant" (Carver) **8**:53
"Philip and Margie" (Jewett) **6**:156
"A Philistine in Bohemia" (Henry) **5**:190, 196
"The Philosopher's Stone" (Andersen) **6**:26, 34
Philosophic Studies (Balzac)
See *Etudes philosophiques*
Philosophical Studies (Balzac)
See *Etudes philosophiques*
"The Piazza" (Melville) **1**:303
The Piazza Tales (Melville) **1**:295-97
"Pickman's Model" (Lovecraft) **3**:261-62
A Picture-Book without Pictures (Andersen) **6**:4, 15, 30
"The Picture in the House" (Lovecraft) **3**:262, 275-76, 292-95
"A Piece of Advice" (Singer) **3**:368
"A Piece of News" (Welty) **1**:468, 478, 487, 496
"A Piece of Steak" (London) **4**:253, 262-63, 291
"A Piece of String" (Maupassant)
See "La ficelle"
"Pierre Grassou" (Balzac) **5**:18
"Pierre Menard, Author of Don Quixote" (Borges)
See "Pierre Menard, autor del quijote"
"Pierre Menard, autor del quijote" ("Pierre Menard, Author of Don Quixote") (Borges) **4**:15, 26, 30, 34-5
"Pierrette" (Balzac) **5**:9
"Pierrot" (Maupassant) **1**:277-78
"The Pig" (Lessing) **6**:196-97, 212-17
"Pig Hoo-o-o-o-ey!" (Wodehouse) **2**:346, 348
"A Pinch of Salt" (Jewett) **6**:158
"The Pine Tree" (Andersen) **6**:12, 40-1
"The Pines" (Bunin) **5**:100
"The Pink Corner Man" (Borges)
See "Hombre de la esquina rosada"
"Pink May" (Bowen) **3**:31-2, 41
"The Pit and the Pendulum" (Poe) **1**:405-06
"The Pixy and the Grocer" (Andersen)
See "The Goblin at the Grocer's"
"Plagiarized Material" (Oates) **6**:237, 242
Plain Tales (Kipling)
See *Plain Tales from the Hills*
Plain Tales from the Hills (*Plain Tales*) (Kipling) **5**:273-74, 278, 288
"Planchette" (London) **4**:265, 294-95
"Plants and Girls" (Lessing) **6**:217
"The Plattner Story" (Wells) **6**:359, 364-66, 394, 405
The Plattner Story, and Others (Wells) **6**:366-67, 380, 388
Play Days (Jewett) **6**:165-66
"Pleasure" (Lessing) **6**:197
"The Pleasure-Cruise" (Kipling) **5**:284
"The Pleasures of Solitude" (Cheever) **1**:88
"The Ploughman" (Dinesen) **7**:177
"A Plunge into Real Estate" (Calvino)
See "La speculazione edilizia"
"Po' Sandy" (Chesnutt) **7**:5-7, 10, 13, 42
"The Poet" (Dinesen) **7**:167-68, 180, 203, 209
The Poet and the Lunatics (Chesterton) **1**:124-26, 132
"Poet and the Peasant" (Henry) **5**:194
"A Point at Issue" (Chopin) **8**:70, 73
"A Point of Law" (Faulkner) **1**:177
Pointed Firs (Jewett)
See *The Country of the Pointed Firs*
The Poisoned Kiss (Oates) **6**:236, 241-43
"Polar Bears and Others" (Boyle) **5**:54
"Polaris" (Lovecraft) **3**:288
"Polarities" (Atwood) **2**:2-5, 7-8, 10, 13-14
"The Policeman's Ball" (Barthelme) **2**:31, 45
"Pollock and the Porroh Man" (Wells) **6**:388
"Polydore" (Chopin) **8**:93
"Polzunkov" (Dostoevski) **2**:170, 192-93
"Pomegranate Seed" (Wharton) **6**:426-27, 431-32
"Un pomeriggio Adamo" (Calvino) **3**:97
The Ponder Heart (Welty) **1**:474, 477, 483, 494-95, 497
"The Pool" (Maugham) **8**:369-71
"The Poor Bird" (Andersen) **6**:4
"A Poor Girl" (Chopin) **8**:69
"Poor John" (Andersen) **6**:4
"Poor Little Black Fellow" (Hughes) **6**:118, 121-22, 134
"Poor Little Rich Town" (Vonnegut) **8**:436
"Poor Man's Pudding and Rich Man's Crumbs" ("Rich Man's Crumbs") (Melville) **1**:303, 323
"Poor People" (O'Flaherty) **6**:262, 264, 280, 283
"The Poor Thing" (Powers) **4**:368, 372-73
"Poor Thumbling" (Andersen) **6**:4, 7
"Pope Zeidlus" (Singer) **3**:364
"Popular Mechanics" (Carver) **8**:14, 18, 26, 30, 44-5
"Porcelain and Pink" (Fitzgerald) **6**:59
"Porcupines at the University" (Barthelme) **2**:56
"Porn" (Walker) **5**:412-14
"Le port" (Maupassant) **1**:264
"The Porter's Son" (Andersen) **6**:11-2
"Portrait" (Boyle) **5**:54
"The Portrait" (Gogol) **4**:102-03, 116, 122, 125
"The Portrait" (Wharton) **6**:414
Portrait of the Artist as a Young Dog (Thomas) **3**:394-97, 399, 402-04, 410-13
"Poseidon and Company" (Carver) **8**:50-1
"The Possessed" (Clarke) **3**:132, 135, 143-44, 148
"Posson Jone'" (Cable) **4**:48, 56, 58, 62, 64-5, 67, 77-80
"The Post" (Chekhov) **2**:130, 156
"The Post Office" (O'Flaherty)
See "Oifig an Phoist"
"Postcard" (Munro) **3**:322
"Posy" (Lavin) **4**:166
"The Pot-Boiler" (Wharton) **6**:435
"The Pot of Gold" (Cheever) **1**:89, 99
"The Pot of Gold" (O'Flaherty) **6**:271
"Potter" (Gallant) **5**:136-37
"The Powder Blue Dragon" (Vonnegut) **8**:432-33
"Powder-White Faces" (Hughes) **6**:118, 122
"Powerhouse" (Welty) **1**:466, 488, 494
"Powers" (Singer) **3**:360
"Pranzo con un pastore" (Calvino) **3**:97
"The Precipice" (Oates) **6**:247
"A Predicament" (Poe) **1**:405-06
"A Premature Autobiography" (Oates) **6**:232
"The Premature Burial" (Poe) **1**:407
"The Presence of Grace" (Powers) **4**:370, 381
The Presence of Grace (Powers) **4**:372-73
"Preservation" (Carver) **8**:26, 32
"The President" (Barthelme) **2**:31
"Press Clippings" (Cortázar)
See "Recortes de prensa"
"The Pretender" (O'Connor) **5**:386, 390
"Pretty Mouth and Green My Eyes" (Salinger) **2**:290, 293, 298, 300
"Prey" (O'Flaherty) **6**:281
"The Price of the Harness" (Crane) **7**:104
"The Pride of the Cities" (Henry) **5**:159, 194
"The Pride of the Village" (Irving) **2**:240-41, 245, 251
"The Priest of Shiga Temple and His Love" (Mishima) **4**:313, 315-17, 322-23
"Priestly Fellowship" (Powers) **4**:376, 381-82
"The Priestly Prerogative" (London) **4**:282
"Prima Belladonna" (Ballard) **1**:68
"Prime Leaf" (Warren) **4**:387-90, 393, 395, 400
"The Primrose Path" (Lawrence) **4**:234-37
"Un Prince de la Bohème" (Balzac) **5**:31-3
"Prince Hamlet of Shehrigov Province" (Turgenev)
See "A Russian Hamlet"
"Prince of Darkness" (Powers) **4**:370, 383
Prince of Darkness, and Other Stories (Powers) **4**:369-71
"The Princess" (Chekhov) **2**:130, 144
The Princess (Lawrence) **4**:238-40, 242
"The Princess and the Pea" ("The Princess on the Pea") (Andersen) **6**:7, 13, 18, 26, 30
"The Princess Baladina—Her Adventure" (Cather) **2**:100
"The Princess Bob and Her Friends" (Harte) **8**:216
"The Princess on the Pea" (Andersen)
See "The Princess and the Pea"
"Priscilla" (Calvino) **3**:95-6
"The Private Life" (James) **8**:280-81
"The Private Life of Mr. Bidwell" (Thurber) **1**:419
"Privilege" (Munro) **3**:334
"The Privy Counsilor" (Chekhov) **2**:130
"Problem No. 4" (Cheever) **1**:99
"The Problem of Art" (Gardner) **7**:226
"Problems of Adjustment in Survivors of Natural/Unnatural Disasters" (Oates) **6**:225
"The Procession of Life" (Hawthorne) **3**:181, 190
"The Procession of Life" (O'Connor) **5**:381, 393
"Prodigal Father" (Gallant) **5**:138
"The Prodigal Father" (London) **4**:256
"La prodigiosa tarde de Baltazar" ("Balthazar's Marvelous Afternoon") (García Márquez) **8**:185, 187-91
"The Prodigy" (Singer) **3**:374
"Professor" (Hughes) **6**:112, 118, 122, 131-32
"The Professor's Commencement" (Cather) **2**:99, 103, 113
"The Profile" (Cather) **2**:98, 103-04
"The Progress of Love" (Munro) **3**:347, 349
The Progress of Love (Munroe) **3**:346-48
"Prologue to an Adventure" (Thomas) **3**:399, 401
"Promenade" (Maupassant) **1**:260, 274
"The Promoter" (Dunbar) **8**:122, 147
"Proof of the Pudding" (Henry) **5**:165
"Propavšaja gramotax" ("The Lost Letter") (Gogol) **4**:117, 121
"Property" (Singer) **3**:374

Title Index

"The Prophet Peter" (Chesnutt) **7**:17
"The Prophetic Pictures" (Hawthorne) **3**:158, 181, 185-86, 190-91
"A Prospect of the Sea" (Thomas) **3**:394, 399, 401, 407-09
"Le protecteur" (Maupassant) **1**:280
"A Protégée of Jack Hamlin" (Harte) **8**:249
"The Prussian Officer" (Lawrence) **4**:197-99, 210, 212, 214-18, 235
The Prussian Officer, and Other Stories (Lawrence) **4**:196-98, 202, 230, 235-36
"Psyche" (Andersen) **6**:36, 38
"Psyche and the Pskyscraper" (Henry) **5**:162
"Psychiatric Services" (Oates) **6**:232
"Public Opinion" (O'Connor) **5**:374
"Publicity Campaign" (Clarke) **3**:134, 150
"Puck of Pook's Hill" (Kipling) **5**:272
Puck of Pook's Hill (Kipling) **5**:271, 273, 292
"Punin and Barbarin" (Turgenev) **7**:321, 323-24, 326, 337, 358, 360
"The Pupil" (James) **8**:291, 316
"The Pure Diamond Man" (Laurence) **7**:245
"The Purloined Letter" (Poe) **1**:387-88
"The Purple Hat" (Welty) **1**:468-69, 471, 479
"The Purple Pileus" (Wells) **6**:360, 383, 389, 404
"The Purple Wig" (Chesterton) **1**:131
"The Pursuer" (Cortázar)
See "El Perseguidor"
"A Pursuit Race" (Hemingway) **1**:216, 219
"Purun Bhagat" (Kipling)
See "The Miracle of Purun Bhagat"
"Put Yourself in My Shoes" (Carver) **8**:9, 13, 20, 46, 49
"Pyetushkov" (Turgenev) **7**:320
"Pytor Petrovich Karataev" (Turgenev) **7**:313
"Quanto scommettiamo" (Calvino) **3**:92
"que sepa abrir la puerta para ir a jugar" ("May you learn to open the door to go out to play") (Cortázar) **7**:95
"Queen Louisa" (Gardner) **7**:233
"Queen of the Night" (Oates) **6**:246
"The Queen's Twin" (Jewett) **6**:152
"The Queer Feet" (Chesterton) **1**:119, 125, 127, 130
"A Queer Heart" (Bowen) **3**:33, 41, 43, 49-50
"The Queer Streak" (Munro) **3**:347
Queremos tanto a Glenda (*We Love Glenda So Much*) (Cortázar) **7**:64, 68, 71-2, 79, 90
"The Quest of Iranon" (Lovecraft) **3**:274
"A Question of Re-Entry" (Ballard) **1**:68
"Qui sait?" (Maupassant) **1**:273
"The Quicksand" (Wharton) **6**:424
"A Quiet Spot" (Turgenev) **7**:328
Quite Early One Morning (Thomas) **3**:392
"The Rabbit" (Barnes) **3**:6-7, 22-4
"The Rabbit-Pen" (Anderson) **1**:52
"The Rabbits Who Caused All the Trouble" (Thurber) **1**:431
"The Race Question" (Dunbar) **8**:122, 147
"Rags Martin-Jones and the Pr-nce of W-les" (Fitzgerald) **6**:46, 56
"Raid" (Faulkner) **1**:170
"Railway Accident" (Mann) **5**:323-24, 330, 348-50
"Rain" (Maugham) **8**:356-61, 371, 373, 375, 377, 381-84
"The Rain Child" (Laurence) **7**:246, 248, 250, 253, 272
"Raise High the Roofbeam, Carpenters" (Salinger) **2**:291-93, 298, 307, 314
"Raise High the Roofbeam, Carpenters and Seymour: An Introduction" (Salinger) **2**:318
"Ralph Ringwood" (Irving) **2**:241
"A Ramble Among the Hills" (Irving) **2**:266
"The Ransom of Red Chief" (Henry) **5**:193
"Rape Fantasies" (Atwood) **2**:3-4, 6-8, 10-12
"Rappaccini's Daughter" (Hawthorne) **3**:159, 171, 173-74, 179-80, 189, 191-92
"Raspberry Spring" (Turgenev) **7**:341
"Rasskaz ottsa Aleksaya" ("Father Alexey's Story"; "The Story of Father Alexis") (Turgenev) **7**:324, 338, 361-62
"The Rats in the Walls" (Lovecraft) **3**:258, 262, 267, 269, 275, 277
"Rattlesnake Creek" (Cather) **2**:106
"The Ravages of Spring" (Gardner) **7**:214-15, 218, 222, 228-29, 232-33
"The Raven" (Bunin)
See "Voron"
"Raw Materials" (Atwood) **2**:17-19
"Rawdon's Roof" (Lawrence) **4**:220
Reach for Tomorrow (Clarke) **3**:124, 129
"Reading a Wave" (Calvino) **3**:113
"A Real Discovery" (Chesterton) **1**:140
"The Real Thing" (James) **8**:296-98, 302
"Really, Doesn't Crime Pay?" (Walker) **5**:401, 405, 408-09, 419
"The Reaping Race" (O'Flaherty) **6**:264, 281
"Recent Photograph" (Bowen) **3**:40
"The Reckoning" (Wharton) **6**:425-26
"Recollections of the Gas Buggy" (Thurber) **1**:431
"The Record of Badalia Herodsfoot" (Kipling) **5**:261
"Recortes de prensa" ("Press Clippings") (Cortázar) **7**:69, 71, 83, 87, 91
"The Recovery" (Chopin) **8**:99
"The Recovery" (Wharton) **6**:414, 420, 423, 428-29
"The Recrudescence of Imray" (Kipling)
See "The Return of Imray"
"Red" (Maugham) **8**:370
"Red Barbara" (O'Flaherty) **6**:260, 262, 271, 277-78, 285
"Red-Headed Baby" (Hughes) **6**:109, 118-19, 121, 123-25, 129-30, 141
"The Red Inn" (Balzac) **5**:18
"Red Leaves" (Faulkner) **1**:147, 162, 168-70, 180
"The Red Moon of Meru" (Chesterton) **1**:129
"The Red Petticoat" (O'Flaherty) **6**:271
"The Red Room" (Wells) **6**:366, 383, 388
"The Red Shoes" (Andersen) **6**:4, 7, 34, 37-8
"Redemption" (Gardner) **7**:224-27, 235-36, 238, 240-41
"Reduced" (Bowen) **3**:33
"Reena" (Marshall) **3**:300, 303, 308, 310, 313, 315, 317
Reena, and Other Stories (Merle: A Novella, and Other Stories) (Marshall) **3**:*313, 315-17*
"The Reference" (Barthelme) **2**:55
"The Refuge of the Derelicts" (Twain) **6**:339
"Regret" (Chopin) **8**:72-3, 84, 93, 111
"The Reincarnation of Smith" (Harte) **8**:254
"Rejuvenation through Joy" (Hughes) **6**:109, 128
"Relato con un fondo de agua" (Cortázar) **7**:58
Los Relatos (Cortázar) **7**:91
"The Reluctant Orchid" (Clarke) **3**:133-34
"Remainders at Bouselham" (Bowles) **3**:66
"The Remarkable Case of Davidson's Eyes" (Wells) **6**:364-66, 376, 393-95, 405
"The Rembrandt" (Wharton) **6**:414
"The Remission" (Gallant) **5**:135-38
"Remnants" (Singer) **3**:385, 387
"Le remplacant" (Maupassant) **1**:256
"Rena Walden" (Chesnutt) **7**:19, 21, 33, 35
"Renner" (Powers) **4**:368, 370, 372-73
"Renunciation" (Barnes) **3**:16
"A Report" (Gållant) **5**:138
"Report on the Barnhouse Effect" (Vonnegut) **8**:428-29
"Report on the Threatened City" (Lessing) **6**:188
"A Report to an Academy" (Kafka) **5**:215-16, 220, 231
"The Reptile Enclosure" (Ballard) **1**:68-9
"The Requiem" (Chekhov) **2**:155
"Requiescat" (Bowen) **3**:40
"Le réquisitionnaire" (Balzac) **5**:16
"Rescue Party" (Clarke) **3**:124-26, 135-36, 148-49
"Respectability" (Anderson) **1**:18, 53, 58
"A Respectable Woman" (Chopin) **8**:72, 96-7, 110, 113
"The Resplendent Quetzal" (Atwood) **2**:3, 5, 7, 10-11, 15-16, 19, 22
"Rest Cure" (Boyle) **5**:55
"The Resurrection of Father Brown" (Chesterton) **1**:129, 137-38
"Le retour" (Maupassant) **1**:285
"Retreat" (Faulkner) **1**:170-71
"Retreat from Earth" (Clarke) **3**:148
"A Retrieved Reformation" (Henry) **5**:158, 170, 193
"The Return" (Anderson) **1**:31, 39, 50
"The Return" (Bowen) **3**:40, 53
"The Return of Imray" ("The Recrudescence of Imray") (Kipling) **5**:262, 273-75, 285
"Return of the Native" (Thurber) **1**:424
"Return Trip Tango" (Cortázar) **7**:69
"Reunion" (Cheever) **1**:100
"Reunion" (Clarke) **3**:133
"Reunión" ("The Meeting") (Cortázar) **7**:83, 89-90
"Reunión con un círculo rojo" (Cortázar) **7**:85
"Rêveil" (Maupassant) **1**:274
"Revelation" (O'Connor) **1**:341-42, 344
"Revenge" (Balzac)
See "La vendetta revenge"
"The Revenge" (Gogol) **4**:85
"The Revenge of Hannah Kemhuff" (Walker) **5**:401, 403, 405-06
"Revenge of Truth" (Dinesen) **7**:177, 180
"The Reversed Man" (Clarke)
See "Technical Error"
"The Revolt of 'Mother'" (Freeman) **1**:192, 196-97, 200
"The Revolutionist" (Hemingway) **1**:244
Rewards and Fairies (Kipling) **5**:273, 283, 285, 292
"Rhobert" (Toomer) **1**:445, 450, 458-59
"The Rich Boy" (Fitzgerald) **6**:46-7, 76, 86-9, 95, 100-03
"Rich Man's Crumbs" (Melville)
See "Poor Man's Pudding and Rich Man's Crumbs"
"A Ride with Olympy" (Thurber) **1**:431
"The Right Eye of the Commander" (Harte) **8**:245-46
"Rikki-Tikki-Tavi" (Kipling) **5**:293

"El río" ("The River") (Cortázar) **7**:59, 70, 79, 81-3
"Rip Van Winkle" (Irving) **2**:239-51, 253, 256-60, 262-64
"Ripe Figs" (Chopin) **8**:93
"The Rise of Capitalism" (Barthelme) **2**:37, 39, 47
"The River" (Cortázar)
See "El río"
"The River" (O'Connor) **1**:344-45, 356
"River Rising" (Oates) **6**:227-28, 230, 249-50
"The Road to the Sea" (Clarke) **3**:135-36
"Roads of Destiny" (Henry) **5**:163
"The Roads Round Pisa" (Dinesen) **7**:164, 167-68, 171, 175, 179-80, 182, 187, 198, 208
The Robber Bridegroom (Welty) **1**:471-72, 483, 489-90, 496
"Robert Kennedy Saved from Drowning" (Barthelme) **2**:31, 36, 42, 46-7
"The Robin's House" (Barnes) **3**:12
"Rock, Church" (Hughes) **6**:133
"The Rockfish" (O'Flaherty) **6**:260-61, 267-69, 280
"The Rocking-Horse Winner" (Lawrence) **4**:200-01, 206, 212, 221, 229-30, 233, 238
"Roger Melvin's Burial" (Hawthorne) **3**:157, 164, 166-67, 171, 185-86, 189
Rolling All the Time (Ballard) **1**:72
"Roman Fever" (Wharton) **6**:423-24
"The Romance of Madrono Hollow" (Harte) **8**:225
"The Romance of the Busy Broker" (Henry) **5**:158, 181-82, 194
Romans et contes philosophiques (*Contes philosophiques*) (Balzac) **5**:22-3, 31
"The Romantic Adventures of a Milkmaid" (Hardy) **2**:211, 215-18, 221, 224
"A Romantic Young Lady" (Maugham) **8**:380
"Rome" (Gogol) **4**:83
"A Room" (Lessing) **6**:200-01
"Rope" (Porter) **4**:327-28, 339-40, 342
"Rosalie Prudent" (Maupassant) **1**:286
"The Rose-Elf" (Andersen) **6**:12, 30
"A Rose for Emily" (Faulkner) **1**:147-52, 158, 162, 165, 180-81
"The Rose of Dixie" (Henry) **5**:159, 171
"A Rose of Glenbogie" (Harte) **8**:217, 222, 252
"The Rose of Jutland" (Dinesen) **7**:169
"The Rose of Tuolumne" (Harte) **8**:223, 233
"Roselily" (Walker) **5**:401-02, 405, 408-09
"Rosendo's Tale" (Borges) **4**:18, 20
"Le rosier de Madame Husson" (Maupassant) **1**:280
"Rothschild's Fiddle" (Chekhov)
See "Rothschild's Violin"
"Rothschild's Violin" ("Rothschild's Fiddle") (Chekhov) **2**:157-58
"Rouge High" (Hughes) **6**:112, 118
"The Rough Crossing" (Fitzgerald) **6**:61, 100, 103-04
"La rouille" (Maupassant) **1**:256, 272, 274
"The Round Dozen" (Maugham) **8**:364, 378-79
"The Rout of the White Hussars" (Kipling) **5**:260
"A Rude Awakening" (Chopin) **8**:88, 103
"La ruinas circulares" (*The Circular Ruins*) (Borges) **4**:5, 10, 18-19, 28-9, 33, 35-6
"Runaways" (Vonnegut) **8**:433
"Rural Life in England" (Irving) **2**:244
"Rus in Urbe" (Henry) **5**:191
"Rusia" ("Rusya") (Bunin) **5**:113
"A Russian Hamlet" ("Prince Hamlet of Shehrigov Province") (Turgenev) **7**:316, 344
"Rusya" (Bunin)
See "Rusia"
"Ruthie and Edie" (Paley) **8**:411
"Sabbath in Gehenna" (Singer) **3**:389
"Sabbath in Portugal" (Singer) **3**:376
"Sacks" (Carver) **8**:14-15, 18, 20-1, 37-8
"The Sacred Marriage" (Oates) **6**:254
"A Sacrifice Hit" (Henry) **5**:184
"The Sad Horn Blowers" (Anderson) **1**:23, 27, 30
Sadness (Barthelme) **2**:37-40, 46-7, 49
"The Sailor and the Steward" (Hughes) **6**:131
"Sailor Ashore" (Hughes) **6**:122, 132
"The Sailor Boy's Tale" (Dinesen) **7**:199
"St. John's Eve" (Gogol)
See "Večer nakanune Ivana Kupala"
St. Mawr (Lawrence) **4**:205, 211-12, 238-29, 241-42
"The Salad of Colonel Cray" (Chesterton) **1**:131
Salmagundi (Irving) **2**:241, 250-53
"Salome Müller, the White Slave" (Cable) **4**:49, 59
"The Salt Garden" (Atwood) **2**:21
"La salud de los enfermos" (Cortázar) **7**:61
"Salvatore" (Maugham) **8**:366
"Samson and Delilah" (Lawrence) **4**:202, 232-36
"Samuel" (London) **4**:254-55
"Sanatorium" (Maugham) **8**:369, 380
"The Sand Castle" (Lavin) **4**:178-81
"The Sandman" (Andersen)
See "Ole Luköie"
"The Sandman" (Barthelme) **2**:52
"A Sappho of Green Springs" (Harte) **8**:247-48, 255
"Sarah" (Lavin) **4**:167, 184
"Saratoga Rain" (Hughes) **6**:112
"Sarrasine" (Balzac) **5**:33-4
"Satarsa" (Cortázar) **7**:91
"Saturday" (Gallant) **5**:141
"Saturn Rising" (Clarke) **3**:132
"Saved from the Dogs" (Hughes) **6**:121
"The Scandal Detectives" (Fitzgerald) **6**:49
The Scandal of Father Brown (Chesterton) **1**:128, 139
"The Scapegoat" (Dunbar) **8**:122, 129, 132, 137, 141-43
"Scarlet Ibis" (Atwood) **2**:18, 22
"An Scáthán" (O'Flaherty) **6**:289
Scènes de la vie de campagne (Balzac) **5**:9
Scènes de la vie de province (*Scenes of Provincial Life; Scenes of Country Life*) (Balzac) **5**:3, 5, 7-9, 13
Scènes de la vie militaire (*Scenes of Military Life*) (Balzac) **5**:7-9
Scènes de la vie Parisienne (*Scenes of Parisian Life*) (Balzac) **5**:3, 5, 7-9
Scènes de la vie politique (*Scenes of Political Life*) (Balzac) **5**:7-9, 13
Scènes de la vie privée (*Scenes of Private Life*) (Balzac) **5**:3-4, 7, 9, 21-2, 25, 28-31
Scenes from Russian Life (Turgenev)
See *Sportsman's Sketches*
Scenes of Country Life (Balzac)
See *Scènes de la vie de province*
Scenes of Military Life (Balzac)
See *Scènes de la vie militaire*
Scenes of Parisian Life (Balzac)
See *Scènes de la vie Parisienne*
Scenes of Political Life (Balzac)
See *Scènes de la vie politique*
Scenes of Private Life (Balzac)
See *Scènes de la vie privée*
Scenes of Provincial Life (Balzac)
See *Scènes de la vie de province*
"Scholar with a Hole in his Memory" (Cortázar) **7**:59
"The School" (Barthelme) **2**:53
"The School by Night" (Cortázar)
See "La escuela de noche"
"The School for Witches" (Thomas) **3**:399, 408-09
"The Schoolmistress" (Chekhov) **2**:128
"Schwallinger's Philanthropy" (Dunbar) **8**:122, 132, 137, 147
"The Scorn of Women" (London) **4**:286
"The Scorpion" (Bowles) **3**:59, 61, 68, 70-2, 79
"A Scrap and a Sketch" (Chopin) **8**:98
"The Scream" (Oates) **6**:248-49
"The Sculptor's Funeral" (Cather) **2**:90, 94-5, 98, 100, 103, 105
"Scylla and Charybdis" (Lavin) **4**:183
"Sea Constables" (Kipling) **5**:270
"The Sea-Farmer" (London) **4**:254
"The Sea of Hesitation" (Barthelme) **2**:51
"The Sea of Lost Time" (García Márquez)
See "El mar del tiempo perdido"
"The Sea Raiders" (Wells) **6**:361, 365, 367, 389, 393, 406
"The Seal" (O'Flaherty) **6**:282
"The Séance" (Singer) **3**:369
The Séance, and Other Stories (Singer) **3**:362, 369-70, 373
"The Searchlight" (Woolf) **7**:377, 390, 392, 396
"A Seashore Drama" (Balzac) **5**:11-13
"The Seaside Houses" (Cheever) **1**:100, 105
"The Season of Divorce" (Cheever) **1**:99
"Season of the Hand" (Cortázar)
See "Estación de la mano"
"The Secession" (Bowen) **3**:40
"Second Best" (Lawrence) **4**:197
"Second Dawn" (Clarke) **3**:131, 135, 144, 150
"Second Hand" (Lavin) **4**:167, 183
"The Second Hut" (Lessing) **6**:186, 189, 191
The Second Jungle Book (Kipling) **5**:287, 295
"Second Time Around" (Cortázar)
See "Segunda vez"
"Second Trip" (Cortázar)
See "Segundo viaje"
"The Secret" (Singer) **3**:385-86
"The Secret Garden" (Chesterton) **1**:119, 134, 137
"The Secret Life of Walter Mitty" (Thurber) **1**:420, 422, 424, 427, 431-32, 435
"The Secret Miracle" (Borges) **4**:29-30, 37
"The Secret Mirror" (Oates) **6**:237
The Secret of Father Brown (Chesterton) **1**:128, 131
"The Secret of Flambeau" (Chesterton) **1**:126
"A Secret of Telegraph Hill" (Harte) **8**:233
"Secret Weapons" (Cortázar)
See "La armas secretas"
Secret Weapons (Cortázar)
See *Las Armas Secretas*
"Les secrets de la Princesse de Cadignan" (Balzac) **5**:31

Title Index

"See the Moon?" (Barthelme) **2**:35, 42-3, 53
"The Seed of Faith" (Wharton) **6**:422
"Seeds" (Anderson) **1**:20, 27, 46
"Un segno" (Calvino) **3**:92
"Segunda vez" ("Second Time Around") (Cortázar) **7**:83-5, 90-1
"Segundo viaje" ("Second Trip") (Cortázar) **7**:89
Seis problemas para don Isidro Parodi (Borges) **4**:25
"A Select Party" (Hawthorne) **3**:181
Selected Stories (Lavin) **4**:163, 186
Selected Works of Djuna Barnes (Barnes) **3**:5, 7, 13, 20, 22
Selected Writings of Truman Capote (Capote) **2**:72, 74
"A Self-Made Man" (Crane) **7**:108-09
"Semper Idem" (London) **4**:263
"Senility" (Lavin) **4**:182
"Señor Ong and Señor Ha" (Bowles) **3**:59, 61, 69, 79
"A Sense of Responsibility" (O'Connor) **5**:372
"The Sensible Thing" (Fitzgerald) **6**:46
"The Sentence" (Barthelme) **2**:38, 41, 44
"Sentiment" (Parker) **2**:273-74, 280, 285
"A Sentimental Education" (Oates) **6**:246-47
A Sentimental Education (Oates) **6**:246-47
"Sentimental Journey" (Oates) **6**:251-52
"A Sentimental Soul" (Chopin) **8**:72, 95, 108, 110, 112
"The Sentimentality of William Tavener" (Cather) **2**:101
"The Sentinel" (Clarke) **3**:124, 127, 135, 145-46, 149-50
"The Sentry" (O'Connor) **5**:369, 372
"Senza colori" (Calvino) **3**:92
"September Dawn" (O'Connor) **5**:385, 391-92
"The Sergeant" (Barthelme) **2**:53
"Sergeant Prishibeev" (Chekhov) **2**:155
"A Serious Talk" (Carver) **8**:14, 18-19, 53
"The Serpent of Fire" (Bunin) **5**:87
"A Service of Love" (Henry) **5**:171, 185
A Set of Variations (O'Connor) **5**:373-74, 378
"A Set of Variations on a Borrowed Theme" (O'Connor) **5**:373
"The Seven Bridges" (Mishima) **4**:313, 315, 317, 322
Seven Gothic Tales (Dinesen) **7**:161, 166, 170, 172, 175, 180, 191, 196-98, 200-03, 208-09
"Seventh Street" (Toomer) **1**:443, 450, 458
"Sex Ex Machina" (Thurber) **1**:431
"The Sexes" (Parker) **2**:273, 281, 283
"Seymour: An Introduction" (Salinger) **2**:296, 307-09
"The Shades of Spring" (Lawrence) **4**:197-98, 219
"The Shadow" (Andersen) **6**:7, 24, 30, 35, 41
"Shadow, a Parable" (Poe) **1**:379
"The Shadow of a Crib" (Singer) **3**:361
"The Shadow of the Shark" (Chesterton) **1**:124
"The Shadow out of Time" (Lovecraft) **3**:258-61, 263, 266, 268, 271-72, 274-75, 279, 290
"The Shadow over Innsmouth" (Lovecraft) **3**:259. 263, 271-77, 291
"The Shadowy Third" (Bowen) **3**:54
"The Shaker Bridal" (Hawthorne) **3**:185-86
"Shame" (Crane) **7**:104
"A Shameful Affair" (Chopin) **8**:71, 86
"The Shape of the Sword" (Borges)
See "La forma de la espada"
"The Shape of Things" (Capote) **2**:65
"She Was Good for Nothing" (Andersen)
See "Good-for-Nothing"
"She Was No Good" (Andersen)
See "Good-for-Nothing"
"The Shepherdess and the Chimney Sweep" (Andersen) **6**:6, 18, 36
"The Shepherd's Pipe" (Chekhov) **2**:130, 156
"The Sheriff of Kona" (London) **4**:269
"The Sheriff's Children" (Chesnutt) **7**:13, 16, 18-19, 21-6, 29, 32-5, 37
"The Shilling" (O'Flaherty) **6**:271
"Shin Bones" (London) **4**:256, 270
"Shingles for the Lord" (Faulkner) **1**:178
"The Shining Houses" (Munro) **3**:321, 336, 343
"The Shining Ones" (Clarke) **3**:132
"The Ship That Found Herself" (Kipling) **5**:279
"A Shipload of Crabs" (Calvino) **3**:116
"The Shipwrecked Buttons" (Jewett) **6**:157
"The Shirt Collar" (Andersen) **6**:30, 32, 35
"The Shocks of Doom" (Henry) **5**:182, 184
"Shoes: An International Episode" (Bowen) **3**:30, 49
"The Shooting of the Cabinet Ministers" (Hemingway) **1**:208, 238
"The Shooting Party" (Woolf) **7**:375, 390, 392
"The Shore and the Sea" (Thurber) **1**:430
"The Shore House" (Jewett) **6**:150, 157, 167, 170
"Short Feature" (Cortázar)
See "Cortísimo metraje"
"Short Friday" (Singer) **3**:355, 360, 363-64, 383
Short Friday, and Other Stories (Singer) **3**:357, 370, 373, 376
"The Short Happy Life of Francis Macomber" (Hemingway) **1**:217, 230, 232, 234
The Short Stories of Thomas Hardy (Hardy) **2**:212
"A Short Trip Home" (Fitzgerald) **6**:47-8, 60, 62
"A Shower of Gold" (Barthelme) **2**:27-8, 38, 42, 52, 55
"Shower of Gold" (Welty) **1**:483, 485, 493
"The Shrine" (Lavin) **4**:183
The Shrine, and Other Stories (Lavin) **4**:181
"The Shunned House" (Lovecraft) **3**:262, 276, 282
"Shut a Final Door" (Capote) **2**:61-2, 64, 66, 69, 72-6, 83
"A Sick Collier" (Lawrence) **4**:202
"The Sickness of Lone Chief" (London) **4**:287
"Siestas" (Cortázar) **7**:57
"'Sieur George" (Cable) **4**:50, 52, 65-7
"A Sign in Space" (Calvino)
See "Sign of Space"
"Sign of Space" ("A Sign in Space") (Calvino) **3**:104, 109
"The Sign of the Broken Sword" ("Broken Sword") (Chesterton) **1**:127, 136-37, 142
"Significant Moments in the Life of My Mother" (Atwood) **2**:17, 21-3
"Silas Jackson" (Dunbar) **8**:122, 128, 133, 135, 147
"Silence, a Fable" (Poe) **1**:379
"Silence Please" (Clarke) **3**:133
"The Silences of Mr. Palomar" (Calvino) **3**:113
"Silent Samuel" (Dunbar) **8**:122, 128
"The Silver Key" (Lovecraft) **3**:258, 262, 276, 286
"Silvia" (Cortázar) **7**:57
"Simmering" (Atwood) **2**:19-20
"A Simple Enquiry" (Hemingway) **1**:216
"Simple Simon" (Andersen) **6**:30
Simple Speaks His Mind (Hughes) **6**:110-11, 113, 137
Simple Stakes a Claim (Hughes) **6**:143
Simple Takes a Wife (Hughes) **6**:113
"Simulacra" (Cortázar)
See "Simulacros"
"Simulacros" ("Simulacra") (Cortázar) **7**:92
"The Sin Eater" (Atwood) **2**:15, 18, 22
"The Sing-Song of Old Man Kangaroo" (Kipling) **5**:287
"The Singers" (Turgenev) **7**:316
"A Singer's Romance" (Cather) **2**:101
"A Single Lady" (Lavin) **4**:166
A Single Lady, and Other Stories (Lavin) **4**:164
"The Sinner" (O'Flaherty) **6**:277, 280
"Sir Rabbit" (Welty) **1**:474, 480, 486, 495
"Sis' Becky's Pickaninny" (Chesnutt) **7**:7, 10, 40, 42
"Sister Liddy" (Freeman) **1**:199-200
"Sister Peacham's Turn" (Jewett) **6**:156
"The Sisters" (Joyce) **3**:201, 205-06, 208, 211-12, 216-17, 225, 230, 232, 234-35, 237, 244-47, 249
"The Sisters" (O'Connor) **5**:392
"Siwash" (London) **4**:286
Six Stories Written in the First Person Singular (Maugham) **8**:356, 364, 378
Six Trees (Freeman) **1**:194
"Sixty Acres" (Carver) **8**:3, 10, 34
Sixty Stories (Barthelme) **2**:46, 51, 56
The Sketch Book (Irving)
See *The Sketch Book of Geoffrey Crayon, Gent.*
The Sketch Book of Geoffrey Crayon, Gent. (*The Sketch Book*) (Irving) **2**:238-46, 250-55, 257-59, 262, 265, 267
"Sketches from Memory" (Hawthorne) **3**:157
"A Sketching Trip" (Welty) **1**:480
"Skirmish at Sartoris" (Faulkner) **1**:170-71
"The Slashers" (Kipling) **5**:277-78
"Slater's Pins Have No Points" (Woolf)
See "Moments of Being:"Slater's Pins Have No Points'"
"The Slaughterer" (Singer) **3**:358, 384
"Slave on the Block" (Hughes) **6**:119, 121-22, 128, 134
"Sleeping Beauty" (Clarke) **3**:134
"Sleeping like Dogs" (Calvino) **3**:112
"Sleepy" (Chekhov) **2**:130, 146-49
"Slice Him Down" (Hughes) **6**:118, 132
"A Slice of Life" (Wodehouse) **2**:347
"A Slip under the Microscope" (Wells) **6**:360, 381, 384, 393
"Small Avalanches" (Oates) **6**:231
"A Small Bequest" (Lavin) **4**:167
"A Small, Good Thing" (Carver) **8**:19-26, 30, 39, 56-9
"A Small Paradise" (Cortázar)
See "Un pequeño paraíso"
"The Smile" (Ballard) **1**:79
"Smile" (Lawrence) **4**:219
"The Smilers" (Fitzgerald) **6**:56-7

Smog (Calvino)
See *La nuvola di smog*
"Smoke" (Barnes) **3**:18
"Smoke" (Faulkner) **1**:178-80
Smoke, and Other Early Stories (Barnes) **3**:17, 19
Smoke Bellew Tales (London) **4**:289
The Smoking Mountain: Stories of Postwar Germany (Boyle) **5**:56
"The Smuggler" (Singer) **3**:389
"The Snail and the Rose-Tree" (Andersen) **6**:7
"The Sniper" (O'Flaherty) **6**:261, 280
"A Snobbish Story" (Fitzgerald) **6**:50
"Snow Bound at the Eagle's" (Harte) **8**:254
"The Snow Image" (Hawthorne) **3**:159, 177, 183
The Snow Image, and Other Twice-Told Tales (Hawthorne) **3**:184
"The Snow Queen, a Folk Tale in Seven Parts" (Andersen) **6**:4, 6-8, 13, 18-20, 24-8, 30, 36-7, 40
"The Snows of Kilimanjaro" (Hemingway) **1**:214-15, 217-18, 229, 234
"So Much Water So Close to Home" (Carver) **8**:5, 14-15, 19, 21, 29, 42, 53, 57-60
"The Social Triangle" (Henry) **5**:198
"A Society" (Woolf) **7**:368, 371, 374, 377, 392-93, 396, 400-02, 404
"Les soeurs Rondoli" (Maupassant) **1**:256, 259, 270, 274, 283, 288
"The Soft Moon" (Calvino) **3**:94, 108-09
"Un soir" (Maupassant) **1**:274, 280
"Soldier's Home" (Hemingway) **1**:208, 244
"Soldiers of the Republic" (Parker) **2**:276, 281-82
"Soldiers Three" (Kipling) **5**:269
Soldiers Three (Kipling) **5**:259
"Solid Objects" (Woolf) **7**:373, 377, 387, 397
"The Solitary" ("Gregory's Island") (Cable) **4**:50, 72-4
"A Solitary" (Freeman) **1**:197
"Solitude" (Maupassant) **1**:262
"Solnechnyy udar" ("Sunstroke") (Bunin) **5**:91, 93, 104-06, 114, 119
"Some Facts for Understanding the Perkians" (Cortázar)
See "Datos para entender a los perqueos"
"Some Get Wasted" (Marshall) **3**:303
Some People, Places, and Things That Will Not Appear in My Next Novel (Cheever) **1**:92, 100
"Some Words with a Mummy" (Poe) **1**:402
"Someone Has Disturbed the Roses" (García Márquez)
See "Alguien desordena estas rosas"
Someone Walking Around (Cortázar)
See *Alquien que anda por ahí*
"Someone Walking Around" (Cortázar)
See "Alquien que anda por ahí"
Something in Common, and Other Stories (Hughes) **6**:122-23, 127, 133
Something I've Been Meaning to Tell You (Munro) **3**:328, 331, 335, 339, 346
"Something Squishy" (Wodehouse) **2**:355-56
"Something to Write About" (Andersen) **6**:36
"Somewhere Else" (Paley) **8**:420
"The Son" (Bunin) **5**:81, 103-04, 106, 108-10
"Son" ("The Dream") (Turgenev) **7**:321, 325-28, 338, 361
"The Son From America" (Singer) **3**:374
"The Son of God and His Sorrow" (Oates) **6**:237
"A Son of the Celestial" (Cather) **2**:100, 102
"A Son of the Sun" (London) **4**:259
A Son of the Sun (London) **4**:265
"The Son of the Wolf" (London) **4**:267
The Son of the Wolf: Tales of the Far North (London) **4**:250-52, 258, 264, 278-79, 281-82, 284-87, 290
"The Song of the Flying Fish" (Chesterton) **1**:129, 138
"Song of the Shirt, 1941" (Parker) **2**:277, 280-81, 285-86
"The Song of the Triumphant Love" (Turgenev)
See "Pesn' torzhestruyushchey lyubvi"
"Song without Words" (O'Connor) **5**:365, 371, 383, 398
"Songs My Father Sang Me" (Bowen) **3**:41
"The Songs of Distant Earth" (Clarke) **3**:135-36
"The Son's Veto" (Hardy) **2**:215-16, 223
"Sophistication" (Anderson) **1**:30, 42, 44-5
"The Sorcerer's Apprentice" (O'Connor) **5**:371-72
"Sorcières espagnoles" (Mérimée) **7**:283
"Soročinskaja jamarka" ("The Fair at Sorotchintsy") (Gogol) **4**:85, 118, 121
"Sorrow" (Chekhov) **2**:128
"Sorrow-Acre" (Dinesen) **7**:164, 167, 170-71, 174, 177, 185-86, 188-90, 196, 205-08
"The Sorrows of Gin" (Cheever) **1**:100
"Sosny" (Bunin) **5**:98-9
Soul Clap Hands and Sing (Marshall) **3**:299-304, 307-08, 316-17
"A Soulless Corporation" (Chesnutt) **7**:14
"Souls Belated" (Wharton) **6**:423-25
"The Souls in Purgatory" (Mérimée)
See "Les âmes du purgatoire"
"The Sound of the Singing" (Laurence) **7**:254, 259-60, 268
"Sound Sweep" (Ballard) **1**:68
"Soup on a Sausage Peg" (Andersen) **6**:13-4
"The Source" (Porter) **4**:339, 352, 363
"The South" (Borges) **4**:31
"South of the Slot" (London) **4**:254
South Sea Tales (London) **4**:266, 283
"Spanish Blood" (Hughes) **6**:118, 132
"The Spanish Lady" (Munro) **3**:339
"A Spanish Priest" (Maugham) **8**:380
The Spark (The 'Sixties) (Wharton) **6**:439-40
"Speck's Idea" (Gallant) **5**:147
"The Spectacles" (Poe) **1**:407-08
"The Spectre Bridegroom" (Irving) **2**:240-41, 246, 251, 255-56
"The Speculation of the Building Constructors" (Calvino)
See "La speculazione edilizia"
"La speculazione edilizia" ("A Plunge into Real Estate"; "The Speculation of the Building Constructors") (Calvino) **3**:91, 111-12, 117-18
"Spelling" (Munro) **3**:339
"The Sphynx Apple" (Henry) **5**:162
Spillway (Barnes) **3**:4-5, 12-14, 16, 22
"Spillway" ("Beyond the End") (Barnes) **3**:8-10, 24
"The Spinoza of Market Street" (Singer) **3**:361, 368, 375, 384
The Spinoza of Market Street, and Other Stories (Singer) **3**:370
"The Spiral" (Calvino)
See "La spirale"
"La spirale" ("The Spiral") (Calvino) **3**:92, 103-04, 108-09
"Sport: The Kill" (O'Flaherty) **6**:261
The Sportsman's Sketches (Turgenev)
See *Sportsman's Sketches*
Sportsman's Sketches (*The Sportsman's Sketches*; *Scenes from Russian Life*; *The Memoirs of a Sportsman*; *Notes of a Hunter*) (Turgenev) **7**:313-15, 321, 323, 337, 341-46, 359, 362-63
"Spotted Horses" (Faulkner) **1**:167, 177
"A Spring Evening" (Bunin) **5**:90, 92, 102
Spring Freshets (Turgenev)
See *The Torrents of Spring*
"The Spring Running" (Kipling) **5**:287
"Spring Song of the Frogs" (Atwood) **2**:22
"Spring Sowing" (O'Flaherty) **6**:260-62, 264, 269, 271, 273, 281, 283
Spring Sowing (O'Flaherty) **6**:261-65, 278, 281, 283
"A Spring Sunday" (Jewett) **6**:156-57
Spring-Torrents (Turgenev)
See *The Torrents of Spring*
"A Sprinkle of Comedy" (Barnes) **3**:18
"Spunk" (Hurston) **4**:135-37, 150, 152
Spunk: The Selected Stories of Zora Neale Hurston (Hurston) **4**:155
"La srta. Cora" (Cortázar) **7**:62
"The Stage Coach" (Irving) **2**:245
"A Stage Tavern" (Jewett) **6**:159
Stalky and Co. (Kipling) **5**:277-78, 282
"The Standard of Living" (Parker) **2**:278, 281, 283
"The Stanton Coachman" (Dunbar) **8**:122
"The Star" (Clarke) **3**:125-27, 130, 136-38, 141-42
"The Star" (Wells) **6**:360-61, 365, 367, 382, 385-89, 393, 403, 406
"The Star That Bids the Shepherd Fold" (O'Connor) **5**:383
"Starosvetskie Pomeščiki" ("Old-World Landowners") (Gogol) **4**:86, 119-20
"Starye portrety" ("Old Portraits") (Turgenev) **7**:327, 362-63
"The Statement of Randolph Carter" (Lovecraft) **3**:258-60, 262, 282
"The Steadfast Tin Soldier" ("The Constant Tin Soldier"; "The Hardy Tin Soldier") (Andersen) **6**:7, 16, 18-19, 36, 40-1
"Stepnoy Korol 'Lir" ("A Lear of the Steppes"; "A Village Lear"; "A King Lear of the Steppes") (Turgenev) **7**:318-23, 336, 338, 358, 360-61
"The Steppe" (Chekhov) **2**:129-30, 143, 146, 151, 156
"The Steward" (Turgenev) **7**:313, 342
"Stigmata" (Oates) **6**:224, 226
"A Still Moment" (Welty) **1**:467-69, 482
"Stillness" (Gardner) **7**:223, 226, 235, 237, 240
"The Stolen Bacillus" (Wells) **6**:360, 374-75, 381-83, 395-99, 403
The Stolen Bacillus, and Other Incidents (Wells) **6**:364-66, 380, 388, 403
"The Stolen Body" (Wells) **6**:381, 404
"Stolen Pleasures" (Jewett) **6**:156-58
"The Stone" (O'Flaherty) **6**:281
"Stoney Batter" (O'Flaherty) **6**:280-81
Stories (Andersen)
See *Eventyr, fortalte for bøorn*
Stories (Bowen) **3**:39

Title Index

"Stories I Tell Myself" (Cortázar) **7**:69
The Stories of F. Scott Fitzgerald (Fitzgerald) **6**:60
The Stories of Frank O'Connor (O'Connor) **5**:365
The Stories of John Cheever (Cheever) **1**:105-06, 108-09
The Stories of Liam O'Flaherty (O'Flaherty) **6**:260, 265
Stories of Three Decades (Mann) **5**:308-09, 311
Stories Told for Children (Andersen)
See *Eventyr, fortalte for bøorn*
"The Storm" (Bowen) **3**:38-9
"The Storm" (Chopin) **8**:80, 84, 86, 91, 95
"The Storm Ship" (Irving) **2**:254
"The Storming of the Redoubt" (Mérimée)
See "L'enlèvement de la redoute"
"A Story from the Dunes" (Andersen) **6**:18-9, 34
"The Story Hearer" (Paley) **8**:420
"Story in Harlem Slang" (Hurston) **4**:139
"The Story of a Mine" (Harte) **8**:216
"The Story of a Mother" (Andersen) **6**:6-7, 18-9, 30, 35
"The Story of a Non-Marrying Man" (Lessing) **6**:188, 211
"The Story of an Hour" ("The Dream of an Hour") (Chopin) **8**:72-3, 79-80, 84, 87, 99, 102, 108
"The Story of Bras-Coupé" (Cable) **4**:61
"The Story of Father Alexis" (Turgenev)
See "Rasskaz ottsa Aleksaya"
"The Story of Jees Uck" (London) **4**:271
"The Story of Keesh" (London) **4**:253
"The Story of Lahcen and Idir" (Bowles) **3**:80
"The Story of Lieutenant Ergunov" (Turgenev)
See "Istoriya leytenanta Ergunova"
"The Story of Muhammad Din" (Kipling) **5**:296
"A Story of the Days to Come" (Wells) **6**:389, 390, 403-04, 406-08
The Story of the Gadsbys (*The Gadsbys*) (Kipling) **5**:260, 264-65, 274
"The Story of the Late Mr. Elvesham" (Wells) **6**:361, 363, 366, 383, 388, 405
"A Story of the Stone Age" (Wells) **6**:389-90, 403-04
"Story of the Warrior and the Captive" (Borges) **4**:29
"The Story of the Year" (Andersen) **6**:30
"The Story of the Young Italian" ("The Young Italian") (Irving) **2**:260-61, 268
"The Story of the Young Robber" ("The Young Robber") (Irving) **2**:255, 257, 262
"The Story of Two Dogs" (Lessing) **6**:198, 200, 203-04, 206, 208
"A Story with a Pattern" (Lavin) **4**:163, 167-69, 184-85
"Story with Spiders" (Cortázar) **7**:69
"A Story without a Title" (Chekhov)
See "An Anonymous Story"
"The Stout Gentleman" (Irving) **2**:250-51, 254, 259
"La strada di San Giovanni" (Calvino) **3**:97
"The Strange Crime of John Boulais" (Chesterton) **1**:138
"The Strange Disease" (O'Flaherty) **6**:262
"The Strange High House in the Mist" (Lovecraft) **3**:262, 277
"The Strange Ride of Morrowbie Jukes" (Kipling) **5**:262, 265, 273, 278, 299
"Strange Stories by a Nervous Gentleman" (Irving) **2**:251, 261
"A Strange Story" (Turgenev)
See "Strannaya istoriya"
Strange True Stories of Louisiana (Cable) **4**:49, 51, 53, 58-62, 75
"Strannaya istoriya" ("A Strange Story") (Turgenev) **7**:315, 321, 324, 337, 358-59
"Strašnaja mest" ("A Terrible Vengeance") (Gogol) **4**:103-04, 118-19
"The Strategy of the Were-Wolf Dog" (Cather) **2**:100
"Stratford-on-Avon" (Irving) **2**:245
"The Stream" (O'Flaherty) **6**:265, 277-78
"The Street" (Lovecraft) **3**:292
"Streetcorner Man" (Borges)
See "Hombre de la esquina rosada"
"The Strength of Gideon" (Dunbar) **8**:128, 136, 141, 144
The Strength of Gideon, and Other Stories (Dunbar) **8**:120-21, 124-25, 127, 131, 144-45
"The Strength of God" (Anderson) **1**:18
"The Strength of the Strong" (London) **4**:255
The Strength of the Strong (London) **4**:254-55, 283
Strictly Business (Henry) **5**:171
"The String Quartet" (Woolf) **7**:368-69, 374-75, 390, 392, 399
"Strong as Death is Love" (Singer) **3**:386
Strong Hearts (Cable) **4**:50, 62, 75
"Strong Horse Tea" (Walker) **5**:401, 403
"The Struggle" (O'Flaherty) **6**:264, 269
"The Student" (Chekhov) **2**:158
"The Student of Salamanca" (Irving) **2**:251, 254, 259
"The Student's Wife" (Carver) **8**:11, 46, 50-1, 53
"The Study of History" (O'Connor) **5**:376
"Stuk...stuk...stuk" ("Toc...toc...toc"; "Knock...Knock...Knock") (Turgenev) **7**:319, 321, 324-25, 338, 358-59
"A Subject of Childhood" (Paley) **8**:396, 398, 407
"The Subliminal Man" (Ballard) **1**:68-9, 77-8
"Subpoena" (Barthelme) **2**:37, 39
"The Successor" (Bowles) **3**:64-5, 80, 83
"A Sudden Trip Home in the Spring" (Walker) **5**:414
Sukhodól (Bunin) **5**:81, 87
"Summer" (Boyle) **5**:54
"Summer" (Cortázar)
See "Verano"
"The Summer Farmer" (Cheever) **1**:99, 106
"Summer Night" (Bowen) **3**:39, 41, 46, 51
"Summer Theatre" (Cheever) **1**:99
"Summertime on Icarus" (Clarke) **3**:130, 138, 147
"The Summing Up" (Woolf) **7**:376, 381, 390, 392, 411
"Sun" (Lawrence) **4**:238, 240-42
"The Sun between Their Feet" (Lessing) **6**:198-99, 203, 212
"The Sun-Dog Trail" (London) **4**:253, 290
"Sunday Afternoon" (Bowen) **3**:41, 53
"Sunday Afternoon" (Gallant) **5**:141
"Sunday Afternoon" (Munro) **3**:343
"Sunday at Home" (Hawthorne) **3**:189
"Sunday Brings Sunday" (Lavin) **4**:176
"Sunday Evening" (Bowen) **3**:53
"Sunjammer" (Clarke) **3**:132
"Sunlight/Twilight" (Oates) **6**:236-37
"The Sunrise" (Atwood) **2**:17-18, 21-2
"A Sunrise on the Veld" (Lessing) **6**:186
"Sunset" (Faulkner) **1**:177
A Sunstroke (Bunin) **5**:90
"Sunstroke" (Bunin)
See "Solnechnyy udar"
"The Superintendent" (Cheever) **1**:99, 107
"Superiority" (Clarke) **3**:126, 150
"The Superstitious Man's Story" (Hardy) **2**:217
"The Supper at Elsinore" (Dinesen) **7**:168, 177, 186, 190, 203-04
"A Supper by Proxy" (Dunbar) **8**:122, 135, 139
"Sur l'eau" (Maupassant) **1**:261-62, 265, 278
"Surgery" (Chekhov) **2**:130
"The Survival of Childhood" (Oates) **6**:224
"Susy" (Harte) **8**:222, 251-52
"Suzette" (Chopin) **8**:100
"Svajatye gory" (Bunin) **5**:98
"Swaddling Clothes" (Mishima) **4**:313, 317, 322-23
"The Swan's Nest" (Andersen) **6**:4
"The Sway-Backed House" (Chesnutt) **7**:33
"Sweat" (Hurston) **4**:136-38, 151, 155
"The Sweethearts" (Andersen) **6**:28, 30, 36
"Swept and Garnished" (Kipling) **5**:275, 282
"The Swiftest Runners" (Andersen) **6**:10
"The Swimmer" (Cheever) **1**:94, 100, 102, 106, 108
"The Swineherd" (Andersen) **6**:7, 18, 24, 26, 30-1, 34
"The Swing" (Bunin)
See "Kacheli"
"Sympathy" (Woolf) **7**:409
"A Symphony in Lavender" (Freeman) **1**:199
"The System of Doctor Tarr and Professor Fether" (Poe) **1**:407
"t zero" (Calvino) **3**:93
t zero (Calvino)
See *Ti con zero*
"Taibele and Her Demon" (Singer) **3**:375, 384
"Tain't So" (Hughes) **6**:121, 131
"The Taking of Lungtungpen" (Kipling) **5**:260, 265
"Taking of the Redoubt" (Mérimée)
See "L'enlèvement de la redoute"
Un tal Lucas (*A Certain Lucas*) (Cortázar) **7**:91-4
"The Tale of Astolpho on the Moon" (Calvino) **3**:101
"The Tale of How Ivan Ivanovich Quarrelled with Ivan Nikiforovich" ("The Two Ivans"; "About How Ivan Ivanovič Quarreled with Ivan Nikiforovič") (Gogol) **4**:82, 84, 86, 105
"A Tale of Jerusalem" (Poe) **1**:407
"The Tale of the Ingrate and His Punishment" (Calvino) **3**:101-02
"A Tale of the Ragged Mountains" (Poe) **1**:400, 402
"A Tale of the White Pyramid" (Cather) **2**:100
"A Tale of Two Liars" (Singer) **3**:375
"A Tale of Two Sisters" (Singer) **3**:377
Tales by Edgar A. Poe (Poe) **1**:388
Tales from Bective Bridge (Lavin) **4**:170-72, 185

Tales from the White Hart (Clarke) **3**:131, 133
Tales of a Traveller (Irving) **2**:241, 244, 246, 250-51, 254-55, 258-62, 268
Tales of Men and Ghosts (Wharton) **6**:421, 435
Tales of Space and Time (Wells) **6**:366-67, 380, 389
Tales of the Grotesque and Arabesque (Poe) **1**:389-90
Tales of the Jazz Age (Fitzgerald) **6**:45-6, 56, 58-9, 74, 101
Tales of the Long Bow (Chesterton) **1**:133
"Tales of Two Old Gentlemen" (Dinesen) **7**:173
Talk (Carver)
See *What We Talk about When We Talk about Love*
"The Tall Men" (Faulkner) **1**:151, 162
"Tamango" (Mérimée) **7**:280-81, 283, 287-89, 300
"The Taming of the Nightmare" (Chesterton) **1**:140
"Tanhum" (Singer) **3**:380
"Tania" ("Tanya") (Bunin) **5**:113
"Tante Cat'rinette" (Chopin) **8**:94
"Tanya" (Bunin)
See "Tania"
"An tAonach" (O'Flaherty) **6**:287-88
"Tapiama" (Bowles) **3**:64-5, 80, 83
Taps at Reveille (Fitzgerald) **6**:46-7, 56, 60
Taras Bulba (Gogol) **4**:83, 85-6, 117-19
"Tarquin of Cheapside" (Fitzgerald) **6**:58, 60
"The Tartarus of Maids" (Melville)
See "The Paradise of Bachelors and the Tartarus of Maids"
"A Taste of Honey" (Freeman) **1**:196
"The Taxidermist" (Cable) **4**:50
"Tea" (Gallant)
See "Thank You for the Lovely Tea"
"Tea on the Mountain" (Bowles) **3**:61, 72, 79
"The Teacher" (Anderson) **1**:18, 45, 52
"The Teacher of Literature" (Chekhov) **2**:128, 131-32, 155
"Teacher's Pet" (Thurber) **1**:422-23
"The Teachings of Don B.: A Yankee Way of Knowledge" (Barthelme) **2**:40
"Teangabháil" (O'Flaherty) **6**:286-89
"Tears, Idle Tears" (Bowen) **3**:33, 41, 47
"Tears—Idle Tears" (O'Connor) **5**:371, 395
"The Tears of Ah Kim" (London) **4**:257, 270
"Technical Error" ("The Reversed Man") (Clarke) **3**:124-25, 129
"A Technical Error" (Henry) **5**:165
"Teddy" (Salinger) **2**:293, 295, 300-01, 307, 309, 311-12, 316
"Telemachus, Friend" (Henry) **5**:179
"A Telephone Call" (Parker) **2**:274, 278, 280, 285
"A Telephone Call on Yom Kippur" (Singer) **3**:385-86
"Tell Me Yes or No" (Munro) **3**:335
"The Tell-Tale Heart" (Poe) **1**:384, 393-94, 408
"Tell the Women We're Going" (Carver) **8**:14, 30
"Telling" (Bowen) **3**:30, 33, 40
"Tema del traidor y del héroe" ("The Theme of the Traitor and the Hero") (Borges) **4**:10, 23, 30, 39
"The Temperate Zone" (Wharton) **6**:428
"Tempests" (Dinesen) **7**:171, 197
"The Temple" (Lovecraft) **3**:282, 289
"A Temple of the Holy Ghost" (O'Connor) **1**:343
"The Temptation of Jack Orkney" (Lessing) **6**:188
The Temptation of Jack Orkney, and Other Stories (Lessing) **6**:188
"Temptation of St. Anthony" (Barthelme) **2**:37, 54
"The Temptation of St. Ivo" (Gardner) **7**:214, 222, 229-30, 232
"The Tempter" (Oates) **6**:227
"Tennessee's Partner" (Harte) **8**:210, 219, 221, 226, 230, 232-33, 236, 244, 255-56, 258-59
"The Tent" (O'Flaherty) **6**:262, 282
The Tent (O'Flaherty) **6**:262-65, 278-79, 283
"The Tents of Kedar" (Kipling) **5**:261
"La tercera resignación" ("The Third Resignation") (García Márquez) **8**:154-55, 169, 182
"The Terminal Beach" (Ballard) **1**:69, 76, 80
The Terminal Beach, and Other Stories (Ballard) **1**:68-70, 73
"The Terrible Old Man" (Lovecraft) **3**:292
"A Terrible Vengeance" (Gogol)
See "Strašnaja mest"
"Terror" (Anderson) **1**:30
"The Terrorist" (O'Flaherty) **6**:262, 284
"The Terrorists" (Barnes) **3**:19
"El tesoro de la juventud" ("The Treasure of Youth") (Cortázar) **7**:95
"The Test of Courage" (O'Flaherty) **6**:281
"Testament of Flood" (Warren) **4**:389, 394
"Los testigos" ("The Witnesses") (Cortázar) **7**:95
"Text in a Notebook" (Cortázar) **7**:69
"Texturologías" ("Texturologies") (Cortázar) **7**:93
"Texturologies" (Cortázar)
See "Texturologías"
"Thanasphere" (Vonnegut) **8**:428
"Thank You for the Lovely Tea" ("Tea") (Gallant) **5**:138, 142
"Thanks for the Ride" (Munro) **3**:322, 329, 331, 336, 343
"That Evening Sun" (Faulkner) **1**:147, 162, 181, 183
"That Good May Come" (Wharton) **6**:424
"That Sophistication" (Anderson) **1**:50
"That Tree" (Porter) **4**:327-28, 330, 339-40, 349
"Theater" (Toomer) **1**:441, 443-45, 450, 452, 458, 460-61
"Theatre of War" (Ballard) **1**:79, 82
"Theft" (Porter) **4**:327, 329, 337-40, 342, 349, 360
"The Theme of the Traitor and the Hero" (Borges)
See "Tema del traidor y del héroe"
"Then It All Came Down" (Capote) **2**:81
"The Theologians" (Borges) **4**:5-6, 25, 28, 30
There and Now (Cortázar)
See *Ahí y ahora*
"There Are No Thieves in This Town" (García Márquez) **8**:185
"There Is No Hope for That" (Cortázar)
See "Ya no quedan esperanzas de"
"There She Is—She Is Taking Her Bath" (Anderson) **1**:50
"Thermos Bottles" ("Thermos Flasks") (Mishima) **4**:313-14, 316-18, 322
"Thermos Flasks" (Mishima)
See "Thermos Bottles"
These Thirteen (Faulkner) **1**:180-81, 184
"These Walls Are Cold" (Capote) **2**:65
"They" (Kipling) **5**:266, 271-72, 275, 279-82, 284
"They called for more structure" (Barthelme) **2**:50
"They Weren't Going to Die" (Boyle) **5**:63
"They're Not Your Husband" (Carver) **8**:9, 34
"The Thief" (O'Connor) **5**:371
"Thieves' Ears" (Bunin)
See "Petlistye ushi"
"The Thimble" (Lawrence) **4**:235, 237
"Thimble, Thimble" (Henry) **5**:159, 171
"A Thing for Nothing" (O'Connor) **5**:365
"The Thing on the Doorstep" (Lovecraft) **3**:259, 263, 272, 274-75, 283
"Things" (Lawrence) **4**:219
"The Thinker" (Anderson) **1**:43-5
"The Third Cock-Crow" (Bunin) **5**:82-3
"The Third Ingredient" (Henry) **5**:181-82
"The Third Person" (James) **8**:325
"The Third Resignation" (García Márquez)
See "La tercera resignación"
"The Third Thing that Killed My Father Off" (Carver) **8**:14
The Thirteen (Balzac)
See *Histoire de treize*
Thirty Stories (Boyle) **5**:56, 63
"The $30,000 Bequest" (Twain) **6**:303, 328-30, 343-45
"This Mortal Coil" (O'Connor) **5**:386, 389
"This Son of Mine" (Vonnegut) **8**:432, 438
This Was the Old Chief's Country (Lessing) **6**:186, 196
"The Thorn in the Flesh" (Lawrence) **4**:197, 202
"The Thorny Path of Honor" (Andersen) **6**:4, 34
Those Days (Carver) **8**:51
"Thou Art the Man" (Poe) **1**:406
"A Thousand Deaths" (London) **4**:277
"The Three-Day Blow" (Hemingway) **1**:208, 219, 244
"Three Encounters" ("Three Meetings") (Turgenev) **7**:314-15, 324-25, 328, 335
"Three Fat Women of Antibes" (Maugham) **8**:379
"The Three-Fold Destiny" (Hawthorne) **3**:160, 177-78, 182-83, 189
"Three Lambs" (O'Flaherty) **6**:264, 274
"Three Meetings" (Turgenev)
See "Three Encounters"
"Three Million Yen" (Mishima) **4**:313-14, 316-18, 322
"Three Miraculous Soldiers" (Crane) **7**:103, 106
"Three Partners" (Harte) **8**:216, 222, 248
"Three Pictures" (Woolf) **7**:408, 410-12
"Three Portraits" (Turgenev) **7**:313, 318, 320, 323
Three Stories and Ten Poems (Hemingway) **1**:206
"The Three Strangers" (Hardy) **2**:202-03, 205, 208, 212-15, 218, 220, 223, 226-27
"Three Thousand Years among the Microbes" (Twain) **6**:333, 336, 338, 350-53
"Three Tools" (Chesterton) **1**:136
"Three Vagabonds of Trinidad" (Harte) **8**:245, 251

"Three Versions of Judas" (Borges) **4**:24, 28-9
"Three Years" (Chekhov) **2**:131, 155-57
"Throat of a Black Cat" (Cortázar)
See "Cuello de gatito negro"
"Through the Gates of the Silver Key" (Lovecraft) **3**:262, 267, 272-73, 286, 294
"Through the Looking Glass" (Oates) **6**:228
"Thrown Away" (Kipling) **5**:261
"Thumbelina" (Andersen) **6**:27-8, 36
The Thurber Carnival (Thurber) **1**:416, 426
Ti con zero (*t zero*) (Calvino) **3**:92, 94-6, 98-9, 107, 117
"Ti Démon" (Chopin) **8**:100
"Ti Frére" (Chopin) **8**:72
"Tickets, Please" (Lawrence) **4**:222-23, 226, 228, 231, 233-35, 242-46
"The Tide" (O'Flaherty) **6**:262, 279, 285
"The Tie" (Kipling) **5**:278
"A Tight Boat" (Chesnutt) **7**:13
"The Time of Death" (Munro) **3**:329-30
"The Time of Friendship" (Bowles) **3**:63-7, 81-2
The Time of Friendship (Bowles) **3**:63-5, 70, 79-81, 84
"Time's Arrow" (Clarke) **3**:133-34, 142
"A Tin Can" (O'Flaherty) **6**:276
"The Tinderbox" (Andersen) **6**:4, 18, 23, 26-7, 30-2, 36-7
"Tišina" (Bunin) **5**:98
"Tite Poulette" (Cable) **4**:52, 62, 67-8, 76-7
"Tlön, Uqbar, Orbis Tertius" (Borges) **4**:6-7, 10-12, 15, 18, 25, 29, 33, 35, 43
"To Build a Fire (1908)" (London) **4**:265, 267, 272-76, 278, 280-82, 289-93
"To Build a Fire (1902)" (London) **4**:272-74
"To Da-duh, in Memoriam" (Marshall) **3**:301, 303, 307, 313-15, 317
"To Hell with Dying" (Walker) **5**:403, 406, 419, 422
"To Room Nineteen" (Lessing) **6**:198, 201-02, 208, 214, 218, 220
"To Set Our House in Order" (Laurence) **7**:252, 262, 264-65, 269
"To the Man on Trail" (London) **4**:250, 267, 277, 279
"Tobias Mindernickel" (Mann) **5**:322, 334, 336
"Toc...toc...toc" (Turgenev)
See "Stuk...stuk...stuk"
"Der Tod in Venedig" ("Death in Venice") (Mann) **5**:307, 309-11, 313-14, 319, 323-27, 331, 338-40, 342-45, 348, 355-56
"Today is Friday" (Hemingway) **1**:228-29
Todos los fuegos el fuego (*All Fires Are Fire*; *All Fires the Fire*) (Cortázar) **7**:52-4, 60, 62, 64
"Todos los fuegos el fuego" ("All Fires the Fire") (Cortázar) **7**:61, 69
"Together and Apart" (Woolf) **7**:376, 381, 388
"Told in the Drooling Ward" (London) **4**:255-56, 266
"Told in the Tavern" (Jewett) **6**:159
"The Toll-Gatherer's Day" (Hawthorne) **3**:158
"The Tomb of His Ancestors" (Kipling) **5**:266
"Les tombales" (Maupassant) **1**:263
"The Tommy Crans" (Bowen) **3**:33, 41
"Tommy, the Unsentimental" (Cather) **2**:100, 105
"Tomorrow" (Faulkner) **1**:165, 179, 181
"Tomorrow and Tomorrow and Tomorrow" (Vonnegut) **8**:425, 429-31
"The Tomorrow-Tamer" (Laurence) **7**:249, 261
The Tomorrow-Tamer (Laurence) **7**:245-50, 260-61, 272
"Tom's Warm Welcome" (Chesnutt) **7**:14
"Tonio Kröger" (Mann) **5**:307, 310-11, 316, 318, 324, 331, 342-44, 355
"Tony Kytes, the Arch Deceiver" (Hardy) **2**:206-07
"Too Bad" (Parker) **2**:274, 280, 285
"The Top and the Ball" (Andersen) **6**:18, 32
"Torch Song" (Cheever) **1**:89, 99, 106, 109-10
"Torito" ("Little Bull") (Cortázar) **7**:54, 88-9
"A Torrent Dammed" (O'Connor) **5**:387
The Torrents of Spring (*Spring-Torrents*; *Spring Freshets*) (Turgenev) **7**:316-17, 320-21, 324-25, 327-29, 334, 336-38, 357-58, 361-62
"The Touch" (O'Flaherty) **6**:265, 285
The Touchstone (Wharton) **6**:413
"A Tour in the Forest" (Turgenev)
See "A Tour of the Forest"
"A Tour of the Forest" ("A Tour in the Forest") (Turgenev) **7**:320, 337-38
A Tour of the Prairies (Irving) **2**:244
"The Town Poor" (Jewett) **6**:151
"Track 12" (Ballard) **1**:68
"A Tradition of 1804" (Hardy) **2**:215, 220-21
Traffics and Discoveries (Kipling) **5**:266, 272, 283
"A Tragedy" (Lavin) **4**:165, 176, 183
"The Tragedy at Three Forks" (Dunbar) **8**:121-22, 125, 136
"A Tragedy of Error" (James) **8**:302
"A Tragedy of Two Ambitions" (Hardy) **2**:205-06, 214-17, 223
"The Train" (Carver) **8**:25-6, 34
"Training" (Atwood) **2**:3-4, 7-8, 10, 12-13, 16
"The Traitor" (Maugham) **8**:368, 377
"Traitors" (Lessing) **6**:217
"The Tramp" (O'Flaherty) **6**:275, 285
"La transaction" (Balzac) **5**:24
"The Transformation of Martin Burney" (Henry) **5**:197
"The Transformation of Vincent Scoville" (Oates) **6**:230
"Transience" (Clarke) **3**:127, 135, 142
"Transients in Arcadia" (Henry) **5**:158, 189
"Transit Bed" (Calvino) **3**:112
"Transit of Earth" (Clarke) **3**:147
"The Transposed Heads" (Mann) **5**:312-13, 315, 323, 326
"Trapped" (O'Flaherty) **6**:273, 276, 279, 283
"Trastevere" (Lavin) **4**:183, 185
"A Travel Piece" (Atwood) **2**:3-4, 6-7, 10, 12, 15-16
Traveller's Samples (O'Connor) **5**:371
"The Travelling Companion" (Andersen) **6**:18-9, 30-1, 35
"The Treasure" (Maugham) **8**:380
"The Treasure of Youth" (Cortázar)
See "El tesoro de la juventud"
"The Tree" (Thomas) **3**:399, 402, 408-09
"The Tree of Justice" (Kipling) **5**:292
"The Tree of Knowledge" (James) **8**:301
"A Tree of Night" (Capote) **2**:61-3, 66, 69, 72-5
A Tree of Night, and Other Stories (Capote) **2**:61-4, 72, 74, 83
"The Trees of Pride" (Chesterton) **1**:122
Treize (Balzac)
See *Histoire de treize*
The Trembling of a Leaf (Maugham) **8**:370-72
"The Trial of the Old Watchdog" (Thurber) **1**:426
"The Trial Sermon on Bull-Skin" (Dunbar) **8**:118, 121, 127, 136
"Tribuneaux rustiques" (Maupassant) **1**:259, 286
"The Trimmed Lamp" (Henry) **5**:171, 185, 198
The Trimmed Lamp (Henry) **5**:155, 192
"The Trinket Box" (Lessing) **6**:196-97, 212-20
"A Trip to Chancellorsville" (Fitzgerald) **6**:47
"Tristan" (Mann) **5**:311, 321, 323-24
Tristan (Mann) **5**:307
"The Triumph of Night" (Wharton) **6**:418, 428, 431-32
The Triumph of the Egg (Anderson) **1**:19-20, 22, 26-7, 30, 32, 34, 46-7, 50
"The Triumph of the Egg" ("The Egg") (Anderson) **1**:20, 23, 26, 30, 34, 37-8, 40, 47, 52, 54-5
"The Triumphs of a Taxidermist" (Wells) **6**:380, 384, 388
The Troll Garden (Cather) **2**:90, 93, 96, 103, 113
"The Trouble" (Powers) **4**:368-69, 372
"The Trouble about Sophiny" (Dunbar) **8**:122
"The Trouble of Marcie Flint" (Cheever) **1**:90
"Trouble with the Angels" (Hughes) **6**:112, 118-19, 122, 131
"Trouble with the Natives" (Clarke) **3**:124, 149
"The Trousers" (Dunbar) **8**:122
"The Truant" (Irving) **2**:265
"Trumpeter" (Gardner) **7**:225-26, 233, 235
"Trust" (London) **4**:265
"The Trustfulness of Polly" (Dunbar) **8**:122, 128, 147
"The Truth about Pyecraft" (Wells) **6**:360, 392, 404
"The Tryst" (Oates) **6**:251-52
"The Tryst" (Turgenev) **7**:342-43
"A Tryst at an Ancient Earthwork" (Hardy) **2**:210, 214-15
"Tu más profunda piel" ("Your Most Profound Skin") (Cortázar) **7**:95
"Tubal-Cain Forges a Star" (García Márquez)
See "Tubal-Cain forja una estrella"
"Tubal-Cain forja una estrella" ("Tubal-Cain Forges a Star") (García Márquez) **8**:154, 156
"Tuesday Siesta" (García Márquez) **8**:183, 185
"Tuman" (Bunin) **5**:98
"A Turkey Hunt" (Chopin) **8**:88
"The Turkey Season" (Munro) **3**:346
The Turn of the Screw (James) **8**:271-76, 283, 291-96, 298, 316, 318, 320, 325-26
"The Turn of the Screw" (Oates) **6**:225
"The Turtles of Tasman" (London) **4**:255-56
The Turtles of Tasman (London) **4**:255-56, 266
"Tutto in un punto" (Calvino) **3**:92
"Twelve O'Clock" (Crane) **7**:108

Twelve Stories and a Dream (Wells) **6**:366-67, 380, 391, 400
"Twenty-Four Hours in a Strange Diocese" (Powers) **4**:380
"29 Inventions" (Oates) **6**:225
Twice-Told Tales (Hawthorne) **3**:154-55, 157-61, 180, 184-85, 190
"Two" (Singer) **3**:381
"Two Blue Birds" (Lawrence) **4**:220
"Two Corpses Go Dancing" (Singer) **3**:370
"Two Friends" (Cather) **2**:100, 109, 115, 117-18
"Two Friends" (Turgenev) **7**:327
"Two Gallants" (Joyce) **3**:200-01, 205-06, 209, 214, 220-21, 225, 231-34, 237, 246
"The Two Ivans" (Gogol)
See "The Tale of How Ivan Ivanovich Quarrelled with Ivan Nikiforovich"
"The Two Kings and Their Two Labyrinths" (Borges) **4**:28, 30-1, 35
"Two Lovely Beasts" (O'Flaherty) **6**:269-70, 274, 281-82, 285
Two Lovely Beasts, and Other Stories (O'Flaherty) **6**:262-63, 265, 276, 278, 281-83, 285
The Two Magics (James) **8**:296
"Two Markets" (Singer) **3**:377
"Two Old Lovers" (Freeman) **1**:197, 200-01
"Two Old-Timers" (Fitzgerald) **6**:71
"Two Portraits" (Chopin) **8**:72, 87, 98, 110
"Two Potters" (Lessing) **6**:200
"Two Sides to a Tortoise" (Melville)
See "The Encantadas; or, The Enchanted Isles"
"Two Soldiers" (Faulkner) **1**:151
"Two Summers and Two Souls" (Chopin) **8**:99
"The Two Temples" (Melville) **1**:303, 323
"Two Thanksgiving Day Gentlemen" (Henry) **5**:187
"Two Wrongs" (Fitzgerald) **6**:51, 60, 61
"The Tyrant" (O'Flaherty) **6**:264
"U istoka dnej" (Bunin) **5**:98-9
"The Ugly Duckling" ("The Duckling") (Andersen) **6**:5, 7, 10-1, 18, 30-1, 35, 40
"Uglypuss" (Atwood) **2**:18, 22
"Uisce faoi Dhraíocht" (O'Flaherty) **6**:287-88
"Ukridge Sees Her Through" (Wodehouse) **2**:354
The Ultimate City (Ballard) **1**:72, 74, 83-4
"The Ultimate Melody" (Clarke) **3**:133-34
Ultimo round (*Last Round*; *El último round*) (Cortázar) **7**:53, 70-1, 80, 91, 94-5
El último round (Cortázar)
See *Ultimo round*
"El último viaje del buque fantasma" ("The Last Voyage of the Ghost Ship") (García Márquez) **8**:154, 160, 167-68, 170-72, 186
Ultimo viene il corvo (*Adam, One Afternoon, and Other Stories*) (Calvino) **3**:106, 116
"Unapproved Route" (O'Connor) **5**:371
"Uncertain Flowering" (Laurence) **7**:271-72
"Uncle Anne" (Boyle) **5**:54
"Uncle Jim and Uncle Billy" (Harte) **8**:227, 244
"Uncle Peter's House" (Chesnutt) **7**:12, 27
"Uncle Simon's Sunday Out" (Dunbar) **8**:122, 127, 144
Uncle Tom's Children (Wright) **2**:360-61, 363, 365-68, 370-71, 373-75, 379, 381-84, 386-88
"Uncle Valentine" (Cather) **2**:98, 113-15
"Uncle Wellington's Wives" (Chesnutt) **7**:3, 16, 23, 28-9, 33, 37
"Uncle Wiggily in Connecticut" (Salinger) **2**:290, 292, 295, 299, 305-06, 313-14
"Uncle Willy" (Faulkner) **1**:151
"Unclean" (O'Flaherty) **6**:259
"Uncle's Dream" (Dostoevski) **2**:164, 172, 184
The Uncollected Short Stories (Jewett) **6**:156, 166
The Uncollected Wodehouse (Wodehouse) **2**:343
"The Unconquered" (Maugham) **8**:380
"Uncovenanted Mercies" (Kipling) **5**:271, 283
"The Undefeated" (Hemingway) **1**:209, 216, 218-19, 224, 230, 234
"Under Glass" (Atwood) **2**:3, 6, 10, 13, 16
"Under the Deck Awnings" (London) **4**:291
Under the Deodars (Kipling) **5**:265
"Under the Jaguar Sun" (Calvino) **3**:118-19
Under the Jaguar Sun (Calvino) **3**:119
"Under the Knife" (Singer) **3**:362
"Under the Knife" (Wells) **6**:360, 389, 393-94, 405
"Under the Sky" (Bowles) **3**:59, 61-2, 67, 79
"Under the Willow-Tree" (Andersen) **6**:4
"The Underground" (Dostoevski) **2**:187
"Undertakers" (Kipling) **5**:293
"Unearthing Suite" (Atwood) **2**:17, 22
"The Unexpected" (Chopin) **8**:72, 100
"The Unexpected" (London) **4**:253, 260-62
"An Unfinished Collection" (Wodehouse) **2**:343
"An Unfinished Story" (Henry) **5**:163, 171, 178-79, 182, 185
"An Unhappy Girl" (Turgenev)
See "Neschastnaya"
"The Unicorn in the Garden" (Thurber) **1**:427-28, 431
A Universal History of Infamy (Borges)
See *Historia universal de la infamia*
"The Unknown Masterpiece" (Balzac)
See "Le chef d'oeuvre inconnu"
"The Unknown Quantity" (Henry) **5**:197
"Unlighted Lamps" (Anderson) **1**:27, 30, 39, 46-7, 53, 55
"An Unmarried Man's Summer" (Gallant) **5**:122, 130-31
"The Unnameable" (Lovecraft) **3**:262, 276, 293-94
"Unpaid Consultant" (Vonnegut) **8**:436
"The Unparalleled Adventure of One Hans Pfaall" (Poe) **1**:400, 402, 406
"The Unparalleled Invasion" (London) **4**:255
"An Unpleasant Predicament" (Dostoevski) **2**:166, 184
"Unprofessional" (Kipling) **5**:285
"Unready to Wear" (Vonnegut) **8**:434
"The Unseen" (Singer) **3**:358, 362, 383-84
"Unser Karl" (Harte) **8**:220
Unspeakable Practices, Unnatural Acts (Barthelme) **2**:29-31, 35, 37-8, 51
"The Untold Lie" (Anderson) **1**:21, 34, 39, 41-2, 44, 52
"'Unused'" (Anderson) **1**:23, 27, 30, 39-40, 46-7, 53, 55
The Unvanquished (Faulkner) **1**:151, 170, 177, 180
"The Unvexed Isles" (Warren) **4**:387, 389-90, 395, 400
"Unwelcome Words" (Bowles) **3**:85-6
Unwelcome Words: Seven Stories (Bowles) **3**:85
"The Unworthy Friend" (Borges) **4**:18
"An Unwritten Novel" (Woolf) **7**:368, 371-72, 375-76, 378, 382, 388, 392, 397-99, 405, 408-09
"Uomo nei gerbidi" (Calvino) **3**:96
"Up, Aloft in the Air" (Barthelme) **2**:38
"Up in Michigan" (Hemingway) **1**:207, 219
"Upon the Sweeping Flood" (Oates) **6**:224-25
Upon the Sweeping Flood, and Other Stories (Oates) **6**:224-25
"Uprooted" (Chekhov) **2**:130
"Uprooted" (O'Connor) **5**:369, 371, 375-77, 383, 397
"The Upturned Face" (Crane) **7**:109, 143-45
"Das Urteil" ("The Judgment") (Kafka) **5**:225-26, 228-29, 232, 240, 243-45, 252-55
"The Used-Boy Raisers" (Paley) **8**:399, 406-07
"Vacation Time" (Boyle) **5**:54
"The Valet" (Barnes) **3**:22-4
"The Valiant Woman" (Powers) **4**:380-81, 383
"The Valley Between" (Marshall) **3**:303, 308-09, 312, 315, 317
"The Valley of Childish Things" (Wharton) **6**:427
"The Valley of Spiders" (Wells) **6**:361
Valley of the Moon (London) **4**:254
"The Valley of the Shadow" (Kipling) **5**:261
"The Vanishing of Vaudrey" (Chesterton) **1**:131
"The Vanishing Prince" (Chesterton) **1**:122
"Vanity and Some Sables" (Henry) **5**:187
"Vánka" (Chekhov) **2**:130
"The Vanvild Kava" (Singer) **3**:383
"Varieties of Exile" (Gallant) **5**:134-35, 143
"Le vase étrusque" (Mérimée) **7**:278, 280-81, 283, 286-91, 300, 304
"Večer nakanune Ivana Kupala" ("St. John's Eve") (Gogol) **4**:88, 119-21
"Vechera no xutore bliz Dikan'ki" ("Evenings on a Farm Near Dikanka") (Gogol) **4**:85-7, 98, 117
"Velga" (Bunin) **5**:98
"Vendée" (Faulkner) **1**:171
"Une vendetta" (Maupassant) **1**:277
"La vendetta revenge" ("Revenge") (Balzac) **5**:4, 22, 29, 31
"The Vengeance of 3902090" (Thurber) **1**:419
"The Venturers" (Henry) **5**:159, 190-91
"La Vénus d'Ille" (Mérimée) **7**:276, 279-80, 283-86, 288, 290, 293-95, 297, 301, 306
"Verano" ("Summer") (Cortázar) **7**:61-3
"The Verdict" (Wharton) **6**:435
"El verdugo" (Balzac) **5**:21, 31
Vermilion Sands (Ballard) **1**:78
"Die Verwandlung" ("The Metamorphosis") (Kafka) **5**:210-13, 215, 217-20, 224-25, 231, 234, 239-40, 245, 252
"A Very Fine Fiddle" (Chopin) **8**:88, 103
Very Good, Jeeves (Wodehouse) **2**:346
"A Very Old Man with Enormous Wings" (García Márquez) **8**:160, 167-70, 182, 186
"The Very Proper Gander" (Thurber) **1**:431
"Veselyi dvor" (Bunin) **5**:87
"The Vessel of Wrath" (Maugham) **8**:375, 378
"Vesti iz rodiny" (Bunin) **5**:98
"A Veteran Falls" (Hughes) **6**:122

Title Index

"Veteran of the Private Evacuations" (Ballard) **1**:70
"Il viccolo di Madama Lucrezia" (Mérimée) **7**:283-84, 290, 295-96, 306-07
"Victory" (Faulkner) **1**:148
"The Victory Burlesk" (Atwood) **2**:19
"The Viennese Opera Ball" (Barthelme) **2**:28
"A View of the Woods" (O'Connor) **1**:342-45, 356
"Views of My Father Weeping" (Barthelme) **2**:31, 42, 46, 48, 55
The Viking Portable Library Dorothy Parker (Parker) **2**:276, 278
"Villa Violetta" (Lavin) **4**:183, 185
"A Village Lear" (Turgenev)
See "Stepnoy Korol 'Lir"
"The Village of Stepanchikovo" ("The Friend of the Family"; "The Hamlet of Stepanchikovo"; "The Manor of Stepanchikovo") (Dostoevski) **2**:164, 172, 175, 176
"A Village Singer" (Freeman) **1**:197, 200
"The Village That Voted the Earth Was Flat" (Kipling) **5**:277, 280, 282
"The Vindication of Jared Hargot" (Dunbar) **8**:138
"Viney's Free Papers" (Dunbar) **8**:122, 127, 131, 133, 144
Vinter-Eventyr (Dinesen)
See *Winter's Tales*
"The Virgin and the Gipsy" (Lawrence) **4**:205-06
"Virgin Violeta" (Porter) **4**:341, 350
"Virtue" (Maugham) **8**:378
"A Virtuoso's Collection" (Hawthorne) **3**:171
"Virus X" (Gallant) **5**:139
Il visconte dimezzato (*The Cloven Viscount*; *The Nonexistent Knight and the Cloven Viscount*) (Calvino) **3**:90-1, 94, 99, 106, 117
"La vision de Charles XI" (Mérimée) **7**:287, 289
"A Vision of Judgment" (Wells) **6**:360, 391
"The Vision of the Fountain" (Hawthorne) **3**:178, 182
"A Vision of the World" (Cheever) **1**:93-6, 105
"Visions" (Turgenev) **7**:315
"A Visit Next Door" (Jewett) **6**:158
"A Visit of Charity" (Welty) **1**:470
"A Visit to America" (Thomas) **3**:393
"A Visit to Avoyelles" (Chopin) **8**:72, 84
"A Visit to Grandpa's" (Thomas) **3**:397, 402, 405, 410, 412
"A Visit to the Cemetery" (Lavin) **4**:164-66, 168-69
"The Visiting of Mother Danbury" (Dunbar) **8**:127
"The Visitor" (Bowen) **3**:40
"The Visitor" (Thomas) **3**:400, 407, 409
"Visitors" (Barthelme) **2**:56
"Vitamins" (Carver) **8**:26, 32
"La viuda de Montiel" (García Márquez) **8**:187-90
"Viy" (Gogol) **4**:82, 86, 102-03
"Vizitnye kartochki" ("Calling Cards") (Bunin) **5**:114
"Vlemk the Box-Painter" (Gardner) **7**:223-26, 238-41
"A Vocation and a Voice" (Chopin) **8**:72, 78, 100, 102
A Vocation and a Voice (Chopin) **8**:93, 97, 99
"The Voice of the City" (Henry) **5**:171, 191, 194
The Voice of the City (Henry) **5**:155, 192
"The Voice of the Turtle" (Maugham) **8**:379
"Voices Lost in the Snow" (Gallant) **5**:135, 139
"The Voices of Adamo" (Laurence) **7**:245, 249-50
"The Voices of Time" (Ballard) **1**:71, 80
"Von Kempelen and His Discovery" (Poe) **1**:402
"Vor dem Gesetz" ("Before the Law") (Kafka) **5**:254
"Voron" ("The Raven") (Bunin) **5**:113
"The Voyage to Rosewood" (Oates) **6**:231
La vuelta al día en ochenta mundos (*Around the Day in Eighty Worlds*) (Cortázar) **7**:53, 61, 91, 94
"A Wagner Matinée" (Cather) **2**:90-1, 96, 103, 105, 108
"A Waif of the Plains" (Harte) **8**:222, 251
"The Waiting" (Borges) **4**:5, 37-9
"Waiting" (Oates) **6**:232
"The Waiting Grounds" (Ballard) **1**:68, 76
"The Waiting Supper" (Hardy) **2**:211, 215-16, 219, 223
"Wakefield" (Hawthorne) **3**:154, 159, 161-62, 178, 189, 191
"Waldemar Daa and His Daughters" (Andersen)
See "The Wind Tells of Valdemar Daae and His Daughters"
"A Walk in the Dark" (Clarke) **3**:124, 147-49
"A Walk in the Woods" (Bowen) **3**:54
"Walker Brothers Cowboy" (Munro) **3**:321, 329, 343, 347
"A Walking Delegate" (Kipling) **5**:279
"Walking on Water" (Munro) **3**:331, 346
"Die Walkuere" (Mann) **5**:310
"The Wall of Darkness" (Clarke) **3**:125, 129, 147
"Walled City" (Oates) **6**:251-52
"The Walls of Jericho" (Dunbar) **8**:122, 136, 149
"The Waltz" (Parker) **2**:274, 281, 283, 285-86
"Wan Lee, the Pagan" (Harte) **8**:249
"The Wanderers" (Welty) **1**:479, 493
"Wants" (Paley) **8**:397, 399, 416
"The War in the Bathroom" (Atwood) **2**:4, 6-8, 10
"Ward No. 6" (Chekhov) **2**:126, 131-32, 143, 152, 157
"A Ward of Colonel Starbottle's" (Harte) **8**:249
"The Warden" (Gardner) **7**:213-14, 218, 222, 231
"The Wardrobe" (Mann) **5**:330
"The Warehouse" (Singer) **3**:358, 360
"Was" (Faulkner) **1**:148, 173-74, 182
"Wash" (Faulkner) **1**:166, 180
"The Watch" (Turgenev)
See "Chasy"
"Watch This Space" (Clarke) **3**:133
"The Watcher" (Calvino)
See "La giornata d'uno scrutatore"
The Watcher, and Other Stories (Calvino) **3**:98-9
"The Water Baby" (London) **4**:270
"The Water Hen" (O'Flaherty) **6**:268
"The Water of Izli" (Bowles) **3**:68
"The Wave" (O'Flaherty) **6**:261, 264, 268, 285
"The Way of a Woman" (Dunbar) **8**:122, 128, 136
"The Way of the World" (Cather) **2**:102-03
The Way Some People Live (Cheever) **1**:87-8, 92, 98-100
"The Way to the Churchyard" (Mann) **5**:322, 328-29, 334-37
"A Way You'll Never Be" (Hemingway) **1**:218, 245, 247
The Ways of White Folks (Hughes) **6**:109-10, 121-23, 126-29, 131-34, 136-38, 140-42
"The Wayside Inn" (Turgenev)
See "The Inn"
"We Drink the Wine in France" (Walker) **5**:401
"We Love Glenda So Much" (Cortázar) **7**:69
We Love Glenda So Much (Cortázar)
See *Queremos tanto a Glenda*
"A Weak Heart" (Dostoevski)
See "A Faint Heart"
"A Weary Hour" (Mann) **5**:330
"The Weaver and the Worm" (Thurber) **1**:428
"The Web of Circumstance" (Chesnutt) **7**:3, 16, 19, 22-3, 29-33, 37
"The Wedding" (O'Flaherty) **6**:260, 265, 277-78, 285
"Wedding Day" (Boyle) **5**:54-5, 65, 70-2
Wedding Day, and Other Stories (Boyle) **5**:54
"A Wedding in Brownsville" (Singer) **3**:360, 363, 376
"The Wedding Knell" (Hawthorne) **3**:154
"Wednesday's Child" (Oates) **6**:225
"Wee Willie Winkie" (Kipling) **5**:269
Wee Willie Winkie (Kipling) **5**:273
"The Welcome Table" (Walker) **5**:401, 403, 406, 410-11
"Welcome to the Monkey House" (Vonnegut) **8**:425, 427-30
Welcome to the Monkey House: A Collection of Short Works (Vonnegut) **8**:424-28, 435-36
"The Well of Days" (Bunin) **5**:100
Wessex Tales (Hardy) **2**:202-03, 205, 212, 214-15, 220, 223, 225-26, 229
"A West Indian Slave Insurrection" (Cable) **4**:59, 75
"The Westbound Train" (Cather) **2**:102
The Western Stories of Stephen Crane (Crane) **7**:153
"Westminster Abbey" (Irving) **2**:244-45, 250-51
"Whacky" (Clarke) **3**:134
"The Whale Tooth" (London) **4**:266
"What Death with Love Should Have to Do" (Oates) **6**:224, 226
"What Do You Do in San Francisco?" (Carver) **8**:32, 34
"What Do You Mean It Was Brillig?" (Thurber) **1**:428
"What Do You See, Madam?" (Barnes) **3**:18
"What Father Does is Always Right" (Andersen) **6**:18, 26, 30
"What Goes Up" (Clarke) **3**:134
"What Is It?" (Carver) **8**:4, 10, 32
"What the Shepherd Saw" (Hardy) **2**:210
"What We Talk about When We Talk about Love" (Carver) **8**:15, 18, 20, 34, 41-2, 47, 51
What We Talk about When We Talk about Love (*Talk*) (Carver) **8**:13, 15, 17-23, 26, 30, 32, 37-40, 43-4, 46, 48, 56-9
"What You Want" (Henry) **5**:187

"What's in Alaska?" (Carver) **8**:7, 10-11, 32, 34, 53
The Wheel of Love, and Other Stories (Oates) **6**:247
"When Alice Told Her Soul" (London) **4**:257, 270
"When God Laughs" (London) **4**:253
When God Laughs, and Other Stories (London) **4**:253-54
"When It Happens" (Atwood) **2**:4, 6-7, 10, 13, 16
"When the Light Gets Green" (Warren) **4**:389-90, 394, 396, 399, 401
"When the Waters Were Up at Jules" (Harte) **8**:214
"When We Were Nearly Young" (Gallant) **5**:148
"Where Are You Going, Where Have You Been?" (Oates) **6**:238, 244-46
"Where I Lived, and What I Lived For" (Oates) **6**:225, 234-35
"Where I'm Calling From" (Carver) **8**:17, 26-8, 32, 51
Where I'm Calling From: New and Selected Stories (Carver) **8**:41, 45-6, 48-50, 55, 57, 59-61
"Where is Everyone?" (Carver) **8**:18, 32, 59-60
"Where Tawe Flows" (Thomas) **3**:397, 406, 411-12
"Where the Trail Forks" (London) **4**:258, 286
"Which Was It?" (Twain) **6**:331-34, 337, 350
"Which Was the Dream?" (Twain) **6**:331-34, 337, 340, 350
"While the Auto Waits" (Henry) **5**:158, 189
Whilomville Stories (Crane) **7**:104
"The Whip-Poor-Will" (Thurber) **1**:422
Whirligigs (Henry) **5**:182
"The Whisperer in Darkness" (Lovecraft) **3**:258-60, 263, 269-71, 274-75, 278-80, 284, 291, 294
"The Whistle" (Welty) **1**:468
"Whistling Dick's Christmas Stocking" (Henry) **5**:161, 170
"The White Counterpane" (Dunbar) **8**:127, 134
"White Dump" (Munro) **3**:347-49
"The White Eagle" (Chopin) **8**:99
"A White Heron" (Jewett) **6**:157, 160, 170-73
A White Heron, and Other Stories (Jewett) **6**:171
"The White Horses of Vienna" (Boyle) **5**:63-4
"The White Man's Way" (London) **4**:253
"White Nights" (Dostoevski) **2**:171-72
"The White Old Maid" (Hawthorne) **3**:154, 159, 180-81
"The White Rabbit Caper" (Thurber) **1**:431
"The White Sea" (Kipling) **5**:293
"The White Silence" (London) **4**:250-51, 258, 267, 277, 281-84, 287-88
"White Spot" (Anderson) **1**:52
"The White Stocking" (Lawrence) **4**:198, 202, 230
"Who Am I This Time?" (Vonnegut)
See "My Name is Everyone"
"Who Do You Think You Are?" (Munro) **3**:343
Who Do You Think You Are? (*The Beggar Maid: Stories of Flo and Rose*) (Munro) **3**:333, 335-40, 342-43, 345-47
"Who Do You Wish Was With Us" (Thomas) **3**:395, 398, 403, 406, 411-12
"Who Is This Tom Scarlett?" (Barnes) **3**:18
"Who Stands for the Gods" (Dunbar) **8**:122
"Whoever Was Using this Bed" (Carver) **8**:43
"The Whole World Knows" (Welty) **1**:474, 479-80, 483
"Who's Passing for Who?" ("Passing") (Hughes) **6**:132, 141
"Who's There" (Clarke) **3**:134
"Why Don't You Dance?" (Carver) **8**:32, 37, 42-3, 47-8, 51
"Why Heisherik Was Born" (Singer) **3**:385, 387
"Why Honey?" (Carver) **8**:32
"Why I Live at the P. O." (Welty) **1**:465, 468-69, 471, 476-79, 482, 489, 494, 497
"Why I Want to Fuck Ronald Reagan" (Ballard) **1**:70, 75, 82
"Why the Little Frenchman Wears His Arm in a Sling" (Poe) **1**:407
"Why the Waves Have Whitecaps" (Hurston) **4**:140
"Why, You Reckon?" (Hughes) **6**:118, 132
"The Wide Net" (Welty) **1**:467, 469, 471, 494
The Wide Net (Welty) **1**:466-68, 471, 482, 496
"The Widow and Her Son" (Irving) **2**:240-41, 251
"The Widow's Ordeal" (Irving) **2**:241
"The Wife" (Irving) **2**:240-41, 243, 245, 251
"The Wife-Killer" (Singer) **3**:358
"The Wife of a King" (London) **4**:258, 282, 284, 286
"The Wife of Another and the Husband under the Bed" (Dostoevski) **2**:171, 193
"The Wife of His Youth" (Chesnutt) **7**:2, 15-16, 23, 33-7
The Wife of his Youth, and Other Stories of the Color Line (Chesnutt) **7**:2-3, 15, 19, 21-3, 26, 30,33, 37-8
"The Wild Goat's Kid" (O'Flaherty) **6**:260, 262, 264, 268-69
"The Wild Palms" (Faulkner) **1**:159-61
The Wild Palms (Faulkner) **1**:159-61, 167-68
"The Wild Swan" (O'Flaherty) **6**:268
The Wild Swan, and Other Stories (O'Flaherty) **6**:259, 271
"The Wild Swans" (Andersen) **6**:13, 19, 30, 35, 40
"The Will" (Lavin) **4**:165-66
"The Will to Happiness" (Mann) **5**:322-23
"Will You Please Be Quiet, Please?" (Carver) **8**:3-4, 7, 10-11, 18-19, 22, 32
Will You Please Be Quiet, Please? (Carver) **8**:3-6, 17-18, 26, 29, 32, 34, 45, 50, 54
"Will You Tell Me" (Barthelme) **2**:27
Willa Cather's Collected Short Fiction (Cather) **2**:103, 105
"Willi" (Gallant) **5**:138
"William the Conqueror" (Kipling) **5**:283
"William Wilson" (Poe) **1**:378, 385-86, 394-97, 407
"William's Wedding" (Jewett) **6**:180
"Willie Winkie" (Andersen) **6**:24
"The Willing Muse" (Cather) **2**:98, 103
"The Wind at Beni Midar" (Bowles) **3**:64, 85
"The Wind Tells of Valdemar Daae and His Daughters" ("Waldemar Daa and His Daughters"; "The Wind Tells the Story of Valdemar Daa and his Daughters"; "The Wind's Tale") (Andersen) **6**:12, 15, 18, 24
"The Wind Tells the Story of Valdemar Daa and his Daughters" (Andersen)
See "The Wind Tells of Valdemar Daae and His Daughters"
"The Winds" (Welty) **1**:472
"The Wind's Tale" (Andersen)
See "The Wind Tells of Valdemar Daae and His Daughters"
Winesburg, Ohio (Anderson) **1**:17-19, 22, 24-35, 38-46, 48, 51-2, 55, 57-8
Winner Take Nothing (Hemingway) **1**:211, 216-17
"Winter Cruise" (Maugham) **8**:380
"Winter Dreams" (Fitzgerald) **6**:46, 59, 66, 69, 76, 88, 90-1, 100, 102, 104
"Winter in July" (Lessing) **6**:186, 191, 213-14, 217-18
"Winter Night" (Boyle) **5**:55
"Winter Wind" (Munro) **3**:331
"The Winters and the Palmeys" (Hardy) **2**:207, 209
Winter's Tales (*Vinter-Eventyr*) (Dinesen) **7**:164, 166, 170-71, 175, 180, 193, 195-96, 199-200, 205, 208
"Wintry Peacock" (Lawrence) **4**:231, 234-35
"Wireless" (Kipling) **5**:266, 275, 280
The Wisdom of Father Brown (Chesterton) **1**:120-21, 124
"The Wisdom of Silence" (Dunbar) **8**:122, 126, 132, 135, 146
"The Wisdom of the Trail" (London) **4**:282-85, 288
"The Wise Men" (Crane) **7**:101, 126
"Wiser than a God" (Chopin) **8**:69-70, 73, 84, 99
"The Wish House" (Kipling) **5**:275, 280-81
"The Witch" (Singer) **3**:377
"The Witch a la Mode" (Lawrence) **4**:220
"Witches Loaves" (Henry) **5**:184
"With Justifiable Pride" (Cortázar)
See "Con legítimo orgullo"
"With the Night Mail" (Kipling) **5**:268
"The Withered Arm" (Hardy) **2**:202-03, 205, 208, 213-14, 217-20, 227-28, 231-34
"Without Benefit of Clergy" (Kipling) **5**:262, 291, 295-97, 299
"Without Colors" (Calvino) **3**:104, 108-09
"The Witness" (Porter) **4**:339-40, 358
"The Witnesses" (Cortázar)
See "Los testigos"
"The Wives of the Dead" (Hawthorne) **3**:159, 164, 186
Wodehouse on Crime (Wodehouse) **2**:352
"Wolf Lonigan's Death" (O'Flaherty) **6**:261, 276, 280
"Wolfert Webber" (Irving) **2**:241, 247, 249, 251-52, 262, 266, 268
"Wolfert's Roost" (Irving) **2**:246
"A Woman of Fifty" (Maugham) **8**:380
"A Woman on a Roof" (Lessing) **6**:199, 206
"The Woman Who Came at Six O'Clock" (García Márquez) **8**:172, 183, 185
"The Woman Who Rode Away" (Lawrence) **4**:219, 226, 239
The Woman Who Rode Away, and Other Stories (Lawrence) **4**:230
"A Woman with a Past" (Fitzgerald) **6**:50
"A Woman without a Country" (Cheever) **1**:95, 100
"A Woman, Young and Old" (Paley) **8**:388, 390, 396, 398
"A Woman's Kingdom" (Chekhov) **2**:156-57

"Women" (Singer) **3**:358
Wonder Stories Told for Children (Andersen)
See *Eventyr, fortalte for bøorn*
Wonder Tales (Andersen)
See *Eventyr, fortalte for bøorn*
Wonder Tales for Children (Andersen)
See *Eventyr, fortalte for bøorn*
"The Wonderful Old Gentleman" (Parker) **2**:274, 281, 283
"The Wood Duck" (Thurber) **1**:414, 422
"The Work on Red Mountain" (Harte) **8**:231, 254
"The Working Party" (Bowen) **3**:30, 40, 49
"The World and the Door" (Henry) **5**:182
"The World of Apples" (Cheever) **1**:112
The World of Apples (Cheever) **1**:97-8, 101
"A Worn Path" (Welty) **1**:466, 470, 491-92, 494
"Worship" (Atwood) **2**:20
"The Worst Crime in the World" (Chesterton) **1**:129, 138
"The Wounded Cormorant" (O'Flaherty) **6**:260, 262, 268, 282-83
Wounds in the Rain: War Stories (Crane) **7**:104, 108
"The Wreath" (O'Connor) **5**:372, 389
"Wrens and Starlings" (Powers) **4**:380
"The Wren's Nest" (O'Flaherty) **6**:274, 279
"Wressley of the Foreign Office" (Kipling) **5**:279
"The Wrong Shape" (Chesterton) **1**:121, 129-30, 136
"Xingu" (Wharton) **6**:418, 422, 428-29, 437
Xingu, and Other Stories (Wharton) **6**:417-19, 421, 435
"Ya no quedan esperanzas de" ("There Is No Hope for That") (Cortázar) **7**:95
"Yah! Yah! Yah!" (London) **4**:266
Yakov Pasynkov (*Jacob Pasinkov*) (Turgenev) **7**:314, 320, 324
"The Yelagin Affair" (Bunin)
See "The Elaghin Affair"
"The Yellow Beret" (Lavin) **4**:167
"The Yellow Bird" (Chesterton) **1**:124-25, 133
"A Yellow Flower" (Cortázar)
See "Una flor amarilla"
"The Yellow Gown" (Anderson) **1**:52
"The Yellow Streak" (Maugham) **8**:367, 372
"Yentl the Yeshiva Boy" (Singer) **3**:359, 384
"Yermolai and the Miller's Wife" ("Ermolai and the Miller's Wife") (Turgenev) **7**:342
"You Are Not I" (Bowles) **3**:59-61, 66, 68-9, 72, 76-7
You Can't Keep a Good Woman Down (Walker) **5**:412-14
"You Have Left Your Lotus Pods on the Bus" (Bowles) **3**:69
"You Touched Me" (Lawrence) **4**:203-04, 231, 233-36
"You Were Perfectly Fine" (Parker) **2**:272, 278, 281
"The Young Aunt with the White Hair" (Cable) **4**:49
"The Young Glory of Him" (Hughes) **6**:127
"Young Goodman Brown" (Hawthorne) **3**:164-68, 171-74, 177-78, 180, 182-83, 185-87, 189, 191-93
"The Young Italian" (Irving)
See "The Story of the Young Italian"
"The Young Man with the Carnation" (Dinesen) **7**:164, 191-92, 194, 198
Young Men in Spats (Wodehouse) **2**:325, 328
"The Young Robber" (Irving)
See "The Story of the Young Robber"
"Young Robin Gray" (Harte) **8**:223
"A Young Woman in Green Lace" (Parker) **2**:273, 283
"Your Most Profound Skin" (Cortázar)
See "Tu más profunda piel"
Youth and the Bright Medusa (Cather) **2**:91-2, 94, 98, 103, 111-13
"Yveline Samoris" (Maupassant) **1**:283
"Yvette" (Maupassant) **1**:263, 275, 283
"Z. Marcas" (Balzac) **5**:27, 31, 33
"Zagrowsky Tells" (Paley) **8**:412
"The Zahir" (Borges) **4**:10, 25
"Zakoldovannoe mesto" ("The Bewitched Spot") (Gogol) **4**:117, 121
"Zeal" (Powers) **4**:370
"Zeitl and Rickel" (Singer) **3**:359
"Lo zio acquativo" ("The Aquatic Uncle") (Calvino) **3**:92-3, 109
"Zodiac 2000" (Ballard) **1**:79
"Zone of Terror" (Ballard) **1**:68
"Zooey" (Salinger) **2**:291, 293-94, 296-97, 302-05, 308